Nineteenth-Century Literature Criticism

Guide to Gale Literary Criticism Series

For criticism on	Consult these Gale series
Authors now living or who died after December 31, 1999	*CONTEMPORARY LITERARY CRITICISM (CLC)*
Authors who died between 1900 and 1999	*TWENTIETH-CENTURY LITERARY CRITICISM (TCLC)*
Authors who died between 1800 and 1899	*NINETEENTH-CENTURY LITERATURE CRITICISM (NCLC)*
Authors who died between 1400 and 1799	*LITERATURE CRITICISM FROM 1400 TO 1800 (LC)* *SHAKESPEAREAN CRITICISM (SC)*
Authors who died before 1400	*CLASSICAL AND MEDIEVAL LITERATURE CRITICISM (CMLC)*
Authors of books for children and young adults	*CHILDREN'S LITERATURE REVIEW (CLR)*
Dramatists	*DRAMA CRITICISM (DC)*
Poets	*POETRY CRITICISM (PC)*
Short story writers	*SHORT STORY CRITICISM (SSC)*
Black writers of the past two hundred years	*BLACK LITERATURE CRITICISM (BLC)* *BLACK LITERATURE CRITICISM SUPPLEMENT (BLCS)*
Hispanic writers of the late nineteenth and twentieth centuries	*HISPANIC LITERATURE CRITICISM (HLC)* *HISPANIC LITERATURE CRITICISM SUPPLEMENT (HLCS)*
Native North American writers and orators of the eighteenth, nineteenth, and twentieth centuries	*NATIVE NORTH AMERICAN LITERATURE (NNAL)*
Major authors from the Renaissance to the present	*WORLD LITERATURE CRITICISM, 1500 TO THE PRESENT (WLC)* *WORLD LITERATURE CRITICISM SUPPLEMENT (WLCS)*

ISSN 0732-1864

Volume 89

Nineteenth-Century Literature Criticism

Excerpts from Criticism of the Works of Novelists, Philosophers, and Other Creative Writers Who Died between 1800 and 1899, from the First Published Critical Appraisals to Current Evaluations

Juliet Byington and Suzanne Dewsbury
Editors

Detroit
New York
San Francisco
London
Boston
Woodbridge, CT

STAFF

Lynn M. Spampinato, Janet Witalec, *Managing Editors, Literature Product*
Kathy D. Darrow, *Product Liaison*
Juliet Byington, Suzanne Dewsbury, *Editors*
Mark W. Scott, *Publisher, Literature Product*

Mary Ruby, Patti A. Tippett, *Technical Training Specialists*
Deborah J. Morad, Kathleen Lopez Nolan, *Managing Editors, Literature Content*
Susan M. Trosky, *Director, Literature Content*

Maria L. Franklin, *Permissions Manager*
Edna Hedblad, Kimberly F. Smilay, *Permissions Specialists*
Sarah Tomasek, *Permissions Assistant*

Victoria B. Cariappa, *Research Manager*
Tracie A. Richardson, *Project Coordinator*
Andrew Guy Malonis, Barbara McNeil, Gary J. Oudersluys, Maureen Richards, Cheryl L. Warnock, *Research Specialists*
Tamara C. Nott, *Research Associate*
Tim Lehnerer, Ron Morelli, *Research Assistants*

Dorothy Maki, *Manufacturing Manager*
Stacy L. Melson, *Buyer*

Mary Beth Trimper, *Composition and Prepress Manager*
Gary Leach, Carolyn Roney, *Composition Specialists*

Randy Bassett, *Image Database Supervisor*
Robert Duncan, *Imaging Specialist*
Michael Logusz, *Graphic Artist*
Pamela A. Reed, *Imaging Coordinator*
Kelly A. Quin, *Imaging Editor*

Library of Congress Catalog Card Number
ISBN 0-7876-4544-3
ISSN 0732-1864
Printed in the United States of America

10 9 8 7 6 5 4 3 2 1

Contents

Preface

Since its inception in 1981, *Nineteeth-Century Literature Criticism* (*NCLC*) has been a valuable resource for students and librarians seeking critical commentary on writers of this transitional period in world history. Designated an "Outstanding Reference Source" by the American Library Association with the publication of is first volume, *NCLC* has since been purchased by over 6,000 school, public, and university libraries. The series has covered more than 300 authors representing 29 nationalities and over 17,000 titles. No other reference source has surveyed the critical reaction to nineteenth-century authors and literature as thoroughly as *NCLC.*

Scope of the Series

NCLC is designed to introduce students and advanced readers to the authors of the nineteenth century and to the most significant interpretations of these authors' works. The great poets, novelists, short story writers, playwrights, and philosophers of this period are frequently studied in high school and college literature courses. By organizing and reprinting commentary written on these authors, *NCLC* helps students develop valuable insight into literary history, promotes a better understanding of the texts, and sparks ideas for papers and assignments. Each entry in *NCLC* presents a comprehensive survey of an author's career or an individual work of literature and provides the user with a multiplicity of interpretations and assessments. Such variety allows students to pursue their own interests; furthermore, it fosters an awareness that literature is dynamic and responsive to many different opinions.

Every fourth volume of *NCLC* is devoted to literary topics that cannot be covered under the author approach used in the rest of the series. Such topics include literary movements, prominent themes in nineteenth-century literature, literary reaction to political and historical events, significant eras in literary history, prominent literary anniversaries, and the literatures of cultures that are often overlooked by English-speaking readers.

NCLC continues the survey of criticism of world literature begun by Gale's *Contemporary Literary Criticism* (*CLC*) and *Twentieth-Century Literary Criticism* (*TCLC*).

Organization of the Book

An *NCLC* entry consists of the following elements:

- The **Author Heading** cites the name under which the author most commonly wrote, followed by birth and death dates. Also located here are any name variations under which an author wrote, including transliterated forms for authors whose native languages use nonroman alphabets. If the author wrote consistently under a pseudonym, the pseudonym will be listed in the author heading and the author's actual name given in parenthesis on the first line of the biographical and critical information. Uncertain birth or death dates are indicated by question marks. Single-work entries are preceded by a heading that consists of the most common form of the title in English translation (if applicable) and the original date of composition.

- The **Introduction** contains background information that introduces the reader to the author, work, or topic that is the subject of the entry.

- A **Portrait of the Author** is included when available.

- The list of **Principal Works** is ordered chronologically by date of first publication and lists the most important works by the author. The genre and publication date of each work is given. In the case of foreign authors whose works have been translated into English, the list will focus primarily on twentieth-century translations, selecting those works most commonly considered the best by critics. Unless otherwise indicated, dramas are dated by first performance, not first publication. Lists of **Representative Works** by different authors appear with topic entries.

- Reprinted **Criticism** is arranged chronologically in each entry to provide a useful perspective on changes in critical evaluation over time. The critic's name and the date of composition or publication of the critical work are given at the beginning of each piece of criticism. Unsigned criticism is preceded by the title of the source in which it appeared. All titles by the author featured in the text are printed in boldface type. Footnotes are reprinted at the end of each essay or excerpt. In the case of excerpted criticism, only those footnotes that pertain to the excerpted texts are included. Criticism in topic entries is arranged chronologically under a variety of subheadings to facilitate the study of different aspects of the topic.

- A complete **Bibliographical Citation** of the original essay or book precedes each piece of criticism.

- Critical essays are prefaced by brief **Annotations** explicating each piece.

- An annotated bibliography of **Further Reading** appears at the end of each entry and suggests resources for additional study. In some cases, significant essays for which the editors could not obtain reprint rights are included here. Boxed material following the further reading list provides references to other biographical and critical sources on the author in series published by Gale.

Indexes

Each volume of *NCLC* contains a **Cumulative Author Index** listing all authors who have appeared in a wide variety of reference sources published by the Gale Group, including *NCLC*. A complete list of these sources is found facing the first page of the Author Index. The index also includes birth and death dates and cross references between pseudonyms and actual names.

A **Cumulative Nationality Index** lists all authors featured in *NCLC* by nationality, followed by the number of the *NCLC* volume in which their entry appears.

A **Cumulative Topic Index** lists the literary themes and topics treated in the series as well as in *Classical and Medieval Literature Criticism, Literature Criticism from 1400 to 1800, Twentieth-Century Literary Criticism,* and the *Contemporary Literary Criticism* Yearbook, which was discontinued in 1998.

An alphabetical **Title Index** accompanies each volume of *NCLC*, with the exception of the Topics volumes. Listings of titles by authors covered in the given volume are followed by the author's name and the corresponding page numbers where the titles are discussed. English translations of foreign titles and variations of titles are cross-referenced to the title under which a work was originally published. Titles of novels, dramas, nonfiction books, and poetry, short story, or essay collections are printed in italics, while individual poems, short stories, and essays are printed in roman type within quotation marks.

In response to numerous suggestions from librarians, Gale also produces an annual paperbound edition of the *NCLC* cumulative title index. This annual cumulation, which alphabetically lists all titles reviewed in the series, is available to all customers. Additional copies of this index are available upon request. Librarians and patrons will welcome this separate index; it saves shelf space, is easy to use, and is recyclable upon receipt of the next edition.

Citing *Nineteenth-Century Literature Criticism*

When writing papers, students who quote directly from any volume in the Literary Criticism Series may use the following general format to footnote reprinted criticism. The first example pertains to material drawn from periodicals, the second to material reprinted from books.

Kim McQuaid, "William Apes, Pequot: An Indian Reformer in the Jackson Era," *The New England Quarterly,* 50 (December 1977): 605-25; excerpted and reprinted in *Nineteenth-Century Literature Criticism,* vol. 73, ed. Janet Witalec (Farmington Hills, Mich.: The Gale Group, 1999), 3-4.

Richard Harter Fogle, *The Imagery of Keats and Shelley: A Comparative Study* (Archon Books, 1949), 211-51; excerpted and reprinted in *Nineteenth-Century Literature Criticism,* vol. 73, ed. Janet Witalec (Farmington Hills, Mich.: The Gale Group, 1999), 157-69.

Suggestions are Welcome

Readers who wish to suggest new features, topics, or authors to appear in future volumes, or who have other suggestions or comments are cordially invited to call, write, or fax the Managing Editor:

Managing Editor, Literary Criticism Series
The Gale Group
27500 Drake Road
Farmington Hills, MI 48331-3535
1-800-347-4253 (GALE)
Fax: 248-699-8054

Acknowledgments

The editors wish to thank the copyright holders of the excerpted criticism included in this volume and the permissions managers of many book and magazine publishing companies for assisting us in securing reproduction rights. We are also grateful to the staffs of the Detroit Public Library, the Library of Congress, the University of Detroit Mercy Library, Wayne State University Purdy/Kresge Library Complex, and the University of Michigan Libraries for making their resources available to us. Following is a list of the copyright holders who have granted us permission to reproduce material in this volume of *NCLC*. Every effort has been made to trace copyright, but if omissions have been made, please let us know.

COPYRIGHTED EXCERPTS IN *NCLC*, VOLUME 89, WERE REPRODUCED FROM THE FOLLOWING PERIODICALS:

American Literary Realism 1870-1910, v. 24, 1992. Copyright © 1992 by the Department of English, The University of New Mexico. Reproduced by permission of the publisher.—***American Literature,*** v. 69, December, 1997. Copyright © 1997 Duke University Press, Durham, NC. Reproduced by permission.—***Amerikastudien,*** v. 22, 1977 for "Melville's Cosmopolitan: Bayard Taylor in 'The Confidence-Man'" by Hans Joachim Lang. © J. B. Metzlersche Verlagsbuchhandlung und Carl Ernst Poeschel Verlag GmbH in Stuttgart 1977.—***CLA Journal,*** v. 18, 1974; v. 18, 1975; v. 23, 1980. Copyright, 1974, 1975, 1980 by The College Language Association. All used by permission of The College Language Association.—***College English,*** v. 56, November, 1994 for "The Function of Matthew Arnold at the Present Time" by Timothy Peltason. Copyright © 1994 by the National Council of Teachers of English. Reproduced by permission of the publisher and the author.—***Comparative Literature,*** v. 46, Winter, 1994 for "Philhellenism and Antisemitism: Matthew Arnold and his German Models" by Lionel Gossman. © copyright 1994 by University of Oregon. Reproduced by permission of the author.—***Critical Survey,*** v. 4, 1992. Reproduced by permission.—***Dickens Studies Annual,*** v. 20, 1991. Copyright © 1991 by AMS Press, Inc. Reproduced by permission.—***English Studies in Canada,*** v. IV, Spring, 1978 for "Arthur's Misuse of the Imagination: Sentimental Benevolence and Wordsworthian Realism in 'Adam Bede'" by Mason Harris. © Association of Canadian University Teachers of English 1978. Reproduced by permission of the publisher and the author.—***English Studies in Canada,*** v. IX, June, 1983 for "Infanticide and Respectability: Hetty Sorrel as Abandoned Child in 'Adam Bede'" by Mason Harris. © Association of Canadian University Teachers of English 1983. Reproduced by permission of the publisher and the author.—***Genre,*** v. IX, Spring, 1976 for "'Adam Bede' as a Pastoral" by Kenny Marotta. Reproduced by permission of the publisher and the author.—***The Kenyon Review,*** Summer, 1987 for "Delicate Beauty Goes Out: 'Adam Bede's' Transgressive Heroines" by Lori Lefkovitz. Copyright © 1987 by Kenyon College. All rights reserved. Reproduced by permission.—***The Markham Review,*** v. 3, May, 1973; v. 9, Fall, 1979. Both reproduced by permission.—***Mosaic,*** v. 22, Fall, 1989. © Mosaic 1989. Acknowledgment of previous publication is herewith made.—***Papers on Language & Literature,*** v. VIII, Winter, 1972. Copyright © 1972 by The Board of Trustees, Southern Illinois University at Edwardsville. Reproduced by permission.—***Studies in the Novel,*** v. XXIV, Winter, 1992. Copyright 1992 by North Texas State University. Reproduced by permission.—***Textual Practice,*** v. 8, Summer, 1994. Reproduced by permission of Taylor & Francis, Ltd., PO Box 25, Abingdon, Oxfordshire, OX14 3UE.—***Victorian Poetry,*** v. 18, 1980 for "Iseult of Brittany: A New Interpretation of Matthew Arnold's 'Tristram and Iseult'" by Barbara Fass Leavy. v. 34, Summer, 1996 for "Arnold's 'The Scholar-Gipsy': The Use and Abuse of History" by Alan Grob. © West Virgina University, 1996. Reproduced by permission of the author.—***Victorians Institute Journal,*** v. 22, 1994. Reproduced by permission.—***Women's Writing,*** v. 3, June, 1996 for "Women or Boys? Gender, Realism, and the Gaze in 'Adam Bede'" by Caroline Levine. Reproduced by permission of the author.

COPYRIGHTED EXCERPTS IN *NCLC*, VOLUME 89, WERE REPRODUCED FROM THE FOLLOWING BOOKS:

Cary, Richard. From ***The Genteel Circle: Bayard Taylor and His New York Friends.*** Cornell University Press, 1952. Copyright © 1952 by Cornell University, renewed 1980 by Richard Cary. Used by permission of the publisher, Cornell University Press.—Collini, Stefan. From ***Victorian Thinkers.*** Oxford University Press, 1993. Arnold © Stefan Collini 1988. Reproduced by permission of the author.—Gara, Larry. From an introduction to ***The Narrative of William W. Brown A Fugitive Slave, and a Lecture Delivered Before the Female Anti-Slavery Society of Salem, 1847.*** Addison-Wesley Publishing Company, 1969. Copyright © 1969 by Addison-Wesley Publishing Company, Inc. All rights reserved.

Reproduced by permission.—Holtze, Elizabeth. From ***Hamartia: The Concept of Error in the Western Tradition.*** Edited by Donald V. Stump et al. The Edwin Mellen Press, 1983. Copyright © 1983, Donald V. Stump. Reproduced by permission.—Jefferson, Paul. From an introduction in ***The Travels of William Wells Brown.*** Edited by Paul Jefferson. Markus Wiener Publishers, Inc., 1991. © Copyright 1991 for the introduction and commentary by Paul Jefferson. All rights reserved. Reproduced by permission.—La Salle II, C. W. From ***The Story of Kennett by Bayard Taylor.*** College & University Press, 1973. Copyright © 1973 by College and University Press Services, Inc. All rights reserved. Reproduced by permission of NCUP, Inc.—Mulvey, Christopher. From "The Fugitive Self and the New World of the North: William Wells Brown's 'Discovery of America'," in ***The Black Columbiad: Defining Moments in African American Literature and Culture.*** Edited by Werner Sollors and Maria Diedrich. Harvard University Press, 1994. Copyright © 1994 by the President and Fellows of Harvard College. All rights reserved. Reproduced by permission.—Riede, David G. From ***Matthew Arnold and the Betrayal of Language.*** University Press of Virginia, 1988. Copyright © 1988 by the Rector and Visitors of the University of Virginia. Reprinted with permission of the University Press of Virginia.—Schneider, Mary W. From ***Poetry in the Age of Democracy: The Literary Criticism of Matthew Arnold.*** University Press of Kansas, 1989. © 1989 by the University Press of Kansas. All rights reserved. Reproduced by permission.—Sterner, Douglas W. From ***Priests of Culture: A Study of Matthew Arnold & Henry James.*** Peter Lang, 1999. © 1999 Peter Lang Publishing, Inc., New York. All rights reserved. Reproduced by permission.—Stone, Donald S. From ***Communications with the Future: Matthew Arnold in Dialogue.*** The University of Michigan Press, 1997. Copyright © by the University of Michigan 1997. All rights reserved. Reproduced by permission.—Wermuth, Paul C. From an introduction to ***Selected Letters of Bayard Taylor.*** Edited by Paul C. Wermuth. Bucknell University Press, 1997. © 1997 by Associated University Presses, Inc. All rights reserved. Reproduced by permission.—Wermuth, Paul C. From ***Bayard Taylor.*** Twayne Publishers, Inc., 1973. Copyright © 1973 by Twayne Publishers, Inc. All rights reserved. Reproduced by permission of the author.—Whelchel, Jr., L. H. From ***My Chains Fell Off: William Wells Brown, Fugitive Abolitionist.*** University Press of America, 1985. Copyright © 1985 by University Press of America, Inc. Reproduced by permission of the author.

PHOTOGRAPHS APPEARING IN *NCLC*, VOLUME 89, WERE RECEIVED FROM THE FOLLOWING SOURCES:

Arnold, Matthew, engraving. The Library of Congress.—Brown, William Wells, drawing. Fisk University Library Collection.—"Clotel" by William Wells Brown, title page, 1853, London.—Eliot, George, photograph of a engraving. National Portrait Gallery. Reproduced by permission of National Portrait Gallery (London).—From a title page of "Adam Bede" by George Eliot. Edinburgh & London: Blackwood, 1859, 1 volume, New York: Harper, 1859. The Graduate Library, University of Michigan. Reproduced by permission.—Ricketts, Charles, artist. From the title page of "Empedocles on Etna; A Dramatic Poem" by Matthew Arnold. London, Sold by Hacon & Ricketts, 1896. Special Collections Library, the University of Michigan. Reproduced by permission.—Taylor, Bayard, photograph. The Library of Congress.

Matthew Arnold
1822-1888

English poet, critic, and essayist. For more information on Arnold's life and works, see *NCLC,* Volumes 6 and 29.

INTRODUCTION

Arnold is considered one of the most significant writers of the late Victorian period in England. He initially established his reputation as a poet of elegiac verse, and such poems as "The Scholar-Gipsy" and "Dover Beach" are considered classics for their subtle, restrained style and compelling expression of spiritual malaise. However, it was through his prose writing that Arnold asserted his greatest influence on literature. His writings on the role of literary criticism in society advance classical ideals and advocate the adoption of universal aesthetic standards.

BIOGRAPHICAL INFORMATION

Arnold was the eldest son of Thomas Arnold, an influential educator who served as headmaster of Rugby School for a number of years. Arnold himself attended Rugby from 1837 to 1841, and it was while he was a student there that he composed the prize-winning poem *Alaric at Rome,* which was published in 1840. After graduating from Balliol College at Oxford in 1844, Arnold accepted a teaching post at the university and continued to write verse, publishing *The Strayed Reveller, and Other Poems* in 1849. Two years later he was appointed inspector of schools, a position he held until shortly before his death.

Arnold focused his energies on poetry until 1853, when he became critical of Romantic expressions of emotion in poetry. For the remaining thirty-five years of his literary career, Arnold wrote numerous essays and reviews on literary, educational, and cultural issues; his controversial perspective on Christianity provoked the outrage of conservative politicians and religious thinkers. He died of heart failure on April 15, 1888.

MAJOR WORKS

In 1852, Arnold released a collection entitled *Empedocles on Etna, and Other Poems.* The following year, he reissued the collection without its title poem. Explaining his actions in his preface to the reissued collection, an essay that has become one of his most significant critical statements, Arnold denounced the emotional and stylistic excesses of late Romantic poetry and outlined a poetic theory derived from Aristotelian principles of unity and decorum. He also stated that some of his own works, most notably the dramatic poem "Empedocles on Etna," were flawed by Romantic self-absorption, and that he had therefore decided to suppress those most affected. Critics suggest that Arnold's recognition of the pervasive Romantic tendencies of his poetry, which conflicted dramatically with his classicist critical temperament, ultimately led him to abandon poetry as a form of self-expression.

Arnold's first major prose works, *On Translating Homer* and *The Popular Education of France, with Notices of That of Holland and Switzerland,* both published in 1861, inaugurated his career as a highly visible and sometimes controversial literary and social critic. With the appearance of *St. Paul and Protestantism, with an Essay on Puritanism and the Church of England* in 1870, Arnold's focus shifted to theological issues, particularly what he viewed as a crisis of religious faith in Victorian society. Arnold attributed this crisis to the conflict between the prevailing influence of scientific rationalism and the intransigence of conservative theology. His solution was a liberal, symbolic interpretation of biblical scripture, presented in *Literature and Dogma: An Essay towards a Better Apprehension of the Bible* (1873), the publication of which caused an immediate uproar among conservative Church leaders and religious theorists. Two years later Arnold answered his critics in *God and the Bible: A Review of Objections to "Literature and Dogma"* (1875), affirming his rejection of religious orthodoxy. During his final years, Arnold made two tours of the United States and recorded his overwhelmingly negative assessment of American culture in *Civilization in the United States: First and Last Impressions of America* (1888).

Arnold's prose writings articulate his desire to establish universal standards of taste and judgment. In his highly regarded *Essays in Criticism* (1865), he elaborates on this key principle, defining the role of critical inquiry as "a disinterested endeavor to learn and propagate the best that is known and thought in the world, and thus to establish a current of fresh and true ideals." For Arnold this endeavor should not be limited to literature, but should embrace theology, history, art history, science, sociology, and political theory, with pertinent standards drawn from all periods of world history. Arnold's approach was markedly eclectic, and in "The Literary Influence of the Academies," the second of the *Essays in Criticism,* he pointedly contrasts the isolation of English intellectuals with European urbanity, hoping to foster in his own country the sophisticated cosmopolitanism enjoyed by writers and critics on the European continent. Similarly, *Culture and Anarchy: An Essay in Political and Social Criticism* (1869), widely viewed as one of Arnold's most important works, was motivated by his desire to redress what he saw as the smug provincialism and arrogance of English society. The essay is a sociopolitical analysis of England's class structure in which Arnold identifies three major classes: Barbarians (the aristocracy), Philistines (the middle class), and the Populace (the lower class). While Arnold praised the aristocracy for their refined manners and social assurance, he also condemned them for their conservatism. "Philistines" Arnold considered hopelessly uncouth though innovative and energetic. The lower class he dismissed as an ineffectual, inchoate mass. Arnold argued that as the middle class gradually assumed control of English politics, they must be transformed from their unpolished state into a sensitive, sophisticated, intellectual community. The alternative, he contended, would be a dissolution of England's moral and cultural standards. Arnold also endorsed the eventual creation of a classless society in which every individual would subscribe to highly refined ideals based on the culture of ancient Greece.

CRITICAL RECEPTION

Critics generally view Arnold's poetry as a reflection of a spiritual dilemma that was innately Victorian, experienced by people who, in the words of Arnold's "Scholar-Gipsy," "were caught" between "two worlds, one dead / the other powerless to be born." The "dead" world is widely interpreted as a metaphoric evocation of the early Romantic movement, during which Western culture was reinvigorated by newly developed humanist and democratic ideals, while the "unborn" world is considered to be a not-yet-realized society in which the scientific materialism of industrialized nations would be tempered by a highly developed state of cultural enlightenment. Although Arnold strove to imitate classical Greek and Roman models in his poetry, critics agree that his work manifests Romantic subjectivism. Many of his poems assume the form of a soliloquy or confession in which the narrator communicates feelings of melancholy or regret. However, Arnold's essentially Romantic sentiments are praised for the precisely wrought and measured manner in which they are expressed.

Critical scholarship attests to Arnold's prescience in his prose writings, in forecasting the problems and possibilities that would arise with the transition from an aristocratic society to a democratic one. Arnold's conception of culture, frequently read as strongly conservative, has recently been reevaluated as suggesting a model of critical and "imaginative reason" that continues to guide literary theory. In discussing Arnold's place in modern literature studies, Timothy Peltason notes that although Arnold's name has long been considered "shorthand . . . for . . . cultural conservatism," there is a misunderstanding among many scholars and critics regarding what Arnold actually wrote and said. According to Peltason, Arnold did not endorse "received cultural values," nor did he passively accept the value of accredited masterpieces. Instead, contends Peltason, Arnold focused his writing and scholarship on an examination of how things "work for us here and now." This interest in maintaining the value of culture and using criticism to stress that value to society was a central theme in Arnold's prose works. In an essay comparing Arnold's "The Function of Criticism" to T. S. Eliot's essay of the same name, critic Terence Hawkes notes that both writers consider criticism a seminal tool in helping society objectively examine its failures and successes. Hawkes relates that the role of criticism as described by Arnold and his contemporaries is often haunted by the notion that it is secondary to the actual happening. Instead, says Hawkes, Arnold himself viewed criticism as a necessary and complementary act to the primary text or idea it was examining, often serving to illustrate uncanny and noteworthy aspects not inherent in the original text or incident. Recent scholarship on Arnold has acknowledged that Arnold's writing reflects the tensions of modern literature, particularly his remarks on aesthetic judgment, and his attempts to formulate a theory of the role of criticism in culture. His integration of social criticism and literary analysis, says Stefan Collini, is acknowledged as his most significant and lasting achievement. In Collini's words, Arnold "characterized in unforgettable ways the role that criticism—that kind of literary criticism that is also cultural criticism, and thus . . . a sort of informal political theory—can and must play in modern societies."

PRINCIPAL WORKS

Alaric at Rome (poetry) 1840
The Strayed Reveller, and Other Poems (poetry) 1849
Empedocles on Etna, and Other Poems (poetry) 1852
Poems (poetry) 1853
Poems: Second Series (poetry) 1855
Merope (verse drama) 1858
On Translating Homer (lectures) 1861
The Popular Education of France, with Notices of That of Holland and Switzerland (essay) 1861
Essays in Criticism (criticism) 1865
New Poems (poetry) 1867
On the Study of Celtic Literature (criticism) 1867
Culture and Anarchy: An Essay in Political and Social Criticism (essay) 1869
St. Paul and Protestantism, with an Essay on Puritanism and the Church of England (essay) 1869
Literature and Dogma: An Essay towards a Better Apprehension of the Bible (essay) 1873
God and the Bible: A Review of Objections to "Literature and Dogma" (essay) 1875
Mixed Essays (essays) 1879
Discourses in America (lectures) 1885
Civilization in the United States: First and Last Impressions of America (essay) 1888
Essays in Criticism: Second Series (criticism) 1888
Letters of Matthew Arnold, 1848-1888 (letters) 1895
Matthew Arnold's Notebooks (notebooks) 1902
The Works of Matthew Arnold 15 vols. (criticism, essays, lectures, and poetry) 1903-04
The Letters of Matthew Arnold to Arthur Hugh Clough (letters) 1932
The Poetical Works of Matthew Arnold (poetry) 1950
Complete Prose Works (criticism, lectures, and essays) 1960-77

CRITICISM

Barbara Fass Leavy (essay date 1980)

SOURCE: "Iseult of Brittany: A New Interpretation of Matthew Arnold's *Tristram and Iseult*," in *Arthurian Women: A Casebook,* edited by Thelma S. Fisher, Garland Publishing, 1996, pp. 205-28.

[*In the following essay, originally published in 1980, Leavy argues that Arnold's sympathetic portrayal of Iseult, especially the fantasy world she has created for herself to help cope with the monotony of her existence, is an astute example of "female fantasy in nineteenth-century literature."*]

Matthew Arnold was pleased with his version of the Tristram and Iseult legend. He was especially proud of having gotten to the story before Richard Wagner popularized it, and Arnold thought that he himself had done the better job. An audience unfamiliar with Wagner, however, did not find ***Tristram and Iseult*** easy to read. Such narrative details as the drinking of the love potion are only alluded to, and the story, told in flashbacks from the deathbed of the hero, was not easy to follow. Modern readers are less likely to face such difficulties. Nevertheless, critics of Arnold's poetry find themselves in much the same situation today that his general readers did in the past: "***Tristram and Iseult,*** though it will stand as the most brilliant of Arnold's poems on love, is not an easy work to approach or to comprehend."[1] The major problem concerns Part III, the conclusion of the poem. In it, a widowed Iseult of Brittany tells her children an ancient tale from her country. She relates how Merlin and Vivian were traveling together in a forest, how they stopped to rest (and, implicitly, to make love), and how Vivian imprisoned Merlin in a magic plot of ground from which she left him to follow her own way. The end of Iseult's story is also the end of Arnold's poem.

Explanations for the presence of this tale in ***Tristram and Iseult*** vary, as do opinions about whether Arnold added Part III as an afterthought or whether it was part of his plan from the outset. Some critics find the story added merely to provide comic relief in a tragic poem, but this is a rather lame interpretation—especially since the story of Merlin and Vivian is far from comic in any sense of that word. Others find a parallel between Tristram and the Irish Iseult on one hand, and Merlin and Vivian on the other, but at least one Arnold scholar admits that the analogy is inept.[2] Nothing but a consuming love unites Tristram and Merlin. In their *Commentary,* Tinker and Lowry even suggest a parallel between Iseult of Brittany and Merlin: both have been the victims of a "disastrous love."[3] Tinker and Lowry argue that the final episode of the poem may "be interpreted as her conscious, though indirect, presentation of her own case to Tristram's children" (p. 124).

In their reading, Tinker and Lowry emphasize the central role Iseult of Brittany plays in Arnold's poem. In the legend, as in Wagner, the usual heroine is Tristram's mistress, Ireland's Iseult, and the triangle involves her husband, King Mark of Cornwall. Iseult of Brittany plays but a minor role in the drama, a role that portrays her as a deceitful woman. Quite different is Arnold's triangle; according to G. Robert Stange, the "whole tendency of Arnold's treatment of the legend is toward a balanced opposition, a contrast between two kinds of women and two kinds of love, an issue which is not even suggested in earlier versions." Stange expresses surprise that through a startling "shift of emphasis Iseult of Brittany becomes the central figure of the poem" (p. 257). In fact, critics generally find themselves wondering whom the poem *is* about. It is divided according to the subtitles "Tristram," "Iseult of Ireland," and "Iseult of Brittany." I will argue with Paull F. Baum that from "beginning to end the poem is her poem, the Breton Iseult's."[4] But I will also offer an entirely new reading of the poem to explain the significance of Arnold's unique focus of interest.

Arnold's ***Tristram and Iseult*** portrays a young wife and mother who has spent her youth at stereotyped female tasks while the men she knew were occupied with more exciting pursuits. As she tends her dying husband in the dutiful fashion that would be expected of her, he, in turn, longs only for his mistress, who is herself bored with a tedious marriage. Moreover, in a Shelleyan fashion, Tristram expects his wife to accept calmly his passion for another. After he dies, she does continue to care for their children in a faultlessly maternal fashion, living an existence whose monotony and emptiness are described so emphatically that the description cannot possibly be read as a minor element in the poem. But here the narrative takes a surprising direction: the stoical, long-suffering wife has an extraordinarily rich fantasy life, one in which she reveals what the poet in another work calls the "buried life," a fantasy existence in which she can draw on a legend of her own country, the story of Merlin and Vivian, to project herself imaginatively into the role of her rival and conceive of a relationship in which she is the adventurous and dominating rather than passive and submissive partner. In short, Arnold's poem offers one of the most extraordinarily astute examples of female fantasy in nineteenth-century literature.

The basis for identifying Iseult of Brittany with Vivian exists in a source for Arnold's version of Merlin's tale, the essay by Villemarqué in the *Revue de Paris.*[5] Baum has analyzed this source in detail, but has failed to take up Villemarqué's depiction of the Druidesses who inhabit the Brittany forest in which legend has it that Merlin is buried. Vivian is one of these shape-changing fairies about whom Villemarqué has a great deal to say. A major theme in his discussion is of crucial importance to a reading of Arnold's ***Tristram***: the Druidesses of Brittany are very unhappy about their *inability to bear children.* Villemarqué refers to them as "ces vierges du druidisme, á qui une loi fatale refussait les noms de mére et d'épouse" (p. 55). For this reason, they frequently serve as nurses to other women's babies, for they are also the "bonnes fées auxquelles on voue les petits enfans, et qui veulent parfois leur servir de mére pour se consoler de ne pouvoir l'être" (p. 48). One of the longer stories about them that Villemarqué relates comes from a thirteenth-century manuscript, "Le Roman de Brun de la Montagne," and it is important because—as will be seen later in this essay—it describes one of these frustrated would-be mothers in details that Arnold would later employ to portray Iseult of Brittany, a real mother who could in her buried life imagine herself a Vivian. In the medieval tale, Butor de la Montagne decides to take his newborn infant to be blessed by the fairies. One of these is so taken with the child that she is not content merely to hold and bless it, relinquishing it as she must when the cock crows. The next day she arrives at the castle where the baby lives, and, claiming that she has lost her own child, begs to be allowed to serve as a nurse to the newborn. Villemarqué describes at some length her tender ministrations towards the child, whom she "baisa toujours en chantant" (p. 52), returning to her forest after he slept, but then only until she could once again return to offer him her attentions. Arnold plays a variation on this theme when the children of Iseult are asleep at night and their mother's imagination is free to roam in ways that are not revealed until she expresses her own visions of the forests of Brittany and the legendary lovers, Merlin and Vivian, who are associated with them.

In short, it is the thwarting of a Vivian's maternal instincts that Arnold read about in Villemarqué. Would it take much of an imaginative sleight of hand in an age that recognized only too ruefully the existence of "two voices" and "divided aims" to toss the coin and conversely imagine that a mother might be a frustrated Vivian? The shape-changing motif itself would sustain this double vision.

A proper Victorian wife could never openly confess to a secret longing to be Vivian. A clue to the response she might receive were she to reveal her buried life can be found in a note added to a later edition of another source for Arnold's poem, John C. Dunlop's *History of Fiction.* A footnote to Tristram's story records Robert Southey's dismay at learning that the Arthurian hero whom some legends praise is reported in others as an adulterer. Southey's moral disgust is reflected in his question, "Who could bear Desdemona represented as an adulteress?"[6] Who indeed! The question itself hints at buried longings that dare not be exposed to conscious awareness. Arnold would not have read this note, added to Dunlop more than forty years after his poem was written. Nevertheless, Southey's reaction remains interesting within the context of Arnold's poems. First, it recalls the passage in **"The Terrace at Berne"** in which the beautiful Marguerite is unaccountably depicted as a prostitute. Second, it reflects both the antithesis and the synthesis that exist in the Iseult of Brittany-Iseult of Ireland duality. (Was there ever a more Desdemona-like heroine than the Breton Iseult?) Was Arnold himself indulging in a common Victorian fantasy? For Southey's disgust also points to the popular (although now disputed) assumptions about Victorian female sexuality. Wives were expected to be uninterested in sex, and the innocence of young girls was assiduously guarded. Is it not possible, then, that part of the Victorian "buried life" could be described by a popular, if distasteful, saying that every man wants his wife to be a whore in bed, and that Iseult's projection of herself as Vivian represents a corresponding female fantasy?

Again, the desire to have a wife who behaved as a courtesan was hardly a wish that the well-bred Victorian man could admit to, and it is ironic that his projection of the wish on to her might be unwittingly accurate. The wife and the courtesan formed polar opposites, and as Peter Cominos expresses it, there was an "unbridgeable gulf formed between the chaste and the unchaste."[7] And yet the very denial of shared sexual impulses between the proper lady and her fallen sister is evidence that the idea had occurred to someone. In *The Other Victorians,* Steven Marcus quotes from William Acton that

> it is a delusion under which many a previously incontinent man suffers . . . to suppose that in newly married life he will be required to treat his wife as he used to treat his mistresses. It is not so in the case of

> any modest English woman. He need not fear that his wife will require the excitement, or in any respect imitate the ways of a courtezan.[8]

From this statement, one is hardly surprised to read further in Marcus that in Victorian pornography, wives as well as prostitutes are sexually excitable and active. The suppression of such an idea so that pornography becomes its only medium of expression is significant for a reading of ***Tristram and Iseult*** and an understanding of how Iseult of Brittany sees herself in Vivian. To quote from Cominos once more, in Victorian times "the respectable ideal of purity represented unadulterated femininity; her opposite represented the *projection* of those rejected and unacceptable desires and actions that must be destroyed to keep women pure beings."[9]

Sex is not the entire story. Many aspects of the proper Victorian wife's personality had to be repressed and her lack of freedom is reflected in the constrained life of Brittany's Iseult. It is ironic that the only essay given over to Mrs. Matthew Arnold (a corrective to the usual scholarly attention to the mysterious Marguerite), an article that purports to establish Arnold's contentment within his marriage, also reveals how many of her husband's needs Frances Lucy Arnold could not satisfy. In addition, the reader is left with the distinct impression that she was damned with faint praise: "Several contemporaries have left general one-sentence estimates of her."[10] It does not matter then whether Arnold's Marguerite was fact or fiction. Indeed, if she were but a figment of his imagination, as he claimed, all the more significant. No wonder Arnold was drawn in the Villemarqué essay to the motif of the shape-changing fairies, Vivians who also longed to be gentle mothers. And when he created in ***Tristram and Iseult*** a wife most critics think represents Mrs. Arnold, she was not one who stayed in the background, but was rather the center of his poem. In light of the conclusion of the poem, this seems less an homage to his marriage partner than a recognition of the implications of choosing a wife about whom no one cared to write more than one line. But in projecting his fantasy onto her, Arnold succeeded in providing an uncannily accurate depiction of female fantasy.

To read Part III of ***Tristram and Iseult*** as a projection of the Breton Iseult's fantasies has the virtue of clearing up the difficulties critics almost unanimously admit to in interpreting the poem. The remainder of this essay will undertake an exposition of ***Tristram*** that focuses both upon the organic relationship of Part III to the rest, specifically Part I, and the way in which Part III parallels Part I as it provides the contrast between Iseult's real life and her imagined existence as Vivian.

One of the links between the parts is the relationship of both the Tristram legend and the story of Merlin to Keats's "La Belle Dame sans Merci." In both Arnold and Keats an ailing knight is introduced with a similar question: "What Knight is this so weak and pale" (Arnold, 1. 9)[11] "Ah, what can ail thee knight at arms, / Alone and palely loitering" (Keats). The image of Keats's "wretched wight"[12] can be found in Tristram, who is called a "fever-wasted wight" (I. 107), and in the portraits of both Iseults, each of whom at some point in the poem is described as pale and wasted. More significant is the comparison between Iseult of Brittany, whose "looks are mild, her fingers slight" (I. 30), and Keats's fairy, whose "foot was light, / And . . . eyes were wild." Arnold has preserved Keats's rhyme while modifying his diction in a manner that will prove significant.

Despite the change of meaning, the contrast between Iseult's mildness and the fairy's wildness, the allusion to Keats's poem is but one of many. But the allusion does *not* make the seemingly logical connections, that is between La Belle Dame sans Merci and Iseult of Ireland, each a temptress who has lured the hero away from the world to which he belongs. Instead, Arnold has drawn his reader's attention—even if by way of contrast—to La Belle Dame and Iseult of Brittany, preparing the way for the conclusion of the poem, in which Tristram's wife imagines herself a temptress, a Vivian whose resemblance to the light foot of Keats's fairy lies in her freedom: "But she herself whither she will can rove—/ For she was passing weary of his love" (III. 223-224).

This developing identification between Iseult of Brittany and Keats's fairy is reinforced by a reading of Villemarqué's description of the Breton Druidesses (e.g. Vivian). Again, one would expect Arnold to pick up details from their portraits for his own of Tristram's mistress. But once again the reverse is true; it is his hero's wife who resembles them. According to Villemarqué, "leur peau était plus pure que neige; elles portaient de blanches robes de soie et des couronnes d'or" (p. 51). Arnold's depiction of Iseult of Brittany seems almost an expanded translation of this passage:

> What Lady is this, whose silk attire
> Gleams so rich in the light of the fire?
> The ringlets on her shoulders lying
> In their flitting lustre vying
> With the clasp of burnish'd gold
>
> . . . . .
>
> I know her by her mildness rare,
> Her snow-white hands, her golden hair;
> I know her by her rich silk dress.
>
> (I. 24-28, 50-52)

The Druidesses possess skin "plus pure que neige"; Iseult of Brittany is known in legend, Malory, and in Arnold's poem by her "snow-white hands." In both passages the ladies wear robes of silk; and in both instances, gold (crowns or clasps) adorn their persons. Now admittedly, white skin, silk robes, and gold ornament are hardly original to either Villemarqué or Arnold. Yet the poet has spent much time on the description of Iseult of Brittany's appearance, and very little on that of her rival. More crucial, if Vivian in Part III is to be linked with Iseult of Ireland, as she is by those critics who read the final story as an analogue to Tristram's fated love affair with his uncle's wife, then it is very strange that Arnold has gone out of his way to endow Tristram's wife rather than his mistress with Vivian's physical appearance. But in so doing, he prepares the way in Part I for her final fantasy, her vision of herself as the woman whose appearance she has possessed all along.

Other structural resemblances between Arnold's and Keats's poems illuminate Iseult's fantasy, for, as will be seen later, they help explain the meaning of her imagined transformation. One of the changes that Arnold made in Villemarqué's story of Merlin and Vivian brings his own poem still closer to Keats's. In Villemarqué, Merlin and Vivian are walking in a forest when she imprisons him. In ***Tristram and Iseult*** she is riding on horseback, a detail which again invokes Keats's analogue to the legendary Arthurian material. In both poems the man falls asleep with his enchantress, either to dream of thralldom or to wake up literally imprisoned. Finally, a recurrent image in ***Tristram*** evokes the concluding image of Keats's knight, who, awakened from his dream, wanders disconsolate about the scene of his tryst: "And this is why I sojourn here, / Alone and palely loitering." Arnold's Tristram, similarly "Thinn'd and paled before his time" (I. 108), is more than once portrayed as a sojourner—"Whither does he wander now?" (I. 189)—also searching for a lost love:

Ah! he wanders forth again;
We cannot keep him; now, as then,
There's a secret in his breast
Which will never let him rest.

(I. 243-246)

In summary, Keats's "La Belle Dame sans Merci" is reflected both in Parts I and III of ***Tristram,*** providing a link between the beginning and the end of the poem. But the significance of Arnold's borrowing from Keats does not stop here. Keats's ballad, and its many sources and analogues so popular in England, form a pattern into which ***Tristram and Iseult*** easily fits. The story of the man who leaves the world (and often a wife in it) to seek a more blissful existence with a supernatural mistress in her magic realm was commonly told in nineteenth-century Europe.[13] Such stories depicted man's dilemma in being torn between mundane reality and a more carefree or more passionate existence. It was not unusual to conceive of his split psyche as embodied in two women (in this sense Arnold had ample precedent for his conception of the Tristram triangle), his wife representing the seemingly inferior part of himself:

There were two Iseults who did sway
Each her hour of Tristram's day;
But one possess'd his waning time,
The other his resplendent prime.

. . . . .

She is here who had his gloom,
Where art thou who hadst his bloom?

(I. 68-71, 76-77)

Arnold's contribution to this basic story in his time, however, is less obvious in ***Tristram and Iseult*** than it is in one of his most popular poems, **"The Forsaken Merman."** And it will be significant to note that in this well-known work, the protagonist is a woman. For Margaret there is no merging of reality with yearning imagination, but only an oscillation between the productive demands, not always unhappy, of her everyday existence on the one side, and the symbolic world of her musings on the other. During the day she spins and sings joyfully,

Till the spindle drops from her hand,
And the whizzing wheel stands still.
She steals to the window, and looks at the sand,
And over the sand at the sea;
And her eyes are set in a stare;
And anon there breaks a sigh,
And anon there drops a tear,
From a sorrow-clouded eye,
And a heart sorrow-laden,
A long, long sigh;
For the cold strange eyes of a little Mermaiden
And the gleam of her golden hair.

(ll. 96-107)

When, a few years later, Arnold depicted a similar scene in Part III of ***Tristram,*** its unique applicability to the life of women, rather than the plight of mankind in general, was emphasized. Iseult of Brittany, left alone to care for her children, peacefully if not joyfully fulfills the duties of each day. The embroidery she takes up each night has much in common with Margaret's spinning, and she too pauses or stops at times, although the exact cause of her distraction, other than concern for her children, is left deliberately vague:

and there she'll sit
Hour after hour, her gold curls sweeping it;
Lifting her soft-bent head only to mind
Her children, or to listen to the wind.
And when the clock peals midnight, she will move
Her work away, and let her fingers rove
Across the shaggy brows of Tristram's hound
Who lies, guarding her feet along the ground;
Or else she will fall musing, her blue eyes
Fixt, her slight hands clasp'd on her lap.

(III. 82-91)

It is ironic that Margaret, who has deserted her children in the otherworld, and Iseult, who is so irrevocably bound to hers in this, should enact so similar a routine. But the important question is raised only in ***Tristram:***

And is she happy? Does she see unmoved
The days in which she might have lived and loved
Slip without bringing bliss slowly away,
One after one, to-morrow like to-day?

(III. 64–67)

This question, and its relation to Arnold's choice of a female heroine in poems whose traditional conflicts are usually centered on a male figure, pick up added meaning from a very important influence on the poet, Homer. For behind the image of Margaret's weaving and Iseult's embroidery (there is also an image of a woman darning in **"The Scholar Gipsy"** and weaving is crucial to the Philomela story) stands the classical and archetypal figure of Penelope, the virtuous and faithful wife. She, in turn, easily becomes the ideal Victorian housewife as the latter has been recently described: "Sentiment's favorite domain in Victorian times was near the warm cozy hearth of the home where the wife, sweet, passive and long-suffering, waited patiently for the return of her husband."[14] Homer's epic bears a noteworthy relationship to Arnold's work as a whole, and to ***Tristram and Iseult*** in particular,[15] mainly because of the prominence in his poetry of the wanderer image. But as clear as it is in his poems that Odysseus was a more important symbol to Arnold than critics acknowledge,[16] so is it equally clear that "Penelope" was ordinarily to remain at home. His wanderers are invariably men, whether they are on long journeys, eternal quests, or short hunting trips.

"The Church of Brou" provides the typical example of the male-female relationship that forms the central conflict in ***Tristram and Iseult:***

> In the bright October morning
> Savoy's Duke had left his bride.
> From the castle, past the drawbridge,
> Flow'd the hunters' merry tide.
>
> Steeds are neighing, gallants glittering;
> Gay, her smiling lord to greet,
> From her mullion'd chamber-casement
> Smiles the Duchess Marguerite.
>
> (I. 5-12)

Even Iseult of Ireland leaves on her sea journey only when she is so commanded by her father or summoned by Tristram. In only three poems is a woman conceived of as a wanderer, and significantly in all three are joined the themes of her wandering and of illicit sexual passion. One instance has drawn much critical attention; it is, again, the puzzling treatment of Marguerite that is at issue:

> Or hast thou long since *wander'd* back,
> Daughter of France! to France, thy home;
> And flitted down the flowery track
> Where feet like thine too lightly come?
>
> (**"The Terrace at Berne,"** ll. 17-20; italics added)

In another instance, Philomela, victim rather than perpetrator of her eternal travels, is, like Odysseus, a "wanderer from a Grecian shore." It would not be going too far to say that Arnold's **"Philomela,"** with its theme of rape, incest, and infanticide, could be read as a nightmarish inversion of respectable Victorian domesticity. The horrendous outcome of the story was, moreover, the personal nightmare of a poet for whom stoic acceptance and quietude were a precious goal: eternal passion, eternal pain.

For a man to be an Odysseus was to be for Arnold immature, unsettled, alienated; and the famous letter he wrote to his sister shortly before he married makes clear that for him family life was a haven for a wandering spirit that threatened his stability, however reluctantly he might relinquish his freedom. But for a woman to be an Odysseus was far worse, especially since the respectable Victorian woman was raised not only to curb her own instincts, but ultimately to help her husband curb his. Hence it is significant that in Part III of ***Tristram and Iseult*** the substance of Iseult's fantasy lies not so much in her love affair, but in her freedom to end love affairs when she pleases—in short, in her freedom to wander, to abandon her role as Penelope, and to assume that of a female Odysseus.

In Part I of ***Tristram and Iseult*** the Odysseus-Penelope motif is worked out through the reiterated themes of Tristram's wandering and the steadfastness of Iseult of Brittany. His journeys are both actual and symbolic, as various time levels interact within this portion of the poem. The narrator describes not only the present scene in which a dying Tristram awaits his mistress, but presents as well the flashbacks in which the legend of Tristram and the two Iseults is recounted. At times the flashbacks and his memories merge to become one, and it is Tristram's wandering mind that we follow back through the years. His early and tranquil love for his "timid youthful bride" (I. 214) is described so that at first she seems less a Penelope than a Naussica:

> —Whither does he wander now?
> Haply in his dreams the wind
> Wafts him here, and lets him find
> The lovely orphan child again
> In her castle by the coast;
> The youngest, fairest chatelaine
> Whom this realm of France can boast
> Our snowdrop by the Atlantic sea,
> Iseult of Brittany.
>
> (I. 189-197)

Such memories of these early years soothe him in his feverish state, and the narrator encouragingly begs,

> Hither let him wander now;
> Hither, to the quiet hours
> Pass'd among these heaths of ours
> By the grey Atlantic sea;
> Hours, if not of ecstasy,
> From violent anguish surely free!
>
> (I. 228-233)

But this second best will not long content Tristram, and the lure of ecstasy causes him to "[wander] forth again," to follow the "secret in his breast / Which will never let him rest" (I. 243-246).

In contrast to Tristram's wandering,

> Thy lovely youthful wife grows pale
> Watching by the salt sea-tide
> With her children at her side

For the gleam of thy white sail.
Home, Tristram, to thy halls again!

(I. 269-273)

Her role as Penelope is one for which Brittany's Iseult has been trained since childhood. Once again the time sequence in the poem is deliberately blurred as youthful and adult reality merge while she sorrowfully hovers over her ill husband:

Is it that a deep fatigue
Hath come on her, a chilly fear,
Passing all her youthful hour
Spinning with her maidens here,
Listlessly through the window-bars
Gazing seawards many a league,
From her lonely shore-built tower,
While the knights are at the wars?
Or, perhaps, has her young heart
Felt already some deeper smart,
Of those that in secret the heart-strings rive
Leaving her sunk and pale, though fair?

(I. 37-48)

Of all the emotions in this poem of tragic passion, those of Brittany's Iseult remain the most complex, because they are the least specifically articulated. The passage is fraught with merely suggestive possibilities. First of all, it depicts a young woman trapped in her role, gazing "listlessly" through barred windows, her separation from the active life emphasized. In contrast, the men in her life are free to roam, to follow the adventures that war represented in the Arthurian tales. Second, the source of her fear is left deliberately vague. The imminent death of her husband revives emotions long familiar to her, associated with her maiden years and buried deep in her unconscious.

To repeat, it is the blurring of past and present that creates the mood of the passage, for the final impression is of a young woman experiencing deep emotional conflict that saps all vitality as she buries her secret desires. The nature of this conflict may have to do with the battle Cominos has described as perpetually ongoing in the personality of the Victorian lady as she "waged her battle between sensual desire and duty at an unconscious level." For respectable Victorians "'Innocence' or 'pure-mindedness' or 'inherent purity' was an exalted state of feminine consciousness, a state of unique deficiency or mindlessness in their daughters of that most elementary, but forbidden knowledge of their own sexuality" (pp. 156-157).

Innocence is probably the most emphasized characteristic of Iseult of Brittany in Part I. There is, again, the reference to Tristram's "timid youthful bride," with its unmistakable sexual implications. Her looks further emphasize her purity, the whiteness of her skin and hands an almost clichéd symbol. Also stressed is her youth; and she is named the "sweetest Christian soul alive." Moreover, her beauty is not such as would imply passion, but is rather the "fragile loveliness" of a "patient flower" or "snowdrop," an image of frigidity as well as delicacy (I. 49-55, 72). The asexual childishness that these descriptions imply is at one point in the poem made explicit: "Sweet flower! thy children's eyes / Are not more innocent than thine" (I. 325-326).

This juxtaposition of sexual innocence and motherhood would not have seemed at all unusual to the Victorian mind. William Acton wrote that the "best mothers, wives, and managers of households, know little or nothing of sexual indulgences. Love of home, children, and domestic duties are the only passions they feel" (Marcus, p. 31). In addition, Victorian man, trained to view his own fleshly desires as part of his lower nature, would depend upon his wife's innocence to help him conquer his animal instincts. Or so the scholarship on the subject tells us. But D. H. Lawrence, much of whose writing is directed against the remnants of Victorian sexual attitudes, has warned us to heed the tale and not the teller. What is noticeable in ***Tristram and Iseult*** is that Arnold depicts the effect of Iseult's purity in such a way that her innocence seems almost the wound from which Tristram is dying.

To pursue this subject it is necessary to quote more fully a passage partially quoted in another context:

There were two Iseults who did sway
Each her hour of Tristram's day;
But one possess'd his waning time,
The other his resplendent prime.
Behold her here, the patient flower,
Who possess'd his darker hour!
Iseult of the Snow-White Hand
Watches pale by Tristram's bed.
She is here who had his gloom
Where art thou who hadst his bloom?
One such kiss as those of yore
Might thy dying knight restore!

(I. 68-79)

The diction—"prime," "waning," "bloom," "restore"—suggests that what is at stake is actual sexual potency; Iseult of Ireland possessed Tristram's prime, his wife merely his waning time. And sexual potency is no less than a matter of life and death. Iseult of Brittany watches ineffectually by (not in) Tristram's bed as the life ebbs out of him. One might argue that this is the appropriate place for the wife of a sick man: at his bedside. But the poem suggests that the scene has another significance. The passion of a kiss from Ireland's Iseult might arouse enough energy in Tristram to save his life. Finally, then, innocence is death and only sexuality bestows life:

Does the love-draught work no more?
Art thou cold, or false, or dead,
Iseult of Ireland?

(I. 80-82)

The theme of impotence was explicitly presented by Dunlop in an appendix to the 1816 edition of his *History of Fiction* (too explicitly for the Philadelphia editors of the book, who omitted the passage in their 1842 edition). In the brief passage, a beautiful and even seductive Iseult lies asleep in the arms of her husband. He kisses her, but then memories of his mistress keep him from going any further:

> Tristan se couche avec Yseult sa femme. Le luminaire ardoit si cler, que Tristan pouvoit bien voir la beauté d'Yseult: elle avoit la bouche vermeille et tendre, yeux pers rians, les sourcils bruncs et bien assis, la face claire et vermeille comme une rose a l'aube du jour. Sy Tristan la baise et l'acolle; mais quante il lui souvient de Yseult de Cornouailles, sy à toute perdue la voulonté du surplus. Cette Yseult est devant lui, et l'autre est en Cornouailles qui lui defent que à l'autre Yseult ne fasse nul riens que a villeinie lui tourne. Ainsi demeure Tristan avec sa femme; et elle qui d'acoller et de baiser ne savoit riens, s'endort entre les bras de Tristan.
>
> ["Tristan lies down with Yseut, his wife. The light burned so clearly that Tristan could see Yseut's beauty: she had a red and tender mouth, merry blue eyes, brown and well-arched eyebrows, a face that was bright and pink like a rose at dawn. Tristan kisses and hugs her; but when he remembers Yseut of Cornwall, he lost all desire for lovemaking. This Yseut is before him, and the other is in Cornwall, who prevents him from doing anything to the other Yseut that might turn into vileness. Thus Tristan remains with his wife; and she, who knew nothing of hugging and kissing, falls asleep in Tristan's arms," I, 491.]

The passage weakens arguments, such as Stange's, that earlier versions of the Tristram and Iseult legend did not present a balanced contrast between two kinds of women and two kinds of love. In addition, the passage suggests that Arnold quite consciously altered his sources and that what is noticeably original in his version is the innocence of Brittany's Iseult, who—again—is pictured by but never in her husband's bed. What Arnold has depicted in this poem is the double tragedy, for man and for woman, of Victorian attitudes towards sexuality. For Iseult of Brittany, repressed desire is associated with the symbolic barred windows through which she can only gaze listlessly at a life closed to her forever. Her education and upbringing have fitted her for no tasks beyond motherhood, so that in Part III of the poem it is said of her unhappy existence that a "noisier life than this / She would find ill to bear, weak as she is" (III. 100-101). Critics have found in Tristram's wife an example of that stoic acceptance Arnold is supposed to have extolled, but it is impossible to applaud an acquiescence on her part to a life in which playing games with her children—that is, a perpetuation of her own childhood—is her only recreation.

On the other side, her husband has also been victimized by the assumptions that governed her life, his own sexuality being thwarted by the role he is forced to play with respect to his wife. The Tristram legend embodied within it not only the dualism between duty and love, but a social system which in Victorian England created polar opposites in woman, the one side denied the desires that were in reaction projected so emphatically on to her opposite that she could be conceived of as a diabolical temptress.

The dichotomization of women into the Eve and Mary prototypes is hardly unique to Victorian times. But something new had been added: the century was particularly aware of the existence of two voices. They were, for Arnold, the cause of "this strange disease of modern life, / With its sick hurry, its divided aims" (**"The Scholar Gipsy,"** ll. 203-204). His desire for unity in such a world is reflected in much of his prose writing as well as his poetry. It is a desire particularly noteworthy in ***Tristram and Iseult*** because of lines that do not appear in the final version of the poem in a passage he obviously had some difficulty with. In Part II, after Iseult of Ireland has come to Tristram's side too late to save his life, he asks her to approach his wife and request that she, Iseult of Ireland, be allowed to stay at his side. Counting on the obedience as well as the goodness of his wife, he orders, "Say, I will'd so, that thou stay beside me" (II. 95). Two other versions of this line, however, suggest a quite different meaning: "Say I charg'd her, that ye live together. / Say, I charg'd thee, that thou stay beside her" (p. 145n). What has finally been discarded depicts the strong desire that somehow a union be established between the two Iseults. Why did Arnold reject this conception? Of course, one can only speculate. The rejected lines do have a Shelleyan ring which might have led Arnold's audience to unfortunate conclusions. Even a relatively modern, enlightened reader probably finds it difficult to read the Romantic poet's letter to his first wife, in which he asks Harriet to come and live with him and Mary as their sister, without thinking that Shelley was insensitive, mad, or both. To expect your wife and mistress to live in harmony and become friends is asking, for most people in any event, too much. Yet the request is highly significant, for it reflects the yearning on the part of the man that somehow his life might be fulfilled if only he could find one who combined the qualities of both wife and mistress, who thus might allow him a deeper satisfaction than life had bestowed by forcing him to choose between them.

What is striking in ***Tristram and Iseult*** is that Tristram's dying wish, that somehow wife and mistress would unite as one, is fulfilled after his death through his wife's own fantasy. Pragmatically, she is the only one left alive in the poem to satisfy his wishes and is specifically referred to as the "young surviving Iseult" (III. 5). But this pragmatism has happy dramatic results for the poem: the dream of a temptress to be a mother, as was the case in the stories recounted by Villemarqué, is nowhere near as enthralling to the reader as the dream of a mother to be a temptress. In addition, a "fallen" woman can quite openly and consciously long to be a respectable member of society, since her very dream would thus suggest a conscience at least potentially pure. The contrary is not true. The desire of a "good" woman to lead the life of her counterpart involves feelings that must be so deeply repressed that they surface only through unconscious fantasy.

Cominos writes of the repressed Victorian woman that she "became subject to motives and desires of which she was not aware. . . . Repressed Victorian sexuality reasserted itself in indirect ways in the symbolic disguises of dreams and fantasies and in the symptoms of commissions wherein acts alien to the actors themselves were carried out" (p. 164). One of the resultant patterns of behavior that Cominos emphasizes is what he calls the "urge towards domination," which is a reaction against the usual submissiveness and passivity experienced by the Victorian woman. Interestingly, there are two themes in Part III of ***Tristram and Iseult,*** particularly in the Merlin and Vivian story: one of these has to do with freedom; the other, quite explicitly, with Vivian's domination and control over Merlin, he becoming literally her prisoner.

The beginning of Part III of ***Tristram*** establishes a crucial context for the tale of Merlin and Vivian, a tale not actually told until the climax and end of the poem. A seemingly unimportant change that Arnold made in an earlier conception of the poem is significant. Originally the wording of the fifth and sixth lines was a description of how "one bright day, / Drew Iseult forth" to play with her children out of doors. The revision of what can be found in the Yale manuscript of the first sixty-three lines of Part III establishes Iseult as one of Arnold's rare female wanderers: "The young surviving Iseult, one bright day, / Had wandered forth. Her children were at play" (III. 5-6). Now it has been noted that when Arnold's women explicitly "wander," as in the case of Marguerite or Philomela, they do so within the negative context of illicit sexual passion, unsettled lives, and alienation. If Tristram's wife were merely on an aimless walk now, Arnold would probably have chosen another word to describe her sojourn. That Iseult "wandered" forth now suggests her uneasy state of mind and Arnold's commentary on a potentially dangerous mood. It is at this point that she calls her children to her to narrate "an old-world Breton history" (III. 37).

There are two noteworthy aspects to the telling itself. First, the story elicits from the children a reaction that is vague enough to create some ambiguity as to what Arnold intended:

> From Iseult's lips the unbroken story flow'd,
> And still the children listen'd, their blue eyes
> Fix'd on their mother's face in wide surprise
>
> . . . . .
>
> And they would still have listen'd, till dark night
> Came keen and chill down on the heather bright.
>
> (III. 45-47, 50-57)

What is it that has so surprised the children? Merely the story of Merlin and Vivian? Unlikely, for children are with ease able to suspend their disbelief in a world of fairy tales. Their "wide surprise" may more likely be attributed to their having caught something of their mother's uncharacteristic mood; they may be reacting, that is, more to the teller than to the tale.

Significantly, the story itself is told in motion, Iseult wandering with her children, although on safely warm, dry roads. But reality eventually beckons:

> when the red glow on the sea grew cold,
> And the grey turrets of the castle old
> Look'd sternly through the frosty evening-air
> Then Iseult took by the hand those children fair,
> And brought her tale to an end, and found the path,
> And led them home over the darkening heath.
>
> (III. 58-63)

The end of the yet untold (for the reader) tale coincides with the journey homewards, with Iseult's abandonment of her wanderer role and her assumption once more of her role as mother providing the safety of a home that "look'd sternly" at her to remind her of her responsibilities.

Once home, mother and child-woman again merge to become one; no longer free to wander, Iseult

> moves slow; her voice alone
> Hath yet an *infantine* and silver tone,
> But even that comes languidly; in truth,
> She seems one *dying in a mask of youth*
> And now she will go home, and softly lay
> Her laughing children in their beds, and play
> Awhile with them before they sleep.
>
> (III. 72-78, italics added)

But there is a crucial difference between the once-child and the still child-woman. She is no longer really innocent; it is clear that she has crossed the line into the realm of experience, her voice alone retaining its "infantine and silver tone." Marriage to Tristram, suffering his passion for another, her *experience* with sexuality and motherhood have to have awakened in her some of those buried impulses that made her maidenhood trapped and languid. And thus it is not really true, as the poem says, that the stories she tells her children mean for her now what they may have meant when, a child, she learned them. Her innocence is indeed but a "mask of youth," a lie perpetrated to keep her imprisoned in her status as child-woman:

> the tales
> With which this day the children she beguiled
> She gleaned from Breton grandames, when a child,
> In every hut along this sea-coast wild.
> She herself loves them still, and, when they are told,
> Can forget all to hear them as of old.
>
> (III. 106-111)

As of old? Only so if one can attribute special meaning to the "Breton grandames." Such figures play a significantly ambiguous role in the literature Arnold would have known. For example, the influence on ***Tristram*** of Keats's "The Eve of St. Agnes" has been noted by some critics, although restricted to the pictorial imagery in the poem, especially the description of the tapestry in Part II. In Keats's poem, Angela, intended to protect Madeline's purity, actually cooperates in the young virgin's seduction by Porphyro. Angela is modeled on the nurse in *Romeo and Juliet,* who similarly cooperates with Romeo and his designs on Juliet. Shakespeare's nurse, in turn, is thought by some to be modeled on Chaucer's Wife of Bath, a woman of unrestrained sexual impulses, whose main target for abuse is a treatise extolling virginity. Angela, Juliet's nurse, and the

Wife of Bath all have stood on end the role each would have been expected to play as the experienced guardians of young women's chastity, just as the fallen woman would be seen as the resultant counterpart of unguarded innocence, seduced unawares.

Therefore it is possible that Iseult of Brittany, hearing the story of Merlin and Vivian from Breton grandames, might have been made aware all along of the sexual implications of the tale. If so, then her education has not been entirely pure, and her fantasy life may have been fed from the outset by the legends of her country, legends whose meaning she has recognized from the start.

The tale of Merlin and Vivian itself forms a striking contrast with the description of Iseult of Brittany in Part I of ***Tristram.*** Whereas Iseult stares listlessly out of barred windows while the men of her court are at war, Vivian travels with Merlin, the two of them wanderers together. He is on foot and she is on horseback, but lest it be thought that the difference suggests her helplessness, to which he is chivalrously deferring, a special point is made of how, after he suggests a resting place, she "Nodded, and tied her palfrey to a tree" (III. 212). Her control of her own horse, her independence in action, prepare the way for her final imprisonment of him. Vivian, of course, has won her dominance over Merlin through typically feminine beauty and wiles, and that "he grew fond, and eager to obey / His mistress, use her empire as she may" (III. 183-184), does not imply more than that the battle of the sexes involves inequality from the outset. Cominos points out that "in the Victorian battle of the sexes, women were disarmed of the weapon of their sexuality" (p. 163). Not so Vivian, and her passive assent to Merlin at this point in the poem seems but a pose intended to disarm him.

The next section of the passage is properly demure, less suggestive, for example, than the corresponding section of "La Belle Dame sans Merci," where, to the extent that Keats could make it clear, the sleep of his knight follows upon sexual satisfaction. Merlin's deep sleep is not so explicitly described, although a reference is made to Vivian's "sleeping lover" (III. 218). What thereupon ensues is an incantatory description of Vivian's spell, in lines evocative of the magic conclusion to "Kubla Khan":

> Nine times she waves the fluttering wimple round,
> And made a little plot of magic ground.
> And in that daisied circle, as men say,
> Is Merlin prisoner till the judgment-day.
>
> (III. 219-222)

The final lines in this episode are also the climactic lines of the entire poem: "But she herself whither she will can rove—/ For she was passing weary of his love" (III. 223-224).

And this is the story Iseult of Brittany told her children, as she wandered with them from their home, which finally beckoned her with stern reminders of duty and responsibility. It is a story in which the contrasts to her own life are clear. She is bound in her role as Penelope. She was so bound in her youth, yearning after the adventuring heroes she knew; she was so bound in her marriage, waiting on her homebound shore for Tristram's sails to appear; and she is so bound now in an existence where every day will be "To-day's exact repeated effigy" (III. 95). Is it any wonder that she is drawn by a tale of one who "whither she will can rove"? Moreover, she has been the passive partner in her love relationship, suffering a martyr's role, expected even to tolerate her husband's love for another. Vivian, in contrast, chooses her lovers as she will, discarding them as she pleases, for it is she who dominates in her affairs with men. She is also sexually free, her travels with her lover an expression of desires she has no need to repress, her role as a temptress one in which she has no need or inclination to deny her sexuality. As Cominos writes, women in Victorian England "were either sexless ministering angels or sensuously oversexed temptresses of the devil" (p. 167). In Iseult's fantasy, the imprisonment of Merlin by such a temptress is no less than the revenge exacted by the ministering angel whose enforced asexuality was, again, symbolically represented by her own prison, the barred windows by which she was constrained.

It has already been suggested that Arnold may have projected upon Iseult of Brittany Victorian man's forbidden desire for synthesis, his wish that his wife share the attributes of his mistress (real or imagined), an idea vehemently denied in such popular works as Acton's. This psychological mechanism has been made part of the theory involved in a recent anthropological study of "Gypsy Women: Models in Conflict"—a study that bears comparison to ***Tristram and Iseult*** because the Carmen-Micaela dichotomy that arises from myths of the gypsy woman as temptress corresponds to the motif of the two Iseults. Bizet's librettist and Arnold were working out the same pattern. But the reality, notes Judith Okely, is that gypsy women are in fact bound by sexual codes more stringent than women outside their group, and she argues that each woman projects upon the other characteristics her own culture insists be repressed. Okely's depiction of this interrelationship between gypsy and female outsider corresponds to the interrelationship between the fairies of Brittany who long for the motherhood denied them, while mothers constrained by domestic duties long for the life of the footloose Vivian. In addition, Okely extends this mutual projection to relations between the sexes, and what she has to say may illuminate the division that took place in Arnold's poem and in his age as women were divided into the mutually incompatible temptress and angel: "Just as men may be dissatisfied by the ideal woman and ideal role they have created for themselves, so may women be troubled by alternative images and tendencies within themselves. Both men and women protect themselves by giving these tendencies, oversimplified, to an alien people."[17]

The battle of the sexes, as Cominos has described its manifestation in Victorian culture, does divide men and women, husband and wife, into alien camps. Yet, Arnold's depiction of the fantasy life of Brittany's Iseult is too astute and too sympathetic to be only a projection on to her of his own forbidden impulses. It is, however, difficult to speculate about what might account for this unusual insight into the female psyche. Arnold was extremely circumspect about his personal life, and if ***Tristram and Iseult*** does reveal some of his conflicts about married life, he would have endeavored to bury the clues as well as the feelings. In addition, Arnold did not write on the question of woman's role in society. Thus one can only be tentative about the source of the poet's insight into woman's repressed fantasies.

A. Dwight Culler has provided a source of help in his study of "Monodrama and the Dramatic Monologue," for although Arnold's poem does not fit perfectly the genres Culler is studying, ***Tristram*** can nevertheless be viewed in the same context. As Culler writes,

> One may say that there arose in the decades immediately before and after the turn of the century several related art forms that focused on a solitary figure, most frequently a woman, who expressed through speech, music, costume, and gesture the shifting movements of her soul. That the figure was solitary and that virtually the entire text consisted of her utterance was evidence of an attempt to focus on her subjectivity; that she was feminine was a further indication that the drama was one of passion.[18]

Two points about the classical tradition behind many of these monodramas are significant here. First, figures from ancient literature who served as models for such treatments of feminine passion were often deserted or betrayed women—Œnone and Dido, for example. Second, Culler has noted the part that the prosopopoeia played in the education of students during this period. As part of their training in rhetoric, they wrote speeches in which they took the part of persons not themselves (and, presumably, frequently quite alien to themselves) whose feelings they were nevertheless encouraged to depict and whose cause they were to plead. From these points alone one could partially account for Arnold's portrait of Iseult of Brittany and for his attempts to reconstruct sympathetically her emotions as a betrayed wife. In addition, "passion" was Arnold's theme in ***Tristram*** much as it was the theme of the monodrama:

> And yet, I swear, it angers me to see
> How this fool passion gulls men potently;
> Being, in truth, but a diseased unrest,
> And an unnatural overheat at best.
>
> (III. 133-136)

This passage is, however, puzzling. What, specifically, is the source of the passion from which Arnold's narrator is recoiling? Has it to do with the illicit love of Tristram, which is about to be recounted through Merlin and his enthrallment by Vivian? Or, perhaps, is the passion Iseult's, a temporary welling up of strong feelings which, were they to find no utterance, would result in her failure to achieve the quietism Arnold seems to have advocated?

For there is one other possibility that can be explored to show that Arnold might have recognized (as the result of personal experience or imaginative projection) and even sympathized with the repressed desires of women to live existences quite different from the ones allowed them, but that this recognition and sympathy do not necessarily imply approval. One of the functions of storytelling is to supply the medium through which emotions otherwise forbidden can find outlet. This compensatory feature of the narrative has in recent years drawn the attention of folklorists who try to determine what role folktales play in the societies that retain them as part of their culture. One theory, propounded by anthropologist J. L. Fischer, is that it is in the best interests of a society to allow its people some outlet for the tensions built up in the conflict between personal desires and the "demands of other members of the society that the individual pursue his personal goals only in ways which will also contribute to, or at least not greatly harm, the welfare of the society."[19] There is evidence in ***Tristram and Iseult*** that Iseult's final story serves the function that many folklorists attribute to the folktale.

The articulation of her repressed fantasies by Iseult of Brittany through the story of Merlin and Vivian does not, in fact, come in the poem until the reader has some assurance that all is well with the teller and with her family. Nothing specific about Iseult's inner-life is at first known except that it is allowed to surface only after her children have been put to sleep each night. The reader nevertheless learns from the outset that Iseult has told them a story and that she "brought her tale to an end, and found the path, / And led them home over the darkening heath" (III. 63-64). Having been assured that some disequilibrium expressed earlier through Arnold's use of the wanderer image has been restored, the reader then learns the source of Iseult's tension through Arnold's poignant description of her bleak day-to-day existence. And then—only then—the story itself is told, with its final climactic protest. But Iseult's fantasy life has already been rendered harmless, for Arnold has established for the reader, as well as for himself, that the status quo has remained undisturbed. It is perhaps within the haven of this security that Arnold can retain enough sympathy for his heroine to allow himself to explore her buried life, creating as a result one of the most sympathetic, insightful portraits of female dependency and resultant fantasy to come to us from his age.

Notes

1. G. Robert Stange, *Matthew Arnold: The Poet as Humanist* (Princeton Univ. Press, 1967), p. 254.
2. Howard W. Fulweiler, *Letters from the Darkling Plain: Language and the Grounds of Knowledge in the Poetry of Arnold and Hopkins* (Univ. of Missouri Press, 1972), p. 77.
3. C. B. Tinker and H. F. Lowry, *The Poetry of Matthew Arnold: A Commentary* (Oxford Univ. Press, 1940), p. 124.

4. *Ten Studies in the Poetry of Matthew Arnold* (Duke Univ. Press, 1985), p. 39.
5. Theodore de la Villemarqué, "Visite au Tombeau de Merlin," *Revue de Paris,* 41 (1837), 45-62.
6. (London, 1888), I, 207.
7. "Innocent Femina Sensualis in Unconscious Conflict," in *Suffer and Be Still: Women in the Victorian Age,* ed. Martha Vicinus (Indiana Univ. Press, 1972), p. 166.
8. (New York, 1966), p. 29.
9. "Innocent Femina," p. 168. Cominos' views have been disputed by Carl Degler in "What Ought to Be and What Was: Women's Sexuality in the Nineteenth Century," *The American Historical Review,* 79 (1974), 1477. For the purposes of this essay, however, the controversy is not important; as I will try to show, Arnold's poem seems almost an illustration of Cominos' essay.
10. Patrick J. McCarthy, "Mrs. Matthew Arnold," *TSLL* [*Texas Studies in Literature and Language: A Journal of the Humanities*], 12 (1971), 647.
11. Citations are to *The Poems of Matthew Arnold,* ed. C. B. Tinker and H. F. Lowry (Oxford Univ. Press, 1963).
12. Arnold could have known Keats's other version of line 1.
13. Lionel Trilling is only one of the critics who have pointed out, for instance, that Arnold was probably familiar with the popular tale of *Undine. Major British Writers,* ed. G. B. Harrison (New York, 1959), II, 597.
14. Helene E. Roberts, "Marriage, Redundancy or Sin: The Painter's View of Women in the First Twenty-Five Years of Victoria's Reign," *Suffer and Be Still,* p. 48.
15. To argue for the importance of the *Odyssey* in Arnold's poems is counter to prevailing scholarly opinion. Warren D. Anderson contrasts Arnold with Joyce, citing Arnold's Oxford lectures to prove that Arnold "ignored" this particular Homeric work. See *Matthew Arnold and the Classical Tradition* (Univ. of Michigan Press, 1965), pp. 89-90. Also see Ellen S. Gahtan, "'Nor help for pain': Matthew Arnold and Sophocles' *Philoctetes,*" *VN* [*Victorian Newsletter*], No. 48 (Fall. 1975), pp. 21-26. The resemblance between the Philoctetes and Tristram stories is striking; in the former, Odysseus plays a major role and may have contributed to some of the motifs in *Tristram and Iseult.* Arnold was sensitive to any comparisons between himself and Tennyson, and for this reason he might have muted the obvious evidence for the influence on his own poetry of Odysseus' wanderings. For evidence of this sensitivity see the *Letters of Matthew Arnold 1848-1888,* ed. George W. E. Russell (New York, 1896) I. 375: "I am rather troubled to find that Tennyson is at work on a subject, the story of the Latin poet Lucretius, which I have been occupied with for some twenty years."
16. Subtle identifications between himself and Odysseus can be found in the letters. One of these can be seen in the famous letter to his sister in which he describes the "aimless and unsettled" nature of youth, which for him threatens a gulf across which he fears he may never again be able to have close personal contact with his family. He intends to fight these tendencies within himself that isolate him from those he loves, although to leave the freedom of youth "is a melancholy passage from which we emerge shorn of so many beams that we are almost tempted to quarrel with the law of nature which imposes it on us" (*Letters,* I, 17). The sea journey here is but a metaphor for his state of mind; in another letter he writes to his wife that he is on his way home from one of the journeys his work as school inspector has necessitated: "My face is now set steadily homewards," he writes his Penelope, "Chamouni, Geneva, Dijon, Paris, London, Fox How. Kiss my darling little boys for me" (*Letters,* I, 86). Years later, in another letter to his sister, he reveals that these business trips hardly satisfied his wanderer impulses: "Much as I could have desired to see Greece, too, and the East, I know that my time is not yet come" (*Letters,* 1, 230).
17. In *Perceiving Women* (London, 1975), p. 79.
18. *PMLA* [Publications of the Modern Language Association of America], 90 (1975), 375.
19. "The Sociopsychological Analysis of Folktales," *Current Anthropology,* 4 (1963), 259.

David G. Riede (essay date 1988)

SOURCE: "Love Poetry: Sincerity and Subversive Voices," in *Matthew Arnold and the Betrayal of Language,* University Press of Virginia, 1988, pp. 163-203.

[*In the following essay, Riede discusses Arnold's love poetry and his frustration with the inadequacy of human speech.*]

The conventions and consolatory purposes of elegy put enormous pressure on poetic language to say the utmost that can be said about life, death, and the hereafter. Indeed, elegy tempts the poet to say more than can be justly said, excuses the flattering fictions and the consoling lie. Similarly, love poetry involves sets of conventions that may tempt the poet to excess, to flattery, seductive deception of the beloved, and even self-deception. The love poem is, in one tradition, a tissue of transparent fictions, specious logic, and false spirituality designed seriously to woo or playfully to seduce—the beloved is a divinity, love is eternal, union is paradise. An important convention of love poetry, of course, is that both author and reader recognize and accept the hyperboles as pleasant fictions, exercises in troping on the simple idea of being in love. But the hyperbolic descriptions of love can be taken seriously as an attempt to express insatiable desire and aspiration, especially when no higher ideal than human love is to be found. Consequently, for many nineteenth-century writers, love comes to replace religious faith as the primary source of value and meaning in life. Agnostic poets eager to find and utter the largest possible truths about human life wrote a good deal of love poetry in the nineteenth century, attempting to use the old conventions with a new earnestness and sincerity, attempting in love poetry even more than in the elegy to utter absolute truth, to communicate genuinely in language. Without a divine word to order the phenomenal world and give its expression meaning, Byron, Shelley, and Keats among the romantics, and Swinburne, Rossetti, and Arnold among the Victorians persistently attempted to look within, to read the language of the heart. Shelley, in the brief essay "On Love," described love in part as a desire that one's language be precisely understood, that one be able to escape isolation in the self by perfect communion with another human being.

Other Victorian poets were more obviously love poets than Arnold was, but for none was it so absolutely clear that love presented the ultimate challenge to sincere self-expression. **"The Buried Life"** is from beginning to end concerned with whether "even lovers" can "reveal / To one another what indeed they feel" (ll. 14-15), and the poems of the **"Switzerland"** series examine the possibilities of escaping isolation within the self through passionate love. But over and over again the poems arrive at the conclusion that even love cannot enable the speaker to say what he means, to find an effective—let alone a magical or definitive—language. As E. D. H. Johnson said, Arnold's love poetry makes clear "that in the modern world there no longer exists any channel for communication between one individual and another on the level of the deeper sensibilities. The impossibility of true love is thus emblematic of a general breakdown in human intercourse."[1] With the notable exception of **"Dover Beach,"** Arnold's best love poems are preoccupied with the failure of language to express honest feelings, to utter the most important truths of human relationships. But even beyond the thematic expression of the difficulty, the poems necessarily enact the failure of language that they only partially understand and describe—not because Arnold planned it that way, but because he was right in his sense of the incapacity of language, and especially of highly conventional poetic language, to express unmediated truth. That is, the poems cannot simply speak "from the heart"—to achieve any meaning or significance at all, they must refer to the whole Western discourse about love, must accept, reject, qualify, or in any case *respond* to prior utterances about love and the language of love. The poems are particularly interesting as studies in intertextuality because they so clearly seek to transcend discourse while engaging in it, a feat as impossible as picking oneself up by the seat of the trousers. Because they are, as poems, deliberately placed within a tradition of obviously artificial conventions, they of course make the effort to speak "naturally" all the more clearly futile. For this reason T. S. Eliot said that the proper language of love is prose, not the public and artificial language of poetry[2]—but of course Eliot was further than Arnold from the romantic notion that poetry is the natural language of the passions. Yet to be natural, poetic language must avoid its unavoidable conventionality. Robert Browning, faced with this difficulty, adopted the unusual idea that if the artist is to speak sincerely to his love, he must do so in a language of which he has not mastered the conventions:

> no artist lives and loves, that longs not
> Once and only once, and for one only,
> (Ah, the prize!) to find his love a language
> Fit and fair and simple and sufficient—
> Using nature that's an art to others,
> Not, this one time, art that's turned his nature.
>
> ("One Word More," ll. 59-64)

But a language that is "sufficient" (Arnold would have preferred "adequate") is not to be had—there are simply no words (or signs of any other kind) to denote the fine shades of individual feeling. And a language that is "simple" cannot be had, since to be comprehensible at all language must take its place in the increasingly complex discourse of a chaotic civilization. The poems of the **"Switzerland"** series, **"The Buried Life,"** and **"Dover Beach"** are all relatively short lyrics, and evidently less ambitious than ***Empedocles on Etna,*** or ***Sohrab and Rustum,*** or ***Merope,*** but they represent in its clearest and most urgent form Arnold's longing to find an authentic and authoritative language, and they demonstrate emphatically the impossibility of doing so.

"Switzerland"

Over the past quarter-century it has become critical standard practice to lament the inordinate amount of biographical criticism of Arnold's two series of love lyrics and to wish the poems could be treated as works of art. Critics complain that, for our understanding of the poems, it does not matter whether the "Marguerite" of the **"Switzerland"** poems was a real woman, let alone who she was, and that it similarly does not matter whether the five poems of **"Faded Leaves"** describe a crisis in Arnold's courtship of Frances Lucy Wightman. Perhaps now that the biographical events behind the poems have been somewhat sorted out in Park Honan's masterful biography, critics will no longer feel the need to scrutinize **"Switzerland"** for clues to Arnold's life.[3] Yet it is important to note that it *does* very much matter to our understanding of the poems whether Arnold was writing autobiography or was generating a fictive construct out of whole cloth. If we assume, as William Buckler does, that each poem is to be read on New Critical grounds, divorced from biographical considerations, we are likely to argue—as Buckler does—that the **"Switzerland"** series is a monodrama analogous to Tennyson's *Maud* and that "Arnold places at the center of this drama a hero so fallible that he brings to his lyrics the exacerbated stresses suggestive of a species of madness."[4] The interest of the poems in such a case, and Buckler draws this out very well, is in the controlled dramatization and analysis of certain morbid states of mind, and in the skill with which Arnold manipulates the ironic distance between author and speaker. It is assumed that the poet controls his language absolutely. But if the poems are at all self-analytical, as the biographical evidence strongly suggests, Arnold and his speaker are less easily disentangled, ironic distances diminish, and the gap between what is said and what the poet feels is a function of the "sad incompetence of human speech" not of controlled authorial detachment. The argument is not whether Arnold was a great poet who knew what he was doing or a poor one who could not handle his materials but whether the poems transcend the romantic ideology they dramatize or enact the entrapment within that ideology of a major poet. Reading the lyrics from a New Critical perspective that would have been alien to Arnold makes him seem a more "modern" poet but obscures our sense of the controlling personal, historical, and ideological pressures that frame and control his discourse. And among these was the belief, fostered by Wordsworth in particular and romanticism in general, that the poet should speak sincerely and from his own experience. Arnold shifted his ground on this point, but in 1848, not long before writing the **"Switzerland"** poems, he was praising Goethe (and, to a lesser extent, Wordsworth) for "his thorough sincerity—writing about nothing that he had not experienced."[5] The poems are best understood not as autonomous artifacts dislocated in time but as manifestations of how a particular mind at a particular historical time and place could enter the vast and complex Western discourse about love.

Nevertheless, Buckler is undoubtedly right to the extent that whatever autobiographical materials the poems may discuss, the finished **"Switzerland"** series is indisputably a work of art in which speaker and author cannot be simply identified. Transforming personal experience into art necessarily involves a certain aesthetic distance precisely because the personal and idiosyncratic must be rendered conventional in order to be understood. But it is important to realize that this need to conventionalize and so to falsify personal experience is not just a speaker's problem but Arnold's. Still, the poems do take their place within a well-established literary tradition of attempting to analyze and understand fundamental human problems through a series of love lyrics. In a general sense the tradition can be traced to the lyric sequences of the Italian *stilnovisti* or the sonnet sequences of the English Renaissance, though G. Robert Stange finds more immediate precedents in Wordsworth's "Lucy poems" and the German *Liedercyklus.*[6] As Stange and others have argued, Arnold's careful arrangement and rearrangement of the sequence make it clear that he was attempting to fuse them into an aesthetically satisfying whole, and not just to pour out his soul in heartfelt utterance, and this is yet more evidence that the speaker is not *simply* Arnold, but at most a tidied up, orderly, more conventionalized Arnold.[7] Still, there is no doubt that though the speaker is not precisely Arnold, his problems are profoundly Arnoldian, and chief among his problems is the impossibility of direct communication through efficient speech, the impossibility, in a sense, of Arnold's presenting himself as unequivocal, unadulterated, unmistakable Arnold.

Among the most fundamental Arnoldian difficulties, as we have repeatedly seen, is the ever-frustrated need to find an authoritative voice, a voice that can utter truth. Perhaps more conspicuously than anywhere else in Arnold's poetry, the feebleness and inadequacy of human speech is illustrated in the **"Switzerland"** series by the sudden intrusions of an infallible utterance from on high. In **"Meeting,"** for example, the speaker begins the poem, and the series, with calm self-assurance:

> Again I see my bliss at hand,
> The town, the lake are here;
> My Marguerite smiles upon the strand,
> Unaltered with the year.
>
> I know that graceful figure fair,
> That cheek of languid hue;
> I know that soft, enkerchiefed hair,
> And those sweet eyes of blue.

The tranquil tone is achieved partly by the very first word, "Again," which suggests the comfortable continuation of a smooth, continuous discourse (even without knowing what was before, the reader accepts as a poetic convention that there *is* a "before") and by the direct appeals to experience, "I see," and to certainty, "I know . . . I know." But as soon as contemplation gives way to action, a more authoritative voice breaks in to destroy the confidence of the earlier one:

> Again I spring to make my choice;
> Again in tones of ire
> I hear a God's tremendous voice:
> "Be counselled, and retire."
>
> (ll. 9-12)

Here as elsewhere in Arnold's poetry the voice of God rings hollow. It is not even really the voice of God but of a vague, unspecified divinity, "*a* God," and however "tremendous," it is utterly unconvincing except as a projection of the speaker's own latent reservations. Simply by representing an unconvincing voice of God the poem suggests that there is no genuine, authoritative voice but only the wish for one. Yet even this specious authority is enough to collapse the calm of the previous lines, and looking back at them we see how vulnerable they are. The appeal to experience, "I see," is unfounded—he *sees* Marguerite, but perhaps is indulging in an unfounded assumption when he translates this into the language of love: "I see my bliss." Bliss, to make the obvious point, cannot be seen. Further, the possessive, even proprietary "My Marguerite" and the implication that she is "unaltered" in affections as well as in appearance make unsupported claims about the relationship, and even the repetition of "I know . . . I know" turns out to assert no more than superficial recognition. Not surprisingly, the poem that began with the calm of simple indicative sentences ends with an open question to mysterious powers and an exclamatory plea for peace:

Ye guiding Powers who join and part,
What would ye have with me?
Ah, warn some more ambitious heart,
And let the peaceful be!

(ll. 13-16)

The poem, understood most simply, is about a sense of foreboding that erupts into a too complacent anticipation of bliss, but it is also the enactment of the eruption of one inadequate form of discourse into another to generate, in the final stanza, a rhetoric of nervous uncertainty.

It is too simple, however, to say that the mysterious "God" and the "guiding Powers" are simply metaphoric projections of the speaker's forebodings. In **"Human Life,"** which was never a part of the **"Switzerland"** series but was written at about the same time and involved similar concerns, the "guiding Powers" reappear as "some unknown Powers" (l. 26) that guide us, even against our will, to some predetermined end. These "Powers" do not simply "warn," but rule, and they deny us

The joys which were not for our use designed;
The friends to whom we had no natural right,
The homes that were not destined to be ours.

(ll. 28-30)

In the **"Switzerland"** poems, as is anticipated in **"Meeting,"** the "Powers" will eventually deny the speaker his beloved. In **"To Marguerite—Continued"** the "Powers" appear once again as "a God," not to warn, but to decree:

Who ordered, that their longing's fire
Should be, as soon as kindled, cooled?
Who renders vain their deep desire?—
A God, a God their severance ruled!
And bade betwixt their shores to be
The unplumbed, salt, estranging sea.

(ll. 19-24)

The authoritative presence of the God provides a concise explanation of human misery, but within the emotional context of the poems it even more clearly provides an excuse for the speaker's failure in love. Since all is destined and decreed, the individual is not responsible for his actions. If the love affair with Marguerite went wrong, it was not the speaker's fault—it just was not meant to be. The God is presented as an absolutely authoritative voice, but this voice emerges from the thoroughly questionable source of the speaker's psychological need for justification. Ultimately this God cannot be taken seriously as more than the wish for certainty, the wish for absolute dictates to explain and justify human behavior. Once again he is only "*a* God," asking to be understood as definitive but remaining vague and unconvincing. The more authoritative the discourse attempts to become, the more hollow it in fact becomes. The introduction of a mysterious God as an explanation of human suffering becomes a cheap and easy evasion—not transcendence—of the difficulties and uncertainties of unauthorized human discourse.

The evasions are, to be sure, the speaker's, and the speaker is not simply Arnold, so it would be wrong to conclude that Arnold in fact believed in "a God" as more than a metaphoric simplification of all the unknown, indescribable forces that obstruct human happiness. Nevertheless, the simplification is itself an evasion that enables Arnold as well as the speaker to make pithy, resonant, seemingly authoritative statements about the human condition. Yet this evasion is essential to the inner dramatic tension of both **"Meeting"** and **"To Marguerite—Continued."** The generation of transcendental terms from a cry of desire indicates the hollowness of those terms as the poems enact the development and dependence on essentially empty words. Also, the sheer desperation to find a definitive form of utterance demonstrates the perceived inadequacy of ordinary, referential speech. In **"Meeting"** the seemingly authoritative transcendental speech forced a reassessment of the seemingly empirical discourse that preceded it. In **"To Marguerite—Continued"** the "God" confirms rather than contradicts the preceding ideas about the inevitability of human isolation, but even so the evident need to introduce a new, supposedly more authoritative, mode of discourse implies that the preceding mode had been perceived as insufficiently authoritative. In both cases the juxtaposition of human utterance with purportedly divine truth results in a tension that calls into question the adequacy of *both* modes of speech.

The "divine" confirmation of human utterance at the end of **"To Marguerite—Continued"** is all the more remarkable since the poem begins—as the title implies—as a continuation and confirmation of a still earlier discourse. It begins, in fact, with an emphatic "Yes!" presumably in response to the preceding poem, **"Isolation. To Marguerite."**[8] The need for such doubly emphatic confirmation of the initial poem would seem to suggest a lack of confidence in it as an authoritative statement. As in the opening stanzas of **"Meeting,"** the discourse in **"Isolation"** is apparently based on empirical evidence, though in this case the poem analyzes experience more fully. The first two stanzas establish the "lesson" of the poem, and explain how it was learned:

We were apart; yet, day by day,
I bade my heart more constant be.
I bade it keep the world away,
And grow a home for only thee;
Nor feared but thy love likewise grew,
Like mine, each day, more tried, more true.

The fault was grave! I might have known,
What far too soon, alas! I learned—
The heart can bind itself alone,
And faith may oft be unreturned.
Self-swayed our feelings ebb and swell—
Thou lov'st no more;—Farewell! Farewell!

The diction and syntax are simple, straightforward, declarative. The speaker had been able to communicate with his own heart ("I bade my heart . . . I bade it . . .") but not with that of his beloved. He had presumptuously assumed a union of hearts, a sympathetic and corresponding constancy, but he has learned from experience that love is not always reciprocated, that love does not necessarily enable one to escape isolation in the self by communion with the beloved. The movement, from innocence to experience, naiveté to disillusionment, implies that the lesson learned and the discourse engaged in are based empirically. Cultural illusions about two hearts beating as one are jettisoned in the face of contradictory personal experience. But of course the empirical evidence is woefully insufficient, since the evident fact that the speaker's love is unreciprocated can hardly prove that love is *never* reciprocated, and the overblown romantic posturings that follow demonstrate that the speaker has not been chastened by experience, but seduced by another set of conventional cultural assumptions. Like Byron or Obermann, he bids a dramatic "Farewell!" to the world of deceived mortals and bids his "lonely heart" (l. 13) retreat: "Back to thy solitude again" (l. 18). Literary and cultural imitation, not unmediated experience of life, now informs the poem's language, and leads it even to what Buckler has called the "superbly literary moment" when the speaker compares himself to the mythically personified moon: "Back! with the conscious thrill of shame / Which Luna felt" (ll. 19-20) when she longingly gazed on Endymion.[9] The language of the poem, at first so simple, becomes increasingly inflated as the speaker justifies and magnifies his cosmic sorrow. The mythic interlude, rather like the eruption of a divine voice in other poems, indexes the speaker's dissatisfaction with a language based merely on experience, but it is almost irrelevant to his real situation. In the first place, Luna is described as moving *toward* love, not away from it, and in the second place, as the speaker soon recognizes, she can hardly be used as an analogy to his experience because she has never experienced human love. With this realization the speaker moves once more, with greater urgency, back to the empirical basis of his discourse:

> Yet she, chaste queen, had never proved
> How vain a thing is mortal love,
> Wandering in Heaven, far removed,
> But thou [his heart] hast long had place to prove
> This truth—to prove, and make thine own:
> "Thou hast been, shalt be, art, alone."
>
> (ll. 25-30)

The desire for *proof* is of course characteristic of Arnold's poetry, and here it is interestingly based on experiential evidence—but also on the ambiguity of the word *prove.* In the first line "proved" means "experienced" but in the next two uses "prove" equivocally means both "try" and "definitively confirm." The experiential evidence remains extremely limited, but the verbal quibble leads to an authoritatively stated, dogmatic maxim about human isolation. Empirical language has not described the way *things* are in life but has become enmeshed in ideological and cultural assumptions and in vacillating, uncertain meanings of words. Consequently, the seemingly definitive maxim does not hold up even for the duration of the poem but is immediately qualified: "Or, if not quite alone" (l. 31), he will have the company of nature and of those "happier men" who

> at least,
> Have *dreamed* two human hearts might blend
> In one, and were through faith released
> From isolation without end
> Prolonged; nor knew, although not less
> Alone than thou, their loneliness.
>
> (ll. 37-42)

The ending does not reverse the empirically grounded observation that all men are alone, but severely qualifies it. Even the speaker may have the "love, if love, of happier men" (l. 36), and others at least *seem* to escape their isolation. The speaker's assertion that they are lonely but do not know it seems almost absurd since one can hardly be said to *be* lonely but not *feel* lonely. The dream is dismissed as an illusion, but the illusion is most people's reality. And of course, the speaker's "reality," as we have seen, is at least as culturally determined as the "dream" of "happier men." Buckler is convinced that Arnold is manipulating a self-deluded speaker throughout this poem, and to an extent that is undoubtedly true, but the uncertainties about what is empirically verifiable and what is not are characteristically Arnoldian, and the fruitless attempt to achieve a clear, authoritative statement epitomizes Arnold's continual struggle for a univocal utterance.

The problem is even more obvious in another **"Switzerland"** poem, **"Parting,"** in which two different lyric forms and voices confront each other and eventually issue in yet a third. The poem is not exactly a dialogue of Arnold's mind with itself—it cannot be, because he is unable simply to express his mind. Rather it is a dialogue of different culturally determined voices. One is the voice of Sturm und Drang romanticism, as Byronism at its stormiest impels the speaker to seek the mountain solitudes:

> There the torrents drive upward
> Their rock-strangled hum;
> There the avalanche thunders
> The hoarse torrent dumb.
> —I come, O ye mountains!
> Ye torrents, I come!
>
> (ll. 29-34)

The next presents an ideal of gentle romance, the sweetly domestic charms of the angel in the house:

> But who is this, by the half-opened door,
> Whose figure casts a shadow on the floor?
> The sweet blue eyes—the soft ash-coloured hair—
> The cheeks that still their gentle paleness wear—
> The lovely lips, with their arch smile that tells
> The unconquered joy in which her spirit dwells—
> Ah! they bend nearer—
> Sweet lips, this way!
>
> (ll. 35-42)

And the final voice ultimately opts for the solitude of a Byron or Obermann, not by resolving the conflict between the prior perspectives, but by introducing the stern patriarchal tones of a puritanically repressive ideology:

To the lips, ah! of others
    Those lips have been pressed,
And others, ere I was,
    Were strained to that breast.

(ll. 67-70)

It is this fastidious sentiment that leads to the poem's sententious moral:

Far, far from each other
    Our spirits have grown;
And what heart knows another?
    Ah! who knows his own?

(ll. 71-74)

The rhetorical questions suggest the idea of isolation, estrangement from others and even from oneself, that dominates the **"Switzerland"** poems, but it has been unearned. More clearly than in **"Isolation. To Marguerite"** the lesson supposedly learned from experience in love is actually based on juxtaposed and unreconciled literary representations of stock romantic and Victorian attitudes. Yet the poem does demonstrate formally that the speaker does not know his own heart—it is self-ignorance that leads him into the various inadequate poses and patterns of speech. The disjunctive discourse can hardly be said to prove that true knowledge of ourselves or of others is impossible, but it dramatically enacts the plight of a mind divided against itself and unable even to differentiate between superficial, imitative posing and a "true" self. In strictly literary terms, the poem illustrates its entrapment within the inherited codes and conventions of poetic discourse—it can bounce among various forms of conventional discourse but cannot escape or transcend them. Of course the speaker is never simply Arnold, if only because the poet can never be simply himself. The failure of the poems to find a unified, coherent discourse is, in a sense, a measure of the poet's, or speaker's, creditable recognition that the "true" self, like the "best self" of Arnold's prose, is a merely hypothetical construct representative of the desire for an impossible wholeness. The incoherence of these love poems is movingly analogous to Arnold's recognition that consciousness itself is inevitably fragmented, that the various components of the self can never be fully grasped. Indeed, neither Arnold nor anyone else could ever succeed in accurately representing himself if only because, as Jacques Lacan argues, the attempt to construct the self verbally is paradoxically self-alienating: in the labor that one "undertakes to reconstruct *for another,* he rediscovers the fundamental alienation that made him construct it *like another,* and which has always destined it to be taken from him *by another.*" The danger of attempting to construct the self in language is that all that can be caught of the shifting complexities of consciousness would be an imaginary "objectification . . . of his static state or of his 'statue,' in a renewed status of his alienation."[10] Ironically, it is Arnold's failure to present such a neatly packaged self that saves the **"Switzerland"** poems—and **"The Buried Life"**—from suffering the fate of his inert attempts in classical form.

"Parting" and **"Isolation. To Marguerite"** both demonstrate the extreme difficulty of speaking of personal experience rather than writing variations on literary themes. **"To Marguerite—Continued"** is evidently intended to be read as a confirmation of the preceding poem's dictum that individuals are hopelessly alone, estranged from their fellows, but in demonstrating a need to bolster the argument it also demonstrates the perceived weakness of the empirical argument. Interestingly, **"To Marguerite—Continued"** completely abandons the appeal to personal experience and evolves a stronger, more resonant voice than the individual can muster by bolstering itself with countless echoes from the literary tradition. Kathleen Tillotson, who finds echoes of Horace, Lucretius, Donne, Coleridge, Thackeray, Keble, Carlyle, Browning, Collins, and Foscolo in the poem, has argued that the opening "Yes!" is not a reaffirmation of reality felt along the pulses but is, "finally, something like 'I know now the truth of what so many have written,'" and she argues that "some part of the poem's power consists in its waking of echoes from our reading, and that these also lay within Arnold's reading."[11] Similarly, Roper declares that the poem is characterized by an "imprecise allusiveness" so that "while no one gloss is especially pertinent, the whole complex of glosses—analogues, sources, allusions, reminiscences—greatly contributes to the almost majestic inevitability" of the work.[12] In some sense "imprecise allusiveness" is characteristic of every poem, since literature inevitably gains its significance by generalized intertextualized reference to the codes and conventions established in the entire body of literary work and, indeed, of language generally, but such poems as **"To Marguerite—Continued"** draw deliberate attention to the tradition by an ostentatiously literary allusiveness, by echoing literary images so familiar as to have almost become clichés.[13] In **"Isolation"** the most obviously "literary" exclamations, the Byronic posturings, tended accidentally to displace the speaker's direct experience, but in the opening of **"To Marguerite—Continued"** the speaker does not even try to describe individualized experience but fuses complex echoes of traditional voices to generalize about human experience:

Yes! in the sea of life enisled,
With echoing straits between us thrown,
Dotting the shoreless watery wild,
We mortal millions live *alone.*
The islands feel the enclasping flow,
And then their endless bounds they know.

Pointing out specific possible allusions would be redundant after Tillotson's essay, and would be almost beside the point, since the passage is characterized by "imprecise allusiveness" and no one citation can serve as a gloss or even a source—Arnold may or may not have had any of the possible sources in mind when he exploited the general tradition. But it is important to note, as Tillotson has, that Arnold's resonant statement is achieved by implicit refutation of some possible predecessors (Donne's "No man is an *Iland,*" for example), confirmation of others (most clearly Thackeray's "How lonely we are in the world! . . . you and I are but a pair of infinite isolations, with some fellow-islands a little more or less near to us"),[14] and qualification and variation of yet others. The contentious voices of his predecessors are subdued to Arnold's purposes and seem to speak univocally with the ponderous weight of the whole literary tradition. The passage epitomizes what Arnold later called the "grand style severe," which "comes from saying a thing with a kind of intense compression, or in an allusive, brief, almost haughty way, as if the poet's mind were charged with so many and such grave matters, that he would not deign to treat any one of them explicitly" (1:189).

Yet this near perfect blending of multitudinous voices seems somewhat to counter the stanza's premise—such grand concord contrasts with, or at least greatly qualifies, the prevailing idea that "We mortal millions live *alone,*" in total isolation. The description of "echoing straits between us thrown" reinforces the sense that the islands are not wholly desolate—like Prospero's, these islands are "full of noises, / Sounds and sweet airs that give delight and hurt not." The second stanza confirms the idea that human isolation is eased by communication in song, for on each island

> The nightingales divinely sing;
> And lovely notes, from shore to shore,
> Across the sounds and channels pour.
>
> (ll. 10-12)

The nightingale is among the most traditional of images for the solitary, grieving singer, but it is a symbol of the transmutation of pain to beauty, not of barren isolation. Arnold's own later **"Philomela,"** of course, makes use of the traditional and mythic symbol in this sense, and in **"To Marguerite"** the song is evidently itself a "balm," even a "divine" alleviation of mortal pain, and a form of communication among the scattered isles of human misery. The song of the nightingale, like the perfectly blended voices of the cultural inheritance, suggests that human beings must have some deep primal connection to one another, that once we were "Parts of a single continent!" (l. 16). In short, both the comprehensive allusiveness of Arnold's "grand style" and the symbolic implications of the traditional images imply that the lost human solidarity is recoverable.

The discourse that makes use of the tradition to find a language of plenitude tends toward the contradiction and refutation of the lone individual voice of **"Isolation"** as **"To Marguerite—Continued"** develops, but the blending of disparate voices into a univocal utterance may be perceived in a less reassuring way. One may, after all, perceive the hubbub and Babel of countless suppressed, misinterpreted, disagreeing individual utterances beneath the apparent serenity of the poem's unruffled surface—taking only the voices that make themselves most insistently heard, one can argue that Donne, Keble, Horace, Thackeray, and Carlyle can hardly be brought into agreement. The univocity of the grand style is, in this sense, an illusion brought about by ignoring, not reconciling, the vast and perhaps unbreachable differences among isolated individuals. The serenity disguises but does not wholly conceal the tensions brought about by conflating different ideologies, tensions that are most obviously and nakedly present in **"Isolation"** when the ideal of Byronic solitude is pitted against the ideal of blended human hearts. Further, the manifest reliance on intertextual echoes for resonance and a full range of implication may be seen as evidence that the poem can be no more than "conventional," and so cannot express the fully personal feelings of the speaker, who therefore is indeed isolated. The allusive method is strangely double-edged—it seems to break down the barriers between individuals, to draw all humanity together in a common voice and sentiment, but at the same time it seems to deny the possibility of simple self-expression. The pessimistic outlook is dominant in the poem, of course, since the evident loss of human solidarity results not in hope for reunion but only in a "longing like despair" (l. 13), an unsatisfiable desire to escape the confines of the self, to communicate with another human being.

The failure, ultimately, of the allusive style to provide a satisfying and definitive form of expression accounts for the sudden eruption of a God's voice into the poem. The ambiguity and ambivalence of merely mortal language is swept aside and replaced by divine fiat: "A God, a God their severance ruled!" But the God is an empty signifier, and his decrees are hollow, so his insertion at this point is only an index of the poet's "longing like despair" for a language that expresses truth. Taken together, the **"Switzerland"** poems epitomize Arnold's various efforts to find an authoritative voice. The personal voice of **"Parting"** and **"Isolation,"** speaking from the heart of anguished experience, can never be genuinely personal, and gives way to the fuller, more freely literary speech of **"To Marguerite—Continued."** Liberally drawing on traditional symbols and echoing past voices enabled Arnold to produce one of his greatest, weightiest, most apparently authoritative poems. But this lyrical grand style gives way, as the personal style of **"Meeting"** did, to an attempt at a still more authoritative speech when a divine decree, a voice of God, is introduced. The effect of bringing in what can only be an empty signifier for the agnostic is jarring not only because it is abrupt and unwarranted but because it shows a lack of confidence in the humanistic mode that would draw strength from the tradition. The various modes of discourse, then, do not reinforce one another, as would seem to be the design, but deconstruct one another, leaving Arnold without an effective language.

The highly allusive condensed style of **"To Marguerite—Continued"** would certainly seem to be Arnold's strongest and the best suited to his later ideas about the soothing and saving powers of the literary tradition. But one further example, from a mediocre poem, will reveal some of the dangers involved in awaking echoes of dead poets. In Arnold's first arrangement of "Marguerite" poems into a series for **"Switzerland"** (1853), the opening poem was **"To My Friends,"** which was later dropped from the series and retitled **"A Memory Picture."** The original title of the poem when it was first published in 1849, however, was **"To my Friends, who ridiculed a tender Leave-taking."** The original title suggests a specific biographical origin, and Honan's reconstruction indicates that the source of the poem was Arnold's romantic disappointment with Mary Claude ("Marguerite"), and his friends' mockery upon seeing the usually serene and supercilious dandy put down.[15] The epistolary title, moreover, suggests that the poem is a justification or a self-defense, that at least in a general way the poet is portraying himself in the speaker. The theme reinforces Arnold's projected image of a sophisticated young man, able to rise above even heartbreak—he has been wounded in love but wisely realizes that time erases all wounds and obliterates even the occasion of them, and so he attempts to sketch his beloved in verse in order to avoid forgetting her entirely. The cultured, poised stance is communicated by the poem's most notable feature, an allusive refrain that concludes all but one of the eight stanzas: "Ere the parting hour go by, / Quick, thy tablets, Memory!" The unmistakable allusion is to Hamlet, who sought his "tables" to set down the message of the Ghost. The speaker's reference to Hamlet, another superior man in disarray ("Th' observ'd of all observers, quite, quite down!") not only invites a flattering comparison but shows a cultivated mind solacing itself with the best that has been said and thought in the world. But the danger of awaking echoes is that they may stir an uncontrolled chain of associations by summoning their larger context. Hamlet's words are in response to a revelation from beyond the grave, a revelation that negates the easy wisdom to be had by a cultivated reading:

> Yea, from the table of my memory
> I'll wipe away all trivial fond records,
> All saws of books, all forms, all pressures past,
> That youth and observation copied there.
>
> (1.5.98-101)

What Arnold sets down on his tablets is a picture of a human countenance that transparently reveals the inner goodness of his beloved:

> Paint, with their impetuous stress
> Of inquiring tenderness,
> Those frank eyes, where deep I see
> An angelic gravity.
>
> (ll. 43-46)

But Hamlet records just the reverse: "My tables! Meet it is I set it down, / That one may smile, and smile, and be a villain" (1.5.107-8). The allusion superficially supported the self-image projected in Arnold's poem, but at a deeper level, in context, it flatly contradicts Arnold's premises and his stylistic recourse to "all saws of books." And as an extra fillip, the Shakespearean context is precisely about the untrustworthiness of the images people project.

It would seem highly unlikely that Arnold intended his allusion to be read as a subversive subtext, but it nevertheless sets up uncontrolled chains of association. All language has a life of its own in triggering endless series of associations, but Arnold's highly allusive language demonstrates with special force that attempts to channel those associations may lead to unexpected hazards. **"To My Friends"** is a slight poem and perhaps not too much should be made of it, but its evidently accidental generation of a subversive subtext provides a model with which to compare Arnold's most ambitious attempts to write wholly sincere love poetry in **"The Buried Life"** and **"Dover Beach."**

Sincerity and Buried Voices

"The Buried Life" and **"Dover Beach"** are Arnold's clearest and most earnest efforts to find an entirely sincere poetic language. Without the dramatic framework and romantic posturings of **"Switzerland,"** they present themselves as direct addresses from a speaker to his beloved. Indeed, the presence of such an auditor in the poems, as Dorothy Mermin points out, creates a situation "in which the speaker can speak absolutely freely" and unselfconsciously.[16] But his language, however sincere, is not unmediated utterance from the heart. Rather, as in **"Switzerland,"** it is highly allusive, mediated by other texts that are evidently meant to strengthen the language, to provide authority. The two poets most interestingly echoed in the poems, in fact, are Wordsworth and Milton, authors of sublime authority—Arnold had only half-jokingly written to Clough that "those who cannot read G[ree]k sh[ou]ld read nothing but Milton and parts of Wordsworth: the state should see to it."[17] Arnold's invocations of earlier poets, however, are often for the purpose of debunking them. His elegies, as Culler has argued, do not call the dead back to some form of life, but rather attempt to lay the spirits (Arnold once defined *spirit* as "influence" [6:290]) of the threateningly undead to deprive even the surviving words of their potency.[18] And as John Hollander and Harold Bloom have both noted in passing, Arnold's allusions and echoes frequently empty the predecessor's language of its meaning.[19] At their most extreme, Arnold's deflating allusions call into question the status of his own language, of poetic language generally; they generate uncontrolled intertextual reverberations and become subversive subtexts that undermine his ostensible purpose but add a deeper pathos to his poetry. They may constitute, in fact, a kind of demonic buried life beneath the surface stream of his diction.

Even more clearly than in **"Switzerland,"** Arnold's most ostentatiously allusive discourse in **"The Buried Life"** erupts into a discourse in which the speaker is evidently struggling for an austere, plain diction that can strip words down to pure denotation and so arrive at unadorned truth and avoid any illusions in love. **"The Buried Life"** is overtly concerned with the limitations of language from its opening lines:

Light flows our war of mocking words, and yet,
Behold, with tears mine eyes are wet!
I feel a nameless sadness o'er me roll.
Yes, yes, we know that we can jest,
We know, we know that we can smile!
But there's a something in this breast,
To which thy light words bring no rest,
And thy gay smiles no anodyne.
Give me thy hand, and hush awhile,
And turn those limpid eyes on mine,
And let me read there, love! thy inmost soul.

The speaker's dissatisfaction with "mocking words" is sufficiently evident in his injunction to his beloved to "hush." But the inefficacy of language is also enacted through a kind of imitative form in the presumably accidental bathos of "Behold, with tears mine eyes are wet!" and the reiterative assertions ("Yes, yes" and "we know . . . / We know, we know") that seem to protest too much. The problem is not in the levity of "light words" but in a general incapacity of language to name emotional states, to communicate feeling—the "sadness" is "nameless" and the language that states only what it can honestly name is able to state almost nothing: "But there's a something." The difficulty is that Arnold is seeking a language purged of metaphorical or connotative meanings as he attempts to describe not what the sadness, or the soul, or the something is *like* but what it *is*. Such a purely denotative language might describe an object as in itself it really is, might even describe an object that inspires a state of feeling (Wordsworth, in an analogous situation, had been able to say "But there's a Tree"),[20] but can hardly describe a feeling.

The speaker is quick to admit his failure, in a pair of rhetorical questions:

Alas! is even love too weak
To unlock the heart, and let it speak?
Are even lovers powerless to reveal
To one another what indeed they feel?

(ll. 12-15)

The questions signal a change in linguistic procedure formally as well as thematically precisely because they are rhetorical (they must be—as in **"Thyrsis"** the sole auditor, having been hushed, is not expected to reply). The figure of rhetoric as well as the sudden burst of metaphor—apparent in the personification of love, the lock on the heart, and the potentially speaking heart—both indicate that the speaker is willing to try a figurative language. Unfortunately the slightly mixed metaphor anticipates the considerable confusion that metaphoric language will encounter in this poem, and the section ends with an assertion that manages simultaneously to be a platitude, and to be unconvincing: "and yet / The same heart beats in every human breast!" (ll. 22-23). Ironically, the assertion would be hopelessly trite if it made sense within the context of the poem, but as Alice Stitelman has noted, it "contradicts the emphasis of all which has preceded it, and gains its emotional impact by standing as a desperate plea against the weight of the speaker's documented experience."[21] Or put another way, the statement, in the middle of a poem that is trying to establish a completely honest, sincere language, is effective precisely because it is untrue, a lie. Metaphoric language had led to an emotionally effective poetry, but only by betraying truth, or as the poem later puts it, it "Is eloquent, is well—but 'tis not true!" (l. 66).

The dubious assertion leads to the central metaphor of the poem, that of the "buried life," and significantly, the central metaphor, based on a lie, leads to a tangled web. In what follows it is not clear whether our hearts and voices are benumbed by a magical "spell" (ll. 24-25) or are enchained (ll. 26-27), and what we most assuredly cannot know is stated with absolute assurance: "that which seals them hath been deep-ordained!" (l. 29). As always, the ordinance is unauthored; the passive voice allows Arnold to avoid strict mention of a God's voice, but does not provide any other authoritative legislator. The horror of emotional and verbal incapacity is set forth as a boon:

Fate, which foresaw,
How frivolous a baby man would be—
By what distractions he would be possessed,
How he would pour himself in every strife,
And well-nigh change his own identity—
That it might keep from his capricious play
His genuine self, and force him to obey
Even in his own despite his being's law,
Bade through the deep recesses of our breast
The unregarded river of our life
Pursue with indiscernible flow its way;
And that we should not see
The buried stream, and seem to be
Eddying at large in blind uncertainty,
Though driving on with it eternally.

(ll. 30-44)

The cluttered syntax of this one long sentence, the numerous qualifications, the seven lines between the subject and the predicate, the clashing metaphors of the buried self and the river of life—all of this almost, but not quite, conceals the remarkable central statement: fate decreed that we should not know ourselves so that we cannot betray ourselves. My point, however, is not to sort through the tangle of these lines but only to note how the attempt at absolute honesty, apparent in the qualifications and explanations, leads not to an austere, plain diction and a lucid statement but to an absurd assertion uttered by a disembodied voice and couched in a language that approaches inarticulateness as its complex structures begin to collapse under their own weight.[22]

The poem does not, however, end with a bang as the tower of Babel collapses, but—and this is the important point—just as it approaches inarticulateness, it becomes densely allusive, and far more lucid:

But often, in the world's most crowded streets,
But often, in the din of strife,
There rises an unspeakable desire
After the knowledge of our buried life

(ll. 46-49)

The language unmistakably summons Wordsworth's "Tintern Abbey": "But oft, in lonely rooms, and 'mid the din / Of towns and cities"[23] and just a few lines later, the speaker's "longing to inquire / Into the mystery of this heart which beats" (ll. 51-52) may call to mind Wordsworth's famous phrase "the burthen of the mystery" in conjunction with his efforts to lift the burdens that "Have hung upon the beatings of my heart" (ll. 38, 54). Further, as the speaker listens carefully for some sound of his buried life, he hears strange resonances:

vague and forlorn,
From the soul's subterranean depth upborne
As from an infinitely distant land,
Come airs, and floating echoes, and convey
A melancholy into all our day.

(ll. 72-76)

The echoes are echoes of echoes, recollections of Wordsworthian recollections:

Those shadowy recollections,
Which, be they what they may,
Are yet the fountain-light of all our day.[24]

As in **"Isolation. To Marguerite,"** the allusiveness introduces a new, weightier level of discourse, and the authoritative presence of Wordsworth, especially, in the poem's subtext is at least initially reassuring. Wordsworth's experience would seem to confirm the possibility of easing "the burthen of the mystery" and, more, his reassuring resonance within the breast reveals that the buried life and language, especially poetic language, may not be incompatible after all. Also, Wordsworth is the poet best suited to help the speaker, for as Arnold stated in **"Memorial Verses,"** Wordsworth's "soothing voice" (l. 35) had the "healing power" (l. 63) to set free just such benumbed souls and enchained hearts:

He found us when the age had bound
Our souls in its benumbing round;
He spoke, and loosed our heart in tears.

(ll. 45-47)

Certainly with Wordsworth's "soothing voice" running in a deep subtextual stream, the surface currents of **"The Buried Life"** smooth out—the syntax becomes clear and the rhythms are no longer tortuous. It would seem that Arnold is indeed using allusions, as one might have conjectured, to provide voices of reassurance and authority, to give resonance and plenitude to his language.

Allusions are rarely so unambiguously reassuring, however, and a brief consideration of Arnold's responses to Wordsworth's influence reveals how troubled the subtextual stream of **"The Buried Life"** is likely to be. Arnold, of course, had known Wordsworth as a neighbor in the Lake district, and respected him as the greatest English poet since Milton, but as his numerous critical comments on the matter reveal, he was in some ways ambivalent about the older poet's achievement. Wordsworth had "natural magic," could show a "grand style," and often showed "moral profundity," but his "eyes avert their ken / From half of human fate," presumably because like the other romantics he did not "know enough," had not read enough books.[25] Arnold's complex response to Wordsworth's work has been exhaustively studied, and it is not necessary to review it here in detail, but a look at how he laid Wordsworth's perturbed spirit to rest in **"Memorial Verses"** will help to show how Arnold's having read enough books complicates his allusions to Wordsworth in **"The Buried Life"** and in **"Dover Beach."** The allusions in fact open up general problems of intertextuality that complicate matters far beyond, for example, a Bloomian agon in which Arnold combats his ghostly predecessor face to face.

The sense that Wordsworth's voice in Arnold's poem might be reassuring is encouraged by a passage from **"Memorial Verses"** in which Wordsworth is said to restore our innocence:

He laid us as we lay at birth
On the cool flowery lap of earth. . . .

Our youth returned; for there was shed
On spirits that had long been dead,
Spirits dried up and closely furled,
The freshness of the early world.

(ll. 48-49, 54-57)

Since Arnold consistently blamed the complexities of the age—its "multitudinousness," its rush, its "unpoetrylessness"—for benumbed senses and failures of communication, this return to Eden would seem a perfect cure for the ills of **"The Buried Life."** Moreover, the return to Eden is still more suggestive when read in conjunction with Arnold's somewhat later comments on "natural magic" as a kind of Adamic naming that accomplishes the goal of the speaker in **"The Buried Life"** by perfectly expressing its object. The idea that Wordsworth's language has "magical" restorative powers associated with a kind of hidden, underground life is, moreover, strengthened by Arnold's association of it with "the clear song of Orpheus" in Hades. Once again, such words of power drifting upward from the buried life ought to be heartening.

And yet the full implications of **"Memorial Verses"** raise disturbing questions about echoes of Wordsworth elsewhere. In the first place, Orpheus almost, but only almost, redeemed Eurydice from Hades—he was able to get only himself out of hell, and not to help others. Also, "natural magic" names only the "outward world" (3:33) so that Wordsworth's ability to say "But there's a Tree" will not provide an alternative to the feeble utterance of the man looking inward, who can still say only "but there's a something." Further, **"Memorial Verses,"** as Culler has argued, does not ultimately affirm the continued potency of Wordsworth's voice but rather denies it by characterizing Wordsworth as "the last survivor of an idyllic age which has long since passed away."[26] Wordsworth can no longer restore the freshness of the early world; he is left well dead and, as the opening lines of the poem make clear, well silenced: "The last poetic voice is dumb— / We stand today by Wordsworth's tomb" (ll. 4-5). The notion of a dumb and entombed voice rising from its buried life begins to take on macabre implications, and the flat statement that Wordsworth's "voice is dumb" seems a direct answer to the fundamental question of **"The Buried Life"**: "But we, my love!—doth a like spell benumb / Our hearts, our voices? must we too be dumb?" (ll. 24-25).

Intriguingly, and pertinently, **"Memorial Verses"** has a buried life of its own that still further erodes the possibility of genuine poetic communication. In the very lines that seem to place Wordsworth in a primal state of innocence, the subtext reaches back to a still earlier predecessor. Arnold's lines "He laid us as we lay at birth / On the cool flowery lap of earth" recall Gray's description of Shakespeare, a still earlier, still more magical voice: "Far from the sun and summer gale, / In thy green lap was Nature's Darling laid."[27] And the general sentiment of the whole, that the age of poetry is past partly because, benumbed, we can no longer feel deeply, recalls eighteenth-century lamentations of the loss of feeling and lyric power, and in particular Collins's "Ode to Fear," in which the belated poet echoes Milton's "Il Penseroso" as he seeks from Fear the emotional intensity of Shakespeare: "Hither again thy fury deal, / Teach me but once like him to feel" (ll. 68-69). Collins's lines are a subversive undercurrent beneath Arnold's lament that in these latter days "Others will teach us how to dare" and how to bear, "But who, ah! who, will make us feel?" (ll. 64-67). Arnold does not summon the voices of Shakespeare and Milton to show that those reassuring voices do indeed survive; rather he echoes fruitless pleas for the return of those potent spirits. But their absence indicates that they are silenced, as Wordsworth is. The voices that do survive are the ineffectual voices of Gray and Collins, Arnold's kindred spirits as the talented victims of an unpoetical age.[28]

The displacement of Milton by Collins is especially disturbing since Arnold apparently considered his poem in some sense Miltonic, for he wrote (albeit somewhat facetiously) to Clough that he had "dirged W. W. *in the grand style,*"[29] a style that he associated almost exclusively, in English poetry at least, with Milton. Further, the Miltonic grand style, as Arnold defined it, is the perfect vehicle for a modern poetry that should be able to overcome the problem of belatedness and the consequent unavailability of natural magic by resorting to extreme allusiveness. Arnold divides the grand style into two types, the "simple" and the "severe," of which the "simple" is the more "magical" but is unfortunately not available to modern poets. The "grand style severe," best seen in Milton, "is much more imitable" (though "this a little spoils its charm") and it "comes from saying a thing with a kind of intense compression, or in an allusive, brief, almost haughty way" (1:189-90). Still more pertinently, Arnold described Miltonic style in 1849 as designed "to compose and elevate the mind by a sustained tone, numerous allusions, and a grand style."[30] The style would seem to enable the poet to make a positive use of the "multitudinousness" of his age, the "height to which knowledge is come," rather than being burdened by it.[31] And, indeed, Arnold suggested in a letter to Clough that he was making an effort to achieve such a style: "The poet's matter being *the hitherto experience of the world, and his own,* increases with every century. . . . For me you may often hear my sinews cracking under the effort to unite matter." Yet within the same letter he made two observations that suggest why Milton and Shakespeare are not heard in **"Memorial Verses,"** in his version of the grand style. In the first place, they are too "*curious* and exquisite" because they did not have to contend with "the multitude of new thoughts and feelings" that "a modern has" (they are, presumably, like Wordsworth in this), and second, imitation of the great masters is to be avoided as a sign of "the Decadence of a literature": "One of the factors of its decadent condition indeed, is this—that new authors attach themselves to the poetic expression the founders of a literature have flowered into, which may be *learned* by a sensitive person, to the neglect of an inward poetic life."[32] To save his own "inward poetic life" from decay, the modern must keep out the spirits (influences!) of the dead. The weaker spirits of Collins and Gray may be allowed in as reassurance that the ghosts of Wordsworth and Milton have been well laid.

All of this leads us back to the disturbing implication of Wordsworth's voice suddenly entering into **"The Buried Life"** to save it from inarticulateness and even to introduce a loftiness that seems to approximate a grand style. Wordsworth's resurrection in the buried life ought surely to constitute not a healing power but a threat to the speaker's "inward poetic life." A closer look at the passage shows that this is so:

> But often, in the world's most crowded streets,
> But often, in the din of strife,
> There rises an unspeakable desire
> After the knowledge of our buried life.

Wordsworth's presence seems, at first, innocent enough. The passage from "Tintern Abbey" describes how the inward life of the mind is restored to tranquility as the remembered past, a kind of buried life, wells up into present consciousness. But in opening up his verse to Wordsworth's voice, Arnold's "inward poetic life" suddenly begins to be crowded out by other, possibly more dangerous voices. The next voice, in fact, is Satan's, as the Father of Lies speaks of his "Unspeakable desire to see and know / All these his wondrous works, but chiefly Man."[33] The lines occur as Satan is lying to Uriel, in an incident that Milton used to emphasize the dangers of hypocrisy, of dissembling words. The situation is peculiarly akin to the echo of Hamlet's horror of hypocrisy in **"A**

Memory Picture"—in both cases the speaker is aiming at complete sincerity while his language is ineluctably summoning references to hypocrisy as a hidden, often indiscernible evil. Even the most sincere speech may veil a lurking evil. Within Arnold's poem about his desire to speak the unspeakable, to name what is nameless, Satan's precedent must be unsettling.

Perhaps Milton's voice drowning out Wordsworth at this point should not be surprising since Arnold argued, much later, that Wordsworth had "no assured poetic style of his own, like Milton" (9:52) but often seemed to take on Milton's style. Written long after Arnold had himself stopped writing poetry, long after he had ceased to be troubled by the anxieties of poetic influence, Arnold's comment betrays no sense that Wordsworth's poetic integrity might have been threatened by Milton's influence. Yet the young poet of **"The Buried Life,"** aware that he did not have Wordsworth's power of natural magic, of writing as though "Nature not only gave him the matter for his poem, but wrote his poem for him" (9:52), might well have felt threatened by the spectacle of one poetic voice welling up from his buried text only to be inundated by yet another. Indeed the Miltonic voice does not merely follow the Wordsworthian, but from the first is a still more deeply buried subtext beneath the Wordsworthian subtext, for the Wordsworthian lines may have conjured in Arnold's mind the famous simile that compares Satan in Eden to "one who long in populous City pent" (*Paradise Lost* 9.445) has temporarily, but only temporarily, escaped from hellish confinement to pastoral innocence and freedom. It is impossible to say to what extent any of these echoes are deliberate, but certainly in this case the Miltonic lines had made an impression on Arnold, who once jokingly wrote to Clough that his "present Labours may be shadowed forth under the Figure of Satan, perambulating, under the most unfavorable circumstances, a populous neighborhood."[34] The reference, however submerged it may be in **"The Buried Life,"** is extremely telling, for like the echo of Satan's hypocrisy, it calls to mind the last moments before the language of the "early world" is corrupted, the last moments before Satan's convincing lies seduced Eve and put an end to the simplicity and magic of Adamic naming. Further, the particular lines from Milton were especially apt to set a chain of echoes dinning in Arnold's ear for, as John Hollander has shown, the lines resound through Coleridge and Keats and, significantly, become explicitly associated with writers in crowded cities as Coleridge addresses "Bards in city garret pent" ("To the Nightingale") and Charles Lamb pining for nature while "In the great City pent" ("This Lime-Tree Bower My Prison").[35] The moment Arnold chooses to tap the grand style of allusive poetry, the moment he allows poets and poetry to surface in his text, he is inundated by lies and a Babel of ancestral voices. In the next fifty lines he will repeatedly echo the voices of his poetic forefathers, Coleridge and Wordsworth and, possibly, even Thomas Arnold.[36]

My allusion to the ancestral voices of "Kubla Khan" is, of course, deliberate, for "Kubla Khan" emerges as yet another precursor of **"The Buried Life."** The central metaphor of both poems is a subterranean river that casts up mysterious voices. In both poems the river seems harmless so long as it can be placed in a comfortable pastoral setting—"meandering with a mazy motion" in "Kubla Khan" and gliding through the meadows with a "winding murmur" in **"The Buried Life"**—on its way to a reassuringly quiet end in a "lifeless ocean" in Coleridge's poem and in "the sea where it goes" in Arnold's. But also in both poems the river is associated with a frightening underworld that casts up disturbing voices. In "Kubla Khan" the sounds are of a "woman wailing for her demon lover!" and of a general "tumult" in which can be discerned "Ancestral voices prophesying war!" The Arnoldian river murmurs less dramatically, but disturbingly nevertheless:

> vague and forlorn,
> From the soul's subterranean depth upborne
> As from an infinitely distant land,
> Come airs, and floating echoes, and convey
> A melancholy into all our day.
>
> (ll. 72-76)

Further, both poems are ultimately concerned at a deep level with the speaker's capacity to control these voices, and so to be able to express himself fully, even magically.

Like the other voices making themselves heard in the poem, Coleridge's dishearteningly suggests that mankind is fallen away from the state in which perfect language is possible, that poetic language is fallen, a hubbub of contending voices from the underworld. Also, to make room for his own voice, Arnold must clear away Coleridge's by revising the prior poem, by showing that it is not the ultimate statement that would make Arnold's redundant. Arnold swerves from the Coleridgean perspective in a fundamentally important respect. Coleridge's speaker considers the demonic voices of the underworld as the sources, if only he could revive them, of a visionary power; Arnold's, with a Victorian distrust of the visionary, hears them as seductively attractive lies that can only bring "A melancholy into all our day."

The extent to which Arnold rejected the demonic lies of poetry, and the consequence of this rejection, can best be appreciated by considering his conclusion, which claims a triumph, but in such carefully honest language that it undoes itself. The speaker claims to have found a language that perfectly expresses inward states ("And what we mean, we say, and what we would, we know" [l. 87]), but in fact he makes no attempt to communicate his feelings. Rather he simply returns to the metaphor of the buried stream, spells it out as his "life's flow" (l. 88), and affirms that he can now not only hear it but even "sees / The meadows where it glides, the sun, the breeze" (ll. 89-90). The actualization of the metaphor is forced, since the speaker is not willing to let it stand as an objective correlative for a state of feeling but insists on placing the physical stream inside the breast. Obviously the speaker does not in fact see such a stream, even though his eyes are apparently turned around in his head ("the eye sinks inward" [l. 86])—and in fact the pretense at seeing is betrayed by the forced rhyme that obliges him to claim even that "he sees . . . the breeze." The closing section, unable to build on such a shaky basis, claims much less:

And there arrives a lull in the hot race
Wherein he doth for ever chase
That flying and elusive shadow, rest.
An air of coolness plays upon his face,
And an unwonted calm pervades his breast.
And then he thinks he knows
The hills where his life rose,
And the sea where it goes.

(ll. 91-98)

Though this ending has been called a "moment of joy and insight,"[37] it seems to me far from joyful. The lines achieve their calm not by coming to terms with the murmurs of the buried life but by silencing them. Unlike the speaker of "Kubla Khan," who wants to become the vehicle for the subterranean song, to achieve a language of plenitude and redemptive power, the speaker here wants only to silence it and so, by implication, to empty language of its seductive poetical delusions. The calm is not achieved through a full inner life, but rather through an acceptance of death. The goal of life is the "elusive shadow, rest," and the poem ends with the anticipation of life itself and the buried stream emptying themselves into the sea, into the final calm of death. Further, the speaker, fighting to be honest, cannot claim to have achieved even the minimal goal of rest, but only a "lull in the hot race," and cannot claim knowledge of his origin or end, but only that "he thinks he knows." In short, there is no insight, and there certainly is no joy, only calm. The most that can be said of such calm is said at the close of **"Youth and Calm"**:

Youth dreams a bliss on this side death.
It dreams a rest, if not more deep,
More grateful than this marble sleep;
It hears a voice within it tell:
Calm's not life's crown, though calm is well.
'Tis all perhaps which man acquires,
But 'tis not what our youth desires.

(ll. 19-25)

"Calm," here, is found "in the tomb" (l. 15), and the calm of **"The Buried Life"** is not much better. What is more, the speaker, as has been frequently noted, has completely abandoned the attempt to read his lover's "inmost soul" (l. 11), and in his futile attempt to understand even his own soul he is left entirely alone, isolated by his failure to find an adequate language. In spite of itself, the poem expresses a sense of solipsistic entrapment, or entombment, and anticipates Pater's famous assertion that "each one of us" is bound within "that thick wall of personality through which no real voice has ever pierced on its way to us, or from us to that which we can only conjecture to be without."[38] Emptying the language of his predecessors of its power, Arnold ends by emptying his own, ends with a return to silence. Seeking a calm of Wordsworthian repletion, the poem ends with a calm that, fully examined, is far more akin to the Tennysonian calm of deep grief, or death:

And in my heart, if calm at all,
If any calm, a calm despair;

Calm on the seas, and silver sleep,
And waves that sway themselves in rest,
And dead calm in that noble breast
Which heaves but with the heaving deep.

(*In Memoriam,* section 11)

I am by no means contending that Arnold intended to deconstruct his own poem, or intended to include a subtextual current of allusion that would undermine his own language and poetic language generally. Indeed, Arnold presumably saw **"The Buried Life"** as a fairly tranquil poem about the power of love to unlock the heart and lips. But poetic language has a life of its own, and beneath the surface the poem becomes a subtextual battle that ends in universal casualties. **"The Buried Life"** is consequently a confused poem that gains its genuine pathos in large measure by its valiant, if losing, struggle for a language of affirmative power. But Arnold's greatest lyric, **"Dover Beach,"** exhibits none of this confusion because, though it fights the same battle as **"The Buried Life,"** it never assumes a victory.

Like **"The Buried Life," "Dover Beach"** is addressed to a beloved in a situation that demands, and seems to make possible, sincerity. According to Mermin's excellent discussion of the poems from this perspective, in **"The Buried Life"** the speaker realizes that "all he can sincerely say is that he would like to be sincere," but in **"Dover Beach,"** she argues, Arnold produced his "one poem in which he shows communication from speaker to auditor as open, direct, complete, and wholly unproblematic."[39] I will argue, however, that like **"The Buried Life," "Dover Beach"** ends with a desolating sense of aloneness, and that its attempted austerity of diction is similarly undermined by the subtextual voices of Wordsworth and Milton. Also like **"The Buried Life,"** it is a poem that in subtle ways is about its own decomposition. In what is probably the best essay to date on **"Dover Beach,"** Ruth Pitman has convincingly argued that even the landscape—the cliffs and the shoreline—is not as solid as it at first appears. The opening description of the cliffs "glimmering," the light that "gleams and is gone," and the "grating" of pebbles on the shore suggests an erosion of the shoreline, a reminder of what the geologists had been telling the Victorians about the impermanence of the solidest features of the earth itself. The passage is analogous to Tennyson's description of geological transformations in *In Memoriam:*

The hills are shadows, and they flow
From form to form, and nothing stands;
They melt like mist, the solid lands,
Like clouds they shape themselves and go.

(section 123)

Further, Pitman argues, the physical decomposition of the landscape suggests an analogous decomposition of meaning in the Victorian worldview—the changed sense of time, the general sense of impermanence, the idea of living in a world in a constant state of flux and decay not only undermined Christian faith but left nothing at all solid to lean on. The decaying shoreline is precisely the spot to ponder the withdrawal of faith from the world, and the loss of a stable worldview. And finally, Pitman adds, erosion of the land and the decay of faith are both reflected in an analogous erosion of poetic form. The poem, she points out, "is made up of a series of incomplete sonnets: erosion of form matches erosion of meaning."[40] I will not recapitulate her perceptive and thorough analysis of the poem's prosody to support this claim, except to note the obvious. The first two sections each consist of fourteen lines that suggest but do not achieve strict sonnet form, and except for a short (three foot) opening line, the last section emulates the octave of a sonnet, but closes with a single, climactic line instead of a sestet—as though the final five lines had been eroded.

Not only is the form decomposing but, as in **"The Buried Life,"** the poem's metaphors tend to be self-destructive. As Elizabeth Gitter has pointed out, Arnold introduces Sophocles' metaphorical interpretation of the sea only to reject it and replace it with a thought independent of the actual sound: "The vehicle of this new metaphor is not the 'tremulous cadence' of the waves of Dover Beach, but a steady, 'melancholy, long, withdrawing roar.' And the metaphor of the continuously ebbing Sea of Faith is suggested to the poet by the meaning of the note of sadness he hears, not by the way it sounds."[41] Though Gitter's interpretation of her excellent observation is different from mine, it seems to me that this severance of the mind's metaphoric creation from external actuality, this breakdown of metaphoric connection of mind and other, signals the same kind of solipsistic isolation as in **"The Buried Life."** Arnold's speaker listens to the rising sound of distant waters but hears only what is already within him. He contrasts sharply with the figure of Wordsworth on Mount Snowdon, hearing in the rising sound of waters a proof of a universally and benevolently meaningful world outside of the self. Indeed, as U. C. Knoepflmacher has pointed out, Arnold draws Wordsworth into the poem from its very first lines. And this time the allusion is so sustained, and so pertinent, that Arnold must surely have intended it to be noted.

The allusion in the opening section is to Wordsworth generally and, as Knoepflmacher has noted, is in particular to the sonnet "It Is a Beauteous Evening."[42] Within his sonnet Wordsworth is describing the sounds and significance of the sea to a child (though it is not mentioned in the poem, the setting is, significantly, the shore of the English Channel, though on the French side):

> It is a beauteous evening, calm and free,
> The holy time is quiet as a Nun
> Breathless with adoration; the broad sun
> Is sinking down in its tranquillity;
> The gentleness of heaven broods o'er the Sea:
> Listen! the mighty Being is awake,
> And doth with his eternal motion make
> A sound like thunder—everlastingly.

The echoes in the opening lines of **"Dover Beach"** are immediately obvious:

> The sea is calm to-night.
> The tide is full, the moon lies fair
> Upon the straits; on the French coast the light
> Gleams and is gone; the cliffs of England stand,
> Glimmering and vast, out in the tranquil bay.
> Come to the window, sweet is the night-air
> Only, from the long line of spray
> Where the sea meets the moon-blanched land,
> Listen! you hear the grating roar
> Of pebbles which the waves draw back, and fling,
> At their return, up the high strand,
> Begin, and cease, and then again begin,
> With tremulous cadence slow, and bring,
> The eternal note of sadness in.

The opening "calm," the stylistic recourse to flat copulative verbs, the importance of the sea's sound, and especially the request to the companion to "Listen!" are all caught up in Arnold's lines. In the diction, the choice of such words as "calm," "full," "sweet," and "tranquil," the lines invoke a general Wordsworthian sense of epiphany. But the undertow is treacherous. The "grating roar" calls in a note of sadness utterly unlike the Wordsworthian undersong of the "sad music of humanity" that, Knoepflmacher notes, is described in "Tintern Abbey" as "Nor harsh, nor grating."[43] Further, in this particular context, the meaningless "grating roar" displaces the powerful and holy presence of a "mighty Being" whose bang is replaced with a whimper, whose eternal motion and everlasting thunder are replaced by an "eternal note of sadness." For this reason—because the world and Wordsworth are emptied of their mythic presence—the calm of Arnold's lines is, as in **"The Buried Life,"** a calm not of repletion but of emptiness. In fact, even the simplest words are emptied of their meaning in Arnold's poem. Wordsworth's serenity is characteristically achieved by the plenitude of his verbs of being—in the first six lines of his octave the word *is* is used four times, and is reinforced by the word *Being*. The word *is* is not a mere linking verb, but an affirmation of divine presence, a transcendental signifier. It is akin, indeed, to the word *broods* that summons up the transcendent and creative presence of the Holy Spirit. But Arnold's four uses of *is* in his opening six lines cannot have this force. As we have seen, Arnold later scorned the idea that *is* and *be* were meaningful metaphysical terms, and he mocked the notion that "*being* was supposed to be something absolute, which stood under all things,"[44] but even within **"Dover Beach"** it is clear that *is* is not informed with transcendental presence but simply links nouns to adjectives, making the minimal verbal statement. Indeed, in three cases, "The sea is calm," "The tide is full," and "sweet is the night-air," the verb is unnecessary and the adjectives could be used directly: the calm sea, the full tide, the sweet night-air. And in the fourth case the *is* signifies no presence, but absence: "the light . . . is gone." The metaphysical emptiness of Arnold's language is, of course, analogous to the poem's general description of the emptiness of faithless Victorian life, an emptiness most emphatically stated near the end of the poem in a desolating series of denials:

> the world, which seems
> To lie before us like a land of dreams,
> So various, so beautiful, so new,
> Hath really neither joy, nor love, nor light,
> Nor certitude, nor peace, nor help for pain.
>
> (ll. 30-34)

As John Hollander has recently argued, verbal echoes may be a sign not of repletion but of reverberations in hollow or empty landscapes,[45] and certainly the resounding of Wordsworth's voice in the meaningless landscape of **"Dover Beach"** seems to be just that.

Even in these negations the voices of Milton and Wordsworth reverberate hollowly. The "world, which seems / To lie before us," Ronald A. Sharp has recently noted,[46] is a skeptical, attenuated version of Milton's

> The World was all before them, where to choose
> Thir place of rest, and Providence thir guide:
> They hand in hand with wandring steps and slow,
> Through *Eden* took thir solitarie way.
>
> (*Paradise Lost,* 12.646-49)

Not surprisingly, by this time, mediating between Milton and Arnold is the voice of Wordsworth from the 1850 *Prelude:* "the earth is all before me" (1.14) and "the road lies plain before me" (1.641). But these voices and visions from the grand style are denied; Arnold is cut off not only from Providence, and from the clarity of Wordsworthian purpose, but also, of course, from the language of affirmation that contributes to their grandeur. Yet the prior voices do make themselves heard, and not always to be simply rejected. Whether deliberately or not, the voice of Milton—or more accurately Milton's Satan—is heard in a devastatingly subversive subtext. As Martin Bidney has recently pointed out, the words "neither joy nor love" are lifted directly from *Paradise Lost.* The loss of Wordsworthian joy[47] is associated with Satan's description of Hell as he enviously sees the embrace of Adam and Eve, who

> shall enjoy their fill
> Of bliss on bliss, while I to Hell am thrust,
> Where neither joy, nor love, but fierce desire,
> Among our other torments not the least,
> Still unfulfill'd with pain of longing pines.
>
> (4.507-11)

Bidney effectively notes the significance of this: "Now that the world has become Hell, the embrace of two lovers stranded amid the dark expanse of aimless fury is a very precarious Eden indeed—an Eden internal, vulnerable, isolated, intermittent at best. The poet tenderly holds out to his beloved the prospect of hope, but in the same sentence, almost in the same breath, he depicts their earthly world in the very words used by a despairing Devil to describe an eternal Hell."[48] The allusion also has a dark significance for the possibilities of language. Arnold, who in a very different context once asked where, in a contaminated language, he could "find language innocent enough" to express the "spotless purity of [his] intentions" (3:275), now cries "Ah, love, let us be true / To one another!" (ll. 29-30) and ironically mouths the words of the Father of Lies, of an archfiend agonizing over the frustration of an unsatisfied sexual desire. Once again, though the Wordsworthian voice may be neutralized, demonic voices will continue to rise from the abyss and subvert the language.

But anterior even to the voice of Satan is another voice, yet more devastating in its implications. As Culler and Pitman have both noted, the speaker of **"Dover Beach"** is not actually situated on the beach, but on the cliff known—and known to Arnold—as "Shakespeare's cliff" after the cliff scene in *King Lear.*[49] The cliff scene has been lurking in the background all along, but *King Lear* is brought into the verbal texture of the poem by only one word—though a highly charged poetic one—in the closing simile:

> And we are here as on a darkling plain
> Swept with confused alarms of struggle and flight,
> Where ignorant armies clash by night.
>
> (ll. 35-37)

Pitman, who notes how thoroughly the closing lines are a tissue of poeticisms, how the plain is "made up of literary allusion and [is] itself a simile," sees a faint hope in the speaker's ability to use the literary tradition to rebuild after all other meaning has been lost: "All that is left is what the mind can construct, from *King Lear,* perhaps, or from Thucydides, not a secure or certain physical place: 'And we are here as on a darkling plain.' The coast lights, gleaming or glimmering, have gone out, like the Fool's candle and left us without a guide, unable to discern the perspective of landscape outside ourselves, confined to the 'darkling plain' of our own minds. ('So out went the candle, and we were left darkling'; *King Lear* 1.4.226)."[50] But the situation is even grimmer than this, for the subtext of the poems has consistently implied that our building blocks, those fragments of the tradition, may be all we have, but they are lies.

Indeed, the situational allusion to the cliff scene makes this painfully clear. Arnold has been listening to the "grating roar / Of pebbles which the waves draw back" but Edgar has told Gloucester that

> The murmuring surge
> That on th' unnumber'd idle pebble chafes
> Cannot be heard so high.
>
> (4.6.21-23)

Arnold has once again echoed a precursor to correct his lie—and of course Edgar *is* a liar. He was not at the top of a cliff, but was standing on a flat plain, a "darkling plain" for poor blinded Gloucester, weaving an elaborate poetical lie to save the inhabitant of the darkling plain from utter despair and suicide. Gloucester, of course, thinks he is on the cliffs of Dover, and after he thinks he has jumped off them, he presumably thinks he is on Dover Beach—but in fact there is no escape from his plight, from his darkling plain. The implication of Arnold's allusion is that the lies of poetry may save us from despair, as they saved the deluded Gloucester, but lies they remain and cannot alter our existential state, which is always "as on a darkling plain." The allusiveness of **"Dover Beach"** helps to make it one of the most powerful and compelling poems in the language, but not because the voices of past poets provide the kind of authoritative language Arnold usually sought. Rather, the poem is compelling in its courageous struggle to set aside the lies, the false consolations of such precursors as Wordsworth (a kind of Edgar figure) and to battle for a true standing ground, however barren and desolate. Even if he is "as on a darkling plain," the speaker wants to be able to state, with an existential truth unavailable to the blind and duped Gloucester, that "we are here."

In his 1863 essay on Maurice de Guérin, Arnold quoted a passage that demonstrates his awareness of the extreme difficulties of finding a language unadulterated by the words of previous authors: "'When I begin a subject, my self conceit,' (says this exquisite artist) 'imagines I am doing wonders; and when I have finished, I see nothing but a wretched made-up imitation, composed of odds and ends of colour stolen from other people's palettes, and tastelessly mixed together on mine.' Such was his passion for perfection" (3:35). The problem is not with deliberate allusions, but with a language so overused that uncontrollable echoes and chains of association are inevitable. And perhaps Arnold's turn from poetry to prose resulted in part from his recognition of an element of "wretched made-up imitation" in his poetry, of his inability to forge a language entirely his own. Certainly when he made a point of deliberately exploiting the tradition by mimicking past poets in such works as ***Sohrab and Rustum, Balder Dead,*** and ***Merope*** he was able to achieve little more than lifeless pastiche. The echoes and allusions in his love poetry, however, are extremely vital, uncontrollably so. Nevertheless, Arnold does not use the voices of the poetic tradition as words of power and authority to confirm his own vision. In fact, **"Dover Beach"** contrasts sharply with such a poem as Swinburne's "On the Cliffs," also about hearing the sea and other voices on an eroding cliff by a "distant northern sea," for whereas Swinburne heard the voices of Sappho—and of Wordsworth, and even of Arnold's **"Dover Beach"**—as filling the landscape with meaning, Arnold heard the voices of Sophocles and Wordsworth only to reject and deny them, to empty the landscape of their presence. Paradoxically, in his greatest poem the greatest of all defenders of the poetic tradition found himself encumbered by it, and struggled to clear it away. But perhaps it was precisely the resistance against a living and recalcitrant language, the battle to control intertextual echoes and subordinate them to his own purposes, that enabled Arnold to produce his finest poems. The model for Arnold's battle with his poetic forefathers, then, is not a Bloomian agon, an armed battle against a single combatant, but a much harder, less glorious encounter with the protean, many-voiced forces of a seductive and betraying poetic tradition.

Notes

1. [E. D. H.] Johnson, [*The Alien Vision of Victorian Poetry: Sources of the Poetic Imagination in Tennyson, Browning, and Arnold* (Princeton: Princeton Univ. Press, 1952)], p. 151.
2. Eliot, "The Three Voices of Poetry," in *On Poetry and Poets* (New York: Farrar, Straus and Cudahy, 1957), pp. 97-98.
3. [Park] Honan, *Matthew Arnold: A Life* (New York: McGraw-Hill, 1981), chap. 7. For more on the Marguerite debate, see Miriam Allott, "Arnold and 'Marguerite'—Continued," in *Victorian Poetry* 23 (1985):125-43, and in the same issue, Honan, "The Character of Marguerite in Arnold's *Switzerland,*" pp. 145-59.
4. Buckler, [*On the Poetry of Matthew Arnold: Essays in Critical Reconstruction* (New York: New York Univ. Press, 1982)] p. 68.
5. *Letters of Matthew Arnold, [1848-1888,* 2 vols., ed. George W. E. Russell (New York: Macmillan, 1896)] 1:11.
6. [G. Robert] Stange, [*Matthew Arnold: The Poetas Humanist* (Princeton: Princeton Univ. Press, 1967),] p. 222.
7. For the publication history of the poems, see Paull F. Baum, *Ten Studies in the Poetry of Matthew Arnold* (Durham: Duke Univ. Press, 1958), pp. 79-84, and Stange, pp. 216-32.
8. How the two poems were originally related is not entirely clear. "Isolation. To Marguerite" was not published until 1857 (as "To Marguerite"—the present title was not bestowed until 1869), and "To Marguerite—Continued" was not given its present title until 1869 but was originally entitled "To Marguerite, in Returning a Volume of the Letters of Ortis" (1852), then "To Marguerite" (1853, 1854), and then "Isolation" (1857). Still, the identical stanza forms, the overlapping titles, the publication in sequence from 1857 on, and the final titles all indicate their eventual relationship, and strongly imply an initial connection.
9. Buckler, p. 65.
10. *Écrits: A Selection,* trans. Alan Sheridan (New York: Norton, 1977), pp. 42-43.
11. Tillotson, "Yes: In the Sea of Life," *Review of English Studies,* n.s. 3 (1952):364, 346.
12. Roper, [*Arnold's Poetic Landscapes* (Baltimore: Johns Hopkins Univ. Press, 1969),] p. 156.
13. The poems thus admirably fit the theoretical model of Michael Riffaterre's *Semiotics of Poetry*

(Bloomington: Indiana Univ. Press, 1978), in which the completed poem is seen as a series of variations on a "pre-existent word group" (p. 23) called a "hypogram."

14. Tillotson, p. 347. According to Kenneth Allott, Saintsbury, who first pointed out the reference to *Pendennis,* chap. 16, called the poem "simply an extension of a phrase in *Pendennis.*" Notes in *Poems,* p. 129.
15. Honan, pp. 149-58.
16. [Dorothy] Mermin, [*The Audience in the Poem: Five Victorian Poets* (New Brunswick: Rutgers Univ. Press, 1983),] p. 97.
17. [*The Letters of Matthew Arnold to Arthur Hugh Clough,* ed. Howard Foster Lowry (London: Oxford Univ. Press, 1932)], p. 97. According to J. B. Broadbent, Arnold's echoes of Milton, Wordsworth, and the Bible provide, at least in *Sohrab and Rustum,* precisely the desired tone of authority and, moreover, reveal the poet as "a man confident—for all he may say elsewhere—in the value of his own civilization." Broadbent also quotes Arnold's admission that he had indeed imitated Milton's manner, "but Milton is a sufficiently great master to imitate." See his "Milton and Arnold," *Essays in Criticism 6* (1956):406.
18. See the chapter entitled "The Use of Elegy" in *Imaginative Reason* [*: The Poetry of Matthew Arnold* (New Haven: Yale Univ. Press, 1966)], pp. 232-86. Culler characteristically remarks of some that "they are not so much elegies as attempts on Arnold's part to exorcise an evil spirit which had formerly dwelt within him" (p. 246).
19. Hollander, *The Figure of Echo: A Mode of Allusion in Milton and After* (Berkeley: Univ. of California Press, 1981), p. 90. Bloom, [*The*] *Anxiety* [*of Influence: A Theory of Poetry* (New York: Oxford Univ. Press, 1973)], p. 56.
20. "Ode: Intimations of Immortality from Recollections of Early Childhood," l. 51.
21. Stitelman, "Lyrical Process in Three Poems by Matthew Arnold," *Victorian Poetry* 15 (1977):136.
22. Others have commented on this confusion. See, for example, Allott's note in *Poems,* pp. 287-88, and for a more extended discussion, Roper, pp. 173-77.
23. Noted in *Poems,* p. 289.
24. "Ode: Intimations of Immortality," ll. 151-53. The allusion is noted in *Poems,* p. 290.
25. "But surely the one thing wanting to make Wordsworth an even greater poet than he is,—his thought richer, and his influence of wider application,—was that he should have read more books" (3:262).
26. Culler, p. 235.
27. The allusion to Gray's "The Progress of Poesy," ll. 84-85, is noted in *Poems.*
28. The point about Gray is made in "The Study of Poetry" (9:181) and Collins is drawn into it in the essay "Thomas Gray" (9:204), but for an earlier comment to the same effect see Arnold's 1849 letter in *Letters to Clough,* p. 99.
29. *Letters to Clough,* p. 115.
30. Ibid., p. 100.
31. Ibid., p. 111.
32. Ibid., pp. 64-65.
33. The echo of *Paradise Lost* 3.662-63 is noted in *Poems.*
34. Quoted by Culler, p. 52.
35. Hollander, p. 80.
36. For the possible allusion to Thomas Arnold, see *Poems,* p. 291.
37. Strange, p. 176.
38. Pater, Conclusion, *The Renaissance,* p. 187.
39. Mermin, pp. 97, 106.
40. Pitman, "On Dover Beach," *Essays in Criticism* 23 (1973):129.
41. Gitter, "Undermined Metaphors in Arnold's Poetry," *Victorian Poetry* 16 (1978):278.
42. [U. C.] Knoepflmacher, ["Dover Beach Revisited: The Wordsworthian Matrix in the Poetry of Matthew Arnold," *Victorian Poetry* 1 (1963):] pp. 21-22. Michael Timko also discusses the poem as a response to Wordsworthian poetry and thought—he sees it as "Arnold's strongest poetic declaration of his break with the Romantics, especially Wordsworth, and his most direct and explicit denunciation of Wordsworth's 'Ode: Intimations of Immortality.'" ("Wordsworth's 'Ode' and Arnold's 'Dover Beach': Celestial Light and Confused Alarms," *Cithara* 13 [1973]:53).
43. Knoepflmacher, pp. 21-22.
44. See pp. 15-17.
45. Hollander, p. 12.
46. Sharp, "A Note on Allusion in 'Dover Beach,'" *English Language Notes* 21 (1983):53. Sharp points out the echoes of *The Prelude* as well.
47. In his "Address to the Wordsworth Society," Arnold referred to "what is perhaps Wordsworth's most distinct virtue of all—his power of happiness and hope, his 'deep power of joy'" (10:133). For Arnold's consistent association of Wordsworth with joy, see [Leon] Gottfried, [*Matthew Arnold and the Romantics* (Lincoln: Univ. of Nebraska Press)] chap. 2.
48. Bidney, "Of the Devil's Party: Undetected Words of Milton's Satan in Arnold's 'Dover Beach,'" *Victorian Poetry* 20 (1982):89.
49. Culler, p. 39.

50. Pitman, p. 124.

Mary W. Schneider (essay date 1989)

SOURCE: "The Great Work of Criticism," in *Poetry in the Age of Democracy: The Literary Criticism of Matthew Arnold,* University Press of Kansas, 1989, pp. 103-34.

[*In the following essay, Schneider reviews the major themes in Arnold's* Essays in Criticism, *including the role of literary criticism, modernity, and the distinctive natures of poetry and prose.*]

When Arnold collected the best of his articles for ***Essays in Criticism*** (1865), he wrote an introductory essay that in its general theory sought to explain his own recent criticism and to work out new answers to the old questions. **"The Function of Criticism at the Present Time"** asserted once more his faith that the intellectual movements of the Enlightenment were returning to full vigor and that free inquiry in all branches of human knowledge was promising once more to sweep away the old and false ideas. In this essay, however, in setting out a theoretic basis for his criticism, Arnold no longer emphasized the power of criticism to destroy the encumbrances on human thought. Now he showed the power of criticism not only to discover or to recognize worthy ideas but also to preserve what was true or good in the past. Emphasizing the work that criticism was to perform, he also began to see criticism as an activity performed, not so much for a further end, social or aesthetic, but as an activity worthwhile in itself. In the "present time" to which Arnold was speaking in the essay, the revival of romanticism—with a renewed enthusiasm for creative genius and the power of the imagination, the poetic temperament, and the ordinary life—was met by the rigorous inquiry that Arnold had begun in the essays. What Arnold now tried to show was not only that the criticism or examination of these notions indicated the limits of poetry and criticism but also that the activity of criticism—in its broadest sense the examination of ideas and of life itself—is a productive work. Arnold now answered Wordsworth's claim for the superiority of poetry over criticism and Shairp's assertion that the new spirit of imagination had led to the great age of Romantic poetry. Arnold sets out to show the defects of this argument and to find a theoretical basis for his criticism of the Romantic poets in the earlier essays, which were collected in this volume and formed the bulk of his first major criticism. Arnold found his theoretical basis in ideas suggested by Aristotle's *Ethics;* he developed the notion of criticism as an activity, as in his essays on the Romantic poets he had turned to Aristotle for his analysis of the Romantic temperament and the provincial mind.

Arnold did not intend so much to show the deficiencies of the Romantics as poets as to show the inadequacy of their criticism, above all the danger of elevating the folk as the standard of taste and reason. Arnold's insistence on the function of criticism in finding the best that is thought and said was meant for the coming age of the people: the people were not, in his view, to be cheated by being handed ideas or poetry that were thought to be good enough for them. Arnold, it may be said, was offering a new declaration of the rights of humankind—the right to know the best that is thought and said. Arnold's declaration of an equality of such rights did not mean that Arnold naîvely supposed that the best was necessarily within the reach of all people. One must also keep in mind here his practical work for an improved public education. In practice, he tended to aim at an educated middle class rather than at the populace or at an aristocracy that was indifferent, or so he thought, to ideas. But there is nothing in Arnold's thought that assumed that the common people were by nature incapable of intelligent reflection and comprehension. Preceding Arnold's insistence on the work of criticism in finding and making known the best that is thought and said was his criticism of Homer, in which he had insisted that Homer was not a ballad poet and that the ballad poets were not Homer; Arnold's essay on the modern, in which he held that the contemporary was not always new or fresh, let alone the best; and his essay on the discoveries of Bishop Colenso, which was essentially naïve and uninformed Biblical criticism. Arnold's praise of the Romantic poets was reserved for Shelley and Byron, who neither lost their faith in the democratic revolution nor fell into a sentimental view of the folk.

In emphasizing criticism as work or activity, I should say at the outset that Arnold did not have in mind Carlyle's notion of work as duty or an economic or utilitarian view of work as useful labor. Arnold's emphasis was on the activity itself as the end, on the happiness found in the performance. Arnold insisted, in opposition to Emerson and Carlyle, that the end of human life was happiness, and he located happiness in performing an activity well. Moreover, Arnold, like Aristotle, was to find the highest human activity in thinking—*theoria,* or theoretical activity, and this aspect of Arnold's criticism explains his emphasis in these essays on ideas, on the best that is thought and said, and his lack of interest in judging the value of literary works—his eye was on the activity, on the question of whether the activity of criticism was one in which the critic might find the good life, or happiness—on what criticism does when it is done well. Although he thought about theoretical more than practical criticism, he did not neglect practical criticism, nor did he neglect the effect that criticism could have on society. He saw that the effect was not different from the activity but extended its scope—that is, made it possible for more, if not all, to share in the activity of knowing the best that was being thought and said.

In spite of Arnold's emphasis on thought in the activity of criticism—on judgment and theory—it would be wrong to think of Arnold's idea of literary criticism as severely "intellectualist," a criticism that was rigorously logical or that relied on the application of unvarying principles. The "free play of mind" was the phrase that best indicated the kind of inquiry that criticism undertakes; the qualities of flexibility and "sweet reasonableness" that Arnold later would develop and define were necessary to the best criticism, the best that is written. Arnold's own critical essays did not offer a body of abstract ideas or principles; they were literary essays, nearer to art than to scientific treatises. At its best, Arnold's own criticism exemplified his own description of criticism as "ardent" and "flexible." If one compares, for example, an essay by Arnold with one by Shairp on a similar theme, one can see how often Shairp fell back on critical abstractions, how often he relied on a numerical order of points in a way that is alien to art and how he made his way, in rather plodding fashion, through the life and works of his subjects. Arnold, on the other hand, conveyed always the sense of a curious mind that was observing and exploring the life and work of his subjects, a mind that was responding in various ways to what he saw, perceiving, ordering, and judging, not according to a plan, but as his subject led him to fresh and original ideas.

In inquiring into the function of criticism in the introductory essay, Arnold consciously set out on the kind of inquiry that Aristotle had undertaken in the *Nicomachean Ethics.* Thinking about the function of criticism, Arnold adapted for his own purpose certain terms and ideas from the *Ethics.* Arnold did not appeal to Aristotle as an authority, but he kept in mind Aristotle's discussion of the moral and intellectual virtues and the appeal to the "judicious" in determining the best. Arnold's inquiry into the activity of criticism, especially into the relation of criticism to creation, appears to go beyond the *Ethics,* but Arnold did begin with the idea of the activity that is proper to a human being, in order to find the correct place for criticism in the good life.

Throughout the essay, Arnold kept the emphasis on criticism as an activity. When Arnold spoke of the "function" of criticism, he was asking what the essential *work (ergon)* of criticism should be. By means of various synonyms for *function,* he kept before his readers this essential idea of criticism as an activity: thus "a critical effort" is "'the endeavor, in all branches of knowledge, theology, philosophy, history, art, science, to see the object as in itself it really is'" (***PW,*** [***The Complete Prose Works of Matthew Arnold,*** Edited by R. H. Super. 11 vols. Ann Arbor: University of Michigan Press, 1960–77] 3:258, 261). Again, "a great critical *effort* is necessary for a creative epoch": "Goethe's [poetry] was nourished by a great critical *effort* providing the true materials for it" (***PW,*** 3:262; emphasis added). Arnold predicted that "a time of true creative *activity*" would come "when criticism has done its *work*" (***PW,*** 3:269). By such words as *function, effort,* and *endeavor,* Arnold kept the focus on the *work* of criticism.

Although the idea of work or function was important to Aristotle, what is distinctive in his thought is *energeia,* activity—roughly, the performance of the work—as Clough said in *The Bothie,* to find and to *do* the *ergon.* For a human being, Aristotle concluded in his inquiry in the *Ethics,* the highest activity is contemplation, or theoretical activity: at the highest level, the level of *arete* or excellence, this is the good for mankind, and in this activity is to be found the greatest happiness.[1] While it is now generally agreed that by *theoria* Aristotle meant mathematics, physics, and metaphysics, earlier commentators in the nineteenth century included aesthetic and divine thought.[2] Arnold included in critical thought nearly all branches of knowledge; it is likely that Arnold at this point would have seen *theoria* as inclusive. Criticism, certainly, is a mode of inquiry that is not restricted to any discipline.

Arnold went on to connect thought or inquiry with disinterestedness. Criticism, he said, follows "the law of its own nature, which is to be a free play of mind on all subjects which it touches" (***PW,*** 3:270), and the definition of criticism at which Arnold ultimately arrived is that criticism is *"a disinterested endeavor to learn and propagate the best that is known and thought in the world"* (***PW,*** 3:283). To what extent Aristotle's idea of *energeia* implied either what Arnold called "a free play of mind" or *disinterestedness* is a question. Alexander Grant, in a note on individuality, saw in *energeia* "a sense of life and free action," and later he used the phrase "play of mind" in commenting on *energeia.*[3] Arnold made a similar connection when he said that criticism requires a "disinterested love of a free play of the mind on all subjects, for its own sake" (***PW,*** 3:268). In saying that the activity is pursued for its own sake, Arnold was keeping in mind what Aristotle had said on theoretical activity: "And this activity alone would seem to be loved for its own sake; for nothing arises from it apart from the contemplating, while from practical activities we gain more or less apart from the action" (*NE,* x.7.1177b1-4, trans. Ross). Arnold also defined the proper end of criticism as being essentially theoretical, "to create a current of true and fresh ideas" (***PW,*** 3:270). In this respect, criticism has no end beyond itself. Arnold was here especially concerned to show that criticism does not aim at the practical application of the ideas that it examines but that it belongs in the "pure intellectual sphere" (***PW,*** 3:271). As a theoretical activity, criticism cannot leave the intellectual sphere for practical action without becoming another kind of activity; otherwise it would cease to be free, and it would no longer be disinterested.

When Arnold asserted that criticism has the end of "creating a current of true and fresh ideas," he indicated still the activity of criticism as he had defined it, and the result or product of criticism is more or less the same as the activity. When, however, Arnold said that criticism provides the materials for poetry, he seems to have been saying that criticism exists, not for itself, but for the sake of poetry. When he spoke earlier about the effect of a current of ideas, he seems to have been suggesting a further end, for, according to Arnold, as criticism does its work, ideas stimulate in society "a stir and growth," and out of this growth develop "the creative epochs of literature" (***PW,*** 3:261). Certainly, Arnold wanted to argue that criticism has an effect, and indeed his apology for criticism depends largely on the argument that criticism does have this particular effect.[4] One may suggest, however, that criticism may have an effect without aiming at any end beyond its own activity—the disinterested endeavor to know the best that is thought and said. Thus, so far as criticism is an intellectual activity, it is free.

Clearly, Arnold was trying to include the work of the critic in theoretical activity. Therefore he distinguished between theory and practical criticism, again following Aristotle's distinctions. Indeed, Arnold's idea that criticism is knowing and communicating the best that is thought and said takes no account of what is considered the usual business of criticism, as Arnold recognized: criticism as the "mere judgment and application of principles," whether to literary works of other kinds of work, is, he said, not "the most satisfactory work to the critic" (***PW,*** 3:283). But here, too, Arnold turned to Aristotle. The literary criticism that sorts out the good from the bad depends, Arnold thought, on what Aristotle called *phronesis,* now generally translated as "practical wisdom," but what Arnold called "judgment." As Arnold had said in ***On Translating Homer,*** after quoting the passage from the *Ethics,* "'As the judicious would determine'—that is a test to which every one professes himself willing to submit his works" (***PW,*** 1:99).[5] Arnold referred such questions to the instructed human reason.

As a young poet struggling for self-discipline, Arnold had hoped to get some measure of judgment; now, Arnold, in his analysis of such poets as Maurice de Guérin and Keats, argued essentially that the nature poets lack practical wisdom and, unable to keep in bounds either their emotions or their fancies, fall into melancholy. Nature poets, Arnold theorized, have a certain temperament which is related to "a faculty of naturalistic, not of moral interpretation"; such poets have "an extraordinary delicacy of organization and susceptibility to impressions" (***PW,*** 3:30). Arnold moreover saw an opposition between this temperament and moral activity: "Assuredly it is not in this temperament that the active virtues have their rise" (***PW,*** 3:32). In this analysis Arnold drew on Aristotle's discussion of melancholy, on the melancholics who are among those who lack practical wisdom: "It is keen and excitable people [melancholics] that suffer especially from the impetuous form of incontinence; for the former by reason of their quickness and the latter by reason of the violence of their passions do not await the argument, because they are apt to follow their imagination."[6] That this passage was considered a locus for the theory of melancholy is indicated by Grant's comment on Aristotle's treatment of melancholy; Grant showed that the classical account attributed melancholy to an excess of passion, and he cited Tennyson's *Maud:* "'The passionate heart of the poet is whirl'd into folly and vice."[7] What the melancholics lack is judgment, and Arnold found that the nature poets and the critics alike could fall into this Greek kind of melancholy—a passionate and impetuous excitability.

In the essay on academies, Arnold pointed out that the absence of a high standard is evident in what he called provinciality; the provincials are also those who lack judgment; they are indeed melancholics: "The provincial spirit . . . exaggerates the value of its ideas for want of a high standard at hand by which to try them. Or rather, for want of such a standard, it gives one idea too much prominence at the expense of others; it orders its ideas amiss; it is hurried away by fancies; it likes and dislikes too passionately, too exclusively" (***PW,*** 3:249). Thus Aristotle's melancholics, Arnold's nature poets, and Arnold's provincial critics have these characteristics in common: they are too passionate, they follow their fancies, they are impetuous, they cannot order their ideas—they lack, in short, judgment. Judgment is also what the practical critic must have; and literary work, in Arnold's theory, is to be referred to the judicious critic.

Neither Aristotle's *phronimos* nor Arnold's critic are, perhaps, entirely satisfactory solutions to the way in which the good or the best is to be determined. Grant pointed out that Aristotle's ethics was saved from relativism by the concept of the *phronimos,* as his idea of justice is by the *epieikes* or the equitable man (1857 ed., 2:118, 4th ed., 2:91). Arnold would continue to think about the question in **"The Study of Poetry,"** but his solution would remain much the same—the standard found in human reason and experience, practically, in a critic.

In saying that in discovery of fresh knowledge lies "the sense of creative activity" (***PW,*** 3:283), Arnold addressed another question—the relative importance of critical and creative activity. He began the essay on the function of criticism by acknowledging the Romantic claim of the superiority of genius, creative genius, or original genius. Arnold offered the Romantic claim, however, in the form of the classical definition, putting "creative power" in the place of theoretical activity as the proper activity for humankind. Whether Arnold meant to raise creative power to the level of *theoria* or whether he meant ironically to note the magnitude of the Romantic claim are questions that can best be answered by noting first that all such questions are subordinate to the main question—namely, whether criticism can be as important as poetry or even whether it is in some ways the same kind of activity.

Arnold began by answering Wordsworth's assertion that poetry is of higher worth than literary criticism. It is evident, however, that Arnold had in mind not only Wordsworth but also current revivals of Romantic thought and criticism, particularly those of Shairp. Arnold said in this essay that it was Shairp's essay on Wordsworth that had drawn his own attention once more to Wordsworth; and while there may be some truth in this, it is more important to see that Shairp had attacked some of the major positions that Arnold had taken. Shairp had begun by tracing the operation of the "new birth of imagination" in Europe and its flowering in the English Romantic poets.[8] Shairp's emphasis on the new spirit of imagination was exactly the opposite of Arnold's emphasis on the new critical spirit in **"On the Modern Element in Literature"** and such later essays as **"Heinrich Heine."**

Because Arnold in **"The Function of Criticism"** was clarifying the theoretic basis of the earlier essays, he had to make a case for criticism. Thus Arnold, although he praised the essay on Wordsworth, actually set out to show that Shairp was mistaken in his estimate of the Romantic poets and in his view that the "new birth of imagination" alone could bring about a new age of poetry. Shairp had assumed that the Romantic imagination, as a kind of inspired intuition, was sufficient for great poetry. Arnold, although advancing no theory of the imagination, intended to show the necessity of criticism to poetry, to say that the poets, including Wordsworth, had failed because they did not know enough. In a subsequent essay, Shairp defended the polymath Coleridge against this charge but did not fully answer Arnold's arguments until his own Oxford lecture, "Criticism and Creation" (1878). In Plato's *Ion,* Shairp found authority for a theory that the poet is "inspired and possessed": "Plato's few words on this in the *Ion* are worth all Aristotle's methodical treatise on Poetry."[9] Shairp went on to describe Plato's metaphor of the chain of rings suspended from a magnet, from which inspiration flashes out from the magnet—or the muse—to the poet, the actors, and the spectators. Shairp missed the irony in Plato's satire of the "inspired" or irrational poet and his audience. Shairp made explicit, correctly, what Arnold himself had not claimed—namely, that his criticism was based on Aristotle. Shairp, on the other hand, aligned himself with Plato, as Shairp understood the *Ion,* and asserted not only that creation was superior to criticism, because it had the spark of divine truth received by the inspired poet, but also that it was independent of criticism. Indeed, the so-called Arnoldian Concordat, which Geoffrey Hartman has found in **"The Function of Criticism at the Present Time,"** described the work of Shairp, rather than that of Arnold, insofar as this "concordat," as Hartman has said, "assigns to criticism a specific, delimited sphere detached from the creative (which remains superior and the object of millenial hopes)."[10] But it was Shairp, not Arnold, who separated criticism and creation and who argued most strongly for the supremacy of poetic creation. Arnold's problem, in **"The Function of Criticism,"** was, rather, to defend criticism against those who argued for the supremacy of poetry and to claim for criticism, at its best, a share in creative activity.

Arnold began the essay by agreeing that the creative power was higher than the critical power, ostensibly accepting the proposition offered by Wordsworth; but Arnold then looked for reasons why criticism might be considered a creative activity. First he took the high Romantic notion of creation, with its implications of inspiration, prophecy, and visionary power, and confined it within the Aristotelian formula for theoretical activity, putting "free creative power" in the place of *theoria* as the activity or *energeia* that leads to happiness: "It is undeniable that the exercise of a creative power, that a free creative activity, is the highest function of man; it is proved to be so by man's finding in it his true happiness" (***PW,*** 3:260). Whatever Arnold intended to say in this passage, whether to go beyond Aristotle and to say that the proper activity for human kind is creative, not theoretical, or to extend *theoria* to include creative activity, he put the question in the Aristotelian form. In what follows, Arnold made the terms inclusive, when he said that creative power may be exercised in several ways. And he followed Aristotle in the emphasis on "well-doing," when he said that creative power may be exercised in "well-doing . . . in learning, . . . even in criticising" (***PW,*** 3:260). In adding well-doing to the list of creative activities, Arnold was showing that he understood that well-doing was not the same thing as doing good or even doing well but that the Greek *eudaimonia* or happiness carried the sense of living the life of a good person, or living a good life, in the sense that the person was performing an activity that was satisfying. Arnold thus seems to have included criticism among the other kinds of activities that belong to the general category that he called creative activity.

When Arnold said that the critic may have "the sense of exercising this free creative activity" (***PW,*** 3:260), it should be made clear that by "sense" he was referring, not to an illusory sensation, but to something like an awareness. Aristotle had argued that pleasure in friendship lay not only in being engaged in an activity but in being aware that one is engaged in the activity. Grant extended this notion to make *energeia* not only the activity but also the consciousness of the activity; he saw consciousness as something like the inspired visionary moment of the Romantics.[11] Although Arnold was not thinking of the critic as a visionary, he acknowledged that the awareness of an activity was necessary if one were to be happy in performing it. So far, then, Arnold did claim that the critic could exercise free creative power; the question then became one of the limits or conditions under which this power may be exercised.

At the end of the essay, Arnold set up, not so much definite limits, as a scale in which criticism may share in creative activity and be "genuine" creation. Criticism could be creative, he said, when it was "sincere, simple, flexible, ardent, ever widening its knowledge"; then the critic could have "a joyful sense of creative activity" (***PW,*** 3:285). Since Arnold had defined criticism as knowing the best that is thought and said, it would follow that such criticism was, as he said, "ever widening its knowledge" as was thus far creative. In the last paragraph of the essay, however, Arnold qualified what he had said earlier: "in full measure, the sense of creative activity belongs only to genuine creation" (***PW,*** 3:285). Arnold did not, however, draw a clear boundary line between the two activities.

When Arnold spoke here of "genuine creation," he was clearly referring to literary creation—more narrowly, poetry. Furthermore, Arnold distinguished between creative literary genius and philosophy and, significantly, did not assign to creation the discovery of new ideas:

> . . . creative literary genius does not principally show itself in discovering new ideas, that is rather the business of the philosopher. The grand work of literary genius is a work of synthesis and exposition, not of

> analysis and discovery; its gift lies in the faculty of being happily inspired by a certain intellectual and spiritual atmosphere, by a certain order of ideas, when it finds itself in them; of dealing divinely with these ideas, presenting them in the most effective and attractive combinations,—making beautiful works with them, in short.
>
> (***PW,*** 3:260-61)

The work of literary genius is making a work of art, as Aristotle had made clear in the *Poetics* and as Arnold had argued earlier in his letters to Clough and in the 1853 Preface. Originality, so important to the Romantic idea of genius, does not figure in Arnold's definition; indeed, much of his criticism had insisted instead on the importance of tradition and imitation in poetry. Nor does the poet have the function of the seer or the philosopher; the materials of literary art, Arnold said, are ideas. But the creative literary genius does not discover ideas; the genius makes works of art with them. The philosopher does discover ideas, but it is not evident that Arnold was thinking of philosophic thought as belonging to what he called creative activity. Originality, then, was not for Arnold a defining characteristic of creativity. Creativity belonged, rather, to making, to "poetics" in the radical sense. Thus, if criticism was to aspire to being a creative activity, it must do so, not by approaching philosophy, but by becoming a work of art.

Whether creative activity included more than poetry and critical thought was another question; Arnold did not ordinarily speak of philosophy as being creative, but in the essays he did talk about the "inventive power" of science. In **"The Literary Influence of Academies,"** Arnold discussed energy and genius: "Genius is mainly an affair of energy, and poetry is mainly an affair of genius; . . . Again, the highest reach of science is, one may say, an inventive power, a faculty of divination, akin to the highest power exercised in poetry" (***PW,*** 3:238). By *energy,* Arnold here was implying the ordinary meaning of power or force. Indeed, "inventive power" in Arnold's criticism was much the same as creative power, and Arnold used both in **"The Function of Criticism"** (***PW,*** 3:259) and further equated energy with "creative force" (***PW,*** 3:262).

If creative and inventive power are more or less synonymous, then Arnold thought that both the poet and the scientist were engaged in creative activity; he implied the same thing by attributing to both "the faculty of divination." While we may more readily have opposed the poet to the scientist, Arnold tended to think of the scientist as one like Lucretius, who was also a poet.

As a critic, however, Arnold was engaged not so much in synthesis as in analysis, in sorting out the functions of the poet and the critic. In this essay, Arnold set the intellectual, including the critical, power below the genius of the poet and of the scientist. He acknowledged, in response to Wordsworth's ranking of criticism, the superiority of creative or inventive genius: "Everybody, too, would be willing to admit, as a general proposition, that the critical faculty is lower than the inventive" (***PW,*** 3:259). Thus in **"The Function of Criticism,"** Arnold, although he was primarily arguing that the critic could have a sense of creative activity, separated the poet from the critic in that the poets had a power of "divination" and the critic had intellectual power. Arnold did not resolve the Romantic idea that creation is inspiration, which in some degree is suggested by "divination," and the classical idea of poetry as art, a thing made.

Certainly Arnold did not find a solution in imaginative reason, a phrase that he used at the end of the essay on **"Pagan and Medieval Religious Sentiment"** (1864). Some have found a key to Arnold's poetry and even to his criticism in the phrase; others have looked for the origins of the phrase.[12] In this essay, Arnold used "imaginative reason" to suggest his idea of Hellenism, the particular quality of Greek thought that would renew the "modern spirit" in the nineteenth century:

> But the main element of the modern spirit's life is neither the senses and understanding, nor the heart and imagination; it is the imaginative reason. And there is a century in Greek life,—the century preceding the Peloponnesian War, from about the year 530 to the year 430 B.C.,—in which poetry made, it seems to me, the noblest, the most successful effort she has ever made as the priestess of the imaginative reason, of the elements by which the modern spirit, if it would live right, has chiefly to live.
>
> (***PW,*** 3:230)

The limits of meaning that Arnold assigned to "imaginative reason" are suggested when he went on to say that "no other poets, who have so well satisfied the thinking-power, have so well satisfied the religious sense" (***PW,*** 3:231). Arnold's "thinking-power" seems to be close to scientific, logical, or analytic reason, and what satisfies the "religious sense" is most likely to have to do with intuition, or what Arnold called "divination" (which both poets and scientists have).

Certainly, in the two lectures, which were given three months apart, Arnold was clearly thinking about the connection between knowledge and intuition and between imagination and reason. It is even possible that Arnold was again following Aristotle and that "imaginative reason" corresponded to *sophia* (wisdom), which combines scientific knowledge *(episteme)* and intuitive reason *(nous)* (*NE* 1139a15-20).[13] Arnold took his illustration of "imaginative reason" from Sophocles' chorus on divine law in *Oedipus Tyrannos.* Arnold had used Sophocles as the ideal poet from the 1853 Preface to the essay on **"Pagan and Medieval Religious Sentiment"** and had seen Sophocles as the ideal poet of the age of Pericles. Arnold had seen in the age of Pericles the critical spirit in 1857; now he saw in it imaginative reason; and in 1868 he would see in the age the great example of creative activity. Either the shifting emphasis marks only Arnold's particular concern at the moment, or else these terms are closely related in his thought and there is a close connection between the critical spirit and imaginative reason.

At this point in the development of his criticism, Arnold was arguing for the importance of criticism, of the "critical spirit," which he made the chief characteristic of a modern age. Because throughout the ***Essays in Criticism,*** Arnold was arguing for the revival of a critical method in dealing with ideas, the emphasis in the phrase "imaginative reason" surely has to be kept on *reason;* it may even be a synthesis of two kinds of reason, as in Aristotle—intuition and scientific knowledge. One may follow Grant in noting that Aristotle had no theory of the imagination (1857 ed., 2:255, on VI. 4 and 5). But this, too, is evidence that Arnold was identifying a kind of reason.

In any case, Arnold was answering Shairp's claims for the imagination—namely, that imagination can bring about a new age; not imagination, Arnold replied, but imaginative reason. It will be useful, in exploring further the sense of the term, to place it in the context of the writing of the Balliol scholars. Grant said that "with Plato, philosophy was a higher kind of poetry, in which reason and imagination both found their scope" (1857 ed., 1:89). Conceivably Grant was influenced on this point by Jowett, but clearly it was a standard reading of Plato. According to Müller's literary history, which Arnold had consulted on Greek drama, "In Plato the powers of the imagination were just as conspicuous as those of reasoning and reflexion; he had all the chief characteristics of a poet, especially of a dramatic poet."[14] On the side of science and poetry, Lucretius also had a claim to imaginative reason.

Sellar, in his discussion of Lucretius in *The Roman Poets of the Republic* (1863) spoke about the imaginative power of Lucretius in the invocation to Venus, in the association of Venus and Mars, which achieved "a symbolical representation of the philosophical idea of Nature, as creating and sustaining the harmonious process of life, by destruction and dissolution in union with a productive and restoring principle."[15] Lucretius, through his "conception of Nature," was able, Sellar thought, to bring his "abstract philosophical system" into "complete harmony with his poetical feelings and his moral convictions. . . . The contemplation of Nature satisfies the imagination of Lucretius by her aspects of power and life, order, immensity, and beauty"; Sellar also said that there was a difference between what the understanding (or analytical reason) and the "higher speculative faculty" could see:

> Though the mechanical view of the universe may be accepted by the understanding, it has never been acquiesced in by the higher speculative faculty which combines the feeling of the imagination with the insight of the reason. The imagination, which recognizes the presence of infinite life and harmony in the world, rises to the recognition of a creative and governing Power, which it cannot help endowing with consciousness and will.
>
> (*Roman Poets,* pp. 279-80)

Although Sellar did not use the term "imaginative reason" here—instead he used the "higher speculative faculty"—in some ways he was very close to Arnold in the distinctions that he made; the "higher speculative faculty" was separated from the understanding, or analytical reason; this faculty combined imagination and reason; and it was in some sense a faculty of "divination" which satisfied the religious sense, to use Arnold's terms, in the contemplation of Nature.

It is another question whether Arnold meant that to associate poetical feeling or feeling with imagination and insight with reason, as Sellar did, is to achieve imaginative reason. Arnold had read Sellar's *Roman Poets of the Republic,* because he had been asked to recommend Sellar for the professorship of Latin at Edinburgh.[16] Both men may, however, have been drawing from a shared knowledge of the group.

Certainly Sellar later attributed to Lucretius the quality of imaginative reason when, in comparing Vergil to Lucretius, he described the analogies of Lucretius: "The apprehension of these analogies between great things in different spheres proceeds from the inventive and intellectual faculty in the imagination,—that by which intuitions of vast discoveries are obtained before observation of reason can verify them."[17] Here Sellar clearly was connecting what he called "the faculty of imaginative reason" to the "inventive faculty," as it seems that Arnold may have done, and to "intuition"; Sellar distinguished between "imaginative reason" and the analytic reason connected with "observation." Even more clearly, Sellar thought of several kinds of reason—imaginative, scientific, inventive, intuitive—and connected "imaginative reason" to what would nowadays be called the creative imagination, as the faculty by which, through metaphor and symbol, scientific theories are grasped before they can be described and proved by scientific method. Sellar's linking of the poet and the scientist is very close to what Arnold had done in **"The Literary Influence of Academies,"** as we have seen, in assigning to the scientist "an inventive power, a faculty of divination, akin to the highest power exercised in poetry" (***PW,*** 3:238). Yet Arnold's discussion of the great Romantic concepts of the creative imagination, original genius, and inspiration was, like Sellar's, grounded in Aristotelian ideas of reason and was illustrated by the example, not of Wordsworth, but of Lucretius.

The principal idea in Arnold's theory of creation was not that criticism is creative but that the critic knows the best that is thought and said and that he makes this known. Further, given the idea that criticism is an activity, the critic, the poet, and the reader may share in the activity, so that the kind of happiness to be found in the discovery of new ideas or in theoretical activity is open to everybody. Practically, in his own criticism, Arnold illustrated how ideas were to be shared, not so much by the rigor of his arguments or the difficulty of his exposition as by the grace of his prose. Arnold used all the art of his magnificent prose—which is supple, ingenious, witty, graceful—to elucidate the kinds of questions that Shairp, in his somewhat heavy-handed way, made abstract, or "philosophical." Arnold was vivid, particular, varied, interesting;

he seems lightweight, but he touches difficult problems with his clarifying intellect. Again, practically, the subjects that Arnold touched upon in these essays were not exclusively literary; they further draw attention to writers who were distinguished for their literary as well as for their social importance. The list of writers has caused some to question Arnold's own judgment: Are these the best that have written in modern Europe? But that was not Arnold's intention; others could write on Goethe, Kant, Voltaire; on Shakespeare and Milton; on Lucretius and Thucydides; on Sophocles and Plato. Arnold, in these essays, turned to the little-known writers or to those who had lived ordinary lives. Thus he wrote about the brother and sister Maurice and Eugénie de Guérin, about Joseph Joubert, about Marcus Aurelius, but also about Epictetus. In other essays he wrote about those who had taken up the cause of the people, such as Heinrich Heine; and in an essay on a classical writer, not about Sophocles but about Theocritus, not so much about Theocritus as about the ordinary people of the Hellenistic age. Further, his subjects included not only these particular writers but also the common subjects—of nature, man, and society; of the nature poets; of the French Revolution; even of the ordinary life of ancient Rome. This is not to say that Arnold had now accepted the criticism of his friends and turned his prose to the illumination of ordinary life in modern times. Rather, his intention was to show the deficiency of the contemporary, the mistake of relying upon the inspired but uninstructed imagination; he showed that the critical intelligence is needed everywhere.

Although the essays that Arnold collected for ***Essays in Criticism*** do not deal directly with democracy, Arnold had once intended to include his essay **"Democracy"** (1861) in the collection. Certainly, the theme winds in and out of the essays as a connecting thread. So far as there is any visible plan for the whole, it is in the idea of the modern which was the subject of the lectures from about 1857 to 1863, an idea that is certainly attached to Arnold's idea of democracy. Although the chronological order shows to some extent the development of Arnold's aesthetic ideas (as we have seen), the arrangement of the essays in the collection, beginning with **"The Literary Influence of Academies"** and ending with **"Marcus Aurelius,"** shows how Arnold presented his theme of poetry in a democratic age. Arnold was here concerned with the question, which is central for literature in a democracy, of how to keep to a high standard of art yet reach the many. Thus, Arnold began with an examination of an academy in a democratic society and ended with the emperor who, although he thought about the idea of a democracy, attempted to crush the "new spirit" of his own time.

The first essay, **"The Literary Influence of Academies,"** takes up the question of setting a high standard for a national literature. At first glance, Arnold seems to have set aside his essay **"Democracy"** and declared instead for an authoritarian society or at least for a society of artists ruled by a national academy, a high tribunal of artists. An academy, Arnold suggested, is not necessarily inconsistent with a democratic society, and he pointed out that the French Academy had continued to exercise a beneficial influence on the national literature of a people who possessed some of the characteristics of the ancient Athenians, "openness of mind and flexibility of intelligence" (***PW,*** 3:233-35, 237).[18] These qualities of mind are especially necessary in a democracy, as Arnold pointed out in the essay **"Democracy"**: "democracy has readiness for new ideas, and ardour for what ideas it possesses"; but ancient Athens was also the model for a great popular culture: "the spectacle of ancient Athens has such profound interest for a rational man [because] it is the spectacle of the culture of a *people*" (***PW,*** 2:25).[19] As Arnold said, "It was the *many* who relished those arts, who were not satisfied with less than those monuments" (***PW,*** 2:25). Although Arnold did not always use the terms *democracy* and *people* as synonymous and although he sometimes meant by *democracy* the lower classes, here by *people* he clearly meant both the middle and the lower classes of Athens. Thus, Arnold found no inherent conflict between a democratic society and a high standard of art or literature.

Thus, in looking at the French Academy, Arnold considered whether an academy could work in a modern democratic society. Arnold began by showing the difficulty of the critic in England, who must speak from "the critic's isolated position." Citing as an example Palgrave's *Handbook to the Fine Arts Collection of the International Exhibition of 1862,* Arnold noted that Palgrave had adopted a style that was intended to reach the multitude:

> Mr. Palgrave . . . feels himself to be speaking before a promiscuous multitude, with the few good judges so scattered through it as to be powerless; therefore, he has no calm confidence and no self-control; he relies on the strength of his lungs; he knows that big words impose on the mob, and that, even if he is outrageous, most of his audience are apt to be a great deal more so.
>
> (***PW,*** 3:254-55)

There are other ways to reach the multitudes, Arnold implied, than by impressing them with big words. An academy that enforces a high standard in intellectual work, as Arnold thought the French Academy did, encourages good prose, prose without the note of "provinciality" that is the mark of the lonely critic speaking to the crowd. Arnold's ideal was of a classical prose: "the problem is to express new and profound ideas in a perfectly sound and classical style" (***PW,*** 3:247-48). But as Arnold showed in a complex argument, this was true for prose, for intellectual work, but not for poetry.

Poetry—and here Arnold was true to his earliest critical principles—required freedom, the free activity of genius: "And what that energy, which is the life of genius, above everything demands and insists upon, is freedom; entire independence of all authority, prescription, and routine,—the fullest room to expand as it will." And this energy, "the life of genius," which naturally resists authority, also reaches "splendid heights in poetry and science" (***PW,*** 3:238). Thus, poetry and science require freedom; prose, an intellectual work that depends upon flexibility and quickness of mind, profits from the authority both of a form and of an academy (although even the best poetry requires the structure of form). Arnold, with an unexpected chauvinism in a critic who had deplored provinciality, declared that the English were greater in poetry than were the French. His problem then became whether democracy would in fact nourish poetry. If freedom or liberty was necessary to poetry and to the free activity of genius, then the question was whether democracy would allow such freedom or whether democracy (as John Stuart Mill later thought) would restrict individual liberty or stifle individual genius. Arnold had already examined this question in **"Democracy,"** where he had argued that political freedom could be established as well by an aristocracy as by a democracy; here Arnold was thinking about the English barons (***PW,*** 2:7-8). Arnold argued that what democracy certainly established was social freedom: "Social freedom,—equality,—that is rather the field of the conquests of democracy" (***PW,*** 2:8). The effect of living amidst a society of equals was liberating:

> Can it be denied, that to live in a society of equals tends in general to make a man's spirits expand, and his faculties work easily and actively; while, to live in a society of superiors, although it may occasionally be a very good discipline, yet in general tends to tame the spirits and to make the play of the faculties less secure and active?
>
> (***PW,*** 2:8)

Arnold, following Alexis de Tocqueville, thought that equality in France had "given to the lower classes, to the body of the common people, a self-respect, an enlargement of spirit, a consciousness of counting for something in their country's action, which has raised them in the scale of humanity" (***PW,*** 2:9). Still, Arnold was not sure about the changes that would take place as the English lower class became part of a democratic society. The class, which Arnold saw as remarkable for individualism and self-reliance, would give up something to a sense of community or cooperation, though it would gain, as others had, an increased self-respect through belonging to a class that would now have greater importance and through losing a sense of deference to superiors. Certainly, Arnold concluded that although an academy had worked well in France, it would not work so well in England, and it would not encourage poetry, which indeed required individual freedom. Arnold did not, in this essay, answer the question of how one can assure, without an academy, a high standard of art and literature in a democratic society.

Nonetheless, the example of the French Academy, which is set before us in the first essay, is followed by essays on French writers of the nineteenth century. Arnold's two essays on Maurice de Guérin and Eugénie de Guérin serve as examples of the influence of the French Academy; they also illustrate the distinction achieved by almost-ordinary writers working in minor forms—the journal and the letter. Arnold's further purpose was to make these two authors known to English readers through his own lively and vivid translations and through quoting at length from their works. Arnold, then, was making known to the common reader the works of two rather ordinary writers, but ones who were working in a country in which a high standard prevailed. Indeed, commenting on Maurice de Guérin's sure taste in his reading, Arnold observed, "His literary tact is beautifully fine and true" (***PW,*** 3:20).[20] Although what now seems most interesting about Arnold's criticism is the comparison to Keats and the analysis of the romantic or poetic sensibility, in the context of the democratic society one must keep in mind that the Tory reviewers had attacked Keats as an apothecary who was trying to be a poet. Arnold's criticism was disinterested. Like the Romantics, Arnold said, Maurice de Guérin withdrew from society to contemplate Nature: "So he lived like a man possessed; with his eye not on his own career, not on the public, not on fame, but on the Isis whose veil he had uplifted" (***PW,*** 3:34). Yet Guérin had held to a high standard, because of "his *passion for perfection,* his disdain for all poetical work not perfectly adequate and felicitous" (***PW,*** 3:35). Through his style, Maurice de Guérin had achieved distinction: "The magic of expression, to which by the force of this passion he won his way, will make the name of Maurice de Guérin remembered in literature" (***PW,*** 3:35).

Turning to Eugénie de Guérin, Arnold again showed what could be done in the minor forms of the journal and the letter by a woman who was like Blaise Pascal mainly in "the clearness and firmness of her intelligence, going straight and instinctively to the bottom of any matter she is dealing with" (***PW,*** 3:89)[21] The only essay in which Arnold dealt with the writing of a woman, he, much like the feminists of the present time, did not leave out of account "femininity" and the difference that this made to her writing. Unhappily, at least to those of us who are too Americanized or just plainly too American (as we have lately been reminded by an eminent historian) and who are looking for something like equality, the "difference" that Arnold saw lay mainly on the side of inferiority of talent. Thus, in natural description, Maurice reached the sublime but Eugénie only the picturesque; Eugénie suffered from an ennui that arose from her situation and thus differed from Pascal: "Pascal is a man, and the inexhaustible power and activity of his mind leave him no leisure for ennui. . . . Eugénie de Guérin is a woman, and longs for a state of firm happiness, for an affection in which she may repose" (***PW,*** 3:89). Arnold found in Eugénie's prose "a feminine ease and grace, a flowing facility" (***PW,*** 3:89). Arnold noted in Eugénie's journal a perennial concern of women, the conflict between "'a life of household business'" and "this life of reading, thinking, and writing" (***PW,*** 3:92, 93). Arnold noted her resolution to do her household tasks without complaining, to keep "in her proper sphere"; "'I feel that I cannot go beyond my needlework and my spinning without going too far'" (***PW,*** 3:94). As Arnold compared Maurice to the English Romantic Keats, so he might have compared Eugénie to the Romantic Emily Brontë, especially when he saw "something primitive, indomitable in her, which she governs, indeed, but which chafes, which revolts" (***PW***, 3:88). Instead, Arnold brought in for comparison the poet Emma Tatham, the better to make a point about the narrowness of Philistinism in England (***PW***, 3:97) and, by implication, the limits placed in such a society on the genius of women as well as men.

Arnold ended the essay by noting the quality of distinction in the work of Maurice and Eugénie de Guérin: "It procures that the popular poet shall not finally pass for a Pindar, nor the popular historian for a Tacitus, nor the popular preacher for a Bossuet" (***PW***, 3:106). Arnold's use of intrusive alliteration had a function here. As in a heroic couplet, it showed that he had assumed the role of the heroic satirist: the "popular poet" and the "preacher" are contrasted to Pindar and are measured against the great writers who set the standard. Thus, Arnold at the end brought his essay around to his central theme, the high standard set by criticism; at the same time he showed that distinction could be achieved by writers like the isolated brother and sister even in the minor forms.

The essay **"Heinrich Heine"** seems to stand at the center of the collection, announcing the central theme of the age of democracy and defining the task of literature in the new age. Certainly the idea of democracy is central: Heine was "a most effective soldier in the Liberation War of humanity" (***PW***, 3:107).[22] The essay carried on Arnold's speculation about the modern, which he had begun in **"On the Modern Element in Literature."** As there he had asserted that poetry must offer an adequate interpretation of life, so here he said that poetry in the "main current" must "apply modern ideas to life" (***PW***, 3:122). Although "modern ideas" may have a wide reference, as in the opening of **"The Function of Criticism at the Present Time,"** where all branches of knowledge were included, actually Arnold seems here to be thinking of political ideas, of democracy, literally "the liberation of humanity" by the ideas of 1789. Thus he said that Byron and Shelley, the great revolutionary poets, though they failed as artists, did apply "modern ideas" to life, whereas the other Romantic poets retreated from life—Wordsworth to "the inward life," Scott to the feudalism of the past (***PW***, 3:121-22). It could not be said that either Coleridge or Wordsworth were not aware of modern philosophical ideas, but they did turn away from their early enthusiasm for democratic ideas.

Although Arnold denied that poetry aims at "direct political action" (***PW***, 3:118) and would develop in the later essays the principle of disinterestedness, still he continued to say that poetry must offer an "intellectual deliverance"—that is, an adequate interpretation of the age. Equally, the critic must "ascertain the master current in the literature of an epoch" (***PW***, 3:107). And in the modern times (whether past or present) both poets and critics were alive to what Arnold called the "modern spirit," were aware that inherited institutions were not rational and no longer worked. True, as in the essay on the French Academy, Arnold noted the limits of living by reason: the English Revolution, which had been practical rather than theoretical and had made no appeal to reason or to principles, did gain for England a remarkable degree of liberty and prosperity (***PW***, 3:114). But the future, Arnold warned, would require something more. All of Arnold's talk about a modern spirit, about adequate interpretation of an age, about master-currents, really amounted to saying that this was the age of democracy or that it was coming and that it was the task of the critic to make ready for it.

The essay is the source of some remarkable and striking images, definitions, and epigrams of the sort that work well for a lecture but later prove to be more baffling than clarifying. There is the great metaphor about the prison of Puritanism: "the great English middle class . . . entered the prison of Puritanism, and had the key turned on its spirit there for two hundred years" (***PW***, 3:121). Although the image is striking, the history seems suspect. Some definitions are remarkable for their simplicity: "Poetry is simply the most beautiful, impressive, and widely effective mode of saying things, and hence its importance" (***PW***, 3:110). There are also firm pronouncements: "Direct political action is not the true function of literature" (***PW***, 3:118). There are sweeping profundities, as on the great religious poets: "These spirits reach the infinite, which is the true goal of all poetry and all art,—the Greek spirit by beauty, the Hebrew spirit by sublimity" (***PW***, 3:128). In effect, the essay aimed at a "thoroughly modern" criticism, with neat definitions and usable phrases such as "mainstream" and "main-currents" to supply critics and literary historians for another fifty years.

Yet the statements cannot be put together into a coherent theory. If poetry is saying things effectively, why may it not be used for propaganda or for direct political action? Or why should poetry reach for the infinite? And if it does so, then why are not Keats and Wordsworth the great poets of the Romantic age, rather than the Revolutionary poets Byron and Shelley? Arnold would return to each of these points in his later essays on the Romantic poets and would modify these definitions of poetry.

Here what gave Arnold the greatest difficulty was the practical or the political use of literature, especially of poetry. As in all of his essays on the "modern," beginning with the lecture **"On the Modern Element in Literature,"** Arnold wanted to say that the *modern* lies, not in the contemporary or the new, but in a critical or a rational habit of mind. To some extent Arnold also wanted to say that a truly modern literature responds in some way to *modern ideas;* indeed it may offer a historical or a philosophical interpretation of events. Not until **"The Study of Poetry"** did Arnold successfully disentangle poetry from philosophy and from history. Because a democratic people had to respond to ideas, poetry had in some way to satisfy this need. Arnold tended at times to imply that a poetry of ideas was what democracy needed, yet he realized that poetry could not aim at direct political action.

In the following essays, the emphasis shifts from what might seem to be the necessity of the intellectual appeal of poetry to its emotional appeal, the question now being how poetry can reach and move the people. Strictly speaking, Arnold held to the idea that people in a fully developed democracy would be like the Athenians—that is, lively, open-minded, flexible, and demanding the very greatest art and poetry. Nevertheless, this remained an ideal to be attained in the future; and for the present, Arnold thought that the lower classes in England were nearer to the state of the populace in the late Hellenistic Age or the early Middle Ages. Thus, in the essay **"Pagan and Medieval Religious Sentiment,"** the question was how poetry in each age could reach the people.[23] Arnold's method was to compare a popular (religious) poem by Theocritus to a poem written by Saint Francis, choosing these as typical. Arnold offered the hymn to Adonis in the "Fifteenth Idyll" by Theocritus as "a representative religious poem of paganism" (***PW,*** 3:216). Setting the hymn in the context of its audience—the chattering housewives—Arnold translated the idyll and the hymn and offered his own commentary. He contrasted the treatment of the Adonis story in the popular hymn to the symbolic treatment that would have been found in the Eleusinian mysteries: the hymn presents a "story as prepared for popular religious use, as presented to the multitude in a popular religious ceremony" (***PW,*** 3:222). Arnold found that the poem made its appeal to the senses; it was not consoling but was wearying.

From Theocritus, Arnold turned to Saint Francis, the saint who "brought religion to the people": "Poverty and suffering are the condition of the people, the multitude, the immense majority of mankind; and it was towards this *people* that his soul yearned" (***PW,*** 3:223). Saint Francis's *Canticle of the Sun* was "designed for popular use" (***PW,*** 3:224). Arnold found, however, that neither poem appealed to the whole human mind: "Now, the poetry of Theocritus's hymn is poetry treating the world according to the demand of the senses; the poetry of St. Francis's hymn is poetry treating the world according to the demand of the heart and imagination" (***PW,*** 3:225). Nonetheless, the appeal to the heart was preferable to the appeal to the senses. Returning once more to Heine, the subject of an earlier essay, Arnold reflected now on what he saw as Heine's own religion of pleasure, a religion that gave no comfort to "the mass of mankind" (***PW,*** 3:229). In contrast, Arnold now decided that "a religion of sorrow" had the power to reach the "many millions"; it had the "power to be a general, popular, religious sentiment, a stay for the mass of mankind, whose lives are full of hardship" (***PW,*** 3:229-30). Not entirely satisfied with the idea of a religion of sorrow, Arnold reflected that Christianity was also a religion of joy, "drawing from the spiritual world a source of joy so abundant that it ran over upon the material world and transfigured it" (***PW,*** 3:230). The appeal of such poetry as that by Saint Francis was, in any case, to the emotions, and this was an appeal that could be made to the "many millions."

In a modern age, as in the Athenian age of Pericles or in an age of democracy, poetry must make yet another appeal, which Arnold here specified as the appeal to the "imaginative reason." Beyond the popular poetry that speaks to the heart and the imagination, such as the *Canticle of the Sun,* or the poetry that speaks to the senses and the imagination, such as the hymn to Adonis, was the poetry of Simonides, Pindar, Aeschylus, and Sophocles, which speaks to the imaginative reason. Here Arnold tried to discover the appeal that popular poetry makes in a democratic age, to people such as the Athenians. Arnold did not, I think, try to offer a synthesis of the heart and the senses, the imagination and the understanding. Rather, he tried to define another faculty—the imaginative reason—a reason, as I have suggested, of the kind that poetry and science use in reaching for an analogy or a metaphor as a way of explaining an insight. He developed this idea in his next essay, on the French Academy. Such a poetry, which makes an appeal both to reason and to feeling, may be the best poetry for a democratic age.

In the following essay, **"Joubert,"** Arnold advanced another theory of the way in which poetry reaches the reader, using still the Romantic idea of creative genius: "And yet what is really precious and inspiring, in all that we get from literature, except this sense of an immediate contact with genius itself, and the stimulus towards what is true and excellent which we derive from it?" (***PW,*** 3:183)[24] The idea of sharing, in a sense, the inspiration of the genius corresponds to Arnold's theory of the way in which an audience delights in the "high art" of the drama. To Aristotle's principle that all men desire to know, Arnold added the delight in novelty: "from what is new to us we in general learn most"—his argument for noticing a minor author. Arnold, near the end of the essay, defended his choice of Joubert. Arnold had asserted that "a criticism of life" was "the end and aim of all literature" (***PW,*** 3:209). He went on to note the difference between the criticism of "men of ability" and that of "men of genius." Here, again, is Arnold's defense of the "modern" as against the merely contemporary: his "modern" is what "is permanently acceptable to mankind"; it possesses "inherent truth" (***PW,*** 3:209), in contrast to the ideas that make a great appeal in their time. "But the taste and ideas of one generation are not those of the next" (***PW,*** 3:209)—and here Arnold sketched the energetic march of the leaders of the new generation as it sweeps away the old, saving the great men—the Homers and the Shakespeares—and those of their family—the Jouberts—protecting them from the destroying hordes that follow. Arnold commented on those who spoke to their age alone, "What a fate, . . . to be an oracle for one generation, and then of little or no account for ever" (***PW,*** 3:211). Arnold's paradoxical definition of *modern* was an answer to those who held that the writer could only speak to his own age.

Although Arnold abandoned his series of lectures on the modern element before he wrote the essay **"Joubert,"** he had not abandoned the idea of the modern, which is central in **"The Function of Criticism at the Present Time."** Nor had Arnold changed in finding the "modern" in ancient Greece, whether in the "critical spirit," in "imaginative reason," or in a "criticism of life." Rather, Arnold dramatized once more his defense of what he would later call the classic against Shairp and others who had declared that the classical poet was irrelevant to the Victorian world. Arnold's "modern" meant what is permanently true, whether this be an idea discovered in ancient Greece or in the nineteenth century. On the other hand, as he had said in the essay **"On the Modern Element in Literature,"** the historian or the poet must have an adequate understanding of his own age and of new ideas, which might include radically different ways of looking at the world.

In taking up the works of Marcus Aurelius, Arnold in fact considered the consequence of failing to grasp a radical "new spirit" in the history of the world. The essays of the Roman emperor had always had a popular appeal, and in translation, they continued to make an appeal to the common reader, like the essays of Epictetus. True, Arnold here expressed doubt that moral ideas as such could reach the many: "The mass of mankind have neither force of intellect enough to apprehend them clearly as ideas, nor force of character enough to follow them strictly as laws. The mass of mankind can be carried along a course full of hardship for the natural man, can be borne over the thousand impediments of the narrow way, only by the tide of a joyful and bounding emotion" (***PW,*** 3:134).[25] Like religious poetry, moral discourse must appeal to emotion: and Arnold here included pagan with Christian, Empedocles with Paul, as those who "have insisted on the necessity of an inspiration, a joyful emotion, to make moral action perfect" (***PW,*** 3:134). Once more, Arnold saw in religion the clue to reaching the multitude; here Arnold compared the wisdom of Epictetus and that of the Old Testament to the "warmth" of the New Testament. Again, it appears that Arnold had forgotten the "idea-moved" masses; he saw the multitudes as being nearer to those of the Middle Ages than to the Athenians of the Age of Pericles.

Yet, when Arnold took up the modernity of the Roman emperor Marcus Aurelius, he saw him as "a man like ourselves, a man in all things tempted as we are" (***PW,*** 3:140); indeed, Arnold made a strong case for seeing parallels between the age of Marcus Aurelius and the Victorian. Indeed, Arnold's interest lay in just this parallel. Discussing the mistakes for which the Roman emperor had been criticized, the worst being his persecution of the Christians, Arnold clearly kept before him the modern parallel. The new spirit in Rome at the time of Marcus Aurelius was Christianity, the new "dissolvent" of the old order: "It was inevitable that Christianity in the Roman world, like democracy in the modern world, like every new spirit with a similar mission assigned to it, should at its first appearance occasion an instinctive shrinking and repugnance in the world which it was to dissolve" (***PW,*** 3:144). The modern sage, Arnold implied, must take warning from the example of Marcus Aurelius and therefore not impede the new spirit of democracy. Marcus Aurelius, according to Arnold's account, meditated on the idea of equality and freedom: "'The idea of a polity in which there is the same law for all, a polity administered with regard to equal rights and equal freedom of speech, and the idea of a kingly government which respects most of all the freedom of the governed'" (***PW,*** 3:147). Arnold saw Marcus Aurelius as the Roman emperor who could imagine equality and freedom in an ideal state yet who dealt with the new spirit of Christianity as others in later times would deal with the new spirit of democracy.

As to whether the emperor in his own writing could move the reader, whether he could, like the Christian moralist, reach the emotions, Arnold finally said that the emperor could, although not so powerfully, with something "less than joy and more than resignation"; "the sentences of Marcus Aurelius find their way to the soul" (***PW,*** 3:149). Although Marcus Aurelius was not a poet, Arnold did deal with the question of how literature reached the multitudes. Certainly in writing about the late Roman Empire, the age of Trajan, Arnold could see the division (as Sellar was to show) between the aristocrats and the populace in Rome. Marcus Aurelius, in suppressing a popular religion, could not cross this division—to the greater loss of Rome and to European civilization, which would have benefited from a Christianity that learned from Roman culture. This is the parallel, and this is the lesson: the Victorians had to recognize that the new spirit of democracy was inevitable, and in order to assist its development, they must make available the best of the old civilization. Thus, Arnold ended his collection of essays with the example of Rome, as he had begun it with the example of Greece in **"Democracy."**

Notes

1. *Ethica Nicomachea* (cited in the text and notes as *NE*), ed. Ingram Bywater (Oxford: Clarendon Press, 1949), pp. 212-13; William David Ross, *Aristotle,* 5th ed. (1949; reprint, New York: Barnes & Noble, 1964), pp. 232-34; W. F. R. Hardie, *Aristotle's Ethical Theory,* 2nd ed. (Oxford: Clarendon Press, 1980), pp. 336-57.

2. Ross, *Aristotle,* p. 234; Hardie, *Aristotle's Ethical Theory,* pp. 338-40, quoting J. Burnet, *The Ethics of Aristotle* (London: Methuen, 1900), p. 438. Hardie says: "It may be suggested, however, that some of Aristotle's reasons for commending theoretical activity, in contrast with practical and political pursuits, are applicable to artistic and aesthetic as well as to scientific interests" (p. 340).

3. *Ethics of Aristotle,* ed. Alexander Grant, 2 vols. (London: John W. Parker, 1857), 2:153; see also the 4th ed., 2 vols. (London: Longmans, Green & Co., 1885), 2:335, hereafter cited as *Ethics.* See Frank M. Turner, *The Greek Heritage in Victorian Britain* (New Haven, Conn.: Yale University Press, 1981), pp. 326-27, 340-52. Turner sees Grant's work as a dividing point in studies of Aristotle during the nineteenth century. It seems evident to me that Arnold's reading of Aristotle in "The Function of Criticism at the Present Time" belongs to the earlier

interpretations, especially of "activity"; but the presence of Grant in the circle of the friends of Benjamin Jowett, who was so important to Arnold and his friends as a guide to Greek studies, cannot be ignored. I have found Grant's commentary on certain words to be a useful illustration of points that Arnold made in his criticism.

4. Peter Allan Dale, *The Victorian Critic and the Idea of History: Carlyle, Arnold, Pater* (Cambridge, Mass.: Harvard University Press, 1977), pp. 10, 107-9.

5. See *Ethics,* 1857 ed., 2:83, 256-57.

6. *NE* 1150b25-28, p. 144; *The Works of Aristotle,* vol. 9, ed. W. D. Ross (Oxford: Clarendon Press, 1925).

7. *Ethics,* 4th ed., 2:223-24; *The Poems of Tennyson,* ed. Christopher Ricks (London: Longman, 1969; reprint, New York: Norton, 1972), p. 1050.

8. John Campbell Shairp, "Wordsworth: The Man and the Poet," in *Studies in Poetry and Philosophy* (Boston and New York: Houghton Mifflin, 1872), pp. 1-4; this first appeared in *North British Review* 41 (Aug., 1864): 1-54.

9. John Campbell Shairp, "Criticism and Creation," *Aspects of Poetry, Being Lectures Delivered at Oxford* (Oxford: Clarendon Press, 1881), pp. 49-53; this essay was first published in *Macmillan's Magazine* 38 (July, 1878): 246-56. On the *Ion* as satire see Gerald F. Else, *Plato and Aristotle on Poetry,* ed. Peter Burian (Chapel Hill: University of North Carolina Press, 1986), pp. 5-9.

10. Geoffrey Hartman, *Criticism in the Wilderness* (New Haven, Conn.: Yale University Press, 1980), p. 6.

11. *NE* 1170; see Ross's note; Turner, *Greek Heritage,* pp. 350-51; *Ethics,* 1857 ed., 1:193-94, 200-201.

12. David J. DeLaura, "Arnold's Imaginative Reason: The Oxford Sources and the Tradition," *Prose Studies* 1 (1977): 7-18, "Imaginative Reason: A Further Note," ibid., 2 (1979): 103-6, and "Imaginative Reason: Yet Again," ibid., 188-89.

13. Ross, *Aristotle,* pp. 216-18; Hardie, *Aristotle's Ethical Theory,* pp. 345-57; on difficulties of *nous* in Aristotle's theory see *Ethics,* 1857 ed., 1:261-63 ("a union of reason and science").

14. Karl Otfried Müller, *A History of the Literature of Ancient Greece,* trans. George Cornewall Lewis and John William Donaldson, 3 vols. (London: John W. Parker, 1858), 2:258.

15. William Young Sellar, *The Roman Poets of the Republic* (Edinburgh: Edmonston & Douglas, 1863), p. 279.

16. *The Note-Books of Matthew Arnold,* ed. Howard Foster Lowry, Karl Young, and Waldo Hilary Dunn (London: Oxford University Press, 1952), p. 571, July, 1863; William Bell Guthrie, "Matthew Arnold's Diaries: The Unpublished Items: A Transcription and Commentary" 4 vols. (Ph.D. diss., University of Virginia, 1957; Ann Arbor, Mich.: University Microfilms, 1981), 2:402-4: Arnold entered "Sellar's Roman Poets" on July 23, 25, 27, 28, 29, and 30 and Aug. 4 and 5, 1863; on August 7 he wrote "finish Sellar's Roman Poets." The letter that Arnold wrote to Shairp is included in E. M. (Eleanour Denniston) Sellar's *Recollections and Impressions* (Edinburgh and London: William Blackwood & Sons, 1907), pp. 164-65. Arnold wrote, "I have now read every word of it, some of it more than once, and with extreme satisfaction" (p. 164); on Lucretius, he wrote: "The delicacy and interestingness of the criticism in certain places I say little about, because these are chiefly shown in the chapters on Lucretius, most of which I had read and liked, as such criticism deserved to be liked, before"; Arnold thus indicated that he had read the essay on Lucretius in the *Oxford Essays* of 1855.

17. William Young Sellar, *The Roman Poets of the Augustan Age: Virgil,* 3d ed. (London: Oxford University Press, 1908; reprint, New York: Biblo & Tannen, 1965), p. 240.

18. The lecture "The Influence of Academies on National Spirit and Literature" was given on June 4, 1864, and was revised for *Cornhill.* In chronological order, it thus immediately precedes "The Function of Criticism at the Present Time," but in the order of the essays in the collection, Arnold placed it immediately after the introductory essay, in part to show a function of the "critic" ([*The Complete Prose Works of Matthew Arnold,* Edited by R. H. Super. 11 vols. Ann Arbor: University of Michigan Press, 1960–77. Cited in the text and notes as] *PW,* 3:463).

19. See Super's notes on *PW,* 2:331; the essay was composed as an introduction to *The Popular Education of France* (1861) and was considered in 1864 as part of the collection of *Essays in Criticism.*

20. The lecture "A Modern French Poet" was given on Nov. 15, 1862; it appeared in *Fraser's Magazine* in Jan., 1863 (See Super's notes on pp. 407-8).

21. The essay was first published in June, 1863, in *Cornhill* (see Super's notes *PW,* 3:428). "The French Academy voted a prize to her [Eugénie de Guérin's] posthumously published *Journal*" (ibid.). Eugénie de Guérin died in 1848.

22. Super notes that the lecture "The Modern Element in Romanticism" was not published; it was delivered on Mar. 26, 1863. The lecture "Heinrich Heine" was given on June 13 and was subsequently published in *Cornhill* (*PW,* 3:433).

23. *PW,* 3:215. The Oxford lecture "Pagan and Christian Religious Sentiment," which was given on Mar. 5, 1864, was published in *Cornhill* in April (see Super's notes in *PW,* 3:458). Between this essay and the earlier one on Heine, Arnold had published

"Marcus Aurelius," "Spinoza and the Bible," and "Joubert"; that is, he had given considerable thought to popular religion, as well as to Stoic morality, and to the emotional appeal of morality and religion.

24. The lecture "A French Coleridge" was delivered on Nov. 28, 1863, and was published in the *National Review* in Jan., 1864 (*PW,* 3:452).

25. The essay first appeared in *Victoria Magazine* in Nov., 1863; see Super's notes in *PW,* 3:440.

Tony Pinkney (essay date 1992)

SOURCE: "Matthew Arnold and the Subject of Modernity," in *Critical Survey,* Vol. 4, No. 3, 1992, pp. 226-32.

[*In the following essay, Pinkney emphasizes the continuities between Arnold's account of the detached subject of literature's emergence and more recent elaborations on the death of the subject.*]

One thing which traditionalist and radical literary critics tend to agree on, however bitterly they fight over everything else, is the idea that a decisive transformation or what the French Marxist Louis Althusser might have termed a *coupure épistémologique* has taken place in English studies over the last twenty or so years. Both sides, naturally, have a vested interest in the notion of such a 'break': it suits the traditionalists to draw a sharp distinction between the wholesome and commonsensical discipline English once used to be and the florid, jargon-ridden elitism it has collapsed into, and it suits the radicals to dismiss everything prior to (say) 1968 as boring and outmoded, and to celebrate everything after it as dynamically state-of-the-art and intellectually adventurous. A few bold and flexible spirits, of whom Frank Kermode is probably the most eminent, have tried over the years to work across both sides of this divide—without, however, ceasing to view it *as* a divide and thus requiring particularly acrobatic feats of straddling and bridging. 'Only connect' might be the Forsterian motto of Kermode's long and admirable critical career, but then you have to have two diametric opposites and a gaping *coupure épistémologique* between them to do your connecting in the first place.

What I want to suggest in this article is that traditional English studies and radical literary theory are by and large the same thing. This is a view which gives cold comfort to both sides of the current debate over the 'crisis of English'. Traditional critics will presumably not take kindly to discovering that they were 'always-already' Jacques Derrida in disguise, while post-1968 radical theorists, in the grip of a modernist compulsion to 'Make It New' (usually mediated through Bertolt Brecht rather than Ezra Pound), will hardly welcome a postmodern claim that, after all, they're only doing what's been done before, that they're in the grip of a Freudian *Wiederholungszwang* or compulsion to repeat which they cannot bring to consciousness though it governs their every gesture. Of course the English studies that already *is* contemporary literary theory isn't the whole of traditional Eng Lit; there are indeed aspects of the latter which are just incompatible with theory and must now be abandoned. But it is an important and widely influential version of English Studies. I first came across this version of English as an undergraduate between 1975 and 1978 in what was possibly the very last militant Leavisite English Department in the country. And once you'd intellectually taken on board the strongest version of Leavisism, that which aligns him with T. S. Eliot (the stress on 'dissociation of sensibility'), D. H. Lawrence (the lost 'organic community') and the romantic anti-capitalist impulse of modernism in general, then the leap one had to make, as a postgraduate, to Michel Foucault, Walter Benjamin, Jacques Derrida and others did not seem very great at all. As a signal of continuity rather than *coupure,* the journal of literary theory that I help edit is titled *News from Nowhere,* and it seeks precisely to elicit the links between that powerful project of utopian cultural studies implicit in the term 'Gothic' in the work of John Ruskin and William Morris and developments in the field of cultural theory today.[1]

To trace through the connections between Leavisite English studies and the radical literary theory of recent years would be a long task, and a crucial mediating figure would be the German philosopher Martin Heidegger. In the brief compass afforded to me by this article, I want rather to focus on the relations between contemporary theory and a figure who, for a certain F. R. Leavis (what I am here calling the 'strong', Lawrence-orientated Leavis), would be the critical arch-enemy—Matthew Arnold. One of the signs of the impact of theory throughout English Departments has been the way in which it has drawn even more traditional, 'period' courses into its orbit, giving them a distinctly conceptual rather than author-based framework. So it is, for example, that one increasingly teaches 'Modernism' rather than 'English Literature 1890-1930', or 'Postmodernism' rather than 'Contemporary Literature'. Indeed, the debate over the whole cluster of cultural, theoretical and social issues implicit in the terms 'modernity', 'modernisation', 'modernism' and 'postmodernism' is extremely active in most English Departments today, constituting one of their liveliest points of contact with such adjoining disciplines as Sociology, History and Philosophy. But if literary theory has made such concepts and issues highly visible over the last decade, we should not assume that English Studies before that—'traditional' English Studies, if you will—was not passionately concerned with such topics. Leavis's own work would be a rich field for demonstrating the truth of that claim; but I shall here argue it through an analysis of a seminal text of Matthew Arnold's, **'On the Modern Element in Literature'**, which he delivered at Oxford as his inaugural lecture as Professor of Poetry on 14 November 1857. Arnold's title is so germane to our current debates around modernity that literary theory would surely have been obliged to invent it if Arnold hadn't conveniently used it himself in the first place.

Undergraduate literary theory courses can be organised in many different ways to many different institutional ends. Some are topic based (Language, Intertextuality, Meaning, etc.), and some are school and -ism based (Russian Formalism, Structuralism, Feminism, etc.); some concentrate on the commanding heights of 'pure' theory, others put a premium on the 'application' of theory to literary and other texts; and the most successful courses probably involve a nimble, opportunistic blend of all these possibilities. But there is perhaps a single fundamental insight which a theory course must communicate, a single governing principle which, once the student has grasped it, justifies one in calling the course a success, even if its clientele can't recall every single one of Vladimir Propp's thirty-one functions or haven't followed every last wrinkle of Jacques Derrida on masturbation in Rousseau. This principle is, in Roland Barthes's phrase, the 'death of the author' or, as I prefer to call it for my purposes here, the 'death of the subject'. Traditionalist criticism is founded on the notion of the author as transcendental subject, a pinpoint of lucid self-consciousness who exists outside and before language, history, gender, race, class. The act of writing is then a 'secondary' act whereby this 'author-God' (Barthes's phrasing again) externalises the inner contents of his or her psyche. The very first task of a literary theory course is to dislodge this model. It must 'situate' the subject, as Derrida once put it, demonstrating that the conscious subject is not 'master in its own house' as it would like to think itself, but is rather the product of systems and forces which it does not control. Consciousness or the subject is, on this showing, an effect of *un*conscious systems—whether we conceive of the unconscious as sexual (Freud), linguistic (Saussure, semiotics) or political (Marxism, feminism). The subject as thus conceived is 'decentred', dislodged from the centrality it claims for itself; it is not, however, eradicated altogether, as some traditionalist fantasies of literary theory as a Dalek-like process of extermination might suggest. Roland Barthes's death of the author, need one say, is *not* the Ayatollah Khomenei's.

Now all this might sound abstract and alien, even 'theory-mad beyond redemption', to borrow a fine phrase of Edgar Allen Poe's. None the less, it is what English Studies has *always* been arguing about, in its own idiom, on its own occasions. One such occasion was Arnold's 1857 inaugural lecture at Oxford, though his concern is more with the *con*struction rather than deconstruction of the subject. Modernity, as Arnold defines it here, involves a relation of 'adequacy' (a key term in this text) between subject and object:

> This, then, is what distinguishes certain epochs in the history of the human race, and our own amongst the number;—on the one hand, the presence of a significant spectacle to contemplate; on the other hand, the desire to find the true point of view from which to contemplate this spectacle.[2]

But the establishment of this 'point of view', this modern subject, is a far from easy task. In modern epochs the object, the social world itself, is 'copious and complex', 'a vast multitude of facts', 'an immense, moving, confused spectacle'—to the point, indeed, where it totally swamps the subject, which can achieve no distance or autonomy from its frenetically developing environment. What is accordingly required is a strenuous process of 'intellectual deliverance' whereby the subject hoists itself out of the ruck of the multitudinous modern world, distancing and mastering an object which is now defined as distinctly *other* than it:

> The deliverance consists in man's comprehension of this present and past. It begins when our mind begins to enter into possession of the general ideas which are the law of this vast multitude of facts. It is perfect when we have acquired that harmonious acquiescence of mind which we feel in contemplating a grand spectacle that is intelligible to us.
>
> (20)

The task of Arnold's lecture is thus to give substance and detail to this abstract notion of an 'intellectual deliverance', of the emergence of the detached subject.

Arnold aims to do this through a comparison and contrast between a 'modern' and a 'premodern' epoch. His instance of the latter is 'the age of Elizabeth in our own country' (23), particularly as represented by Sir Walter Raleigh's *History of the World;* the inaugural lecture thus extends that critique of the Elizabethan age that is already implicit in his assault on Shakespeare's poetic language and influence in the 1853 Preface to his ***Poems.*** His instance of modernity is 'the life of Athens in the fifth century before our epoch' (23), above all as represented by Thucydides's *History of the Peloponnesian War.* In the 1853 Preface, too, the Greeks had been counterposed to the Elizabethans and 'moderns', their self-effacing devotion to poetic subject-matter and their practice of the harmonious aesthetic totality being favourably contrasted with Shakespeare's fetishism of 'expression' and Keatsian poetic fragmentation. Now, however, in a crucial shift of terms, what counts as 'modern' in the 1853 Preface—the excess of signifier over signified, of language over that which it ought transparently to express—is defined as *non*-modern; and the 'ancients' of the 1853 text have become the very paragons of modernity itself in the 1857 lecture. The contrast is now between Elizabethan 'barbarism' or primitivism and a 'modernity' which oddly happens, in the inaugural lecture, to be illustrated by the Greeks. In his *Matthew Arnold: A Life,* Park Honan describes Arnold as 'England's first great comparative critic'.[3] This isn't strictly true, others had been there first; but it is none the less a crucial emphasis. From Arnold's work on, the comparison between the Elizabethan epoch and its 'modern' successor, between Shakespearean English and 'modern prose', becomes the fundamental substance of English criticism. In many ways, it still is today, and it is a comparison rich in literary-theoretical consequences.

The central characteristic of the modern subject, as exemplified by Thucydides, is its autonomy: in separating itself off from the 'object', the social world, it achieves mastery over the latter. Whereas Thucydides displays 'rational appreciation and control of his facts', the Elizabethan historian, Raleigh, writing in an epoch in which subjectivity has not yet been constituted, 'wanders among them helplessly and without a clue' (27-8). Thucydides's prose is '*modern* language . . . the language of a thoughtful philosophic man of our own days', while Raleigh's is 'a language wholly obsolete and unfamiliar to us' (26-7). The Greek's history evinces what Arnold considers modernity's 'supreme characteristic of all': 'the tendency to observe facts with a critical spirit; to search for their law, not to wander among them at random' (24)—this last phrase, of course, once again describing Raleigh's practice.

Where does such a 'critical spirit' or modern subjectivity come from? How is it constituted? Arnold's text gives us the materials for an answer, though it does not formulate the answer itself; and once we have articulated it, reading the inaugural lecture 'against the grain', we shall discover a remarkable convergence of views between Matthew Arnold and Michel Foucault. 'To begin with what is exterior', as Arnold puts it: 'One of the most characteristic outward features of a *modern* age, of an age of advanced civilization, is the banishment of the ensigns of war and bloodshed from the intercourse of civil life' (23). On this criterion Elizabethan England, in which 'the wearing of arms was universal', is not modern, while ancient Greece, in which 'the Athenians first left off the habit of wearing arms', is. But if violence, in modernity, is indeed banished from daily social life, where does it go *to?* Is it truly negated without remainder, or does it infiltrate itself into other areas of human existence, in forms which may look very different indeed from the bloodthirsty duelling of Raleigh and his contemporaries? To answer this question we must attend to the 'violence' of Arnold's own language as he describes Thucydides's practice as historian.

Violence still operates within the modern, but it is *internalised* and no longer takes the spectacular, external form of the street brawl. Modernity's violence is felt repeatedly in Arnold's verbs, and is first exercised in Greece against the very surfaces of the body, since one of the key features of a modern culture is 'that propriety of taste which *proscribes* the excess of ornament, the extravagance of luxury' (24—my italics). But if modernity exercises aggression against its own body rather than that of others, it at once takes the internalising process a stage further and directs violence against layers of the inner self. The historian must dislodge 'men's habit of *uncritical* reception of current stories'; he must '*strip* these facts of their exaggeration . . . examine them critically' (25—my italics). Such naive gullibility is, in the first place, a feature of his own psyche as well as that of others; it is a psychic capacity he inherits from a culture in which tradition, custom, prejudice, legend are all important social forces. Only by turning upon and destroying his *own* gullibility, his own tendency to submit to tradition, can he later, as author, hope to wean his readers away from their dependency on custom. To become a modern historian, a modern subject, an archaic layer of one's psyche must first be annihilated. Walter Raleigh might get his nose bloodied in a street fight, but the subject of modernity must exercise a ceaseless, invisible, internalised violence within the self. Only by violently breaking up the inherited 'heteronomous' self can a truly modern, autonomous one come into being.

But this is very much the tale that Michel Foucault has to tell in the unforgettable opening pages of *Discipline and Punish,* where he contrasts the gruesome public dismembering and execution of Damiens the regicide in 1757 with a 'modern' prison timetable drawn up by Léon Faucher some eighty years later. Foucault's contrast of medieval 'barbarism' and modern 'humanitarianism' serves the very same purpose as Carlyle's social contrasts in *Past and Present* or Ruskin's contrast of Gothic architecture and contemporary industrialism in 'The Nature of Gothic'. In all three cases, a supposedly 'humane' modernity is shown to be more, not less, cruel than the 'barbarism' it claims to have left behind. The violence inflicted on the body of Damiens, we come slowly to realise as we work through Foucault's book, is at least less insidious than that exercised upon the souls of nineteenth-century prison inmates: medieval violence shatters the body but leaves the 'inner man' intact, but 'modern' violence bypasses the body in order permanently to reprogramme the very psyche of its victim. Its ultimate achievement, as Foucault shows in his discussion of the Panopticon, is to get the victim to *internalise* his own repression, so that instead of being policed from outside he emerges, finally, as an apparently autonomous but in fact self-policing subject; his very subjectivity, paradoxically, *is* his subjection.

That Foucault and Arnold differ profoundly in their valuations of what they describe—Arnold speaking for modernity, Foucault problematising it—should not blur the fact that they are both describing, from their own specific angles, the same general historical process: the emergence of modernity, of the subject of modernity. But what about the non-subject of premodernity, represented by the hapless Sir Walter Raleigh in **'On the Modern Element in Literature'**? As we have seen, Raleigh as historian is characterised by 'helplessness' before the facts: unable to master them, he is their victim; they write him, rather than he them. But since Arnold is essentially developing a contrast of modes of *language*—Thucydides's, we recall, was '*modern* language . . . the language of an intelligent man of our own days' (26-7)—it is to the discussion of Shakespearean English in the 1853 Preface that we should turn for Arnold's more developed thoughts on premodern language and its consequences for the subject. The 'school of Shakespeare' in English poetry is distinguished, according to the Preface, by its preference for fragment rather than totality, for 'separate thoughts and images' rather than crisply delineated subject-matter or overall aesthetic unity:

> A modern critic would have assured him [the poet] that the merit of his piece depended on the brilliant things which arose under his pen as he went along. We have poems which seem to exist merely for the sake of single

> lines and passages; not for the sake of producing any total impression. We have critics who seem to direct attention merely to detached expressions, to the language about the action, not to the action itself.
>
> (7)

Within the Shakespearean poetic tradition, that is to say, language achieves a materiality and autonomy of its own: it cannot be reduced to the signified or content, but rather obtrudes its own ungainly bulk between reader and subject-matter, and cannot be reduced to the intention of an author, but instead 'arises under his pen' almost by its own will as he goes along. Greek poetic practice, as described in the Preface, involves a violent effort of will whereby language is reduced to purely secondary status: in classical Greek poetry the style is 'so simple and so well subordinated', 'the tone of the parts was to be perpetually kept down' (5-6).

If we transpose all this into the terms of the 1857 lecture, where the Greeks are the very exemplars of the 'modern element' and the Elizabethans of premodern barbarity, then we can see that Arnold is articulating what I have argued is the central principle of an undergraduate literary theory course: the 'death of the subject', the notion of the subject as an effect of language and the unconscious. Only, whereas for literary theory this is the necessary condition of subjectivity as such, for Arnold it is (a) a bad thing, (b) only characterises 'primitive' epochs, and (c) with the help of Greek poetics and literary Academies can be avoided entirely by a transcendental modern subject. If I had space here, I would seek to show that throughout both Arnold's and Leavis's work, throughout whole areas of 'traditional' English studies, the term 'Shakespearean English' operates as a shorthand, nontheoretical way of referring to the idea of a 'situated', decentred subject, while 'modern prose' (whether of the Greeks or of eighteenth-century England) is a codeword for what theory would today term the transcendental subject. Arnold's classicist assault on Shakespearean English and Elizabethan historiography, T. S. Eliot's defence of the 'undissociated' sensibility and language of the Jacobean dramatists in 'The Metaphysical Poets', Leavis's great attack on Dryden's classicist rewriting of *Antony and Cleopatra* in *The Living Principle*—all these are profound meditations, through the focus of contrasted modes of language, on modernity and the nature of the modern subject. But contemporary literary theory is *also* that, above all in the epoch of the postmodern. It should not, then, in terms of undergraduate teaching, be a matter of externally 'applying' theory to literary texts, but rather of aiming to demonstrate that literature itself for many centuries, English studies as we have known them for the last hundred or so years, and the literary theory of the last two decades have a single, obsessive object of concern: the condition and costs of modernity. That being so, the findings of any one of these three traditions can, with a little patience and ingenuity, be fruitfully transcoded into those of the others. To communicate that insight, to give students the resources they need to come to their own judgments on the whole epoch of Western modernity, is, in my view, the central responsibility of an undergraduate English degree today.

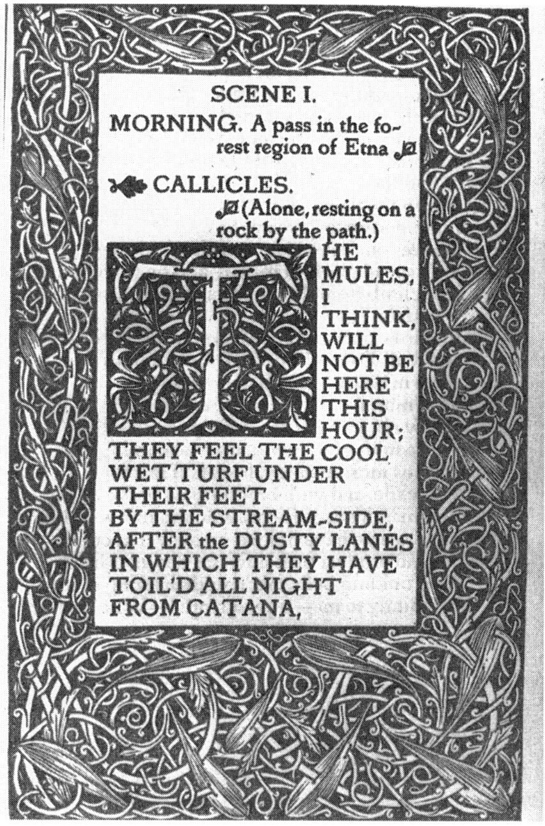
SCENE I.
MORNING. A pass in the forest region of Etna
CALLICLES.
(Alone, resting on a rock by the path.)
THE MULES, I THINK, WILL NOT BE HERE THIS HOUR; THEY FEEL THE COOL WET TURF UNDER THEIR FEET BY THE STREAM-SIDE, AFTER the DUSTY LANES IN WHICH THEY HAVE TOIL'D ALL NIGHT FROM CATANA,

Page one of Arnold's "Empedocles on Etna: A Dramatic Poem."

Notes

1. See my 'Editorial: In Praise of Gothic', *News from Nowhere,* no. 9, Special Issue on 'Utopias and Utopianism', Autumn 1991, 3-5.
2. R. H. Super (ed.), *The Complete Prose Works of Matthew Arnold. I: On the Classical Tradition* (Ann Arbor: University of Michigan Press, 1960), p. 20. References to this volume are hereafter included in my text.
3. Park Honan, *Matthew Arnold: A Life* (London: Weidenfeld and Nicolson, 1981), p. 291.

Stefan Collini (essay date 1993)

SOURCE: "Arnold," in *Victorian Thinkers,* Oxford University Press, 1993, pp. 27-47.

[*In the following essay, Collini surveys Arnold's poetic achievements, focusing on such works as "Empedocles on Etna," the* Switzerland *poems, and "Dover Beach."*]

The collected prose works of Matthew Arnold occupy eleven fat volumes; the complete poetry, even when fleshed out with notes, variants, and appendices, fits easily into one volume in any of the several modern editions in which it has appeared. Though any rounded account of his achievement must to some extent reflect these proportions, such crude quantities tell us little about the relative value or enduring appeal of his various compositions in the two genres. In fact, the reputation of his poetry has been more stable and more generally favourable over the past hundred years than that of his prose, even though, as I have suggested, I think it is now the latter which has the greater claim on our attention. But certainly there may still be some readers who, vaguely recalling **'Dover Beach'** or **'The Scholar-Gypsy'** from school anthologies, are surprised to find he 'also' wrote prose.

Arnold's poetry, as we have seen, belongs very largely to the earliest stage of his adult life; most of his best pieces are contained in three slim volumes he published in 1849, 1852, and 1853, all written before his thirtieth birthday. It is true that in the mid- and late 1850s Arnold wrote some of his longest dramatic and narrative poems, but these have never found much favour. In 1867 he published a volume entitled ***New Poems,*** which contained several fine individual pieces, but even some of these (including **'Dover Beach'** and **'Stanzas from the Grande Chartreuse'**) had almost certainly been largely written before 1853. Much of his poetry recounts an inner struggle to find some equilibrium, but its conclusion, both discursively and in practice, was that balance was only to be found, or only came upon him (since it was not so entirely a matter of will as the poems at times suggest), when he committed himself to the world, to action, to mundane existence—to, in short, prose, with all the overtones that word can carry of the ordinary, the practical, the flat. Part of the poignancy of Arnold's biography comes from the fact that he never ceased to have the sensibilities and yearnings of a poet, though he largely ceased to write poetry. He lived the greater part of his life knowing that 'the Muse be gone away' (578).

Despite both the limited quantity and, in a sense to be explained in a moment, the restricted range of Arnold's poetry, he has always been regarded as one of the major poets of the nineteenth century, and has indeed usually been accorded a secure place in the second rank of English poetry, no inconsiderable achievement for one who devoted the greater part of his creative energies to other genres. In the best of his lyrics and elegies the experience of reflective sadness is rendered with touching melodic aptness, while even those poems which are uneven wholes sometimes contain lines that make us want to read on and to know more about a poet of such intriguingly erratic gifts.

Moreover, Arnold's poetry continues to have scholarly attention lavished upon it, in part because it seems to furnish such striking evidence for several central aspects of the intellectual history of the nineteenth century, especially the corrosion of 'Faith' by 'Doubt'. No poet, presumably, would wish to be summoned by later ages *merely* as an historical witness, but the sheer intellectual grasp of Arnold's verse renders it peculiarly liable to this treatment. In an exceptionally frank, but not unjust, self-assessment in a letter to his mother in 1869, Arnold himself almost predicted this historical role for his poetry:

> My poems represent, on the whole, the main movement of mind of the last quarter century, and thus they will probably have their day as people become conscious to themselves of what that movement of mind is, and interested in the literary productions which reflect it. It might be fairly urged that I have less poetical sentiment than Tennyson, and less intellectual vigour and abundance than Browning; yet, because I have perhaps more of a fusion of the two than either of them, and have more regularly applied that fusion to the main line of modern development, I am likely enough to have my turn, as they have had theirs.
>
> (***L*** [***The Letters of Matthew Arnold 1848–1888,*** collected and arranged by George W. E. Russell, 2 volumes, London: Macmillan, 2nd edn., 1901] ii. 9)

Those who find Arnold's poetry unsympathetic might be inclined to respond that its chief defect lies precisely in the way it arises too exclusively from a movement of *mind.*

'The Dialogue of the Mind with Itself'

Although he wrote in several poetic genres—sonnets, lyrics, elegies, extended narrative poems, verse drama and so on—Arnold's range as a poet was limited in two ways: he largely dealt with a confined set of themes, and to a great extent he wrote in one readily recognizable register or voice. Before considering certain particular aspects of his poetic achievement, it may be well to try to characterize the nature of these themes and this voice in very general terms.

The dominant note of Arnold's best poetry is reflection on loss, frustration, sadness. It is important from the start to draw attention to 'reflection', because his poems nearly always are, even if now explicitly, second-order reflections on the nature or meaning of certain kinds of experience, rather than expressions or records of that experience itself. When Arnold spoke, famously, of modern poetry as 'the dialogue of the mind with itself' (i. 1), he coined a phrase that irresistibly asks to be applied to his own writing. At the same time, and in a spirit with which later generations have become more rather than less familiar, the poetry frequently expresses a desperate, eternally self-defeating desire to escape from this unending round of intellection, from being 'prisoners of our consciousness' (200).

A recurrent symbolic landscape operates both as a backdrop and a load-bearing metaphorical structure in Arnold's chief lyrics and elegies, a landscape which, when reduced to its bare elements, maps the three stages of life's journey. That journey is characteristically represented by a river, which rises in a cool, dark glade, flows out on to the fierce, hot plain, and then finds its way to the wide, calm sea. These are three periods of the individual's life, but also three stages in historical growth more generally: as described in the standard modern commentary on the three phases of this symbolism, 'the first is a period of joyous innocence when one lives in harmony with nature, the second a period of suffering when one is alone in a hostile world, and the third a period of peace in which suffering subsides into calm and then grows up into a new joy, the joy of active service in the world'.[1]

But Arnold's poetry also returns to certain favoured settings which are symptomatic rather than symbolic in this sense. For example, the implied or explicit location of the persona speaking a particular poem frequently turns out to be on a mountain-top or other lofty place, the natural habitat of reflection and of those searching for the wide comprehending view. 'From some high station he looks down', as he says of 'the poet' in the early **'Resignation'** (95), but of course both 'lofty' and 'looking down' also suggests a relation to the world which is not purely a matter of altitude, and Arnold has been accused of viewing suffering humanity a little too much *de haut en bas.* Similarly, his marked taste for ambience of cool, moonlit settings (a staple of Romantic poetry that becomes almost a cliché with Arnold) reveals as well as represents. In Arnold's symbolic economy, such settings are obviously intended to contrast with or provide an escape from the hot, dusty scenes of bustling workaday life, but their coolness and brightness can easily start to seem chill, the light a little too clinical. We are reminded that in this setting the yearned-for transforming emotion which would enable us to escape ourselves can only be reflected upon, not experienced.

Another way to consider the limits of Arnold's range (tastes vary on whether these should also be regarded as limitations) is to observe how much of his poetic diction depends upon a kind of Romantic thesaurus: much use is made of stage-properties like moons and graves, tears flow a little too freely (no less than 68 times, according to one count), and there is embarrassingly frequent resort to the mannered interjection 'Ah!'. It is also noticeable, especially in some of his less successful pieces, how much of the weight of tone and meaning is carried by the adjectives, often in the form of past participles, rather than by the verbs, where he relies a good deal on the blandest or least energizing forms like 'was', 'had', and (an Arnoldian favourite) 'seemed'. These combine with the past participles to reinforce the elegiac sense of a world in which nothing is now happening: it is already all over before the poem starts, whether through death or loss or—not a trivial feature of Arnold's dominant poetical mood—simple belatedness.

Arnold was a self-conscious poet, arguably a learned poet, and thus inevitably preoccupied with his relation to his great predecessors. 'Predecessors', for the young poet of the 1840s, meant, overwhelmingly, the English Romantics. Needless to say, Arnold's poetic sympathies and, in certain senses, debts were wide: he felt the length of the shadow of the Greeks as much as any Englishman in his Greece-obsessed century; he displayed a responsive affinity to Virgil's gentle pastoral melancholy; he, somewhat exceptionally, was selectively appreciative of Goethe's verse, as well as holding him in something like awe as a cultural hero; and the list could be extended. But the English Romantics, perhaps Byron and Keats even more than Shelley or Coleridge, were his mind's familiar companions and left permanent echoes in his ear. Above all, the inescapable poetic presence for Arnold was Wordsworth. In literary terms, his relationship to Wordsworth bordered on the filial, a connection strengthened by early visits to him from the Arnolds' neighbouring family home in the Lake District, but more significantly intensified by Arnold's implicit association of Wordsworth with the early stage of human innocence, and with the simple, joyful song which that age still allowed. This surfaced most visibly in the **'Memorial Verses'** Arnold wrote following Wordsworth's death in 1850, where it is 'The freshness of the early world' which Wordsworth, the poet of childhood recollected in maturity, is credited with restoring to us.

> He laid us as we lay at birth
> On the cool flowery lap of earth. . . .

But the power to re-create the immediacy of this primitive experience is one which Arnold's 'time-ridden' consciousness[2] now regards as irrecoverably lost. Possibly others may arise to do for later generations what Byron and Goethe did for theirs,

> But where will Europe's latter hour
> Again find Wordsworth's healing power?
> Others will teach us how to dare,
> And against fear our breast to steel;
> Others will strengthen us to bear—
> But who, ah! who, will make us feel? (242)

The slight awkwardness of the syntax of 'against fear our breast to steel' is characteristic of Arnold's verse, though for once the interjection 'ah!', complete with its over-insistent exclamation-mark, manages not to seem affected here, or introduced merely to accommodate the rhythm.

The relation to Wordsworth has an interpretative as well as biographical significance, and it helps us fix the sense in which Arnold should be regarded as a post-Romantic as well as, more straightforwardly, a late-Romantic poet. For example, although he pays homage to some of the same aspects of nature's 'healing power', and even celebrates some of the same associations of the English countryside, the relation to nature revealed in Arnold's poetry is quite different from that characteristic of Wordsworth's. In Arnold's work, nature figures either as a reinforcing backdrop for the dialogue of the mind with itself, or else as a set of symbols on to which man's travails and hopes are transposed. It is never immediately at one with man, nor is it infused with a deeper life of its own. In fact, Arnold tries to make nature, too, into a good Stoic: the nature that 'seems to bear rather than rejoice' has learned to keep a stiff upper lip. For all its recourse to the standard Romantic scenery, Arnold's poetry is pre-eminently that of emotion recollected indoors.

Moreover, where memory, in Wordsworth's poetry, can refresh by bringing back the flavours of a more nourishing or soothing moment, thus easing our passage through an uncongenial world, for Arnold memory itself is usually a painful reminder of the utter unrecoverability of experience: far from refreshing, it merely provides another occasion for self-conscious wistfulness. There are, of course, many possible sources of the feeling that, poetically, one has come too late, but it is particularly characteristic of the post-Romantic sensibility in general and Arnold's in particular to blame the curse of reflectiveness for making certain kinds of pure or unmeditated satisfaction permanently unattainable.

Of Love and Loss

The two poetic forms in which Arnold is commonly held to have excelled are the lyric and the elegy. That traditional division is, however, somewhat misleading in Arnold's case: exaggerating to bring out the point, one could say that most of his lyrics are really elegies too. That is, his characteristic preoccupation as a poet is so much with transience and loss that he writes in a recognizably elegiac manner even when not formally writing about the dead. But, more suggestively, there is a sense in which many of his finest lyrics are not really about what they seem to be about. The point can be made most tellingly by considering the set of poems Arnold wrote on that most traditional of themes for the lyric—love.

Those short pieces which Arnold later grouped as a sequence under the heading **'Switzerland'** ostensibly record successive stages of the love-affair with **'Marguerite'.** They do, certainly, contain many of the conventional tropes of the genre, such as the lover's fond inventory of his loved one's attributes:

> The sweet blue eyes—the soft, ash-coloured hair—
> The cheeks that still their gentle paleness wear—
> The lovely lips with their arch smile that tells
> The unconquered joy in which her spirit dwells . . .
>
> (**'Parting'**, 125)

But as we reread these poems, the unsettling thought comes over us that they are not really about Marguerite, nor even about the experience of being in love. They are reflections upon how even this kind of experience—it is part of their unsatisfactoriness as love poems that Arnold didactically classifies it as a *kind* of experience, rather than being overwhelmed by its uniqueness—affords no real escape from the self and its oppressive sense of isolation. Although they effectively exploit the lightness and vigour of crisp mountain air and rushing, snow-fed streams, the Switzerland sequence is ultimately dark in tone, a sombre reflection about the inconsolable spiritual isolation which had hoped to find a cure in love, but which, chastened by failure, has now been thrown back upon a deeper self-examination.

Revealingly, several of the poems in this set are doubly retrospective: they are not only, in an obvious sense, reflections on a past experience, but it turns out that that experience itself is already one of rumination prompted by some event subsequent to the experience being ruminated upon. Meeting **'Marguerite'** a year later is the most obvious of these reflection-provoking events: the 'still' in the above lines marks both the passage of time and a reflective awareness of the shifting relation of memory and reality. This soon develops into a more comprehensive reflection, in which the focus retreats from the outer world of the lovers' situation to the inner world of self-knowledge:

> Far, far from each other
> Our spirits have grown;
> And what heart knows another?
> Ah! who knows his own?
>
> (126)

Even in these relatively early poems, we can see that love figures as what has been nicely termed 'a sort of mournful cosmic last resort', but one that is, like all earlier possible refuges, ultimately doomed to prove unsatisfactory.

Where, at their best, the **'Marguerite'** poems excel is in conveying the poignancy of these sentiments by certain simple yet haunting rhythms rather than by explicit argument. Despite its somewhat mannered title, **'To Marguerite—Continued'** constitutes a particularly happy example of this quality. The first stanza states the Arnoldian preoccupation succinctly:

> Yes! in the sea of life enisled
> With echoing straits between us thrown
> Dotting the shoreless watery wild
> We mortal millions live *alone.*
>
> (130)

Among the details that contribute to the effect here, we may particularly remark the randomness suggested by 'dotting', the homeless infinity behind 'shoreless', the unnerving transfer of the 'wild', trackless and inhospitable, from land to sea, and the brilliant near-oxymoron of the 'millions' who live 'alone'.

The subtle effect of the rhythms tells to even greater effect in the last stanza, which concludes with one of the most beautiful lines that Arnold every wrote:

> Who ordered that their longing's fire
> Should be, as soon as kindled, cooled?
> Who renders vain their deep desire?
> A God, a God their severance ruled!
> And bade betwixt their shores to be
> The unplumbed, salt, estranging sea.
>
> (130-1)

The iambic beat of this is at first regular and almost clipped, with a faintly Augustan flavour to the neat antithesis of 'kindled/cooled'. But the minor caesura at mid-line following 'salt' is, in both senses, arresting; the effect at first seems angular, but then registers as a lightly-sustained diminuendo. This, together with the fathomless 'unplumbed', the unwelcoming 'salt', the discordant 'estranging', all call up dimensions of loneliness in a line that has a wonderful sense of inevitability to it.

The second, much shorter and generally less successful, sequence of love poems (entitled, banally, **'Faded Leaves'**) moves even further away from the experience itself in its meditation on the tantalizing power of recalled emotion. The additionally elegiac note here comes from the anguished sense that even memory is only an imperfect reminder that there was, once, an emotion which briefly impinged on our isolation, but that *no* feeling can be preserved or re-created, not even the feeling of love. The most effective of this set is the simple **'Too Late',** where larger reflections on transience and the unarrestability of experience do not choke a more directly expressed pain:

> Each on his own strict line we move,
> And some find death ere they find love;
> So far apart their lives are thrown
> From the twin soul which halves their own.
>
> And sometimes, by still harder fate,
> The lovers meet, but meet too late.
> —Thy heart is mine!—*True, true! ah, true!*
> —Then, love, thy hand!—*Ah no! adieu!*
>
> (245)

But the immediacy of this last stanza is rare among Arnold's so-called 'love poems', a further indication that they are not essentially *about* love (a point I shall return to at the end of this chapter). Whatever may have been true of Arnold the man, the poet almost seems to treat his ideal of love as a state of *diminished* rather than of heightened emotion:

> How sweet to feel, on the boon air,
> All our unquiet pulses cease!
> To feel that nothing can impair
> The gentleness, the thirst for peace.
>
> (134)

In the same poem, in which the speaker imagines being re-united in another life with the woman for whom he has experienced an unrequited or unsatisfactory love in this life, the deeper sympathy which the lovers might then discover between themselves is referred to as being 'Ennobled by a vast regret'. That 'regret' provides the keynote of these lyrics, and it is revealing of the sensibility that can turn even love-poems into elegies that Arnold should choose to dwell upon its 'ennobling' power.

This sensibility found less problematic expression in the best-known of Arnold's actual elegies, such as the pastoral **'The Scholar-Gipsy'** (composed in 1852-3) and its companion piece **'Thyrsis'** (probably written 1864-5, in commemoration of Clough, who had died in 1861). Extended discussion of these poems is not possible here, but it is worth remarking that they, too, share with the love-poems the quality of having a deeper preoccupation than their ostensible subjects. What unites them, apart from Arnold's explicit commentary and their use of the same unusual Keats-inspired stanza form, is their celebration of the countryside around Oxford and its association with the untrammelled responsiveness of the young poets who roamed the hills together in the early and mid 1840s. But in fact both poems constantly return to meditating upon the unrecoverability of this youthful aestheticism, and around both poems, but especially **'Thyrsis',** there hovers the suggestion of sentimental indulgence in nostalgia and regret for its own sake—'let me give my grief its hour' (543). In a letter to one of their mutual friends, Arnold acknowledged a little defensively that 'one has the feeling, if one reads the poem as a memorial poem, that not enough is said about Clough in it' (***L*** i. 327). As this suggests, the poem is less an elegy for a dead friend, than a lament for a lost youth, the poet's *own* youth. The meditation soon takes on the stylized pathos of youth-recollected-in-maturity, with

> The heart less bounding at emotion new
> And hope, once crushed, less quick to spring again.
>
> And long the way appears, which seemed so short
> To the less practised eye of sanguine youth;
>
> (545)

'Thyrsis' was the last of Arnold's really successful major poems, but its theme, and even to some extent its mood, had been evident in his poetry from the start. Arnold may have written his best poetry when young, but, given his sustained preoccupation with transience and loss, there is a sense in which he never was a young poet.

'Empedocles on Etna'

A special place in Arnold's poetic *œuvre* is occupied by his long dramatic poem **'Empedocles on Etna'.** This is partly because it is such a brilliant dramatization of Arnold's own internal conflicts (though it would be a mistake, of course, simply to reduce the poem to such biographical elements, or to identify the author too closely with any one of its characters); but it is also because he thrust additional significance on the poem by withdrawing it almost immediately after its first publication in 1852. The austere classicism of the Preface to the 1853 collection was in part a justification of his decision to omit **'Empedocles'** from that volume; he treated it as the epitome of that modern dwelling upon one's own hesitations and uncertainties whose fruitlessness could only be remedied by returning to the portrayal of great actions. Thereafter, Arnold did not republish the poem until 1867, when he expressly included a note explaining that it now appeared 'at the request of a man of genius . . . Mr Robert Browning' (156). It is a sign of the intensity of Arnold's eddying struggles over his identity in the early 1850s, which found expression in the perversely self-repudiating 1853 Preface, that should omit what has since come to be regarded as a major part of his poetic achievement and one of the most significant long poems of the nineteenth century.

Although Arnold subtitled **'Empedocles'** 'a dramatic poem', 'dramatic' is something of a misnomer. Despite being divided into two 'acts' and being put into the mouths of three 'characters', there is really no 'action', but rather an uninterrupted series of discursive monologues. (Actually, something similar could be said of many of Arnold's so-called 'narrative poems' too, which are really extended reflections only very loosely hung on a narrative frame.) In effect, **'Empedocles'** takes the usual Arnoldian 'dialogue of the mind with itself' and puts the different sides of the discussion into the mouths of different speakers. Empedocles himself, who speaks the greater part of the poem, attempts, despite the contrary promptings of his own creative aspirations, to represent in an attractive light the stoicism necessary to confront the increasing burden of joyless life that comes with maturity. He preaches this message to his disciple, Pausanias, who, as a physician and therefore someone who lives in the world of action, is able to confront the prospect fairly cheerfully, which Empedocles himself is notably unable to do. The third character, a young poet named Callicles, expresses the untroubled joy of the creator living entirely in the realm of the aesthetic, a position Empedocles moodily regards as incompatible with increasing maturity.

The three scenes are set at successively higher points on the slopes of Mount Etna, until, in the final scene, Empedocles, unable to resolve the conflicting demands of his sensibilities and his reason into a livable life, throws himself into the crater of the volcano. The meaning of Empedocles' suicide for the interpretation of the poem as a whole has continued to divide commentators, some seeing it as an endorsement of Empedocles' analysis of the irreconcilable conflicts within existence, while others take it as a more robust condemnation of his inability to engage with the world as it is. Perhaps a more detached, philosophic, reading of the outcome is suggested by the obviously important fact that the last lines of the poem are given to Callicles, who sings of the continuing, impersonal, existence of the whole of creation, 'What will be for ever; / What was from of old', concluding with the cosmic closure of

> The day in his hotness,
> The strife with the palm;
> The night in her silence
> The stars in their calm.
>
> (206)

Significantly, the last word of this whole troubled poem is thus 'calm', the quality which Arnold at this point so uncalmly sought and failed to find.

Part of the fascination of the poem lies in the way the verse constantly signals that Empedocles cannot give his real emotional assent to the stoic resignation he ostensibly commends. His official creed is essentially that of the ancient Stoic philosopher Epictetus (an author whom Arnold had recently been reading with growing sympathy), laced with a dash of the work-ethic of Carlyle. It offers deliberately low-key satisfactions: man must not 'fly to dreams, but moderate desire', and so

> I say: Fear not! Life still
> Leaves human effort scope.
> But, since life teems with ill,
> Nurse no extravagant hope;
> Because thou must not dream, thou need'st not then
> despair!
>
> (182)

Empedocles himself, however, is cursed with a kind of intellectual nostalgia, a yearning for (and reluctance to accept the disappearance of) more animating creeds, held with livelier conviction. He is still tormented by the memory, and sometimes more than the memory, of the struggle between the 'impetuous heart' and the 'contriving head'. Callicles observes that Empedocles' railing is not adequately accounted for by the state of the world:

> There is some root of suffering in himself,
> Some secret and unfollowed vein of woe,
> Which makes the time look black and sad to him.
>
> (163)

One source of Empedocles' 'secret and unfollowed vein of woe' is his sense of his 'dwindling faculty of joy'. Suffocated by the inescapable nightmare of consciousness, he fears he is 'a living man no more',

> Nothing but a devouring flame of thought—
> But a naked, eternally restless mind.
>
> (200)

He searches for that sense of 'poise' that was, when characterized a little differently, to be such a crucial value in Arnold's critical writings, but in his most anguished moments Empedocles knows that

> . . . only death
> Can cut his oscillations short, and so
> Bring him to poise.
>
> (196)

In one of the fiercest passages in the whole poem, Empedocles bitterly ruminates on how, though the body may die and return to the elements whence it came, mind and thought will live on:

> Where will *they* find their parent element?
> What will receive *them,* who will call *them* home?

And so

> . . . we shall unwillingly return
> Back to this meadow of calamity,
> This uncongenial place, this human life;
> And in our individual human state
> Go through the sad probation all again,
> To see if we will poise our life at last,
> To see if we will now at last be true
> To our only true, deep-buried selves,

Being one with which we are one with the whole
world;
Or whether we will once more fall away
Into some bondage of the flesh or mind,
Some slough of sense, or some fantastic maze
Forged by the imperious lonely thinking power,
And each succeeding age in which we are born
Will have no more peril for us than the last;

(201-2)

Pausanias, a more robust, active figure, can cheerfully accept the limitations of such a creed and implicitly live by it. Empedocles' own broodings drive him inexorably to a choice between a spirit-numbing, poetry-killing compromise with a drab world—or death, which allows the preservation of at least some kind of integrity of passion. Finally, he works free from the toils of reflection: he knows that he 'breathes free', if only a moment, and to (as it were) commit himself to that moment 'ere the mists of despondency and gloom' begin to choke him once more, he throws himself into the crater (204).

But Arnold, of course, does not. By this I mean not only the rather obvious point that what Arnold 'does' is to write **'Empedocles on Etna',** thus attempting to shape some whole in which these conflicting choices can be realized and held in a satisfying tension; but also that Arnold *did* 'turn to the world'. His acceptance of the all-too-mundane post of school-inspector in order to get married can be seen, in this light, as something of a 'philosophic act'. Auden famously quipped that Arnold the poet 'thrust his gift in prison till it died'. But it may be nearer the mark to suggest that it was precisely during his poetically creative years that Arnold most acutely *felt* trapped in 'the hot prison of effortless life', and that the poetry was a kind of protest against the possibility that mind and thought will forever 'keep us prisoners of our consciousness' (200). The poetry and the unresolved unhappiness went together; it was accepting the prison that ultimately provided some release. Arnold did not throw himself into the crater; rather, he turned to writing prose.

'Wandering between Two Worlds'

After the inner turmoil that accompanied his transition from dandyish young late-Romantic poet to burden-shouldering man of affairs in the early and mid 1850s, Arnold tried various poetic experiments which, it now seems clear, were forced against the grain of his talent. Following the injunction of his 1853 Preface to leave behind the crippling introspection of modern thought, he took his subjects from Norse sagas and Greek history. The first issued in his rather leaden epic **'Balder Dead'** (damned for ever by one wag as 'Balder Dash'); the second in his attempt to reproduce the grandeur of ancient tragedy in his verse-drama ***Merope.*** This last has been universally judged a poetic failure, though an impressive technical achievement: a skilful re-creation of original instruments but a lifeless pastiche of early music. Swinburne long ago set the tone of subsequent response to the piece when he teased, 'The clothes are well enough, but where has the body gone?'[3] ***Merope*** pays homage to, but only limply embodies, some of the qualities that Arnold most admired in Greek literature (a topic to be discussed more fully in Chapters 4 and 5 below), and it has some of the smooth coolness and clear lines of an alabaster statue; but, as with most things in alabaster, one is constantly aware that one is looking at a reproduction.

Although the 1867 volume ***New Poems*** is generally thought to include much that fell below the standard of Arnold's earlier volumes, it did contain a few poems that have since become among his best-known pieces, notably **'Dover Beach'** (probably written as early as 1851, though the evidence is inconclusive), and the thematically linked but poetically more discursive **'Stanzas from the Grande Chartreuse'** (largely composed in 1852). Familiar as these poems may be, they demand discussion here not only on account of their intrinsic merits, but also because they are such representative expressions of some of Arnold's deepest preoccupations.

It is, of course, hard now to see **'Dover Beach'** with anything like fresh eyes, so much a part of our familiar poetic stock has it become. The organizing trope of the poem, the way in which the retreat of the tide-driven sea suggests the withdrawing of 'the Sea of Faith', employs a favoured Arnoldian metaphor. A sequence of monosyllables joined by simple verbs establishes the encompassing peacefulness of the setting.

The sea is calm tonight.
The tide is full, the moon lies fair
Upon the straits; on the French coast the light
Gleams and is gone; the cliffs of England stand,
Glimmering and vast, out in the tranquil bay.

(254)

The very stillness of the scene invites that mood of reflective sadness at which Arnold excelled. Indeed, the 'grating roar' of the shingle on the beach, and the movement of the waves themselves as they 'Begin, and cease, and then again begin', brings 'The eternal note of sadness in'. It leads the speaker to reflect, as the poem gathers intellectual and rhythmic intensity, how 'The Sea of Faith / Was once, too, at the full'; and then, in a haunting evocation of bleak absence, come the famous lines:

But now I only hear
Its melancholy, long, withdrawing roar,
Retreating, to the breath
Of the night-wind, down the vast edges drear
And naked shingles of the world.

(256)

Ostensibly, love is then invoked as the only solace, but almost immediately this comes to seem something of a perfunctory gesture, as it is swallowed up by the gathering momentum of the poem's powerfully dark picture of our homelessness in a cold, indifferent world.

> . . . for the world, which seems
> To lie before us like a land of dreams,
> So various, so beautiful, so new.
> Hath really neither joy, nor love, nor light,
> Nor certitude, nor peace, nor help for pain;
> And we are here as on a darkling plain
> Swept with confused alarms of struggle and flight,
> Where ignorant armies clash by night.
>
> (257)

Interestingly, though the rhythm and cadence of **'Dover Beach'** have cast their spell even over some of the unwillingly-conscripted readers of school anthologies, the poem is unusually hard to analyse in formal terms. It is, as the standard edition describes it, 'a lyric consisting of four unequal verse-paragraphs, irregularly rhymed. Lines vary between two and five stresses, but more than half the lines are five-stressed' (254). This dry, technical description cannot take us very far, but since there is no doubt that Arnold's ear could at times let him down very badly, his command of the emotion-sprung rhythm of **'Dover Beach'** is all the more striking precisely for *not* being able to take its structure from one of the established verse-forms. Is it significant or merely curious that it should be Arnold, advocate of an austere classicism and polished cultivator of the most traditional genres, who should thus be credited with the first major 'free-verse' poem in the language?

With **'Stanzas from the Grande Chartreuse',** it is hard not to feel that Arnold's relation to 'the Age of Faith' is a little more equivocal than it may at first appear. While the poem laments the impossibility of ever again inhabiting an animating faith in the way his imagined monks did, it also condescends a little to the credulity of earlier ages, and thus introduces a slight note of self-congratulation. We may be deprived, but we are not deceived. The monks, 'Last of the people who believe', are no doubt fortunate, but at least those like Arnold, 'Last of the race of them who grieve', can savour the bitter-sweet taste of a yet more exquisite emotion, that special pathos that attaches to being the last of a line. Though the poet famously characterizes himself as

> Wandering between two worlds, one dead,
> The other powerless to be born,
>
> (305)

he surely takes a subtle, if perverse, pleasure in his stranded state, and would not, now, exchange his lot for that of the credulous monk or the indifferent unbeliever. R. H. Hutton, always the most perceptive of Arnold's contemporary critics, was pointing in the same direction when he unfavourably contrasted 'the true humility of the yearning for faith' with Arnold's 'grand air of tearful Virgilian regret'.[4]

For this as well as other reasons, Arnold may be a more doubtful, or perhaps just a more subtle, witness of the intellectual dilemmas of his age than historians have always allowed. But certainly some of the deepest spirits of his own and the immediately succeeding generation, not least among them George Eliot, found that Arnold's poetry spoke to their anxieties and yearnings with a special power. Hutton again forces his way to the front with the rhetorical excess of the natural spokesman:

> When I come to ask what Mr Arnold's poetry has done for this generation, the answer must be that no one has expressed more powerfully and poetically its spiritual weaknesses, its craving for a passion it cannot feel, its admiration for a self-mastery it cannot achieve, its desire for a creed that it fails to accept, its sympathy with a faith it will not share, its aspiration for a peace it does not know.[4]

'Heroic Egotism'

We have already seen that the ostensible subject-matter of many of Arnold's lyrics and elegies proves, on closer examination, not really to be the governing preoccupation of the poems. The love poems are not 'about' Marguerite, nor are they actually about love; similarly the elegies are often not about the dead, whether people or faiths, nor even quite about transience and mutability as such. It is rather the poet's own self-conscious melancholy, aroused by reflection on these themes, that determines the emotional force and direction of these pieces. If the experience of love yielded the poet any positive conclusion, it was that at the moments of most intense communion with another, 'A man becomes aware of his life's flow',

> And then he thinks he knows
> The hills where his life rose
> And the sea where it goes.
>
> (291)

But even here, in **'The Buried Life',** one of his more optimistic poems, the significance of the experience, its beneficiary, as it were, is a kind of reflective self-centredness. More generously, one might observe how much of Arnold's work, in prose as well as poetry, expresses his sustained, though not showily strenuous, search for self-knowledge. In a revealing letter to Clough, written in 1849 when still roused and disoriented by his love for 'Marguerite', he characterized himself as somebody 'whose one natural craving is not for profound thoughts, mighty spiritual workings etc etc but a distinct seeing of my way as far as my own nature is concerned' (***C*** [***The Letters of Matthew Arnold to Arthur Hugh Clough,*** edited by Howard Foster Lowry (London: Oxford University Press, 1932)] 110). This should remind us that, although Arnold is often taken as a representative of 'the Victorian crisis of faith' and similar large-scale intellectual shifts, he was not attempting to construct an alternative system or synthesis, in the way in which several nineteenth-century doubters and self-declared 'humanists' were trying to do; rather, more modestly, he was trying to 'see his way'.

But the more immediate conclusion to which the argument of this chapter pushes us is to see that the voice of Arnold's poetry is inherently reflexive: his poems are nearly always fundamentally about himself, not just in the sense in which any artist's work is the expression of something about himself, but rather in that, by a series of covert mechanisms and sly stratagems, Arnold's poetry so often contrives to make the mood and temperament of the poet the focus of attention. Something of this was caught by Hutton when, in another of his perceptive comments on Arnold's work, he referred to the 'clear, self-contained, thoughtful, heroic egotism'[5] of much of the poetry. There *was* an element of heroism in Arnold's struggle to come to terms with the intensity of his dissatisfaction, but that, too, was egotistical, promoting to centre-stage the poet's sensitivity and visible effort to accommodate himself to a grating world.

This is surely partly accounted for by the deep but neglected truth that melancholy is inescapably self-important, whereas there is a relative impersonality about cheerfulness. Perhaps Arnold arrived at an intuitive recognition of this truth; certainly, much of the 'dialogue of the mind with itself' that took place in the early 1850s suggests an attempt to convince himself of the possibility of rising to the level of cheerfulness, a development, as we shall see in subsequent chapters, that he only really achieved, and then fitfully, in his prose. In replying to Clough's favourable comments on **'The Scholar-Gypsy'**, Arnold expressed his own dissatisfaction with the merely self-indulgent aspect of his poetry.

> I am glad you like the Gipsy Scholar—but what does it *do* for you? Homer *animates*—Shakespeare *animates*—in its poor way I think Sohrab and Rustum [Arnold's narrative poem of that name, first published in 1853] *animates*—the Gipsy Scholar at best awakens a pleasing melancholy. But this is not what we want.
>
> The complaining millions of men
> Darken in labour and pain—
>
> [lines from his own 'The Youth of Nature'] what they want is something to *animate* and *ennoble* them—not merely to add zest to their melancholy or grace to their dreams.
>
> (**C** 146)

In the Preface to the 1853 volume of his poems (to be considered further in the next chapter). Arnold's curious repudiation of **'Empedocles on Etna'** and the whole mood of anguished self-absorption he took it to represent, was part of his struggle to resist the charms of this 'pleasing melancholy'. That Preface was certainly not a successful way, and its programmatic recommendations stood at odds with Arnold's own best poetic practice. But he could not achieve in poetry what he recommended: it was not a register he commanded. When he tried to escape from himself to impersonal subjects like Nordic myth and Greek drama, he only succeeded in producing the lifeless husks of **'Balder Dead'** and ***Merope.*** They are too willed: his gift did not run so far so freely. In much of Arnold's poetry we see the disconsolate Romantic trying to turn himself into the resolute Stoic: his partial success has a pathos of its own, though we may wonder whether it is the small element of failure or the large degree of success which is the sadder sight. Yet there is a kind of self-indulgence here, too: genuine stoicism does not keep calling attention to its achievement in this way.

It is not the least of the reasons for which Arnold has been called 'the poet of our modernity' that this consuming self-consciousness was from the start allied to a note of precocious weariness. Although the theme of loss—loss of joy, loss of youth, loss of faith—is, as we have seen, at the heart of Arnold's lyrics and elegies, there is a sense in which what they register is absence rather than loss. That is, they mourn the fact that the poet—but also we, fellow-victims of history and the corrosion worked by its attendant self-consciousness—have never really known, can never know, the immediacy of real joy, real faith, or even—the precociousness returns in another role here—real youth. In a celebrated phrase, Arnold was later to charge that the Romantic poets were not 'adequate' to their age because, ultimately, they 'did not know enough' (iii. 262), but it could be said that his own poetry movingly expressed the existential plight of those upon whom history has imposed a choking burden of knowledge.

Increasingly, the loss of which he sang was the loss of the power of song itself. The drying-up of 'The fount that shall not flow again' (585) becomes just another of the grey truths to be, more in sorrow than in *angst,* accepted and lived with. The fact that 'the Muse be gone away' (578) was, as I suggested earlier, an enduring source of sadness to Arnold, and it left an undertow of regret and wistfulness occasionally discernible through the urbanity of the later prose. It is possible that he was for once overtly voicing this regret when he wrote of Sainte-Beuve's transition from an early dabbling in verse to his mature critical work:

> Like so many who have tried their hand at *œuvres de poésie et d'art,* his preference, his dream, his ideal was there; the rest was comparatively journeyman-work, to be done well and estimably rather than ill and discreditably, and with precious rewards of its own, besides, in exercising the faculties and keeping off ennui; but still work of an inferior order.
>
> (v. 305)

But even if Arnold did share this feeling, his own objectivity led him immediately to deny that Sainte-Beuve would have been justified in this self-assessment, given the immense value of his critical *œuvre* set alongside the work of even some of the most creative writers of his time. In the following chapters I shall try to show that, despite the undeniable, if patchy, glories of his poetry, *our* objectivity requires that, whatever sadness it may have brought to Arnold himself, we cannot regret that the greater part of his achievement was to be in prose.

Notes

1. A. Dwight Culler, *Imaginative Reason: The Poetry of Matthew Arnold* (New Haven, 1966), p. 4.

2. William A. Madden, *Matthew Arnold: A Study of the Aesthetic Temperament in Victorian England* (Bloomington, 1967), p. 83.

3. A. C. Swinburne, quoted in Frederic E. Faverty (ed.), *The Victorian Poets: A Guide to Research* (Cambridge, Mass., 1956; 2nd edn 1968), p. 200.

4. [R. H.] Hutton, *Literary Essays* [(London, 1888)] pp. 352, 350.

5. Hutton, *Literary Essays,* p. 313.

Lionel Gossman (essay date 1994)

SOURCE: "Philhellenism and Antisemitism: Matthew Arnold and his German Models," in *Comparative Literature,* Vol. 46, No. 1, Winter, 1994, pp. 1-39.

[*In the following essay, Gossman claims that Arnold's criticisms of "Hebraism" obscure a vision of society that is inclusive of both culture and religion and that his work cannot be equated with antisemitism.*]

> No one says it, but every one knows that pantheism is an open secret in Germany. We have, in fact, outgrown deism. We are free and don't want any thundering tyrant. We are of age and need no parental care. Nor are we the botches of any great mechanic. Deism is a religion for servants, for children, for the Genevese, for watchmakers . . . and every deist is, after all, a Jew.
>
> —Heinrich Heine[1]

With some notable exceptions, such as George Eliot, virtually everyone who put pen to paper in the nineteenth century, it seems, is vulnerable to the charge of antisemitism. It is not easy to draw any other conclusion from Leon Poliakov's rich compendium of opinions about Jews and Judaism from Voltaire to Wagner. Interest in Jews, it appears, almost invariably had an antisemitic slant.

Antisemitism has many strands, however, and the term may be too broad to be usefully applied. As there are degrees of racism—the residual prejudice that emerges in an occasional tasteless remark or traditional ethnic joke being of a different order from deliberately espoused, programmatic racism—so there are degrees of antisemitism. This is unlikely to have been any less the case at a time when Jews enjoyed full civil rights only in very few places and were known to many people chiefly through folk legends about their religious practices and popular accounts of their alleged part in the Crucifixion. It may even be that modern antisemitism—antisemitism as an ideology—developed only *after* the emancipation of the Jews in the course of the nineteenth century. Isolated, derogatory remarks about Jews should thus probably be viewed as the common currency of a time when Jews were in fact barely tolerated strangers and there was less incentive than now to curb inconsiderate language or to check the expression of unreflected prejudice.

There are probably good grounds, moreover, for distinguishing between anti-Judaism and antisemitism. The former, I would argue, is a philosophical and ideological position that might well be shared by emancipated Jews themselves and that often went hand in hand with enthusiasm for the culture of ancient Greece. Antisemitism, in contrast, is directed toward living Jews as a social and ethnic group and, in the nineteenth century, usually implied resistance to granting them equal civil rights with Gentiles and recognizing them as citizens. Both the young Hegel and Nietzsche, for instance, were anti-Judaic but arguably not antisemitic in the sense described. The young Hegel disliked Judaism as a religion, but supported Jewish emancipation. Nietzsche's contempt for the popular and demagogic antisemitism of his time is well known. Nevertheless, contempt for Judaism as a religion of servitude, resentment, mechanical obedience to precept, and hair-splitting, dry-as-dust rabbinical scholarship was not always distinct from distaste for certain alleged physical and moral characteristics of Jews.[2] Nor did support for Jewish emancipation imply respect for or even tolerance of Jewish religious beliefs and practices. Anti-Judaism easily spilled over into antisemitism. A fairly convincing case could even be made for the proposition that anti-Judaism was only the respectable mask of an unavowed antisemitism. It is all the more striking that despite the vehemence of his well-known criticism of excessive English and American "Hebraising," Matthew Arnold turns out to be considerably more attached to the values of "Hebraism" and considerably less vulnerable to the appeal of antisemitism than most of the German writers from whom he borrowed not only his celebrated antithesis of Hellenism and Hebraism but also the twin ideals—which seem to have been always associated with the first term in that antithesis, never with the second—of the fully developed harmonious individual and of the state as the embodiment of culture.

Arnold's criticism of the "excess" of "Hebraism" in England and his advocacy of a stronger dose of "Hellenism" in the famous fourth chapter of ***Culture and Anarchy*** put us on the track of what appears to be a historical connection between philhellenism and anti-Judaism.[3] Normally, the term "philhellenism" is used to describe the upsurge of support among liberal and educated Europeans, of whom Byron was the most illustrious, for the Greek independence movement against the Ottoman Empire in the third decade of the nineteenth century. I use it here in a broader sense to include not only the revival of interest in and enthusiasm for ancient Greece, which began in Germany in the second half of the eighteenth century with Winckelmann and Wolf, and which no doubt laid the foundations of the political philhellenism of the nineteenth, but also the entire "neohumanist" movement in German literature, education, and politics. Growing out of the work of Winckelmann and Wolf, "neohumanism" took deeper root in Germany than in any other European country and resulted in the sweeping educational reforms enacted by the Prussian Department of Education under Wilhelm von Humboldt and his assistant Johann Wilhelm Süvern. Goethe, Schiller, Hölderlin, the Humboldts, and Hegel were all nourished at the neohumanist source and contributed to it. Its effects were felt in Germany into the early twentieth century, when there was a remarkable renewal of interest in Winckelmann in the famous *George-Kreis,* the circle of writers, artists, scholars, and philosophers that had formed around the poet Stefan George.

The basis of German philhellenism or neohumanism was the conviction that ancient Greece represented an ideal condition of freedom and harmony: free and harmonious development of all human capacities in each individual and free and harmonious development of the *polis* or community. Having fallen away from that original condition, modern man must strive to recover it by eliminating everything that stood between him and it, including the distortions of a misguided (predominantly Roman Catholic) baroque and rococo classicism that imitated the external forms of antiquity without penetrating to the original spirit that had animated them. This new Reformation would result, it was hoped, in the overcoming of all the destructive dualisms that characterize the life of modern man—matter and spirit, the ethical and the aesthetic, substance and form, reason and passion, the sacred and the profane—and the restoration of freedom, beauty, and harmony to the individual and the community.[4] Winckelmann's cult of antique statuary, and in particular of the male nude, marked his rejection of the distinction between the inner and the outer, spirit and matter. In their plastic representations of the free, self-sufficient male body, the Greeks had symbolized for Winckelmann the unity and harmony of man and nature, the human and the divine. The symbol itself, being both the sign *and* the thing signified—in contrast to traditional neoclassical allegory, in which sign and signified are clearly distinguished—was an expression of the new ideal of unity as opposed to the old dualisms.[5] Beauty was nothing other than that harmonious unity of inner and outer, spirit and form, the divine and the human, which the ancients alone had achieved. "The foundation of higher study," Hegel declared in his rectorial address at the Nürnberg Gymnasium in 1809,

> must be and remain Greek literature in the first place, Roman in the second. The perfection and glory of those masterpieces must be the spiritual bath, the secular baptism that first and indelibly attunes and tinctures the soul in respect of taste and knowledge. For this initiation a general, perfunctory acquaintance with the ancients is not sufficient; we must take up our lodging with them so that we can breathe their air, absorb their ideas, their manners, one might even say their errors and prejudices, and become at home in this world—the fairest that ever has been. While the first paradise was that of human *nature,* this is the second, the higher paradise of the human *spirit,* the paradise where the human spirit emerges like a bride from her chamber, endowed with a fairer naturalness, with freedom, depth, and serenity . . . The human spirit manifests its profundity here no longer in confusion, gloom, or arrogance, but in perfect clarity. Its serenity is not like the play of children; it is rather a veil spread over the melancholy which is familiar with the cruelty of fate but is not thereby driven to lose its freedom and moderation . . . If we make ourselves at home in such an element, all the powers of the soul are stimulated, developed, and exercised.
>
> ("On Classical Studies" 324-25)

In the reconstruction of man and the polis proposed by the neohumanists—partly, no doubt, as an alternative to the purely "material" political ideals of the French Revolution[6]—the study of Greek language and culture was to play a crucial role. For the old grammatical study of the ancient languages, which concentrated on "external" forms, the neohumanists wanted to substitute the study of language as a unity of form and creative spirit. "The works of the ancients," Hegel explained, "contain the most noble food in the most noble form: golden apples in silver bowls. They are incomparably richer than all the works of any other nation and of any other time . . . These riches, however, are intimately connected with the language, and only through and in it, do we obtain them in all their special significance. Their content can be approximately given us by translations, but not their form, not their ethereal soul." What the student was to appropriate was not the rules of Greek grammar or composition, but the creative genius of the Greek people which was held to be chiefly accessible through their language. "Imitation" of the Greeks, in art, in language, in ethics and politics would thus result not in the mechanical and slavish reproduction of the old, but in the production of new and original work in the spirit of the Greeks, that is to say, in that spirit of beauty and harmony that centuries of alienated culture had all but eradicated from the human consciousness. "It is necessary," in Hegel's view, "that we appropriate the world of antiquity not only to possess it, but even more to digest and transform it" ("On Classical Studies" 326-27).

How Christianity, or even Enlightenment deism, or the Kantian philosophy which strongly influenced a number of the neohumanists could be made compatible with this fundamentally immanentist vision of man and the world was not always clear. To some, like Heine, it could not. In "Concerning The History of Philosophy and Theology in Germany" he denounced not only Christianity but deism as fundamentally hostile to beauty, joy, and man's inner harmony. But the irreconcilable enemy of Greek harmony and of the Greek sense of beauty was Jewish spiritualism and dualism. "The Jews looked on the body as something inferior, as a wretched cloak for the *ruach hakodesh,* the holy breath, the spirit, and only to the latter did they award their attention, their reverence, their worship." No wonder "the Jews, the Swiss guard of deism," had been "inexorable" in their hounding of the pantheist in their midst, Benedict Spinoza. As for the Christians, they "went much further" even than the Jews and "regarded [the body] as something objectionable, something bad, as evil itself." Inevitably, in the art and literature influenced by Christianity, "there is no obvious harmony between form and idea as with the Greeks" (177, 174, 177, 163).

The young Hegel of "The Spirit of Christianity" found a way of accommodating Christianity by representing it as the reconciliation of Greek religion, the soul of which is beauty, and Kantian reason, the core of which is morality. Love, the moral principle of the Gospel, is the beauty of the heart, a spiritual beauty combining the Greek soul and Kant's moral reason. In this conception it was Judaism that became the "villain of the piece," as Richard Kroner put it (9). "Abraham wanted *not* to love," Hegel tells us, "wanted to be free by not loving" ("The Spirit of Christianity" 185). While Hegel recognizes that for culture to exist, man must be able to work on "nature" and "spirit" and must therefore transform them into his "object," he distinguishes between a radical and destructive alienation—that of the Jews—and a mild and productive one, that of the Greeks.

> The substance of Nature and Spirit must have confronted us, must have taken the shape of something alien to us, before it can become our *object.* Unhappy he whose immediate world of feelings has been alienated from him—for this means nothing less than the snapping of those bonds of faith, love, and trust which unite heart and head in a holy friendship. The alienation which is the condition of theoretical erudition does not require this moral pain, or the sufferings of the heart, but only the easier pain and strain of the imagination which is occupied with something not given in immediate experience, something foreign, something pertaining to recollection, to memory and the thinking mind.
>
> ("On Classical Studies" (327-28)

The patriarch of Judaism appears in Hegel's early writings as having deliberately chosen the most extreme and inhuman form of alienation:

> Abraham, born in Chaldea, had in youth already left a fatherland in his father's company. Now, in the plains of Mesopotamia, he tore himself free altogether from his family as well, in order to be a wholly self-subsistent, independent man, to be an overlord himself. He did this without having been injured or disowned, without the grief which after a wrong or an outrage signifies love's enduring need, when love, injured but not lost, goes in quest of a new fatherland in order to flourish and enjoy itself there. The first act which made Abraham the progenitor of the nation is a disseverance which snaps the bonds of communal life and love. The entirety of relationships in which he had hitherto lived with men and nature, these beautiful relationships of his youth (Joshua 24.2), he spurned.
>
> ("The Spirit of Christianity" 185)

As a result, the world was forever disenchanted. The Jews never knew the harmonious "second paradise" of the Greeks. They lived in a world that they regarded as utterly alien to them, to which they had no ties, and for which they had no love. With no sense of the immanence of the divine, they had no feeling for beauty. "An image of God was just stone or wood to them; . . . they despise the image because it does not manage them, and they have no inkling of its deification in the enjoyment of beauty or in a lover's intuition" ("The Spirit of Christianity" 192). Judaism so understood might well seem to be in league with modern science or with the utilitarianism of the despised, practical, "philistine" English.

Hegel constantly contrasts the Greeks and the Jews, invariably to the disadvantage of the latter. In their representations of man's struggle with nature, the Greeks seek reconciliation, an end to dualism: "Deucalion and Pyrrha, . . . after the flood in their time, invited men once again to friendship with the world, to nature, made them forget their need and their hostility in joy and pleasure, made a peace of *love,* were the progenitors of more beautiful peoples, and made their age the mother of a newborn natural life which maintained its bloom of youth." Noah, in contrast, sought mastery over nature at the price of submission to an all-powerful force alien to both himself and nature. Likewise Abraham, as we saw, left his fatherland but refused to become attached to any new land. "The groves which often gave him coolness and shade he soon left again; in them he had theophanies, appearances of his perfect Object on High, but he did not tarry in them with the love which would have made them worthy of the Divinity and participant in Him. He was a stranger on earth, a stranger to the soil and to men alike . . . He entered into no ties . . . He steadily persisted in cutting himself off from others, and he made this conspicuous by a physical peculiarity imposed on himself and his posterity." Cadmus and Danaus, in contrast, who also forsook their fatherland, "went in quest of a soil where they would be free and they sought it that they might love . . . In order to live in pure, beautiful unions, as was no longer given to them in their own land, [they] carried their gods forth with them . . . [and] by their gentle arts and manners won over the less civilized aborigines and intermingled with them to form a happy and gregarious people" ("The Spirit of Christianity" 182-86).

Since the Jews insist on maintaining their distance from nature and others and have removed their "perfect Object on High" far out of the world, the divine for them is never incarnate, it is never *present* in the world, even in the holiest of holies. For them, according to Hegel, the sacred and the profane are two unconnecting realms, whereas for the Greeks the one informs the other. "The concealment of God in the Holy of Holies had a significance quite different from the arcanum of the Eleusinian gods. From the pictures, feelings, inspiration, and devotion of Eleusis, from these revelations of god, no one was excluded; but they might not be spoken of, since words would have desecrated them. But of *their* objects and actions, of the laws of *their* service, the Israelites might well chatter (Deuteronomy 30.11), for in these there is nothing holy. *The holy was always outside them, unseen and unfelt*" (italics added). Even the holy days of the Jews in no way signified a transformation of the mundane; sacred time is *another* time. The day of rest is kept "in a complete vacuum, in an inactive unity of spirit" and "the time dedicated to God is an empty time" ("The Spirit of Christianity" 193). Finally, equality as envisaged by the Jews is the equality Montesquieu attributed to the subjects of a tyrant, not the equality of the free citizens of the ancient republics. "The Greeks were to be equal because all were free, self-subsistent; the Jews equal because all were incapable of self-subsistence" ("The Spirit of Christianity" 198). Hegel also subscribed, as one might expect, to what had already been a criticism of Jewish religious practice in antiquity and was to become a commonplace of all nineteenth-century discussion of the Jews: their dry, mechanical legalism, which contrasted unfavorably with both the life-giving charity of the Christians and the natural spontaneity and creativeness of the Greeks. "An essential of their religion was the performance of a countless mass of senseless and meaningless actions"; "the holiest of things, namely, the service of God and virtue, was ordered and compressed in dead formulas"; and lives were "spent in a monkish preoccupation with petty, mechanical, spiritless, and trivial usages" ("On Christianity" 69, 178).

Judaism, in short, with its *deus absconditus,* its radical alienation, its stark dualisms, and its rigid, inflexible obedience to the letter of the law, is identified with lifeless mechanism, repression, and death; youth, life, and the harmony of beauty belong, in contrast, to Christianity, but especially to the Greeks, with their feeling for the continuity of the divine, the human, and the natural and their emphasis on freedom rather than punctual fulfillment of commands. Judaism represents the dead world of allegory in contrast to the living world of symbol: "It is true only of objects, of things lifeless," Hegel notes in a passage of "The Spirit of Christianity" concerning the Trinity, "that the whole is other than the parts; in the living thing, on the other hand, the part of the whole is one and the same as the whole. If particular objects, as substances, are linked together while each of them yet retains its character as an individual (as numerically one), then their common characteristic, their unity, is only a concept, not an essence, not something being. Living things, however, are essences, even if they are separate, and their unity is still a unity of essence. What is a contradiction in the realm of the dead is not one in the realm of life" ("The Spirit of Christianity" 261).

By the middle of the nineteenth century, according to the authors of an illuminating study of antisemitism in Nietzsche, the antithesis of "Hellenes and Jews" was part of the repertory of antisemitism among the educated classes in Germany. "Over against plastic art, the beauty of youth, eroticism, and creativity were set the prohibition of images, original sin, the mortification of the body; over against the noble and heroic life, elevated by dyonisiac extasy and the sense of the tragic, was set everything that could be disparaged as democratic, philistine, plebeian" (Hubert Cancik and Hildegard Cancik-Lindemaier).

Like the young Hegel, a number of writers sought to distinguish between Judaism and Christianity, so as to save the latter from the condemnation of the former. Some, like Wagner and Lagarde in Germany or Emile Burnouf in France, imagined a Christianity completely cleansed of Judaism (Uriel Tal 223-89). This movement culminated in the heresy of the so-called *Deutsche Christen* in the 1930s. By the end of the nineteenth century, the criticism of monotheism and its repressive and "servile" moral code had become so vocal and pervasive that, to defend Christianity from it, even highly respected liberal theologians, such as Adolf von Harnack, argued for the independence of Christianity from a petrified and legalistic Judaism and advocated the removal of the Old Testament from the Bible.[7]

Another group, which included Feuerbach and Nietzsche, as well as the notoriously antisemitic Eugen Dühring, lumped Christianity with Judaism and rejected both. For Dühring, the struggle against Judaism was bound up with the struggle against monotheistic religion and hence also against the forces suppressing the free and natural impulse in life itself. "The religious systems," he wrote in *Wert des Lebens* (1877), "are a chapter in the study of the diseases of the universal history of the spirit, for religion, including Christianity, is the quintessence of the 'hatred of life' . . . and the eradication of the natural instincts." There was no point in combatting Judaism with Christianity. Christian antisemitism "ignores the basic truth that Christianity itself is semitic, a truth which should be the point of departure of all true anti-Hebraism."[8] That was also, basically, Nietzsche's view, according to Hubert and Hildegard Cancik. Nietzche's antisemitism, they claim, must be understood as antisemitism "raised to the second power, more subtle, less vulgar, deepened by historical and philosophical arguments and expressed in brilliant language." Nietzsche's position was "that Christian antisemitism is a pure and simple stupidity, since Christianity itself is a heightened Judaism . . . Whoever would combat Judaism and its morality, cannot, in Nietzsche's view, be Christian" (42).[9]

Increasingly, the attacks on "Semitic" repression of the "natural instincts" and on the servile morality of Jews and Christians alike were made in the name of "Aryan" or "Nordic-Germanic" heroism and manliness. Dühring argued that "the Nordic idols and the Nordic God contain a natural kernel and no thousand-year-old distraction can remove it from the world . . . Here has reigned an imaginative spirit incomparably superior to the Jewish slave imagination" (quoted in Tal 266). But the underlying reference was ultimately to the ancient Greeks, with whom, since Winckelmann and Wolf, the Germans had felt a special affinity. To this affinity the early sociologist Wilhelm Heinrich Riehl bears unaffected testimony in his recollections of student life at a German Gymnasium around mid-century:

> We regarded Greece as our second homeland; for it was the seat of all nobility of thought and feeling, the home of harmonious humanity. Yes, we even thought that ancient Greece belonged to Germany because, of all the modern peoples, the Germans had developed the deepest understanding of the Hellenic spirit, of Hellenic art, and of the harmonious Hellenic way of life. We thought this in the exuberance of a national pride, in virtue of which we proclaimed the German people

> the leading culture of the modern world and the Germans the modern Hellenes. We announced that Hellenic art and nature had been reborn more completely in German poetry and music than in the poetry and music of any other people of the contemporary world . . . Our enthusiasm for Greece was inseparable from our enthusiasm for our fatherland . . . We looked back to classical antiquity as to a lost paradise.[10]

In Nietzsche's *Anti-Christ* the link is between the Hyperborean creed of power, strength, and joy, on the one hand, and, on the other, the archaic, aristocratic Greece of the Dorians, rather than the popular and liberal Hellenism beloved of early philhellenes like Winckelmann.[11]

The identification of Germans and Hellenes was thus an essential aspect of the struggle for the German soul against "Hebraism" in the nineteenth century. Feuerbach claimed that science and art originated only in polytheism, since "polytheism is the open, unresentful feeling for everything that is good, without differentiation; the feeling for the world, for the universe." Whereas "the Greeks contemplated nature with the theoretical senses . . . heard heavenly music in the harmonious course of the stars . . . and saw pictures emerge in the shape of Venus Anadyomene from the foam of the ocean," the Jews "only enjoyed nature through their palate. They only became men of God through the enjoyment of manna. Eating is the most solemn act . . . of the Jewish religion . . . In eating man declares nature to be a nullity in itself."[12]

If Judaism and Christianity had "stupefied" the Germans and "blunted their senses," "impaired the understanding and the spirit," vigor and life would be restored to them through the aristocratic and tragic culture of ancient Greece. That was the essential message of Nietzsche and of his followers. The attack on Wilamowitz by Nietzsche and his sympathizers was an attack on a classical scholar who, it was alleged, was incapable of understanding the glorious, heroic, and tragic culture of Greece and who kept importing into his interpretation of it alien, "philistine" notions of virtue, sin, and repentance. "Sin is Wilamowitz's favorite word," one critic declared in a review of Wilamowitz's translation of the Greek tragic writers. "He uses it to translate a whole range of Greek terms. It can be said a priori that this is a mistake in the case of the older classical tragedy. The idea of sin is so closely bound up for us with notions of punishment and the injunction to repent, that it ought to be kept well away from this tragic art. A contrite and submissive heart may have been pleasing to the Jewish-Christian god. The tragic sense is quite different. Repentance and penance would have seemed entirely out of place to the tragic hero. The hero is not a bourgeois in theatrical costume; and the heroic ethos . . . has nothing to do with our official morality" (Kurt Hildebrand 143; my translation).

Nineteenth-century criticism of the repressive aspects of Christian and bourgeois culture sometimes claimed affinities with an earlier tradition of opposition to the authority of Church and State in the *ancien regime*. (In fact, that opposition was bourgeois as well as aristocratic.) Hence Nietzsche's admiration for certain writers of the age of French classicism—La Rochefoucauld, Chamfort, and even Pascal. Hence also the link that the George-Kreis forged between itself and Winckelmann. The tone of serenity and confidence that marks the earlier writing is absent from the later, however, while the philosophical nihilism and the emphasis on the role of exceptional individuals and leaders are new. In an important review of *Der Dichter als Führer in der deutschen Klassik* by Stefan George's favorite disciple, Max Kommerell (1928), Walter Benjamin demonstrated how the basic undertaking of Kommerell's book was to co-opt German classicism by reinterpreting it as "the first canonical case of a German uprising against the times, of a holy war of Germans against the age, such as George was later to call for." German classicism was thus presented as a precursor of George's politico-poetical program. In this way, according to Benjamin (252-59), Kommerell hoped to conceal the Romantic roots of George's project.

Philhellenism, in sum, seems to have been one of the more ingenious and deceptive guises adopted by the Romantic revolt against the Enlightenment, and it seems also to have been one of the more enduring: the intoxicating Romantic topos of the special link between Hellas and Germania, of German culture as the fulfillment of Greek culture, remained vigorously alive as late as the post-World War II writings of Heidegger.[13] And one may legitimately consider in what measure the "postmodern" rejection of the transcendent nature of truth and the contemporary emphasis on the ludic as against the ethical are the outcome of an authentic coming to grips with the failures of the modernist project—and of rationalism in general—and in what measure they are yet another version of the same Romantic revolt that was once presented as the struggle of Judaism and Hellenism.

I would like now to turn back to Matthew Arnold. England had also known a Greek revival. As in Germany, it appears to have been closely connected with a desire to overcome the dualism of man and nature and to rehabilitate the body and the senses. Wordsworth swore he would rather be

> A Pagan suckled in a creed outworn;
> So might I, standing on this pleasant lea,
> Have glimpses that would make me less forlorn;
> Have sight of Proteus rising from the sea;
> Or hear old Triton blow his wreathed horn.

Byron grieved over the death of the old gods:

> Oh! where, Dodona! is thine aged grove,
> Prophetic fount and oracle divine?

The Chorus in Shelley's *Hellas* laments the defeat of Apollo, Pan, and Jove by the "killing Truth" of Christianity:

> The Powers of earth and air
> Fled from the folding-star of Bethlehem:

Apollo, Pan, and Love,
And even Olympian Jove
Grew weak, for killing Truth had glared on them;
Our hills and seas and streams,
Dispeopled of their dreams,
Their waters turned to blood, their dew to tears,
Wailed for the golden years.

Leigh Hunt wrote to Hogg—in jest, it is true—that "if you go on so, there will be a hope that a voice will be heard along the water saying 'The great God Pan is alive again'[14]—upon which the villagers will leave off starving, and singing profane hymns, and fall to dancing again."[14] Hunt's reference to Pan is noteworthy. More than the Olympian Gods, "Pan," as Richard Jenkyns observes, "had become the god of the pantheists" (179). Even Ruskin, who warned against investing the Ancients' religious view of nature with modern sentiment, sometimes thought it could be revived. "With us," he wrote, ". . . the idea of the Divinity is apt to get separated from the life of nature; and imagining our God . . . far above the earth, and not in the flowers or waters, we approach those visible things with a theory that they are dead; governed by physical laws, and so forth." Ruskin longed to repeople with divine spirits the rivers and hills of an England already scarred by the industrial revolution. The scientific, utilitarian, exploitative relation to nature "fails." In Jenkyns's words: "Christian beliefs in transcendence and monotheism seem inadequate" (184-85). Philhellenism was thus, at least in part, a rejection of Enlightenment rationalism and deism, Judeo-Christian monotheism, religious and philosophical dualism, and the mixture of prosaic utilitarianism and literalist Christian fundamentalism that Victorian Englishmen saw as the prevailing ideology of hard-nosed middle-class businessmen and industrialists.

Though an implicit opposition of Hellenism and Hebraism was thus already in the air in his own Victorian world, most scholars who have studied the matter are in agreement that Arnold took the basic idea of the fourth chapter of ***Culture and Anarchy*** from Heine. Heine was well aware, of course, of Hegel's comments on Judaism and subscribed to them in large measure:

> As the prophet of the East called them [the Jews] the "People of the Book," so the prophet of the West, in his *Philosophy of History,* characterizes them as the "People of the Spirit." Already in their earliest beginnings—as we observe in the Pentateuch—they manifest a predilection for the abstract, and their whole religion is nothing but an act of dialectics, by means of which matter and spirit are sundered, and the absolute is acknowledged only in the unique form of Spirit. What a terribly isolated role they were forced to play among the nations of antiquity, which, devoting themselves to the most exuberant worship of nature, understood spirit rather as material phenomena, as image and symbol! What a striking antithesis they represented to multicolored Egypt, teaming with hieroglyphics; to Phoenicia, the great pleasure-temple of Astarte, or even to that beautiful sinner, lovely fragrant Babylonia—and, finally, to Greece, burgeoning home of art!
>
> ("Ludwig Börne: A Memorial" 265)

Heine's poem "Die Götter Griechenlands" ("The Gods of Greece"), with which Arnold was almost certainly familiar, communicates the ambivalence of the German-Jewish poet's relation to both the Greeks and the Judeo-Christian tradition. The poet laments the passing of the ancient gods, now "verdrängt und verstorben" ("driven out and wasted away") and reflects that even the gods are subject to the iron law of historical existence. "Auch die Götter regieren nicht ewig, Die jungen verdrängen die alten" ("Even the gods do not rule forever; the young drive out the old"; my translation, as are the other excerpts from this poem). As Zeus drove out the Titans, he has in turn been dethroned, his thunderbolts extinguished. The Virgin has displaced once haughty Juno: "Hat doch eine andre das Zepter gewonnen," the poet tells the ancient goddess,

Und du bist nicht mehr die Himmelskönigin,
Und dein grosses Aug ist erstarrt,
Und deine Lilienarme sind kraftlos,
Und nimmermehr trifft deine Rache
Die gottbefrüchtete Jungfrau
Und den wundertätigen Gottessohn.

(Another has won the sceptre,
And you are no longer the queen of heaven,
And your great eye is glazed,
And your lily-white arms without strength,
And your vengeance will never reach
The divinely impregnated virgin
And the miracle working son of the god.)

For centuries now the inextinguishable laughter of the gods of Greece has been extinguished.

The lament is suddenly interrupted by the startling lines: "Ich habe euch niemals geliebt, ihr Götter! Denn widerwärtig sind mir die Griechen . . ." ("I have never loved you, you gods! For the Greeks are repugnant to me"). The fact is, the poet recalls, that the Greek gods had little compassion for human suffering and always sided with the victors. Man, however, can be more generous than they and may feel compassion for them—"Tote, nachtwandelnde Schatten" ("Dead, nocturnally wandering shades")—in their abandonment. Especially, the poet cries, in yet another shift in position,

. . . wenn ich bedenke, wie feig und windig
Die Götter sind, die euch besiegten,
Die neuen, herrschenden, tristen Götter,
Die schadenfrohen im Schafspelz der Demut.

(. . . When I reflect how cowardly and insubstantial
Are the gods who conquered you,
The new, ruling, joyless gods,
Wearing the sheepskin of humility and exulting in
suffering.)

At such moments of awareness, overcome with anger, the poet would gladly destroy the new temples, take up arms on behalf of the ancient gods and their "ambrosial law," and sink down in prayer before their altars, his arms outstretched in supplication.

Many scholars believe that the immediate source of Arnold's Hellenism-Hebraism opposition is a critical passage in Heine's Memorial to Ludwig Börne, the left-wing German-Jewish writer and publicist.[15] "In his comments on Goethe as in his judgments of other writers," Heine writes,

> Börne betrays the narrowness of mind of the Nazarene. I say "Nazarene," in order to use neither the term "Jewish" nor the term "Christian," although the two terms are synonymous for me and are used by me to designate not a faith but a natural disposition. "Jews" and "Christians" are for me closely related in opposition to "Hellenes," by which I likewise do not mean a particular people, but a turn of mind and an outlook, both inborn and acquired. From that point of view, I could say that all men are either Jews or Hellenes, men motivated by asceticism, hostility to graven images, and a deep desire for the spiritual, or men whose essential being is delight in life, pride in the development of their capacities, and realism. In this sense, there have been Hellenes among those German pastors who come from families of pastors and among Jews born in Athens and perhaps descended from Theseus.
>
> ("Ludwig Börne: Eine Denkschrift" 94-95; my translation)

Heine speculated whether the "harmonious fusion of the two elements" might not be "the task of all European civilization." But while there were "rare instances" in which a reconciliation appears to have occurred ("Shakespeare is at once Jew and Greek"), in general "we are still very far removed from this goal. Goethe the Greek (and the whole poetic party along with him) has in recent times expressed his antipathy to Jerusalem in an almost passionate manner" ("Ludwig Börne: A Memorial" 270-71). Though Heine's position was complex, as can be seen from "The Gods of Greece," and though in later years especially, bed-ridden and racked by pain, he described himself as "disillusioned with metaphysics" and "clinging fast to the Bible" (*Geständnisse* 138), he also always considered himself a "Hellene in secret" ("A Memorial" 264). There was no doubt whose side he was on in the account he gave of Börne's judgments of Goethe, which he read as a new skirmish in the "*unresolved and perhaps never to be resolved duel* between Jewish spiritualism and Hellenic glorification of life" (italics added). Börne is presented here, with almost Nietzschean vehemence, as "the little Nazarene full of hate for the great Greek, who was a Greek god into the bargain!" (*Werke und Briefe* 6:94). And while longing for the return of "Harmony," Heine never questioned that it meant above all "making the world healthy again by curing it of the one-sided striving for spiritualization, the crazy error that makes soul as well as body sick!" In reawakening a feeling for Greek art in his countrymen and creating works of great solidity and concreteness to which they could cling, "as if to marble representations of the Gods," Goethe—according to Heine—had done his bit to achieve this end (*Werke und Briefe* 6:120).

In Arnold's view of him, Heine was certainly on the side of Hellenism. "No man has extolled . . . the pagan extreme more rapturously" (***Essays in Criticism*** 207). Yet one of the reasons for Arnold's enduring admiration for Heine may well have been that he found in Heine *both* the Hellenic and the Hebraic. "No account of Heine is complete which does not notice the Jewish element in him," he wrote in the Heine essay.

> His race he treated with the same freedom with which he treated everything else, but he derived a great force from it, and no one knew this better than he himself. He has excellently pointed out how in the sixteenth century there was a double renascence,—a Hellenic renascence and a Hebrew renascence,—and how both have been great powers ever since. He himself had in him both the spirit of Greece and the spirit of Judaea; both these spirits reach the infinite, which is the true goal of all poetry and all art,—the Greek spirit by beauty, the Hebrew spirit by sublimity. By his perfection of literary form, by his love of clearness, by his love of beauty, Heine is Greek; by his intensity, by his untamableness, by his "longing which cannot be uttered," he is Hebrew.
>
> (***Essays in Criticism*** 179)

What Arnold seems to be pointing to in the combination of "Greek" and "Hebrew" elements he discerned in Heine is a coming together or reconciliation (admittedly an imperfect one, as his criticisms of Heine suggest) of classical beauty of form and Enlightenment wit with Romantic imagination. For Heine himself, however, as the passages just quoted indicate unequivocally, such a reconciliation could be expected—at very best—only in the distant future, at the far end of a long dialectical process. The relation of the two elements was one of "unresolved and perhaps never to be resolved" conflict. In addition, the meanings Arnold attributed to "Greek" and "Hebrew" or to "Hellenism" and "Hebraism" are not quite those that the terms "Greek" and "Nazarene" had for Heine.

The parallel between the title Arnold gave to the collection of articles known as ***Culture and Anarchy*** and the title he gave to the fourth of the articles in the collection, **"Hebraism and Hellenism,"** inevitably invites reflection on the possible relations among the four terms in the two titles. Is "Culture" connected with "Hellenism," for instance, and "Hebraism" with "Anarchy"?

Culture and Anarchy was Arnold's response to the overwhelming sense, which he shared with earlier poets like Byron and Shelley as well as with contemporaries like Ruskin, of living in a withered and decaying world. When he took over the ideal of the harmonious, fully developed human person from Humboldt and the German neohumanists, it was in order to hold it up against what he felt was the pressing, ugly reality of mid-Victorian England: misshapen, parochial individuals removed from intercourse with nature and the experience of beauty, enslaved to specialized tasks—be it running a business or serving a machine—and fanatically committed to idiosyncratic and—in his eyes—arbitrary varieties of religion. But it was no longer simply the disenchantment of the world, the radical separation of the sacred from the profane, and the alienation of men from nature and from their own humanity that disturbed Arnold. It was an intense conviction that the center was already, visibly, not holding, that the world increasingly lacked, in his own words, not only unity but "a sound centre of authority" (***Culture and Anarchy*** 119).

Unlike most of his liberal countrymen, who were traditionally far more concerned with individual freedoms than with "culture" or "totality" or "the State," Arnold was haunted by the specter of order disintegrating into "anarchy." In fact, there is probably an element of challenge or provocation in the very title of his volume. With their inveterate empiricism and pragmatism, Arnold's English contemporaries—on the critic's own admission—viewed "culture" with suspicion. Frederic Harrison, the distinguished legal scholar and champion of trade union legislation, derided "the cant about culture."[16] Perhaps the mockers of "culture" saw it as a foreign concept in tune with abstruse German philosophies and alien political regimes and having nothing to do with familiar British concerns such as moral and religious truth, the principles of political economy, or the Englishman's right to think as he likes, say what he likes, worship as he likes, and, above all, trade as he likes. Arnold can only have reinforced their suspicions by constantly praising Continental practices as superior to British ones and flaunting his Continental connections: with the German neohumanists in the first instance—Goethe, Wilhelm von Humboldt, Schiller, and Schleiermacher (whom he had learned to admire in the house of his father, Thomas Arnold, the celebrated headmaster of Rugby and a strong Germanophile), but also with French writers such as Michelet, Renan, Sainte-Beuve, and Tocqueville. In the end, Arnold was questioning the idiosyncratic and—according to him—increasingly provincial path of the native tradition in politics and religion since the time of the Puritan revolution. Radical, consistent, English-style liberalism, he was arguing, can only lead to anarchy, the dissolution of all traditional social bonds and institutions.

Culture, in contrast, is the cement that holds society together and founds it. Neither the rational, natural-law principles of the Enlightenment—ideas of justice or equality—nor the pragmatic principles of the Utilitarians—ideas such as the greatest happiness of the greatest number—can provide a firm foundation for social life, according to Arnold. On the contrary, they are likely to tear it apart, by setting one group against another, one interpretation against another, one interest against another. Culture, in contrast, is not debatable: it is not based on principles that can be disputed. It is an accumulated, historically produced, and shared tradition which, despite its being a product of historical development, claims universal validity. In this respect it is fundamentally at odds with the narrow, one-sided concerns of particular moments and particular groups. Nothing could be further from the ephemerism and pseudo-culture of politics and the newspaper (a particular target of Arnold's, as it was also of his contemporary Jacob Burckhardt, who in far-off Basel was struggling with the same threat, as he perceived it, to the "old culture of Europe"). In addition, for Arnold—who in this respect is far closer to the German neohumanists than to the Romantics—culture is the result of a careful process of selection, enhancement, and preservation by an elite, a priesthood or clergy of humanity. For that reason, culture is not national. It is catholic and universal—"the best that has been thought and written" by all human beings in all times and all languages (though, with the single exception of the Bible, Arnold's culture is effectively restricted to the Greek, Latin, and other Western European languages and literatures). Arnold appears to have expected this "culture," man-made and historically produced, to substitute for a no longer attainable Truth (whether religious or philosophical) as the foundation of individual conduct and social order. From this perspective, British science, British literature, and especially British politics and British religion (which far from being unifying were conceived as an arena of debate and clashing convictions and interests) had to appear narrow, provincial, divisive, even aberrant, and above all destructive of that "centre of authority" which was so important to the critic and which he believed was no longer provided by reason or even by faith.

Arnold's view of his own countrymen was strikingly similar to that of Michelet—notoriously no Anglophile. The English, according to Michelet, are the "aristocratic" people of world history: the people whose idea of liberty is anarchic, arrogant, exclusive, Byronic, and daemonic, and whose heroic struggle to win liberty was, and continues to be, marked by violence, parricide, revolt, and exploitation both of nature and of their weaker fellows. In Michelet's vision of history, the English—like the Jews—represent an essential and recurrent moment in the evolution of society, but one that is destined to be overcome by a less austere and exclusive, more harmonious and comprehensive form of sociability, a form of sociability which Michelet, drawing on Vico, considered "democratic." For Michelet, as to a large extent for Arnold, that higher form of sociability was represented by France, which, since the Revolution, had harmonized better than any other society the competing claims of the part and the whole, the individual and the state. The argument of ***Culture and Anarchy*** was, in short, that British individualism—"the dissidence of dissent and the Protestantism of the Protestant religion," as Arnold put it disdainfully (***CA*** 56 *et passim*)—would have to yield to a more comprehensive vision of society and that a greater role would have to be conceded to both the state and a national church if Britain was not to collapse in "anarchy."

It is essential to Arnold's understanding of culture that in modern times it must inevitably be the product of formal education. The withered, sickly condition of society can be cured. Culture can be restored. But for a while at least, until it is so reintegrated into the life of society that it again becomes a second nature, culture, as something learned and acquired rather than organically connected with all aspects of life in the way it once was, will be second-best—not so much an ersatz of the real thing as a kind of forced hot-house seedling which might be expected to grow sturdier later in the open air. In this important respect, as already noted, Arnold is far closer to the German neohumanists than to the Romantics, for while the Romantics looked back nostalgically to organic folk-cultures or tried to preserve them, the neohumanists aimed to resurrect ancient culture through education by having students progressively internalize Greek culture along with the inner forms and energies of the Greek language. Arnold in fact refers explicitly to Goethe in one of several fine passages where he discusses the difference between "organic" culture and culture as he understands it in the modern world:

> In the Greece of Pindar and Sophocles, in the England of Shakespeare, the poet lived in a current of ideas in the highest degree animating and nourishing to the creative power; society was, in the fullest measure, permeated by fresh thought, intelligent, and alive. And this state of things is the true basis for the creative power's exercise, in this it finds its data, its materials, truly ready for its hand; all the books and reading in the world are only valuable as they are helps to this. Even when this does not actually exist, books and reading may enable a man to construct a kind of semblance of it in his own mind . . . This is by no means equivalent to the artist for the nationally diffused life and thought of the epochs of Sophocles or Shakespeare; but, besides that it may be a means of preparation for such epochs, it does really constitute, if many share in it, a quickening and sustaining atmosphere of great value. Such an atmosphere the many-sided learning and the long and widely combined critical effort of Germany formed for Goethe . . . There was no national glow of life and thought there as in the Athens of Pericles or the England of Elizabeth. That was the poet's weakness. But there was a sort of equivalent for it in the complete culture and unfettered thinking of a large body of Germans. That was his strength.
>
> (**"The Function of Criticism"** 240)

Arnold implies that the aim of education is to bring about the eventual return of the "nationally diffused life and thought" which he associated with the glorious days of Pindar and Shakespeare. The realization of that goal could only be expected in a remote and rather ideal future, however. So while Arnold has "no doubt" that ages like those "are the true life of literature . . . the promised land, toward which criticism can only beckon," he is no less certain of the melancholy reality that "that promised land . . . will not be ours to enter, and we shall die in the wilderness (**"The Function of Criticism"** 267). On many occasions, in fact, the goal he presents is not so much the restoration of the "true life of literature" as the achievement of a more modest general culture, a middle-class *aurea mediocritas.* Over and over again, whether he is writing about the virtue of academies or about democracy, he argues for the superior merit of a more even distribution of culture, in the French manner, over an unruly combination of virtually "uncultured" masses and idiosyncratic geniuses, in the English manner. It even seems that it was such a general distribution of "culture" that he had in mind when he wrote about democracy, rather than any notions of political or economic rights or freedoms.[17] His chief concern in the essay on **"Democracy"** was not how to achieve democracy (following Tocqueville, whom he quotes approvingly as "a philosophic observer, with no love for democracy, but rather with a terror of it," he simply saw it as inevitable) but how to "prevent the English people from becoming, with the growth of democracy, *Americanised*"—in other words, how to ensure that democracy would not result in the overthrow or radical transformation of culture, as Arnold had defined it. It was necessary to find an accommodation of culture and democracy, just as it was necessary to find an accommodation of culture and religion, of "Hellenism" and "Hebraism" (**"Democracy"** 443-44, 452).

As Dover Wilson makes abundantly clear in the introduction to his edition, ***Culture and Anarchy*** was in fact a response to a particular political situation. It was not just the disenchantment of the world that had prompted Arnold to take up his pen: it was the enfranchisement of vast new sectors of the British population proposed in the Second Reform Bill of 1867; the violent agitation, provocative flouting of authority, and rioting (at Kidderminster, Hyde Park, and elsewhere) that accompanied the parliamentary debates; and the prospect of a spate of further radical legislation following passage of the bill. This was the time, Dover Wilson reminds us, of Carlyle's notorious essay "Shooting Niagara" with its call for a well-armed elite of "heroes" to defend culture against the advancing hordes. A concrete political situation is thus the context of Arnold's work at least as much as the more general problem of the "alienation" of the modern world. It is not hard to identify the ignorant armies clashing by night on the darkling plain of **"Dover Beach."** Certainly they are the mindless forces of historical action in a world revealed as purposeless, but they are also the liberal and dissenting commercial class and the increasingly aggressive proletariat of mid-Victorian England.[18]

It was in the face of this disturbing situation, which to many seemed to mark a real crisis of culture and society, that Arnold proposed his solution: a re-emphasizing of "culture and totality," as he put it,[19] against the destructive forces of individual enterprise, the mechanistic spirit of positivist and materialist thought, the alienating, impoverishing effects of liberal economics and industrialism, the parochialism of dissent and protestant sectarianism, the ephemerism of politics and the culture of the newspaper, the narrowness, ignorance, and vulgarity of democracy in the English-speaking countries.[20]

Arnold's critique of liberal optimism, like Heine's, is often effective and in the post-Thatcher and post-Reagan years, still surprisingly pertinent. He points with unerring perceptiveness to the weak spots of both economic liberalism—it has created *publice egestas, privatim opulentia,* he declares, quoting Sallust (***CA*** 186-87)—and political liberalism: demagoguery and populism, libertarianism at home and oppression abroad—in Ireland, for instance (***CA*** 80-81). The pathos of some of his descriptions of the lives of the poor reinforces the effectiveness of the critique of liberalism as a whole.[21] As usual with Arnold, the argument is conducted on a high plane of generality and spiritual significance. The class conflicts of nineteenth-century England are represented in idealized, universalized form as conflicts between different universal values or tendencies of the human psyche. Thus the "populace" is not exactly the proletariat; it is an eternal aspect of humankind—its cruelty and animality—which happens to dominate among proletarians (***CA*** 107). The terms "Barbarians," "Philistines," "Populace" transform a concrete historical struggle into a psychomachy, an allegory of the "eternal" conflict in human history between competing forces.[22]

Culture and Anarchy turns essentially on the conflict between two opposing sets of values: the whole and the part, order and absolute individual freedom, the state and the individual. On one side: the total, harmonious, fully developed individual human being of the German neohumanists, the ideal of Goethe, Schiller, Wilhelm von Humboldt (***CA*** 11, 126-27); the State—"organ of our collective best Self, of our national right reason" (97) viewed as standing above all particular interests and classes and embracing them all, as essentially classless (70); the Sacred ("the very framework and exterior order of the state," we are told, is sacred, 204); "Humanity" as a kind of universal Church or Communion (192); eternal Truth;[23] universal and unchanging norms; a classically trained elite of disinterested servants of the state, concerned only for the common weal, such as Humboldt had hoped to create for Prussia; finally, the idea of a hierarchy or sacred order, which excludes nothing, but on the contrary includes everything *in its proper place.*[24] On the opposite side: against the aesthetic neohumanist ideal of the harmonious, fully rounded individual, the moral ideal of the individual passionately dedicated to a single overriding imperative, a single calling or task, the specialist, the religious fanatic, the dissenter, the protestant; against the State as the organ of our collective best Self, the idea of society as an arena of competition, debate, and struggle between rival classes and interests, out of which the best solution is supposed to emerge, but which Arnold tended to see as a "darkling plain . . . where ignorant armies clash by night"; against the view of the State as sacred, in some way still invested with the power and authority of the divine, a mechanical and profane conception of society as pure historical fact in a postlapsarian world from which God has withdrawn; against the ideal of "Humanity" as a Communion, a fragmented vision of individuals, generations, and peoples isolated from each other in both space and time; against the notion of eternal Truth, the relativism or pragmatism of adaptation to the demands of the particular time and occasion (***CA*** 120); against eternal norms, the value of continuous research and experimentation (***CA*** 124); against the ideal of a classical elite, the practice of "representational democracy," in which "every one of our governors has all possible temptation, instead of setting up before the governed who elect him, and on whose favor he depends, a high standard of right reason, to accommodate himself as much as possible to their natural taste for the bathos" (***CA*** 113-114); and finally, against hierarchy or sacred order, anarchical competition and distorted overdevelopment of particular individual traits and tendencies.

The opposition of "Hellenism" and "Hebraism" is part of this more comprehensive set of oppositions in Arnold's text, and in his work in general. As a result, its meaning, though not entirely unrelated to the meaning it had for Heine, is by no means the same as it was for Heine. "Hellenism" designates for Arnold not so much sensualism, worldliness, and love of life as the contemplative, playful, free consideration of all aspects of reality. It is an ideal of aesthetic comprehensiveness, closely related to theory and intellectual speculation (***CA*** 132). "Hebraism," in contrast, is closer to *praxis.* It is the term used to designate not so much otherworldliness and spirituality as the primacy of moral commitment, of the existential moment of choice or decision, which is always, by definition, exclusive and limiting or narrowing. It has to do with conduct and action. Arnold's "Hellenism" is related to "culture and totality," his "Hebraism" to division and conflict.

Whereas the two terms, as we saw, are in an unending and unresolvable dialectical relation to each other for Heine, Arnold's thesis is that it is necessary, and possible, to find a golden mean that will accommodate both. His advocacy of "Hellenism" against "Hebraism," he makes clear, is pragmatic and tactical, by no means principled. It is entirely a matter of adjustments and degrees, of balancing competing and equally justified claims rather than resolving a dialectical opposition by means of some Hegelian "Aufhebung."[25]

> For *the days of Israel are innumerable;* and in its blame of Hebraising too, and in its praise of Hellenising, culture must not fail to keep its flexibility, and to give to its judgments that passing and provisional character which we have seen it impose on its preferences and rejections of machinery. Now, and for us, it is a time to Hellenise, and to praise knowing; for we have Hebraised too much, and have over-valued doing. But the habits and discipline received from Hebraism remain for our race an eternal possession; and, as humanity is constituted, one must never assign to them the second rank to-day, without being prepared to restore them to the first rank to-morrow.
>
> (***CA*** 37)

Had Arnold been writing about Prussia, rather than England, in other words, he might have chosen a different emphasis.[26] After the debacle of 1870, he did in fact fault the French, whom he normally held up as models to his countrymen, for their lack of "Hebraism." Reviewing Renan's *La Réforme intellectuelle et morale* in 1872, he took issue with Renan's view that France's defeat was the result of *le manque de foi à la science.* "No one feels more than we do the harm which the exaggeration of Hebraism has done in England; but [Renan's proposal to concentrate more on schooling] is Hellenism with a vengeance! . . . Moral conscience, self-control, seriousness, steadfastness, are not the whole of human life certainly, but . . . without them—and this is the very burden of the Hebrew prophets . . . —nations cannot stand. France does not enough see their importance" (***Complete Prose Works*** 7:44-45). The implication of this argument is that "Hebraism," if it can be curbed and brought into harmony with "culture," will make Protestant England a more successful nation and a better model for others, in the end, than Catholic and Revolutionary France.

Though Arnold sometimes presents Hellenism and Hebraism, in the manner of Heine or Michelet, as the twin motors of history and civilization—by their "alternations," he suggests, "the human spirit proceeds; and each of these two forces has its appointed hours of culmination and seasons of rule" (***CA*** 139)—his most persistent tendency is to try to strike a balance between them. His deepest longing is to reconcile everything: the whole and the part, community and individual freedom, tradition and individual talent, pragmatism and principle, harmony and truth, culture and religion, culture and democracy, the dominance of the elite and the moral and physical well-being of the masses. It could be said that he is as "English" in this pursuit of compromise as the dissenters he attacked for their stubborn individualism. In a passage like the following, which is fairly typical, the provocative tensions of Hegel, Heine, and later Nietzsche are relaxed in what the last would almost certainly have characterized as an insipid optimism. It is only the baser forms of Hellenism and Hebraism that are irreconcilable, we are assured. At their noblest, the two are entirely compatible. In "beauty and charm" their opposition is smoothed away:

> Hebraism strikes too exclusively upon one string in us; Hellenism does not address itself with serious energy enough to morals and righteousness. For our totality, for our general perfection, we need to unite the two; now the two are easily at variance. In their lower forms they are irreconcilably at variance; only when each of them is at its best, is their harmony possible. Hebraism at its best is beauty and charm: Hellenism at its best is also beauty and charm. As such they can unite; as anything short of this, each of them, they are at discord, and their separation must continue. The flower of Hellenism is a kind of amiable grace and artless winning good-nature . . . ; the flower of Christianity is grace and peace by the annulment of our ordinary self through the mildness and sweet reasonableness of Christ. Both are eminently *humane,* and for complete human perfection both are required; the second being the perfection of that side in us which is moral and acts, the first, of that side in us which is intelligent and perceives and knows.
>
> (***Complete Prose Works*** 6:125)

In some texts the two poles usually represented in Arnold's writing by Hebraism and Hellenism are situated entirely within the Greek world. In a speech to the students at Eton, for instance—where in the speaker's own words "the Greek and Latin classics continue to fill the chief place in [the students'] school-work"—a somewhat doubtful contrast developed by many German scholars between "manly" Aryan Dorians on the one hand, and "Asiatic Greeks of Ionia" on the other, is picked up and serves as the basis of an opposition between the "moral ideas of conduct and righteousness" strenuously cultivated by the "less gay and more solitary tribes in the mountains of Northern Greece," and the "brilliancy and mobility," the "gay lightness" characteristic of the "Ionians of Asia." Conflict is resolved, however, and the right balance struck by the Athenians. The latter, though they were Ionians, "were Ionians transplanted to Hellas, and who had breathed, as a Hellenic nation, the air of Delphi, that bracing atmosphere of the ideas of moral order and of right. In this atmosphere the Athenians, Ionian as they were, imbibed influences of character and steadiness, which for a long while balanced their native vivacity and mobility, distinguished them profoundly from the Ionians of Asia, and gave them men like Aristides." In this way, the Athenians—whose relation to the severe and alien Dorians strikingly resembles that of the English to the people of the Book—found the right middle ground between the extremes of the Ionians on the one hand and of the Dorians on the other. (The defects of the latter are described, incidentally, in the exact terms Arnold always used to describe the limitations of Hebraism: "stiffness, hardness, narrowness, prejudice, want of insight, want of amiability.") The Athenians thus come to represent that synthesis of "Hellenism" and "Hebraism" that was Arnold's ideal. "With the idea of conduct, so little grasped by the Ionians of Asia, still deeply impressed on their soul, they freely and joyfully called forth also that pleasure in life, that love of clear thinking and of fearless discussion, that gay social temper, that ease and lightness, that gracious flexibility, which were in their nature."[27]

It might seem, in light of the argument developed here, that Hellenism has a definite edge over Hebraism in that it is capable of containing and subsuming Hebraism in the same way that the culture of the Athenians included the best of the Dorians as well as the best of the Ionians. Hellenism at its best, in other words, could be conceived to be identical with "culture" or "totality." Arnold never gives any indication that Hebraism has the same capacity. At the same time, a totality that is defined as a well-balanced mixture, flexible enough to accommodate seemingly contradictory values, is not the same as the concept of a totality, the essential characteristic of which is that it cannot be understood simply as an aggregate of parts and which is held to be superior to any and all of its parts. What Arnold proposes, in the end, is a watered-down—if practical and manageable—version of both culture or totality and of religion or the moral imperative of choice. For in the same way that his version of an achieved "totality" seems more like a balance of competing elements than a resolution of differences, so too the one-sided and fanatical concern with righteousness, which is what "Hebraism" stands for, becomes acceptable by losing the intransigent transcendentalism that is its special force and that underlies its capacity to generate the most radical and uncompromising criticism of all worldly institutions.

Where "flexibility" is the highest virtue, and undeviating obedience to divine law is seen as "stiffness, hardness, narrowness, prejudice, want of insight, want of amiability," fundamental conflicts of principle are unlikely to arise. It is not in the least surprising that Arnold consistently rejects Judeo-Christian messianism and eschatology—"the turbid Jewish fancies about 'the great consummation,'" as he liked to say[28]—or that he responds impatiently to criticism of his own milder view of Christianity. "People talk scornfully of a 'sublimated Christianity,' as if the Christianity of Jesus Christ himself had been a materialistic fairy-tale like that of the Salvation Army or of Messrs Moody and Sankey" (***Complete Prose Works*** 7:372). The intransigence of the old Jewish and Christian rejection of this world, the excessiveness of the longing for its total transformation, are alien to Arnold, and he does not see that there are only two alternatives: absolute alienation from the divine or absolute oneness with it, damnation or salvation. To the advocate of a proper balance between "Hebraism" and "Hellenism" the world does not present itself in those stark terms.

For the same reason, he has no sympathy with the literalism of orthodox Jews and fundamentalist Christians, for whom Holy Scripture has "a talismanic character," as he says disparagingly. Paul "Judaises," we are told, when he "uses the letter of Scripture in [an] arbitrary and Jewish way" to back up a point, for that use of the sacred text is "due to a defect in the critical habit of himself and his race." Arnold cannot conceive a direct relation to the language of Scripture, only a relation mediated and eased by historical interpretation. "To get . . . at what Paul really thought and meant to say, it is necessary for us modern and Western people to translate him" (***Complete Prose Works*** 6:22-23). In fact, it sometimes seems as though Arnold is prepared to carry interpretation beyond the point at which the religion of the nineteenth century can be considered the same as that of its early adherents. In one of his ***Last Essays*** he explains that "the partisans of religion" in England and America "do not know . . . how decisively the whole force of progressive and liberal opinion on the Continent has pronounced against the Christian religion." Nor do they know "how surely the whole force of progressive and liberal opinion in this country tends to follow, so far as traditional religion is concerned, the opinion of the Continent. They dream of patching up things unmendable." And once again, Arnold looks for a compromise. "One cannot blame the rejection . . . The religion of tradition, Catholic or Protestant, *is* unsound and untenable." The only question that remains is whether "to claim for the Bible the direction, in any way, of modern life, is . . . as if Plato had sought to found his ideal republic on a text of Hesiod." Does the irrelevancy of the Bible to the conduct of modern life follow necessarily from the view that traditional religion is obsolete? It is because Arnold would save the Bible not as Truth, but as an important element in Western culture, that he finds it "so all-important to insist on what I call the natural truth of Christianity."[29]

If Arnold's Hebraism balks at the "turbid fancies" of eschatology and at the "Judaising" reading of Scripture by fervent Jews and Christians alike, his Hellenism is brought up short before what he sees as the unresponsiveness of the Greek gods and of paganism in general to suffering: "The ideal, cheerful, sensuous, pagan life is not sick or sorry."[30] That had been, in Heine's view too, the fatal flaw of the Greek gods and it had cost them their throne: "What a refreshing spring for all sufferers was the blood that flowed on Golgotha! . . . The white marble Greek gods were bespattered with this blood, and sickened with horror, and could never more recover . . . The first to die was Pan" ("Ludwig Börne: A Memorial" 269). But whereas Greek sensualism and Jewish spiritualism were engaged, for Heine, in an unrelenting "war between matter and spirit, which began with the world and would only end with the world" (as his Parisian friend Michelet put it in the opening paragraph of his *Introduction to Universal History* of 1831); whereas Nietzsche embraced joyfully the reality of tragedy, the acceptance of which he considered the core of Greek culture, and his colleague and close friend at the University of Basel, Franz Overbeck, denounced the attempt to reconcile Christianity and Culture as ruinous to both,[31] Arnold still hoped that a sensible compromise might be realized: a bit of Judeo-Christian religion watered down to morality and charity and a bit of Greek culture reduced to the free play of form and ideas, but no excess of either.

Arnold's relation to the social class he was addressing in ***Culture and Anarchy*** is characteristic of his search for compromise and inclusiveness and his distaste for conflict. Heine and Nietzsche were radically critical of the culture of the middle class; Arnold, in contrast, hoped to correct and improve the English middle class, to which all his essays were addressed and to which he himself belonged. His goal was to get it to reform, to save itself from its own defects, to confront the consequences, for its own political power and prosperity, of dogmatic adherence to laissez-faire social, cultural, educational, and economic policies. His concern for the poor, his lifelong championship of public education, and his advocacy of state power were inspired less by visions of a democratic society than by expediency. His interest in democracy was in fact quite weak, and his compassion for the poor was more than equalled by his fear of an increasingly vocal and aggressive working class. Not surprisingly, perhaps, the model he often invited his own countrymen to borrow from—though characteristically he did not recommend that they adopt it as a whole—was the German culture and state that Nietzsche tirelessly denounced. One can speculate that if Nietzsche had known Arnold's work, he would most likely have judged that the English critic of English "philistinism" was as irremediably "philistine" as the dissenting free-trading businessmen who were the object of his reforming efforts or, for that matter, as irremediably philistine as English writers and thinkers were, in Nietzsche's view, in general.

Arnold's very lack of intellectual rigor and decisiveness—which makes his work so much less stimulating and provocative than Heine's or Nietzsche's—has probably a great deal to do with his tolerance on most subjects. Arnold's reasoning, his way of bringing competing claims to our attention, is not so much dialectical as rhetorical, and the solutions he comes up with are pragmatic rather than theoretical. His views of Judaism and Jews are no exception to this general rule. Arnold's totality, as we saw, is an empirical accommodation of competing values, not a unity resulting from their *Aufhebung* or sublation. Judaism, consequently, was not for him something that had to be overcome either by Christianity or by an ideal culture more comprehensive than Christianity. "The days of Israel are innumerable." In practical terms, neither conversion nor assimilation of the Jews was necessary. Nor, on the other hand, was Mosaic Law or Sacred Scripture the first and last word of all faith and morality. They were subject to interpretation, in Arnold's view, in the light of other, equally valid demands and values.

Thomas Arnold had not been well disposed to Jews. In 1838 he had resigned from the senate of the newly founded University of London when he failed to convince his colleagues that Jews should not be admitted (Alexander 91). Matthew Arnold, in contrast, defended both Judaism and Jews. There are unflattering references in his work to Jews as "unattractive, nay, repellent, . . . a petty, unsuccessful, unamiable people, without politics, without science, without art, without charm."[32] (Arnold's descriptions of the ancient Dorians and of modern Puritans and Dissenters were strikingly similar, however, and hardly less negative). And occasionally he allows himself to be influenced by current racial theories concerning the superiority of "Aryans" to "Semites," as in a notable passage of ***Culture and Anarchy*** concerning the controversy over legislation about marriage between a man and his deceased wife's sister:

> Who, that is not manacled and hoodwinked by his Hebraism, can believe that, as to love and marriage, our reason and the necessities of our humanity have their true, sufficient, and divine law expressed in them by the voice of any Oriental and polygamous nation like the Hebrews? Who, I say, will believe . . . that where the feminine nature, the feminine ideal, and our relations to them, are brought into question, the delicate and apprehensive genius of the Indo-European race, the race which invented the Muses, and chivalry, and the Madonna, is to find its last word . . . in the institutions of a Semitic people, whose wisest king had seven hundred wives and three hundred concubines?
>
> (184)

In **"Literature and Dogma,"** however, Arnold makes a spirited defence of the ancient Jews against modern claims that they were "perpetually oppressive, grasping, slanderous, sensual," worshippers of a "tribal God," blind followers of "a positive traditionary code, . . . a mechanical rule which held them in awe," incapable of conceiving evil in any but an external way, as "oppression, theft, or riotous excess," and insensitive to the idea of "internal faults." He insists on the "deeper personal religion" that "constantly breaks in," on the importance in Judaism of following God's law out of love rather than blind obedience, on the crucial discovery of the idea of righteousness. To those who question the special moral insight of the ancient Hebrews by asking, "Why, if the Hebrews of the Bible had eminently the sense for righteousness, does it not equally distinguish the Jews now?" he responds by pointing out that a modern people that has endured centuries of persecution and oppression cannot be expected to have the grandeur of its ancestors. Modern Jews are not any further removed from the Jews of Biblical times than modern Greeks from the Greeks of the age of Aeschylus and Sophocles.[33]

In practice, moreover, Arnold's support of modern Jews was solid. To the high-minded and serious Louisa Montefiore, Lady de Rothschild, to whom he became closely attached, and who was fervently interested in the traditions of her people, he owed not only the acquaintance of Disraeli but, in all probability, a deeper and more sympathetic understanding than he might otherwise have had of the Jews of his own time (Honan 316-18). As a result, he was instrumental in getting the Jews' Free School in Bell Lane, near Liverpool Street Station, included among the state-aided schools. Invited to propose the toast at a banquet in aid of the school in 1884, he recalled his early association with it: though he is no public orator, he says, "it is less difficult to speak among old friends—and, gentlemen, the Free School and I—as by your kind cheers you have shown me that you are aware—are old friends. I may almost adopt Grattan's famous words, and say that I sat by the Free School's cradle." A few years earlier, in 1872, he had sent the headmaster of the School a copy of an introduction he wrote to the last 27 chapters of the Book of Isaiah, which was intended for use in schools, "as a sort of expression of gratitude," as he wrote to Lady de Rothschild, "for the ideas your great Bell Lane schools have awakened in me" (***Complete Prose Works*** 10:245-46 and 538n).

But it is in his almost instinctive resistance to anti-Judaic tendencies in continental scholarship that Arnold's own "Hebraism" is most visible. He is suspicious of the application of Hegelian philosophy to the interpretation of Scripture and notably cool to German attempts to demonstrate the anti-Petrine, universalist character of the Third and Fourth Gospels. In the eagerness of some scholars to prove that from very early on "the peaceable coexistence of a Jewish and a Gentile Christianity no longer satisfies the religious consciousness" and that "it will be satisfied with nothing less than a Catholic Church one and indivisible"—in other words that Christianity almost immediately sought to "transcend" its Jewish roots—he smells a rat. These scholars, he objects, are pursuing their Hegelian agenda with such zeal that they try to pass off as hard facts interpretations which are at best only possible. One theologian claims, for instance, "that by two crucified thieves, one converted, the other impenitent, the writer of the Third Gospel meant to contrast Jew and Gentile, the obstinate rejection of Christ by the former, the glad acceptance by the latter." A possible reading, Arnold comments: "No doubt this may be called an 'ingenious conjecture,' but what are we to think of the critic who confidently builds upon it?" (***Complete Prose Works*** 7:273-74). Though Arnold's sympathy with the Oxford movement is well documented and he himself repeatedly voiced his support for the idea of a national church—an idea consonant with his view of religion as part of culture and his belief that "our only real perfection is our totality" (***Complete Prose Works*** 6:126)—the reference here to the peaceable co-existence of a Jewish and a Gentile Christianity is a reminder that his vision of totality did not require assimilation or the "resolution" of difference.

Perhaps the most telling sign of the authenticity of Arnold's "Hebraism" is his unequivocal recoil from the racist antisemitism of Emile Burnouf. In a time of increasing attacks on the religion of the Bible, Arnold wrote in **"Literature and Dogma,"**

> even what the most modern criticism of all sometimes does to save it and to set it up again, can hardly be called very flattering to it. For whereas the Hebrew race imagined that to them were committed the oracles of God . . . there now comes M. Emile Burnouf . . . [who] will prove to us in a thick volume that the oracles of God were not committed to a Semitic race at all, but to the Aryan; that the true God is not Israel's God at all, but is "the idea of the absolute" which Israel could never properly master. This "sacred theory of the Aryans," it seems, passed into Palestine from Persia and India, and got possession of the founder of Christianity and of his greatest apostles St. Paul and St. John . . . So that we Christians, who are Aryans, may have the satisfaction of thinking that "the religion of Christ has not come to us from the Semites," and that "it is in the hymns of the Veda, and not in the Bible, that we are to look for the primordial source of our religion." The theory of Christ is accordingly the theory of the Vedic Agni, or *fire.* The Incarnation represents the Vedic solemnity of the production of *fire,* symbol of force of every kind, or all movement, life, and thought. The Trinity of Father, Son, and Spirit is the Vedic Trinity of Sun, Fire, and Wind; and God, finally, is "a cosmic unity."
>
> (***Complete Prose Works*** 6:239).

Arnold's reaction is incredulous astonishment at the audacity of these claims in a work that purports to offer *La Science des Religions.* "Such speculations almost take away the breath of a mere man of letters," he comments with characteristic irony. He proceeds not to dispute Burnouf on scholarly grounds, but to challenge his entire understanding of religion. The un-metaphysical Englishman makes common cause with the allegedly un-metaphysical Hebrews to defend the religion of Israel:

> Admitting that Israel shows no talent for metaphysics, we say that his religious greatness is just this, that he does *not* found religion on metaphysics, but on moral experience; . . . and that, ever since the apparition of Israel and the Bible, religion is no longer what, according to M. Burnouf, to our Aryan forefathers in the valley of the Oxus it was,—and what perhaps it really was to them,—metaphysical theory, but is what Israel has made it.
>
> (***Complete Prose Works*** 6:241).

Compared with the young Hegel's or with Nietzsche's philhellenism, Arnold's vision of a culture that can embrace both Homer and the Bible must inevitably appear timid, conservative, somewhat schoolmasterish. No doubt it is closer in spirit to British parliamentarism than to the ancient *polis* or to more recent attempts to establish unified national cultures. Like Parliament, Arnold's "culture" aims at accommodating more than one party rather than at unity, and like Parliament, its inclusiveness is selective. Still, it has its modest advantages. It was, after all, to Parliament that Disraeli was elected and through Parliament that he rose to become the first Jewish prime minister of a major Western European nation.[34] There appears likewise to be an inner compatibility between Arnold's inclusive, pluralistic vision of "culture" and the form taken by the emancipation of the Jews in Britain. Though legal disabilities and restrictions on Jews were less severe in Britain than in most continental countries before emancipation, full emancipation came later than it did in France, for instance. On the other hand, as the most recent historian of the emancipation in England has explained, "in Britain, civil rights were granted to Jews and other religious minorities unconditionally. They were not asked to make concessions at the expense of their religion, unlike the requirements made in France, Germany or Italy. Even though certain religious beliefs, such as prohibition of marriage with non-Jews, were incompatible with the expectations of modern citizenship, Jews were not told to reform such tenets. Similarly, Quakers were not forced to give up religious imperatives such as refusal to take oaths, to pay for or fight in wars, though these principles could clash with the modern notion of citizenship. During the process of emancipation, Britain legitimized religious pluralism by leaving the peculiarities of each sect untouched."[35] This pragmatic and in the end conservative solution, by which the complete secularization of public life was avoided and the Church of England maintained as the established Church, has not been without its drawbacks, especially for British Jews,[36] but, like Arnold's "culture," it seems to have allowed for more peaceful coexistence, in the short term anyway, than the more radical emancipation policies pursued in several continental states.

Notes

1. "Religion and Philosophy in Germany" (1834) 181, 223.
2. See Elisabeth de Fontenany 55 (where the claim is made that "anti-judaisme," in the sense of a critique of Judaism as a religion, may go hand in hand with "philo-sémitisme," in the sense of support for Jewish emancipation), and 104 (where the distinction between "Juifs philosophiques" and "Juifs sociologiques," between "anti-judaisme" and "anti-sémitisme" is hedged round with the caveat

that "ces deux perspectives, l'une plus métaphysique, l'autre plus sociologique, se recoupent toujours en même temps qu'elles divergent." Fontenay evokes the example of Hegel, who "parlant péjorativement du judaisme, en vient insidieusement à mentionner le malheur hérité des Juifs actuels, lui qui d'ailleurs défend leur droit à l'émancipation." The reference is no doubt to the passage in "The Spirit of Christianity" (written 1798-99, unpublished in Hegel's lifetime) where Hegel writes that "the subsequent circumstances of the Jewish people up to the mean, abject, wretched circumstances in which they still are today, have all of them been simply consequences and elaborations of their original fate" (*On Christianity* 199). Fontenay's attempt to spirit away Marx's antisemitism by presenting "Jews" in Marx as a "metonymy of bourgeois society" is criticized by Francis Kaplan (61-62), who also emphasizes the ease with which the "philosophical" critique of Judaism as a religion can shade off into plain antisemitism. When Marx asks rhetorically "Quel est le fonds profane du judaisme?" and answers "Le besoin pratique, l'utilité personnelle . . . l'abaissement effectif de la nature, le mépris de la théorie, de l'art, de l'histoire, de l'homme considéré comme son propre but," at least part of that reply, according to Kaplan, can feed into the popular stereotype of the Jew as selfish, greedy, and indifferent to others (45).

3. For a brief general account of ancient Greek and Roman hostility to Judaism and Jews, see Carlos Lévy.

4. For a short overview of the essentials of neohumanism, see my article, "The 'two cultures' in nineteenth century Basle" (99-105).

5. See the invaluable study of Bengt Sørensen.

6. "We are fighting not for the human rights of the people but for the divine rights of mankind," Heine was to write in the early thirties; "we do not want to be sansculottes, nor simple citizens, nor venal presidents; we want to found a democracy of gods, equal in majesty, in sanctity, and in bliss" ("Religion and Philosophy in Germany" 180).

7. Robert P. Ericksen; see also Tal 191-92, 200-201, 217-18. According to Jenkyns (72), Newman in England held a somewhat similar position at one point in his career: "Newman's perversely systematic mind had not only divided Hellenism sharply from Hebraism, but had separated Christianity no less sharply from both. Christ was neither Greek nor Jew . . ." Jenkyns also quotes a comment by George Eliot about her contemporaries: "They hardly know that Christ was a Jew."

8. Both passages, the second from a text of 1882, are quoted by Tal (264-65). In the early decades of the twentieth century in France, the views of Charles Maurras, chief ideologist of the radical right-wing and antisemitic *Action française*, were similar, though Maurras's emphasis falls more on restraint and order (which he associated with classical antiquity) than on energy and life: "Admirateur de l'antiquité classique, Maurras ne se sent à l'aise que dans le paganisme. Il connaîit Lucrèce par coeur. Le polythéisme grec lui a toujours paru un chef d'oeuvre de mesure, d'ordre et d'harmonie puisqu'il assigne à chaque désir humain une divinité précise. Ainsi l'orientation du désir, dûment canalisée ne risque-t-elle pas de prendre le chemin de l'Infini. Dans le paysage méditerranéen, la lumière du soleil dessine nettement les contours et les ombres: à l'homme d'y prendre sa place, sans rêves ni chimères insensées, en acceptant de se soumettre à cet ordre préétabli. C'est la condition du bonheur. L'esprit biblique, les Evangiles de 'quatre juifs obscurs,' Jérusalem et la synagogue sont venus rompre ce bel équilibre. Le christianisme est aussi dangereux que le judaisme pour le maintien de la civilisation . . . L'aire de l'humanité civilisée ne déborde guère les rivages de la Méditerranée (encore faut-il préciser Méditerranée occidentale jusqu'à la Grece incluse, mais pas au-delà)" (Jacques Prévotat 250-52).

9. As the implications of late nineteenth-century anti-Judaism and antisemitism became unmistakably clear in the twentieth century, many Christians came to the defense of Judaism. Nicolas Berdyaev, for instance, emphasized the Judaic roots of Christianity, arguing that "in its human origins, [Christianity] is a religion of messianic and prophetic type, the spirit of which, as utterly foreign to Graeco-Roman spiritual culture as to Hindu culture, was introduced into world religious thought by the Jewish people. The 'Aryan' spirit is neither messianic nor prophetic . . ." (1-2). On the other hand, some Jewish thinkers have maintained that the dualism which the German philhellenes so detested is Christian, not Jewish. Rosenzweig claimed that the Jew is destined by his religion to remain in the Jewish world of his birth and is expected only to perfect his Judaism. The Christian, on the other hand, being by nature pagan, has to withdraw from the world to which he belongs, repeal his nature, and break with his original paganism, in order to carry out the precepts of his faith (see Berdyaev 23). Josué Jehonda claims that the Christians are rebellious, the Jews traditional. The Christians created the opposition between Jerusalem, the city of God's justice, and Athens and Rome, the political city. Thus "la vraie cause de tout anti-sémitisme est le dualisme chrétien." Pagan antisemitism was in reality directed against the Christians. They were seen as subversives. The Jews, in contrast, were recognized as a national group. Thus in our own times, Nazi antisemitism "aimed to destroy, through the Jews, the entire Christian world" (Jehonda 108-110).

10. *Kulturgeschichtliche Charakterköpfe* (1891), quoted in Fritz Blättner 161-62.

11. The point is made forcefully by Hubert Cancik, "Philhellenism and Anti-Semitism in Germany (II)" 7-10. The rehabilitation of the Dorians began toward the close of the eighteenth century with the Greek Revival in architecture, for which Winckelmann himself had prepared the ground. In England, the second volume of Stuart and Revett's *Antiquities of Athens* (1787) revealed a Greek architecture unlike anything men had imagined, and the vogue of the "Greek style" to which it gave rise prompted established architects like Sir William Chambers to attack the "gouty columns" and "disproportionate architraves" of the Doric. The editor of the third volume, Willey Reveley, leaped to the defense of the style that possessed, he claimed, "a masculine boldness," "an awful dignity and grandeur" (see Jenkyns 12). But it was in Germany that the Doric and then the Dorians enjoyed the greatest vogue. Goethe recorded his disorientation and awe before the ruins of Paestum in a well-known passage of the *Italian Journey*: "In the distance appeared some huge quadrilateral masses, and when we finally reached them, we were at first uncertain whether we were driving through rocks or ruins. Then we recognized what they were, the remains of temples . . . Kniep quickly choose a favourable spot from which to draw this very unpicturesque landscape . . . At first sight [the temples] excited nothing but stupefaction. I found myself in a world which was completely strange to me. In their evolution from austerity to charm, the centuries have simultaneously shaped and even created a different man. Our eyes and, through them, our whole sensibility have become so conditioned to a more slender style of architecture that these crowded masses of stumpy conical columns appear offensive and even terrifying . . ." (209-10). In the work of Carl Otfried Müller (*Die Dorier,* 1824) and in that of his student, Ernst Curtius, the author of a much translated and widely read *History of Greece* (1857-61), it was the invading Northern Hellenes or Dorians (the name Dorian is said to be derived from Dorus, one of the sons of Hellen), who, thrusting south toward the Peloponnese, were the active, "manly" power that fecundated the somnolent, "feminine" Pelasgians, and forged the greatness of ancient Greece. "From the Hellenes sprang entirely new currents of life," according to Curtius. "The Pelasgian times lie in the background—a vast period of monotony: impulse and motion are first communicated by Hellen and his sons; and with their arrival history commences. Accordingly we must interpret them to signify tribes which, endowed with special gifts, and animated by special powers of action, issue forth from the mass of a great people, and extend themselves in it as warriors" (41). Müller's and Curtius's view of the Dorians was taken over in Britain, where there was a strong temptation to associate the Dorian "highlanders" with the Scots (see Jenkyns 167).

12. *Wesen des Christentums,* ch. 12, quoted in Poliakov 415.

13. See the striking article by Nicholas Rand.

14. All four passages quoted in Jenkyns 177-78. The Shelley passage is cited more fully here than in Jenkyns.

15. The essay on Heine (read as a lecture in 1863) in *The Function of Criticism* and the poem "Heine's Grave" (probably completed by 1863 but not published until 1867) are eloquent testimony to Arnold's long-standing admiration for Heine. The exact relationship of Arnold's contrast of Hellenism and Hebraism to Heine's writings is, however, a matter of some scholarly dispute. Lionel Trilling, R. H. Super (the editor of Arnold's *Complete Prose Works*), and most other English-speaking scholars (but not, apparently, David J. DeLaura in his now-classic study) hold that Arnold derived the Hellenism-Hebraism opposition from Heine's memorial essay on Börne. But it has been questioned whether Arnold had read that essay, and some of Trilling's assertions in particular have been effectively invalidated. More pertinently, it has been argued that Arnold altered the meaning that the opposition of Jews and Hellenes had for Heine, while retaining Heine's idea that history is marked by the struggle and alternance of forces represented by the two terms Hebraism and Hellenism. See Ilse-Maria Tesdorpf, especially 43-36, 138-69.

16. Quoted by Arnold himself in *Culture and Anarchy* 39 (hereafter *CA*). See also 72.

17. "Democracy is a force in which the concert of a great number of men makes up for the weakness of each man taken by himself; democracy accepts a relative rise in their condition, obtainable by this concert for a great number, as something desirable in itself, because *though this is undoubtedly far below grandeur,* it is yet a good deal above insignificance" (italics added), in "Democracy" 448.

18. See Dover Wilson's Introduction to *CA,* xxii-xxxiv.

19. *CA* 19. See also 21: "Culture . . . and what we call totality . . ."

20. See *CA* 48-49; also 17-18, 19, 22 on North America. America, "that chosen home of newspapers and politics," is "without general intelligence," according to Renan, and Arnold believes "it likely from the circumstances of the case, that this is so; and that, in the things of the mind, and in culture and totality, America, instead of surpassing us all, falls short" (19). To Arnold, only the first generation of Puritans—Milton, Baxter, Wesley—had had any greatness, chiefly because they still enjoyed the legacy of the catholic culture that they rejected ("were trained within the pale of the Establishment"). Since then, they had all been mediocrities (13).

21. See, for instance, *CA* 189-98.

22. Michelet, whom Arnold admired, tended to do the same thing in his histories, most blatantly in his powerfully schematic *Introduction à l'histoire universelle* of 1831.

23. One thinks of Burckhardt's expression: "Unzeitung."

24. Thus "culture" admits the necessity of "fortune making and industrialism," "culture does not set itself against games and sports" (*CA* 61).

25. Jenkyns underlines the deliberately non-dialectical nature of Arnold's thought on the subject of Hellenism and Hebraism. "It was characteristic of the age, or of its more enquiring members, to feel that between faith in Christianity and the love of Greece there must be a tension. Arnold was being consciously heterodox when he argued that Hellenism and Hebraism could be painlessly combined" (70). The contrast between the dialectical character of Heine's opposition of Greeks and Nazarenes and the undialectical character of Arnold's opposition of Hellenism and Hebraism is one of the chief themes of Ilse-Maria Tesdorpf's *Die Auseinandersetzung Matthew Arnolds mit Heinrich Heine*. Tesdorpf argues convincingly that while Arnold's Hellenism and Hebraism is not the same as Heine's Greeks and Nazarenes, his philosophy of history is borrowed from Heine. As a result there is a significant degree of inconsistency in Arnold's ideas (see especially 168).

26. See Park Honan 331 on Arnold's reservations about Prussia.

27. "A Speech at Eton," in *Complete Prose Works* 9:28-29. Arnold develops the idea of a tension within Greek culture similar to that between Hebraism and Hellenism in other texts also, notably "God and the Bible," in *Complete Prose Works* 7:208-11, and "Pagan and Medieval Religious Sentiment," in *Essays in Criticism* 212.

28. "Literature and Dogma," in *Complete Prose Works* 6:260. See also 225, 259-60 on "the turbid Jewish fancies . . . ," 281-82, 302-303 on "the turbid phantasmagory" that filled the thoughts of the Jews at the coming of Jesus Christ; and "God and the Bible," in *Complete Prose Works* 7:370-71, where we are told that the influence of Christ gradually transformed "the turbid elements among which it was thrown."

29. *Complete Prose Works* 8:151-52. My conclusions coincide with those reached by Edward Alexander several decades ago in his excellent study of *Matthew Arnold and John Stuart Mill* 52: "Arnold did his best . . . to maintain an equilibrium between the two adversaries [Hellenism and Hebraism] . . . But he could not help letting the cat out of the bag. Hellenism, after all, represented all of Arnold's hopes for the perfection of mankind, and Hebraism his scepticism about the capacity of men for perfection and his consciousness of their inherent weakness. Whereas Hellenism is a positive ideal, investing human life 'with a kind of aerial ease, clearness, and radiancy, [Hebraism] has always been severely pre-occupied with an awful sense of the impossibility of being at ease in Zion.' Hebraism and Hellenism are committed, ultimately, to opposite conceptions of human nature. For the ideal of culture as a harmonious human perfection which Arnold espoused throughout *Culture and Anarchy* was the ideal of Hellenism; and just as culture, in Arnold's theory, ultimately encompasses religion, so is Hellenism ultimately to encompass Hebraism."

30. "Pagan and Mediaeval Religious Sentiment" (first delivered as a lecture at Oxford, 1864) in *Essays in Criticism* 201. See also 205: "It is natural that man should take pleasure in his senses. But it is natural, also, that he should take refuge in his heart and imagination from his misery. And when one thinks what human life is for the vast majority of mankind, how little of a feast for their senses it can possibly be, one understands the charm for them of a refuge offered in the heart and imagination."

31. On Overbeck, see Walter Nigg; see also my "Anti-Theologie und Anti-Philologie."

32. "Literature and Dogma," in *Complete Prose Works* 6:199.

33. CA 196-99. See also "Equality," in *Complete Prose Works* 8:286-87: "the power of conduct . . . was so felt and fixed by Israel that we can never with justice refuse to permit Israel, in spite of all his shortcomings, to stand for it." Admiration for the Jews as a people is found even in the English translation of Houston Stewart Chamberlain's notoriously antisemitic *Foundations of the Nineteenth Century*. The author of the introduction to this translation, Lord Redesdale, finds Chamberlain's testimony to the "nobility" of the Sephardic Jews the more convincing as "Chamberlain is a strong anti-Semite," but he challenges Chamberlain on the latter's disparagement of the Ashkenazim or German Jews: "Chamberlain is unjust . . . They are born financiers and the acquisition of money has been their characteristic talent. But of the treasure which they have laid up they have given freely. The charities of the great cities of Europe would be in a sad plight were the support of the Jews to be withdrawn; indeed many noble foundations owe their existence to them. Politically too they have rendered great services . . ." (xxxv-xxxvi). Redesdale later notes his "appreciation of the stubborn singleness of purpose and dogged consistency which have made the Jew what he is. The ancient Jew was not a soldier . . . He was no sailor like his cousins the Phoenicians . . . He was no artist . . . neither was he a farmer nor a merchant. What was it then that gave him his wonderful self-confidence, his toughness of

character, which could overcome every difficulty, and triumph over the hatred of the other races? It was his belief in the sacred books of the law, the Thora . . . The influence of the books of the Old Testament has been far-reaching indeed, but nowhere has it exercised more power than in the stablishing of the character of the Jew. If it means so much to the Christian, what must it not mean to him? It is his religion, the history of his race, and his individual pedigree all in one. Nay! it is more than all that: it is the attesting document of his convenant with God" (xxxix).

34. It is true, of course, that Disraeli, though he flaunted his Jewish roots, had been baptised, and could therefore take the oath that was offensive to Jews and that prevented them, even when they had been duly elected, from taking their seats in Parliament until the final passing of the Jews' Act Amendment Bill in 1859. This fact hardly diminishes the extraordinary character, in the European context of the mid-nineteenth century, of Disraeli's role in British politics and public life.

35. Abraham Gilam ii. Gilam points out that, in contrast to Germany and France, "Jewish communal autonomy and separateness remained untouched in Britain. The Board of Deputies retained control over marriages, education, welfare and other domestic concerns. In 1836 it was given statutory recognition by Parliament as the marriage registrar for the Jewish community and in 1852, the chief rabbi and head of the Portuguese congregation were entrusted with the responsibility of supervising educational grants allocated from parliamentary endowments . . . British politicians constantly refused to intervene in internal Jewish disputes even when asked to do so by Jewish dissidents . . . England was the only European country where Jews continued to retain an autonomous management of their domestic affairs during a process of emancipation." (151) Gilam contrasts this with the Napoleonic interrogation of the Sanhedrin to determine whether the Jewish creed was sufficiently universalistic and whether Jews were ready to alter it when ever it seemed anti-social. (152) The British road to Jewish emancipation was in fact a compromise between liberal and conservative interests: "English statesmen wanted to establish freedom of conscience in the country while retaining the privileged position of the Anglican Church. In order to retain Church establishment, British legislation had to recognize the uniqueness of other creeds. They did not wish to separate church and state, disestablish Anglicanism or secularize public life. They did not confine religion to the sphere of individual privacy. If England wanted to retain an inequality before the law in favor of Anglicans, it had no right asking other minorities to make concessions in return for their own civil rights" (ii; see also 152).

36. For a sense of what these might be, from the point of view of the Jewish community in Britain itself, see Howard Cooper and Paul Morrison.

Works Cited

Alexander, Edward. *Matthew Arnold and John Stuart Mill.* London: Routledge and Kegan Paul, 1965.

Arnold, Matthew. *Complete Prose Works.* Ed. R. H. Super. 11 vols. Ann Arbor: University of Michigan Press, 1961—.

———. *Culture and Anarchy.* Ed. J. Dover Wilson. Cambridge: Cambridge University Press, 1969.

———. "Democracy." *The Portable Arnold* 436-69.

———. *Essays in Criticism.* London: Macmillan, 1865.

———. "The Function of Criticism at the Present Time." *The Portable Arnold* 234-67.

———. *The Portable Arnold.* Ed. Lionel Trilling. New York: Viking Press, 1949.

Benjamin, Walter. *Gesammelte Schriften.* Ed. Rolf Tiedeman and Herman Schweppenhäuser. Vol. 3. Frankfurt a. M.: Suhrkamp, 1972. 7 vols.

Berdyaev, Nicolas. *Christianity and Anti-Semitism.* New York: Philosophical Library, 1954.

Blättner, Fritz. *Das Gymnasium.* Heidelberg: Quelle & Meyer, 1960.

Bourel, Dominique and Jacques Le Rider, eds. *De Sils-Maria à Jerusalem: Nietzsche et le judaisme—Les intellectuels juifs et Nietzsche.* Paris: Cerf, 1991.

Cancik, Hubert. "Philhellenism and Anti-Semitism in Germany (II): 'Anti-Judaism Squared'—Toward a Historical and Literary Interpretation of Friedrich Nietzsche, 'Der Antichrist.'" Unpublished paper read to the Institute for Advanced Study, Princeton, N.J., February 1992.

Cancik, Hubert and Hildegard Cancik-Lindemaier. "Philhellénisme et antisémitisme en Allemagne: Le cas Nietzsche." Bourel and Le Rider 21-46.

Chamberlain, Houston Stewart. *Foundations of the Nineteenth Century.* London: John Lane, The Bodley Head, 1912.

Cooper, Howard and Paul Morrison. *A Sense of Belonging: Dilemmas of British Jewish Identity.* London: Weidenfeld and Nicolson, in association with Channel Four Television, 1991.

Curtius, Ernst. *History of Greece.* Trans. A. W. Ward. Vol. 1. New York: Charles Scribner's Sons, 1891. 5 vols.

DeLaura, David J. *Hebrew and Hellene in Victorian England: Newman, Arnold, and Pater.* Austin and London: University of Texas Press, 1969.

Ericksen, Robert P. "Theologian in the Third Reich: the Case of Gerhard Kittel." *Journal of Contemporary History* 12(1977): 595-622.

Fontenay, Elisabeth de. *Les Figures juives de Marx.* Paris: Editions Galilée, 1973.

Gilam, Abraham. *The Emancipation of the Jews in England 1830-1860.* New York and London: Garland, 1982.

Goethe, Johann Wolfgang von. *Italian Journey 1786-1788.* Trans. W. H. Auden and Elizabeth Mayer. San Francisco: North Point Press, 1982.

Gossman, Lionel. "Anti-Theologie und Anti-Philologie: Overbeck, Bachofen und die Kritik der Moderne in Basel." *Franz Overbecks unerledigte Anfragen an das Christentum.* Ed. Rudolf Brändle and Ekkehard Stegemann. Munich: Kaiser, 1988. 17-46.

———. "The 'two cultures' in nineteenth century Basle: between the French *'Encyclopédie'* and German neohumanism." *Journal of European Studies* 20(1990): 95-133.

Hegel, Friedrich. *On Christianity: Early Theological Writings.* Trans. T. M. Knox and Richard Kroner. New York: Harper Torchbooks, 1961.

———. "On Classical Studies." *On Christianity* 321-30.

———. "The Spirit of Christianity." *On Christianity* 182-301.

Heine, Heinrich. "Concerning the History of Religion and Philosophy in Germany." Trans. Helen Mustard. *The Romantic School* 128-244.

———. "Geständnisse." *Werke und Briefe* 7:95-179.

———. *Heinrich Heines Werke und Briefe.* Ed. Kans Kaufmann. 10 vols. Berlin: Aufbau-Verlag, 1962.

———. "Ludwig Börne: A Memorial." Trans. Frederic Ewen and Robert C. Holub. *The Romantic School* 261-83.

———. "Ludwig Börne: Eine Denkschrift." 1841. *Werke und Briefe* 6:83-229.

———. *The Romantic School and Other Essays.* Ed Jost Hermand and Robert C. Holub. New York: Continuum Books, 1985.

Hildebrand, Kurt. "Hellas und Wilamowitz." *Die Grenzboten* 69(1910). Rpt. in *Der George-Kreis: eine Auswahl aus seinen Schriften.* Ed Peter Landmann. Cologne and Berlin: Kiepenhauer und Witsch, 1965. 141-49.

Honan, Park. *Matthew Arnold: A Life.* New York: McGraw Hill, 1982.

Jehonda, Josué. *L'Antisémitisme, miroir du monde.* Geneva: Editions Synthesis, 1958.

Jenkyns, Richard. *The Victorians and Ancient Greece.* Cambridge, Mass.: Harvard University Press, 1980.

Kaplan, Francis. *Marx Anti-Sémite.* Paris: Editions Imago, 1990.

Kroner, Richard. Introduction. Hegel, *On Christianity* 1-66.

Levy, Carlos. "L'Antijudaisme paien: essai de synthèse." *De l'Antijudaisme antique à l'antisémitisme contemporain.* Ed. Valentin Nikiprowetsky. Lille: Presses universitaires de Lille, 1979. 51-86.

Nigg, Walter. *Franz Overbeck: Versuch einer Wurdigung.* Munich: Beck, 1931.

Poliakov, Leon. *The History of Anti-Semitism.* Trans. Miriam Kochan. Vol. 3. London: Routledge and Kegan Paul, 1975. 4 vols.

Prevotat, Jacques. "L'Antisémitisme de l'Action Française: Quelques repères." Levy 249-75.

Rand, Nicolas. "The Political Truth of Heidegger's 'Logos': Hiding in Translation." *PMLA* 105 (1990): 436-47.

Sørensen, Bengt. *Symbol und Symbolismus in den ästhetischen Theorien des 18. Jahrhunderts und der deutschen Romantik.* Copenhagen: Munksgaard, 1963.

Tal, Uriel. *Christians and Jews in Germany: Religion, Politics, and Ideology in the Second Reich, 1870-1914.* Trans. N. J. Jacobs. Ithaca and London: Cornell University Press, 1975.

Tesdorpf, Ilse-Maria. *Die Auseinandersetzung Matthew Arnolds mit Heinrich Heine.* Frankfurt a. M.: Athenaeum Verlag, 1971.

Terence Hawkes (essay date 1994)

SOURCE: "The Heimlich Manoeuvre," in *Textual Practice,* Vol. 8, No. 2, Summer, 1994, pp. 302-16.

[In the following essay, Hawkes analyzes Arnold's understanding of the role of criticism in culture, asserting that, like T. S. Eliot, Arnold views the role of English literature criticism as the mirror that reflects the "true nature of English national culture."]

I In Custody

I will focus on two eruptions. The first occurs in the middle of Matthew Arnold's essay of 1864, **'The Function Of Criticism At The Present Time'.** Arnold has been addressing the linked questions of the true nature of English literary criticism on the one hand and the true nature of English national culture on the other. If the first is ever to engage fruitfully with the second, literary criticism must become, he says, a de-politicized 'absolutely and entirely independent' activity. Only then will it be able to confront and finally defeat what he calls the 'retarding and vulgarizing' accounts of current Englishness recently put forward by two home-grown journalist/politicians, Sir Charles Adderley and Mr John Arthur Roebuck.

Then, casting round for an example of something concrete to set against the fatuous self-satisfaction of these apologists, with their cant about 'our unrivalled happiness' as members of 'the old Anglo-Saxon race . . . the best breed in the whole world', he quite suddenly and out of the blue quotes from a newspaper account of a specific criminal case:

> A shocking child murder has just been committed at Nottingham. A girl named Wragg left the workhouse there on Saturday morning with her young illegitimate child. The child was soon afterwards found dead on Mapperley Hills, having been strangled. Wragg is in custody.[1]

The impact of that, even today, is considerable. A nugget of genuine domestic Englishness, the case of Wragg is curiously disturbing at a number of levels. *Nomen est omen.* The 'hideous' name *Wragg,* Arnold comments, itself challenges the pretensions of 'our old Anglo-Saxon breed . . . the best in the whole world' by showing 'how much that is harsh and ill-favoured' there is in that best. A literary criticism which 'serves the cause of perfection' by insisting on these contrasts between pretensions and reality in society must begin precisely here, at home. And although Mr Roebuck may not think much of an adversary who 'replies to his defiant songs of triumph only by murmuring under his breath *Wragg is in custody*', in no other way (says Arnold) will these songs of triumph be induced gradually to moderate themselves.[2] He doesn't consider whether Mr Roebuck (*nomen est omen* indeed) might have been more effectively challenged by the murmuring of what a local newspaper reports to have been Wragg's own piteous, yet oddly piercing cry at her trial, setting her present state of custody tellingly against its opposite: 'I should never have done it if I had had a home for him.'[3]

II Homeboy

Wragg's is a voice—and a name—that could easily have issued, a generation later, from the depths of T. S. Eliot's *The Waste Land.* Like the snatches of conversation about pregnancy and marriage, and the drunken demotic pub-talk of that poem, her words somehow manage to speak from the domestic centre of a culture, indeed literally of house and 'home', whilst at the same time signalling a fundamental estrangement from it. But the second eruption I have in mind occurs in fact in a critical essay of Eliot's: one that has something of the same purpose as Arnold's, signalled by the fact that it has the same title: 'The Function of Criticism' (1923).

In response partly to the vaporizings of the critic John Middleton Murry, Eliot here also takes up the question of literary criticism and the nature of genuine Englishness. Murry has argued that the latter is to be found vested in something which he terms the 'inner voice' of the nation: 'The English writer, the English divine, the English statesman, inherit no rules from their forebears; they inherit only this: a sense that in the last resort they must depend on the inner voice.'[4] Eliot's carefully honed New England sensibility, with its precise *commitment* to the inheritance of rules from forebears, immediately recoils from this 'inner voice' of Old England. Admitting, coldly, that the statement appears 'to cover certain cases', he begins a withering attack:

> The inner voice, in fact, sounds remarkably like an old principle which has been formulated by an elder critic in the now familiar phrase of 'doing as one likes'.

—and then the ice cracks and a most startling and memorable image suddenly erupts:

> The possessors of the inner voice ride ten in a compartment to a football match at Swansea, listening to the inner voice, which breathes the eternal message of vanity, fear, and lust.[5]

Moral revelations vouchsafed in the corridor of a train of the Great Western Railway (as it then was) whilst pulling out of Paddington Station are no doubt few and far between. But even if they lack the force of holy writ, their impact can apparently be considerable. Faced with what might be called an excluding plenitude of rowdy Englishness, Eliot's criticism here starts to draw on rhythmic and metaphorical skills developed in the cause of the modernist aesthetic. What suddenly surfaces here is nothing less than the nucleus of a kind of *imagist* poem, something that Ezra Pound characterized as 'an intellectual and emotional complex in an instant of time'.

Characteristically, like Pound's own famous 'In a station of the Metro':

> The apparition of these faces in the crowd;
> Petals on a wet, black bough.

it involves modern urban transport systems, with their enclosed spaces and vivid, if ephemeral visual contacts. Ultimately, it offers an image which is both fleeting and concrete, confirming—as Richard Aldington put it—that an imagist poem properly manifests a 'hardness, as of cut stone'.[6] Yet it is also clear and concise, mimicking the episodic glance of the male urban *flâneur.* It meets, almost precisely, the requirement of T. E. Hulme for a 'visual, concrete language' which '. . . always endeavours to *arrest* you and to make you continuously see a physical thing' (*Speculations*).[7] And when the undoubtedly arrested Eliot inspected that intensely physical railway compartment, what he saw was an Englishness which, in a suddenly disturbing mode, seemed to have no resting place, no room, no home to offer him.

III Easily Freudened

The concept of 'home' in that expanded sense is of course crucial to Freud's well-known paper of 1919, *Das Unhe-*

imliche.[8] Its aim is to distinguish a particular class of, or core of feeling within, the general field of 'the frightening', which could justify the use of a special name for it. Freud's immediate target is the apparently stable opposition between the *heimlich,* the 'intimate' or 'domestic', and the *unheimlich,* the strange or 'uncanny'.[9] His central tactic is to unpick and ultimately to dissolve that opposition.

Freud's case is that the 'uncanny' is not simply the new and the unfamiliar. Something has to be added to it in order to give it its 'uncanny' quality, and that something is, disturbingly, already well known to us: 'the uncanny (*unheimlich*) is that class of the frightening which leads back to what is known of old and long familiar'.[10] More disturbingly, 'the *unheimlich* is what was once *heimisch,* familiar; the prefix "un" is the token of repression'. Thus the uncanny, says Freud, invariably involves something 'which ought to have remained hidden, but has come to light'.[11]

One key to the mystery lies in 'an examination of linguistic usage'.[12] This reveals that the apparent polarities *heimlich/ unheimlich* are not truly opposed. The 'familiar' begins to reveal surprising links with the 'not known'. Indeed, as the different shades of meaning derived from *heimlich* develop, they start to exhibit qualities identical with their opposites until, on the one hand, the word 'means what is familiar and agreeable, and on the other, what is concealed and kept out of sight'.[13] This migration of meaning finally reveals, as Freud puts it in a classic deconstructive manoeuvre, the interdependence of the terms: 'Thus *heimlich* is a word the meaning of which develops in the direction of ambivalence, until it finally coincides with its opposite *unheimlich. Unheimlich* is in some way or other a subspecies of *heimlich.*'[14]

It is obviously tempting to try to situate Matthew Arnold's notion of a *heimlich* English culture in this context. His essay not only considers Englishness in terms of what Edward Said calls 'an aggressive sense of nation, home, community and belonging', of being 'at home' or 'in place' in a particular sphere.[15] He defines it at last and most powerfully by pointing to the boundary beyond which the 'placeless' or the 'homeless' or the 'uncanny' begins. This is exactly where we encounter Wragg. She erupts in Arnold's text as a horrific, homeless spectre, revealing a suppressed dimension of the culture which a properly directed criticism will force us to confront. Such a criticism's last, and best function, Arnold seems to be saying, is to tell us what our 'home' culture is really like, and it does that by enabling us to see Wragg clearly, as a powerful signifier whose reiteration is enough to puncture the pomposities of Messrs. Adderley and Roebuck. Criticism's very detachment from the political, practical and polemical enables it, says Arnold, to confront these gentlemen with what their vision occludes: it points to an *unheimlich* suppressed by, but unavoidably included within, the English *heimlich.* Once more the focus is on nomenclature:

> *Wragg*! If we are to talk of ideal perfection, of 'the best in the whole world', has any one reflected what a touch of grossness in our race, what an original shortcoming in the more delicate spiritual perceptions, is shown by the natural growth amongst us of such hideous names—Higginbottom, Stiggins, Bugg! In Ionia and Attica they were luckier in this respect than 'the best race in the world': by the Ilissus there was no Wragg, poor thing![16]

Recognition of Wragg and her plight is not only seen as the central concern and duty of responsible criticism, but, in the course of Arnold's analysis, it becomes clear that her homelessness, like the plight of the homeless everywhere, serves to define what we mean by 'home'. Wragg acts as a boundary marker, a gibbet and a dangling body which proclaims the limit of civilization as we know it, the absolute distinctions of an 'English' discourse, the end of the real, the natural, the 'inside', the 'superior', and the domestic, and the beginning of the strange, the unnatural, the 'outside', the 'inferior' and the uncanny. Wragg, in short, marks the spot where the *heimlich* is defined by the fact that the *unheimlich* appears.

The spectre continually haunting the notion of 'criticism', as described by Arnold and many others since, is that of its apparently essential *secondariness:* its status as something merely repetitive, something that is always already *preceded.* Michel Foucault's disingenuous statement that the hierarchical relationship primary/secondary, text/commentary is permanent, regardless of the nature of the documents which take on these functions, offers a classic formulation. He grants that 'This differentiation is certainly neither stable, nor constant, nor absolute. There is not, on the one side, the category of fundamental or creative discourses, given for all time, and on the other, the mass of discourses which repeat, gloss, and comment.'[17] Nonetheless he claims that the 'principle of a differentiation will continuously be 'put back into play'. We can annul one or other of the terms of the relation, but we cannot 'do away with the relation itself'.

Foucault goes on to argue that 'in what is broadly called commentary', the hierarchy between primary and secondary texts plays two complementary roles. The 'dominance of the primary text, its permanence, its status as a discourse which can always be re-actualised' seems to make for an 'open possibility of speaking'. On the other hand, the 'only role' open to commentary is to repeat: 'to say at last what was silently articulated "beyond", in the text'. Caught in a paradox, the commentary must 'say for the first time what had, nonetheless, already been said, and must tirelessly repeat what had, however, never been said'. It offers a 'repetition in disguise', at whose furthest reach there lurks the spectre of 'mere recitation'.

The first casualty of any probing of the notion of an unchallengeable relationship between primary and secondary will of course be that idea of repetition. Repetition presupposes a primary to which it is itself inevitably secondary. However, Freud's notion of the *unheimlich* immediately brings that relationship into question. Repetition of the same thing, he argues, is a major source of the uncanny, and it can finally be defined in terms which stress exactly that: it is that class of frightening things 'in which the frightening element can be shown to be something repressed which *recurs*'.[18] Freud's larger theory of repetition is of course fully developed in *Beyond The Pleasure Principle* on which he was working concurrently with his revision of *Das Unheimliche.* There, as part of a fundamental 'need to restore an earlier state of things', repetition achieves a kind of primary initiating status as it comes to be linked to the death drive.[19] And certainly when *heimlich* and *unheimlich* merge, the Foucauldian 'secondary' seems to mingle with and almost to usurp its 'primary'. Here, at least, the so-called 'relation itself' between them starts to seem collusive, rather than 'given', and the persistent sense that the one lies at the heart of the other hints at a potential obliteration of the distinction between the two.

For Arnold, it is clear that literary criticism is the activity which, drawing the uncanny to the attention of the domestic, or pointing out Wragg to Adderley and Roebuck, demonstrates their interdependence and insists upon it. If this is its function at the present time, then criticism (which may appear to be secondary, merely repetitive) has at least a *prima facie* case also to be seen as primary. Or rather, the whole primary-secondary relationship begins to seem ungroundable: perhaps there is, in respect of the literature/criticism nexus, no primary, no resting place, no home?

IV Mein Irisch Kind

If we were looking for an area of repression, in which unspeakable *unheimlich* secrets recurrently haunt the *heimlich* texts of British culture and prove to be their foundation as much as their undoing, the secondary that worryingly questions the standing of their primary, then we would do well to look slightly more closely at Matthew Arnold's account of the case of Wragg. The Victorian period broadly encouraged the operation of a complex system of social distinction which finally confined most of those determined as the 'lower' orders within the limits of what can be seen as a specific, unifying 'race'. The common characteristics supposedly shared by the labouring classes, Jews, Southern Europeans and non-Europeans subjugated by empire, included moral degeneracy, physical uncleanliness and, in consequence, a systematic tendency towards desecration of the unified holy shrine of domesticity and hygiene. In Britain, any one instance of inferiority could readily be taken as a sign of the others and there are plenty of examples of a kind of 'network of affinities'[20] supporting a programme of racial totalization which constructed foreigners—and the working class in general—as hovel-dwelling, bathroom-subverting, low-browed, dirty, cunning, dark-skinned 'savages'.

In Britain, one of the chief objects of this kind of derision was of course the Irish. As early as the mid-seventeenth century, Irish servants who had been summarily shipped to service in the British West Indies were liable to join forces with black slaves in rebellions against their common masters.[21] By the nineteenth century the word 'Irish' functioned broadly in English as a term signifying the wild, intemperate, aggressive behaviour and illogical untutored argument deemed characteristic of savagery in general. That many of the poorest sections of Britain's industrial cities could be nominated 'Irishtown' or 'Irish Court' without demur is a telling detail in respect of the degrading, grubby context in which Arnold is at pains to locate Wragg:

> by the Ilissus there was no Wragg, poor thing! And 'our unrivalled happiness'—what an element of grimness, bareness, and hideousness mixes with it and blurs it; the workhouse, the dismal Mapperly Hills—how dismal those who have seen them will remember—the gloom, the smoke, the cold, the strangled illegitimate child! . . . And the final touch—short, bleak, and inhuman: *Wragg is in custody.* The sex lost in the confusion of our unrivalled happiness; or (shall I say) the superfluous Christian name lopped off by the straight-forward vigour of our old Anglo-Saxon breed![22]

Wragg's context, involving dirt, labour, poverty, moral irresponsibility and the defilement of domesticity in the form of her illegitimate child and her infanticide, surely presents her in this sense not as Anglo-Saxon, but as something Anglo-Saxons have 'lopped off' in an attempt to dispose of it: as Irish, a representative of that ubiquitous, emasculated, and by now thoroughly 'feminized' Celtic culture whose apparent nature Arnold, in his writings elsewhere, had done much to characterize.[23] We need make nothing of the fact that, not five miles from the dismal Mapperley Hills (how dismal those who have seen them will remember) the map shows a quite separate, 'lopped off' town called—exquisitely—Arnold. For Wragg's anarchic, anti-patriarchal, *unheimlich* eruption in Arnold's text as the Other repressed by a self-satisfied Anglo-Saxon bourgeois and colonial ideology, invites us by its own force to see her as a version of an immemorial displaced figure. It is one which, despite the demands of and for Home (Ireland's claims for 'Home' Rule climax in 1870, with the founding of the Home Rule movement) seems forever doomed to wander homelessly in the English psyche:

> *Frisch weht der Wind*
> *Der Heimat zu*
> *Mein Irisch Kind*
> *Wo weilest du?*

That these lines, for English speakers, urge a return to Eliot as much as to Wagner is not accidental. *The Waste Land*'s use of the sailor's song from *Tristan und Isolde* is a significant part of the poem's focus upon wandering, rootlessness and homelessness as a feature of the Western experience in the twentieth century. And when we return to Eliot's essay 'The Function of Criticism', his diatribe against the 'inner voice' seems to spring from similar concerns. The central objection to the 'inner voice' is that it is exclusive. If its presence defines true Englishness, in a sense that *Heimat* points to, then its absence must bar the American Eliot from that company, however successful had been his elocutionary exertions over the years in sedulous pursuit of the English 'outer voice'.

Eliot's overriding critical notion was always of course of an adjustable 'order' or tradition of truly great Western writers, in which the advent of newcomers made a regular realignment necessary: the 'outsider' is thus accommodated, domesticated, put 'in place' and made 'at home'. Eliot's conversion to the established church starts after the publication of *The Waste Land* and perhaps represents, as Edward Said has suggested, a turning away from the difficulties of *filiation* (natural continuity between generations: something prohibited by his exile and the difficulties of his marriage to Vivien) and towards the alternative involvements available through *affiliation,* that is the bondings offered by 'institutions, associations and communities'.[24] This would certainly encourage a sense of the weaving of the individual talent into the web of connections afforded by the great Western 'tradition', so that an inherited American, Republican, and Protestant commitment might eventually be transformed into the infamous English affiliative trio of Royalism, Classicism, and Anglo-Catholicism.

Natural justice suggests that the strenuous pursuit of such strange Gods should be rewarded by a modicum of acceptance. Eliot's uncomprehending resentment when the 'inner voice' of Englishness turns out to be vested elsewhere is correspondingly acute. Its monument is the sudden eruption into the text of **'The Function of Criticism'**—garnished for better effect with a broad range of modernist poetic devices—of that over-full railway carriage, whose denizens can be derided for asserting their insufferably boisterous, fully affiliated Englishness as football supporters on a trip to foreign parts (i.e. Swansea) at the expense of the exclusion from their number of a would-be fellow-traveller.

European readers will of course be aware of the phenomenon of football as the focus of riotous affiliative nationalism in the twentieth century. In this, as in other regards, the United States retains an unviolated innocence (at least until the World Cup arrives there) so that Eliot's American experience can hardly have prepared him for behaviour of this sort. That perhaps confirms—despite his best efforts at Anglicization—how American he had remained. By their football supporters shall ye know them, and indeed it seems to have been precisely by those means that his discovery is made of an *unheimlich* spectre of exclusion located at the very heart of the English *heimlich* (what offers to be more *heimlich* for a Harvard educated traveller in pursuit of the great Western tradition than a seat in a carriage of the Great Western Railway?)

But let me be entirely outrageous. The eruption that confronts Eliot in that carriage is a phenomenon for which we English have a particular and revealing name: *hooliganism.* The provenance of the word 'hooligan' is clear, disturbing, and once more involves nomenclature. It probably derives from an account (published in 1899) of the exploits of a fictitious denizen of Irish Court in East London, 'Patrick Hooligan'.[25] In short, 'hooligan' carries the clear connotation 'Irish'. It offers a classic displacement of violent disorderly behaviour on to a despised and supposedly 'savage' subculture, with the implication that it is racially characteristic. Throughout the twentieth century, the increasingly broad deployment of the term in Britain has been part of a series of complex ideological manoeuvres by which the British have tried to negotiate an engagement with what they still presume to call the 'Irish problem'—that is, by writing off the activities of an anti-colonial movement as the typical behaviour of degraded barbarians. That the rise in what is now firmly perceived and routinely denounced as 'football hooliganism' in Britain increasingly parallels the rise of violent rejection of British rule in Ireland no doubt warrants further investigation in these terms.

Of course from time immemorial there has been a tradition in Britain and throughout Europe of Carnivalesque behaviour which, with its riotous upturning of accepted values and hierarchies, its commitment to 'rough music' and the crude extra-legal settling of scores, has appeared to override civil authority and has sometimes fostered serious political challenge to it. And more recently in Britain there has been a tradition of rowdy, law-breaking behaviour which—if practised by, say, undergraduates at the universities of Oxford or Cambridge—could be safely written off as 'high spirits', or part of the tradition of the undergraduate 'Rag'. But this kind of boisterousness has increasingly—once it is seen to attract lesser breeds without the law—invited the moralizing tendencies of magistrates and sociologists as a prelude to its denunciation as the work of 'football hooligans'.

The brief but memorable eruption of football hooliganism into Eliot's 'The Function of Criticism' is a matter of some moment; not least because it resonates with the eruption in Matthew Arnold's **'The Function of Criticism'** of a similar, violently disorderly force. Linked to Eliot's not only by a potential Irish dimension, but by a name—Wragg—in which, as Arnold (quintessentially an Oxford Man) would know, the spectre of youthful disruptive behaviour also lurks—this side of Ionia, Attica and the Ilissus at least—it stands as a factor with which British culture—and its literary criticism—has had to come to terms.

V First Aid for the Choking Victim

However, at what Foucault calls the 'preconceptual' level, Arnold's essay and Eliot's perhaps share much more extensive common ground. Together they tell us a good deal about the ideological freight carried by literary criticism at the moment of its installation as a key component of Anglo-American culture. Both promote and reinforce a fundamental division between the 'domestic' and the 'foreign', between 'home' and 'away', 'us' and 'them', in which the complexities surrounding the *heimlich* are actively at work. For Arnold, 'foreignness' involves the 'free play of ideas' which can only influence for the good an English insularity committed to the merely practical. For Eliot, the 'foreign' offers an ordered, hierarchical stability to shore against what he sees as the disorder likely to flow from the chaotic and potentially revolutionary 'inner voice' on which John Middleton Murry and later D. H. Lawrence seem to insist.

Of course, that is only the crudest sketch of the terrain in question, but in general terms it seems to confirm that the subject position offered by both examples of this discourse—and I am taking Arnold's and Eliot's essays as crucially definitive locations and formulations of a discourse that will for a generation supply the common coin of academic literary criticism in the English-speaking world—systematically presents the critic in terms of a sophisticated 'foreignness' projected as part of the cool appraising stance of the outsider. Coleridge's notion of a praetorian cadre of teachers operating within society as a select 'clerisy', or Arnold's idea of the recruitment of an elite fifth column of trained academic 'aliens', comes disturbingly to mind. The Arnold-influenced *Newbolt Report* (1921), direct precursor in Britain of professionalized academic literary criticism, speaks chillingly of University teachers of English as Missionaries.

Of course, Arnold professes sympathy for Wragg, whilst Eliot maintains a frigid scorn for the possessors of the 'inner voice'. But both accept—as colonizing 'outsiders' who claim to be able to see what the savage aboriginal 'insiders' cannot—the necessity of recognizing the paradoxical Englishness of each eruption. Eliot's essay is important because it sanctions the transfer of aspects of its own eruption to Arnold's and establishes a resonance—albeit deeply submerged—with the case of Wragg. Freud's point is confirmed in both: the *unheimlich* represents a repressed dimension of the *heimlich.* Meanwhile, the links of football hooliganism with an older tradition of Carnival, and even the 'psychological onomatopoeia' of Wragg's name (of which Arnold as we have seen makes a great deal) begin to hint at a sanctioned loosening of moral strictures. And that disturbing prospect starts, darkly, and surprisingly, to suggest the Mapperley Hills and Paddington Station as unlikely locations of a long-hidden and unified *unheimlich* that literary criticism, at its academic inception in Britain, feels it has somehow to engage with.

In short, I am suggesting that the essays of Arnold and Eliot *cohere* around the eruptions of this Wragg-Hooligan nexus. Its vague roots lie, I would also suggest, in a forgotten—or repressed—dimension of British culture. In proposing its consideration as a single unit, I do so with only residual misgivings about the reduction and false clarity this imposes on its shadowy complexity. It is hardly counter-intuitive, after all, to suggest that the *unheimlich* lying within the *heimlich* in the modern English psyche has something to do with Ireland. And this is no more than to say that Ireland can always be perceived by an inherent prejudice as the Anarchy to a Culture whose presuppositions are and always have been English.

What confronts both Arnold and Eliot, as they consider the function of literary criticism in its post-industrial setting, is thus the stirring of a pre-industrial ghost: a wholly disconcerting prospect in which that which is 'away' in football terms, startlingly erupts into that which is 'home'. As Missionaries, their project is nothing less than the imposition of a law and order on this savage chaos. Their central aim is to 'map' it, to establish the contours of 'home', by imposing an apellation which we have perhaps for too long endorsed: English. As part of the process, both offer to speak on behalf of a complex and hitherto covert, but none the less authentic Englishness, an *'inside'* which apparently reluctantly agrees to emerge in order to take on the policing role of *'outside'*. But by the stratagem of backing thus humbly into the limelight, 'authentic' Englishness—Wragg, the absurd claims of the 'inner voice'—manages in my view to obscure something far more radical, far more deeply 'inside' and implicated with itself. In calling up this deep-seated internal challenge to the 'law and order' of English literary criticism and nominating it, however rawly, as 'Irish', I suppose I am finally trying to outline a principle which out-Arnolds Arnold and out-Eliots Eliot: one which challenges fundamental 'English' presuppositions in the most fundamental way; which ultimately refuses their very logic, their very ordering of the world, their very notion of causality, of the plausible in scholarship, the very oppositions on which this depends—and which refuses in the end the distinction between 'literature' and 'criticism', and between those modes of 'primary' and 'secondary' on which—as in Arnold and Eliot—it apparently insists.

The voice which has most relentlessly made this challenge over the years is inevitably an Irish one. It is of course that of Oscar Wilde. It speaks most cogently in the essay which presents his astonishing reply to Arnold and, as it were in advance, to Eliot: 'The Critic as Artist' (1891). In effect, what this essay awards to criticism is a primary not a secondary role:

> Without the critical faculty, there is no artistic creation at all, worthy of the name . . . criticism demands infinitely more cultivation than creation does. . . . Anybody can write a three volumed novel. It merely requires a complete ignorance of both life and literature . . . criticism is itself an art. . . . It is to criticism that the future belongs. . . . There was never a time when Criticism was more needed than it is now. It is only by its means that Humanity can become conscious of the point at which it has arrived.[26]

The work of a true—albeit dandified—Hooligan, this polemic effortlessly reverses the apparently immutable hierarchy identified by Foucault, just as Wilde's whole life from the level of a paradoxical literary style to that of committed sexual role, seems to have been geared to the reversal at all levels and in all respects of the English sense of how things are and should be. 'Considered as an instrument of thought,' he writes, 'the English mind is coarse and undeveloped. The only thing that can purify it is the growth of the critical instinct.'[27] For reversals on that scale, of course, he paid the price that Hooligans pay.

The principle at stake may nevertheless be allowed finally to challenge the notion of 'mere' repetition which lies at the heart of traditional ideas of literary criticism, certainly in its professionalized form in the Academy. I hope to have suggested that a different notion of repetition might finally engage us. It is one whose aim is the generation of the new in terms of the only kind of newness we can recognize because its source is the old. I am speaking of a criticism anxious, not merely to raise the spectre of the *unheimlich,* but also intent, not on nullifying it, but on somehow including and promoting the *unheimlich* within the material it examines—indeed of openly scrutinizing those elements that its initial impulse is to try to occlude or swallow. When such a criticism then takes the criticism of the past as its raw material—puts Arnold's and Eliot's criticism, that is, on the syllabus, with a standing equal to that of their so-called 'creative' writing, it will be releasing repetition from its servitude to precedence, and presenting it as a vital source of the new.

What we can retain from Foucault is surely the notion that, as part of the project of modernity, the essence of a truly modern criticism will not involve the reinforcement of so-called transcendental standards or structures, or any of the other lineaments of a tired, not to say oppressive scholarly tradition. It will rather call for a kind of principled and self-inventing betrayal of that tradition whose investigation of criticism's own presuppositions will wilfully promote the, by traditional standards, bogus connections and parallels of the sort that I have been shamelessly deploying: their aim an expansion of the possibilities of our *use* of criticism as a material intervention into history rather than the prosecution of what we misguidedly think of as scholarly 'facts' or 'truth'.

Such a project absolves Criticism from any commitment to the tetchy pursuit of true judgement or, worse, the soul-gelding aridity of *quellenforschung.* Instead it turns into a creative genre in its own right; one whose fundamental mode is a sort of pre-emptive repetition: a matter (I begin, I dare say, to sound 'Irish') of getting the repetition in first, its central feature the active identifying, confronting and *using* of the *unheimlich,* the pressing home of Freud's deconstructive proposal that the *unheimlich* is in some way or other a sub-species of the *heimlich,* until those positions are virtually reversed. Until, that is, the *heimlich* appears almost as a sub-species of the *unheimlich,* and we begin to face the possibility that 'home' is only the tamed and taming doll's house we construct as a poor bulwark against the apparitions that permanently haunt us.

That the various rooms of one's home may be comfortably lined with books, plays and poems perhaps just intensifies an unease which lies at the heart of that vision of domesticity. And perhaps it serves finally to confront us with a prospect which is genuinely frightening because truly known of old and, though long repressed, long familiar: the appalling possibility that home is where the art is: that, in terms of the *unheimlich* critical vision, what we think of as home and what we think of as art are in some way shockingly coterminous in their role as mere vehicles for the most paltry of human comforts.

It is a view whose implications have undergone a crucial probing in those numerous voices which have spoken and continue to speak of the homelessness, expropriation, expatriation and exile that are central features of life in our century. The range is vast, and perhaps the case of Wragg, for whom custody clearly stands in a deeply ironic opposition to the 'home' which would have prevented her crime, lies at one end of it. At the other, a hundred years, two world wars, revolutions and holocausts on, lies the work of Theodor Adorno. His judgement that 'Dwelling, in the proper sense, is now impossible. The traditional residences we grew up in have grown intolerable' concludes, at its uttermost bitter reach, that 'Today . . . it is part of morality not to be at home in one's home'.[28]

In respect of art, the sort of homeless, 'hooligan' criticism that I am advocating must eventually subscribe to a morality of that sort. And if it is finally able to plumb the deepest entrails of a culture, beyond the level at which any way of life feels itself to be 'at home', bringing to the surface—or, better, bringing the surface down to—whatever inhibits that culture's genuine nourishment, then it may aptly, and in the name of a more beneficial notion of eruption, be finally linked to a strategy whose simple design, I have lately observed, seems, astonishingly, to be outlined on the walls of every American restaurant. For there, in that most portentous of modern locations, an exotic rubric suddenly and darkly speaks of 'First Aid For The Choking Victim'.

Central to the welfare of any Choking Victim (and surely most of us will from time to time have felt included in that company) is the principle that there is a sort of eruption which can be good for you, and that in its most benign form—that of regurgitation—lies the basis of a new beginning. In the circumstances—and to mention nomenclature for the last time—it strikes me as only slightly uncanny that the name given to this most radical of critical gambits happens to be 'The Heimlich Manoeuvre'.

Notes

1. Matthew Arnold, *Lectures and Essays in Criticism,* ed. R. H. Super, *The Complete Prose Works of Matthew Arnold,* vol. III, (Ann Arbor: University of Michigan Press, 1962), p. 273.
2. ibid., p. 274.
3. ibid., p. 479.
4. See T. S. Eliot, *Selected Essays,* 3rd edn (London: Faber, 1951), p. 27.
5. ibid., p. 27.
6. I am here and in what follows drawing extensively on Andrew Thacker's provocative argument in his 'Imagist Travels in Modernist Space', *Textual Practice,* 7, 2 (Summer 1993), pp. 224-46.
7. See Thacker, art. cit., pp. 239-40.
8. Usually translated as 'The Uncanny'. See Sigmund Freud, *Complete Psychological Works,* vol. XVII,

Standard Edition, ed. James Strachey (London: Hogarth Press, 1963), pp. 217-56.

9. I am aware that the modern German word *heimlich* does not necessarily carry the sense that the Austrian Freud seems to ascribe to it. His detailed philological analysis covers several pages and is none the less remarkably thorough. Its aim, of course, is less to specify individual meanings than to focus on the spurious 'opposition' of *heimlich* and *unheimlich.*
10. Freud, op. cit., p. 220.
11. ibid., pp. 241-5.
12. ibid., p. 220.
13. ibid., pp. 224-5.
14. ibid., p. 226. This classic deconstructive analysis perhaps lingered to haunt the German language in the twenty years following Freud's paper. At its furthest reach, *heimlich* has links not only with *Heimat,* the 'homeland', but even perhaps—via *geheim*—with the secret forces of terror raised to exclude the *Heimat*'s enemies. This generates a kind of oxymoron whose grim climax occurred when Freud joked of the *Geheime Staatspolizei,* after they had ransacked his *heimlich* Vienna home, that he could 'heartily recommend the Gestapo to anybody'. See Ernest Jones, *The Life and Work of Sigmund Freud* (Harmondsworth: Penguin Books, 1964), p. 642.
15. Edward Said, *The World, the Text, and the Critic* (London: Faber, 1984), p. 12.
16. Arnold, op. cit., p. 273. Christopher Ricks has commented on Eliot's no less intense interest in such matters. Certainly, Eliot's inventions for the correspondence columns of *The Egoist* include names that would have confirmed Arnold's despair: 'Charles James Grimble (The Vicarage, Leays)' and 'Helen B. Trundlett (Batton, Kent)', to say nothing of 'Muriel A. Schwarz (60, Alexandra Gardens, Hampstead NW)'. Note also Eliot's constant invention of names in the spirit of *nomen est omen:* Professor Channing-Cheetah, Nancy Ellicott, and supremely, J. Alfred Prufrock. Of course Eliot also had his *trouvailles* to match Arnold's Wragg and Roebuck, such as Sir Alfred Mond. See Christopher Ricks, *T. S. Eliot and Prejudice* (London: Faber, 1988), pp. 1-24 and 242-3.
17. Michel Foucault, 'The order of discourse' in Robert Young (ed.), *Untying the Text* (London: Routledge, 1981), pp. 52-64. See also Foucault's *The Order of Things: An Archaeology of the Human Sciences* (London: Tavistock Publications, 1970), pp. 78-81.
18. Freud, op. cit., p. 234.
19. *Das Unheimliche* itself presents a valuable complication of the matter for the actual writing of it is so saturated with the issues of repetition that they begin to call into question the very principles on which parts of the argument seem to rest. The War itself had of course decisively undermined linear notions of sequence and consequence. It is, Freud says, as a result of the 'times in which we live', that he presents his paper 'without any claim to priority' (op. cit., p. 220). In a letter to Ferenczi in May 1919 he indicates directly that he has dug an old paper out of a drawer and is rewriting it (p. 218), whereupon the editors of the Standard Edition admit that 'Nothing is known as to when it was originally written or how much it was changed.' They even contribute the straight-faced comment that 'The passages dealing with the "compulsion to repeat" must in any case have formed part of the revision' (p. 218). In short, Freud's revisionary return to the paper means that a crumbling of the primary-secondary relationship characterizes the very composition of the argument before surfacing as one of its most disturbing features.
20. I take the phrase from Luke Gibbons's invaluable, 'Race against time: Racial discourse and Irish history', *Oxford Literary Review,* vol. 13, 1991, p. 98.
21. See Christopher Hill, *People and Ideas in 17th Century England* (Brighton: Harvester, 1986), pp. 169-70.
22. Arnold, op. cit., pp. 273-4.
23. See Luke Gibbons, op. cit. There was a notable rise in cases of recorded infanticide in Britain in the 1860s, together with a tendency to regard the crime as an 'Irish' solution to the problem of poverty—a point of view informed perhaps by recollections of Swift's *A Modest Proposal.* See R. Sauer, 'Deadly motherhood: Infanticide and abortion in 19th century Britain', *Population Studies,* vol. 32 (1978) pp. 81-93. I am indebted to Dr Jo McDonagh of the University of Exeter for this and a great deal more information on the topic.
24. See Edward Said, op. cit., pp. 8 and 17.
25. See Clarence Rook, *The Hooligan Nights* (1899) (Oxford University Press, 1979), especially pp. 14-20.
26. See Richard Ellmann (ed.), *The Artist as Critic: Critical Writings of Oscar Wilde* (London: W. H. Allen, 1970), pp. 355-403, *passim.*
27. ibid., p. 403.
28. Theodor Adorno, *Minima Moralia: Reflections from Damaged Life,* 1951, trans. E. F. N. Jephcott (London: New Left Books, 1951), pp. 38-9. Edward Said has recently drawn attention to these passages in his BBC Reith Lectures (1993).

Timothy Peltason (essay date 1994)

SOURCE: "The Function of Matthew Arnold at the Present Time," in *College English,* Vol. 56, No. 7, November, 1994, pp. 749-65.

[In the following essay, Peltason contests the characterization of Arnold as a cultural conservative and emphasizes his continued significance as a literary theorist.]

In recent debates about cultural politics, Matthew Arnold's name regularly appears as a kind of shorthand for a familiar and long discredited form of cultural conservatism. Sometimes it is not Arnold's name, but just a phrase, "the best that is known and thought" or "sweetness and light," quoted without attribution and taken to represent an uncritical endorsement of received cultural values and a passive receptivity to accredited masterpieces. My project in this essay is to show how and why Arnold should be recuperated, indeed to show how insistently he is still with us. More broadly, I wish to illustrate the dangers of literary and cultural misunderstanding that arise when a major literary figure is invoked in the culture wars, but not actually read with precision and care.

In addition to the enemies who put him to such uses, Arnold has had a full complement of the friends who makes enemies superfluous. Champions like William Bennett and Lynne Cheney have invoked Arnold as a fellow savior of the humanities and joined his least discriminating detractors in writing as if there were one orthodoxy to restore (or to ridicule), a blandly affirming humanism of which Arnold and Robert Maynard Hutchins, Lionel Trilling and F. R. Leavis, were equally and similarly representative. Not that Arnold's writings fail to cooperate in such acts of appropriation. When Arnold writes in **"The Function of Criticism at the Present Time"** that "the elements with which the creative power works are ideas; the best ideas on every matter which literature touches, current at the time" (***CPW*** 3:260), he seems to stand in need of a first course in formalism. What are these "ideas" that are the building blocks of the *Iliad* and *King Lear, Paradise Lost* and *Anna Karenina,* and in what form did they exist before their embodiment in the language of these texts? Are they the same ideas that will restore us to the prelapsarian cultural health of some other time and place, and, if so, why will nobody say what they are?

A further charge against Arnold, but also the first item to offer in his defense, is that he devotes very little space to answering these questions or others like them, which inquire about "the best that has been known and thought" as if that best were the separable and summarizable content of a row of great books. The apparent essentialism of Arnold's position, with its reference to the fixed nature of the object "in itself" and its occasional stress upon the "ideas" that literary works hold in readiness for the qualified reader, is belied and counterbalanced by another emphasis in his writings, on process and on particularity: "Not a having and a resting, but a growing and a becoming, is the character of perfection as culture conceives it" (5:94). The modern cant of "personal growth" taints for us this remark from ***Culture and Anarchy,*** a remark that itself threatens to freeze into a slogan, a phrase to have and to rest in, rather than an act of the writer's and the reader's mind. But Arnold does live and write by this slogan and everywhere stresses "the deed of writing," to borrow a phrase from Thoreau to which Richard Poirier has recently drawn attention (3-66). Just the title of Arnold's greatest essay ought to make clear that his interest is not in what things timelessly and essentially *are,* but in how they work for us here and now. Indeed, one measure of the influence of **"The Function of Criticism at the Present Time"** is the extraordinary number of times that its title has been copied or appropriated by later essayists inquiring into the function not just of criticism, but of a host.of other activities and institutions.

This emphasis on "function" brings with it a correspondent stress on activity, and the nearest and most insistent activity under observation in Arnold's prose writings is the activity of criticism itself. Another persistent charge against Arnold is that he assigns to criticism too modest and secondary a role. But if we recognize the continuity between his creative and his critical writing and respond fully to the performative and evocative powers of his criticism, we will not linger long with this error. Wendell Harris's impatient remark is to the point here: "One would feel it unnecessary to rehearse the evidence that Arnold neither sharply divided criticism from creativity nor conceived criticism to be simply a commentary on literature if such skewed readings of Arnold by eminent critics were not so prevalent" (120). In spite of his notorious unresponsiveness to the great fiction of his time, Arnold is among the most influential advocates and, in his prose writings, one of the distinguished practitioners of Victorian realism—realism as it is redefined by the idiosyncratic practice of such diverse writers as Carlyle, Dickens, Ruskin, Trollope, and Eliot. Of the many mottos and keywords with which Arnold is associated—"the best that is known and thought in the world," "to make reason and the will of God prevail," "sweetness and light"—the ones that still matter and persuade are those clustered around his central statement of the function of criticism, "to see the object as in itself it really is." This realist injunction, for all its susceptibility to deconstruction and demystification, has hardly been dislodged by any competing formula. It is hard to find an interpreter of texts or events who does not at some point ground his or her authority in the claim to have gotten things *right.* Even when the claim is downgraded to one of provisional rightness, a standard of accuracy has been invoked. And Arnold, from his side, makes more provision for the flux and contingency of judgment than is generally acknowledged.

This is both lucky and appropriate, since so many of Arnold's own judgments now seem limited and idiosyncratic. Even those writers who think of themselves as Arnoldians hardly defend many of his likes and dislikes, and, in fact, read him more for the flux and contingency—for the companionship of a distinctive and vividly rendered personality—than for the judgments. But this division of faculties is itself misleading, since one of the lessons to be learned from Arnold's writings is that personality and judgment are inseparable. Judgment, for Arnold, is an activity of the whole person, the source of a pleasure that differs in degree, but not in kind, from the pleasures of creation. The making of judgments, and thus the practice of criticism, springs from "a curiosity,—a desire after the things of the mind simply for their own sakes and for the pleasure of seeing them as they are,—which is in an intelligent being, natural and laudable" (5:91). Kindred passages to this one from ***Culture and Anarchy*** appear throughout Arnold's writings, asserting both the primacy of this pleasure and its availability to all intelligent beings. In this significant and characteristic passage from his essay on **"Maurice de Guerin,"** he describes "the grand power of poetry" in a vocabulary that stresses the continuity between creation and the activities of the critically alert mind of any "intelligent being":

> The grand power of poetry is its interpretative power; by which I mean, not a power of drawing out in black and white an explanation of the mystery of the universe, but the power of so dealing with things as to awaken in us a wonderfully full, new, and intimate sense of them, and of our relations with them. When this sense is awakened in us, as to objects without us, we feel ourselves to be in contact with the essential nature of those objects, to be no longer bewildered and oppressed by them, but to have their secret, and to be in harmony with them; and this feeling calms and satisfies us as no other can.
>
> (3:12-13)

For a twentieth-century analogue to this remarkable passage we can turn to Edmund Wilson, writing on "The Historical Interpretation of Literature" in *The Triple Thinkers*: "The writer who is to be anything more than an echo of his predecessors must always find expression for something which has never yet been expressed, must master a new set of phenomena which has never yet been mastered. With each such victory of the human intellect, whether in history, in philosophy, or in poetry, we experience a deep satisfaction: we have been cured of some ache of disorder, relieved of some oppressive burden of uncomprehended events" (270). Wilson has begun this paragraph trying to describe the greatness of great art, but in the course of it, and in the last two clauses especially, he has come to a succinct formulation of his own ambitions as a critic. In Arnold's passage, too, the critic's task and the creator's are merged, and it would require only a few substitutions to make his passage a central statement on the interpretive powers of criticism.

Perhaps this is why the passage stands out as one of Arnold's finest on the powers of poetry. More often, when Arnold describes what great art should do or be, he is maddeningly, culpably vague. The accent of "high seriousness," the capacity to produce "Joy"—these are not useful criteria and they tell us little about the writing of the last few centuries that readers have most valued. Arnold was so strikingly wrong about the coming age of creation that it can be hard to see why he is now more than a footnote in cultural history, a figure on the margins of Victorian discourse pointing off to a promised land that nobody, in fact, entered. But when he describes the functions of criticism, he is exemplary and current, a champion of the artistic virtues of which he is elsewhere so suspicious, and thus a kindred spirit to the Victorian poets and novelists he depreciates or ignores.

Arnold's best criticism is at once a succession of exact judgments and observations and an allegory of the critic's own mind. This combination evaporates the opposition between "subjective" and "objective" on which Arnold's criticism at first seems to depend and unites him with the Victorian modernism he aims to deplore, a modernism for which "realism" is an inevitable, if also an inadequate, label. I understand that this reading of Arnold will hardly satisfy those Marxist and historicist detractors for whom the tradition of Victorian realism is more notable for its bankruptcy than for its greatness. But a return to Arnold's texts may nevertheless clarify the terms of disagreement between the liberal tradition and the varieties of historicism now ascendant, by separating out the genuinely liberal strain in Arnold's writing from the reactionary misjudgments of which Arnold himself is occasionally guilty and the reactionary uses to which his grander pronouncements are regularly put.

The distinguishing marks of this Victorian realism are at once an attention to sensuous particulars and a fidelity to the particulars of the writer's own personality, a realism of the outer and the inner worlds together. It happens again and again in Arnold's writings that the critic's interest in things as they really are reveals itself suddenly as an interest in the workings of the critic's own mind and spirit. In ***Culture and Anarchy,*** for instance, Arnold first establishes the need for a principle of cultural authority and then turns to locate that authority in a "best self." The first cultural imperative—"to make reason and the will of God prevail" (5:91)—gives way gradually, in the course of argument, to a second: "The great thing . . . is to find our *best* self, and to seek to affirm nothing but that" (5:135). Something similar happens in **"The Function of Criticism at the Present Time,"** which begins and ends by suggesting that the function of criticism is to prepare the way for a new age of creation by propagating "the best that has been known and thought," but which asserts along the way that the truer function of criticism is to afford the critic the sure pleasures and the enhanced life of this knowing.

This stress on the personal and the particular seems a reversal of the inaugural movement of Arnold's criticism. In his first prose work of any significance, the Preface to the 1853 edition of his poems, Arnold begins by alluding to the common human pleasure in mimesis, in representations that are "particular, precise, and firm" (1:2). But the burden of his argument is to suggest that though those were good qualities and good words, he will offer us better. In this new hierarchy of literary values, vividness of representation is a necessary, but not a sufficient, accomplishment, and it is one of the signal failures of modern literature and criticism to believe otherwise. In the lost land of cultural and personal health that Arnold beckons us to return to, literature is concerned less with externals than with essentials, less with "ingenious expression" than with clearly delineated actions. It seeks to offer its readers not just the shock of recognition that an accurate and detailed representation can give, but the cleansing joy that is produced by the representation of a great action.

The Preface is a peculiar and contradictory performance, in which Arnold feelingly praises the qualities of mind and art that he has set out to rate as insufficient and describes only from a distance that art that he admires and recommends. "The modern dialogue of the mind with itself"; "an allegory of the state of the poet's own mind"—these memorable terms of dismissal, the second a quotation from David Masson, describe Arnold's own poetry well, as many readers have noticed and as Arnold himself acknowledges in casting the Preface as an explanation of his decision not to reprint **"Empedocles on Etna."** But these phrases also describe the Preface itself, which is studded with ingenious turns of phrase throughout the changeable and hard-to-follow course of its argument. Poor history and worse prophecy, the Preface nevertheless presents a tempting allegory of the state of Arnold's own mind, with its troublous turns and confusions, its yearning after a phantom objectivity. Turning from poetry to prose, Arnold does not turn from the inner world to the outer, from subjective to objective, but rather finds in his prose a more satisfactory mode of refusing these easy divisions and of coming to life in language.

The Preface strikingly begins Arnold's new career as a writer of prose, but if he had stopped with that essay, we would not now trouble to reclaim its confusions. Over the next ten years, in the lectures **"On Translating Homer,"** and then, triumphantly, in 1864, in **"The Function of Criticism at the Present Time,"** Arnold emerged fully as a critic. The latter essay begins with the central and celebrated assertion that the object of criticism is "to see the object as in itself it really is." The assertion is typical in its over-insistence, an exhortation "to see the object" that has built by accretion—"to see the object as it is," "as it really is," "as in itself it really is"—to its final form, a symptom that rhetoric, rather than logic, is the chosen mode of persuasion. Everyone has noticed Arnold's habit of repetition. The redundancies of this famous phrase constitute a kind of conceptual repetition. And the phrase is a repetition in another typically Arnoldian sense because it is a self-quotation, from the essay **"On Translating Homer."** Here as elsewhere, Arnold's self-quotations are more than an evidence of self-regard. He makes up for the perceived poverty of the modern tradition by constituting a tradition in himself, a vocabulary of handed-down words and values that are established as cultural presences if only by their ubiquity. Whether we meet such tag phrases as "the best that has been known and thought in the world" or "the disinterested free play of the mind" as old friends or old irritants, they have been established as points of reference.

To say this is to acknowledge the ways in which Arnold's criticism constitutes less a window on the world than a world in itself, an enclosed and unique space. It is both at once, of course, and in **"The Function of Criticism at the Present Time,"** as elsewhere in his writings, Arnold shifts without commentary from a vocabulary of objectivity to one of inwardness. For all his emphasis on attending to the object, Arnold speaks often of the purely intransitive pleasures of clear-sightedness. As in the passage from **"Maurice de Guerin"** above, Arnold holds that certain acts of the mind are self-evidently valuable. When he speaks of the "disinterested love of a free play of the mind on all subjects, for its own sake" (3:268), we notice first about this oddly over-packed phrase that the play of the mind is valued for its own sake rather than for the sake of the subjects, and then that the object of "disinterested love" is the mind's own activity.

In the Preface, Arnold established "joy" as a key term, quoting and endorsing Schiller's assertion that "all Art is dedicated to Joy," and proposing a test for great art that seemed more theological than aesthetic or psychological. Arnold's puzzling and irritating assertion in **"The Function of Criticism at the Present Time,"** that the Romantic poets "did not know enough" makes a kind of sense only in the context of this emphasis upon joy. What Arnold misses in the Romantics is the secure basis for affirmation that he quests after throughout his writings on religion, the "joy whose grounds are true," in the quotable phrase from the late poem **"Obermann Once More."** In such works as ***Literature and Dogma,*** however, Arnold's religious faith remains a matter of assertion and hopefulness, a joy whose ground is joy, as one might call it to expose its failure of logic and argument or, to assert its failure as rhetoric, a joy that is willed and recommended rather than felt or communicated.

The great accomplishment of **"The Function of Criticism at the Present Time"** is to substitute for this unconvinced and unconvincing rhetoric of "joy" a rhetoric of pleasure that has behind it the weight of Arnold's own evident pleasure in observing and writing. The function of criticism, for the first few pages of the essay, is to prepare the way for a great renaissance of creation, creation that will be nourished and animated by the unspecified ideas that the critic will make current, ideas that Wordsworth and Coleridge, Shelley, Keats, and Byron apparently did not have enough of. But Arnold's own current of thought in this essay shifts quickly from the Romantics to the French Revolution to Edmund Burke and then to the unhealthy climate of opinion and expression in mid-Victorian Britain. The free play of his mind leaves behind the sharper division between creation and criticism and, along with it, the sense that literature is the uniquely fit object of criticism. For the rest of the essay, criticism is not the handmaiden of artistic creation, but a mode of living. The function of criticism is at once to perform a very broadly defined cultural service and to offer to the critic, in the fullest measure possible, "the great happiness and the great proof of being alive" (3:285).

The celebrated account of Burke's "return upon himself" provides an important instance of this shift of attention.

Arnold has praised Burke's undeflectable clarity of vision—"disinterestedness" is the key term just about to enter the essay—and he cites a passage in which Burke recognizes and accepts the inevitability of "a great change in human affairs" brought about by the French Revolution, a change that Burke has long deprecated. Leaving aside the question of whether "disinterestedness" is the right word for this recognition—it would seem a better instance of disinterestedness if Burke saw something good about the change as well as something inevitable—we can observe that Arnold has offered in evidence, as "one of the finest things in English literature," a triumph of critical vision, a triumph, furthermore, that relocates the space of criticism within the experience of the critic. Burke's accuracy of observation has its cultural and political value, but it is first and unarguably, for Arnold, an intrinsic good, an exercise of human faculties both pleasurable and valuable in itself.

This intrinsic good leads on to other goods, and criticism serves the cause of cultural and personal hygiene at once. The "best spiritual work" of criticism "is to keep man from a self-satisfaction which is retarding and vulgarising" (3:271), beginning the work of cultural reform from within. This language of inwardness suggests Arnold's affinity with another of his contemporaries, Walter Pater, who begins his *Studies in the Renaissance* by substituting the critic's own impression for the object in itself as the primary datum of criticism. Arnold has already taken several steps in Pater's direction in his account of the right operation of critical judgment: "Here the great safeguard is never to let oneself become abstract, always to retain an intimate and lively consciousness of the truth of what one is saying, and, the moment this fails us, to be sure that something is wrong" (3:283). If judgment is not quite, on this account, a mode of introspection, it does depend on introspection for its self-assurance, as if the critic's relations with consciousness were more trustworthy, or at least more testable, than relations with the object.

In his distrust of the habitual, his endorsement of criticism as both an antidote for complacency and a form of quickened consciousness, Arnold is even closer to Pater and, curiously, anticipates the definition of "success in life" Pater offers in the "Conclusion" to *Studies in the Renaissance.* Arnold's repeated injunctions to the critic to avoid abstraction, to remain vigilant, "perpetually dissatisfied" and thus alive, constitute his own version of the hard gem-like flame. At times in the essay, the critic's own hunger after life seems the first motive for criticism. Arnold anticipates Pater in this, and also echoes the triumphantly frustrated questers of Victorian poetry, figures like Childe Roland and Tennyson's Ulysses who are animated and drawn forward by the foreknowledge of failure. Like Browning and Tennyson in their greatest and most characteristic lyrics, Arnold writes in celebration of a perpetual striving and as if a yearning after perfection were itself a form of accomplishment and of enhanced life. This strain in the essay comes to a climax in its poignant and yet excited conclusion. Conceding the promised land to poets, Arnold nevertheless claims for criticism a stylistic freedom essayed by few modern critics:

> In an epoch like those [of Aeschylus and Shakespeare] is, no doubt, the true life of literature; there is the promised land, towards which criticism can only beckon. That promised land it will not be ours to enter, and we shall die in the wilderness: but to have desired to enter it, to have saluted it from afar, is already, perhaps, the best distinction among contemporaries; it will certainly be the best title to esteem with posterity.
>
> (3:285)

In sentences like these Arnold both describes and occupies the imaginative space of the post-Romantic writer. Absorbing the energies and the concerns of his own poetry, as well as that of his contemporaries, Arnold's prose tries to find a function not just for criticism, but for the imagination itself in a time of limited possibilities. This is projection, of course, and the limitations that Arnold perceived were at least partly his own, at a time when Tennyson and Browning and the great mid-century novelists were working out their own forms of fidelity to Victorian circumstance. Arnold was of their party without always knowing it, and he works out in his criticism a necessary defense of the Victorian imagination, of a collectedness that can be misconstrued as retreat, but that is actually the condition of genuinely engaged observation. In the following passage for instance, Arnold borrows the vocabulary of **"The Buried Life"** to assert that the critic serves others by serving himself:

> The rush and roar of practical life will always have a dizzying and attracting effect upon the most collected spectator, and tend to draw him into its vortex; most of all will this be the case where that life is so powerful as it is in England. But it is only by remaining collected, and refusing to lend himself to the point of view of the practical man, that the critic can do the practical man any service; and it is only by the greatest sincerity in pursuing his own course, and by at last convincing even the practical man of his sincerity, that he can escape misunderstandings which perpetually threaten him.
>
> (3:274-75)

Misunderstandings still threaten, and this passage has been read by many as a counsel of retreat. After being scorned by one academic generation as a naïve objectivist, Arnold is scorned now by another as an accomplice in the aestheticist denial of history. But even a quick survey of Arnold's topics of discussion and his range of contemporary reference ought to give pause to modern critics whose writings are far less conversant with the events of contemporary public life than his. (And this is to say nothing of his daily descent into the material as a traveling, composition-grading, report-writing school inspector.) If Arnold sometimes deserves to be called Mr. Kidglove Cocksure, as in his distastefully fastidious distaste for Keats's love letters or Coleridge's private life (in his essay in **"Joubert"**), it needs to be said that he is being judged by his own standards and found guilty of a betrayal of his own best self, a contamination of judgment by local interests and private needs. When Raymond Williams, always a shrewd and respectful reader of Arnold, faults him in a late interview for his sensationalized and prejudiced account of the Hyde Park riots in ***Culture and Anarchy,*** he is accusing Arnold, and very persuasively, of a failure of disinterestedness (406-7).

But Arnold's misjudgments are not a principled retreat from the world. He wanted to make a difference, he spoke out directly on public affairs, and he would not have been shocked or undone to hear from a Marxist critic that he was a partisan for non-partisanship, a highly interested champion of disinterestedness. That he was a reactionary, a defender of vested material interests, he would have disputed, and both his overtly political judgments and the political consequences of his cultural judgments are available topics for debate. But it won't do simply to dismiss disinterestedness as a bourgeois fantasy or to declare, as Robert von Hallberg does, that "the Arnoldian notion that criticism or even poetry is ever disinterested is now fully discredited in American academic circles" (2). It is hard to know whether the putatively Arnoldian notion here is that critics have no vested interests or that they can ever be judged to have transcended them. In either case, such confident assertions are as magisterally self-assured as any of Arnold's that they intend to rebuke. And they fail to explain by what means critics can first come to know their interests and their allegiances, if not by some effort at disinterested judgment. To think that "disinterested" is simply a synonym for "a member of my party" is to accept consignment to a windowless prison far more confining than the Palace of Art.

If much of Arnold's poetry remains stuck in a mode of defeated Romanticism, his prose is more resourceful, and in his account of the contemporary language of politics Arnold avails himself of another tradition than that of Romantic interiority. The example of Burke suggests that the critic's experience may be personal without being private or claustrophobic and that the collected observer is not therefore disengaged. Arnold's distrust of the practical, which may at first seem to ally him only with Pater and Wilde, starts from this praise of Burke and also allies him, somewhat unexpectedly, with another commentator who will not be accused of a retreat into aestheticism, John Stuart Mill.

In his 1840 essay, "Coleridge," written to complement the critique of his mentor, Jeremy Bentham, that he had published in 1838, Mill describes that unlikely pair as "the men who, in their age and country, did most to enforce, by precept and example, the necessity of a philosophy" and remarks "the insufficiency for practical purposes of what the mere practical man calls experience" (120-21). One of the signal failings of the practical man, for Arnold, is his disinclination to subordinate his practical interests to the demands of disinterested judgment. And John Stuart Mill, in spite of the failure of respect for religion that Arnold could never excuse or overlook, ought to have represented to Arnold a model of disinterestedness. In his care to discover the strengths and the true value of opposing points of view, in his avowal in the essay on Coleridge that "'Lord, enlighten thou our enemies,' should be the prayer of every true Reformer" (163), in the strength and clarity of mind that carried him, in his *Autobiography,* through one of the great returns upon the self in Victorian literature, Mill largely succeeded in earning the trust of "the practical man" that Arnold saw as the reward of criticism rightly practiced. And not just of his contemporaries. When Charles Peirce sets out to criticize Mill's logic, he stops to acknowledge the "natural candour" that made Mill a reliable observer even where he was a faulty logician (219).

Edward Alexander presents a comprehensive examination of the relationship between these two writers in his book, *Matthew Arnold and John Stuart Mill,* and he quotes a passage in which Arnold praises Mill as "a singularly, acute, ardent, and interesting man," a praise earned largely by the fact that Mill "was capable of following lights that led him away from [his] regular doctrine of philosophical radicalism" (31). I would stress particularly this shared interest in disinterestedness, a shared sense that clarity of vision and judgment is both rare and indispensable, the only foundation of all reasoning and reform. Both Arnold and Mill reserve special praise for the moral and cognitive heroism that can see and hear the truth even amidst the smoke and clamor of received and unexamined opinion. This is at the heart of Arnold's praise of Burke and of his counsel of collectedness. It is also the great positive accomplishment of Bentham to which Mill turns with pleasure after a clear-eyed accounting of his limitations. The subject is the chaos of the English legal system:

> It may be fancied by some people that Bentham did an easy thing in merely calling all this absurd, and proving it to be so. But he began the contest a young man, and he had grown old before he had any followers. History will one day refuse to give credit to the intensity of the superstition which, till very lately, protected this mischievous mess from examination or doubt—passed off the charming representations of Blackstone for a just estimate of the English law, and proclaimed the shame of human reason to be the perfection of it.
>
> (103)

Casting Bentham as the brave boy in "The Emperor's New Clothes," Mill not only does honor to his mentor, but describes the critical vantage that Dickens will occupy in the great public satires of *Bleak House* and *Little Dorrit.* In the last sentence of this extract, Mill's language acquires a Dickensian force. And the founding notion—that prejudice and habit operate with such force that the clear-sighted will often be accused of fantastic exaggeration—underlies Dickens's whole project and method. "When people say Dickens exaggerates," says Santayana, "it seems to me they can have no eyes and no ears. They probably have only *notions* of what things and people are; they accept them conventionally, at their diplomatic value" (65).

Arnold's refusal of the merely practical point of view is intended not to deny the world, but to see it as it is. Among the many odd twists and turns of argument in **"The Function of Criticism at the Present Time"** is one that takes Arnold into a brief discussion of "this charming institution," the English Divorce Court, "an institution which perhaps has its practical conveniences, but which in the ideal sphere is so hideous" (3:281). For the reform of this institution Arnold looks forward to a time when criticism has done its work so well that it "may, in English literature be an objection to a proposition that it is absurd," and thus a time when "it will in the English House of Commons be an objection to an institution that it is an anomaly" (3:282). The critic's task is not to say what form the divorce law should take, but to see and say clearly how the actual falls short of the ideal. When the actual, for all its absurdity, has come to seem natural and inevitable to one party, and when the merely practical persons of another party are bent on the quickest form of possible triumph, the difficult and necessary business of keeping the ideal in view falls to the critic. And here, to repeat a central assertion, "the great safeguard is never to let oneself become abstract, always to retain an intimate and lively consciousness of the truth of what one is saying, and, the moment this fails us, to be sure that something is wrong."

Intimacy, liveliness, truth: and, by implication, concreteness. These form an alternative vocabulary of praise to the joy-talk of the Preface to ***Poems*** and a return to the language of "particularity, precision, and firmness." Accuracy may be enough, after all, and so may be the full, intimate, and lively presentation of the critic's own mind and experience. The most memorable of the instances of concrete observation in **"The Function of Criticism at the Present Time,"** and an odd companion to its other tag phrases, is the newspaper fragment that Arnold seizes and repeats as an incantation: "Wragg is in custody." He introduces this grim account of a poor girl from the workhouse, accused of murdering her illegitimate child, as an antidote to the "exuberant self-satisfaction" of contemporary political rhetoric. It's a story that Arnold's poetry could not have accommodated (though Tennyson's might have—the world of "Rizpah" is not so remote), and Arnold draws in telling it upon the combined resources of realistic fiction and Carlylean declamation. He brings Wragg and the dismal Mapperley Hills before us in a few short strokes, and along with them the impoverished and coarsened sensibility that must grow accustomed to such stories in reporting them.

Any undistinguished novelist could have written the few, evocative sentences in which Wragg and her environs are described. But when these sentences are combined with the dithyrambs of Roebuck and Adderley, quoted and placed to such devastating effect, and then with Arnold's own commentary, returning over and again to the bass-note, *"Wragg!"* the result is a remarkable and powerful passage of criticism. Shaken free of context, the words of Roebuck and Adderley and of Wragg's anonymous chronicler acquire new force and are taken up together into a new structure of feeling:

> And "our unrivalled happiness";—what an element of grimness, bareness, and hideousness mixes with it and blurs it; the workhouse, the dismal Mapperley Hills,—how dismal those who have seen them will remember;—the gloom, the smoke, the cold, the strangled illegitimate child! "I ask you whether, the world over or in past history, there is anything like it?" Perhaps not, one is inclined to answer; but at any rate, in that case, the world is very much to be pitied. And the final touch,—short, bleak and inhuman: *Wragg is in custody.* The sex lost in the confusion of our unrivalled happiness; or (shall I say?) the superfluous Christian name lopped off by the straightforward vigour of our old Anglo-Saxon breed! There is profit for the spirit in such contrasts as this; criticism serves the cause of perfection by establishing them.
>
> (3:273-74)

"Wragg is in custody." The phrase serves Arnold as a kind of negative touchstone, a substance of known value to hold up against corrupted uses of language and to expose their true nature. He goes on to suggest that the reader might respond to any future hymns of national self-praise "only by murmuring under his breath, *Wragg is in custody.*" The phrase is offered as a talisman against canting falsehood, as if some political commentator in the course of the 1984 Presidential campaign had fixed in the public mind the image of one wretched homeless person, to be called up and contemplated at every repetition of the Reagan campaign's "Morning in America" TV-spot. But the same commentator, had he or she wished to act in the spirit of Arnoldian criticism, would have resisted every effort to incorporate the image into an answering Democratic advertisement. The testimony of the critic, though it might incidentally speak for one party or the other, must not abandon to party interest an obligation to bear witness that will outlast the election year. To focus upon the proximate goals of political success is to sacrifice credibility, and, more important, to let oneself become abstract, to submit one's statement to some other test than the intimate conviction of truthfulness. But to recognize this does not constitute either a claim or an ambition to political inconsequence.

It may seem a long way from Wragg to the "touchstones," which appear by name in the late essay **"The Study of Poetry,"** and are among the most easily and often mocked of Arnold's critical devices. Few readers can have found these touchstones the handi-kit for critical evaluation that Arnold actually does seem to suggest that they are, and many readers have noted the circularity of the argument that produces them as grounds for judgment. But the touchstones are not dispensed with when their arbitrariness is exposed, and Arnold's use of them in **"The Study of Poetry"** is more interesting and defensible than our current epistemological sophistication may permit us to see.

Whatever essentialist or ahistorical claims Arnold may seem to make merely by positing the existence of the touchstones, his use of them suggests that value and meaning are always differential. We come into full possession of texts and events, according to Arnold, only by placing them in relationship to what we know already, either by long experience or because this knowledge has imposed itself on us with the undeniable force of Wragg's fate. Wherever the touchstones appear, they are terms of comparison, and wherever Arnold sets himself to describe their value, the emphasis again is upon difference. "If we are thoroughly penetrated by their power," he says of the touchstones, "we shall find that we have acquired a sense enabling us, whatever poetry may be laid before us, to feel the degree in which a high poetical quality is present or wanting there" (9:170).

Not the "high poetical quality" itself, but a feeling for the degree of its presence or absence. The peculiarity of this emphasis is even more striking in an earlier passage in the essay, before the notion of touchstones has been introduced. "But if [a poet] is a real classic . . . then the great thing for us is to feel and enjoy his work as deeply as ever we can, and to appreciate the wide difference between it and a work which has not the same high character. This is what is salutary, this is what is formative; this is the great benefit to be got from the study of poetry" (9:165). For this passage, which clearly asks to be read as central and summarizing, the reader's consciousness is the exclusive theater of operations—and the emphasis, again, is on feeling the difference between different orders of poetic accomplishment, as if value were realized only through difference, and as if the animating effects of true judgment were more important than any purely passive benefit to be drawn from a great work in isolation.

These passages return to the many in **"The Function of Criticism at the Present Time"** that locate the value of criticism in the awakened consciousness of the critic. And they echo other, more unstable moments, where Arnold's language undergoes a similar slippage toward idealism. There is a strange sentence, for instance, in the essay on **"Wordsworth,"** so filled with images of holding fast and coming to rest, with the sense that Wordsworth's poetry offers a stay and a support to the reader. After describing the several forms of delusion that might draw us away from a true sense of what great poetry is, Arnold suggests "the best cure for our delusion," which "is to let our minds rest upon that great and inexhaustible word *life,* until we learn to enter into its meaning" (9:46). It seems subversive, though maybe it should not where poetry is the topic, to remind readers so sharply that the only ground they are being offered to rest upon is a *word.* The invitation to enter into the meaning of "life" stands revealed suddenly as an encounter not with shepherds, or with rocks and stones and trees, or even with Wordsworth, but with a single word, meditated upon and told over.

And yet it is not one word, but many, that the readers of Arnold's **"Wordsworth"** are offered, in an essay that introduces that practical and substantial accomplishment of criticism, a selection of poems. The touchstones, too, are noteworthy not only for their arbitrariness but for the faith they express in practice over precept. At every turn in **"The Study of Poetry,"** precepts are obliged to retire before examples, and the final test is to see what works. The touchstone method is an homage to pragmatism, not because readers can take over Arnold's list of passages and set up shop with them, but because it recognizes, in gross terms, that this is how judgment works if it works at all. The circularity of Arnold's reasoning is not a logical mistake, but a recognition that judgment has to start somewhere, and that we start from where we are. Readers with no conscious affinity for Arnold nevertheless proceed by a version of these methods, illustrating by extract what a work under examination is capable of rising or falling to, measuring the value of new work by the internalized standards of other works read and admired. It is possible to set aside a great deal of Arnold's program in **"The Study of Poetry,"** and nearly all of his prophecies, and still find its condensed account of critical judgment truer to experience than those of any number of canon-busting exposés. More to the point, most of those same exposés, to the extent that they engage in literary interpretation and advocacy at all, can be shown to proceed by methods of demonstration and evaluation that are recognizably Arnoldian.

Late in his career, Arnold turned explicitly to the novel, to Tolstoy's *Anna Karenina,* and his essay on that novel affords him an opportunity for an impressive, if unacknowledged, return upon himself. The whole essay bears belated witness to the fact that literary greatness in the nineteenth century has taken a new and shaggy form. Arnold praises the practice of Tolstoy's fiction over his later philosophy, taking a position consistent with the essay on **"Wordsworth"** and **"The Study of Poetry,"** but also demonstrating his own readiness to respond to greatness where he finds it, even if it does not fit the literary-historical scheme that he has mapped out elsewhere in his writings. In one passage, he describes the greatness of Tolstoy's novel in terms that amount to a simple retraction of most of the argument of the Preface to ***Poems***. "But the truth is we are not to take *Anna Karenina* as a work of art; we are to take it as a piece of life. A piece of life it is. The author has not invented and combined it, he has seen it; it has all happened before his inward eye, and it was in this wise that it happened" (11:285). A contemporary reader will notice first the lack of theoretical sophistication with which Arnold comes to rest upon that word "life" and sets it over against mere art. "History" now, rather than "life," is the preferred honorific and the master term of invidious comparison. But Arnold's "life" functions rather differently, and the invocation of the "inward eye" makes it clear that he is distinguishing between two kinds of art. His homage to the "life" of *Anna Karenina* is noteworthy not just as a relatively early attempt to define the Tolstoyan, but as an abandonment of the classical standard of great ideas embodied in great actions. Arnold describes in this passage the characteristic method of contemporary literature, a realism for which the crucial distinction is located somewhere else than between realms presumptively within and without. And he confesses implicitly his indebtedness to another contemporary, John Ruskin, echoing closely this passage from Book 3 of *Modern Painters:*

> All the great men *see* what they paint before they paint it,—see it in a perfectly passive manner,—cannot help seeing it if they would; whether in their mind's eye, or in bodily fact, does not matter; very often the mental vision is, I believe, in men of imagination, clearer than the bodily one; but vision it is, of one kind or another,—the whole scene, character, or incident passing before them as in second sight, whether they will or no, and requiring them to paint it as they see it . . . it being to them in its own kind and degree always a true vision or Apocalypse, and invariably accompanied in their hearts by a feeling correspondent to the words,—"Write the things *which thou hast seen,* and the things which *are.*"
>
> (5:114)

Or, as Arnold had said in praising Burke: the true critic, like Balaam, must be "unable to speak anything *but what the Lord has put in [his] mouth*" (3:267-68).

Such inspired accuracy of vision is rare, and it is the *sine qua non* of literary greatness, its presence or absence rendering secondary the distinctions between criticism and creation, or between the mirror and the lamp. Even when the objects of description are one's own thoughts, it is no easy matter to get them down as they really are. Thirty years earlier, struggling to write out his feelings to Arthur Clough, Arnold had complained in a letter of the difficulty of plain statement: "One endeavors to write deliberately out what is one's mind, without any veils of flippancy levity metaphor or demi-mot, and one succeeds only in putting on the paper a string of dreary dead sentences that correspond to nothing in one's inmost heart or mind, and only represent themselves" (129-30). Sentences that only represent themselves: this might be a postmodernist complaint, or, more likely, a postmodernist boast, but it is closer in time and spirit to the modernist rebellion against poetic diction. A relevant passage for comparison is from Yeats's "Reveries over Childhood and Youth": "I tried . . . to write out of my emotions exactly as they came to me in life, not changing them to make them more beautiful. . . . Yet when I re-read those early poems which gave me so much trouble, I find little but romantic convention, unconscious drama" (*Autobiography* 68-69). Both of these passages describe the young writer's struggle for a voice of his own. The point of placing Arnold at the scene of this struggle is not just to place his critical prose more clearly into the context of Victorian literature, but to underline the intimacy and continuity between Victorian and modern realisms, between the mysteriously difficult critical and novelistic project of seeing things as they are and the mysteriously difficult lyric project of saying things as they are.

I am not an Arnoldian, and there is much in his collected works that I cannot read with pleasure or agreement. But he is by no means the predictable and doctrine-mongering writer of many recent polemics, and reading him is a more varied and surprising experience than could be inferred from most recent accounts. In his effort to describe the awkward predicaments of modern literature and criticism, Arnold is exemplary and, in many ways, unsuperseded. He cannot establish for us the sure grounds of judgment that we might want, but perhaps he can cure us, if not of wanting them, then of thinking that we must have them in order to proceed. Here is a final passage, from Robert Garis writing about the ballets of George Balanchine: "There is something not merely subjective, something connected with our own survival, in trying to establish the identity of things that interest us, including works of art" (34). For those who cannot abandon the desire to get things right, even after the embarrassing acknowledgment that this rightness will always rest on the shaky, contested ground of private judgment, Arnold is the prose laureate of both our ambition and our embarrassment.

Works Cited

Alexander, Edward. *Matthew Arnold and John Stuart Mill.* New York: Columbia UP, 1965.

Arnold, Matthew. *Collected Prose Works.* 11 vols. Ed. R. H. Super. Ann Arbor: U of Michigan P, 1960-77.

———. *The Letters of Matthew Arnold to Arthur Hugh Clough.* Ed. H. F. Lowry. London: Oxford UP, 1983.

Garis, Robert. "The Dancer and the Dance; Balanchine: Change, Revival, and Survival." *Raritan* 5 (1985): 1-34.

Harris, Wendell. "The Continuously Creative Function of Arnoldian Criticism." *Victorian Poetry* 26 (1988): 117-34.

Mill, John Stuart. *Essays on Ethics, Religion, and Society.* Toronto: U of Toronto P, 1969.

Peirce, Charles Sanders. *Philosophical Writings of Peirce.* Ed. Justus Buchler. New York: Dover P, 1955.

Poirier, Richard. *The Renewal of Literature.* New York: Random House, 1988.

Ruskin, John. *The Works of John Ruskin.* 39 vols. Ed. E. T. Cook and Alexander Wedderburn. London: George Allen, 1903.

Santayana, George. *Soliloquies in England.* New York: Charles Scribner's Sons, 1923.

von Hallberg, Robert. *Politics and Poetic Value.* Chicago: U of Chicago P, 1987.

Williams, Raymond. *Politics and Letters.* London: New Left Books, 1979.

Wilson, Edmund. *The Triple Thinkers.* New York: Oxford UP, 1948.

Yeats, William Butler. *The Autobiography of William Butler Yeats.* New York: Macmillan, 1965.

Alan Grob (essay date 1996)

SOURCE: "Arnold's 'The Scholar-Gipsy': The Use and Abuse of History," in *Victorian Poetry,* Vol. 34, No. 2, Summer, 1996, pp. 149-74.

[*In the following essay, Grob contends that Arnold's later poetry and his prose represent a fundamental break from a "predominantly metaphysical mode . . . of explanation" of the human condition to a philosophy of cyclical history that was closely aligned with prevailing Victorian intellectual tendencies.*]

After the publication in 1849 of ***The Strayed Reveller, And Other Poems,*** Arnold's poetry conceptually underwent something of a midcourse correction, a tentatively taken turn from predominantly metaphysical modes of explanation for our unhappy human predicament to what clearly seems a more overtly historicist analysis of our situation, a turn, it should be added, that brought Arnold as poet and later as prose writer more closely in line with the prevailing intellectual tendencies of the Victorian age. In **"Resignation,"** a kind of philosophic summing up and position paper for those poems of negation and despair that largely fill Arnold's volume of 1849, he had plainly ascribed our sufferings to an apparently atemporal cosmic agency, a "something that infects the world" (l. 278), which in its blind but all-encompassing indifference destructively afflicts nature as well as ourselves. To mitigate the effects of this metaphysically conceived source of infection he had counseled resignation, withdrawal, and even a renouncing of the very life of consciousness itself—he enjoins Fausta, indeed, to emulate those who would "Draw homeward to the general life" (l. 252), a mode of existence characterized earlier in **"Resignation"** by its chillingly austere minimalness:

> That life, whose dumb wish is not missed
> If birth proceeds, if things subsist;
> The life of plants, and stones, and rain.
>
> (ll. 193-195)[1]

Elsewhere I have argued that **"Resignation"** provides us with what is philosophical most original and fundamental in Arnold's poetry, that it is the most clearly articulated statement in Victorian poetry of nineteenth-century metaphysical pessimism, a poetic analogue to the philosophy of Schopenhauer (a likeness, I hasten to add, that is the result of a shared *Weltanschauung* rather than any direct influence by the philosopher upon the poet).[2] For Arnold, like Schopenhauer, the world oppositionally divides into noumenal will and phenomenal idea, with an overridingly omnipotent blind cosmic impulse metaphysically determining our human fate to our ultimate detriment. Such a conception of metaphysical agency, I would add, helps shape not only the poems that appear in ***The Strayed Reveller, and Other Poems,*** but many of those written afterwards, even poems as different as **"Human Life," "The Buried Life," "To Marguerite—Continued"** and ***Empedocles on Etna.***

Nonetheless, as some of Arnold's most prominent critics have noted, not long after the publication of the 1849 volume, a discernible and in many ways contradictory turn to history is evident, a turn that would provide the governing intellectual paradigm not only for most of Arnold's later prose but even for some of the most notable poems written in the immediately ensuing years—**"Dover Beach," "Stanzas from the Grande Chartreuse,"** and **"The Scholar-Gipsy."**[3] In these poems we are led to believe that we are as we unhappily are, not because some metaphysically determining cause mandates unremitting misery but because unluckily we are temporarily caught between worlds, born to dwell in the bottoming out of a historical cycle that has only one direction in which to move. Thus, while the poetry of historicism might lament present circumstances, it should contain the seeds of an inherent optimism and be amenable to hopes that present misery will be alleviated in that better future that awaits us when the historical cycle reverses itself, when a now withdrawing Sea of Faith cyclically turns shoreward as the logic of the figure dictates it must, or a spark from heaven finally falls or the world now powerless to be born completes its period of gestation and comes into being. Yet as readers of Arnold's poetry know, **"Dover Beach," "Stanzas from the Grande Chartreuse,"** and **"The Scholar-Gipsy,"** for all of their historically implicit cyclical expectancy, convey little optimism and belong no less than **"Resignation"** or the **"Marguerite"** poems to Arnold's poetry of negation, carrying forward much of the melancholy and anxiety from that metaphysical pessimism that Arnoldian historicism might be thought to have supplanted.

"The Scholar-Gipsy" is a striking case in point. Born in a better and happier phase of the historical cycle, "when wits were fresh and clear, / And life ran gaily as the sparkling Thames" (ll. 201-202), provided with a seeming exemption from the historically determined evils of the unhappy present—at least for as long as he remains faithful to his quest—and granted the possibility of surviving into that better and happier future to be called into being when "the spark from heaven" (l. 171) shall fall, the poem's title character should stand as a beacon of hope, a guide beckoning us toward that inevitable improvement necessarily mandated by the foreordained reversal of the historical cycle. Yet by poem's end the most resonant notes finally struck in **"The Scholar-Gipsy"** express nothing so much as desperation, denial, and despair, with any progressively conceived historical expectations repeatedly undermined and undone by the strategies and tactics of Arnoldian representation.

Though born "when wits were fresh and clear, / And life" (ll. 201-202) still gay, the scholar-gipsy had apparently presciently fled society at virtually the very point when the historical cycle began its downward turn toward a grim and dreary modernity. As we know from Arnold's subsequent prose, the mid-seventeenth century is the appropriate starting point for our historical epoch of cyclical decline and therefore an especially fortuitous moment for just such a flight from the prevailing culture as, we are told by Glanvill, the scholar-gipsy had chosen. It was then that Renaissance Hellenism with its free play of intellect and spontaneity of consciousness, its clarity of wit and gaiety of life, received a seemingly fatal check in England from the Hebraizing spirit of Puritanism; and an essentially Protestant Philistinism, with its twin impulses (as we have learned from Weber and Tawney) toward strictness of conscience and the making of money, began to dominate English life, so that one who was born when "life ran gaily as the sparkling Thames" (l. 202) and who has become "tired of knocking at preferment's door" (l. 35) might well choose to leave behind him a society increasingly Protestant and acquisitive. Moreover at the same historical moment a scientifically grounded skepticism had begun to put in question the supernatural tenets of a Christianity that even in the early phases of the Renaissance served as the basis for much of the seeming cohesiveness of European culture. Apparently foreseeing the future that these culturally dispiriting changes would produce, on the one hand, the rise of a socially stultifying Protestant Philistinism and, on the other, the emergence of that scientifically generated "languid doubt" (l. 164) that would typify the intellectual life of modernity, the young Oxford scholar had chosen to opt out of this transitional epoch, this unhappy, between-worlds span of history, and to keep himself in readiness instead for the reversal of the cycle, the advent of that happier age waiting to be born.

As to when that better world will be born and what it will be like, Arnold tells us very little. But as with any cyclically conceived historicism, the future we await should come about not through any merely contingent human endeavor but by the workings of some immanent necessity, inexorable historical laws that no individual or individuals can hasten, impede, or alter. The triggering signal for the upward turn of the historical cycle is to be the fall of a "spark from heaven" (l. 171), a heralding event that would seem to perform the same kind of annunciatory function in the cyclical changes of **"The Scholar-Gipsy"** that the birth of a god does in the regular and necessary two-thousand-year reversals of the Yeatsian gyre. Yet human agency does apparently collaborate in this Arnoldian schema of change, with the scholar-gipsy himself assigned a leading role in the working out of this historically transformative process. When the "heaven-sent moments" (l. 50) come he "will to the world impart" (l. 49) the arts he has learned from the gipsies, arts presumably indispensable to humanity's long awaited betterment but which until now had remained a closely guarded secret supposedly possessed by the gipsies alone who are apparently under no like obligation to disseminate it to humanity at large.

From Arnold's earliest considerations of the scholar-gipsy as a subject for poetry, the special and secret art he had acquired from the gipsies—hypnotism or mesmerism as the Victorians termed it—had been a principal reason for the poet's interest in the little known tale from Glanvill; indeed, as a notebook entry of 1848 tells us, the title originally contemplated by Arnold for a poem on the scholar-gipsy was "The first mesmerist."[4] Taken literally, the scholar-gipsy's explanation of what he will do with "the secret" of the gipsy's "art" (l. 48)—that is, mesmerism—at that critical juncture when the new world stands on the verge of being born is that he will "impart" it "to the world" (l. 49): he will transmit the secret of the gipsies to everyone, thereby apparently making all humans mesmerists. But since the end of mesmerism for those possessed of hypnotic powers is "to rule as they desired / The workings of men's brains" (ll. 45-46) so that "they can bind them to what thoughts they will" (l. 47), it is more likely that it is submission to rather than the acquisition of such powers by the generality of humankind that is to be culturally transformative. To have all humans mesmerized rather than all humans mesmerists—figuratively speaking—would thus seem the goal implicit in this admittedly imprecise formulation of that better future called into being by the fall of "the spark from heaven" (l. 171).

Since Glanvill himself attributes the hypnotic wonders performed by the gipsies to "the power of imagination" (*Poems,* p. 357), it seems reasonable, following Culler, to take the story of the scholar-gipsy as Arnold retells it a step further and read it as "a myth of the Romantic imagination."[5] And taking our hint from Arnold himself, we may further infer that the cultural function Arnold speculatively contemplated for the mesmerizing imagination at that momentous point at which the historical cycle begins its upward turn is probably much like that high destiny he will later assign to poetry itself in **"The Study of Poetry."** There he tells us that at a date not far in the future "most of what now passes with us for religion and philosophy will be replaced by poetry" (***CPW,*** 9:162), a poetry that will then be employed "to interpret life for us, to console us, to sustain us" (***CPW,*** 9:161), as religion and philosophy had once done. Caught on the horns of one of the nineteenth-century intellectual's major dilemmas, certain that the metaphysical explanations of Christianity had been exploded once and for all by the scientific rationalism and philosophic skepticism of the Enlightenment, and yet hopeful, as many nineteenth-century historicists were, that the unity of culture which Christianity had once fostered might be reconstituted under essentially secular auspices, Arnold apparently saw in a poetry more generally disseminated to a better educated public a vehicle for restoring that cultural and ultimately spiritual cohesiveness now lost. In **"The Scholar-Gipsy"** too these later conclusions are already intimated: that is, when the falling of "the spark from heaven" (l. 171) signals the emergence of a new epoch, the human community shall find its "thoughts" again bound into cohesiveness, this time by succumbing to the mesmerizing powers acquired by the scholar-gipsy, which themselves symbolically represent those powers widely ascribed in the nineteenth century to the poetic imagination, especially given its axiomatically assumed mythopoeic capabilities.

One major feature of **"The Scholar-Gipsy"** long noted by commentators is its strong though uncharacteristic resemblance to the great odes of Keats, especially "Ode to a Nightingale."[6] In **"The Scholar-Gipsy"** Arnold imitates both the meter and stanzaic form of the odes, and the first half of his poem displays an atypical lushness of natural description of a kind usually associated with Keats. But the most semantically interesting of Arnold's borrowings from the odes in **"The Scholar-Gipsy"** is his appropriation of their highly distinctive dramatic design, that process in which the desiring self imaginatively reaches out towards empathic communion with some implicitly sacralized symbolic object, a nightingale or a Grecian urn, only to find its efforts ultimately thwarted because the imagination has ascribed to those objects attributes and powers that cannot be empirically justified or because it has wildly overestimated its own power and reliability. Thus at poem's end the desiring speaker is essentially returned to the "sole self" ("Ode to a Nightingale," l. 72) wiser perhaps but immeasurably sadder and more "forlorn," though the reader is finally left with a highly problematized hope that things may be otherwise through the interrogatory possibilities raised in the closing lines of "Ode to a Nightingale" and the encapsulated summation with which the "Ode on a Grecian Urn" ventriloquistically concludes. For the first half of **"The Scholar-Gipsy,"** Arnold's argument too follows a roughly Keatsian trajectory. Having invested the scholar-gipsy with special mesmerizing powers of inestimable future usefulness, the speaker, anxious to claim these benefits for himself and his own age, embarks on an imagined pursuit that culminates with surprising ease in his astonishingly improbable claim to having "once, in winter," (l. 121) actually seen the scholar-gipsy on a "wooden bridge" (l. 123) near Oxford, thereby achieving for himself something analogous to the empathic union with the symbolic object that is the comparable goal of the desiring self in the odes of Keats. But in Arnold, as in Keats, the empathic trajectory concludes with the admission of the wishful imagination's defeat, vanquished in this case by acknowledgment of the brute fact of human mortality, the limited life span allotted mortal man which renders any sighting of the scholar-gipsy by the speaker utterly impossible because "Two hundred years are flown / Since first thy story rang through Oxford halls" (ll. 131-132).

But the most radical departure by Arnold from his Keatsian precursors is in the remarkable unqualifiedness of his denial, his sudden reversal of that seemingly commonsense conclusion that since "Two hundred years are flown" (l. 131), the scholar-gipsy, presumably a mortal man like all others, must now be "in some quiet churchyard laid" (l. 137). Going far beyond the problematic but tentatively hopeful closings of the great odes, Arnold, in the parallel recovery of **"The Scholar-Gipsy,"** simply flies in the face of the seeming fact of human finitude and, wholly reversing himself, declares that the scholar-gipsy "hast not felt the lapse of hours" (l. 141) like the rest of us but rather possesses "an immortal lot" (l. 157). And because he has never died but is presumably destined to live forever, he can have been seen not many winters past and perhaps can be seen again by and even give instruction to the speaker and that modernity he represents.

Yet more seems less in this case and, despite the bold assurance with which Arnold asserts the immortality of the scholar-gipsy, his is a claim that implies considerably less than what is usually attached to such a claim in nineteenth-century poetry. For it is a strange and ultimately inconsequential immortality that emerges from **"The Scholar-Gipsy,"** and no critic and perhaps no reader either has probably ever taken its argument for immortality very seriously, at least in anything like the sense in which it is a serious and central concern of other major Victorian poems. Surely none of us reads **"The Scholar-Gipsy"** as we read *In Memoriam* and "Cleon," for example, where the claim that the soul of Hallam now lives, or the intimation that the spirits of Cleon and Protos might continue to exist even after their deaths through the saving grace of Christ, is implicitly understood to have general human applicability, to be crucial evidence for the larger, essentially theological claim that the human soul survives beyond the grave. Nor does Arnold even go as far as Keats, who, by leaving open the speculative possibility that the nightingale might be an "Immortal Bird" ("Ode to a Nightingale," l. 61) or the Grecian urn (and possibly even the individuals depicted there) might endure forever plainly encourages us to draw noumenal inferences, crucial conclusions about the possible eternality of the ultimately real, conclusions from which humanity, by extension, can derive for itself the hope of a life after death.[7]

But in **"The Scholar-Gipsy"** the prospect of immortality is obviously confined to the scholar-gipsy himself. His "immortal lot" (l. 157) is not by inference our "immortal lot," an instance of the general laws governing our ultimately human destiny but is rather an apparently unique case of one man's exemption from these otherwise general laws of human mortality. Moreover, "The generations of thy peers" (l. 155), men who, like the scholar-gipsy, were "born in days when wits were fresh and clear, / And life ran gaily as the sparkling Thames" (ll. 201-202) have certainly been granted no such exemption and are, as Arnold delicately puts it, "fled" (l. 155), gone to the grave and presumably to that death which is extinction. And alluding to the members of his own generation, Arnold ominously adds, "we ourselves shall go" (l. 156). (Nor does he ever offer the slightest hint that the inhabitants of the world that is to be born with assistance from the scholar-gipsy's mysteriously acquired arts shall be spared the mortality that, apart from the poem's one critical exception, seems the inescapable destiny of every human individual.)

Thus, the significance of this extravagantly asserted claim of immortality derives, I would suggest, not from its applicability to the essentially religious problem of death and the life hereafter but from its usefulness as a vehicle for carrying forward Arnold's argument about history. What the scholar-gipsy seems to have gained by remaining alive though "Two hundred years are flown" (l. 131) is for the poem's purposes not eternal life but a longevity sufficient to bridge the positive phases in the cyclical movement of a highly deterministic historical process, if only he can keep himself free from that inevitably fatal contamination by the contagiously tainting modernity that comes between these phases. And to achieve that narrower and implicitly fictive end of establishing the scholar-gipsy's exceptional longevity, Arnold, it would appear, does not feel that he needs anything like the complexly elaborated evolutionary arguments of Tennyson in *In Memoriam* nor even the scriptural authority that Browning draws upon in "Cleon." In this case all that would seem required is the authorizing presence of a literary precedent of incontestable greatness, Keats's odes, which recollected by Arnold's reader might at least encourage him to suspend disbelief momentarily and by an act of poetic faith accept at something like face value Arnold's asserted but virtually unargued analogous claim that Arnold's scholar-gipsy, like the nightingale of Keats, was "not born for death" ("Ode to a Nightingale," l. 61), but possessing an "immortal lot" (l. 157) remains similarly "exempt from age / And living as thou livs't on Glanvill's page" (ll. 158-159).

But there is another and perhaps more pertinent reason for Arnold's connecting the matter of **"The Scholar-Gipsy"** with the figure and poetry of Keats. As Culler has shown, the scholar-gipsy displays manifest symbolic affinities with other representatives of a recurrent Arnoldian type, especially figures like Callicles and the strayed reveller (the general designation which Culler applies to this Arnoldian type). While Arnold's strayed revellers are usually known by the symbolic locale associated with them, the shaded grove, and by their general disposition toward solitude and even reclusiveness, two of them, Callicles and the strayed reveller himself, are identified as poets and given songs to sing or poems to recite of a very special character. Unlike Arnold's other and greater poets, Sophocles and Shakespeare, sages who dwell upon seemingly impregnable mountain-tops from which they are able to comprehend life either in its vastness or to its depths, the strayed reveller as poet is essentially a celebrator of natural magic and concomitantly a purveyor of myth, a teller of quasi-religious tales designed to render human existence with all of its enigma and pain somehow intelligible, if possible bearable, and, at rare moments perhaps, even pleasurable as it would seem to have become in the orgiastic bacchic celebrations with which **"The Strayed Reveller"** itself concludes. (Probably nowhere in Arnold's poetry is the mythopoeic disposition and power of the strayed reveller as poet more strikingly displayed than in Callicles' great hymn to Apollo which follows the suicide of Empedocles in ***Empedocles on Etna,*** for by the poet's mythopoeic sleight-of-hand, Callicles manages to produce an explanation and ordering of the most inexplicable and painful of cosmic mysteries, converting them into a scenario not only of meaning but beauty.)

Of the poets who meant most to Arnold, Keats was clearly the one most closely associated with natural magic and the mythmaking imagination, thus with the poet as strayed reveller. (Even before Culler proposed his *dramatis personae* of basic Arnoldian types, Leon Gottfried in *Matthew Arnold and the Romantics* had astutely entitled his chapter on Keats and Arnold, "The Strayed Reveller: Keats.")[8] Admittedly, in the 1853 preface Arnold does single out Keats's *Isabella, or the Pot of Basil* as a bad example, a modern instance of the harmful influence of Shakespeare upon modern poetry, an influence Arnold saw as the precipitating cause of its misguided emphasis upon felicity of expression and its no less misguided disregard of "*Architectonicè* in the highest sense; that power of execution, which creates, forms, and constitutes" (***CPW,*** 1:9). But as that homage which is imitation in **"The Scholar-Gipsy"** clearly shows, by 1853 Arnold also had almost certainly already recognized that quality in Keats on which he would base his 1880 encomium: "that in one of the two great modes by which poetry interprets, in the faculty of naturalistic interpretation, in what we call natural magic, he ranks with Shakespeare" (***CPW,*** 9:214).[9]

Magic, indeed natural magic, its possession by those most profoundly in contact with the natural order, the gipsies, whose magical art of mesmerism can control "The workings of men's brains" and ultimately "bind them to what thoughts they will"; its acquisition by the Oxford scholar who would apparently keep it wholly to himself until he could direct it to socially useful ends; and finally its projected deployment by him at a propitious and seemingly sanctified moment for the sake of a new cultural cohesiveness: these in a sense constitute the greater subject and conceptually generate the principal action in **"The Scholar-Gipsy."** And even as the figure of the scholar-gipsy possesses certain discernible affinities with Keats, so too, as I have already suggested, does the magic the scholar-gipsy has acquired bear a certain obvious likeness to the poetic imagination at its most magical, that is, as it manifests itself in poems like those in which Keats himself most brilliantly employed it. Carrying this same analogy a step further, I would maintain too that just as the magic of mesmerism will be imparted by the scholar-gipsy "to the world" (l. 49) at a moment designated by heaven for its deployment, so too, at a similarly fated moment, will the signified counterpart to his gipsy magic, the poet's power of imagination, be similarly deployed to bind men to the poet's imaginative will and bring humankind into that new cultural and spiritual cohesiveness that awaits it in that coming epoch whose unifying agency shall be not religion but poetry.

Thus it is to fulfill the high destiny assigned to poetry and the poetic imagination in the world that is to be born that the scholar-gipsy has been exempted from death and granted immortality (though a longevity sufficient to bridge the cycles might have sufficed). To keep the imagination inviolate, to preserve intact for the future those powers handed down from the past for their designated employment in that culturally transformative "project" that in his closely guarded solitude he nurses "in unclouded joy" (l. 199)—it is for these ends that the scholar-gipsy has chosen to lead a life apart and flee those who would seek him out to persuade him to disseminate his magic prematurely, before the arrival of the "heaven-sent moments" when the secrets of his art are to be imparted. From the very first, the scholar-gipsy would seem to have already adopted the artist's self-alienating strategy of "silence, exile, and cunning" as his way of guarding his special and ultimately indispensable powers. With the least sophisticated, those most like the gipsies in their relationship with nature, he may maintain a certain contact, remaining apparently unperturbed at being observed by the housewife who quietly darns "At some lone homestead in the Cumner hills" (l. 101) or by the "Children, who early range these slopes / And late for cresses from the rills" (ll. 105-106) and even handing flowers to "Maidens, who from distant hamlets come / To dance around the Fyfield elm in May" (ll. 82-83). But on these occasions, the scholar-gipsy keeps essentially to himself, remaining "pensive and tongue-tied" (l. 54), maintaining that self-imposed state of alienation, the artist's exile projected in his bearing. And when those he encounters are at all likely to upset that equanimity, to draw him away from his chosen pensiveness and silence, whether they are noisy shepherds at some lonely country alehouse or "Oxford riders blithe" (l. 72), his strategy is already one that shall become even more pronounced in the poem's second half, an even more urgent flight into a still deeper solitude.

In fact, in the poem's second half the scholar-gipsy is never again seen with another person but is either depicted in solitary flight or encouraged to continue so; hence David Riede's suggestion that we look upon the second part of **"The Scholar-Gipsy"** as a "misreading" of the first part, resulting in an all-too-arbitrary transformation of the scholar-gipsy's character from "happy wanderer" to "zealous quester."[10] What is most remarkable though about the second half of **"The Scholar-Gipsy"** is not any change in the scholar-gipsy's character but that after the poem's great reversal—the denial and then reassertion of the scholar-gipsy's immortality—it is the self-designated pursuer himself, the speaker whose ruminations during the poem's first half were only intended to pass the time until nightfall when he could "again begin the quest," who most strenuously exhorts the scholar-gipsy to persist in a flight that must leave the goals of the speaker's quest unattained if its object were to heed his counsel. For success by the speaker in overtaking the scholar-gipsy would mean not the imparting of a special wisdom by that exemplary figure to his would-be disciple, but its destruction before its possessor could fulfill the special purpose of his mission to the future; and for the scholar-gipsy personally, success in the quest would mean exposure to the fatal contagion of modernity—its feverishness and, above all, "the infection of our mental strife" (l. 222)—endangering one who up to this time had remained free of that contagion by living (at least for the duration of the modern period) within a natural order that seemingly stands outside the historical process altogether. While the speaker may be compelled by his own historical predicament to persist in his quest after the scholar-gipsy, he knows that the least he can do if he truly is concerned with the scholar-gipsy's well-being is to warn him away, implore him to "fly our paths, our feverish contact fly!" (l. 221). And if the scholar-gipsy were to be unlucky enough to come within sight of his ardent pursuers, he is urged to remain "Averse" (l. 208), to "Wave us away, and keep thy solitude!" (l. 210) because contact would mean transmission of that endemic and inevitably fatal ailment, "this strange disease of modern life" (l. 203), with the result that "thy glad perennial youth would fade, / Fade, and grow old at last, and die like ours" (ll. 229-230).

At this point, it is probably useful to reconsider our governing analogy which connects **"The Scholar-Gipsy,"** its titular figure, and his mesmerizing magic with Keats and poetry and the poetic imagination. And carrying that analogy to its logical conclusion, we would undoubtedly wish to argue that just as success by the speaker in his quest, his overtaking of the scholar-gipsy and appropriation of his powers, would fatally impair the efficacy of those magical powers whose proper application is to make the world now waiting to be born as healthy and whole as that better world which existed prior to modernity, so too would the allegorically comparable pursuit of poetry by the modern poet (and most especially by Arnold himself) impair the analogously magical powers of the poetic imagination and prevent it from realizing the high destiny that awaits it in that better future which it will help to bring about. In fact, a danger very much like this would seem to have been on Arnold's mind in the preface to the ***Poems*** of 1853, an essay probably written in the same year as **"The Scholar-Gipsy"** and Arnold's first full-scale prose attempt at literary criticism. While written largely to admonish his critics in their preference for subject matter from the present age over imitation of the ancients, that preface also contains a substantial element of self-admonishment, especially in his strictures against his own ***Empedocles on Etna,*** which, though his most ambitious poem until now, was to be excluded from the ***Poems*** of 1853. And in the closing paragraphs of his essay he explains that his purpose in commending the ancients as the best model for the modern poet is not so that the modern poet may equal them in excellence but that he may do as little harm as possible to the art with which he has, for so brief a time, been entrusted before turning it over to those generations that will succeed his.

Not the advancement of poetry but its transmission undamaged and intact to the coming epoch is thus the most satisfactory outcome Arnold can foresee for the poets of his own age (among whom he must doubtlessly include himself), those who because of their historical situation, "these damned times," can never become more than dilettanti. Appealing to Goethe as the final authority on the question of modernism, Arnold writes:

> Two kinds of *dilettanti,* says Goethe, there are in poetry: he who neglects the indispensable mechanical part, and thinks he has done enough if he shows spirituality and feeling; and he who seeks to arrive at poetry merely by mechanism, in which he can acquire an artisan's readiness, and is without soul and matter. And he adds, that the first does the most harm to art, and the last to himself."
>
> (***CPW,*** 1:15)

For Arnold, that the poets of his time, living as they do in "an age wanting in moral grandeur" (***CPW,*** 1:14) and amid "bewildering confusion" (***CPW,*** 1:14), cannot be anything other than dilettanti seems indisputable; and therefore the only real choice they are allowed, that is, which of the two kinds of dilettanti they are to become, should be decided not by what they perceive to be their own private desires or interests but by what Arnold takes to be their larger obligations to their art and to that posterity who shall be its future practitioners and beneficiaries:

> If we must be *dilettanti:* if it is impossible for us, under the circumstances amidst which we live, to think clearly, to feel nobly, and to delineate firmly: if we cannot attain to the mastery of the great artists;—let us, at least, have so much respect for our art as to prefer it to ourselves. Let us not bewilder our successors; let us transmit to them the practice of poetry, with its boundaries and wholesome regulative laws, under which excellent works may again, perhaps, at some future time, be produced, not yet fallen into oblivion through our neglect, not yet condemned and cancelled by the influence of their eternal enemy, caprice."
>
> (***CPW,*** 1:15)

Reading these cautionary instructions to modern poets from the contemporaneous preface back into the figurative argument of **"The Scholar-Gipsy"** requires surprisingly little modification. The speaker himself provides a self-rebuking admission of what must be judged his own dilettantism, of his having been condemned by the historical process, by "the circumstances amidst which we live," to that waywardness and "caprice" inherent in a modernity in which "each strives, nor knows for what he strives, / And each half-lives a hundred different lives" (ll. 168-169). Though doubtlessly inclined to seek another way, to aspire to the "spirituality and feeling" the scholar-gipsy apparently enjoys, the speaker understands that his own obligation to the future mandates restraint, compels him to sound the warning signal and urge the object of his pursuit to speedier flight, to more cunning evasions. Here too we sense a fear that the good that the scholar-gipsy carries forward for dissemination when the time is ripe will be fatally impaired if he should unluckily come into contact with any of those unhappily condemned by the circumstances of history to an age to which moral grandeur has been denied. To take the final leap, we may say that **"The Scholar-Gipsy"** itself may be read as a set of self-constraining instructions to poets lest they spoil the future, the upward phase of the historical cycle, and, more poignantly, it may be read as a set of self-constraining instructions which Arnold, engaged "in the dialogue of the mind with itself" (***CPW,*** 1:1), addresses to himself as well, instructions that can be seen to have taken hold in that petering out of Arnold as modern poet in the years that follow the writing of **"The Scholar-Gipsy."** Indeed, what Arnold as poet and the poets of his own poetically ill-starred age have been entrusted to do, according to the preface of 1853, is ensure that no harm befalls poetry in their own unpoetical age, that what has been handed on to them from a more inspiriting and morally superior past will be passed on intact—uncontaminated by the modern poet's own hunger for "spirituality and feeling"—to that more inspiriting and morally superior future which paradoxically, and perhaps contradictorily, will make possible the very poetry whose emergence shall serve as enabling agency for bringing that future into being. And yet it is clear from all that has been said in **"The Scholar-Gipsy"** that if these modern poets (and most especially Arnold himself) do persist in pursuing their vocation, the probable outcome will be not just failure in their obligation to the future but the very ruin of its hopes.

But to account for a disease so pandemically contagious and devastatingly virulent that contact with those who carry it must undo the seemingly inexorable course of historical necessity and prevent the poetry and society of the future from coming into being, the reader conditioned by the personal and private melancholy of Arnold's earlier poetry is probably best advised to seek the ultimate source of that disease not in history per se, in any event or events, no matter how momentous, but in deeper and more primal longings, in the latent psychological conflicts and anxieties that determine so much of the manifest content of Arnold's poetry prior to 1853. (Certainly the cataclysmic infectedness in **"Resignation,"** whose source Arnold traces to an unspecified metaphysical "something" [l. 278], has significant psychological connections with the family relationships with sister and father that provide the autobiographical context of that poem.) And in **"The Scholar-Gipsy"** just as in Arnold's earlier poetry, that latently determining psychological matter would seem to lie closest to the surface of consciousness in just such troublingly unassimilable materials as the two notoriously perplexing similes with which **"The Scholar-Gipsy"** closes.

In the first of these, the scholar-gipsy is implored to turn away from his pursuers from modernity as absolutely as Virgil's Dido had turned away from Aeneas, the man who, having wronged her and driven her to suicide, would, nonetheless, in the netherworld call her back:

> Still fly, plunge deeper in the bowering wood!
>   Averse, as Dido did with gesture stern
>   From her false friend's approach in Hades turn,
> Wave us away, and keep thy solitude!
>
> (ll. 207-210)

Commentators on **"The Scholar-Gipsy,"** following the lead of G. Wilson Knight, have been quick and correct in seeing in this a reassertion of the most basic thematic oppositions in Arnold's poem and a reaffirmation of its most fundamental values in its siding with Dido, "a figure of feminine appeal and oriental glamour" who, in a final, heroic show of integrity, rebuffs the young Aeneas, even then on his way to "fulfilling his destiny as the founder, through Rome, of western efficiency and organization."[11] But Arnold's sympathy for Dido almost surely carries implications that resonate far beyond the poem's manifest cultural oppositions and choices.

With that Rome and its values, Arnold would almost certainly have associated his father as scholar and teacher and advocate, an association that may help to understand why at so crucial a moment in his own poem Arnold would recall the *Aeneid.* **"The Scholar-Gipsy"** had, of course, been written at what would seem to have been a highly stressful moment in Arnold's life, when the decision to marry and to work as a school inspector would have stood most obviously in opposition to his diminishing hopes for himself as a poet, so that this particular episode from the *Aeneid* in which he had doubtlessly been thoroughly drilled as a schoolboy must have presented itself to him as a psychologically compelling way of expressing such conflict. On the one hand, there was the figure of Aeneas, the embodiment of the masculine spirit and its associated values of duty to and involvement in the world, the idea of Rome, a notion forever identified for Arnold with his father and his father's teachings; on the other, Dido, clearly associated here with a countervailing and deeply seductive image of poetry that to Arnold's discomfort presented itself to him as not merely unmanly but dangerously feminized. Yet Arnold's own inclinations seem abundantly clear, with the paternally identified Aeneas castigated as "false friend" (l. 209) and the injured and abandoned Dido granted an austere and defiant integrity that leaves little doubt where our sympathies are to lie. But a second and psychologically still more disturbing resonance can be seen to attach itself to this encounter, through its framing context, the larger love story of Dido and Aeneas themselves, a narrative which in all of its compulsions, resistances, interweavings, and overdeterminations provides one of the most complexly rich instances in all of literature of the scarcely displaced oedipal masterplot.

The love story of Dido and Aeneas is above all else a tale of primal sexual transgression and contamination. Initially it is the widowed Dido herself who insists that self-pollution and desecration must follow if her dead husband were to be supplanted in a marriage bed in which love now would be trespass. Though Aeneas may be the "only one" since her husband's death "who has stirred my senses and sapped / My will" (4.22-23),[12] the divine ordinance which commands sexual abstinence in widowhood must, Dido knows, still be obeyed:

> I feel once more the scars of the old flame.
> But no, I would rather the earth should open and swallow me
> Or the Father of heaven strike me with lightning down to the shades
> The pale shades and deep night of the Underworld—before
> I violate or deny pure widowhood's claim upon me.
>
> (4.23-27)

And never questioning the rightness of that divine ordinance, Dido herself reiterates the inviolability of the claim of her first and therefore only husband: "He who first wedded me took with him, when he died, / My right to love: let him keep it, there, in the tomb, for ever" (4.28-29).

Taboos against the desecration of widowhood are themselves, as Freud tells us in *Totem and Taboo,* readily assimilable to fantasized oedipal prohibitions against killing off and then supplanting the mother's husband in that position of privilege he occupies as her sexual partner. But even more germane to the oedipal scenario are the night terrors Aeneas himself recounts after attaining his sexual ends and becoming Dido's lover, the appearance to him of "the troubled ghost of my father, Anchises" (4.352), who "Comes to me in my dreams, warns me and frightens me" (4.353). Only after Aeneas has entered upon that love which so troubles the ghost of his father does Virgil, in fact, mention those political and patriotic responsibilities to the founding of Rome which we are accustomed to regard as the real grounds for the abandonment of Dido by Aeneas. And even this act of duty on behalf of the state is rooted in more narrowly patrilinear obligations passed on to him from his father and which Aeneas, in his turn, believes he owes to his son, Ascanius. "Disturbed no less by the wrong I am doing Ascanius" (4.354), Aeneas fears he is "Defrauding him of his destined realm in Hesperia" (4.355) by dallying for the sake of a pleasure desired (and indeed enjoyed) but impermissible.

All of this, of course, forms the overarching context for the encounter in Hades between Aeneas and the ghost of Dido alluded to in **"The Scholar-Gipsy,"** and it must have been a context deeply etched into the cultural memory of Arnold's educated readers, since study of the *Aeneid* had been so prominent a staple of their early education and especially that of Arnold himself, the son of the schoolmaster. Moreover, that scene of encounter in Hades itself picks up many of the compulsions, inhibitions, and pained ambivalences seen earlier in Book 4 of the *Aeneid,* undoubtedly complicating and, to some degree, undermining the manly and patriotic resolution that apparently had been negotiated earlier with the flight of Aeneas and the seeming removal by death of the temptation Dido represents. Pained at seeing the ghost of Dido, Aeneas tearfully insists in "tender, loving tones" (6.455) that the decision to leave her "was not of my own will" (6.460) but was rather an involuntary yielding to some implacable external agency, "Heaven's commands" (6.461) that "drove me / Imperiously from your side" (6.462-463). (It is an explanation worthy of the Marguerite poems, where that speaker too seeks to exonerate himself from the charge of disloyalty to his former lover by attributing his apparent forsaking of her to the overruling of love by the seemingly arbitrary ordinances of a god.) But when Aeneas tearfully pleads with Dido to "let me see you a little longer" (6.465), Dido, contemptuous of his excuses, coldly rejects him and returns to the husband she had earlier forsworn:

> She would not turn to him; she kept her gaze on the ground,
> And her countenance remained as stubborn to his appeal
> As if it were carved from recalcitrant flint or a crag of marble.
> At last she flung away, hating him still, and vanished
> Into the shadowy wood where her first husband,

Sychaeus,
Understands her unhappiness and gives her an equal love.

(6.469-474)

Thus Arnold introduces into his narrative of his poet-speaker's feared betrayal of the scholar-gipsy (represented as the unintended though unavoidable consequence of impersonal historical forces) a disquieting and undermining subtext in which the poet-speaker's figurative counterpart, Aeneas, clearly must bear personal responsibility for a seemingly analogous betrayal, whose apparent source, however, is not history but the inevitable transgressiveness that resides in the deepest recesses of the sexual life. And giving that unanticipated and seemingly anomalous allusion a still more personal reference is its striking resemblance to that paradigmatically shaping sequential structure found repeatedly in the Marguerite poems, where the poet as lover on the very verge of embracing the loved object, reaches out only to find fulfillment almost instantaneously thwarted by what often seem oedipally charged prohibitions. Sometimes the impeding obstacle would seem to be the corruptness that resides in sexuality itself, and especially in the passions of women—"things that live and move / Mined by the fever of the soul" (**"A Farewell,"** ll. 21-22)—a passionateness likely to have flowed over into a contaminating infidelity as in **"Parting"** where the speaker as lover, his arms stretched to embrace, finds himself compelled to draw back from imminent gratification, immobilized as lover by the fact of Marguerite's alleged past debasement: "To the lips, ah! of others / Those lips have been pressed" (ll. 67-68). And in other poems in the sequence, that impeding obstacle presents itself to the speaker in even more overtly oedipal terms as the inhibiting presence of the superego, projected through that strange Arnoldian God whose "tremendous voice" (**"Meeting,"** l. 11) in ireful tones commands the lovers to "Be counselled, and retire" (**"Meeting,"** l. 12) or whose severing ordinance "bade betwixt their shores to be / The unplumbed, salt, estranging sea" (**"To Marguerite—Continued,"** ll. 23-24).

Moreover, that profoundly troubling apprehension of desire aroused and frustrated in near simultaneity, what Arnold will term "a longing like despair" (**"To Marguerite—Continued,"** l. 13) in his most memorably encapsulating formulation of that experience, in displaced form infiltrates other texts as well, poems built around significant but presumably less libidinally charged relationships. So in **"Shakespeare,"** for example, the speaker who imploringly "ask[s] and ask[s]" (l. 2) knows, even as he reaches toward, that the special wisdom the smilingly enlightened Shakespeare possesses is a knowledge transcendently "Out-topping knowledge" (l. 3), and therefore destined forever to remain inaccessibly beyond the speaker's grasp. And in **"To a Gipsy Child by the Sea-Shore,"** despite hints of mutual recognition—"With eyes that sought thine eyes thou did converse, / And that soul-searching vision fell on me" (ll. 15-16)—the ardently searching speaker similarly knows from the outset that the empathic communion he seeks will never take place: because by comparison with the earth-enhancing glooms of the gipsy child, his own shallow glooms are "Moods of fantastic sorrow, nothing worth" (l. 18), he immediately recognizes that the grim visionary understanding granted the precociously enlightened gipsy child—this infant Shakespeare—lies far beyond the speaker's own limited depths of comprehension. (It is clearly worth noting that these two early poems in which some exemplary character possessed of a special and saving knowledge is zealously but unsuccessfully pursued by a diffidently unworthy Arnoldian speaker share obvious affinities with **"The Scholar-Gipsy."**)

These narratives of desire aroused only to trigger almost instantaneously a counter-narrative of desire thwarted, perhaps the most fundamental of Arnoldian scenarios, would seem strikingly to conform in major respects to Freud's enduringly influential final formulation of the concept of anxiety. In the relatively late *Symptoms, Inhibitions, and Anxiety* Freud had concluded that anxiety was not to be understood as undischarged libido, as he had earlier believed, but rather in its functional role as a warning signal (hence the designation of this account of anxiety as the theory of "signal anxiety"), a signal alerting the ego helpless in the face of an "accumulation of excitation"[13] to the presence of danger from that excitation against which it must mobilize those familiar defenses—repression, regression, isolation, undoing—defenses that often dictated neurotic flight from or neurotic transformation of the source of instinctual danger. Nor should we be surprised that anxiety so conceived generally occurs, according to Freud, as a reoccurrence of "affective states" that "have been incorporated into the mind as precipitates of primaeval traumatic experiences" (p. 93). And predictably these experiences are most likely to have arisen during our earliest relations with our mother—on occasions "of missing someone who is loved and longed for" (a condition that Freud will break down even more finely into those closely resembling situations of anxiety he terms the loss of the loved object and fear of the loss of the loved object's love), occasions in which, as a result of our oedipal fantasies, we are prone to blame our own guilty desires for that loss (p. 137).

In **"The Scholar-Gipsy,"** then, we have a primary narrative that is itself an enactment of the scenario of anxiety, the familiar Arnoldian gesture of reaching toward by the poet-speaker being in reality a signal of warning, a set of instructions to the imagined object longed for and pursued (though in reality a set of instructions to the ego itself), urging that defenses be mobilized, that the appropriate response to the quester's desires be aversion and flight. And inserted into that narrative is a reinforcing simile that in effect reiterates the scenario of anxiety, presenting in the tale of Dido and Aeneas in Hades another episode of reaching toward that similarly concludes in aversion and flight, but in this case with the psychosexual and oedipal origins of that scenario, by its Virgilian context, more overtly exposed. But that reinforcing simile, even as it reiterates, also undermines the primary narrative's manifest content. It unmistakably insinuates that history alone, these "damned times," cannot explain Arnold's surely traumatic decision to put his career as a poet behind him so that he might pursue other less psychologically equivocal goals. Indeed the regendering of the scholar-gipsy through the figure of Dido in the course of that simile can only lead one to suspect that the Arnoldian speaker's frantic urging of the scholar-gipsy to flee modernity's fatally contaminating infectedness is itself a precipitate of "primaeval traumatic experiences," a means of reinscribing in adult life a guilt-laden childhood encounter whose sexual overtones had come to be identified with the mother or some surrogate for her. And extrapolating still further from that simile and allusion which, with its oedipal resonances, both amplifies and undermines, one can also reasonably infer that to forsake that vocation as poet for which the scholar-gipsy apparently imaginatively stands is for Arnold not just to keep faith with his obligations to poetry and the better future it makes possible but, more compellingly, to obey a dead father's repressed but now remembered wishes and commands and to avoid once again putting at risk a loved and idealized maternal presence.

The more extended simile of the Tyrian trader similarly provides a kind of mirroring image of the poem's primary narrative that more closely observed also discloses undermining traces of the psychologically transformative. Plainly the ostensible intent of the simile is to have us regard the flight by the Tyrian trader from the advancing civilization of the Greeks and his heroic voyage to the edge of the world and to the margins of culture in quest of some unspecified form of traditional wisdom as a historically distant but essentially parallel enactment of the poem's primary narrative, the scholar-gipsy's abandonment of seventeenth-century Oxford to live with and like the imaginatively empowered gipsies, acquiring and husbanding their arts until he can use them for socially beneficial ends at that eagerly awaited moment when the cycle of history reverses itself once more. By insinuating a figurative likeness between the Tyrian trader voyaging "O'er the blue Midlands water with the gale" (l. 244) and, beyond that, "To where the Atlantic raves" (l. 246) and the scholar-gipsy as he wanders in the tame woods of the Oxford countryside, Arnold might at first glance seem to be doing little more than endowing a very timid referent with something of the heroic character of the seafarer's courage. Moreover, in identifying the story of the Tyrian trader with that of the scholar-gipsy, Arnold also lends credibility to the primary narrative's claim that an essentially cyclical history does repeat itself and, by extension, to the hope that the distressful present of modernity shall give way to a better future when the spark from heaven falls, just as the irreverent science and demoralizing skepticism of Antiquity finally gave way to the epoch of Christian faith, an epoch that Arnold would perhaps have us believe was prepared for by transmission of something like the traditional faith of the shy Iberians.

Yet from that preliminary assertion of likeness stipulated by the "As" (l. 232) of the simile, we might logically expect each of the major figures in the primary narrative to have a clearly resembling counterpart within the simile: that the scholar-gipsy, for example, can be matched with the Tyrian trader (as, in fact, they grammatically are by the connecting subordinating conjunction of the simile); the inhabitants of a now ascendant modernity from whom the scholar-gipsy flees similarly matched with those "young light-hearted masters of the waves" (l. 241), the encroaching Greeks; and, rounding out the design, the aloofly reclusive gipsies with the still more mysterious inhabitants of the little-known regions beyond the western straits, those "shy traffickers, the dark Iberians" (l. 249).

Yet while the Iberians and gipsies, both of whom lead traditional lives close to nature, seem enough alike to make sense of the simile, neither of the other two parallels really holds. Even Culler, while strongly committed to the simile's expressly stated logic of likeness, is forced to admit that the scholar-gipsy, "as we originally knew him, more closely resembles the Grecian coaster than the Tyrian trader" (p. 191). Indeed, the figure from the primary narrative that the "grave Tyrian trader" (l. 232) seems most to resemble is not the scholar-gipsy in his "glad perennial youth" (l. 229) to whom he is expressly likened but the speaker himself, similarly grave in his forebearance, in his "Sad patience, too near neighbor to despair." Nor finally do "The young light-hearted masters of the wave" (l. 241) who man the "merry Grecian coaster" (l. 237) in the concluding simile seem at all like their tacitly designated counterparts from the primary narrative, those neurasthenic moderns who in their wretchedness and misery exemplify Arnold's own phase of the historical cycle, which, following the logic of the simile, is supposedly the phase that most closely parallels the epoch of Greek ascendancy.

What these intimations of difference amid claims of a signifying likeness suggest is that what Arnold has given us by means of this simile is not a mirroring narrative but a covert counterplot, not merely divergent but, in truth, oppositional. But that is not too surprising, since in **"Stanzas from the Grande Chartreuse,"** a poem written not very long before **"The Scholar-Gipsy,"** he had used his closing simile in much the same way, to undermine, indeed even to undo, those implicitly historicist premises which that simile had been ostensibly designed to elaborate. There his strategy had been to take his speaker and those for whom he purports to speak, the between-worlds generation forlornly awaiting that cyclical reversal through which "may dawn an age, / More fortunate, alas! than we" (ll. 157-158), and, in the most unexpected of transformations, reconstitute them literally as children, desiring and perhaps destined to live out their lives in regressive changelessness "Beneath some old-world abbey wall" (l. 170). And standing in opposition to the speaker and the "we" he speaks for in the simile's reconceptualizing of the argument of the primary narrative of **"Stanzas from the Grande Chartreuse"** are a surprisingly attractive set of very different figures, men of action, apparently able to live successfully in the world and who, with banners flying, vigorously step forward in quick time "To life, to cities, and to war" (l. 180). Nor are those thus able to live in the world therefore men of the future, beneficiaries of that reversal of the historical cycle which shall free humanity from the burden imposed by its downward turn; instead, they are plainly men of the present, living cheerfully in the here and now, seemingly unconstrained by the between-worlds limitations of historical circumstance which Arnold and those for whom he speaks must passively endure, unless they choose that implicitly neurotic course of an immobilizingly regressive flight.

In the coda to **"The Scholar-Gipsy"** there are also suggestions of regressive flight but a flight more complex, more highly displaced, and less fully effectuated than the immediate and absolute transformation of speaker into child that we find in **"Stanzas from the Grande Chartreuse."** The regressive implications of the voyage of the Tyrian trader do not in this case manifest themselves by the reversion to childhood of the voyager himself. They are rather to be found in the object of his voyage, in his projected transaction with the reclusive and presumably childlike Iberians from whom the Tyrian trader apparently hopes to acquire, as a return for his own unspecified offerings, some good that bespeaks their own innocently uncorrupted nature, some profoundly elemental antidote to the spiritually devastating effects of a dangerously encroaching civilization. Of course, whether there is to be a successful outcome to the trader's heroic voyaging remains highly problematic. Whereas in the poem's initial and far more confidently viewed quest, the scholar-gipsy had made contact with those he sought out, had gleaned what their crucial secret was, and had begun instruction in their art, in the concluding lines the Tyrian trader does no more than set out the commodities he would barter, uncertain whether or not the contents of his "corded bales" (l. 250) will prove acceptable items of trade to these "shy traffickers" (l. 249) and, more important, whether those greatly desired goods (though goods never identified nor seen) he has come so far and through such dangers to obtain will be offered in exchange. Thus that desperate yearning to return to and to recapture origins, the presumptive object of that regressive impulse, is represented in the heroic voyage of the closing simile as both desperately sought after and yet uncertain of attainment.

But the more striking and significant point of likeness between the similes is the prominence in both of a set of resembling figures, light-hearted, adventuresome, and seemingly masterful men, the "passing troops" (l. 177) whose entreaties the children of **"Stanzas from the Grande Chartreuse"** refuse and, correspondingly, the Grecian sailors of **"The Scholar-Gipsy"** from whose intrusion the Tyrian trader actually takes flight. They are, of course, figures for whom there is no real precedent within the primary narratives to which the similes refer and whose presence therefore is probably our most promising clue to that counterargument to the original that the simile covertly puts forward. Where the poet-speaker in each poem had initially cast himself as spokesman for his generation, those listlessly unhappy men and women accidentally cast adrift in the between-worlds circumstances that are the inescapable lot of everyone born into the joylessly transitional epoch of modernity, the similes seem to alter drastically that historically deterministic argument. The passing troops and Grecian sailors are clearly members of the child-speaker's and Tyrian trader's own generation and yet they still manage to exhibit energy in abundance, an energy enabling them to create history rather than passively remain its wholly suffering victims. In fact, the real contrast in the concluding similes of the two poems is not between hypothesized representatives of two diametrically opposed phases of the historical cycle, but rather between two sharply differentiated segments of contemporary humanity, the strivers and doers and makers of the world, whether soldiers or seafarers, and those who find themselves held in check from any commitment to action by an innate diffidence, remaining wary and anxious, desirous only of evading or escaping the claims upon them of life and the world.

In effect, in the similes Arnold seems to put the assumptions of historicism behind him, to rule out the cyclical movements of the *Zeitgeist* as the ultimate determinant of human behavior in a process that renders all individuals alike who at any given time fall under—as they necessarily must—its inescapable causal influence. Instead, he seems to indicate that human behavior must inevitably depend upon the intrinsic attributes and characteristics each individual brings to the historical circumstances under which he lives. Thus, in these two final similes, the Arnoldian speaker, who up to that point in these poems has represented himself as spokesman for the unhappy collective humanity of the transitional epoch, suddenly and unexpectedly reverts to type, becoming once again—whether he depicts himself as child or trader—that melancholy, solitary "I" so often observed in Arnold's earlier poetry. Essentially isolated and estranged from others, not for reasons of history but from causes that we can assume lie within, he too seems beset by the usual Arnoldian amalgam of desire and anxiety, the prospect of contact with another calling forth the stock psychological defenses of regression or flight. Moreover, with the appearance of "the merry Grecian coaster" (l. 237) manned by "The young light-hearted masters of the waves" (l. 241) there are intimations that the earlier theory of history with its despairing sense of the present and its relegation of hope to an unattainable future was badly misconceived. From the confidence and evident mastery of these heroic voyagers, we would guess that the future is now, that the turn that advances civilization has, in fact, already been taken by these men of action (whose similarly confident and similarly masterful Victorian counterparts Arnold was only too well aware of), and that it is from the men of his own time who most resemble them, those who are most likely to be agents of progress and potential benefactors of their society, that the speaker of **"The Scholar-Gipsy"** is actually and perhaps culpably most profoundly estranged.[14]

Thus, the simile with which **"The Scholar-Gipsy"** closes, in effect, impels the poem in radically new directions, revising its apparently historicist and forward looking referent in ways that actually bring **"The Scholar-Gipsy"** into intellectual and psychological alignment with what is bleakest and most personally painful in Arnold's earlier and avowedly pessimistic poetry. With the Tyrian trader having displaced the speaker as the poem's point of subjective reference, human life is once again imagined as a solitary voyage as it was in **"Human Life"** and **"A Summer Night."** And even if, unlike the madman of **"A Summer Night,"** this particular voyager averts shipwreck in his desperately headlong and incautious journey, and even if journey's end proves to be not "some false, impossible shore" (**"A Summer Night,"** l. 69) but those lands beyond the Pillars of Hercules, "where down cloudy cliffs, through sheets of foam, / Shy traffickers, the dark Iberians come" (ll. 248-249), nevertheless, the outcome of the trader's heroic voyaging remains highly problematic, with the Tyrian trader uncertain whether or not what is contained within his "corded bales" (l. 250) will prove acceptable items of trade to these "shy traffickers" (l. 249) and, more important, whether they will offer in exchange those desired goods he has undergone such dangers to obtain. And taking the assumed parallel between simile and referent a step further, we are entitled to read this account of the Tyrian trader in terms of that quasi-allegory that seemingly follows from the narrative of the scholar-gipsy, an allegory of poetry and myth (or a poetry that is myth) collaboratively working to effect at a historically propitious moment nothing less than the imaginative regeneration of humanity. But from the fact that, unlike the scholar-gipsy, the Tyrian trader never actually completes his crucial transaction with those he has abandoned civilization to seek out, we can only conclude that by poem's end Arnold has, if not renounced, at least drawn back from his earlier faith that the shattered culture of historical man shall, through the imaginative magic of poetic myth, be restored again to something approaching its lost unity or, still worse, that he has come to doubt that the poet will ever really affect a world that is ruled over by men of energy and power, "The young light-hearted masters of the waves" (l. 241).

But while these two major similes put much in question, they do in one major respect reiterate and amplify what is already present in the narrative of the quest for the scholar-gipsy, its psychologically underlying plot of reaching toward that is thwarted, of desire forestalled by anxiety's arousal of the ego's defenses. Indeed, viewed sequentially, the two concluding similes of Dido and the Tyrian trader provide an almost textbook illustration of signal anxiety: a reaching out toward the loved object, an object implicitly feminized by the allusion to Dido and therefore a suitable substitute for some yearned-for lost original, with that movement toward the object immediately short-circuited by fears that success will bring only feelings of debasement and shame. It is this preemptive anxiety which impels the Arnoldian speaker in the Marguerite poems to flight, his only effective recourse against instinctual danger, a flight whose necessity and urgency is surely reflected in the Tyrian trader's abruptly undertaken and frenetically driven voyage beyond "the western straits" (l. 247). Moreover, at the center of this triad of narratives, standing between the story of the scholar-gipsy and that of the Tyrian trader as the fulcrum upon which the reiterated plots of signal anxiety turn, is the recollected tale of Aeneas and Dido, Rome and Carthage, a legendary evocation of male responsibility and female enticements which Arnold more than likely associated with childhood memories of his father as teller and as modern-day advocate of the Roman virtues and, deeper still, with that family romance which lies at the heart of our earliest childhood impulses and anxieties.

And reading back from this simile of transgression and betrayal in love with its deeply oedipal resonances, we are surely encouraged to impute other, more intrinsically private and disturbingly regressive origins than simply modernity to the speaker's fear in the primary narrative that he carries a fatal contagiousness that would undo the mission that the scholar-gipsy has embarked upon in behalf of a world waiting to be born. It is as if Arnold, by employing the simile, had determined to say manifestly what had been latently present in the tale of the scholar-gipsy all along: that to quest after the scholar-gipsy is to abdicate manly responsibilities, to violate a father's wishes by pursuing a goal inimical to the need to work in the world. And considering the identification of the scholar-gipsy with the Romantic imagination and the idea of poetry, we should not be surprised if one of the unstated objects of these implicitly paternal strictures is poetry itself, a vocation that from a father's perspective might be looked upon as mere dalliance, a self-indulgent abdication of obligations to assist in the work of reconstituting the world not at the hypothesized end of some far-fetched historical cycle dependent upon poetry for its spiritual health but during one's own lifetime, indeed at this very moment. Given this latent counterargument surreptitiously compounded of the most troubling elements of the primary narrative and the materials of the two equally troubling closing similes, **"The Scholar-Gipsy"** can be seen finally for what it proves to be: a kind of valedictory to the major part of Arnold's poetic career, a turning away from a poetry that until now has primarily been made out of the profoundly conflicted but courageously authentic products of "the mind's dialogue with itself" (***CPW,*** 1:1) and a turning instead toward a poetry and prose more responsible, more dedicated to ameliorating the social needs of the larger community, more in keeping with paternal wishes and commands.

Notes

1. *The Poems of Matthew Arnold,* ed. Miriam Allott (New York: Longmans, 1979). All subsequent quotations from Arnold's poems are to this edition, hereafter cited in the text. All quotations from Arnold's prose are from *The Complete Prose Works of Matthew Arnold,* ed. R. H. Super, 11 vols. (Ann Arbor: Univ. of Michigan Press, 1960-77), hereafter cited as *CPW.*

2. Alan Grob, "The Poetry of Pessimism: Arnold's 'Resignation,'" *VP* [*Victorian Poetry*] 26 (1988): 25-44.
3. For a fuller discussion of Arnold's historicism, see Fraser Nieman, "The Zeitgeist of Matthew Arnold," *PMLA* 72 (1957): 977-996; Peter Allan Dale, *The Victorian Critic and the Idea of History* (Cambridge: Harvard Univ. Press, 1977), pp. 91-168; A. Dwight Culler, *The Victorian Mirror of History* (New Haven: Yale Univ. Press, 1985), pp. 122-151; and especially David DeLaura, "Matthew Arnold and the Nightmare of History" in *Victorian Poetry,* Stratford-upon-Avon Series 15 (London: Edward Arnold, 1972), pp. 37-57.
4. See the headnote by Kenneth Allott to "The Scholar-Gipsy" in *Poems,* p. 356.
5. A. Dwight Culler, *Imaginative Reason: The Poetry of Matthew Arnold* (New Haven: Yale Univ. Press, 1966), p. 182.
6. Culler, in fact, chooses the famous penultimate line of "Ode to a Nightingale" as an epigraph for his chapter on "The Scholar-Gipsy" in *Imaginative Reason,* p. 178. For a searching and sensitive examination of Keats as precursor poet for Arnold in "The Scholar-Gipsy," see William A. Ulmer, "The Human Seasons: Arnold, Keats and 'The Scholar-Gipsy,'" *VP* 22 (1984): 247-261.
7. For a discussion of Keats, immortality, and metaphysics see my essay "Noumenal Inferences: Keats as Metaphysician," in *Critical Essays on John Keats,* ed. Hermione de Almeida (Boston: G. K. Hall, 1989), pp. 292-317.
8. Leon Gottfried, *Matthew Arnold and the Romantics* (London: Routledge and Kegan Paul, 1963), pp. 116-150.
9. As early as 1862, in "Maurice de Guérin," Arnold had already said that in Keats "the natural magic is perfect" (*CPW,* 3:34).
10. David G. Riede, *Matthew Arnold and the Betrayal of Language* (Charlottesville: Univ. of Virginia Press, 1988), p. 142.
11. G. Wilson Knight, "The Scholar-Gipsy," in *Matthew Arnold,* ed. Harold Bloom (New York: Chelsea House, 1987), p. 65.
12. *The Aeneid of Virgil,* trans. C. Day Lewis (Oxford: Oxford Univ. Press, 1952). All quotations from *The Aeneid* are from this edition.
13. James Strachey, intro. to Sigmund Freud, *Inhibitions, Symptoms, and Anxiety,* in *Complete Psychological Works,* 24 vols., ed. James Strachey (London: Hogarth Press, 1959), 20:81. Anxiety seems to me the shaping psychological issue in Arnold's poetry. For a good discussion of anxiety in Arnold's poetry in relation to his audience and particularly to his female readers, see Mary Ellis Gibson, "Dialogue on the Darkling Plain: Genre, Gender, and Audience in Matthew Arnold's Lyrics," in *Gender and Discourse in Victorian Literature and Art,* ed. Anthony H. Harrison and Beverly Taylor (DeKalb: Northern Illinois Press, 1992), pp. 30-48.
14. Robert Langbaum, in *Mysteries of Identity* (Chicago: Univ. of Chicago Press, 1982), also suggests that these "joyous Greeks could stand well enough for modern men of *action*" (p. 60).

Donald D. Stone (essay date 1997)

SOURCE: "Arnold and the Pragmatists: Culture as Democracy," in *Communications with the Future: Matthew Arnold in Dialogue,* University of Michigan Press, 1997, pp. 139-74.

[*In the following essay, Stone claims that despite Arnold's largely unfavorable view of American culture, he appealed to American intellectuals and that his philosophy has been an inspiration for many American pragmatists, including John Dewey and William James.*]

> I am more and more convinced that the world tends to become more comfortable for the mass, and more uncomfortable for those of any natural gift or distinction—and it is as well perhaps that it should be so—for hitherto the gifted have astonished and delighted the world, but not trained or inspired or in any real way changed it—and the world might do worse than to dismiss too high pretentions, and settle down on what it can see and handle and appreciate.
>
> Arnold to Arthur Hugh Clough, January 7, 1852

> I am finite once for all, and all the categories of my sympathy are knit up with the finite world *as such,* and with things that have a history.
>
> William James, *A Pluralistic Universe*

> Our neglect of the traditions of the past, with whatever this negligence implies in the way of spiritual impoverishment of our life, has its compensation in the idea that the world is recommencing and being remade under our eyes.
>
> John Dewey, "The Development of American Pragmatism"

> *Here or nowhere is America!*
>
> Goethe, *Wilhelm Meister's Apprenticeship*

While pleased that Clough liked **"The Scholar-Gipsy,"** Arnold persisted in asking his friend, "but what does it *do* for you?" The greatest poets—Homer, Shakespeare—*animate;* and "'The complaining millions of men [who] / Darken in labour and pain'" (Arnold is quoting from his **"The Youth of Nature"**) desire "something to *animate* and *enoble* them—not merely to add zest to their melancholy or grace to their dreams." In 1853 Arnold called this feeling "the basis of [his] nature—and of [his] poetics."[1] What does poetry—or, for that matter, criticism or culture—*do* for you? The utilitarian-sounding question may seem strange coming from an Oxford-trained idealist; but, as I have argued in the preceding chapter, Arnold's idealism is inextricably linked to his emphasis on practice. Like his hermeneuticist descendant Hans-Georg Gadamer, Arnold sees knowledge and action, Hellenism and Hebraism, as incomplete without the other. By now we have seen an Arnold who upholds principles of unity and authority coexisting with an Arnold who praises diversity and who questions dogmas and traditions. There is the Arnold who defers to Burke and Newman, and the Arnold who identifies with Byron and Heine. And yet all these seemingly contradictory selves are part of an individual totality—the personal equivalent of what William James called our "multiverse"—and this polyphonic self pursues a pragmatic goal. If a pragmatist may be defined as a pluralist with standards—someone who believes in subjecting the doctrines inherited from the past, and the unexamined presumptions of the present, to critical reflection; one whose aim is the improvement of the kingdom of this earth, bolstered by humanist ideals that promote social solidarity and individual transformation—then Arnold must be seen as an important precursor of pragmatism.

While acknowledging it to be a "vague, ambiguous, and overworked word," Richard Rorty nevertheless names pragmatism as "the chief glory of [America's] intellectual tradition. No other American writers have offered so radical a suggestion for making our future different from our past, as have James and Dewey." In recent years, in large part owing to Rorty, pragmatism has enjoyed a resurgence of popularity,[2] having become a philosophical refuge and sounding board for a variety of fin de siècle intellectuals: frustrated liberals and enraged radicals, post-Marxists and anti-Marxists, individualists and communitarians, aesthetes and social activists. At a time when many intellectuals feel themselves at odds with the establishment, and at the same time oppose the nihilism and fatalism implicit in some recent academic trends, pragmatism has offered a belief both in the potential for change and in the power of ideas and ideals to effectuate change. And yet, despite Arnold's tendency to regard "America" as symbol of what should be avoided by lovers of culture, this most American of philosophies restates, in many ways, and builds upon some of the Arnoldian attitudes I have been examining for the past four chapters.

Arnold has had an extraordinary appeal for American intellectuals, from *North American Review* editor Charles Eliot Norton down to the editor of Arnold's ***Complete Prose Works,*** R. H. Super. He has been admired by, and inspired, some of America's best minds, beginning with Emerson and Henry James. In recent years, he has attracted such New York intellectuals as Lionel Trilling, Irving Howe, and Morris Dickestein.[3] It should not be a surprise, then, that American pragmatists have seen in Arnold a useful ally or a valuable adversary. Rorty includes him among the literary critics whose example he thinks philosophers may profit from. William James drew on Arnold's religious writings and (surprisingly, given his patriotism) praised Arnold's final and harshest piece on **"Civilisation in the United States"** as "very sensible and good."[4] And Dewey conducted a dialogue with Arnold that extended over six decades. In 1890, two years after Arnold's death, Dewey devoted the major portion of a lecture on "Poetry and Philosophy" to a sensitive and highly revealing analysis of Arnold—all the more surprising coming from a philosopher often accused of being indifferent to the arts, but who, early on, showed sympathetic awareness of Arnold's depiction of mankind's tragic plight.

Dewey's apostle Sidney Hook has characterized pragmatism in terms both of its "melioristic" thrust and its "tragic sense of life." The hopeful aspect of pragmatism is contained within three of its premises: first, that "the universe [is] open," with the result that human "possibilities [are] real"; second, that "the future [depends] in part upon what" we do or leave undone; and, third, that ideas are "potentially plans of action." Rather than supporting a materialistic status quo, as some have charged, pragmatism must be seen as "a method of clarifying ideas" and thus as "a method of *criticism*." But along with this sense of the "efficacy of human ideals and actions" comes an awareness of "their inescapable limitations." For it is a finite world that we inhabit—one cut off from divine support or guidance—and living with finitude means accepting a world of "inescapable tragedy."[5] Hook's emphasis on the tragic side of pragmatism is supported by a look at Dewey's 1890 lecture. Dewey begins by quoting the opening of Arnold's **"The Study of Poetry,"** with its account of how, in a time of dying creeds and dissolving traditions, people are increasingly "turning to poetry for consolation, for stay, for interpretation." Speaking as one for whom philosophy and science should provide the "method and standard" for truth, Dewey nonetheless notes that Arnold's poetry—with its awareness of man's "isolation from nature, his isolation from fellow-man"—sounds a chord of authenticity that cannot be denied. Comparing Arnold's "Stoic" stance with Browning's more optimistic verses (Browning's sense that "the world was made for man, and that man was made for man," which Dewey would obviously prefer to be closer to the truth than Arnold's view), Dewey contends that "Arnold's message has weight and penetration with us, . . . because that message conveys something of the reality of things." What the philosophy of 1890, by contrast, lacks is just such an awareness of the *Zeitgeist* held by such poets as Arnold and Browning. What is needed, then, is a bridging of "this gap of poetry from science," of a uniting of the poet's sense of reality with the philosopher's and scientist's method for transforming that reality.[6]

Even with his hopeful conclusion—and from the latter part of the nineteenth until the middle of the twentieth century, Dewey was remarkable for his hopefulness—Dewey's recital of all those Arnold passages that undermine optimism ("Wandering between two worlds, one dead / The other powerless to be born"; "The sea of faith / Was once, too, at the full"; "Thou hast been, shalt be, art alone"; and so on) indicate how closely he had studied the poet. But he had also absorbed the hopeful side of Arnold the critic, the Arnold who looked to education and the forces of culture to release humankind from its tendency to anarchy, intolerance, and provinciality. In a fragment of autobiography dating from 1930, Dewey, judging the present from the point of view of the future, dismissed "the whole of western European history [as] a provincial episode," and he called on philosophers "to help get rid of the useless lumber that blocks our highways of thought, and strive to make straight and open the paths that lead to the future." Not for the first time in his work, Dewey is echoing the theme of **"The Function of Criticism at the Present Time"**; and to underscore the resemblance, he concludes with Arnold's image of the forward-looking critic as he wanders through the wilderness: "Forty years spent in wandering in a wilderness like that of the present is not a sad fate—unless one attempts to make oneself believe that the wilderness is after all itself the promised land."[7] It was Dewey's goal no less than it had been Arnold's to counter the individual sense of isolation with a social vision of solidarity.

In this chapter I will be exploring Arnold's affinities with the pragmatists: with William James, himself eminently Victorian in many of his conflicting attitudes, and not least in his desire to reconcile individual and religious needs with societal and scientific claims; with Rorty, whose mixture of private aestheticism and public liberalism, as well as whose ironic stance, bears some resemblance to that of the Arnoldian artist-critic; and finally with Dewey, whose faith in education as the instrument best capable of nourishing a cultivated and creative democracy resembles Arnold's own abiding faith. Arnold's description of himself, in the Introduction to ***Culture and Anarchy,*** as "a Liberal tempered by experience [and] reflection," as, "above all, a believer in culture" (***CPW,*** 5:88) is not a bad description of Dewey too. For if Arnold's keyword *culture* gives way to Dewey's keyword *democracy,* the two terms were intertwined from the beginning in Arnold's mind. Arnold's culture was never meant to be a defense against democracy but was meant rather to be a preparation for, and safeguard of, democracy.[8] Apostles of culture, he repeatedly argued, are necessarily proponents of equality; and no culture is worth its name, he felt, that did not contain all its citizens ("all our fellow-men, in the East of London and elsewhere" [5:216]) in the goal of individual and societal transformation ("progress towards perfection"). As prelude to my last set of Arnoldian dialogues, therefore, I will be looking at perhaps the most pragmatic in tone of all his volumes, the fine and often overlooked collection of ***Mixed Essays*** (1879), which brings together his important essays on **"Democracy"** and **"Equality,"** as well as his eloquent tributes to Falkland and George Sand.

The author of the ***Mixed Essays*** is a more earnest and appealing Arnold than the combative author of the more quotable ***Culture and Anarchy.*** The years spent inspecting schools, reevaluating literary and religious texts, and reflecting on the spirit of the age had all intensified Arnold's belief in the need for ideals and in the value of conduct. Without ceasing to be a Hellenist, an advocate of beauty and intelligence ("sweetness and light"), he is more passionate now in his defense of "civilization"—a term that has displaced "culture" in the Preface to the new volume. Arnold has, in part, returned to literary subjects—to George Sand, to the French critic Edmond Scherer (and, through him, to Milton and Goethe)—but in order to examine what part literature plays in the "whole" of civilization, whose aim is the "humanisation of man," all men, "in society." To signal the continuity of his interests, Arnold includes in his new book the essay on **"Democracy"** that had served, two decades earlier, as Introduction to ***The Popular Education of France*** (1861). To it he added essays on Clarendon's (and Thomas Arnold's) beloved **"Falkland,"** on **"Equality,"** on **"Irish Catholicism and British Liberalism,"** and on the woeful state of British education (**"Porro Unum Est Necessarium"**). A "mixed" collection, indeed, and yet each essay illustrates Arnold's principle: "Whoever seriously occupies himself with literature will soon perceive its vital connection with other agencies" (***CPW,*** 8:370).

The radical nature of Arnold's **"Democracy"** is evidenced if we put it in the context of the authors on the subject who preceded him, Tocqueville and Mill, and the pragmatists who succeeded him. *On Liberty* (1859) had appeared just two years before Arnold's ***Popular Education***; but whereas Mill's argument is made in behalf of the "highly gifted" individual's right to develop himself, free from the dictates of the unreflecting "mass," Arnold's plea is in behalf of that mass's right: "no longer individuals and limited classes only, but the mass of a community—to develop itself with the utmost possible fulness and freedom" (***CPW,*** 2:8). Mill shares Tocqueville's fear of the "tyranny of the majority," and he celebrates, in romantic fashion, the right of genius to resist and reshape public opinion. (Mill bristles, however, at the thought that he is "countenancing . . . 'hero worship'" of a Carlylean nature; the Millite genius must not force the public into doing his bidding, but he does claim "freedom to point out the way.")[9] But Tocqueville had warned not only of the conformist power of public opinion but also of the excesses of individualism in America, where "Everyone shuts himself up tightly within himself and insists upon judging the world from there." To the French observer, "individualism is of democratic origin": it encourages a self-reliance that prides itself on "contempt for tradition" and disregard for the past, but that also occasions an alienation between man and man, throwing "him back forever upon himself alone and [threatening] in the end to confine him entirely within the solitude of his own heart."[10] From Emerson to William James to Rorty, the individual has remained the romantic intellectual's focus of attention; and this romantic impulse has often pulled against pragmatism's activist streak. Thus, as a liberal of the laissez-faire school, Mill opposes state intervention in public education. He does not oppose the state's requiring that its children be educated, but he demands that parents be free "to obtain the education where and how they pleased." To his mind, a state-run education will only mould "people to be exactly like one another," and is thus to be resisted.[11] Mill's text has become a secular bible for conservatives and radicals alike, all those for whom freedom to go one's own way takes precedence over what Arnold, in ***Popular Education,*** called "the strong bond of a common culture" (2:89). In **"My Countrymen,"** Arnold assailed his fellow Liberals for failing to see that "Freedom . . . is a very good horse to ride;—but to ride somewhere" (5:22). And, like Dewey, he suggests that the worship of individual freedom is often done at the expense of the other two principles of the French Revolution, equality and fraternity.

Arnold begins **"Democracy"** with a glance at Mill's position that no amount of state action is permissible; but, unlike Mill, he accepts the fact that a new force is coming to power—that "democracy" is now in the process of "trying *to affirm its own essence;* to live, to enjoy, to possess the world, as aristocracy has tried, and successfully tried, before it" (***CPW,*** 2:7). Supporting the legacy of the French Revolution, Arnold notes how in France democracy has flourished with the aid of a massive state-run educational system, and how the French support the state because they see it working in their name. (As Dewey will say of democracy, it is the one political system in which the dualism between governor and governed disappears.)[12] In England, however, with its traditions supporting self-reliance, there is no rallying point to provide the uneducated masses with a sense of ideals existing beyond the self. "Nations are not truly great solely because the individuals composing them are numerous, free, and active," Arnold maintains; "but they are great when these numbers, this freedom, and this activity are employed in the service of an ideal higher than that of an ordinary man, taken by himself" (2:18). Arnold is not setting up the state as an authoritarian ideal. Rather, he is positing an ideal of the solidarity of men, "a true bond of union," in which the "best self" of each citizen finds a "rallying-point for the intelligence and for the worthiest instincts of the community" (2:19). To those who demand, *"Leave us to ourselves!"* Arnold suggests that they look at the present state of England, to the widespread indifference to beauty, the paucity of intelligence, the scarcity of essential services that such an attitude has prompted: "The State can bestow certain broad collective benefits, which are indeed not much if compared with the advantages already possessed by individual grandeur, but which are rich and valuable if compared with the make-shifts of mediocrity and poverty. A good thing meant for the many cannot well be so exquisite as the good things of the few; but it can easily, if it comes from a donor of great resources and wide power, be incomparably better than what the many could, unaided, provide for themselves" (2:21). To charge Arnold with elitism (as so many do) is to ignore where he stands when it comes to the sharing of education, culture, even health care.

It is in Arnold, not Mill, that Dewey's faith in democracy finds its true forebear. Dewey's early "The Ethics of Democracy" (1888) builds upon Arnold's position that each individual in a democracy is not to be seen as a "disorganized fragment" (as Sir Henry Maine claimed in his attack on *Popular Government*) but rather as a member of an "organism." There is no such thing in reality as a "non-social individual," Dewey maintains, and the Platonic (and liberal) notion that "democratic freedom" means "doing what one likes," without respect for ideals, is wrongheaded. ("For men are solidary, or co-partners; and not isolated," Arnold says in a late religious essay [***CPW,*** 8:43].) For Dewey, democracy is itself an ideal, an ideal allowing for each person's right to fulfill himself; and the "democratic ideal includes liberty, because democracy without initiation from within [without that is, in Arnoldian terms, regard for one's "best self"], without an ideal chosen from within and freely followed from within, is nothing." Dewey's democracy is thus "a social, that is to say, an ethical conception"; "it is a form of government only because it is a form of moral and spiritual association." Dewey's vision of democracy is more idealized than Arnold's; but for both educators, the goal of their vocation is the guidance of the masses toward ideals of self-fulfillment (affirming "one's *own essence*") and solidarity. Only a democracy enables every individual to follow the Nietzschean injunction to become what one is; only with "equality," Dewey and Arnold agree, do we have an "ideal of humanity." Dewey ends his essay on the same note with which Arnold ends his essay on George Sand: his may be an ideal, but (to cite James Russell Lowell) "'I am one of those who believe that the real will never find an irremovable basis till it rests upon the ideal.'"[13]

The pragmatist thrust of Arnold's and Dewey's essays rests upon their belief in the efficacy of the ideal to move us forward. ("Perfection will never be reached," Arnold says in the conclusion to **"Democracy"**; "but to recognize a period of transformation when it comes, and to adapt ourselves honestly and rationally to its laws, is perhaps the nearest approach to perfection of which men and nations are capable" [***CPW,*** 2:29].) And they share an awareness that "civilisation" or "culture" is connected to "character," to conduct. The Arnoldian sense of culture as *Bildung* (which I discussed in the last two chapters) is also Dewey's; and Dewey's democratic ideal (what he later calls "Creative Democracy") is precisely that which Arnold advocated in **"A French Eton,"** wherein the transformation, the "growth in perfection," of the individual is paralleled by the transformation of society as well (2:312-13). To turn from Arnold to a contemporary pragmatist like Rorty is to see how tenaciously this faith in democracy as *Bildung* has persisted, even in one for whom *ideals* and *values* are merely localized and transitory terms.

Rorty's career as philosopher has been the attempt, by turns ironical and serious, to justify both the aesthetic doctrine of self-fulfillment and the liberal appeal to solidarity—despite his sense that there is no foundation to support either belief. In "The Priority of Democracy to Philosophy" (in the Cambridge University Press reprint, capital letters are coyly dispensed with), Rorty's position is that the democratic society we live in is a worthy one even if he cannot offer philosophical reasons to support the claim. (Elsewhere, he celebrates "bourgeois capitalist society as the best polity actualized so far, while regretting that it is irrelevant to most of the problems of most of the population of the planet.") Rorty supports a Rawlsian view of democratic society, in which the "Socratic commitment to free exchange of views [exists] without the Platonic commitment to the possibility of universal agreement"; and he is willing to accept an image of the self as a "centerless web of historically conditioned beliefs and desires." Any attempt to speak of enduring values existing outside or within the self is clearly a waste of time. Claiming Dewey as his source, Rorty argues that "communal and public disenchantment is the price we pay for individual and private spiritual liberation," and that this "liberation" is worth any regressive return to the realm of "philosophical reflection" or "religion." And yet, one can only marvel at the tenacity whereby this disbeliever in all absolutes (Rorty describes his procedure as a kind of Socratic slapstick, a "joshing" of his fellow citizens out of their earnestness) clings, with the sincerity of a romantic pragmatist, to the belief in "individual liberation" and to a faith in democracy as affording "experiments in cooperation."[14] Even without the capital letters, democracy retains a metaphysical sense of priority.

In the ***Mixed Essays*** Arnold readily admits the lack of absolute standards, and he denies the value of all systematic judgments ("altogether unprofitable"). Still, he points to the examples of Falkland and Goethe and George Sand for having reflected lucidly and acted generously. Together, they embody an ideal of civilization whose components (in Arnold's view) are the liberty that allows for human "expansion" and a sense of "equality" that encourages human *civility* (***CPW,*** 8:371-72). Falkland's personal civility during the time of the English civil wars makes him "a martyr of sweetness and light" (8:206) to Arnold. Choosing to fight on the Royalist side, despite his awareness of its aristocratic "vices" and "delusions," Falkland realized that the alternative was an unsound Puritan cause that promoted religious "narrowness" and "intellectual poverty" (201). In giving "himself to the cause which seemed to him least unsound" (204) because its opponent was opposed to the progressive spirit of the age, but which contained no more "truth" than its antagonist, Falkland found himself in a "tragic"—and, for Arnold, *modern*—dilemma. A pragmatist's "tragic sense," Hook argues, derives precisely from this sense that one is often forced in practice to choose between what is "good" and what is "right."[15] For Arnold, looking at the unsoundness of the Liberal and Conservative positions of his own time, the individual can only act in behalf of what is right for the *future.* Falkland's "lucidity of mind and largeness of temper," Arnold declares ". . . link him with the nineteenth century. He and his friends, by their heroic and hopeless stand against the inadequate ideas dominant in their time, kept open their communications with the future, lived with the future . . .

> To our English race, with its insularity, its profound faith in action, its contempt for dreamers and failers, inadequate ideals in life, manners, government, thought, religion, will always be a source of danger. Energetic action makes up, we think, for imperfect knowledge. We think that all is well, that a man is following "a moral impulse," if he pursues an end which he "deems of supreme importance." We impose neither on him nor on ourselves the duty of discerning whether he is *right* in deeming it so.
>
> Hence our causes are often as small as our noise about them is great.
>
> (8:204-5)

If the "impassioned seekers of a new and better world" such as Falkland fail, Arnold notes, paraphrasing George Sand, that "proves nothing . . . for the world as it is. Ineffectual they may be, but the world is still more ineffectual, and it is the world's course which is doomed to ruin, not theirs" (***CPW,*** 8:223). Calling himself a liberal not of the present but "of the future," Arnold identified with the French novelist. In the eloquent essay devoted to her, he speaks of the power of ideals to form "a purged and renewed human society" (220). Sand's idealism is based on intense love—for nature, for the past, for all mankind, beginning with the French peasantry. He sees her as a Wordsworth devoid of any post-Wordsworthian Romantic egoism: "She regarded nature and beauty, not with the selfish and solitary joy of the artist who but seeks to appropriate them for his own purposes [but] . . . as a vast power of healing and delight for all" (226). But she is also a daughter of the Revolution, dismayed by the ideological hatreds of French intellectuals. Rorty has written, without irony, of the ethical power of "edifying" novelists. For Arnold, no novelist was more edifying than Sand, none more committed to what she called "the sentiment of the ideal life, which is none other than man's normal life as we shall one day know it" (219).[16]

Having invoked a pre-Deweyan faith in idealism in the pieces on Falkland and Sand, Arnold argues elsewhere in the ***Mixed Essays*** the pragmatic view that human development requires a critical examination of the defects of the present. (Pragmatism means "death on bunkum and pretentious abstractions," Hook says, "especially when they are capitalized as Success or Historical Destiny or Reality.")[17] In **"Irish Catholicism and British Liberalism,"** Arnold blames the English, including his fellow Liberals, for failing to see the justice of Irish grievances; and he lambasts the middle class, which prides itself on "knowing how to make money, but not knowing how to live when they have made it" (***CPW,*** 8:338). In **"Porro Unum Est Necessarium,"** he points up once again (as Dewey will devote his life to arguing) the value of public education in creating a sense of "social solidity" (8:361), a solidarity that in France translates into an agreeable social life. "If there is one need more crying than another," he says, "it is the need of the English middle class to be rescued from a defective type of religion, a narrow range of intellect and knowledge, a stunted sense of beauty, a low standard of manners. And what could do so much to deliver them and to render them happier, as to give them proper education, public education, to bring them up on the first plane; to make them a class homogeneous, intelligent, civilised?" (369).

In the great essay **"Equality"** (a remarkable act of confrontation on Arnold's part, since his first audience was the Royal Institute, "'the most aristocratic and exclusive place out'" [***CPW,*** 8:283]), Arnold attributes the lack of civilization in England to its "religion of inequality" (8:303). Civilization, "the humanisation of man in society," requires that we "make progress towards this, our true and full humanity" (286); but England, with its materialized upper class, its vulgarized middle class, and its brutalized working class, perpetuates a condition in which incivility rules. It is not by the widespread possession of material goods but "by the humanity of their manners that men are equal," Arnold contends. "'A man thinks to show himself my equal,'" says Goethe, "'by being *grob,*—that is to say, coarse and rude; he does not show himself my equal, he shows himself *grob.*' But a community having humane manners is a community of equals, and in such a community great social inequalities have really no meaning" (289). However, to attain a community of civility, there must be political equality. No one, Arnold daringly (and pragmatically) argues, has "natural rights"—neither peasant nor nobleman (285). Democratic France, thanks to its "spirit of society" (286), has produced an atmosphere in which people of all conditions feel a sense of companionship with, not alienation from, each other. And thus, Arnold notes (looking to the Liberals as they grapple with the Irish Question), the Alsatians *want* to be part of the affable French "social system," whereas "we offer to the Irish no such attraction" (291).

Acknowledging democracy to be the political power of the future, Arnold deplores the examples of the two classes who have hitherto held power: the aristocracy, incapable of ideas or an aesthetic sense ("They may imagine themselves to be in pursuit of beauty," he scoffs; "but how often, alas, does the pursuit come to little more than dabbling a little in what they are pleased to call art, and making a great deal of what they are pleased to call love!" (***CPW,*** 8:301]); the middle-class heirs to Puritanism, drugged with religion and business, not knowing, "good and earnest people as they were, that to the building up of human life there belong all those other powers also,—the power of intellect and knowledge, the power of beauty, the power of social life and manners" (294). In what is perhaps the most passionately argued of all his essays, Arnold charges "that we are trying to live on with a social organisation of which the day is over. Certainly equality will never of itself alone give us a perfect civilisation. But, with such inequality as ours, a perfect civilisation is impossible" (304). More than fifty years later, across the ocean, Dewey would make a case similar to Arnold's about the inefficacy of present-day (1935) liberalism, and would argue that it "must now become radical, meaning by 'radical' perception of the necessity of thoroughgoing changes in the set-up of institutions and corresponding activity to bring the changes to pass." And, for both writers, education is the "first object" of a "renascent liberalism," education's task being the encouragement of "the habits of mind and character, the intellectual and moral patterns, that are somewhere near even with the actual movements of events."[18] For the genuine "well-being of the many," as Arnold argues in **"Equality,"** "comes out more and more distinctly . . . as the object we must pursue" (289).

Arnold's pragmatism is, in some respects, more progressive-minded than William James's. On the subject of democracy, for example, James resembles Carlyle more than he does Arnold or Dewey. "If democracy is to be saved," James avowed in 1907, "it must catch the higher, healthier tone" that intellectuals trained in the humanities possess. The aim of the humanities, he says, is to teach stimulating "biographies"—to show what great men have achieved so that we may be provided with diverse "standards of the excellent and durable." History, for Carlyle (for whom democracy meant "despair of finding any Heroes to govern you"), was synonymous with biography, the biographies of heroes. James's Carlylean hero worship is evident in the essays "Great Men and Their Environment" and "The Importance of Individuals" (1880) and in his celebration of those who act, who practice the "strenuous mood," who break the rules, and who exert their free will in defiance of deterministic philosophies. Philosophy itself, James states in *A Pluralistic Universe* (1909), is not the expression of a man's "reasons" but of his "vision": "all definitions of the universe are but the deliberately adopted reactions of human characters upon it."[19]

James's strong individualistic streak—a compound of Emerson's self-reliance, Carlyle's hero worship, and Mill's libertarianism—is accompanied by an unidealized view of the masses. Arnold's disgusted reaction to the Hyde Park rioters of 1866 (a prime example of "doing as one likes," in ***Culture and Anarchy***) pales in comparison to James's reaction to demos in action, whether illustrated in the imperialist war fever occasioned by the Spanish-American War or in the "lynching epidemic" that occurred in Massachusetts in 1903. James's tribute to the college-bred ("the only permanent presence that corresponds to the aristocracy in older countries") as a bulwark "in our democracy, where everything else is so shifting," is in keeping with his fear of that human "carnivore," the uncivilized multitude. In 1892 James urged teachers to "wean" students "from their native cruelty"; and in his outcry against the lynchings, he gives way to a Darwinian pessimism absent (perhaps to their loss) in Arnold or Dewey: "The average church-going Civilizee realizes, one may say, absolutely nothing of the deeper currents of human nature, or of the aboriginal capacity for murderous excitement which lies sleeping even in his own bosom. Religion, custom, law and education have been piling their pressure upon him for centuries mainly with the one intent that his homicidal potentialities should be kept under."[20]

Nearly two decades prior to these remarks, James took issue with Ernest Renan's virulently antidemocratic sentiments. While admitting his own "dislike" for the Commune (Arnold, in contrast, had sympathized with "that fixed resolve of the [French] working class to count for something and *live*"), James maintained that the new "Democratic religion which is invading the Western world" would probably provide for a "political or spiritual hero" to stand "firm till a new order built itself around him." In the *Talks to Teachers,* he described his "pluralistic or individualistic philosophy" as one whose "practical consequence . . . is the well-known democratic respect for the sacredness of individuality," that is to say (with a nod to Mill), "the outward tolerance of whatever is not itself intolerant." James renamed his philosophy on several occasions—calling it, variously, "pragmatism" (in lectures dedicated to Mill, "our leader were he alive today"), "meliorism," "pluralism," and "radical empiricism"; but in all its incarnations, he sought to balance a "personal and romantic view of life" with a scientific regard for the *"facts of experience."* Dewey perhaps intended to minimize the confusions occasioned by such a balancing act when he described James as being "possessed of the spirit of the artist." One need not be too critical of a thinker who "sees the functions of the mind in terms of drama, and records his insights as though he were writing for the theatre." But Dewey recognized that if James veered toward singularity at times—a kind of romantic-aesthetic waywardness—he also aimed at making artists of his auditors and readers. Paradoxically, the Carlylean individualist promoted a "radical liberalism," a "philosophy which invites each man to create his own future world."[21]

In the lectures on *Pragmatism* James elaborates on the "creative" aspect of "cognitive" life. "The world stands really malleable," he declares, "waiting to receive its final touches at our hands" (*P,* 167). Truth, hence, is not something we find, but something we make and test: "Truth *happens* to an idea. It *becomes* true, is *made* true by events" (133). It is for remarks of this sort that Rorty has celebrated Jamesian pragmatism for having rejected all truths or values existing prior to the self (truths of science, religion, or "Philosophy") or pertaining to the self—for having promulgated the modernist "sense that there is nothing deep down inside us except what we have put there ourselves, no criterion that we have not created in the course of creating a practice, no standard of rationality that is not an appeal to such a criterion, no rigorous argumentation that is not obedience to our own conventions." What we are left with, thus, is a "post-Philosophical culture—in which men and women [feel] themselves alone, merely finite, with no links to something Beyond."[22] But Rorty's reading ignores the way in which James's pragmatism, like Arnold's, contains a wistful dialogue between the finite and the "Beyond"; it ignores the ways in which James is very much a man of his time, the late Victorian period, and in some respects even behind his time.

Born only twenty years after Arnold (in 1842), James found himself caught in the same dilemma as other Victorians, having seen the grounds for belief eroded by scientific discoveries and yet clinging to a "will to believe." James's pragmatism puts itself forward as a "solution" to those who want *both* "the scientific loyalty to facts . . . , but also the old confidence in human values and the resultant spontaneity, whether of the religious or of the romantic type" (*P,* 33, 26). Hence, F. C. S. Schiller, James's English disciple (who preferred the name "humanism" to "pragmatism"), speaks of the "middle path" this philosophy offers between naturalism and idealism: "it will neither reject ideals because they are not realised, nor yet despise the actual because it can conceive ideals."[23] To a considerable degree, James is updating Carlyle's own "solution," his "Natural Supernaturalism," which redirects human attention to this world and this time sphere. James's focus on the finite and the temporal restates Carlyle's view (expressed as early as 1831, in "Characteristics") that we are "beings that exist in Time, by virtue of Time, and are made of Time." One might call James's philosophy a version of the Goethean idea, translated and preached by Carlyle in *Sartor Resartus,* "that your 'America is here or nowhere.' . . . Yes here, in this poor, miserable, hampered, despicable Actual, wherein thou even now standest, here or nowhere is thy Ideal."[24] James correctly labels pragmatism "a new name for some old ways of thinking" (empiricist methods, in his case, that extend back to Socrates and Aristotle), but he also sees his efforts as part of a "new dawn" in which the acceptance of our finitude allows us to decide what we are going to make of ourselves and our world (*P,* 45, 18, 86). "I am finite once for all," he affirms in *A Pluralistic Universe,* "and all the categories of my sympathy are knit up with the finite world *as such,* and with things that have a history" (*APU,* 48). Yet it is a characteristic of our historical natures to reach beyond ourselves, James avows—not to a Deweyan sense of community but toward God. Using his pragmatic argument that whatever "works satisfactorily in the widest sense of the word" is "true," James is able to accept the divine hypothesis as one that "certainly does work" (192).

Gerald Myers has compellingly argued that James's "pragmatism was developed to make room for faith."[25] Indeed, if "democracy" is the thread in Dewey's writings and "culture" in Arnold's, then, "religion" is the omnipresent theme in James. "The most interesting and valuable things about a man," James proclaims, "are his ideals and over-beliefs" (*WB,* xiii). In this respect, James is echoing Arnold's view, in his religious writings, that "the chief exercise of [mankind's] higher thought and emotion which they have, is their religion" (***CPW,*** 7:117); and James would scarcely dispute Arnold's sense that "the chief guide and stay of conduct, so far as it has any at all, is their religion" (117). Given his sense of humanity as "carnivores," James might appear to be adopting a utilitarian defense of religion as an instrument of control. But that is by no means the intention of the essays that make up *The Will to Believe* (1897) or of the lectures that pay tribute to *The Varieties of Religious Experience* (1902). His idol Mill had modified his position on the "utility of religion": having argued in the 1850s that "those great effects on human conduct, which are commonly ascribed to motives derived directly from religion, have mostly for their proximate cause the influence of human opinion," Mill suggested, two decades later in "Theism," that the "hope" born of religion might well promote a sense of fellow-feeling and duty in believers.[26] Mill's view (startling to his fellow Liberals, for whom, as Arnold complained, "religion is a noxious thing . . . that . . . must die out" [***CPW,*** 7:117]), which denies certainty to both believer and atheist, is James's starting point in *The Will to Believe* volume. But James quickly makes it clear that what Mill condoned, and Arnold praised, as an aid to mankind's social well-being, was for himself the most *personal* of concerns.

In the Preface to *The Will to Believe,* James agrees, with Arnold, that most men lack a sense of Hellenism ("criticism") rather than a sense of Hebraism ("faith"), but the "academic audiences" he is addressing (and of which he is a member), "fed already on science, have a very different need" (*WB,* x). For such people, "criticism" is not what is wanted; and, for James in particular, the Hellenizing that Arnold brought to bear on the Bible is inadequate in certain respects. Where Arnold, for example, treats *Aberglaube* (the belief in miracles or immortality) as "a kind of fairy-tale," part of the Bible's "poetry" but not something subject to scientific verification (***CPW,*** 6:212), James accepts this "extra-belief." He calls it "over-belief" in *The Varieties of Religious Experience,* and affirms that this "over-belief on which [he is] ready to make his personal venture" persuades him that "divine facts . . . exist."[27] Preeminent among these divine facts is God Himself; and here James rejects Arnold's abstract definition in *God and the Bible.* James wants "A power not ourselves, . . . which not only makes for righteousness, but means it, and which recognizes us" (*WB,* 122), a personal God, in short. In *A Pluralistic Universe,* James concedes "that the only God worthy of the name *must* be finite" (125) if human beings are to exert their freedom of will (an article of faith to Jamesian pragmatism). Elsewhere, James maintains, "The gods we stand by are the gods we need and can use, the gods whose demands on us are reinforcements of our demands on ourselves and on one another" (*VRE,* 264). Yet James wants to be true to the "unseen world" no less than to the "seen world" (295).

A guiding principle of the French critics admired by Arnold was "ne pas être dupe." James, by advocating the "right to believe" (the title he claims he should have given his famous essay), contends "that worse things than being duped may happen to a man in this world" (*WB,* 19). In an early essay on Renan (1876), James criticized the "dandified despair" flaunted by this favorite of his brother Henry and of Arnold; and his subsequent references to Renan are startling in their ferocity.[28] In *Varieties,* he assaults Renan's "Who cares?" attitude, the French critic's willingness to treat life as an ironic spectacle rather than a strenuous activity (46-47). "The name of Renan," he later notes, "would doubtless occur to many persons as an example of the way in which breadth of knowledge may make one only a dilettante in possibilities, and blunt the acuteness of one's living faith" (380). In "The Dilemma of Determinism," James assails this Renanian attitude as "subjectivism," a spectator's view of life that inevitably degenerates into "the corruptest curiosity," and whose worst sin is "ethical indifference" (*WB,* 170-71). Condemning the "romanticism" of Renan and his aesthetic kind, James invokes Carlyle to say for him, "Hang your sensibilities!" But if the Carlylean message is one Arnold would support ("It says conduct, and not sensibility, is the ultimate fact for our recognition" [174]), James implicates Arnoldian culture, in debased form, among his villains: "if the stupid virtues of the philistine herd do not then come in and save society from the influence of the children of the light," he snarls, "a sort of inward putrefaction becomes its inevitable doom" (172).

The James who pits Carlyle against Renan is not an author one might expect to appeal to another connoisseur of "irony," Richard Rorty. And Rorty is indeed uncomfortable with the James who writes (defying Rorty's antifoundationalism), "If this life be not a real fight in which something is eternally gained for the universe by success, it is no better than a game of private theatricals, from which we may withdraw at will." Rorty has written movingly of the pragmatist enterprise as a matter of "our loyalty to other human beings clinging together against the dark, not our hope of getting things right,"[29] yet he has also praised the Renanian aesthetic antihumanists, Nietzsche and Foucault, who mock such presumptions of solidarity. For James, our ethics and our sanity depend upon our having a something Out-there "which recognizes us." Never mind, he argues, the possibility that we may be duped: "The universe is no longer a mere *It* to us, but a *Thou,* if we are religious" (*WB,* 27). Despite Nietzsche's scorn for saintliness (an attitude James finds "itself sickly enough" [*VRE,* 295]), James compares the visions of saints to "Utopian dreams of social justice" (dreams like those Arnold found in George Sand) that "help to break the edge of the general reign of hardness and are slow leavens of a better order" (*VRE,* 285). In the conclusion to *Varieties,* James asserts that "we belong to" a region beyond self (call it "the mystical region, or the supernatural region") "in a more intimate sense than that in which we belong to the visible world, for we belong in the most intimate sense wherever our ideals belong" (399). In the last resort, he avows, we belong to the supreme "other," to whom James gives the name of God: "We and God have business with each other; and in opening ourselves to his influence our deepest destiny is fulfilled" (399).

James's pragmatist ethics requires a religious sphere, as well as a Carlylean work ethic, to draw mankind out of its isolation and potential murderousness. The melancholy tone of much of Arnold's poetry—the sense, that so haunted Dewey, that "We mortal millions live *alone*"—finds expression in the famous description, in James's *Principles of Psychology,* of the "stream of consciousness": "Absolute insulation, irreducible pluralism, is the law." What the scientist in James and the poet in Arnold had deduced required a counterweight: religion for James, culture for Arnold. For both, what the facts of "experience" reveal, the values emanating from something that transcends the self must counteract. In James's case, science may speak in support of determinism, but "ethics makes a counter-claim" to the effect that "our wills are 'free.'"[30] Comparing Arnold and James, one notes this paradox: while the stoical Englishman trusts to the future (what else is culture but an ideal guiding us forward?), the optimistic American instinctively retreats to the emotional position of a Carlyle or to the Tennyson of *In Memoriam,* who answers the voice of scientific determinism with a confident "I have felt." Whereas the melancholy poet in Arnold gave way to the critic speaking of social solidarity, the scientist in James inevitably bowed to the "personal and romantic" voice. Perhaps even more so than his brother or Arnold, William James was indeed "possessed by the spirit of the artist."

Of Rorty, too, it has been said that he writes with "A Touch of the Poet." One might describe Rorty's career to date as an attempt to redefine philosophy along the lines of romantic poetics, which Rorty sees as the progenitor of pragmatism. In an era when many English professors routinely profess their distaste for "literature"—seeing it as an agent of hegemonic forces, or else essaying to deconstruct its authorial pretensions—it is touching to find a philosopher who praises the power of literature so unstintingly and who draws on credos of literary modernism (such as "Make it new") that have become virtually threadbare through overuse. Lacking James's Victorian confidence in the seriousness of "this life," Rorty has occasionally taken refuge in an ironic posture (he calls it "light-minded aestheticism") that resembles Arnold's notorious "vivacity." Both have been criticized accordingly.[31] One thinks of the famous Max Beerbohm cartoon of Arnold being addressed by his earnest niece (the future novelist Mary Augusta Ward), "Why, Uncle Matthew, Oh why, will not you be always serious?" Arnold's reply ("My vivacity is but the last sparkle of flame before we are all in the dark, the last glimpse of colour before we all go into drab,—the drab of the earnest, prosaic, practical, austerely literal future" [***CPW,*** 3:287]) is prelude to Rorty's apologia in "The Priority of Democracy." Here he claims that his aim of "joshing" his "fellow citizens . . . out of the habit of taking these [traditional philosophical] topics so seriously" is not without a "moral purpose."[32]

Arnold's targets were the enemies of enlightenment, the latter-day Philistines; and his goal, as he told his mother, was to do "what will sap them intellectually." But where Arnold saw Protestant Dissent, with its opposition to culture and state-run education, as the leading obstacle standing in the way of England's necessary transformation, Rorty initially saw "Philosophy," with its pretensions of having discovered universal truth, as the first obstacle to be cleared away. At most, according to Rorty, philosophers can provide an edifying conversation for the benefit of the *Zeitgeist.* Rorty's recent criticism of neo-Marxist ideologues resembles Arnold's criticism of the Dissenters—both groups sharing a naive faith in the truth of dogma; both incapable of appreciating beauty or art, but seeing them only as forms of "ideology." (Interestingly, Rorty, like Arnold, wrote poetry in his youth.) Attracted initially to the fashionably antifoundationalist views of Wittgenstein and Heidegger, Rorty soon realized that his closest affinity was to the unfashionable Dewey, whose hope had been "that philosophy will join with poetry as Arnold's 'criticism of life.'"[33]

As Rorty's enthusiasm for Heidegger has ebbed, his enthusiasm for Dewey has intensified. "What seems to me most worth preserving in Dewey's work," Rorty has recently affirmed, "is his sense of the gradual change in human beings' self-image which has taken place in recorded history—the change from a sense of their dependence upon something antecedently present to a sense of the utopian possibilities of the future, the growth of their ability to mitigate their finitude by a talent for self-creation." Beginning with *Philosophy and the Mirror of Nature* (1979), Rorty has praised Dewey's democratic vision: "in his ideal society, culture is no longer dominated by the ideal of objective cognition but by that of aesthetic enhancement."[34] Rorty's first book also draws on Gadamer's preference for "edifying" philosophy over "systematic" philosophy (a preference shared by Arnold), and he invokes Gadamer's substitution of "the notion of *Bildung* (education, self-formation) for that of 'knowledge' as the goal of thinking." However, this crucial German term, so important to Arnold's sense of culture and Gadamer's sense of the humanities (a term, for both of them, *linked* to knowledge), is translated by Rorty to mean "edification," a term that departs from Gadamerian hermeneutics to include personal projects that may be poetically "edifying" without being socially "constructive." And here one can see a source of tension between Rorty's Deweyan allegiance and his romantic-aesthetic predilections. Dewey, after all, sought to break down dualisms—as Arnold implicitly did when he defined knowledge in terms of practice, Hebraism in terms of Hellenism—particularly the dichotomy between self and society. For Rorty, aesthetic delight in the workings of the self (a mixture of Hellenism, Emersonian self-reliance, Germanic *Bildung,* and Bloomian genius-worship) coexists with, but does not necessarily interpenetrate his liberal Deweyan faith in the advancement of the community. For art, as Rorty realizes (to the dismay of the ideologues), does not necessarily serve the people. Like the poetic (but not the critical) Arnold, Rorty sees finite man as inescapably isolated—detached from anything "out there." Perhaps with Arnold's reversal of attitude in mind, Rorty contends, in *Consequences of Pragmatism* (1982) that there is *no* "something, not ourselves, which makes for rigor." "Both the Age of Faith and the Enlightenment seem beyond recovery." The modern self must give up any pretense of seeing "things steadily and [seeing] them whole," he says, and instead must "take a nominalistic, ironic view of oneself."[35]

Rorty's rejection of a humanistic hermeneutics in favor of aesthetic pragmatism has social and ethical "consequences," as he makes clear in his second book. Discussing the transformation of "Nineteenth-Century Idealism" into "Twentieth-Century Textualism," he traces the establishment of a romantically imbued cultural criticism (a critical dynasty extending from Coleridge to Arnold to Trilling) that uses literature to fill up the space left by the disappearance of metaphysical certainties. But humanistic "culture," for all its benign intent, lacks a unifying center; and the inevitable result of literature's displacement of religious or Enlightenment certainties has been the emergence of the private vocabularies of a Nietzsche or Foucault. The "strong" modernist textualist (admired by Harold Bloom) becomes, thus, for Rorty a heroic pragmatist whose goal is to cultivate novelty, privacy, and sometimes (in the case of Nietzsche and Foucault) contempt for humanity—all contrary to the ideal of the Arnoldian culture-critic. (In *Twilight of the Idols,* Nietzsche expressed contempt for the spread of higher education, what he called the "democratism of *Bildung.*") "The stimulus to the intellectual's private moral imagination provided by his strong misreadings [the inevitable consequence of making things new], by his search for sacred wisdom," Rorty observes, "is purchased at the price of his separation from his fellow-humans." It is to Rorty's credit that he does not minimize the "moral cost" of the Nietzschean-Foucauldian enterprise; yet, as a believer in democracy, Rorty champions a democratic society "in which there is room for subjectivity and self-involvement, room for the kind of private spiritual development that politically irrelevant philosophers and novelists help us to achieve." Rorty's reverence for creative genius resembles James's infatuation with heroism; but Rorty's democratic principles temper his wilder romantic flights. For just as Rorty is almost unique among academics in his faith in literature, he is also unique in his refusal to hate the democratic society that allows such creativity and self-creation to flourish.[36]

Dewey figures in Rorty's pantheon as a liberal who championed solidarity and aesthetic self-creation, but who was perhaps too idealistic to see a potential conflict between the two aims, who saw them rather as interdependent. In the nineteenth century, Mill had similarly proposed a marriage of Coleridgean and Benthamite "half-truths," an alliance of romantic ethics (true for all time) with a liberal faith in progress (the *Zeitgeist* at work). For Rorty, liberalism and romanticism make for necessary, if sometimes unwilling, bedfellows; and in place of Coleridge and Bentham, he offers us Foucault and Habermas, the former "an ironist who is unwilling to be a liberal," the latter "a liberal who is unwilling to be an ironist." By embracing both figures, Rorty concedes that Foucault may provide "a very bad model for a society," yet he deserves a "poet's privileges." For it is incumbent upon liberal democrats that they support a society in which all voices are heard: "The point of a liberal society is not to invent or create anything, but simply to make it as easy as possible for people to achieve their wildly different private ends without hurting each other." (Elsewhere, he notes the usefulness of Foucault's work.)[37] Rorty's most unsatisfactory book, *Contingency, Irony, and Solidarity* (1989), speaks in behalf of private and public vocabularies, the Foucauldian language of ironic detachment and the Habermasian language of communitarian goals. But having jettisoned, in his early writings, any reason why we should sustain *either* vocabulary, let alone both, he can offer little more here than his personal vision of a "liberal utopia" in which "we ironists" cultivate private gardens while, at the same time, the social-minded dream of a "solidarity" that remains little more than a dream. Rorty's utopia contains an ivory tower for the ironists, plus a stable of writers below who produce edifying novels to sensitize the "nonintellectual" masses. Having reduced all intellectual positions to fictions alone, Rorty has no way to justify the value of his own distinctive fiction, his utopian vision.[38]

In recent years, perhaps in response to the charge of aesthetic detachment, Rorty has strenuously demonstrated his liberal allegiances, often in defiance of the pervasive antiliberalism coming from left and right. He has also spoken in favor of the cultural canon, again in defiance of academic trendiness. "One good reason for having a high culture," he maintains, in support of E. D. Hirsch, Jr.'s defense of a communal heritage, "is to provide an alternative set of fantasies to those current in mass culture"—fantasies that serve as "stimuli to social change." Like Arnold assailing his fellow-liberals for their lack of vision, Rorty has criticized the new left for clinging to an outmoded set of dogmas and for regarding itself as "a saving remnant which despises its opponents too much to argue with them." In *Objectivity, Relativism, and Truth* (1991), he attacks the ideologues within the American academy who preach hatred against the democratic society that supports them, and he criticizes the "Foucauldian left" for "its failure to offer such visions and such suggestions" for change as the Deweyan liberals once did. Only a democratically based culture, he argues (as did Dewey and Arnold), offers room for hope, room for change: "if there is social hope," he affirms, "it lies in the imagination—in people [like Dewey and Roberto Unger] describing a future in terms which the past did not use."[39]

"The School of Resentment," Rorty wittily observes, "made up of people who can single-handedly deconstruct a large social theory faster than a Third World village can construct a small elementary school, does not take kindly to romance." It prefers a "fruitless exercise in nostalgia" (Marxism) to the Deweyan faith in liberal democracy with its hope for the future. And yet, Rorty notes elsewhere, Dewey's philosophy of education does provide a vision and a method that have enabled society to move forward. At times Rorty's disdain for the past exceeds Dewey's own disdain. ("We think that Dewey and Weber absorbed everything useful Plato and Aristotle had to teach, and got rid of the residue.")[40] But because Dewey felt that certain "traditions of the past" stood in the way of progress, he was willing to accept a certain "spiritual impoverishment" in exchange for his pragmatist faith "that the world is recommencing and being remade under our eyes." "For the past as past is gone," Dewey declares in *Liberalism and Social Action* (1935), "save for aesthetic enjoyment and refreshment, while the present is with us. Knowledge of the past is significant only as it deepens and extends our understanding of the present." Such Deweyan disregard for the past might seem to mark a considerable gap between Dewey and Arnold, the former fixated (as Santayana complained) on the "foreground,"[41] the latter supposedly enmeshed (in the eyes of detractors) in a flimsy web called "culture." But many of Dewey's views are extensions or restatements of Arnoldian ideas, especially Arnold's views on education, culture, and democracy. The two men shared a common task as liberals and educators, and they shared a common faith in the efficacy of a democratic culture that included (or came to include, in Dewey's case) the fruits of science, religion, and art. For the remainder of the chapter, hence, I will be focusing on the Arnoldian side of Dewey, while underscoring, at the same time, Arnold's pragmatic side.

With regard to the past, Arnold is by no means animated by the nostalgia of Newman or Carlyle. "The past in itself has no attraction for him." Peter Keating observes; "it is only in so far as the past illuminates, guides, or acts in any way as a model for the present, that he speaks with approval of its study." Hence, Arnold looks for the "modern element" in past history (and literature), and he accuses liberals and Dissenters of failing to follow the spirit of the time. Dewey, too, takes a pragmatic view of the past. "We live," he writes, ". . . in a haphazard mixture of a museum and a laboratory. Now it is certain that we cannot get rid of the laboratory and its consequences, and we cannot by a gesture of dismissal relegate the museum and its specimens to the void. There is the problem of selection, of choice, of discrimination. What are the things of the past that are relevant to our own lives and how shall they be reshaped to be of use?"[42] What, in other words (to rephrase Arnold's question to Clough), can the past *do* for us, and what can we, thus edified, do for the future?

Dewey was born in the year of Mill's *On Liberty* and Darwin's *The Origin of Species* (1859)—the year also of Arnold's first inspection of the superior state-run schools on the Continent—and he quickly found himself in the position of Arnold's pilgrim, "wandering between two worlds." Although Dewey claimed that the loss of his religious beliefs did not affect his philosophic views, he nevertheless admitted to having undergone a "trying personal crisis." From his college days, he retained a strong residue of Hegelian idealism, allied with what he later called the Hegelian "glorification of the here and now."[43] Very early on, Dewey found in science one of the "articles" that constituted his "creed of life." Like Arnold (as well as like William and Henry James), the young Dewey was fascinated by the example of Renan, the seminarian turned science-lover turned ironic aesthete. For Dewey, Renan was fully justified in having put his faith in science: the youthful French author of *The Future of Science* (*L'Avenir de la science*) had seen that, thanks to the French Revolution, ideals were set forth in "practice [in Dewey's words]; knowledge into action." The "development of science" had allowed for that legacy of the Revolution that Arnold praised in **"The Function of Criticism at the Present Time"**: it put "intelligence," for the first time, in the controls.[44]

Despite Dewey's disagreement with Arnold over the superiority of a scientific to a literary education, it should be noted here that in Dewey's earliest descriptions of the scientific method, science plays a role analogous to Arnold's "criticism" (a term Arnold himself partly owed to Renan). Indeed, for Dewey the terms *science, intelligence,* and *criticism* are often interchangeable. As Robert B. Westbrook notes, Dewey regarded science as "a strictly *methodological* conception. . . . The scientific attitude of mind, he said, was apparent whenever beliefs were not simply taken for granted but established as the conclusions of critical inquiry and testing." Arnold's description of criticism as "a free play of the mind on all subjects" (***CPW,*** 3:270) suits the experimental role of the Deweyan scientist no less than the (Henry) Jamesian literary critic. In the late essay "Construction and Criticism" (1930), Dewey restates Arnold's thesis of the necessary connection between criticism and creation ("Critical judgment is . . . not the enemy of creative production but its friend and ally"), and he defines criticism as a universal task whereby we discover how much our beliefs are still "validated and verified in present need, opportunity, and application."[45]

In "Science as Subject-Matter and as Method" (1909), Dewey does take issue with what he interprets to be Arnold's underestimation of a scientific education. (Although Dewey often defers to Arnold, here he sides with Arnold's friendly opponent, T. H. Huxley.) "Without ignoring in the least the consolation that has come to men from their literary education," Dewey argues, "I would even go so far as to say that only the gradual replacing of a literary by a scientific education can assure to man the progressive amelioration of our lot. Unless we master things, we shall continue to be mastered by them; the magic that words cast upon things may indeed disguise our subjection or render us less distinguished with it, but after all science, not words, casts the only compelling spell upon things." That philosophy or criticism should be (in Wittgenstein's memorable phrase) "a battle against the bewitchment of our intelligence by means of language"[46] was an idea shared by Arnold and Dewey. But the notion that science provided the only key to a more humane future was doubted by Arnold. In ***Friendship's Garland,*** Arnold humorously notes how the well-intending utilitarian "educational creed" of "Archimedes Silverpump, Ph.D" ("We must be men of our age. . . . Useful knowledge, living languages, and the forming of the mind through observation and experiment"), becomes perverted into the illiberal views of Silverpump's pupil, the businessman Bottles: "Original man, Silverpump! fine mind! fine system! None of your antiquated rubbish—all practical work—latest discoveries in science—mind constantly kept excited—lots of interesting experiments—lights of all colours—fizz! fizz! bang! bang! That's what I call forming a man" (***CPW,*** 5:70-71). Without disputing the importance of science (he invokes science in his religious writings),

Arnold foresaw the possibility that the language of science might become yet another bewitching jargon. At its best, however, science, by liberating mankind from past errors, cleared the way so that "the value of humane letters, and of art also," might "be felt and acknowledged, and their place in education be secured" (10:68-69).

As Dewey gradually came to see the importance of art and religion—and as the twentieth century gave increasing evidence of the potential misuse of science—he qualified some of his earlier scientific optimism. But just as Arnold saw in culture the means of prodding his countrymen toward the future, Dewey saw in the scientific method the means of encouraging us to deal with a universe not "closed" but rather "infinite in space and time, having no limits here or there," a world capable of being transformed by our own efforts and intelligence. Science, he argues in *The Quest for Certainty* (1929), allows us to become artists, working on the inexhaustible "material" afforded by nature (*QC,* 100). Here too, Renan may have affected the young Dewey by having developed a principle of "evolution" (a decade before Darwin's *Origins*) as the law for individuals and society alike. "'Each individual travels in his turn,'" Dewey in 1890 quotes from Renan's early work, "'along the line which the whole of mankind has followed, and the series of the development of human reason is parallel to the progress of individual reason.'" To a professional educator, this was a pregnant idea indeed; and by 1893 Dewey was praising "Self-Realization as the Moral Ideal," arguing that the unending activity of education is not a means but "an end in itself."[47] ("There is nothing which a scientific mind would more regret," Dewey says in *The Quest for Certainty,* "than reaching a condition in which there were no more problems" [101].) In practice, Dewey is drawing upon Arnold's activist sense of culture as continuous *Bildung*. For if the author of ***Culture and Anarchy*** described the sense of "a growing and a becoming [as] the characteristic of perfection as culture conceives it," he also noted that the aim of culture is to beget "a dissatisfaction" with the status quo "which is of the highest value in stemming the common tide of men's thoughts in a wealthy and industrial society" (***CPW,*** 5:94, 98).

Only in a democracy, Dewey felt, could the principles of *Bildung* be applied to everyone. But while he defined "Culture and Culture Values" in the Germanic-Arnoldian sense of their aiding the individual expansion of one's talents, Dewey also adopted Arnold's sense of culture as something that prepares the individual for society. (He questions Arnold's "humanistic notion, . . . not in its end, but in its exclusive reliance upon literature and history as means of reaching this end"—missing Arnold's repeated inclusion of science among the ingredient of culture.) "From the broader point of view," Dewey states, "culture may be defined as the habit of mind which perceives and estimates all matters with reference to their bearing on social values and aims." In one of his most suggestive phrases, Arnold calls "education . . . the road to culture";[48] and in one of his last works, a **"Special Report"** on Continental **"Elementary Education"** (1886), based on a recent inspection tour, he praises the humanities-centered schools abroad for *humanizing* their students. The fault of English elementary education, he complains, is "that it is so little formative; it gives the children the power to read the newspapers, to write a letter, to cast accounts, and gives them a certain number of pieces of knowledge, but it does little to touch their nature for good and to mould them." Why shouldn't *all* English children, Arnold asks, have the right (hitherto reserved for the privileged classes) to a "fuller cultivation of taste and feeling?" (***CPW,*** 11:28).

Dewey's philosophy of education expands upon three basic Arnoldian premises: that in a democracy all students should have access to the best, that critical thinking should be encouraged, and that education should instill a sense of social solidarity. "Education must have a tendency, if it is education, to form attitudes," he asserted in 1936. But "The tendency to form attitudes which will express themselves in intelligent social action is something very different from indoctrination"; education consists, for Dewey, in learning not what to think, but rather in learning to think critically and to think as part of a social dialogue. In response to Walter Lipmann and others who felt (in the 1920s) that democracy had failed to create an enlightened, responsible public, Dewey argued that it was education's task to do just this. "We are born organic beings associated with others," he contends in *The Public and Its Problems* (1927), "but we are not born members of a community. The young have to be brought within the traditions, outlook and interests which characterize a community by means of education; by unremitting instruction and by learning in connection with the phenomena of overt association."[49] The fullest expression of Dewey's pedagogic views is found in *Democracy and Education* (1916); here, he combines Mill's sense of a progressive society as one that allows for "the play of diverse gifts and interests" with an Arnoldian sense of culture as something that encourages solidarity as well as free play of mind ("the capacity for constantly expanding the range and accuracy of one's perception of meanings") for everyone. In a brief account of "The Aims and Ideals of Education," Dewey in 1921 condensed the Arnoldian program into two goals: to transmit "the 'best of what has been thought and said'" and to work for the reformation of society.[50]

Arnold's views on education came out of his experience as inspector of schools and his fight with the Liberal Party's tendency to favor individual rights at the expense of communal responsibilities. He took issue, moreover, with the insensitivity of Liberal leaders like Robert Lowe, for whom public education was treated as little more than a means of training students to pass examinations (Lowe's policy of "payment by results") rather than a means of instructing them in the "power of reading." As a future-oriented liberal, Arnold deplored the negative strain of his party, which permitted, under the slogan of "doing as one likes," a widespread national neglect of minds and bodies. In his reports on English schools, Arnold called attention to the lack of "humanizing" instruction. Unlike "rich" children, who had opportunities to read good books outside of class, the working-class children Arnold inspected were at the mercy of "second or third-rate literature," which would remain henceforth their "principal literary standard"; they (and their middle-class counterparts) received an education that reflected the national obsession with "mechanical processes" at the expense of "intelligence." (Arnold cites, approvingly, Bishop Butler's comment, "Of education, . . . *information itself is really the least part.*") To those skeptical of his "high estimate of the value of poetry in education," Arnold retorts, pragmatically, "Good poetry does undoubtedly tend to form the soul and character; it tends to beget a love of beauty and of truth in alliance together, it suggests, however indirectly, high and noble principles of action, and it inspires the emotion so helpful in making principles operative."[51] In ***Culture and Anarchy,*** Arnold called for a rethinking of Liberal premises ("turning a stream of fresh and free thought upon our stock notions and habits" [***CPW,*** 5:233]) in order to promote an inward and social change. Instead of praising the fruits of industrialism (as Liberals tended to do), we should, he argues, be tending to the increase of education, thereby advancing common goals of "increased sweetness, increased light, increased life, increased sympathy" (5:109).

Arnold's political essays of the 1880s harp on the theme of Liberal irresponsibility. In **"The Future of Liberalism"** (1882), he derides the Liberal celebration of "heroes of industrial enterprise," who, in their hurry to make a fortune, "have not made the fortunes of the clusters of men and women whom they have called into being to produce for them" (***CPW,*** 9:146), and who have left behind a legacy of slums ("hell-holes") and widespread illiteracy. And he mourns the Liberal coddling of the badly educated middle class, with its "effusion and confusion," its lack of ideas and its addiction to empty phrases. (The natural human instinct for "beauty . . . , intellect and knowledge has been maltreated and starved; because the schools for this class, where it should have called forth and trained this instinct, are the worst of the kind anywhere" [9:147-48].) Elsewhere, Arnold laments the English mistreatment of Ireland and the specious (as he sees it) Liberal support for Home Rule as a way of ensuring continued Irish misery. If in the early lectures on Celtic literature Arnold had highlighted the indispensible Celtic components of the English imagination, in his later writings he was incapable of imagining a political disjunction of the two countries that would not be harmful to both sides. Supporting political separatism, he felt, was equivalent to supporting the negative Liberal sense of human beings as detached atoms.

However questionable Arnold's views on Ireland may seem in hindsight, they are consistent with his sense of himself as a "Liberal of the future," one believing in solidarity within nations and codependency between nations. (He believed that Ireland and England were as codependent, and mutually supportive, as Alsace and France or Alabama and the Northern States.) Arnold held an organic view of society in which classes and individuals could rise above partisan interests "to the idea of the whole community" (Arnold's idealized "state" [***CPW,*** 5:134]). And so did Dewey, whose faith in democracy was sustained from the beginning by his sense "that men are not isolated non-social atoms, but are men only when in intrinsic relations to men."[52] Dewey's faith in democracy is Arnold's belief in culture writ large. If Dewey inherits Arnold's future-oriented liberalism, he does so, like Arnold, in revolt against the outmoded view of liberalism as the party of laissez-faire individualism. Democracy, like culture, provides for the liberation of creative energies; but, Dewey cautions, "Doing as one pleases signifies a release from truly *intellectual* initiative and independence, unless taste has been well developed as to *what* one pleases." And just as the school provides, in Dewey, the educational means for the development of taste (with the help of teachers who "guide the child," as Westbrook notes, "in the subject matter of science and history and art"), so too does the democratic community provide lessons in cooperation and interdependence. The future-oriented liberal, hence, is not one who is "jealous of every extension of governmental activity," but rather one "committed to the principle that organized society must use its powers to establish the conditions under which the mass of individuals can possess actual as distinct from merely legal liberty." But liberalism, according to Arnold and Dewey, must also wean the public and itself from the addiction to "claptrap" (Arnold's term), from the force of "party politics" wherein (in Dewey's phrase) "words not only take the place of realities but are themselves debauched." It is because of such debasement that Dewey looked to scientific "intelligence"—just as Arnold had appealed to "criticism"—to create a climate of "greater honesty and impartiality [Arnold's "disinterestedness"], even though these qualities be now corrupted by discussion carried on mainly for purposes of party supremacy and for imposition of some special but concealed interest."[53]

Rorty has characterized Dewey's educational philosophy as one "calculated to change the character of American institutions—to move society to the political left by moving successive generations of students to the left of their parents." But this is another way of saying that Dewey was a lifelong liberal, believing (with Arnold) in the promise of the future despite all the blunders of the present. Dewey himself maintained, in 1936, that the "new social ideals" implicit in his educational views were only "a new version of the very same ideals that inspired the Declaration of Independence," the ideals of democracy forever-renewing themselves, and those of liberty and equality finally being applied to all people. As liberals of the future, Dewey and Arnold saw that the real strength of liberal ideals remained to be tested. Both trusted to the idea of liberalism, despite the inevitable debasement of the term, and despite jeers from left and right alike at liberal pretensions.[54] They never lost sight of a liberal vision of society and its inhabitants in constant development, always moving toward the unreachable goal Arnold called "perfection." But liberalism also meant, for both, a communal ideal, a dream of associations of men and women (what John Rawls, the most recent defender of the liberal ideal, calls "the idea of overlapping consensus") forming common bonds, as Dewey says, "for the better realization of any form of experience which is augmented and confirmed by being shared." In the end, they invoke a sense of liberalism implicit in the word's original meaning: this is what Arnold's heir Lionel Trilling means when he calls the "job of criticism" a recalling of "liberalism to its first essential imagination of variousness and possibility"; and it is what Rawls means when he describes the ideal social union in terms of an orchestra whose various musicians need one another's complementary gifts in order to flourish individually. Like the Arnold of ***Essays in Criticism,*** with its appeal "To try and approach truth on one side after another" (***CPW,*** 3:286), Dewey in his eighties defined the liberal mission as the "quiet and patient pursuit of truth, marked by the will to learn from every quarter."[55]

What is obvious in even a brief examination of Dewey's and Arnold's views on education and liberalism is the fact that these terms run into each other, and that they keep ending up in Arnold's "culture" and in Dewey's "democracy." Their common mentor, here, is Emerson, whose concept of culture as something that combines the principles of *Bildung* (cultivation of the "best") with a corrective to human isolation anticipates both Arnold's culture and Dewey's democracy. "Culture," says Emerson, "is the suggestion, from certain best thoughts, that a man has a range of affinities through which he can modulate the violence of any master-tones that have a droning preponderance in his scale, and succor him against himself. Culture redresses his balance, puts him among his equals and superiors, revives the delicious sense of sympathy and warns him of the dangers of solitude and repulsion."[56] Arnold's culture and Dewey's democracy resemble each other because they are both processes and ideals, something to steer by and something to steer toward. As Dewey moved toward his own journey's end, he never lost his democratic faith, but, increasingly, he saw democracy as a cultural ideal that needed more than the stimulus supplied by science. By the 1920s, even as he rebutted Lipmann's critique of democracy, Dewey was replacing the pragmatic trust in "experience" with the larger term of *culture.* He realized, soon after its publication, that *Experience and Nature* (1925) should have been titled *Culture and Nature*—the term referring, he explained, to more than what Arnold and his followers meant by *culture:* "the whole body of beliefs, attitudes, dispositions which are scientific and 'moral'"; a world in which facts and values are no longer at odds and in which the "scientific" coexists with the "'ideal' (even the name 'spiritual,' if intelligibly used)."[57]

The later Dewey, hence, turns increasingly to the world of art and religion to extend the range of experience available in a democratic culture. And here his Arnoldian affinities cause him to adopt a rather different position from the one Rorty claims for Dewey—"following [in the unlikely company of Foucault and Derrida] through on Enlightenment secularization by, roughly, pragmatizing and demetaphysicizing culture." On the contrary, Dewey, as early as 1920, in *Reconstruction in Philosophy,* imagined a revival of "the religious spirit," set within the kingdom of the earth (this resembles Arnold's position in his religious writings) and inspiring a poetry and religion that arise out of hope, not fear. That the "old beliefs have dissolved" (*QC,* 71) Dewey knew no less than did the Arnold of **"The Study of Poetry"** ("not a creed which is not shaken, not an accredited dogma which is not shown to be questionable" [***CPW,*** 9:161]), but that does not prevent the desire for "standards, principles, rules." Like Arnold, he redefines these standards as "hypotheses" that are endlessly "tested and confirmed—and altered," losing "all pretence of finality—the ultimate source of dogmatism" (*QC,* 277). In *Reconstruction* Dewey updates Arnold's appeal to "criticism," calling for a new "poetry and religious feeling," born of the union between "science and emotion" that has been facilitated by a new, clearsighted "philosophy."[58]

Arnold's massive attempt at Hellenizing the Bible led him to the conclusion that, in spite of the efforts of "modern liberalism," people "cannot do without" religion, even as "they cannot do with it as it is." In wanting the joy provided by religious faith, they "are on firm ground of experience" (***CPW,*** 7:378-81). Mill came round to this position (which William James never lacked), and eventually, in his own way, so did Dewey. In *Human Nature and Conduct* (1922) Dewey questions Arnold's habit of treating cognition and righteous action, Hellenism and Hebraism, as separate faculties. (In the conclusion to ***Literature and Dogma,*** Arnold, somewhat disingenuously, claimed that "In praising culture, we have never denied that conduct, not culture, is three-fourths of human life" [***CPW,*** 6:407].) "Potentially," Dewey retorts, "conduct is one hundred per cent of our acts." In *A Common Faith* (1934), his Jamesian defense of the religious impulse (as opposed to organized religion), Dewey again challenges the Arnoldian "opposition between Hellenism and Hebraism," not realizing that Arnold himself had implicitly been arguing all along that knowledge and action, the love of truth and beauty and right conduct, are interlinked. Arnold was pleased by the popular success of these rhetorical terms, and while he spoke of their being a "distinction on which more and more will turn,"[59] he nevertheless did not doubt "the old and true Socratic thesis of the interdependence of virtue and knowledge" (8:162). For, as Dewey argues, "Intelligence becomes ours in the degree in which we use it and accept responsibility for consequences" (*HNC,* 314). But humanity requires "symbols" to draw forth their "reverences, affections, and loyalties," and perhaps the most potent symbol of the "communal sense" (330) is that which finds expression in the religious impulse.[60]

As much as Dewey would have liked for the democratic community to constitute the only needful source of faith, and as much as he might have wished for science to provide the only earthbound hypotheses, he was obliged to recognize, in *A Common Faith,* the psychological need for a belief that links the real world and the ideal. "I should describe this faith," he offers, "as the unification of the self through allegiance to inclusive ideal ends, which imagination presents to us and to which the human will responds as worthy of controlling our desires and choices" (*ACF*, 33). "In a distracted age," there is a particular need for an "*active* relation between ideal and actual to which [Dewey gives] the name 'God'" (51), and such a name "may protect man from a sense of isolation and from consequent despair or defiance" (53). In the end, however, Dewey's own faith is in the union of knowledge and conduct that (like Arnold in the ***Mixed Essays***) he calls "civilization." "The things in civilization we most prize," he says, "are not of ourselves. They exist by grace of the doings and sufferings of the continuous human community in which we are a link. Ours is the responsibility of conserving, transmitting, rectifying and expanding the heritage of values we have received that those who come after us may receive it more solid and secure, more widely accessible and more generously shared than we have received it" (87).

In *Art as Experience* (1934) the Arnoldian faith in the humanizing power of civilization reaches its Deweyan climax. Here, the man accused by Lewis Mumford of having no aesthetic sense, no appreciation of the imagination, writes knowingly, and sometimes eloquently of art as the consummate human "experience." Dewey describes art's capacity to imagine a better world as the consummate "criticism of life." (The book's wealth of citations reveals that Dewey, in 1934, was as familiar with Cezanne, van Gogh, and Matisse as he was with Goethe, Johnson, Keats, Shelley, George Eliot, Tolstoy, Pater—and, of course, Arnold.) Arnold's "dictum that poetry is criticism of life" is true, Dewey contends, because art imagines "possibilities that contrast with actual conditions. A sense of possibilities that are unrealized and that might be realized are when they are put in contrast with actual conditions, the most penetrating 'criticism' of the latter that can be made." Moreover, in a world in which "mortal millions live *alone*," "works of art are the only media of complete and unhindered communication between man and man that can occur in a world full of gulfs and walls that limit community and experience."[61] There are other (and nonpragmatic) ways to describe and defend artistic experience, but Dewey here provides perhaps the fullest answer to the Arnoldian query, "What does it *do* for you?"

In stressing areas where Arnold and Dewey have shared interests, I have underplayed their differences in taste and sensibility. Arnold makes more of the internal dimension of culture and education than does Dewey, although both ultimately agree on the social ends of these two forces. And even though his aesthetic sensibility is less refined and more utilitarian than, say, Pater's or Henry James's, Arnold had a far deeper awareness than Dewey of the qualitative nature of beauty and art (of poetry's "natural magic," for example [***CPW***, 3:33]). In the essay on Wordsworth, Arnold faults those who prize the "philosophy" over the "poetry" (9:48). Still, Arnold and Dewey were critics active in the public arena, fighting in behalf of a liberal society that they saw beckoning in the future. "That promised land it will not be ours to enter," Arnold realized; ". . . but to have desired to enter it, to have saluted it from afar, is already, perhaps, the best distinction among contemporaries" (3:285). Opposing (like Falkland) "the inadequate ideals dominant in their time," Arnold and Dewey "kept open their communications with the future, lived with the future."

All his life, Dewey sought a way for philosophy to bridge the gap between the old order and the new, between a feudal and a democratic world. In 1946 (Dewey's eighty-seventh year), with yet another terrible reminder of man's cruelty to man recently experienced, he once more cited Arnold in connection with the fate of humanity, "Wandering between two worlds, one dead, / The other powerless to be born." But he remained confident in the possibility of philosophy—a philosophy that transmuted Arnold's belief in civilization into his own faith in "creative democracy"—to project pragmatic ideals sufficient to "give intelligent direction to men in search for ways to make the world more one of worth and significance, more homelike, in fact. There is no phase of life, educational, economic, political, religious, in which inquiry may not aid in bringing to birth that world which Matthew Arnold rightly said was as yet unborn."[62]

Notes

1. Arnold, *The Letters of Matthew Arnold,* ed. Cecil Y. Lang (Charlottesville: University Press of Virginia, 1996-), 1:233, 282.
2. Rorty, "Pragmatism, Relativism, and Irrationalism," *Consequences of Pragmatism* (henceforth *CP*) (Minneapolis: University of Minnesota Press, 1982), 160. See, for example, Richard J. Bernstein, "The Resurgence of Pragmatism," *Social Research* 59 (Winter 1992): 813-40, and *Philosophical Profiles: Essays in a Pragmatic Mode* (Philadelphia: University of Pennsylvania Press, 1986); John Patrick Diggins, *The Promise of Pragmatism* (Chicago: University of Chicago Press, 1994); Giles Gunn, *Thinking Across the American Grain: Ideology, Intellect, and the New Pragmatism* (Chicago: University of Chicago Press, 1992); John J. McDermott, *The Culture of Experience* (New York: New York University Press, 1976) and *Streams of Experience* (Amherst: University of Massachusetts Press, 1989); John Rajchman and Cornel West, eds., *Post-Analytic Philosophy* (New York: Columbia University Press, 1985); Cornel West, *The American Evasion of Philosophy: A Genealogy of Pragmatism* (Madison: University of Wisconsin Press, 1989).
3. See John Henry Raleigh, *Matthew Arnold and American Culture* (Berkeley: University of California Press, 1957). "Ever since Arnold found that reflecting upon the place of poetry in an industrial society led him to worry about 'a girl named Wragg,'" Irving Howe writes in *A Margin of Hope* (San Diego: Harcourt Brace Jovanovich, 1982), "the most valuable critics have often doubled

as cultural spokesmen, moral prophets, political insurgents" (147). The finest recent contribution to Arnoldian criticism is Morris Dickstein's *Double Agent: The Critic and Society* (New York: Oxford University Press, 1992). Arnold "believed not simply in the spread of knowledge and the free play of mind," Dickstein observes, "but above all in usable knowledge, knowledge that could take on flesh and blood and make a difference, knowledge that was also poetry" (11). Cornel West, in *American Evasion,* dubs Trilling a "Pragmatist as Arnoldian Literary Critic" (164-81); but Diggins, in *Promise of Pragmatism,* finds divergencies as well as affinities between Trilling and Dewey (3-4, 382-84).

4. Rorty, "Private Irony and Liberal Hope," *Contingency, Irony, and Solidarity* (henceforth *CIS*) (Cambridge: Cambridge University Press, 1989), 81. James, quoted in Ralph Barton Perry, *The Thought and Character of William James,* 2 vols. (Boston: Little, Brown, 1935), 1:407.

5. Hook, *Pragmatism and the Tragic Sense of Life* (New York: Basic Books, 1974), 3-5, 22.

6. Dewey, "Poetry and Philosophy," in *John Dewey: The Early Works, 1882-1898,* ed. Jo Ann Boydston. 5 vols. (Carbondale: Southern Illinois University Press, 1969-72), 3:110, 123, 115, 120, 122, 123.

7. Ibid., 114-15; Dewey, "From Absolutism to Experimentalism," in *The Philosophy of John Dewey,* ed. John C. McDermott, 2 vols. (New York: Putnam's, 1973), 1:13.

8. "To read Arnold as the foe of democracy is false," observes Ruth apRoberts. "Democracy is the spring and the motive of *Culture and Anarchy* and of Arnold's whole career" ("Nineteenth-Century Culture Wars," *American Scholar* 64 [Winter 1995]): 147.

9. Mill, *On Liberty,* in *Autobiography and Other Writings,* ed. Jack Stillinger (Boston: Houghton Mifflin, 1969), 413-14. For Arnold on Mill, see Arnold, *Letters,* ed. Lang, 1:468. Edward Alexander compares the two in *Matthew Arnold and John Stuart Mill* (New York: Columbia University Press, 1965).

10. Alexis de Tocqueville, *Democracy in America,* ed. Philips Bradley, 2 vols. (New York: Vintage Books, 1960), 2:4, 104, 42, 106.

11. Mill, *On Liberty,* 452-53. Herbert Spencer, following Mill, attacked the "tyrannical system" of state-run education in "From Freedom to Bondage," 1891 (reprinted with *The Man versus the State,* ed. Donald MacRae [Harmondsworth: Penguin, 1969], 325). For a splendid recent account of Mill's position, see Stefan Collini, *Public Moralists: Political Thought and Intellectual Life in Britain, 1850-1930* (Oxford: Clarendon Press, 1991).

12. Dewey, "The Ethics of Democracy," *Early Works,* 1:237.

13. Ibid., 235, 232, 244, 245, 240, 246, 249.

14. Rorty, "The Priority of Democracy to Philosophy," *Objectivity, Relativism, and Truth* (henceforth *ORT*) (Cambridge: Cambridge University Press, 1991), 191, 188, 194, 193, 196.

15. Hook, *Pragmatism and the Tragic Sense of Life,* 13-14.

16. For Arnold's attachment to Sand, see Patricia Thomson, *George Sand and the Victorians* (New York: Columbia University Press, 1977), chap. 6.

17. Hook, *Pragmatism and the Tragic Sense of Life,* 4.

18. Dewey, *Liberalism and Social Action,* in *John Dewey: The Later Works, 1925-1953,* ed. Jo Ann Boydston, 17 vols. (Carbondale: Southern Illinois University Press, 1981-91), 11:45, 44.

19. James, "The Social Value of the College-Bred," in *Works of William James: Essays, Comments, and Reviews* (henceforth *ECR*) (Cambridge: Harvard University Press, 1987), 111, 118; Carlyle, *Past and Present,* in *The Works of Thomas Carlyle,* ed. H. D. Traill, 30 vols., Centenary Edition (London: Chapman and Hall, 1898-1901), 10:25; "Biography," *Works,* 28:46; James, *A Pluralistic Universe* (henceforth cited as *APU* in text) (1909; reprint, New York: Longman's, 1920), 20.

20. See James's letters to various newspapers on "The Philippine Tangle" (etc.), *ECR,* 154 ff.; "The Social Value of the College-Bred," *ECR,* 110; *Talks to Teachers* (New York: Norton, 1950), 131; "A Strong Note of Warning Regarding the Lynching Episode," *ECR,* 171.

21. For Arnold on the Paris Commune, see *Letters,* ed. George W. E. Russell, 2 vols. (New York: Macmillan, 1895), 2:65-66; James, "Renan's Dialogues," *ECR,* 330-31; *Talks to Teachers,* 19; *Pragmatism* (henceforth cited in text as *P*) (1907; reprint, New York: Meridian Books, 1955), 11; *The Will to Believe and Other Essays in Popular Philosophy* (henceforth cited in text as *WB*) (1897; reprint, New York: Dover, 1956), 325; Dewey, *Three Contemporary Philosophers,* in *John Dewey: The Middle Works, 1899-1924,* ed. Jo Ann Boydston, 15 vols. (Carbondale: Southern Illinois University Press, 1976-83), 12:206, 250.

22. Rorty, *CP,* xlii-xliii.

23. Schiller, *Humanism: Philosophical Essays* (1903; reprint, Freeport: Books for Library Press, 1969), xxiv.

24. Carlyle, "Characteristics," *Works,* 28:37; *Sartor Resartus, Works,* 1:156.

25. Myers, *William James: His Life and Thought* (New Haven: Yale University Press, 1986), 305. And see Hilary Putnam with Ruth Anna Putnam on Jamesian ethics in *Philosophy with a Human Face* (Cambridge: Harvard University Press, 1990), 217-31.

26. Mill, "The Utility of Religion," *Three Essays on Religion* (New York: Henry Holt and Co., 1874), 87; "Theism," Ibid., 249, 255-56. Noting the similarity between Arnold's and James's religious views, Lionel Trilling remarks, in *Matthew Arnold* (1939; reprint, New York: Meridian Books, 1955), "had James not read Arnold, we might have argued that Arnold had read James, for the earlier writer argued the pragmatic position with which the name of the latter is more intimately associated" (291).

27. James, *The Varieties of Religious Experience* (henceforth cited in text as *VRE*) (1902; reprint, New York: Collier Books, 1961), 401; and see *WB*, 89 (on "what Matthew Arnold likes to call *Aberglaube*").

28. James, "Renan's Dialogues," *ECR*, 331. R. W. B. Lewis suggests, in *The Jameses: A Family Narrative* (New York: Farrar, Straus and Giroux, 1991), that the real target of the Renan review is brother Henry ("William discerned in [Renan's *Dialogues*] an exaggerated version of everything that . . . he most feared about Henry: priggishness, fussy self-regard, and a disdainful—by implication, an anti-American—elitism"; 269-70). Henry James's re-sponse to William's Renan review was to agree with his brother about French "superficiality" (see Gay Wilson Allen, *William James: A Biography* [New York: Viking Press, 1967], 206). Perhaps William was taking the occasion, in the Renan review, to scourge his own aesthetic leanings.

29. Rorty, *CP*, 174, 166.

30. James, *Psychology, Briefer Course* (1892; reprint, New York: Fawcett, 1963), 148, 402. In the first passage James seems to echo the words of Arnold's follower, Walter Pater, in *The Renaissance:* "Every one of [our] impressions is the impression of the individual in his isolation, each mind keeping as a solitary prisoner its own dream of a world" (Oxford: Oxford University Press, 1986; 151).

31. Rorty, *ORT*, 193. Among those disturbed by Rorty's aesthetic turn are Richard J. Bernstein, in "One Step Forward, Two Steps Backward: Richard Rorty on Liberal Democracy and Philosophy," *Political Theory* 15 (Nov. 1987): 538-63; Nancy Fraser, "Solidarity or Singularity? Richard Rorty between Romanticism and Technology," *Unruly Practices: Power, Discourse, and Gender in Contemporary Social Theory* (Minneapolis: University of Minnesota Press, 1989); Jürgen Habermas, *The Philosophical Discourse of Modernity*, trans. Frederick Lawrence (Cambridge: MIT Press, 1990), 206-7; Frank Lentricchia, *Criticism and Social Change* (Chicago: University of Chicago Press, 1983), 15-19; the various contributors to the collection *Reading Rorty*, ed. Alan R. Malachowski (Oxford: Basil Blackwell, 1990); and Cornel West in *American Evasion* (194-210) and his afterward to *Post-Analytic Philosophy* (deploring Rorty's unashamed "ethnocentrism" and his non-Marxism: 259-72). For Alexander Nehamas, on the other hand, Rorty is insufficiently Nietzschean, insufficiently ironic ("A Touch of the Poet," *Raritan* 10 [Summer 1990]: 101-25).

32. See R. H. Super, "Sweetness and Light: Matthew Arnold's Comic Muse," in *Matthew Arnold in His Time and Ours*, ed. Clinton Machann and Forrest D. Burt (Charlottesville: University Press of Virginia, 1988), 183-96; Rorty, *ORT*, 193.

33. Arnold, *Letters*, ed. Russell, 2:20; Rorty, *CP*, 45.

34. Rorty, *ORT*, 17; *Philosophy and the Mirror of Nature* (Princeton: Princeton University Press), 13.

35. See Arnold, *CPW*, 3:53, 179 (on Spinoza's "edifying" versus Strauss's unedifying views); 9:254; Rorty, *Philosophy and the Mirror of Nature*, 359-60; *CP*, 24, 175; *Essays in Heidegger and Others* (henceforth *EH*) (Cambridge: Cambridge University Press, 1991), 152.

36. Rorty, "Nineteenth-Century Idealism and Twentieth-Century Textualism," *CP*, 148-49, 158; Nietzsche, *Twilight of the Idols*, in *The Portable Nietzsche*, trans. and ed. Walter Kaufmann (New York: Viking Press, 1954), 510; Rorty, "Thugs and Theorists," *Political Theory* 15 (Nov. 1987): 573; (Rorty deploring the sense of "alienation" in Lentricchia and others) "Two Cheers for the Cultural Left," *South Atlantic Quarterly* 89 (Winter 1990): 228, 223 n; "The Unpatriotic Academy," *New York Times* (Feb. 13, 1994), 15.

37. Rorty, *CIS*, 61; *EH*, 196-98. Foucault's emergence as a human rights advocate in the late 1870s and early 1880s is touched on in chapter 2.

38. See "Private Irony and Liberal Hope," *CIS*, esp. pp. 87-95. "Why language that is not stable enough to support truth," Diggins wonders in *Promise of Pragmatism*, "can be clear enough to forge solidarity as a unifying principle held by different people remains unexplained" by Rorty (476).

39. Rorty, "Two Cheers," pp. 234 n, 229; *ORT*, 15-16; *EH*, 186.

40. Rorty, *EH*, 183; "Thugs and Theorists," 571. Rorty's fondness for Harold Bloom (who coined the phrase "School of Resentment") has led him to the dubious position that "strong modern" authors are always better than their predecessors. "Once we had Yeats's later poems in hand," Rorty says (*CIS*, 20), "we were less interested in reading Rossetti's." It is this kind of crassness that gives pragmatism a bad name in aesthetic matters.

41. Dewey, "The Development of American Pragmatism," in *Philosophy of John Dewey*, 1:56; *Liberalism and Social Action*, in *Later Works*, 11:52; George Santayana, "Dewey's Naturalistic Metaphysics," in *The Philosophy of John Dewey*, ed. Paul Arthur Schilpp (Evanston, Ill.: Northwestern University Press, 1939), 251.

42. Keating, "Arnold Social and Political Thought," in *Writers and Their Background: Matthew Arnold,* ed. Kenneth Allott (Athens: Ohio University Press, 1976), 222; Dewey, "Construction and Criticism," *Later Works,* 5:142.

43. Dewey, "From Absolutism to Experimentalism," 7, 8-9; *The Quest for Certainty* (henceforth cited in text as *QC*) (1929; reprint, New York: Perigree Books, 1980), 62. James, in 1903, noted in a letter to Dewey that while he had come "from empiricism," his fellow pragmatist had reached "much the same goal" even though proceeding "from Hegel" (Perry, *Thought and Character,* 2:521).

44. Dewey, "Science as Subject-Matter and as Method," *Middle Works,* 6:78; "Two Phases of Renan's Life," *Early Works,* 3:174-79; "Renan's Loss of Faith in Science," *Early Works,* 4:11-18. Dewey supports Renan's position (which Renan later abandoned) that science, in supplanting religion, presents "us with a deeper truth," and that the "practical outcome" of science should be "made the possession of all men" (4:14-15). See Arnold, *CPW,* 3:264-65.

45. Westbrook, *John Dewey and American Democracy* (Ithaca: Cornell University Press, 1991), 141. And see Richard J. Bernstein, *John Dewey* (New York: Washington Square Press, 1967), esp. chap. 9. In "Science as Solidarity," Rorty suggests that Dewey saw the community of "scientific inquirers" as a noteworthy example of democracy in action (*ORT,* 43). Dewey, "Construction and Criticism," 134, 142.

46. Dewey, "Science as Subject-Matter," 78; Ludwig Wittgenstein, *Philosophical Investigations,* trans. G. E. M. Anscombe (New York: Macmillan, 1968), 47e.

47. Dewey, *Reconstruction in Philosophy, Middle Works,* 12:114; "Two Phases of Renan's Life," 174-75; "Self-Realization as the Moral Ideal," *Early Works,* 4:50.

48. Dewey (defining "Culture" for *A Cyclopedia of Education*), *Middle Works,* 6:406; Arnold, canceled passage from *Culture and Anarchy, CPW,* 5:527.

49. Dewey, "The Challenge of Democracy to Education," *Later Works,* 11:189; *The Public and its Problems* (1927; reprint, Athens: Ohio University Press, 1991), 154. See Lipmann, *The Phantom Public* (New York: Harcourt, Brace, 1925).

50. Dewey, *Democracy and Education* (New York: Macmillan, 1916), 357, 145; "The Aims and Ideals of Education," *Middle Works,* 13:399-405.

51. See W. F. Connell, *The Educational Thought and Influence of Matthew Arnold* (London: Routledge & Kegan Paul, 1950); G. H. Bantock, "Matthew Arnold, H. M. I.," *Scrutiny* 18 (1951): 32-44; Vincent L. Tollers, "A Working Isaiah: Arnold in the Council Office," in *Matthew Arnold 1988: A Centennial Review,* ed. Miriam Allott, *Essays and Studies* 41 (John Murray, 1988): 108-24; Peter Smith and Geoffrey Summerfield, eds., *Matthew Arnold and the Education of the New Order* (Cambridge: Cambridge University Press, 1969), 239, 215-16, 223-24, 227 (selections from Arnold's inspector reports). Bantock notes Arnold's emphasis on "the value of the [student's] inner life" (which Dewey neglects), and he applauds "Arnold's insistence that the teachers should have a high standard of culture" (35, 39). Connell points to Arnold's and Dewey's joint stress on individual "growth" for the sake of social progress (279). In their goods anthology (and introduction), Smith and Summerfield demonstrate Arnold's commitment to his task as school inspector, his anxiety over the deprivations endured by working-class children, and his sense that teachers were undervalued. The most stinging of Arnold's published rebukes of the Liberal mishandling of British education is his tract on "The Twice-Revised Code" (the policy dictating, for example, payment to schools on the basis of examination results): *CPW,* 2:212-43.

52. Dewey, "Ethics of Democracy," 231. Trilling pertinently notes that Arnold "demanded that men think not of themselves but of the whole of which they are a part" (52).

53. Dewey, "Construction and Criticism," 132; Westbrook, *Dewey And Democracy,* 100 (Westbrook also notes that "Dewey clearly differentiated his pedagogy" from that of "child-centered" educators who failed "to connect the interests and activities of the child to the subject matter of the curriculum"; 99); Dewey, *Liberalism and Social Action,* 21, 51-52.

54. Rorty, introduction to *Dewey: Later Works,* 8:xi-xii; Dewey, "Education and Social Ideals," *Later Works,* 11: 167. Two recent assaults on liberalism from within the academy emanate from Stanley Fish, who, in *There's No Such Thing as Free Speech and It's a Good Thing, Too* (New York: Oxford University Press, 1994), claims that "Liberalism Doesn't Exist" (like pragmatism, in Fish's view, it has no right to offer opinions that have a claim on us since it lacks a foundation, a center, to argue from); and from John Kekes, in *The Morality of Pluralism* (Princeton: Princeton University Press, 1993), who derides the notion that there are "overriding values." From the left, liberals such as Dewey and Rorty (and Arnold) have been attacked for their adherence to old-fashioned values (Kekes prefers what he calls a "reasonable immorality"; 163); from the right, they have become a convenient target for those opposing tolerance and public-mindedness.

55. Dewey, *Reconstruction in Philosophy,* 197; Trilling, *The Liberal Imagination* (Garden City: Doubleday Anchor Books, n.d.), xii; Rawls, *Political Liberalism* (New York: Columbia University Press, 1993), see chap. 4 ("Overlapping Consensus"), 321 (social

union as an orchestra); Dewey, "The Meaning of the Term: Liberalism," *Later Works,* 14: 254. Arnold's forward-looking liberalism is well treated by R. H. Super in *The Time-Spirit of Matthew Arnold* (Ann Arbor: University of Michigan Press, 1970); a welcome recent defense of Dewey's liberalism is Alan Ryan's *John Dewey and the High Tide of American Liberalism* (New York: Norton, 1995). The development of nineteenth-century English liberalism from an individualistic to a more collectivist position is considered by Stefan Collini in *Public Moralists.* J. W. Burrow, in *Whigs and Liberals: Continuity and Change in English Political Thought* (Oxford: Clarendon Press, 1988), stresses the traditional liberal concerns with individuality and diversity. Nancy L. Rosenblum's collection, *Liberalism and the Moral Life* (Cambridge: Harvard University Press, 1989), includes authors like Charles Taylor and Judith Shklar, who consider liberalism's moral purpose. See also Richard Bellamy, ed., *Victorian Liberalism* (London: Routledge, 1990); John Gray, *Liberalisms: Essays in Political Philosophy* (London: Routledge, 1989) and *Postliberalism: Studies in Political Thought* (New York: Routledge, 1993).

56. Ralph Waldo Emerson, *The Conduct of Life* (1860), in *Selected Writings of Emerson,* ed. Donald McQuade (New York: Modern Library, 1981), 724.
57. Westbrook, *Dewey and Democracy,* 345.
58. Rorty, "Thugs and Theorists," 571; Dewey, *Reconstruction in Philosophy,* 200-201.
59. Dewey, *Human Nature and Conduct* (henceforth cited in text as *HNC*) (New York: Henry Holt and Company, 1922), 279; *A Common Faith* (henceforth cited in text as *ACE*) (New Haven: Yale University Press, 1934), 54; Arnold, *Letters,* ed. Russell, 2:37.
60. Steven C. Rockefeller, in *John Dewey: Religious Faith and Democratic Humanism* (New York: Columbia University Press, 1991), discusses the uses of religion in Dewey's thinking. And see West's advocacy of "Prophetic Pragmatism" (Dewey applied to Christian Marxism) in *American Evasion,* chap. 6. "Symbols control sentiment and thought," Dewey observes in *The Public and its Problems,* "and the new age has no symbols consonant with its activities" (142).
61. "I recollect eulogies of Bacon in Mr. Dewey's works," Mumford complains in *The Golden Days* (1926; reprint, New York: Dover, 1968), "but none of Shakespeare; appreciations of Locke, but not Shelley and Keats and Wordsworth and Blake" (134). Dewey, *Art as Experience* (1934; reprint, New York: Perigree Books, 1980), 346, 105.
62. Dewey, Introduction to *Problems of Men,* in *Later Works,* 15: 156, 169.

Douglas W. Sterner (essay date 1999)

SOURCE: "Matthew Arnold, The Apostle of Culture," in *Priests of Culture: A Study of Matthew Arnold and Henry James,* Peter Lang, 1999, pp. 23-67.

[*In the following essay, Sterner studies Arnold's conception of culture and the implications of this ideal for his evaluation of modernity.*]

> Culture is then properly described not as having its origin in curiosity, but as having its origin in the love of perfection; it is *a study of perfection.* It moves by the force, not merely or primarily of the scientific passion for pure knowledge, but also of the moral and social passion for doing good. . . . there is no better motto which it can have than these words of Bishop Wilson: "To make reason and the will of God prevail!"
>
> —Matthew Arnold

> Poor Matt, he's gone to Heaven, no doubt—but he won't like God.
>
> —Robert Louis Stevenson

The smile of paradox may be glimpsed in the conjunction of Stevenson's affectionate joke with Matthew Arnold's sober proclamation of culture's destiny: "to make reason and the will of God prevail!"[1] If Arnold has indeed "gone to Heaven," I am sure that he would smile with us, for paradox suited his mind. The balancing in tension of opposing tendencies, the moderation of extremes, the mind turning on itself—these are quintessential traits of Arnold's habit of mind and of the "modern spirit" he grew to celebrate. This effort to rest in tension is itself paradoxical and points to one of the outstanding contrasts of his life's works: the "sad lucidity" reflecting upon "the something that infects the world"[2] of the early, poetical Arnold set against the blithe assurance and cheerful urbanity of the later critical prose. The presence of this contrast has been a challenge to his critics, and I believe it contains the secret of his continuing relevance and appeal.

More than a century after Arnold's death in 1888, there has been no waning of that appeal.[3] His most recent biographer, Park Honan, calls him "the Victorian who matters the most" and goes on to quote Arnold writing of Oxford and of himself in ***Culture and Anarchy*** that "we have kept up our communications with the future."[4] Oddly enough, part of the success of his communication, not only to his contemporaries but to subsequent generations of critics, lies in the very ambiguity and vagueness for which he has been criticized. "In Arnold's prose," Honan points out, "a verbal term throws out its magnetic field and is modified by the field of an opposing word."[5] Since for Arnold the needle of truth would fluctuate somewhere midway between these polarities, he was able to exasperate his critics by hopping back and forth across his compass with an agility rivaled only by his bland assurance that he was, after all, only disinterestedly pointing the way to truth. William Robbins has expressed Arnold's ability to maneuver amid the ambiguities of his thought in graphic terms:

> It is true, as John Holloway says, that Arnold "had no metaphysics which might form apparent premises for

> the moral principles he wished to assert." Whether this is a damaging criticism is another matter; to Arnold it was not. . . . The fact is that Arnold has continued to worry both the theologian and the philosopher, turning up all over again after he has been put in his place or disposed of for the last time. . . . Roped in by dogma, padlocked by logic, and shut up in a dark metaphysical cupboard, he would always escape Houdini-like, stroll back to the footlights, and urbanely tell the audience that such conventional bonds were child's play to a supple man of culture.[6]

However vague or doubtful in substance his doctrine of culture might be, moreover, there is no doubting its hopefulness. In his prose Arnold holds out to the uncertain and doubting reader the hope of reason. Beaming with fatherly good humor, he patiently assures us that with a little good will and pragmatic perseverance we can make our way through any uncertainty; he offers to save us even the consolation of faith once faith itself is gone. His air of calm superiority, once infuriating to his opponents, can be strangely reassuring to a reader fresh from the wastelands of modernity. His proffered "culture" is after all, as Honan says, a process of "psychological becoming" whereby one "moves towards realizing his mental, emotional, and creative potential, or his humanity,"[7] and so what if it is a bit vague and uncertain?—its uplifting tone promises that, however blurred at the edges or soft at the center, in time it will become what it promises and carry us along in its triumph. Offering this genial reassurance, Arnold's temper and style thus combine to disguise a vagueness of definition, while the vagueness of definition itself protects his doctrine of culture from definitive assault; its very vagueness in a curious way becomes its masterful touch. Together with his hopeful temper and genial style, it has contributed to his continued appeal.

But surely the most important reason for his enduring relevance to us, as "the Victorian who matters the most," is that, as Homan goes on to summarize, "His poetry seems to give us to ourselves, even as it portrays a modern mind, sensitive to the historic past and to its own past. . . ."[8] Robert Langbaum, writing on the problem of identity in modern literature, strikes a similar note, declaring that what "Arnold as a poet can give us that the romanticists cannot, and that even Tennyson and Browning cannot, is a convincing rendition of modern urban numbness and alienation"; he was, Langbaum adds, "the first Victorian poet to deal with the modern problem of loss of self."[9] Whatever the vagueness or inconsistency to which Arnold succumbs in the course of his efforts, it is in grappling with modernity that he matters most to us. I remarked at the outset that he "grew to celebrate" modernity because his early poetry could hardly be characterized as a celebration. "Perhaps more than any poet of his time," Lionel Trilling writes, "Arnold saw what was happening"; but his poetic response to what was happening, Trilling adds, "is a threnody for the lives of men smirched by modernity, of men who have become, in the words of Empedocles, living men no more, nothing but 'naked, eternally restless mind.'"[10] This phrase of Arnold's, taken from **"Empedocles on Etna,"**[11] portrays the plight of modern man, which for Arnold is a condition of mind and not limited to recent time; it points to the central characteristic of modernity for Arnold: the unanchored mind.

Seen positively, a mind "unanchored" is free from past errors and the constraint of custom; no longer bounded by ignorance or narrow prejudice, the mind expands its quest for truth with a new freedom and critical maturity, guided by "one irresistible force, which is gradually making its way everywhere, removing old conditions and imposing new, altering long-fixed habits, undermining venerable institutions, even modifying national character: *the modern spirit.*"[12] The positive features of this modern spirit Arnold first identified in his inaugural lecture after being elected at 34 to the Chair of Poetry at Oxford in 1857; the first to deliver the lecture in English, he fittingly entitled it **"On the Modern Element in Literature"**:

> One of the most characteristic outward features of a *modern* age . . . is the banishment of the ensigns of war and bloodshed from the intercourse of civil life. . . . With the disappearance of the constant means of offense the occasions of offense diminish; society at last acquires repose, confidence, and free activity. An important inward characteristic, again, is the growth of a tolerant spirit; that spirit which is the offspring of an enlarged knowledge; a spirit patient of the diversities of habits and opinions. Other characteristics are the multiplication of the convenences of life, the formation of taste, the capacity for refined pursuits. And this leads to the supreme characteristic of all: the intellectual maturity of man himself; the tendency to observe facts with a critical spirit; to search for their law, not to wander among them at random, to judge by the rule of reason, not by the impulse of prejudice or caprice.[13]

While possible survivors of the twentieth century might question the "banishment of the ensigns of war and bloodshed" as the modern age's "characteristic outward feature," it is really the "inward" features that are important to his definition of modernity. They include that inner flexibility of consciousness, the widening of possibilities consequent upon freedom from convention, that Arnold stressed in another key passage for understanding his conception of modernity from an essay on Heinrich Heine:

> Modern times find themselves with an immense system of institutions, established facts, accredited dogmas, customs, rules, which have come to them from times not modern. In this system their life has to be carried forward; yet they have a sense that this system is not of their own creation; that it by no means corresponds exactly with the wants of their actual life, that, for them, it is customary, not rational. The awakening of this sense is the awakening of the modern spirit. The modern spirit is now awake almost everywhere; the sense of want of correspondence between the forms of modern Europe and its spirit, between the new wine of the eighteenth and nineteenth centuries, and the old bottles of the eleventh and twelfth centuries, or even of the sixteenth and seventeenth. . . . To remove this

want of correspondence is beginning to be the settled endeavor of most persons of good sense. Dissolvents of the old European system of dominant ideas and facts we must all be, all of us who have any power of working; what we have to study is that we may not be acrid dissolvents of it.[14]

The hint at the end of this passage that the dissolution of the old order may not be without its dangers is echoed a little further on in the essay in Arnold's tribute to "that grand dissolvent," his cherished Goethe:

> Goethe's profound, imperturbable naturalism is absolutely fatal to all routine thinking; he puts the standard, once for all, inside every man instead of outside of him; when he is told, such a thing must be so, there is immense authority and custom in favor of its being so, it has been held to be so for a thousand years, he answers with Olympian politeness, "But *is* it so? is it so to *me?*" Nothing could be more really subversive of the foundations on which the old European order rested; and it may be remarked that no persons are so radically detached from this order, no persons so thoroughly modern, as those who have felt Goethe's influence most deeply.[15]

With the standard placed inside each man, he may look out upon the world from within his own self to question (with "Olympian politeness"), "Is it so to *me?*" But his *detachment* is equally Olympian; and this detachment and isolation, so hauntingly captured for generations of moderns in **"To Marguerite—Continued"** and **"Dover Beach,"** characterize the negative features of modernity, its element of pain:

> Yes! in the sea of life enisled,
> With echoing straits between us thrown,
> Dotting the shoreless watery wild,
> We mortal millions live *alone.*
>
> . . . . .
>
> Oh! then a longing like despair
> Is to their farthest caverns sent;
> For surely once, they feel, we were
> Parts of a single continent!
> Now round us spreads the watery plain—
> Oh might our marges meet again![16]
>
> . . . for the world, which seems
> To lie before us like a land of dreams,
> So various, so beautiful, so new,
> Hath really neither joy, nor love, nor light,
> Nor certitude, nor peace, nor help for pain;
> And we are here as on a darkling plain
> Swept with confused alarms of struggle and flight,
> Where ignorant armies clash by night.[17]

Here that modern world—"so various" and "so new" as to deprive the speaker of "joy" and "peace" along with "certitude" (which has dwindled with the sea of faith)—shows its depressing and frightening dimensions. It is a world against which Arnold as a young man himself cried out when he wrote to his close friend Arthur Clough:

> These are damned times. Everything is against one—the height to which knowledge is come, the spread of luxury, our physical enervation, the absence of great *natures,* the unavoidable contact with millions of small ones, newspapers, cities, light profligate friends, moral desperadoes like Carlyle, our own selves, and the sickening consciousness of our difficulties.[18]

Arnold was then 26, a struggling young poet, and much of his poetry would express this negative response to modernity and attempt to find escape from or an answer to the disorienting flux of freedom.

The "damned times" in which Arnold found himself witnessed, in the inner life of its heart and mind, the decline of the authority and unity of Christianity, the collapse of what historians are fond of calling the "medieval synthesis." Arnold perceived that collapse, as Park Honan observes, to be the "chief fact about modern Europe":

> Since no Christian church could reassert its authority or enforce its dogmas, a psychological vacuum remained. In consequence, Arnold concluded, man lacks a deep identity; he suffers from disorientation and ennui, shifting and unsatisfying feelings, shallowness of being, dissatisfaction with his own endeavors—from debilities caused by the lack of any compelling authority for the spiritual life.[19]

Or as Arnold himself writes, in contrast to the time of Dante or even of Shakespeare, for whom "the basis of spiritual life was given," by the time of Goethe "Europe had lost her basis of spiritual life. . . ."[20]

Cut loose from traditional anchors, prejudice, and custom, modern consciousness is cut loose from meaning and purpose in life, for it is in the connections one makes or perceives to exist between oneself, others, and the world that meaning consists. Moderns play a price for their freedom from those vital connections:

> The predominance of thought, of reflection, in modern epochs is not without its penalties; in the unsound, in the over-tasked, in the over-sensitive, it has produced the most painful, the most lamentable results; it has produced a state of feeling unknown to less enlightened but perhaps healthier epochs—the feeling of depression, the feeling of *ennui.*[21]

Writing from a positive, more hopeful outlook than had been his at an earlier point in life, Arnold neglects to add in this essay that he is here describing his own earlier condition. It is a condition in which one's "feelings" are in conflict, characterized by anxiety and frustration, because one's life is given no clear direction or meaning by one's confused and restless "thoughts": reason *questions* and feeling *desires,* but those desires find *no answers in reason.* This disjunction is the very same as that to be identified later in T. S. Eliot's famous phrase as a "dissociation of sensibility"; its tendency is to reduce the artist into neurotic forms of self-expression and generally to cripple the modern self with alienation from within (Langbaum's "loss of self").[22]

The other historical dimension of modernity, paralleling the decline of Christianity, is the rise of industrial and materialistic civilization, which adds its outer pressures to the alienation within the modern mind. It is these pressures that Arnold cites in his litany of complaints in the letter to Clough (the "spread of luxury," "physical enervation," "newspapers," "cities"). In their divorce of life from the physical presence and routines of nature, they parallel the modern mind's metaphysical divorce of values from nature represented in the rise of scientific consciousness. Finally, the social and political stress accompanying all of these changes, and democracy's rising challenge to structures and customs inherited from the disintegrated medieval world view, add further dimensions of stress and uncertainty to modern life.

From this state of alienation and detachment, occasioned by the decline of the unified Christian cosmos and the rise of scientific naturalism and critical reason amid the changing social and political environment of urban industrial and commercial civilization, the modern spirit cries out for "deliverance." And since the root difficulty is the inner experience of the unanchored mind—the self freed from traditional supports and connections giving purpose and meaning to life—it is an "intellectual deliverance" that is most needed:

> An intellectual deliverance is the peculiar demand of those ages which are called modern. . . . Such a deliverance is emphatically, whether we will or no, the demand of the age in which we ourselves live. All intellectual pursuits our age judges according to their power of helping to satisfy this demand; of all studies it asks, above all, the question, how far they can contribute to this deliverance.
>
> . . . The demand arises, because our present age has around it a copious and complex present, and behind it a copious and complex past; it arises, because the present age exhibits to the individual man who contemplates it the spectacle of a vast multitude of facts awaiting and inviting his comprehension. The deliverance consists in man's comprehension of this present and past.[23]

In effect, a *reconnection:* if not precisely a new anchor, at least a positioning of the self in a significant cosmos so as to constitute a modern *ethos* which would serve to reconnect the self to that cosmos; and by reconnecting him to the world outside himself, to restore the sense of meaning and purpose to his life, to offer his feelings a hopeful direction on which to fix their desires and his mind an intelligible cosmos on which to exercise its rule of reason. Then the poet would find words to unite his heart and mind; together with other men of culture similarly "delivered," they would be able to "see life steadily, and see it whole."[24]—which means to see it integral and harmonious, no longer fragmented in lonely isolation, adrift without meaning.

Whether the world was ever as integrated and "whole" as Arnold envisions it to have been is problematic at best. But the point here is not the accuracy of his historical estimate; it is his identification of modernity with both that loss of unity and that gain of critical independence. Arnold felt both the pain of the former and the promise of the latter. He not only identifies the key features of modernity but also represents in himself a range of possible responses to that condition of *being* modern, felt sometimes as a "sickness" and then again as a hopeful opportunity. In sympathetically representing both reactions to a condition in which we still find ourselves, Arnold has continued ever since to stir responses across a wide intellectual spectrum.

Modernity and the Continuity of Arnold's Thought

Joseph Carroll in his study of *The Cultural Theory of Matthew Arnold* focuses on Arnold's response to modernity as the key variable in distinguishing the early Arnold's poetical achievement from the later Arnold of the critical prose. In the early poetry, Carroll argues, Arnold succeeds in establishing "the problems to which all of his later, critical work responds,"[25] but he is nonetheless unable to reach a satisfactory resolution of them, since none of his tentative responses (stoic withdrawal, mystical union in nature, pragmatic moderation of desire) succeeds in resolving the plight of modern consciousness: the mind's unanchored state, its awareness of its own freedom and the absence of any prescriptive or authoritative relation to the world outside of it, of any connection affording purpose or enduring value. This dilemma is most thoroughly explored in **"Empedocles,"** and Carroll's superb summary merits extensive quotation:

> **"Empedocles"** is Arnold's most thorough exploration of the spiritual malaise of his own times. The problems it describes and the various solutions or alternatives it proposes subsume those of the shorter poems and, by subsuming them, implicates them in the final, suicidal frustration of Empedocles himself. Arnold repudiates this poem because it has no resolution; the suffering of Empedocles "finds no vent in action" (I, 2).
>
> . . . There is no possibility of union between the animated life of nature and the divisive, intrusive, and distorting character of the intellect. This conclusion comes near the end of the poem, and it reveals to us, beyond the scope of Arnold's intentions, the real source of Empedocles' despair.
>
> Since mentality is the defining quality of humanity, our "human side," spiritual frustration appears as the culmination of all human experience, and from this human condition there is no escape. Once the intellect becomes "the master part of us," once we have identified ourselves with our own conscious recognitions, we must then remain "prisoners of our consciousness," unable ever to "clasp and feel the All" but through "forms, and modes, and stifling veils" of thought. After he reaches this conclusion, Empedocles recognizes that death cannot provide the resolution he seeks. Mind remains an alien element, and death only gives the stamp of finality to spiritual futility: "the ineffable longing for the life of life / Baffled for ever."
>
> Carried to its logical extreme, Empedocles' problem is not merely personal and social but epistemological and metaphysical. The problem is not his alone, and is not

> limited to one anomalous phase of history. It appears to him rather as an inevitable and recurrent progression of intellectual alienation that provides a prototype for all of cultural history.[26]

Arnold will continue to be drawn to the various forms of attempted escape from the agony of modern consciousness, but his best poems, as Carroll points out, are those which confront it directly while providing "some vent for distress" or some "appeal to elementary passions that transcend the modern condition," as in the cry for love in **"Dover Beach"** ("Ah, love, let us be true / To one another!").[27]

But even these poems are "compromises," in Carroll's view, "between his *a priori* aesthetic criteria [laid out in the 1853 preface] and his actual experience given to him in his historical situation [of modernity]."[28] In fact, poetry cannot resolve the underlying problem, which is intellectual (or spiritual); it is not the function of poetry, Arnold writes to Clough, "to *solve* the Universe."[29] So that after exhausting "the ideas of the world accessible to him in poetry," and finding that "they did not add up, in his own view, to that grand unity of vision he found in the best of ancient literature."[30] Arnold turns from poetry to prose—a turn which, far from being a "defeat" for Arnold's talent, represents a maturer recognition of where his talent would achieve its greatest success in addressing his overriding concern (which is, in fact, precisely to *"solve"* modernity). Arnold's shift from poetry to prose prepares the way for the exercise of his talents to their greatest effect; Carroll thus concludes that Arnold's poetic stream "did not so much dry up as become diverted into another channel; that is, the spring was not basically poetic but literary, and so convertible to Arnold's needs as he felt them change."[31]

This shift in Arnold's basic orientation dates from the time of his opening Oxford lecture, **"On the Modern Element in Literature,"** in 1857, in which Arnold "announces his critical mission, to find an 'intellectual deliverance' from spiritual distress."[32] At the heart of Arnold's new approach is a redefinition of the idea of the "modern," associated now with the idea of criticism and offering the hopeful prospect of a progressive intellectual "deliverance" from the previous dead end of a stagnant emotional quandary. Whereas in his earlier phase the term "modern" implied *decline,* a loss of unity, Arnold's new departure, elevating the creative function of "criticism," highlights the positive and hopeful features of modernity whereby freedom is not simply a *loss* of moorings but an opportunity to construct new ones, to progressively reconstruct a unity in harmony with modern forces (rather than seeking to escape them). Arnold has moved beyond his initial critical doctrine of "aesthetic withdrawal from the modern world" to a more aggressive stance, centered around this redefinition of "modern":

> . . . The querulous passivity of the letters to Clough and of **"Empedocles"** is suppressed through the assumption that the course of culture is in some measure subject to intelligible control. This is the central redefinition of "modern." A modern age is one in which the critical intelligence rises above the blind forces of history and by grasping them gains freedom over them.[33]

It is the formulation of this theory of cultural progress, Carroll argues, "that enables Arnold to satisfy his deepest and most abiding intellectual need—the need for wholeness, that is, unity and completeness."[34]

The essence of this cultural theory is the dialectic of cultural forces (Hebraism and Hellenism) which correspond to innate traits of human nature and social prerequisites (order, or "conduct," and freedom, or "expansion"). Whereas the Hebraistic tendency represents a concern for morality and conduct according to its standards, the tendency of Hellenism is for spontaneity of consciousness, for beauty and rationality, for seeing things as they are, in *all* spheres of life, not simply the moral. What is needed, in Arnold's view, is a proper balance of these forces, both in the individual and in society. "Culture" becomes the advocate for and instrument of this balance. All this is familiar terrain. However, Carroll finds a logic and unity to Arnold's exposition and development of it that, while occasionally compounded of scattered insights made before, appears to be original in its synthesis of them into a coherent thesis covering the entire span of Arnold's career and thought as a unified whole. Arnold's cultural theory is seen to evolve, as he is forced by his need for wholeness and purpose to add to it gradually, so that its systematic comprehensiveness emerges over the course of Arnold's career, rather than being definitively or systematically *presented.* But the scattered method of presentation ought not to prevent us, Carroll argues, from recognizing the systematic, comprehensive result.

There are several steps along the way to this result.[35] One is an adjustment in Arnold's understanding of how any "bridge" connecting one's consciousness to formless "life," "nature," or "world" is to be experienced. In an early essay (**"Heinrich Heine"**) Arnold seems to reflect "the Romantic assumption that 'the All' is a formless infinity inaccessible to the divisive analytical categories of the mind."[36] Both Hebraism and Hellenism reach to connect with that "beyond" through some kind of merger—Hellenism via "beauty," Hebraism through "sublimity." However, by the time of ***Culture and Anarchy,*** the notion of *merger* has been replaced by that of *order,* so that the "goal of both Hebraism and Hellenism is no longer 'the infinite' but the universal order, an order accessible to rational intuition." Here enter in Arnold's ideas of "right reason," as the human capacity to perceive (and by cooperating, to advance) that order, and of "God," not as a person but as "a summary term of that order."[37] Perfection as the goal of Arnold's "culture" thus becomes, as will be seen, not a closed condition capable of definitive analytical description, but an open-ended process of cultural and individual becoming, a progressive apprehension and approximation of an order inherent in the universe.

To make that process of becoming purposive, however, Arnold has to evolve, first, an historical understanding according to which each pole of the dialectical process generates its opposite tendency as a corrective, and, second, an overriding goal or principle according to which the process may be seen to progress. Hence, the Hebraic tendency of Christianity cannot be viewed simply as a mistaken fable, dismissed of no use to a "modern" perspective, but rather must be seen as contributing its needed corrective to a prior Hellenic phase, as well as itself requiring further correction from a subsequent Hellenic phase. This historical view is presented in ***Culture and Anarchy,*** wherein Arnold positions his own period as one in need of the Hellenizing corrective, following as it does upon the heels of the Hebraisizing Reformation. Moreover, as Carroll convincingly argues,[38] Arnold implicitly (though never explicitly) crowns this historical progression with an overall goal and principle of progress by elevating the Hellenic principle as the higher and more inclusive ideal of the two. With this elevation of the Hellenic ideal of perfection, history and man's place in it become purposive, with culture both perfection's instrument (seen as critical method) and its goal (seen as an ideal of balanced character, both individual and national).

In order to arrive at this view, of course, Arnold has to adopt some assumptions which are not strictly compatible with what would today pass for a "modern" view. He must believe in the existence of objectively valid universal moral and aesthetic laws, and that these laws progressively reveal themselves to govern history. The insertion of these assumptions into Arnold's "system" occurs gradually, almost imperceptibly, in response to his underlying drive for "unity and completeness." They enter in (as noted above) through the ideas of "right reason" and of "God." ("Imaginative reason," in Arnold's lexicon, would appear to be an analogue of "right reason" applied to literature.) While these assumptions appear to vitiate the "modern" dimension of Arnold's thought and are allied to vague and often inconsistent definitions (which form the basis for much of the debunking of Arnold's inaptitude for systematic thought), in fact, Carroll notes, Arnold "finds a modern philosophical grounding for these views in Spinoza," though he also departs from Spinoza in his own conception of the universal order which "unlike that of Spinoza . . . , is of a progressive historical character [allowing for] only one absolute principle of value: the idea of human perfection as a harmonious expansion of all the faculties."[39]

However vague or inconsistent in their formulation at different times in different places in Arnold's work, these assumptions are essential to the construction of Arnold's "comprehensive vision of man's place in nature and in history"[40] by which his life is anchored once again to a significant cosmos, a universe with an ideal goal (transcending the present, but not the natural order) to which the individual can intelligibly relate himself and which (as the pursuit of perfection) provides his life with moral meaning. However naive his reading of history might seem today, moreover, the important point is that Arnold *believed* his view to be "verifiable," based on experience, and so freed from the death grip of what he believed to be a moribund form of Christianity; it was thus capable of providing that "deliverance" which eluded Empedocles, overcoming "the division of mind and nature and the consequent sense of futility in the cultural progression."[41] In contrast to his earlier period, when the lonely eminence of human consciousness was felt to leave man adrift without purpose or significance, that height of consciousness is now deemed capable of objectively identifying history's progression in harmony with an ideal of perfection which man can now—by virtue of that same critical intellect which separates him from nature—actively seek and foster. Arnold, in erecting an ideal of "culture" as part of a redefined, positive conception of "modern," thus enables modernity to triumph over its own malaise.

I have elaborated extensively the main part of Carroll's thesis, partly because he correctly identifies the overall shape of Arnold's career, the progress and structure of his thought, and partly as background for a subsequent discussion in which I depart from Carroll's views. Suffice it to comment at this point that what Carroll terms a "redefinition" of modernity in Arnold's thought I refer to as a difference of *response* to a conception of the modern condition which Arnold accurately perceived in his early period.[42] In his later writing Arnold finds new and more hopeful applications for features of modernity that had once left him discouraged, but he does not thereby *redefine* the nature of modernity itself.

Arnold's Doctrine of Culture

Having explored the meaning of modernity for Arnold and introduced the most significant recent scholarly contribution to understanding the pivotal role of that concept in his thought, we must now turn to consider more directly Arnold's central doctrine of "culture." The enclosure in quotation marks is meant to mark a recognition that we are here dealing with a major nebula of modern thought. Raymond Williams calls it "one of the two or three most complicated words in the English language"; surely it is one of the few to have an entire book devoted to collecting and analyzing its definitions.[43] There is no need here to rehearse the complex history of its derivation and usage, except to note that its three most common usages today (disregarding its specialized use in biology and agriculture) are significantly interrelated: (1) use of the term in anthropology and sociology to indicate "the totality of socially transmitted behavior patterns, arts, beliefs, institutions, and all other products of human work and thought characteristic of a community or population"[44] is the most inclusive, but still distinct from (2) the use of "culture" to indicate intellectual or artistic activity or achievements (including what is sometimes called "high culture") and from (3) "culture" used to refer to a more general process of formation and development of the mind and character of an individual.

A significant distinction affecting the second two usages in contrast to the first points to the role of value judgments. While an anthropologist studying a particular culture in the first sense would certainly take account of expressions of "culture" in the other two senses, his study would not equip him to make value judgments of the intrinsic moral worth of the various elements of the culture under study (though he could make judgments of their utility to the harmonious functioning and survival of the society); the term "culture" as used by the anthropologist is not laden with implicit value judgments, even though values comprise an essential part of any given culture. When the term "culture" is used in either of the other two senses, however, it typically carries a heavy freight of normative meaning. This implicit moral dimension is especially true of its use in the third sense, since the development of mind and character is not normally considered a morally neutral process; but even in the second usage, there is usually a presumption that intellectual and artistic achievement is a good thing (unless of course it is used derogatorily to challenge the pretensions of "high culture," in which the moral judgment is merely reversed). Most confusion in the use of "culture" involves a failure to distinguish this element of moral judgment—a lack of clarity about when it is present and when it is not. In ordinary usage the "magnetic fields" (to borrow Honan's metaphor) of these three meanings overlap; a speaker may use the word in one sense with a vague sense of its qualification in relation to the other two meanings or without any awareness at all—in either case an illicit association with either objectivity or moral value may be introduced by mere use of the word without its ever being made clear or justified.

When Arnold began writing of "culture," the anthropologist's sense of the word was not fully established; but it was formally introduced by Tylor in his *Primitive Culture* in 1871, and it was also used by the mid-nineteenth century generally to describe a particular way of life of a people or period (as was "civilization"). Moreover, Arnold was certainly aware of the idea (if not the terminology) of cultural relativity: he had read Herder's *Ideas on the Philosophy of the History of Mankind,* in which Herder challenges the notion of "universal" history and stresses the importance of the local conditioning of culture, making it necessary to speak of "cultures" in the plural.[45] Arnold in his own criticism also places great emphasis on the importance of a comparative knowledge of literature and history as part of his emphasis on the value of culture. So that it seems clear that the idea of "culture" affording a perspective of relativity, or the objectivity fostered by comparative knowledge of cultures, was familiar to him. So familiar to him, indeed, that it became one of the ingredients on the basis of which he recommended his famous "culture": its flexibility, its offering a current of "fresh ideas." Arnold also had available to him, as we do, its other two uses, and they too were admirable features of "culture." But Arnold did not always distinguish these various uses; to the contrary, possessed of a mighty weapon by which to redeem modernity and slay the Philistines (which for him meant educating them), he took full promiscuous advantage of the illicit association of meanings detailed above. This talented polemicist and poet instinctively knew a good symbol when he had one in hand, and Matthew Arnold, apostle of "culture," rode the term for all its worth.

"Culture" for Arnold is the means of our "intellectual deliverance" from the ills of modernity. Developed and used ambiguously, the concept is intended to provide the source of authority both for the life of the individual and for the social order. For the individual it offers an ideal of "perfection" fostering intellectual as well as emotional and moral growth; for society it provides a standard of judgment and a stabilizing perspective, a means of promoting harmony and order along with the necessary and inevitable changes in the social order. In association with other key Arnoldian phrases—"sweetness and light," "study of perfection," "spontaneity of consciousness," "free play of ideas," "reason and the will of God," "imaginative reason" and its twin "right reason," and, simplest of all, "the best"—the central term *culture* becomes in Arnold's hands a *symbol* promising a rational and human solution to doubt and disorder.

Defending Arnold against the critical consensus "that Arnold is not to be regarded as a systematic thinker," Joseph Carroll argues for the comprehensive "unity" of Arnold's thought as a kind of "synthesis."[46] But if Carroll is right in calling our attention to the overall unity of Arnold's work—and I believe he is—it remains true that there is inconsistency, ambiguity, a lack of analytic rigor, in his "unity." Carroll admits as much, while claiming at the same time a "consistency" in Arnold's pursuit of the "synthesis": "Despite variations and reversals in his theoretical formulations, the consistency with which Arnold pursues this ideal of perfection gives unity to his whole body of thought."[47]

Here he is close to the truth. The truth is that the "unity" of Arnold's thought is his *desire for unity* which took on objective reality for him in the symbolism of culture; his "synthesis" of culture comes to represent both the *means* to fulfill the desire, to achieve unity, *and the goal itself*—a vision of culture containing the promise of unity achieved, desire harmonized, so as to motivate and inspire with hope the purposeful effort to achieve it. The "unity" of Arnold's thought is symbolic, not analytic, in character. When subjected to the rigors of analytic scrutiny, the unity breaks down: a confusion of means and ends in its key term, culture, is fatal to its coherence; but this same blur of meaning or logical ambiguity is the dynamic heart of a functioning symbol, which can both represent a goal achieved and inspire an effort to achieve it. Ambiguity, or a blur of associated meanings reinforcing one another, can add power to a symbol where it would muddy an attempt at systematic doctrine. Thus the very vagueness and ambiguity for which Arnold has been often criticized (correctly, but missing the point), far from being a "weakness," is the very secret of the success and power of Arnold's appeal to culture. In appealing to culture he is appealing to a symbol promising hope and cohesion, purpose and peace, "reason and the will of God"—*deliverance* from the ills of the modern world; it is a symbol owing considerably to his own efforts at creating it and to his success in resisting its analytic reduction or precise formulation. Carroll is right in claiming for Arnold's thought a "unity" and "cohesion," but it is not a systematic intellectual cohesiveness or "system." The terms Carroll uses, "complete cultural system" and "synthesis," are too strong, suggesting an analytic rigor which Carroll himself admits is not present. Rather, it is the unity and cohesion afforded by culture functioning symbolically both to embody desired goals as ideally present within itself and to inspire the effort towards those goals through its own means.

Arnold's "definition" of culture, such as it is, begins as a definition of the function of criticism: "to know the best that is known and thought in the world, and by in its turn making this known, to create a current of true and fresh ideas."[48] As the role of criticism grows in scope and responsibility, Arnold eventually adopts the term "culture," but the definition is virtually the same:

> The whole scope of this essay is to recommend culture as the great help out of our present difficulties; culture being a pursuit of our total perfection by means of getting to know, on all matters which most concern us, the best which has been thought and said in the world; and through this knowledge, turning a stream of fresh and free thought upon our stock notions and habits. . . .[49]

The job of criticism, operating not in literature alone but surveying the entire breadth and depth of culture past and present, is to mine these sources to identify *"the best"* in every aspect of individual and social life to serve as standards of excellence and sources of authority. By seeking after and adhering to these models of excellence, pearls of "sweetness and light," we grow towards *perfection* (Arnold elsewhere refers to culture as "the study of perfection"[50]). Since perfection is an ideal standard and goal, imperfections abound, and the partisan of culture must be *disinterested* in detecting and correcting them. Hence the importance of *flexibility* to culture, of an inward attitude of openness and balance:

> . . . culture directs our attention to the natural current there is in human affairs, and to its continual working, and will not let us rivet our faith upon any one man and his doings. It makes us see not only his good side, but also how much in him was of necessity limited and transient; nay, it even feels a pleasure, a sense of increased freedom and of an ampler freedom, in so doing.[51]

It is this pleasure that Arnold takes in the close of Burke's *Thoughts on French Affairs* where, having argued and struggled against the Revolution, Burke suggests (incorrectly as it turns out) that he is through arguing with it, that if in fact the current of history is for it, to oppose it is folly:

> That return of Burke upon himself has always seemed to me one of the finest things in English literature, or indeed in any literature. That is what I call living by ideas: when one side of a question has long had your earnest support, when all your feelings are engaged, when you hear all round you no language but one, when your party talks this language like a steam-engine and can imagine no other—still to be able to think, still to be irresistibly carried, if so it be, by the current of thought to the opposite side of the question. . . .[52]

This open-minded and flexible attitude—the mind questioning itself—is essential to a disinterested apprehension of "the best"; it precludes routine, mechanical actions or hasty, "practical" (but ill-considered) solutions over thoughtful, considered ones (however delayed their results). But this disinterested flexibility of mind does not mean that culture is aloof from social or political questions. Culture is concerned not only to discover "the best," but also to *propagate* it, to make it *prevail.* "It is not satisfied till we *all* come to a perfect man; it knows that the sweetness and light of the few must be imperfect until the raw and unkindled masses of humanity are touched with sweetness and light."[53] Or, as Arnold says elsewhere, the perfection aimed at must be both a general and a harmonious "expansion of *all* the powers which make the beauty and worth of human nature":

> . . . culture, which is the study of perfection, leads us . . . to conceive of true human perfection as a *harmonious* perfection, developing all sides of our humanity; and as a *general* perfection, developing all parts of our society. For if one member suffer, the other members must suffer with it; and the fewer there are that follow the true way of salvation, the harder that way is to find.[54]

The overall contribution of culture to social harmony is to recognize and to "establish an order of ideas"[55]—the truest, the best ideas available. Just as in criticism these ideas provide the basis for growth of "creative epochs of literature," so in the realm of culture they tend

> to draw towards a knowledge of the universal order which seems to be intended and aimed at in the world, and which it is a man's happiness to go along with or his misery to go counter to—to learn, in short, the will of God . . .[56]

The fostering of this *order of ideas* in society, tending to promote individual happiness and social harmony, requires the allegiance and support of the "best self" in each individual. While the state has a role in supporting the growth in the number of "best selves" in the population, its action in behalf of culture depends on culture's prior appeal to a select number of "best selves" already existing across class lines. This "best self," capable of recognizing an order of "best ideas," Arnold identifies as "right reason."

Right reason is the intuitive recognition of where one's "perfection" lies. It presumes a structure or "law" to characterize human nature (hence society); it is this law that right reason intuits, and it is in following it that perfection is approached.[57] It is "right" because it accords with our true nature and results in our happiness; it is rational because it is open to discovery by our reason, is verifiable in human experience. It becomes for Arnold a principle of authority sanctioning and defining "the best":

> If we look at the world outside us we find a disquieting absence of sure authority. We discover that only in right reason can we get a source of sure authority; and culture brings us toward right reason . . . by enabling ourselves, by getting to know, whether through reading, observing, or thinking, the best that can at present be known in the world, to come as near as we can get to the firm intelligible law of things, and thus to get a basis for a less confused action and a more complete perfection than we have at present.[58]

This "less confused action" is both personal and social, for the "enabling" authority of right reason provides an ordering sanction for both personal and social life:

> Now, if culture, which simply means trying to perfect oneself, and one's mind as part of oneself, brings us light, and if light shows us that there is nothing so very blessed in merely doing as one likes, . . . that the really blessed thing is to like what right reason ordains, and to follow her authority, then we have got a practical benefit out of culture. We have got a much wanted principle, a principle of authority, to counteract the tendency to anarchy which seems to be threatening us.[59]

Yet "right reason" is not to be confused with conscience, which for Arnold is a narrower moral term implying literal-minded observance of rules of conduct. Indeed, he contrasts "belief in right reason" with the Hebraistic emphasis, "as the one thing needful," on a

> *strictness of conscience,* the staunch adherence to some fixed law of doing we have got already, instead of *spontaneity of consciousness,* which tends continually to enlarge our whole law of doing. They have fancied themselves to have in their religion a sufficient basis for the whole of their life fixed and certain for ever, a full law of conduct and a full law of thought. . . .[60]

This emphasis on *spontaneity of consciousness* as part of the functioning of right reason within us recalls the emphasis on flexibility and disinterestedness as elements of culture. Right reason is not narrow rationality, reducible to formula or capable of charting our course with scientifically experimental precision (in our sense of these terms); that is why I characterized it above as an "intuitive recognition" which Arnold nonetheless believes to be rational. It is rational, not in being scientifically or logically demonstrable, but in being "apparent" or "reasonable" to a man of culture looking at the available evidence.

Here again we are confronted with the centrality of *culture.* Its defining elements are elaborated in an effort to explain its workings; accordingly, we have *right reason* exercised in a *disinterested* and *flexible* manner apprehending *the best* so as to establish an *order of ideas* which will engender, with the aid of *imaginative reason* and a *spontaneity of consciousness,* the *perfection* of humankind in society. Yet none of these terms succeeds in escaping the invocation of culture itself in order to explain their own workings. Like altar regalia, they surround and suggestively enhance the central mystery, but the mystery remains. The regalia and vestments borrow dignity and significance from the mystery they are presumed to surround, at the same time that the mystery is made present to those assembled through the ceremonial adornments. It is ever thus when it is symbols, or symbolic actions, that are set before us on the altar. Supernatural transubstantiations having become impossible for him to believe in (and soon, he believes, for most others), Arnold has placed before us on the bare altar table a resplendent vision of culture; he entertains us with its varied allurements and invites us to share in his reverence for it. If we ask him for a closer look at this object of our invited devotion, he tells us it is "the best" we can ever obtain, "perfection" itself is its destination; if we ask him how we shall recognize it, he tell us that our "right reason" will show us. But how, then, shall we gain this pearl of "right reason"?—why, *culture* will bring it![61] If, sensing contradiction, we press him yet further, he cautions us to be "flexible," that dogmas and doctrines or narrow systems cannot touch the holy of holies wherein culture resides, to be approached only by the "imaginative reason."[62]

If I am here having fun at Arnold's expense, it is not to belittle his achievement but to expose its true character, to portray the symbolic working of his *culture.* That working is disguised in Arnold's thought because he did not intend it to be taken as a symbol; he believed in his offer of culture, believed himself to be offering us real sustenance (*real food*). Quite simply, Arnold believed in his own symbol, so that it was to his own mind not symbolic at all, but substantial—just as to the orthodox Christian believer of his day, the Eucharist or other supernatural tenets of the faith were not mere "symbols" or "metaphors" so touching one's imaginative reason as to inspire Christian conduct (as Arnold saw them), but were real and substantial. Arnold, while disagreeing with these believers and pointing out the looming inadequacy of that faith for the society as a whole, honored those for whom this was an adequate faith in their own lives; so we must honor his.

How, then, if unintended, and without suggesting any insincerity or inadequacy on Arnold's part, might this symbolic functioning of culture be demonstrated? If Arnold did not intend his culture concept as a symbol, but believed in its "content" as a substantive aid to thought and a solution to the modern plight of consciousness, two questions must be addressed in offering this "symbolic functioning" as an explanation for the simultaneous vagueness and power of Arnold's doctrine of culture: (1) where precisely in Arnold's own writing can evidence be found of this symbolic treatment? and (2) how can we account for Arnold's failure himself to awaken to this element in his thought?—or more precisely (since who among us knows his own mind?), what enabled Arnold to treat culture in this symbolic fashion, without its hollowness (from an analytic point of view) being exposed to his full view? In the process of answering these questions we shall have to review and evaluate more critically Arnold's doctrine of culture.

The Symbolic Function of Culture

The role of Arnold's style in promoting his doctrine of culture has been noted by numerous critics and referred to previously in this chapter. T. S. Eliot has written that, in spite of the vagueness of Arnold's prose, which will not stand "very close analysis," yet "Arnold does still hold us . . . by the power of his rhetoric and by representing a point of view which is particular though it cannot be wholly defined." Eliot goes on to point out that a lack of clarity in ideas is "one reason why Arnold, Carlyle, and Ruskin were so influential, for precision and completeness of thought do not always make for influence."[63] But it was the *particular combination* of a vague idea of culture with a style suggesting a genial worldliness, prudent cosmopolitanism, and a casual temper of assurance, of confident knowing (which were themselves what his culture promised) that was one of the secret's of Arnold's success. His own style, in a sense, seems to stand as witness for his recommended culture; it breathes with the voice of culture, repetitiously chanting culture's key words, and by its self-assured, genial, unruffled tone seems to say to the reader, "This is what culture does for you: it makes you whole, secure, serene, free."

John Holloway has analyzed one of the devices by which Arnold's prose style works this effect in a discussion of its "value frames." In scrutinizing a number of different instances of Arnold rendering judgments, he notes that they "influence us less because they describe than because they exemplify the right habit of mind; that is to say, they effect the reader less through their meaning than through their tone."[64] This "right habit of mind" is of course the habit of culture, and it is the invocation of culture that is the consistent feature of these value frames: "Surely culture is useful in reminding us . . ." or "The aspirations of culture are not satisfied unless . . ."—to cite only two instances of Arnold's recommending a quality of culture by first "framing" it with an invocation of the central symbol.[65] This repetitious invocation of culture (only vaguely defined previously) enhances the term's positive content by associating it with the various goods recommended in these more specific judgments, or by contrasting it to things condemned, so that these value frames not only "recommend [particular] assertions and offer grounds for them" but also "elucidate and recommend the temper of mind to which they seem true"[66]—which is to say *they* recommend *culture* while at the same time *culture* validates *them*—and all of this kept swimmingly afloat by Arnold's tone and temper, his characteristic "urbanity and amenity . . . so pervasively recommended to the reader by the whole texture of his writing."[67]

It is this blurred associative value of the term that is at work in its "symbolic functioning": its repetitious use and varied associations give it what Eliot calls "a kind of illusion of precision and clarity"[68] while the enormous appeal of the qualities and state of mind associated with it protect its vagueness by surrounding it with an aura of ultimate value. The most concrete evidence of the term's functioning in this manner in Arnold's thought is the transformation that occurs in the use of the term. In his definition and early use of "culture," Arnold is referring to a habit of mind and of human inquiry, to a process at the end of which a human judgment invoking value is needed for it to have an effect. But very quickly this use of "culture" is transformed into another, subtly and significantly different: "culture" becomes in Arnold's usage an abstract noun of force, used in much the same way a layman might refer to "gravity," as a power of its own—still a process, but now capable of generating its own results, *with the element of human value silently subsumed into the concept!* It is only this rhetorical shift in his use of the term that enables Arnold to write sentences like "culture brings us toward right reason" and get away with it!—because he is implicitly using the term in two different senses: culture in the sense he began with requires the exercise of right reason in order to reach its judgments, it is dependent upon it; but now culture—in the grander sense, with value judgments subsumed within it—is freed from that dependence upon right reason: it will in fact create right reason within us. This unmarked dual use of "culture" in Arnold's prose is effective and highly infectious; it seduces the mind of the reader to believe in its promises even as he remains vaguely unsure what "it" is or how it can accomplish them. To oppose culture, once Arnold is through ringing her changes, would constitute a kind of sacrilege:

> The pursuit of perfection, then, is the pursuit of sweetness and light. He who works for sweetness and light, works to make reason and the will of God prevail. He who works for machinery, he who works for hatred, works only for confusion. Culture looks beyond machinery, culture hates hatred; culture has one great passion, the passion for sweetness and light. It has one even greater!—the passion for making them *prevail*. It is not satisfied till we *all* come to a perfect man; it knows that the sweetness and light of the few must be imperfect until the raw and unkindled masses of humanity are touched with sweetness and light.[69]

Here we have all the blessed realms of England, the heights of poetry, the wisdom of Oxford, the rustic sagacity of Wordsworthian nature, the light of Heaven, and the will of God Himself, gathered up into one sweet cuddly bundle together with "the raw and unkindled masses"—all drawn close to the bosom of culture! Surely our apostle has chosen the side of God and the angels in trumpeting his cause!

So long as one is content to bask in the sweetness and light of Arnold's deft style, the trumpet's call sounds serenely oblivious to the underlying theoretical difficulties in the culture concept. Once Arnold gets down to specific cases, however, and considers how his culture might be fostered concretely in society and politics, the tune strains and cracks, as those difficulties sound their discordant notes.

Inadequacy of Arnold's Doctrine of Culture

As the title of ***Culture and Anarchy*** suggests, Arnold's interest in advancing the cause of culture arose not simply out of some abstract Platonic conception of the ideal human condition. Throughout his long career as Inspector of Schools beginning in 1851, Arnold was in close touch with social and educational conditions in England among the middle and lower classes; moreover, ***Culture and Anarchy*** was written amid agitation for suffrage extension, including mass meetings and occasional outbreaks of violence, as well as continuing disputes over Ireland. Arnold's endorsement of the maintenance of order in response was unequivocal. For those "who believe in right reason" and "the progress of humanity towards perfection," Arnold wrote (and here we note Holloway's "value frame" in action),

> the framework of society, that theater on which this August drama has to unroll itself, is sacred; and whoever administers it, . . . we steadily and with undivided heart support them in repressing anarchy and disorder; because without order there can be no society, and without society there can be no human perfection.[70]

The latter part of this statement is no mere window dressing intended to conceal a harsh repressiveness; that much is clear from Arnold's other statements in support of promoting equality through the reduction of class distinctions and the alleviation of oppressive economic conditions. Arnold was not a partisan of any of the three classes into which he divided English society; from the standpoint of culture, all were deficient. The upper class he calls "Barbarians" because they are impervious to ideas, settled in inherited patterns stemming from the feudal era of dissolution during which their elevated position served a unifying social function; later, their privileges lingered on without functional justification. The middle classes are "Philistines," intent on immediate practical (and often material) benefits and committed to their "freedom" to grow in personal power and comfort. The lower class (that part of the working class not identifying with the middle class) he calls simply the "Populace"; it is the unleavened mass, "that portion . . . of the working class which, raw and half-developed, has long lain half-hidden amidst its poverty and squalor" but which is now beginning to do as it likes too, which means (in its benign mood) drinking and (in its menacing mood) "brawling, hustling, and smashing."[71] What all classes lack is a standard of excellence to summon them out of their "ordinary selves" and to stimulate their growth in the direction of culture.

With Tocqueville, Arnold believed the inevitable trend of the age to be toward equality, because inequality constrains man's "instinct of expansion" which is "as genuine an instinct in man as the need in plants for the light. . . ."[72] But this tendency is not, in Arnold's view, merely unavoidable; in the providence of culture it is a necessary and desirable step toward that ideal of perfection which, given the nature of man, is both individual *and* social, which cannot rest in the elevation of the few but must extend the benefits of culture to all. Culture is inherently evangelistic; its vision is unitary:

> [Culture leads us] to conceive of true human perfection as a *harmonious* perfection, developing all sides of our humanity; and as a *general* perfection, developing all parts of our society. For if one member suffer, the other members suffer with it; and the fewer there are that follow the true way of salvation, the harder that way is to find.[73]

Arnold is saying something more here than what man's status as a "social" animal obviously implies (that human interaction is an essential by-product of his nature; therefore, what we do affects others in such a way that even the achievement of individual goals requires the cooperation of others). Alongside this obvious argument lies his belief that human nature contains a "vital instinct of expansion," an innate tendency of life "*to affirm one's own essence;* meaning by this, to develop one's own existence fully and freely, to have ample light and air, to be neither cramped nor overshadowed."[74] In a social creature like man this instinct of life toward expansion implies a drive toward *unity,* a desire to be in agreement, in harmony, with others.[75] This presumptive goal of unity is the buried axiom in Arnold's definition of the ideal culture, or civilization, according to our "true humanity":

> Civilization is the humanization of man in society. Man is civilized when the whole body of society comes to live a life worthy to be called *human,* and corresponding to man's true aspirations and powers.[76]

And again:

> To be humanized is to comply with the true law of our human nature. . . . To be humanized is to make progress towards this, our true and full humanity. And to be civilized is to make progress towards this in . . . civil society "without which," says Burke, "man could not by any possibility arrive at the perfection of which his nature is capable, nor even make a remote and faint approach to it."[77]

The ideal of culture, or civilization,[78] thus presupposes not only an "order of ideas" (see page 44 above), but also social organization to embody those ideas in such a way that men's (and women's—though Arnold has little to say of them) "powers" of expansion may be exercised both freely and harmoniously.

What is needed, then, both as a principle of organization for such a society and to elevate members of all classes to its level, is a harmonizing standard, a "source of authority," as well as a means to make it prevail. In attempting to meet this provision, Arnold's concept of culture is strained beyond its capacity. Culture, Arnold tells us,

> seeks to do away with classes; to make the best . . . current everywhere; to make all men live in an atmosphere of sweetness and light, where they may use ideas . . . *freely*—nourished, and not bound by them.

> This is the *social idea;* and the men of culture are the true apostles of equality.[79]

The clarion call here is impeccable. The existing classes are, after all, so badly flawed that what is wanted is not the rule of any one of them, nor more aristocrats and fewer populace, but a new species—the man of culture. Happily he already exists; within each class there are—Arnold's chosen term here is striking—*"aliens."* These blessed beings are "persons who are mainly led, not by their class spirit, but by a general *humane spirit,* by the love of human perfection. . . ."[80]; in a word, they are, as the flashing of those key words tell us, men of *culture.* These are the ones who have risen above the "ordinary selves" of their classes and have found their "best selves." And it is in that "best self," the self of culture, that Arnold finds his "source of authority" and unity answering to the "difficulty of democracy" which is "how to find and keep high ideals."[81]

But has he found an organizing principle for social order? There have always been elite souls, and it is at least arguable that at times they have gained the upper hand in a governing class and wielded power over the society as a whole. But this is not Arnold's vision; he is not attempting to reinvest the aristocracy; he wants a free, equal, and harmonious order. He admits that conditions are not such at that time "to help and elicit our best self," but he claims that those conditions can be mended and the number of "aliens" increased. How? By the action of the *State*—and here the trumpet falters.

Arnold first tries to escape the difficulty by redefining "the State," conceived in Burke's sense as "the nation in its collective and corporate character," as a "center of light and authority"[82]:

> The question is . . . whether the nation may not thus acquire in the State an ideal of high reason and right feeling, representing its best self, commanding general respect, and forming a rallying-point for the intelligence and for the worthiest instincts of the community, which will herein find a true bond of union.
>
> . . . Only, the State-power which [the nation] employs should be a power which really represents its best self, and whose action its intelligence and justice can heartily avow and adopt. . . . To offer a worthy initiative, and to set a standard of rational and equitable action—this is what the nation should expect of the State. . . .[83]
>
> Providence . . . generally works in human affairs by human means; so when we want to make right reason act on individual inclination, our best self on our ordinary self, we seek to give it more power of doing so by giving it public recognition and authority, and embodying it, so far as we can, in the State. . . .
>
> . . . we are all afraid of giving to the State too much power, because we only conceive of the State as something equivalent to the class in occupation of the executive government, and are afraid of that class abusing power to its own purposes. . . . By our everyday selves . . . we are separate, personal, at war; we are only safe from one another's tyranny when no one has any power; and this safety, in its turn, cannot save us from anarchy. And when, therefore, anarchy presents itself as a danger to us, we know not where to turn.
>
> But by our *best self* we are united, impersonal, at harmony. We are in no peril from giving authority to this, because it is the truest friend we all of us can have; and when anarchy is a danger to us, to this authority we may turn with sure trust. Well, and this is the very self which culture, or the study of perfection, seeks to develop in us; at the expense of our old untransformed self, taking pleasure only in doing what it likes or is used to do, and exposing us to the risk of clashing with everyone else who is doing the same! So that our poor culture, which is flouted as so unpractical, leads us to the very ideas capable of meeting the great want of our present embarrassed times! We want an authority, and we find nothing but jealous classes, checks, and a deadlock; culture suggests the idea of *the State.* We find no basis for a firm State-power in our ordinary selves; culture suggests one to us in our *best self.*[84]

It is this reconstituted "State," acting on culture's behalf as the "organ of our collective best self, of our national right reason,"[85] that Arnold charges with the task of creating conditions conducive to the growth of culture, augmenting the number of "best selves" within each of the existing classes. The primary field in which Arnold seeks this state harvest of culture is, not surprisingly, education—and especially education of the dominant middle class whose lead, he believes, the lower class will follow. Arnold has seen the educational system at first hand and has also had the opportunity to compare it with those on the Continent; he finds the English middle classes "are among the worst educated in the world" and strongly urges the adoption of a system of state-supported public schools for them.[86] Other state actions he urges include "a reduction of those immense inequalities of condition and property amongst us" and "a genuine municipal system."[87]

Raymond Williams in *Culture and Society* has focused succinctly on the "breakdown" in Arnold's thought at this point. In essence, Williams's point is that Arnold's "State" is reconstituted only in theory, so that the "State for which Burke was an actuality has become for Arnold an idea."[88] Arnold may redefine the state as a "collective best self," but saying so does not make it so. Lionel Trilling makes an interesting comparison of Arnold's position to Rousseau's: just as Rousseau was driven to posit a "General Will" to embody the good, "to place power and reason in the same agent," so Arnold creates a theoretical "State" as a last resort given the inadequacy of the existing state. "In short," Trilling concludes, "where Rousseau writes 'general will' we may, with no violence to his idea or Arnold's, read 'best self.'"[89] Though Trilling does not make note of it in his discussion of the points of similarity, even Arnold's language in places is reminiscent of Rousseau. In writing of the "ordinary self" of the existing classes, he says that it is "wholly occupied . . . with the things of itself and not its *real self,* with the things of the State, and not the *real State.*"[90] Arnold is left, as Trilling and Williams both point out, with the same dilemma that confronts

Rousseau: how to use the existing state to reconstitute the "real" or "true State"? This question goes begging in Arnold, as Williams neatly points out:

> . . . the position in which [the general argument is left] is this: that the State itself must be the principal agent through which the State as a "center of authority and light" is to be created. Yet the existing State, loaded with such an agency, is in fact, on Arnold's showing, subject to the deadlock of the existing and inadequate social classes.[91]

This kind of thinking is, in Trilling's phrase, "confusion in a circle." Yet as Trilling also points out this confusion "lies not only in Arnold's thought but in the nature of the problem": "The way in which society is ordered determines the moral life of individuals and classes, but the moral life of individuals determines the way in which society is ordered."[92] One may question as a practical matter—which was, in spite of the vagueness and idealism of his language, the level to which Arnold addressed his argument in ***Culture and Anarchy***—whether this theoretical dilemma is all that staggering. Arnold in fact does take note of it, in a passage unmarked by either Trilling or Williams. Answering a contemporary critic's question—"how you can be certain that reason will be the quality which will be embodied in [the State]?"—Arnold replies:

> You cannot be certain of it, undoubtedly, if you never try to bring the thing about; but the question is, the action of the State being the action of the collective nation, and the action of the collective nation carrying naturally great publicity, weight, and force of example with it, whether we should try to put into the action of the State as much as possible of right reason or our best self, which may, in this manner, come back to us with new force and authority . . . ?[93]

In this passage we seem to see Arnold the pragmatist escaping the theoretical straitjacket into which his critics seek to confine his argument. For in spite of Williams's argument that "it is not merely the influence of the best individuals that Arnold is recommending; it is the embodiment of this influence in the creation of a State,"[94] it appears that it is precisely "the influence of the best individuals" that Arnold is recommending as the practical means to "the creation [technically a reconstituting] of a State." Without denying the absence of a theoretical guarantee of the workability of his proposals, Arnold doggedly insists that we must do what we can and see what happens. He is savvy enough to realize that a state composed of Philistines and Barbarians is not going to adopt his proposals for culture unless, through an act of persuasion, their own "best selves" are called forth first; that being the case, what is involved is a simultaneous process of education to foster the growth of individual "best selves," in and out of government, and a gradual adaptation of the state in exercising its influence in harmony with this slower, piecemeal process. Arnold is not proposing a wholesale revamping of the state according to a theoretical blueprint; he specifically rejects the radicalism and folly of such schemes as "Jacobinism." Surprisingly, given his sensitivity to the idea of organicism in *Culture and Society,* Williams seems to miss the point where Arnold is concerned. Lionel Trilling is closer to an understanding of Arnold here, recognizing that Arnold's conception of the state is "essentially mythic . . . like a Platonic myth." "The value of the myth"—in this case Arnold's ideal conception of the state—"cannot depend on its demonstrability as a fact," Trilling writes, "but only on the value of the attitudes it embodies, the further attitudes it engenders and the actions it motivates."[95]

This assessment is surely closer to Arnold's intention, yet it does not wholly obviate the dilemma underscored in Williams's more abbreviated treatment. The fact remains that the *influence* even of Arnold's *idea* of the state depends to some extent on its theoretical integrity. Ultimately, what Arnold is attempting to create is an idea, or inner standard, which will hold people's loyalty and unite them in common purpose. If in illustrating the application of this standard to the social order, a crack appears in the internal consistency of the ideal, if the standard shows itself to be ambiguous, then even though a practical effort to urge its adoption may yet continue, its ultimate value and status as a standard is thrown into question. Even if one succeeded in converting a nation to Arnold's doctrine of culture, if the concept itself be flawed, then attempts to follow it, whether embodied in a state or not, would eventually falter. Thus even an analysis of Arnold's attempt to conceive a state or social order is thrown back onto an analysis of the integrity of his concept of culture. What the question comes down to is whether there is any real content to the concept, whether one can say what a "best self" *is?* If not, one may appeal to people's "best selves" and urge upon them a "collective best self" as much as one wants—and even accomplish some good results with this moralizing—but measured against Arnold's intentions, in the final analysis such efforts will be no more than "vain repetitions" babbled in the wind to no purpose.

"The best," after all, is a relative term, a term of comparison. Arnold even admits its relativity, recognizing that what appears "best" is one era fades in another, giving way to a different or more advanced "best." But if one cannot locate a consistent principle which defines what is "best" in each instance, then culture conceived as "the best" becomes a standard that undermines itself in ludicrous succession. A striving for "perfection" may unite people harmoniously in shared devotion to a common cause; it may also foment revolution and war. It all depends on the content of the "perfection" envisioned, on whether we are all devoted to the same cause in the same way. "Culture" urges one to strive for the "best," and not to settle for the routine, to seek one's "best self" and to seek its embodiment in the state; this same culture is advanced as a harmonizing standard of unity. Yet this striving for the ideal, without any further qualification of the relativity of the standard proposed, breeds conflict and disunity as readily as harmony and peace. Conceived abstractly, with value judgments implicit but not spelled out, "culture" unifies, harmonizes; it seems to do so easily precisely because of Arnold's failure to spell out the hidden values. Conceived relatively and historically, "culture" breeds change and reform, frees us from routine and tradition; in Arnold's hands it seems to do so without conflict, still harmoniously, because it is now promiscuously joined to the other, more absolute but abstract, meaning of "culture." This equivocality, I take it, is what Williams means when he comments that Arnold's "confusion of attachment was to be masked by the emphasis of a word":

> Culture was a process, but he could not find the material of that process, either, with any confidence, in the society of his own day, or, fully, in a recognition of an order that transcended human society. The result seems to be that, more and more, and against his formal intention, the process becomes an abstraction. Moreover, while appearing to resemble an absolute, it has in fact no absolute ground. . . . His way of thinking about institutions was in fact relativist, as indeed a reliance on "the best that has been thought and written in the world" (and on that alone) must always be. Yet at the last moment he not only holds to this, but snatches also towards an absolute: and *both are Culture.* Culture became the final critic of institutions, and the process of replacement and betterment, yet it was also, at root, beyond institutions. This confusion of attachment was to be masked by the emphasis of a word.[96]

In this "emphasis of a word" we see the symbolic function of that word, *culture*: it functions both to focus commitment and to cloud the object of that commitment, just as a symbol both conceals and reveals the reality it mediates.

But even to speak of Arnold's "culture" (or of symbols in general) in this way presupposes a reality to be mediated; otherwise Arnold's "culture" becomes nothing but a subjective grab bag of relative preferences, just as symbols deprived of realities to mediate become an endless maze of self-reflecting mirrors, reducing thought and analysis to vain subjective babble. It seems clear, as in Williams's finding above, that Arnold "snatches toward an absolute," that Arnold did admit into his thought a belief in an order of reality transcending reason. He appears to have done so without being fully aware of it; indeed, if challenged on this point, he would argue that the realities in question are fully "rational" and "verifiable." But to our later perspective, his "rational" seems merely "conventional"; and deprived of the consensus that sustained (no doubt unconsciously) his reason, what appears to him as reasonably "verifiable" seems to us only "arguable."

William Robbins has thoroughly detailed this buried content in Arnold's thought; he finds there, ultimately sustaining the content of all those relative terms clustering about it ("the best," "perfection," and so on), an implicit idealism which he identifies with the philosophical tradition of "ethical idealism."[97] Though Robbins is more concerned with the invasion of the transcendent into Arnold's moral and religious thought, there seems little doubt that it also affects his doctrine of culture. Indeed, it is the hidden content of Arnold's "culture" that enables it to function successfully as a symbol in his thought, disguising even from himself its fatal ambiguity (considered from an analytic point of view). That implicit content provides the necessary basis of a presumed *reality* which allows "culture" to function as a symbol in both obscuring the nature of and heightening commitment to that reality.

In one sense this content, the ultimate "source of authority" in the ideas of the "best self," "right reason," and "perfection" that Arnold advances, is not hidden at all. He makes repeated references to the "true law of human nature," "the law of human life," and the "intelligible law of things."[98] Arnold clearly believed in the existence of a *moral order* in individual life and in the life of society in history; while he denied supernatural status to that order, in the form of a personal God willing and enforcing that order, he believed that it was built into the nature and structure of the cosmos, pointing the path to human achievement and happiness. How or why it came to be does not seem to concern Arnold; he insists merely on reason's capacity to recognize that such *is* the order and to discover in it the direction to human life and history. "Right reason" is the spontaneous, intuitive recognition of that order, an appreciation of "the idea that the world is in a course of development, of *becoming,* towards a perfection infinitely greater than we now can even conceive, the idea of a *tendance a l'ordre* present in the universe."[99] "Perfection" is being in accord with that order, just as the "best self" is the self awakened to the existence of such an order and desiring it. The "verifiable" or experimental "proof" of the existence of this order is the experience of satisfaction or happiness one experiences in seeking to follow it. While progress toward it is a process, both individually and socially, and although Arnold recognizes that the process is not automatic, still the impulse driving us to seek that order is built into human nature:

> Such an effort to set up a recognized authority, imposing on us a high standard in matters of intellect and taste, has many enemies in human nature. We all of us like to go our own way. . . . But if the effort to limit this freedom of our lower nature finds, as it does and must find, enemies in human nature, it finds also auxiliaries in it. . . . Man alone of the living creatures, [Cicero] says, goes feeling after ". . . the discovery of an *order,* a law of *good taste,* a *measure* for his words and actions." Other creatures submissively follow the law of their own nature; man alone has an impulse leading him to set up some other law to control the bent of his nature.[100]

To say that there is in human nature and history a built-in tendency toward the ideal, toward "perfection," does provide hope and incentive for the mission of culture in bringing us toward the ideal. It is also true, as Joseph Carroll notes, that for Arnold culture has replaced God as that in which he trusts to bring us toward that ideal—"culture" here being "spiritual progress in accordance with right reason . . . the 'absolute' not as state or substance but as the historical process of growth."[101] But a belief in an inherent tendency in human nature and in the universe toward such an order still does not define for us the nature of that order; without specifying the values endorsed by that order, the character of Arnold's "absolute" remains abstract, his "source of authority" unworkable.

When we turn to examine precisely with what values Arnold does in fact invest this universal order, we find that they turn out to be those of a traditional and humane Christianity—the values, by and large, of his own culture and class. The clue is dropped in the above passage by the reference to our "lower nature"; the duality of our nature—high and low, spirit and flesh—is here presumed, requiring only a reference to enlist the reader's acceptance of its truth. The principle of order in human nature leading to happiness thus turns out to be—*righteousness!* The supreme model of our "best self" turns out to be—*Jesus!* The values endorsed by the order of the universe and culture turn out to be—"self-renouncement," "purity," "mildness," "charity."

In truth, Arnold hardly needs to describe the values he has culture endorse because he leans so heavily upon and adopts so uncritically the prevailing moral consensus. He can write of "ideas of moral order and of right" that "are in human nature"[102] without pausing to detail or attempt to argue for them because he can presume that no "reasonable" person questions them; everyone knows what "righteousness" and "conduct" are (he needn't even prefix "moral" here), and when he does write "moral" the word can have only one meaning—the morality of the Judeo-Christian tradition. Where other religions overlap, whether pagan or Moslem, it is the Judeo-Christian tradition to which they are seen to correspond, which provides the standard by which *they* are measured; and where they fail to coincide, they are judged accordingly. The "relativity" of Arnold's standard of culture is dangerous and subversive of traditional order only in the abstract (or only to emphasize one part of that traditional order as against another, to right an imbalance). Even the "Judeo" part of the moral consensus can be dismissed readily with a smug blast of rhetorical questions where it conflicts with the Christian order (which at its best incorporates the Hellenic as well); thus the voice of righteousness can thunder its questions in full confidence of an answering moral consensus:

> . . . immense as is our debt to the Hebrew race and its genius, incomparable as is its authority on certain profoundly important sides of our human nature, worthy as it is to be described as having uttered, for those sides, the statutes of the divine and eternal order of things, the law of God—who, that is not manacled and hoodwinked by his Hebraism, can believe that, as to love and marriage, our reason and the necessities of our humanity have their true, sufficient, and divine law expressed for them by the voice of any Oriental and polygamous nation like the Hebrews? Who I say, will believe, when he really considers the matter, that where the feminine nature, the feminine ideal, and our relations to them, are brought into question, the delicate and apprehensive genius of the Indo-European race, the race which invented the Muses, and chivalry, and the Madonna, is to find its last word on this question in the institutions of a Semitic people, whose wisest king had seven hundred wives and three hundred concubines?[103]

Arnold is here arguing against a literal-minded interpretation of Scripture (forbidding a man to marry his deceased wife's sister on the basis of the book of Leviticus), for leavening a narrow Hebraism with Hellenic culture; but notice that culture's liberal method ends by endorsing conventional morality, with which no serious argument is presumed to be possible, as Basil Willey has pointed out:

> And this righteousness, what is it? We have already seen that it involves renouncement of self, dying to sin, and rising to new life on the spiritual plane. In this Preface [to ***Last Essays on Church and Religion***], Arnold reduces it to a yet simpler formula: *kindness* and *pureness,* or charity and chastity. I think a reader of today . . . will especially notice Arnold's sense of security on this subject; he can appeal to an almost unbroken consensus of opinion about what righteousness meant. There might be, and of course there were, the widest possible divergences in credal beliefs, but everybody knew perfectly well what was the right thing to do on any occasion, and what was wrong. A man might not do what he knew he ought to do, or he might do what he ought not; but conscience and universal agreement pointed unfailingly in the right direction.[104]

How fortunate that the grand labor of culture, ranging comparatively over the whole of human experience and history, should find at its conclusion that "the best" lay, after all, pretty much in one's own back yard!

The content of "culture" turns out, then, to be in large measure the content of Christian character, with the added qualification that character be united to reason, conduct to intellect, Hebraism to Hellenism: "Culture without character is, no doubt, something frivolous, vain, and weak; but character without culture is, on the other hand, something raw, blind, and dangerous."[105] In sum, as Trilling concludes succinctly, "Culture may best be described as religion with the critical intellect superadded."[106] But if "culture goes beyond religion," as Arnold believed in did,[107] it does not contradict its moral content; rather, that content is subsumed into the standard of "the best" along with an intellectual attitude of openness or flexibility, or not presuming any particular embodiment of that "best" to be immutable or incorruptible. True, "culture begets a dissatisfaction," but only in behalf of "its spiritual standard of perfection"; culture opposes anarchy, and its dissatisfaction is a disciplined striving, not an indulgent liberty or nihilistic whim.[108] Arnold belonged, in Robbins's words, "to a generation which, though learning to do without God, could not be without absolutes, especially in the moral sphere."[109]

The concept of culture gave Arnold a perspective from which simultaneously to endorse and to critique his own particular culture. Able to draw upon a received consensus of moral values, which his concept confidently subsumed without questioning, he could proceed with his critique on a secure footing, without facing the unsettling possibility that the critique could be turned against the traditional Christian values presumed by his own concept of culture. Thus the delicate balance between the maintenance of the *standards of perfection* of culture, on the one hand, and the challenging, questioning, seeking, inconclusive attitude of *flexibility,* on the other—the balance between order and freedom—though difficult, was still theoretically possible to Arnold, because both rested on an unquestioned consensus of values. Once those values are called into question, however, both the integrity of this concept of culture and the unity it serves to symbolize collapse. Deprived of its implicit content of values, the standard becomes abstract, ultimately subjective in actual content; "the best" becomes a point of dispute instead of a unifying goal. Deprived of a moral consensus to endorse his tone in rhetorically dismissing "the voice of any Oriental polygamous nation like the Hebrews," Arnold's presumption of the superior wisdom of monogamous family structures is left exposed, fair game for anthropologists of all races and cultures to dispute. Just as a nation's flag, to function successfully as a symbol, presumes a prior loyalty to the country symbolized, so Arnold's "culture," functioning to represent in a word both the goal and method of "perfection," "the best," presumes an existing consensus about the *nature* of that goal, the *moral content* of that perfection.

Even with that moral consensus intact, however, Arnold's attempt to construct a unifying principle for modern society around his conception of culture faces a serious difficulty in his assumption that the ideal quest for culture could be spread throughout the society, that its excellence is sufficiently apparent to win endorsement in a democratic society when promoted through education. From the perspective of the late twentieth century, Arnold's hopes for the spread of his culture through education seem naive, even aside from the breakdown of traditional moral patterns. Arnold himself seems to have been ambivalent about the elitist implications of his appeal to culture. He argues of course for the extension of that appeal by education and by holding aloft its standard wherever it might be made visible (through the established church, the state, or the influence of example of those already responding to its call); and he states that it is part of culture's goal to extend itself to *all.* Yet at other times he evidences an awareness that not all can attain its sublime heights. In **"Numbers"** he places his hopes for culture in the leading influence of a significant minority, a saving "remnant," and admits that the majority, while its action may be "good occasionally,"

> lacks principle, it lacks persistence; if today its good impulses prevail, they succumb tomorrow; sometimes it goes right, but it is very apt to go wrong. . . . the world being what is it, we must surely expect the aims and doings of the majority of men to be at present very faulty. . . .[110]

We may perhaps reconcile these divergent strands in Arnold's conception of culture's operation and say that Arnold envisions culture extending its reach to all in the sense of prevailing in defining and setting the standards which all would at least honor, and to which all would aspire in the varying degrees of their capacities; but that the exercise of this dominant influence in society would always depend on an active, exemplary minority.

But even this partial resolution of conflict between culture's democratic and elitist tendencies leaves the question of how that influence could be exercised so as to prevail over the whole of society. It was Arnold's understanding of the importance of religion and the Bible in forming the standards and behavior of "the masses" that led him to focus his attention on religious questions almost exclusively for ten years (and four books) following the publication of ***Culture and Anarchy*** in 1869. By bringing the perspective of culture to bear upon religion, he hoped to strengthen and preserve an essential Christianity against a skepticism occasioned by the conflict felt to exist between the modern outlook of science and the rigid claims of a doomed dogmatic orthodoxy. He believed such a redefinition of Christian truth—focusing on the example of Christ (a paragon of the "best self") and on a common institutional embodiment in a national church with shared rituals of worship, rather than on supernatural elements (occasioning doubt) and points of metaphysical dogma (occasioning institutional divisions)—would preserve the moral influence of the Bible and the institutional supports of the church for those standards which culture also endorsed. The continuity of Christianity thus appears as part of the overall program for the human advance toward the ideal of perfection presided over by culture. Since the dependence of culture upon Christianity for more than its influence in preserving a moral consensus (i.e., its dependence on Christianity as a source of values to subsume within its claim to be an ideal standard of its own) does not surface explicitly in Arnold's thought, he is quite comfortable in detaching the moral lessons and examples of Christianity from their traditional supernatural foundation. It is not merely that he does not believe in that foundation himself; equally important, he believes that he has in "culture" an adequate basis for authenticating values independently, apart from supernatural religion. Given the dependence of Arnold's doctrine of culture upon his understanding of religion, the following chapter will examine his attempt at redefining Christianity and evaluate the consequences of that redefinition for his ideal of culture.

Notes

1. The Arnold passage is from *Culture and Anarchy* in R. H. Super, ed., *The Complete Prose Works of Matthew Arnold,* 11 vols. (1960-77), 5:91. All subsequent citations of Arnold's prose are to this authoritative standard edition, but for the convenience of those referring to other editions I have retained references to the original titles of volumes published by Arnold. The Stevenson line is from *Quotations of Wit and Wisdom,* edited by John Gardner and Francesca Gardner Rease (1975), 4.
2. "Resignation," in Kenneth Allott and Miriam Allott, eds., *The Poems of Matthew Arnold,* 2d ed. (1979), 97, 100 (lines 198, 278).

3. Three recent studies illustrate the diversity of Arnold's thought and the range of his continuing relevance: Joseph Carroll's *The Cultural Theory of Matthew Arnold* (1982) and Ruth apRoberts's *Arnold and God* (1983) offer contrasting but ultimately complementary interpretations of Arnold's thought. Carroll's book in particular is an excellent synthesis, taking issue with debunkers of Arnold's "unsystematic" thinking and proposing as Arnold's primary achievement the construction of a "complete cultural system." Ruth apRoberts challenges the neglect of Arnold's religious writings; and while her study proceeds at a more pedestrian pace than Carroll's, it offers a worthwhile contrasting perspective and is useful in identifying sources of influence in the evolution of Arnold's thought. A third study, James C. Livingston's *Matthew Arnold and Christianity: His Religious Prose Writings* (1986) approaches Arnold's religious writings from a more rigorous theological perspective than does either Carroll or apRoberts, arguing counter to the critical mainstream for an interpretation of Arnold's religious beliefs as authentically Christian—indeed, as "in accord with the mainstream of liberal and modernist Christian theology of the past century" (xi).
4. Honan, 424, 425.
5. Honan, 349.
6. William Robbins, *The Ethical Idealism of Matthew Arnold* (1959), 139-40.
7. Honan, viii.
8. Honan, 424.
9. Robert Langbaum, *The Mysteries of Identity: A Theme in Modern Literature* (1977), 51, 52.
10. Lionel Trilling, *Matthew Arnold* (1939), 112.
11. "Empedocles on Etna," II, line 330, in Allott and Allott, 200.
12. Matthew Arnold, "Democracy," in Super, 2:29. "Democracy" was originally published as the introduction to *The Popular Education of France* in 1861 and later included in a collection of *Mixed Essays* (1879).
13. Arnold, "On the Modern Element in Literature," in Super, 1:23-24.
14. Arnold, "Heinrich Heine," *Essays in Criticism* (1865), in Super, 3:109-10.
15. Arnold, "Heinrich Heine," *Essays in Criticism,* in Super, 3:110.
16. "To Marguerite—Continued," in Allott and Allott, 130, 131, lines 1-4, 13-18. Whether intended by Arnold or not, I find here a poignant reversal of John Donne's "no man is an island" imagery in his "Meditation 17."
17. "Dover Beach," in Allott and Allott, 256-57, lines 30-37. The reinforcing, echoing imagery of these two poems when read in conjunction in their entirety (and not simply the fragments given here) has always seemed to me to enhance both poems.
18. Howard Foster Lowry, ed., *The Letters of Matthew Arnold to Arthur Hugh Clough* (1932), 111 (September 23, 1849).
19. Honan, 140.
20. Arnold, *On the Study of Celtic Literature* (1867), in Super, 3:381.
21. Arnold, "On the Modern Element in Literature," in Super, 1:32.
22. Langbaum calls attention to what appears to be an echo of Arnold's line from "Stanzas from the Grande Chartreuse" ("Silent—the best are silent now") in W. B. Yeats's classic characterization of the modern age ("The best lack all conviction") in "The Second Coming" (Langbaum, 5).
23. Arnold, "On the Modern Element in Literature," in Super, 1:19, 20.
24. This expression was often used by Arnold to describe the wholesome vision of Sophocles, which Arnold admired as a model of what "culture" seeks (*cf.* "To a Friend" in Allott and Allott, 111, and "On the Modern Element in Literature," in Super, 1:28 and 35).
25. Carroll, xiv.
26. Carroll, 2, 7-8.
27. Carroll, 15.
28. Carroll, 16.
29. Lowry, 63.
30. Carroll, 30.
31. Carroll, 34. Though expressed in somewhat different terms, Honan's view of the shift in Arnold's career supports Carroll's. Honan writes that Arnold's "prose is an adjunct to his best poetry—and especially to *Empedocles on Etna*—since in his social and literary essays he seeks a middle ground between the aridity of fact (or the world of scientific positivism which really destroys Empedocles) and the truths in religion and myth (or the world implicit in the songs of Callicles, the nightmare boy myth-maker)" (Honan, 210). David DeLaura in an essay on Arnold's "Critical Ideas" also notes that the "mature" Arnold condemns a whole set of "modern" attitudes (melancholy, isolation, gloom, morbidity, etc.) which in themselves "represent the deepest attitudes and temptations of Arnold's early career" (Kenneth Allott, ed., *Matthew Arnold* [1975], 147).
32. Carroll, xiv.
33. Carroll, xvii, 42-43.
34. Carroll, xiv, xv.
35. Carroll distinguishes four "phases" in Arnold's career: the initial phase of discontent in the early

poetry, establishing the problems to which his critical phases respond; the second "Hellenizing" phase extending from the early critical and political essays through *Culture and Anarchy,* in which Arnold develops the main outlines of his cultural theory serving as a "deliverance" from the modern spiritual dilemma; a third phase devoted almost exclusively to reinterpreting Christianity and the Bible in an effort to render them harmonious with the new "modern spirit" and so to preserve their moral influence; and a fourth phase of critical essays in Arnold's final decade in which he attempts to integrate his efforts of the previous two phases in a unified vision of intellectual "expansion" and moral "concentration" and in which poetry serves an elevating moral or religious function similar to that of his redefined (as poetry) religion.

36. Carroll, 75.
37. Carroll, 76.
38. Carroll, 83.
39. Carroll, 81. William Robbins argues along similar lines in *The Ethical Idealism of Matthew Arnold* for the philosophic seriousness of Arnold's views. He also suggests that Arnold might have found a more consistent philosophical position for his "experimental" approach, stopping short of adopting idealist assumptions, in William James's pragmatism, had the latter been available to him. However, given Arnold's evident desire for "unity and completion," it is debatable whether he would have been content with a Jamesian universe; forced to admit he had inadmissibly reintroduced into his system elements he began by purging, he might instead have been plunged back into Empedoclean despair.
40. Carroll, xiii.
41. Carroll, 14.
42. See pages 26*ff* above. Carroll does recognize that in Arnold's "redefinition" of modernity, Arnold "still takes account of the intellectual neurasthenia . . . previously marked as peculiarly modern"; but this negative feature is now simply overshadowed by the positive uses of modernity (Carroll, 44).
43. Raymond Williams, *Keywords: A Vocabulary of Culture and Society* (1976), 76. The book of definitions and explanatory discussion is A. L. Kroeber and Clyde Kluckholm's *Culture: A Critical Review of Concepts and Definitions* (1952).
44. This definition is taken from *The American Heritage Dictionary of the English Language* (Boston, Houghton Mifflin Co., 1969). It may be compared with a "condensed" definition offered by Kroeber and Kluckholm: "Culture consists of patterns, explicit and implicit, of and for behavior acquired and transmitted by symbols, constituting the distinctive achievements of human groups, including their embodiments in artifacts; the essential core of culture consists of traditional (i.e., historically derived and selected) ideas and especially their attached values; culture systems may, on the one hand, be considered as products of action, on the other as constituting elements of further action" (357).
45. See Raymond Williams in *Keywords* (76-82) and Ruth apRoberts in *Arnold and God* (especially pages 37-47 where she traces a significant influence of Herder on Arnold).
46. Carroll, xi.
47. Carroll, 39.
48. Arnold, "The Function of Criticism at the Present Time," in *Essays in Criticism,* in Super, 3:270.
49. Arnold, *Culture and Anarchy,* in Super, 5:233.
50. Arnold, *Culture and Anarchy,* in Super, 5:235.
51. Arnold, *Culture and Anarchy,* in Super, 5:110.
52. Arnold, "The Function of Criticism at the Present Time," *Essays in Criticism,* in Super, 3:267.
53. Arnold, *Culture and Anarchy,* in Super, 5:112.
54. Arnold, *Culture and Anarchy,* in Super, 5:94, 235.
55. Arnold, "The Function of Criticism at the Present Time," *Essays in Criticism,* in Super, 3:261.
56. Arnold, *Culture and Anarchy,* in Super, 5:93.
57. It is true that we often need aid in following even that which we know to be right. Arnold attempts to locate this aid in what he calls "imaginative reason"—a concept loosely allied with "right reason." To some extent they are interchangeable; both imply an intuitive (but rational) apprehension of the truth of human nature and the character of its ideal perfection. "Imaginative reason," however, is more often used in Arnold's discussion of poetry, whereas "right reason" is invoked for social or political concerns; imaginative reason adds to those intuitions it shares with right reason elements of feeling and of the senses, sympathetically representing its vision of perfection so as to inspire the loyalty and dedication of the corresponding "best self" within us. It is akin to that "grand power of poetry" Arnold describes in his essay on "Maurice de Guerin": ". . . the power of so dealing with things as to awaken in us a wonderfully full, new, and intimate sense of them, and of our relations with them. When this sense is awakened in us, as to objects without us, we feel ourselves to be in contact with the essential nature of those objects, to be no longer bewildered and oppressed by them, but to have their secret, and to be in harmony with them; and this feeling calms and satisfies us as no other can ("Maurice de Guerin," *Essays in Criticism,* in Super, 3:13). While Arnold here refers to "objects without us," because Guerin's poetic gift is to represent the natural world, poetry can also imaginatively awaken us to the moral world within

and without us, allowing us to glimpse "reason and the will of God" at work in life and calling forth our "best self."

58. Arnold, *Culture and Anarchy,* in Super, 5:190-91.
59. Arnold, *Culture and Anarchy,* in Super, 5:123.
60. Arnold, *Culture and Anarchy,* in Super, 5:176-77.
61. See passage quoted above ("culture brings us toward right reason") on pages 45-46.
62. William Robbins has similar fun with Arnold's attempt to forge a synthesis of Hellenism and Hebraism, the practical and the transcendent, by conceiving their reciprocal relation in "imaginative reason": "When Arnold fuses this 'reciprocal relation' by means of 'the imaginative reason,' he reaches the climax of his endeavor, the completion of his critical doctrine. The synthesis has been achieved, the dialectic successfully resolved. The phrase is persuasive and challenging. Yet it is a phrase that defies precise definition, that vaguely suggests transcendent mysteries, a departure from the horizontal to the vertical. The critic has left the plains and foothills of historical experience and for the moment stands tip-toe on the misty mountain-tops" (Robbins, 162-63).
63. T. S. Eliot, "Arnold and Pater," in *Selected Essays, 1917-1932* (1932), 346-48.
64. John Holloway, *The Victorian Sage: Studies in Argument* (1953), in David J. DeLaura, ed., *Matthew Arnold: A Collection of Critical Essays* (1973), 121.
65. Holloway, in DeLaura, 121, 120.
66. Holloway, in DeLaura, 121.
67. Holloway, in DeLaura, 119.
68. Eliot, "Arnold and Pater," in *Selected Essays, 1917-1932,* 347.
69. Arnold, *Culture and Anarchy,* in Super, 5:112.
70. Arnold, *Culture and Anarchy,* in Super, 5:222-23.
71. Arnold, *Culture and Anarchy,* in Super, 5:143, 145.
72. Arnold, preface to *Mixed Essays,* in Super, 8:371.
73. Arnold, *Culture and Anarchy,* in Super, 5:235. The echoing of Biblical language here is characteristic of Arnold's rhetoric.
74. Arnold, "Democracy," in Super, 2:7.
75. Arnold does not make this connection between these strands of his thought explicit, but it seems to me clearly implicit as the link between his emphasis on *expansion* on the one hand and on *harmony* on the other.
76. Arnold, preface to *Mixed Essays,* in Super, 8:370.
77. Arnold, "Equality," *Mixed Essays,* in Super, 8:286.
78. "Civilization" is the term Arnold uses in his later writing to describe the organization of society according to the ideal of culture. It involves four "powers," or manifestations of the desire for "expansion" or "life" in human behavior: the power of social life, or manners; the power of conduct; the power of intellect and knowledge, or science; and the power of beauty. In his preface to *Mixed Essays* Arnold adds "expansion" as a presiding fifth power, comprehending the "love of liberty" and the "love of equality" and reigning over the other four because civilization "presupposes this instinct, which is inseparable from human nature; presupposes its being satisfied, not defeated" (Super, 8:372).
79. Arnold, *Culture and Anarchy,* in Super, 5:113.
80. Arnold, *Culture and Anarchy,* in Super, 5:147.
81. Arnold, "Democracy," in Super, 2:17.
82. Arnold, *Culture and Anarchy,* in Super, 5:117, 134.
83. Arnold, "Democracy," in Super, 2:19, 28.
84. Arnold, *Culture and Anarchy,* in Super, 5:159, 134-35.
85. Arnold, *Culture and Anarchy,* in Super, 5:136.
86. Arnold, "Porro Unum Est Necessarium," *Mixed Essays,* in Super, 8:349.
87. Arnold, "Ecce, Convertimur ad Gentes," *Mixed Essays,* in Super, 9:7. Arnold was impressed with both the American and the French systems of municipal government which "provide people with the fullest liberty of managing their own affairs, and afford besides a constant and invaluable school of practical experience" ("A Word More About America," in Super, 10:197).
88. Raymond Williams, *Culture and Society, 1780-1950* (1958), 123.
89. Trilling, 253, 281.
90. Arnold, *Culture and Anarchy,* in Super, 5:143 (my emphasis).
91. Williams, 254.
92. Trilling, 254.
93. Arnold, *Culture and Anarchy,* in Super, 5:158.
94. Williams, 122.
95. Trilling, 255.
96. Williams, 127-28.
97. See Robbins, 165-75.
98. I have drawn three such references here at random: "Civilization in the United States" in Super, 11:352; *Culture and Anarchy* in Super, 5:207; and "Ecce, Convertimur ad Gentes" (*Mixed Essays*) in Super, 9:5.
99. Arnold, "Theodore Parker," in Super, 5:83.
100. Arnold, "The Literary Influence of the Academies," in Super, 3:235-36.
101. Carroll, 84.
102. Arnold, *God and the Bible* (1875), in Super, 7:208.

103. Arnold, *Culture and Anarchy,* in Super, 5:208.

104. Basil Willey, "Arnold and Religion," in Allott, 255-56.

105. Arnold, "Democracy," in Super, 2:24.

106. Trilling, 266.

107. Arnold, *Culture and Anarchy,* in Super, 5:94.

108. Arnold, *Culture and Anarchy,* in Super, 5:97-98.

109. Robbins, 164.

110. Arnold, *Discourses in America* (1885), in Super, 10:144-45.

Works Cited

Allott, Kenneth, ed. *Matthew Arnold.* London: G. Bell & Sons, 1975.

Altick, Richard D. *Victorian People and Ideas.* New York: W. W. Norton & Co., 1973.

Anderson, Quentin. *The American Henry James.* New Brunswick, NJ: Rutgers University Press, 1957.

———. "Henry James and the New Jerusalem." *Kenyon Review* 8, no. 4 (Autumn 1946): 414-566.

Annan, Noel. "The Intellectual Aristocracy." In *Studies in Social History: A Tribute to G. M. Trevelyan,* ed. by J. H. Plumb, 243-84. London: Longmans, 1955.

apRoberts, Ruth. *Arnold and God.* Berkeley: University of California Press, 1983.

Arnold, Matthew. *The Complete Prose Works of Matthew Arnold.* Edited by R. H. Super. 11 vols. Ann Arbor: University of Michigan Press, 1962-77.

———. *The Letters of Matthew Arnold to Arthur Hugh Clough.* Edited by Henry Foster Lowry. London: Oxford University Press, 1932.

———. *The Note-Books of Matthew Arnold.* Edited by Henry Foster Lowry, Karl Young, and Waldo Hilary Dunn. London: Oxford University Press, 1952.

———. *The Poems of Matthew Arnold.* 2nd ed. Edited by Kenneth Allott and Miriam Allott. New York: Longman, 1979.

Auden, W. H. Introduction to *The American Scene,* by Henry James. New York: Charles Scribner's Sons, 1946.

Baumer, Franklin L. *Modern European Thought: Continuity and Change in Ideas, 1600-1950.* New York: Macmillan Publishing Co., 1977.

———. *Religion and the Rise of Scepticism.* New York: Harcourt, Brace & Co., 1960.

Beach, Joseph Warren. *The Method of Henry James.* Philadelphia: Albert Saifer, 1954, rev. ed. Originally published by Yale University Press in 1918.

Berger, Peter L. *The Sacred Canopy: Elements of a Sociological Theory of Religion.* Garden City, NY: Doubleday & Co., 1967; Anchor Books, 1969.

Berland, Alwyn. "The Ambiguities of Culture." In *The New Pelican Guide to English Literature.* Vol. 9, *American Literature,* ed. Boris Ford, 228-50. New York: Penguin Books, 1988.

———. *Culture and Conduct in the Novels of Henry James.* New York: Cambridge University Press, 1981.

Berman, Morris. *The Reenchantment of the World.* New York: Bantam Books, 1984. Originally published by Cornell University Press in 1981.

Black, C. E. *The Dynamics of Modernization.* New York: Harper and Row, 1966.

Blackmur, R. P. *Studies in Henry James.* Edited with an introduction by Veronica A. Makowsky. New York: New Directions, 1983.

Boorstin, Daniel J. *The Americans: The Democratic Experience.* New York: Random House, 1973.

———. *The Americans: The National Experience.* New York: Random House, 1965.

Brennan, Stephen C. and Stephen R. Yarbrough. *Irving Babbitt.* Twayne's United States Authors. Boston: G. K. Hall, 1987.

Buckley, Vincent. *Poetry and Morality: Studies on the Criticism of Matthew Arnold, T. S. Eliot, and R. F. Leavis.* London: Chatto & Windus, 1961.

Capra, Fritjof. *The Tao of Physics: An Exploration of the Parallels Between Modern Physics and Eastern Mysticism.* New York: Bantam Books, 1977. Originally published by Shambhala Publications in 1976.

Carroll, Joseph. *The Cultural Theory of Matthew Arnold.* Berkeley: University of California Press, 1982.

Carter, Paul A. *The Spiritual Crisis of the Gilded Age.* DeKalb: Northern Illinois University Press, 1971.

Cockshut, A. O. J. *The Unbelievers: English Agnostic Thought, 1840-1890.* London: Collins Publishing Co., 1964.

Collins, Robert M. "David Potter's People of Plenty and the Recycling of American History." *Reviews in American History* 16, no. 2 (June 1988): 321-335.

Coulling, Sidney. *Matthew Arnold and His Critics: A Study of Arnold's Controversies.* Athens: Ohio University Press, 1974.

DeLaura, David J., ed. *Matthew Arnold: A Collection of Critical Essays.* Englewood Cliffs, NJ: Prentice-Hall, 1973.

Dickens, Charles. *Dombey and Son.* The Laurel Dickens. Edited with an introduction by Edgar Johnson. New York: Dell Publishing Co., 1963. First published in serial form in 1846-48.

Dupee, F. W., ed. *The Question of Henry James: A Collection of Critical Essays.* New York: Henry Holt & Co., 1945.

Edel, Leon. *Henry James.* 5 vols. Philadelphia: J. B. Lippincott Co., 1953-1972.

Eliot, T. S. *Selected Essays, 1917-1932.* New York: Harcourt, Brace and Co., 1932.

———. *Collected Poems, 1909-1962.* New York: Harcourt, Brace & World, 1963.

Frederick, John T. *The Darkened Sky: Nineteenth-Century American Novelists and Religion.* Notre Dame, IN: University of Notre Dame Press, 1969.

Fromm, Erich. *Psychoanalysis and Religion.* New Haven: Yale University Press, 1950.

Gardner, John W. and Francesca Gardner Reese, eds. *Quotations of Wit and Wisdom.* New York: W. W. Norton & Co., 1975.

Gregor, Ian. Introduction to *Culture and Anarchy,* by Matthew Arnold, ed. Ian Gregor. Indianapolis, IN: Bobbs-Merrill Co., 1971: xiii-xxxviii.

Hall, David D. "The Victorian Connection." *American Quarterly* 27, no. 5 (December 1975): 561-74.

Hoeveler, J. David., Jr. *The New Humanism: A Critique of Modern America, 1900-1940.* Charlottesville: University Press of Virginia, 1977.

Holloway, John. *The Victorian Sage: Studies in Argument.* London: Macmillan, 1953.

Honan, Park. *Matthew Arnold: A Life.* Cambridge: Harvard University Press, 1983. Reprint, New York: McGraw-Hill, 1981 (pagination is the same in both editions).

Houghton, Walter E. *The Victorian Frame of Mind, 1830-1870.* New Haven: Yale University Press, 1958.

Howe, Daniel Walker. "American Victorianism as a Culture." *American Quarterly* 27, no. 5 (December 1975): 507-32.

Jaki, Stanley L. *The Road to Science and the Ways of God.* Chicago: University of Chicago Press, 1978.

James, Henry. *The American.* Edited with introduction by Richard Poirier. New York: Bantam Books, 1971. Originally published in 1877.

———. *The American Scene.* Edited with introduction by Leon Edel. Bloomington: Indiana University Press, 1968. Originally published in 1907.

———. *Autobiography: A Small Boy and Others, Notes of a Son and Brother, The Middle Years.* Edited with introduction by Frederick W. Dupee. New York: Criterion Books, 1956. Originally published by Charles Scribner's Sons as three separate volumes in 1913, 1914, and 1917.

———. *The Bostonians.* Modern Library edition. With an introduction by Irving Howe. New York: Random House, 1956. Originally published in 1886.

———. *English Hours.* With an introduction by Leon Edel. New York: Oxford University Press, 1981. First published in book form in 1905.

———. *Essays in London and Elsewhere.* New York: Harper & Brothers, 1893.

———. *French Poets and Novelists.* London: Macmillan and Co., 1878.

———. *The Future of the Novel: Essays on the Art of Fiction.* Edited with an introduction by Leon Edel. New York: Vintage Books, 1956.

———. *Hawthorne.* With a preface by William M. Sale, Jr. Ithaca, NY: Cornell University Press, 1956. Originally published in 1879.

———. "Is There a Life After Death?" In *In After Days: Thoughts on the Future Life,* by William Dean Howells and others, 199-233. New York: Harper and Bros., 1910.

———. *Italian Hours.* New York: Grove Press, 1959; Black Cat Edition, 1979. First published in book form in 1909.

———. *The Letters of Henry James.* Edited by Percy Lubbock. 2 vols. New York: Charles Scribner's Sons, 1920.

———. *Literary Reviews and Essays on American, English and French Literature.* Edited with an introduction by Albert Mordell. New York: Grove Press, 1957; Black Cat Edition, 1979.

———. *A Little Tour of France.* Boston: Houghton Mifflin Co., 1912. Originally published in 1884.

———. *The Notebooks of Henry James.* Edited by F. O. Matthiessen and Kenneth B. Murdock. Phoenix Edition. Chicago: University of Chicago Press, 1981. Originally published by Oxford University Press in 1947.

———. *Notes and Reviews,* Edited by Pierre Chaignon La Rose. Cambridge, MA: Dunster House, 1921.

———. *Notes on Novelists.* London: J. M. Dent & Sons, 1914.

———. *Parisian Sketches: Letters to the* New York Tribune, *1875-1876.* Edited with an introduction by Leon Edel and Ilse Dusoir Lind. New York: New York University Press, 1957.

———. *Partial Portraits.* Ann Arbor: University of Michigan Press: 1970. First published in book form in 1888.

———. *Portraits of Places.* Boston: James R. Osgood & Co., 1884.

———. *A Question of Our Speech & The Lesson of Balzac.* Boston: Houghton, Mifflin Co., 1905.

———. *Transatlantic Sketches.* Boston: Houghton, Mifflin Co., 1882. First published in book form in 1875.

———. *Views and Reviews.* Edited with an introduction by LeRoy Phillips. Boston: Ball Publishing Co., 1908.

———. *William Wetmore Story and His Friends.* New York: Grove Press, 1957. Reprint in 1 vol., Boston:

Houghton Mifflin Co., 1903, 2 volumes (page references are to the reprint edition).

———. *Within the Rim and Other Essays, 1914-1915.* London: W. Collins Sons & Co., 1918.

James, Henry, Sr. *The Literary Remains of the late Henry James.* Edited with an introduction by William James. Boston: Houghton, Mifflin & Co., 1885.

Jastrow, Robert. *God and the Astronomer.* New York: W. W. Norton & Co., 1978.

Jones, Howard Mumford. *The Age of Energy: Varieties of American Experience, 1865-1915.* New York: Viking Press, 1971.

Kroeber, A. L. and Clyde Kluckhom. *Culture: A Critical Review of Concepts and Definitions.* New York: Vintage Books, n.d. Originally published as *Papers of the Peabody Museum of American Archaeology and Ethnology* 47, no. 1. Cambridge, MA: Harvard University, 1952.

Krook, Dorothea. *The Ordeal of Consciousness in Henry James.* Cambridge: Cambridge University Press, 1962.

Langbaum, Robert. *The Mysteries of Identity: A Theme in Modern Literature.* New York: Oxford University Press, 1977.

Lears, T. J. Jackson. *No Place of Grace: Antimodernism and the Transformation of American Culture, 1880-1920.* New York: Pantheon Books, 1981.

Lightman, Bernard. *The Origins of Agnosticism: Victorian Unbelief and the Limits of Knowledge.* Baltimore, MD: Johns Hopkins University Press, 1987.

Livingston, James C. *Matthew Arnold and Christianity: His Religious Prose Writings.* Columbia: University of South Carolina Press, 1986.

Marcus, John T. *Heaven, Hell, and History: A Survey of Man's Faith in History from Antiquity to the Present.* New York: Macmillan Co., 1967.

Matthiessen, F. O. *The James Family: Including Selections from the Writings of Henry James, Senior, William, Henry, & Alice James.* New York: Alfred A. Knopf, 1947.

———. *Henry James: The Major Phase.* New York: Oxford University Press, 1944.

Meyer, D. H. "American Intellectuals and the Victorian Crisis of Faith." *American Quarterly* 27, no. 5 (December 1975): 585-603.

Morris, Wright. *The Territory Ahead: Critical Interpretations in American Literature,* rev. ed. New York: Atheneum, 1963. Originally published by Harcourt, Brace & World in 1961.

Nevin, Thomas R. *Irving Babbitt: An Intellectual Study.* Chapel Hill: University of North Carolina Press, 1984.

O'Dea, Thomas F. *The Sociology of Religion.* Englewood Cliffs, NJ: Prentice-Hall, 1966.

Panichas, George A. and Claes G. Ryn, eds. *Irving Babbitt in Our Time.* Washington: Catholic University Press, 1987.

Perry, Lewis. *Intellectual Life in America: A History.* New York: Franklin Watts, 1984.

Persons, Stow. *The Decline of American Gentility.* New York: Columbia University Press, 1973.

Potter, David M. *People of Plenty: Economic Abundance and the American Character.* Chicago: University of Chicago Press, 1954.

Raleigh, John Henry. *Matthew Arnold and American Culture.* Berkeley: University of California Press, 1961. Originally published as *University of California Publications: English Studies* 17. Berkeley: University of California Press, 1957.

Reilly, Robert J. "Henry James and the Morality of Fiction." *American Literature* 39, no. 1 (March 1967): 1-30.

Roberts, J. M. *The Pelican History of the World,* rev. ed. New York, Penguin Books, 1983. First published in United States as *History of the World.* New York: Alfred A. Knopf, 1976.

Robbins, William. *The Ethical Idealism of Matthew Arnold: A Study of the Nature and Sources of His Moral and Religious Ideas.* Toronto: University of Toronto Press, 1959.

Ross, Ralph and Ernest van den Haag. *The Fabric of Society: An Introduction to the Social Sciences.* New York: Harcourt, Brace and Co., 1957.

Rowe, John Carlos. *Henry Adams and Henry James: The Emergence of a Modern Consciousness.* Ithaca, NY: Cornell University Press, 1976.

Santayana, George. *Winds of Doctrine.* London: J. M. Dent & Sons, 1913.

Sherman, Stuart P. *Matthew Arnold: How To Know Him.* Indianapolis, IN: Bobbs-Merrill Co., 1917.

Tomisch, John. *A Genteel Endeavor: American Culture and Politics in the Gilded Age.* Stanford, CA: Stanford University Press, 1971.

Trilling, Lionel. *Matthew Arnold,* uniform ed. New York: Harcourt Brace Jovanovich, 1977. Originally published by W. W. Norton in 1939; 2nd ed., 1949.

———. Introduction to *The Portable Matthew Arnold,* ed. Lionel Trilling. New York: Viking Press, 1949.

Turner, James. *Without God, Without Creed: The Origins of Unbelief in America.* Baltimore, MD: Johns Hopkins University Press, 1985.

Willey, Basil. *Nineteenth Century Studies: Coleridge to Matthew Arnold.* New York: Columbia University Press, 1949.

Williams, Raymond. *Culture and Society, 1780-1950.* Harper Torchbooks. New York: Harper & Row, 1966. Originally published by Columbia University Press in 1958.

———. *Keywords: A Vocabulary of Culture and Society.* New York: Oxford University Press, 1976.

Yeats, W. B. *The Collected Poems of W. B. Yeats,* 3d ed., rev. New York: Macmillan Co., 1956.

Zabel, Morton Dauwen. Introduction to *The Art of Travel: Scenes and Journeys in America, England, France and Italy from the Travel Writings of Henry James,* ed. Morton Dauwen Zabel. Garden City, NY: Anchor Books/Doubleday & Co., 1962. Originally published by Paul R. Reynolds & Sons, New York, in 1958.

FURTHER READING

Bibliography

Tollers, Vincent L., ed. *A Bibliography of Matthew Arnold, 1932-1970.* University Park: Pennsylvania State University, 1974, 172 p.

Compiles primary and secondary sources on Arnold's poetry and prose writings. Coverage of secondary sources is limited to 1932-1970.

Biographies

Honan, Park. *Matthew Arnold: A Life.* Cambridge, Mass.: Harvard University Press, 1983, 496 p.

Definitive biography aimed at both Arnold specialists and general readers.

Rowse, A. L. *Matthew Arnold: Poet and Prophet.* London: Thames and Hudson, 1976, 208 p.

Comprehensive biography.

Trilling, Lionel. *Matthew Arnold.* New York: Norton, 1939, 465 p.

A sympathetic and insightful analysis of Arnold's life and literary career.

Criticism

Allott, Miriam. "'Both/And' or 'Either/Or'?: Arnold's Mind in Dialogue with Itself." In *The Arnoldian* 15, No. 1 (Winter 1987-88): 1-16.

Assesses the formal and aesthetic implications of Arnold's juxtaposition of differing or opposing ideas that shapes his work.

apRoberts, Ruth. *Arnold and God.* Berkeley and Los Angeles: University of California Press, 1983, 299 p.

Study of Arnold's writings on religion and the Bible, emphasizing their integral relation with his poetry and critical essays.

Bell, Bill. "The Function of Arnold at the Present Time." In *Essays in Criticism* 47, No. 3 (July 1997): 203-19.

Surveys recent scholarly appropriations of Arnold's literary and cultural criticism.

Buckler, William E. *Matthew Arnold's Prose: Three Essays in Literary Enlargement.* New York: AMS Press, 1983, 116 p.

Three essays on Arnold's literary criticism that seek to increase the reader's understanding of the author by showing how his critical effectiveness is dependant upon his literary art.

Bush, Douglas. *Matthew Arnold: A Survey of His Poetry and Prose.* New York: The Macmillan Co., 1971, 202 p.

Traces the "main lines and attitudes" of Arnold's career, reflected in his works.

Carroll, Joseph. *The Cultural Theory of Matthew Arnold.* Berkeley and Los Angeles: University of California Press, 1982, 275 p.

Analysis of Arnold's theories on culture and religion, asserting that his critical importance arises from "his own sense that literary theory must not be isolated from other types of knowledge."

Corr, Chris. "Matthew Arnold and the Younger Yeats: The Manoeuvrings of Cultural Aesthetics." In *Irish University Review* 28, No. 1 (Spring/Summer 1998): 11-27.

Focuses on Arnold's "pervasive influence" on Yeats' views in literary criticism.

Dawson, Carl, ed. *Matthew Arnold: The Poetry.* The Critical Heritage Series, edited by B. C. Southam. London: Routledge & Kegan Paul, 1973, 466 p.

A comprehensive compilation of critical commentary written on Arnold's poetry between 1849 and 1900. In addition, the editor's introduction provides a concise overview of critical reaction to the poetry.

Dawson, Carl and Pfordresher, John, eds. *Matthew Arnold: Prose Writings.* The Critical Heritage Series, edited by B. C. Southam. London: Routledge & Kegan Paul, 1979, 458 p.

A companion to *Matthew Arnold: The Poetry* providing a thorough selection of critical commentary written on Arnold's prose between 1861 and 1899. The volume also contains an introductory overview of the criticism.

Dickstein, Morris. "Cultural Criticism: Matthew Arnold and Beyond." In *Double Agent: The Critic and Society,* pp. 8-34. New York: Oxford University Press, 1992.

Discusses Arnold's influential blending of literary and social criticism.

Eliot, George [pseudonym of Mary Ann Evans]. *Westminster Review* n.s. LXIV, No. VII (July 1855): 297-99.

A brief commentary on *Poems, Second Series.* Eliot finds Arnold's earlier poems superior to those in his second collection, and, while she praises the powerful effect of Arnold's verse, she considers his rhythm flawed.

Fulweiler, Howard W. "Literature or Dogma: Matthew Arnold as Demythologizer." In *The Arnoldian* 15, No. 1 (Winter 1987-88): 37-47.

Considers Arnold's thought on the relative importance of literature and religious doctrine in modern society.

Gooder, Jean. "Matthew Arnold and the Idea of the Modern." In *Cambridge Quarterly* 24, No. 1 (1995): 1-16.

Discusses Arnold's views on cultural progress and education.

Gottfried, Leon. *Matthew Arnold and the Romantics.* Lincoln: University of Nebraska Press, 1963, 277 p.

Explores and evaluates the full range of Arnold's reaction to the major Romantic poets.

Grob, Alan. "The Poetry of Pessimism: Arnold's 'Resignation'." In *Victorian Poetry* 26, Nos. 1-2 (Spring/Summer 1988): 25-44.

Argues that Arnold's poem "Resignation" is the first and possibly the fullest example of metaphysical pessimism in nineteenth-century English poetry.

Madden, William A. *Matthew Arnold: A Study of the Aesthetic Temperament in Victorian England.* Bloomington: Indiana University Press, 1967, 242 p.

Contextualizes Arnold's position in the debate that accompanied the emergence of aesthetic consciousness in England.

Miller, J. Hillis. "Matthew Arnold." In his *The Disappearance of God,* pp. 212-69. Cambridge, Mass.: The Belknap Press, 1963.

An approach to Arnold's poetry and poetic theory as a reflection of the nineteenth-century's struggle with godlessness.

Mulhern, Francis. "Culture and Authority." In *Critical Quarterly* 37, No. 1 (Spring 1995): 77-89.

Argues that Arnold's linking of culture and criticism remains a vital resource for contemporary society.

Phillips, Jerry. "Culture, the Academy, and the Police: Or Reading Matthew Arnold in 'Our Present Unsettled State'." In *College Literature,* 25, No. 3 (Fall 1998): 109-32.

Evaluates "the contemporary ideological significance of the Arnoldian tradition" with specific reference to commodification, education, and state authority.

Raleigh, John Henry. *Matthew Arnold and American Culture.* Berkeley: University of California Press, 1957.

Explores Arnold's critical influence in the United States.

Riquelme, J. P. "Aesthetic Values and Processes in Eliot, Arnold, and the Romantics." In *T. S. Eliot: Man and Poet,* edited by Laura Cowan, pp. 277-301. Orono, Maine: University of Maine Press, 1990.

Analyzes Eliot's modernist engagement with Arnold and the Romantic poets.

Stange, G. Robert. *Matthew Arnold: The Poet as Humanist.* Princeton, NJ: Princeton University Press, 1967, 300 p.

Thematic discussion of Arnold's poetry.

Thorpe, Michael. *Matthew Arnold.* London: Evans Brothers, 1969, 176 p.

Biographical and critical overview of Arnold's literary career, placing it within the context of Arnold's own time.

Additional coverage of Arnold's life and career is contained in the following sources published by the Gale Group: *DISCovering Authors; DISCovering Authors: British; DISCovering Authors: Canadian; DISCovering Authors Modules: Most-Studied Authors* and *Poets; Poetry Criticism,* Vol. 5; and *World Literature Criticism, 1500 to the Present.*

William Wells Brown
1813-1884

American novelist, playwright, and historian. For further discussion of Brown's life and career, see *NCLC,* Volume 2.

INTRODUCTION

After growing up a slave in Kentucky, Brown escaped to freedom in Ohio and became a noted abolitionist and writer in both the United States and England. Though in his time Brown was primarily appreciated as an antislavery speaker and as the author of the notorious *Clotel; or, The President's Daughter: A Narrative of Slave Life in the United States* (1853), he is now recognized as an important historian of black experience in America. Brown's importance to American literary history also stems from the fact that he was the first published American black novelist and playwright.

BIOGRAPHICAL INFORMATION

Born the son of a white slave owner and a black slave, Brown spent the first twenty years of his life as a slave on a plantation in Lexington, Kentucky. He escaped to freedom in Cincinnati, Ohio, in 1834 and became passionately devoted to the abolitionist cause. He was befriended by a Quaker, Wells Brown, whose name the former slave took as his own. Brown first settled in Cleveland, where he worked as a handyman and continued to aid in the escape of other slaves. He eventually moved to Buffalo, New York, where he came to the attention of William Lloyd Garrison, who enlisted him as a lecturer in the abolitionist cause.

MAJOR WORKS

Brown's first publication, *Narrative of William W. Brown, a Fugitive Slave, Written by Himself* (1847), was a great success and established him as an important social reformer. The success of the *Narrative* encouraged Brown, and in 1848 he collected a group of antislavery songs and published them under the title *The Anti-Slavery Harp: A Collection of Songs for Anti-Slavery Meetings.*

Because of his exceptional ability as a speaker, Brown was chosen by the American Peace Society as its representative to the Paris Peace Congress of 1849. These activities, as well as his extensive travels in England as an antislavery lecturer, are chronicled in his next publication, *Three Years in Europe; or, Places I Have Seen and People I Have Met* (1852). Brown, at this time, was still a fugitive slave, and it was not until several English friends raised the money to pay his indenture that he became a free man.

While in England he completed *Clotel; or, The President's Daughter: A Narrative of Slave Life in the United States,* which proved to be a popular success and something of a scandal. Drawing on the legend that Thomas Jefferson had fathered many children by his slave mistresses, Brown cast his heroine, Clotel, as Jefferson's slave daughter. Brown shows, simply and effectively, both the horror and the irony of the institution of slavery in a system which would allow the daughter of a president to be sold into bondage. For the American version of the novel, which came out eight years later, Brown chose not to suggest presidential parentage for his heroine, concentrating instead on the heroism of his black characters in their fight for freedom.

Brown also wrote the first play by a black American to be published, *The Escape; or, A Leap for Freedom* (1858) (his earlier drama,*Experience; or, How to Give a Northern Man a Backbone* [1856] was never published). Though

The Escape was never performed, Brown gave many readings of the play, largely to antislavery gatherings in the North. It was not a dramatic success, marred, as was much of Brown's work, by his didacticism. Brown was passionate and polemical in all that he wrote, and strove to impress his audience with the content, rather than the literary form, of his work.

It is perhaps as a historian of the black American experience that Brown is best remembered. In such works as *The Black Man: His Antecedents, His Genius, and His Achievements* (1863), Brown illustrates the importance of blacks to American culture in the years following the Civil War. In his last work, *My Southern Home; or, The South and Its People* (1880), Brown presents essays of a nostalgic nature, combining his political and social concerns in a reminiscence of the South.

CRITICAL RECEPTION

Critics have noted that, from a literary standpoint, Brown's achievement is weak. His fiction and drama are sensational and crafted for uncritical audiences. Arthur P. Davis echoes many critics when he says "If the subject is admittedly not an outstanding writer, why bother?" But he explains, as many scholars have come to realize, that Brown is an important subject of study because he chronicled a turbulent period of history from a perspective that rarely had a public voice at the time—that of the black slave. Brown committed his life and his work to the freedom and dignity of his people and to the abolitionist cause. Self-educated and strong-willed, he defied the barriers of racial prejudice to contribute the first novel, first play, and some of the first notable works of history to be published by a black American, enriching the lives of all Americans through his explication of the black experience.

PRINCIPAL WORKS

A Lecture Delivered before the Female Anti-Slavery Society of Salem (essay) 1847

Narrative of William W. Brown, a Fugitive Slave, Written by Himself (autobiography) 1847

The Anti-Slavery Harp: A Collection of Songs for Anti-Slavery Meetings [editor] (songs) 1848

Three Years in Europe; or, Places I Have Seen and People I Have Met (travel essays) 1852 [published in the United States as *The American Fugitive in Europe: Sketches of Places and People Abroad* (1855)]

Clotel; or, The President's Daughter: A Narrative of Slave Life in the United States (novel) 1853 [revised as *Miralda; or, The Beautiful Quadroon* (1861-62)] [also revised as *Clotelle: A Tale of the Southern States* (1864)] [also revised as *Clotelle; or, The Colored Heroine* (1867)]

St. Domingo: Its Revolutions and Its Patriots (essay) 1855

**Experience; or, How to Give a Northern Man a Backbone* (drama) 1856

**The Escape; or, A Leap for Freedom* (drama) 1858

The Black Man: His Antecedents, His Genius, and His Achievements (history) 1863

The Negro in the American Rebellion, His Heroism and His Fidelity (history) 1867

The Rising Son; or, Antecedents and Advancement of the Colored Race (history) 1874

My Southern Home; or, The South and Its People (narrative essays) 1880

*Dates given for first publication rather than first performance.

CRITICISM

Larry Gara (essay date 1969)

SOURCE: "Introduction," in *The Narrative of William W. Brown, A Fugitive Slave, and a Lecture Delivered Before the Female Anti-Slavery Society of Salem, 1847,* Houghton Mifflin Company, 1969, pp. ix-xvii.

[*In the following introduction, Gara presents an overview of Brown's life and explains that many elements of his philosophy can be found in modern Black Nationalism.*]

"It is a terrible picture of slavery," commented Edmund Quincy about William Wells Brown's newly written manuscript, "told with great simplicity. . . . There is no attempt at fine writing, but only a minute account of scenes and things he saw and suffered, told with a good deal of skill, propriety and delicacy." Quincy was an abolitionist editor and the son of Harvard's president. When Brown asked him to read the manuscript, he intended only to glance at a few pages, but found it so good he could not put it down until interrupted by a call to dinner. He readily agreed to write a letter to be prefixed to the book, and suggested to the author only "one or two alterations and additions."[1]

Brown's narrative quickly became a best seller and took its place with the memoirs of Frederick Douglass, Moses Roper and other former slaves whose writings contributed to the growing antislavery sentiment in the northern states. Whatever their literary merits, the works of ex-slaves had the ring of authenticity. Unlike the white abolitionists, these men could not be accused of speaking without knowledge and experience of the South's "peculiar institution." A contemporary writer said of the slave narratives that they were "calculated to exert a very wide influence on public opinion" because they contained "the *victim's* account of the workings of this great institution."[2] An abolitionist editor saw in them an "infallible means of abolitionizing" the North. "Argument provokes argument," he said, "reason is met by sophistry; but narratives of slaves go right to the hearts of men."[3]

For William Wells Brown, born a slave in Kentucky around 1816, publication of his memoir brought fame and probably some monetary compensation. The first edition of a thousand hardbound and two thousand paperbound copies cost him less than eleven cents a copy, and it was quickly out of print.[4] Within two years he sold out four editions totalling eight thousand copies.[5] With its personal approach and vivid pictures of slave life, Brown's narrative quickly found a receptive audience. In addition to the American versions, it was translated into several foreign languages and circulated in European editions. The book was only the first of a notable series of literary productions from Brown's pen. In 1848 he published a short anthology of antislavery songs, ***The Anti-Slavery Harp,*** and in 1852 his travel book, ***Three Years in Europe,*** appeared in London and Edinburgh. The following year he published a novel, ***Clotel, or the President's Daughter,*** whose main character was an alleged mulatto child of Thomas Jefferson. Though it could not compete successfully with *Uncle Tom's Cabin,* it was one of the first novels published by an American Negro, and as such was a significant work. Brown wrote several dramas about slave life and published one in 1858: ***The Escape; or, a Leap for Freedom.*** In ***The Black Man, His Antecedents, His Genius, and His Achievements*** Brown traced Negro history back to its African origins and included short biographical sketches of notable colored persons. Other writings included ***The Negro in the Rebellion,*** and several historical volumes expanding on the material first presented in ***The Black Man.*** The number of his publications is impressive and contemporary critics were nearly unanimous in praising their quality.

It is the second, or 1848, edition of Brown's memoir which is reprinted in this volume. He made very few changes from the first edition, but he added several appendices and this new edition contains as well a transcript of a speech he made in November, 1847 to the Female Anti-Slavery Society of Salem, Massachusetts. The narrative was written thirteen years after Brown's escape from slavery and reflects, therefore, both the conditioning of his long contact with abolitionists and the vagaries of detail implicit in writing from distant memory. Nevertheless, it is full of insights about slavery and the antebellum South which only a former slave could know. Furthermore it is important both because of the impact it had on thousands of readers and because of the wealth of material it contains.[6]

Even before publishing his narrative William Wells Brown was known as an effective antislavery speaker, one of a number of former slaves whose message reached many northerners untouched by the white abolitionist crusader.[7] In his talks Brown emphasized the terrible injustice of slavery as an institution which deprived individuals of their humanity, and he also included impressive eyewitness accounts of the cruelties which were sometimes practiced in the South. His lectures were well written and eloquently delivered, and he often drew large audiences both in America and in Great Britain, where he sometimes appeared in company with William and Ellen Craft, a famous fugitive slave couple from Georgia. Brown's lectures were occasionally illustrated with his own panorama of slavery, and after he wrote his antislavery plays he often substituted a dramatic reading for the usual lecture. In 1857 William Lloyd Garrison attended one of Brown's readings in Philadelphia and he reported it was "well delivered and well received" though the audience on that occasion was disappointingly small.[8] A Vermont reporter commented that Brown held an audience breathless for nearly two hours with his wit and speaking ability. "His dignity of manner, his propriety of expression were more than we had expected to see in one who had spent the early part of his life as a slave," he commented.[9] A New York reporter found one of Brown's dramas, "in itself, a masterly refutation of all apologies for slavery, and it abounds in wit, satire, philosophy, arguments and facts. . . ."[10] Although early in Brown's career antagonistic mobs sometimes interrupted his meetings, for the most part he was greeted with enthusiasm. He continued to give lectures on Negro history after the Civil War ended slavery. In 1868 the *New York Evening Post* described one of his historical lectures as "intensely interesting" and an "able and manly vindication of his race from the charge of natural inferiority."[11]

Unlike Frederick Douglass, his more famous contemporary, Brown never broke with William Lloyd Garrison and the moral suasion school of abolitionists, though their reactions to him and his contribution varied considerably. "It is a long time since I have seen a man, white or black, that I have cottoned to so much as Brown, on so short an acquaintance," said Edmund Quincy. Brown, he said, was an "extraordinary fellow," with "no meanness, littleness, no envy or suspiciousness about him."[12] An English abolitionist reported to Garrison that a whispering campaign regarding Brown's personal life involving an alleged love affair was wholly without foundation and that he was a "sensible, excellent fellow."[13] On the other hand some of the abolitionists were suspicious of the former slave's motives. Samuel May, Jr., when he learned of Brown's impending trip to England, noted that he was "a very good fellow, of very fair abilities and has been quite true to the cause. But he likes to make popular and taking speeches, and keeps a careful eye upon his own benefit." Brown owed everything to the Garrisonian cause, said May, "and he ought to be true to it." As it turned out, Brown consistently defended the Garrisonians during his stay in England.

Still the Garrisonians were concerned that certain of Brown's actions would hurt the cause. When his marriage seemed in danger, they urged reconciliation with his wife.[14] When Brown undertook to buy his freedom, they were further troubled. In 1847 Brown sent a copy of the first edition of his memoir to Enoch Price, his former master, who wrote Edmund Quincy expressing a willingness to free Brown for three hundred and twenty-five dollars. To the Garrisonians it was a matter of principle not to pay a slaveholder anything to manumit a person who was already free by natural and divine right. Brown agreed and wrote his former master that he could not accept the offer. "God made me as free as he did Enoch Price," he wrote, "and Mr. Price shall never receive a dollar from me or my friends with my consent."[15] Nevertheless, English friends, worried about Brown's safety under the new Fugitive Slave Law, apparently persuaded him to allow the transaction, for on July 7, 1854 it was completed for three hundred dollars.[16] While some of the American abolitionists were able to sympathize with Brown's dilemma and eventual decision, others were appalled. Sarah Pugh, a Philadelphia Quaker, asked an Irish friend if Brown had consented to be bought. "I hope he has not," she added, "for he would lose half his manhood."[17]

Despite the misgivings of his antislavery friends, William Wells Brown suffered no loss of manhood or of courage as a result of his manumission. Indeed, it gave him a new sense of security which freed him to continue his labors for antislavery and other reform causes. For in addition to abolition, Brown actively supported the peace crusade and the temperance movement. It was partly to participate in an International Peace Congress in Paris that he first traveled to Europe in 1849. He spoke at the meeting but found little support for his introducing antislavery matters into the proceedings, and left the Congress disillusioned with its results.[18] He gave longer service to the cause of temperance, organizing a temperance society among the colored population of Buffalo during his nine-year stay there. After the Civil War Brown joined several temperance groups and in 1871 at the Boston meeting of the National Division of the Sons of Temperance of North America he presented strong arguments in favor of admitting the colored delegates from Maryland to its deliberations. He also helped organize and became president of the National Association for the Spread of Temperance and Night Schools among the Freed People of the South.[19]

For William Wells Brown, however, the plight of America's colored people, whether slaves or nominally free, was always uppermost. The unique contribution of the fugitive slave speakers was to personalize slavery and remove its operations from the realm of abstract ideas. But for Brown and the others the battle against slavery was only half the war—the other was the battle against prejudice and discrimination in the North as well as in the South. In his books and in the letters he wrote to newspapers Brown called attention to the indignities suffered by colored people in the free states. A letter from England recalled the discrimination he had encountered on steamers, in hotels, in coaches, railways, and even in churches where he was forced to sit in a "Negro pew." When he arrived in Britain, he said, for the first time in his life he felt truly free.[20] In his first travel book he wrote, "our country is the most despotic in the wide world, and to expose and hold it up to the scorn and contempt of other nations, is the duty of every coloured man who would be true to himself and his race."[21]

Prejudice, he believed, was clearly a corollary of slavery. "One of the bitterest fruits of slavery in our land," he wrote, "is the cruel spirit of caste . . ." It was a most foolish prejudice, without a "single logical reason to offer in its defence." Black people were mistreated in America only because "of their identity with a race that has long worn the chains of slavery." Black in itself was not bad. Brown pointed out that black clothing was often preferred to either white or colors, that black eyes and black hair in women often attracted men, and that men and women dyed their hair black, only to "curse the negro for a complexion that is not stolen."[22]

Brown was determined that all Americans should recognize the falsity of the doctrine of the natural inferiority of colored people. In his study ***The Black Man*** he met and refuted this misrepresentation, calling attention to the early black civilizations of Ethiopia and Egypt, as well as to many colored Americans "who, by their own genius, capacity, and intellectual development," surmounted the obstacles created by slavery and prejudice and "raised themselves to positions of honor and influence." Benjamin Banneker he described as a man of African parents whose blood was never corrupted "by a drop of Anglo-Saxon." Nat Turner, like Napoleon, "regarded himself as a being of destiny." He compared Toussaint L'Ouverture with George Washington, and said Samuel R. Ward was "never ashamed of his complexion, but rather appeared to be proud of it." Brown's list of Negro notables included poets, preachers, rebel slave leaders, painters, educators, actors, lawyers, and rulers of Haiti and Liberia. It was an impressive volume and, though some of his sources and conclusions would not pass the test of modern scholarship, he made his point and in the process he revived a virtually forgotten Negro past. Negroes, he said, should be proud of their heroes whose achievements proved the doctrine of inferiority a lie. "All I demand for the black man," he asserted, "is that the white people shall take their heels off his neck, and let him have a chance to rise by his own efforts."[23]

To the Negroes, Brown preached a mixed gospel of self-respect, hard work and self-improvement. In his last book, ***My Southern Home,*** published in 1880, he viewed slavery in a more benevolent light than he ever had before. The postwar plight of the colored people of the South he blamed on their religion and mode of living. There was an entire disregard of the laws of physiology, a tendency towards extravagant dress and an almost total lack of organized efforts to improve their lot. "Those who do not appreciate their own people will not be appreciated by other people," he declared. The black people must take up their own struggle for elevation, exhibit pluck and use all available spare time, day and night, to educate themselves. He advised Negroes to emigrate from the South as a first, necessary step in their improvement, and above all, he admonished, "black men, don't be ashamed to show your colors, and to own them."[24]

William Wells Brown took his goal of full equality from the American dream stemming back to the Declaration of Independence, yet much that he wrote foreshadowed some of the ideas of twentieth century Black Nationalism. His passionate resentment of all forms of discrimination and his repeated insistence on the need for colored people to cultivate self-respect and dignity on their own terms are clearly an aspect of current thinking. Yet only a few scholars have recognized his many contributions.[25] Saunders Redding, the noted Negro writer, described Brown as the first Negro novelist, playwright and historian whose list of accomplishments "argues his place."[26] Nevertheless, Brown's name remains unknown to many who are familiar with the writings and achievements of his contemporary, Frederick Douglass. When he died in Chelsea, Massachusetts in 1884 he was buried in an unmarked grave.

An unusually effective reformer, writer of history, fiction and drama, and an individual whose own life was an irrefutable argument against racial inferiority, William Wells Brown deserves a better fate than history has accorded him. Hopefully, the publication of his narrative and one of his antislavery talks will stimulate a new interest in this remarkable man and his many contributions to the American heritage.

Notes

1. Edmund Quincy to Caroline Weston, July 2, 1847 in the Weston Papers, Boston Public Library.
2. Ephraim Peabody, "Narratives of Fugitive Slaves," in the *Christian Examiner,* 47:64 (July, 1849).
3. Quoted in Charles H. Nichols, "Who Read the Slave Narratives?," *Phylon,* 22:153 (1959).
4. Samuel May, Jr. to Dr. John Bishop Estlin, January 13, 1848 in the May Papers, Boston Public Library.
5. Peabody, "Narratives," 64.
6. Some of the basic factual material of Brown's life remains obscure, and the details differ in the several editions of his memoirs. At various times, for instance, Brown gave three different birthdates and also varying versions of his parental background. In one account Brown claimed that his mother was Daniel Boone's daughter.
7. Larry Gara, "The Professional Fugitive in the Abolition Movement," *Wisconsin Magazine of History,* 48:196-204 (Spring, 1965).
8. William Lloyd Garrison to his wife, May 18, 1857 in the Garrison Papers, Boston Public Library.
9. New York *Anti-Slavery Standard,* October 20, 1855.
10. William Wells Brown, *The Escape; or, A Leap for Freedom. A Drama in Five Acts,* Boston, 1858, p. 52.
11. Printed circular advertising Brown's lecture on the "Origin and Early History of the African Race," to be delivered in Boston's Tremont Temple, May 10, 1858, in the Garrison Papers.
12. Edmund Quincy to Caroline Weston, July 2, 1847 in the Weston Papers, Boston Public Library.
13. John Bishop Estlin to Garrison, June 7, 1852 in the Garrison Papers.
14. Samuel May, Jr. to John Bishop Estlin, May 21, 1849 in the May Papers, Boston Public Library; Amy Post to Wendell Phillips, June 20, 1850, and William Wells Brown to Garrison, September 15, 1848 in the Garrison Papers. Brown was never reconciled with his wife, who died while he was in Europe. He later remarried.
15. Quoted in William Farmer's "Memoir of William Wells Brown," in Brown, *Three Years in Europe,* London and Edinburgh, 1852, p. xxi.
16. Josephine Brown, *Biography of an American Bondman by his Daughter,* Boston, 1856, pp. 96-98.
17. Sarah Pugh to Richard Webb, May 22, 1854, in the Garrison Papers.
18. W. Edward Farrison, "William Wells Brown," *Phylon,* 9:16 (First Quarter, 1948).
19. William Wells Brown, *The Rising Son; or, The Antecedents and Advancement of the Colored Race,* Boston, 1874, p. 25.
20. "Memoir of William Wells Brown" in Brown's *Clotel; or, The President's Daughter,* London, 1853, p. 41.
21. William Farmer, "Memoir of William Wells Brown," in Brown's *Three Years in Europe,* p. 311.
22. William Wells Brown, *The Negro in the American Rebellion: His Heroism and His Fidelity,* Boston, 1867, pp. 39, 361-362.
23. William Wells Brown, *The Black Man, His Antecedents, His Genius, and His Achievements,* New York and Boston, 1863, pp. 5-6, 51, 59, 285, 49.
24. William Wells Brown, *My Southern Home: or, The South and Its People,* Boston, 1880, pp. 188, 237, 253.
25. For many years Professor W. Edward Farrison of the English Department of North Carolina College has been collecting material for a Brown biography and publishing articles on aspects of Brown's career.
26. Quoted by Arna Bontemps in "The Negro Contribution to American Letters," in John P. Davis, Ed., *The American Negro Reference Book,* Englewood, N. J., 1966, p. 869.

Bernard W. Bell (essay date 1974)

SOURCE: "Literary Sources of the Early Afro-American Novel," in *CLA Journal: Official Publication of the College Language Association,* Vol. 18, No. 1, 1974, pp. 29-43.

[In the following essay, Bell traces the roots of the African-American aesthetic to the oral tradition, slave narratives, and the Bible.]

With the resurgence of Black cultural nationalism in the 1960's, the question of a Black aesthetic became a vital issue for many students of American literature. On one side of this issue were distinguished critics like J. Saunders Redding, who insisted that "aesthetics has no racial, national or geographical boundaries" and who saw no future for a school of writers that sought to establish a Black aesthetic.[1] On the other side were Black cultural nationalists such as Imamu Amiri Baraka (LeRoi Jones) and Laurence Neal, who indicted Afro-American writers for their imitation of white middle-class models yet maintained that "there is no need to establish a 'black aesthetic.' Rather it is important to understand that one already exists. . . . The models for what Black literature should be are found primarily in our folk culture, especially in the blues and jazz."[2]

In terms of militancy, the seeds of a Black aesthetic were sown in the Afro-American novel as early as 1859 with the serialization of Martin Delany's *Blake; or, The Huts of America* (1970). The more crucial questions to ask at this juncture of the debate over a Black aesthetic is: Where does the Afro-American novelist find the literary sources for his art? And what are the special characteristics of this offshoot of the Euro-American novel? It is common knowledge that from the birth of the Peculiar Institution to the premature death of the Great Society Black Americans have been restricted in their exposure to the written word, the chief mode of socialization in Euro-American culture. "In white American," Charles Keil notes in the *Urban Blues,* "the printed word—the literary tradition—and its attendant values are revered. In the Negro Community, more power resides in the spoken word and the oral tradition—good talkers abound, and the best gain power and prestige, but good writers are scarce."[3] Afro-Americans have historically relied on the oral tradition for models to express their vision of the world. As Richard Dorson has observed:

> Only the Negro, as a distinct element of the English-speaking population, maintained a full-blown storytelling tradition. A separate Negro subculture formed within the shell of American life, missing the bounties of general education and material progress, remaining a largely oral, self-contained society with its own unwritten history and literature.[4]

The implications of this statement for the tradition of the Afro-American novel can best be understood by an examination of its folk roots and literary sources. Because of limitations of time and space, however, my discussion will be restricted to the latter.

By virtue of social conditions and cultural exigencies, most Black novelists felt compelled to use their art as a weapon. "In giving this little romance expression in print," Pauline Hopkins writes in her preface, "I am not actuated by a desire for notoriety or for profit, but to do all that I can in a humble way to raise the stigma of degradation from my race."[5] Much of this stigma was perpetuated in the fiction of Kennedy, Tucker, Simms, Page, and Dixon—not to mention major writers like Cooper, Poe and Melville—where one finds a gallery of Sambos and Babos, characters who run the gamut from obsequious lackeys to diabolic savages. In reacting to the grotesque manners and speech of these stereotypes and projecting their own vision of the Black American identity, Hopkins and fellow novelists drank deeply from the literary fountains at hand, especially abolitionist literature, the Bible and popular fiction of the day.

Abolitionist Literature

Abolitionist literature—letters, newspapers, periodicals, journals, pamphlets, verse and fiction—was by far the most compelling tradition for the propaganda purposes of Black novelists. Its formal diction, rhythmic cadences, balanced syntax, stark metaphors, and elevated tone provided the sophisticated vehicle necessary for their initial moral and political assaults on white public opinion. By their adaptation of the conventions of abolitionist literature, William W. Brown, Martin Delany, James Howard, Frances E. W. Harper and others exploited the opportunity to strike a blow at American racism while at the same time demonstrating their assimilation into Euro-American culture.

More important than *Uncle Tom's Cabin* (1852) to the neophyte Black novelist, however, were the slave narratives, for they provided a natural bridge between the oral and literary worlds. The pioneers of the Afro-American novel were either former slaves and abolitionist lecturers or the children of free parents and able spokesmen in the civil rights movement. In one way or another they were all familiar with the techniques of the lecture platform and the process for translating this oral performance into the slave narratives. Anti-slavery meetings would generally begin with introductory remarks by a local abolitionist in preparation for the appearance of a seasoned guest lecturer like Garrison or a fugitive slave to provide a dramatic first-hand account of life in bondage. This performance would be followed by an impassioned, critical analysis of the evils of the peculiar institution and, on occasion, either a few songs or poems. Finally, a collection for the cause would be taken up, abolition publications sold and the meeting adjourned.[6]

The transformation of folksay (i.e., oral history) into romance is a matter of literary history. By definition, the slave narratives are the personal accounts of physical and psychological bondage. Some, like *Narratives of the Sufferings of Lewis and Clarke* (1846) and *The Life of Josiah Henson* (1849), were dictated to white amanuenses, but many were written by the fugitives themselves after telling their stories dozens of times from the antislavery platform. The pattern of narratives by Frederick Douglass, William Wells Brown, J. W. C. Pennington, Solomon Northup, and William and Ella Craft begin with the fugitive slave's realization of the evils of the institution, his first attempts at resistance, his cunning victories over oppression, detailed descriptions of different phases of bondage, the successful flight to the North, and an activist role in the "true" religion and abolitionist politics.[7] All of the personal histories are characterized by a unity of purpose, Christian values and moral fervor. Many read like morality plays. Their style is essentially derived from the pulpit, the lectern, the soapbox, the Good Book, and anti-slavery materials. Even though most are devoutly Christian, they carefully distinguish between "true" Christianity and the religion their masters used to justify slavery. And though by and large their appeal is to white pity and piety, they clearly express a resolute faith in the humanity of Blacks and the righteousness of their struggle for freedom and dignity.

One of the most popular features of the slave narratives was the melodrama and romance of the perilous journey to freedom. The ingenuity of the escape stratagems and the bold manner in which they were carried out—incidents first related from the abolitionist platform in the form of anecdotes and legends—gradually became stock conventions of the form. Many light-skinned slaves passed for white in their flight North, occasionally stopping at the best restaurants and hotels along the way. Some disguised themselves as master and slave as did the well-known fugitives William and Ellen Craft. Others employed more elaborate devices such as shipping themselves North in packing crates or barrels. The courage and imagination of the fugitives won the respect of white abolitionists. "They are among the heros of our age," wrote Charles Sumner. "Romance has no stories of more thrilling interest than theirs. Classical antiquity has preserved no examples of adventurous trial more worthy of renown."[8]

The heroic figure of the rebel looms large in the slave narratives. He might be political in nature like Toussaint L'Ouverture and Frederick Douglass or metaphysical (i.e., intensely religious) like Nat Turner and Harriet Tubman. In either case, he is invariably an activist in the struggle for justice and freedom. That these dominant types were not always mutually exclusive is dramatically illustrated by unique references to John Brown in several novels. Yet the core of their identities as rebel leaders seems to gravitate around one or the other of these poles. And the values they represent—an indomitable will to be free, unshakable faith in the justice of their cause, extraordinary genius, and irrepressible bravery—are thematically important to the tradition of the Afro-American novel.

The Bible

Equally important is the Bible. Through sayings, sermons, songs and stories, its moral lessons were passed on by word of mouth and the printed page from generation to generation. Like the slave narratives, Paul Laurence Dunbar's *The Uncalled* (1898), Jean Toomer's *Cane* (1923), Countee Cullen's *One Way to Heaven* (1932), Zora Neale Hurston's *Jonah's Gourd Vine* (1934), Waters Edward Turpin's *O Canaan* (1939), Ralph Ellison's *Invisible Man* (1952), James Baldwin's *Go Tell It on the Mountain* (1953), and Margaret Walker's *Jubilee,* among others, draw heavily on the Bible for language and subject matter. Traditionally, Blacks have recognized parallels between their experience of oppression and that of the Children of Israel. Aside from allusions to the Hebrew patriarchs and prophets, the most frequent adaptations are of the myths of Moses and the Second Coming of Christ. "Weevils and wars are pest that God sends against the sinful," says Lewis, one of the central characters in *Cane.* "People are too weak to correct themselves: the Redeemer is coming back. Get ready, ye sinners, for the advent of Our Lord."[9] In the wake of the Civil War, Vyry Brown the heroine of *Jubilee,* sings joyously of her earthly salvation and the divine judgment to come:

> I'll be dar, I'll be dar
> When de muster roll am calling, I'll be dar
> Sure's yer born.
> I'll be dar, I'll be dar
> When de muster roll am calling
> I'll be dar, sure's yer born!
> Oh, come you sinners, go wid me
> Oh, I'll be dar
> I'll take you down to Tennessee
> Oh, I'll be dar
> Com and jine de silver band
> Oh, I'll be dar
> I'se gwine to fly to Canaan's land
> Oh, I'll be dar.[10]

In *Moses, Man of the Mountain* (1939) Miss Hurston reinterprets the legend of Moses in terms of the Black experience. Seth Stanley, the messiah figure in *Appointed,* is white; but Henry Holland in *Blake,* Tucker Caliban in *A Different Drummer* (1962), Jesse Jacobs in *Many Thousand Gone,* Chuck Chaney in *'Sippi* (1967), Dan Freeman in *The Spook Who Sat by the Door,* and all modern day messiahs in the Afro-American novel are Black.

Perhaps a word or two about the differences between the eschatology of Jews and Black Christians would be appropriate here.[11] As derived from the Old Testament the Judaic outlook links closely the coming of the anointed of God with the restoration of the dispersed House of Israel and of the peace of Paradise. African converts to Christianity, on the other hand, derived their eschatological vision mainly from the New Testament where the end of the world precedes the Second Coming of Christ and the Last Judgment, with its concomitant salvation for the righteous and damnation for the wicked. What was looked for in both redemptive views of history, however, was not an escape from the world time, and history, but a new world rising out of the ruins of the first. "For, behold," says Isaiah lxv: 17-18, "I create new heavens and a new earth: and the former shall not be remembered, nor come into mind. But be ye glad and rejoice for ever *in that* which I create: for, behold, I create Jerusalem a rejoicing, and her people a joy." The mediator for this salvation is the Messiah and His appointed messenger, Moses.

Within the tradition of the Afro-American novel there is also a significant difference between Pharisaic orthodoxy and the Apocalyptic visionaries. The Pharisees, which best describes the vast majority of early Black exhorters, preached the gospel of piety and humility in the present age while hoping for the advent of the Messiah, the Day of Judgment and the Age-to-Come. In contrast, the Apocalyptics, like the biblical Daniel and historical Nat Turner, wrote off the present age as irredeemably evil, saw the new age as abruptly replacing, not redeeming, this age and claimed to have a revealed scheme of things. These ideological and strategic tensions became a major force in the Afro-American novel with the publication of *Blake,* whose protagonist is hailed by his people as the "messenger of light and destruction."

The influence of the Bible is also seen in the tensions between the most common heroes in the Afro-American novel: the preacher and hustler. Andy, a slave exhorter, is one of the principal organizers of the rebels in *Blake.* In another nineteenth century novel, James Howard's *Bond and Free* (1886), Brother Belden, the folk preacher, is a gifted man:

> He was blessed or gifted with a stentorian pair of lungs, a very active and original imagination, and could read the bible with the lids closed, with as much satisfaction to himself as he could when open, because Brother Belden could not read at all. He had, however, been called to preach and . . . he responded. . . . They were all equally deprived, both the called and the uncalled. . . . In him they confided; him they honored; in him they saw the messenger of the Lord bearing the only consolation which was like balm to their hearts in their deepest sufferings.[12]

The hustler is another gifted man who lives by his wits and the power of his oratorical ability. Like Sadness in *The Sport of the Gods,* he might be a confidence man and belong to that "set which lives, like the leech, upon the blood of others,—that draws its life from the veins of foolish men and immoral women, that prides itself upon its well-dressed idleness and has no shame in its voluntary pauperism."[13] Or he might be like Rinehart in *Invisible Man* and become at will "Rine the runner and Rine the Gambler and Rine the briber and Rine the lover and Rinehart the Reverend."[14] The list of hustlers in the Black novel—including many musicians and preachers as well as criminals—and the masks they wear to manipulate an ever-changing reality are legion.

In addition to the dialectical tensions between the preacher and hustler types, the tradition of the Afro-American novel reveals a conflict between the stories and supernatural forces of the Bible and the reinterpretations of African deities, sorcerers and beliefs. Faith in dreams, the mysterious powers of the Lord, and a New Jerusalem contend with conjuration, hoodoo, root doctors and other residual African forces. Having lost the sanctions of religion and social custom they formally held in Africa, conjuring or hoodoo (the syncretistic blend of Christian and African religious traditions in the United States) mingled in time with the witchcraft and ghost lore of whites and the ritualistic customs of Indians.[15] That the potency of hoodoo, considered mere superstition by the more literate social classes, is well-established among the Black masses can be traced in the Afro-American novel from ***Clotel*** to Ishmael Reed's *Mumbo Jumbo* (1972).

Popular Fiction

While abolitionist literature and the Bible provided their most vital mythological system, the popular fiction of nineteenth century America was also a useful source for early Black novelists. Beginning in 1833, the humor of Seba Smith, the creator of the letters of Jack Downing, and his many followers flourished among the masses. The popularity of Yankee rustics commenting on political affairs in racy idiomatic language and awkwardly apt metaphors was not lost on Black novelists in search of appropriate vehicles for their own satirical commentary on American democracy, Christianity, and racism. Nor were the early novelists beyond the influence of the Southwestern frontier humor of Augustus Longstreet's *Georgia Scenes* (1835) and Joseph Baldwin's *Flush Times in Alabama and Mississippi* (1853). Like the crackerbox philosophy of Yankee types, the sketches of Longstreet and Baldwin were provincial but honest attempts at recording native comedy. Although frequently given to caricature and burlesque, their emphasis was on the common man, oral tale, colloquial speech, local mores and humorous character types. In ***Clotel*** we see how Brown draws on this vein of humor when his heroine is traveling in disguise as a man on a Cincinnati stagecoach:

> The coach stopped to take in a real farmer-looking man, who no sooner entered than he was saluted with "Do you go for Clay?" "No," was the answer. "Do you go for Van Buren?" "No." "Well, then, of course you will go for Harrison." "No." "Why, don't you mean to work for any of them at the election?" "No." "Well, who will you work for?" asked one of the company. "I work for Betsy and the children, and I have a hard job of it at that," replied the farmer, without a smile. . . . "Are you an Odd Fellow?" asked one. "No, sir, I've been married more than a month." "I mean, do you belong to the order of Odd Fellows?" "No, no; I belong to the order of married men." "Are you a mason?" "No, I am a carpenter by trade." "Are you a Son of Temperance?" "Bother you, no; I am a son of Mr. John Gosling."[16]

We also overhear an exchange between a Southerner and Northerner:

> "You are from Connecticut, are you?" asked the Southerner. "Yes, and we are an orderly, pious peaceable people. Our holy religion is respected, and we do more for the cause of Christ than the whole Southern States put together." "I don't doubt it," said the white hat gent. "You sell wood nutmegs and other spurious articles enough to do some good. You talk of your 'holy religion'; but your robes' righteousness are woven at Lowell and Manchester; your paradise is high per centum on factory stacks; your palms of victory and

> crowns of rejoicing are triumphs over a rival party in politics on the questions of banks and tariffs. If you could, you would turn heaven into Birmingham, make every angel a weaver, and with the eternal din of looms and spindles drown all the anthems of the morning stars. Ah! I know you Connecticut people like a book. No, no, all hoss; you can't come it on me."[17]

Critics generally overlook this satirical dimension of the early Afro-American novel.

Instead, they point to the more obvious influence of the plantation tradition. Ante-bellum writers like George Tucker, Nathaniel B. Tucker, William A. Caruthers, John P. Kennedy, Caroline H. Ingraham and Joseph H. Ingraham helped to establish idyllic pictures of plantation life and the peculiar endowments of Black people. Subsequent local colorists and regionalists such as Harris, Page and Dixon—the classic literary apologists for slavery—glorified the Old South even more. Harris' *Uncle Remus: His Songs and Sayings* (1880) and *Gabriel Tolliver* (1902), Page's *In Ole Virginia* (1887) and *Red Rock* and Dixon's *The Leopard's Spots* (1902) and *The Clansmen* (1905) celebrated the beauty of an orderly feudal society and decried its destruction by rapacious Unionists and Blacks. Although Harris and Page's use of extensive monologues and tall tales within a framework suggests their influence by the humorists, melodrama was the dominant form of the Southern apologists. The melodramatic conflict was both sectional and racial. The Good Guys in this conflict were the chivalrous, white Bourbon aristocrats, their chaste, dazzlingly beautiful belles and their devoted abject slaves or freedmen. The Bad Guys were the malevolent white Union Leaguers, carpetbaggers and scalawags and the struggling Black freedmen. In retrospect, the moral absolutism of melodrama was highly suited for the tide of white nationalism that swept the country after Reconstruction.

More instructive than critic Robert Bone's approach to melodrama as an illustration of "the uncultivated sensibilities of the early Negro novelist" and "his firm allegiance to the American success ideology"[18] is an exploration of how melodrama served his philosophical and aesthetic needs. According to culture historian David Grimstead, melodrama was basically religious drama, "wherein surface detail, psychological or social, was firmly subordinated to a world view" and "the 'real' truth had to be that which affirmed the optimism of tomorrow over the frequent bleakness of today."[19] The last minute rescues, numerous reunions of long separated families and lovers and projected ultimate triumph of virtue over villainy in the early Black novels were a metaphysical necessity in a universe ruled by moral laws. Many of the sorely tried older Black characters, like the Lockleys in George Pryor's *Neither Bond Nor Free,* believed "that in the world about them all things worked together for good."[20] Even though for many the hand of Providence insured the triumph of the good eventually, it moved too slowly for some. Spurning his father-in-law's pious counsel, Delany's hero responds:

> "It is not wickedness, Daddy Joe; you don't understand these things at all. If a thousand years with us is but a day with God, do you think that I am required to wait all that time?"
>
> "Don't, Henry, don't! De wud say 'stan' still an 'see de salbation'."
>
> "That's no talk for me, Daddy Joe; I've been 'standing still' long enough—I'll 'stand still' no longer."[21]

Viewed from the subjugated economic and political position of Blacks, the basic goodness of Providence, man and society was being perverted on a grand scale by white devils. Most often, then, the serpent in the Edenic imagery of the Afro-American novel is white oppression.

In addition, the dime romances with domestic felicity and female chastity at their matrix seemed heaven sent for the treatment of illicit relations between Black women and white men. Refined heroes and heroines in elaborate disguise, mistaken identity, passwords, and violent episodes were keys to the formulaic packaged Beadle Dime Novels. In developing their forbidden fruit theme nineteenth century Black novelists found these melodramatic conventions irresistible. Contrary to popular belief, however, the mulatto heroines of ***Clotel*** and *Iola Leroy* are not mere carbon copies of white feminine purity. True, as Ellen Morton's suicide suggests, death before sexual dishonor was also the unwritten code for Black writers. But as in the case of Clotel and Althesa, virtue, when thwarted by man-made laws prohibiting interracial marriage, could be satisfied by "a marriage sanctioned by heaven." That both women die before the end of the novel is less important to the plot than their exploitation—Horatio's infidelity and Henry's failure to manumit Althesa—by a perverse society. In contrast, blue-eyed, near-white Iola survives triumphantly as she repeatedly rejects a persistent aristocratic white suitor and dutifully dedicates her life to family and race.

Loyalty to race or region often clashes with loyalty to country in melodrama, for nationalism was another cardinal virtue of the form. "Faith in the goodness of the United States, its government, and its destiny," Grimsted notes, "was modulated only by association with principles of liberty, justice, and equality which were assumed to be the birthright of all men."[22] While Belton Piedmont, the protagonist in *Imperium in Imperio,* has faith in white people and chooses patriotism over Black nationalism when it comes to outright revolution, Dan Freeman in *The Spook Who Sat by the Door* acts on the principle that Blacks must use guerilla warfare to attain their rights. By and large, the emphasis in the tradition of the Afro-American novel is not on my country right or wrong but, as in Ellison's *Invisible Man,* on my country because despite economic and political perversions it is based on principles common to all men: Liberty, Justice and Equality.

Allegiance to these principles, of course, influenced characterization and plot. Convinced that the cause of justice and equality was not served when the birth rights, patriotism and civil rights of Blacks were subordinated to those of poor whites, immigrants, and anarchists, postbellum novelists depicted this travesty with righteous indignation. "The Negro is not plotting in beer-saloons against the peace and order of society," we hear a character protesting in *Iola Leroy.* "His fingers are not dripping with dynamite, neither is he spitting upon your flag, nor flaunting the red banner of anarchy in your face."[23] In contrast, Iola is characterized as a Black feminist who insists on being self-reliant and holding a job as a saleswoman. And sobriety, thrift, honesty, hard work, property ownership and education are portrayed as the keys to dignity and freedom in a puritan, capitalistic system. Understandably, during an age when industrialism ran rampant, many Black novelists saw middle class values as the most realistic guarantors of racial justice and equality. "Greater industry, skill, the sticking quality, honesty and reliability will open the way . . ." writes Pryor. "If we will only cultivate the saving spirit, cut loose from extravagant habits, work the year round, encourage and assist one another in business, we will acquire wealth, and this will effectively dissipate race prejudice."[24] If, as Bone claims, "the early Negro novelist has the soul of a shopkeeper,"[25] he also represented the unfulfilled promise of the nation and an unrelenting struggle for Black power, i.e., economic, political, and cultural self-determination.

On the other hand, the double-consciousness which W. E. B. Du Bois so eloquently expressed in *The Souls of Black Folk,* "this sense of always looking at one's self through the eyes of others, of measuring one's soul by the tape of a world that looks on in amused contempt and pity,"[26] produced a corresponding ambivalence toward the literary traditions of the day. Under the influence of popular fiction, for example, most early novelists included at least one farcical episode and minstrel figure in their novels. Brown's Sam, the "Black Doctor" with a flair for wearing ruffled shirts and a half pound of butter in his hair, and Griggs' church member, who flings her white charge across the room and swings on the preacher's neck in religious ecstasy, fall into this category. But the folk are not simply viewed in a comic perspective as Bone argues.[27] Some, like Griggs' Hannah Piedmont are self-sacrificing Black matriarchs; others, like Dunbar's Sadness are surrogate fathers; and still others, like Chesnutt's Josh Green, are Black Avengers.

Earlier I asked: Where does the Afro-American novelist find the literary sources for his art? And what are the special characteristics of this offshoot of the Euro-American novel? If the outline I have given has any validity at all, it is clear that the tradition of the Afro-American novel is much more complex and diverse than we have been led to believe. Contributing to this complexity is the fact that early Afro-American novelists did not rely solely on folklore for creative inspiration and form, but drew heavily on abolitionist literature—especially the slave narratives—the Bible, and popular fiction. Although such diverse literary influences suggest the difficulty of defining a Black aesthetic, I have discovered that from William Wells Brown to Cecil Brown the primary unifying metaphor in the Afro-American novel is the quest for identity as free men. This archetypal journey, usually cast in a Christian framework, begins metaphorically in the Valley of the Shadow of Death and leads its hero to salvation: the City of God, Self-Awareness, or Social Equality. The Promised Land may be the North as in ***Clotel*** and *The Garies and Their Friends;* the South as in *The Marrow of Tradition* (1901) and *Cane;* the West as in *The Conquest* (1913) and *Yellow Back Radio Broke-Down* (1969); or in another country as in *Blake, The Life and Loves of Mr. Jiveass Nigger* and *Dunfords Travels Everywheres.* Then, again, the Promised Land may be in neither time nor space but in a state of mind, a longing to attain self-conscious manhood by merging one's double self into a better, truer self, as in *The Autobiography of an Ex-Coloured Man* (1912), *Native Son* (1940), *Invisible Man,* and *Go Tell It on the Mountain.* Whatever the case, the path is strewn with snares and pitfalls: the Peculiar Institution, Jim Crow, the Urge to Whiteness, False Prophets, the Almighty Dollar, the Machine Age, and the Siren of Success. But guided by faith in the American Dream and the Second Coming the heroes and anti-heroes of the Afro-American novel struggle up the Mountain, from whose summit they behold the immanence of the Apocalypse and Canaan.

Besides illustrating that the Afro-American novelist explores both the supernatural and natural worlds in his art, this little allegory makes clear that the basic values of the Afro-American tradition are inextricably linked with the Christian principles of Faith, Hope and Charity, albeit a faith that is often sorely tried to the breaking point, a hope that must struggle to overcome the despair of material setbacks, and a charity that irrationally affirms the power of love in a world of human waste and destruction. I find, in short, that the major tendencies in the tradition of the Afro-American novel are romantic, protestant, and messianic.

Notes

1. "Black Writers' Views on Literary Lions and Values," *Negro Digest,* XVII (January, 1968), 12.
2. *Ibid.,* pp. 35 and 81.
3. (Chicago: University of Chicago Press, 1966), p. 17.
4. *American Negro Folktales* (Greenwich: Fawcett Premier Book, 1967), p. 12.
5. *Contending Forces: A Romance Illustrative of Negro Life North and South* (Boston: The Colored Co-operative Publishing Company, 1900), p. 13.
6. For a useful description of the Brown and Craft lectures, see William Edward Farrison, *William Wells Brown: Author and Reformer* (Chicago: University of Chicago Press, 1969), pp. 136-137.
7. See Frederick Douglass, *Narrative of the Life of Frederick Douglass: An American Slave,* ed., Benjamin Quarles (Cambridge: The Belknap Press, 1967); Gilbert Osofsky, ed., *Puttin' on Ole Massa:*

The Slave Narratives of Henry Bibb, William Wells Brown, and Solomon Northup (New York: Harper Torchbooks, 1969); Arna Bontemps, ed., *Great Slave Narratives* (Boston: Beacon Press, 1969); and William Loren Katz, ed., *Five Slave Narratives* (New York: Arno Press; 1969). See also Charles Nichols, *Many Thousand Gone: The Ex-Slaves Account of Their Bondage and Freedom* (Leiden: E. J. Brill, 1963); George P. Rawick, *The American Slave: A Composite Autobiography* (Westport: Greenwood Publishing, 1972), I; and Stephen Butterfield, "Black Autobiography: The Development of Identity, Language and Viewpoint from Douglass to Jackson," Diss. University of Massachusetts, 1972.

8. *The Liberator,* October 22, 1852; quoted in *Puttin' On Ole Massa,* ed. Gilbert Osofsky (New York: Harper Torchbooks, 1969), p. 29.
9. Jean Toomer, *Cane* (New York: Perennial Edition, 1969), p. 199.
10. Margaret Walker, *Jubilee* (Boston: Houghton Mifflin, 1966), pp. 264-265.
11. This information was culled from the following sources: John Hastings, *A Dictionary of the Bible,* Vol. I (New York: Charles Scribners, Sons, 1901), 734-757; *Encyclopedia Britannica,* Vol. VIII (Chicago: William Benton, 1965), 694-697; John S. Mibiti, *African Religions and Philosophy* (Garden City: Anchor Books, 1970), pp. 1-129, 195-216, 266-281, 299-342; E. Franklin Frazier, *The Negro Church in America* (New York: Schocken Books, 1964), pp. 1-19; and W. E. B. Du Bois, *The Negro* (New York: Oxford University Press, 1970), pp. 62-85.
12. (Miami: Mnemosyne, 1970), pp. 24-25.
13. (New York: Dodd, Mead and Co., 1902), p. 150.
14. (New York: Signet Books, 1953), p. 326.
15. See Charles W. Chesnutt, "Superstitions and Folklore of the South," *Modern Culture,* Vol. 13, 1901, 231-235; reprinted in *Mother Wit from the Laughing Barrel,* ed. Alan Dundes (Englewood Cliffs: Prentice Hall, Inc., 1973), p. 371. As this article and his short stories indicate, Chesnutt was a serious, sensitive student of folklore.
16. (New York: Collier Books, 1970), p. 155.
17. *Ibid.,* pp. 159-160.
18. *The Negro Novel in America,* rev. ed. (New Haven: Yale University Press, 1965), p. 25.
19. "Melodrama as Echo of the Historically Voiceless," *Anonymous Americans,* ed. Tamara K. Hareven (Englewood Cliffs: Prentice-Hall, Inc., 1971), pp. 82-83.
20. (New York: J. S. Oglive Publishing Co., 1902), p. 12.
21. *Blake; or, The Huts of America* (Boston: Beacon Press, 1970), p. 21.
22. *Op. cit.,* p. 87.
23. Frances E. W. Harper, *Iola Leroy; or, Shadows Uplifted* (Boston: James H. Earle, 1892), p. 223.
24. *Op. cit.,* p. 81.
25. *Op. cit.,* p. 15.
26. (Greenwich: Crest Book, 1961), pp. 16-17.
27. Bone, p. 26.

W. Edward Farrison (essay date 1975)

SOURCE: "*The Kidnapped Clergyman* and Brown's *Experience,*" in *CLA Journal: Official Publication of the College Language Association,* Vol. 18, No. 4, 1975, pp. 507-15.

[*In the following essay, Farrison looks at an anonymous play,* The Kidnapped Clergyman, *as a possible source for Brown's lesser known play,* Experience.]

In 1839 an anonymous antislavery drama entitled *The Kidnapped Clergyman; Or, Experience the Best Teacher* was published in Boston with the imprint of Dow and Jackson. In the next year it was reprinted with the imprint of G. N. Thomas, also of Boston. Each of these printings consists of a duodecimo volume of 123 pages. The only difference between them is in the names of the publishers. The fact that there were two printings of the drama in a short time may lead one to suppose that it had become a popular work. If it had, most probably its popularity did not remain extensive in either time or locales. At least only a few copies of the two printings seem to be extant. The drama was probably written after the spring of 1836, perhaps not long before it was first published. At the end of the scene next to the last one in it, there is a reference to the atrocious burning alive in Saint Louis of Francis McIntosh, a free mulatto steamboat employee, who had been accused of murdering a white deputy sheriff. This burning occurred late in April, 1836, so that its date was presumably the *terminus ante quem* for the writing of the drama.

It is inferable from the contents of the volume that in addition to being a confirmed abolitionist, its author was familiar with the iniquities of American slavery as well as with the legal dialectics involved in it. Possibly he had spent some time as a private teacher in the South, as many graduates of Northern colleges of his time did, and most probably he was also a student of law if not possessed of some experience in the practice of it. Whoever he was, apparently his major purpose was, not to produce a great artistic work especially adaptable to the exigencies of the stage, but to dramatize a comprehensive, persuasive argument against slavery, with special reference to the pronouncements of preachers and opportunist politicians who pretended to abhor slavery in the abstract but condoned it on specious grounds as a reality. In accordance with its purpose, the drama abounds less in action than in dialogue, much of which consists of complicated legal arguments. Because of this fact a considerable part of the drama is much more effective when carefully read than it would be if recited.

In a preface of five pages, the author refuted the arguments that slavery did not concern the Northern people, that Southern slavery was tolerated by Christianity, and that it was the mildest system of slavery ever established. Summarily dismissing the first argument on the principles of humanity, Christianity, and American citizenship, he concentrated on the other two. In doing this he devoted most of his efforts to a scrupulous interpretation of the story of Saint Paul, Onesimus, and Philemon—a story of which apologists for slavery had made too much in their attempts to harmonize Christianity and slavery. "Would Paul have sent Onesimus in chains," the author queried, "to a Philemon, who had offered a reward for him, dead or alive, and who was hunting for him with blood-hounds and rifles?" (P. 5.) According to the author, implicitly at least, the bondage to which the apostle remanded Onesimus was incomparably mild in contrast to American slavery with its inherent inhumanities; and it was the author's conviction that Christian nations needed to abolish slavery and thus to remove "one of the stumbling-blocks to the spread of Christianity."

The drama is divided into nine unnumbered scenes, the first of which constitutes more than one-third of the text, and which graphically exposes various evils inherent in slavery. The story told in these scenes is as follows:

It is a warm Sunday afternoon in summer. The Reverend David Dorsey, a pastor in a town near Boston, has just returned to his well-furnished library after preaching what he considered a masterful antiabolitionist if not altogether pro-slavery sermon. As he soliloquizes with lofty satisfaction concerning it, he is sure that Francis Atterbury (1662-1732), the distinguished, controversial British bishop of Rochester, could not have done better. He is also sure that if the "profound and methodical" John Tillotson (1630-1691), who was briefly archbishop of Canterbury, could have heard the sermon, he too would have been pleased with it. Ambivalently Dorsey admits to himself that he dislikes slavery in the abstract but finds it consistent with Christianity, and sees "no hardship to the blacks to be kept at work." For to him "Negroes [are] a degraded race, it is to be feared, different from white people, altogether inferior" (p. 11). His conscience is pricked withal by his severity on the abolitionists, but he is sure that his sermon will please his parishioners, win compliments from the Southern clergy, and generally enhance the already bright prospects for himself and his family.

Meanwhile, en route from church homewards, Dorsey and his wife stopped to visit Mrs. Marjoram, presumably one of his parishioners. Upon that good lady's insistence, Dorsey ate indulgently of her pound cake regardless of his wife's warning winks—pound cake which he now suspects had lard in it. Now at home alone, he becomes uncomfortable and drowsy as a result of his overeating, falls asleep, and has a long and eventually horrible nightmare. At the beginning of this event, Tillotson, a London bookseller named Lackington, and Dr. John Abernathy (1764-1831), a London authority on digestive disorders, appear in visions. Tillotson praises Dorsey's sermon, the bookseller promises to publish it and make it a best seller, and Abernathy diagnoses Dorsey's present ailment as temporary indigestion.

Still on Dorsey's mind when he falls asleep are the "horrid slave stories" he has recently and regretfully read—"stories of cruelty exaggerated, made up," he suspects, stories of the remanding of fugitives to slavery and of free persons kidnapped and sold into slavery. It is these stories which become the basis of his nightmare, in which he, his wife, and their six children are kidnapped, separated, and sold into slavery. Dorsey thinks that his kidnappers have mistaken him for a Negro. He admits that he has "a dark, swarthy complexion," but he has never thought that he would ever "be mistaken for a colored man." And although Dinah, an elderly slave of one of his purchasers, notices that he is "very dark," she is convinced that he is a white man. (Pp. 91-92 and 27.) What Dorsey seems not to know, however, is that ever so many slaves are whiter than he is, and that slavery is no respecter of complexions—that it is basically concerned, not with the racial identity of the enslaved, but with his strictly legal status as such. Dorsey is not long, nevertheless, in learning these facts, and also that it is incomparably more difficult to get out of slavery than to get into it. Despite his contention that he is a white preacher, he is sold and resold in Maryland, Virginia, and Kentucky and is repeatedly subjected to the process (mainly brutal whippings) of breaking recalcitrant slaves. Goaded by this process, to which he has lost three front teeth, and by the all-inclusive harshness of slave life, he runs away but is captured "in a deep wood" after one of his ears is shot off by one of his pursuers.

At an opportune time Dorsey escapes from Kentucky and returns to Massachusetts. There his owner discovers and claims him and appeals to three magistrates in succession for the authority to remove the fugitive from the state. The first magistrate, an abolitionist who considers slavery "wicked and abominable," summarily denies the claimant's appeal. The second magistrate, who is also an abolitionist, interprets the Constitution so as to legally deny the appeal. The third magistrate, whose attitude is proslavery, interprets the Constitution so as to authorize the claimant's appeal. He tells the fugitive that "You are merely free, *in the abstract,* which is perfectly consistent with the most abject slavery, in reality" (p. 84). Finally, with the help of an abolitionist lawyer, the fugitive appeals to the judge of the superior court on a writ of habeas corpus; and that official, a strict constructionist of the law, denies the fugitive's appeal and orders him remanded to the claimant. The long, technical, and often specious arguments carried on during these juridical proceedings vividly illustrate the legal dialectics which slavery involved.

En route with his fugitive back to Kentucky, the claimant stops at a tavern, where coincidentally he sells the fugitive to a Saint Louis slaveholder. Upon arriving at the home of his new purchaser, Dorsey discovers that his daughter Clara, erstwhile a beautiful, amiable, and accomplished young lady, but alas no longer that, is now owned by the same man. In a fight that ensues when, in violation of the slave code, Dorsey forcefully attempts to protect his daughter from the slaveholder's abuse, the slaveholder wounds Dorsey and is immediately killed by him. Just as a mob arrives threatening to burn the slave alive for killing a white man, Mrs. Dorsey and Clara return home and end his nightmare by awaking him.

Much to his relief, Dorsey finds that none of the horrors of his nightmare were real, even though they were so vivid as to leave his mind momentarily unhinged after he awakes. When he comes fully to his senses, he resolutely tears up the manuscript of his sermon, with the determination never to write another like it. He confesses that his nightmare has aroused his conscience against slavery, and he vows that not "for the applause of men, the hope of riches and honors, or the fear of poverty and reproach" will he ever again "speak complacently of a system of shocking cruelty and injustice" (pp. 122-123). As an unforgettable, crucial experience, albeit only a nightmare, it has proved to be an excellent teacher.

Historically interesting though it is, *The Kidnapped Clergyman* might have remained forgotten if a similar drama written seventeen years later and soon afterwards also forgotten had not been brought to light within the last twenty years. The later drama is William Wells Brown's ***Experience; Or, How to Give a Northern Man a Backbone. The Escape, Or, A Leap for Freedom,*** by the way, has been frequently and incorrectly called Brown's first drama, which it was not. His first drama was ***Experience,*** which he wrote early in 1856, before he wrote ***The Escape,*** but which he seems never to have published. Meanwhile he published ***The Escape*** in 1858, thus making it apparently the first drama to be published by an American Negro. Brown's own synopsis of ***Experience*** and reports of his public readings of it are given in my *William Wells Brown: Author and Reformer* (Chicago, 1969), Chapter XVIII.

The similarities as well as the differences between *The Kidnapped Clergyman* and ***Experience*** are remarkable. The general purpose of Brown's drama was essentially the same as the previously noted purpose of the earlier work. Consonant with this purpose, the two works share a general plan whose theme is the reformation of a proslavery preacher into an abolitionist. There is, however, an important difference in the motivation of the action in their plots, as will appear later in this discussion. The plots of the two dramas involve a considerable amount of the same kinds of action because of the similarity of the purposes and plans of the two works, and because the kinds of wrongful practices represented in the action were common in slavery as it indisputably was. More action is indicated in Brown's synopsis than in the earlier drama, but it could have been fully realized only if his drama had been performed by a full complement of actors, as it seems never to have been. In Brown's public readings of the drama, much of this action could only have been suggested by Brown and left to the imagination of the members of his audiences.

The protagonists in both dramas are Massachusetts proslavery preachers who are too solicitous about their prospects for success and public approval. The author of the earlier drama might or might not have had a specific preacher in mind, but Brown certainly did. The Reverend Dr. Jeremiah Adderson, his protagonist, was easily identifiable as the Reverend Dr. Nehemiah Adams (1806-1878), a Boston Congregational preacher, who had published in Boston in 1854 his *A South-Side View of Slavery.* Adams's book, which is one of the most specious works ever written about American slavery, was based on his sojourn of three months mainly in Georgia, South Carolina, and Virginia early in the year just mentioned. Ultimately, far from brightening his prospects, his book did more to alienate Northerners than to ingratiate him with Southerners.

Although Brown kept his protagonist in the central position throughout his drama, it could not have been his intention to develop that protagonist into either an admirable, heroic character or a perfect villain. If it had been, he would hardly have chosen Adams as the prototype of his protagonist; for to him Adams was not even reverable, to say nothing of being heroic, and was indeed more of a hypocrite and theological harlequin than a villain. As far as Adams himself mattered, it was simply Brown's intention to satirize him efficaciously for his apparently apologetic but really proslavery position concerning slavery.

It was Adams's visit to the South, doubtless—a visit during which he learned only superficially about slavery or ignored what he saw—that prompted Brown to motivate the action in his drama by having Adderson visit the "Sunny South" a second time. During this visit, Adderson is kidnapped and sold into slavery in Richmond, Virginia, subjected to the usual slave-breaking process sometimes called with grim humor "a course of sprouts," and burdened with the drudgery of slave labor in particular and slave life in general. Like Dorsey, Adderson finds himself suddenly enslaved in spite of the fact that he is as white as his enslavers. Like Dorsey he also learns that there are numerous white slaves, that slavery is no respecter of complexions, that it is basically concerned, not with the racial identity of bondmen, but with their strictly legal status as such, and that it is much easier to be forced into slavery than to get out of it.

From his experience as a slave, Adderson learns to hate slavery and firmly resolves to oppose it when he gets out of it, as he eventually does. Upon his return home he evidences his determination to keep his resolution by taking the first opportunity available to succor a fugitive slave, Marcus, who is on his flight to freedom. Experience has indeed proved to be an excellent teacher for Adderson as well as for Dorsey; and what is more, it has given Adderson a backbone—moral courage to violate the infamous Fugitive Slave Law, which Adams along with others who shared his views had tried to enshrine in Constitutional sacrosanctity. Thus at the end of the action, as a new convert to the antislavery cause, Adderson, even more than Dorsey, finishes by winning the sympathy of the audience.

From the standpoint of both realism and the credible motivation of the action, putting Adderson in a position to fully experience as well as observe slavery as it actually prevailed was a much more valid and much more effective device than the dream-nightmare scheme of *The Kidnapped Clergyman.* As Brown presumably knew, however horrible nightmares resulting from overeating may be, they are less powerful to reform individuals than actual experiences are. If they were not, most probably fewer people would eat themselves into their graves.

Unlike Dorsey, Brown did not need to refer to the slave stories he had read for details with which to develop the plot of his drama. During his twenty years as a slave and twenty years as an aggressive antislavery leader, he had become so familiar with the usages of slavery that he could authoritatively and vividly exemplify Adderson's experiences in it without relying on the assertions of others.

By his familiarity with dramatic literature and stage presentations, Brown was enabled to invest his drama with a plot more compact than that of the earlier work—a plot possessed of dynamic dramatic situations, as are indicated in his previously mentioned synopsis. Doubtless, being cognizant from the beginning, however, of the nonexistence of prospects for the production of his work as a theatrical performance, he knew that he would have to keep within the limits prescribed by the only way in which he could present it, namely, as a dramatic reading. This meant that with the aid of whatever variations in tones and gestures he could convincingly employ, he had to make it interesting to audiences. From the numerous accounts of his reading of the drama on lecture platforms, it appears that his presentations of it were quite effective.

An intriguing question still remains: Was Brown familiar with *The Kidnapped Clergyman*? It is possible, of course, that he might have seen a copy of one of the printings of the drama sometime before he wrote ***Experience.*** If he did he must have been one of the few if not the only one among his contemporary fellow-abolitionists to see it, since none of them are definitely known even to have referred to it during the years that immediately preceded his writing of ***Experience*** or during the time of his public readings of it. Now it seems quite probable that anyone familiar with both dramas would have been moved at some time to comment on their similarities.

There is still another pertinent consideration. In his writing, Brown commonly drew upon the general store of antislavery literature for material. When he did so he usually acknowledged his indebtedness, although he did not accurately identify his sources. For instance, in his ***Clotel; Or, The President's Daughter*** (London, 1853), he used freely Mrs. Lydia Maria Child's "The Quadroons," a short story. In the "Conclusion" to his novel, he acknowledged his indebtedness to Mrs. Child for his use of her story but did not give its title, as he should have done. At the end of Chapter XXV of the novel, he quoted with some changes a poem of Grace Greenwood's which had been included in her *Poems* (Boston, 1851). As his source for the poem, he referred, not to Miss Greenwood's volume, but vaguely to "one of the newspapers." And in fact he might have taken his version of the poem from a newspaper—but which one? The summary point here is that if Brown was sufficiently familiar with the earlier drama to be influenced by it, he might have been expected to indicate in some way that he was; and perhaps he would have done so if he had published ***Experience.***

Considerations to the contrary notwithstanding, the similarities between the two dramas render it easier to believe that Brown was familiar with the earlier one than to believe that he was not. Perhaps he found in that work at least some exemplary suggestions for the plan of his own drama—suggestions on which his knowledge of his subject and his originality enabled him to improve. Anyway he produced a drama which apparently proved to be more interesting and more popular, at least for a while, than the earlier one seems ever to have been.

Gerald S. Rosselot (essay date 1980)

SOURCE: "*Clotel,* A Black Romance," in *CLA Journal: Official Publication of the College Language Association,* Vol. 23, No. 3, 1980, pp. 296-302.

[*In the following essay, Rosselot defends* Clotel *against criticism for its romanticism, explaining that the novel embraced the romance tradition of its time and succeeded in its political purpose.*]

Clotel (1853), "generally considered the first novel written by an American Negro," has often been a disappointment because the romance elements in it have been unrecognized. Although Farrison, William Wells Brown's biographer, calls the slave narrative based on the legend of Thomas Jefferson's black children the "memorable effort of a pioneer among Negro authors," he notes that the book "abounds in imperfections."[1] Then there is Loggins' classic complaint: "The great weakness of ***Clotel*** is that enough material for a dozen novels is crowded into its two hundred and forty-five pages."[2] Farrison, agreeing that ***Clotel*** contains too much material for full treatment in a single novel, believes that besides stylistic problems "the novel suffers from sketchiness . . . in the portrayal of characters. . . ."[3] Loggins feels that because the novel moves so rapidly "we never see any one person in the

CLOTEL;

OR,

THE PRESIDENT'S DAUGHTER:

A Narrative of Slave Life

IN

THE UNITED STATES.

BY

WILLIAM WELLS BROWN,

A FUGITIVE SLAVE, AUTHOR OF "THREE YEARS IN EUROPE.

With a Sketch of the Author's Life.

"We hold these truths to be self-evident: that all men are created equal; that they are endowed by their Creator with certain inalienable rights, and that among these are LIFE, LIBERTY, and the PURSUIT OF HAPPINESS." — *Declaration of American Independence.*

story at any time long enough to get a clear impression of his character."[4] Presumably the limited characterization in ***Clotel*** prompts Davis' charge that "Brown's greatest weakness is that he doesn't know how to make his characters come alive."[5]

However, the characters in ***Clotel*** particularly illustrate Brown's indebtedness to the romance tradition that pervaded the American novel in the nineteenth century.[6] Since Brown's purpose is to show as many horrors of slavery as he can, hoping to bring "British influence to bear upon American slavery,"[7] he subordinates his characters, both black and white, to an eventful and sensational, rapidly moving plot wherein those horrors are detailed. Thus his characters, inadequately motivated and developed, are hurriedly and directly presented by a romancer, not a novelist. Brown offers his reader little opportunity to judge the characters or even to watch them acting out the business of their miserable lives. Rarely are they allowed to think or feel, and flattened by the author's sincere intention to persuade his audience of slavery's outrage, the characters seem a static group in which conversation is infrequent and dialogue that distinguishes and reveals character and temperament and furthers action is rarer. Brown's method is not then the indirect presentation of the novelist who shows his characters in action. Rather Brown steadily tells about his characters, what happens to them, what they mean to him. Consequently, his less than rounded characters, if they do seem real, emerge as significant symbols in the violence and anguish that slavery fostered.

Occasionally characters in the narrative make speeches, usually abolitionist arguments, which seem illogical and incongruous unless Brown's appeal to British readers is recalled. For example, in Chapter XX Henry Norton, the white Vermont physician who is, so Brown tells us, a violent opponent of slavery because of his Northern education and his marriage to Clotel's sister, speaks in solitary argument against slavery. It is a stilted and unrealistic performance; Morton, like his message, is admirable, and if not persuasive, he does advance the author's abolitionist logic. But Morton's speech neither defines nor enlarges his character more than we had known it previously since he had, without prejudice and with great love and charity, rescued and married a slave girl. At this point his speech seems to make him an ironic figure. Certainly as a man of wealth, position, and intelligence, Morton might have made some provision for the protection of his family, but Brown claims Morton was "unacquainted with the laws of the land," i.e., the laws of "the Southern States [wherein] the children follow the condition of the mother. If the mother is free the children are free; if a slave, they are slaves" (p. 165). On the death of Morton and his wife, Althesa, their daughters are sold at auction to settle the estate, and his brave speech seems quite hollow and pointless. Thus the well-intentioned Morton, revered by Brown as "A True Democrat," the title of Chapter XX, becomes in Brown's plot not a consistent and plausibly motivated character but another hapless victim of slavery and his family's tragedy one of its horrors.

While Brown's political purpose may have outweighed any concern for carefully plotting the destinies of his characters, he did not, unlike the novelist, want us to see his characters in any great detail or complexity, for ***Clotel*** is not and never pretends to be a story about only the title character, her sister, and their mother. In fact, the title is misleading. ***Clotel*** is really "A Narrative of Slave Life in the United States"; that is the subtitle of Brown's romance that moves abruptly through three generations from Richmond to Natchez to New Orleans to Ohio, Canada, and Dunkirk, France. Covering so much time and distance, cataloguing so many aspects of slavery, Brown's perspective had of necessity to be broad and his method of characterization that of assertion rather than dramatization. While he describes an abundance of potentially dramatic situations, his scenes lack the intensity that rounded and carefully motivated characters could give them. Like other writers of romance, Charles Brockden Brown and Cooper, for instance, Brown emphasizes an elaborate and extended action-packed plot in which a wide range of flat characters are carried through several generations, but never casually presented. It is not, as Davis charges, that Brown fails to take seriously his "look-alike females" and "simply kills them off when his invention flags. . . ."[8] Rather, the plot demands brisk movement from episode to episode, and deaths are necessary horrors if Brown is to keep to his purpose.

Of the slave women Clotel is the most important character and the richest symbol. Though she shares with other black characters a common goodness and a longing for freedom, even as they nobly bear the various abuses of slavery, Clotel is still an ideal in the extreme. At the auction where she is sold for fifteen hundred dollars, she is described not only as beautiful and white, but also as Christian, trustworthy, chaste, virtuous and moral (p. 43). Later, in her alliance with Horatio Green, her white lover and owner, Clotel's genuine feeling for Green, her tender conscience and "her high poetic nature" (p. 57) combine with anguish and "indwelling sadness" when she considers "the unavoidable and dangerous position which the tyranny of society had awarded her . . ." (p. 58) and the child she has borne Green.

Clotel represents several aspects of slavery. She is Brown's first victim of sexual exploitation that accompanied the peculiar institution, and she is the victim, as a near-white slave, of cruel treatment by both whites and blacks. Brown regards her ironically as "a devoted Christian" sold "in a city thronged with churches, whose tall spires look like so many signals pointing to heaven, and whose ministers preach that slavery is a God-ordained institution!" (p. 43). Finally she symbolizes enduring love, courage, and heroism after she is arrested and doomed as a fugitive while attempting to find her daughter.

Ultimately Brown sees Clotel as a tragic heroine, one whose death had been determined by God to be enacted "within plain sight of the President's house and the capital of the Union. . . ." Her death is "evidence . . . of the inconquerable [sic] love of liberty the heart may inherit; as well as a fresh admonition to the slave dealer, of the cruelty and enormity of his crimes" (p. 177). In Clotel's "appalling tragedy" (p. 177) Brown senses the inevitable, ironic waste: "Such was the life and such the death of a woman whose virtues and goodness of heart would have done honour to one in a higher station of life, and who, if she had been born in any other land but that of slavery, would have been honoured and loved" (p. 178).

If Clotel symbolizes tribulation, separation, and loss, her daughter, Mary, the only near-white slave girl whose life is not a tragedy since she escapes to France, symbolizes the fragile hope for the future; freedom and the happiness it brings are possible for slaves only as fugitives in Europe.

George Green, Mary's lover, is the last of three slave men appearing in the latter part of the book who illustrate the theme of survival and so counter the numerous horrors in the narrative. The trio, sharing a certain high spirit, contrasts markedly with the doomed slave women (except Mary Green), particularly Currer, Clotel, Althesa, and Althesa's daughters, all of whom die, and with the exception of Althesa, die as slaves.

Because these men have talents, virtues, and perceptions that enable them to cope successfully with life, they seem to be survivors much as Brown himself was. Indeed, Brown's **"Narrative of the Life and Escape of William Wells Brown,"** the memoir of the author preceding the novel, suggests several similarities between the characters and Brown as a slave and as a fugitive. Like Brown, they are sympathetic to others, responsible, industrious, intelligent, and shrewd. Like Brown, they have known separation and trial, loneliness and suffering, fear and frustration, and the longing for freedom and escape. They seem to be drawn out of Brown's understanding of his "new existence" after his escape to freedom, for as a slave he felt he had not been a man. The title of "freeman" sounded, he says, in his ears "like charm." He writes: "I wanted to see Captain Price [his owner], and let him learn from my own lips that I was no more a chattel, but a MAN" (p. 16). Free at last with the Quaker who befriends him, Brown questions his own identity: "The fact that I was a freeman—could walk, talk, eat, and sleep as a man, and no one to stand over me with the blood-clotted cowhide—all this made me feel that I was not myself" (p. 16). In this last respect, Brown's uncertainty of his *self,* we are reminded that not only for his three survivors but for all his slave characters the loss of liberty meant an even more basic loss of personality, the lack of identity, the submersion of self.

The heroic George Green is a sentimental, almost Byronic figure who compensates for all the humiliation and deprivation endured by slaves. His heroism and his chivalry (he hesitates to flee from prison, preferring death rather than an escape that would incriminate and endanger his beloved Mary) seem attempts by Brown to establish, quickly and without adequate motivation, nobility and the potential for greatness in a character who closes the novel on a positive, if ironic, note. Young Green, one of Nat Turner's rebels and a fiery defender of that revolt, ultimately appears as the epitome of worldly success when he accidentally meets Mary in France after a ten-year separation. George and Mary, probably the first fictional black expatriates in the American novel, are the best characters Brown can muster to engage that awful, inevitable irony—that while the rest of the world would honor them, the Greens "cannot return to their native land without becoming slaves" (p. 200). Such is the final horror of slavery in Brown's catalogue.

The other two survivors are presented as examples of heroism and shrewdness. In the chapter which follows his final reference to Black Sam and offers the fleeting glimpse of William escaping to Ohio with Clotel, Brown says that "no country has produced so much heroism in so short a time, connected with escapes from peril and oppression, as has occurred in the United States among fugitive slaves, many of whom show great shrewdness in their endeavors to escape from this land of bondage" (p. 131). William encounters and triumphs over what Brown calls "another form of slavery" (p. 138), prejudice against blacks in the Free States. Though William must ride in the luggage van of a train because of Jim Crow custom, he successfully insists on paying only freight rates for himself rather than the first-class passenger rates the conductor attempts to extort. "Slavery is a school in which the victims learn much shrewdness, and William has been an apt scholar" (p. 138).

Black Sam, though initially presented as a comic character on the Natchez farm of the cruel Rev. John Peck, is revealed as a shrewd slave when he sings of his true feelings on the death of his un-Christian master. Sam's shrewdness extends to his role as Cupid when he slyly encourages Georgiana Peck's reluctant suitor to propose marriage, thus assuring the farm community "good times den" (p. 125). Later, Sam emerges, because he is experienced, reliable, responsible, and intelligent, as a positive leader when he supervises ninety-eight slaves working successfully under his direction in a system of gradual emancipation. When the slaves are freed, Sam charitably and responsibly remains behind to care for the dying Georgiana, who had secured their freedom. Sam is Brown's most rounded black character, and intriguingly he suggests that Brown could develop character. While it is regrettable that there is not more of Sam or more characters like him, still that would not have suited Brown's purpose.

Clotel is best read as a romance in which reality is rendered in less volume and detail than in a novel. The rendering, of course, is Brown's, and though he attests to the truth of the "incidents and scenes" (p. 201) in his narrative, his method has been that of the romancer, preferring flat characters and rapid action in an exciting plot and interpreting it all for his reader. Behind each character and scene we understand the presence of the fugitive slave writer, himself a willing symbolist, who, ever mindful of his purpose, responds passionately to every horror and outrage in his plot. It is his feeling that charges the narrative, making it at once more personal, more urgent, more dramatic, and more symbolic.

Notes

1. William Edward Farrison, *William Wells Brown: Author and Reformer* (Chicago: University of Chicago Press, 1969), p. 231.
2. Vernon Loggins, *The Negro Author: His Development in America to 1900* (1931; rpt. Port Washington, N.Y., 1964), p. 166.
3. Farrison, p. 230.
4. Loggins, p. 166.
5. Arthur Davis, "Introduction" to *Clotel, or The President's Daughter* (New York: Collier Books, 1970), p. xv.
6. The romance tradition has been treated by Richard Chase in *The American Novel and Its Tradition* (Garden City, N.Y.: Doubleday Anchor Books, 1957). For his distinction between the novel and the romance, see pp. 12-13.
7. William Wells Brown, "Preface" to *Clotel, or The President's Daughter* (New York: Collier Books, 1970), p. xx. Subsequent references are to this edition; page numbers are given parenthetically in the text.
8. Davis, p. xvi.

L. H. Whelchel, Jr. (essay date 1985)

SOURCE: "A Mighty Pen," in *My Chains Fell Off: William Wells Brown, Fugitive Abolitionist,* New York: University Press of America, 1985, pp. 45-50.

[*In the following essay, Whelchel provides a summary of Brown's first novel,* Clotel, *interpreting Brown's purpose as both entertaining and political.*]

William Wells Brown's commitment to the struggle for freedom and equality for the blacks was a consuming passion that found expression, not alone in effort to effect his goals through legislation and political activity. He expressed himself, as well, in the idiom of literature.

Brown continued his relentless endeavor to crusade against slavery through writing novels and plays. He is recognized as the first black American male to publish a novel and a play. His first novel entitled ***Clotel, or The President's Daughter,*** was published in 1853, and a revised version, called ***Clotelle: A Tale of the Southern States,*** was published in 1864. In his original version, Thomas Jefferson is the father of the slave heroine in his novel. The president's name was offensive to some of the abolitionist sympathizers. To broaden the appeal, Brown substituted an "unnamed senator" for the name of President Jefferson. The revised edition had also the expressed purpose of entertaining the Union Army in their quest for "Universal Emancipation."

After experiencing the horrors of slavery and delight in freedom, Brown expressed empathy with the slaves in a poem in the preface of his novel:

> Is true freedom but to break;
> Fetters for our own dear sake,
> And with leathern hearts forget;
> No, true freedom is to share!
> All the chains our brothers wear, and with heart
> And hand to be earnest to make others free.[1]

The novel touches on slavery in Richmond, Natchez, New Orleans, and in areas along the Ohio and Mississippi Rivers. The plot treats a situation all too familiar in the antebellum south. The heroine, Clotel, is the daughter of one of the first families of the region. Clotel resided in Richmond, Virginia. Earlier she had lived with members of her family; but Currer, Clotel's mother, was sold to a resident modeled after James Walker, the notorious slave trader of Natchez, Mississippi. Althea, the sister of Clotel, was purchased by a slaveholder in New Orleans, Louisiana.

In the novel the sale of the two heroines was advertised in a Richmond newspaper:

> Thirty eight Negroes will be offered for sale on Monday, November 10, at twelve o'clock, being the

> entire stock of the late John Graves, Esq. Also several mulatto girls of rare personal qualities; two of them very superior. Any gentleman or lady wishing to purchase can take any of the above slaves on trial for a week.[2]

The two referred to in the advertisement as "very superior" were Clotel and Althea. While Currer was the official property of John Graves, Esq., she also served as the housekeeper of a "young slaveholder named Thomas Jefferson." Jefferson—having taken Currer as a mistress, at least on occasion—had, according to Brown, fathered her two daughters, Clotel and Althea. Jefferson moved from Virginia to Washington to serve the government but he left Currer and their two daughters behind in Richmond. Following the departure of Jefferson, Currer was hired out by her master as a laundress. Currer was industrious and proud and she made every effort to instill the dignity of womanhood in her daughters.

According to Brown, "nearly all the Negro parties in the cities and towns of the southern states are made up of quadroon and mulatto girls and white men." The beautiful daughters of Currer attracted much attention at these parties. It was at one of these gatherings that Clotel won the admiration of Horatio Green. At the time Horatio met Clotel he was a college student. He frequently visited Currer's house to see her daughter. Green promised to purchase Clotel for his mistress and to provide her with a home. Clotel awaited the fulfillment of Horatio's promise with great anticipation.

> It was a beautiful moonlight night in August, when all who reside in tropical climes are eagerly grasping for a breath of fresh air, that Horatio Green was seated in the small garden behind Currer's cottage, with the object of his affections by his side. And it was here that Horatio drew from his pocket the newspaper, wet from the press, and read the advertisement for the sale of the slaves to which we have alluded; Currer and her two daughters being of the number. At the close of the evening's visit, and as the young man was leaving, he said to the girl, "you shall soon be free and your own mistress."[3]

Horatio purchased Clotel at a public slave auction for fifteen hundred dollars. Brown observed that the sale of Clotel occurred in a southern city "thronged with churches . . . and whose ministers preach that slavery is a God-ordained institution!"

Horatio provided his slave mistress with a beautiful cottage on the outskirts of Richmond. Clotel was conscious of the fact that her relationship with Horatio had no legal sanction. "If the mutual love we have for each other, and the dictates of your affections fall from me," she told Horatio, "I would not, if I could, hold you by a single fetter." To this union was born a baby daughter, named Mary. The child brought new happiness and joy to their home. Clotel was sensitive to the hostility of a slave society and the possibility of her returning to slavery and separation from her child. To escape the restriction and cruelties of American slavery, Clotel asked "Horatio to remove to France or England, where both [sic] and her child would be free, and where colour was not a crime," Horatio did not oppose the idea in principle but his political aspirations overpowered Clotel's proposal.

> He still loved Clotel, but he was now becoming engaged in political and other affairs which kept him oftener and longer from the young mistress, and ambition to become a statesman was slowly gaining ascendancy over him.[4]

To enhance his political career, Horatio arranged a diplomatic marriage with the daughter of one of the wealthiest and most influential families in Richmond. When Clotel heard of Horatio's approaching marriage she despaired. The novel then becomes a tragic portrayal in the brutal melodramatic tradition that figures so largely in the abolitionist literature of the times. The form is naturalistic. Like *Uncle Tom's Cabin* it owes much to *Oliver Twist* and the works of Charles Dickens. Clotel, like Eliza, is a mulatto, a tragic character, for whom we sympathize more because she is part white than because she is colored. The quadroon is tarred by her slave ancestry; and she represents the irrational persecution brought about by a color caste.

For Brown, ***Clotel*** becomes the stock method of abolitionist propaganda. His characters are clear-cut, simple and artificial. They make natural vehicles for moral extremes, cast as either right (Clotel) or wrong (Horatio). Action is emphasized to the expense of in-depth depiction of character. In all charity Clotel and other characters are stereotypes in a stable, moral and fanciful world.

Brown's moral thus contains the well-used triangle of hero, heroine and villain. The plot material does not venture beyond the excitement of miscegenation and slavery's oppressive features, since the moral natures of hero and villain are fixed and without possibility of development. There is no inner conflict. The reader is sustained by the thriller-like aspect of the story in action revolving about a romantic projection between the classes. And ***Clotel*** is fully a novel of social aspiration as much as it is propaganda.

The period of the novel is well after the importation of African slaves had ceased in the United States. The slave had to structure his life in a culture to which he was denied full access. The process of assimilation was deliberately obstructed by whips. And shortly after American independence was won there were Afro-Americans who were native Americans by several generations.

By this time, too, Clotel's people were already losing their racial identity. Countless white males had been trying to wash her whole race whiter than snow. There was even a premium on "white slaves." This illegitimate offspring was creating new problems and moral ambiguities. From the start miscegenation was the congenital weakness in slavery's biological defense.

In Brazil and Cuba the importation of African slaves replenished the attrition of slaves lost to biological assimilation. But in North America manumission from interracial liaisons was legally impossible. But interracial ancestry created a privileged group of mulatto house servants, thereby resulting in a division of labor that corresponded to complexion.

In Brown's view the color line, and not just slavery, is unjust because it suppresses natural human instincts of affection. His novel is an argument for freedom and also for assimilation. For Currer, the mulatto mistress of President Thomas Jefferson, is just like other white mistresses. She is attractive and an expert laundress. Her children, Clotel and Althea, are descendant of quality, as much like "cultured" and refined white women as possible. After Clotel is sold, her jealous white mistress makes the slave cut off her beautiful hair. The edict for Clotel to cut her hair won the approval of the other slaves. After her hair was cut, the other servants laughed, "Miss Clo needn't strut round so big, she got nappy har well as I," said Nell, with a broad grin that showed her teeth.

> "She tinks she white, when she come here wid dat long har of hers," replied Mill.
>
> "Yes," continued Nell; "Missus make her take down her wool so she no put it up today."

Brown observed that Clotel's fair complexion was despised with envy by the other servants as well as the white mistress. In addition to the hostilities Clotel encountered, she was still grief-stricken over the separation from her only child, Mary. The heartfelt grief of Clotel was perceived by her master and her refusal to eat caused him to sell her to a young man for housekeeper.

The audience for ***Clotel*** was the parochial one of the dime store novel. It appealed to the new literate class of quality white folks and freedmen. Brown's aim was not to attack the character of Thomas Jefferson but to exploit an entertaining story as an argument against American slavery.

Brown's novel is an anthology of anti-slavery material which he employs to expose the tragedy of human bondage. "The blood of the first American statesmen coursing through the veins of the slaves" is a central theme of the novel. The increasing mulatto population of slaves caused Henry Clay to predict that the abolition of slavery would be brought about by the amalgamation of the races. The careers of Currer and her two daughters demonstrate that slaves, regardless of physical attraction and ability, are entirely subject to the will of their master. The institution of slavery is sanctioned by law, and even the religious leaders are mere echoes of public sentiment rather than correctors of wrongs perpetrated by human bondage.

Brown's writings demonstrate that the members of slave families encountered tremendous emotional suffering and stress. Brown cited in his autobiography that his mother had seven children fathered by seven different men. The major decisions and provisions for the slave family were made by the master, and the slave father was left with little or no authority. The master's lust for pretty black women jeopardized the development of family morality and stability.

The fear of separation from their loved ones caused many slaves not to want to establish family ties. Rather than see their loved ones beaten, insulted, over-worked and abused, many slaves preferred living on a different plantation from their mates. Henry Bibb felt that way: "If my wife must be exposed to the insults and licentious passions of wicked slavedrivers and overseers; if she must bear the stripes of the lash laid on by an unmerciful tyrant; if this is to be done with impunity, which is frequently done by slaveholders and their abettors, Heaven forbid that I should be compelled to witness the sight."

From the accounts of Brown and other fugitive slave narrators, slaves were made to feel inferior and degraded from the cradle to the grave.

The inherent limitations of Brown's melodrama are sketchiness in the development of the plots and in the portrayal of characters. Of necessity his story foundered within the artistic framework of 19th century Romanticism. At the same time, ***Clotel*** detracted nothing from the horrors of slavery as Brown had witnessed them. It is the most important of his works with the exception of his own narrative. As a publishing venture ***Clotel*** was unspectacular. Published the year after *Uncle Tom's Cabin,* Brown's novel could only suffer by comparison.

Although its shelf life was brief, ***Clotel*** was widely read and received positive reviews in England and among antislavery critics. To paraphrase Charles Sumner, romance has no story of more thrilling interest than his. Classical antiquity has preserved no examples of adventurous trial more worthy of renown. His novel goes to the heart of men.

Notes

1. William Wells Brown, *Clotel, or, The President's Daughter: A Narrative of Slave Life in the United States.* (London: Partridge and Oakey, 1853), Preface.

   Noel Hermance. *William Wells Brown and Clotel: A Portrait of the Artist in the First Negro Novel.* (Archon Book, 1969), Preface VII-VIII. See "New York by W. W. Brown." *Liberator,* Feb. 3, 1854, p. 191.

   William Wells Brown, *Clotelle: A Tale of the Southern States.* (Boston and New York, 1864), p. 104. See Herbert Ross Brown, *The Sentimental Novel in America, 1789-1860.* (Durham, North Carolina: Duke University Press, 1940), pp. 278-79.

2. Ibid., pp. 66-67. See Sterling Brown, *The Negro in American Fiction.* (Washington, D.C.: The Associates in Negro Folk Education, 1937), p. 63.

Ibid., pp. 63-64. The rumor about Jefferson's slave mistress was bandied about by some of the abolitionists. See Levi Gaylord, "A Scene at New Orleans," *Liberator,* September 21, 1838. See *The Liberator,* February 3, 1854. Early political enemies of Jefferson had not ignored the scandal. See William Cullen Bryant, "The Embargo or, Sketches of the Times," 1808.

3. See Buron Edward Reuter, *The Mulatto in the United States,* (Boston: Richard G. Badger, 1918), p. 65.
4. Ibid., p. 84. See Bernard N. Bell, "Literary Sources of the Early Afro-American Novel," *College Language Association Journal* (18 September, 1974), p. 85.

L. H. Whelchel, Jr. (essay date 1985)

SOURCE: "The Color of Ham and Cain," in *My Chains Fell Off,* New York: University Press of America, 1985, pp. 63-66.

[*In the following essay, Whelchel summarizes Brown's teachings on slavery and its effects.*]

William Wells Brown, a productive and published writer of American literature, was one of the first black American authors to support himself through writing. He first published in 1847, only thirteen years after his escape from human bondage. Over the next forty years, Brown published nine major books and at his death in 1884, his works had appeared in over thirty editions. Primarily known as a writer, he was also an effective lecturer for the abolition of slavery.

Brown's initial publication, his ***The Narrative of William Wells Brown,*** was an effective attack upon slavery. His narrative was widely read and over a two-year period, 8,000 copies (four editions) were sold. The slave narrative presented the side of slavery as seen by its victims. To make a fair-minded and objective appraisal of American slavery, it is imperative to hear the side of the slave as well as the slave master. It is as important to know what the institution meant to Brown the slave, as what it meant to Dr. Young his master.

The fugitive slave presented the institution as having a degrading and negative effect on both black and white. Brown argues that by denying education to the slaves, the slaveholders kept their own children in ignorance.

Brown countered the pro-slavery claim that Negroes are morally inferior, inherently lazy and slothful with the charge that the human bondage inevitably degraded not only slave, but slaveholders and their sympathizers as well. He describes one of his slave masters as a "horse-race, cockfighter, gambler and withal an inveterate drunkard whose fits and anger would cause him to throw chairs at his servants and put them in the smoke house."

According to Brown's testimony, he was the private property of only three slaveholders, but he worked for seven different employers during the twenty years he was in captivity. The frequent change in employers and varied positions acquainted Brown with the many facets of slavery, and prepared him to speak and write from a broad and knowledgeable background.

His knowledge and exposure were not restricted to the United States. He tells of his travels in Europe where his itinerary took him more than twenty thousand miles lecturing on American slavery and pleading the cause of abolition. While Brown was abroad, he seized every opportunity to consolidate international public opinion against the institution of slavery. Brown's treatment of slavery transcends the provincial idiom.

Brown's consuming passion for freedom grew even more intense after the enactment of the Fugitive Slave Law. The Fugitive Slave Law was enacted while he was abroad, and his abolitionist position changed from "moral persuasion" to a "new militancy." He warned his audiences that if the moral struggle for freedom failed, a physical one would be inevitable.

Brown's commitment to the struggle for freedom for the blacks was a consuming passion that found expression through the idiom of literature. His novel, ***Clotel or the President's Daughter,*** revolves around a mulatto woman and her two beautiful daughters who are sold as slaves after the mother has been deserted by her white lover. The separate careers of the three women are traced, but the main character is Clotel, the President's daughter, who finally ends her tragic life by drowning in the Potomac River as she is pursued by slave catchers, who anticipated capturing her and returning her to the deep south.

The fact that Clotel dies in sight of the White House, occupied by Thomas Jefferson, is more than a coincidence, as the title of the novel suggests. Brown said that the tragedy of Clotel "should be an evidence wherever it should be known, of the unconquerable love of liberty the heart may inherit; as well as a fresh admonition to the slave dealer, of the cruelty and enormity of his crime."[1]

Brown consistently argued that the institution of slavery was a sad commentary on American society. He uses the novel to expose the evils of slavery and to refute the claims of the plantation tradition. The plantation tradition stereotyped the Negro as inherently inferior and happy only under supervision and protection of the white master on the plantation.[2]

Seventeen years after the Civil War, Brown published ***My Southern Home, or The South and Its People.*** In this, his final book, Brown shifted from simply describing the horrors and cruelties of slavery to analyzing and examining the race problems beyond abolition.

Brown observed that some of the most vocal abolitionists were paternalistic and discriminated against the people they were fighting to emancipate. Many abolitionists were incapable of proposing a program because they saw slavery as a moral abstraction and not as a social problem. Brown's constant contention and imaginative understanding of the problem which emancipation alone did not address outran the understanding of even so ardent an abolitionist as William Lloyd Garrison.

Brown, in contrast to many other abolitionists, maintained that the struggle for equality would be long and tedious, because the anti-slavery crusade succeeded in abolishing slavery but failed to alter the image of the Negro in the eyes of White America, or measurably improve the Negro's position in society.

Possibly, the most important message Brown ever delivered to blacks is the final sentence in ***My Southern Home:*** "Black men, don't be ashamed to show your colors and to own them!" Brown was aware of the fact that the Negro, as any American, must grapple with the universal "who am I?" However, unlike other ethnic groups, who brought their cultures, languages, and traditions with them to America, the Negro was virtually stripped of his past. Nevertheless, Brown saw as did DuBois, the eminent black scholar, that "there is nothing so indigenous, so completely 'made in America' as we [blacks]."

Brown's writings argue that American slavery was developed in such a way as to convince the whites that Negroes were inherently inferior and incapable of freedom. Equally important, the system of slavery was administered in a fashion to make the Negroes behave as if they were inferior—to distort their personalities and suppress their mentalities in such a way as to make them incapable of utilizing the "freedom" that finally became theirs after two-and-a-half centuries of enslavement. He attacked prejudice, not only because it was wrong, but because if accepted, it postponed the acceptance of the Negro and his establishment in his rightful place.

Understanding the peculiarity of slavery in America is the key to understanding both the white man's and black man's Negro problem. Tocqueville pointed out nearly a hundred and twenty-eight years ago that: "In the ancient world men could move from slavery to freedom without great difficulty because former slaves could not be distinguished from those who had always been free. The Negro by contrast, transmits the eternal mark of his ignominy to all his descendants; and although the law may abolish slavery, God alone can obliterate the trace of its existence." Although Brown, understandably, argued that "No people had borne oppression like the Negro, and no race had been so much imposed upon," he looked beyond the dimensions of the now toward the prospect of ultimate equality for the blacks.

Lacking some religiously oriented Moses to lead them, blacks came to freedom via political and military developments. Following emancipation, the American freedmen were left with the aftermath of war, terrors of the ex-slaveholders, the lies of carpet-baggers, and the contradictory advice of friends and foes. Undaunted by the complexity and difficulty of post-war life, Brown continued to offer analysis and understanding of the problem and to exhort the blacks with challenge and courage.

Notes

1. William Wells Brown, *Clotel; or, The President's Daughter. A Narrative of Slave Life in the United States.* (London: Partridge and Oakey, 1853), p. 177.
2. Sterling Brown defines the plantation tradition in the following manner: "The pattern seldom varied: scenes of bliss on the plantation alternated with scenes of squalor in the free North. The contented slave, the down and the wretched freedman are the Negro stereotype. . . . A plantation with a kindly master was basis for generalizing about all plantations, of whatever type, in whatever sections. A pampered house-servant, who refuses uncertain freedom for a comparative easy place, becomes the Negro slave; a poor unemployed wretch becomes the freedman. Miscegenation is missing in spite of the proofs walking about in great houses or the fields or the slave pens. Slavery is shown as a beneficent guardianship, never as a system of cheap and abundant labor that furnished the basis of a few large fortunes (and assured an impoverished, disfranchised class of poor whites)." Sterling Brown, *The Negro in American Fiction* (New York: Atheneum, 1969), p. 28.

Paul Jefferson (essay date 1991)

SOURCE: An introduction to *The Travels of William Wells Brown,* Markus Wiener Publishing, 1991, pp. 1-20.

[*In the following essay, Jefferson contextualizes Brown's literary accomplishments by providing background information on his life.*]

I

William Wells Brown, the black nineteenth-century man of letters, is best known for the ***Narrative of William Wells Brown, A Fugitive Slave*** (Boston, 1847), a once popular and now classic autobiography;[1] ***Clotel; or, The President's Daughter*** (London, 1853), the first novel published by an African-American;[2] and several works of history, among them ***The Rising Son; or, The Antecedents and Advancement of the Colored Race*** (Boston, 1873), the most important book by a black historian until George Washington Williams' *History of the Negro Race in America, 1619-1880* (New York, 1883). Brown's other writings include a compilation of anti-slavery songs, published lectures, a five-act play, and English and American editions of the first travel sketches published by a black American.

Brown's writings exhibit the thematic richness and formal variety of nineteenth century black literature at its best. As a pioneering architect of a black counter-discourse, an ambiguously subversive literary tradition whose complexity is now appreciated, his work warrants the closer reading it is beginning at last to receive.

II

The future William Wells Brown was born a slave in Lexington, Kentucky in 1814. His mother, Elizabeth, was one of forty slaves owned by Dr. John Young, a gentleman farmer and practising physician who had migrated from Virginia. Brown's father, George Higgins, was his master's cousin. In 1816, when William was two years old, Young moved his goods and chattels to Saint Charles County in the Missouri Territory. Eleven years later, Young relocated his household to St. Louis, after buying a farm near the city. Here William was hired out successively as a tavern-keeper's helper, a steward on a Mississippi River steamboat, a servant to a hotel-keeper, and a boy Friday in the printing office of Elijah P. Lovejoy, then part-owner and editor of the *St. Louis Times*.[3] Before he escaped from slavery, three years and two owners later, William would work once more as a steamboat steward, a fieldhand, a house-servant and general factotum, a part-time physician's assistant, a carriage-driver, and a gang-boss for his nemesis, the slave-trader James Walker.

On January 1, 1834 the young Missouri bondsman slipped off a steamboat at Cincinnati, Ohio, and set out toward Canada and freedom. Taking the name of Wells Brown, a Quaker benefactor who assisted him on his way, he entered history as William Wells Brown, Fugitive Slave, a *persona* he exploited professionally until his freedom was certified in 1854.[4]

Brown reached Cleveland by the end of January 1834 and made it through the winter doing odd jobs. He had exhausted his scanty funds, and felt secure enough to bide his time. By spring he had obtained work on a Lake Erie steamboat, a position he exploited to help other fugitive slaves reach Canada by way of Buffalo, New York and Detroit, Michigan. In the summer of 1836 Brown himself moved to Buffalo, which had a larger black population, was closer to Canada, and was the terminus of the Lake Erie steamboat lines on which he worked each year from thaw to freeze. In Buffalo he made his home an important station on the Underground Railroad, and he got more deeply involved in the welfare of the free black community. He organized a black temperance society—one of the first in western New York—which became, in effect, an omnibus local reform association.

Brown met Frederick Douglass for the first time in August 1843 when the latter came to Buffalo to hold a series of anti-slavery meetings. He encountered Douglass again at a national convention of free Negroes which met in Buffalo later that month. At this tumultuous five-day gathering Brown was introduced to a wider network of black leaders and anti-slavery workers. That fall Brown became a traveling lecturer for the Western New York Anti-Slavery Society. He was soon one of its most successful agents.

In May 1844 he attended an interstate convention of abolitionists in New York City. At this meeting the American Anti-Slavery Society officially took the position that the Constitution was a pro-slavery document, and reaffirmed its opposition to attacking slavery through political action. Brown extended his widening contacts with white abolitionists, meeting William Lloyd Garrison and Wendell Phillips for the first time, and coming away committed more strongly than ever to the Garrisonian strategy of "moral suasion."[5] He continued his work for the Western New York Anti-Slavery Society over the next three years, recounting his experiences as a slave to audiences throughout New York State.

In May 1847, at the annual meeting of the American Anti-Slavery Society in New York City, arrangements were made for Brown to lecture in New England under the auspices of the Massachusetts Anti-Slavery Society. That summer he moved to Boston, which he made his permanent home.

In turning his precarious legal status as fugitive to personal profit, first on the lecture circuit and then in print, Brown followed the example of Frederick Douglass, with whom he was inevitably compared. His autobiography, the ***Narrative of William Wells Brown, A Fugitive Slave*** (Boston, 1847), was published two years after the success of Douglass' *Narrative of the Life of Frederick Douglass, An American Slave* (Boston, 1845) demonstrated the utility of such a venture. Boston abolitionist Edmund Quincy asserted, following its appearance, that Brown was the most valuable recruit to the cause since Douglass. "I do not know," he wrote, "that his intellectual power is equal to that of Douglass, but he is of a much higher character."[6]

In June 1849 Brown was selected by the American Peace Society as a delegate to an International Peace Congress to be held in August in Paris. He was so honored because one of the leaders of the American Peace Society had established in 1846 a sibling organization, the League of Universal Brotherhood, thus linking the peace and anti-slavery movements.[7]

At this time the American anti-slavery fraternity learned that an agent of the American Colonization Society was in England winning support for its cause—the mass emigration of free American Negroes to Africa. This utopian program—subsidized privately by national benevolent associations and church groups, and publicly by grants from state legislatures—was being marketed to different constituencies, white and black, northern and southern, as a solution to the "Negro problem" of the day. The

American Colonization Society insisted that the United States was a white man's country, that free blacks would fare better elsewhere, and that, were owners financially compensated and the nation assured that mass emigration would follow emancipation, slavery itself could be gradually abolished and the national honor restored. The program was a dangerously seductive one which had won wide support.[8]

In July 1849, a meeting of black and white abolitionists in Boston voted to have Brown counter the propaganda of the American Colonization Society's overseas agent when Brown went abroad in his official capacity as American Peace Society delegate.[9]

In a note to the fourth edition of the ***Narrative*** (Boston, 1849), Brown recalls that in visiting Great Britain he had two related objects in view—to parade his person widely, and to explain his point of view. In demonstrating by his presence as Peace Society delegate that a black person and fugitive slave could be elected to so honorable a position, he could dramatize the progress of abolitionist principles. At the same time, Brown indicates, "I wished to follow up the work of my friends and fellow-labourers, Charles Lenox Remond[10] and Frederick Douglass, and to lay before the people of Great Britain and Ireland the wrongs that are still committed upon the slaves and the free colored people of America."

The importance of Brown's dual function was emphasized by British journalist William Farmer in introducing ***Three Years in Europe: or Places I Have Seen and People I Have Met*** (London, 1852), the original English edition of Brown's travel sketches. Speaking on behalf of the trans-Atlantic abolitionist community, Farmer wrote that "[i]t was thought desirable always to have in England some talented man of colour who should be a living lie to the doctrine of the inferiority of the African race; and it was moreover felt that none could so powerfully advocate the cause of 'those in bonds' as one who had actually been 'bound with them.'"[11]

The utility of such living witness had been originally demonstrated by Frederick Douglass in his own visit to England four years before. As the second fugitive slave to function professionally as an anti-slavery publicist at home and abroad, William Wells Brown was as instrumental as his more famous contemporary in establishing the multiple parameters of the role.

The passage of the 1850 Fugitive Slave Law prolonged Brown's stay abroad by making it too dangerous for him to return to the United States.[12] Ironically, the threat the law posed caused him to recant a principle he had once invoked to distinguish himself from Douglass. In 1847 Brown had sent a copy of the ***Narrative*** to Enoch Price, the owner from whom he had escaped. Price wrote Edmund Quincy in reply, acknowledging that Brown was in fact who he claimed to be, and offering to provide Brown with free papers were Price's Boston agent remitted half of Brown's original purchase price. This letter—which worked to confirm Brown's identity and establish his veracity as author—was included in the third edition of the ***Narrative*** (Boston, 1848), along with Brown's response.

Unlike Douglass who had been prevailed upon to allow well-wishers to buy his freedom, Brown would not, he said, "accept Mr. Price's offer to become a purchaser of my body and soul. God made me as free as he did Enoch Price, and Mr. Price shall never receive a dollar from me or my friends with my consent." However, the Fugitive Slave Law caused Brown to rethink this admirable position. In 1854, like Douglass, he allowed his freedom to be purchased by friends abroad, so that he could return to the United States.[13] Though he might have remained in England, Brown felt that he could not in conscience do so while his countrymen languished in bondage. He returned as a moral soldier, he later explained, "for the express purpose of joining in the glorious battle against slavery, of which . . . Negrophobia is a legitimate off-spring."[14]

For the next two years Brown traveled and lectured as an agent for the Massachusetts and the American Anti-Slavery Societies. He began to try his hand at other forms of anti-slavery argument. After presenting an earlier version on the lecture circuit, he wrote ***The Escape; or, A Leap for Freedom: A Drama in Five Acts*** (Boston, 1858), the first play to be published by an African-American. Four years later the first of four editions of an historical work, ***The Black Man, His Antecedents, His Genius, and His Achievements*** (Boston/New York, 1863), appeared.[15] In his preface, Brown made the rhetorical purpose of the book explicit. Targeting the "calumniators and traducers" of black Americans, the book was meant to counter assertions of the natural inferiority of the Negro by providing sketches of "individuals who, by their own genius, capacity, and intellectual development," Brown explained, "have surmounted the many obstacles which slavery and prejudice have thrown in their way, and [have] raised themselves to positions of honor and influence."[16]

During the Civil War—following the Emancipation Proclamation and Lincoln's decision to enlist black troops in the Union army—Brown helped recruit enlistees for the famous Massachusetts 54th and 55th Regiments, which were led by white officers.[17] At the same time, he lobbied energetically but unsuccessfully for the right of black soldiers to be led by officers of their own race. During the war, he worked to secure equal pay for black and white troops alike, and he called attention to the need for improved medical services for black units too often used as shock troops.

Following the Civil War—from a black point of view, the conflict was brought to a conclusion only upon the ratification of the 15th Amendment in 1870—Brown again took up the temperance cause. He continued to lecture and write, publishing his most ambitious work of history, ***The Rising Son; or, The Antecedents and Advancement of the***

Colored Race (Boston, 1873), three years later. After a unique variety of experiences as a fugitive and a free man, Brown's later years were less eventful. He died quietly in Boston, Massachusetts on November 6, 1884, a respected elder statesman for his race. Having been successively a temperance reformer, an anti-slavery lecturer, a versatile man of letters, and ultimately also a practising physician,[18] Brown lived—against all odds—a rich and instructive life.[19]

III

The texts reprinted here—the ***Narrative of William Wells Brown, A Fugitive Slave*** (Boston, Second Enlarged Edition, 1848) and ***The American Fugitive in Europe: Sketches of Places and People Abroad*** (Boston, 1855), the American edition of his account of his travels—are good examples of first-person retrospective prose narratives,[20] the most eloquent of forms in nineteenth century black literature. They reveal the development of the author's distinctive voice and point of view as he fashions differently managed accounts of successive stages in his life. Reprinting them side by side enables the reader to follow the development of William Wells Brown from a humiliated slave to a racial ambassador and an eloquent man of letters.[21]

From one point of view, the first text—Brown's ***Narrative***—may be read as travel literature, as well as autobiography. Mapping changing spiritual and physical geographies, the ***Narrative*** first chronicles Brown's life in bondage—disclosing aspects of slavery more various and disturbing than those registered in the *Narrative of the Life of Frederick Douglass*—and then follows Brown's pilgrim's progress north to freedom.

Read as autobiography, the ***Narrative*** witnesses a double act of self-creation. Brown invents himself both in making the escape the narrative recounts, and in recounting the escape he makes. In the first instance, he makes good his resolve to change his fate by becoming a fugitive slave. The act of fleeing is an existential act of self-creation. In the second instance, he recreates himself as author and as free man in the very act of constructing the ***Narrative.***

For the reader, the larger story Brown tells includes as well the wonder of his hard-won capacity to tell it—like Frederick Douglass, he had no formal schooling.[22] In blurring the distinction between Brown as subject, the teller of a generic "free story,"[23] and Brown as fugitive slave, the object of the story he tells, the first-person ***Narrative*** increases our appreciation of the double achievement.

Just as the ***Narrative*** may be read as travel literature. ***The American Fugitive*** may also be read as autobiography. But in contrast to the ***Narrative,*** in the latter work Brown plays his *persona* as fugitive slave off against his achieved self, especially in his encounters with European philanthropists and *literati.* As simultaneously author and object of a brief for emancipation, Brown functioned abroad as the professional man of letters and anti-slavery lecturer, on the one hand, and as the fugitive slave as case in point, on the other. Strategically exploiting his anomalous identity, as an acknowledged fugitive Brown was a living refutation of the very assumptions of black incapacity and the justice of slavery that he challenged discursively as publicist.

IV

The ***Narrative*** is constructed in a distinctive way, and its framing is an integral aspect of its desired effect. Structurally, Brown's autobiography proper is only one of the constituents of the *Narrative* as an affective and cognitive whole. The reader encounters first an open letter to the Quaker, Wells Brown, in which the author demonstrates a becoming gratitude to his "earliest benefactor" and "first white friend." This letter is followed by another from Edmund Quincy to the author Brown himself. Quincy, a Boston abolitionist, has been asked by Brown to serve as his editor and intermediary, and has been given permission by Brown to blue pencil the narrative. However, he would "be a bold man, as well as a vain one," Quincy tells the author, who would presume to improve upon the other's first-person testimony. Finally, there is a conventional preface by J. C. Hathaway, president of the Western New York Anti-Slavery Society, Brown's first employer in his capacity as anti-slavery lecturer.

This mode of external framing does double duty. It is meant to confirm the truthfulness of the account and to suggest in advance how to read it. The issues the ***Narrative*** is presumed to raise are clearly spelled out, and the reader's feelings are manipulated without apology. Edmund Quincy functions implicitly as Everyman, suggesting that only one response is possible to the facts Brown recounts. "[A] man must be differently constituted from me," Quincy asserts, "who can rise from the perusal of your Narrative without feeling that he understands slavery better, and hates it worse, than he ever did before." The reader is moved to sympathize with Brown the slave, Brown the fugitive, and Brown the man, whose authority as witness must be vindicated. To this end, J. C. Hathaway comments on the author's "simplicity and ingenuousness which carries with it," he says, "a conviction of the truthfulness of the picture [the author paints]." Hathaway then addresses the reader directly—Reader, are you an Abolitionist? are you a Christian? are you a friend of the Bible?—and stipulates unequivocally how Brown's text is to be read. To understand slavery better is to understand it as theft and as sin, he insists; and to hate it worse than before is to join the crusade to eliminate it.

The distinction between the textual substance of the ***Narrative*** and its external packaging—even if editorially imposed—is not always a clear one. This is truer still of the internal framing of the ***Narrative,*** which—being Brown's own architecture—is more obviously a vehicle for his argument. Such structural elements include the generic themes, memorable human types, and significant incidents or rites of passage which would soon become conventions of the form. Brown, following Douglass, is working to invent an insider perspective on the "peculiar institution" by establishing the parameters of the literary genre, the slave narrative, which is its privileged vehicle.

Typically, slave narratives dramatize a juxtaposition of the facts surrounding the cultural status of slaves as objects, and the fictions by which masters monopolize the status of human subjects. The meta-themes of the genre involve, on the one hand, the fundamental contrast between slavery and freedom—a contrast so stark as to achieve metaphysical resonance—and, on the other hand, the contradictions of principle and practice in a society determined to expropriate the humanity of others and to spare its own feelings while doing so.

The contrast between slavery and freedom is often represented, implicitly or explicitly, as that between life and death. This occasionally has the textual consequence of yielding a pivotal narrative episode, a probative "dark night of the soul,"[24] through which the author must pass. Brown refers obliquely to such an episode in the first paragraph of chapter 11 of the ***Narrative***: "The love of liberty that had been burning in my bosom, had well nigh gone out. I felt as though I was ready to die . . . my thoughts were so absorbed in what I had witnessed [here alluding to the last time he would see his mother], that I knew not what I was about half of the time. Night came, but it brought no sleep to my eyes." The final paragraphs of chapter 13 link the notions of physical and spiritual death in another fashion: "I have ever looked upon that night as the most eventful part of my escape from slavery. Nothing but the providence of God, and that old barn, saved me from freezing to death. . . . The thought of death was nothing frightful to me, compared with that of being caught, and again carried back into slavery."[25]

The theme of the contradiction of principle and practice is typically exploited by turning the languages nineteenth century America used to explain itself—the languages of natural law, moral philosophy, and republicanism, on some occasions; and the languages of religion, liberal or evangelical, on others—against the idealized norms, sacred and secular, those cultural languages presumed. Brown's references in the ***Narrative*** to "slavery with its Democratic whips—its Republican chains—its evangelical bloodhounds, and its religious slave-holders" and his ironic invocations of the "paraphernalia of American Democracy and Religion" are unique only in their energy and pointedness.

There are particular human types whose strutting and fretting on stage also helps to structure the ***Narrative.*** The obscenity of slavery is dramatized, for example, in the persons of the Yankee overseer, the Christian slave-holder, and the predatory slave-driver—figures whose contradictory spiritual and cultural identities point up the unnaturalness of a social institution that reproduces human mutants. For example, Brown mentions the overseer, Friend Haskell, "a regular Yankee from New England," early in chapter 3, and suggests without comment that Yankees in that role were noted for their cruelty. He concludes chapter 4 with an eloquently spare account of the on-the-ground meaning of religion as but an alternative language of power. In this connection, he dryly notes that during the visit of Mr. Sloan, a young Presbyterian minister from the North, "[i]nstead of his teaching my master theology, my master taught theology to him." Having earlier "got religion," Brown observes, identifying the practical consequences of slave-holder Christianity, his master proceeded to regiment his slaves more strictly in the name of the Lord.

Finally, Brown's distaste for the "soul-driver" James Walker is so profound as to evoke a tortured lyricism. Walker represents the acme of villainy in the ***Narrative.*** He forces the chaste quadroon, Cynthia, into his bed; fathers four children on her; then sells both children and mother down the river. While driving a coffle of slaves to St Louis, Walker tears a crying child from a mother who is unable to sooth her. To spare himself annoyance, he leaves the child behind. In reporting this scene, Brown can capture the horror it inspires only by resorting to poetry. His time in Walker's service, he later reports, "was the longest year I ever lived." Introduced first by Douglass and Brown in their master narratives, figures of this sort stalk the pages of the genre.

The physical violence inherent in the relation of master-as-subject and slave-as-object is evident throughout the ***Narrative.*** Of the ten incidents witnessed in the brief text, the most unsettling involve deliberate attempts to bring male slaves to heel, that is, in the revealing words of an irate owner. "to tame the d---d nigger." The first such incident involves breaking the spirit of the slave Randall, a man of great strength who has not before been flogged. It takes the combined efforts of three white men and a pistol shot to overpower him. Just as the beating then administered by the overseer, Mr. Cook, puts Randall himself in his place, witnessing the incident through young William's eyes fixes an indelible impression of slavery in the reader's mind.

A second incident, described more briefly, is equally telling. The slave John, purchased by one Robert More for the express purpose of repaying an earlier slight, is thrown into irons and whipped three times a week for two months. There was no "more noble looking man" than John before he fell into More's hands, Brown reports; but after undergoing this taming process, there was no "more degraded and spirit-crushed" being on a southern plantation. In the zero-sum game logic of the master-slave relation—a logic at once political and psychological—the need to break the spirit of the slave was a systemic one. Making discussions of "slave-breaking" a convention of the genre becomes a useful means of deciphering the obscene logic of the "peculiar institution."

Finally, two incidents function in concert as devices of internal framing in the ***Narrative,*** to mark a rite of passage. Together suggesting what's in a name, they signal Brown's coming of age. In the first incident, young William is deprived of his given name as a child, when his master's nephew moves into their household. Because the white William preempts their common name, the black William is henceforth known as Sandford. Though Brown enjoys no property in himself in more basic ways, his resentment at being so brusquely expropriated remains alive throughout his years as a slave.

Brown's perspective on his double predicament as a slave appears later in the ***Narrative*** in a wry allusion to the distinction between appearance and reality, name and fact. I was "not only hunting for my liberty," he says, "but also hunting for a name; though I regarded the latter as of little consequence, if I could but gain the former." Depending on how it is taken, as the reader comes to see, this statement is both true and not true.

Following his escape, Brown represents himself in the ***Narrative*** as free in fact, when he is legally still a fugitive. In his characteristic few words, he suggests that this new state took some getting used to. At first "[t]he fact that I was a freeman—could walk, talk, eat and sleep as a man, and no one to stand over me with the blood-clotted cowhide—all this," he says, "made me feel that I was not myself." But his physical liberty is consolidated and confirmed by an assertion of spiritual autonomy.

In the second incident, William becomes his own man in the encounter with the Quaker, Wells Brown, when he chooses a name for himself. He repossesses his given name and takes on the name of this early benefactor. Staking his claim to the past and the future, Sandford becomes William Wells Brown. That acquiring the name of a free man was in fact a matter of some consequence is confirmed by the author's grateful dedication of the ***Narrative*** to Wells Brown, his "first white friend."

V

The external framing of the second text, ***The American Fugitive in Europe*** (Boston, 1855), serves in similar ways to reinforce and focus its argument. The book opens with the preface to the original English edition in which Brown makes ritual apology for the shortcomings of the text, reminding the reader that he had been twenty years a slave and was without formal schooling. Thus, the *persona* he assumes is thrown into high relief.

A note to the American edition follows. Here Brown confesses that he had published an earlier book of travels while abroad because it was "advantageous to my purse." However, this curious announcement is less off-putting than it appears. It anticipates mention of a circumstance in the "Memoir of the Author"—which introduces the text proper of ***The American Fugitive***—that Brown thought was entirely to his credit.

Written by the British journalist, William Farmer—here unnamed—the "Memoir" was based closely on Brown's ***Narrative.*** It told readers who the fugitive slave was whose adventures they would share, and it brought the story of Brown's life as anti-slavery worker fully up to date. Farmer recounts that Brown had been careful to stress that unlike those who had preceded him to England—he meant unlike Frederick Douglass and Charles Lenox Remond, with whom he was associated in the minds of the trans-Atlantic anti-slavery fraternity and from whom he hoped to distinguish himself—he went as a professional man of letters, who as a matter of principle would be self-supporting. Brown thus implied that he disdained charity and would take his chances. By mentioning this fact Brown insinuated that it was an exercise of will—the mental faculty most highly esteemed by the moral philosophy of the day—which enabled him to fashion from unpromising materials a self that could move in European society without apology. His achieved self and his assumed *persona* would be simultaneously on display—the one played off the other—throughout his sojourn abroad.

The external framing of the text is completed by four pages of "Opinions of the British Press," which follow Brown's account of his travels and close the book. Here the rhetorical point of the volume is made clear past all mistaking. The very fact of its publication, says *The Literary Gazette,* constitutes "another proof of the capability of the negro intellect." William Wells Brown in person, the *Glasgow Citizen* agrees, is "a full refutation of the doctrine of the inferiority of the negro." Elsewhere there are references to the excitement created by the recent appearance of Harriet Beecher Stowe's *Uncle Tom's Cabin* (1852). The comments of a "real fugitive slave" deserve equal billing, *The Critic* suggests. Finally, the point is made that Brown's is a radical counter-discourse. His "doings and sayings," the *Morning Advertiser* confidently predicts, will be "among the means of destruction of the hideous abomination" of slavery.

As in Brown's ***Narrative,*** certain aspects of the internal structuring of ***The American Fugitive*** also warrant notice. For example, Brown takes particular care to highlight the occasions he encounters other black persons in Europe. He mentions a visit paid to Alexander Crummell, later a famous educator and missionary, then studying at Cambridge University. He indicates that in an hour's walk through London "one may meet half a dozen colored men, who are inmates of the various colleges of the metropolis." Elsewhere, Brown notes with pleasure the three black students he sees "seated upon the same benches with those of a fairer complexion" at the University of Edinburgh.

These encounters do significant rhetorical work in several respects. First, Brown represents the presence of black students at institutions of higher learning as a sign of progress in "the cause of the sons of Africa." Then he draws the appropriate moral lesson, demonstrating the justice—at once interpersonal and cultural—of a state of affairs so foreign to American readers. There "appeared no feeling on the part of the whites toward their colored associates," he said, "except of companionship and respect." Taking the high ground, Brown presses the point home, then twists the knife. "In the sight of God and all just institutions, the whites can claim no precedence or privilege on account of their being white; and if colored men are not treated as they should be in educational institutions in America, it is a pleasure to know that all distinction ceases by crossing the broad Atlantic." The lesson is an emphatic one.

Another encounter with a black person abroad, the most memorable and amusing of all, works rhetorically in an entirely different way. Departing from his normal procedure, Brown devotes an entire chapter to one Joseph Jenkins. Jenkins is "a good-looking man, [who is] neither black nor white." As a semi-comic figure of uncertain antecedents, he is a nineteenth-century *picaro,* a man on the move who has learned to make do. Brown encounters Jenkins in London in the successive guises of Cheapside bill distributor; Chelsea street sweeper; street musician and vendor of religious tracts; Shakespearean actor; spellbinding store-front preacher, who inveighs against "the sale and use of intoxicating drinks and the bad habits of the working classes;" kidnapped putative African prince; and sometime professional band-leader. Jenkins is a protean figure, a benign early incarnation of the urban hustler, and, withal, "the greatest genius," Brown wryly observed, "that I had met in Europe." Brown has just spent the greater part of ***The American Fugitive*** dropping famous names; the point is well taken and seriously intended.

This chapter works rhetorically by counterpoint. In light of the myriad tasks Brown had performed as a slave, and the promiscuous talent he had displayed; in light of the revealing description of Jenkins as "a good-looking man, neither black nor white," a description which could fit Brown himself; and in light of his current obligation to be a model "race man," and its possible spiritual costs, it is as if Brown recognizes in Jenkins a repressed *alter ego.* Whether this is so or not, his whole-hearted response to Jenkins complicates the reader's sense of the author more than he might have wished. Appreciation of the picaresque Jenkins appears to compromise Brown's commitment to the middle-class values he elsewhere consistently espouses.

On the other hand, recall that Jenkins inveighs against "the sale and use of intoxicating drinks and the bad habits of the working classes." What Brown celebrates in Jenkins is not the negative "fact" that a black man will do everything he might want to do, but the positive "fact" that—if permitted—a black man is able to do anything he may have to do. Joseph Jenkins, like Benjamin Franklin, is a very well-educated man. Read in this way, this chapter points up Brown's conventionality on social issues apart from that of race. Education and character—their sociological vacuity notwithstanding—are, for Brown, terms to conjure with. Like most of his nineteenth-century counterparts, he looks to individual transformations rather than institutional ones when he seeks for social remedies.

Alain Locke's penetrating twentieth-century observation that "the Negro is radical on race matters, conservative on others, . . . a 'forced radical,' a social protestant rather than a genuine radical" quickly comes to mind.[26] Though the African-American counter-discourse Brown has a hand in creating is culturally subversive from the point of view of race, from other points of view it is ambiguously so.

We may wonder, for example, whether Brown's acceptance of a "divide and rule" model of social injustice is the price of lack of class-consciousness. He alludes repeatedly in ***The American Fugitive*** to differences in the material conditions of life of American slaves and European workers. On three occasions he explicitly challenges the proto-Marxist argument that the poverty and insecurity of the white working class in Europe—and, by implication, that of the factory worker in the northern United States—make wage slavery harsher than the plantation slavery of the American South.

Brown's need to challenge a staple pro-slavery argument of the day is understandable. But by addressing the question in the terms in which it is framed, he mistakes what is really at issue. Because the languages at his disposal—the languages of natural law, moral philosophy, and republicanism, on the one hand; and of religion, on the other—yield no structural insights, Brown does not understand that the question of relative victimization is beside the point. The implications of the fact that hierarchies of race and class alike are institutionally reproduced, and might at times be usefully analyzed together, are lost on him.

Elsewhere, the device of contrast serves Brown as well in ***The American Fugitive*** as it did in the ***Narrative.*** He again plays England off against the United States, ironically juxtaposing Enlightenment ideals and reactionary racial attitudes. He marvels at one point that "no sooner was I on British soil, than I was recognized as a man, and an equal." On another occasion, he wryly suggests how curious it is that monarchical England rather than Christian republican America should be the home of freedom. The liberating difference distance makes is dramatized in a more human idiom as well. Snubbed at home and on the trip over by a fellow American, Brown has the pleasure of snubbing him in turn when he seeks an introduction to *literati,* like Victor Hugo, with whom Brown himself freely mingles.

Finally, Brown opens and closes ***The American Fugitive*** with an eloquent ambivalence, the grounds for which have been established throughout the account. The book opens with his anxiety at leaving his native land—whose evils at least are familiar—for the hazards of foreign travel. It closes with his uncertainty about returning to the land of his birth five years later—where now he feels a stranger—from an England which has made him feel at home. Going and coming, Brown strikes the perfect note.

VI

The ***Narrative*** and ***The American Fugitive*** are extended cultural arguments. Printing them side by side invites the reader to consider more closely the ways they affect their audiences. On the page, the texts work rhetorically in a double or hybrid manner. They function at once epistemically—by mirroring the world of slavery and picturing the impact of racism; and politically or ideologically—by undermining their rationales.

One effective example of this occurs in the ***Narrative*** when William dupes a free black man into receiving a beating meant for himself, a slave. Brown recounts what happened, as an unimpeachable first-person witness. Then he interprets what happened. By commenting astutely on his own unseemly behavior, he indicts the "peculiar institution" itself for producing slaves to pattern. "This incident shows," he suggests—at once conceptualizing and subverting a "blame the victim" point of view—"how it is that slavery makes its victims lying and mean, for which vices it afterwards reproaches them, and uses them as arguments to prove that they deserve no better fate."

As arguments deriving from a single parent form—that of the first-person retrospective prose narrative—the ***Narrative*** and ***The American Fugitive*** exhibit a certain kinship. But as distinct species of a common genus—as an autobiography and a travel account—they work on the reader in ways peculiar to themselves. Brown's ***Narrative,*** for example, is simpler on the surface, but more sharply focused, and more deftly subversive of reader expectations.[27] ***The American Fugitive,*** in contrast, works rhetorically by attrition, painting a broader canvas, and multiplying opportunities to show Brown at his best in good company.

Were one to exaggerate the differences between the two books, one might read them as examples of alternative modes of representation, that of metaphoric realism and that of mimetic realism, respectively. So phrased, however, the distinction is ultimately misleading. What is more to the point is their common rhetorical function. The ***Narrative*** and ***The American Fugitive*** are extended cultural arguments. As fully accessible first-person narratives—however they achieve their effects—they are best appreciated on their own terms, without further preliminaries.

Notes

1. Following its publication in July 1847, the *Narrative* went through three editions and eight thousand copies in less than eighteen months. A fourth American edition of two thousand copies was printed in August 1849. Between 1849 and 1853, while abroad, Brown arranged the publication of four English editions—one an illustrated version—and one Irish edition of the *Narrative,* bringing the total number of copies in print to more than fifteen thousand. See William Edward Farrison, *William Wells Brown: Author and Reformer* (Chicago: University of Chicago Press, 1969), pp. 114, 155-157.
2. Harriet Wilson's *Our Nig; or Sketches of the Life of a Free Black* (Boston, 1859) was the first novel published in the United States by an African-American. Brown's *Clotel* was published six years earlier, but published abroad.
3. Seven years later the Reverend Elijah P. Lovejoy became the first white abolitionist martyr. He was killed in Alton, Illinois in 1837 when a pro-slavery mob destroyed the printing presses of his paper, the *Alton Observer.*
4. See Farrison, *William Wells Brown* (1969), p. 8.
5. William Lloyd Garrison inaugurated the radical phase of the anti-slavery movement in the United States. The first issue of his Boston-based anti-slavery paper, the *Liberator,* appeared on January 1, 1831 and the New England Anti-Slavery Society was organized later that year. In 1833 the American Anti-Slavery Society—its Declaration of Sentiments written by Garrison—was founded in Philadelphia. In 1835 the patrician Wendell Phillips joined the movement. The Garrisonian position was that slave-holding was a sin, and that abolition should be immediate and unconditional. Because the Constitution was seen as a pro-slavery document, radical abolitionists were not to compromise their principles by working politically to end slavery. Garrison's unbending posture and his commitment to public agitation and "moral suasion" as a tactic are reflected in the famous words with which he closed the opening number of the *Liberator:* "I will not equivocate—I will not excuse—I will not retreat a single inch—and I WILL BE HEARD."
6. See Edmund Quincy to Caroline Weston, July 2, 1847, Anti-Slavery-Weston Papers, Boston Public Library; cited in Farrison, *William Wells Brown* (1969), pp. 113.
7. The American Peace Society, founded in 1828, brought together within a national organization most of the existing state and local peace societies of the day. Its membership was made up largely of Congregational, Baptist, and Methodist ministers. Strangely, the Society of Friends as a body did not associate itself with the peace movement, perhaps because the American Peace Society equivocated on the admissibility of "defensive war." Elihu Burritt, a leader of the American Peace Society and prime mover behind the International Peace Congresses of 1848 and 1849, organized the League of Universal Brotherhood in 1846. See Merle Eugene Curti, *The American Peace Crusade, 1815-1860* (Durham: Duke University Press, 1929), *passim.*
8. The American Colonization Society was established in 1817. By 1830 its goals had been endorsed by national conventions of the Presbyterian, Methodist, Baptist, and Dutch Reformed Churches, as well as by regional conferences of Episcopalians, Congregationalists, and Quakers. Its wide support was reflected in the approval voted its program by the state legislatures of Connecticut, Delaware, Indiana, Kentucky, Maryland, Massachusetts, New

Jersey, New York, Ohio, Pennsylvania, Rhode Island, Tennessee, Vermont, and Virginia. The best single expression of the Society's program and rationale is the letter written by Robert Goodloe Harper to Elias B. Caldwell, August 20, 1817. Caldwell was the first secretary of the American Colonization Society. See William H. Pease and Jane H. Pease, eds., *The Antislavery Argument,* (Indianapolis: Bobbs-Merrill Company, 1965); pp. 18-32.

9. In his official capacity as American Peace Society delegate, Brown gave a speech at the Paris Congress the following month protesting the war spirit by which slavery was maintained in the United States. Interestingly, his lecture was favorably noticed in the Paris newspapers, but sarcastically reviewed in the *London Times.* Brown would keep good company abroad. At the Paris Peace Congress, for example, he was introduced to the celebrated novelist and playwright, Victor Hugo, and to the wife of Alexis de Tocqueville, French Minister for Foreign Affairs.

10. Charles Lenox Remond was a free black anti-slavery lecturer renowned for his eloquence. He was the most widely heralded black spokesman of the early-mid nineteenth century, until Frederick Douglass upstaged him.

11. William Wells Brown, *Three Years in Europe; or, Places I Have Seen and People I Have Met* (London, 1852), p. xxi.

12. By multiplying the mechanisms for recapturing fugitives available under the original Fugitive Slave Law of 1793, the Fugitive Slave Law of 1850 endangered the security of free blacks as well. Under the later act putative slaves could be seized either with a federal warrant, as under the act of 1793, or without legal process, by oral affidavit. The certificates of rendition thus secured could be issued not only by federal judges, but also by a new class of "commissioners" appointed for the purpose, who earned a larger fee if they ruled that the fugitive was a slave than if they decided he was free. Alleged fugitives were prohibited from testifying in their own behalf and were denied *habeas corpus.* Those obstructing slave-catchers were liable to heavy fine and imprisonment. Federal marshalls were authorized to form posses of bystanders to help recapture fugitives, for whose safe return once apprehended said marshalls were personally liable.

13. It was to a Miss Ellen Richardson of Newcastle—ironically, a member of the family which had earlier purchased Douglass' freedom—that Brown was "mainly indebted for the redemption of my body from slavery." See William Wells Brown, *The American Fugitive in Europe: Sketches of Places and People Abroad* (Boston, 1855), p. 304; Farrison, *William Wells Brown* (1969), pp. 238-241.

14. Brown, *The American Fugitive in Europe* (1855), p. 314.

15. The book appeared in December 1862, the printed date of publication notwithstanding.

16. William Wells Brown, *The Black Man, His Antecedents, His Genius, and His Achievements* (Boston/New York, 1863), pp. 5-6.

17. Brown was joined in this task by Martin R. Delany, Frederick Douglass, Henry Highland Garnet, John Mercer Langston, and Charles Lenox Remond, arguably the six most celebrated and influential black leaders of the day. However, it is significant that only Douglass' role as recruiter is dramatized in the recent movie *Glory.* (1989).

18. Having spent much of his spare time since 1860 reading medicine and attending lectures, Brown set up shop as a physician in Boston in 1865. No state agencies then existed to set conditions for admission to the profession. Though the Harvard Medical School offered lectures and some clinical instruction, aspiring physicians were not obliged to attend a medical college. The usual route into the profession was through apprenticeship with an established practitioner. Brown's interest in medicine probably grew out of his experience while still a slave as a part-time physician's assistant to his master, Dr. Young. See Farrison, *William Wells Brown* (1969), pp. 24, 399-401.

19. Brown's life is historically instructive precisely because, from today's point of view, he was a rather conventional person—notwithstanding the myriad things to which he turned his hand. Temperamentally and ideologically—apart from the issue of race—he was emphatically not a revolutionary. His attitudes and opinions were solidly middle-class. He believed in education, character, and hard work. The only fault he found with the structure and functioning of American society was the fact that black Americans were not allowed to participate freely in it. But in the nineteenth-century context, to be black, on the one hand, and to be sufficiently successful and to command enough cultural literacy to mouth plausibly the platitudes of the day, on the other hand, was so thoroughly to confound expectations as to be in its way revolutionary. In this respect, Brown's life was instructive for his white contemporaries as well.

20. William L. Andrews has recently distinguished seven forms of antebellum first person retrospective prose narratives—forms, we suggest, which are not entirely and invariably distinct. These include slave narratives, spiritual autobiographies, criminal confessions, captivity narratives, travel accounts, interviews and memoirs. See his *To Tell a Free Story: The First Century of Afro-American Autobiography, 1760-1865* (Urbana and Chicago: University of Illinois Press, 1988), p. 19.

21. Brown's later confidence and assertiveness are memorably captured in an incident he recounts in *The American Fugitive.* He spent one winter's night in an English hotel which supplied him with damp bedding. The next morning he threw his sheets out the window. When the landlady threatened to charge him for the ruined bedding, Brown threatened to send the bill to the *London Times,* so its readers would learn how poorly-run the establishment was. The landlady backed down, and apologized.
22. Like Douglass, Brown was largely self-taught. He reports in the *Narrative* that he acquired what little learning he obtained while in slavery working in the St. Louis printing office of Elijah P. Lovejoy. This was in 1830. However, two years later Brown is obliged to have a literate free black man read a note for him. Clearly, whatever "learning" he had acquired earlier as a slave was ephemeral. After escaping to Cleveland, Brown reports that in the spring of 1834 he purchased several books and subscribed to an anti-slavery newspaper. His biographer suggests that Brown taught himself to read at this time by working his way doggedly through such material. However, no fully trustworthy information is available. For Brown's implausible later accounts of how he first learned to read and write, see Farrison, *William Wells Brown* (1969), pp. 61-62. However, we can assume that having somehow acquired a basic literacy by 1843, Brown's finishing school was the organized anti-slavery movement. The comments of a fellow matriculant, Frederick Douglass, at the National Negro Convention in Cleveland, Ohio in 1848 were autobiographical, as well as hortatory: "We ask you to devote yourselves to this [anti-slavery] cause, as one of the first, and most successful means of self-improvement. . . . Many of the brightest and best of our number, have become such by their devotion to this cause, and the society of white abolitionists." See "An Address to the Colored People of the United States," *Report of the Proceedings of the Colored National Convention, Held at Cleveland, Ohio* (Rochester, 1848), pp. 18-19, reprinted in Howard Holman Bell, ed., *Minutes of the Proceedings of the National Negro Conventions, 1830-1864* (New York: Arno Press, 1969).
23. See Andrews, *To Tell a Free Story* (1988), pp. xi-xii, 1-31.
24. See Andrews, *To Tell a Free Story* (1988), pp. 8-9.
25. A related consequence of this reading of slavery—less in evidence in the laconic Brown text than in other slave narratives—is that resurrection imagery abounds. Negotiating a dark night of the soul may constitute a form of purgation and presage spiritual rebirth. At other times, talk of being a "new man"—an evangelical locution—may follow either the symbolic assertion of autonomy in resisting an overseer, or an actual escape from bondage.
26. Alain Locke, ed., *The New Negro* (New York: Albert and Charles Boni, Inc., 1925), p. 11. Chapter XXX of *The American Fugitive,* which describes a day in the House of Commons, highlights Brown's conventionality. In his stereotyped references to future Prime Minister Benjamin Disraeli as "the Jew," in his admiration for the splendid fortunes and social polish of the land-owning aristocracy, and in his vicarious pride in "this assembly of senators" of an expanding British Empire, we see that he has internalized the political and social prejudices of his day.
27. See Andrews, *To Tell a Free Story* (1988), pp. 22-29, 144-151, 176, 273-274, whose use of "speech-act theory" to explore how slave narratives, generally, and Brown's *Narrative,* in particular, work on their readers is unexcelled.

Angelyn Mitchell (essay date 1992)

SOURCE: "Her Side of His Story: A Feminist Analysis of Two Nineteenth-Century Antebellum Novels—William Wells Brown's *Clotel* and Harriet E. Wilson's *Our Nig,*" in *American Literary Realism, 1870-1910,* Vol. 24, No. 3, 1992, pp. 7-21.

[*In the following essay, Mitchell argues that Brown and Wilson differed in their depiction of female characters because of their own gender biases and experiences.*]

The first four novels by African Americans were published after the Fugitive Slave Act of 1850 and after the publication of Harriet Beecher Stowe's consciousness-raising novel, *Uncle Tom's Cabin, or Life Among the Lowly* (1852).[1] Two of these four novels, William Wells Brown's ***Clotel or The President's Daughter: A Narrative of Slave Life in the United States*** (1853) and Harriet E. Wilson's *Our Nig; or, Sketches from the Life of a Free Black, in a Two-Story House, North. Showing That Slavery's Shadows Fall Even There* (1859), examine, as one would expect, the major historical concern of their time—slavery. The primary issues for Black and White abolitionists—the paradoxical tenets of Christianity, the monstrous physical treatment of enslaved Blacks, and the psychological devastation of slavery on Black men, women, and children—are all interrogated by both novelists. However, and perhaps not surprisingly, Brown and Wilson approach these subjects from different perspectives. While both novels are undoubtedly propaganda novels, Brown and Wilson render their respective propagandistic notions through different subgeneric forms. Whereas Brown propagandizes within the constructs of a romance, Wilson propagandizes within the constructs of a sentimental novel. Brown, an escaped slave, an historian, and a professional abolitionist, gives a depiction of slavery in ***Clotel*** which is highly romanticized, dramatic, and political. Wilson, an indentured servant in the antebellum North, provides a perspective which is also highly romanticized and political, as she too borrows heavily from the literary tradition of the nineteenth-century English and American Romantics, with her emphasis on justice, sentimentality, and the Gothic. But Wilson's novel springs, it seems to me, from what might be called a "secret well of immanent femininity," to borrow an expression from Jane Gallop.[2] In keeping with the tradition of the sentimental novel, Wilson portrays her female characters' quest for freedom through hyperbolic renderings of interpersonal, familial, and social interactions. Brown is also concerned with women and their quest for freedom; however, his female characters seek freedom through heroic deeds such as daring escapes and other adventures. Therefore, in what follows I contend that although both novelists are concerned with enslaved females and their quests for freedom, their novels differ significantly in their characterizations of women, a difference mediated by each author's intent and gender.

The search for the female's voice and demand that the voice be heard is central to much of feminist methodology in the study of literary texts. It is a response to the fact that women have either been left out of or included in demeaning, disfiguring, and misleading ways in what has been for the most part an exclusively male account of the world. But when women are allowed to speak for themselves, as Mary Helen Washington says of Black female writers, their literature takes the trouble to record the genuine "thoughts, words, feelings, and deeds of black women, experiences that make the realities of being black in America look very different from what men have written."[3] And as recent discourse theory has made clear, the ability to talk, to give utterance, about one's life and to interpret it, is integral to leading that life rather than being led through it. This explains in part the feminist critic's distrust of a male voice who narrates a woman's story.

The opening of Brown's linearly rendered romance establishes the historical moment of narrative. Set in Richmond at the beginning of the nineteenth century, the novel "dwells in possibilities" by presenting a fictional account of what could be Thomas Jefferson's actual slave daughter. According to Brown, Currer, the slave woman who for a time in her youth had been the housekeeper and mistress of Thomas Jefferson, lives peacefully with the two daughters she has borne him, Clotel and Althesa.[4] Brown employs Jeffersonian rhetoric as a propagandistic device, but Thomas Jefferson is physically absent from the narrative. Although all three are slaves, the property of a wealthy Virginian, Currer and her daughters enjoy a kind of liberty. Known as the most skillful laundress in Richmond, Currer pays—in currency rather than in labor—her master for her pseudo-freedom as well as for her daughters' freedom. The daughters are provided with a tutor and grow up as ladies. All runs smoothly until the master dies and his seventy-nine slaves are auctioned for sale. The plot then moves rapidly and is developed along two main lines—the continuous adventures and the tragic fates of each of the mulatto daughters. Northrop Frye explains in *Anatomy of Criticism* that "the essential element of plot in romance is adventure, which means that romance is naturally a sequential and processional form."[5] Indicative perhaps, too, of the expatriate Brown's diverse life experiences, the shifting, episodic scenes bring the reader in contact with slavery in Virginia, in Washington, on a plantation near Natchez, in New Orleans, and on the Ohio and Mississippi River steamboats. There are slave auction blocks, bloodhounds, indentured Whites, murders, and suicides. The devastating yellow fever epidemic in New Orleans in 1831 and Nat Turner's fateful insurrection in Virginia in 1832 are both described with the harrowing horrors that accompanied them. Brown purposefully and consistently quotes the ideals expressed in the Declaration of Independence and in Jefferson's antislavery speeches, i.e., "that all men are by nature equal" and "endowed by the Creator with certain rights, which are irrefragable" to show to the world the inconsistencies of democratic ideology in the United States. That Clotel's final catastrophe is acted out in Washington, an environment metonymically linked to Jefferson and to the constructs of liberty and justice, constitutes one of the novel's main ironies. The fleeing Clotel, cornered by slave trappers on the "Long Bridge," drowns herself in the Potomac, "within plain sight of the President's house and the Capitol of the Union."[6]

In the preface to ***Clotel,*** Brown states his polemical intentions:

> If the incidents set forth in the following pages should add anything new to the information already given to the Public through similar publications, and should thereby aid in bringing British influence to bear upon American slavery, the main object for which this work was written will have been accomplished. (p. 16)

To demonstrate that the "system of chattel slavery in America undermines the entire social condition of man" (p. 62), Brown employs Clotel as "the archetype of the beautiful heroine whose mixed blood, noble spirit, and poetic nature make her a tragic figure."[7] Thus, Brown introduces the theme of the tragic mulatto to the African-American literary tradition. That Clotel's function is primarily as an abolitionist instrument is clear from the nature of Brown's plot and characterization; the narrative movement is so rapid and episodic that readers never see her at any one time long enough to get a clear impression of her character and feelings. All too often, a scene which might provide such insight is incompletely sketched in only a few sentences. For example, in the short four pages of narration when Horatio Green betrays Clotel's love by marrying another, an act that radically changes Clotel's life, Brown reveals simply the facts of this perfidy. This flatness of character may well be a result of Brown's choice of genre as Frye explains that "the essential difference between novel and romance lies in the conception of characterization. The romancer does not attempt to create 'real people' so much as stylized figures which expand into psychological archetypes."[8] Additionally, Brown's inability to illuminate and to interrogate the true nature of the enslaved female's plight in slavery, i.e., how could he give witness to what he personally had not lived, and his own explicitly stated political agenda may be responsible.

In ***Clotel,*** Brown not only provides character sketches rather than full characterizations, but most of these sketches are of women as heroic figures. Clotel, for instance, is portrayed as struggling against all odds to be reunited with her daughter. It is also her role as mother that inspires her adventurous quest for freedom, her escape, which ultimately leads to her death.

Brown's heroic treatment of Althesa, Clotel's sister, provides the reader with a monentary ray of hope. When the three are sold into bondage, Althesa's plight takes an unexpected hopeful turn. While a slave, she meets and marries the white physician Henry Morton and creates for herself a new identity. This particular illumination of the uncontrollable ebb and flow of the slave's destiny is later examined in Frances E. W. Harper's *Iola Leroy* (1892) as her protagonist also experiences the same escape from and subsequent return to slavery. Leaving slavery behind her by passing as a white woman, Althesa is finally the wife and mother of her mother's dreams. But subsequently, Althesa heroically gambles with fate. Sadly, her marriage to Morton is as illegal as was Clotel's marriage to Green. Although Morton becomes a leading spokesperson for abolition, he naively fails to manumit his wife and daughters. Although Althesa achieves Currer's dream, she and her daughters are not allowed to sustain it. After Morton and Althesa die during the Yellow Fever epidemic, their daughters, Ellen and Jane, are sold into slavery. Unable to cope with their horrendous situation, the two girls die in bondage. Brown laments, "And no one wept at the grave of her [Jane] who had been so carefully cherished, and so tenderly beloved" (p. 210). Thus, Brown poignantly depicts the elusive nature of the slave's freedom as well as the degradations suffered by slaves in bondage.

The only triumphant female character to remain in the story is Clotel's daughter, Mary, who counts among her many adventures impersonating a man as her mother did in order to escape bondage, and who lives freely and happily with her husband and son in France. Before her good fortune, however, Mary had courageously saved the life of her slave lover, sentenced to die as an insurgent, by taking his place in the cell. Love does conquer as Mary and George are reunited after her husband's death in France, where they both live freely.

It is clear that Brown saw no dichotomy between art and propaganda and that he championed the argument that art must be instrumental in liberating people from social evils. This objective, prevalent throughout this propaganda novel, situates him as a moral propagandist. Any device that would damage the "peculiar institution" of slavery—sentimentality, melodrama, contrived plots, or newspaper articles—was employed. In light of this purpose, the sexual licentiousness of the slave owner and the control he and his family wielded over Black women receive particular attention. For Brown, illegitimacy, the result of the ravaging of Black women and the inevitable destruction of the family structure, is a corrupt principle upon which slavery is founded. To give his thesis validity, he peoples his novel with females like Currer, Clotel, and Althesa, who are victims of that licentiousness. Currer is separated, never to be reunited, from her daughters when they are teenagers. Her daughters' attempts to reunify the family are unsuccessful. Horatio Green reneges on his promise to reunite the family, and when Althesa is financially able, Currer's owner refuses to sell her. The separation of Clotel and her daughter leads to Clotel's death; Althesa's daughters, separated by slavery, die apart. In short, slavery's greatest atrocity, according to Brown, is the fracture of the enslaved African American's family. He writes, "Husbands and wives were separated with a degree of indifference that is unknown in any other relation of life, except that of slavery. Brothers and sisters were torn from each other; and mothers saw their children leave them for the last time on this earth" (p. 65). Even in contemporary literature, novelists still grapple with this unforgettable and unforgivable phenomenon of cruel familial separation. In *Beloved* (1987), Toni Morrison compares this separation to a game of checkers and describes what she refers to as "the nastiness of life"—that the players did not stop playing checkers just because the pieces happened to be someone's child.[9]

Again, Brown's ***Clotel*** is by no means an unsophisticated novel about women in slavery. The major difficulty with his treatment of females in ***Clotel*** lies in its reductiveness, i.e., its tendency to reduce the female characters merely to symbols of oppression. This explains the necessity of the female voice, for as Elizabeth Fox-Genovese points out in her essay "My Statue, My Self: Autobiographical Writings of Afro-American Women," autobiographies written by Black women "resist reduction to either political or critical pieties and resist even more firmly reduction to mindless empiricism."[10] She argues for a more adequate understanding of women's autobiographies in terms of "discourse." Some would even argue, she says, that "the self is a function of discourse—a textual construct—not of experience at all. Others, including many black feminist critics, would emphasize black women's writing as personal testimony to oppression, thus emphasizing experience at the expense of text."[11] This attention to discourse or rhetoric helps to explain, in part, how a writer like Brown could so easily privilege his abolitionist "text" over his female slaves. Instead of focusing on their experiences as such, he focuses on their fixed condition as victims in an interlocking structure of gender, class, and race.

The mistake that authors like Brown and critics like Fox-Genovese make is repeated by the noted African-American critic, Henry Louis Gates, Jr. In this 1982 introduction to Harriet E. Wilson's *Our Nig; or, Sketches from the Life of a Free Black,* Gates states:

> Let us, at last, read closely Harriet Wilson's novel. I propose, in the remainder of this essay, to describe the text's own mode of presentation, to gloss its echoes, to establish its plot structure and compare this to those details we have been able to glean of Mrs. Wilson's biographical "facts," then to compare these elements of the plot of *Our Nig* to a typology of "Woman's Fic-

tion" published in this country between 1820 and 1870, which Nina Baym has so carefully devised.[12]

After being informed of Gates' decision to acquaint the audience with the way in which Wilson's novel wrote itself, i.e., "to describe the text's own mode of presentation," the reader should not be surprised that Gates attempts to dismiss the significance of Wilson's unsustained first-person narrative voice:

> What are we to make of the first person lapses in the chapter titles? We can conclude . . . that the novel is indeed "an Autobiography," of sorts, an autobiographical novel. Whether the lapses are a sign of an inexperienced author struggling with or *against* the received conventions of her form, or the result of the imposition of a life on the desires of a text to achieve the status of fiction, these first-person traces point to the complexities and tensions of basing fictional events upon the lived experiences of an author. . . . Curiously enough, the first-person proprietary consciousness evinced in the titles of the early chapters does not parallel events that we have been able to document. . . . Since these early chapters describe events far removed from the author's experiences closest in time to the period of writing, the first-person presences perhaps reveal the author's anxiety about identifying with events in the text that she cannot claim to recollect clearly, and some of which she cannot recollect at all, such as the courtship and marriage of her mother, and the protagonist's ultimate abandonment by her widowed parent. . . .[13]

A detailed commentary upon Gates' approach to Wilson's narrative would far exceed the boundaries of my present endeavor. Suffice it to say here that Gates reads the novel not merely as a "structuralist" critic, but as one who operates out of a classical epistemology which concentrates on the knowledge of objects and not living persons and their unobservable "desires." It is, accordingly, not surprising that he is drawn to an intellectualist and rationalistic critical position such as structuralism which seeks to banish the nature of experience. The structuralist's establishment of an identity between language (text) and experience is unwittingly reproduced in the talk of discourses as constituting human experience. "A signifier," Lacan explains,

> is that which represents a subject: for whom?—not for another subject, but for another signifier. . . . In order to illustrate this axiom, suppose that in the desert you find a stone covered with hieroglyphics. You do not doubt for a moment that, behind them, there was a subject who wrote them. But it is an error to believe that each signifier is addressed to you—this is proved by the fact that you cannot understand any of it. On the other hand, you define them as signifiers by the fact that you are sure that each of these signifiers is related to each of the others. And it is this that is at issue with the relation between the subject and the field of the Other. . . . The subject is born insofar as the signifier emerges in the field of the Other. But by that very fact, this subject—which was previously nothing if not a subject coming into being—solidifies into a signifier.[14]

By accepting the view that experience is produced by language, we are left powerless to appreciate the insight given by Brown's ***Clotel*** that propaganda, discourse, rhetoric, and other structures of thought can and do in actuality silence reality, making it possible to miss the "truth" entirely.

This is the case with Wilson's *Our Nig*. In the preface to her novel, Wilson reveals her motives for writing: "Deserted by kindred, disabled by failing health, I am forced to some experiment which shall aid me in maintaining myself and child without extinguishing this feeble life."[15] Of particular interest is Wilson's prefatory request for patronage from her "colored brethren" when one considers the lack of available funds among the African-American slave communities and among the small African-American free communities. "Our Nig," a term later employed derogatorily in Nella Larsen's *Passing* (1929), is Alfrado ("Frado"), another tragic mulatto and one of two children born from a marriage between a poor White woman, Mag Smith, and a Black man, Jim. Prior to the racially mixed union, Mag has already been ostracized, like Hawthorne's Hester Prynne, by her own people because she has given birth to an illegitimate child who dies soon after birth. To escape this disgrace, she moves away, only to discover that the "publicity of her fall" (p. 7) has followed her. Living a wretched existence marked by poverty and loneliness, she accepts the offer of marriage by Jim, a "kind-hearted African" (p. 9) who pities her plight. Of this liaison, Wilson comments that Mag "has descended another step down the ladder of infamy" (p. 13). The two manage to live comfortably until Jim dies of consumption. Once more, Mag finds it difficult to survive and marries another Black man, Seth Shipley, Jim's business partner. Because of difficult times, they decide, at Seth's insistence, to abandon the children and leave town.

Pretty and spirited, Alfrado is, at the age of six, abandoned at the big, white, two-story house owned by the Bellmonts, a White family. She grows up as an indentured servant and is ruled by the evil Mrs. Bellmont and her equally demonic daughter, Mary. Alfrado is overworked, constantly beaten, and deprived not only of clothing but also of her long curly hair, like Clotel's, which Mrs. Bellmont spitefully shears. From time to time but not often enough, Alfrado is rescued from her maltreatment by the kindly Mr. Bellmont, his sister Abby, and his two sons, Jack and James.

Upon reaching the age of eighteen, Alfrado is free to leave her servitude. She attempts to be self-sufficient as a seamstress, but the long years of abuse and deprivation have taken their toll, leaving her in fragile health. She is shuffled between charity homes whenever she is sick and unable to care for herself. Finally, she marries a Black man, Samuel, a fugitive slave and abolitionist lecturer. When she is pregnant with their first and only child, Samuel abruptly leaves her to go to sea. Once again abandoned, Alfrado has her baby, a son. Samuel then returns and leaves again. Alfrado later learns that he has died from yellow fever in New Orleans. Ill and with no means of support, Wilson (Alfrado) writes her narrative in order to earn money to reclaim her son who is in foster care; despite her attempts to save him through her creative endeavors, county records show the death of Wilson's son at the age of seven.[16]

In his assessment of Wilson's narrative, Gates, who does acknowledge the debt of the African-American literary tradition to Wilson, asserts:

> And if Allida's letter suggests that "Alfrado's tale" is that of love betrayed, a glance at the text suggests the contrary. The subplot of love, marriage, childbirth, and betrayal only appears in the text's final chapter, Chapter XII, "The Winding Up of the Matter," which unfolds in scarcely five pages of a one-hundred-and-thirty-one page novel.[17]

But love, in the broadest sense of caring and desiring care, is precisely what informs Wilson's text. Like William Wells Brown, Wilson is obviously concerned with the sociopolitical dimensions of slavery; her very title condemns Northern slavery. However, the major difference is that Wilson's concern resonates reciprocally with her desire for love and with her desire for personal and economic freedom—a reality which Brown was unable or perhaps unwilling to stress in his treatment of ***Clotel.***

A quick glance at Wilson's circuitous plot clearly reveals that Wilson follows the sentimental novel tradition by placing her analysis of slavery and American cultural values directly within the context of familial relationship, again just as Toni Morrison would do over one hundred and twenty years later in *Beloved,* with emphasis on the plight of women and children. What is of primary importance in the novel's opening scenes is not, as some critics have maintained, the author's blunt discussion of her White mother, but rather, as Claudia Tate suggests in her essay "Allegories of Black Female Desire; or, Rereading Nineteenth-Century Sentimental Narratives of Black Female Authority,"[18] Alfrado's (Wilson's) tender expression of love and sympathy for her mother:

> Lovely Mag Smith! See her as she walks with downcast eyes and heavy heart. It was not always thus. She *had* a loving, trusting heart. Early deprived of parental guardianship, far removed from relatives, she was left to guide her tiny boat over life's surges alone and inexperienced. As she merged into womanhood, unprotected, uncared for, there fell on her ear the music of love, awakening an intensity of emotion long dormant. (p. 1)

American culture has maintained a preference for myths which define African Americans and Anglo-Americans in extreme binary oppositions. Wilson demystifies and deconstructs the myth of the paragonic nature of White womanhood, i.e., as depicted in Harriet Beecher Stowe's Mrs. Shelby, as well as other myths by portraying her White mother as poor, lonely, and fallen, indicating that Black female slaves were not the only concubines and jezebels. The White female's fallen status was in many cases even more of a handicap and a burden because she was White—and female. As Deborah White reveals this sentiment in *Ar'n't I a Woman? Female Slaves in the Plantation South*: "If white women behaved like either white men or black women . . . they would be 'ridiculed,' 'abandoned,' and sent out of any decent house."[19]

The concern for and characterization of women and children of all races in *Our Nig* is one of the novel's features that marks it as a maternal text. Tate notably argues that "motherhood both motivates and justifies Wilson's authorship, and *Our Nig* appropriates the discourse on motherhood as its mode of literary representation."[20] For instance, Mag feels, as an unclean woman, that she must live in unclean places. She therefore confines herself to a "hovel" which she had often passed in her "better days" (p. 8). "Who can tell what numbers . . . ," the narrator interjects, "have chosen to dwell in unclean places, rather than encounter these 'holier-than-thou' of the greater brotherhood of man!" (p. 7). Mag's "hovel" can be said to represent what Jane Gallop refers to as the "rubbish-heap," the place for "trash," or the "cloaca" (sewer), a place, says Gallop, "beneath our consideration or notice."[21] Mag lives in the hovel, rubbish-heap, or cloaca because she is a woman who has chosen to exercise her sexuality. But as Gallop contends, female sexuality is "not to be recognized but rather consigned to the cloaca."[22] Additionally, Wilson's description of Mag's "fall" does not imply that, for Mag, her sexual initiation was a lewd form of vagrancy; instead, Wilson writes, Mag

> knew the voice of her charmer, so ravishing, sounded far above her. It seemed like an angel's alluring her upward and onward. She thought she could ascend to his and become an equal. She surrendered to him a priceless gem, which he proudly garnered as a trophy, with those of other victims, and left her to her fate. (p. 6)

It is little wonder then that when Mag's illegitimate baby girl dies at birth, Mag's reaction is a joyful one:

> "God be thanked," ejaculated Mag, as she saw its breathing cease; "no one can taunt *her* with my ruin."
>
> Blessed release! may we all respond. How many pure, innocent children not only inherit a wicked heart of their own, claiming life-long scrutiny and restraint, but are heirs also of parental disgrace and calumny, from which only years of patient endurance in paths of rectitude can disencumber them. (pp. 6-7).

In short, Wilson insinuates the notion of better dead than lonely, abandoned, unclean—and female.

Not only does Wilson confront the myth of the pure, moral White woman in the figure of Mag, but also its antithesis in Mrs. Bellmont, who lives not in a hovel but in the big, white, two-story house she inhabits with her husband and four children. But the Bellmonts represent another equally important nineteenth-century American cultural myth—the myth of the domestic madonna or angel, i.e., the myth of the happy home and family flawlessly nurtured by saintly matrons. Mrs. Bellmont is anything but saintly. Although hyperbole is characteristic of the sentimental novel, Wilson writes of Mrs. Bellmont's extreme cruelty to Alfrado. Mrs. Bellmont constantly exercises her arbitrary dominion over Alfrado by beating and kicking her, and on one occasion, she props Frado's mouth open with a piece of wood and hangs Frado by her thumbs. Most of the torture takes place significantly in the kitchen as Wilson reveals:

> It is impossible to give an impression of the manifest enjoyment of Mrs. B in these kitchen scenes. It was her favorite exercise to enter the appartment [sic] noisily, vociferate orders, give a few sudden blows to quicken Nig's pace, then return to the sitting room with such a satisfied expression, congratulating herself upon her thorough house-keeping qualities. (p. 66)

So terribly abused, Alfrado despairingly wishes her own death. She is forced to live in the "L chamber" of the house; to get there she has to crawl through a dark, unfinished passageway, a Gothic scene that prefigures Harriet Jacobs' narrative of a few years later. The roof slants nearly to the floor, and the sun is a constant source of discomfort. Although quite young, Alfrado knows that she is living in hell and often thinks of fleeing; however, she resolves "to tarry, with the hope that mother would come and get her some time" (p. 28).

Although Mag never returns, many people represent the mother for Alfrado in the novel. If Mrs. Bellmont and her daughter, Mary, are indeed devils, Wilson balances her novel by providing Alfrado with good and decent White individuals like her teacher, Miss Marsh with her kind words for Alfrado. There is also Mr. Bellmont, "a kind, humane man, who would not grudge hospitality to the poorest wanderer, nor fail to sympathize with any sufferer, however humble. The child's desertion by her mother appealed to his sympathy, and he felt inclined to succor her" (p. 24). Mr. Bellmont is, in fact, more nurturing than Mrs. Bellmont in his gentle compassion for Alfrado, while cruelty and insensitivity are Mrs. Bellmont's essence. Mr. Bellmont's sister, Abby, his sensitive sons, Jack and James, as well as his invalid daughter, Jane, also love, mother, and protect Alfrado.

Much could be made of the title's ironic and negative connotation, but if read in terms of the novel's motherly characters, "Our Nig" as a title can also be read as a formal acceptance of Alfrado by a family which provides her with a number of surrogate mothers, some of them evil and devouring, some of them kind and loving. In terms of narrative strategy and political hegemony, Tate congently elucidates that

> as their "nig," she could tell her own story of racial abuse seemingly from their point of view and possibly arouse the sympathy of white readers as well as demonstrate that her life was not substantially different from those who were born in bondage. This authorial strategy would also allow her to abort much of the criticism from readers who might regard her story as atypical or exaggerated because technically she was not a slave.[23]

One similarity that should be noted between William Wells Brown and Harriet E. Wilson is their willingness to credit some of the White females with loving Christian attitudes toward their slaves or servants. Both novelists are critical in general of the Christianity practiced by their masters. An epigram from the poetry of John Greenleaf Whittier at the beginning of chapter six of ***Clotel,*** "The Religious Teacher," vividly reveals Brown's attitude:

> What! preach and enslave men?
> Give thanks—and rob thy own afflicted poor?
> Talk of thy glorious liberty, and then
> Bolt hard the captive's door? (p. 91)

Not only is Christianity used to validate the captivity of Blacks, but it is also used to re-enforce slave-holding on the plantations. One slave owner, Reverend Peck, maintains that slave-holding is divinely ordained, and his slaves are literally taught that "the Lord intended them for slaves" (p. 102). Reverend Peck's daughter, however, believes that "true Christian love is of an enlarged, disinterested nature. It loves all who love the Lord Jesus Christ in sincerity, without regard to colour or condition" (p. 96). She practices the true teachings of Christianity, at least by Anglo-American ethical standards, by heroically emancipating her slaves at her death.

Wilson's suspicions of Christianity are intimated in the novel through Alfrado's voice. Early in the novel, she despairingly questions her existence, saying, "'Oh, I wish I had my mother back; then I should not be kicked and whipped so. Who made me so?'" (p. 51). In the end, it is the good Aunt Abby who unties Alfrado's "knotty queries" of spirituality (p. 51) by introducing her to the Bible and by taking her to Bible classes.

In addition to interrogating the myth of White women as the bearers of true Christian and/or egalitarian ethics, Wilson destroys yet another myth about White women during slavery. When Alfrado leaves the Bellmonts and becomes ill as a result of her many years of abuse and hard labor, she shuffles between charitable homes not occupied by the stereotypic Black "mammy." Rather, the caring and mothering she receives are given by the White women. Deborah White reveals the sentimental tradition's view of women during the period:

> Although women were also idealized as virgins, wives, and Christians, it was above all as mothers that women were credited with social influence as the chief transmitters of religion and moral values. Other female roles—wife, charity worker, teacher, sentimental writer—were in large part cultural defined as extensions of motherhood, all similarly regarded as nurturing, empathetic, and morally directive.[24]

In *Our Nig,* Mrs. Moore, "a plain, poor, simple woman," provides the invalid Alfrado with foster care, which once again confirms Deborah White's thesis that

> White women also played a role in slave child care, and while a legend has been built around the black nurses who helped raise Southern white children, the role that white women played in raising slave children has largely been ignored. If there was no elderly or disabled slave woman to supervise slave children during the day when their parents worked in the field, the responsibility fell to the white mistresses. White women also played an important role in the health care of slave children.[25]

If *Our Nig* is to be remembered as a novel of great significance, it must be rescued from critics of a narrowly structuralist and a narrowly ethnic persuasion and must be placed in its proper context as a sentimental novel about women, mothering, children, and humanity as well as about hatred, indifference, bondage, and inhumanity. Although both are primarily propaganda novels, to conflate *Our Nig,* a sentimental novel, with William Wells Brown's ***Clotel,*** a romance novel, without acknowledging significant distinctions, and to suppress *Our Nig*'s numerous maternal subplots and themes in favor of formal and textual matters are to miss much of the work's value. While recognition and acceptance of the female voice in the sentimental tradition is the first step in expanding our understanding and sensibility, perhaps in the final analysis it is simply not enough to write, as Helene Cixous suggests, with breast milk.[26] We must read as women as well.

Notes

1. The other two novels are Frank Webb's *The Garies and Their Friends* (1857) and Martin R. Delany's *Blake; or The Huts of America: A Tale of the Mississippi Valley, the Southern United States and Cuba* (1859).
2. Jane Gallop, *Thinking Through the Body* (New York: Columbia Univ. Press, 1988), p. 170.
3. Mary Helen Washington, *Invented Lives: Narratives of Black Women 1860-1960* (New York: Anchor Press, 1987), p. xxi.
4. For further information concerning *Clotel* and William Wells Brown, see W. Edward Farrison's biography of Brown, *William Wells Brown: Author and Reformer* (Chicago: Univ. of Chicago Press, 1969), and also his article, "Clotel, Thomas Jefferson, and Sally Hemings," *CLA Journal* 17 (December 1973), 147-174.
5. Northrop Frye, *Anatomy of Criticism: Four Essays* (1957; Princeton: Princeton Univ. Press, 1973), p. 186.
6. William Wells Brown, *Clotel or The President's Daughter: A Narrative of Slave Life in the United States* (1853; New York: Carol Publishing Group, 1969), p. 219. Subsequent references to *Clotel* are to this edition and will be cited in parentheses within the text.
7. Bernard W. Bell, *The Afro-American Novel and Its Tradition* (Amherst: Univ. of Massachusetts Press, 1987), p. 40.
8. Frye, p. 304.
9. Toni Morrison, *Beloved* (New York: Knopf, 1987), p. 23.
10. Elizabeth Fox-Genovese, "My Statue, My Self: Autobiographical Writings of Afro-American Women," *Reading Black, Reading Feminist,* ed. Henry L. Gates, Jr. (New York: Meridian, 1990), p. 179.
11. *Ibid.,* p. 178.
12. Henry Louis Gates, Jr., introduction to *Our Nig; or, Sketches from the Life of a Free Black, In a Two-Story White House, North. Showing that Slavery's Shadows Fall Even There,* by Harriet E. Wilson (New York: Vintage Books, 1983), p. xxxiv.
13. *Ibid.,* p. xxxvii.
14. Jacques Lacan, *The Four Fundamental Concepts of Psycho-analysis* (London: Hogarth Press, 1977), pp. 198-99.
15. Harriet E. Wilson, preface to *Our Nig; or, Sketches from the Life of a Free Black, In a Two-Story White House, North. Showing that Slavery's Shadows Fall Even There* (1859; New York: Vintage Books, 1983), n. p. Subsequent references to *Our Nig* are from this edition and will be cited in parentheses within the text.
16. Gates, p. xii.
17. *Ibid.,* p. xxvii.
18. Claudia Tate, "Allegories of Black Female Desire; or Rereading Nineteenth-Century Sentimental Narratives of Black Female Authority," *Changing Our Own Words: Essays on Criticism, Theory, and Writing by Black Women,* ed. Cheryl A. Wall (New Brunswick: Rutgers Univ. Press, 1989), pp. 111-12.
19. Deborah Gray White, *Ar'n't I a Woman? Female Slaves in the Plantation South* (New York: Norton and Co., 1985), p. 40.
20. Tate, p. 116.
21. Gallop, p. 146.
22. *Ibid.*
23. Tate, p. 114.
24. White, p. 56.
25. *Ibid.,* p. 53.
26. Helene Cixous, Madeleine Gagnon, and Annie Leclerc, *La Venue a l'ecriture* (Paris: Union Generale d'Editions 10/18, 1977), p. 37.

    Employing the metaphor of milk to represent ink, Cixous, in "The Laugh of the Medusa," defines feminine writing as

    an act which will not only "realize" the decensored relation of woman to her sexuality, to her womanly being, giving her access to her native strengths; it will give her back her goods, her pleasures, her organs, her immense bodily territories which have been kept under seal. (Marks and Courtivron, *New French Feminisms* [Harvester Press: Brighton, 1981], p. 250.)

Christopher Mulvey (essay date 1994)

SOURCE: "The Fugitive Self and the New World of the North: William Wells Brown's Discovery of America," in *The Black Columbiad: Defining Moments in African American Literature and Culture,* Harvard University Press, 1994, pp. 99-111.

[*In the following essay, Mulvey explicates Brown's interest in the paradox of the European "discovery" of America.*]

Columbia is the poetical name for America, and the Columbiad is the poetical name for the journey to the New World. This journey is a quest, but it is a quest for special prizes, special riches which represent both the idea of a New World and the idea that that New World should be one distinct from a world known, explored, and exhausted. For the inhabitants of the New World that is Columbia, the Old World that is Europe is a place of tyranny and imprisonment, a world that denies to all but kings, emperors, and popes expression of self and ambition. The air of the New World is believed to be fuller, richer, cleaner, more exhilarating than the air of the Old World. Breathing that air makes possible the realization of dreams—dreams most powerful when they have been expressed as dreams of liberty.

Columbia is also that name for America which refers to the image of the continent as a land discovered by a European. Christopher Columbus is more present in the name Columbia than is Amerigo Vespucci in the name America. America has overwhelmed Amerigo, but Columbia has not overwhelmed Columbus. He remains the great figure, the great father, the great author. There is a tension between the image of the authoritative father figure, giving the law and siring the children, and the image of the land possessed by those children, the daughters and the sons of Columbia, a land of American freedoms and American dreams. A dilemma confronts anyone approaching Christopher Columbus and his particular discovery of America because it is plain that the Columbiad of Christopher Columbus was a journey not of dreaming and freedom but of calculation and enslavement. Knowing this seems to make little difference to the magical quality of the worlds Columbia and Columbiad. They resist their historical interpretations and insist on their mythological, mythopoeic meanings, which associate them with the human spirit. These conflicts of language and symbols, the paradox of Columbus, are felt everywhere through what has often been called the first black American novel, ***Clotel***[1] by William Wells Brown, published in London in 1853.

William Wells Brown was born in Lexington, Kentucky, about the year 1816, and he died in Chelsea, Massachusetts, in 1884. He is described in the *Concise Dictionary of American Biography* as a "negro reformer," as a man who "escaped from slavery," and as one "celebrated in his own time as a lecturer and a historian of his race." Like other artists of his time, William Wells Brown used the name Columbia to represent a poetical America, and his America was discovered, like the traditional Columbia, by three ships; but William Wells Brown's three ships are not the *Santa Maria,* the *Nina,* and the *Pinta,* commanded by Christopher Columbus. For Brown, Columbus discovers the continent, but it is two later ships that discover America. In chapter 21 of ***Clotel*** Brown describes these three ships. First, there is the *Santa Maria,* Columbus's ship, a ship of "moral grandeur." Second is the *Mayflower*: "Next in moral grandeur, was this ship to the great discoverer's: Columbus found a continent: the *Mayflower* brought the seed-wheat of states and empire" (***Clotel,*** 183). The third ship is the first Jamestown slaver, which in Brown's historical vision made land on the same day as the *Mayflower*: "But look far in the Southeast and you behold, on the same day, in 1620, a low rakish ship hastening from the tropics, solitary and alone, to the New World. What is she? She is freighted with the elements of unmixed evil . . . Listen to those shocking oaths, the crack of the flesh-cutting whip. Ah! it is the first cargo of slaves on their way to Jamestown, Virginia" (***Clotel,*** 184). Brown did not call these slaves "Pilgrim Fathers," but this is the term which suggests itself from the moral construct that evolves in his vision of the *Santa Maria,* the *Mayflower* and the slaver, the founding ships of the land that was to become the United States of America. Brown makes no reference at all to the thousand intervening landings between 1492 and 1620 which created the cultures of South, Catholic, and Latin America. Brown was an American Protestant and he wrote like one, but he was also a black American Protestant. He matched the moral event which founded white America with the moral event which founded black America.

"Behold the Mayflower anchored at Plymouth Rock, the slave-ship in James River. Each a parent" (***Clotel,*** 184). Brown saw in these two ships two Americas which would attempt to occupy the mythical space of Columbia. This vision presented American history as tragic from its outset, a history leading directly from the landings of 1620 to the struggles of the 1850s which consumed Brown's life and writing. "These ships are the representation of good and evil in the New World, even to our day," he wrote in ***Clotel.*** "When shall one of those parallel lines come to an end?" (***Clotel,*** 184). In 1853, when he published ***Clotel,*** he was of the opinion that the United States was moving, by way of the Fugitive Slave Act and the increasing violence against the antislavery movement, more toward the parentage of the slaver than of the *Mayflower.* William Wells Brown himself had had to compromise his resolution not to traffic in his own "body and soul." He had had to agree to his American freedom being bought from the man who claimed to own him.[2] Had he not done so, he would have returned as a slave in 1854 to the land that he had left as a freeman in 1849.

The historical vision of ***Clotel*** looked at both the white *Mayflower* and the black slave ship and saw "each a parent" (***Clotel,*** 184). Brown's father was a white man and his mother was a slave, and he could see in each of the ships an ancestor. Here was a conflict and a union for William Wells Brown more primary even than that of the United States itself. It generated a pattern of contradictions and affirmations that created the central story of his fictions as much as it created the actual fact of his life. The most complete working out of this theme was in the first version of ***Clotel*** and was made clear by the subtitle of the 1853 London edition of the novel, ***Clotel; or the President's Daughter.*** The president was Thomas Jefferson, and his role in the novel is to father the heroine and her sister before removing to Washington to take up office. Jefferson becomes in Brown's fiction the author of the Declaration of Independence and Clotel.

The epigraph on the title page of ***Clotel*** reads: "We hold these truths to be self-evident: that all men are created equal; that they are endowed by their Creator with certain inalienable rights, and that among these are Life, Liberty, and the Pursuit of Happiness." Thomas Jefferson's language promised a universal meaning for the Declaration of American Independence. But for William Wells Brown that meaning had been canceled. He puts it simply in the first sentences of his autobiography: "Chapter 1. I was born in Lexington, Ky. The man who stole me as soon as I was born, recorded the birth of all infants which he claimed to be born his property, in a book which he kept for that purpose."[3] The ledger recorded an original act of theft; the Declaration recorded the original act of liberty. The Declaration of American Independence might have taken moral precedence over the plantation ledger, but the Declaration did not protect William Wells Brown the man when he was William the slave. The text quoted on the title page of ***Clotel*** had to be denied as often as it was affirmed. William Wells Brown's life and writings contained a continuing but quite unresolved confrontation with the fact that the Declaration of Independence was written by a slave owner. The moral authority and the human author could not be brought into the same focus. It was as if a Zionist had to look to a Nazi philosopher for the highest statement of Jewish aspiration.

In the opening chapter of the novel William Wells Brown quotes John Randolph. Randolph had represented Virginia in Congress almost continuously from 1799 to 1829, and he was remarkable for, among many other things, declaring that "the blood of the first American statesmen coursed through the veins of the slave of the South" (***Clotel,*** 55). This fantastical piece of southern rhetoric contained as a boast one of Brown's main indictments of the South and one of the major elements of the American paradox: American fathers were using and selling their own children as slaves. This was not only an actual fact, it was an attested and unashamed fact. From Brown's point of view the case against men like Randolph was so well made by men like Randolph that moral indignation and action were all but nonplussed. The result was Brown's constant representation of the American paradox and the constant disintegration of his argument. He was appealing for moral outrage but could not establish the moral indictment.

The Fugitive Slave Act of 1850 made the paradox "more perfect" because it explicitly involved the North in the Jeffersonian contradiction of a constitution designed for freedom being used to enslave people. "On every foot of soil, over which Stars and Stripes wave," Brown wrote in the preface to ***Clotel,*** "the negro is considered common property, on which any white man may lay his hand with perfect impunity. The entire white population of the United States, North and South, are bound by their oath to the Constitution, and their adhesion to the Fugitive Slave Law, to hunt down the runaway slave and return him to his claimant, and to suppress any effort that may be made by the slaves to gain their freedom by physical force" (***Clotel,*** iii-iv). This insistence reinforced a further point, one central to the moral action of the novel: the whole South was to be held accountable for the worst excesses of any one part of the South. "It does the cause of emancipation but little good," Brown wrote, "to cry out in tones of execration against the traders, the kidnappers, the hireling overseers, and brutal drivers, so long as nothing is said to fasten the guilt on those who move in the higher circle" (***Clotel,*** iv). The Fugitive Slave Act had extended that higher circle effectively to the whole people of the United States of America.

In the Fugitive Slave Act, William Wells Brown had a symbol for the constitutional outrage of the American paradox; in his own person he had a more immediate symbol for the human outrage of the American paradox. In the "Memoir of the Author," which William Wells Brown attached to his work ***The Black Man,*** he says: "My fair complexion was a great obstacle to my unhappiness both with whites and blacks, in and about the great house."[4] The great house was the home of Dr. and Mrs. Young, and since Brown was the son of a close relative of the doctor, there were occasions when visitors to the house took him to be Mrs. Young's child. For this Mrs. Young had him whipped. His fellow slaves mocked him.[5] The vulnerability of the fair-skinned Negro in the slave world is central to the tragedy of ***Clotel.*** In chapter 15, "To Day a Mistress, to Morrow a Slave," Brown gives an account of Clotel's fate when her owner-lover and sham husband, Mr. Horatio Green, takes a legal wife, Gertrude, a blond-haired but less beautiful woman than Clotel. The new and legal Mrs. Green makes it her business to end her husband's bachelor arrangements and insists on the sale of Clotel and Mary, Clotel's daughter by Mr. Green.

The dynamics of Brown's novel required continuous intensification of the American paradox so that the dual authorities of Thomas Jefferson could be seen to be more and more in profound self-contradiction. The moral authority of the Declaration of Independence had to be defied in the case of a woman who not only was Jefferson's daughter but was to all appearances white. If Brown was not certainly saying that it was better to enslave one of another race than to enslave one of your own, he was certainly saying that it was morally more abhorrent to enslave your own child than to enslave another's. "Nature abhors it; the age repels it; and Christianity needs all her meekness to forgive it," he wrote (***Clotel,*** 61), but southern custom had so altered values that the sale of an American president's daughter did not excite those reactions. "The appearance of Clotel on the auction block created a deep sensation amongst the crowd. There she stood, with a complexion as white as most of those who were waiting with a wish to become her purchasers; her features as finely defined as any of her sex of pure Anglo-Saxon; her long black hair done up in the neatest manner; her form tall and graceful, and her whole appearance indicating one superior to her position" (***Clotel,*** 62-63).

The full-length description of the heroine of this Victorian novel, seen in as vulnerable a posture as Hester Prynne or Tess of the D'Urbervilles, enables Brown to confront his white Anglo-Saxon and Protestant readers with the fact that, like the purchasers at the auction, they are dealing with one of their own kind as well as one of Brown's kind. The auctioneer's cry emphasises the point: "How much, gentlemen? Real Albino, fit for a fancy girl for any one" (***Clotel,*** 63). William Wells Brown matches the bidding to her attributes, and the price rises as the auctioneer draws attention to her health, her looks, her education, her Christianity, her virginity. "This," says Brown in summary, "was a Southern auction, at which the bones, muscles, sinews, blood and nerves of a young lady of sixteen were sold for five hundred dollars; her moral character for two hundred; her improved intellect for one hundred; her Christianity for three hundred; and her chastity and virtue for four hundred dollars" (***Clotel,*** 63-64). William Wells Brown had now established his main charge against America, and it led him once again to restate the American paradox: "Thus closed a negro sale, at which two daughters of Thomas Jefferson, the writer of the Declaration of Independence and one of the presidents of the great republic, were disposed of to the highest bidder" (***Clotel,*** 64).

With her dark hair and fine eyes, Clotel is no albino. When Brown carries Clotel's romance with her purchaser to its next stage, she reappears in chapter 4 living in an idyllic rural cottage, in an idyllic "outward marriage," blessed with a daughter yet more white than Clotel herself. This is the daughter Mary, of whom Brown says only her eyes were African: "The iris of her large dark eyes had the melting mezzotinto, which remains the last vestige of African ancestry, and gives that plaintive expression, so often observed, and so appropriate to that docile and injured race" (***Clotel,*** 80). Mary's whiteness eventually enables her to live happily ever after in England. The effect of the final twist of the paradox leaves the heroines of this black drama effectively white. Indeed, William Wells Brown makes them appear to be white, in part because his plot requires it. Clotel is able to make her escape from New Orleans to the North and then return to Richmond because she can pass as white. Althesa, Clotel's sister, must be able to pass as white if she is to take advantage of the protection offered by the moral sensitivity of her husband. Mary similarly needs to be able to pass if she is to live in England as a white woman. Nonetheless, alternative plot devices were available, and Brown had an unusually rich knowledge of the ways in which fugitives escaped from the South, a knowledge gained from his own work: "In one year alone, I assisted sixty fugitives in crossing to the British queen's dominions" (***Black Man,*** 25). In choosing to have Clotel's escape depend on her fair skin, Brown was as much emphasizing Clotel's mulatto state as he was obliged to make her mulatto in order to have her escape.

In ***The Black Man: His Antecedents, His Genius, and His Achievements,*** his biographies of fifty-seven black men and women, Brown speaks with pride about his African heritage and its claim to a culture antecedent to that of the Anglo-Saxon. "I admit," he wrote in the introductory essay, "that the condition of my race, whether considered in a mental, moral, or intellectual point of view, at the present time cannot compare favorably with the Anglo-Saxon. But it does not become the whites to point a finger of scorn at the blacks, when they have so long been degrading them. The negro has not always been considered the inferior race. The time was when he stood at the head of science and literature. Let us see" (***Man,*** 32). He gave a history of the Ethiopians and the Egyptians, assuming it "as a settled point that the Egyptians were black" (***Black Man,*** 32). He quoted with pleasure a comment by Cicero, writing to his friend Atticus, advising "him not to buy slaves from England, 'because,' said he, 'they cannot be taught to read, and are the ugliest and most stupid race I ever saw'" (***Black Man,*** 34). William Wells Brown did not distinguish between the Anglo-Saxons and the ancient Britons, but the point was a good one.

Brown's history showed that racial prejudice varied the object of its contempt, but not the grounds of the contempt so that now one race and then another would become despised and persecuted. A race that had been up at one point in history would be down in another. The Anglo-Saxons had once been considered contemptible barbarians but were now considered the most civilized of people; the Africans had once led civilization and were now considered contemptible. Of his collection of black biographies Brown wrote: "If this work shall aid in vindicating the Negro's character, and show that he is endowed with those intellectual and amiable qualities which adorn and dignify human nature, it will meet the most sanguine hopes of the writer" (***Black Man,*** 6). Although Brown spoke of the amiable qualities of human nature, he did not mean to stress the docility of the black man. Several of his portraits celebrate militant and military black heroes. He concludes his account of Nat Turner with the remark that "every eye is now turned towards the south, looking for another Nat Turner" (***Black Man,*** 75). Brown admired the slave-insurgent, and in addition to Nat Turner, he included lives of Toussaint L'Ouverture, Denmark Vesey, Madison Washington, and others. This was a theme that he included in ***Clotel.***

Chapter 24 of the novel, titled "The Escape," deals not with the escape of Clotel but with the story of George, the house slave who is the lover of her daughter, Mary. George has been imprisoned for taking part in Nat Turner's rebellion. He had done so because he "had heard his master and visitors speak of the down-trodden and oppressed Poles; he heard them talk of going to Greece to fight for Grecian liberty." Inspired by this dinner table conversation, George joined the slave revolt (***Clotel,*** 222). For this he is eventually condemned to death but is given the freedom of the court to speak after he has heard his sentence. Brown uses this as an opportunity to state again the central paradox of American liberty. "I will tell you why I joined the revolted negroes," says George. "I have heard my master read in the Declaration of Independence 'that all men are created free and equal,' and this caused me to inquire of myself why I was a slave" (***Clotel,*** 224). George goes on to say that if he and his companions had succeeded in establishing their liberty, they "would have been patriots too," and he asks the court to think about the meaning of Independence Day celebrations in a slave state: "You make merry on the 4th of July. Yet one sixth of the people of this land are in chains and slavery" (***Clotel,*** 225).

George moves his listeners to tears, but he does not move the law to compassion. His sentence is not commuted, and he escapes death only by the intervention of his lover, Mary, who sets in train a pattern of events that lead to life and freedom in England. In due course, and several years later Mary too escapes and makes her way to England. By complete coincidence the lovers unite, embrace, marry, and live happily ever after. George, says Brown, "being somewhat ashamed of his African descent" (***Clotel,*** 231), has told no one that he is a fugitive, and so the couple are able to disappear into the English crowd and escape the persecution of their race. But they escape only through the fantasies of fairy-tale and romance fiction and through George's denial of a self which had led him earlier to speak as powerfully at the bar of history as any European freedom fighter.

For the climactic chapter of ***Clotel,*** in which the heroine takes her own life rather than return to slavery, the moral and topographical scene has been fully set. Clotel is imprisoned, says Brown, "midway between the capitol at Washington and the president's house" (***Clotel,*** 215). When she jumps to her death from the Long Bridge over the Potomac, this formula is repeated. Clotel hopes to escape: "But God by his Providence had otherwise determined. He had determined that an appalling tragedy should be enacted that night, within plain sight of the President's house and the capitol of the Union" (***Clotel,*** 217). Clotel is midway between the president's house, where once her father had lived, and the Capitol, which gives expression in stone and mortar to the Declaration of Independence. This irony leads William Wells Brown to repeat once again, as he never tires of doing, the American paradox: "Thus died Clotel, the daughter of Thomas Jefferson, a president of the United States; a man distinguished as the author of the Declaration of American Independence" (***Clotel,*** 218). Brown's anger and frustration spill over once he has killed his heroine. He takes up the theme that Americans have the greatest admiration for all the world's freedom fighters, except for black American freedom fighters. "Had Clotel escaped from oppression in any other land, in the disguise in which she fled from the Mississippi to Richmond, and reached the United States, no honour within the gift of the American people would have been good enough to have been heaped upon the heroic woman," he writes (***Clotel,*** 218). He is angry that having no tears for Clotel, the American people "have tears to shed over Greece and Poland; they have an abundance of sympathy for 'poor Ireland'; they can furnish a ship of war to convey the Hungarian refugees from a Turkish prison to the 'land of the free and the home of the brave'" (***Clotel,*** 218). His heroine is buried in a riverbank without inquest or religious service; and yet, he says, she is a woman who, "if she had been born in any other land but that of slavery, would have been honoured and loved" (***Clotel,*** 218-219).

The energy Brown brought to the expression of this paradox arose from the moral contexts which conditioned his own narrative and life. These can now themselves be seen to be paradoxical. He had learned his ideals within the world of the plantation and of hired service, where he found these ideals systematically violated; but having adopted them under such adverse conditions, he would not abandon his ideals about the nature of men and women, about heroes and heroines, about the virtues of love, loyalty, generosity, and sacrifice, about the life well led. When in 1834 the man escaped from the morally bleak world of the slave owner, William Wells Brown carried with him little more than this orthodox moral freight, which endorsed a traditional right and wrong, a traditional virtue and vice. The Declaration of American Independence remained his statement of the politically ideal. Brown quoted Jefferson against Jefferson, but Brown did not propose to devalue the language of the American creed he was resolved by insistent use to defend the right of force against American violations of the creed, to give the creed its full meanings, and to make its language include black as well as white.

Perhaps William Wells Brown should have resisted these meanings and this language and worked with a mythology that did not lead him constantly to contradiction and paradox. But his writings insist that he was an American, and he would not forgo that rich poetry, language, and rhetoric which any American could and can adopt. The language went before him and made him what he was. He could no more remake the language than any other user could remake the language. More important, he did not *want* to remake the language. He wanted to talk about America in America's language, and he did so always with a sense of how it mocked him even as it spoke. One hundred and fifty years later the language has been remade by history and by politics and by the accumulation of personal interventions. These amount to little on their own, but in time and with sufficient number they can reshape the moral dialect of a language. The twentieth-century reader can then see the limitations that the language had for Brown perhaps more clearly than he could himself. What today's reader cannot see are limitations of contemporary language which will no doubt be obvious to readers in another one hundred and fifty years' time.

For students of American studies, the American paradox is so familiar that it has become a truism, and no student is without a ready explanation of how Jefferson could say one thing and live another. But William Wells Brown did not work out any solution to the paradox, nor did he seem to want to. Rather he seemed to wish to exist at the center of the contradiction, to continue to experience its anger, grief, and frustration, and constantly to expose his white readership to this moral anguish. Perhaps he believed that this witness to suffering should, would, must bring about the conversion of his readers. In the preface to ***Clotel*** Brown pitted one set of white readers against another, hoping that British readers would be so moved by the moral paradox of their former colony that British public opinion would move to influence American public opinion. Brown believed the English to be free of racial prejudice. "Hatred to oppression is so instilled into the minds of the people in Great Britain," he wrote in ***Three Years in Europe,*** "that it needs little to arouse their enthusiasm to its highest point; yet they can scarcely comprehend the real condition of the slaves of the United States." (***Europe,*** 247).

But there was a lesson here that Brown was not learning, both about the British and to some extent about the Americans. His inference that the British were not racists in the 1850s was not borne out by their behavior in India and Africa. William Wells Brown's was a strong test, and the willingness of the British to shake his hand, welcome him to their homes, and have him at their tables could not be denied, but it was at the same time a partial test. It might mean that the British were free of racial prejudice, but it might also mean that the British rarely met cultivated Americans of African descent, that they did not feel any immediate interest threatened by Brown's presence, and that they could gain considerably in moral and political capital by investing in his friendship. This is not to say a lot about the British or any other people. It has the perhaps unpalatable consequence that the Americans are to be judged as no better and no worse than the British in general, though they were far worse to William Wells Brown in particular.

He was angered on the one hand by the American celebration of European liberationists such as John Mitchel of Ireland and Louis Kossuth of Hungary and on the other hand by American persecution of fugitive liberationists such as himself and Frederick Douglass. Yet William Wells Brown appeared to share the prejudice of the English against Disraeli, whom he called, as they did, "the Jew," and of whom, in ***Three Years in Europe,*** he gave a pointed present-tense description in a midnight sitting of the House of Commons: "There sits Disraeli, amongst the tories. Look at the Jewish face, those dark ringlets hanging round that marble brow. When on his feet, he has a cat-like, stealthy step; always looks on the ground when walking . . . is believed to be willing to support any measures, however sweeping and democratical, if by doing so he could gratify his ambition" (***Europe,*** 288, 292). Brown's hostility can be accounted for on political grounds, but his expression of it resorted to stereotypical comments on Jewish looks and behavior. The admiration for liberty expressed by those who gave receptions for Louis Kossuth in 1851 were less abstract celebrations of political ideals than Americans celebrating what they thought were mirror images of themselves, so that they could once again celebrate their own worth and history. It was the establishment of their own republic and the overthrowing of their own tyrant that made them wild for Louis Kossuth, though neither they nor he would have been too conscious of this.

By 1854 William Wells Brown had been five years in England. Of this exile he wrote: "I had become so well acquainted with the British people and their history, that I had begun to fancy myself an Englishman by habit, if not by birth" (***Europe,*** 303). Brown was becoming an Englishman by self-adoption, and in so doing he was repeating a process of self-discovery, self-creation, and self-invention that had been a vital part of his life as a slave and as an American. Identification with his native land was always one that he made with difficulty. "I recommenced," he wrote of that period when he was steeling himself to cross the Atlantic, "with palpitating heart the preparation to return to my nativeland. Nativeland! How harshly that word sounds to my ears" (***Europe,*** 303). Indeed, earlier in this book he had begun to refer to England as his "fatherland," exactly as many a white New Englander or Virginian did. (***Europe,*** 161). William Wells Brown identified nationally with the English because they did not reject him racially. Brown had a white father and English ancestors, and there was no reason why he should not claim the link, along with New Englanders, with what Nathaniel Hawthorne called their "Old Home."

On his arrival in Philadelphia after his return from London in 1854, he was told that he could not board the omnibus with his two white companions when they left the ship. "Had I been an escaped felon, like John Mitchel, no one would have questioned my right to a seat in a Philadelphia omnibus," he wrote (***Europe,*** 312). John Mitchel, the Irish agitator and the author of *Jail Journal,* a text beloved of Irish freedom fighters, had just escaped to the United States, where he was eventually to buy a farm and slaves in the South and settle down to a more prosperous and less arduous life than the English had allowed him in his native land. Almost from the day of his arrival in the United States, Mitchel declared himself a strenuous opponent of abolition. One country's freedom fighter was another's tyrant. Brown constantly pointed up the paradox that men and women are inconsistent in their heroism. It troubled him deeply, as it troubles all idealists who want to make out of single human beings consistent persons to admire consistently. It remains a fact that in 1834 William Wells Brown's Black Columbiad into the New World of the northern United States brought him from the moral clarities of slavedom and into the moral contradictions of freedom. It still remains a fact that in 1776 it was a slave owner who wrote the Declaration of Independence. And it still remains a fact that in 1492 Columbus did not know where he had arrived and was forever to believe that he had found the edge and the boundary of Asia, the continent of tyranny, whereas in fact he had stumbled upon the edge and the boundary of America, the continent of liberty.

Notes

1. William Wells Brown, *Clotel; or the President's Daughter: A Narrative of Slave Life in the United States* (London: Partridge & Oakey, 1853). All further references will be cited by page in the text.
2. William Wells Brown, *Three Years in Europe; or, Places I Have Seen and People I Have Met* (London: C. Gilpin, 1853), p. 297. All further references will be cited by page in the text.
3. William Wells Brown, *Narrative of William Wells Brown, an American Slave. Written by Himself. With Additions by the Rev. Samuel Green,* (London: W. Tegg & Co., 1853), p. 13. All further references will be cited by page in the text.
4. William Wells Brown, *The Black Man: His Antecedents, His Genius, and His Achievements* (Boston: James Redpath, 1863), pp. 18-19. All further references will be cited by page in the text.
5. William Edward Farrison, *William Wells Brown: Author and Reformer* (Chicago: University of Chicago Press, 1969), p. 14.

Paul Gilmore (essay date 1997)

SOURCE: "'De Genewine Artekil': William Wells Brown, Blackface Minstrelsy, and Abolitionism," in *American Literature,* Vol. 69, No. 4, December, 1997, pp. 743-80.

[*In the following essay, Gilmore examines how the popular minstrel show became for Brown a forum for constructing a "viable representative black manhood" and analyzes* Clotel *for its representations of race and gender.*]

In 1856, in addition to continuing to deliver lectures, former slave and "professional fugitive" William Wells Brown began to read dramatic pieces of his own composition at antislavery meetings.[1] His first play—the first play known to have been written by an African American—was entitled either ***The Dough Face*** (a common epithet for "Yankees") or ***Experience; or, How to Give a Northern Man a Backbone*** and provided a satirical reply to Boston clergyman Nehemiah Adams's proslavery *A South-Side View of Slavery* (1854).[2] There is no extant text of this play, but two years later Brown published ***The Escape; or, A Leap for Freedom,*** another dramatic piece he often delivered to antislavery audiences. One of the central characters of ***The Escape*** is Cato, a slave characterized in the first two acts as a comic buffoon who toadies to his master and spies on his fellow slaves. In the second scene of the first act, Brown dramatizes Cato in an incident that he claimed was autobiographical and that he had already used in his novel ***Clotel*** (1853): when Cato is left to treat slaves for his doctor-owner, in a bit of slapstick humor he accidentally pulls out the wrong tooth of a fellow slave. In the third act, however, Brown reveals a different side of Cato when the slave is left alone: "Now, ef I could only jess run away from ole massa, an' get to Canada wid Hannah, den I'd show 'em who I was." At this point in his dramatic readings, the light-skinned and eloquent Brown would, after a soliloquy full of malapropisms and dialect, break into an antislavery song set to the minstrel standard "Dandy Jim"—Cato's "moriginal hyme"—which Brown had already published as part of his ***Anti-Slavery Harp*** (1848):[3]

> Come all ye bondmen far and near,
> Let's put a song in massa's ear,
> It is a song for our poor race,
> Who're whipped and trampled with disgrace.
>
> CHORUS
> My old massa tells me, Oh,
> This is a land of freedom, Oh;
> Let's look about and see if it's so,
> Just as massa tells me, Oh.[4]

As one contemporary reviewer put it, at such moments "you lose sight of the speaker" and in place of the educated Brown see the caricatured Cato.[5] This moment epitomizes Brown's performance of blackness—essentially a putting on of blackface—and is emblematic of how black abolitionists like Brown were necessarily engaged with blackface minstrelsy, the most popular entertainment form of the time.[6] Whether in narratives, lectures, or fiction, professional fugitives were called upon to prove their authenticity by providing, as Frederick Douglass recalled his white supporters putting it, "a *little* plantation manner of speech."[7] At the same time, however, black abolitionists were expected to mirror the ideal traits of white manhood—intelligence, literacy, eloquence, and self-restraint—in order to exemplify black capacity for freedom. The professional fugitive was, in essence, required to embody simultaneously the social meanings of blackness and whiteness—to be both the illiterate plantation darkey of the minstrel stage and an eloquent defender of his race.

I will use this episode from ***The Escape*** as a starting point for reading Brown's ***Clotel***—the first novel by an African American—as a reworking of the ways both the minstrel show and the antislavery movement constructed strict racial definitions through their display of race as a matter of masquerade. As in Cato's scene from ***The Escape,*** Brown "blacks up" in ***Clotel*** by invoking minstrel show stereotypes when fictionalizing incidents from his own life through dark black male characters. Through multiple blackface characters, Brown links antislavery and minstrelsy, highlighting the antislavery possibilities in minstrelsy. Brown defended his appropriation of such theatrical effects as a way to gain financial and popular support: "People will pay to hear the Drama that would not give a cent in an anti-slavery meeting."[8] Nevertheless, he did not turn to the minstrel show simply because of its popularity, but because in the early 1850s minstrelsy provided perhaps the best forum through which to construct a viable representative black manhood. For Brown, the minstrel show offered particularly expansive representational possibilities because its commercialized images foregrounded the slippage between performative and essential notions of blackness and manliness.

In both abolitionism and the minstrel show, ideas about gender were intrinsic to the production of race as a sort of mask. The minstrel show was obsessed with the "black" male body, producing it as the embodiment of both a hypermasculine bestiality and a sentimental, effeminate childishness; antislavery rhetoric consistently circulated around one of two notions: either the proposition that slavery's chief crime was the destruction of "true" gender relations based in the domestic family unit or the idea that the effeminate, more spiritual African race should be saved from the masculine, aggressively materialistic Anglo-Saxon one. Despite important political and iconic differences, the economies of race and gender at play in the minstrel show and the most prominent antislavery forms similarly equated manhood with whiteness; in this way, both forums attempted to use gender distinctions to anchor the slipperiness of race. But both also depended on displaying gender as a matter of performance. Through his redeployment of minstrel tropes, Brown reveals how the markers of manliness and whiteness were dependent upon and constantly in play with those of blackness and femininity, so that gender and racial markers were at once strictly defined and, to a limited extent, transmutable. In writing the first African American novel, Brown turns to fiction not to escape stereotyped black representations, but to negotiate the objectification and commodification of the black image by revealing its instability. In doing so, he turns the abolitionist platform into a minstrel stage and the minstrel stage into an abolitionist platform, thus revealing the logic of each.[9]

"The Blacking Process"

The parallel courses of the minstrel show and abolitionism begin in the early 1830s. White actors had appeared in blackface on the American stage as early as a 1769 production of *The Padlock,* but the minstrel craze did not begin in earnest until T. D. Rice "jumped Jim Crow," first in the old northwest (perhaps Cincinnati, Pittsburgh, or Louisville), sometime between 1829 and 1831, and then on the New York stage in 1832. At essentially the same time that Rice was first performing Jim Crow, the immediate emancipation movement emerged onto the political scene, inaugurated by William Lloyd Garrison's founding of *The Liberator* in 1831 and following on the heels of David Walker's *Appeal* (1829) and Nat Turner's revolt (1831).[10] By the late 1830s, the demand for "black" male bodies had increased significantly—in the slave markets of the old southwest as laborers, in theaters and other entertainment sites as blackface performers, and in the abolitionist movement as antislavery lecturers.[11] What these sites had in common was a focus upon the black male body in slavery, on its status as an economic "article." Both the abolitionist platform and the minstrel stage attempted to invoke the "reality" of the Southern plantation by capturing and reproducing the "truth" of black life in the slave South. Neither minstrel shows nor abolitionism, however, focused exclusively on blacks in the South. Minstrel shows combined representations of the plantation slave Jim Crow with those of the Northern dandy Zip Coon; abolitionists demonstrated the connection between slavery in the South and racial prejudice in the North. Yet when defending their claims to authenticity by citing experience as the basis for their testimony or representations, both abolitionism and the minstrel show consistently set that experience either in the South or in some border region that granted access to the South.

In attempting to reveal "American Slavery As It Is," both the minstrel show and the antislavery movement produced and exploited what one abolitionist called "the public['s] . . . itching ears to hear a colored man speak, and particularly a *slave.*"[12] As antislavery groups began to employ black men to give "authentic" testimony about slavery in the late 1830s and early 1840s, minstrel performers began to claim that they gave a "true" picture of African American life through skits and "genuine" songs and dances.[13] In 1842 and 1843 western New York witnessed both the beginning of William Wells Brown's career as an antislavery agent and what Edwin Christy claimed was the first complete minstrel show. While Brown and other fugitive slaves tried to represent black manhood to white Northern audiences through their experiences in the slave South, ads and reviews proclaimed that white performers like Christy, Rice, and Dan Emmett were "the negro, par excellence," "the best representative of our American negro," "the perfect representative of the Southern Negro Character."[14] The minstrel show spectacularized "black" bodies for commercial purposes; antislavery groups put ex-slaves on display—"curiosit[ies] from the South," "specimen[s] of the fruits of the infernal system of slavery"—primarily for political ends.[15] Yet the representations of black character staged by each were often similar. The minstrel show has most often been characterized as an extremely racist caricature of blacks and black lifeways that served to legitimate slavery and racial prejudice, but as scholars like Eric Lott and Robert Toll have argued, despite its racist content the minstrel show was a complicated production in which various, at times contradictory, racial and political logics came into play. In fact, as Toll has pointed out, the minstrel show, at least prior to 1850 or so, "presented virtually every argument abolitionists used."[16] The emergence of these arguments in the minstrel show points towards a deeper connection between the minstrel show and abolitionism, specifically, the way in which both the minstrel show and antislavery rhetoric linked the construction of racial and gender distinctions to racial and gender confusion.

It was these representational limitations and possibilities that Brown faced in writing the first African American novel. Inspired by the phenomenal success of Harriet Beecher Stowe's *Uncle Tom's Cabin* (1852), Brown wrote ***Clotel*** in 1853 while living in England as an exile from the Fugitive Slave Law of 1850.[17] Rather than being, as its title implies, a coherent narrative consistently centered on Clotel, the president's daughter, Brown's novel is a fragmented, episodic overview of slavery from Virginia to New Orleans to Mississippi.[18] Part of its patchwork quality is due to Brown's incorporation of stories from his ***Original Panoramic Views*** of slavery (1850) and his travel book, ***Three Years in Europe*** (1852), incidents from his slave narrative (1847), and whole sections lifted verbatim from Lydia Maria Child's "The Quadroons" (1842). While Brown ostensibly focuses on the histories of Currer, her daughters by Thomas Jefferson, Clotel and Althesa, and her granddaughters—all beautiful mulattas who, with one exception, come to tragic ends—he does so through a series of often disconnected (or only slightly connected) scenes reminiscent of the segmented program of a minstrel show. In these episodes Brown not only recalls the minstrel show's formal aspects but also introduces a number of minstrel-like male characters who form a thematic line parallel to the tragic mulatta stories. While the impact of slavery on the "fairer" sex—and in this novel they always are fairer—provides Brown's starting point, he doubles the racial confusion caused by his apparently white but really black heroines through a number of black male characters who, by invoking and reworking the minstrel show, similarly reveal the markers of their blackness as a matter of performance.[19] By incorporating the more "masculine" form of the minstrel show into his sentimental tragic mulatta stories, Brown uncovers the performative nature of race and gender in both abolitionism and minstrelsy while negotiating the ways in which such constructions both created strict equations of gender and race and allowed a certain space within which to rearticulate those equations.

Following an introductory third-person **"Narrative of the Life and Escape of William Wells Brown,"** Brown opens the novel itself by setting up these two narrative lines, distinguishing between the "fearful increase of half whites" like his heroines and himself and "the real Negro," who "does not amount to more than one in every four of the slave population."[20] This distinction first arises in the diegesis following the sale of Currer and her daughters in an auction block scene set in Virginia. When taken south via the Mississippi River, Currer meets Pompey, the personal slave of the slave trader Walker. Pompey's duties include "getting the Negroes ready for market" as they are transported down the river (70). In his introductory narrative, Brown recounts how he was hired out to a slave trader—also named Walker—who would buy gangs of slaves in Missouri and then transport them down the river to New Orleans. One of Brown's jobs under the "soul-driver" was "to prepare the old slaves for market." In doing so he had to shave old men and "pluck out the grey hairs where they were not too numerous; where they were, he coloured them with a preparation of blacking. . . . After having gone through the blacking process, they looked ten or fifteen years younger" (21). Pompey, who "clearly showed that he knew what he was about," has similar duties and instructs the slaves that they "must grease dat face an make it look shiney" when they go into the market (70). Neither Brown's "blacking process" nor Pompey's "greas[ing]" up is exactly equivalent to the corking of the minstrel show, but in his narrative Brown goes on to recount having to set slaves in the New Orleans market "to dancing, some to jumping, some to singing, and some to playing cards . . . to make them appear cheerful and happy" (*N,* 194). What Pompey's "greas[ing]" up and Brown's "blacking process" indicate is the constructedness of the black body as a commodity form. Slaves are not simply what they appear to be on the auction block; rather, they must be coerced into performing their roles as valued (because of their youth, demeanor, and strength) objects.

Yet this implicit recognition of the performative nature of those traits most valued in the marketplace does not reveal race as an illusion. Instead, it seems to lead to strict racial distinctions.[21] Brown notes that Pompey is, like all other male slave characters in ***Clotel*** (with one exception), "of real Negro blood." He "was of low stature, round face, and, like most of his race, had a set of teeth, which for whiteness and beauty could not be surpassed; his eyes large, lips thick, and hair short and woolly." Pompey "would often say, when alluding to himself, 'Dis nigger is no countefit; he is de genewine artekil'" (70-71). Yet Pompey, like Brown, is a master of counterfeiting, especially the counterfeiting of such valuable "articles" as slaves. This episode demonstrates that *appearing* as the "genewine artekil," like Pompey, involves masquerade, essentially putting on blackface; it reveals race as an illusion, as a mask that one puts on, while acknowledging the ways in which that mask makes race very real. What then does it mean for the light-skinned Brown to fictionalize himself in basically the same way, blacking himself up as a character (Pompey) described as a minstrel caricature? In narrating his own complicity with a slave driver in the form of a caricatured black figure, Brown could be, and often has been, accused of being "colorist"—of espousing the idea that the worst slaves were the "real Negro[es]" and that the ones most deserving and capable of freedom and its responsibilities were light-skinned, like his mulatta heroines and himself.[22] I think that Brown is pursuing a much subtler point. While Pompey's actions show no resistance to slavery, other blackface characters in the novel complicate the idea of his complicity by forming a composite representative black male character who resists slavery through acts of subterfuge and masquerade. By describing the submission and resistance of his male slaves as different masks—as different ways of blacking up—Brown demonstrates both how masquerade creates them as "genewine artekil[s]" through strict racial definitions and how the performative nature of that masquerade allows them to redefine what it means to be a "genewine" black man.

Through these multiple black men, Brown reveals a different face of the caricature of the happy black slave. Jean Fagan Yellin places Brown's characterization of these figures within the trickster tradition in African American culture.[23] I am more interested in the ways in which Brown was invoking and critiquing the minstrel show. This is not to say that Brown was not drawing upon African American traditions of the trickster figure; rather, it is to insist on the ways in which representations of such "folk" figures were already mediated by mass cultural representations.[24] Because of this mediation, the slave per se could not be represented. Brown frequently described this problem in his lectures: "I may try to represent to you Slavery as it is . . . yet we shall all fail to represent the real condition of the Slave. . . . Slavery has never been represented; Slavery never can be represented. . . . The Slave cannot speak for himself." At the same time, however, Brown realized that on the abolitionist stage he "represent[ed]" the "system of Slavery."[25] Or, as he put it in another lecture, "I stand here as the representative of the slave to speak for those who cannot speak for themselves."[26] In attempting to "speak for" the slaves still in bondage, the ex-slave entered into public debates over race and slavery. But to do so he had to cast off the markers of both his past enslavement and his racial difference and take up the language and figures of the dominant culture.[27] Through the minstrel show, Brown was able to reclaim the blackness that he had had to abandon in order to enter the public sphere.[28] In this way, he was able to produce a model of black manhood that could be read as representative of slaves in general, even while undermining any simple notion of "the Slave." In ***Clotel,*** Brown recognizes and demonstrates the possible uses and limitations of reappropriating minstrel figures for explicitly antislavery purposes, but his appropriation does not amount to the complete transformation of a monolithically negative form. Instead, Brown is able to use minstrelsy for his antislavery purposes because of the ambivalence within the form itself—because of the ways in which the minstrel show, in both negative and positive ways, mirrored the representational logic and problematic of the abolitionist platform. Brown does not undermine the minstrel show in order to reveal a "true" representation of black manhood; rather, he undermines the idea of one authentic representation of black manhood by insisting on the instability of both white and black manhood and by pointing to the ways in which race and gender were always being performed and being performed together.[29]

"And So Did I Pretend"

Although not strictly a masculine affair, the minstrel show centered on the interplay between markers of black and white manhood. As Eric Lott has demonstrated, the "main achievement" of the minstrel show's white male audiences and performers was the "simultaneous production and subjection of black maleness."[30] Lott and historians such as David Roediger have described how the minstrel show engendered the formation of a Northern white working-class male subculture that gave voice to some distinctly working-class concerns.[31] I am primarily concerned, however, with how Brown was able to use the minstrel show for antislavery ends because of the ways in which it staged blackness in conjunction with characteristics of dominant (white middle-class) ideas of manhood, which, according to a certain antislavery logic, blacks had to demonstrate in order to prove their humanity.[32]

Many blackface acts and performers did begin in working-class oriented theaters in areas like the Bowery in New York. But by the end of the 1840s, as Carl Wittke argues, minstrel shows had begun "to attract the patronage of the most respectable citizens," in part because they had become one of the chief attractions of the more bourgeois environs—like Barnum's American Museum—of Broadway.[33] In fact, discourse around the minstrel show is striking for its emphasis on how everybody was under its spell: "Mr. T. D. Rice made his debut in a dramatic sketch entitled 'Jim Crow,' and from that moment everybody was 'doing just so,' and continued 'doing just so' for months, and even years afterward. Never was there such an excitement in the musical or dramatic world"; "Next day found the song of Jim Crow, in one style of delivery or another, on everybody's tongue. Clerks hummed it . . . artisans thundered it . . . boys whistled it . . . ladies warbled it . . . and house-maids repeated it"; "The schoolboy whistled the melody. . . . The ploughman checked his oxen. . . . Merchants and staid professional men . . . were sometimes seen . . . to unbend their dignity. . . . [It was] sung in the parlor, hummed in the kitchen, and whistled in the stable."[34] Still others emphasized the minstrel show's appeal to both cultural elites and the working class: "Many of the most fashionable families attend. . . . Negro melodies are the very democracy of music."[35]

While it appears that working-class men often did make up the majority of the audience in antebellum minstrel shows, and minstrel shows often did serve to enunciate working-class concerns and interests, minstrel shows were far from exclusively working-class forums. Although some diversification along class and gender lines did occur in New York (more "respectable" shows on Broadway catered to a more middle-class audience with Stephen Foster-type sentimental tunes, rowdier shows in the Bowery retained more sexual double entendre and humor), the minstrel show and its basic conventions, its racial masquerade and caricatures of simple, happy slaves, had by 1850 come to structure the ways in which a broad cross section of white Northerners confronted and constructed ideas of black character and understood and lived their own raced and gendered identities. Even though middle-class reformers attacked minstrel shows for their rowdiness and lurid humor, the minstrel show, as Roediger acknowledges, not only served as a site for the production of working-class manhood but also made "special appeals to those in the West and some in the respectable middle classes and above."[36]

Specifically, contemporary critics celebrated the minstrel show as an antidote to or an escape from the increasingly complex and disciplined world arising with industrial market capitalism and urbanization.[37] By providing white audiences with models of "African nature . . . full of poetry and song," minstrel shows could revitalize an overly refined and business-oriented white existence. Because "[African] joy and grief are not pent up in the heart, but find instant expression in their eyes and voice," "these simple children of Africa," though "[i]nferior to the white race in reason and intellect," offer a valuable "lesson" in "lighten[ing] the anxiety and care which brood on every face and weigh on every heart."[38] In the figure of the simple plantation darky, audience members could appreciate the joys of a bodily existence undisciplined by the market and developing ideals of decorum, while at the same time maintaining the distance from that bodily enjoyment mandated by the emerging discourse of bourgeois manhood.[39]

In order to maintain the bodily (dis)engagement necessary to appreciate the pleasures associated with these images of natural freedom in slavery without succumbing to them, the minstrel show oscillated between acknowledging its performative nature and claiming unmediated authenticity. Although critics admitted that "We at the North hear these songs only as burlesqued by our Negro Minstrels," commentary on the minstrel show often obscured the distinction between "Negro Minstrels" and "actual" "African[s]."[40] Numerous stories circulated about naive viewers who believed that the performers were "actually" black, a confusion that could easily spring from the ubiquitous references to white performers as "Negro songsters" or "Negro dancers."[41] But at the same time, performers and audiences emphasized the artifice of performances, the fact that underneath the burnt cork were white men: lyrics, skits, and sheet music illustrations made frequent references to the white identity of performers.[42] Accordingly, minstrel performers simultaneously displayed characteristics that marked them as black and white. And by extension, in attending minstrel shows and learning the "lesson[s]" of "black" bodily and emotional freedom from such "Negro" entertainers, white audience members were imagined to replicate this logic by internalizing the characteristics of blackness while remaining "white" themselves: audience members "lighten[ed]" their "brood[ing]" "face[s]" by vicariously "blacking up." In this way, minstrelsy was driven by an oscillation between the celebration and denigration of black men, a dance of identification and differentiation that simultaneously foregrounded and disavowed the interpenetration of notions of white and black manhood.

Accounts of the most famous black minstrel entertainer of the period, William Henry Lane, demonstrate how this oscillation between authenticity and artifice produced strict racial distinctions and at the same time rendered those distinctions nonsensical. The story of Lane, who like Brown lived in England from 1848 to 1852, exemplifies the dual movement of the minstrel show that allowed Brown to articulate his antislavery argument. In the early 1840s, because audiences would "have resented . . . the insult of being asked to look at the dancing of a real negro," Lane "greased" and "rubbed" his face "with a new blacking of burnt cork" before appearing on stage. According to this contemporary account, although "a genuine negro"—"the genuine article"—Lane needed to become a "seeming counterfeit" in order to gain a place on the minstrel stage.[43] This description highlights the way in which the minstrel show produced authenticity through "counterfeit[s]."[44] Lane could only be accepted as black on the minstrel stage if he appeared to be a white man in blackface. Just as Pompey had to "grease" the faces of slaves and use a little "blacking" to make his owner's slaves "de genewine artekil[s]" for the slave market, Lane had to become a "counterfeit" in order to reveal himself as "the genuine article." In order to appear real—and gain commercial success—Lane had to perform the blackness that he supposedly embodied naturally.

As Lane's fame grew, his "actual" race became well known, and apparently he began to appear on stage without blacking up. But even without blackface, the type of imitation and repetition staged by the minstrel show rendered Lane's race simultaneously a mask and his essential identity. According to flyers from the period, at the climax of his performances, Lane would perform an "Imitation Dance . . . in which he will give correct Imitation Dances of all the principal Ethiopian Dancers in the United States. After which he will give an imitation of himself—and then you will see the vast difference between those that have heretofore attempted dancing and this Wonderful Young Man."[45] In this series of imitations, as he imitates white men in blackface who claim they are imitating black men, Lane ends up imitating himself, conflating the authentic and the counterfeit and making any idea of the authentic appear bankrupt. This multiplication of Jim Crow-like images is at the center of the most famous description of Lane's dancing, that of Charles Dickens. In his *American Notes* (1842), Dickens describes seeing Lane during a trip into the underworld of the Five Points district of New York: "the greatest dancer known. He never leaves off making queer faces . . . dancing with two left legs, two right legs, two wooden legs, two wire legs, two spring legs—all sorts of legs and no legs. . . . He finishes . . . with the chuckle of a million of counterfeit Jim Crows, in one inimitable sound!"[46] In Lane's performances, his legs begin multiplying until it seems he has no legs at all, and his multiple "queer faces" leave him with no "real" face, making him at once "inimitable" and "a million of counterfeit Jim Crows."

Lane's performances verge on the unreal, as he becomes a counterfeit of a counterfeit and his body both multiplies and disappears. This is not to say, however, that the unreality created through this multiplication of images undermines the idea of authenticity. Rather, while it does deconstruct the possibility of finding a stable center of authenticity, it also enables the authentic to be re-invoked. Reviews used Lane's imitations of imitations not to reveal how the blackness he represented was also an imitation, but to argue for the purity of previous dancers: "the Nigger Dance is a reality. . . . [Otherwise] how could Juba enter into their wonderful complications so naturally?" Lane was able to copy other dancers "so naturally" because they had reproduced "real" black dancing practices in their "Nigger Dance[s]" so well. Lane's performances were "far above the common performances of the mountebanks who give imitations of American and Negro character" because he embodied "an ideality . . . that makes his efforts at once grotesque and poetical, without losing sight of the reality of representation."[47] Through his performances, Lane both places the idea of authentic black identity into question and provides a possible site for its reinterpretation. His example points up how the minstrel show produced race and gender as authentic—as real—by repeatedly staging their defining traits as matters of masquerade.[48]

As Lane's story also demonstrates, the minstrel show simultaneously produced black men as white and white men as black, thus making the differential markers of white and black manhood interchangeable while creating notions of essential racial difference and authentic racial identity. Because minstrel performers embodied characteristics of both black and white manhood, the minstrel show at times staged "black" men who displayed characteristics of white manliness that blacks supposedly lacked. In particular, this slippage produced minstrel representations of the possibility of slave resistance even while the minstrel show as a whole actively discounted such possibilities. A number of minstrel songs actually constructed black resistance to slavery in a positive light. Early versions of "Jim Crow" raised the possibility of emancipation and slave revolt in reference to the Nullification crisis:

> Should dey get to fighting,
> Perhaps de blacks will rise,
> For deir wish for freedom,
> Is shining in deir eyes.
>
> . . . . .
>
> I'm for freedom,
> An for Union altogether,
> Aldough I'm a black man,
> De white is call'd my broder.[49]

This desire for freedom, by whatever means necessary, including violence, often appeared in the lyrics of early minstrel songs like "The Raccoon Hunt": "My ole massa dead and gone, / A dose of poison help him on / De debil say he funeral song."[50] Such moments depended upon racial slippage. In singing of slave resistance, the performer of "Jim Crow" is at once "black"—"I'm a black man"—and "white," or at least the white man's equal, his "broder."[51]

First performed in New York less than a year after Nat Turner's failed revolt, "Jim Crow" evokes the image of "the Spartacus of the Southampton revolt."[52] Turner's rebellion is explicitly celebrated in the song "Uncle Gabriel, the Darkey General," which conflated Turner's revolt and the Gabriel Prosser-led conspiracy of 1800: "He was the chief of the Insurgents, / Way down in Southampton. / Hard times in old Virginny." By simply invoking the memory of two of the best known American slave revolts, such songs gave evidence against the image of the happy plantation darky so central to Southern propaganda and many minstrel skits. Yet by referring to the slave leader as an "Uncle," and by focusing on his punishment—"And there they hung him and they swung him"—the song attempts to contain the specter of slave revolt by reinscribing black manhood as either submissive or disempowered.[53] In staging race and manliness as fluid and performed, the minstrel show, at least temporarily, enabled the union of blackness and manhood, pointing to a way of constructing an "authentic" black manhood through the instability of race and gender. In the slippage created by this constant repetition and performance of difference, the constant oscillation between whiteness and blackness, Brown was able to produce a representative black manhood through his "million of counterfeit Jim Crows."

In ***Clotel,*** Brown foregrounds the possibility of using the minstrel show to enunciate slave resistance in his characterization of Sam, the novel's second black male character. Pompey "*appeared* perfectly indifferent to the heartrending scenes" (70, emphasis added) of slavery and seemed simply to submit to its structures while displaying the stereotyped characteristics of the minstrel slave; yet Brown's description of him points toward the elements of masquerade in his appearance. With Sam, Brown turns that masquerade into an explicit critique of slavery. A slave with Currer on Reverend Peck's plantation in Mississippi, Sam is an earlier incarnation of ***The Escape***'s Cato. In the chapter "A Night in the Parson's Kitchen," Sam seems to be nothing more than comic relief in the form of a minstrel burlesque: he wishes he were lighter ("He was one of the blackest of his race" [131]), fawns over his master and mistress, treats his position in the household with an excess of pride and dignity, and is overly concerned with his dress ("he was seldom seen except in a ruffled shirt" [131]). Despite his ability to read, Sam still believes in fortune tellers, and Brown explicitly links his prejudice against blacks (he claims his mother was a mulatta) to "ignorance" (133). Finally, "A Night in the Parson's Kitchen" ends with Sam telling of his experience as a doctor's assistant, including the story of pulling the wrong tooth that Brown later used in ***The Escape***: "We once saw Sam taking out a tooth for one of his patients, and nothing appeared more amusing" (134). Through an illustration of minstrelized blacks and the use of the communal "we," Brown's novel stages a scene that could have come directly from a minstrel show, a skit that represents blacks as inherently comic and incapable of performing the more intellectual tasks involved in professions such as medicine.[54]

Up to this point Brown has shown his black male characters as buffoons and toadies who accept the master's ideology. Yet as he develops Sam more fully, "we" realize that we have seen only the stereotypical laughing black face, not the critical, freedom-yearning face that coexists with it. We next encounter Sam after Reverend Peck's death. As Peck's abolitionist daughter Georgiana and her friend Carlton walk over the plantation grounds trying to decide what to do with the slaves, they hear "[h]ow prettily the Negroes sing." After Georgiana informs Carlton that the slaves will stop singing if they realize they have an audience, the pair decide to remain secluded and "stop, and . . . hear this one." Leading the singing is Sam, and at first it seems that he is still the simple plantation darky who is "always on hand when there's any singing or dancing" (154). The setting of this song recalls Stephen Foster's minstrel standard "Massa's in De Cold Ground" (1852): "Down in the corn-field / Hear that mournful sound; / All de darkies am a weeping— / Massa's in de cold, cold ground."[55] But instead of expressing their sorrow and love for their master as Foster's song seems to do and as both the lovers and "we" the readers might expect, Sam and the other slaves celebrate their master's death, recounting his many cruelties and their own pretended sadness:

> He will no more trample on the neck of the slave;
> For he's gone where the slaveholders go.
>
> . . . . .
>
> Mr. Carlton cried, and so did I pretend;
> Young mistress very nearly went mad;
> And the old parson's groans did the heavens fairly rend;
> But I tell you I felt mighty glad.
>
> . . . . .
>
> He no more will hang our children on the tree,
> To be ate by the carrion crow;
> He no more will send our wives to Tennessee;
> For he's gone where the slaveholders go. (154-55)

Here, Brown redeploys the standard conceits of the minstrel show—slaves singing and dancing on the plantation—to uncover its antislavery possibilities. Brown's rewriting of Foster's song makes its possibly subversive meaning explicit. In Foster's song, "all de darkies am a weeping," yet the natural world, and specifically the mockingbird, with which blacks were often aligned in minstrel songs, is joyous—"mockingbird am singing, / Happy as de day am long." And though the "days were cold / . . . [and] hard" while master was still alive, now, "summer days am coming." Finally, Foster's song raises the possibility that the slaves are faking their sorrow in order to gain respite from work: "I cannot work before tomorrow, / Cayse de tear drops flow." Like other minstrel songs, "Massa's in De Cold Ground" depends on the slippage between characterizing its singers as childishly sentimental—as "black"—and cunningly subversive—as intelligent and courageous (or at least treacherous) *men.*[56] By making explicit this implied critique within minstrelsy, Brown shows another side of both the minstrelized Sam and the minstrel show itself. In particular, this scene demonstrates that the slave's submission cannot be taken at face value and that representations of the male slave depend on occasionally revealing his unexpected resistance to oppression. But what Brown also makes clear is that "from these unguarded expressions of the feelings of the Negroes" his two white abolitionist characters can "learn a lesson" (156). Specifically, what Carlton, Georgiana, and other abolitionists can learn is a different way of approaching one of the central problems of antislavery rhetoric, the problem of representing black manhood.

"A White Man . . . Within"

Antislavery rhetoric consistently spoke of the debilitating effects of slavery in gendered terms. During the antebellum period, rising bourgeois ideologies of the family foregrounded gender—as defined by strictly distinguished traits—as an essential quality of humanity. Being human meant being either a "true woman" or a "real man." Hence, as Kristin Hoganson has argued, despite its radical sexual politics, Garrisonian abolitionism attempted to show both how slavery deformed "true" gender relations and how blacks demonstrated their humanity by still maintaining these gender roles.[57] These contradictory impulses come together in the most famous antislavery topos—the ubiquitous "am I not a man and a brother"—which Brown used in both his ***Panoramic Views*** pamphlet and his ***Anti-Slavery Harp.*** The emblem emphasizes that the slave is a man—is human—while making its declaration in the form of a question that focuses on the disempowered and enchained figure of the unmanned male slave.[58] Although the accompanying text implies the slave's common manhood, the illustration strips the black man of the markers of manhood; with his body exposed both to the gaze of all onlookers and to the whips at his feet, his hands chained, his head turned up in supplication, the figure represents the black male as dependent upon the sympathy and good will of others, an object to be pitied and acted upon rather than a subject who acts. According to this logic, under slavery a man could not be a true man and a woman could not be a true woman. Yet abolitionists needed to show that blacks were capable of such gender identities. As Richard Yarborough has argued, "the crucial test of black fitness" for freedom came "to be whether or not black men were, in fact, what was conventionally considered 'manly.'"[59]

Abolitionists faced two primary problems in representing black manhood: first, slavery was constructed as antithetical to ideal manhood; second, because ideas of enslavement were intrinsic to the construction of blackness, blackness itself came to be seen as unmanly. The position of ex-slave orators highlights this first problem.[60] Professional fugitives like Brown displayed the markers of genteel middle-class manhood—intelligence, eloquence, and especially literacy—but in becoming educated they were seen as less and less representative of the majority of the slave population.[61] As Frederick Douglass recounts in his 1855 autobiography, "People doubted if I had ever been a slave. They said I did not talk like a slave, look like a slave, nor act like a slave. . . . '[H]e is educated, and is, in this, a contradiction of all the facts we have concerning the ignorance of the slaves.' Thus, I was in a pretty fair way to be denounced as an impostor."[62] And it was not just that the ex-slave did not mirror accepted images of the slave; ex-slaves themselves often interpreted their acquisition of freedom as a complete transformation of their old selves. Douglass's paradigmatic narrative underlines the gendered nature of this transformation. There he recounts that his resistance to Edward Covey not only "rekindled the few expiring embers of freedom" but also "revived within [him] a sense of [his] own manhood." For Douglass, regaining manhood meant that "however long I might remain a slave in form, the day had passed forever when I could be a slave in fact" and "that the white man who expected to succeed in whipping, must also succeed in killing me."[63] Through active, physical resistance to slavery, Douglass becomes a man by ceasing to be a slave.

Brown narrates similar feelings in his introduction to ***Clotel***: "I was no more a chattel, but a MAN. . . . The fact that I was a freeman—could walk, talk, eat, and sleep as a man, and no one to stand over me with the blood-clotted cowhide—all this made me feel that I was not myself" (34). But Brown also critiques Douglass's construction of a black voice and black manhood through physical resistance. In the second chapter of his 1847 narrative, Brown recounts his memories of a slave named Randall, who, like Douglass, "declare[d], that no white man should ever whip him—that he would die first" (*N,* 181). Randall staked his claim to manhood on physical resistance and thus was a slave only "in form." Yet rather than eventually escaping to freedom, Randall is finally "subdued" (*N,* 182) by the cruel overseer. In Brown's narrative, active resistance to the mechanisms of slavery does not make one a man, as Douglass insisted; instead it leads to one's being completely unmanned. Brown's critique of Douglass's model of black manhood points up the problem of representability. Douglass proves his own manhood through his resistance and eventual escape, but his narrative also emphasizes his exceptionalism. And this exceptionalism characterizes the majority of slaves as "brute[s]" who demonstrate their "want of manhood" in not making "at least one noble effort to be free."[64] As Douglass phrased it in his 1855 autobiography, "I was *nothing* before; I WAS A MAN NOW. . . . A man, without force, is without the essential dignity of humanity." Importantly, in this version of Douglass's autobiography his reclamation of manhood and freedom erases racial distinctions—"I now forgot my *roots,* and remembered my pledge to *stand up in my own defense.* . . . The very color of the man was forgotten."[65] At the moment of becoming a man, race disappears because achieving middle-class attributes of manliness—autonomy, freedom, self-control—was seen as antithetical to the servitude with which blackness had become so forcefully bound. It is only by denouncing his slave past that Douglass can fully become a man. In achieving freedom and the literacy and eloquence required to gain access to the public stage, the ex-slave was able to prove his manliness, but by doing so he could no longer be representative of black manhood; he might be black, but he was not "really" black, not like most blacks. As Frantz Fanon phrased it a century later, white acceptance was premised on the idea that "At bottom you are a white man," "You have nothing in common with real Negroes."[66]

In trying to prove black humanity by demonstrating black manhood, antislavery rhetoric did not simply face the problem that slavery seemed antithetical to physical self-possession, family protection, and powerful activity; rather, the supposed absence of these traits among slave men was consistently seen—often even by antislavery advocates—as characteristic of black men. According to this logic, blacks were not submissive because slavery made them so; they were naturally submissive.[67] The focus in antislavery fiction and forums on light-skinned characters and speakers highlights this problem. Certainly one of the reasons Brown and Douglass became so influential was because white abolitionists viewed their light complexions as both potentially more acceptable to the unconverted and proof of the sexual degradations of slavery.[68] But, as often happened in Brown's case, the light black spokesman's manly attributes—especially his eloquence and intelligence—were explained as coming simply from his white blood: "He is far removed from the black race, being just the 'color of mahogany,' and his distinct enunciation evidently showed that a white man 'spoke' within, although the words were uttered by the lips of a redeemed slave"; "eloquent, humorous and interesting, showing clearly the white blood of his father."[69] As Douglass put it, "an intelligent black man is always supposed to have derived his intelligence from his connection with the white race. To be intelligent is to have one's negro blood ignored."[70] In being recognized as intelligent and eloquent, the professional fugitive was accepted as manly, but his manhood made him "white."

This logic of mulatto exceptionalism—the idea that blacks displayed admirable traits because of their "Anglo-Saxon blood"—appears in gendered terms in abolitionist fiction. Attempts to reveal slaves as either true women or real men—attempts to engender the black body—often ended up turning that body white.[71] As Karen Sánchez-Eppler has put it more generally, "The problem of antislavery fiction is that the very effort to depict goodness in black involves the obliteration of blackness."[72] The central role of tragic mulatta figures in antislavery fiction in general and in ***Clotel*** in particular illustrates this problem. Such characters embodied the ideals of middle-class true womanhood and illustrated the dangers of slavery to the virtue and modesty deemed essential to this idealized femininity. Yet in rendering female slaves true women, such stories erased all but the most minute trace of their blackness.[73] A similar problem obtained in depicting male slaves in antislavery fiction. As Nancy Bentley has shown, black heroes of antislavery fiction who displayed the "masculine" traits of self-reliance and physical resistance to the degradations of slavery were almost invariably nearly white, like George Harris in Harriet Beecher Stowe's *Uncle Tom's Cabin.*[74] The contrast between such mulatto characters and black slaves distinguished fully gendered white slaves from more androgynous black characters. Specifically, mulatto heroes underlined a gendered racial distinction between the more active, masculine white race and the more passive, feminine black race.[75]

Even when writers characterized black men as heroes, they were burdened by this equation of race and gender. In

"The Heroic Slave" (1853), a fictionalized account of the 1841 slave revolt on board the *Creole,* Frederick Douglass attempts to depict Madison Washington as a traditional hero who retains a black identity. Douglass's story underlines, however, the ways in which the display of manliness racially transformed even an explicitly *black* man. Douglass first introduces Madison Washington by his voice, a move that denies his black body. When Washington appears, Douglass's first narrator describes him as "'black, but comely,'" with a "sable" "manly form."[76] While these descriptions stress the blackness of Washington's skin, the first begins to feminize his "manly form" with an adjective usually reserved for women and its allusion to the bride of Solomon.[77] More telling, in the second narrator's depiction of the key moment of the revolt aboard the *Creole,* Washington's heroism all but transmogrifies him into a white man: "I forgot his blackness. . . . It seemed as if the souls of both the great dead (whose names he bore) had entered him" (75). While this second white narrator's point has been to correct the "ignorance of the real character of *darkies* in general" (70) by showing their true nobility and courage, at the moment of these traits' clearest manifestation he erases not only Washington's black body but also his black soul. Douglass might be emphasizing the racism of his second narrator, but this moment clearly echoes Douglass's 1855 account of achieving manhood by fighting Covey: "[t]he very color of the man was forgotten." As the commentator on Brown's oratory might put it, both Douglass's and Washington's manliness reveal a white man acting from within.

In the early 1850s, to depict a black man as a man required either painting him white—as with mulatto heroes—or stripping off his blackness to reveal a white interior—as with Madison Washington.[78] But both solutions replicated the racial distinctions they attempted to question—whiteness made one a man, blackness, by itself, left one less than a man. In ***Clotel,*** however, Brown uses his mulatto hero, George Green, to point towards a way out of this conundrum. Specifically, George's story helps Brown expand and elaborate his understanding of race and gender as masquerade by revealing the performative nature of white manhood. Yet as with his black male slaves and mulatta heroines, Brown uses his mulatto hero not only to render racial lines fluid but also to demonstrate the ways in which the performance of race and gender made them real. By demonstrating the fictive nature of race and gender, Brown is able to construct black manhood as a reality. Brown introduces George Green near the end of the novel as both a participant in Nat Turner's rebellion and the betrothed of Clotel's daughter Mary. Like Stowe's rebellious George Harris, Green "was as white as most white persons" (224). Whereas Stowe saw slave rebellion arising from an "infusion of Anglo Saxon blood," Brown offers a more environmentalist understanding of his mulatto hero's rebelliousness.[79] Green's mixed blood does, in part, enable him to become an insurgent. But it does so because his complexion makes "his condition still more intolerable" (224)—both blacks and whites treat him harshly—and because it grants him greater opportunities for realizing what freedom means: "George's opportunities were far greater than most slaves'. Being in his master's house, and waiting on educated white people, he had . . . heard his master and visitors speak of the down-trodden and oppressed Poles. . . . [F]ired with love of freedom, and zeal for the cause of his enslaved countrymen, [he] joined the insurgents" (224).

Brown further undermines the idea that black rebelliousness arises from an "infusion of Anglo Saxon blood" by making it clear that Nat Turner—"respected by the whites, and loved and venerated by the Negroes"—was "a full-blooded Negro" (213). And, the only other slave rebel Brown mentions is the Maroon Picquilo, "a large, tall, full-blooded Negro, with a stern and savage countenance" (213). But Picquilo points up yet another problem of representing black male resistance. George—whether because of his greater educational opportunities or because of his "Anglo Saxon blood"—can denounce the slave system and cite European wars of liberation as examples for his own activities. Picquilo stands mute, "a bold, turbulent spirit" whose "revenge imbrued his hands in the blood of all the whites he could meet" (214). George rebels because of his "love of freedom"; Picquilo fights for "revenge" because of his "barbarous . . . character" (213-14). Picquilo becomes an animalistic spirit rising out of the Virginia swamps, the black, atavistic Nat, the mirror image of the submissive Sambo.[80] While white men became men by waging war for their freedom, black men who did the same were irrational primitive brutes.[81] Middle-class manhood was based upon the ideal of control over one's own body, and fighting for one's freedom—as Frederick Douglass did—could demonstrate this power. But unless it could be defended in rational terms, physical conflict came too close to undisciplined bodily expression, an attractive but threatening prospect. Because Picquilo cannot speak for himself, because he must always be represented, he cannot account for his actions. Readers might temporarily identify with Picquilo's embodiment of primitive manliness, his "savage" rebellion—as minstrel show audiences might have identified with the singer of "Uncle Gabriel"—but emerging discourses of manhood encouraged them to disavow such embodiment. While minstrel show representations of black resistance might similarly be interpreted as displaying blackness as atavistic, the minstrel show undermined any easy reading of this form of embodiment as essentially black, as anything more than yet another mask. Through its constant interplay of blackness and whiteness, the minstrel show made it unclear whose atavism was whose, whose body was out of control through rebellion and whose was the tool of rational and righteous revolt.

Brown uses George to point toward this kind of racial (and gender) confusion as an alternative to equating manhood with resistance—an equation that eventually turned the black male into a white man or a primitive brute. After George is sentenced to death for his part in the rebellion, Mary, while visiting him in prison, suggests that they exchange clothes so that he can leave the prison unnoticed as a woman. When eventually discovered, Mary will be punished but not executed, and George will have escaped. George finally accepts Mary's plan and succeeds in escaping (Mary is sold south for her part in the plan), but he tellingly must remain "in the dress of a woman" (229) until well into the free states.[82] Eventually George emigrates to England, where he becomes a successful clerk while passing for white. Through improbable plot twists, George meets Mary in France soon after she has become a widow, and the two are finally married. Brown's denouement underlines masquerade—both of a gendered and racial nature—as a route to achieving a freedom that regrounds the basis of manhood. It is by putting on a feminine face of obsequiousness and acceptance that the black man can eventually gain the markers of (white) manhood: economic and political freedom and a family truly his own. Brown shows that George's "white" manhood—his ability to resist slavery—depends on being a "black" woman, his ability to act as a "slave woman" (229). Through George's escape Brown underscores the ways in which race and gender—specifically white manhood—are matters of masquerade, while using that masquerade to create a representative black manhood.

Though antislavery rhetoric and conventions, like the minstrel show, relied on destabilizing racial and gender distinctions, their logic of revealing black men as truly "white" (whether spiritually or physically) maintained a basic racial equation of gender. Douglass's Madison Washington troubles distinctions between blackness and whiteness by containing both, but his whiteness still marks his manhood and resistance to slavery, his blackness his emasculating inability to escape. Brown, through his multiple minstrel "heroes" and through George Green's story of masquerade, not only destabilizes notions of blackness while conjuring up "authentic" representations of it; he also reveals the instability of whiteness and the dependence of white manhood on blackness. Brown suggests this interdependence not just through George Green's escape but also in his characterization of Sam. Sam acts as a matchmaker between Georgiana and Carlton, enabling a marriage that he knows must take place for their plan of emancipation to come to fruition. By standing in for the desire that Carlton's "high spirit" (161) will not allow him to speak of, Sam enables Carlton to escape pauperism and take possession of the markers of middle-class manhood: economic independence and a beautiful, religious wife. By granting him access to the body (the desires of which he cannot speak) as the minstrel show was imagined to do, Sam's agency allows Carlton to become a man. But Sam's actions also grant him access to manhood. By steering the couple together, Sam reveals his "general intelligence" (165) and is rewarded for his work by gaining a position of power in the new economic dispensation—he becomes the foreman over the incredibly productive, soon-to-be-freed slaves. Sam's intelligence and work earn him economic success and freedom, replicating the dream of self-made manhood upon which middle-class manhood was founded. By figuratively putting on blackface, Sam not only enables the flowering of white manhood but also demonstrates the possibilities of black manhood.[83]

Brown's multiple black male characters in ***Clotel*** reveal how the performative nature of both race and gender allowed the negotiation of a type of black manhood dependent upon covert resistance and isolated moments of subversion rather than on heroic but fatal attempts to prove manhood through physical rebellion. The masquerades of George, Sam, and other black male characters do not enable Brown's novel to escape the need to oscillate between blackness and whiteness in order to create black manhood; Sam, for example, sings his subversive song without a touch of dialect. Rather, ***Clotel*** emphasizes, through its invocation of the minstrel show, the way in which white manhood was similarly indebted to an oscillation between whiteness and blackness, thus demonstrating the instability of both race and manliness as markers of identity. While in early chapters Sam and Pompey appear to be simple buffoons, as the novel continues Brown shows that such a reading is one-dimensional because it neglects the critical, at times almost rebellious, side of these characters. By keeping both masks in play, Brown does not denounce the minstrelized face as untrue but prompts us to look beyond the buffoonery of such acts and see them as more than evidence of black inferiority or effeminacy. Like Lane's performances as Juba, Brown produces a plethora of "counterfeit Jim Crows"—Pompey, Sam, William, Jack, Cato—all of whom seem to be unreal reflections of one another while simultaneously being "de genewine artekil." Rather than attempting to substitute a singular "real" picture of slavery for the minstrel show's depiction, Brown multiplies minstrel images ad infinitum, rendering blackness unreal even as he redefines it. Through "real Negro" men—who are "real Negro" men through masquerade—Brown reveals to his white audience the numerous minute ways in which black men in slavery grasped power, if only temporarily, and hence reveals the ways in which black men conformed to middle-class ideas of manliness—and thus proved their humanity—even while remaining slaves. In this way he mirrors both the constant interplay of artifice and authenticity within the minstrel show *and* the minstrel show's own critique of slavery. By turning to the minstrel stage, Brown demonstrates the inherent instability of representations of race and gender and points towards the possibility of a representative black manhood that, while depending upon the instability of blackness and manhood, denies neither.

Notes

1. I take the term and idea of the "professional fugitive" (a way of designating former slaves who supported themselves through abolitionist activity) from Larry Gara, "The Professional Fugitive in the Abolition Movement," *Wisconsin Magazine of History* 48 (spring 1965): 196-204. The best overall study of black abolitionists is still Benjamin Quarles's *Black Abolitionists* (New York: Oxford Univ. Press, 1969). For a general history of free blacks in the antebellum North, see Leon F.

Litwack, *North of Slavery: The Negro in the Free States, 1790-1860* (Chicago: Univ. of Chicago Press, 1961).

2. See William Edward Farrison, *William Wells Brown: Author and Reformer* (Chicago: Univ. of Chicago Press, 1969), 277-80.
3. Brown entitled this song "A Song for Freedom" in his *The Anti-Slavery Harp: A Collection of Songs For Anti-Slavery Meetings* (Boston: Bela Marsh, 1848), 37-38. This volume compiles a range of abolitionist songs (only a few of which Brown wrote), including "Get off the Track" (set to "Dan Tucker") and, in later editions, "The North Star" (set to "O, Susannah").
4. William Wells Brown, *The Escape; or, A Leap for Freedom* (1858), in *Black Theater, U. S. A.: Forty-Five Plays by Black Americans, 1847-1974,* ed. James V. Hatch (New York: The Free Press, 1974), 47. Further references will be to this edition and will be given parenthetically.
5. Quoted in Farrison, *William Wells Brown,* 281.
6. As Robert C. Toll (along with numerous other historians) has noted, minstrelsy "swept the nation in the 1840s," becoming the "most popular entertainment form in the country" and the "first American popular entertainment form to become a national institution" (*Blacking Up: The Minstrel Show in Nineteenth-Century America* [New York: Oxford Univ. Press, 1974], v, vi).
7. Frederick Douglass, *My Bondage and My Freedom* (1855; reprint, New York: Arno, 1969), 362.
8. Quoted in Farrison, *William Wells Brown,* 294.
9. Brown's construction of race as performance prefigures later formulations of black racial consciousness as a matter of double-consciousness (W. E. B. DuBois, *The Souls of Black Folk* [1903]) and as a matter of masquerade (Frantz Fanon, *Black Skin, White Masks* [1952]). For a reading of DuBois that has influenced my understanding of the relationship between cultural (or sociohistorical) and biological understandings of race, see Anthony Appiah, "The Uncompleted Argument: DuBois and the Illusion of Race," *Critical Inquiry* 12 (autumn 1985): 21-37.
10. Eric Lott notes this historical conjunction and other connections between abolitionism and minstrely in *Love and Theft: Blackface Minstrelsy and the American Working Class* (New York: Oxford Univ. Press, 1993), 111. In his afterword, Lott moves toward investigating black appropriations of the minstrel show, citing Martin Delany's *Blake* (1859-1861) as a text that "devises a complex reinvention of the minstrel tradition" (236). My work attempts to complicate and expand Lott's theorization of the ambivalence of the minstrel show in the direction in which this brief discussion points.
11. Despite my characterization of the abolitionist movement as "white" (which is generally true of its early leadership), the movement depended on the support of free blacks from the beginning. For example, Garrison's *Liberator* would have failed in its first years but for black subscriptions. It was not until the late 1830s, however, that blacks began to gain positions as speaking agents for abolition societies. Apparently Charles Lenox Remond, a native of Salem, Massachusetts, became the first black antislavery agent in 1838. While he provided "a living refutation of the stereotyped falsehood of inferiority," he could not speak of slavery from his own experience; see Robert C. Dick, *Black Protest: Issues and Tactics* (Westport, Conn.: Greenwood, 1974), 207. See also Leon F. Litwack, "The Emancipation of the Negro Abolitionist," in *The Antislavery Vanguard: New Essays on the Abolitionists,* ed. Martin Duberman (Princeton: Princeton Univ. Press, 1965), 137-55.
12. Letter from John A. Collins to William Lloyd Garrison, January 1842, quoted in Gara, "The Professional Fugitive," 196. See also Theodore Dwight Weld, *American Slavery As It Is: Testimony of a Thousand Witnesses* (New York: American Anti-Slavery Society, 1839). Weld's record, which became one of the sources for Harriet Beecher Stowe's *Uncle Tom's Cabin* (1852), reports an incident—a slave being drowned by a mob in New Orleans—that Brown claimed to have witnessed; see *Narrative of William Wells Brown, A Fugitive Slave, written by himself* (1847), in *Puttin' On Ole Massa,* ed. Gilbert Osofsky (New York: Harper and Row, 1969), 200-01. Further references to this work will be to this edition and will be noted parenthetically as *N.*
13. The antebellum minstrel show was not primarily based on anything that could be called "authentically" African American. Rather, it drew from conventions of representing Irish and frontier characters, popular Euro-American songs (already influenced by African American culture), and some elements of an already hybridized African American slave culture. The minstrel show became a place where elements of American culture already marked as "black" or "white" (although, in both cases, already a mixture of "African" and "European" influences) came together and influenced one another. For one interesting case study of the way minstrelsy emerged through a constant play of cross-racial cultural appropriation, see Howard L. Sacks and Judith Rose Sacks, *Way Up North in Dixie: A Black Family's Claim to the Confederate Anthem* (Washington, D.C.: Smithsonian Institution Press, 1993).
14. "Editor's Table: Bowery Theatre," *Knickerbocker,* July 1840, 84; advertisement quoted in Carl Wittke, *Tambo and Bones: A History of the American Minstrel Show* (Durham, N.C.: Duke Univ. Press, 1930), 37.

15. Both quoted in Gara, "The Professional Fugitive," 198.

16. Toll, *Blacking Up,* 101.

17. In a letter to William Lloyd Garrison dated 17 May 1853, which recounts the fanfare accompanying Stowe's arrival in England and criticizes her husband for his reconciliatory rhetoric, Brown declared that "*Uncle Tom's Cabin* has come down upon the dark abodes of slavery like a morning's sunlight, unfolding to view its enormities in a manner which has fastened all eyes upon the 'peculiar institution,' and awakening sympathy in hearts that never before felt for the slave" (*The Black Abolitionist Papers,* vol. 1, *The British Isles, 1830-1865,* ed. C. Peter Ripley et al. [Chapel Hill: Univ. of North Carolina Press, 1985], 344). See Peter A. Dorsey, "De-authorizing Slavery: Realism in Stowe's *Uncle Tom's Cabin* and Brown's *Clotel,*" *ESQ* 41 (winter 1995): 256-88, for a discussion of the intertextual borrowings of these two novels.

18. The novel has often been criticized for its fragmentary and episodic character. Like M. Giulia Fabi, however, I see the fragmentary nature of Brown's novel as giving him access to a systemic critique of slavery, specifically in the portrayal of male slaves; see M. Giulia Fabi, "The 'Unguarded Expressions of the Feelings of the Negroes': Gender, Slave Resistance, and William Wells Brown's Revisions of *Clotel,*" *African American Review* 27 (winter 1993): 639-54.

19. Fabi focuses on these "two competing plots" (639) while pointing to Brown's failure to depict any *black* female slaves in a positive light. While I am more interested in how these two plots intersect to destabilize the idea that race is legibly inscribed on the body, Fabi's point about the lack of black women is well taken. Alongside a viable representative black manhood, Brown offers multiple mulatta heroines whose mixed racial status stands as evidence of the sexual crimes of slavery as it troubles any easy racial essentialization. While the mulatta heroine can stand in, to an extent, for black women, Brown fails to offer the same critique of—or at least devotes less attention to—constructions of black womanhood as he does constructions of black manhood.

20. William Wells Brown, *Clotel; or, The President's Daughter: A Narrative of Slave Life in the United States* (1853; reprint, New York: Carol, 1969), 59; further references to *Clotel* will be to this edition and will be noted parenthetically. Numerous critics have seen the third-person introductory section as a key moment in African American letters, explicitly marking the shift from the autobiographical slave narrative to fictional forms and acting to displace the "authenticating white abolitionist preface" of slave narratives (Carla L. Peterson, "Capitalism, Black (Under)development, and the Production of the African-American Novel in the 1850s," *American Literary History* 4 [winter 1992]: 563). See also William L. Andrews, "The Novelization of Voice in Early African American Narrative," [*Publications of the Modern Language Association*] 105 (January 1990): 23-34.

21. In regard to gender masquerade, Judith Butler argues that "drag fully subverts the distinction between inner and outer psychic space and effectively mocks . . . the notion of a true gender identity" (137). Thus, "gender parody reveals that the original identity after which gender fashions itself is an imitation without an origin" (138). While my work is indebted to Butler's delineation of the power of masquerade, my point is that while masquerade does reveal the constructedness of race and gender, it also works to substantiate those distinctions. Butler does note that such masquerades "become domesticated and recirculated as instruments of cultural hegemony" (139), but I believe her account (at least here) is overly celebratory of the subversive possibilities of masquerade; see Judith Butler, *Gender Trouble: Feminism and the Subversion of Identity* (New York: Routledge, 1990). In a discussion of Nella Larsen's *Passing* (1929), Butler provides a more nuanced reading of the constitution of racial and gender lines through a movement of acknowledgment and disavowal of their fluidity; see *Bodies That Matter: On the Discursive Limits of "Sex"* (New York: Routledge, 1993), 167-85.

22. I borrow the term "colorist" from Alice Walker. For her critique of Brown as a racist and exist, see *In Search of Our Mothers' Gardens* (San Diego: Harcourt Brace Jovanovich, 1983), 297-303.

23. See Jean Fagan Yellin, *The Intricate Knot: Black Figures in American Literature, 1776-1863* (New York: New York Univ. Press, 1972), 160. Fabi also comments on Brown's "folk characters" (640). Brown's blackface characters could be seen as part of the tradition of signifying that Henry Louis Gates Jr. describes in *The Signifying Monkey: A Theory of African-American Literary Criticism* (New York: Oxford Univ. Press, 1988). My point is that this tradition is always being constructed in dialogue with and through a constant interplay of appropriation and reappropriation from and by both "white" literature and mass cultural forms such as minstrelsy.

24. As Ralph Ellison puts it in a different context, "Without arguing the point I shall say only that if it is a trickster, its adjustments to the contours of 'white' symbolic needs is far more intriguing than its alleged origins, for it tells us something of the operation of American values as modulated by folklore and literature [and, I would add, mass culture]" ("Change the Joke and Slip the Yoke" [1958], in *Shadow and Act* [New York: Random House, 1964], 51-52).

25. William Wells Brown, *A Lecture Delivered Before the Female Anti-Slavery Society of Salem At Lyceum Hall, Nov. 14, 1847,* in *Four Fugitive Slave Narratives,* ed. Larry Gara (Reading, Mass.: Addison-Wesley, 1969), 81-82.

26. "Speech by William Wells Brown, Delivered at the Horticultural Hall, West Chester, Pennsylvania, 23 October 1854," in *The Black Abolitionist Papers,* vol. 4, *The United States, 1847-1858,* ed. C. Peter Ripley et al. (Chapel Hill: Univ. of North Carolina Press, 1991), 248.

27. Brown's statements provide an early articulation of some of the difficulties Gayatri Chakravorty Spivak enunciates in "Can the Subaltern Speak?" in *Marxism and the Interpretation of Culture,* ed. Cary Nelson and Lawrence Grossberg (Urbana: Univ. of Illinois Press, 1988), 271-313.

28. In other words, Brown is able to use the minstrelized black body as, to use Lauren Berlant's term, a prophylactic body in order to remain black even while entering into the essentially white male realm of the public sphere; see Berlant, "National Brands/National Body: Imitation of Life," in *The Phantom Public Sphere,* ed. Bruce Robbins (Minneapolis: Univ. of Minnesota Press, 1993), 173-208.

29. Brown's appropriation of minstrelsy is only one way in which he provides an important contrast in strategy and focus to Frederick Douglass. In 1849 Douglass reported on going to see Gavitt's Original Ethiopian Serenaders, a minstrel troupe "said to be composed entirely of colored people." Douglass remarks that "they, too, had recourse to the burnt cork and lamp black, the better to express their characters, and to produce uniformity of complexion. Their lips, too, were evidently painted, and otherwise exaggerated. Their singing generally was but an imitation of white performers, and not even a tolerable representation of the character of the colored people." By appearing in blackface, and thus producing themselves as "uniform," the black performers fail to give "a tolerable representation of the character of the colored people." Imitating white performers, they do not reveal "the peculiarities of their race," but rather exaggerate them. Douglass states that "[i]t is something gained, when the colored man in any form can appear before a white audience," but he immediately qualifies this gain by arguing that "this company, with industry, application, and a proper cultivation of their taste, may yet be instrumental in removing the prejudice against our race. But they must cease to exaggerate the exaggerations of our enemies; and represent the colored man rather as he is, than as Ethiopian Minstrels usually represent him to be. They will *then* command the respect of both races." According to Douglass, black performers in blackface cannot succeed in fighting racism and slavery because they do not represent the black man "as he is." It is by representing the "true" "character of colored people" that blacks can help in the struggle for equality and freedom. Brown, on the other hand, uses minstrelsy to obscure the very notion of a "true" black character while simultaneously constructing a representative black manhood; see Frederick Douglass, "Gavitt's Original Ethiopian Serenaders," *North Star,* 29 June 1849; reprinted in *The Life and Writings of Frederick Douglass,* vol. 1, ed. Philip S. Foner (New York: International Publishers, 1950), 141-42.

30. Lott, *Love and Theft,* 115.

31. See David R. Roediger, *The Wages of Whiteness: Race and the Making of the American Working Class* (New York: Verso, 1991), 115-32.

32. Generally, middle-class manhood in this period has been identified with rising ideals of decorum and self-restraint—a more spiritualized manhood—while working-class manhood has been identified with a certain rugged, unconstrained physicality; see, for example, E. Anthony Rotundo, *American Manhood: Transformations in Masculinity from the Revolution to the Modern Era* (New York: Basic Books, 1993); and Elliott J. Gorn, *The Manly Art: Bare-Knuckle Prize Fighting in America* (Ithaca: Cornell Univ. Press, 1986). I find it useful here to invoke this idea of middle-class manhood, but, as the middle-class celebration of the physicality of the minstrel show indicates, I think middle-class manhood was actually more complicated in its attempt to balance bourgeois decorum with a more physical manliness.

    Lott engages the "class unevenness of minstrel audiences" and suggests the minstrel show's "possible counteruses as a mode of cultural embourgeoisement" in his chapter on Stephen Foster (182). But even there, his focus remains on working-class investment in the minstrel show.

33. Wittke, *Tambo and Bones,* 52. As Alexander Saxton has noted, the major stars of antebellum minstrelsy "were clearly [men] of middle-class background . . . [who] rejected the straight ways of the Protestant ethic and sought escape into the bohemianism of the entertainment world" (*The Rise and Fall of the White Republic: Class Politics and Mass Culture in Nineteenth-Century America* [New York: Verso, 1990], 167). The minstrel show provided a forum in which white men generally could access the pleasures of the body associated with blackness and middle-class whites in particular could access the pleasures associated with both blackness *and* the lower classes.

34. *New York Tribune,* 30 June 1855, quoted as Lott's epigraph, 3; Robert P. Nevin, "Stephen C. Foster and Negro Minstrelsy," *Atlantic Monthly,* November 1867, 610; "Negro Minstrelsy—Ancient and Modern," *Putnam's Monthly,* January 1855, 72.

35. From 1847, quoted in Marian Hannah Winter, "Juba and American Minstrelsy," *Dance Index,* February 1947, 27.
36. Roediger, *The Wages of Whiteness,* 116.
37. As Toll puts it, "By focusing on caricatures of frolicking Negroes in the idealized plantation family, minstrelsy created a state of perpetual childhood that audiences could vicariously participate in and feel superior to at the same time" (*Blacking Up,* 86).
38. "Songs of the Blacks," *Dwight's Journal of Music,* 15 November 1856; reprinted in *What They Heard: Music In America, 1852-1881,* ed. Irving Sablosky (Baton Rouge: Louisiana State Univ. Press, 1986), 264-65.
39. Frantz Fanon quotes "a friend who was a teacher in the United States, [who said,] 'The presence of the Negroes beside the whites is in a way an insurance policy on humanness. When the whites feel that they have become too mechanized, they turn to the men of color and ask them for a little human sustenance'" (*Black Skin, White Masks* [1952], trans. Charles Lam Markmann [New York: Grove Weidenfeld, 1967], 129).
40. "Songs of the Blacks," 264.
41. The most famous account of viewers misperceiving minstrel performers as actually black is Mark Twain's story of taking his mother and aunt to a show; see *The Autobiography of Mark Twain,* ed. Charles Neider (1924; reprint, New York: Harper, 1959), 58-63.
42. For discussions of sheet music covers, see Toll, *Blacking Up,* 40, and Lott, *Love and Theft,* 20-21.
43. Thomas L. Nichols, *Forty Years of American Life,* vol. 2 (London: John Maxwell and Co., 1864), 231-32.
44. See Lott, *Love and Theft,* 113-18, for a discussion of this point and others related to accounts of Lane's performances.
45. Quoted in Winter, "Juba and American Minstrelsy," 33. Winter and Lott provide the best overviews of Lane's career.
46. Charles Dickens, *American Notes* (1842; reprint, London: Oxford Univ. Press, 1957), 90-91.
47. Both comments quoted in Winter, 36.
48. As Homi Bhabha puts it in his discussion of the ambivalence of stereotypes, "in order to be effective, mimicry must continually produce its slippage, its excess, its difference. The authority of . . . mimicry is therefore stricken by an indeterminacy." This "recognition and disavowal of 'difference' is always disturbed by the question of re-presentation or construction" (*The Location of Culture* [New York: Routledge, 1994], 86, 81).
49. Quoted in Sam Dennison, *Scandalize My Name: Black Imagery in American Popular Music* (New York: Garland Publishing, Inc., 1982), 56.
50. Quoted in Saxton, *Rise and Fall of the White Republic,* 177.
51. Toll hypothesizes that the dearth of antislavery material he sees in the minstrel show after 1850 or so was related to a move away from slave sources: the antislavery jokes on masters performed on the minstrel stage "may be among the authentic folk materials that minstrels borrowed" (*Blacking Up,* 73). Saxton, while seeing less antislavery rhetoric in minstrelsy, goes further in accrediting such subversive messages to minstrelsy's appropriation of African American cultural elements: "[T]he early borrowings of African American music and dance carried antislavery connotations that sometimes persisted subliminally in traditional verses" (*Rise and Fall of the White Republic,* 176). Again, my point is not to deny that some "authentic" black folk material containing antislavery elements might have persisted in the minstrel show, but to foreground how the minstrel show's structure required the retention (or production) of such material.
52. This phrase is from Brown's description of Turner in his lecture on St. Domingo in 1854; see William Wells Brown, *St. Domingo: Its Revolutions and Its Patriots. A Lecture* . . . (1855; reprint, Philadelphia: Rhistoric, 1969), 23.
53. *Christy's Plantation Melodies #2* (Philadelphia: Fisher and Brothers, 1852), 44-45.
54. Minstrel shows were rife with this kind of characterization. Stump speeches depicting blacks as incompetently trying to follow the white examples of famous speakers like Daniel Webster and scenes involving blacks failing to act as lawyers, doctors, and such were central to minstrel shows. See, for example, "Sambo's Address to his Bred'ren," in Dennison, 41-45; the selections on the minstrel show in *Dramas from the American Theatre, 1762-1909,* ed. Richard Moody (Cleveland: World Publishing Co., 1966), 475-500; and skits such as "The Quack Doctor," in *This Grotesque Essence: Plays from the American Minstrel Stage,* ed. Gary D. Engle (Baton Rouge: Louisiana State Univ. Press, 1978).
55. *The Music of Stephen C. Foster: A Critical Edition,* ed. Steven Saunders and Deane L. Root (Washington: Smithsonian Institution Press, 1990), 1: 216-18.
56. Foster's song has a different antislavery connotation without being read against the grain, as I have done. In Stowe's *Dred* (1856), the slaves sing "Mas'r's in the cold, cold ground" to the abolitionist lovers as part of a minstrel-like entertainment in which they express their love for their owners; see Harriet Beecher Stowe, *Dred, A Tale of the Great Dismal Swamp* (1856; reprint, Boston: Houghton Mifflin, 1884), 342-43. Foster's song here serves to demonstrate the humanity of black slaves by underlining their capacity for genuine affection and emotional attachment.

57. Kristin Hoganson, "Garrisonian Abolitionists and the Rhetoric of Gender, 1850-1860," *American Quarterly* 45 (December 1993): 558-95.

58. Jean Fagan Yellin reads this emblem as representing the slave as "powerful and athletic," on the verge of "bursting his fetters and asserting his freedom" (*Women and Sisters: The Antislavery Feminists in American Culture* [New Haven: Yale Univ. Press, 1989], 8). I concur with Hoganson, however, that in such contexts "black men's bare bodies represented impotence, . . . an impotence caused by the inability to resist the master" (567).

59. Richard Yarborough, "Race, Violence, and Manhood: The Masculine Ideal in Frederick Douglass's 'The Heroic Slave,'" in *Frederick Douglass: New Literary and Historical Essays,* ed. Eric J. Sundquist (New York: Cambridge Univ. Press, 1990), 167-68.

60. At least early on, white abolitionists focused on finding black men to serve as lecturers. While black women such as Sojourner Truth had denounced slavery in public forums at least as early as the 1830s, black women did not, it seems, become antislavery agents per se until the 1850s. For black women lecturers, writers, and workers in the antislavery movement, see Carla L. Peterson, *"Doers of the Word": African-American Women Speakers and Writers in the North (1830-1880)* (New York: Oxford Univ. Press, 1995); and Yellin, *Women and Sisters.* Two quintessential texts of ex-slave women negotiating middle-class gender expectations are Harriet Jacobs's *Incidents in the Life of a Slave Girl* (1861) and Sojourner Truth's perhaps fictional "A'n't I a Woman" speech (1851).

61. Henry Louis Gates Jr. explores the importance of literacy in the fight for recognition of black humanity in *Figures in Black: Words, Signs, and the "Racial" Self* (New York: Oxford Univ. Press, 1987). Janet Duitsman Cornelius has argued that literacy was actually far more common among slaves than previously believed; see her *When I Can Read My Title Clear: Literacy, Slavery, and Religion in the Antebellum South* (Columbia: Univ. of South Carolina Press, 1991). My point is that slaves, correctly or incorrectly, were perceived as illiterate and ignorant.

62. Douglass, *My Bondage and My Freedom,* 362.

63. *Narrative of the Life of Frederick Douglass, An American Slave. Written by Himself* (1845), in *The Classic Slave Narratives,* ed. Henry Louis Gates Jr. (New York: Mentor, 1987), 298-99.

64. Douglas, *Narrative,* 293, 305. The most conspicuous calls for black resistance during the period forcefully play out this logic. David Walker's *Appeal* (1829) is particularly telling on this account. Walker declares that "we are *men,* notwithstanding our *improminent noses* and *woolly heads*" (25), yet like the antislavery emblem, Walker's declaration repeatedly becomes a question: "Are we MEN!!—I ask you, O my brethren! are we MEN? . . . How could we be so *submissive?*" (36). If the enslaved blacks are truly men, they would chance death rather than submit to the degradations of slavery (34, 42, 46). Only by actively resisting slavery, "meet[ing] death with glory," will they prove to themselves and "the Americans, who are waiting for us to prove to them ourselves, that we are MEN" (*David Walker's Appeal, In Four Articles* . . . [1830 (3rd ed.); reprint, Baltimore: Black Classic Press, 1993], 48). See also Henry Highland Garnet, *Address to the Slaves of the United States of America* (1848), in *The Ideological Origins of Black Nationalism,* ed. Sterling Stuckey (Boston: Beacon Press, 1972), 165-73. Garnet's address was originally delivered at the National Colored Convention at Buffalo in 1843, where Douglass and Brown helped to defeat its adoption.

65. Douglass, *My Bondage and My Freedom,* 246-47, 242. Douglass plays on the word *root* by referring both to the charm he was given by a fellow slave and his roots as a slave. In both cases, he is breaking explicitly with what becomes constructed as a feminized and ineffectual slave past.

66. Fanon, *Black Skin, White Masks,* 38, 69.

67. As Herbert Aptheker has shown, violent slave rebellions were more common than has often been recognized. See, for example, his *American Negro Slave Revolts* (1943; reprint, New York: International Publishers, 1983). Although the majority of slaves did not take part in such uprisings, as Eugene D. Genovese has shown in his Gramscian study of slavery and hegemony, blacks did exert a limited amount of control over their own lives in slavery and actively partook in both symbolic and covert resistance to white power; see Genovese, *Roll, Jordan, Roll: The World The Slaves Made* (New York: Random House, 1974).

68. See Frances Smith Foster, "Racial Myths in Slave Narratives," in *Witnessing Slavery: The Development of Ante-bellum Slave Narratives* (Westport, Conn.: Greenwood Press, 1979), 127-41, for an account of the importance of mulatto spokesmen in abolitionism.

69. Both quoted in Farrison, *William Wells Brown,* 259 (December 1854), 288 (September 1857). Because eloquence in light-skinned black speakers called into question their "blackness," white abolitionists not only desired more "plantation manner" from spokesmen like Brown, but also actively sought out the "full, unmitigated, unalleviated and unpardonable blackness" of men like Henry Highland Garnet; see Jane H. Pease and William H. Pease, *They Who Would Be Free: Blacks' Search for Freedom, 1830-1861* (New York: Atheneum, 1974), 43.

70. Frederick Douglass, "The Claims of the Negro Ethnologically Considered: An Address Delivered in Hudson, Ohio, on 12 July 1854," in *The Frederick Douglass Papers,* Series One, *Speeches, Debates, and Interviews, Volume 2: 1847-1854,* ed. John W. Blassingame (New Haven: Yale Univ. Press, 1982), 510.

71. For an account of how the black body was constructed as ungendered and at the same time hypersexualized, see Hortense J. Spillers, "Mama's Baby, Papa's Maybe: An American Grammar Book," *Diacritics* 17 (summer 1987): 64-81.

72. Karen Sánchez-Eppler, "Bodily Bonds: The Intersecting Rhetorics of Feminism and Abolition," in *The Culture of Sentiment: Race, Gender, and Sentimentality in Nineteenth-Century America,* ed. Shirley Samuels (New York: Oxford Univ. Press, 1992), 102.

73. See Judith R. Berzon, *Neither White Nor Black: The Mulatto Character in American Fiction* (New York: New York Univ. Press, 1978), especially chapter 2, "Racist Ideologies and the Mulatto," for a rehearsal of the critiques of the tragic mulatta as a racist figure. For a defense of its effectiveness in antislavery literature, see Jules Zanger, "The 'Tragic Octoroon' in Pre-Civil War Fiction," *American Quarterly* 18 (spring 1966): 63-70. While the mulatto character was almost always imagined to be the product of a union between a black slave woman and a white man (frequently a close relative), as Sánchez-Eppler has demonstrated, the mulatta heroine could also stand in for the most unspeakable cross-racial desire, that of a white woman for a black man.

74. See Nancy Bentley, "White Slaves: The Mulatto Hero in Antebellum Fiction," *American Literature* 65 (September 1993): 501-22.

75. Stowe's novel is the essential text for mapping out this notion of gendered racial traits, which George Fredrickson has termed "romantic racialism"; see Fredrickson, "Uncle Tom and the Anglo-Saxons: Romantic Racialism in the North," in *The Black Image in the White Mind: The Debate on Afro-American Character and Destiny, 1817-1914* (New York: Harper & Row, 1971), 97-129. Cynthia Griffin Wolff has attempted to qualify readings of *Uncle Tom's Cabin* that see Tom as effeminate by correctly showing how Stowe calls for a type of manhood in which being "brave, manly" is equated with being "gentle, domestic." Wolff, however, fails to take into account the ways in which Stowe bases this idea of a more "domestic" manhood on the notion that blacks *naturally* have a more "feminine" disposition that white men need to learn; see Wolff, "'Masculinity' in *Uncle Tom's Cabin,*" *American Quarterly* 47 (December 1995): 595-618.

76. Frederick Douglass, "The Heroic Slave" (1853), in *Violence in the Black Imagination,* ed. Ronald T. Takaki (New York: G. P. Putnam's Sons, 1972), 40, 41. All further citations will be to this edition and will be given parenthetically.

77. Richard Yarborough, whose reading of "The Heroic Slave" has influenced my own thinking about the story, argues that Washington's blackness is also called into question from this opening description (173-74). For more positive accounts of "The Heroic Slave" and its obviously important reconceptualization of black manhood, see Eric J. Sundquist, *To Wake the Nations: Race in the Making of American Literature* (Cambridge, Mass.: Harvard Univ. Press, 1993), 115-24; and Maggie Sale, "To Make the Past Useful: Frederick Douglass' Politics of Solidarity," *Arizona Quarterly* 51 (autumn 1995): 25-60.

78. Shirley Samuels explores the ways in which sentimental antislavery fiction worked on the premise of revealing the "white" inside of black slaves; see Samuels, "The Identity of Slavery," in *The Culture of Sentiment,* 157-71.

79. Harriet Beecher Stowe, *Uncle Tom's Cabin, or, Life Among the Lowly* (1852; reprint, New York: Penguin, 1981), 392.

80. For more on the Nat/Sambo dichotomy in the Southern imagination and in the slave community, see John W. Blassingame, *The Slave Community: Plantation Life in the Antebellum South* (New York: Oxford Univ. Press, 1972). Brown invokes the image of black atavism again in his lecture on St. Domingo from 1854. While Brown stresses that the educated, rational French started the violence and were far worse in their cruelties, when he explicitly connects this revolt to the Southern states, his point is clear: "Let the slave-holders in our Southern States tremble when they shall call to mind these events" (25).

81. This construction of black resistance and rebellion as irrational or prerational was a commonplace. Perhaps the best example of this constant shift between seeing the rebel slave as admirable and as insane is T. R. Gray's *Confessions of Nat Turner* (1831).

82. Brown notes that upon escaping George went "but a short distance before he felt that a change of his apparel would facilitate his progress" (228), but he makes it clear that George remains in women's clothes until in the North. Both Bentley and Fabi misread this passage as indicating that George immediately reclaims his masculine appearance. Bentley argues that Brown uses the scene to set up a "contrast between the female and male Mulattoes," so that "White male bodies are spared and female bodies are sacrificed" (507); Fabi argues that George must reclaim his manliness immediately because of Brown's "evaluation of passing as unheroic" and feminine (645). My point is that Brown *stresses* George's escape through masquerade because of the

impossibility of heroic action and because of his desire to emphasize the performative nature of white manhood.

83. Brown reiterates this logic in the story of Clotel's escape with William, a dark black slave. In their escape Clotel poses as an invalid white man and William poses as her faithful servant. Not only does Brown point to the instability of white manhood—a "black" woman can become a white man—but William achieves manhood, thus demonstrating that he is "as good as white folks" (177), by reconfiguring his status as a "Jim Crow"-like slave (176).

FURTHER READING

Braga, Thomas. "Castro Alves and the New England Abolitionist Poets." In *Hispania: A Journal Devoted to the Interests of the Teaching of Spanish and Portuguese* 67, No. 4. (December 1984): 585-93.

Compares and contrasts Brazilian abolitionism with New England abolitionism, finding some interesting parallels but not influences.

Clark, Margaret Goff. *Their Eyes on the Stars: Four Black Writers.* Champaign, Ill.: Garrard Publishing Co., 1973, 174 p.

General biography, appropriate for young readers.

Farrison, William Edward. *William Wells Brown: Author and Reformer.* Chicago: University of Chicago Press, 1969, 482 p.

Farrison provides a thorough biography of Brown, paying special attention to historical context.

Heermance, Noel J. *William Wells Brown and Clotelle: a Portrait of the Artist in the First Negro Novel.* Archon Books: Shoe String Press, 1969, 309 p.

Emphasizes Brown's importance to the genre of slave narratives.

Additional coverage of Brown's life and career is contained in the following sources published by the Gale Group: *Black Literature Criticism,* Vol. 1; *Dictionary of Literary Biography,* Vols. 3, 50, and 183; *DISCovering Authors Modules: Multicultural Authors*; and *Drama Criticism,* Vol. 1.

Adam Bede
George Eliot

The following entry presents criticism of Eliot's novel *Adam Bede* (1859). For discussion of Eliot's complete career, see *NCLC,* Volume 4; for discussion of the novel *Middlemarch,* see *NCLC,* Volume 13; for discussion of the novel *Daniel Deronda,* see *NCLC,* Volume 23; for discussion of the novel *Silas Marner,* see *NCLC,* Volume 41; for discussion of the novel *The Mill on the Floss,* see *NCLC,* Volume 49.

INTRODUCTION

Following the critical and popular success of *Scenes of Clerical Life* in 1858, George Eliot (pseudonym of Mary Ann, or Marian, Evans) published *Adam Bede* to further acclaim. Having gained recognition for the realistic characters and situations in the three sketches comprising *Scenes,* Eliot again sought to create complex characters who display a range of traits, neither all good nor all bad. A pastoral novel, *Adam Bede* is set at the turn of the nineteenth century and presents realistic images of daily life in a quiet rural community. However, within this apparently peaceful, simple country world, Eliot's character-narrator tells a story of unfulfilled love and selfishness resulting in tragedy and hard-won self-awareness. Through the narrator, the middle-class reading audience is encouraged to look upon the novel's lower-class characters with the same sensibility and sensitivity as they would their peers. Rather than expressing superiority or contempt for the rural people in the novel, readers are invited by the narrator to set aside class or economic biases and view the characters in *Adam Bede* in light of their humanity and goodness.

Discussing *Adam Bede* in her personal journals, Eliot cautiously confessed that the character of Adam was inspired by her own father's early life, and the character of Dinah was drawn from her Methodist Aunt Samuel. She insisted, however, that the novel was not biographical beyond those initial inspirations. These same journals, along with her published essays and reviews, have led critics to argue that *Adam Bede* reflects themes in other literary works with which she was familiar, including Milton's *Paradise Lost,* Hawthorne's *The Scarlet Letter,* and the Greek Tragedies, among others. However, according to Eliot, she did not intend *Adam Bede* as a memoir or even as historical fiction; it was her most earnest intent to write realistic fiction at a time when realism was "out of fashion." *Adam Bede,* considered by her contemporaries to display "a touch of genius," has been overshadowed in twentieth-century criticism by the more mature *Middlemarch.* Nevertheless, its reputation has remained untarnished and many scholars regard *Adam Bede* as one of the finest examples of realistic fiction of its time.

PLOT AND MAJOR CHARACTERS

Adam Bede is set in the rural community of Loamshire, England, in the summer of 1799. Adam Bede, the eponymous main character, and his younger brother Seth are employed as carpenters. Seth is well-meaning and generous while Adam, who serves as foreman to the crew of rustics who assist him, is serious and hard-working. Outwardly, Adam is a role model for the community, but inwardly he is plagued by resentment towards his alcoholic father and annoyance with his ever-complaining mother. Seth is a devout Methodist who practices his religion over the objections of both his family and the larger community. He is in love with Dinah Morris, a solemn Methodist preacher who, though demure and feminine, refuses to allow her religious mission to be compromised by her gender. Her quiet confidence attracts significant attention in Loamshire, and, in part, fuels Seth's affection. Meanwhile, Adam hopes one day for the financial security to be able to ask Hetty Sorrel, a distractingly beautiful and childishly self-centered young woman, to be his wife. While Dinah refuses Seth's romantic affections believing her duty is to minister to the unsaved, Hetty is deliberately distant and coquettish, while at the same time encouraging Adam's hopes for an eventual union. Although the two women are entirely different in character and morals, their lives are nevertheless entwined; both are orphaned cousins staying with their relations, the Poysners, a prominent tenant farming family.

Like the Poysners, the entire community operates under the patronage of the elderly landowner, Squire Donnithorne. His grandson Arthur, without an income of his own as long as his grandfather remains alive, looks benevolently upon Loamshire as his birthright. He imagines himself making improvements to the land and gaining the love of all his tenant farmers through his generosity and earnestness. But until he gains his inheritance, he is powerless and becomes bored and frustrated with his grandfather's mismanagement of the land. Seeking distraction, he discovers Hetty. While he is drawn to her beauty, she is equally drawn to his social position and the promise of being rescued from domestic servitude to live as the wife of a wealthy, respected man.

Hetty becomes deluded about the nature of their relationship, and Arthur is torn between his determination to live up to his social position and his desire for the young woman. At a pivotal moment, the couple is caught in an embrace by Adam who, despite his inferior social standing, challenges Arthur over the indiscretion. Adam, heartbroken, loses his faith in his long-time friend Arthur, but becomes more protective of Hetty. Shortly after Adam's discovery, Arthur ends the affair and leaves town, and Hetty turns to Adam for comfort. He takes her back, and joyously plans their life together. However, haunted by her scandalous behavior, Hetty discovers that she is pregnant and, unable to take responsibility for her actions, runs away.

Alone, Hetty gives birth to a child, whom she abandons in the wilderness. Her crime is discovered, and she is sentenced to death for infanticide. Adam refuses to believe she could have committed such a crime, and Hetty herself refuses to confess. Arthur, who left the country immediately following the affair, has not been heard from, and Hetty is left with only the comfort of her cousin Dinah. Arthur returns with a stay of execution just in time to save Hetty from death. Through the course of his love and loss of Hetty, Adam learns sympathy and forgiveness, and thus becomes a better person than he was at the start of the novel. With this change, Adam is rewarded with marriage to Dinah, who gives up her ministry in favor of domestic life.

MAJOR THEMES

While *Adam Bede* centers around the title character's progress from a calloused sense of moral superiority to a state of sympathy and understanding for others, there are several other significant themes. *Adam Bede* is widely recognized as a pastoral novel dealing with rural farm life and country people. Attention to the everyday details of butter-making, berry-picking, and cattle-herding, far away from the political and economic changes of an industrialized society, lend the story a sense of innocence and peacefulness. However, as England crossed from the eighteenth to nineteenth century, the pastoral peace enveloping the Loamshire countryside is disrupted by Hetty and Arthur's affair. The pastoral setting underscores the transition of English society from relative innocence to experience, leaving Eliot's readers nostalgic for simpler times.

In addition, issues of religion, while not at the forefront of the novel, are nonetheless present. Dinah's evangelical Methodist preaching is set against Reverend Irwine's staid traditional church leadership. In the midst of this doctrinal difference, moral weaknesses abound and neither religious leader is able to save Hetty and Arthur from their lack of moral judgement. While Eliot avoids religious sermonizing, the lack of spiritual intervention on behalf of the lovers demonstrates her greater concern with the state of religion in nineteenth-century England and hints at her own religious dissent.

Eliot's use of realism in the novel is also significant. The realistic portrayal of both her characters and situations is reinforced by her pointed description of Dutch genre painting in Chapter 17 of the novel. Dutch painting was considered a low art form by Eliot's contemporaries, not because the technique was inferior, but because the subject matter failed to conform to the aesthetic ideal of beauty so favored by critics and consumers alike. By embracing this genre of painting, where commoners engaged in common tasks were presented in great detail, Eliot attempted to justify her own representation of "common, coarse people."

CRITICAL RECEPTION

Immediately recognized as a significant literary work, *Adam Bede* has enjoyed a largely positive critical reputation since its publication. An anonymous review in *The Athenaeum*in 1859 praised it as a "novel of the highest class," and *The Times* called it "a first-rate novel." Contemporary reviewers, often influenced by nostalgia for the earlier period represented in *Bede,* enthusiastically praised Eliot's characterizations and realistic representations of rural life. Charles Dickens wrote: "The whole country life that the story is set in, is so real, and so droll and genuine, and yet so selected and polished by art, that I cannot praise it enough to you." (Hunter, S. 122) In fact, in early criticism, the tragedy of infanticide has often been overlooked in favor of the peaceful idyllic world and familiar personalities Eliot recreated.

Other critics have been less generous. Henry James, among others, resented the narrator's interventions. In particular,

Chapter 15 has fared poorly among scholars because of the author's/narrator's moralizing and meddling in an attempt to sway readers' opinions of Hetty and Dinah. Other critics have objected to the resolution of the story. In the final moments, Hetty, about to be executed for infanticide, is saved by her seducer, Arthur Donnithorne. Critics have argued that this deus ex machina ending negates the moral lessons learned by the main characters. Without the eleventh hour reprieve, the suffering of Adam, Arthur, and Hetty would have been more realistically concluded. In addition, some scholars feel that Adam's marriage to Dinah is another instance of the author's/narrator's intrusiveness. These instances have been found to directly conflict with the otherwise realistic images and events of the novel.

PRINCIPAL WORKS

"The Life of Jesus, Critically Examined. Translated from the Fourth German Edition." 3 vols. [translator; as Marian Evans] (essay) 1846
"The Essence of Christianity" [translator; as Marian Evans] (essay) 1854
**Scenes of Clerical Life* (novel) 1858
Adam Bede (novel) 1859
"The Lifted Veil" (short story) 1859
The Mill on the Floss (novel) 1860
Silas Marner, the Weaver of Raveloe (novel) 1861
Romola (novel) 1863
Felix Holt, the Radical (novel) 1866
The Spanish Gypsy (poetry) 1868
Middlemarch: A Study of Provincial Life. 4 vols. (novel) 1871-72
The Legend of Jubal, and Other Poems (poetry) 1874
Daniel Deronda. 4 vols. (novel) 1876
Impressions of Theophrastus Such (essays) 1879
The George Eliot Letters. 9 vols. (letters) 1954-78
Essays of George Eliot (essays) 1963

*All of Eliot's novels were originally published serially in magazines.

CRITICISM

Geraldine Jewsbury (review date 1859)

SOURCE: "*The Athenaeum,* 26 February 1859," in *George Eliot and Her Readers: A Selection of Contemporary Reviews,* edited by John Holmstrom and Laurence Lerner, The Bodley Head, 1966, p. 21.

[*Originally published in 1859, this early favorable review of* Adam Bede *recommends the novel for its realism and power.*]

Adam Bede is a novel of the highest class. Full of quiet power, without exaggeration and without any strain after effect, it produces a deep impression on the reader, which remains long after the book is closed. It is as though he had made acquaintance with real human beings: the story is not a story, but a true account of a place and people who have really lived; indeed, some of them may even be living yet, though they will be rather old, but that everything happened as here set down we have no doubt in the world. The duty of a critic in the present instance is almost superseded by the reader. ***Adam Bede*** is a book to be accepted, not criticized. . . . It is very seldom we are called on to deal with a book in which there is so little to qualify our praise.

W. L. Collins (review date 1859)

SOURCE: "*Blackwood's Edinburgh Magazine,* April 1859," in *The Critical Response to George Eliot,* edited by Karen L. Pangallo, Greenwood Press, 1994, pp. 37-38.

[*The following excerpt of a review originally published in 1859 discusses Eliot's portrayal of religion and praises her for her rendering of common working class people.*]

The great merit of ***Adam Bede*** consists in the singular grace and skill with which the characteristic detail of country life are rendered. To say of such a book that it does not depend for its main attraction on the development of a carefully-constructed plot, is little more than saying that it is a novel of character rather than action. With one great exception, the masters of fiction of our own day—and among these Mr. Eliot has incontestably made good his place—either fail in the constructive power, or will not condescend to write a story. They throw all their force into the delineation of character, and the enunciation of their own favourite philosophy by the actors whom they place upon the stage. This Mr. Eliot has done, and done it admirably. The story itself is simple enough, and the interest of a very quiet order, until the commencement of the third volume, when it is worked up with great power of detail, and becomes even painfully absorbing. The whole account of Hetty Sorrell's night-wandering in the fields is as strong an instance of the author's power in vivid melodramatic description, as the lighter parts of the book are of genuine humour and truth. . . .

One of the most real things in these volumes, which will at once strike all those who have had any experience of its truth, is the picture they give of the state of religious feeling in country villages—as it was fifty years ago, and as it is now, for there has been little change.

Adam Bede is not "a religious novel." It would hardly be recommended without reservation to that large class of readers who take Miss Yonge and Miss Sewell for their high-priestesses; and will run some risk of being placed in the *index expurgatorius* of the Evangelicalism. The author has a presentiment that to some minds the Rector of Broxton will seem "little better than a pagan." Yet for both parties it would be a very wholesome change to lay aside for an hour or two the publications of their own favourite school, and to read Mr. Eliot's story. For its religious principle is a large-hearted charity. And this, after all, is surely the right ground on which to treat religious questions in a work of fiction. . . . The author of ***Adam Bede*** is not one of those who, in the eloquent words of a late preacher, "have restricted God's love, and narrowed the path to heaven." No one handles Scripture more reverently; none with better effect; because it is not as a weapon against opponents, but as armour of proof.

It is very cheering too, setting the religious question apart, to read a book in which the writer has the courage to say that "by living a great deal among people more or less commonplace and vulgar," he "has come to the conclusion that human nature is lovable"—and has the ability to maintain his thesis. He does not conceal or palliate the weaknesses of humanity; there is no attempt to paint rural life as an Arcadia of innocence; we have Hetty's silly vanity, and young Donnithorne's weakness of principle, and Lisbeth's petulance, all truthfully set before us; and even Adam, the hero, has quite enough of his old namesake about him to be far from perfect; yet we part from all of them at last with an honest sympathy, or, at the worst, a mild and tearful pity. It is encouraging, as it is unfortunately rare, in fiction, to find ourselves watching the operations of a skilful anatomist, as he lays bare the secrets of our quivering frame, and to feel that the hand is not only sure and steady, but gentle as a woman's. It is pleasant to find, combined with all the power of the satirist, the kindly warmth of human charity, and to mark the light which it throws upon human failings; not concealing them, but softening the harsher outlines, mellowing the glaring tones, and bringing out beauties of which we were before unconscious. We have here no morbid dwelling upon evil, nor yet an unreal optimism which dresses out life in hues of rose-colour; but a hearty manly sympathy with weakness, not inconsistent with a hatred of vice. The "common, coarse people" shame us sometimes, as they do in actual life, by the delicacy of their moral organization; the outwardly gentle and refined shame us no less by their coarse selfishness. It is no small praise to Mr. Eliot, that he has described to us the attractions of sense without allowing them to influence our judgment.

Eneas Sweetland Dallas (review date 1859)

SOURCE: "*Adam Bede,* from *The Times,*" in *A Century of George Eliot Criticism,* edited by George Haight, Houghton Mifflin Company, 1965, pp. 2-8.

[*Originally published in 1859, the following review praises* Adam Bede *for demonstrating that despite social differences, people are more similar than not, and recommends the author for imbuing her characters with goodness.*]

There can be no mistake about ***Adam Bede.*** It is a first-rate novel, and its author takes rank at once among the masters of the art. Hitherto known but as the writer of certain tales to which he gave the modest title of ***Scenes,*** and which displayed only the buds of what we have here in full blossom, he has produced a work which, after making every allowance for certain crudities of execution, impresses us with a sense of the novelist's maturity of thought and feeling. Very seldom are so much freshness of style and warmth of emotion seen combined with so much solid sense and ripened observation. We have a pleasant feeling of security in either laughing or crying with such a companion. Our laughter shall not be trifling, and our tears shall not be maudlin. We need not fear to yield ourselves entirely to all the enchantments of the wizard whose first article of belief is the truism which very few of us comprehend until it has been knocked into us by years of experience—that we are all alike—that the human heart is one. All the novelists and all the dramatists that have ever lived have set themselves to exhibit the differences between man and man. Here, they seem to say, are circumstances precisely similar, and yet mark how various are the characters which grow out of these circumstances. . . . It is in the enunciation of this difficult truism that Mr. Thackeray differs from all previous novelists. It is the supreme motive of all that he has written, and the key to all the criticism that has been poured upon him. . . . A novelist, writing in accordance with this philosophy, has a most difficult task to perform. It is comparatively easy to draw a character so long as we dwell mainly on points of difference and contrast. But when the object is to touch lightly on mere peculiarities, and to dwell mainly on those traits which we have all in common, and, which, therefore, are anything but salient, the difficulty of the task is enormously increased.

We do not mean for one moment to detract from Mr. George Eliot's originality when we say that after his own fashion he follows this difficult path in which Mr. Thackeray leads the way. He has fully reached that idea which it is so easy to confess in words, but so hard to admit into the secret heart, that we are all alike, that our natures are the same, and that there is not the mighty difference which is usually assumed between high and low, rich and poor, the fool and the sage, the best of us and the worst of us. In general, it is only matured minds that reach this state of feeling—minds that have gone through a good deal and seen through a good deal, and our author has precisely this broad sympathy and large tolerance combined with ripe reflection and finished style, which we admire in Mr. Thackeray. Here the comparison ends. Mr. Eliot differs so widely from Mr. Thackeray in his mode of working out the philosophy which is common to both that some of our readers may wonder how we could ever see a resemblance between him and the great painter of human vanities and weakness. Whereas Mr. Thackeray is, to the great disgust of many young ladies, continually asserting that we have all got an evil corner in our hearts, and little deceitful ways of working, Mr. Eliot is good enough to tell us that we have all a remnant of Eden in us, that people are not so bad as is commonly supposed, and that every one has affectionate fibres in his nature—fine, loveable traits, in his character. . . . But, although tending to such opposite results, the principle upon which both novelists work is the same. . . .

The story is simple enough, and as far as the mere skeleton is concerned, soon told. For the sake of introducing a fair young Methodist who has the gift of preaching, the date of the incidents is thrown to the end of last century, but the time is not strictly observed, and we are not very much surprised to be informed that Bartle Massey "lighted a match furiously on the hob," which is far from being the only anachronism in the tale. Mrs. Poyser, the chatty wife of a well-to-do farmer, is the pivot on which the plot revolves. She is the chorus who is continually intervening with her opinions.

[A long summary of the plot follows.]

There is not much of a story it will be seen. The great charm of the novel is rather in the characters introduced than in the action which they carry on. All the characters are so true, and so natural, and so racy that we love to hear them talk for the sake of talking. They are so full of strange humours and funny pretty sayings that we entirely overlook the want of movement in the story. Besides which, when the dialogue ceases, the author's reflections are so pointed, and his descriptions are so vivid, that we naturally think more of what we have than of what we have not. There is not a character in the novel which is not well drawn, and even if the portrait is but a sketch still it is a true one. We have not mentioned the name of Mr. Irwine, the parson, who is very carefully drawn, nor of his mother, who is touched off in a more rapid manner; and yet the former is a very important personage in the dialogue, and is a fine moral influence throughout the tale. He is a very favourable specimen of the moral preachers of the close of last century, and the author has placed him in contrast to the more Scriptural style of which Dinah Morris, the young Methodist, is the representative. He sympathizes strongly with both, but leans most to the side of those moral teachers who have been somewhat harshly judged, he thinks. Comparing Mr. Irwine with the curate of an "evangelical" turn who succeeded him, he makes Mrs. Poyser pronounce this judgment:—"Mr. Irwine was like a good meal o' victual; *you are the better for him without thinking on it;* but Mr. Ryde is like a dose o' physic; he gripes you and worrets you, and after all he leaves you much the same." Irwine is a noble man, with a fine presence and a kindly catholic nature. He was a silent influence, who did not trouble his parish much with theological "notions," but gave them the example of a kind heart, and demanded from them the reward of honest lives. "It's summat like to see such a man as that i' the desk of a Sunday," says that rattling Mrs. Poyser. "As I say to Poyser, it's like looking at a full crop o' wheat, or a pasture with a fine dairy o' cows in it; it makes you think the world's comfortable-like." The tolerance with which an author who is able to conceive the character of Dinah Morris, and to sympathize with her religious views, is thus pleased to regard a very opposite type of the religious character—a type which many worthy people, no doubt, would be disposed to brand as utterly irreligious, is one of the finest things in the novel, and affords a very good illustration of the tendency of the author to beat down all external differences, and bring into the light the grand points of genuine resemblance. . . .

It will be evident that in order to establish the identity of man with man an author must travel a good deal into the region of latent thoughts, and unconscious or but semi-conscious feelings. There is infinite variety in what we express; there is a wonderful monotony in that great world of life which never comes into the light, but moves within us like the beating of the heart and the breathing of the lungs—a constant, though unobserved influence. It is in this twilight of the human soul that our novelist most delights to make his observations. . . . Like Mr. Thackeray, he takes a peculiar pleasure in showing the contrariety between thought and speech, the heart within and the mask without, which we call a face. He is always showing that we are better than we seem, greater than we know, nearer to each other than, perhaps, we would wish. It is a fertile theme of immense interest, and through the three volumes the author has handled it with rare skill. His dissection of all the motives at work in Arthur Donnithorne's mind when he is pleased to trifle with the affections of Hetty is very masterly—how he was tempted, how he struggled with the temptation, and what a strange under-current of feeling was carrying him on to his purpose, while he took note only of the feeble ripple on the surface. In the case of poor Hetty we have a similar analysis, but one still more difficult, owing to the utterly thoughtless character of the girl. She, perhaps, might be accepted as a fair example of the truth of Pope's very unjust saying, "Most women have no characters at all." Not that she is unreal—she is drawn to the life; but she is one of those who are so much less than they seem to be, whose most significant acts mean so little, that it is not easy to fix upon any central principle in their nature, any strong point of thought, or word, or act which belongs to them. "Hetty's face had a language that transcended her feelings," says the novelist. . . .

All through the work the same train of thought runs, and at the very opening of the novel we have a curious illustration of it in a remark uttered by Joshua Rann, the parish clerk, . . . on the occasion of a crowd collecting on the village-green to hear the young Methodist preach. Many were the comments more or less appropriate, of the village worthies on the audacious act which Dinah Morris was about to commit, but, surely, if there was one comment more unmeaning than another, it was that of old Joshway, who in a resounding voice exclaimed, "Sehon, king of the Amorites; for His mercy endureth for ever; and Og, the king of Basan, for His mercy endureth for ever." Mr. George Eliot points out, with great gusto, the unconscious associations which led to this extraordinary speech—how Mr. Rann felt the necessity of maintaining the dignity of the Church, how, further, he felt that this dignity was bound up with his own sonorous utterances of the responses, and how, in accordance with this theory, he volleyed forth a quotation from the Psalm of the previous Sunday, in order to give a practical illustration of the Church's dignity.

The gem of the novel is Mrs. Poyser, who, for that combination of shrewd remark and homely wit with genuine kindliness and racy style which is so taking in Mr. Samuel Weller, is likely to outvie all the characters of recent fiction, with the single exception of the hero we have named. Mrs. Poyser, in her way, is as amusing as Mrs. Gamp or Mrs. Nickleby, and much more sensible. Wife of a rough and ready farmer, she is a great woman. She is the firstling of the author's mind, which he is not likely to surpass, even as that glorious Sam Weller, the firstling of Mr. Dickens's pen, has not been outshone by any successor. Mrs. Poyser pervades the novel. Her wisdom is always coming out, either spoken by herself, or quoted by somebody else, or mentioned by the author. On one occasion, the author, unable to express himself in his own words, introduces Adam Bede to express the thought in his words, and Adam Bede, finding his own language inadequate, is obliged to fall back upon the expressions used by Mrs. Poyser, whom accordingly he quotes. "You're mighty fond o' Craig," says Mrs. Poyser to her husband, speaking of a certain Scotch gardener; "but for my part, I think he's welly like a cock as thinks the sun's rose o' purpose to hear him crow." This is the Poyser style, a good pungent style, remarkably effective when it is necessary to scold her husband, to subdue her nieces, or to lash the maids. It is a fine thing to hear her out of the goodness of her heart and the fullness of her wisdom abuse her household. . . . Her style runs into proverbs. "Folks must put up wi' their own kin, as they put up with their own noses—it's their own flesh and blood"—she says. "If the chaffcutter had the making of us, we should all be straw, I reckon," she says again. "I'm not one o' those as can see the cat i' the dairy an' wonder what she's come after" is another of her sayings. . . . Of mankind she says, "The men are mostly so slow, their thoughts over-run 'em, an' they can only catch 'em by the tail. Howiver, I'm not denyin' the women are foolish; God Almighty made 'em to match the men." She adds a little further on, "Some folks' tongues are like the clocks as run on strikin', not to tell you the time o' the day, but because there's summat wrong i' their own inside." A good homely woman, it will be observed, who knows how to keep her own, and doing her duty well, has a wonderful supply of self-complacency. . . . In some respects, also, Mrs. Poyser is repeated in another good lady with a querulous twist in her,—old Lisbeth Bede, mother of Adam. When her husband is dead, Adam proposes to go to the village to have the coffin made, fearing that if he worked at it himself it would pain his mother. "Nay, my lad, nay," Lisbeth cries out in a wailing tone, "thee wotna let nobody make thy feyther's coffin but thysen? Who'd make it so well? *An' him, as know'd what good work war,* an's got a son as is th' head o' the village, an' all Treddles'on too, for cleverness." . . . We might go on quoting these speeches until at last we transfer half the novel to our columns. The hero of the work, Adam Bede, is not so remarkable for his speeches as for what he does. He speaks out in a strong, manly way, but not very often with that sharp epigrammatic force which is so characteristic of Mrs. Poyser, Lisbeth Bede, and the schoolmaster, Bartle Massey. . . . The speeches of Seth Bede and of Dinah Morris, though excellent as illustrations of character, are, like those of Adam, not of the epigrammatic sort. Dinah's sermon is very fine, and she herself is a most beautiful piece of portraiture—a perfect chrysolite. The minor sketches are superabundant; they crowd the canvass. We have not here one great and real character in the midst of a mob of lay figures. The subordinate personages are in their way quite as well pictured as the leading one. The whole work, indeed, leaves upon us the impression of something highly finished and well matured, and we close the volumes wondering whether the author is to do better in his next novel,—curious, also, to know who the author really is. Nobody seems to know who is Mr. George Eliot, and when his previous work appeared it was even surmised that he must be a lady, since none but a woman's hand could have painted those touching scenes of clerical life. Now, the question will be raised, can this be a young author? Is all this mature thought, finished portraiture, and crowd of characters the product of a 'prentice hand and of callow genius? If it is, the hand must have an extraordinary cunning, and the genius must be of the highest order.

The Westminster Review (review date 1876)

SOURCE: "*The Westminster Review,* October 1876," in *George Eliot and Her Readers: A Selection of Contemporary Reviews,* edited by John Holmstrom and Laurence Lerner, The Bodley Head, 1966, pp. 22-23.

[*Originally published in 1876, the following excerpt lauds Eliot's characterization of Hetty Sorrel for its artful power and poignance.*]

(This review of ***Daniel Deronda*** prefaced its unfavourable notice of the book with a leisurely survey of G. E.'s other novels, and selected Hetty Sorrel as one of her masterpieces.) . . .

The figure of Hetty is like nothing that art had before developed out of nature, and yet it is profoundly true, with a reality in it which makes the heart ache. The very landscape, hitherto so broad and large and calm, changes and intensifies round this being, so tragical in her levity and shallowness. Never was the hapless simpleton, strange mixture of innocence and that self-love which is the root of ill, deserving of her fate, yet not deserving, in her lightness and reckless ignorance, of any such tremendous encounter with destiny and the powers of evil, so wonderfully set forth. In most cases, when a human soul, either in history or fiction, is brought face to face with the darker passions and calamities, it is of a nature lofty enough to cope with and combat them; but George Eliot was the first to thrill the spectator with the sight of a helpless, frivolous, childish creature, inadequate even to understand, much less to contend with, those gigantic shadows, confronted all at once by despair, crime, remorse, and destruction—things with which her soft childlike foolishness and baby character had nothing to do. The effect produced is much like that which would be roused in us did we see a child set in motion, by some heedless touch, a whole system of grim machinery, such as must crush it into a thousand pieces, and before which we stand trembling and appalled, not only by the horror itself, but by the shock of those tremendous forces employed for such a result. The anguish of pity in such a case is not mingled with any of those nobler sentiments which make the heart swell when we watch a worthy struggle, but is sharp and sore with our inability to assist, and with yearning over the helpless victim. There is nothing finer in modern literature than the power with which this contrast is kept up, and the slightness and frivolity of poor Hetty's being, preserved consistent through all the tempest of woe that comes upon her. A lesser artist would have made this trifling country girl develop into a heroine in face of the terrible emergency; but genius knows better; and the tragedy gains in depth and solemn force from the helpless weakness of the central figure. We have seen a spotless Desdemona, a lovely dream like Juliet perish with a less pang and shiver of feeling than that with which we watch this poor, pretty, self-regarding fool crouch helpless and dumb before the awful fates. . . .

Joseph Wiesenfarth (essay date 1972)

SOURCE: "*Adam Bede* and Myth," in *Papers on Language and Literature,* Vol. VIII, No. 1, Winter, 1972, pp. 39-52.

[*In the following essay, Wiesenfarth looks at the roles Hebrew, Greek, and Christian mythology play in Eliot's presentation of realism in* Adam Bede.]

George Eliot told John Blackwood that ***Adam Bede*** was filled with "the breath of cows and the scent of hay."[1] She never said a word about its being filled with Adam, Prometheus, and Jesus. ***Adam Bede,*** however, is impregnated with allusions to Hebrew, Greek, and Christian mythology. The reviewer of Stahr and Mackay, the translator of Strauss and Spinoza, the disciple of Feuerbach and Müller, the student of Sophocles and Aeschylus is as present in ***Adam Bede*** as the house- and dairy-keeper of Griff House, Nuneaton.[2] But the fact remains that George Eliot chose to speak of the realism of her work.[3] So the question must be: how does myth contribute to realism in the novel?

In ***Adam Bede*** George Eliot dramatizes man's physical and moral-emotional condition. She shows life the way it is and suggests the way it should be so that it actually can become better. Her art blends a realism of presentation (breath of cows and scent of hay) with a realism of assessment (the human need for fellow-feeling).[4] In a phrase, George Eliot creates a meliorist realism in ***Adam Bede:*** one which begins with man and his world the way they actually are and which shows what, through human effort and intelligence, they can become.[5] To be significant in ***Adam Bede,*** myth must effectively support this meliorist theory of reality.

The theory that myth itself portrayed a reality of human existence was Otfried Müller's, and George Eliot had it constantly before her while she was translating *Das Leben Jesu.* For Müller, myth was an expression of the true aspirations, sentiments, and ideals of a community and was given poetic form by one of its more capable members who acted as spokesman for all.[6] Strauss used this sense of myth and demythologized the four gospels on the basis of it. Human feeling for the divine was the reality that the evangelists articulated into a poetic gospel. Under Strauss's scrutiny, Christ became in the nineteenth century the symbol of man's striving for divinization.[7] George Eliot found a similar emphasis on the truth of enduring human feeling in myth when she began translating Spinoza's *Tractatus Theologico-Politicus* in 1849. Spinoza, writing on the Old Testament, insisted that one had to distinguish between truth and meaning in Scripture. Truth is governed by reason; meaning by textual analysis. Truth and meaning come together in vital ethical imperatives. Therefore "the Word of God which we find in the prophets coincides with the Word of God written in our Hearts."[8] Once again myth pointed to the truth of human feeling. George Eliot's own conception of myth was inseparable from her sense of its connection with the persistence of patterns of human feeling in poetic form. Thus her admiration for the classics: "The Greeks were not taking an artificial, entirely erroneous standpoint in their art—a standpoint which disappeared altogether with their religion and art. They had the same elements of life presented to them as we have, and their art symbolized these in grand schematic forms."[9]

"At any given period of literature the conventions of literature are enclosed within a total mythological structure, which may not be explicitly known to anyone, but is nevertheless a shaping principle," writes Northrop Frye; and accepting his dictum, one must recognize that the first and most important thing to say about ***Adam Bede*** is that it articulates a modern myth.[10] It is a story that details one woman's deepest feelings about a world without God—or, more specifically, about a world in which Love substitutes for God, work defines man's social and moral condition, suffering due to selfishness his emotional agony, and fellow-feeling his redemption. George Eliot is the gifted spokesman of a community that more or less consciously shares these convictions. As narrator she "is an all-embracing consciousness," says J. Hillis Miller, and she sees her characters "in terms of their relations to one another and in terms of the universal facts of human nature which they exemplify."[11] ***Adam Bede*** is the Genesis of a community that read George Eliot through four editions of her first novel the year it was published. That community's heritage was Judaeo-Christian and Greco-Roman in origin. Accordingly, this new Genesis incorporates these ancient traditions in the account of modern man that it renders.

Adam Bede contains many of the same elements that the biblical Genesis does, but it rearranges them. The novel gives us an Adam, but he is a Bede—who "justified his name" (5).[12] He shares in the first Adam's curse: he must work. But he is found working before he loses his innocence by seeing Hetty, the woman formed from his imagination, kissing Arthur and violating his trust in her. God is not betrayed in a garden, but Love is betrayed in a wood. The betrayal brings the most intense suffering to Adam, and he is not redeemed until Love again governs his life. His redemption comes through the Christlike Dinah, who marries Adam only after he himself is accommodated to the suffering and risen Jesus—only after the Old Adam becomes the New.

Two basic elements run through these ancient and modern stories. They are love and work. Work is the bond between the gentry and the lower class in the novel. The Poysers are the Donnithorne tenants on the Hall Farm, and Adam is the manager of the Donnithorne timber. The old squire tampers with the bond when he tries to change the working of the farm, but Mrs. Poyser has her "say out" and stops him. Arthur tampers with the bond by making love to Hetty, and Adam gives him a thrashing in the wood. It is Arthur's duty to respect the bond of work between the classes, but he does not. Rather, he attempts love where love is impossible: "No gentleman, out of a ballad, could marry a farmer's niece" (206). Arthur prefers the romance of life to the reality that Adam articulates: "We're like enough to find life a tough job—hard work inside and out" (182).

To characterize Arthur's passion for Hetty, George Eliot goes to Aeschylus for analogues. From *The Libation Bearers* she takes the phrase unloving love, [*aperotos eros*], and then dramatizes the nature of such love by reference to *Prometheus Bound.* These allusions to Aeschylus do not make ***Adam Bede*** a tragedy, but they do give depth and dimension to the characters of Irwine and Adam, Arthur and Hetty.[13] They also foreshadow the pathos inherent in the events subsequent to the seduction.

Mr. Irwine, who invokes the shade of Aeschylus, sits in judgment on Arthur and Hetty. His is the voice of a morality that is Greek in origin and characterized by nemesis. With a Ceres as mother, Juno as a dog, Aeschylus as a breakfast companion, and Sophocles and Theocritus as favorite authors, it is altogether suitable that Irwine's learning should allow him to see life and judge conduct in a classical context. When Arthur comes to him and they speak about love and marriage, Irwine refers Arthur to the chorus of *Prometheus Bound* in which the passion of Zeus for Io is detailed and judged. The chorus's words bear directly on the story of Arthur and Hetty, though they refer explicitly to Zeus and Io.

> Wise was the man who declared, "like is fitly coupled
>   with like, and let equal pair with equal."
> Not for grimy craftsman the hand of a rich man's
>   daughter, nor must
> Simple maid plight troth with purse-proud nobleman.
>
> May it be mine to enjoy youth and beauty far from
>   the eyes of the gods; may Zeus not name me
> Bride nor call me up to his couch on Olympus,
>   where malignant
> Hera looks down on Io's misery!
>
> For me a match within my own degree,
> Not the glance from eyes invisible
> Weaving around me inescapably
> Magical miseries and miracles of wrong,
> Caught in the irresistable
> Cunning of Zeus Almighty.[14]

In ***Adam Bede*** Arthur is like Zeus and Hetty like Io. She even looks upon him as an "Olympian god" (148). Their love is consummated in a Hermitage set in a semienchanted wood, is clearly unreal, and is certainly headed for disaster: "He may be a shepherd in Arcadia for aught he knows, he may be the first youth kissing the first maiden, he may be Eros himself, sipping the lips of Psyche—it is all one" (204). Like Psyche, Hetty is deserted. Like Io, she is doomed to a journey in despair (bk. 5, chap. 37).

Adam is likened to Prometheus by his action and his suffering. Actively, like Goethe's Prometheus, he works and scorns idleness: "what we can *do,* we *are:* our strength is measured by our plastic power. Thus the contempt of Prometheus for the idleness . . . of the gods is both deep and constant."[15] Passively, like the chained Prometheus, who listens to the sad story of the wandering and despairing Io, Adam must hear of Hetty's fate without being able to rescue her from it.[16] Adam is unable to act; he is only able to suffer. Like Prometheus, Adam does not die, but he must suffer for his sympathy with those who do die—Hetty and her child. Prometheus's rage against Zeus is ineffectual, and so is Adam's against Arthur. Were it to be effectual—with individual and societal justice colliding head on—***Adam Bede*** would have been a tragedy, not a tragicomedy.

In revenge there is no chance for amelioration. Revenge breeds death upon death, as George Eliot showed in her analysis of the *Oresteia.*[17] And nothing could have been clearer to her when she was writing ***Adam Bede*** because she was simultaneously reading the Aeschylean trilogy in the Greek. From her Autograph Journal and from Cross's biography, one can determine the exact chronology of her reading of Aeschylus and her writing of ***Adam Bede.***[18] She began reading the *Agamemnon* on August 1, 1857, and she started to write ***Adam Bede*** on October 22. She finished the play on December 6, 1857, and had begun reading *The Libation Bearers* (the *Choephoroe*) by the 17th. She finished reading this play by January 20, 1858, while she was writing chapter 5 of the novel. She immediately began the *Eumenides.* On February 10, chapter 9 of ***Adam Bede*** was completed, and George Eliot began the *Prometheus.* On March 4, 1858, she gave Blackwood the manuscript of the novel to the end of chapter 13. The overlapping of the reading of Aeschylus with the writing of ***Adam Bede*** shows the imaginative resonance that Greek myth gave to a story that first came to George Eliot as a recollection from the life of a Methodist aunt.[19]

Many elements that she must have noticed in the Aeschylean trilogy appear in ***Adam Bede.***[20] Unloving love is transformed into Arthur's passion for Hetty; murder within a bloodline is turned into Hetty's fatal neglect of her child; nemesis shows itself in unpitying consequences: Hetty's trial, transportation, and eventual death; Arthur's ostracism from his home and inheritance; Adam's excruciating suffering. The Furies show themselves in the haunted imagination of Hetty, who sees and hears her dead child: "Dinah, do you think God will take away that crying and the place in the wood, now I've told everything?" (2: 252). Arthur is similarly haunted by Hetty: "I feel sometimes as if I should go mad with thinking of her looks and what she said to me . . ." (2: 275).[21] Perhaps taking a hint from Lewes's analysis of Goethe's *Iphigenia,* George Eliot makes the Furies in ***Adam Bede*** "phantasms moving across the stage of an unhappy soul, . . . visible only to the inward eye."[22]

Adam narrowly avoids entering into the pattern of tragedy. He seeks to revenge himself on Arthur, and only the intervention of Irwine—who understands Aeschylus all too well—prevents him. Consequently, the revenge element of the *Oresteia* works itself out in the novel with a moral wisdom not unlike that which Athena brings to the *Eumenides* itself. Trial by one's peers replaces a cycle of personal revenge. Hetty is judged guilty by a court, and Arthur becomes an exile from a community that cannot tolerate his presence. In the Greek drama, at the end, the Furies are welcomed into Athens as respected guardians of the city and given a new name. In ***Adam Bede,*** ultimately, the hope is that through fellow-feeling the Eumenides (the "workers of grace") will replace the Furies (the "disturbers of sleep") in the heart of man, as they have in the heart of the new Adam.[23]

Had Arthur and Hetty been less callow characters, George Eliot could have created a modern tragedy on an ancient model. Clearly, however, she did not choose to do this. She used Aeschylus to show how, ancient and modern, life demonstrates and demands the same imperative.

> The divine yea and nay, the seal of prohibition and of sanction, are effectually impressed on human deeds and aspirations . . . by that inexorable law of consequences, whose evidence is confirmed instead of weakened as the ages advance; and human duty is comprised in the earnest study of this law and patient obedience to its teaching. . . . Every past phase of human development is part of that education of the race in which we are sharing; every mistake, every absurdity into which poor human nature has fallen, may be looked on as an experiment of which we may reap the benefit."[24]

For Adam to revenge himself on Arthur would be for Adam to have learned nothing and to have called down upon himself that inexorable law which he himself had quoted to Arthur: "... You can never do what's wrong without breeding sin and trouble more than you can see" (250). Or as Irwine puts it more succinctly, "Consequences are unpitying" (258). The consequences of Arthur and Hetty's sin are visited upon Adam, and his suffering is Promethean; but Adam, the only character capable of tragic actions, does not become the architect of a tragedy. On the contrary, taking the advice of Irwine to heart, he prevents further disaster and prepares himself for redemption.

Northrop Frye has shown that comedy and tragedy use the same basic archetypal characters but reverse their functions. In tragic structures, the hero is self-deceived and unwittingly an impostor. The heroine, excluded from society, becomes a picture of unmitigated hopelessness and destitution. The friend of the hero is a plain-speaker and thus a critic of events. And the nature of the irrefragable law that governs man is explicated by a self-effacing individual. These different characters are part of an action that is so plotted that it paradoxically combines "a fearful sense of rightness (the hero must fall) and a pitying sense of wrongness (it is too bad that he falls)."[25] It moves to a moment when what might have been and what will be are seen simultaneously. In ***Adam Bede*** Arthur and Hetty are hero and heroine of a tragedy *manqué.* Adolphus Irwine is a self-effacing wise man who details the operation of nemesis. Adam is Arthur's friend and, as a rival for Hetty's love, his outspoken and hard-hitting critic. The plot moves to Arthur and Hetty's inevitable fall and makes her trial correspond with the day she should have married Adam and the day that Arthur should have taken over the Donnithorne estate.

"The action of comedy moves toward a deliverance from something which . . . is by no means invariably harmless. We notice too how frequently a comic dramatist tries to bring his action as close to a catastrophic overthrow of the hero as he can get it, and then reverses it as quickly as possible."[26] When Dinah's gospel of love—introduced as early as chapter 2 of the novel—emerges as a major moral force in the action, a second self-effacing character appears and the ground-work for a comedic resolution of the novel is laid.[27] With fellow-feeling comes love, and with love amelioration. Thus a new human structure can be built and can reverse a course of action previously governed by the law of nemesis alone. In this comedic strand of action, Adam's friends are his brother and his teacher. Seth, who himself loves Dinah, rejoices in his brother's happiness; Bartle Massey, an incorrigible misogynist, praises Dinah.[28] The heroine changes from a helpless outcast to one who possesses the clue to life and happiness, so Hetty gives way to Dinah. Adam changes from the friend of the false hero to the real hero himself; having lost Hetty (certainly a blessing in disguise), he wins Dinah. Adam, undeceived, passes from ignorance to knowledge and from hardness to love, retaining the stewardship of the property Arthur must leave and finding his love for Dinah as well. The Poysers, shamed by Hetty, approve and celebrate this turn of fortune. Around the hero and heroine, in true comedic fashion, a new society grows up. And the novel ends with Adam and Dinah's two children playing with their Uncle Seth.[29]

This interweaving and developing of a structure akin to tragedy with one of true comedy is accompanied by a gradual emphasis on a new law—the law of love. The consequences of selflessness and fellow-feeling are seen to be as inevitable as the nemesis of selfishness and give hope to the future of a new society. The mythic archetype changes too. George Eliot has shown Bede as an Adam-figure and as a Prometheus-figure. But as his work and suffering move him toward a truly redemptive love, Adam becomes closely associated with Jesus. Adam is purified by suffering in order to learn love.[30] The words of Dinah's letter become the drama of his human development: "Surely it is not true blessedness to be free from sorrow, while there is sorrow and sin in the world: sorrow is then a part of love, and love does not seek to throw it off. It is not the spirit only that tells me this—I see it in the whole work and the word of the gospel. Is there not pleading in heaven? Is not the Man of Sorrows there in that crucified body wherewith he ascended? And is He not one with the Infinite Love itself—as our love is one with our sorrow?" (2: 59). In his suffering, the narrator says of Adam, "the power of loving was all the while gaining new force within him" (2: 303). Adam is brought to this change of heart and mind, which leads to his forgiveness of Arthur and Hetty, by a dramatic entry into the sufferings of Jesus from his agony to his resurrection. If, as Barbara Hardy says, "George Eliot's interest lies in modes of suffering which are moral and exemplary,"[31] Jesus is the moral exemplar for Adam.

The eve of the trial finds Adam a haggard and worn man, bearing within himself the sorrow of his friend's deceit and his beloved's wickedness: "You would hardly have known it was Adam without being told. His face has got thinner this last week: he has the sunken eyes, the neglected beard of a man just risen from a sick-bed" (2: 200). Adam's face—like the "sad face" of a Christ George Eliot saw in Nuernberg—makes the Man of Sorrows seem "a very close thing—not a faint hearsay."[32] On the morning of the trial, Bartle Massey comes to Adam in an "upper room" to get him to eat some lunch: "I must see to your having a bit of the loaf, and some of that wine Mr. Irwine sent this morning" (2: 210). Only after deciding to go to Hetty and to stand beside her does Adam eat: "Nerved by an active resolution, Adam took a morsel of bread, and drank some wine" (2: 214). Adam next suffers with Hetty the agony of her trial and imprisonment.

Later in the novel Eliot relates Adam to the risen Christ. Reading the Bible one Sunday morning, Adam comes upon a picture—"that of the angel seated on the great stone that has been rolled away from the sepulchre" (2: 319).[33] The angel reminds him, with Lisbeth's help, of Dinah. George Eliot here provides the reader with a classically comedic recognition scene: "the person whom the hero is seeking turns out to be the person who sought him."[34] A few moments later his mother intimates to Adam Dinah's love for him, and the narrator returns us to the picture in the Bible: "the blood rushed to Adam's face, and for a few moments he was not quite conscious where he was: his mother and the kitchen had vanished for him, and he saw nothing but Dinah's face turned up towards his. It seemed as if there was a resurrection of his dead joy" (2: 322). This is certainly an accommodation of Adam to the resurrected Christ. Keeping in mind, then, the relation of Adam to Jesus, one might well say that Dinah is, at the mythical level, correct in finally refusing to distinguish between her love for Jesus and her love for Adam.

Dinah presides over the resurrection of Adam's joy as surely as Hetty presided over its death. She rewards Adam's work and love as surely as Hetty disappointed them. This tragic and comedic complexity in Adam's life George Eliot found mirrored in the Old Testament story of Jacob and Rachel. She uses it in ***Adam Bede*** as the overarching analogue of the novel's tragicomic structure. Her use of it stands as "an exemplar of the adaptation of an antique symbol to modern meanings, not [as] the idle imitation of a bygone creed."[35]

If ***Adam Bede*** is to be likened to Jacob, it must be in terms of his own situation. The biblical Jacob is never in doubt about whom he loves. It is Rachel, even though he is tricked into marrying Leah. But Adam first loves Hetty, then Dinah. He must come to find his true Rachel. At one point in the story—an event that seems to have little relevance outside an attempt to suggest Jacob's story—Hetty is equated with Dinah. When walking with Hetty, who has just put a rose in her hair, Adam says, "If a woman's young and pretty, I think you can see her good looks all the better for her being plain dressed. Why, Dinah Morris looks very nice, for all she wears such a plain cap and gown" (336). Shortly after, Hetty appears looking like Dinah: "The little minx had found a black gown of her aunt's, had pinned it close round her neck to look like Dinah's, and made her hair flat as she could, and had tied on one of Dinah's high-crowned borderless net-caps" (342-43).

Jacob's relation to Rachel is defined by love and work. Seth, who himself loves Dinah, delineates that relation nicely: "It's a deep mystery—the way the heart of man turns to one woman out of all the rest he's seen i' the world, and makes it easier for him to work seven year for *her*, like Jacob did for Rachel, sooner than have any other woman for th' asking. I often think of them words, 'And Jacob served seven years for Rachel; and they seemed to him but a few days for the love he had to her!'" (46-47). From the very first chapter, "The Workshop," Adam is characterized by his work. Relating it to Hetty, he muses, "I'd make her life a happy 'un, if a strong arm to work for her, and a heart to love her, could do it" (431). The narrator says of Adam that "he had done the extra work cheerfully, for his hopes were buoyant again about Hetty" (2:

5). He tells Martin Poyser, "I'm a poor man as yet, but she shall want nothing as I can work for" (2: 106). And in great indignation, Adam reminds Arthur when he sees him kissing Hetty, "And I never kissed her i' my life—but I'd ha' worked hard for years for the right to kiss her" (2: 16).

In addition, one specific piece of extra work that Adam undertook was a screen for Arthur's Aunt Lydia. He was supposed to fasten onto it a piece of "very fine needlework, Jacob and Rachel a-kissing one another among the sheep, like a picture" (365). This passage was carefully amended in the manuscript of the novel: what had read "a lady and gentleman" was made to read "Jacob and Rachel."[36]

The relation between work and love is undeniable in Adam's connection with Hetty, but that work finds its fruition in love only when the true Rachel appears in Dinah (a fact emphasized by the scene in which Dinah is played by Hetty in a Methodist dress and netcap). Just as Jacob finds the blessing of his labors in finally winning Rachel, Adam finds his in finally winning Dinah: "What greater thing is there for two human souls, than to feel that they are joined for life—to strengthen each other in all pain, to be one with each other in silent unspeakable memories at the moment of the last parting?" (2: 369).

In ***Adam Bede*** the human world is finally embraced fearlessly unto death. The biblical Adam sinned against God and became the archetypal working man. Prometheus defied Zeus to bring man fire and became the archetypal suffering man. Jesus left heaven for earth and became the archetypal loving man. Jacob wrestled with God and became the archetypal blessed man, though no man before him had seen God and lived. Each of these prototypes of Adam Bede in some way achieves distance from God and identity with man. The characteristics of these prototypes become the characteristics of Adam Bede and are dramatized consistently in relation to a wood, suggesting lack of order, rather than a farm, suggesting order. Adam is placed in charge of that wood by Arthur, but resigns after fighting Donnithorne in the very place Arthur had earlier seduced Hetty. When Arthur leaves Loamshire, however, Adam again assumes the management of the wood and undertakes to give it order. The wood relates to Adam's own life, which he undertakes to reorder after Hetty betrays him. Adam in this way is different from the Poysers. They are disgraced by Hetty and do not forgive her. The unalterable condition of the Hall Farm contrasts with the alterable condition of the Donnithorne wood. The Poysers stand by what was; Adam develops what will be. He has come by the path of suffering from the rigid rules of Burge's workshop to creativity in Dinah's love. Working within the ambience of that love, Adam finds a new hope for life.

I suggested at the beginning of this essay that myth was an essential element of realism in ***Adam Bede.*** This point should no longer be in doubt. Clearly, George Eliot presents the reader of ***Adam Bede*** a new world made out of age-old things carefully arranged and newly interpreted. Whereas the Fall and Redemption once suggested the limits of man's earthly life, work and love now suggest the condition of man's only life. Heaven and hell give way to joy and sorrow, and eternal law to an ethic of consequence and fellow-feeling. Myths, divested of their mystery, are placed in an elemental tragicomic pattern and made to reveal the pain and pleasure of human existence. The ancient and sacred become the ground of the modern and secular, the former impressing on the latter the dignity of ageless wisdom and the preciousness of human life. Adam Bede, consequently, stands forth as a new man in a new world—a new world which work and love make not a paradise but a carefully delineated human possibility.[37]

Notes

1. *The George Eliot Letters,* ed. Gordon S. Haight (New Haven, Conn., 1954), 2:387.

2. Adolf Stahr's *Torso. Kunst, Künstler, and Kunstwerk der Alten* was reviewed by George Eliot in the *Leader,* 17 March 1855, pp. 257f. R. W. Mackay's *The Progress of the Intellect, as Exemplified in the Religious Development of the Greeks and the Hebrews* she reviewed in *Westminster Review* 54 (January 1851): 353-68. David Friedrich Strauss's *Das Leben Jesu kritisch bearbeitet* (1835) George Eliot translated and John Chapman published as *The Life of Jesus, Critically Examined* in 1846. Benedict de Spinoza's *Tractatus Theologico-Politicus* she began translating in 1849; the whereabouts of the manuscript, presuming it is extant, is unknown. Ludwig Feuerbach's *Das Wesen des Christhentums* (1841), which George Eliot translated in 1854, and Karl Otfried Müller's *Prolegomena zu einer wissenschaftlichen Mythologie* (1825), which Strauss used, both had a profound influence on George Eliot's art, as this essay will subsequently demonstrate.

3. The cows and hay have suggested to Ian Gregor not a realistic country world, but an Arcadian one: Ian Gregor and Brian Nicholas, *The Moral and the Story* (London, 1962), chap. 1, pp. 13-32. Gregor argues that George Eliot dramatizes a pastoral world into which the moral tragedy of Hetty Sorrel does not fit: "Hetty feels the impossibility of returning to Hayslope" (27). I do not agree with Gregor's analysis: he recreates Hayslope in his own nostalgic prose, which strings together selected passages in *Adam Bede* that do not give the total picture of George Eliot's community; moreover, he establishes a false dichotomy, demanding of the novel either the tragic irony of Hardy's *Tess* or the pastoral convention of Shakespeare's *Winter's Tale,* a dichotomy that does not allow for George Eliot's doing something quite different from both; finally, he insists on Hetty's story as tragedy, too powerful a genre—in my opinion—for so feeble a character. Gregor's analysis supports his more general thesis that *Adam Bede* is a watershed novel, as in English fiction community and individual interests were vitally and morally more closely interrelated before

the novel's publication and were more separated in other novels after it appeared. In *Adam Bede,* Gregor produces the pastoral community this theory requires. In addition, he cites previous scholarship that views *Adam Bede* "as primarily belonging to a pastoral convention" (32). But Foakes, Hussey, Van Ghent, and Creeger recognize that a country setting does not necessarily produce a pastoral ethic. To Gregor's question, "Can the tree of good and evil grow in Arcadia?" they answer that Hayslope is not Arcadia. Contrary to Gregor, I maintain with Gordon S. Haight (*George Eliot: A Biography* [New York, 1968], pp. 249f) that *Adam Bede* is a novel of realistic effect.

4. This terminology is borrowed from Ian Watt, *The Rise of the Novel* (Berkeley and Los Angeles, 1959).
5. In "The Ethical Revolt against Christian Orthodoxy in Early Victorian England," *The American Historical Review* 60, no. 4 (1955), Howard Murphy writes that "meliorism refers to the notion . . . that the life of man on this earth both can and should be progressively improved through a sustained application of human effort and intelligence. Because it served as a substitute for the otherworldly-salvation motif that has so dominated the history of Christianity, it tended to bring Christianity itself into question, and to put all forms of orthodoxy on trial" (p. 701, n. 2).
6. See C. O. Müller, *Introduction to a Scientific System of Mythology,* trans. John Leitch (London, 1844), p. 111; *The Life of Jesus Critically Examined,* trans. George Eliot (London, 1902 [1st ed. 1846]), p. 81; and "Janet's Repentance," where Bill Powers is made "to issue forth with his companions" at the Bear and Ragged Staff and, "like the enunciator of the ancient myth, make the assemblage distinctly conscious of the common sentiment that had drawn them together (*The Works of George Eliot: Scenes of Clerical Life* [Edinburgh, n.d.], 2:96). This concept of myth appears again in George Eliot's article "Three Months in Weimar," *Fraser's Magazine* 51 (June 1855): 699-706, in which she discusses the classical statue depicting a serpent devouring cakes placed as an offering on top of a column inscribed *Genio loci.* The citizens of Weimar, ignoring Virgil's *Aeneid,* gave a meaning all their own to this statue; see *Essays of George Eliot,* ed. Thomas Pinney (New York, 1963), pp. 85f. Curiously enough, G. H. Lewes had discussed the same statue and myth in *The Life and Works of Goethe* (London, 1959 [1st ed. 1855: *The Life of Goethe*]), p. 201. Though factually inaccurate, the myth had an emotional truth all its own for the citizens of Weimar. *"Et voilà, comme on écrit l'histoire,"* remarks Lewes.
7. *The Life of Jesus* (1902 ed.), pp. 779f.
8. *The Chief Works of Benedict De Spinoza,* trans. and intro. R. H. M. Elwes, 2 vols. (New York, 1955 [1st ed. 1883]), 1:197.
9. John Walter Cross, *George Eliot's Life,* 3 vols. (Edinburgh, n.d.), 3:37. Hereafter cited as *Life.*
10. *A Study of English Romanticism* (New York, 1968), p. 5.
11. *The Form of Victorian Fiction* (South Bend, Ind., 1968), p. 83.
12. *The Works of George Eliot: Adam Bede* (Edinburgh, n.d.), 2:379. Quotations from vol. 1 will be cited in parentheses by page only; from vol. 2 by volume and page.
13. Barbara Hardy argues that Eliot "makes us see a tragedy which is too big for her characters" (*The Novels of George Eliot* [1959; reprint ed., New York, 1961], p. 25). But precisely because Arthur and Hetty are not "big enough," and also because Adam finds love and redemption in Dinah, I think *Adam Bede* is better seen as tragicomedy than as tragedy.
14. Aeschylus, *The Oresteia Trilogy* (*Agamemnon, Choephoroe, Eumenides*). *Prometheus Bound,* ed. Robert W. Corrigan, trans. and intro. George Thompson (New York, 1965), p. 143.
15. Lewes, *Goethe,* p. 184.
16. There are many echoes of *Faust* in *Adam Bede.* Arthur and Hetty are the rich man and the poor maid that Faust and Gretchen were. Hetty and Gretchen are both shown with earrings before a mirror, pregnant out of wedlock, imprisoned for child-murder, given a chance to live just as the hangman approaches: Gretchen refusing Faust's offer and Hetty being swept melodramatically from the scaffold with Arthur's pardon.
17. *Life,* 3:37.
18. George Eliot's manuscript Autograph Journal, 1854-1861 is in the Beinecke Rare Book and Manuscript Library at Yale. See *Life,* 1:374-87; 2:6-11.
19. *Letters,* 2:502-04; see also Gordon S. Haight, "George Eliot's Originals" in Robert C. Rathburn and Martin Steinmann, eds., *From Jane Austen to Joseph Conrad* (Minneapolis, Minn., 1958), pp. 182-86.
20. Robert A. Colby has suggested Dinah Mulock's *A Woman's Thoughts about Women* as a source for the seduction, child-murder, and social attitudes in *Adam Bede* ("Miss Evans, Miss Mulock, and Hetty Sorrel," *English Language Notes* 2 [1964-65]: 206-11). There is, however, no evidence that George Eliot read Dinah Mulock's book, whereas the evidence that she read Aeschylus is unimpeachable. The influence of Aeschylus is also more certain and specific than that of Milton, which U. C. Knoepflmacher argues for in *George Eliot's Early Novels* (Berkeley and Los Angeles, Calif., 1968), chap. 4.
21. George Eliot likened the haunted and haunting look of Hetty to "the wondrous Medusa face, with the

passionate, passionless lips" (*Adam Bede,* 2:145), that is, to the Medusa Rondanini, which she saw in the Glyptothek in Munich on April 17, 1858, while she was writing *Adam Bede* (*Letters,* 2:451).

22. Lewes, *Goethe,* p. 281.
23. Some of my terminology here is taken from Rollo May's discussion of the *Oresteia* in *Love and Will* (New York, 1969), pp. 175-77.
24. *Essays of George Eliot,* p. 31.
25. *Anatomy of Criticism* (New York, 1967), pp. 214-19.
26. Ibid., p. 178.
27. See William M. Jones, "From Abstract to Concrete in *Adam Bede,*" *College English* 17 (1955): 88f, for a discussion of Dinah's sermon in relation to the structure of the novel.
28. Seth's role as Dinah's lover has been mistakenly attributed to George Eliot's reading of Otto Ludwig. Lawrence M. Price, "Otto Ludwig's *Zwischen Himmel und Erde* and George Eliot's *Adam Bede,*" *Dichtung und Deutung,* ed. Karl S. Guthe (Bern, 1961), pp. 113-16, suggests George Eliot's indebtedness to Ludwig because at the end of *Adam Bede* there is "a situation reminiscent of *Zwischen Himmel und Erde*: Two brothers love a woman living near at hand." The problem with Price's hypothesis is that the composition of *Adam Bede* shows that George Eliot saw both Seth and Adam as Dinah's lovers before she read Ludwig's novel. Seth is in love with Dinah from the first chapter of the novel. G. H. Lewes suggested Adam's love for Dinah after George Eliot had read the first thirteen chapters of the novel to him (see *Letters,* 2:435-36, 503). After she had written thirteen chapters of *Adam Bede,* therefore, George Eliot knew that both Seth and Adam would love Dinah. But she did not read Ludwig's novel until after she had written chapter 20 of her own work; consequently Price's theory is untenable. In terms of the structure of *Adam Bede,* a more convincing hypothesis emerges: Arthur's conduct in relation to Hetty and Adam is set in contrast with Seth's conduct in relation to Dinah and Adam—Arthur's being selfish, Seth's generous.
29. "In comedy the erotic and social affinities of the hero are combined and unified in the final scene; tragedy usually makes love and the social structure irreconciliable and contending forces, a conflict which reduces love to passion and social activity to a forbidding and imperative duty" (Frye, *Anatomy,* p. 218).
30. "Christ on the cross," wrote Strauss in paraphrase of De Wette, "is the image of humanity purified by self-sacrifice; we ought all to crucify ourselves with him, that we may rise with him to new life" (*The Life of Jesus,* p. 775).
31. *The Novels of George Eliot,* p. 32.
32. *Life,* 2:19.
33. George Eliot carefully prepared for this recognition scene. In chapter 6 she had written of Dinah's "seraphic gentleness of expression" (p. 107). In chapter 14 Lisbeth tells Adam, "I could be fast sure that pictur was drawed for her i' thy new Bible—th' angel a-sittin' on the big stone by the grave" (p. 208).
34. Frye, *Anatomy,* p. 173.
35. Lewes, *Goethe,* p. 181.
36. British Museum Additional Manuscript 34, 021, MS Adam Bede, 2:114.
37. U. C. Knoepflmacher speaks of *Adam Bede* as an "analogue of an ideal world" (p. 90). I think that this description is not precise. Only *Silas Marner,* with its mixture of fairy tale and comedy, ends with an ideal world. *Adam Bede* ends with a real possibility, not an ideal reality.

Kenny Marotta (essay date 1976)

SOURCE: "*Adam Bede* as a Pastoral," in *Genre,* Vol. IX, No. 1, Spring, 1976, pp. 59-72.

[*In the following essay, Marotta outlines the characteristics of a pastoral, and discusses the limitations of analyzing the pastoral elements in* Adam Bede.]

Many critics have attempted to account for the pastoral element in ***Adam Bede,*** with varying success. These discussions of the novel as a pastoral are of two kinds, which correspond to two ways of defining the genre. The first, which I will call the "simple" definition, offers a list of pastoral items (the theme of retreat and return, the depiction of a *locus amoenus,* etc.). The author of the pastoral either presents the items in order to identify the genre to which they contribute, or employs the genre in order to present the items; in both cases, the genre is its own justification, and the motive for its use can be pursued no farther than the author's nostalgic delight in the pastoral world. What I will call the "allegorical" definition, on the other hand, begins with a meaning, a purpose which the pastoral subserves. Here, pastoral is one particular kind of allegory, a kind that, in Empson's broad definition, puts the complex into the simple. These different definitions can be seen to arise from the problematic nature of the genre: they can be easily translated as the Nature and Art of Renaissance pastoral debate, such as that conducted in Marvell's poetry.[1] But in the opposition of things meaningful in themselves to things meaningful by their attributed significances, these different views of pastoral correspond to oppositions that nearly always arise in discussions of Eliot's works: "art" and "ideology," "realism" and "moralism." And the views of ***Adam Bede*** that arise out of these contrary definitions also correspond to the traditional contraries of Eliot criticism. This suggests that a discus-

sion of the pastoral element in the novel can only be dubiously illuminating. In fact, however, such discussion can illuminate both Eliot's purposes and a characteristically Victorian use of pastoral.

We may begin by noting the common limitation of the two attempts to describe the pastoral element in ***Adam Bede***: their opposition of the novel's use of pastoral to its claims, stated in Chapter xvii, to the "faithful representing of commonplace things." The "simple" view of pastoral has been put forth most recently and comprehensively by Michael Squires in *The Pastoral Novel.* By his definition, the pastoral novel, of which he discusses specimens by Hardy and Lawrence as well as Eliot, is characterized by some number of the following "elements and techniques of traditional pastoral":

> the contrast between city and country; the recreation of rural life from both urban and rural viewpoints; the implied withdrawal from complexity to simplicity; the nostalgia for a Golden-Age past of peace and satisfaction; the implied criticism of modern life; and the creation of a circumscribed and remote pastoral world.[2]

Critics who apply this kind of definition to ***Adam Bede*** must either ignore certain of the harsher aspects of its world or see a split between these "realistic" aspects and the pastoral aspects.[3] The "allegorical" critics, on the other hand, do not see this opposition, nor do they exclude suffering from their pastoral world. But realism is equally alien to their version of pastoral, which pretends to record no true landscape—which need not even take place in the country.[4] Although one kind of critic sees Eliot's pastoralism as decoration and the other sees it as allegory, both find it inconsistent with Eliot's pretensions to realism, and both see it as a form of self-deception (although what the former critics would call evasion the latter would ultimately call the creation of a religion). Neither of the resultant images of Eliot—as sentimental celebrant or as sibyl—seems just to Eliot or to the kind of realism she sought.

For Eliot herself pointed out this apparent divergence between pastoral and a truthful record of country life, most explicitly in her essay **"The Natural History of German Life."** A life in the fields, she asserts, is no guarantee of happiness, straight teeth, and high morality.[5] The complaint is repeated in ***Adam Bede***: "The bucolic character of Hayslope, you perceive, was not of that entirely genial, merry, broad-grinning sort, apparently observed in most districts visited by artists."[6] Thus, at least in her explicit statements, Eliot objects to the notion of peasants as *putti.*

Yet in that same essay, Eliot's argument for the interest of the true peasantry attributes to that body qualities pertaining to these artificial pastoral conventions. There was less invidious social distinction among the English peasantry of "half a century ago": "the master helped to milk his own cows, and the daughters got up at one o'clock in the morning to brew . . . the family dined in the kitchen with the servants, and sat with them round the kitchen fire in the evening." There was a lack of individuality, a sameness of interests and characteristics which militated against change and preserved peace; even feuds, preserved through history, became ritualized "under the milder form of an occasional round of cudgelling and the launching of traditional nicknames." The material and aesthetic luxuries of civilization are lacking: "In those days, the quarried parlour was innocent of a carpet, and its only specimens of art were a framed sampler and the best teaboard . . . instead of carrying on sentimental correspondence, [the daughters] were spinning their future table-linen."[7]

Eliot seems consciously to bring this ambivalence to our attention in ***Adam Bede.*** The inhabitants of Hayslope can appear to be artless, adherent to custom, in harmony with Nature. The dancing at Arthur's birthday feast is merry, simple, sprightly, in contrast to the "languid men in lacquered boots smiling with double meaning" of our own day, when dancing has lost both its simplicity and its customary function of reaffirming social bonds and social hierarchy: "It'll serve you to talk on, Hetty, when you're an old woman—how you danced wi' th' young Squire the day he came o' age" (xxvi). But this instance of simplicity and custom is charged with a contrary meaning: Hetty has more than danced with the young Squire, whose smiles do carry a double meaning; and just for this reason she will never be an old woman. Nor can the natural comforts of Hayslope hide the different world of Snowfield, an industrial world that will alter Hayslope's future. Even within this pleasant natural world, no benign influence is exerted over Hetty Sorrel. Perhaps the best sign of the deceptiveness of this pastoral appearance is the fact that such conceptions are attributed to characters themselves deceived or deceiving. When Arthur kisses Hetty, "he may be a shepherd in Arcadia for aught he knows" (xiii); and Adam thinks his marriage with Hetty will be "a marriage such as they made in the golden age" (xv).

As these ambiguities suggest, the perception of pastoral attributes depends upon the condition of the viewer. Mrs. Poyser's comments on farm life are perhaps the most characteristic expression of this fact: "Yes; a farmhouse is a fine thing for them as look on, an' don't know the liftin', an' the stannin', an' the worritin' o' th' inside, as belongs to't" (xx). Only at a distance does life take on these ideal simplicities and congruities: "The jocose talk of haymakers is best at a distance; like those clumsy bells round the cows necks, it has rather a coarse sound when it comes close, and may even grate on your ears painfully; but heard from far off, it mingles very prettily with the other joyous sounds of nature" (xix). And, as Squires has shown in convincing detail, the narrator himself at times keeps this distance, designedly sustaining the pastoral illusion.[8]

This ambivalence towards the pastoral is very like Wordsworth's. In Book VIII of *The Prelude,* Wordsworth rejects "literary" pastoral—the classical Arcadia, Shakespeare's pastorals, Spenser's—for "the rural ways / And manners which may childhood looked upon / . . . the unluxuriant produce of a life / Intent on little but substantial needs, / Yet rich in beauty, beauty that was felt."[9] But his description of rustic life in the 1800 Preface to *Lyrical Ballads* as simple, artless, unchanging, and more real than other lives, is like Eliot's in its return to the convention.[10]

Point of view is significant to Wordsworth's pastoral as well: the meaning of his rustics depends on his distance from them. Their eminent reality is an artifice, a willed appearance dependent upon the viewer as much as the mellowness of landscapes was upon the Claude-Lorraines through which eighteenth-century enthusiasts looked. The artificiality is evident in the special style which, Harold Toliver argues, Wordsworth uses to convey the special truth of the rustic life: either an "abstract language" which "allows some sense of place and time to coexist with types of eternity" or a concrete language that points beyond itself to what is lost or hidden.[11]

These two styles are interestingly similar to the two George Eliot's critics see: one relying on the multifarious capacities of language, the other doomed to the flatness of a gilt-framed mirror. What is yet more interesting is that these two styles are employed in ***Adam Bede*** not simply by Eliot trying to infer ideals in the grimmer aspects of life in Hayslope, but by the characters themselves. In the depiction of her characters' efforts, Eliot is regarding critically the transforming act of pastoralizing.

The reality the characters must transform is what appears to them in moments of disillusionment. Barbara Hardy has pointed out the recurrence of such moments in Eliot's works.[12] One locus in ***Adam Bede*** is Hetty's awakening the morning after reading Arthur's letter:

> Every morning to come, as far as her imagination could stretch, she would have to get up and feel that the day would have no joy for her . . . she should always be doing things she had no pleasure in, getting up to the old tasks of work, seeing people she cared nothing about, going to church, and to Treddleston, and to tea with Mrs. Best, and carrying no happy thought with her. (xxxi)

Such quotidian realities can be transfigured by love or religious feeling. The influence of Arthur's affection made Hetty "tread the ground and go about her work in a sort of dream, unconscious of weight or effort, and [showed] her all things through a soft, liquid veil, as if she were living not in this solid world of brick and stone, but in a beatified world" (ix). In the same way Adam sees in Hetty that beauty "beyond and far above the one woman's soul that it clothes . . . he called his love frankly a mystery. . . . He only knew that the sight and memory of her moved him deeply, touching the spring of all love and tenderness, all faith and courage within him" (xxxiii).

Alternatively, reality can be transformed by Mrs. Poyser's combination of memory and prophecy, which can find a tale in everything:

> "Spinning, indeed! It isn't spinning as you'd be at, I'll be bound, and let you have your own way. . . . To think of a gell o' your age wanting to go and sit with half-a-dozen men! . . . And you, as have been here ever since last Michaelmas, and I hired you at Treddles'on stattits, without a bit of character—as I say, you might be grateful to be hired in that way to a respectable place. . . . Why, you'd leave the dirt in heaps i' the corners—anybody 'ud think you'd never been brought up among Christians. . . . You're never easy till you've got some sweetheart as is as big a fool as yourself: you think you'll be finely off when you're married, I daresay, and have got a three-legged stool to sit on, and never a blanket to cover you, and a bit o' oat-cake for your dinner, as three children are a-snatching at." (vi)

Even when she is quoted at such length, as she must be, Mrs. Poyser's effect is difficult to convey. Her speeches do not have limitations, beginnings and endings, like those of other speakers; this is in fact part of the point of this character, as I will suggest below.

I would assert that these two modes of transformation correspond to Wordsworth's two modes of using language. The first mode is an invocation of abstract terms, usually coupled with a lament that all words are futile. The schism between the concrete occasion and the abstract language is obvious, being applied to characters who could not use such language themselves. The passage on Adam's response to Hetty's beauty quoted above includes the remark "our good Adam had no fine words into which he could put his feeling for Hetty," before proceeding, "he could not disguise mystery in this way with the appearance of knowledge." Precisely in Adam's inarticulateness is his closeness to the truth of feeling. The abstractions he could not use thus emphasize the ineffability of the experience, and so paradoxically seem all the better to suggest it.

The second mode is an associative accumulation of concrete facts of past or future which often militates against meaning itself: Mrs. Poyser has so much difficulty keeping to a subject that her original meaning is almost always lost. The only message that succeeds in emerging from her harangues is the need to stave off the ever-encroaching chaos by constant vigilance—an ironic message, surely, when one considers its chaotic vehicle.

The ultimate tendency of the first sort of transformation is visible in a character such as Dinah, whose habit it is "to forget where I am and everything about me, and lose myself in thoughts that I could give no account of, for I could neither make beginning nor ending of them in words" (viii). The tendency of the second sort of transformation is visible in Mrs. Poyser. While Dinah's abstraction tends to a mystical—or self-deceived—silence, Mrs. Poyser's unceasing lectures tend to the opposite, a tendency finally fulfilled in one of the novel's scenes most clearly in the tradition of the simple pastoral: the harvest supper. In this scene, Eliot repeatedly emphasizes the primitive and ceremonial character of the events by ironic comparisons of the participants to Tityrus and Meliboeus and of their song to the Homeric writings. At the end of the scene we reach the long-awaited confrontation between Bartle Massey and Mrs. Poyser, a confrontation whose staged character seems confessed by Mr. Poyser's attitude throughout. This battle of the sexes is brought to a conclusion (as Mrs. Poyser says, "I say as some folks' tongues are like the clocks as run on strikin', not to tell you the time o' the day, but because there's summat wrong i' their own inside") by the sudden uproar of those Homeric ballads being sung all at once at full volume. The various elements of the uproar (at which Dinah is not present, having fled from Adam's avowal of love)—the ceremony, the pastoral echoes, the ritual debate, and Mrs. Poyser's final remark—contribute to a single statement: the language by which we seek to transfigure unordered reality can itself be a further chaos, can be mere noise. The novel's plot conveys the limitations of these different modes of transformation by the failure of both Mrs. Poyser and Dinah to provide proper nurture or comfort for Hetty, and by the insufficiency of Hetty's own version of these attitudes (her dreams of Arthur and the opposing vision of her daily activities).

An equally significant method of criticizing these pastoralizing attitudes is Eliot's own use of them, the limits becoming apparent in the conflict of the two attitudes. We see instances of the simple, descriptive method, apparently rooted in nostalgia, in Eliot's presentation of characters such as the Miss Irwines, "inartistic figures crowding the canvas of life without adequate effect" (v), introduced in the novel apparently for the purpose of asserting the relevance of the irrelevant. The Miss Irwines forestall theoretical objections against Irwine's type of ministry in two ways: by providing an opportunity for Irwine to reveal his charitable principles, they offer evidence against aspersions on his moral character; in addition—and this is what is most important here—by the simple fact of their concreteness and particularity, they offer evidence against all merely theoretical arguments. They are a sort of noise, and this is precisely their value. Mrs. Poyser is herself "noise" like this, the superfluity of the chapter in which she has her "say out" being particularly noticeable (and noticed by critics).

To these instances might be added all that seem irrelevant to the plot of seduction and betrayal: the set-pieces of praise for lost days, the descriptions of Nature, the traditional ceremonies, those intrusions of a first-person narrator conceived not as omnipotent artist but as a man who might have lived in a world like Adam's, whose "we" joins us with him and with the novel's characters. In these instances, too, Eliot is before us in pointing out the irrelevance: denying her shame for "commemorating old Kester" (liii), discussing our participation in Adam's imperfect world in a chapter "in which the story pauses a little," most obviously, perhaps, insisting upon the indifference to her story of the nature she records. Although its cycles are comfortingly invoked and its imagery is confidently used to explain the development of the characters, Nature is ultimately mysterious. Its indifference, the narrator insists, evades any meaning attached to it: "For if it be true that Nature at certain moments seems charged with a presentiment of one individual lot, must it not also be true that she seems unmindful, unconscious of another?" (xxvii). The strongest expression of the natural world's resistance of meaning is Eliot's use of the "et in Arcadia ego" theme whose history has been traced by Erwin Panofsky.[13] "It was a strangely mingled picture—the fresh youth of the summer morning, with its Eden-like peace and loveliness, the stalwart strength of the two brothers in their rusty morning clothes, and the long coffin on their shoulders" (iv). Later the narrator muses again on the landscape of Loamshire:

> What a glad world this looks like, as one drives or rides along the valleys and over the hills! I have often thought so when, in foreign countries, where the fields and woods have looked to me like our English Loamshire—the rich land tilled with so much care, the woods rolling down the gentle slopes to the green meadows—I have come on something by the roadside which has reminded me that I am not in Loamshire: an image of great agony—the agony of the Cross . . . and surely, if there came a traveller to this world who knew nothing of the story of man's life upon it, this image of agony would seem to him strangely out of place in the midst of this joyous nature. (xxxv)

In both instances, Eliot points out the strange inconcinnity between man and his world: Nature has nothing to say to these greatest crises of men's lives. In the second instance, even the symbol on which the rhetoric turns must be imported from the Continent.

The opposite sort of transformation is suggested by the narrator's alternate stance, as one at a distance from what he records—the distance of creator from creation. Those passages that transform reality in an abstract language unavailable to the characters reveal by their imagery the basis of the transformation in the artist's power: "Our caresses, our tender words, our still rapture under the influence of autumn sunsets, or pillared vistas, or calm majestic statues, or Beethoven symphonies all bring with them the consciousness that they are mere waves in an unfathomable ocean of love and beauty" (iii). Such references seem peculiarly incongruous in the context of Hayslope; note, for instance, the different effects of the art-references in Eliot's other novels, where the art-works are part of the characters' environments—Cheverel Manor, fifteenth-century Florence, Rome, London studios. Art is what the narrator knows about and the characters don't. Furthermore, it is what the narrator uses: by his references to art he gives meaning to his created pastoral world, he embodies in it even those kinds of experience it would seem necessarily to exclude. As in Marvell's pastoral, "though art . . . accepts itself as a tour de force, becoming deliberately diminished and artificial in its aims, it will not give up a magical ambition to rival or supplant nature."[14] This ambition is a prime source of the appeal of ***Adam Bede***: we take pleasure both in the simplicity of the pastoral world and in the way in which this simplicity is made to imply complexity. The narrator, who refers to Homeric criticism and tells us of his European travels, thereby reminding us of his superiority in experience, in philosophy, and even in social class to his subjects, also points out how the pastoral world contains the fruit of his experience and is in fact a symbolic expression of that experience. The numerous allegorical interpretations of ***Adam Bede,*** and of ***Silas Marner*** (critically the quickest-dissolving of all of George Eliot's efforts at embodiment), attest to the success with which larger issues, in the most obvious way irrelevant to the novel's remote world, are carried by their pastoral vehicles.

Eliot's primary method of creating her allegory is, like Dinah's, the use of an abstract language provided by Christianity, a language whose limits are, like those of Dinah's vocabulary, confessed: "After our subtlest analysis of the mental process, we must still say, as Dinah did, that our highest thoughts and our best deeds are also given to us" (x). Knoepflmacher has suggested that the allegory is Feuerbachian, offering a natural basis for the supernatural language, as in Eliot's use of bread and water, culminating in Adam's last supper.[15] This interpretation can be further borne out by Eliot's use of religious language for secular concepts (e.g. suffering is a "baptism" [xlii]) and by the implicit correspondences she establishes between secular feelings and events and Christianity. One interesting example of the latter is the juxtaposition of Seth's hymn—"Dark and cheerless is the morn / Unaccompanied by thee: / Joyless is the day's return / Till thy mercy's beams I see"—to the description of Adam's happiness in the morning because of his love for Hetty: "His happy love . . . was to his thoughts what the sweet morning air was to his sensations: it gave him a consciousness of wellbeing that made activity delightful" (xxxviii).

In the allegory of Renaissance pastoral, the artist is a "second God creating a second Nature."[16] The allegorical critic sees Eliot replacing the idea of God with physical and psychological laws, and ultimately with an abstract and unverifiable Law that is really the artist's will. ***Adam Bede*** does suggest, in several ways, a God-like artist. One can go further than Knoepflmacher, who has discussed the futility of foresight and the value of hindsight in the novel, by noting that the narrator's exercise of foresight, borne out by events, places a value on the artistic imagination which Knoepflmacher attributes to memory.[17] The narrator often suggests the potential contained as a seed in any event. Of Arthur's prospects we are told, "many a 'good fellow,' through a disastrous combination of circumstances, has undergone a like betrayal"; of Hetty's, "it is too painful to think that she is a woman, with a woman's destiny before her—a woman spinning in young ignorance a light web of folly and vain hopes which may one day close round her and press upon her, a rancorous poisoned garment" (xii, xxii). The proximity of art and religion, upon which the accuracy of such divination rests, is suggested in those passages which associate the transforming powers of love and of art. In explaining Adam's love for Hetty, Eliot writes, "the beauty of a lovely woman is like music: what can one say more? Beauty has an expression beyond and far above the one woman's soul that it clothes. . . . The noblest nature sees the most of this *impersonal* expression in beauty" (xxxiii). Adam's aesthetic appreciation of his beloved enables him to see beyond her material reality to a higher order.

The author's providence is also implied in the end of the first chapter, "The Workshop," in which an elderly horseman stops to look at "the stalwart workman."

Adam, unconscious of the admiration he was exciting, presently struck across the fields, and now broke out into the tune which had all day long been running in his head:—

> "Let all thy converse be sincere,
> Thy conscience as the noonday clear;
> For God's all-seeing eye surveys
> Thy secret thoughts, thy works and ways."

The lines are thematically significant, demonstrating at once Adam's self-righteousness—his ignorance of the complexity which makes the imputation of blame so difficult—and the futility of the many deceptions and moral subterfuges which do occur in the novel. But the close proximity of the all-seeing eye of God and the unknown stare of the stranger (and of the reader, also permitted to see Adam's secret thoughts) suggests that the higher order in Adam's life, of which he cannot be aware, is his participation in the literary work.

To discover the limits of this point of view, we have to return to the other model for the narrator and the novel, and to attempt for a moment the feat that Eliot sustained throughout ***Adam Bede,*** and that saves her from the errors of her characters: the simultaneous contemplation of the two contradictory pastoralizing attitudes. The suggestions of allegory and of sophisticated artifice we have just explored work to undermine the pretence of irrelevance we first looked at (as do the very metaphors of the passages insisting on their irrelevance—the canvas of life, Eden, the coffin, the cross, all meaningful human artifacts, the last introduced into the landscape only by the memory of the human viewer). And the claims of irrelevance, of an impenetrable Nature, undermine the pretence of a world controlled and made meaningful.

Eliot builds into the plot itself elements which deny the allegorical meaning we have been pressing toward. The fortunate fall which, following the Christian pattern, should be enacted, does not seem to be. Critics who see such a pattern in the novel balk at Eliot's and her characters' insistence that good cannot come out of evil, or at the incommensurate quality of Hetty's plight and Adam's final marriage to Dinah. But these two objections are related, and become answerable once we reject the Christian premise of a fortunate fall. What is lacking to such a premise in this novel is the adumbration of higher order: Hetty's plight and Adam's marriage are intended to be incommensurate.

There is undeniably a sacrifice at the center of the novel. But the pathos of Hetty is integrally related to the final union. Her sacrifice is not quite a Christian sacrifice of self to God; it is rather extorted than not, and it removes obstacles in the way of earthly rather than heavenly fulfillment. Hetty's ruin does incarnate the failure of sheer, egoistic this-worldliness and materialism, and it is of a power almost sufficient to shift the novel's focus. But she is ultimately a fossil, an "unassimilable fragment."[18]

What Eliot achieves by using this sacrifice as a pivot in her pastoral novel is to make clear the minimal, essential fact out of which religion grows—the renunciation life forces on us—and to offer us not the eternal consolations of religion, nor the temporary and delusive consolations of nostalgia, but the temporary and acknowledged consolations of art. The replacement of Providence by the author's providence is an avowed replacement, not a sleight of hand. By keeping before us the two opposing models of pastoral, Eliot makes us realize that the novel's nostalgic descriptions only reiterate Nature's opacity, and that the intimations of meaning only reveal the human need to create such fictions.

Whether regarded as surface or as symbol, the pastoral world of ***Adam Bede*** insists on its distance from a reality independent of human perception. Thus the novel obviates the question of "realism," as Eliot herself does by her metaphor of the defective mirror—a mirror the faintness or blurring of whose reflection says as much about itself as about what is reflected. As in Tennyson's gardens, the "surface" and the "meaning" of ***Adam Bede*** are inseparable: they are equally projected by the perceiver, equally distant from the world of our own immediate knowledge. Thus, the significance of ***Adam Bede,*** and the nature of its realism, can be conveyed in a passage that is simply descriptive: that in which the narrator reminisces about the taste of whey.

> Ah! I think I taste that whey now—with a flavour so delicate that one can hardly distinguish it from an odour, and with that soft gliding warmth that fills one's imagination with a still, happy dreaminess. And the light music of the dropping whey is in my ears, mingling with the twittering of a bird outside the wire network window—the window overlooking the garden, and shaded by tall Gueldres roses. (xx)

His actual distance from that whey is an image of our distance from it: what should be our most intimate experience can only be words on a page. For what in the seventeenth century was the appropriate genre for intimations of higher order, in the nineteenth has become a genre for expressing doubts about any order higher than that of the artist's work, and any ordering consciousness more comprehensive than the individual mind. Yet, within the novel's accepted illusion, we also taste the whey, as we adumbrate a loving presence behind the novel's world, and certainty in Eliot's repeated "surely." It was perhaps this special iridescence of the pastoral genre, its constantly dual possibilities, that led Eliot to use it in her first major novel.

Notes

1. Among the many works on this subject are Frank Kermode's introduction to *English Pastoral Poetry* (London: G. C. Harrap, 1952), pp. 11-44; Leo Marx, *The Machine in the Garden* (New York: Oxford Univ. Press, 1964), especially chapter 2; Edward William Tayler, *Nature and Art in Renaissance Literature* (New York: Columbia Univ. Press, 1964); and Donald M. Friedman, *Marvell's Pastoral Art* (London: Routledge and Kegan Paul, 1970).

2. Michael Squires, *The Pastoral Novel: Studies in George Eliot, Thomas Hardy, and D. H. Lawrence* (Charlottesville: Univ. of Virginia Press, 1974), p. 18.

3. In the former group are R. A. Foakes, "*Adam Bede* Reconsidered," *English,* 12 (1958-59), 173-76; and John Paterson, "Introduction," *Adam Bede,* ed. Paterson (Boston: Houghton-Mifflin, 1968), pp. v-xxxiii (an otherwise commendable introduction). In the latter are Ian Gregor, *The Moral and the Story* (London: Faber and Faber, 1962), pp. 13-32; Jerome Thale, *The Novels of George Eliot* (New York: Columbia Univ. Press, 1959), pp. 14-16; Raymond Williams, *The Country and the City* (New York: Oxford Univ. Press, 1973), pp. 173, 178-80, and Squires. Squires's argument is somewhat ambiguous in this regard. Although at one point he contends that Eliot offers a criticism of the pastoral's idea of the sufficiency of innocence, his

main argument is that Eliot alternates anguish and pastoral in order to persuade the reader "to accept the novel's pastoralism as meaningful rather than escapist, significant rather than artificially pretty, since the novel's fictional world does not seem unreal" (p. 83). But since it is, according to Squires, the "anti-pastoral" elements of the novel's world that give it reality, this acceptance can only be self-deluding, although the substitution of "meaningful" for "realistic" evades this issue. A sympathetic discussion of the Theocritean model for the simple pastoral is Thomas G. Rosenmeyer's *The Green Cabinet* (Berkeley: Univ. of California Press, 1969).

4. The allegorical view of *Adam Bede* is taken by U. C. Knoepflmacher, *George Eliot's Early Novels: The Limits of Realism* (Berkeley: Univ. of California Press, 1968), pp. 90-93; John Bayley, "The Pastoral of Intellect," in *Critical Essays on George Eliot,* ed. Barbara Hardy (New York: Barnes and Noble, 1970), pp. 199-213; and John Goode, "*Adam Bede,*" in *Critical Essays,* pp. 19-41. Bayley's definition of the genre is so broad that it demands neither a rural setting nor a significant landscape.
5. "The Natural History of German Life," in *Essays of George Eliot,* ed. Thomas Pinney (New York: Columbia Univ. Press, 1963), pp. 269-70.
6. *Adam Bede,* Cabinet ed. (Edinburgh: William Blackwood, 1878), II, liii, 349. Further references by chapter to *Adam Bede* in this edition will be given in the text.
7. "The Natural History of German Life," pp. 273, 274-75, 277, 273. Raymond Williams shows how Eliot's very belief in the existence of English peasants at the turn of the nineteenth century is a sign that she shared in the myth of pastoral, which ignored the actual conditions of farm-workers.
8. Squires, pp. 77-84.
9. *Poetical Works,* ed. Thomas Hutchinson, rev. by Ernest De Selincourt (London: Oxford Univ. Press, 1969), pp. 734-35.
10. Squires has also noted this, following David Ferry; see Squires, p. 42; David Ferry, *The Limits of Mortality* (Middletown: Wesleyan Univ. Press, 1959), pp. 94-96, 135-43. See also Herbert Lindenberger, *On Wordsworth's Prelude* (Princeton: Princeton Univ. Press, 1963), p. 249.
11. Harold E. Toliver, *Pastoral Forms and Attitudes* (Berkeley: Univ. of California Press, 1971), p. 254.
12. Barbara Hardy, *The Novels of George Eliot* (New York: Oxford Univ. Press, 1959), pp. 189-200. Compare, in *Adam Bede,* Adam's powerless "counting of the long minutes" as he waits for Hetty's trial (xlii), and the "purposeless tenacity" of Old Poyser's attention to trivial details (xiv).
13. Erwin Panofsky, "Et in Arcadia Ego," in *Pastoral and Romance,* ed. Eleanor Terry Lincoln (Englewood Cliffs: Prentice-Hall, 1969), pp. 25-46; and "Et in Arcadia Ego: On the Conception of Transience in Poussin and Watteau," in *Philosophy and History: Essays Presented to Ernst Cassirer,* ed. Raymond Klibansky and H. J. Paton (1936; rpt. New York: Harper Torchbooks, 1963), pp. 223-54.
14. Geoffrey Hartman, "'The Nymph Complaining for the Death of Her Faun': A Brief Allegory," in *Beyond Formalism* (New Haven: Yale Univ. Press, 1970), p. 179. Compare Kitty W. Scoular, *Natural Magic* (Oxford: Oxford Univ. Press, 1965); and Kathleen Williams, "Courtesy and Pastoral in *The Faerie Queene,* Book VI," *R.E.S. [Review of English Studies],* n.s. 13 (1962), 343.
15. Knoepflmacher, *Religious Humanism and the Victorian Novel* (Princeton: Princeton Univ. Press, 1965), pp. 55-59.
16. Norman Robkin, "The Holy Sinner and the Confidence Man: Illusion in Shakespeare's Romances," in *Four Essays on Romance,* ed. Herschel Baker (Cambridge: Harvard Univ. Press, 1971), p. 52.
17. Knoepflmacher, *George Eliot's Early Novels,* pp. 97-116.
18. The phrase is John Goode's; see "*Adam Bede,*" p. 25.

Mason Harris (essay date 1978)

SOURCE: "Arthur's Misuse of the Imagination: Sentimental Benevolence and Wordsworthian Realism in *Adam Bede,*" in *English Studies in Canada,* Vol. IV, No. 1, Spring, 1978, pp. 41-59.

[*In the following essay, Harris examines Arthur's class consciousness and the psychology of his seduction of Hetty as they are revealed through Eliot's use of Wordsworthian realism.*]

Because ***Adam Bede*** is "a country story—full of the breath of cows and the scent of hay,"[1] it seems to invite oversimplified interpretations. Critics assume that George Eliot's first novel lacks the complexity of her later work, or at least that any complexity it possesses must be in conflict with its pastoral elements. Part of the problem in getting a clear perspective on this novel arises from a tendency to concentrate critical attention on the rather idealized Adam and Dinah as representatives of the author's values, while passing over Arthur, who does not belong to the pastoral community and whose affair with a tenant farmer's niece almost destroys it, as a rather ordinary seducer treated with conventional Victorian moralism. In a recent book on George Eliot, Neil Roberts expresses a widely-held view of the novel when he says that it presents a "static moral drama" enacted in an "absence of social and historical analysis" because Arthur's sin is only "a matter of private morality" unrelated to his grandfather's acquisitiveness as landlord.[2]

I shall argue that this seduction is very much a matter of class, and that Eliot's sense of historical process, if somewhat muted by nostalgia, is still active in the novel. A close study of the psychology behind Arthur's crime will show the vital thematic use Eliot makes of his aristocratic status and his participation in the literary taste of the later eighteenth century (Arthur turns twenty-one in 1799). As the well-intentioned heir to his grandfather's estate, Arthur reveals much about the influence of unconscious snobbery in rationalizing the exploitation of social inferiors, while as a reader of fashionable fiction who scorns the first edition of *Lyrical Ballads* he provides a contrast to the narrator's Wordsworthian realism, revealing what the imagination should not be both in art and life.

This contrast also suggests a turning point in the history of taste and sensibility. The moral vision of Adam, Dinah, and their author has something in common with the Romantic concept of the imagination (in Dinah's case mixed with the best aspects of the religious revival), while Arthur, thoroughly imbued with the aristocratic taste and social attitudes of his period, reflects the limitations of the old order and thus helps to show how the novel's narrative vision looks forward to the needs of Eliot's own time as well as celebrating the virtues of the past.

The timing of the action, with a leisurely account of the rustic community through the summer of 1799, while crime, suffering, and new insight come in the winter and spring of 1800, suggests a sense of transition between past and present. Hetty, the "lost lamb," is rejected by the rustic community but rescued by Dinah, whose Methodism has been nurtured in a bleak industrial town and who recognizes no distinctions of rank.[3] Again, the new insight which enables Adam to bear the pain of Hetty's fall foreshadows Eliot's mid-Victorian religion of humanity.[4] On the other hand, Arthur's ideal vision of his future reign as Squire is based on the world-view of a ruling class soon to become obsolete.

In her depiction of the semi-feudal community of Hayslope, Eliot makes much of the dignity of labour as manifested in the Poysers' farm and Adam's workshop, while old Squire Donnithorne, whose income derives from possession of fields which others till, represents the least admirable aspect of this society; as Mrs Poyser angrily remarks to the Squire, "I know there's them as is born t'own the land, and them as is born to sweat on't" (353). The limitations of the aristocratic world-view are most clearly revealed not through the stingy Squire, but through his amiable grandson Arthur, who intends to improve everything upon inheriting but remains unaware of the injustice implied in Mrs Poyser's distinction.

Squire Donnithorne, who has no sympathy for his tenants but always spoke "in the same deliberate, well-chiselled, polite way, whether his words were sugary or venomous" (350), seems the product of an earlier and harsher period of the eighteenth century. However, his grandson Arthur has become a "man of feeling"—both in taste and sentiment he emulates the humanitarian ideal of a later day: "he had an agreeable confidence that his faults were all of a generous kind—impetuous, warm-blooded, leonine; never crawling, crafty, reptilian . . . he couldn't bear to see anyone uncomfortable . . . his aunt Lydia herself had the benefit of that softness which he bore towards the whole sex" (124-25). This seems almost a paraphrase of the virtues of Tom Jones, whose moral sensibility arises from his "good nature" and who, unlike the crafty Blifil, has only "the vices of a warm disposition."[5] Of course, one difference would be that Tom is not aware of being so virtuous while this is the way Arthur sees himself—as he analyzes his moral nature, he regards with satisfaction "his well-looking British person reflected in one of the old-fashioned mirrors" (124). Tom unconsciously stands for his author's concept of virtue, while Arthur admires himself as the epitome of a literary ideal, extending his "love of patronage" to social inferiors, especially his future tenants and the opposite sex.

Perhaps Arthur's story implies some criticism of Fielding's hero: Hetty's ruin might be more typical of the fate of lower-class females pursued by the Squire than Tom's happy resolution of his affair with Molly Seagrim. Tom's "violent animal spirits" tend to amorous entanglement but his sympathetic concern for the lady makes all well in the end, "for though he did not always act rightly, yet he never did otherwise without feeling and suffering for it."[6] Arthur claims a similar virtue for himself: "I'm a devil of a fellow for getting myself into hobbles, but I always take care the load shall fall on my own shoulders," to which Eliot remarks that "unhappily there is no poetic justice in hobbles" (125). Later Arthur refuses to contemplate the possibility that Hetty might become pregnant because he has "a sort of implicit confidence . . . that he was really such a good fellow at bottom, Providence would not treat him harshly" (322), but the plot of Eliot's novel lends no providential assistance to the young Squire's good intentions. Hetty flees Hayslope to escape the shame of unwed motherhood, abandons her child, and is tried for its murder.

The "gratitude" and "compassion" Tom feels for Molly correspond to Arthur's conscious attitude towards Hetty, but an ironic reduction occurs when Eliot describes him as "a handsome generous young fellow—who . . . if he should happen to spoil a woman's existence, will make it up to her with expensive *bon-bons,* packed up and directed by his own hand" (126). After marrying Sophia, Tom continues his generous financial support of Molly and her family; when Arthur decides to end his affair with Hetty he reflects that "she would owe the advantage of his care for her in future years to the sorrow she had incurred now. *So* good comes out of evil. Such is the beautiful arrangement of things!" (320). Eliot's sarcasm in the last two sentences seems directed at that eighteenth-century notion of cosmic harmony which justifies the social order—and is manifested in the "poetic justice" of the plot of *Tom Jones.*[7]

Eliot has not told us exactly what she thought of Fielding, but she probably liked him; at least in ***Middlemarch*** she admires the "lusty ease of his fine English" (Book I, Chapter XV). As Thomas A. Noble has demonstrated, Eliot is the direct heir of those eighteenth-century thinkers who founded ethics on "the relationship of sympathy and imagination"[8]—a tradition which also inspired *Tom Jones.* Eliot and Fielding both believe that virtue springs from sympathetic identification with others; that, as Fielding puts it, "good nature" consists of a "benevolent and amiable temper of mind which disposes us to feel the misfortunes and enjoy the happiness of others" without assistance from "any abstract contemplation on the beauty of virtue, and without the allurements or terrors of religion."[9]

However, Eliot escapes the limitations of upper-class benevolence by endowing this humanistic morality with a psychological dimension that seems absent in Fielding and his more sentimental successors. Walter E. Houghton observes that Eliot is not a sentimentalist because for her sympathetic feeling must be accompanied by a real understanding of the other person: in her fiction effective sympathy "originates in a clear and compassionate perception of human suffering . . . The sentimental indulgence of pity and love is really self-centered . . . George Eliot's benevolence presupposes a forgetfulness of self in the recognition of our common humanity."[10] No character in Eliot's fiction illustrates self-centered benevolence as clearly as Arthur, for whom "deeds of kindness were as easy . . . as a bad habit; they were the common issue . . . of his egoism and his sympathy. He didn't like to witness pain, and he liked to have grateful eyes beaming on him as the giver of pleasure" (317-18). Fielding's formula does not in itself enable us to distinguish between true sympathy and gratification derived from the "grateful eyes," a shortcoming even more evident in the sentimental fiction of Arthur's day. On the other hand, Arthur's complete identification with his social rank obscures awareness of the "common humanity" he shares with Hetty and thus he fails to appreciate the emotional and physical consequences their romance might inflict on her.

Sentimental benevolence is a transaction that can be carried out entirely within the self: it does not require a distinction between experiencing the other as a "thou"—an individual consciousness different from one's own—or merely as an object of warm-hearted charity. As it appears in eighteenth-century fiction (and many Victorian novels), benevolence usually depends on and is protected by a sense of social superiority to the recipient of one's kindness.

Arthur's dream of future patronage reveals his class-oriented view of his relation to Hayslope and humanity in general. He compensates for his present sense of bored aimlessness by imagining himself as a Squire Allworthy-to-be:

> He was nothing if not good-natured; and all his pictures of the future, when he should come into the estate, were made up of a prosperous, contented tenantry, adoring their landlord, who would be the model of an English gentleman—mansion in first-rate order, all elegance and high taste—jolly housekeeping, finest stud in Loamshire—purse open to all public objects—in short, everything as different as possible from what was now associated with the name of Donnithorne. (125)

His vision of the future actually represents the way he relates to people in the present; this picture of a perfect Squire surrounded by adoring dependents allows no place for the intrusion of an equal. To maintain his ideal self he cannot acknowledge any motive incompatible with "good nature" and thus must convince himself that his interest in Hetty consists only of generous concern for her welfare.

Arthur's "pictures of the future" also ignore the economic basis of his class. The old Squire's wealth must be at least partly the result of his cold-blooded meanness with his tenants, while Arthur, in his "model" world, intends to maintain an expensive establishment while being worshipped because he has so improved his tenants' farms. (The tenants imagine that when he inherits there is to be "a millenial abundance of new gates, allowances of lime, and returns of ten percent" [85].) When Irwine points out that Arthur's neighbour Gawaine has made himself unpopular with his improvements and that one must choose between "popularity or usefulness," Arthur objects: "O! Gawaine is harsh in his manners; he doesn't make himself personally agreeable to his tenants. I don't believe there's anything you can't prevail on people to do with kindness" (173).[11] In this definition of "kindness" the emphasis falls entirely on "manners," on being "personally agreeable," which rather easy form of benevolence also seems a method for insuring that one's inferiors will do "anything" one wishes.

Arthur is as interested as any other Squire in having his way with his tenants but imagines that because he means well he can get what he wants through charm rather than intimidation. He intends to be "different" yet manages to disguise as benevolence a pursuit of a tenant's pretty niece which is quite typical of young Squires. On the other hand, his sentimental vision really does make him a more sympathetic fellow than his grandfather; while his soft-heartedness can rationalize the seduction, it also prevents him from responding to the result with the usual callousness of his class.

In Arthur's drift towards seducing Hetty, Eliot presents her first extensive study of unconscious motivation. She asks whether his failure to confess to Irwine was not due to a "motive . . . which had a sort of backstairs influence? Our mental business is carried on in much the same way as the business of State: a great deal of hard work is done by agents who are not acknowledged" (176). Early in the novel we discover the real motive behind Arthur's pursuit of Hetty; he complains that "It's a desperately dull business being shut up at the Chase in the summer months, when one can neither hunt nor shoot, so as to make oneself pleasantly sleepy in the evening" (63). (Hunting is out of season, and Arthur's physical activity is further curtailed by a broken arm.) If Arthur admitted to himself that frustrated sex was keeping him awake nights, he might also have been more realistic about the consequences of fornicating with the Poysers' niece, but he sublimates this natural need into sentimental musing over Hetty and thus can never acknowledge his real object.

Unable to hunt, Arthur pursues Hetty instead and the horse he rides becomes associated with his runaway feelings. He gallops out to dispel his frustrations: "Nothing like 'taking' a few bushes and ditches for exorcising a demon; and it is really astonishing that the Centaurs, with their immense advantages in this way, left so bad a reputation in history" (129). The Centaurs' famous crime was their attempt to ravish the Lapith women, resulting in a battle which the ancient Greeks considered symbolic of the struggle between rational and animal elements in human nature. When Arthur loses a bout in his own struggle by returning prematurely from his ride, his horse suddenly seems to be controlling him. Eliot remarks that "it is the favorite stratagem of the passions to sham a retreat, and to turn sharp round upon us" (129), and in the next chapter he feels that when he gallops back to meet Hetty after resolving not to, "it was as if his horse had wheeled round from a leap and dared to dispute his mastery" (139). This imagery suggests a disjunction in Arthur's being: he is, like the Centaur, both horse and rider, with the horse secretly in control. The sexuality he sublimates into sentiment takes over at crucial moments, prompting actions opposed to his conscious intent.

We have seen that Arthur, a university man, is concerned to maintain not only high living but "high taste" in his future establishment. In the latter point his imagination has been shaped by the taste of his age—Neo-classical esthetic plus exotic fiction. Eliot subtly relates Arthur's false taste to his capacity for rationalization.

We have already noted that dividing the action between 1799 and 1800 suggests transition between two centuries, and that Dinah's evangelicalism presents one form of new sensibility. A casual reference by Arthur early in the novel reveals a literary event of the previous year which, for Eliot especially, would be of great importance in shaping the thought and feeling of the new era:

> I've got a book I meant to bring you, godmamma. It came down from London the other day. I know you are fond of queer, wizard-like stories. It's a volume of poems, "Lyrical Ballads:" most of them to be twaddling stuff; but the first is in a different style—"The Ancient Mariner" is the title. I can hardly make head nor tail of it as a story, but it's a strange, striking thing . . . and there are some other books that *you* might like to see, Irwine—pamphlets about Antinomianism and Evangelicalism, whatever they may be. (64)

Wordsworth is always an important influence on Eliot's fiction; this novel in particular, with its rustic setting and lower-class characters, seems to partake of his belief that the depiction of ordinary life could serve the highest purpose of art.[12] Eliot marks her affinity with Wordsworth's kind of realism by prefacing her novel with a quotation from *The Excursion* that promises "Clear images . . . Of nature's unambitious underwood / And flowers that prosper in the shade." Both Eliot and Wordsworth refuse to separate art from life: the emphasis both place on the value of everyday experience makes the classical dictum that serious literature must deal with an exalted subject in a heightened style seem not only artistically wrong, but also immoral in its implied contempt for the lives of ordinary people. In her first full-length novel Eliot, already an experienced critic of fiction, is concerned with setting an example of how novels should be written. By emphasizing the importance of the commonplace and pointedly eschewing the exotic, she seeks to exercise the same influence on fiction that Wordsworth had on poetry; her essay on realism in Chapter Seventeen could be taken as the "Preface" to her own career.[13]

In her first novel Eliot provides a striking example of her fondness for using styles of painting as a metaphor for perception.[14] She describes the Wordsworthian esthetic in terms of visual art in that famous passage in Chapter Seventeen where she extols the

> rare, precious quality of truthfulness . . . in many Dutch paintings, which lofty-minded people despise . . . I turn, without shrinking, from cloud-borne angels, from prophets, sibyls, and heroic warriors, to an old woman bending over her flower-pot, or eating her solitary dinner, while the noonday light, softened perhaps by a screen of leaves, falls on her mob-cap, and just touches the rim of her spinning-wheel, and her stone jug, and all those common things which are the precious necessaries of life to her. (180)

Eliot's affection for the jug, spinning-wheel, and other "common things" recalls Wordsworth's description of the rustic interior, supper, and fireside work in *Michael* (lines 80-141). The image of clear light illuminating everyday objects recurs many times in ***Adam Bede***; it is associated with clear vision and the "light of heaven" (182) which falls on the ordinary world "in which we get up in the morning to do our daily work" (179).[15] The subjects turned away from—"prophets, sibyls, and heroic warriors"—are the stock in trade of that Neo-classical style which dominated Arthur's age but which Eliot, as heir to Wordsworth, would find particularly sterile.[16]

When Arthur, blindly following the taste of his age, dismisses *Lyrical Ballads,* he excludes from literature (and from the realm of the serious in general) the whole motivation behind Eliot's novel—before becoming sadder and wiser he would probably have found ***Adam Bede*** as "twaddling" as Wordsworth. Furthermore, his separation of the imagination from everyday life is of great assistance in rationalizing the pursuit of Hetty; a close look at his vision of nature and his literary taste will help explain how he could manage a seduction so opposed to his conscious ideals.

After admiring Hetty at the Poysers' butter churn, Arthur describes her in terms of Neo-classical art: "She's a perfect Hebe; and if I were an artist, I would paint her" (102). Irwine replies, "I have no objection to your contemplating Hetty in an artistic light," but in fact there may be some danger if this is the deceptive light of unreality, at furthest remove from the "noonday light" of Dutch painting.

Arthur arranges a meeting with Hetty in

> the delicious labyrinthine wood . . . called Fir-tree Grove . . . It was a wood of beeches and limes, with here and there a light, silver-stemmed birch—just the sort of wood most haunted by the nymphs: you see their white sunlit limbs gleaming athwart the boughs, or peeping behind the smooth-sweeping outline of a tall lime; you hear their soft liquid laughter—but if you look with a too curious sacrilegious eye, they vanish behind the silvery beeches, they make you believe their voice was only a running brooklet, perhaps they metamorphose themselves into a tawny squirrel that scampers away and mocks you from the topmost bough. (130)

Such a depiction of nature represents Arthur's consciousness rather than Eliot's; as Reva Stump points out, this is one of those scenes associated with Arthur and Hetty "where light is used to heighten shadows, point up darkness, and create a haze—where, in short, it distorts rather than assists vision."[17] Further, it should be noted that contrary to Eliot's usual practice, the actual wood is not described but only used as a backdrop for fantasy—"seeing" here is making-believe—and that the literary imagery seems far-removed from real nature. In a review of Ruskin's *Modern Painters,* Eliot insists that "all truth and beauty are to be attained by a humble and faithful study of nature, and not by substituting vague forms, bred by imagination on the mists of feeling, in place of definite, substantial reality."[18] Arthur's vague nymphs arise from the wrong kind of imagination.

The main force of this description of Fir-tree Grove stems not from what is seen, but from something beneath the surface, an underlying sensuality which the imagery intimates while glossing over. Arthur sees the wood only as a backdrop for his mood, for his real interest lies elsewhere: as he "strolled along carelessly, with a book under his arm . . . his eyes *would* fix themselves on the distant bend in the road, round which a little figure must surely appear before long" (131, Eliot's italics). The motion of the eyes suggests an involuntary element in Arthur's search; he is not free to look about in a disinterested manner.

On the other hand, the brooklet and scampering squirrel possess a life and motion lacking in the imaginary nymphs, but these genuine aspects of the scene can be perceived only by the "too curious sacrilegious eye" which would disrupt this Temple of Nature (later Arthur, trying to deceive Adam, calls it the "sacred grove" [303]) and discover a real nature that "mocks" the fantasist. Arthur is embarking on a love-affair which will result in the birth of a child, but no anticipation of this natural process can intrude on his sentimental view of Hetty.

Eliot's strategy here is to entrance the reader for a moment and then awaken him with the rather blunt observation that on such an afternoon "destiny disguises her cold awful face behind a hazy radiant veil . . . and poisons us with violet-scented breath" (131), a process repeated more subtly at a later meeting with Hetty which Arthur has arranged in order to explain that he does not mean anything serious. He quickly forgets his good intentions: "Ah, he doesn't know in the least what he is saying. This is not what he meant to say . . . his lips are meeting those pouting child-lips, and for a long moment time has vanished. He may be a shepherd in Arcadia for aught he knows, he may be the first youth kissing the first maiden, he may be Eros himself kissing the lips of Psyche—it is all one" (138).

This pagan paradise, independent of space, time, and experience, suggests the mood of a certain style of Neo-classical painting. The breathless prose represents Arthur's state of mind, in which we are temporarily caught up only to come down again when we pause to consider the incongruity of the myth of Eros and Psyche in such a context. With the advent of Freud this myth of Love leading the Soul towards perfection has lost its impact, but it played a significant role in the imagination of the eighteenth and nineteenth centuries and seems to have interested Eliot, who uses it again in ***Middlemarch.***[19] Here, however, Psyche is only the mask for an everyday seduction; in Arthur's imagination Hetty seems to have graduated from Hebe the wine-girl to the beloved of the God of Love.

Cupid and Psyche fascinated Neo-classical artists as a symbol of the ideal, but also underwent a rapid deterioration as decorative pornography, Divine Love being a most acceptable excuse for getting voluptuous representations of naked lovers inside the house. In both Arthur's time and Eliot's the pair could frequently be found embracing not only on canvas, but also in bronze on mantelpieces and over the tops of clocks. Arthur is an ordinary fellow and the "artistic light" in which he views Hetty reveals this lower, more popular use of the myth. The most famous and widely-copied example of this genre, the painting of Cupid and Psyche done by Gérard in 1798, with its pretty surface and sensuous undertones, would be a good example of Arthur's consciousness (as different as possible from Dutch realism).[20]

Two months later, as Adam walks through the woods towards a chance encounter with Arthur and Hetty, his carpenter's vision of the Grove becomes an equivalent to realist painting. He views the Grove under

> the magnificent changes of the light . . . What grand beeches! Adam delighted in a fine tree of all things; as the fisherman's sight is keenest on the sea, so Adam's perceptions were more at home with trees than with

> other objects. He kept them in his memory as a painter does, with all the flecks and knots in their bark, and all the curves and angles of their boughs. (301-2)

As he pauses to examine a tree more closely, Adam catches sight of the lovers "in the eastern light," understanding their relation with a clarity with which they have never seen themselves. Arthur, somewhat befuddled with wine, tries to "laugh the thing off' and throw "dust . . . in honest Adam's eyes," but the "strange evening light" shows things too clearly and Adam experiences an inner illumination: "a terrible scorching light showed him the hidden letters that changed the meaning of the past" (303). Here Adam represents the author's vision as well; the contrast between Adam's Grove and Arthur's could be taken as the difference between true and false perception.[21]

Arthur's taste in literature also has some relevance to the ease with which he yields to temptation. There are signs of interest in the Gothic and exotic: he plans to restore the last remaining "piece of the old abbey" (261) and Hetty succumbs in a summer-house in the Grove dubbed "the Hermitage," in which monastic retreat Adam is surprised to find a "snug room" equipped with brandy and showing "all the signs of frequent habitation" (310). Arthur remarks that as a child "I used to think that if ever I was a rich Sultan, I would make Adam my grand-visier. And I believe now, he would bear the exaltation as well as any poor man in an Eastern story" (61). (The Sultan's ministers were also his slaves.) Arthur enacts this fantasy when he rather fulsomely bestows the management of the woods on Adam at the Birthday Feast (272).

Eliot insists that her novel will have no "heroes riding fiery horses, themselves ridden by still more fiery passions" (36), "romantic criminals," or other exotic characters who are not "half so frequent as your common labourer . . ." (182). However, Arthur, who sometimes rides his grandfather's horses rather hard, seems to enjoy stories of romantic crime and passionate violence.

On the morning of his first secret encounter with Hetty, Arthur decides to spend a week fishing instead, but as he strides towards the stables he sings in his "loudest ringing tenor . . . his favorite song from the 'Beggar's Opera,' 'When the heart of man is oppressed with care.' Not an heroic strain; nevertheless Arthur felt himself very heroic . . ." (124). The second line of this song happens to be "The mist is dispelled when a woman appears." It is sung by Macheath, the heroic highwayman, who observes in the same soliloquy, "What a fool is a fond wench! . . . I must have women. There is nothing unbends the mind like them," and reflects on his prowess in turning virgins into ladies of the town (Act II, Scene iii). Arthur's resolve to ride away from temptation seems half-hearted from the beginning. (After discovering that his favorite horse is lame, Arthur decides to keep away from Hetty by riding to visit his friend Gawaine. This resolution also fails in the "Centaur" episode already discussed.)

A significant reference to Arthur's reading occurs at the crucial moment when he rationalizes spending the afternoon in the Grove where he knows Hetty will pass: "it was just the sort of afternoon for lolling in the Hermitage, and he would go and finish Dr. Moore's *Zeluco* there before dinner" (130)—this is the book under his arm during his first tryst with Hetty. Moore's tale of criminal adventure was published in 1786 and went through several editions, remaining popular into the nineteenth century—another edition came out in 1810. Its main interest lies in the persistent wickedness of the title character, the degraded heir of a noble Sicilian family. Handsome and eloquent, but driven by the lowest passions, which he always indulges without restraint, Zeluco perpetrates an extraordinary series of seductions and betrayals, finally tricking a pure and beautiful maiden into marriage against her will. He abuses her outrageously and strangles their infant in a fit of rage, after which she goes mad, becoming unable to accuse him of the crime: the intrigues which arise from this situation provide the climax of the novel. Moore pauses occasionally to present some flat moral commentary of the kind Eliot deplored in fiction.

In his circumstances Zeluco has some resemblance to Arthur—both are fatherless, spoiled, rich, idle, and go into the army. Their story also concerns seduction and child-murder followed by madness. However, the point is not that Arthur failed to heed Moore's warning, but that such fantastic tales can have no kind of moral impact. Arthur could never identify with the exotic crimes of such a villain, nor learn anything from him about impulses to self-indulgence that might lurk in good intentions. The allusion to *Zeluco* contains a double irony: the novel does foreshadow Arthur's fate but also makes it seem impossible in the real world.[22] *Zeluco* seems a good example of those "frantic novels," designed to gratify a "craving for extraordinary incident," which Wordsworth cites in the "Preface to *Lyrical Ballads*" as evidence of degraded taste in contemporary literature.

U. C. Knoepflmacher has pointed out the many links between Hetty and Martha Ray of "The Thorne," another tale of seduction, infanticide, and madness—and also one of the homeliest of Wordsworth's narratives in *Lyrical Ballads*.[23] Arthur enjoys *Zeluco* while refusing to read a book which contains a realistic representation of his own future sin. Later, in a mood for serious meditation on his problem with Hetty, he comments on the moral relevance of exotic fiction by flinging "*Zeluco* into the most distant corner" (134).

The lovers seem to kiss in a static Arcadia but they are not free from social or biological consequences; as Eliot notes, it is only "for a long moment that time has vanished." When he returns to the temporal world of cause and effect Arthur ponders the incompatibility of their social rank:

> To flirt with Hetty was a very different affair from flirting with a pretty girl of his own station: that was understood to be an amusement on both sides; or, if it became serious, there was no obstacle to marriage. But this little thing would be spoken ill of directly . . . And even if no one knew anything about it, they might

> get too fond of each other, and then there would be the misery of parting after all. No gentleman, out of a ballad, could marry a farmer's niece. There must be an end to the whole thing at once. It was too foolish. (139-40)

The thought of "parting" shows that he has descended from the timeless realm of Eros and Psyche. The reality to which he returns is quite prosaic; his undemocratic concept of a "gentleman" takes absolute class-barriers for granted. Romance with a girl of his "station" might become "serious" but his affair with Hetty can only be seen as entertainment, a "little thing" and "too foolish." His phrase "out of a ballad" makes an ironic contrast to *Lyrical Ballads.* By "ballad" Arthur means the opposite of Wordsworth—a fantastic tale (like the plot of *Zeluco*) in an exotic setting (this aspect of "The Ancient Mariner" seems to appeal to him).[24] Since he takes his role in the social hierarchy for granted, any romantic breaching of class-barriers could occur only in a fantasy of no account in the real world. For Arthur literature is an amusement, yet he often behaves as though he were in a ballad instead of out of one, maintaining a separation between the two states of mind as distinct as his separation of art from life. It is a peculiar element in Arthur's tragedy that he foresees in lucid moments the disaster he seems powerless to avoid—"he should hate himself if he made a scandal of that sort" (140).

Arthur's unconscious often works through his imagination, which for him is the realm of unreal "fancy":

> The desire to see Hetty rushed back like an ill-stemmed current; he was amazed at the force with which this trivial fancy seemed to grasp him: he was even rather tremulous as he brushed his hair—pooh! it was riding in that break-neck way. It was because he had made a serious affair of an idle matter, by thinking of it as if it were of any consequence. He would amuse himself by seeing Hetty today . . . (130)

A surprising force drives him towards an impossible breach of his social mores, but once relegated to the imagination, or "trivial fancy," this impulse becomes only a leisure amusement, an "idle matter" of "no consequence" which can safely be indulged. Arthur could imagine "serious consequences" with a "girl of his own station," but a pastoral milkmaid can only be the object of artistic appreciation and pleasing sentiment.

When they embrace Arthur is not "sensible just then that Hetty wanted . . . signs of high breeding" (113). The "just then" indicates that he is in a special state of mind cut off from normal consciousness; he will later think of this deficiency as the most important aspect of their relationship. The thought of a second meeting that evening can be indulged in the imagination precisely because it is not possible, but then becomes possible after being reduced to sentimental fancy: "He made up his mind not to meet Hetty again; and now he might give himself up to thinking how immensely agreeable it would be if circumstances were different . . . How beautiful her eyes were with the tear on their lashes! He would like to satisfy his soul for a day with looking at them, and he *must* see her again" (135). He resolves to "set things right with her by a kindness which would have the air of friendly civility" (137), but he shall satisfy more than his soul.

Through Arthur, Eliot distinguishes between sentimentalism and genuine feeling. While hardly an intellectual Arthur does see himself as a cultivated "man of feeling"; with his upper-class education and leisure he has developed something of a literary imagination, along with some excess emotion to be indulged in it when hunting is out of season. His sharp distinction between art and "fancy" on the one hand, and everyday life on the other, cuts off communication with his emotional nature, which can find expression only in trivial second-hand disguises.

His separation of art from life results in a split consciousness in which he can alternate between fantasies disconnected from the real world and a reality where such fantasies are, of course, impossible. Yet his exalted fantasy permits the satisfaction of a sexual need his sentimental ego refuses to admit. Arthur's imagination does not express feeling but rather provides a disguise under which it operates as an "agent not acknowledged," prompting actions which he does not have to face up to because they are relegated to an imaginary world. What he does with Hetty in the realm of Eros and Psyche remains separate from time and consequence.

In a moment of clarity Arthur decides to make further flirtation impossible by confessing to his friend Parson Irwine: "There was but one resource. He would go and tell Irwine—tell him everything" (140). For Eliot, the Sacrament of Confession had great psychological value because one's feelings revealed their true nature when given objective existence in the consciousness of another person.[25] However, as Arthur forms this resolve he makes the fatal assumption that "the mere act of telling it would make it seem trivial" (140).

When face to face with Irwine, Arthur decides not to mention his problem because "the conversation had taken a more serious tone than he had intended—it would quite mislead Irwine—he would imagine there was a deep passion for Hetty, while there was no such thing" (176). Arthur justifies his pursuit of Hetty by convincing himself that their relationship is "trivial," yet knows that objectively considered it will seem "serious." By refusing to communicate his feelings he reveals the insincerity of his excuse, while keeping it intact so he can see Hetty again.

Arthur depends on the approbation of others rather than an inner sense of self, and it is only through Adam's rudeness, his refusal to be talked round after seeing Arthur and Hetty together, that Arthur experiences himself as seen disapprovingly through the eyes of another: "The discovery that Adam loved Hetty was a shock that made him for the moment see himself in the light of Adam's indignation . . . All screening self-excuse . . . forsook him for an instant . . ." (315). While Irwine is restrained by good manners from enquiring too far into Arthur's conscience, Adam assumes a moral equality which enables him to disregard class-barriers.[26]

However, Arthur's "instant" of vision is only "for the moment." Later he fends off this humiliating encounter with a fantasy that smacks of *droit du seigneur.* When after his grandfather's death he returns, still unaware of Hetty's disaster, to become master of the estate, he contemplates his intended generosity to the husband of his cast-off mistress: "they were soon to be married: perhaps they were already married. And now it was in his power to do a great deal for them" (450).

In a final encounter in the Grove after Hetty's reprieve, Adam forces Arthur to acknowledge the reality of his victims' feelings. Arthur performs his first genuine service to his former ideal when he pleads with Adam to help him sacrifice himself to keep the community intact: "one of my reasons for going away is, that no one else may leave Hayslope—may leave their home on my account" (477). Adam grimly insists that he has seen through Arthur's benevolence—"When people's feelings have got a deadly wound, they can't be cured with favours"—and will give in only when Arthur explicitly renounces it: "if you would talk to the Poysers . . . I know, of course, they would not accept any favour from me: I mean nothing of that kind" (479). Here Arthur belatedly receives that enlightenment through exposure to the vision of an equal which he rejected in his first confrontation with Adam.

For Eliot, the highest purpose of the imagination is to put oneself in another's shoes and foresee the effect of one's actions on his consciousness. An interesting link between Wordsworth and Eliot's kind of agnostic humanism appears in one of G. H. Lewes's last and best books, *The Study of Psychology,* which she edited after his death. Lewes discusses the evolution of morality, both in the race and the individual, from shame and fear of divine punishment to that highest achievement of civilized man, the sympathetic imagination: "In a mind where the educated tracing of hurtful consequences to others is associated with a sympathetic imagination of their suffering, Remorse has no relation to an external source of punishment for the wrong committed: it is the agonized sense, the contrite contemplation, of the wound inflicted on another."[27] In revising Lewes's manuscript, Eliot adds "Wordsworth has depicted a remorse of this kind," and quotes the following lines from *The Excursion:*[28]

Feebly they must have felt
Who in old times, attired with snakes and whips
The vengeful Furies. *Beautiful* regards
Were turned on me—the face of her I loved;
The wife and mother, pitifully fixing
Tender reproaches, insupportable!

(Book III, lines 850-55)

Arthur, preoccupied with the approbation of others, has a moral sense based mainly on shame, and does not get the point when Irwine warns him that for a sensitive man "inward suffering . . . is the worst form of nemesis" (175). Arthur fails to foresee Hetty's doom and thus shall be "educated" by agony and contrition after the fact.

As we have seen, *Zeluco* and Wordsworth's "The Thorn" both comment ironically on the seduction of Hetty. Arthur's education through remorse seems foreshadowed in "The Rime of the Ancient Mariner," the only poem in *Lyrical Ballads* that arouses his interest. The association Eliot establishes between hunting and Arthur's pursuit of Hetty suggests that he downs her in the same sportive spirit in which the Mariner shot the albatross. Arthur is attracted to the Gothic trappings of Coleridge's poem—"it's a strange, striking thing"—but complains that he "can hardly make head nor tail of it as a story"; he cannot grasp the theme of sin, guilt, and repentance which binds together its apparently illogical events.

The Mariner returns to his "own countree" physically much the worse but spiritually enlightened. After Hetty's trial and reprieve, Arthur joins the army in India instead of assuming his long-anticipated role as Squire. In the "Epilogue" Adam describes him when he returns seven years later: "he's altered and yet not altered . . . his colour's changed, and he looks sadly. However, the doctors say he'll soon be set right in his own country air. He's all sound in th'inside; it's only the fever shattered him so. But he speaks just the same, and smiles at me just as he did when he was a lad" (550). Wordsworthian Nemesis has wrought a change on an "inside" of which Arthur was not aware before his fall. The return of his childhood smile suggests innocence regained, in this case bought dear by becoming sadder and wiser through experience of sin—and its consequences. In "The Ancient Mariner" Coleridge uses the supernatural not merely as a Gothic device, but to create a symbolic vision of the inter-relatedness of an organic universe, a vision in itself emblematic of the Romantic imagination.[29] Both the Mariner and Arthur sin carelessly against the complex relationships of their world and both learn the real nature of these relationships through remorse. Unlike the Mariner, Arthur already knows a good deal about the community he violates, but unfortunately his imagination only provides escape from the social structure he otherwise takes for granted.[30]

Through a subtle web of imagery and allusion, Eliot links Arthur to the main themes of the novel and to her concept of the moral purpose of fiction. She introduces *Lyrical Ballads* as a precedent for the realism discussed in Chapter Seventeen, and as a standard by which to judge Arthur's false vision; in turn, Arthur illuminates her realism by way of contrast. The complexity of his motives shows the uselessness of melodramatic villains and refutes the reader of "enlightened opinions and refined taste" who in Chapter Seventeen demands of the novelist: "Let your most faulty characters always be on the wrong side, and your virtuous ones on the right" (179). Arthur's escapist fantasy reflects on Eliot's belief that the imagination should be used to explore the real world, while the egoism concealed in his "love of patronage" underlines her insistence on a perception which can transcend social barriers.

Eliot's conservative respect for tradition has caused some critics to overlook her effort to free the sympathetic imagination from the limits of class. In terms very like Neil Roberts's interpretation of ***Adam Bede,*** Arnold Hauser states that "George Eliot regards as an essentially psychological and moral problem what is in reality a sociological problem, and looks in psychology for the answer to questions which can only be answered sociologically."[31] Two Marxist-oriented critics, Ian Milner and John Goode, are attracted by the appearance of class-conflict in Arthur's crime, but become frustrated by Eliot's failure to develop this theme consistently.[32] We must remember that as heir to Wordsworth Eliot could combine a tendency to conservative (and sometimes rather confused) politics with an insistence on democratic vision in art.[33] The social contradictions Eliot shies away from on the political level often receive a subtle development in the psychology of her characters.

It is characteristic of Eliot's technique that she concentrates on the details of Arthur's state of mind during his first meetings with Hetty, and yet never lets us forget that he is a prospective landlord committing an offense against a tenant-farmer. Thus as we explore the psychology of sentimental benevolence we also become aware of its limitations as an attitude of the upper class towards the lower. Arthur dreams of replacing his grandfather's avarice with an ideal generosity to his tenants, but we know that this can only consist of giving back a small portion of the wealth derived from their labor.[34] A good part of the income from his estate must go to keep the "mansion in first-rate order, all elegance and high taste—jolly housekeeping, finest stud in Loamshire" (125). This giving which is also a taking appears at its worst in a benevolence towards Hetty which disguises a typical aristocratic use of farm-girls. Through Arthur, Eliot demonstrates to the reader of "enlightened opinions and refined taste" that naive complacency in one's social status is incompatible with genuine sympathy for those who must sweat on fields which others own.

We can conclude that Arthur's story is not a "static moral drama," and that it seems quite different from the usual treatment of seduction in Victorian novels. His error arises not from sexual desire in itself, but from misrepresenting it as sympathetic concern and esthetic appreciation. Eliot cannot be accused of punishing the lovers for their sexual vitality: Hetty is a self-obsessed social-climber and Arthur pursues her in a pseudo-pastoral dream fabricated out of second-hand imagery.[35] His escapist notion of literature and his class-bound belief in "high taste" excuse him from any attempt to understand the subjective consciousness of his victim or the economic reality of her class.

On the other hand, the narrator shows us everything Arthur cannot see and speaks out against the fashionable taste in literature he represents, along with the refined reader of Chapter Seventeen. In her first novel Eliot develops her own version of the difference between fancy and imagination. Convinced that the "ill-stemmed current" of his "desire to see Hetty" is only a "trivial fancy" (130), Arthur sublimates his emotional needs into his vision of himself as ideal Squire, while the narrator combines psychological analysis with social concern by revealing the tragic interaction between Arthur's divided self and the class-divisions of the world he is about to inherit.

Notes

1. *The George Eliot Letters,* ed Gordon S. Haight (New Haven 1954-56), II, 387. The page references which appear throughout are from *Adam Bede,* ed Gordon S. Haight (New York 1967).
2. Neil Roberts, *George Eliot: Her Beliefs and Her Art* (Pittsburgh 1975), pp 63-67.
3. Hayslope represents the past, while Dinah's milieu anticipates social problems of the nineteenth century. She complains of a "deadness to the Word" in the country and says that her religion flourishes amid the industrial privation of "great towns like Leeds" (92). She works in a cotton mill in Snowfield, which is also a mining town.
4. A. O. J. Cockshut notes Adam's mid-Victorian quality and describes him as "a convincing portrait of the serious agnostic in the making" (*The Unbelievers* [New York 1966], p 47).
5. Henry Fielding, *Tom Jones,* Book X, xiii.
6. Ibid, Book IV, vi.
7. John Goode also finds an affinity between Tom Jones and Arthur—*"Adam Bede," Critical Essays on George Eliot* (New York 1970), pp 24-25. This essay has many insights but I strongly disagree when Goode argues that Eliot was influenced by Herbert Spencer's social Darwinism.
8. Thomas A. Noble, *George Eliot's 'Scenes of Clerical Life'* (New Haven 1965), p 57.
9. Henry Fielding, "An Essay on the Knowledge of the Characters of Men," *The Complete Works of Henry Fielding* (New York 1967), XVI, 285.
10. Walter E. Houghton, *The Victorian Frame of Mind* (New Haven 1957), p 278.
11. There is a contradiction in the concept of improvement. Irwine says, "Gawaine has got the curses of the whole neighbourhood upon him about that enclosure." Enclosure was an important aspect of that consolidation of land for "improved" farming which was rapidly eliminating the small tenant farmer and thus the whole feudal community which forms the basis of Arthur's "pictures of the future." Arthur has been influenced by Arthur Young, who strongly supported enclosure but changed his mind dramatically in 1800 when he discovered that it was being applied exclusively in the interests of the landowners.

12. For Eliot's general interest in Wordsworth, see Thomas Pinney, "George Eliot's Reading of Wordsworth: The Record," VN [Victorian Newsletter], 24 (1963), 20-22, and "The Authority of the Past in George Eliot's Novels," NCF [Nineteenth Century Fiction], 21 (1966), 131-47. Jerome Thale, in *The Novels of George Eliot* (New York 1959) and U. C. Knoepflmacher, in *George Eliot's Early Novels* (Berkeley 1968), both discuss the peculiarly Wordsworthian quality of *Adam Bede.* Michael Squires provides a more general discussion of Wordsworth's influence on English fiction in *The Pastoral Novel: Studies in George Eliot, Thomas Hardy, and D. H. Lawrence* (Charlottesville 1974). To my knowledge, the best and fullest discussion of Wordsworth's influence on Eliot's early fiction is Robert Dunham's unpublished dissertation, "Wordsworthian Themes and Attitudes in George Eliot's Novels" (Stanford 1971). I am indebted to Professor Dunham for revealing the importance of Wordsworth for the interpretation of Eliot's fiction.

13. Eliot's argument in Chapter Seventeen also seems to parallel Book Thirteen of *The Prelude,* where Wordsworth rejects fashionable elitism and turns to the depiction of humble rustic characters.

14. See Hugh Witemeyer, "George Eliot, Naumann, and the Nazarenes," VS [Victorian Studies], 18 (1974-75), 145-58, and "English and Italian Portraiture in *Daniel Deronda,*" NCF, 30 (March 1976), 477-94.

15. In an essay entitled "Worldliness and Other-Worldliness: The Poet Young" Eliot attacks Edward Young's grandiose, abstract verse, and presents William Cowper as an example of good poetry (described in terms of clear light): "How Cowper's exquisite mind falls with the warmth of morning sunlight on the commonest objects, at once disclosing every detail and investing every detail with beauty"—*Essays of George Eliot,* ed Thomas Pinney (New York 1963), p 382. Here Eliot uses Cowper as an eighteenth-century representative for Wordsworth. In his *Principles of Success in Literature* (Boston 1894) G. H. Lewes quotes extensively from Eliot's criticism of Young but compares him to Wordsworth rather than Cowper (pp 68-72).

    The painting of the old woman closely resembles *Interior with Old Woman Peeling Apples* by David Teniers the younger, a painter noted for his treatment of light and his detailed depictions of peasant life. Eliot saw and admired the work of some Dutch painters, Teniers among them, when she was writing this part of *Adam Bede*—see Gordon S. Haight, *George Eliot: A Biography* (Oxford 1968), p 259.

16. In a hostile review of the first edition of *Lyrical Ballads,* Southey said that "The Idiot Boy" "resembles a Flemish picture in the worthlessness of its design and the excellence of its execution. From Flemish artists we are satisfied with such pieces: who would not have lamented if Corregio or Rafaelle had wasted their talents in painting Dutch boors or the humours of a Flemish wake?" (*The Critical Review,* vol 24, October, 1798). This review may have suggested Eliot's reference to Dutch painting, and Southey is probably included among the "lofty-minded people" who despise it. Eliot considered Southey an example of the bad taste of the period (see note 30). In Chapter Seventeen Eliot pays tribute to "divine beauty of form" but demands recognition for "that other beauty too, which lies in no secret of proportion, but in the secret of deep human sympathy." Arthur sees Hetty entirely in terms of "beauty of form."

17. Reva Stump, *Movement and Vision in George Eliot's Novels* (Seattle 1959), p 18. I am indebted to Stump's excellent discussion of this scene.

18. George Eliot, *Westminster Review,* 65 (April 1856), 626.

19. See U. C. Knoepflmacher, "Fusing Fact and Myth: The New Reality of *Middlemarch,*" *This Particular Web: Essays on 'Middlemarch'*, ed Ian Adam (Toronto 1975), pp 56-57.

20. See Hugh Honour, *Neo-classicism* (Harmondsworth 1968), p 171.

21. Hetty, who never distinguishes between fantasy and the real world, cannot see the Grove at all. As she walks through the Grove, Eliot describes the light-effects she fails to see because of her preoccupation with an imaginary future (136-37).

22. Irving Buchen—"Arthur Donnithorne and *Zeluco:* Characterization *via* Literary Allusion in *Adam Bede,*" VN, 23 (1963), 18-19—and Jerome Thale—"*Adam Bede:* Arthur Donnithorne and *Zeluco,*" MLN, 70 (1965), 263-65—both assume that Eliot blames Arthur for not heeding Moore's message about the awful fate of seducers. In fact, the novel's seductions are far more interesting than its moral passages, and Eliot disapproves of Arthur for preferring this tale to Wordsworth. Also most Victorian readers would have known that in the preface to *Childe Harold's Pilgrimage,* Byron refers to his sin-wearied hero as "A poetical Zeluco." Byron, a poet whom Eliot intensely disliked, stands for everything she opposes in Chapter Seventeen.

23. U. C. Knoepflmacher, *George Eliot's Early Novels,* p 95.

24. Arthur's reference to gentlemen making improbable marriages in ballads suggests a romantic story like "King Cophetua and the Beggar Maid" in Thomas Percy's *Reliques of Ancient English Poetry* (an enlarged edition was published in 1794). Also Gothic tales in ballad form were very popular in this period. Many translations of Gottfried Bürgher's "Lenore" were published, the best known being

William Taylor's "Ellenore," in the *Monthly Magazine,* 1796.

25. See Ludwig Feuerbach, *The Essence of Christianity,* trans George Eliot (New York 1957), pp 78-79 and 122-24. The most impressive confession-scenes in Eliot's fiction are Janet's confession to Mr. Tryan in "Janet's Repentance," Hetty's to Dinah in *Adam Bede* (xlv), and Lydgate's to Dorothea in *Middlemarch* (lxvi).

26. It is interesting to note that in Chapter Fifteen Dinah, also a member of the working-class, disregards social propriety in a forceful attempt to awaken Hetty's conscience, while in the next chapter Irwine fails through excessive politeness to elicit Arthur's confession.

27. G. H. Lewes, *The Study of Psychology: Its Object, Scope, and Method* (Boston 1879), p 150.

28. See Gordon S. Haight, *George Eliot: A Biography* (Oxford 1968), p 527. In "George Eliot's Reading of Wordsworth: The Record," Thomas Pinney states that Lewes and Eliot read *The Excursion* aloud to each other during the composition of *Adam Bede.*

29. See Humphrey House's interpretation of "The Rime of the Ancient Mariner" in *Coleridge: The Clark Lectures 1951-52* (London 1953). Eliot was certainly capable of understanding the poem on this level.

30. A taste for the exotic seems to be associated with snobbery in Eliot's fiction. In *Felix Holt,* Esther Lyon reads Byron and dreams of genteel romance, while Mrs. Transome in her youth laughed at *Lyrical Ballads,* admired Southey's *Thalaba the Destroyer* (an Arabian fantasy of incredible plot), and married for rank and money. (I am indebted to Dunham's "Wordsworthian Themes and Attitudes in George Eliot's Novels" for the reference to Southey.) Rosamond Vincy, the social climber of *Middlemarch,* copies passages out of *Lalla Rookh,* a series of Oriental romances by Thomas Moore. Lydgate, unconscious snob and Rosamond's victim, has given up reading literature for science, but takes a sentimental view of women and imagines that life with Rosy will bring "ideal happiness (of the kind known in the Arabian Nights, in which . . . everything is given to you and nothing claimed) . . ." (xxxvi). In this case sentimentalism makes the man vulnerable to exploitation.

31. Arnold Hauser, *The Social History of Art* (New York 1957), IV, 136.

32. Ian Milner, "The Structure of Values in *Adam Bede,*" *Philologica Pragensia,* 9 (1966), 281-91, and John Goode, "*Adam Bede,*" *Critical Essays on George Eliot.* What Eliot has to offer a Marxist-oriented approach can best be appreciated if we first analyze her fiction in terms of her own values and only then attempt to assess the limitations of her vision—the latter problem is beyond the scope of the present essay.

33. For perceptive discussion of Eliot's ambivalence towards political reform, see Graham Martin, "'Daniel Deronda': George Eliot and Political Change," *Critical Essays on George Eliot,* and Linda Bamber, "Self-Defeating Politics in George Eliot's *Felix Holt,*" VS, 18 (1975), 419-35.

34. Raymond Williams finds a similar problem in the celebration of aristocratic munificence in the English pastoral tradition—*The Country and the City* (London 1975), pp 38-47. In "The Natural History of German Life," Eliot attacks the sentimental treatment of "the working classes" by contemporary authors and insists that the artist must obliterate the "vulgarity of exclusiveness" through accurate depiction of lower class characters (*Essays of George Eliot,* pp 268-71). This aspect of Eliot's realism is emphasized by the contrast between Arthur's idyllic view of Hetty and the narrator's account of her pathetic naiveté and hopeless flight.

35. Ian Gregor—"The Two Worlds of 'Adam Bede,'" *The Moral and the Story* (London 1962)—and Michael Squires—*The Pastoral Novel*—both view Arthur's affair with Hetty as a genuine pastoral idyll. Many readers have assumed that Eliot was passing a Puritan judgment on sexuality in having the affair end in disaster—most recently Calvin Bedient in *Architects of the Self* (Berkeley 1972).

Elizabeth Holtze (essay date 1983)

SOURCE: "Aristotle and George Eliot: *Hamartia* in *Adam Bede,*" in *Hamartia: The Concept of Error in the Western Tradition,* edited by Donald V. Stump, James A. Arieti, Lloyd Gerson, and Eleonore Stump, The Edwin Mellen Press, 1983, pp. 267-80.

[*In the following essay, Holtze examines Aristotelian tragic influences in* Adam Bede *and the errors or "hamartia" committed by Adam, Arthur, and Hetty.*]

In 1855 George Eliot wrote a review entitled **"The Morality of *Wilhelm Meister*"** in which she concludes:

> ... the tragedian may take for his subject the most hideous passions if they serve as the background for some divine deed of tenderness or heroism, and so the novelist may place before us every aspect of human life where there is some trait of love, or endurance, or helplessness to call forth our best sympathies.[1]

Eliot was defending the morality of Goethe's work at a time before she herself became a novelist. When she began to write fiction two years later, her work reflected some of the ideas suggested in the earlier review: that the proper subject matter for novels is all human life, the common as well as the noble; that the novel can, and should, teach moral lessons; and that there is a kinship between the genres of novel and tragedy.

The last idea is perhaps the most striking. Nevertheless, again and again, in both her letters and her novels, Eliot suggests that she is writing tragedy: "And again, it is my way, (rather too much so perhaps) to urge the human sanctities through tragedy—through pity and terror as well as admiration and delights."[2] No one can read these carefully chosen words without thinking of Aristotle, and how different in form are the novels of Eliot and the plays of the three great Greek dramatists. The subject matter is also different. Eliot's insistence upon the tragedy of common experience does not measure up to the standard of magnitude Aristotle sets by which the protagonist must be a hero or ruler, someone who involves a multitude of others in his fall. Nevertheless, in her first fiction, ***Amos Barton,*** Eliot dares to explain the actions of the frivolous, superficial Countess Czerlaski by quoting a Greek couplet from Sophocles (ch. 4), and on the next page speaks of "the tragedy . . . of a human soul that looks out through dull grey eyes . . ." (ch. 5). Eliot's biographer, Gordon Haight, lists the classical tragedies she read in Greek between 1855 and 1858: *Antigone, Ajax,* the *Oedipus* trilogy, *Electra, Philoctetes,* and the *Oresteia.*[3] In addition, Eliot was primarily concerned with moral problems; she shows a kind of suffering that is not an end in itself, but pain through which the sufferer gains knowledge about himself and his relationship with others.[4]

In the year she was reading the three plays of the *Oresteia,* George Eliot was writing her first full-length novel, ***Adam Bede.*** The novel examines the relationships of three characters: Adam of the title, an upright carpenter; Arthur Donnithorne, a young gentleman with expectations; and the pretty, frivolous girl they both love, Hetty Sorrel. Each of these three makes mistakes and suffers unforeseen consequences. At the beginning of ***Adam Bede,*** Eliot says Nature is "the great tragic dramatist" (ch. 4). How closely does she allow her three protagonists, each more a child of the rural countryside than a hero of classical times, to conform to the Aristotelian model for tragedy?

In addition to requiring a hero of some stature who acts in a plot with reversal and recognition, Aristotle says that "the change in the hero's fortunes must be . . . from happiness to misery; and the cause of it must lie not in any depravity, but in some great error on his part . . ."[5] The word translated as "error" is *hamartia.* I take this word to mean "mistake" rather than "sin" or "culpable offence," a "mental error" which often (but not necessarily) leads to a "wrong action" *(hamartêma),* committed in ignorance of its objects, its circumstances, or its consequences.[6] All three of Eliot's protagonists make a mental error that later results in wrong actions, which in turn have disastrous and far-reaching effects. Each of the three is predisposed to make the mistake because each in a different way takes too little care for the people close to him. Arthur, the young squire, is self-indulgent, presuming that he can please himself without taking responsibility for his actions; Adam is self-assured, setting an inflexible and too harsh standard by which he judges himself and others; and Hetty is self-absorbed, a girl who spends hours in her bedchamber in front of her mirror, "bent on her peculiar form of worship" (ch. 15).

Hetty is by far the least Aristotelian of the three. She is lovely, with "a beauty like that of kittens, or very small downy ducks" (ch. 7), and emptyheaded. "A simple farmer's girl, to whom a gentleman with a white hand was dazzling as an Olympian god" (ch. 9), she feels, and reacts, but does not think. She errs when she thinks Arthur will marry her, take her out of the dairy at Hall Farm, and dress her in lace and linen. Her *hamartia* becomes *hamartêma* when she and Arthur begin their dalliance. Hetty is a fatal combination of weakness and pride when she leaves her home in an attempt to escape the shame of bearing Arthur's illegitimate child. The child, born during her wandering, dies of neglect and exposure, but only the court, which sentences her to death, blames more than pities Hetty. When she is awaiting execution and eager for forgiveness from Adam and her family, Hetty still is capable of only a limited understanding of responsibility and consequences. Any knowledge Hetty may have gained from her suffering is of a very limited sort, and both her own suffering and the suffering she causes others are out of all proportion to her mistake, the dream of becoming gentry. Her suffering from the time she sets out to find Arthur until her stay of execution is so relentless, so disproportionate that pity alone results. George Eliot foreshadows Hetty's fate in a metaphor that combines the terrible fates of Arachne and Glauce:

> it is too painful to think that she is a woman, with a woman's destiny before her—a woman spinning in young ignorance a light web of folly and vain hopes which may one day close round her and press upon her, a rancorous poisoned garment, changing all at once her fluttering, trivial butterfly sensations into a life of deep human anguish. (ch. 22)

Adam Bede is more promising material for a tragic protagonist. Even though he does not have the stature of a king, Adam is idealized, "tall, upright, clever, brave Adam Bede" (ch. 9). He is considerably more substantial than any of the protagonists in the earlier ***Scenes of Clerical Life.*** In addition, Eliot was so convinced of the pervasive "tragedy of human life" (ch. 33), and of the inextricable nature of evil and pain that she felt the tragedy affecting the most lowly human beings inevitably affected many others. No tragedy could be limited or contained. Evil, like spilled ink, spread and stained all it touched. Mr. Irwine tells Adam:

> There is no sort of wrong deed of which a man can bear the punishment alone; you can't isolate yourself and say that the evil which is in you shall not spread. Men's lives are as thoroughly blended with each other as the air they breathe: evil spreads as necessarily as disease. (ch. 41)

Adam's tragedy—or even Hetty's—is more than personal.

Adam's *hamartia* is his self-assured inflexibility: he sets harsh standards by which he judges himself and others, and refuses to change his opinions. He early recognizes this rigidity in himself: "But it isn't my way to be see-saw about anything: I think my fault lies th' other way. When I've said a thing, if it's only to myself, it's hard for me to go back" (ch. 16). Most commentators agree with Adam, and some even use the weighted word "flaw" to describe his failing.[7]

Another word charged with meaning in Eliot's works is "error." "Error" is a common translation for *hamartia,* a closer translation than "flaw," and George Eliot uses it at significant points to describe Adam's (and Arthur Donnithorne's) mistaken thoughts and deeds. Before the climactic chance meeting of Adam and Arthur in the woods, the narrator pauses to discuss Adam's character:

> Perhaps here lay the secret of the hardness he had accused himself of: he had too little fellow-feeling with the weakness that errs in spite of foreseen consequences. Without this fellow-feeling, how are we to get enough patience and charity towards our stumbling, falling companions in the long and changeful journey? And there is but one way in which a strong determined soul can learn it—by getting his heart-strings bound round the weak and erring, so that he must share not only the outward consequence of their error, but their inward suffering. (ch. 19)

Adam begins to learn this lesson through grieving over his father's death, but it is in his relationships with Arthur Donnithorne and Hetty Sorrel that the real testing comes.

At the mid-point of the novel's fifty-six chapters, George Eliot calls Chapter 27 "A Crisis." Adam, walking home from work, surprises Arthur and Hetty in the woods and sees their parting kiss. Adam's trust in two of the people he cared about most is severely shaken. He refuses to be taken in by the cavalier Arthur's explanation. He knows "what isn't honest does come t' harm" and forces Arthur to acknowledge the wrongful nature of his conduct. Nevertheless, he remains deceived by both Arthur and Hetty about the exact nature of their flirtation despite considerable evidence to the contrary. He wants to believe Arthur is more like himself than unlike, capable of honorable actions and incapable of deceitful ones; he wants to believe Hetty really loves him. He continues under both misconceptions until Mr. Irwine stuns him with the news that Hetty has been imprisoned, charged with murdering her newborn child (ch. 39). There is both reversal and recognition in Chapter 39, a coincidence of plot admired by Aristotle when it was also probable and necessary.[8] Adam recognizes the truth about the characters and actions of Arthur and Hetty. There is also the actual reversal of his emotional fortune when all hope of marriage to Hetty is given up forever, and the imminent reversal of his professional fortunes, since neither he nor Hetty's family at Hall Farm could continue to work for the man responsible for such disgrace.

Chapters 41 and 42 continue Adam's education in sorrow. He reaches the nadir of his pain when he groans, ". . . I thought she loved me . . . and was good . . ." (ch. 42). At this point he also recognizes that he cannot allow himself the luxury of being an Orestes. His first reaction to the news of Hetty's misdeeds was a wish to make Arthur suffer: "I'll make him go and look at her misery—he shall look at her till he can't forget it—it shall follow him night and day—as long as he lives it shall follow him—he shan't escape wi' lies this time—I'll fetch him, I'll drag him myself" (ch. 39). Adam, however, listens to Mr. Irwine, who says, "It is not for us men to apportion the shares of moral guilt and retribution" (ch. 41). He passes by the opportunity to cause further evil by exacting revenge on Arthur Donnithorne, and somehow reconciles himself to the great waste and unhappiness that cannot be changed or ameliorated. In doing so, Adam changes and grows. George Eliot describes the process as "a regeneration, the initiation into a new state": "Doubtless a great anguish may do the work of years, and we may come out from that baptism of fire with a soul full of new awe and new pity" (ch. 42).

Awe and pity are not the equivalents of Aristotle's pity and fear, but Adam is not the one of the three protagonists whose intellectual forebearers are most Hellenic. That one is Arthur Donnithorne. Early in the novel he is compared to the planet Jupiter (ch. 5) and an Olympian god (ch. 9); he swears "by Jove" (ch. 5), and feels "very heroic" (ch. 12). Those who meet this very engaging young man think well of him, but like the Athenians with Alcibiades, Mrs. Irwine uses criteria that are too superficial when she says, "You'll never persuade me that I can't tell what men are by their outsides" (ch. 5).

Certainly Arthur's "outsides" are exceptionally attractive. The narrator, however, does not fall into the simplistic mistake of Mrs. Irwine:

> We use round, general, gentlemanly epithets about a young man of birth and fortune; and ladies, with that fine intuition which is the distinguishing attribute of their sex, see at once that he is "nice." The chances are that he will go through life without scandalizing anyone; a seaworthy vessel that no one would refuse to insure. Ships, certainly, are liable to casualties, which sometimes make terribly evident some flaw in their construction that would never have been discoverable in smooth water; and many a "good fellow", through a disastrous combination of circumstances, has undergone a like betrayal.
>
> But we have no fair ground for entertaining unfavorable auguries concerning Arthur Donnithorne. . . . (ch. 12)

So surrounded by epithets and auguries, George Eliot obliquely suggests that Arthur, like the ship, may hide some "flaw." That flaw combines with circumstance[9] to thrust Arthur into the tragedy that will affect so many in Hayslope and set Arthur himself on the path from *koros* to *hubris, atê,* and *nemesis.*

Arthur has a more than ample share of self-satisfaction *(koros)* from the beginning. He sees himself as a fine fellow; but he is too self-indulgent, and he presumes to amuse himself without admitting the responsibility for his actions. Arthur's *hamartia* is his belief that there are no consequences of his flirtation with Hetty beyond his ability to make right. He continues under this misapprehension until almost the end of the novel. Because of Eliot's interest in the psychology of the character of Arthur Donnithorne, the reader sees much of Arthur's struggles against temptation and his persistent, mistaken belief that no serious harm can result *(hamartia);* the reader sees comparatively little of Arthur and Hetty together *(hamartêma).*

Arthur does not continue in his error for lack of warnings. He himself is uneasy about his inability to resist seeing Hetty. Arthur seeks to soothe his conscience by visiting the Rector, Mr. Irwine, an easy remedy because, as the narrator explains, "We take a less gloomy view of our errors now our father confessor listens to us over his egg and coffee" (ch. 16). On the way, Arthur chances to meet Adam and the two talk about temptation. Arthur says, "We may determine not to gather cherries and keep our hands sturdily in our pockets, but we can't prevent our mouths from watering" (ch. 16). Adam the realist replies that it is no use looking upon life as if it were the Treddleston Fair, an array of treats waiting to be chosen. That, however, is exactly how Arthur has been acting, and he repeatedly overestimates his ability to keep his hands sturdily in his pockets.

Arthur's second, stronger warning follows immediately. He finds the Rector at breakfast with the first volume of the Foulis *Aeschylus* at his elbow (ch. 16). Mr. Irwine tells Arthur that he always likes to have a "favorite book" available at the breakfast hour. The conversation between the two men is heavy with irony. Mr. Irwine thinks that mornings are conducive to seeing things more clearly, but he does not see Arthur's guilty secret. Arthur, on his part, tells his mentor that, "It was a tempting morning for a ride before breakfast," but he cannot bring himself to confess what his real temptation is. Arthur says, "But I don't think a knowledge of the classics is a pressing want to a country gentleman." He will soon feel the lack of the knowledge he might have gotten from Mr. Irwine, whom the narrator describes as "little better than a pagan!" (ch. 17). Even Arthur winces when the Rector tells him that his godmother, Mrs. Irwine, has been talking about the kind of woman he might marry; the whole conversation has had the "disagreeable effect of a sinister omen" (ch. 16). Mr. Irwine himself reminds Arthur that the chorus in the *Prometheus* warns against imprudent marriages. When Arthur tries to turn the conversation to generalized comments about good intentions somehow gone astray, Mr. Irwine refuses to excuse the hypothetical wrongdoer with an argument reminiscent of Eliot's comments on the ship at harbor with an undetected flaw: "A man can never do anything at variance with his own nature. He carries within him the germ of his most exceptional action." When Arthur asks if Mr. Irwine thinks the man who struggles against temptation is as bad as the man who never tries to resist, Mr. Irwine answers:

> No, certainly; I pity him in proportion to his struggles, for they foreshadow the inward suffering which is the worst form of Nemesis. Consequences are unpitying. Our deeds carry their terrible consequences, quite apart from any fluctuations that went before—consequences that are hardly ever confined to ourselves. (ch. 16)

Arthur passes up the chance to confess his temptation. The next time the two men talk, Mr. Irwine again refers to Greek tragedy: "Ah, my boy, it is not only woman's love that is [*aperotos eros,*] as old Aeschylus calls it. There's plenty of 'unloving love' in the world of a masculine kind" (ch. 22). By this time Eliot does not need to show us Arthur wince: the reader knows that when Hetty dressed that same day for the birthday feast, she concealed under her clothes the enamel and gold locket Arthur had given her.

Discovery of the liaison occurs when Adam happens upon the lovers kissing in the wood. Hetty hurries away, but Arthur is left to confront Adam. Arthur, unaware that Adam loves Hetty, is sure that he can pass off the incident. He is full of careless self-confidence, but when Adam demands an explanation, Arthur passes from *koros* to *hubris* in his actions toward his loyal friend and retainer: "A patronizing disposition always has its meaner side, and in the confusion of his irritation and alarm there entered the feeling that a man to whom he had shown so much favor as to Adam was not in a position to criticize his conduct" (ch. 27). In quick succession Arthur realizes Adam has silently loved Hetty, recognizes his own conduct as ignoble, and comes to "regard Adam's suffering as not merely a consequence, but an element of his error." Neither Adam nor Arthur can contain such overwhelming emotions for long, and the two men fight until Arthur is knocked unconscious.

The physical confrontation discharges some of the tension between the two men but removes none of the problems. Arthur finds himself "in the wretched position of an open, generous man who has committed an error which makes deception seem a necessity" (ch. 28). He deliberately deludes Adam about the extent to which he and Hetty are involved; he adopts a self-serving attitude that goes so far as to presume to forgive Adam for Adam's injustice to him. Later, in the farewell letter Adam forces him to write to Hetty, he talks of his wrong and his fault, but only in the most complacent language (ch. 31). The reader feels that, in his heart, Arthur is sure that he suffers the most, gives up the most, and in doing so is acting with *noblesse oblige.* It is true that his own conscience and Adam's refusal to shake hands bother him, but not enough: "Nemesis can seldom forge a sword for herself out of our consciences—out of the suffering we feel in the suffering we may have caused: There is rarely metal enough there to make an effective weapon" (ch. 29).

Arthur moves from *hubris* to *atê* when he still refuses to recognize the irrevocable nature of his wrongdoing. He balms his conscience by dreaming of the favors he can bestow upon Hetty in future years and concludes, "*So* good comes out of evil." Adam has already denied the validity of this specious doctrine, and will do so again later.[10] Even the simple Mr. Poyser, as much as his fingers ached to hurry the harvest, would never work on a Sunday because "work on sacred days was a wicked thing" and "money got by such means would never prosper" (ch. 18). But Arthur moves and acts under the delusion that good can and will come from his mistakes, and continues under the influence of that delusion for a long time.

> There is a terrible coercion in our deeds, which may first turn the honest man into a deceiver and then reconcile him to the change, for this reason—that the second wrong presents itself to him in the guise of the only practicable right. The action which before commission has been seen with that blended common sense and fresh untarnished feeling which is the healthy eye of the soul, is looked at afterwards with the lens of apologetic ingenuity, through which all things that men call beautiful and ugly are seen to be made up of textures very much alike. Europe adjusts itself to a *fait accompli,* and so does an individual character—until the placid adjustment is disturbed by a convulsive retribution. (ch. 29)

The "convulsive retribution" overtakes Arthur last of the three protagonists. Hetty is already in prison and Adam sees what he had previously refused to see while Arthur is still lulled by Mr. Irwine's letter telling of Hetty's betrothal to Adam. In ignorance and dreaming of his future as beneficent squire, Arthur travels home to his grandfather's funeral. When he does think of "that affair last summer," he dismisses it: "That was an ugly fault ... but the future will make amends" (ch. 44).

When Arthur arrives at his estate and he reads Mr. Irwine's brief note, he, like Adam, experiences a simultaneous reversal and recognition. His ignorance of the consequences of his actions changes to knowledge, and at the same time all his dreams of playing the role of magnanimous squire on the estate he finally inherited are ruined. Adam is not Arthur's Nemesis, although more than once he threatened to take on that role. The magnitude of the suffering caused to Adam, Hetty, and all their relatives and friends at Hayslope is such that Nemesis now can forge a sword out of Arthur's own conscience. His subsequent actions—obtaining Hetty's pardon, going away for years—are actions finally motivated by what will most ease the insupportable situations of those he has hurt. He is no longer trying to appear good; he is no longer concerned with himself. Arthur the squire is the king of Hayslope. Only by going far away and leaving Mr. Irwine to manage the estate does he prevent the further sorrow that would have been caused if the Poysers and the Bedes had felt compelled by honor to leave his lands.

Arthur stays away for seven long years. He returns tired and ill. He is still troubled by his Nemesis. The novel closes with Adam telling Dinah, his wife, what Arthur has said about Hetty:

> "The first thing he said to me, when we'd got hold o' one another's hands was, 'I could never do anything for her, Adam—she lived long enough for all the suffering—and I'd thought so of the time when I might do something for her. But you told me the truth when you said to me once, "There's a sort of wrong that can never be made up for."'" (Epilogue)

Arthur has learned through suffering, just as the chorus in the *Agamemnon* says man must.[11] But the lesson that "There's a sort of wrong that can never be made up for" is not the only thing Arthur learns. The reader comes away with the impression that this older Arthur will care less about looking good and more about being good. Arthur, and Adam, and even perhaps Hetty learn to look outside themselves. If evil is to be avoided as much as possible, man must learn sympathy for his fellow human beings. Man must have sympathy and seek to do right, not because he will be rewarded, but because it is right. George Eliot wished her novels to teach moral lessons. In the same year she published ***Adam Bede,*** she wrote to a friend:

> If Art does not enlarge men's sympathies, it does nothing morally. I have had heart-cutting experience that opinions are a poor cement between human souls; and the only effect I ardently long to produce by my writings, is that those who read them should be better able to *imagine* and to *feel* the pains and the joys of those who differ from themselves in everything but the broad fact of being struggling erring human creatures.[12]

The genre in which Eliot worked is, like Homeric epic, more expansive than tragedy. The novel ***Adam Bede,*** for example, contains material for more than one dramatic tragedy. Eliot also had more than one literary antecedent in mind, as parallels to Miltonic epic and the pastoral tradition demonstrate.[13] Nevertheless, the classical allusions, the vocabulary of the *Poetics,* and the pattern of Adam's and Arthur's actions make comparisons to tragedy compelling. ***Adam Bede*** is tragedy if a noble carpenter or a frivolous country squire who experiences a reversal of fortune because of a *hamartia* is sufficiently noble to be a tragic protagonist. It is tragedy without actors or a stage, without the unities of time, place, and action, without a chorus. It is tragedy in so far as Eliot sought, like the Greeks, to exalt the nobility of man and show that suffering may bring wisdom. And for Eliot, at this early point in her development as a novelist, the wisdom taught by suffering is a moral truth outside the limits of conventional religion, a sympathy and love for all "struggling erring human creatures."

Notes

1. "The Morality of *Wilhelm Meister,*" reprinted from the *Leader,* VI (21 July, 1855), 703 in *Essays of George Eliot,* ed. Thomas Pinney (New York, 1963), p. 146.
2. In the manuscript, the word "urge" replaced "teach," which was crossed out. "Letter to Frederic Harrison," London, 15 August [1866], in *The George Eliot Letters,* ed. Gordon Haight (New Haven, Conn., 1954-55), IV, 301.
3. Gordon S. Haight, *George Eliot: A Biography* (Oxford, 1968), p. 195. For an extensive review of

George Eliot's use of Greek and Latin literature, see Vernon Rendall, "George Eliot and the Classics," *Notes and Queries,* 192 (13 and 27 December, 1947), 544-46, 564-65; and *Notes and Queries,* 193 (3 April, 26 June 1948), 148-49, 272-74, reprinted in *A Century of George Eliot Criticism,* ed. Gordon S. Haight (Boston, 1965), pp. 215ff.

4. See "The Unheroic Tragedy" and following chapters in Barbara Hardy, *The Novels of George Eliot* (New York, 1959; rpt. 1963); Felicia Bonaparte, *Will and Destiny: Morality and Tragedy in George Eliot's Novels* (New York, 1975); and William E. Buckler, "Memory, Morality and the Tragic Vision in the Early Novels of George Eliot," in *The English Novel in the Nineteenth Century: Essays on the Literary Mediation of Human Values,* ed. George Gordin (Urbana, Ill., 1972), pp. 145-63.

5. Aristotle, *Poetics,* ed. and tr. Richard McKeon (New York, 1941; rpt. 1966), 1453a13-16.

6. See Donald Stump, "Sidney's Concept of Tragedy and the Function of *Hamartia* in the *Arcadia,*" Ph.D. Diss. (Cornell University, 1978), pp. 146-56.

7. See R. T. Jones, *A Critical Commentary on George Eliot's 'Adam Bede'* (New York, 1968), p. 9: "This is the flaw (not a fatal one) in Adam's innocence: his confidence that he is righteous and that it is not too hard for anyone to be so. . . ." See also Hardy, p. 38: "In Adam, as later in Dorothea, egoism is no less a flaw which tragedy has to mend because it happens to take the form of a vision of duty. . . ."

8. See *Poetics,* 1452a22-b13. Reversal is translated "Peripety" and recognition "Discovery" by McKeon. Adam Bede's recognition is more psychological than the examples mentioned by Aristotle, which usually involve disguised identities, tokens, plain facts, and the like.

9. See *The Mill on the Floss,* Bk. 6, ch. 6: "For the tragedy of our lives is not created entirely from within. 'Character,' says Novalis in one of his questionable aphorisms '—character is destiny.' But not the whole of our destiny. Hamlet, Prince of Denmark, was speculative and irresolute, and we have a great tragedy in consequence. But if his father had lived to a good old age and his uncle had died an early death, we can conceive Hamlet's having married Ophelia and got through life with a reputation of sanity, notwithstanding many soliloquies and some moody sarcasms towards the fair daughter of Polonius, to say nothing of the frankest incivility to his father-in-law."

10. Adam to Arthur: "It takes the taste out o' my mouth for things, when I know I should have a heavy conscience after 'em. I've seen pretty clear, ever since I could cast up a sum as you can never do what's wrong without breeding sin and trouble more than you can ever see. It's like a bit o' bad workmanship—you never see th' end o' the mischief it'll do" (ch. 16).

Adam to Arthur: "I don't know what you mean by flirting, . . . but if you mean behaving to a woman as if you loved her, and yet not loving her all the while, I say that's not th' action of an honest man, and what isn't honest does come t' harm" (ch. 27).

Adam to Bartle Massey: "Good come out of it! . . . That doesn't alter th' evil: *her* ruin can't be undone. I hate that talk o' people, as if there was a way o' making amends for everything. They'd more need be brought to see as the wrong they do can never be altered. When a man's spoiled his fellow-creatur's life, he's no right to comfort himself with thinking good may come out of it. Somebody else's good doesn't alter her shame and misery" (ch. 46).

Adam to Arthur: "A man should make sacrifices to keep clear of doing a wrong; sacrifices won't undo it when it's done. When people's feelings have got a deadly wound, they can't be cured with favours" (ch. 48).

11. See Aeschylus, *Agamemnon,* ed. and tr. Richmond Lattimore in *Greek Tragedies,* Vol. I (Chicago, 1960), 11. 176-83:

> Zeus, who guided men to think,
> who has laid it down that wisdom
> comes alone through suffering.
> Still there drips in sleep against the heart
> grief of memory; against
> our pleasure we are temperate.
> From the gods who sit in grandeur
> grace comes somehow violent.

12. "Letter to Charles Bray," Wandsworth, 5 July 1859, in *The George Eliot Letters,* III, 110-11.

13. See "Pastoralism and the Justification of Suffering: *Adam Bede,*" in U. C. Knoepflmacher, *George Eliot's Early Novels: The Limits of Realism* (Berkeley, 1968), pp. 89-127.

Mason Harris (essay date 1983)

SOURCE: "Infanticide and Respectability: Hetty Sorrel as Abandoned Child in *Adam Bede,*" in *English Studies in Canada,* Vol. IX, No. 2, June, 1983, pp. 177-96.

[*In the following essay, Harris examines the character of Hetty Sorrel and her place in the larger narrative of* Adam Bede, *and discusses the realism of her despair and flight.*]

Adam Bede has usually been enjoyed and interpreted as a celebration of pastoral community, a loving backward look at a long-vanished rural world. Yet much of this novel's interest, especially for the modern reader, lies in its combination of nostalgic retrospect with "modern" problems not usually found in a pastoral. In particular, Hetty Sorrel's unwed pregnancy, desperate flight, abandonment of her child, and trial for its murder, seems to many readers the most striking episode in the novel. Eliot's vivid depiction of Hetty's flight has attracted some excellent criticism: both Barbara Hardy and Ian Adam analyze the remarkable way in which the narrator merges with Hetty's consciousness to bring us the immediate experience of a confused and inarticulate character.[1]

Our admiration for Eliot's achievement here, however, has tended to raise questions about Hetty's relation to the novel as a whole. The modern reader is likely to be put off by an apparent harshness in Eliot's commentary on Hetty throughout much of the novel—a harshness which seems oddly in contrast to her sympathy during the flight episode; some have seen Hetty's fate as a severe punishment for sexual love. Most serious, because most threatening to the novel's integrity, is the influential view that the realism of Hetty's "Journey in Despair" simply does not belong to the rest of the novel. In his well-known essay, "The Two Worlds of ***Adam Bede,***" Ian Gregor argues that most of the novel is old-fashioned pastoral, while Hetty's flight represents the intrusion of a modern "fiction of moral and philosophical inquiry" incompatible with the pastoral tradition.[2] If we accept this conclusion then we must consider the character at the centre of the plot and the modern reader's interest an inspired accident, and relegate the rest of the novel to a charming but obsolete literary genre. The vital issues raised by Hetty's disaster become irrelevant to Eliot's depiction of the world of Hayslope, and her fall seems a matter of private sin played off against a background of "immemorial" rustic virtue.[3]

The real question lies not in the rather abstract matter of genre but in the novel's sense of community, especially in the opposition between Hetty and her aunt and uncle Poyser, who represent the best aspects of the respectable tenant farmers of Hayslope. Despite the fine studies of Hetty's flight, surprisingly little criticism has been directed to her relation to the Poysers, and this is the area we must explore if we are to get beyond the inhibiting view of her as a separate case. Only if she belongs to the Poysers can she be shown to belong to the novel as a whole.

In his convincing interpretation—published a quarter of a century ago and still one of the most important essays on ***Adam Bede***—J. R. Creeger takes the novel out of the realm of "pastoral" (in the simple sense intended by Ian Gregor) when he demonstrates that Eliot's admiration for the Poysers is not unqualified, and that Dinah's Methodism provides a critical perspective on the world of Hayslope.[4] Hetty is usually seen as quite different from the apparently warm-hearted Poysers, but in emphasizing the difference between their values and Dinah's Creeger suggests that Hetty does indeed belong to Hayslope: she is "a perfect representative of the Loamshire-Hayslope world: she has its fertility, and she has its beauty, which nevertheless conceals an essential hardness."[5] He argues that the effect of her "ordeal is to externalize the hardness which has hitherto been concealed." Although the inhabitants of Hayslope refuse to forgive her crime and thus cannot help her, "they are implicated in her condition."[6]

Perhaps Creeger's insights have not been followed up in any clear way because of the confusing effect of Eliot's ambivalence both towards the Poysers, who are presented so warmly early in the novel but who later repudiate their erring niece, and Hetty, whom the narrator frequently disparages and yet depicts as sympathetic despite her undeniable crime. Finally, Eliot's affection for the Poysers triumphs in a happy ending which gets rid of Hetty and seems designed to make us forget the shortcomings of Hayslope.

Despite these difficulties, Hetty's role deserves further consideration. She is one of the most convincing depictions of a fallen woman in Victorian literature; as we shall see, she is also a crucial instance of the problems of the relation between individual and community in Eliot's fiction. Criticism has had difficulty in recognizing her full significance because of the mistaken assumption that Eliot intends a complete moral polarity between the novel's community and its main character. If the Poysers are seen to represent an ideal familial togetherness which stands for their whole community, then in her lack of family feeling and her most unfamilial crime Hetty can only be seen as an alien threat which tests the coherence of the community. Since Hetty accomplishes this through sexual indiscretion she can also be seen as the heroine of an erotic idyll set in total contrast to the Puritan virtues of the Poysers, and cruelly punished by an equally Puritan author.[7]

The view of Hetty as a sinful intruder on pastoral innocence involves a misunderstanding of her nature as a character—a misunderstanding which in turn obscures her most obvious link with the Poysers. If we look beneath Eliot's sometimes annoying commentary we will discover that she presents Hetty not as an adult sinner but as a confused child, and that it is through her role as child that her relation to her community can best be understood.

Hetty devastates the traditional family life of the Poysers by killing her child; because of this crime we tend to forget that she is herself an orphaned child for whom they have a parental responsibility. Their unthinking adherence to tradition may have something to do with her failure to grow up, and certainly provides the values which motivate her disastrous flight. In her blind respectability she rejects all possibility of rescue, hiding her child in a forest in a compulsive attempt to recover her position as the Poysers' child. As we shall see, the state of mind in which she commits the "murder" reveals a young child's inability to handle inner conflict. Childishly dependent on the values of her community, she remains trapped in a world which cannot recognize the isolated individual; yet her anguished confusion provides the novel's most intense portrayal of individual experience. As lost child, Hetty also acquires a central, if difficult, role in Eliot's preoccupation with moral education through experience, a concern which itself arises out of the breakdown of community.

In attempting a comprehensive study of Hetty's role, we encounter an interesting problem which may help to explain why such a fragmented picture of her is to be found in criticism. There may be some difficulties in perspective in approaching a character who is thematically at the centre of the novel, but psychologically isolated by her narcissism from all the other characters: to understand her as a character we must study her in relation to her own very narrow world, but to understand the full significance of her role in the novel we must see her in relation to a much larger world of which she has no comprehension—a problem made more difficult by her abrupt disappearance from the story after her confession to Dinah.

To accommodate this dual aspect of Hetty, my essay will move through two stages. I will first concentrate on her relation to the Poysers and her psychological motivation, viewing her abandonment of her child and subsequent mental collapse as a comment on the limitations of the communal world she shares with her foster parents. Then, taking a larger perspective, I will consider her in relation to other characters and the main themes of the novel, finally asking why the author herself abandons the pathetic child for whom she has won so much sympathy. A fuller understanding of the psychological and social aspects of Hetty's role will reveal that Eliot's shift from "pastoral" to "realism" is not a break in the novel's continuity but a result of its natural development. Only in the happy ending do we find a pastoral incompatible with Eliot's realism.

II

We first encounter Hetty as a very self-centred and naive girl competently performing her tasks at the Poysers' farm, but without affection for her foster parents or their way of life. It is the editorial commentary here which offends the modern reader; many have assumed that Hetty is being presented as a monster of egotism, especially in Chapter Fifteen, where she is seen in contrast to her Methodist cousin Dinah, who works in a factory and ministers to the poor in industrial Stonyshire, and occasionally visits the Hall Farm, but refuses to live there because she cannot accept the Poysers' complacent prosperity.

In terms of the novel's Wordsworthian values, Hetty does seem rather unwholesome. The narrator tells us that she hates young animals and children, especially those belonging to the Poysers. We should note, however, that the way the narrator describes Hetty suggests that her problem lies in extreme immaturity rather than in wickedness. Despite her distaste for babies and the natural world she is frequently compared to small and young animals: she has a "beauty like that of kittens, or very small downy ducks . . . or babies just beginning to toddle and to engage in conscious mischief—a beauty with which you can never be angry, but that you feel ready to crush for inability to comprehend the state of mind into which it throws you"; here Hetty seems just at the infantile beginning of consciousness.[8] "She was like a kitten, and had the same distractingly pretty looks, that meant nothing, for everybody that came near her" (xix, 213). Hetty's "look" can mean nothing because it has no recognition of the subjective reality of others. Both her admirers seem attracted by her resemblance to small animals: Adam observes her bad temper with "a sort of amused pity, as if he had seen a kitten setting up its back, or a little bird with its feathers ruffled . . . the prettiest thing in the world" (xxiii, 269), and, when she weeps, Arthur finds her irresistibly like "a bright-eyed spaniel with a thorn in its foot" (xiii, 138).

Before condemning Eliot for moral intolerance towards Hetty, we must remember the problem Eliot faced in retaining the sympathy of a Victorian audience for this character. By criticizing Hetty early in the novel Eliot expresses beforehand the disapproval her audience might be expected to feel later, and also, by the very nature of her criticism, implies that Hetty's problem is really psychological, more deserving of sympathy than harsh judgement. Mentally she is a child, a case of arrested development, not responsible for her actions, and thus a victim no matter what she may finally do. Dinah foreshadows the "Journey in Despair" when she compares Hetty facing a woman's destiny to a "child hugging its toys in the beginning of a long toilsome journey, in which it will have to bear hunger and cold and unsheltered darkness" (xv, 160). Later, Adam repeatedly excuses Hetty on the grounds that "'She's all but a child'" (xxviii, 308). Clearly we are invited to do the same; the more Eliot emphasizes Hetty's childishness the better case she has for sympathy later on.

In considering the Poysers' role as Hetty's foster parents, we should remember that despite Eliot's nostalgia for Hayslope she had a sharp critical understanding of the class to which they belong. As prosperous English yeomen, the Poysers represent the very best of the peasant class Eliot describes in her sociological essay, **"The Natural History of German Life,"** but their world-view reveals that predominance of tradition over individual consciousness which she finds characteristic of the peasantry: with the peasant, "Custom holds the place of sentiment. . . . The peasant never questions the obligation of family ties—he questions no custom [but] with him general custom holds the place of individual feeling."[9] Mr. Poyser habitually displays a "predominant after-supper expression of hearty good-nature" (xxv, 285), but towards a man of whose farming methods he does not approve he is "as hard and implacable as the north-east wind" (xiv, 145). Mrs. Poyser constantly criticizes the housekeeping of neighbouring wives, and her frequent tirades against Hetty and the servants are associated with that compulsive cleanliness which Eliot finds less of a virtue when inflicted on Maggie by the Dodson aunts in ***The Mill on the Floss.*** Mrs. Poyser berates Molly, the all-purpose maid, for having been hired "without a bit o' character" and kept despite her filthy ways (vi, 73-74 and xx, 231-32). It would seem that in her first novel Eliot made humour out of certain characteristics of the respectable peasantry (the origins of her own family) towards which she actually felt ambivalent—if we are to judge by her next novel.

Some bitter remarks by "old Martin," Mr. Poyser's father and Hetty's grandfather, reveal that before Hetty's parents died they disgraced themselves through improvident farming. The senior Poyser has never forgiven his daughter, Hetty's mother, for marrying a poor man against his will; he retains "a long unextinguished resentment, which always made [him] more indifferent to Hetty than to his son's children. Her mother's fortune had been spent by that good-for-nought Sorrel, and Hetty had Sorrel's blood in her veins" (xxxi, 344). The Poysers scrupulously acknowledge their obligation to take care of their niece, but their rigid values might well have a stunting effect on a girl dispossessed at the age of ten when her parents died in poverty. Mrs. Poyser means well towards Hetty, but often berates her along with the servants; it would not occur to her to treat the orphan niece as an equal to her own children. Though they wish the best for Hetty in marriage, the Poysers do not see her as "a daughter of their own," but as a "penniless niece. For what could Hetty have been but a servant elsewhere, if her uncle had not taken her in and brought her up as a domestic help to her aunt?" (ix, 98). Hetty occupies an ambiguous position below the Poysers' children, yet partaking of the Poyser respectability, and thus above the more easygoing world of the servants and farmhands.[10] Despite the contrast between the Poysers' good intentions and Hetty's narcissism, she can be seen as a product of their world—a possible outcome of the narrowness and complacency of their values along with their somewhat impersonal attitude towards her as a "domestic help."

Hetty's state of mind can be consistently interpreted as a case of childhood narcissism accompanied by intense sibling rivalry: having lost her own position as daughter she hates the Poysers' children as rivals and does not care much for the parents who produced them. Chapter Fifteen provides a comprehensive account of Hetty's attitude towards the Poysers' family life. She has no "loving thought of her second parents—of the children she had helped to tend—of any youthful companion, any pet animal, any relic of her own childhood even" and "did not understand how anybody could be very fond of middle-aged people. And as for those tiresome children . . . Hetty would have been glad to hear that she should never see a child again." She also hates "the nasty little lambs" brought in for special care, but at least the lambs, unlike the Poysers' children, "*were* gotten rid of sooner or later." This seems a death-wish; Mrs. Poyser complains that she showed no feeling when the infant Totty was missing and assumed drowned. Hetty's attitude towards young animals suggests repulsion towards anything suggestive of birth or the maternal: "Hetty would have hated the very word 'hatching' if her aunt had not bribed her to attend the young poultry" (xv, 156-58). She resembles the four-year-old Totty in preoccupation with clothing, in her interest in getting presents, and in being compared to young animals by the narrator. We shall see that, despite her lack of affection, Hetty is actually very dependent on her family.

While Mrs. Poyser rails at Hetty and the servants she constantly coddles Totty: she admits, Totty is "spoiled shameful . . . being the youngest, and th' *only* gell" (vii, 87, italics mine). Hetty particularly dislikes this child, who was born after she came to the Poysers. The absence of any attachment to the present or fondness for the past suggests a disturbance associated with that past; Hetty's fantasies deny the existence of time. As we have seen, she hates the thought of birth and babies of any species. When Eliot compares her to young animals she implies that babies do not like other babies, and that a woman who has remained a child is not likely to be a sympathetic mother. Hetty's gentlemen admirers are quite mistaken when they imagine, "How she will dote on her children! She is almost a child herself, and the little pink round things will hang about her like florets round the central flower" (xv, 154).[11]

In her obsession with costume, Hetty is not a temptress but a little girl. She projects her childhood interest in clothes and rivalry into adult relationships, thinking of marriage as an occasion "when she would have a silk gown and a great many clothes all at once" (xxxi, 342). She is preoccupied with dressing better than Mary Burge, daughter of the owner of the local timber yard. Her main interest in both Mary and Adam seems to derive from the fact that Mary likes Adam, while Adam has eyes only for herself: "she felt nothing when his eyes rested on her, but the cold triumph of knowing that he loved her, and would not look at Mary Burge" (ix, 99). At the height of her affair with Arthur she still pauses to give Adam one of her "brightest smiles" because "she knew Mary Burge was looking at them" (xxii, 256).

Hetty's feeling for Arthur is just a Cinderella-fantasy in which he plays a god-like handsome prince who will magically elevate her above all rivals, especially Mary Burge. The extent to which her fantasies about Arthur involve infantile dressing up should dispel any belief that sensual love or romantic passion is involved here. As she parades "with a pigeon-like stateliness" before her bedroom mirror, she dreams of Captain Donnithorne, who thought her "prettier than anybody about Hayslope . . . and prettier than Miss Bacon, the miller's daughter, who was called the beauty of Treddleston . . . he would like to see her in nice clothes, and thin shoes and white stockings, perhaps with silk clocks to them . . . of every picture she is the central figure in fine clothes . . . and everybody else is admiring and envying her" (xv, 152-56). Critics are mistaken who assume that Eliot attacks sensual love in having this affair end in disaster; Hetty is infantile from the beginning, and Arthur likes her that way. Hetty's problem is not sin but a regressive narcissism which, with its concomitant naiveté, sets her up as Arthur's victim and then, given the bad luck of his transfer to Ireland, becomes, along with her intense respectability, the driving force behind her crime. In her case criminal justice seems both cruel and irrelevant.

As we have seen, Hetty projects her feeling of dispossession into very naive fairy-tale aspirations; despite her hostility to her family and longing to rise above it she cannot perceive any reality outside her family life. Thus, when she runs away to hide her shame, her dark journey does not represent an advance in experience of the outside world, but a blind, regressive drive to reassert the respectability she possessed when she lived with the Poysers. In this state of mind she acts out a grim parody of their values.

An important comment on Hetty's motivation links her narcissism with the Poysers' sense of respectability. After reading Arthur's letter putting an end to the affair, she resolves that "nobody should find out how miserable she was. . . . They would think her conduct shameful; and shame was torture. That was poor little Hetty's conscience" (xxxi, 343). The full force of her narcissism is focussed on being seen by others in terms of the respectable standards of her community: "Hetty had a certain strength in her vain little nature: she would have borne anything rather than be laughed at, or pointed to with any other feeling than admiration" (xviii, 202).

The emphasis on being "laughed at" or "pointed to" reveals shame-culture at its most basic. Hetty's obsession with maintaining her respectability is related to the distinction, important to both Eliot and G. H. Lewes, between shame and the sympathetic imagination as the basis of morality—also a distinction between primitive and civilized world-views.[12] The Poysers and their community are still mainly at the level of shame-culture, manifested in extreme form in Hetty's case, while Dinah, the self-denying Methodist from industrial Stoniton, combines the sympathetic imagination with an Evangelical disregard for social status, and thus is able to "save" Hetty when the community condemns her. The parallel Eliot suggests between Mr. Poyser's rejection of his niece and Hetty's child-murder indicates the need for a more conscious morality than that of tradition-bound Hayslope.

Early in her flight Hetty displays a social attitude characteristic of the Poysers' world: "she was most of all afraid of . . . becoming so destitute that she would have to ask for people's charity; for Hetty had the pride not only of a proud nature but of a proud class—the class that pays the most poor-rates, and most shudders at the idea of profiting by a poor rate" (xxxvi, 379). Later she is quick to assure the innkeeper that "I belong to respectable folks" (xxxvii, 389). At the beginning of the "Journey in Despair," Eliot describes Hetty's dread of shame as a class-attitude in a passage which brings some central themes together:

> She thought of a young woman who had been found against the church wall at Hayslope one Sunday, nearly dead with cold and hunger—a tiny infant in her arms; the woman was rescued and taken to the parish. "The parish!" You can perhaps hardly understand the effect of that word on a mind like Hetty's, brought up among people who were somewhat hard in their feelings even towards poverty, who lived among the fields and had little pity for want and rags as a cruel inevitable fate such as they sometimes seem in cities, but held them a mark of idleness and vice—and it was idleness and vice that brought burthens on the parish. To Hetty the "parish" was next to the prison in obloquy; and to ask anything of strangers—to beg—lay in the same far-off hideous region of intolerable shame that Hetty had all her life thought it impossible she could ever come near. (xxxvii, 386)

Here Hetty partakes of the conviction, already enuciated by Mrs. Poyser in her criticism of Methodists (viii, 94), that if you're poor it's your own fault—"idleness and vice" are the leading qualities of those who choose to live at the ratepayers' expense. With the Poysers this attitude is natural because they "live among the fields" where Dinah finds "a strange deadness to the Word" (viii, 92). As Dinah admits, her religion flourishes only in cities; it is through contact with the industrial poor that she has been able to develop her democratic vision of poverty as a "cruel inevitable fate" rather than a comment on one's moral character (viii, 92). For Hetty and her class, people who are not respectable, and thus have no place in the social order, cease to exist morally. "Charity" denotes not Christian love but something so degrading that those who receive it have lost all claim to be considered human. No significant distinction can be made between being on the "parish" and imprisonment for a crime.

When worried about possible eviction by the old Squire, the Poysers think of moving twenty miles away to the next parish as a kind of death: "we shall . . . die o' broken hearts among strange folks" (xxxviii, 359). After Hetty's disaster this move seems necessitated by a loss of status felt quite literally as worse than death. Repeatedly insisting on the Old Testament view that their children and grandchildren must suffer for Hetty's disgrace, the Poyser father and son play the role of Pharisee, while the lost sinner can only be saved by Dinah, whose religion emphasizes forgiveness and universal suffering represented by Christ as the "Man of Sorrows":

> the Hall Farm was a house of mourning for a misfortune felt to be worse than death. The sense of family dishonour was too keen even in the kind-hearted Martin Poyser the younger, to leave any room for compassion towards Hetty. . . . Hetty had brought disgrace on them all—disgrace that could never be wiped out. That was the all-conquering feeling in the mind of both father and son—the scorching sense of disgrace, which neutralized all other sensibility; Mr. Irwine was struck with surprise to observe that Mrs. Poyser was less severe than her husband. We are often startled with the severity of mild people on exceptional occasions; the reason is, that mild people are most liable to be under the yoke of traditional impressions. (xl, 423)

The intensity of feeling which Mrs. Poyser manifests in her role as sharp-tongued defender of Hayslope morality can also grant her a certain independence from that morality: though she thinks on conventional lines she can sometimes experience as an individual. If Martin is more tradition-bound because he has less feeling, then we can conclude that Hetty, who has no feeling for others, is the most likely to be "under the yoke of traditional impressions." With his sensibility "neutralized," Mr. Poyser temporarily enters a state of mind which is permanent with Hetty. Weeping "hard tears" he says that he will pay for her defence at the trial, but "I'll not go nigh her, nor ever see her again, by my own will. She's made our bread bitter to us for all our lives to come, an' we shall ne'er hold up our heads i' this parish nor i' any other" (xl, 423). Mr. Poyser's attitude here is more excusable than Hetty's crime, but both repudiate a child because they equate disgrace with death.

Dinah's implied criticism of Hayslope is dramatized by Hetty's flight. Hetty enjoys fantasies of rising above the Poysers, but her behaviour in the flight reveals that she is childishly dependent on her environment and thus blindly follows its values; she possesses no inner consciousness to oppose the compulsion of respectability. Alienated from family life and isolated by her narcissism, she reproduces the Poysers' values without their feeling for kin and community. Of course, this is a distortion of their world-view, but the analogy between her abandonment of her child and her uncle's attitude towards her implies a repudiation of the human on both sides.

Despite Hetty's "resolute air of self-reliance," her actions during the "Flight in Despair" are completely irrational; like a young child, she can only express conflicting drives in contradictory behaviour. She flees from Hayslope to escape "discovery and scorn" before "familiar eyes," but refuses all offers of help on the journey because she takes the outside world as an extension of her community. She seeks a pool in which to drown herself—a pool deep enough so that her body will not be discovered until summer, by which time no one will be able to recognize her. Yet as she searches for such a pool she maintains a respectable appearance, takes care with her money, and travels back towards home.

When she finds a pool she postpones suicide to eat "eagerly" and fall asleep, awakening terrified in "cold, and darkness, and solitude—out of all human reach" (xxxvii, 395). By contrast she thinks of the Hall Farm: "The bright hearth and the voices of home,—the secure uprising and lying down,—the familiar fields, the familiar people" (xxxvii, 395). This antithesis between lethal solitude, the outcome of her flight from human vision, and home perceived in terms of light, heat, the sound of voices—the impersonality of unvarying routine and "familiar people"—presents an extreme form of communal identification. She seeks to return to no particular relationship, but to merge into a total pattern which will be static and therefore absolute.

After recovering from her panic, she feels "exultation" at still being alive and, in an uncharacteristic display of emotion, kisses "her arms with passionate love of life" (xxxvii, 395). Yet this inherent vitality, evoked by her rejection of suicide, cannot extend to a sense of the value of life in general, not even that of the child to which she will soon give birth. The next morning her "passionate joy in life" (xxxvii, 397) succumbs to a moralistic peasant who calls her a "wild woman," renewing her sense of disgrace so that "she felt that she was like a beggar already" (xxxvii, 395-97).

Hetty passionately loves her own flesh, yet passes sentence of death on her pregnant body. She can resolve this dilemma once the child is born by killing it in order to return to the only life she can imagine—unquestioned acceptance in the community. Hetty resists with her whole being the disruption of her infantile dependence on her kin by the child to which she has given birth; there is only room for one infant in her world and that is herself. Later she tells Dinah of her plan to drown the baby so that she could be once more "safe at home": "I thought I'd find a pool, if I could, like that other. . . . I thought I should get rid of all my misery, and go back home, and never let 'em know why I ran away. . . . I longed so to be safe at home. . . . I seemed to hate the baby—it was like a heavy weight hanging round my neck" (xlv, 462-63). Yet as Hetty resolutely takes the baby into the woods she experiences for the first time a counter-movement of feeling for it. This can only find expression in tactile terms: "the baby was warm against me . . . its crying went through me, and I daredn't look at its little face and hands" (xlv, 463). Instead of experiencing the baby only as a "heavy weight" she recognizes the existence of a face by refusing to look at it.

The child is not saved by this feeling, but Hetty's longing to express it will prompt the confession which returns her to humanity.[13] At present the impulse to kill the child still dominates; rather than weighing alternatives Hetty commits the act, but does it in a way that expresses her ambivalence (xlv, 463-64). By covering up the baby in a hole under a bush in the woods Hetty leaves it to almost certain death by exposure, and signifies her lethal intentions by describing the hole as a "grave"; the child is so well hidden that, as we learn at the trial, a man who searched the spot after hearing it cry couldn't find it (xliii, 444-45). Yet by also leaving an opening for it to breathe she expresses the wish that it "wouldn't die." She thinks only now of abandoning the child so that it might live; yet she had a good opportunity to do this earlier after giving birth in the house of a sympathetic woman. At that time, however, when she was actually in contact with another person, her flight from shame demanded a lonely murder in the woods. By burying the child, but not completely, Hetty tries both to kill it and to let it live, and of course the result is death.

Only after she abandons the child does her feeling for it begin to get the upper hand. At this point most Victorian novelists would have presented a scene of melodramatic remorse, but Eliot is too good a psychologist to let Hetty depart from character. Since her consciousness cannot accommodate conflict, her maternal feeling finds expression in auditory hallucination and a compulsive return to the scene of the crime. Miles away she hears the baby crying, a literal expression of the wish that it might still be alive. The "crying" finally overcomes her flight from shame, forcing her to return to the place where she hid the baby: "I'd left off thinking about going home—it had gone out o' my mind" (xlv, 464). Hetty could never have made this confession had she not finally been able to forget her drive to return home.

Since she has no inner consciousness, this feeling appears only after the fulfilment of her drive towards isolation and murder, and then only as hallucination, paralysis of the will, and psychic fragmentation—she never rejects her original goal but only notes later that it had "gone out" of her mind. It seems that she can experience feelings that conflict with her narcissism only as external forces compelling action against her will. Ironically, her belated feeling for the child brings about her arrest and a disgrace worse than unwed motherhood. Unable to face real suicide, she responds with psychotic withdrawal from humanity. During the "Journey in Despair" her features have already become petrified and petrifying "like that wondrous Medusa face, with the passionate, passionless lips" (xxxvii, 393);[14] now her whole being follows suit: "My heart went like a stone: I couldn't wish or try for anything; it seemed like as if I should stay there for ever, and nothing 'ud ever change. But they came and took me away" (xlv, 465). Here "heart" and time freeze in a repudiation of life-processes.

Her psychic suicide seems another parallel to her uncle's attitude towards her. He casts her out of the family, while she "will not confess her name or where she comes from" (xxxix, 418)—in Hetty's kinship-oriented world to have neither place nor name is to be dead. Mr. Poyser will act as though he never had a niece while Hetty "denies that she has had a child" (xl, 427). Killing one's own child, whether in metaphor or fact, is an extreme way of denying the narrator's assertion that we should "help each other the more" because "we are children of a large family" (xxvii, 298).

We have seen that the experience of abandoning the child opens, for the first time, a breach in Hetty's narcissistic world; confession of this experience to Dinah is a step outside herself which earlier would have been impossible. Dinah attributes this change to divine grace but it really arises from the therapeutic value of confession itself.[15] Hetty cannot conceptualize her experience, but in the course of the confession the persistent "crying" and her return to the child change from hallucination and compulsion to an image of guilt linking the present to the past. In tribute to the honesty of Eliot's characterization, however, we must note that Hetty's account of her new feelings is limited to very concrete terms: "that crying and the place in the wood," which she hopes God will "take away" as though it were a physical pain (xlv, 564). Her confession can only be seen as the beginning of consciousness.

III

Hetty's confession is the emotional climax of the novel; nowhere else do we approach such intense involvement with any of the characters. Yet the confession is also the focal point of our problems with the novel, for we are never to see Hetty again, and thus all the questions raised by this climactic scene remain unanswered. Eliot first turns away from Hetty to concentrate on the sympathetic concern felt for her by other characters, and then, having rescued her from the gallows and shipped her off as a transported convict, forgets her altogether—except for a few cold references in the final Book of the novel, where the sole purpose of the narrative is to celebrate the Poysers' harvest supper and lead towards the happy marriage of Adam and Dinah.

The difficulty presented by Hetty's exile can be seen more clearly by comparison to the easier time Eliot has with her fellow sinner, Arthur. Since both Arthur and Hetty have fallen from the rustic community, any sense of reconciliation on their part must come from self-understanding and a sense of reconciliation with humanity in general. Arthur achieves this in Chapter Forty-Eight, where he reestablishes his friendship with Adam, declares his intent to sacrifice himself by leaving for India so that no one else need leave town, and makes Adam promise to persuade the Poysers to stay. His exile is a healing of his relation with the community: he accepts his guilt, does the best thing for others, and thus prepares for his happier return seven years later.

Arthur's capacity for self-understanding, and his resources as officer, gentleman, and landlord, provide the basis for a conventional expiation. Hetty's exile, however, is not a matter of choice; while we trust she has made a beginning we have yet to see how she will deal with guilt and shame, especially as a transported convict.[16] In this context, Eliot's refusal to say anything at all about Hetty's further development seems unforgivable. When, after Arthur has been welcomed back in "The Epilogue," Dinah rather glibly remarks that "the death of the poor wanderer, when she was coming back to us, has been sorrow upon sorrow" (549), we can only take this as a rather cheap way for the author to fudge unfinished business; it would seem that death is after all the only permissible fate for the fallen woman.

Fortunately, this failure occurs too late to inflict fatal damage on the novel. Despite the incompleteness of her story, Hetty stands out, in the very difficulties she creates, as one of Eliot's great heroines. Her flight from Hayslope brings together the problems of community and individual development, and pushes them to the limits of Eliot's realism. The crime led up to by her journey, coldly investigated at her trial, and finally explained in her confession, is the true centre of the novel because its social and psychological causes include so much of the novel's reality. I will show how the main themes of the novel move towards a climax in her flight and confession, and then are defused by her exile.

The nostalgic affection with which Eliot regards the Poysers, especially on our first tour of the Hall Farm, has blinded many readers to the fact that this novel deals with two problems characteristic of her fiction: the difficulties of growing from confused adolescence to moral maturity, and the virtues and limitations of a tradition-bound community. These concerns are closely related because it is a breach in the community which necessitates individual development, and to learn to think for oneself one must transcend the limitations of one's community.

Although Eliot lovingly depicts the tranquil life of the older generation, represented by the Poysers and their Anglican shepherd Mr. Irwine, the novel is really about the problems of three confused children: Arthur and Hetty, both orphans living with relatives, and Adam, a virtual orphan who assumes responsibility for a drunken father and a foolish, querulous mother. In each case, the moral deficiencies of the child are related to an absence of parental guidance and to feelings of resentment towards inadequate parent-figures: Adam responds to his father's disgrace by incorporating Hayslope's "hardness" into his moral independence, while Arthur compensates for his grandfather's hostility and greed by dreaming how, upon inheriting the estate, he will become an ideal Squire, paternally bestowing largesse on his tenants and beloved by them in return. Both must achieve maturity by learning to see beyond the limitations of their class, Arthur much more painfully than Adam. (Dinah is also an orphan, but we are never shown the experience through which she achieves her sympathetic vision. If she seems too good to be true, this may be because Eliot has not confronted the psychological problems inherent in her ascetic religion—as she does later with Maggie Tulliver and Dorothea Brooke.)

Hetty becomes the most interesting of the orphaned children because she presents the most serious threat to the respectable community and the most extreme case of the difficulties of growing up. Eliot's failure to complete Hetty's story indicates that these problems have not been resolved in the novel. With Maggie Tulliver, the heroine of her next novel, [***The Mill on the Floss,***] Eliot presents a more explicit version of conflict with family and community, but Maggie's sympathy and intelligence also make it easier for Eliot to develop and analyze this conflict within the moral context of the novel.[17] Never again does Eliot give such a central role to so intractable a character as Hetty.

On the psychological level, Hetty is an effective portrayal of a dark aspect of childhood experience; she seems both attractive and alarming because we recognize in her a stage through which we all have passed. Her tragedy reveals the consequences of failure to grow out of childhood, thus incidentally commenting on masculine idealization of childishness in women. The fact that Hetty represents childhood experience is relevant both to the defensive criticism of her early in the novel, and to Eliot's ability to identify with her in the flight. As we leave Hetty on the road at the end of Chapter Thirty-Seven we abruptly return to the sympathetic distance of mature adult vision—"My heart bleeds for her as I see her toiling along on weary feet" (xxxvii, 397)—but parental concern on the part of the narrator, Dinah, and Adam is not in itself an adequate way to deal with the character who emerges from the "journey" and the confession.

Adam provides the moral of the story when he overcomes his own version of Hayslopian hardness and agrees to accompany Bartle Massey to Hetty's trial: "I'll stand by her—I'll own her. . . . They oughtn't to cast her off—their own flesh and blood. We hand folks over to God's mercy and show none ourselves. . . . I'll never be hard again" (xlii, 439). Since Hetty's anguish is, however, more interesting than Adam's, most readers are unwilling to view her fall primarily as payment for his education; whatever the quality of his insights, we really want to know the outcome of her experience. Adam's moral improvement can be taken for granted; the most interesting problem at the end of the novel is how a character as regressive as Hetty can develop at all—a problem made all the more interesting by the fact that her confession does suggest the possibility of change. Eliot's religion of humanity depends on the replacement of Christian revelation with moral education through experience, and it is the confused Hetty, not the clear-headed Adam, who provides the real test case for this. Despite Hetty's lack of sympathy and intelligence, we respond more to the nightmare confusion of her aimless journey than to the morally lucid experience of Adam and Dinah.

While Hetty presents an unanswered challenge to Eliot's moral psychology, she also leads us to the most complex aspects of the novel's social vision. Both the classes which dominate the novel, landowning aristocracy and respectable tenant farmers, are implicated in her crime. The first of these is easier for Eliot to deal with than the second; the indolent young Squire and his miserly grandfather threaten the rustic community from the outside, reinforcing its values by way of contrast, while Hetty, the embarrassing product of this community, threatens it from within. We need not invoke the pastoral tradition to explain Eliot's fondness for Hayslope, for she was here describing the origins of her own family.[18] As the daughter of a man who, like Adam, rose from carpenter to estate-agent, she might well admire hardworking artisans and farmers while feeling a certain hostility towards lazy landlords (of whom we see more in ***Silas Marner***). Yet Dinah's rejection of Hayslope implies a reservation about the Poysers, and this expands as the novel develops; as we have seen, the shortcomings of Hayslope become a major theme after Hetty takes over from Arthur as leading character.

Mrs. Poyser complains that the tenant farmers must sweat on fields which others own (xxxii, 353), but we discover that they in turn are "hard" towards the dispossessed proletariat to which Dinah ministers and into which Hetty falls, sinking all the deeper through her compulsive respectability. Her flight puts her community in a colder perspective; the Poysers are now seen as members of a "proud class," which despises those who "profit" by the poor-rates. Though still sympathetic characters, they are no longer protected by their virtuous role in the enclosing world of Hayslope; after Hetty's flight we see them in ambiguous relation to a larger reality. If Hetty is a case of arrested psychological development, it is also true that the class to which she belongs displays a primitive social vision, in contrast to Dinah, whose moral maturity includes a sympathetic understanding of the industrial poor, and social outcasts in general.

We have seen that a conflict between self and community is implicit in Eliot's portrayal of Hetty (a conflict more clearly developed in her later fiction, but always rendered difficult by her nostalgia for community). In ***Adam Bede,*** one manifestation of this conflict appears in the difference in realism between the early chapters and Hetty's flight—a problem fatally oversimplified by Gregor and others. Ian Adam has demonstrated that this novel contains a variety of "realisms" (see note 1). I would add that there is a logical transition between the very different "realisms" of our first visit to the Hall Farm and of Hetty's anguish and flight, and that the contrast between these is an important aspect of the thematic structure of the novel.

The pleasant pastoral of our first visit to the Hall Farm in Chapters Six and Seven is mainly the result of narrative distance; both narrator and reader are assumed to be tourists from the city enjoying a visit to a rural world remote in time and space: "The dairy was certainly worth looking at: it was a scene to sicken for with a sort of calenture in hot and dusty streets" (vii, 82). At this point we can appreciate the cozy sense of community because we are not threatened with personal involvement.

Eliot encourages us to enjoy the "pastoral" as an entrance to the novel, but does not allow us to remain permanently in a mood which depends on not identifying too closely with the feelings of any one character. As we settle down in the world of the novel, we become aware of something slightly oppressive about the Poysers' way of judging everyone by kin, cleanliness, and farming methods. Adam seems more independent than they, but then he moralizes excessively at his fellow workmen, feels little sympathy for his father, and consoles himself for the latter's death by meditating on the accuracy of arithmetic: "the nature o' things doesn't change. . . . The square o' four is sixteen" (xi, 116). The impersonal, collective quality of the novel gradually becomes less our way of enjoying the characters and more a potentially confining manifestation of the Hayslope world-view.[19] In this clearly illuminated, orderly landscape there is no place for the subjective self. The external quality of this world becomes not only the narrator's way of looking at it, but the confines of the world itself, out of which the narrative now seeks to emerge.

In the imagery of dream, vision, and moonlit darkness associated with Dinah in Chapter Fifteen, Eliot suggests an imagination founded on Wordsworthian feeling, but the subjective self becomes located inside Hayslope only through Dinah's moral opposite, Hetty, who, as the literal-minded product of her community, has no imagination at all (in the Wordsworthian sense). Hetty is no longer seen as an alien in the rural world, but, by the beginning of her flight, as a human reality concealed beneath it: "a human heart beating heavily with anguish . . . hidden behind the apple-blossoms, or among the golden corn" (xxiv, 371).

By undergoing inner conflict with no sense of an inner self, Hetty reveals the deficiencies of the Poysers' world, while the literalness with which she takes everything on her journey parodies their unquestioning common sense. Her flight is not a break in the novel's reality but a meaningful shift in perspective; the community we once saw from the outside as an organic whole is now experienced subjectively from the inside by a character with whom the narrator temporarily merges in unqualified identification. In Hetty's confession the objective world which seemed so solid dissolves into conflicting fragments and hallucination—a borderline madness which is also her truest way of seeing. Since Hetty acts out in extreme form problems we have all experienced, she becomes the novel's most impressive representative of the subjective self—a fact to which the narrator's intense identification with her has already attested.

The communal world, which has so far provided the novel's objective reality, now becomes a prison in which the self is condemned to death, and we feel the need for an inner transformation which will free Hetty from her past and reveal, to her as well as to the reader, a larger world of human possibility.[20] Eliot gives this experience instead to Adam, who has always had an unquestioned place in the community. Paradoxically, Hetty disappears into the outside world, while Eliot, through Adam's happy marriage, invites us to take as the repository of human values a community which has never acknowledged anything outside itself.

We have seen what an important role Dinah's independence of Hayslope plays in the thematic structure of the novel. Now our consolation for Hetty's exile is to see her virtuous cousin inherit her position as Adam's fiancée and the Poysers' niece, along with that trousseau of linen Mrs. Poyser has been laying up for Hetty's marriage. When Dinah gives up preaching to merge with Adam's prospering career and the Poysers' respectability, the values of Hayslope become, for the first time, the unchallenged standard of the novel. Yet the gradual but persistent development of the novel has been away from warm pastoral towards a vision of the limitations of Hayslope and of the need for a more comprehensive sense of humanity. Thus the reconstructed, Hetty-less pastoral of the ending seems to refute the whole process of the novel.[21]

When Adam finally becomes the main character, his enlightened patriarchal authority encourages us to forget the problems of fallen women and the class divisions of Hayslope. In his rather idealized nobility, the mature Adam seems entirely removed from Hetty in character and situation. Eliot's emphasis on his regenerative suffering is not an effective way to incorporate the burden of her experience into the novel, especially when we consider that her fall saves him from the worse suffering of marriage to her and clears the way for an ideal "second love."[22] Adam, unlike both Hetty and George Eliot, can grow up without leaving home, while the girl who has to leave is never heard from again—except for a brief obituary. Yet we know that despite the title, our main character is not the hero but the heroine. In the dark wood of Hetty's ambivalence we find the living centre of the novel, and the problems which point beyond the false pastoral of the ending. Eliot's first novel has many virtues, but owes both its unity and its enduring interest to the mystery of Hetty Sorrel.

Notes

1. Barbara Hardy, *The Novels of George Eliot* (London: Athlone Press, 1963), pp. 25-27, and Ian Adam, "The Structure of Realisms in *Adam Bede,*" *NCF [Nineteenth Century Fiction],* 30 (September 1975), 141-48. Since Hardy and Adam have discussed Eliot's technique in depicting Hetty's flight, I will concentrate on Hetty's psychological motivation.
2. Ian Gregor and Brian Nicholas, *The Moral and the Story* (London: Faber and Faber, 1962), p. 29. Jerome Thale sees Hetty's flight as "the most compelling thing in *Adam Bede* and one of the high points of nineteenth-century fiction," but argues that it is a twentieth-century addition to a Wordsworthian pastoral (*The Novels of George Eliot* [New York: Columbia University Press, 1959], pp. 30-33).
3. Neil Roberts argues that "In *Adam Bede* George Eliot creates the illusion of a stable and immemorial rural world" where Hetty's fall becomes a "static moral drama" (*George Eliot: Her Beliefs and Her Art* [Pittsburgh: University of Pittsburgh Press, 1975], pp. 63-67). I have disputed this view in an article previously published—"Arthur's Misuse of the Imagination: Sentimental Benevolence and Wordsworthian Realism in *Adam Bede,*" *English Studies in Canada,* 4 (Spring 1978), 41-59.
4. George R. Creeger, "An Interpretation of *Adam Bede,*" *ELH,* 23 (1956), 218-38.
5. Creeger, p. 266.
6. Creeger, p. 230.
7. Critics who assume that Eliot is making a Puritan attack on sensual love—David Cecil, *Victorian Novelists* (Chicago: University of Chicago Press, 1958)—or that this affair is a genuine pastoral idyll—Ian Gregor (see note 2) or Michael Squires, *The Pastoral Novel: Studies in George Eliot, Thomas Hardy, and D. H. Lawrence* (Charlotsville: University Press of Virginia, 1974)—make the mistake of taking Arthur's high-flown view of Hetty at face value. I have discussed this problem in an article previously published (see note 3). The most recent view of Eliot as Puritan moralist is Nina Auerbach's "The Rise of the Fallen Woman," *NCF,* 35 (1980), 29-52. Auerbach says that "George Eliot seems to condemn Hetty Sorrel's ambitious sexuality with unyielding austerity" (p. 40). Auerbach sees Hetty as "lush and sensuous" (p. 40), but also remarks that "for all her sexuality . . . Hetty is oddly devoid of erotic life. George Eliot reminds us constantly that she is ambitious, not passionate" (p. 49). Much difficulty about Hetty's "sexuality," and the author's attitude towards her, arises from the assumption that she has both the feelings and the moral responsibility of an adult. In my view Hetty becomes "subversive" to her community not by achieving the status of a rebel, but by acting out a naive version of its values. I will argue that her pathetic social aspirations are akin to childhood rivalry, and that her "sensuality" is self-directed narcissism.
8. George Eliot, *Adam Bede,* ed. Gordon S. Haight (New York: Holt, Rinehart and Winston, 1948), Chapter vii, p. 83. All subsequent references will be from this edition. Hetty's dream-world is described in water-imagery combining a womblike absence of weight with self-reflection and plantlike passivity, which also suggests a regressive narcissism.
9. George Eliot, *Essays of George Eliot,* ed. Thomas Pinney (New York: Columbia University Press, 1963), pp. 279-80.
10. Eliot compares Hetty to two girls of lower social status: Molly the housemaid, whom the children always "called on for her ready sympathy" (xviii, 195), and the "unsoaped" Bessy Cranage, the blacksmith's daughter, who is Hetty's equal in trivial vanity but has the advantage of her "in the matter of feeling" (xxv, 281). Neither has to maintain the Poysers' pretensions to respectability.
11. In this rather bitter editorial aside Eliot accuses both Arthur and Adam of idealizing Hetty's childishness, and implies that Adam wants his wife to be his intellectual inferior (xv, 154). Eliot does not pursue this theme, insisting instead on the nobility of Adam's misplaced love. Hetty's seduction could be seen as a fortunate fall which saves him from the much worse fate of marriage to her. In *Middlemarch* Lydgate takes a view of Rosamond very similar to that suggested in the above-mentioned paragraph, and discovers his error through marriage.
12. See G. H. Lewes, *The Study of Psychology: Its Object, Scope, and Method* (Boston, 1879), p. 150. I discuss this concept in "Arthur's Misuse of the Imagination: Sentimental Benevolence and Wordsworthian Realism in *Adam Bede,*" *English Studies in Canada,* 4 (Spring 1978), 54.
13. Ian Adam is the only critic to note how the events of the journey prepare Hetty for confession to Dinah—in addition to the essay cited in note 1, see Adam's "Restoration Through Feeling in George Eliot's Fiction: A New Look at Hetty Sorrel," *Victorian Newsletter,* 22 (Fall 1962), 9-12. I agree with Adam that Hetty is intended to fit into Eliot's concept of moral regeneration, but differ in my view of her actual impact on the novel.
14. In Greek art Medusa was traditionally portrayed as a hideous demon, but Hellenistic artists gave her a pathetic beauty. Eliot shows that she is aware of the dual nature of the Medusa when she remarks, in her review of Adolf Stahr's *Torso. Kunst, Künstler und*

Kunstwerk der Alten (Brunswick, 1854), that in an early sculpture "the Medusa is a hideous caricature; how far from the terrible beauty of the Medusa Rondanini!" (*Saturday Analyst and Leader,* 6 [17 March 1855], 257). The Medusa Rondanini is a sculpture fragment representing Medusa's head, in a museum in Munich.

During the composition of *Adam Bede* Eliot transcribed in her notebook a paragraph from Stahr's book giving two accounts of Medusa's transformation into a Gorgon: "Medusa . . . dared to compare herself in beauty to Athena, and the goddess, thereby enraged, changed the girl into a horrible monster. According to another version of the story . . . Medusa's fate was yet more undeserved. . . . Poseidon raped the incomparably beautiful princess in Athena's temple. . . . Athena's punishment . . . fell on the innocent victim, because she was powerless to punish the guilty god." See Joseph Wiesenfarth, "George Eliot's Notes for *Adam Bede,*" *NCF,* 32 (September 1977), 148-49 (Wiesenfarth's translation). Both the punishment for rivalry, and the unjust punishment which should have fallen on the male, seem relevant to Hetty's case. Hetty turns herself to stone, but her uncle also reveals the "hardness" of Hayslope in his response to her crime.

15. In his analysis of the secular meaning of religious experience, Ludwig Feuerbach gives special importance to the psychological benefits of Confession (*The Essence of Christianity,* trans. George Eliot [New York: Harper, 1957], pp. 78-79 and 122-24).

16. Hetty would certainly be exposed to temptation in a situation where prostitution was taken for granted and also offered escape from heavy labour in appalling conditions. When the female convicts arrived, the officers, soldiers, and farmers (the latter released male convicts) chose the prettiest women as "servants"; also the peculiarly unpleasant life of those not chosen was hardly conductive to virtue—see Margaret Weidenhofer, *The Convict Years: Transportation and the Penal System, 1788-1868* (Melbourne: Lansdowne Press, 1973), pp. 74-77 and 93-96. Despite Eliot's emphasis on realism, her imagination does not follow Hetty to Australia.

17. The heroine of *The Mill on the Floss* combines the hostility towards family life, the Evangelical religion, and the struggle for moral maturity which are here divided between Hetty, Dinah, and Adam; she also winds up in the painful position of having a moral sensibility like Dinah's while being in disgrace like Hetty. Though Maggie is less of a threat to Eliot's values than Hetty, the flood does seem an abrupt end to her moral education. Perhaps Eliot also had difficulty in imagining Maggie's maturity.

18. See Eliot's account of the novel's origins in "History of 'Adam Bede,'" *The George Eliot Letters,* ed Gordon S. Haight (New Haven: Yale University Press, 1954-55), iii, 502-04. Margharita Laski discusses the relation of the novel, in locale and characters, to Eliot's family in *George Eliot and Her World* (London: Thames and Hudson, 1973), pp. 64-66.

19. Raymond Williams complains that in *Adam Bede* Eliot presents the rustic characters collectively "as a landscape . . . a kind of chorus" which "can emerge into personal consciousness only through externally formulated attitudes and ideas" (*The Country and the City* [London: Chatto and Windus, 1973], p. 206). I argue here that this collective quality is not a defect in Eliot's vision, but an attempt to recreate the world-view of Hayslope and enable us to experience both the pleasant and confining aspects of living there.

20. My discussion of Eliot's realism is indebted to Peter Rees's suggestive argument, in an essay constituting part of an unpublished thesis, that the novel's conclusion requires, but fails to provide, a transformation in Eliot's social vision. Peter Rees, in "The Defective Mirror of *Adam Bede*: The Hall Farm and George Eliot's Unnatural History of English Life" (Simon Fraser University, 1980), agrees with Williams that Eliot's pastoral springs from a defective vision of the Poysers' class.

21. Only at this point does Eliot's ambivalence towards community produce a break in the novel's reality. In an essay relevant to all of Eliot's fiction, Carole L. Robinson has noted that in *Romola* "There is no recognition, much less reconciliation, of the disparity between the idealization of 'community' and the more realistic appraisal of the community itself. (At the heart of the failure of *The Mill on the Floss* is a not dissimilar contradiction)" ("*Romola:* A Reading of the Novel," *VS,* 6 [1962-63], 35). The ending of *Adam Bede* is an example of the same problem, though I would add that the failure of an ending is by no means to be considered the failure of the novel as a whole; otherwise there would be few successes in Victorian fiction.

22. For a more favourable view of the capacity of Adam's crisis and the novel's conclusion to assimilate Hetty's suffering, see Jay Clayton's suggestive essay, "Visionary Power and Narrative Form: Wordsworth and *Adam Bede,*" *ELH,* 46 (1979), 645-72. Clayton sees a transformation, beginning with Hetty's confession, from a narrative driven by grim consequences to a Wordsworthian visionary mode governed by sympathy rather than cause and effect. This essay provides important insights into Eliot's relation to Wordsworth but does not resolve the question as to whether such a conclusion would be appropriate to the novel; a sudden shift in reality could be taken as evasion in a novel so committed to psychological realism. In my

view the grimness of Hetty's story arises not from the narrator's values, but from Hetty's consciousness and the values of her community, and can only be dealt with in terms of its source.

Lori Lefkovitz (essay date 1987)

SOURCE: "Delicate Beauty Goes Out: *Adam Bede*'s Transgressive Heroines," in *The Kenyon Review,* n.s. Vol. IX, No. 3, Summer, 1987, pp. 84-96.

[*In the following essay, Lefkovitz examines the differing qualities of beauty and health that Eliot applies to Hetty and Dinah, and discusses the code of delicacy that these images represent.*]

The language in which George Eliot describes her heroines' beauty in ***Adam Bede*** records a transition in nineteenth-century values. Here, Eliot's physical descriptions facilitate the delicate heroine's going out in two senses of the phrase: going safely out into the market place and going out of fashion. Through her descriptions, Eliot not only frees the delicate heroine to go out without subjecting her to risks that the delicate heroine typically faces, risks of rape or death, but Eliot also attempts to reconcile competing and mutually exclusive styles of beauty by creating healthy delicacy, a beauty that is both spiritual and sexual. She does so by appealing to and undermining literature's codes of delicacy.

Eliot revises the connotations of delicate beauty by doubling and exchanging the Poysers' beautiful nieces for one another, as Hetty Sorrel and Dinah Morris displace one another, not only in the novel's economy and structure of desire but also as meaningful figures of beauty. Eliot changes the tradition of the delicate heroine by recovering a sense of delicacy hidden in the word's linguistic history. In Dinah's and Hetty's names, in the adjectives applied to each, and in the objects with which each is associated, Eliot alludes to a code of delicacy. Among the images in that code are the pet, the bird, the flower, the Medusa, and the corpse.

Insofar as the reader recognizes the connotations of these emblems, we apply the appropriate characteristics to the person described. In this reading of the novel's characterization through its descriptions, I will occasionally trace such an allusion, or pause to add something about the historical background against which references to such things as pets, flowers, and corpses emerge in ***Adam Bede*** as ambiguous figures for the delicate heroine's beauty. My point is that neglect of language's power to negate woman through ambiguous idealizations of her image has resulted in critical failures to understand the meaning of woman's delicate health in the nineteenth century.

Apparently in evidence in ***Adam Bede*** is the positive value of delicate health: Dinah is as morally strong as she is physically frail, Hetty as weak willed as she is robust. Illness seems to be redemptive: the guilty lovers, Hetty and Arthur, are each recovered in the eyes of the reader as they grow morally stronger in illness. One reader accordingly observes that "in Eliot's novels those unacquainted with infirmity . . . tend to have short memories and little imagination."[1] Eliot will, however, exchange these religious values for naturalistic ones by challenging the time-honored dichotomies between sexuality and spirituality, health and delicacy.[2]

Shortly before ***Adam Bede*** begins, Dinah Morris, a Methodist preacher who lives among the poor in Snowfield, comes to visit her aunt and uncle Poyser in the relatively comfortable village of Hayslope. She had come to recover her health, which is naturally frail. Within the novel's first pages, her delicate beauty is the talk of the carpentry shop, where Seth Bede is teased for his affections, and soon the indelicacy of a young woman preaching is the buzz of the village. We see Dinah first through the eyes of a stranger, who is struck by "the absence of self-consciousness in her demeanour" as she preaches. The passage evokes an icon of the spirit; three times the adjective "delicate" is used; she is described as having a face of "uniform transparent whiteness with an egg-like line of cheek and chin"; a "lily" in Quaker dress, she has "one of those faces that make one think of white flowers with light touches of colour on their pure petals."[3] The flower's purity and the egg's fragility define Dinah's characteristic qualities, both superficial and essential: the reader regards Dinah as characteristically pure and fragile.

In the novel's descriptions of Dinah, the references to the lily connect her to the beautiful heroines for whom Richardson is famous. Pamela and Clarissa and their lily-white descendants are, however, impossible contradictions. As one classic formula has it: "If the villain pursues her, she must not show either speed or endurance in her flight. Delicacy holds her helpless; chastity must be defended. It is an unfailing dilemma."[4] Apocryphal literature provides another source for the connotations of floral delicacy. Susannah is a flower (her name means both lily and rose), the innocent beauty upon whom the elders spy, and a favorite subject of visual representation. Although this flower is accused of harlotry, her chastity is proven in a court of law. By the nineteenth century, flowers were *literally* associated with chastity and in the 1860s, flowers were "seriously suggested as a means of reducing the high rate of illegitimacy in Cumbria."[5] While the lily connotes the delicacy of frail pallor, the rose wears the blush and bloom of health. In ***Adam Bede***'s descriptive system, Hetty and Dinah are rose and lily respectively.

As Dinah Morris speaks, vain little Bessy Cranage takes to "studying Dinah's nose, eyes, mouth and hair, and wondering whether it was better to have such a sort of pale face as that, or fat red cheeks and round black eyes like her own." Even small-minded Bessy has a vague notion that types of beauty are legible and that the difference between the look of frailty and the look of health is a difference in meaning.

The Poysers are concerned both for their niece's frail health and her public displays, and when the Reverend Irwine and the young Captain Arthur Donnithorne pay an unexpected visit, Mrs. Poyser fears that Dinah will be duly chastised. Instead the Reverend is so impressed that he concludes to himself, "He must be a miserable prig who would act the pedagogue here," by discouraging her public preaching. When he asks aloud, "And you never feel any embarrassment from the sense of your youth—that you are a lovely young woman on whom men's eyes are fixed?" Dinah replies, "... I've preached to as rough ignorant people as can be in the villages about Snowfield—men that looked very hard and wild—but they never said an uncivil word to me."

By convincing the learned Reverend that only "a miserable prig" would disapprove of Dinah Morris and by emphasizing (several times in the novel) that she goes among "rough, hard and wild men" without provoking disrespect, Eliot undermines a tradition within literature that had long associated the beauty of female delicacy with domestic confinement. The reader, after all, would not wish to be characterized as a "miserable prig." Betrayed in the question that the Reverend asks Dinah is the concern that exposing her beauty may lead to some harm. Eliot has another Dinah in mind, and Irwine's question may be motivated by his own recollection of the Dinah he would have read about in Genesis 34.

Dinah, only daughter born to the matriarchs and patriarchs, is not much of a heroine. We are told merely that she "went out to visit the women of the land; and when Shechem . . . the prince of the land saw her, he seized her and lay with her and humbled her."[6] Shechem is so taken with his victim, however, that he determines to marry her and asks leave of Jacob to do so. The biblical narrator offers only one moralizing sentence: "The sons of Jacob came in from the field when they heard of it; and the men were indignant and very angry, because he had wrought folly in Israel by lying with Jacob's daughter, for such a thing ought not to be done."

Leah's sons, therefore, devise a plot. They agree to the marriage and to dwell as neighbors among Shechem's people on the condition that the Hivites agree to circumcise all of their males. On the third day following the operation, when the men would have been most sore, Simeon and Levi slaughter them and take "Dinah out of Shechem's house." When Jacob declares that his sons' deviousness has jeopardized his own position in the community, they protest: "Should he treat our sister as a harlot?"

In some contemporary biblical criticism, the story is understood as a political and historical parable. It accounts for, among other things, the decline of the tribes of Simeon and Levi. Although Dinah seems to function as the innocent victim of a rape for whose sake her brothers take excessive revenge, classical commentary derives lessons from the story that imply a more aggressive female actress.

In *midrash,* the literature of late antiquity that interpreted the Bible and much influenced artists who gave the Western tradition its images of biblical types, we find an origin for the blame-the-victim paradox. Commenting on the creation myth of Adam and Eve, one midrashist—remembering Dinah—understands why man must subdue woman: "Man must master his wife, that she go not into the market place, for every woman who goes out into the market place will eventually come to grief. Whence do we know it? From Dinah, as it is written, *And Dinah . . . went out,* etc."[7] "To go out," in an age when women acted within the boundaries of the tent, was not an innocent activity.

If Dinah's brothers are loathe to have her treated as a harlot, the rabbis have no such qualms. Because Job says that his wife speaks as a "vile woman," the rabbis conclude that Job must be married to Dinah. Moreover, the rabbis imagine that Dinah is violated to punish *Jacob* for refusing to wed her to Esau and for his other acts of pride.

In the rabbinic imagination, not only is Dinah a harlot, but by extension, so is her mother, Leah: "A woman is not immoral until her daughter is immoral." To the rabbi who expresses reluctance to call the matriarch a whore, Rav Kahana replies, "Even so . . . because it says *Leah went out to meet him* [Jacob], which means that she went out to meet him adorned like a harlot." Dinah, therefore, simply follows in her mother's footsteps. Each and every consequent disaster is blamed upon Dinah's "going out," which proves that in spite of God's best efforts to make women modest, women are "frivolous," "coquettish," "gossiping," and "wanton." Rabbi Samuel ben Nahman explains that when Dinah went out, "her arm became exposed," and that this display of her beauty was a conscious provocation. Given Dinah's seductive designs, the rabbis do not interpret Simeon and Levi's recapturing of Dinah as the welcome rescue that it seems to be in the biblical story; her brothers must drag her by force from Shechem's house because "when a woman is intimate with an uncircumcised person, she finds it hard to tear herself away." For Jacob's sake, the rabbis wish that this only daughter had never been born, and while the Bible makes the point that the rapist did "what ought not to have been done," the rabbis conclude that the moral of the story is that a woman should never "go out." It is a moral with which we are very familiar.

While Dinah Morris's friends have full confidence in her virtue, it is not surprising that they fear for her reputation. Working against a literary tradition in which delicate heroines come to evil, Eliot takes special pains to demonstrate that her Dinah invites no sexual harassment. The forbearance of a Reverend in a competing church is a strong indication to the reader that accusations of indelicacy are inappropriate. Though Eliot allows her model of frail beauty to take uncharacteristic liberties, Dinah's friends wish her to stay comfortably at home.

As matters turn out, real reason for concern lies elsewhere, with the Poysers' other niece, Hetty. Both concern and desire are misplaced in the early chapters of the novel, and Eliot will effect several reversals in order to set matters right.

While Dinah talks with remarkable unself-consciousness to the Reverend, Hetty tosses and pats her butter in the dairy, "slyly conscious that no turn of her head was lost," on Captain Donnithorne. Here Eliot describes Hetty at great length, principally as a "kittenish" beauty who leads her beholder into a bog (pp. 89-91). John Berger reasons that zoos and pets became popular in the middle of the nineteenth century because man felt ambivalent about losing the wild. Thus, the look of a domesticated animal deeply disturbs.[8] Hetty Sorrel's wily beauty is repeatedly likened to that of a delicate pet kitten.

By this point in the novel, Dinah and Hetty are both fully described: both women are distractingly pretty, but Dinah distracts attention from the body and Hetty distracts attention from the soul. Dinah elevates; Hetty debases. As frail preacher and rosy farm girl, Dinah and Hetty are exaggerated antithetical types. Dinah may go out among rough men without incurring any disapproval from the narrator, and Hetty cannot go out even among the most refined gentry. It is only after Eliot fixes in our minds the virtue of the one and the wickedness of the other that she will temper her own commentary on each and humanize them both.

The suffering of Hawthorne's Hester Prynne exemplifies, for Eliot, the problem of portraying feminine delicacy. If Dinah takes her name from the Bible, Hetty and Arthur get their names from *The Scarlet Letter.*[9] Hawthorne expresses a guarded admiration for Hester's tender beauty as he raises her to the status of an angel while condemning her to years of misery for the crime of going out in the "midrashic" sense. Eliot responds to the implication that unprotected women provoke lust in the best of men. Because Hawthorne explicitly uses a dated model of healthy beauty, he succeeds in creating a heroine who is both spiritual and sensual. To a description of Hester's beauty Hawthorne adds: "She was lady-like too, after the manner of the feminine gentility of those days; characterized by a certain state and dignity, rather than by the delicate, evanescent, and indescribable grace, which is now recognized as its indication."[10] Eliot, like Hawthorne, ultimately recovers the beauty of health, but she spares her heroine pain by again distinguishing between sexual and spiritual beauty (Hetty and Dinah, respectively), a distinction that Hawthorne blurs.

That which Van Ghent has called the "leisurely pace" of ***Adam Bede*** affords Eliot the opportunity to describe both women at length.[11] Dinah is often called a lily, a bird—the favorite Christian icon of the spirit—an angel, a sublime corpse. The beautiful corpse develops out of the paradox of delicate beauty. Like Clarissa and Little Nell Trent, Dinah seems to belong on that familiar list of Victorian types who are most beautiful in death. But Eliot qualifies the image. When Dinah first comes to visit Lisbeth Bede, Lisbeth mistakes Dinah for her sister's spirit come back from the dead. Her second guess is that this must be an angel, until Lisbeth is brought down to earth when she notices that Dinah's hands bear "traces of labour." She cannot be an angel if she is a "workin woman."

Recently, several feminist critics have argued that the delicate heroine or somnambulist is a model of strength, with power over the men who *seem* to control her.[12] What these readings miss is that hers is the paradoxical power of the slave. The idealization of frail woman as an angel of the spirit keeps women domesticated, out of the markets. Indoors, the spirituality that is embodied in the asexual angel will come to no harm, and the sexuality embodied in the Medusa will do no harm. In either case, she must stay home.

When Adam hears a female voice in his home, he operates under the illusion that Dinah *is* Hetty until he is impressed "with all the force that belongs to a reality contrasted with a preoccupying fancy." The paradox that Adam will come to appreciate is that Hetty, a palpably robust beauty, is a fancy of her beholder's imagination, while Dinah, whose beauty seems vaporous, carries the force of reality.

Book One ends with a series of thematically paired chapters that structurally reinforce Eliot's twinning of heroine and villainess. The first two of these chapters belong to Dinah. Readers who are surprised by Adam's marriage to Dinah at novel's end miss the impact of the sentences that follow Adam's rude surprise (that Dinah is not Hetty) as Eliot describes Dinah's sexual awakening:

> For the first moment he made no answer, but looked at her with the concentrated examining glance which a man gives to an object in which he has suddenly begun to be interested. Dinah, for the first time in her life, felt a painful self-consciousness; there was something in the dark penetrating glance of the strong man so different from the mildness and timidity of his brother Seth. A faint blush came, which deepened as she wondered at it.

Dinah is explicitly, but only symbolically, penetrated by Adam, while Hetty's literal penetration—which would have taken place at the same moment—passes unremarked.

The next two chapters describe Hetty's sexual awakening, her first kiss and the beginning of her clandestine affair. Two chapters follow which belong to Hetty and Dinah together. As the women return home, they meet one another en route. Dinah selflessly speaks to Hetty on behalf of Adam, but Hetty is preoccupied with fantasies of a future life with Arthur. The narrator comments: "it made a strange contrast to see the sparkling self-engrossed loveliness looked at by Dinah's calm pitying face."

Dinah and Hetty, both motherless girls, the latter a niece to Mr. Poyser, the former a niece to Mrs. Poyser, occupy symmetrical positions in the social structure of the novel's world, though Hetty desires to live above their station and Dinah desires to live below it. Each is adamant, and each is wrong. They return home to occupy adjoining bedchambers.

This chapter begins by presenting Hetty worshiping her image in the mirror, adorning herself in lace and ear-rings, and finally prancing about the room. Dinah is startled out of her spiritual reverie by the noise in Hetty's room. She goes to talk, and the narrator marvels:

> What a strange contrast the two figures made, visible enough in that mingled twilight and moonlight! Hetty, her cheeks flushed and her eyes glistening from her imaginary drama, her hair hanging in a curly tangle down her back, and the baubles in her ears. Dinah, covered with her long white dress, her pale face full of subdued emotion, almost like a lovely corpse into which the soul has returned with sublimer secrets and a sublimer love. They were nearly of the same height.

Eliot might be describing the body and the soul doing battle, as in a metaphysical psychomachia. The juxtaposition exploits the paradox of the psychomachia as the two figures are mutually dependent. One sustains the other. The scene ends with Hetty pale and crying while Dinah "departs like a ghost." Next day Dinah leaves Hayslope. Soon after Hetty will leave as well.

In one of the many conversations on the subject of beauty in ***Adam Bede,*** the wealthy notables sit on high and chat lightly about the relative beauty of Hayslope's farm girls. Their discussion concerns delicacy as Mrs. Irwine remarks of Hetty: "What a pity such beauty as that should be thrown away among the farmers, when it's wanted so terribly among the good families without fortune." Reverend Irwine disagrees, but changes the case in point; of "that pretty Methodist preacher," he says: "Such a woman as that brings with her 'airs from heaven' that the coarsest fellow is not insensible to it." Mr. Gawaine interrupts Irwine, as he laughingly notices Bessy Cranage, a "delicate bit of womanhood." Gawaine undoubtedly uses the word *delicate* in its more rarified sense: plump, rosy Bessy, in her country finery, clearly loves delights.

Delicate has meant both dainty and sumptuous. A delicate aristocrat was once likely to have been a robust glutton, a lover of delights. When Shakespeare's Petruchio finds in the shrewish Katherina, a "Kate," because "dainties are all cates," he teases with a double pun. Once an emblem of sensuality, the deli*cate* became an emblem of spirituality. Eliot, writing at a time when the delicacy that had just recently been a clear sign of feminine beauty and virtue had become increasingly "lamentable," reminds us of the word's older and antithetical connotations of physical strength. (Naturalist fiction creates another ambiguity: the "delicate" woman is *either* dainty and lovely *or* she is weak of mind and body, nervous and unfit.) Images of beauty, like descriptive language, can sustain inherent contradiction. Here Eliot gives the reader to understand that when it comes to bits of womanhood, there is more than one way to be delicate. Irwine emerges as Eliot's touchstone of moral rectitude because when his mother speaks of Hetty's beauty, he reminds the reader of Dinah.

Irwine is not the only one to compare Hetty and Dinah on the basis of appearance. In the very terms that Bessy compared *herself* to Dinah, Mrs. Poyser compares her two nieces. "If Dinah had a bit o' colour in her cheeks and didn't stick that Methodist cap on her head . . . folk 'ud think her as pretty as Hetty." But Mr. Poyser knows better: "The men 'ud never run after Dinah as they would after Hetty." He does not explain why. Mrs. Poyser quotes no less an authority than Scriptures to back up her view that Dinah should eat and fill herself out: "You should love your neighbor as yourself." Eliot agrees but will correct Dinah's figure only after we are sure of her spirituality.

Adam, sensitive to the symptoms of Hetty's vanity, also compares Hetty to Dinah, the woman who has "got the face of a lily": when Hetty puts a flower in her hair, Adam tells her "why Dinah Morris looks very nice, for all she wears such a plain cap and gown. It seems to me as a woman's face doesna want flowers; it's almost a flower itself. I'm sure yours is." Through the image of the flower, Adam associates the women, and his remark provokes the most broadly comic scene in the novel. Hetty puts on Dinah's clothes and frightens Mrs. Poyser who thinks she sees a ghost. The jug breaks, and the children roar with laughter.

As the novel moves from the light trials of farm romance to genuine tragedy, Hetty's appearance begins to change, and her masquerade in Dinah's clothes begins to resonate. Adam sees in Hetty's eyes: "something harder, older, less child-like." When Hetty faints among strangers in her troubles, losing the rosy bloom that typified the farm girl, the narrator uses the same phrase that she had earlier applied to Dinah. Hetty is said to look "like a beautiful corpse."

On the following day, we see a "face sadly different from that which had smiled at itself in the old speckled glass. . . . A hard and even fierce look had come into her eyes, though their lashes were as long as ever, and they had all their dark brightness. And the cheek was never dimpled with smiles now. It had the same rounded, pouting, childish prettiness, but with all love and belief in love departed from it—the sadder for its beauty, like the wondrous Medusa-face, with the passionate passionless lips."

This description alludes not only to the Medusa, the icon of terrifying beauty,[13] but also to *The Scarlet Letter.* The beauty of Hester and Hetty both depends upon love. Just as Hetty's appearance is hardened by absence of love, Hawthorne's Hester is alternately transfigured; she is a radiant beauty in her lover's presence and acquires an austere look in his absence. In this unnatural aspect, Hetty Sorrel commits the most unnatural crime imaginable in the world of ***Adam Bede***: she is guilty of infanticide.

After her baby's death, Hetty increasingly acquires the air of the delicate Romantic heroine. The narrator, who had spared no sarcasm in her earlier descriptions, is now moved to pity, as she emotionally declares "My heart bleeds for her as I see her." The identification of Dinah and Hetty is made explicit during the process of trying to identify the criminal. Irwine tells Adam that,

> the description of her person corresponds but that she is said to look very pale and ill. She had a small red-leather pocketbook . . . with two names written on it—one at the beginning, 'Hetty Sorrel, Hayslope,' and the other near the end, 'Dinah Morris, Snowfield.' She will not see which is her own name.

Eliot devotes most of the novel to contrasting Hetty and Dinah, only to bring them into an embrace. Dinah only acquires power in the presence of the lost soul, and Hetty, who will not confess, needs Dinah for spiritual survival. At the heart of ***Adam Bede*** is the quickening of Hetty's weak spirit and the fortification of Dinah's weak body, as each beauty imparts to the other her characteristic strengths. The two women cling to one another in the scene for the sake of which ***Adam Bede*** was written. Eliot wrote in a letter that Hetty's confession to Dinah in prison provided the starting point for the novel. It was a moment that had been described to Eliot twenty-five years earlier by her aunt.[14]

In prison, Dinah and Hetty face one another and reflect one another's faces: "The two faces were looking at each other; the one with a wild despair in it, the other full of sad yearning love. Dinah unconsciously opened her arms and stretched them out. . . . Hetty rose, took a step forward and was clasped in Dinah's arms." And so they remain, inseparable as body and soul, with overwhelming need for one another.

The crowd of onlookers who line the streets as the criminal is to be brought to justice have a double motivation in this case: "All of Stoniton had heard of Dinah Morris . . . who had brought the obstinate criminal to confess, and there was as much eagerness to see her as to see the wretched Hetty." The voyeuristic crowd sees two pale beautiful women clutching one another.

Adam sees the criminal Hetty as a "statue" of her former self, and Eliot thereby justifies transforming the virtuous heroine Dinah. If Hetty pales to the point of resembling her own corpse, Dinah, in Adam's presence, bears only a family resemblance to herself: she blushed a "deep rose colour. She looked as if she were only a sister to Dinah." Persuaded that God does not mean for her to remain self-denying, Dinah does leave the poor to marry Adam and live more comfortably herself. When we see her in the novel's epilogue, she has acquired the only attribute of beauty that Mrs. Poyser found her lacking, a little extra fleshiness: "We can see the sweet pale face quite well now: it is scarcely altered—only a little fuller, to correspond to her more matronly figure." Hetty dies in exile, and Dinah marries the man who loved them both.

Hetty and Dinah are the two faces of the nineteenth century's Janus-faced woman, until Eliot produces beauty out of the synthesis of the healthy (but fatal, murderous) Medusa and the virtuous (but sickly, vulnerable) angel. Adam Bede, who loves first one woman and then the other, stands in for the reader. The narrator takes every opportunity to ask us to identify with Adam's feelings, motivations, and actions, however misguided they may be. Admirable as he is, we are often told that he behaves typically of men in general when he misreads beauty. Through Adam, therefore, Eliot educates the reader.

Dinah is Eliot's response to the Victorian angel. Like Hawthorne, Eliot persuades us that a healthy heroine can be more virtuous than a frail one because she has a body strong enough for purposeful labor (an ideology for the middle class). Dinah is no angel because she works; Hetty's flawed character is expressed by fantasies of idleness when her strength is needed on the farm. Her end is fitting: Hetty cannot stand on her own feet.

Even as the fashions and ideals of the Victorian Age promoted feminine frailty, even as debility was a sign of beauty, absence of spirit or bloom was unlovely. Women were caught in the ambivalence contained in the idealized images of femininity, such as the images of the caged pet and the flower: beauty had to be fragile as the flower even as it required the bloom of health. Much as they admired frail women, Victorians legislated to ensure health. They associated "sanitary" and "sanity."[15]

The ideology of rugged individualism and survival of the fittest gave the body an edge over the spirit in the latter half of the nineteenth century. One consequence was a new image of man: the desire for, in Herbert Spenser's words, "a nation of healthy animals." Coleridge intimates the change in values that prepared England for the Byronic ideal and Darwinism alike when he observed that to call human vices "bestial" was to libel the animals. While this libel was current, one might suppose that in the realm of metaphor woman was flower to man's beast, but true to the contradiction that is woman, in this religious code, woman is represented as more beast than man. Infants are closest to animals, and women, as "breeders," come second only to the poor, "brutes in understanding."[16]

Victorian medical literature highlights another important contradiction in the age's perception of women. Women were defined by constitutional weakness and were accordingly exempt from the Darwinian Revolution. Michelet characterized the nineteenth century as the age of the womb; one doctor put it that the Almighty took a uterus and "built woman around it."[17] The fashions of the early part of the century were so flimsy that beautiful ladies often had "charming colds," and the corset created the condition of weak backs that it was designed to cure. More importantly, just as the metaphors of the pet and flower were taken literally in their applications, so too "a well-dressed woman whose stays were loose . . . was probably a loose woman."[18]

Eliot, unlike Hawthorne, is guilty of some purposeful anachronisms. In 1799, the year in which ***Adam Bede*** is set, mild Seth would have seemed more handsome than rugged Adam, and a noblewoman like Mrs. Irwine would not have been at all likely to select Hetty as "the perfect beauty." Hetty sports too much peasant "rude health." In

1859, however, the year in which both ***Adam Bede*** and Darwin's *Origin of Species* were published, urbanization made frailty a characteristic quality less of the upper-class beauty than of the sickly factory worker. The nostalgic memory of simple healthy peasant life provided a model for middle-class beauty sixty years later. Adam and Hetty are viable ideals in the time of the novel's publication, while Dinah (before her transfiguration) is an ideal of the time about which Eliot writes. Eliot's novel contrasts then and now.

By playing modern and discarded values off against one another, Eliot may depend upon her readers' discomfort with some of the choices that modernization made on their behalf. Were people ready to give up the spirituality that the delicate ideal embodied? Eliot transfigures the healthy rustic and the frail beauty before our eyes, giving us a healthy angel, a benign Medusa. By story's end, Adam and Dinah satisfy an 1859 readership as the industrious couple that was strong enough to meet the needs of changing times. But Eliot is not entirely satisfied with the compromises that the conventions of realism forced upon her novel. Having to choose between healthy sexuality and the freedom of asexuality as criteria for beauty, Eliot—not without some hesitation—chooses health. The narrator interrupts to qualify her conclusions.

Because Dinah becomes what Hetty had been, a sexual woman, Eliot is forced to impose a conventional morality on her. Having come to possess the health and comfort embodied in her fuller figure, Dinah is prevented from going out to the market as she used to. Mrs. Poyser is thus proven right on another score when Eliot puts a stop to Dinah's objectionable preaching. It is significant that the novel closes with a discussion of women preaching. Adam is given the last word on the subject when he responds to Seth's wish that Dinah had quit the Wesleyans to "join a body that 'ud put no bonds on Christian liberty." Adam approves his wife's decision to be bound, catching the author's resignation when he says, "There's no rule so wise but it's a pity for somebody or other. Most o' the women do more harm nor good with their preaching and she [Dinah] thought it right to set the example o' submitting."

Eliot had been deliberate in her effort to lead the reader to believe that Dinah should be free to preach. By novel's end, Adam and Dinah agree that women should attend to matters of the spirit indoors. While Eliot tried to create a delicate woman who could both go out and not die to prove her virtue, she ends by concluding that some unspecified harm does indeed come of a woman's going out to preach. Irwine had intimated as much at the novel's onset.

In the physical description of heroes and heroines, novelists promote those cultural values that the idealized figure embodies. But because readers of narrative from Aristotle to Ian Watt have been trained to regard description as part of the effect of the real, important for its literal rather than its figurative meaning, little attention has been paid to physical description as a strategy of characterization.[19]

In *Word and Image,* Norman Bryson calls "optical truth" into question, explaining, "[I]t is clear that the term 'realism' cannot draw its validity from any absolute conception of 'the real,' because that conception cannot account for the historical and changing character of 'the real' within differing cultures and periods."[20] Bryson demonstrates that when we study realistic images in visual art, what we can discover is how a culture imagines its own reality, what *it recognizes* as the real.

So too with ideals of personal beauty, which so obviously change to accommodate the values particular to a time and place. On the other hand, portraits of beauty, as distinct from "realistic" images of the ordinary or the ugly, are conservative because beauty is conveyed by appeal to the authority of the tradition: "as beautiful as Adonis, or Venus, or the Madonna or Clarissa." Beauty, to use Roland Barthes's words, "cannot assert itself save in the form of a citation."[21] Barthes does not, however, tell the whole story. He neglects *the story* itself, the fact that Adonis, or Venus, or the Madonna each displays a beauty that derives its meaning from narrative contexts; each is as beautiful as his or her characteristic qualities. Thus does beauty bear truth. Reading the inside by using the evidence of the outside is rhetorically enforced by the adjective's penetrating power, as, for example, clear eyes (whatever that means) signify clarity of vision. And, ironically, Barthes neglects the power of coding, to which he habitually directs our attention: dark hair and eyes, for example, suggest the exotic or the demonic, depths of wisdom or of sorrow. When we read beauty, we trace allusions to the tradition.

Novelists do subject their models to revision. Those characters who are more complex than Theophrastan types are developed by appeal to competing codes and traditions, as fiction attempts to reconcile competing claims to value, competing definitions of humanity. In the invention and description of fictional characters, novelists record the tension between the pulls of the tradition and the urge towards innovation.

Because the values embodied in a character of beauty may be self-contradictory, the beauty of literature's characters is often unvisualizable (which may explain our inevitable disappointment with cinema's casting choices for our favorite fictional characters). Art historians have remarked that even in visual portraiture, the interest of a figure often lies in its subtle incoherence.[22] In linguistic figures incoherence masquerades as complexity or development of character; codes compete, and the outcome of the competitions affects how the body is imagined and treated in the world.

Description transgresses the most fundamental boundary in the discourse of literary criticism, the opposition between the literal and the figurative. A figure is a face, a body, a personage, a metaphor. The fictional body is a playground for multiple shifting significances. Transfiguration is a symbolic operation that occurs on the body. Scarry, in *The Body in Pain,* relates the body's situation with respect to language to its situation in torture and war.[23] Cinderella teaches the desirability of a delicate foot. Freud teaches that the foot, an object of fetishism, displaces the site of female sexuality. Such displacements are endless and often scandalous. In ***Adam Bede*** Eliot succeeds in transposing the value of delicate health and that of healthy delicacy, but in doing so she must bring in the heroine who went out.

Notes

1. Bruce Haley, *The Healthy Body and Victorian Culture* (Cambridge: Harvard University Press, 1978), p. 196.
2. Cf. Peter Cominos, "Innocent Femina Sensualis in Unconscious Conflict," rpt. in *Suffer and Be Still: Women in the Victorian Age* edited by Martha Vicinus (Bloomington: Indiana University Press, 1972).
3. George Eliot, *Adam Bede,* with foreword by F. R. Leavis (New York: New American Library, 1961), p. 34. Subsequent references will be given in the text.
4. Robert Palfrey Utter and Gwendolyn Bridges Needham, *Pamela's Daughters* (New York: Macmillan Co., 1936), p. 41.
5. Keith Thomas, *Man and the Natural World: A History of the Modern Sensibility* (New York: Pantheon, 1983), p. 234.
6. Translation from *The New Oxford Annotated Bible with the Apocrypha,* revised standard edition, edited by Herbert G. May and Bruce M. Metzger (New York: Oxford University Press, 1977).
7. *Midrash Rabbah,* vol. I, edited by H. Freedman and Maurice Simon (New York: Soncino Press, 1983), commentary to *Genesis* 34.
8. John Berger, "Why Look at Animals," in *About Looking* (New York: Pantheon Books, 1980).
9. Cf. F. R. Leavis's foreword to *Adam Bede* (New York: New American Library, 1961).
10. Nathaniel Hawthorne, *The Scarlet Letter* (New York: Bantam, 1965), pp. 50-51.
11. Dorothy Van Ghent, *The English Novel: Form and Function* (New York: Harper & Row, 1953).
12. See for examples, Nina Auerbach, *Woman and the Demon: The Life of a Victorian Myth* (Cambridge: Harvard University Press, 1982), and Elizabeth MacAndrew and Susan Gorsky, "Why Do They Faint and Die—The Birth of the Delicate Heroine," *Journal of Popular Culture* 8 (1974-75), pp. 735-745.
13. Cf. Mario Praz, *The Romantic Agony,* trans. Angus Davidson, 2nd ed. (New York: Oxford University Press, 1971).
14. Philip Fisher, *Making Up Society: The Novels of George Eliot* (Pittsburgh: University of Pittsburgh Press, 1981), p. 58.
15. Cf. Haley, p. 19.
16. Thomas, p. 259.
17. See Sarah Stage, *Female Complaints: Lydia Pinkham and the Business of Women's Medicine* (New York: Norton, 1979), pp. 67-72.
18. Alison Lurie, *The Language of Clothes* (New York: Random House, 1981), pp. 216-220.
19. Ian Watt, *The Rise of the Novel: Studies in Defoe, Richardson and Fielding* (London: Chatto and Windus, 1957).
20. Norman Bryson, *Word and Image: French Painting of the Ancien Régime* (New York: Cambridge University Press, 1981), p. 8.
21. Roland Barthes, *S/Z: An Essay,* trans. Richard Miller (New York: Hill and Wang, 1974), p. 33.
22. See for examples, John Berger, *Ways of Seeing* (New York: Penguin, 1977), p. 60, and E. H. Gombrich, "The Mask and the Face: The Perception of Physiognomic Likeness in Life and in Art," in *Art, Perception, and Reality* (Baltimore: The Johns Hopkins University Press, 1970), p. 21.
23. Elaine Scarry, *The Body in Pain: The Making and Unmaking of the World* (New York: Oxford University Press, 1985).

Peggy Fitzhugh Johnstone (essay date 1989)

SOURCE: "Self-Disorder and Aggression in *Adam Bede:* A Kohutian Analysis," in *Mosaic,* Vol. 22, No. 4, Fall, 1989, pp. 59-70.

[*In the following essay, Johnstone uses Heinz Kohut's psychoanalytic notion of "self-psychology" to discuss the failure of* Adam Bede, *and demonstrates Eliot's failure to recognize her characters' aggressive behavior as reflective of her own unresolved conflicts.*]

Although George Eliot's novels seem to be designed to portray her protagonists' growth from egoism and self-delusion toward self-knowledge and a capacity for empathy, critics have long noted tendencies that undermine this concern. F. R. Leavis, for example, draws attention to a "distinctive moral preoccupation" (28) which, as Barbara Hardy suggests, leads Eliot to idealize certain "charmless" characters in order to provide her readers with a "moral example" (39). Eliot has also been criticized for lack of distance, or as Leavis expresses it, "the direct (and sometimes embarrassing) presence of the author's own personal need" (32). Eliot's moralism and want of objectivity are factors in the ongoing debates concerning the endings of some of her novels, with critics of various schools attempting explanations for the dissatisfaction that so many readers feel.

Especially problematic in this respect is ***Adam Bede,*** Eliot's nineteenth-century reinterpretation of the story of the fallen and redeemed Adam of Milton's epic (Knoepflmacher 91-126). Although the title character is the primary focus of the author's theme of "tragic growth" (Hardy 39), Eliot attempts to show "an enlargement of moral sympathy" (Gregor 24) on the part of all four major characters—Adam, Arthur, Hetty and Dinah. Readers often have difficulty accepting Eliot's message, however, because of her attitude toward Hetty, the character who is convicted of infanticide and banished from the community of Hayslope. Critics who have puzzled over Eliot's harshness toward Hetty include U. C. Knoepflmacher, who calls Hetty's early disappearance from the novel her "execution by her moralistic creator" (124), and George Creeger, who suggests that Hetty is "the victim" of her creator's own "hardness" (231). Mason Harris, who refers to Eliot's "unforgivable" refusal to portray Hetty's further development after her exile, objects to the novel's ending on the grounds that "the reconstructed, Hetty-less pastoral of the ending seems to refute the whole process of the novel" ("Infanticide" 189, 194). Other critics who have objected to the ending of the novel include Michael Edwards, who feels that its power "is diminished by Adam's lack of guilt as regards Hetty" (218), and Murray Krieger, who suggests that our discomfort with the conclusion is our sense that the "transformed pain is not evident enough" (219).

My purpose in this essay is to suggest that Heinz Kohut's "self-psychology" best illuminates the problems that critics have noted in ***Adam Bede.*** After exploring the way Kohut's theories about the relationship between incomplete self-development and rage help to explain the aggressive behavior of Eliot's characters, I will then attempt to show how Eliot's apparent failure to see the extent of the aggression that she portrays in her characters may reflect her own unresolved conflicts.

. . . . .

Kohut's psychology of the self defines psychoanalytic cure as a process of self-structuralization that results in a productive life, rather than simply as the resolution of oedipal conflict (*Cure* 7). His version of the well-known definition of mental health (the ability to work and to love) is "the capacity of a firm self to avail itself of the talents and skills at [its] disposal, enabling [the individual] to love and work successfully" (*Restoration* 284). To Kohut, the role of parents is central in the development of a firm self structure, which he believes depends more upon the effect of the child's total environment than upon "gross events," such as the deaths of parents (*Restoration* 187-91). One step in the formation of the "bipolar self" occurs as a result of the infant's early "mirroring," or interaction with a supportive parent figure; this stage is necessary for the development of a healthy self-esteem. Another step occurs as a result of the child's "idealization" of a parent figure—a stage which precedes the successful internalization of values (*Analysis* 40-49, 106-09). When the process of self-structuralization is left incomplete, the result is a "self-disorder," defined by the persistence of archaic self and parent images that have not become integrated into the mature structures of the personality (Russell 140).

Instead of emphasizing the growth from dependence to autonomy, as does traditional psychoanalysis, Kohut emphasizes the changed nature of the relationship between self and "self-objects" (*Cure* 52). He believes that throughout life human beings need healthy attachments to empathic self-objects which replace their infantile self-objects, their parents. Kohut's view of aggression is also different from the traditional view of it as the manifestation of an innate drive. He sees rage as a reaction to the feeling of loss of connection between self and empathic parental object, or, to put it another way, as a reaction to the sense that the integrity of the self has been violated. Rage results from "the breakup of the primary self-experience in which, in the child's perception, the child and the empathic self-object are one" (*Restoration* 91).

. . . . .

In ***Adam Bede,*** Eliot portrays characters who suffer from varying degrees of disorders of the self, resulting from their lack of the parental and community support that is necessary for the development of a firm sense of identity. Eliot's characters have lost their parent(s), yet at the same time, because of their unresolved need for them, have failed to separate themselves from their infantile parental image(s). In their need to attach themselves to an infantile object, Arthur, Adam and Dinah choose Hetty, who functions in the community both as a fertility/mother figure and as a child figure. As the characters struggle to grow beyond their childhood attachments and find replacements for them, however, they must kill off their old parental images as symbolized by Hetty—hence their banishment of her.

Although Eliot seems to blame Hetty for her flaws, her presentation of the harsh family and social conditions that lie underneath the surface of the Eden-like county of Loamshire shows that Hetty has been victimized by its inhabitants. She has been effectively excluded from the community of Hayslope from the time of her arrival. Orphaned at age ten, she has come to live with her aunt and uncle, the Poysers, who are conscientious about the formalities of caring for her, but who treat her differently from their own children. Hetty's grandfather, who is part of the household, also treats her differently from his son's children, because he still resents her mother's marriage to a man beneath the Poysers' status.

Building on Creeger's view of Hetty's "hardness" as "childish . . . egocentricity" (228), Harris sees Hetty not as an "adult sinner" but as a "confused child" essentially "abandoned" by her relatives; her relatives' rigid incapacity to accept her as part of their "respectable" world has resulted in her "arrested development" ("Infanticide" 179, 180). She has not been able to find an appropriate role in her family or community; her status is somewhere between that of the servants and the Poysers' own children. To Harris, Hetty's lack of parental support has prevented her development of the "sense of an inner self" that she needs to be able to assess the values imposed on her by the Hayslope "shame-culture" ("Infanticide" 193, 184). Extending Harris's analysis, one may note that, as Eliot portrays her, Hetty has not completed the steps in the creation of the constituents of Kohut's bipolar self. Her intense need for mirroring is shown in her Narcissus-like tendency to gaze at length at her reflection, either in a polished surface or a mirror (117, 194, 199, 294-96, 378). Her failure to internalize values is reflected in the way that "shame . . . was poor little Hetty's conscience" and "religious doctrines had taken no hold on [her] mind" (382, 430).

Contrasting the usual view of Hetty as "a temptress" with his own interpretation of her as "a little girl," Harris demonstrates that her feeling for Arthur is not "sensual love," but a "Cinderella-fantasy" ("Infanticide" 183). Hetty's propensity for looking at herself in the mirror, along with her self-defeating involvement with Arthur, who she dreams will provide her with wealth and importance, suggest her need for self-completion. In the scene in her bedchamber, she gazes at her image while imagining that Arthur is with her: "his arm was around her, and the delicate rose-scent of his hair was with her still" (195). Hetty is searching for her identity by attaching herself to Arthur, who has the established place in Hayslope that she longs for.

Hetty's treatment of babies and children reenacts her own sense of abandonment. She hates children as much as she hates the lambs and the baby chickens on the farm. When Hetty gives birth to her own child after she runs away from home, she is not able to behave as a mother normally would. "I seemed to hate it," she confesses to Dinah, having explained: "And then the little baby was born, when I didn't expect it; and the thought came into my mind that I might get rid of it, and go home again. . . . I longed so to go back again." Hetty's already weak sense of self deteriorates further when she leaves Hayslope, the only source of her identity and values. Her primary thought, when she thinks of murdering her child, is to "go home again" (498). In her confusion, however, "by burying the child, but not completely, Hetty tries both to kill it and to let it live" (Harris "Infanticide" 187). Hetty is ambivalent, and rather than actively killing the baby, she abandons it in the woods. Thus the murder takes the form of passive aggression.

. . . . .

The characterization of Arthur, whom Harris calls Eliot's "first extensive study of unconscious motivation" ("Misuse" 45), reveals that his inadequate self-development, although less severe than Hetty's, sets him up for his destructive interaction with her. Although Arthur feels that his future position in Hayslope is secure, his background has some parallels with Hetty's. For one thing, he has no parents. His mother died only three months after his christening, and his father is missing. All we know about his father is that the Irwines have a low opinion of him, just as Hetty's relatives have a low opinion of her father. Like Hetty, Arthur's lack of adequate parental substitutes creates his ongoing need for the firm support that would enable him to complete the process of his self-structuralization.

Just as Hetty is treated with indifference by her grandfather, so Arthur feels at times "positively hate[d]" by his (302). He also feels controlled by him. As he says to Mr. Irwine, "My grandfather will never let me have any power while he lives" (215). In the same conversation Irwine tells him that his mother (Mrs. Irwine) has prophesied that Arthur's "lady-love will rule [him] as the moon rules the tides." Arthur replies after a narrative interlude, "A man may be very firm in other matters and yet be under a sort of witchery from a woman." Arthur's sense of being controlled is easily transferable to other relationships; he is susceptible to "woman's witchery." Furthermore, like Hetty, his lack of family support has resulted in his failure to internalize firm values. Eliot comments that Arthur "lived a great deal in other people's opinions and feelings concerning himself" (216). As Harris says, Arthur "depends on the approbation of others rather than an inner sense of self [and has] a moral sense based mainly on shame" ("Misuse" 53, 54). He shares to a lesser degree Hetty's need for self-completion, yet also like Hetty, chooses a self-defeating relationship.

Arthur is described as having a "loving nature," but Eliot's irony becomes clear in the subsequent description of his treatment of the "old gardener." When Arthur was seven, he impulsively kicked over the old man's pitcher of broth. Finally realizing that it was the man's dinner, he "took his favorite pencil-case and a silver-hafted knife out of his pocket and offered them as compensation. He had been the same Arthur ever since, trying to make all offences forgotten in benefits" (356).

Although Arthur is too concerned about other people's opinions to be openly aggressive, he evidences a pattern of behaving aggressively and then seeking atonement by giving up something he possesses. In the incident with the old gardener Arthur takes out his aggression on someone whose social status is beneath his own. His relationship with Hetty follows the same pattern: it is an assertion of his power over the lower classes. The sequence of events that occurs at the time just before Arthur becomes involved with Hetty suggests that although his actions with Hetty appear to be impulsive, they are actually a reaction to his sense of being controlled by his grandfather. Arthur is disgruntled because "There was no having his own way in the stables; everything was managed in the stingiest fashion" (172). Then he learns that his horse is lame and feels "thoroughly disappointed and annoyed" (173). He goes out for a ride on the other horse that is available to him, and by the time he returns is unable to resist breaking his resolution not to see Hetty. In his dressing room after lunch, he feels that "The desire to see [her] had rushed back like an ill-stemmed current." He rationalizes that he will "amuse himself" by seeing Hetty that day "and get rid of the whole thing from his mind." Then he goes to see Hetty in the wood (174-75).

The affair is not simply a matter of Arthur's failure to recognize his own frustrated sex drive, which has been "sublimated" into "sentimental musing over Hetty" (Harris, "Misuse" 45). Sexual fantasy and behavior can also serve as a defense, against "hostile aggression" (Coen 895). Arthur, feeling controlled and therefore angry at his grandfather, expresses his frustration and need for power in the involvement with Hetty. Yet he also feels under her power, or "witchery." As often as he determines to do so, he is not able to end the affair and separate himself from Hetty, who is as much an extension of his fantasies as he is of hers. Just as Hetty's fantasies are about the luxuries of the social position that would be hers as Arthur's wife (144, 181, 199, 296), so Arthur's are about his life as squire after his grandfather's death (170, 483). Arthur's inadequate sense of his own identity, which depends to such an extent on his future inheritance from his grandfather, makes him susceptible to the need for completing himself in the relationship with Hetty, in which he can act out his fantasy of being loved by the lower classes for his philanthropic works after he takes over his grandfather's position in the community.

Arthur does finally suffer from the pain he has caused Hetty. His atonement, however, follows the pattern of his atonement with the old gardener: an attempt to rectify aggressive action by giving up possessions. He gives up his position as squire and goes away. Yet his exile is only temporary. He is eventually able to return and find a place in Hayslope. Hetty, by virtue of her position in the community, is the one who must bear the full weight of the consequences of their behavior.

. . . . .

Eliot attempts to show her title character Adam undergoing a transformation from an inner "hardness" to a capacity for sympathy for others (Creeger 234-35). The description of Adam's family life points to the source of his hardness as his lost "sense of distinction" as "Thias Bede's lad" since the onset of his father's alcoholism during his late teenage years. Adam's "shame and anguish" (92) had caused him to run away from home, but he had returned because he did not want to leave his mother and brother Seth with the burden of enduring the situation without him. To Kohut, shame frequently results in rage and in the shamed individual's ongoing readiness to seek revenge ("Thoughts" 380-81)—a reaction that Eliot similarly depicts. By the time Adam's story opens, his shame has turned to rage, which shows itself in his propensity for fighting (211) and in his severity toward his father (86). Adam focuses all his anger about his family situation on his father, although it is clear that his mother Lisbeth has her own problem of "idolatrous love" for Adam and her obvious preference for him over Seth (87).

Adam's anger toward his father culminates in his actions on the night of his father's death. He is furious because his father is out drinking when he should have been working on the job of making a coffin for a man in a neighboring village. While Adam stays up to finish the job himself, he thinks of his father's continuously "worsening" behavior (92), but feels determined not to run away from the situation again, although he feels that his father will be a "sore cross" to him for years to come. At that moment he hears a rap "as if with a willow wand" on the house door, goes to the door to look out, sees that no one seems to be there, and thinks of the superstition that the sound of a willow wand rapping on the door means that someone is dying (93). After he hears the sound again and still sees no sign of his father, he reasons that Thias is probably "sleeping off his drunkenness at the [tavern]." Not wanting to succumb to superstitious thinking, he determines not to open the door again, and for the rest of the night hears no more knocking. The next morning, however, Seth discovers that Thias has drowned during the night, "not far from his own door," as Mr. Irwine says later (137).

Carol Christ notes that Thias's death "occurs as a magical fulfillment of Adam's anger" (131); Krieger suggests that "the resentfulness Adam feels . . . brings him close to wishing his father dead" (211). It is possible to interpret Adam's hearing the sound of the willow wand not only as a manifestation of his sense of foreboding, but as his wish for his father's death. It is also possible to interpret Adam's decision not to open the door again despite his father's expected arrival as a form of passive aggression and as an indirect contribution to his father's death. In any case, Thias's death causes Adam to repent his "severity" toward him (97). And this repentance, in Eliot's view, turns out to be the first step of the process "in which Adam learns to overcome his angry severity toward others" (Christ 131).

Adam's attitude toward Arthur and Hetty repeats the pattern of his attitude toward his parents. Even before he realizes that they are actually having an affair, he is openly outraged at Arthur's involvement with Hetty and provokes him into a fight. Yet he has trouble seeing any wrong in Hetty even after it becomes clear that she has abandoned her baby. Adam's reluctance to feel hostile to Hetty is related to his reluctance to be angry with his mother. His dream, which recounts the events in the Bede household shortly after Thias's death, shows Adam's close identification of Hetty with his mother. When his mother approaches, accidentally waking him, he is not startled to see her because she had been present "with her fretful grief" throughout his feverish reliving of the day's events. Yet Hetty, too, had "continually" appeared in the dream, "mingling ... in scenes with which she had nothing to do"; and "wherever Hetty came, his mother was sure to follow soon ..." (152). Adam's dream suggests that he has transferred his attachment to his mother, who has always loved him with "idolatrous love," to his "preoccupying fancy" with Hetty (161-62).

When Adam learns of Hetty's interest in Arthur, he does not express anger toward her openly. Instead his aggressiveness takes the form of an intrusion on her relationship with Arthur. By insisting that Arthur not see Hetty again and that he write her a letter breaking off the relationship, he is cutting off all possibility that Arthur will be able to help her. At the time of the intrusion, Adam is not aware that Hetty is pregnant, nor is he aware that Arthur really does care for her more than he has let Adam know. His intrusiveness, however, is inappropriate and ends up making the situation worse. It is perhaps Adam's bitter jealousy (370), more than an interest in Hetty's welfare, that makes him insist on the letter, which he gives to Hetty himself after he tells her that Arthur "care[s] nothing about [her] as a man ought to care" (367). As Bruce K. Martin argues, "Adam thus indirectly contributes to the child-killing" by "remov[ing] from Hetty's mind the possibility of consulting Arthur until it is too late" (759).

Adam's inner struggles center on his inability to see Hetty realistically. Even before he sees her with Arthur in the woods, her locket (a gift from Arthur) drops to the floor in front of Adam; he fears that she has a lover, but then rationalizes that she "might have bought the thing herself" (333). After he delivers Arthur's letter to her, he still hopes that she will become interested in him: "she may turn round the other way, when she finds he's made light of her all the while" (370). He continues to hope for her love by "creat[ing] the mind he believed in out of his own" (400). When he learns that Hetty has been accused of infanticide, he finds it impossible to believe: "'It's his doing,' he said; 'if there's been any crime, it's at his door, not at hers. . . . I *can't* bear it. . . . it's too hard to think she's wicked'" (455). At the trial, when it becomes clear that Hetty is guilty, "It was the supreme moment of his suffering: Hetty was guilty, and he was silently calling to God for help" (481). Later, in the "upper room" scene with Bartle Massey, Adam is still having trouble accepting the truth about her: "I thought she was loving and tender-hearted, and wouldn't tell a lie, or act deceitful. . . . And if he'd never come near her, and I'd married her, and been loving to her, and took care of her, she might never ha' done anything bad" (504). Adam is struggling to separate himself from his fantasy of Hetty, who symbolizes his lingering parental image of the loving young woman who belongs only to him.

When Adam is forced to face the truth about Hetty's affair and infanticide, and when he finally forgives her and Arthur, he becomes free of her (and his mother's) hold on his mind. The sign of his transformation is his participation in "a kind of Lord's Supper" (Creeger 234) with Bartle Massey in the "upper room" before Hetty's trial. Just before he takes the bread and wine, Adam agrees to go see Hetty in the prison and says, "I'll never be hard again" (475). Finally, in the chapter entitled "Another Meeting in the Wood," he even repents of his "hardness" toward Arthur: "I've no right to be hard towards them as have done wrong and repent" (514).

His own suffering after his father's death, and his vicarious participation in Hetty's suffering after the infanticide, have extended his capacity for "sympathy," which in Eliot's novels must be preceded by "the recognition of difference: between oneself and another . . ." (Ermarth 25), as in the case of Adam's changed view of Hetty. Adam's participation in Hetty's guilt causes him to "look upon every sufferer, regardless of guilt, as worthy of sympathy" (Martin 750). From a psychoanalytic point of view, Adam's identification with Hetty and her suffering is therapeutic because at the same time that he separates himself from his childhood image of his mother, he also transfers his wish for his father's death onto Hetty's murderous act. Through Hetty's suffering, he is cleansed of his own guilt; Hetty is the sacrificial lamb whose suffering makes Adam's redemption possible. Eliot calls his "deep, unspeakable suffering" a "baptism, a regeneration, the initiation into a new state" (471). She tries to suggest that he has become a more complete human being, ready for a mature love for Dinah. Yet Adam's growth occurs at the expense of Hetty, whose murderous act and subsequent punishment are in part a consequence of his aggressive intrusion on her relationship with Arthur; thus Eliot's attempt to portray Adam's transformation in terms of the nineteenth-century "religion of humanity" (Knoepflmacher 112) becomes a perversion, rather than a reinterpretation, of the idea of baptism.

In a scene in his mother's cottage shortly after his father's death, Adam hears a foot on the stairs and imagines that it is Hetty; but instead, Dinah, the "reality contrasted with a preoccupying fancy," enters (161-62). This is the first hint that Dinah will be able to replace Hetty in Adam's affections. His love for her becomes "the outgrowth of that fuller life which had come to him from his acquaintance with deep sorrow" (574). He and Dinah marry and find their place in Hayslope. Painful memories remain, but in Eliot's view Adam has regained his Paradise.

. . . . .

Although Eliot attempts to idealize Dinah, to a Kohutian reader she emerges as a character with unresolved needs which are expressed in destructive interactions with Hetty. Like Hetty and Arthur, Dinah has lost both her parents. She has been raised by her Aunt Judith, Mrs. Poyser's sister. When Dinah visits the Bedes's home early in the novel, she tells Lisbeth about her orphaned background and "how she had been brought up to work hard, and what sort of place Snowfield was, and how many people had a hard life there" (157). Yet Dinah does not appear to suffer any ill-effects from her hard life. Lisbeth tells her, "[Y]e look as if ye'd ne'er been angered i' your life" (156). She is referring to Dinah's apparently compliant nature, which Lisbeth thinks must at least have made the aunt's task of bringing up a child a little easier.

The possibility that Dinah's calm exterior is in part a cover for anger is borne out in her preaching and other aspects of her ministry. During her sermon her voice is all calm and compassion until "she had thoroughly arrested her hearers" (71). Then "her utterance" becomes more "rapid and agitated," as she emphasizes the listeners' "guilt . . . wilful darkness, [and] state of disobedience to God" (72). She begins to single out individuals, focusing in particular on Bessy Cranage, who "had always been considered a naughty girl . . . [and] was conscious of it"

(73). She accuses Bessy of paying more attention to her earrings and clothes than to her "Saviour" and warns her that when she is old, she will "begin to feel that [her] soul is not saved" and "will have to stand before God dressed in [her] sins." Toward the end of Dinah's pointed message, which, as Christopher Herbert suggests, amounts to "an attack" on her (415), Bessy bursts into tears; finally, "a great terror [came] upon her," and she throws her earrings "down before her, sobbing aloud" (75).

Dinah repeats the pattern of her attack on Bessy when she "intrude[s]" (Krieger 205) on Hetty in "The Two Bed-chambers," a chapter intended to show the striking contrasts between Hetty, who is "strutting about decked in her scarf and earrings" in front of her mirror (201), and Dinah, who is looking out the window of her room at a "wide view over the fields" (202). Dinah closes her eyes in prayer, is interrupted by a sound from Hetty's room, and begins to think about her. Feeling "pity" for Hetty's lack of "warm, self-devoting love" and "a deep longing to go now and pour into Hetty's ear all the words of tender warning and appeal that rushed into her mind" (203), Dinah goes to her room and with very little introduction says, "it has been borne in upon my mind tonight that you may some day be in trouble" (205). She offers to help in any future time of need, and in her homiletic style reminds Hetty to seek strength from God, who will support her "in the evil day." When Dinah sees that Hetty is reacting "with a chill fear" to her prophecy, her "tender anxious pleading" becomes "the more earnest" until Hetty, "full of a vague fear that something evil was sometime to befall her, began to cry." Interpreting Hetty's reaction as "the stirring of a divine impulse," Dinah begins to "cry with her for grateful joy," but Hetty becomes "irritated under Dinah's caress," and pushing her away impatiently, sobs, "Don't talk to me so, Dinah. Why do you come to frighten me? I've never done anything to you. Why can't you let me be?" (206).

Dinah's style of ministry is in sharp contrast to Mr. Irwine's, who has more a "live and let live" (103) attitude toward his flock. When Arthur comes to see him about Hetty, Irwine refrains from giving him advice because he has already warned Arthur not to get involved with Hetty. Moreover, Irwine has no idea how close he is to an involvement, and is trying to let Arthur take the initiative in any confession or request for advice. Conversely, he very firmly takes the initiative in advising Adam, who he knows has a propensity for violence, not to get into another fight with Arthur. Irwine speaks to him in a rational tone about the consequences of acting out of blind fury and then leaves him to his own thoughts. His behavior indicates that he believes that Arthur and Adam have the capacity to make the right decision. Dinah's behavior toward Bessy and Hetty indicates that she thinks they are lost souls incapable of any right behavior without her help.

Dinah does not actually see Hetty again until the prison scene, where Hetty's "hardness" is melted (497) as she finally makes her confession to Dinah. Although Eliot tries to show Dinah as facilitating Hetty's breakthrough in this scene, her earlier departure from Hayslope is another indication of Dinah's (in this case, passive) aggressiveness toward Hetty. Dinah repeatedly expresses interest in helping Hetty, but she goes away without leaving an address, and by the time she reappears, it is too late to help, except by listening to her final confession in the prison cell.

Dinah tells Seth that she feels "called" to return to Snowfield, although "[her] heart yearns" over her aunt's family and "that poor wandering lamb, Hetty Sorrel" (78). When she is almost ready to leave, Dinah again expresses interest in Hetty, who she says will be in her intercessions (187), and in "The Two Bed-Chambers" scene, Dinah expresses her fear that Hetty "may someday be in trouble" (205). While Dinah is away, Seth receives a letter from her, which refers to her sense of foreboding about her aunt's household (375). When Adam goes to look for Hetty, however, although he believes she is visiting Dinah in Snowfield, he finds that Dinah is out of town and learns that she has not left any address. After Hetty is accused of infanticide, Dinah is still missing and no one knows for certain where she is. The family tries to send her a letter, but they have no idea whether she receives it. Dinah does not reappear until Hetty has already been sentenced, when she visits her in the prison. Dinah's departure and failure to leave an address at a time when she senses that something might be wrong belie the expressions of concern for her aunt's household. Eliot's seemingly idealized Dinah thus expresses aggression indirectly both in the form of intrusiveness and passivity.

Dinah's anger is not acknowledged, but it is evident in her words and actions. Hetty, like Bessy, is a likely target for Dinah's aggressions because the community already looks down on her, her self-esteem is low, and she is the least capable of fighting back. Yet perhaps more importantly, Hetty represents the side of herself that Dinah is unwilling to acknowledge: the sexual (the affair with Arthur) and the aggressive (the murder of the baby). In attacking Hetty, Dinah is attacking the threatening forces in her own nature. Several times Mrs. Poyser refers angrily to Dinah's asceticism (121, 236, 518), as though she is aware that there is something wrong with Dinah's failure to acknowledge any normal physical needs. Dinah's denial of natural needs suggests that she is "lacking in self," or in a "sense of human identity"; her "fear of accepting full maturity" (Creeger 236, 237) is reflected, in psychoanalytic terminology, in her persistent archaic idealized self-image, and is a sign of defective self-development (Russell 139, 144). Dinah identifies only with her "ideal self" as she splits off and projects her unacceptable traits onto others. Hetty answers Dinah's need to get rid of her "bad self."

After Adam's proposal, Dinah goes away again to think it over. A few weeks later, when Adam goes to see her, Dinah, apparently having undergone a transformation that enables her to accept her feelings for Adam, finally declares her love: "it is the Divine Will. My soul is so knit with yours that it is but a divided life I live without you"

(576). Like Adam, who has gone away and returned, she comes back to Hayslope and finds her place in the community. Like Adam's, however, her new life comes at Hetty's expense. It is only after Hetty's guilt is made clear to the community and she is exiled that Dinah finally replaces her in Adam's affections.

Kohut's view that rage is the reaction to the sense of loss of connection to parental figures is thus well illustrated in the story of Arthur's, Adam's and Dinah's treatment of Hetty. Their scapegoating of her is a transference of anger felt toward missing or disappointing parent(figure)s. Hetty as fallen mother and child-murderer becomes the symbol of failed parenthood who must be banished to make way for her replacements as the characters grow beyond their infantile self and parental images. At the same time, Hetty is the symbol of the abandoned and murdered child, whose suffering enacts the characters' sense of abandonment, along with their unacknowledged murderous wishes toward missing or inadequate parents. Reliving and working through unresolved childhood feelings, as in psychoanalytic therapy, is a way of integrating parental images in the mind. In Kohut's terms, the characters have completed their self-structuralization through a transference, in which they have completed the process of "transmuting internalization" that should normally have occurred in childhood (*Analysis* 49).

. . . . .

Critics have wondered why Eliot seems unable to see her favored characters in ***Adam Bede*** and other novels as they come across to the reader. Dinah, Dorothea, Romola and Daniel Deronda are examples in her fiction of idealized hero(ine)s portrayed in sharp contrast to an extremely self-centered and/or immature character: Hetty, Rosamund, Tito and Tessa, and Gwendolen Harleth. Such contrasting of idealized and villainous characters is in part Victorian literary convention, and in part Eliot's deliberate attempt "to illustrate the moral truths of her religion of humanity" (Fulmer 28). Eliot's blind spots, however, can perhaps best be explained by the psychoanalytic concept of splitting. According to Otto Kernberg, the object relations theorist, splitting is a "central defensive operation of the ego at regressed levels" which occurs when the neutralization of aggression in the mind "does not take place sufficiently"; he explains that "Probably the best known manifestation of splitting is the division of external objects into 'all good' ones and 'all bad' ones" (6, 29). Splitting is manifest in Eliot's art not only in her contrasting characters, but also in their development: although her story is abruptly cut off, Hetty is portrayed in more convincing detail than Dinah, a shadowy ideal who is more often than not offstage. Eliot's failure to see the aggression in her idealized character—in this case, Dinah, and to a lesser degree, Adam (whose aggression is in part acknowledged, in part denied)—perhaps constitutes a denial of aggressive impulses in herself. Hetty, the split off, bad side of herself, is banished from Hayslope, and banished from the novel. The failure of the ending of ***Adam Bede*** (Hetty's disappearance and the marriage of Adam and Dinah) may thus reflect Eliot's failure to detach herself from her own conflicts.

Carol Christ has shown how Eliot's concern with the repression of anger is evident in her repeated use of providential death in her fiction both "to avoid ... and prohibit aggression ... in her characters" (132). My purpose has been to extend such insights by showing how Kohut's self-psychology illuminates the patterns of indirect expression of aggression in ***Adam Bede,*** explains some of the problems noted by critics, and suggests their connection to the author's own unresolved conflicts. The application of Kohut's theories to a study of ***Adam Bede*** also shows how narcissistic rage, a "dangerous feature of individual psychopathology" is transformed into an "equally malignant social phenomenon" ("Thoughts" 382), whereby family and social groups turn innocent victims into scapegoats in order to compensate for their own sense of inadequacy.

Works Cited

Christ, Carol. "Aggression and Providential Death in George Eliot's Fiction." *Novel* 9 (1976): 130-40.

Coen, Stanley J., M.D. "Sexualization as a Predominant Mode of Defense." *Journal of the American Psychoanalytic Association* 29 (1981): 893-920.

Creeger, George. "An Interpretation of *Adam Bede.*" *Journal of English Literary History* 23 (1956): 218-38.

Edwards, Michael. "A Reading of *Adam Bede.*" *Critical Quarterly* 14 (1972): 205-18.

Eliot, George. *Adam Bede.* Ed. Stephen Gill. New York: Penguin, 1980.

Ermarth, Elizabeth. "George Eliot's Conception of Sympathy." *Nineteenth-Century Fiction* 40 (1985): 23-42.

Fulmer, Constance Marie. "Contrasting Pairs of Heroines in George Eliot's Fiction." *Studies in the Novel* 6 (1974): 288-94.

Gregor, Ian. "The Two Worlds of *Adam Bede.*" *The Moral and the Story* by Ian Gregor and Brian Nicholas. London: Faber, 1962. 13-32.

Hardy, Barbara. *The Novels of George Eliot.* London: Athlone, 1959.

Harris, Mason. "Arthur's Misuse of the Imagination: Sentimental Benevolence and Wordsworthian Realism in *Adam Bede.*" *English Studies in Canada* 4 (1978): 41-59.

———. "Infanticide and Respectability: Hetty Sorrel as Abandoned Child in *Adam Bede.*" *English Studies in Canada* 9 (1983): 177-96.

Herbert, Christopher. "Preachers and the Schemes of Nature in *Adam Bede.*" *Nineteenth-Century Fiction* 29 (1975): 412-27.

Kernberg, Otto. *Borderline Conditions and Pathological Narcissism.* New York: Aronson, 1975.

Knoepflmacher, U. C. *George Eliot's Early Novels: The Limits of Realism.* Berkeley: U of California P, 1968.

Kohut, Heinz. *The Analysis of the Self.* New York: International UP, 1971.

———. *How Does Analysis Cure?* Ed. Arnold Goldberg with Paul Stepansky. Chicago: U of Chicago P, 1984.

———. *The Restoration of the Self.* Madison, CT: International UP, 1977.

———. "Thoughts on Narcissism and Narcissistic Rage." *The Psychoanalytic Study of the Child.* 27, Quadrangle Books. New York: New York Times, 1973. 360-400.

Krieger, Murray. "*Adam Bede* and the Cushioned Fall: The Extenuation of Extremity." *The Classic Vision: The Retreat From Extremity in Modern Literature.* Baltimore: Johns Hopkins UP, 1971. 197-220.

Leavis, F. R. *The Great Tradition.* New York: Stewart, 1950.

Martin, Bruce K. "Rescue and Marriage in *Adam Bede.*" *Studies in English Literature* 12 (1972): 745-63.

Russell, Gillian A. "Narcissism and the narcissistic personality disorder: A comparison of the theories of Kernberg and Kohut." *British Journal of Medical Psychology* 58 (1985): 137-49.

James Eli Adams (essay date 1991)

SOURCE: "Gyp's Tale: On Sympathy, Silence, and Realism in *Adam Bede,*" in *Dickens Studies Annual,* Vol. 20, 1991, pp. 227-42.

[*In the following essay, Adams examines the limits of the human ability to express emotion through language in* Adam Bede.]

In Chapter 21 of ***Adam Bede,*** the narrator remarks upon the quiet "drama" of three laborers learning to read: "It was almost as if three rough animals were making humble efforts to learn how they might become human" (281). Commentators on Eliot's novel frequently single out this evocation of an obscure struggle against mystery and dispossession: it has "unmistakably the quality of an allegorical panel," as one critic remarks.[1] But a tribute to the humanizing power of literacy is curiously discordant in a work which so strenuously insists on the inadequacies of formal education. Adam, after all, is not made any more human by his literacy: that hopeful view is gently parodied in Bartle Massey's lament that the catastrophe "might never have happened," if Adam, "poor fellow," had "gone into the higher branches" of mathematics (463). Moral education—that which makes one truly human—rests instead on the "lesson" of sympathy, which is transacted in a very different language, under the silent, often inchoate tutelage of suffering. "That is a long and hard lesson," the narrator remarks after Thias Bede's funeral, "and Adam had at present only learned the alphabet of it in his father's sudden death" (255). Formal literacy is thus subordinated to a language whose "alphabet" has no phonic counterpart, nor any established script.

In an earlier epoch, such language was the province of religious doctrine and ceremony. But for Eliot, it is the novelist who must take up the burden of representing the ineffable—of rendering in words the experience of suffering and moral redemption. Eliot's moral design in ***Adam Bede*** thus offers peculiar challenges to the novelist. If, as the novel eloquently insists, what is most precious in human experience is that which cannot be articulated—"something unspeakably great and beautiful"—then the largest significance of formal education and eloquence, whether spoken or written, will be ironic. Eloquence, like literacy, calls attention to the complexity and significance of that which it cannot adequately articulate. Although it represents a uniquely human power, literacy thus confirms in addition a pronounced bond between man and "rough animals." Indeed, what might seem one of the novel's more hackneyed motifs, the uncannily precocious dog population of Hayslope, is but one facet of Eliot's sustained mediation upon the powers and limits of human expression. In the dogs, Eliot portrays creatures who seem to possess a rudimentary inner life, but who, since they lack speech, must struggle to find an outlet for that life in other forms of expression. Whatever their sentimental value, "the dumb creatures," as Mrs. Poyser calls them, thus assume the role of mute choric figures offering oblique commentary on the eminently *human* struggle to find an adequate language for feeling. That human predicament is most obviously embodied in the form of Adam's dog Gyp, the devoted companion who lacks a tail, and is thus "destitute of that vehicle for his emotions."

In stressing the limits of human expression, however, Eliot also engages in a Carlylean celebration of the ineffable that tends to render eloquence inherently suspect. If what is most truly and richly "human" are those states of mind that resist articulation, then those who trust to eloquence or "notions" to represent their experience are not only doomed to frustration; they are destined to seem emotionally impoverished, insufficiently responsive to the integrity of human feeling, which ultimately can be respected only by silence. Conversely, utterance which is inarticulate and incoherent may confirm the authority of the feeling it cannot directly express. Gyp's missing tail, after all, makes its own eloquence felt in the consequent pathos of Gyp's struggle to express his emotions, a struggle whose intensity humanizes him beyond any other dog in the novel. *With* a tail, Gyp would be less emphatically the object of "fellow-feeling." The inability to articulate one's most profound feelings and thoughts may be an obstacle to heightened consciousness—as Eliot would obviously have it in the case of Hetty Sorrel; yet the same failure may also be evidence of the depth of one's feelings, and thus of one's capacity for sympathy.

Such a stance obviously places peculiar and strenuous burdens on the novelist. More precisely, the mistrust of eloquence lends extraordinary pressure to the problematics of realistic representation. Eliot's rejection of religious doctrine, which impels her appeal to the authority of experience, also renders morally (not merely ontologically) suspect the reliance on language to conjure up "experience" as a realm of immediate, external presence. This tension informs a feature of ***Adam Bede*** often explained away as an awkward device of the inexperienced novelist: the reliance on historical present, which is frequently conjoined with exhortations that the reader "see" the scenes being described. Eliot's predicament as a narrator, along with the moral problematic informing it, is thus projected with particular complexity in the figure of Dinah Morris. Celebrated as the vehicle of a profound sympathetic understanding, Dinah is effectively silenced after her marriage to Adam, when she must renounce her preaching. The ending is frequently criticized as a failure of nerve, a capitulation to the pressures of novelistic convention and male sentiment.[2] But however one accounts for the outcome, Dinah's silencing articulates the novel's equivocal view of eloquence. As an evangelical preacher, Dinah is of all the characters the most vulnerable to the suspicion of eloquence; she is also the most obvious surrogate of a novelist notorious for her moral commentary on the action she narrates. The logic which silences Dinah is central to a novel which, in its effort to faithfully represent the complexities of moral experience, is in effect constantly trying to write itself into silence.

Jane Welsh Carlyle, writing to the as-yet-unknown author of ***Adam Bede*** in 1859, praised the novel in these words:

> In truth, it is a beautiful most *human* Book! Every Dog in it, not to say every man woman and child in it, is brought home to one's "business and bosom," an individual fellow-creature! (Eliot ***Letters*** III: 18)

The canine population of Hayslope may recall the devoted hounds that are a sentimental fixture of Victorian genre painting. But Mrs. Carlyle—no mere sentimentalist—here seizes upon a central concern of the novel. The peculiar emotional sensibility of Hayslope dogs (notable even by mid-Victorian standards) places them within Eliot's sustained exploration of what it *means* to be a "fellow-creature." Their choric role is established in the novel's opening chapter, where Adam's dog Gyp alerts us to the distinctive features of his master's voice. Lest we miss the connection, Seth Bede is there to call it to our attention. "Thee'st like thy dog Gyp," he tells Adam, "thee bark'st at me sometimes, but . . . thee allays lic'st my hand after." Gyp's subsequent entrance offers the narrator occasion to elaborate the analogy:

> ... no sooner did Adam put his ruler in his pocket, and begin to twist his apron round his waist, then Gyp ran forward and looked up in his master's face with patient expectation. If Gyp had had a tail he would doubtless have wagged it, but being destitute of that vehicle for his emotions, he was like many other wordly personages, destined to appear more phlegmatic than nature had made him.
>
> "What! Art ready for the basket, eh, Gyp?" said Adam, with the same gentle modulation of voice as when he spoke to Seth.
>
> Gyp jumped and made a short bark, as much as to say, "Of course." Poor fellow, he had not a great range of expression. (54)

The narrator's commiseration offers a coy but nonetheless suggestive gloss on the distinct limits to Adam's own "range of expression." Adam conveys his rigid sense of duty with a ready eloquence, both in his impatient attack on wiry Ben's mockery, and in his lengthy, impromptu *credo*—"sarmunt," Ben calls it—extolling a religion of hard work. The forthright vehemence of Adam's speech is faithful to his Carlylean creed, but, as Gyp's presence emphasizes, it allows little outlet for an awkward tenderness in his character that is suggested by his words to Seth and Gyp. Adam's subsequent ordeal softens his "iron will" and nurtures his tenderness into a richer and more comprehensive sympathy. That moral development is charted in a struggle to find a more adequate vehicle for his more complex emotions. Ultimately, he arrives at a new form of eloquence that can acknowledge the claims not only of personal duty but of human frailty.

Adam's growth is paradigmatic of the novel's moral action, in which the central characters undergo a kind of Feuerbachian baptism: through suffering, they are led to "a regeneration, the initiation into a new state," which Eliot summarizes as the experience of sympathy, "the one poor word that contains all our best insight and our best love" (531).[3] This "lesson," as the narrator describes it, involves the mastery of a new form of language, and in each of the central characters the new understanding is confirmed by a shift in patterns of speech. This transformation is most starkly presented in the figure of Hetty, whose persistent silence through most of the novel reflects her utter incapacity for sympathetic participation in the world around her. Adam's range of expression may be limited, but Hetty's mute egoism is a powerful emblem of her isolation from other human beings. During her bewildered flight from the exposure of her pregnancy, the narrator's imagery reduces her being almost to the level of a frightened animal; after her arrest, she can only reconfirm her humanity by being brought to speak, to confess her responsibility in a human moral order.

Hetty's ordeal confirms the narrator's tribute to Bartle Massey's students: the mastery of language signifies a new level of humanity. Elsewhere, however, enlarged moral awareness is confirmed by the faltering of a former eloquence. Arthur Donnithorne is Hetty's partner in egoism and vanity, but by virtue of his sex and social position he embodies in more complex fashion the relation between insight and eloquence. Arthur is rarely at a loss for words, but his speech, even in his patronizing tenderness towards Hetty, is a tissue of superficial and evasive pleasantries, the language of a gentleman eager to maintain the regard of himself and others. Of his private thoughts, his vague moral qualms and self-mistrust, he cannot bring himself to speak, even with Mr. Irwine. Arthur's eventual acknowledgment of responsibility obviously parallels Hetty's confession, but since his disgrace has destroyed the foundations of his public rhetoric, he can only convey his new insight through a faltering of his former eloquence, as he struggles to master a vocabulary of sincerity he has never before called upon.

Adam's forthright speech—"I speak plain, sir, but I can't speak any other way" (207)—jars the decorum sustained in Arthur's urbane evasions. But Adam's frankness is the expression of an unyielding sense of duty that similarly limits the capacity to acknowledge the complexities of moral experience. His eloquence, after all, draws its conception of human experience from arithmetic: "Life's a reckoning we can't make twice over; there's no real making amends in this world, any more nor you can mend a wrong subtraction by doing your addition right" (247). This trope chimes with Eliot's insistence on the irrevocability of action, but it also represents a stance that cannot easily adapt to unexpected complexity in human experience.[4] As suffering calls into question the adequacy of Adam's moral arithmetic, his eloquence, like Arthur's, begins to falter. With the discovery that Hetty has murdered her infant, his rigid, "hard" speech finally gives way to broken sobs, and he vows to Bartle Massey, "I'll never be hard again." Finally, "with hesitating gentleness," he even manages to forgive Arthur (455, 475, 516).

Dinah at first glance stands outside this pattern: her immense fund of ready sympathy seems to require no correction or expansion. Yet she, too, ultimately enacts the pattern of faltering eloquence. Throughout most of the novel the conviction and support she derives from her sense of vocation are registered in the unwavering calm of her voice. Her appearance at Stoniton jail is typical: "There was no agitation visible in her, but a deep concentrated calmness, as if, even when she was speaking, her soul was in prayer reposing on an unseen support" (492). Even in response to Seth's declaration of love Dinah retains her composure, as the narrator quietly emphasizes: she replies "in her tender but calm treble notes" (79). Adam's presence alone disturbs this self-possession. Initially she greets him as she does Seth, "in her calm treble," but under the scrutiny of Adam's "dark, penetrating glance" she abruptly experiences "for the first time in her life . . . a painful self-consciousness" (163). As the novel approaches its close, this self-consciousness infuses her voice. When Dinah visits Adam after her night in the prison with Hetty, she recalls their first meeting, and speaks with "a trembling in her clear voice" (501). Later at the farm, when the conversation turns to her future, she speaks, "trying to be quite calm"; with Adam in the cottage, she is "trembling, but trying to be calm;" when he finally proposes, even her tears are "trembling" in response (501, 523, 536).

Dinah's peculiar susceptibility to Adam may seem the stuff of those "silly novels by lady novelists" that Eliot attacked. Still, the motif answers to a more strenuous moral design: Eliot clearly wants to enrich Dinah's character by complicating the forces that govern her single-minded existence. Yet this complication is prepared from the very outset as a resistance to Dinah's vocation, which is made to seem—like Adam's very different sense of vocation—"hard" and peremptory in its demands. So receptive to the divine Word that she strives to convey to her listeners, Dinah is less responsive to the claims of more mundane human needs. Mrs. Poyser seizes upon this theme in exasperation at her inability to persuade Dinah to remain with her relatives in Loamshire: "I might as well talk to the running brook and tell it to stand still" (123). Shortly afterwards, Irwine's conversation with Dinah prompts a similar analogy: "he must be a miserable prig who would act the pedagogue here," Irwine thinks, "one might as well go and lecture the trees for growing in their own shape" (136). While they pay tribute to the integrity of Dinah's vocation, both judgments also align that vocation with the profoundly equivocal character of nature itself. The bounties of Dinah's sympathy, they suggest, are bound up with a spiritual allegiance that, like natural forces, may be utterly indifferent to human needs.[5]

The faltering of Dinah's eloquence thus comes to mark a resistance to the specific character of Dinah's vocation. Such resistance is hardly surprising, inasmuch as she is, after all, a Methodist preacher in a novel permeated by Eliot's own rejection of doctrinal religion. That rejection is most obviously embodied in Irwine, who is largely the mouthpiece of a remarkably secular sympathy. "If he had been in the habit of speaking plainly," the narrator informs us,

> he would perhaps have said that the only healthy form religion could take in such minds was that of certain dim but strong emotions, suffusing themselves as a hallowing influence over the family affections and neighbourly duties. He thought the custom of baptism more important than its doctrine, and that the religious benefits the peasant drew from the church where his fathers worshipped and the sacred piece of ground where they lay buried were but slightly dependent on a clear understanding of the Liturgy or the sermon. Clearly, the rector was not what is called in these days an "earnest" man. (112)

No, but he sounds remarkably like the novel's narrator—even to the gently patronizing note in "such minds."[6] Not surprisingly, Irwine's assessment is borne out by Lisbeth Bede's comic quibbles over interpretation of "the tex"—"thee allays makes a peck o' thy own words out o' a pint o' the Bible's," she tells Seth, Dinah's fellow Methodist (90). The same "healthy" independence of theology is exemplified in the community's church services, at which elderly worshippers who cannot read nonetheless sit contented, "following the service without any very clear comprehension indeed, but with a simple faith in its efficacy to ward off harm and bring blessing" (242).

Most importantly, however, this aversion to religious doctrine is seconded by Adam. His endorsement was evidently of some importance to Eliot: in the famous

Chapter 17, the narrator offers it through the fiction of an encounter with Adam in old age—a cumbersome device, but one which exempts Adam's judgment from qualification by the novel's subsequent action:

> I've seen pretty clear, ever since I was a young un', as religion's something else beside notions. It isn't notions sets people doing the right thing—it's feelings. . . . There's things go on in the soul, and times when feelings come into you like a rushing mighty wind, as the scripture says, and part your life in two almost, so as you look back on yourself as if you was somebody else. Those are things as you can't bottle up in a "do this" and "do that;" and I'll go so far with the strongest Methodist ever you'll find. That shows me there's deep, speritial things in religion. You can't make much out wi' talking about it, but you feel it. (226-27)

Adam thus identifies Dinah's predicament: "talking about it" is precisely her vocation. In presenting her Eliot must confront the problem of separating Dinah's sympathetic power from her doctrinal language, and, more generally, of rendering her an authoritative moral presence *in spite of* the vocation by which she defines her very identity.

Throughout the novel Eliot strives to soften the force of Dinah's Methodism by obscuring its particulars—much in the way Irwine blurs Anglican theology. In every instance, moreover, the resistance to theology entails a check upon her preaching. Thus the narrator dwells on, for example, Dinah's respect for the "mystery" of feeling, which informs her instinctive understanding of when to remain silent, and the sympathetic power she conveys even in that silence. But the most subtle means to this avoidance of doctrine is the description of Dinah's speech as a form of music—most arrestingly, in the account of her sermon on the Hayslope common:

> Hitherto the traveller had been chained to the spot against his will by the charm of Dinah's mellow treble tones, which had a variety of modulation like that of a fine instrument touched with the unconscious skill of musical instinct. The simple things she said seemed like novelties, as a melody strikes us when we hear it sung by the pure voice of a boyish chorister, the quiet depth of conviction; with which she spoke seemed in itself evidence for the truth of her message. (71)

This passage tellingly interrupts—and displaces—that portion of Dinah's sermon exhorting her audience to fear damnation. The musical analogy, along with the subsequent shift into oblique oration, directs the reader's attention away from Dinah's sermon to its effect on her listeners, and refers that effect not to the specific content of her words but to the very sound of her voice. Indeed, "the traveller"—"chained to the spot, against his will"—seems to be introduced here, as elsewhere in the novel, to further register the visceral, sensory impact of the scene before him.[7]

Music in this passage has a particular tactical value rarely noted in all the attention given to music in Eliot's novels.[8] In the account of Dinah's preaching, music incarnates a critical norm much like that ratified in Pater's dictum that all art constantly aspires towards the condition of music (*The Renaissance* 106). Of course Eliot does not share Pater's formalism, but here she clearly does wish to minimize, in Pater's terms, "the mere matter" of Dinah's sermon. Dinah's preaching, the figure urges, resembles music in its expression of exquisite feeling unalloyed by discursive content. The force of Dinah's sympathetic "music" is subsequently borne out when she visits Lisbeth Bede in Chapter 10. Lisbeth's response to Dinah's "nice way o' talkin'"—"it puts me i' mind o' the swallows" (157)—is exemplary in being scrupulously divorced from any clear comprehension of Dinah's "earnest prayer":

> Lisbeth, without grasping any distinct idea, without going through any course of religious emotions, felt a vague sense of goodness and love, and of something right lying underneath and beyond all this sorrowing life. She couldn't understand the sorrow; but, for these moments, under the subduing influence of Dinah's spirit, she felt she must be patient and still. (159)

Dinah's presence thus comes to nourish a "simple faith" of rustic parishioners like Lisbeth, a faith that Eliot celebrates as a vital, enduring emotional sustenance abstracted from any distinctly religious conception. That celebration is a consummately Victorian tribute to continuity in the face of social and spiritual upheaval. It also exemplifies the submergence of theology in psychology that Eliot's critics typically refer to the influence of Feuerbach. On this point, however, ***Adam Bede*** seems equally responsive to Carlyle, whose example T. H. Huxley memorably summed up: "*Sartor Resartus* led me to know that a deep sense of religion was compatible with the entire absence of theology."[9] The congruence is suggestive, because Eliot's tributes to such a "deep sense of religion" in ***Adam Bede*** articulate a dynamic strikingly akin to Carlyle's mistrust of self-consciousness. In the novel, a Carlylean aversion to "notions," as Adam puts it, readily passes into an exaltation of precisely those states of mind that cannot be articulated, or even comprehended. Sympathy, that is, can only be understood as one of those intricate complexes of thought and emotion that must remain, in Eliot's resonant adjective, "unspeakable." We're once again recalled to Gyp's predicament, which embodies a similar gap between feeling and language. But rather than standing as a mark of human inadequacy, Gyp's missing tail begins to seem a sign of moral depth. Hence the unexpected complexity of a passage, for example, that describes Adam "waiting for [Hetty's] kind looks as a patient trembling dog waits for his master's eye to be turned upon him" (399). What purports merely to give words to the reader's disdain for Adam's blind devotion manages at the same time to pay tribute to the depth of his emotional being and to the pathos of a seemingly universal inability to find adequate language for one's feelings. As Kenny Marotta has remarked, "Precisely in Adam's inarticulateness is his closeness to the truth of feeling" (59). The opening chapter's juxtaposition of man and "the dumb creatures" in this sense establishes a kinship that is confirmed, rather than transcended, through moral education.

Early in the novel, Mrs. Poyser broaches this topic comically: "Oh, sir," she tells Arthur, "the men are so tongue-tied—you're forced partly to guess what they mean, as you do wi' the dumb creaturs" (315). A few pages later her barb takes on a more somber resonance when Irwine defends the villagers from his mother's genteel contempt:

> The common people are not quite so stupid as you imagine. The commonest man, who has his ounce of sense and feeling, is conscious of the difference between a lovely, delicate woman and a coarse one. Even a dog feels a difference in their presence. The man may be no better able than a beast to explain the influence the more refined beauty has on him, but he feels it. (320)

Dinah, however, most eloquently seizes upon the affinity; characteristically, she describes it not in condescension but as the recognition of a common bond. When Adam points out Gyp's friendly response to her presence—"he's very slow to welcome strangers"—Dinah's own response confirms the emblematic moral resemblance between Adam and Gyp established in the opening chapter. "Poor dog," she says, patting Gyp,

> I've a strange feeling about the dumb things as if they wanted to speak, and it was a trouble to 'em because they couldn't. I can't help being sorry for the dogs always, though perhaps there's no need. But they may well have more in them than they know how to make us understand, for we can't say half what we feel, with all our words. (163)

Illuminated by Dinah's sympathy, "the dumb things" become emblems of a fundamental human predicament. In acknowledging the inadequacy of human speech, Dinah calls attention to the richness and complexity of the feelings it cannot articulate—to those experiences which, as she tells Irwine, "I could give no account of, for I could neither make a beginning nor ending of them in words" (135).

Yet this same insistence on the richness of the ineffable also redounds upon the authority of Dinah's vocation. Even more than the specific doctrinal content of her preaching, a suspicion of eloquence *per se* ultimately compromises Dinah's authority as an agent of moral redemption. If, as the novel continually suggests, the most profound moments of human experience are those that elude speech, then *any* verbal eloquence claiming moral authority becomes vaguely suspect. Adam's musings in Chapter 17 make this transition more explicitly. Initially Adam questions only the adequacy of "notions" as a source of motivation; after repeating his objection, however, he goes on to suggest that notions reflect a fundamental poverty of experience:

> I've seen pretty clear, ever since I was a young un, as religion's something else besides doctrines and notions. I look at it as if the doctrines was like finding names for your feelings, so as you can talk of 'em when you've never known 'em, just as a man may talk 'o tools when he knows their names, though he's never so much as seen 'em, still less handled 'em. (226-27)

Dinah's preaching may aspire to the condition of music, but her words stubbornly continue to denote, to operate as the "names" Adam mistrusts. Under the pressure of Adam's sentiment, Dinah's preaching not only reinforces her status as an alien in Hayslope; it subtly undermines her claim to moral authority within the novel. The novel's epilogue, in which Dinah marries Adam and gives up her preaching, may ratify popular convention, but it also confirms the logic inherent in the novel's celebration of sympathy.

In her essay, **"The Natural History of German Life,"** Eliot emphasizes the significance of a rural community's dialect as a vehicle of continuity with the past. "This provincial style of the peasant is again, like his *physique,* a remnant of the history to which he clings with the utmost tenacity" (***Essays*** 275). This essay is often cited as a rehearsal of the concerns that govern ***Adam Bede,*** and certainly the novel bears witness to Eliot's care in depicting this "historical language." (Mr. Casson, for example, seems almost wholly designed to underscore Hayslope's linguistic integrity: "I'm not this countryman, you may tell by my tongue sir" [59].) In the novel, however, the history embodied in particular lives and a particular language is ultimately subordinated to the universal language of sympathy, "binding together your whole being past and present in one unspeakable vibration . . . blending your present joy with past sorrow and your present sorrow with all your past joy" (399). It is the inchoate, "unspeakable" experience of sympathy that links the unity of an individual life with the fundamental continuity of human existence itself. When Adam responds to the "language" of Hetty's face, or Dinah acknowledges the claims of Adam's love, a character submits to a knowledge beyond what words, or "notions," can convey.[10] And the novel seems to aim at a precisely congruent transformation in the reader, who would submit to the authority of a sympathy derived from participation in the experience of suffering represented in the novel. In this sense, the entire novel aspires constantly towards the condition of music—music, that is, conceived as the emblematic language of sympathy. If Eliot turned to the life and language of a rural community to affirm moral and spiritual continuity in the face of change, the novel discovers that assurance in a language beyond words.

In its celebration of the ineffable, ***Adam Bede*** complicates received views of Eliot's intellectual allegiance, and does so by locating in Dinah's vocation an image of the novelist's. "He who cannot express himself is a slave," writes Feuerbach, in a comment that, Robert Kiely argues, characterizes Eliot's attitude to the significance of language (103-123). Certainly the claim elucidates the narrator's comment on Bartle Massey's students, as well as the emblematic significance of Hetty's silence. But the rhetoric of silence in ***Adam Bede*** responds to a very different view of language, a view modeled less on Feuerbach than on the *Logos* of St. John. To be sure, Eliot's later novels increasingly abandon this divided allegiance, subordinating the theological paradigm to a view of language as, in Kiely's words, "the regulated product of civilization" (Kiely's essay, significantly, deals almost entirely with ***Middlemarch.***) But ***Adam Bede*** helps to explain this trajectory by suggesting at once the attraction and the costs of the older view. Most obviously, to exalt a language beyond words imposes an enormous burden on the novelist: like Gyp, she lacks an adequate vehicle of expression. Indeed, in the effort to convey moral authority in writing, Eliot is exposed to the very suspicion that implicates Dinah's eloquence. Moreover, the novelist must likewise reconcile her evocation of sympathy with a peculiarly "hard," unsympathetic doctrine of her own—Eliot's central tenet that "consequences are unpitying."[11]

But the affiliation of preacher and novelist, along with the peculiar challenges both confront, is most suggestively conveyed in the various passages where the narrator pauses to call attention to the challenges of representation. Much as Dinah in her preaching attempts, through words, to bring an unseen reality before her listeners' eyes—exhorting her audience to "see" an image of the Lord shining through the visible landscape—so the narrator of ***Adam Bede*** exhorts readers to "see" a world beyond the printed page: "Let me take you into that dining-room. . . ." "See there in the bright sunshine ... what do you see?" "See, he has something in his hand" (98,507). The novelist's technique thus mimes the Methodist style so closely reproduced in Dinah's sermon.[12] Much as this device has exasperated some of Eliot's critics, it is not a mere gesture of sympathetic participation in local color. Rather such exhortation crystallizes a central impulse of the novel's moral design, and indeed of Eliot's aesthetic: it appeals to readers to respond to the words on the page as to experience itself, that language whose "alphabet" is human feeling, and whose "lesson" is the experience of sympathy.[13]

Of course, this appeal is at odds with the strenuous distancing of the subject matter that Eliot cultivates through historical setting and pastoral tradition.[14] So formulated, moreover, the appeal to the reader may seem crudely naive. Indeed, in the novel's opening sentences Eliot wryly acknowledges the leap of faith it embodies. "With a single drop of ink for a mirror, the Egyptian sorcerer undertakes to reveal to any chance-comers far-reaching visions of the past. This is what I undertake to do for you, reader" (49). In a sense, Eliot thus preempts all grammatological critics by conceding that the moral authority of her text is a "sorcery" founded on absence, that the "alphabet" of experience has no existence apart from writing. But what the narrator thus demystifies is more than the awkward yearning of the first novelist, or even the particular moral project undertaken in ***Adam Bede.*** The appeal to experience so plangently made in Eliot's use of the authorial present is, after all, an appeal made with varying degrees of urgency and explicitness in all realistic novels. Gyp's missing tail might thus stand for the problematics of representation that attend the project of "realism" in the broadest sense. The novelist *always* lacks an adequate vehicle for representing a realm located outside of language.

But Gyp's tail—like the tale it so curiously animates—has a more precise historical significance. In "the first major exercise in programmatic literary realism in English literature," as John Goode has called ***Adam Bede,*** a familiar Victorian crisis of moral and religious authority assumes a form more far-reaching in its significance than conventional literary history has recognized.[15] The urgency of the moral dilemma informing ***Adam Bede,*** and the explicitness with which Eliot dwells upon it, allows the novel to encapsulate in unusually suggestive form a historically momentous logic, which leads from a mistrust of specifically religious "notions" to a far more comprehensive and radical skepticism concerning the authority of language. Through a skeptical dynamic central to the realistic novel at large, the authority of the general claim or maxim is subordinated to the more particularized forms of an extra-linguistic "experience," which—as ***Adam Bede*** so powerfully illustrates—in turn urges the novelist towards a still greater restriction of linguistic authority. The particular, immediate apprehension of particular, concrete fact becomes the only truth to which the novelist can appeal. Of course the specifically religious concern recedes in Eliot's subsequent novels, along with the bald appeals to the reader's sympathetic participation. But the raw urgency of the moral burden in ***Adam Bede*** issues in a rhetoric that marks a powerful bridge between Eliot's writings and the work of novelists we are accustomed to consider far more "modern" in outlook and technique. The yearning of Eliot's narrator to make us "see" the reality of the novel's action will be echoed, for example, in James's elaborate insistence on presentation and "solidity of specification," and in Conrad, in his more emphatic claim in the Preface to *The Nigger of the "Narcissus"*: "My task which I am trying to achieve is, by the power of the written word to make you hear, to make you feel—it is, before all, to make you *see*" (XIV). The fictional worlds of Conrad and James may seem remote from that of ***Adam Bede.*** But the novelist's struggle to convey a reality beyond words testifies to the persistent eloquence of Gyp's missing tail.

Notes

1. Herbert 422. The panel, Herbert adds, "makes a powerful comment on the large question of man's relation to Nature." Other critics who comment on Massey's students include: John Goode, "Adam Bede," in Barbara Hardy (ed.) *Critical Essays on George Eliot* (London: RKP, 1970), p. 22; Dorothy Van Ghent, *The English Novel: Form and Function* (New York: Holt, Rinehart, Winston, 1953), 177; Daniel Cottom, *Social Figures: George Eliot, Social History, and Literary Representation* (Minneapolis: U of Minnesota, P, 1987), 12.
2. The ending was G. H. Lewes's suggestion, and has been roundly condemned as inconsistent with what

precedes it; an exception is Barnard Paris, *Experiments in Life: George Eliot's Quest for Values* (Detroit: Wayne State UP, 1965).

3. U. C. Knoepflmacher analyzes the Feuerbachian structures of the novel in *Religious Humanism and the Victorian Novel* (Princeton: Princeton UP, 1965), 52-59.

4. On Adam's arithmetic, see Barbara Hardy, *The Novels of George Eliot: A Study in Form* (London: Athlone, 1985), 41-45, and Sally Shuttleworth, *George Eliot and Nineteenth-Century Science: The Make-Believe of a Beginning* (Cambridge: Cambridge UP, 1984), 37-38.

5. This seeming intractability links Dinah to Adam, who is similarly characterized by Seth: "You may's well try to turn a wagon in a narrow lane" (51). On the crucial significance of "nature" in the novel, see Knoepflmacher, *George Eliot's Early Novels*, 117-18; Herbert, "Preachers and the Schemes of Nature," 419-427, and Philip Fisher, *Making Up Society: The Novels of George Eliot* (Pittsburgh: U of Pittsburgh P, 1981), 43-45.

6. "The very slackness of Irwine's doctrine is the sign in him of an almost saintly moral excellence," remarks Herbert, "Preachers and the Schemes of Nature," 417—an overstatement, but salutary in stressing the inverse relation between doctrine and moral authority.

7. Eliot's crucial appeal to the reader on this point is overlooked by critics who see Dinah's sermon as a departure from her normal patterns of speech. See, for example, Herbert, "Preachers and the Schemes of Nature," 415-16, and Goode, "Adam Bede," 38-39.

8. A recent book on the subject by Beryl Gray, *George Eliot and Music* (New York: St. Martin's Press, 1989), makes no reference to this tactic.

9. Cited in William Irvine, *Apes, Angels, and Victorians: Darwin, Huxley, and Evolution* (New York: McGraw Hill, 1972), 131. Eliot sent a copy of *Adam Bede* to Jane Welsh Carlyle, expressing her hope that "the philosopher" would receive from it a pleasure like that which she had received from *Sartor Resartus* (*The George Eliot Letters*, III, 23); Mrs. Carlyle responded in the letter quoted above.

10. Of course, the "natural" language embodied in beauty is not always readily legible, and can be deceptive; see Dianne Sadoff, "Nature's Language: Metaphor in the Text of *Adam Bede*," *Genre* 11 (1978), 411-426.

11. As Jay Clayton has suggestively argued, in "Visionary Power and Narrative Form: Wordsworth and *Adam Bede*," *ELH* 46 (1979), 645-72, the ending of the novel seems an effort to soften and humanise this doctrine, by in effect breaking the rigorous chain of "unpitying" consequences, passing from narrative to the evocation of sympathetic vision. Clayton's fine reading identifies what might be seen as a narratological counterpart of the repeated faltering of eloquence I have been discussing. But the formalistic bent of Clayton's argument impoverishes the significance of Dinah, who becomes "the representation of an absence . . . an attempt to place within the hard bonds of the narrative the author's choice to disrupt that narrative" (660). Dinah seems more richly viewed as Eliot's representation of the equivocality of moral (as well as narrative) authority in mid-Victorian discourse.

12. Valentine Cunningham, *Everywhere Spoken Against: Dissent in the Victorian Novel* (Oxford: Clarendon Press, 1975), 151-61, studies Eliot's reliance on the Methodist idiom. Knoepflmacher, *George Eliot's Early Novels*, 105, notes in this appeal Dinah's resemblance to the novelist, but sees it as an appeal to an audience's "relation to universals" outside of sensuous perception—an explanation which obscures the link between Dinah's appeals and those of the novelist attempting to conjure up an emphatically visible image.

13. W. J. Harvey, who finds the technique "all the more infuriating because it is unnecessary," nonetheless gestures towards this rationale in noting that Eliot "generally juggles her tenses in this way to introduce us to a new aspect of her subject" (more precisely, to impress upon us a new scene) "or to give greater force to a moment of crisis or climax" (*The Art of George Eliot*, 78). The gentleman spectator—which may seem a similarly extraneous device—is likewise designed to register the palpable sensuousness of a particular moment.

14. On such distancing, see Steven Marcus, "Literature and Social Theory: Starting In With George Eliot," in *Representations: Essays on Literature and Society* (New York: Random House, 1975), 183-213.

15. John Goode, "Adam Bede," 37. "The final interest of Adam Bede is that it casts its shadow before it," Ian Gregor has urged, although he locates that historical significance (as do most commentators) in the image of the narrating consciousness conveyed in the famous "pier-glass" passage in Chapter 17. (*The Moral and the Story* [*London: Faber, 1962*], *30-32*.

Works Cited

Clayton, Jay. "Visionary Power and Narrative Form: Wordsworth and *Adam Bede*." *ELH* 46 (1979) 645-72.

Conrad, Joseph. *The Nigger of the Narcissus* in *Complete Works* vol. 23. Garden City: Doubleday, 1925.

Cottom, Daniel. *Social Figures: George Eliot, Social History and Literary Representation.* Minneapolis: U of Minnesota P, 1987.

Cunningham, Valentine. *Everywhere Spoken Against: Dissent in the Victorian Novel.* Oxford: Oxford UP, 1975.

Eliot, George. *Adam Bede.* Ed. Stephen Gill. Harmondsworth: Penguin, 1980.

———. *The George Eliot Letters.* Ed. Gordon S. Haight, New Haven: Yale UP.

———. *The Essays of George Eliot.* Ed. Thomas Pinney. New York: Columbia UP, 1963.

Fisher, Philip. *Making Up Society: The Novels of George Eliot.* Pittsburgh: U of Pittsburgh P, 1981.

Goode, John. "Adam Bede" in Hardy (ed.) *Critical Essays.*

Gray, Beryl. *George Eliot and Music.* New York: St. Martins, 1989.

Hardy, Barbara. Ed. *Critical Essays on George Eliot.* London: RKP, 1970.

———. *The Novels of George Eliot: A Study in Form.* London: Athlone, 1985.

Herbert, Christopher. "Preachers and the Schemes of Nature in *Adam Bede.*" *Nineteenth-Century Fiction* 29 (1975): 412-27.

Irvine, William. *Apes, Angels and Victorians: Darwin, Huxley and Evolution.* New York: McGraw, 1972.

Kiely, Robert. "The Limits of Dialogue in *Middlemarch.*" In J. H. Buckley Ed. *The Worlds of Victorian Fiction. Harvard English Studies* 6. Cambridge: Harvard, 1975, 103-123.

Knoepflmacher, U. C. *George Eliot's Early Novels:* The Limits of Realism. Berkely: U of Calif. Press, 1968.

———. *Religious Humanism and the Victorian Novel.* Princeton: Princeton UP, 1965.

Marcus, Steven. "Literature and Social Theory: Starting in with George Eliot." In *Representations: Essays on Literature and Society.* New York: Random House, 1975.

Marotta, Kenny. "*Adam Bede* as a Pastoral." *Genre* 9 (1976): 59-72.

Paris, Bernard. *Experiments in Life: George Eliot's Quest for Values.* Detroit: Wayne State UP, 1965.

Pater, Walter. "The School of Giorgione," *The Renaissance: Studies in Art and Poetry* Ed. Donald L. Hill Berkeley: U of California P, 1980.

Sadoff, Dianne. "Nature's Language: Metaphor in the Text of *Adam Bede.*" *Genre* 11 (1978): 411-26.

Shuttleworth, Sally. *George Eliot and Nineteenth-Century Science: The Make-Believe of a Beginning.* Cambridge: Cambridge UP, 1984.

Van Ghent, Dorothy. *The English Novel: Form and Function.* New York: Holt, 1953.

Daniel P. Gunn (essay date 1992)

SOURCE: "Dutch Painting and the Simple Truth in *Adam Bede,*" in *Studies in the Novel,* Vol. XXIV, No. 4, Winter, 1992, pp. 366-80.

[*In the following essay, Gunn examines Eliot's discussion of Dutch genre painting and its relationship to realism in* Adam Bede.]

When George Eliot compared her fiction to the work of Dutch genre painters in chapter 17 of ***Adam Bede,*** admiring the "rare, precious quality of truthfulness" in these "Dutch paintings, which lofty-minded people despise" (1:268), she did more than simply announce her intentions as a realist writer.[1] She also marked off a conventional space for "common coarse people" (1:270) in her novel, using a conspicuous visual precedent to define and imagine the rural artisans and tenant farmers she had chosen to represent. The Dutch painting analogy begins as a gloss on the Reverend Irwine's moral weakness, but it quickly opens into an apology for the presence of characters whose class would traditionally have excluded them from serious treatment in art—"old women scraping carrots with their work-worn hands," for example, or "your common labourer, who gets his own bread and eats it vulgarly but creditably with his own pocket-knife" (1:270, 271). In this essay, I want to examine Eliot's references to Dutch art from the perspective of these figures, concentrating on the relation between aesthetic and ideological meanings in the famous metacritical aside. By placing her working-class characters inside the frame of a Dutch genre painting, I will argue, Eliot paradoxically both dignifies and degrades them, admitting them into the universe of representation but simultaneously keeping them at a distance and cleansing them of threatening social meanings.

1

Eliot was right, certainly, to assume that many "lofty-minded people" did not share her affection for Dutch art in 1859. From the eighteenth century on, neoclassical standards of taste had placed the work of Dutch and other genre painters near the bottom of the scale headed by history painting and "the grand style." Painting was supposed to purify and elevate the spectator, drawing him gently away from what was base and vulgar in nature by concentrating his attention on the ideal and the sublime. The Dutch genre artists of the seventeenth century, who had painted tavern brawls and kitchen scenes with scrupulous accuracy, seemed almost perverse in their refusal to elevate the soul, and their work was considered inferior as a result. As Peter Demetz puts it, "only by painting shells or still-life compositions could one sink even lower."[2] For Sir Joshua Reynolds, the complaint against the Dutch was two-fold: they confined themselves to copying nature, merely "deceiving the eye" instead of "animating and dignifying the figures with intellectual grandeur" and thus appealing to the mind; and they chose to represent low and ignoble subjects, thereby placing themselves at a great distance from the exalted and generalized beauty which is the object of art. Reynolds acknowledges that "the painters who have applied themselves more particularly to low and vulgar characters, and who express with precision the various shades of passion, as they are exhibited by vulgar minds . . . deserve great praise." "But," he adds, "as their genius has been employed on low and confined subjects, the praise which we give must be as limited as its object."[3]

Although Dutch art had its defenders throughout the nineteenth century, a position descended from Reynolds still exerted considerable influence at the time Eliot was writing ***Adam Bede.*** For example, a critic reviewing a large art exhibition for the *Manchester Guardian* in 1857 wrote that, in the work of the Flemish and Dutch painters of the seventeenth century, "art was confined to the most grovelling employment of its rare gifts": "A power of painting seldom equalled, and never surpassed, was lavished on pots and pans, on hedge alehouses and fish-markets, on the quarrels of boors, or the amours of troopers and burghers, almost as coarse and sensual. Nature is never vulgar. But Dutch nature comes as near vulgarity as nature can come."[4] Even John Ruskin, the aesthetic theorist whom Eliot admired most, and from whose work she gleaned the doctrine of "realism," that "truth of infinite value,"[5] had little use himself for a style of painting which limited itself to representation of the sensible world and which wandered so far from the beautiful. In *Modern Painters* (1843-1860), he admitted that he had "never been a zealous partisan of the Dutch School."[6] The imitation of detail for its own sake in Dutch painting was "the lowest and most contemptible art" (1:xxxii), and the "collectors of Gerard Dows and Hobbimas may be passed by with a smile" (3:18). After disparaging "the professed landscapists of the Dutch school," Ruskin proposed that "the best patronage that any monarch could possibly bestow upon the arts, would be to collect the whole body of [Dutch landscapes] into a grand gallery and burn it to the ground" (1:92).

By confessing that she "delight[s] in many Dutch paintings" (1:268) in chapter 17 of ***Adam Bede,*** then, Eliot contradicts a well-established tradition of aesthetic opinion. Certainly she does so in part because she anticipates conventional aesthetic objections to the social and moral inferiority of her characters; she adopts a position in the discourse of art criticism in order to defend, by analogy, what she knows will be perceived as unfashionable in her own practice as a novelist. In fact, one complaint about ***Adam Bede,*** cast in the language of art criticism, had already come by the time Eliot wrote this passage. In a letter commenting on the first fourteen chapters of the novel, which he had read in manuscript, John Blackwood, Eliot's publisher, wrote nervously about her depiction of the Reverend Irwine. "The Vicar is a capital fellow," he says, "and the visit to the sick room is very touching, but I wish for the sake of my Church of England friends he had more of 'the root of the matter in him.' However I hope he is to sublime as the story goes on."[7] By using the word "sublime," Blackwood allies himself with the painterly aesthetics of grandeur and nobility outlined by Reynolds and Burke. He seems to hope that the Reverend Irwine, who is rather indolent, will somehow turn into a more thoroughly exemplary and admirable figure, who will produce in the reader appropriate feelings of awe and exaltation. Writing her first novel, Eliot was unusually sensitive to criticism, and Blackwood's complaint emerges in a cartoonish form at the beginning of chapter 17: "'This Rector of Broxton is little better than a pagan!' I hear one of my readers exclaim. 'How much more edifying it would have been if you had made him give Arthur some truly spiritual advice! You might have put into his mouth the most beautiful things—quite as good as reading a sermon'" (1:265). The reference to "beautiful things" is telling here; the spiritual is seen as an aesthetic category, and the imagined critic faults Eliot for failing to meet the standards of ideal beauty. By invoking and defending Dutch painting, which has been repeatedly criticized on similar grounds, Eliot means to challenge the claim that only what is aesthetically pleasing *as object,* what is somehow inherently sublime, picturesque, or beautiful, physically or spiritually, deserves the dignity of representation.

Eliot's defense through the language of painting is thus primarily an argument about the subject matter of art—about the second of Reynolds's two strictures against the Dutch. When she praises the "truthfulness" of the Dutch painters, she means to indicate not their scrupulous depiction of detail and surface, but their decision to depict that "monotonous homely existence" which is the "fate of so many more among my fellow-mortals than a life of pomp or of absolute indigence" (1:268). Dutch art, for Eliot, tells the *representative* truth about human existence—something other paintings have failed to do because they have concentrated on "pomp" or "indigence," on "a world of extremes" (1:270). In between these extremes, Eliot claims, are "common coarse people" (1:270), "the majority of the human race" (1:269), excluded from representation because they have no conventional aesthetic appeal. As Eliot describes these potentially excluded figures, it is clear that she has their class and their association with labor very much in mind:

> [D]o not impose on us any aesthetic rules which shall banish from the region of Art those old women scraping carrots with their work-worn hands, those heavy clowns taking holiday in a dingy pot-house, those rounded backs and stupid weather-beaten faces that have bent over the spade and done the rough work of the world—those homes with their tin pans, their brown pitchers, their rough curs, and their clusters of onions. (1:270)

These genre images stand, in Eliot's argument, for the "common coarse people" who are represented in ***Adam Bede***: carpenters, factory workers, tenant farmers, laborers.[8] Like the morally weak clergyman, socially inferior characters without picturesque appeal would be "banish[ed] from the region of Art" by conventional aesthetic theory.

2

As we have seen, Eliot uses the example of Dutch painting to argue against this exclusion. For her, Dutch painting seems to represent a kind of art whose subject matter is intrinsically neither beautiful nor sublime—in other words, an art which is not, by ordinary cultural standards, recognizably art-like. Since Eliot wants to define her own subject matter in ***Adam Bede*** as that which has been confined to the margins of culture, in a world far from London and middle-class experience, the marginal status of Dutch art in traditional aesthetics is paradoxically helpful to her. Eliot wants to defend the aesthetic dignity of her common rural characters, to show that they are worthy of representation and sympathy, in spite of the prevailing cultural standards. However, talking directly about the situation of marginalized and rural figures is difficult for her in this chapter, despite her intense sympathy, since the easy narrative discourse shared by author and reader in ***Adam Bede*** is situated at the very center of metropolitan culture, in a community acquainted with *Sartor Resartus* and the Foulis Aeschylus, crinolines, silk boots, shepherds in Arcadia, learned men arguing about Hebrew, pictured Madonnas, frustrated actors with monosyllabic parts, Centaurs, statues of Ceres, boyish choristers and musical instruments.[9] The reference to Dutch painting, an art which is not an art, a cultural artifact which is very nearly excluded from culture, enables her to insert rural laborers and artisans uneasily into this discourse. This is an argument made to museum-goers; pointing to a Dutch genre piece is a way to gesture toward the unfashionable rural world while still remaining inside of the museum.

The presence of Dutch pictorial images in chapter 17 is also helpful in that it gives Eliot a relatively simple way to define and embody her marginal subject matter. Throughout the passage, she collapses social, moral, and intellectual marginality into a single aesthetic category—ugliness—which she then represents (and defends) by describing pictures. The problem is that ugliness, like realism, is a kind of negation. It is the deformation of some previously imagined ideal figure—the human figure as painted by Michelangelo and admired by Reynolds, say—and it emerges only through the repeated and violent *deformation* of that figure, as if it were being defaced. And so we read in chapter 17 of "squat figures, ill-shapen nostrils, and dingy complexions," "irregular noses and lips," "a high-shouldered, broad-faced bride," "clumsy, ugly people," "a wife who waddles" (1:268-69). This is description as a physical beating. The problem is acute: because Eliot can only define her characters by reference to figures with which she and her readers are familiar from other representations, and because she genuinely wants to mark the difference between her figures and those which are aesthetically sanctioned, she can only imagine and describe her characters by doing a kind of violence to the conventional figures, distorting them and rendering them grotesque. But when the ugly man is then identified with the laboring man or the village tradesman, when he becomes our principal image for the common men and women George Eliot wants to represent, we are left still with the effects of the abusive description: a broad gap between narrator and character, a rough and disturbing physical presence, a strong sense of the imagined degradation and otherness of these figures. Against all of this, sympathy must labor. Thus the twin projects of first admitting into the sphere of representation what is insistently seen as vulgar, coarse, and stupid, and then engendering sympathy through this same representation necessarily cause Eliot some difficulty. Partly by making use of the analogy to Dutch painting, she has found a way to admit the figures of common men and women into her narrative—as Raymond Williams says, she "restores the real inhabitants of rural England to their places," filling in some of the gaps left by Austen's loose mesh of "neighboring" families—but she has no narrative or social language which will enable her to make sense of them by any means other than negation.[10]

3

I think the presence of the Dutch paintings in this passage helps to mitigate this problem as well as create it, but in order to see how, we will have to place the paintings in another context. By her own account, George Eliot wrote chapter 17 of ***Adam Bede*** in Munich. She and George Henry Lewes left England for Germany on April 7, 1858, after having handed over two more chapters (making sixteen in all) to Blackwood, and they arrived in Munich four days later, on April 11. Eliot later recalled that she had started the second volume, which begins with chapter 17, "in the second week of [her] stay at Munich, about the middle of April"—more precisely, some time after April 18—and that work was "slow and interrupted."[11] It is thus likely that Eliot had only recently completed the passage we have been considering when she wrote about paintings at the Neue Pinakothek in a May 13 letter to Sara Hennell:

> But alas! I *cannot* admire much of the modern German art. It is for the most part elaborate lifelessness. Kaulbach's great compositions are huge charades, and I have seen nothing of his equal to his own Reineke Fuchs. It is an unspeakable relief, after staring at one of his huge pictures, the Destruction of Jerusalem, for example, which is a regular child's puzzle of symbolism, to sweep it all out of one's mind—which is very easily done, for nothing grasps you in it—and call up in your imagination a little Gerard Dow that you have seen hanging in a corner of one of the cabinets. (***Letters,*** 2:454-55)

Eliot's juxtaposition of Kaulbach and Dou in this letter provides an instructive gloss on her reference to Dutch painting in ***Adam Bede.*** It shows us that at a time very near the composition of the famous passage, Dutch painting meant for Eliot simplicity and "unspeakable relief," a respite from the interpretive labor demanded by iconographic signification. For she complains not just about the falseness of Kaulbach's "Destruction of Jerusalem," but about its heavily encoded status: it is a "huge charade," "a child's puzzle of symbolism."

Kaulbach's enormous painting[12] is certainly crowded with meanings: sacred texts held aloft by prophets in the sky, angels blowing trumpets and wielding swords, winged demons, a shining chalice, broken columns, praying groups and huddled masses, soldiers leading women into bondage, the city burning in the background. And like the gestures in a game of charades, the images here are arbitrary and conventional symbols, which must be referred at once to their iconographical meanings to be read properly. We read *through* the images—we decipher them, as if they were elements in a puzzle—hence they do not "grasp" us, as Eliot thinks they should. As is usually the case in such paintings, we read the images only with the conspicuous aid of verbal texts—here the title and inscriptions from Daniel and Luke (once present in the upper corners of the painting but now lost), which refer us to the huge cultural artifact of Christian tradition, which then in turn enables us to collate several different historical enactments of the destruction of Jerusalem (Babylonian, Roman, Apocalyptic) and see them as types of God's awful and righteous indignation and his enduring promise to the chosen.[13] The "Destruction of Jerusalem" thus opens into a narrative, whose temporality includes not only the separate events which make up a single destruction of Jerusalem in 70 AD by Titus—incursion, fear, flight, madness, desolation—but also the story of God's repeated anger at men and women, stretching from the time of the prophets to the final trumpet of the Apocalypse.

Like Lessing, Eliot finds this opening-up into temporality objectionable. In the same letter to Sara Hennell, she complains that since the success of his "Battle of the Huns," "Kaulbach has been concocting these pictures, in which, instead of taking a single moment of reality, and trusting to the infinite symbolism that belongs to all nature, he attempts to give you at one view a succession of events, each represented by some group which may mean 'whichever you please, my little dear'" (***Letters,*** 2:455). In the sardonic mimicry of this last phrase, there is a real impatience with the indeterminacy and caprice of iconographic art, which seems to authorize multiple and layered meanings, this and that and "whichever you please," especially when "a single moment of reality" is transcended.[14]

After this surfeit of convention and arbitrary signification, Eliot finds it an "unspeakable relief" to "sweep it all out of one's mind" and "call up in your imagination a little Gerard Dow you have seen hanging in a corner of one of the cabinets." As Hugh Witemeyer has pointed out, Eliot may be thinking here of "The Spinner's Grace," one of several Dous she might have seen in Munich in 1858, and a painting which she seems to describe in chapter 17.[15] As Eliot turns to this canvas, or one like it, the phrase, "sweep it all out of one's mind," refers us to a gesture of impatience and radical simplification. Eliot wants to wipe out the elaborate symbolic system suggested by Kaulbach's painting and begin anew, in some fresh and purified realm presumably outside of convention, where there is no puzzling iconography, no surfeit of arbitrary meanings, only a simple Dutch interior: woman, table, chair, bowl and jug, spinning wheel, curved and polished surfaces made to catch the light. In the context of such a gesture, Eliot's preference for Dou over Kaulbach seems to entail a rejection of all signification beyond what occurs at what Erwin Panofsky calls the level of "pre-iconographical" description, in which objects are identified as objects and seen in spatial relation to one another.[16] The Dou is a relief because it does not, Eliot thinks, have to be *read,* it is just there, content and sufficient unto itself.

In the light of this letter, it seems clear that Eliot's extended description of Dou-like paintings in chapter 17 of ***Adam Bede*** carries with it suggestions which go far beyond her sympathy for their vulgar subjects. Dutch painting implies for her an aesthetic of simplicity, in which representation is seen as unmediated by the artificial conventions of art and thus untroubled by superimposed meanings.[17] Eliot recognizes, like Ruskin, that any representation is mediated by the consciousness of the artist; in fact, she thinks such mediation is all to the good, since the consciousness of the artist infuses the material with dignity and shows us what is beautiful in it.[18] However, she insists in **"The Natural History of German Life"** that mediation by artistic convention or tradition constitutes a serious flaw. An artist should not rely on types and symbols from earlier representations, Eliot claims; instead, she should represent what she has actually seen, presumably without reference to the artificial history of literary and pictorial depictions. Consider, for example, these complaints about conventional depictions of English peasants:

> But even those among our painters who aim at giving the rustic type of features . . . treat their subjects under the influence of traditions and pre-possessions rather than of direct observation. The notion that peasants are joyous, that the typical moment to represent a man in a smock-frock is when he is cracking a joke and showing a row of sound teeth, that cottage matrons are usually buxom, and village children necessarily rosy and merry, are prejudices difficult to dislodge from the artistic mind, which looks for its subjects into literature instead of life. The painter is still under the influence of idyllic literature, which has always expressed the imagination of the cultivated and town-bred, rather than the truth of rustic life. Idyllic ploughmen are jocund when they drive their team afield; idyllic shepherds make bashful love under hawthorn bushes; idyllic villagers dance in the checquered shade and refresh themselves, not immoderately, with spicy nut-brown ale. But no one who has seen much of actual ploughmen thinks them jocund; no one who is well-acquainted with the English peasantry can pronounce them merry.[19]

It is worth pointing out, I think, that even in her own essay Eliot can only approach "actual ploughmen" by inverting the idyllic images she finds inadequate—ploughmen are *not* jocund, *not* merry, they have *not* always "a row of sound teeth"—or by resorting, as she does a few lines later, to the metaphor of "that melancholy animal the camel," whose form gives her a way to imagine the "slow gaze," "slow utterance," and "heavy slouching walk" of the peasant. But whether her project is realizable or not—and I think it is not—Eliot means to articulate an aesthetic in which the representational or mimetic image—the figure of a rural laborer in a novel, say, or of an old woman saying grace in a painting—can function on its own, by means of a direct relation to nature, without having to derive its force from a created system of artificial correspondences bound to a particular time and place. She holds up "direct observation" and the personally seen "truth of rustic life" as her models, in direct contrast to "idyllic literature" and "the influence of traditions and prepossessions." What I want to stress is that this position tacitly releases the artist from the burden of creating meanings in the process of representation. If the image is just there, a faithful report of what the artist sees (however fuzzily) in nature, then no additional meanings are necessary. In fact, they will only produce falseness and distortion: the opposite of the natural sign, for Eliot, is the sign bent, like Kaulbach's, on pursuing some arcane symbolism of its own, instead of "trusting to the infinite symbolism that belongs to all nature."

4

George Eliot's invocation of Dutch painting in chapter 17 is thus consistent with what might be called the cult of simplicity in ***Adam Bede.*** Distant from the readers of the novel in time and space, the artisans and tenant farmers in ***Adam Bede*** seem to exist in a pared down and purified world, surrounded by unusually clean and polished surfaces. The windows at Jonathan Burge's house are "bright and speckless," and the door-stone is "clean as a white boulder at ebb-tide." On the door-stone stands "a clean old woman, in a dark-striped linen gown" (1:14). Lisbeth Bede is "an anxious, spare, yet vigorous old woman, clean as a snow-drop," with her hair "turned neatly back under a pure linen cap" (1:54). After the saddler tracks dirt, Mrs. Poyser has her kitchen floor "perfectly clean again" in a matter of hours—

> as clean as everything else in that wonderful house-place . . . Surely nowhere else could an oak clock-case and an oak table have got to such a polish by the hand: genuine "elbow polish," Mrs. Poyser called it, for she thanked God she never had any of your varnished rubbish in her house. Hetty Sorrell often took the opportunity, when her aunt's back was turned, of looking at the pleasing reflection of herself in those polished surfaces, for the oak table was usually turned up like a screen, and was more for ornament than for use; and she could see herself sometimes in the great round pewter dishes that were ranged on the shelves above the long deal dinner table, or in the hobs of the grate, which always shone like jasper. (1:105-06)

This emphasis on the clean and well-scrubbed marks the presence of what Eliot wants to imagine as a simple and uncomplicated way of life, a clean and sharply defined world, one which, unlike our own, need not be fussed over and interpreted, as if it were some kind of allegory. At Arthur Donnithorne's birthday dance, the narrator nostalgically recalls the "simple dancing of well-covered matrons" and the "holiday sprightliness of portly husbands," which she sees as opposed to "low dresses and large skirts, and scanning glances exploring costumes, and languid men in lackered boots smiling with double meaning" (1:429).[20] Earlier, in a conversation with the narrator, Adam describes his dawning conviction, as a young man, that the complexities of religious doctrine might be swept out of one's mind:

> "I thought I could pick a hole or two in their notions, and I got disputing wi' one o' the class leaders down at Treddles'on, and harassed him so, first o' this side and then o' that, till at last he said, 'Young man, it's the devil making use o' your pride and conceit as a weapon to war against the simplicity o' the truth.' I couldn't help laughing then, but as I was going home, I thought the man wasn't far wrong. I began to see as all this weighing and sifting what this text means and that text means, and whether folks are saved all by God's grace, or whether there goes an ounce o' their own will to't, was no part o' real religion at all. You may talk o' these things for hours on end, and you'll only be the more coxy and conceited for't. So I took to going nowhere but to church, and hearing nobody but Mr. Irwine, for he said nothing but what was good, and what you'd be the wiser for remembering." (1:276)

When it is opposed, as it is in these passages, to "double meaning" and "weighing and sifting what this text means and that text means," simplicity takes on an epistemological value. It represents the position that knowledge and truth come not from created human meanings, from argument and human discourse, but from some intuited natural source, with which Irwine, the nondoctrinal preacher, is somehow in touch.[21] As we have seen, Eliot associated this position with Dutch paintings like the one she describes in chapter 17. Her gesture toward the pictorial is thus part of a general tendency throughout most of the novel to repress overt signification in favor of the "simple truth."

It may seem ironic that Eliot should use a collection of works of art—Dutch paintings—to argue for the importance of fidelity to simple nature rather than to the complicated conventions of art. Even as she is decrying the influence of conventional precedents, she is herself invoking a graphic precedent to justify and explain her own practice. Here again, though, the marginal status of Dutch art helps to disguise the contradiction, just as Irwine's marginal status as a clergyman helps to disguise the fact that he is creating particular kinds of human meanings himself. Because Dutch art has been excluded from the culturally privileged canons of representation precisely on account of its excessive regard to nature, Eliot can use it as an emblem of "truthfulness." But because it is still art, after all, however marginal, because there is still the presence of the frame and a tradition of viewing, it both authorizes her practice and gives her readers a conventional context within which to place the artisans and laborers in ***Adam Bede.*** In this second capacity, too, the reference to Dutch painting works to suppress the ascription of cultural meanings to figures, because, as a pictorial context invoked in the course of narrative, it has a necessarily stilling and harmonizing effect, even as the narrative tries to destabilize it. Cultural meanings are at home in narrative, in language, where they are created and understood. We supply them to paintings by telling stories about them, by reading images in the light of texts, as we read Kaulbach's "Destruction of Jerusalem." When painting and narrative are brought together, as they are in chapter 17 of ***Adam Bede,*** they have diametrically opposing effects on one another: the narrative tries to discover the cultural significance of the painting, to unpack it by telling a story; but the painting tries to still and defuse the cultural significance of the narrative, by repressing the impulse toward story, holding it in check.[22]

If we return to Eliot's difficulty in representing figures for whom she has no adequate narrative language, the function of this kind of repression in ***Adam Bede*** can be seen quite clearly. By establishing a pictorial context for her figures in the crucial passage in chapter 17, with meaning and narrative suppressed, and then associating that context with nature and simplicity, Eliot is able to depict her artisans and laborers, and even comment on them directly, without fully responding to their disruptive social presence. The sublimating effect of an invoked pictorial context on verbal representation can be seen in microcosm in Eliot's description of the old woman in Dou's "The Spinner's Grace," who is "eating her solitary dinner, while noonday light, softened perhaps by a screen of leaves, falls on her mob-cap, and just touches the rim of her spinning wheel, her stone jug, and all those cheap common things which are the precious necessaries of life to her" (1:268). The implied presence of a frame here changes our response to what is described in words, just as it does in a poem about a photograph, or in Homer's description of the pictures on Achilleus's shield. It is almost as if the ontological status of the represented world changes; the ordinary temporal impulse of narrative is stilled, for a moment at least, and the old woman exists in a timeless pictorial world, where we do not ask the kinds of questions we might otherwise ask: why is this dinner solitary? why should the woman be limited to "cheap common things," the "necessaries of life"? where does she sell what she spins, and at what price? By moving explicitly into the realm of picture, the description represses and deflects these questions, and with them the cultural and ideological significance of the woman. We are invited to concentrate on the quality of the "noonday light," which makes no distinction between the woman's mob-cap and a stone jug, and which gives the scene a static, impersonal repose, something pure and clean, beyond the ordinary concerns of narrative.

This kind of sublimation is important in ***Adam Bede*** because the narrative as a whole insistently returns to the questions which must be suppressed here. When Arthur says casually to one of his grandfather's tenants, "Do you know, Mrs. Poyser, if I were going to marry and settle, I should be tempted to turn you out, and do up this fine old house, and turn farmer myself" (1:117), it is impossible not to feel the injustice of the social division which makes such a remark possible. The implied threat is eventually put into practice by Arthur's grandfather, who tries to change the condition of the Poysers' rental against their interest in order to attract a desirable new tenant. But the remark points more ominously to the central action of the novel, Arthur's seduction of Hetty Sorrel, in the course of which he uses his position for gain with the same unconsciousness he demonstrates in his remark to Mrs. Poyser. With its tragic consequences—child murder, transportation, the blighting of Adam's love—Arthur's action might be read allegorically, in a narrative repeatedly marked by enclosure plans, poaching incidents, talk of labor and rent, and uneasy glances across the harvest table, as a critique of class division and its effects. In fact, Adam tries to read it that way, in the days following Hetty's arrest, when he is full of vengeance. "Ah, and it's right people should know how she was tempted into the wrong way," he says. "It's right they should know it was a fine gentleman made love to her, and turned her head wi' notions" (2:18). But Eliot's whole tendency, as we have seen, is to sweep out of her mind meanings which seem so bound up with culture in favor of what she would see as the simple, natural truth, which is significantly personal rather than social. Her real message, articulated by Irwine after Adam is soundly rebuked, is that there are many "evil consequences . . . folded in a single act of selfish indulgence"—anyone's, presumably, mine, yours, the King of England's—and "evil spreads as necessarily as disease" (2:204-5). That this moral is drawn from Aeschylus and not nature should come as no surprise; in Eliot's novels, as elsewhere, the appeal to what is natural masks a submerged cultural and ideological project of its own, which must have its textual roots someplace.[23]

Overtly artificial signification has its moment, toward the end of ***Adam Bede,*** but only in a scene which masks Adam's class affiliations almost completely, thereby suppressing the social and political tensions which are present elsewhere in the novel and which make the cult of simplicity necessary. Eighteen months after the trial, Adam has turned the room built for Hetty in the Bede cottage into a kind of study, a place with a table and papers and rulers and an open desk, where he writes and draws plans. When he disturbs Dinah dusting there, he might be a Victorian gentleman, standing in the doorway of his gloomy private room. For a moment, the man whose ordinary language in the novel has been a rough country dialect becomes capable of "What! You think I'm a cross fellow at home, Dinah?" and "You don't know the value I set on the very thought of you" (2:308-09). In this comfortable and familiar scene, sophisticated reading is possible: "Those slight words and looks and touches are part of the soul's language; and the finest language, I believe, is chiefly made up of unimposing words, such as "light," "sound," "star," "music,"—words really not worth looking at, or hearing, in themselves, any more than "chips" or "sawdust:" it is only that they happen to be the signs of something unspeakably great and beautiful" (2:310-11). By emphasizing the arbitrary character of the "soul's language," which affixes "unspeakably great and beautiful" meanings to words as unimposing as "chips" and "sawdust," Eliot suggest that the business of signification may not always be simple or natural after all.[24] But this acknowledgement of conventional meanings and interpretive play takes place only when the class tensions at work throughout ***Adam Bede*** have been surreptitiously removed to allow for a conventional love scene. Under the ordinary conditions of the narrative, the values of simplicity and naturalness prevail.

Indeed, as I have tried to argue, these values are a necessary consequence of Eliot's ideological position in ***Adam Bede.*** In order to create the illusion of natural and universally applicable meaning, she must keep in check the narrative's impulse to emphasize social division and its effects on individuals. But her representational intent, announced in chapter 17, is to include figures who highlight social division by their very presence and their resistance to a narrative discourse situated at the center of culture. This is where the famous gesture towards Dutch painting has a crucial function in the novel. By placing the artisans and laborers inside of a frame which suppresses cultural significance at the moment when their presence is most explicitly in question, and by further defining the subject matter of their world as simple and untroubled by meaning, the Dutch painting analogy allows Eliot to clear a small place in ***Adam Bede*** for the working inhabitants of Loamshire, without acknowledging them, as she might have, as a threat.

Notes

1. References to *Adam Bede* follow the Cabinet Edition of George Eliot's works (Edinburgh: Blackwood's, n.d.), with volume and page numbers cited parenthetically in the text. Largely on account of this passage, Dutch painting has served frequently since the publication of *Adam Bede* as a convenient way of imagining George Eliot's "realism," particularly in the early novels. The tendency has been to highlight the exactness and fidelity of Eliot's descriptions and their concern with minute details, as if her work aspired to duplicate the phenomenal world. However, Darrel Mansell, Jr., and Hugh Witemeyer have argued convincingly that Eliot's attitudes toward representation and Dutch paintings are far more complicated than this standard account would suggest. See Mansell, "Ruskin and George Eliot's 'Realism,'" *Criticism* 7 (1965): 203-16, and Witemeyer, *George Eliot and the Visual Arts* (New Haven: Yale Univ. Press, 1979), pp. 106-07.
2. "Defenses of Dutch Painting and the Theory of Realism," *Comparative Literature* 15 (1963): 99.
3. *Discourses on Art,* ed. Robert R. Wark (New Haven: Yale Univ. Press, 1975), pp. 50-51.
4. *A Handbook to the Gallery of British Paintings in the Art Treasures Exhibition* (London: Bradbury and Evans, 1857), p. 16. Witemeyer (p. 216n) identifies the author of this pamphlet as George Scharf.
5. Rev. of *Modern Painters,* 3, *Westminster Review* 65 (1856): 626. Quoted in Mansell, "Ruskin and George Eliot's 'Realism,'" p. 203.
6. John Ruskin, *Modern Painters* (New York: John Wiley and Sons, 1887), 3:5. The quotations below follow this edition, with references to volume and page number cited parenthetically. Demetz (p. 105n) also concludes that the Dutch are "definitely disparaged" in *Modern Painters,* citing the last of the quotations listed here. In *The Realistic Imagination: English Fiction from Frankenstein to Lady Chatterley* (Chicago: Univ. of Chicago Press, 1981), George Levine points out the paradoxical character of Ruskin's aesthetic judgments in this area: "Ruskin, of course, was not a great admirer of the Dutch school, and he was correspondingly unsympathetic to the best fiction written in his lifetime—even when it was written in what the authors might well have felt was a Ruskinian spirit" (p. 208). Levine's entire discussion of "the landscape of reality" (pp. 204-26) is helpful in illuminating the aesthetic context for Eliot's comments in *Adam Bede.*
7. John Blackwood to George Eliot, March 31, 1858, in *The George Eliot Letters,* ed. Gordon S. Haight (New Haven: Yale Univ. Press, 1954), 2:445. Further quotations from this edition will be cited as *Letters* in the text, with references to volume and page.
8. In *George Eliot* (Atlantic Highlands, NJ: Humanities Press International, 1986), a book written primarily for students which nonetheless contains important and original commentary, Simon Dentith observes with some justice that the figures described in chapter 17 do not very closely resemble the characters with whom we are meant to sympathize in *Adam Bede* (pp. 35-36). (See also Gillian Beer, *George Eliot* [Bloomington: Indiana Univ. Press, 1986], p. 65). However, it is not accurate to conclude, as Dentith does, that Eliot's interest in *Adam Bede* is in "*classes* decidedly more respectable" (p. 36; my italics) or that the passage is "little more than a rhetorical flourish in the novel as a whole" (p. 35). Regardless of their good looks or attractive personal qualities, Adam, Seth, Hetty, and Dinah are all, by virtue of their family situations and the work they do, members of the same social and economic class as the figures described in chapter 17, and their presence at the center of *Adam Bede* is thus very much in question when those figures are invoked. (Only the Poysers aspire to anything approaching a "middle-class" condition, and they are, in spite of their ability to hire a few laborers, still finally tenants who are threatened with arbitrary eviction during the course of the novel.) The gap between noble, hard-working Adam and coarser figures like Wiry Ben or the Poysers' laborers suggests not a refusal to extend sympathy to members of a certain class but rather a difficulty in representing them adequately, as I suggest below.
9. Kenny Marotta notices this same tendency toward sophisticated narrative reference in "*Adam Bede* as a Pastoral," *Genre* 9 (1976): 67-68. "Art," he says, "is what the narrator knows and the characters don't";

the narrator reminds us of "his superiority in experience, in philosophy, and even in social class to his subjects" (p. 68).

10. Raymond Williams, *The Country and the City* (New York: Oxford Univ. Press, 1973), p. 168. For further discussion of Eliot's presentation of common people and the ambiguous political substance of *Adam Bede,* see William J. Hyde, "George Eliot and the Climate of Realism," *PMLA* 72 (1957): 147-64; Ian Gregor, "The Two Worlds of *Adam Bede,*" in *The Moral and the Story* (London: Faber and Faber, 1962), pp. 13-32; John Goode, "*Adam Bede,*" in *Critical Essays on George Eliot,* ed. Barbara Hardy (New York: Barnes and Noble, 1970), pp. 19-41; Marotta, "*Adam Bede* as a Pastoral"; Dentith, *George Eliot,* pp. 30-55; Daniel Cottom, *Social Figures: George Eliot, Social History, and Literary Representation* (Minneapolis: Univ. of Minnesota Press, 1987), pp. 83-88; and Mary Jean Corbett, "Representing the Rural: The Critique of Loamshire in *Adam Bede,*" *Studies in the Novel* 20 (1988): 288-301.

11. *George Eliot's Life as Related in Her Letters and Journals,* ed. J. W. Cross (New York: Harper and Bros., 1885), 2:50-51. See also Gordon S. Haight, *George Eliot: A Biography* (New York: Oxford Univ. Press, 1968), pp. 255-60.

12. See Horst Ludwig, ed., *Münchner Maler im 19. Jahrhundert* (Munich: Brückmann, 1982), 2:286.

13. The inscriptions were in Latin. I cite them here (from the reproduction in Ludwig, *Münchner Maler*) along with English translations from the King James Bible: at the upper left, "ET CIVITATEM ET SANCTUARIUM DISSIPABIT POPULUS CUM DUCE VENTURO, ET FINIS EIUS VASTITAS, ET POST FINEM BELLI STATUTA DESOLATIO, DAN IX XXVI" (And the people of the prince that shall come shall destroy the city and the sanctuary; and the end thereof shall be with a flood, and unto the end of the war desolations are determined—Daniel 9:26); at the upper right, "ET CADENT IN ORE GLADII ET CAPTIVI DUCENTUR IN OMNES GENTES, ET JERUSALEM CALCABITUR A GENTIBUS DONEC IMPLEANTUR TEMPORA NATIONUM, LUC XXI XXIV" (And they shall fall by the edge of the sword, and shall be led away captive into all nations: and Jerusalem shall be trodden down of the Gentiles, until the times of the Gentiles be fulfilled—Luke 21:24).

14. Eliot may be mocking a response made by Kaulbach himself; she had visited his studio on April 27 (Cross, *George Eliot's Life,* 2:23).

15. *George Eliot and the Visual Arts,* p. 108. Witemeyer credits Norma Jean Davis and Bernard Williams with identifying the painting in unpublished dissertations (p. 217n).

16. Erwin Panofsky, *Studies in Iconology: Humanistic Themes in the Art of the Renaissance* (1939; repr. New York: Harper and Row, 1962), p. 5.

17. I don't mean to suggest that Dutch paintings actually are unmediated by artistic convention; what is in question here is the view of Eliot and her contemporaries. In a development which would doubtless greatly have surprised them, art critics have begun to argue that Dutch genre paintings are in fact heavily laden with symbolic and allegorical meanings. See, for example, Otto Naumann's reading of Dou's "Girl Chopping Onions" in *Masters of Seventeenth-Century Dutch Genre Painting,* ed. Peter Sutton (Philadelphia: Philadelphia Museum of Art, 1984), in which "the hanging dead bird symbolized the sexual act . . . the empty bird cage is associated with the loss of virtue . . . even the vegetables being prepared [in this painting and another] can be interpreted sexually" (p. 184). Svetlana Alpers argues for a simpler reading of Dutch art in *The Art of Describing: Dutch Art in the Seventeenth Century* (Chicago: Univ. of Chicago Press, 1983).

18. Mansell, "Ruskin and George Eliot's 'Realism,'" pp. 205-07. See also Elizabeth Deeds Ermarth, *Realism and Consensus in the English Novel* (Princeton: Princeton Univ. Press, 1983), pp. 77-78, 225-30, for comments on the relation between consciousness and the objective world in realist fiction.

19. "The Natural History of German Life" (1856), in *Essays of George Eliot,* ed. Thomas Pinney (New York: Columbia Univ. Press, 1963), p. 270.

20. Of course, as Marotta points out ("*Adam Bede* as a Pastoral," p. 62), there are smiles with double meanings in the pastoral scene Eliot is describing here—and it is worth noting that in the passage quoted above Hetty uses Mrs. Poyser's "polished surfaces" as mirrors. In both cases, the corrupting and complicating presence of sexuality shows itself to be in tension with Eliot's idealizing vision of the "simple" rural world.

21. In "Silence in the Courtroom: George Eliot and the Language of Morality in *Adam Bede,*" *Essays in Literature* 13 (1986): 43-55, Timothy Pace notes that "one imaginative impulse [in *Adam Bede*] depicts the deep truths of man's spiritual and moral experience—truths that define how a society can be united in a shared vision of right moral conduct—as essentially beyond the reach of language" (p. 43).

22. Although I do not think he would put the matter in precisely these terms, Martin Meisel often suggests a tension between narrative and pictorial elements in representational art in *Realizations: Narrative, Pictorial, and Theatrical Arts in Nineteenth-Century England* (Princeton: Princeton Univ. Press, 1983). About a meeting between Arthur and Hetty in *Adam Bede,* for example, he writes: "In George Eliot's scene, a developing relationship is crystallized in a situation, an eloquent tableau, isolated from the flow of time, or rather concentrating that flow into a charged stasis" (p. 60). See also his interesting

discussion of the political implications of narrative and pictorial elements in David Wilkie's paintings and the melodramas based on them (pp. 142-65).

23. For comments on the Aeschylean theme in *Adam Bede,* see F. R. Leavis, Introduction to the Signet *Adam Bede* (New York: New American Library, 1961), pp. x-xi. On Eliot's preference for individual rather than social morality, see Williams, *The Country and the City,* p. 180, and Goode, "*Adam Bede,*" p. 29. Dentith points out suggestively that "in the act of recognition, in the act of seeing 'someone like me' beneath those 'superficial' class differences, their fundamental, material importance can be cancelled" (*George Eliot,* pp. 53-54).

24. Dianne Sadoff treats this passage from a different perspective in "Nature's Language: Metaphor in the Text of *Adam Bede,*" *Genre* 11 (1978): 411-12. See also Pace, "Silence in the Courtroom," p. 45.

Mark Warren McLaughlin (essay date 1994)

SOURCE: "*Adam Bede*: History, Narrative, Culture," in *Victorians Institute Journal,* Vol. 22, 1994, pp. 55-83.

[*In the following essay, McLaughlin examines the historical and ideological foundations of the English middle class, and identifies Eliot's* Adam Bede *as a narrative attempt to normalize and legitimize this growing segment of the population.*]

Late in October 1857, Engels wrote to Marx about the economic crisis then developing in England. Engels, who had predicted "a *dies irae* like no other," now thought the times propitious: "*Nous avons maintenant de la chance,*" he wrote (Marx and Engels 197). Marx agreed that luck was on their side and he wrote that he could do little else besides work on what would become the *Grundrisse* and keep records of the present crisis. Over the next several months the crisis steadily developed into "one of the worst depressions of the nineteenth century" (Hughes, *Fluctuations* 30) and seemed to portend a worldwide economic collapse. Though Marx and Engels looked on expectantly, other middle-class intellectuals were less concerned with revolution—England's survival of 1848 had largely allayed that fear—than they were with a society paralyzed by working-class discontent with middle-class leadership. Out of the famines, depressions, labor unrest, and threat of revolution in the earlier decades, mid-Victorian England was emerging as a cohesive culture organized by middle-class beliefs and practices that appeared genuinely consensual (Briggs; Davidoff and Hall; Hobsbawm; H. Perkin; Stone; Tholfsen). As Engels noted at this time, "the ultimate aim of this most bourgeois of all nations would appear to be the possession, *alongside the bourgeoisie,* of a bourgeois aristocracy and a bourgeois proletariat"(344). The economic crisis, however, renewed the threat to the middle class's project of a consensual culture. The moral and economic values it had promulgated as constitutive of that culture—the values of improvement, of class cooperation and class mobility, and of the gendered division of labor—seemed unmasked by the material facts of falling wages, unemployment, and spreading poverty (Hughes, "Commercial"). By early October 1858, however, the depression had abated. A disappointed and mystified Engels reported to Marx that business had suddenly turned "tremendously good"; all signs of the crisis had disappeared.

George Eliot's ***Adam Bede,*** begun late in October 1857 and completed mid-November 1858, took shape against this background of consensus and crisis, and I will argue that, as a professional member of the middle class, Eliot attempted to mediate the threat of cultural disruption by providing in ***Adam Bede*** a normative moral and political narrative that celebrates the historical origins and ideological foundations of a middle class which would transform class-structured society into its own image. The narrative of Adam's rise from worker to owner articulates the fundamental beliefs and practices of mid-Victorian consensus and stakes Eliot's claim for her narrative as "a real instrument of culture" (***L*** 3: 44). But even as that narrative celebrates middle-class values and circulates images of their culturally constructive powers, inherent ideological contradictions finally disrupt the narrative and mock the celebration. This formal fracture originates in Eliot's emerging critical understanding of the normalizing and regulatory cultural forces that empowered middle-class men and marginalized women. While Eliot's apparent faith in middle-class values led her to resist critical conclusions, her "faithful account" of the cultural contradictions circumscribing women's lives suggests possibilities for transforming—for reconstructing—that culture.

As modern anthropologists and social theorists have argued, narratives are central to the construction of culture.[1] Narratives circulate public images of the way "people in a given social environment organize and give meaning to their lives" (Bellah 39); narratives define and communicate certain norms, values, and behaviors and thus help to organize culture. Recent explorations of narrative's participation in what John Bender calls "the ongoing process of cultural construction" (xv) have focused on the realist novel. The foundational premise of that literary form to offer "a full and authentic report of human experience" (Watt 32) together with its historic entanglement with and replacement of prescriptive conduct books (Gilmour 9; Armstrong 96-160) make the realistic novel a potentially powerful system for structuring social understanding and thereby organizing social behavior. As Bender argues, "Novelistic discourse becomes part of the culture's means of understanding" (3). And this is almost precisely George Eliot's understanding of the powers and purposes of narrative. For Eliot, narratives derive their cultural instrumentality from the representational powers of language. Writing in 1856, in a review essay that works up the aesthetic and political theories that govern her narrative practice, Eliot asserted that language exerts its representational powers by virtue of the "images that are habitually associated with ... collective terms" (***E*** 267). The images that most concerned Eliot here were those represented by the collective terms "'the people,' 'the masses,' 'the proletariat,' 'the peasantry'" (***E*** 268). If the images evoked by those terms were widely informed by experience, she confidently asserts, they could represent "all the essential facts" of the named object (***E*** 267). But Eliot was equally certain that those who "theorize" and "legislate" on behalf of "'the people'" had been misinformed and misled by narrative "misrepresentations"—by the "opera peasants," "idyllic ploughmen," and sentimental hirelings (***E*** 270-71) of narratives that are, for Eliot, ethically and ideologically complicit in the construction of culture. Narratives that circulate artistic conventions in place of an authentic image of "human life" (270), Eliot argues, constitute "a grave evil" in their perverse misdirection of social sympathy. Narratives that truthfully record "the life of the People," on the other hand, possess the power to construct a cohesive culture: such faithful representation, she claims, "will guide our sympathies rightly, . . . check our theories and direct their application" to the linking of "the higher classes with the lower" and thus obliterate "exclusiveness" (270-72). In her affiliative conversion of W. H. Riehl's argument, Eliot suggests that what is needed to counteract misinformed political representation, and so to develop a culture based on a true understanding of difference and on class-transcending sympathy, is a narrative of "the natural history of our social classes" (272). Such a narrative will represent the culture's "vital connexion with the past" by recording the "process of development" in which inherited "social conditions" have intertwined with the "roots" of human nature and so produced the "perfect ripeness of the seed." Truthful narrative will, in Eliot's intricate metaphor, record and assist in the generation of culture.[2]

In ***Adam Bede,*** the procedure by which Eliot will mobilize her images of human life to enact their culturally constitutive functions is signalled by the novel's epigraph:

> So that ye may have
> Clear images before your gladdened eyes
> Of nature's unambitious underwood
> And flowers that prosper in the shade. And
> when
> I speak of such among the flock as swerved
> Or fell, those only shall be singled out
> Upon whose lapse, or error, something more
> Than brotherly love may attend.
>
> (*The Excursion,* 6: 651-58)

Mindful of Bakhtin's claims that such "clear images" are "always ideologically demarcated"—that the action and discourse of characters construct or incarnate a specific ideological order ("Discourse" 335)—we can see that ***Adam Bede***'s "clear images . . . of nature's unambitious underwood" were designed to augment her readers' associative understanding and so to produce social sympathy—an energy urgently needed, during an epoch of contested consensus, to forestall cultural disruption. "We are children of a large family," the narrator avers, and we must learn to "help each other the more" (4, xxvii, 298).

Looked at in this way, ***Adam Bede*** appears as a much more historically engaged narrative than is traditionally recognized. In contrast to an interpretive tradition that construes ***Adam Bede*** as a "relatively static picture of life" which either presents "less a process of development than a restoration of a static order" (Shuttleworth 22, 24) or reaffirms a pastoral image of "traditional community" (Graver 95), I want to show, by developing ideas advanced by feminist critics like Sedgwick, that the narrative is hypermobile: it engages the contested triumph of the middle class even as it circulates images subversive of that consolidation of power. And in contrast to another strong line in ***Adam Bede***'s literary history best epitomized in John Goode's claims that the narrative is a dehistoricized version of historical reality (21), I want to demonstrate that ***Adam Bede*** is thoroughly historicized both in the images it deploys and in the complex of values and beliefs that inform and motivate those images.[3]

. . . . .

> People will not look forward to posterity, who never look backward to their ancestors.
>
> Edmund Burke, *Reflections on the Revolution in France.*

With a drop of ink Eliot begins her narrative and conjures an Egyptian sorcerer. The single drop of ink holds whole worlds, and the sorcerer will disclose before the reader's earnest gaze "far-reaching visions of the past." But as the instability of that phrase suggests, the past is not inert. Mesmerized vision may reach far into the past, but the gaze will reverse itself, and the disclosed vision will reach through implication to the Victorian present. The past reappears with Eliot's necromantic trope, and this re-vision will enable readers to construe its lessons.[4]

Initially the customary community of Hayslope in 1799 appears to be contained and supervised by an "ancient family" and the church: the Donnithorne Arms stand at one entrance to the village and the churchyard at the other (1, ii, 10). But those emblems of power betoken profound cultural changes: this ancient landed family now needs the supplemental income of the inn, and the parsonage lies vacant. Power and cultural vitality are now located elsewhere—in grim Stoneyshire, with its cotton mill, and at the Poysers' Hall Farm, rising, as the narrator's extended commercial simile makes clear, in middle-class prosperity on the estate of a defunct and displaced country squire:

> The history of the house is plain now. . . . Like the life in some coast-town that was once a watering-place, and is now a port, where the genteel streets are silent and grass-grown, and the docks and warehouses busy and resonant, the life at the Hall has changed its focus, and no longer radiates from the parlour, but from the kitchen and the farmyard. Plenty of life there! (1, vi, 70-71)

Mrs. Poyser's "handsome eight-day clock" is a sure sign to Eliot's mid-Victorian readers of the middle-class status of these substantial tenant farmers.[5] So formidable is the

Poysers' middle-class vitality that they will not only face down Squire Donnithorne's threat (4, xxxii, 352-57), they will also come to supplant their landlord as the center of communal rituals. The Poysers' Harvest Supper, having replaced by book's end the cultural function of Donnithorne feasting, provides an apt emblem of the new cultural order. It is, the narrator claims, a goodly sight—that table with Martin Poyser at its head and his workers arrayed around him (6, liii, 527).[6]

This displacement signals Eliot's understanding of the dynamics of mid-Victorian culture formation, less a "restoration of a static order" than a record of cultural disruption (initiated by Arthur's "irrevocable wrong") and cultural transformation (signaled by the Harvest Supper and, as we shall see, Adam's admission of Arthur back into the community), the narrative apparently registers a crucial moment in the suturing of a declining but still powerful gentry with a rising middle class.[7] But, against that, I would point to the ultimately *contestatory* values, practices, and beliefs which structure and sanction the progress of the narrative and which disclose the historical seed and roots of mid-Victorian culture.

At one level, of course, ***Adam Bede*** valorizes class cooperation and endorses the suture of gentry and middle class. Mid-Victorian social discourse authorized the naturalness of the hierarchical social order. As Mrs. Poyser remarks, "there's them as is born t' own the land, and them as is born to sweat on 't" (4, xxxii, 353). This naturalized order was typically invested with sacralized injunctions. Mrs. Poyser continues, "and I know it's christened folks's duty to submit to their betters as fur as flesh and blood 'ull bear it." But Mrs. Poyser registers a middle-class resistance to such ordination of rank, a resistance that becomes visible when we note its total absence in another late 1850s text on the social order, William Sewell's sermon on "Gentlemanly Manners."

> We have, I think, in England, owing to the freedom of our constitution, and the happy providential blessings which God has heaped upon us, followed the division of mankind which God himself has made. . . . Some men He has made to rule and govern; some to be ruled and governed. (Gilmour 89)

Adam initially ratifies this static, cooperative order: he wishes "for no better lot than to work under" Arthur because he believes Arthur fulfills his social role. "He's one o' those gentlemen as wishes to do the right thing, and to leave the world a bit better than he found it, something that every man may do" according to class function: "whether he's gentle or simple, whether he sets a good bit o' work going and finds the money, or whether he does the work with his own hands" (3, xxiv, 275). But the formal dynamics of Eliot's narrative, as they propel Adam's rise from the working to the owning class, ratify instead the middle-class's emerging (and ambivalent) resistance to the gentry.

In this community with "no rigid demarcation of ranks" (1, ix, 97), Adam's image most fully incarnates Eliot's cultural project. Though Eliot is careful to mark him with "the blood of the peasant" (1, iv, 48), his discourse is profoundly inflected by his veneration of "the great works and inventions" of the industrializing culture, and he markedly embodies and enacts middle-class values and beliefs (1, i, 6). While Eliot claimed to have drawn Adam from certain particulars of her father Robert Evans (***L*** 2: 503), Joseph Wiesenfarth has shown that she also drew Adam from Samuel Smiles's biography of George Stephenson, the pioneering railway magnate (163); I would add that Eliot's emplotment of Adam's story matches Smiles's emplotment of Stephenson's life as a bourgeois success story. Both Evans and Stephenson exemplified the entrepreneurial hopes and beliefs of the Victorian middle class. As Smiles proclaimed in *Self-Help,* "What some men are, all without difficulty might be." Smiles's 1859 tract for the middle class (also produced in the face of the mid-century economic crisis) articulates the regulatory ideal of social mobility through hard work and "improvement" that Adam's narrative trajectory exemplifies. When Adam thinks of a future life with Hetty, for example, he pulls back at the prospect of a "growing poverty with a growing family" (2, xix, 214). And he plans to establish a small business to manufacture household furniture, build up his savings, and "get beforehand with the world" (215). The very terms of Adam's "calculations" evoke his association with the entrepreneurial ideal. In the anachronistic language of consumerism, Adam imagines housewives in "raptures" with his products and filled with "melancholy longing" for their possession (215). This investment of Adam's working-class image with middle-class aspirations indicates Eliot's principal historicizing strategy. The "mirror" of history, held in "a single drop of ink," reflexively reveals the present lodged in the past (1, i, 1).

Adam's hopes are pinned to his devotion to work, and he is a Carlylean avatar some thirty years before the fact. "His work, as you know, had always been a part of his religion," the narrator explains, "and from very early days he saw clearly that good carpentry was God's will" (6, li, 498). Throughout, Eliot invests ordinary labor with ennobling and therapeutic powers. As Carlyle had written in *Past and Present* (1843), "even in the meanest sorts of Labour, the whole soul of man is composed into a kind of real harmony" (196). By the lights of the professional middle class, common labor possessed an innate dignity capable of converting even menial tasks to vocation and noble duty. The middle class's idealization of work was a driving force in its discursive struggles to define the emergent culture. By glorifying work it legitimated its own acquisitive entrepreneurial impulses, sanctified "improvement," and attempted to regulate working-class impatience with the filtering process of a putatively open but class-structured society (Briggs; Tholfsen, *Working Class* 140-49).

The success of the middle class's ideological project required as well the wresting of cultural—if not political—power from the upper classes. Eliot participates in this discursive struggle by disclosing the class-bound aspirations and assumptions motivating Arthur's transgression. From Arthur's childhood exchange of a pencil box for a poor man's broth (4, xxix, 318) to his seduction of Hetty, Eliot discloses the failure of this "would be" "model of an English gentleman" (1, xii, 125) to perform his class-defined custodial function. It is not just a Carlylean "abdication on the part of the governors" that Eliot represents, however. Through implicit and explicit comparisons of Adam and Arthur, Eliot proposes the middle class's greater ability to sustain civil community. As Adam commands Arthur to do his proper duty toward Hetty, "in this thing we're man and man" (5, xxviii, 315). Eliot leaves no doubt about which of these two exemplary characters better performs his cultural functions. By book's end Arthur will have been exiled from the community; and as final testament to the triumph of middle-class entrepreneurial values over the gentry's landed values, Eliot offers the image of Adam, the new owner of Jonathan Burge's timberyard, admitting the "shattered" Arthur back into the community. Significantly, Arthur now adopts Adam's language, indicating, as a Bakhtinian analysis would demonstrate, that he has come to accept Adam's cultural values: "But you told me the truth," Arthur tells Adam, "when you said to me once, 'There's a sort of wrong that can never be made up for'" (Epilogue, 551; Bakhtin, "Speech Genres" 95-98).

That triumph, as Sedgwick argues, is accomplished "over the dead, discredited, or disempowered body of a woman" (137). In the final section of this paper, I will explore the initiation of Eliot's critical consciousness of just this feature of the middle class's rise to and consolidation of hegemony. But first I want to focus on the strategies Eliot used to insert her narrative into the cultural contest for authority. Although Eliot's deployment of these narrative devices is motivated by her desire to secure readers' commitment to the triumphal history she narrates, they nonetheless work to expose the cultural truths that ultimately disrupt the narrative.

. . . . .

> But not a polype for a long, long while could even G. detect after all his reading; so necessary is it for the eye to be educated by objects as well as ideas.
>
> "Recollections of Ilfracombe, 1856"

Eliot's narrative celebration of middle-class values powerfully intervened in mid-Victorian social discourse. Readers recorded the profound sense of reality that the narrative produced: Dickens claimed that ***Adam Bede*** had "taken its place among the actual experiences and endurances" of his life (***L*** 3: 114), and Sir Theodore Martin wrote to John Blackwood that "one almost forgets it is a book and loses himself in the reality of the incidents" (***L*** 2: 42). The reviewer for the *Westminster* suggests the cultural functions performed by Eliot's narrative: "[Eliot's] work reads like an authentic history; the actors impress us as real men and women, who, being what they were, could not have spoken or acted other than they did" (269). The "general influence" of this history, wrote E. S. Dallas, is "to draw us nearer to each other by showing how completely we are one"; ***Adam Bede*** reveals, he had written earlier, "that there is not the mighty difference . . . usually assumed between high and low, rich and poor" (Carroll 131-33; 79). ***Adam Bede***'s participation in the construction of just such a middle-class culture as Dallas evokes was achieved through the agency of certain narrative devices—which could be called figurations of reading—that promoted specific interpretive strategies for reading the narrative. We will see that these strategies direct reading outward, into the circumambient cultural context and thus educate readers' eyes to the "objects"—the "real breathing men and women" (2, xvii, 180)—standing behind the "ideas"—the representative "clear images"—circulating in narrative.

Perhaps Eliot's most obvious strategy is her deployment of characterized readers. The most famous of these is the "idealistic friend" who appears in Chapter 17: "'This Rector of Broxton is little better than a pagan!' I hear one of my readers exclaim" (178). Drawing on a familiar literary convention, Eliot here constructs an impugned reader—characterized as deficient in the sympathy or understanding necessary to appreciate the story and thus in need of reading instruction. However, where Thackeray and Sterne admonish their characterized readers to be more attentive, Eliot draws out the political implications of her educative project. The impugned reader here serves not only as a foil directing readers' comprehension of character and action but more importantly as an object lesson in class tolerance. For here the characterized reader is presented not only as objecting to Eliot's realism but as rejecting the "low phase of life" brought before ungladdened eyes. The narrator in direct converse with a resistent reader then must argue for the "faithful representing of common-place things." This phase of life is in itself beautiful and needs representing, as witness Vermeer, Teniers, and de Hooch, but more needful still is the extension of sympathy to all phases of life that this art of the commonplace promotes:

> These fellow-mortals, every one, must be accepted as they are. . . . and it is these people—amongst whom your life is passed—that it is needful you should tolerate, pity, and love: it is these more or less ugly, stupid, inconsistent people, whose movements of goodness you should be able to admire—for whom you should cherish all possible hopes, all possible patience. (2, xvii, 179)

By marking this reader with ethically negative signs of a want of sympathy and by impugning this reader's interpretive strategies and class bias, Eliot promotes a specific strategy for reading that will school readers in the moral exigencies and cultural imperatives of class tolerance.

Eliot also deploys a second kind of characterized reader who, though perceptive and sharing the narrator's moral economy, must nonetheless be carefully directed to the correct interpretation of character and action and, from that point, be coaxed to turn outward an enlarged understanding. This reader is not as fully characterized as the impugned reader. In ***Adam Bede*** and elsewhere, the directed reader is evoked by the narrator's simple reference to "you."[8] Though at times directed readers appear on the verge of a mistake, usually they have come only to a limited perception of a character or action. The narrator, so close to this reader as to be able to read the reader's mind, either quickly dispels the misperception or takes up the reader's thought and then points to the wider human applicability of the represented action.

Adam Bede is freighted with such engagements, but for my purposes the richest appears with the narrator's tour of Adam's working day:

> Adam, you perceive, was by no means a marvellous man, nor, properly speaking, a genius, yet I will not pretend that his was an ordinary character among workmen; and it would not be at all a safe conclusion that the next best man you may happen to see with a basket of tools over his shoulder and a paper cap on his head had the strong conscience and the strong sense, the blended susceptibility and self-command, of our friend Adam. (2, xix, 217)

The political implications of the interpretation fostered by this interaction between narrator and characterized reader are obvious. Although the incalculably diffuse effect of workers like Adam may have produced "no discernible echo" beyond their neighborhood, "you" are sure to find traces of it in "some good piece of road, some building, some application of mineral produce, some improvement in farming practice" by which their "masters" were made "the richer" by their work (217). Working-class heroes like Adam, unless they move upward as does he, are like the dependable "main screw" in the machine of production; and their middle-class masters know their heroic—but ultimately replaceable—worth (218).[9]

By presenting these characterized readers, the narrator elaborates a specific strategy of interpretation that directs readers' attentions beyond the text to the world of class-organized society. Readers are able to read outward, in part, because of the particular narrative contract Eliot has struck with them. Organized by shared "paradigms for understanding reality," ***Adam Bede*** purports to register truthful data of "'the people.'"[10] Eliot's readers learn that by accepting Adam as a veritable representative they will participate in the pleasures of reading a story about life-like characters and they will learn "all the essential facts" about the working class he represents. This way of reading, as I have been arguing, was designed to affirm the emerging middle-class culture. But for this approach to work at all, Eliot needed both to secure the narrator's position as the central means for controlling interpretation and to demonstrate the narrative's power to constitute community.

Eliot secures the narrator's controlling position by raising what we might call the problematics of reading. Eliot represents her characters' attempts to understand each other as attempts to *read* each other. The interpretive operations of this "natural" reading are not always trustworthy, since most often in this novel characters *mis*read each other. As the narrator pointedly reminds readers, "Nature has her language, and she is not unveracious; but we don't know all the intricacies of her syntax just yet, and in a hasty reading we may happen to extract the very opposite of her real meaning" (1, xv, 155). To learn "comprehension," characters must "learn the art of vision," and this through the "hard experience" of life (163). In a narrative of largely tragic effect, comprehension comes through suffering. Adam misreads Hetty's character; Irwine draws incorrect inferences from Arthur's hypothetical narrative of infatuation; and Adam must then learn the language of fellow feeling from the "terrible scorching light" that illuminates at last the "hidden letters" of a suffering caused by multiple misreadings (4, xxvii, 303; 2, xix, 214). Even when characters are engaged in textual reading, that activity too is seriously questioned.[11] Had Arthur comprehended the *Lyrical Ballads,* Wordsworth's "The Thorn" might have instructed him on the likely outcome of his infatuation with Hetty.[12] And when Dinah turns to the Bible for directions, her interpretations invariably prove ineffectual—as when she tries to guide Hetty in "The Two Bedrooms"—or tragically wrong—as when she leaves Hayslope and the troubled Hetty for Snowfield. With reading so insistently questioned, the narrator stands as the central means for controlling interpretive operations.

Perhaps not surprisingly, the narrator, like the characters, is "ideologically demarcated," and this signals, too, Eliot's affirmation of middle-class leadership. Even the most casual pieces of discourse—for example, the description of Mr. Casson, a mere bystander, by reference to astronomy and Milton (1, ii, 10)—reveal the markings of the professed intellectual whose vast learning is a resource for cultural and political guidance. As Harold Perkin and others have demonstrated, this thoroughly middle-class "learned class" functioned, in Carlyle's words, as "the modern guides of Nations" (250-72; *Past and Present* 32). Indeed, the difficulty that we feel in referring to the narrator's gender bespeaks Eliot's own attempt to cover any traces of interestedness. Above the accidents of class, history, and gender, the professional intellectual gives access to "the people" and frames their "natural" social relations.[13]

Demonstrating how such narratives intervene in organizing society, Eliot constructed potent images of narrative's capacity to constitute community. These figurations of narrative power are especially purposeful in a text depicting the threat of communal dissolution and composed in a time of pervasive economic crisis. In the first and most obvious image, Dinah preaching on the unenclosed green, narrative visibly constitutes community. For it is Dinah's simple narration that brings together the diverse inhabitants of Hayslope. Dinah's lesson assembles the community and sustains it by assurance—no communally-generated critique of social oppression here. What Dinah narrates is of course not a message for "the poor workmen," but reassurance that economy is irrelevant, that of the one thing needful there is "'Enough for all, enough for each, / Enough for evermore'" (1, ii, 29).[14]

More powerfully still for the anxious times during which ***Adam Bede*** was composed, narrative is represented as redemptive—as providing the necessary power to reestablish disrupted community. Such a redeeming image appears at a crucial juncture in the novel. Adam, "this brave active man," has been made "powerless" in the face of "irremediable evil and suffering." He awaits news of Hetty's trial when Bartle Massey returns from the court of justice. It is at this point that the novel's famous secular communion takes place. It is crucial to note, however, that Adam will not partake until he has received Bartle's narration of the trial. Adam is insistent. Four times he urges Bartle to "Tell me" (5, xlii, 437-39); and he will hear the story out before he receives the bread and wine. That secularized communion signals Adam's completed rehabilitation from hardness. But what motivates his transformation, at least its final stages, is Bartle's narration of suffering and communal dissolution. For it is the story of the Poysers' failure to "stand by" Hetty that provokes Adam's affiliative claim—"I'll stand by her—I'll own her"—and leads to his vow against hardness.

Images of narrative's power to constitute or to restore community further educate readers' eyes to objects figured by ideas. In apprehending those images, Eliot's Victorian readers would learn that the narratives they share are themselves part of the bindings of community. The political community organized by ***Adam Bede*** would discover the sources of its own community. Gazing at that "far-reaching vision of the past," Eliot's narratively educated readers would see the historical development of the moral and economic determinants of the world they now live in. That "authentic history," by its engagement of readers' emotional and cognitive capacities, reproduced a powerful structure of understanding that gave moral sanction as well as consensual intelligibility to the middle class's hegemonic actions.

. . . . .

But even as Eliot celebrates the triumph of middle-class values, cultural contradictions disrupt the narrative and mock the celebration. As readers have long recognized, the marriage of Adam and Dinah in Book 6 vitiates the narrative's ethical dynamics.[15] Narrative progress—the central organizing plot—is driven by a Feuerbachian growth-through-suffering to Adam's enlarged sympathy and understanding. His affiliative claim to "own" Hetty even in his deepest heartbreak and his "feeling his own pain merged in sympathy for Arthur" at the conclusion of Book 5 mark the completion of Adam's transformation and thus signal the narrative's formal completion.[16] The power of the narrative to instill sympathy and admiration for Adam, as the plot brings him to this point, gives rhetorical force to the values he incarnates and advances. Because Adam's middle-class beliefs have sustained him and ennobled his suffering, readers have been led to entertain those ideologically demarcated values as genuinely virtuous; they have organized, in Alasdair MacIntyre's terms, the *internal* end of Adam's moral and psychological transformation (190-91). Moreover, because these values are mutually intelligible to all classes, their public circulation works to consolidate consensual culture. As we have seen, Eliot has taken great pains to insert her representative images into the discursive practices shaping mid-Victorian culture.

But the addition of Book 6 haunts the narrative, to appropriate Eliot's protesting words, with the "base and selfish, even . . . blasphemous spirit" of compensation (6, liv, 541). As Adam reflects on his growing love for Dinah:

> I should never ha' come to know that her love 'ud be the greatest o' blessings to me, if *what I counted a blessing* hadn't been wrenched and torn away from me, and left me with a greater need, so as I could crave and hunger for a greater and better comfort. (liii, 526; my emphasis)

Adam now discovers that his suffering was based on a miscalculation of love, and that discovery attenuates his pain and provides him with ample compensation in the "greater and better comfort" of Dinah. Those internally defined and directed values are shown now to be merely instrumental to the *external* ends of entrepreneurial success and sexual compensation.[17] Instead of an "irrevocable evil" with radically proliferating consequences, evil is now contained and effaced by Adam's greater happiness and Arthur's return. Instead of living out an authentic and narratively sanctioned vocation, Dinah is reduced to "a convenient household slave" (6, l, 499). Instead of a narrative endorsement of suffering as an agent of personal and cultural transformation, there is now an undeniable sense that Hetty has suffered solely to promote Adam's deeper happiness. These irrepressible reversals countermand both the ethical dynamics of the narrative and Eliot's defense of middle-class values.

Eliot's fracturing of narrative form and disabling of its cultural project derive from her subversive understanding of the cultural contradictions that empowered middle-class men and marginalized women. Whether we argue that Eliot's understanding arose out of the self-divided contest of "the conscious conservative moralist" with "the subconscious subversive" within, as Dorothea Barrett does (32-33), or was part of her incipient critical consciousness, as I do, it is clear that Eliot's "faithful account" of this cultural feature renders it as a cultural problem.[18] Eliot backs away from either resolving or fully critiquing the problem, but we can see in the development of Dinah's and Hetty's plots disturbances that register the emergence of Eliot's more critical assessment of middle-class hegemony.

I want to return now to Sedgwick's argument about the historical transference of power enacted in ***Adam Bede.*** She argues that ***Adam Bede*** records in Dinah's plot the "genealogy of the English middle-class family" (145) as that structure was reorganized by cultural changes produced in England's industrialization. While Sedgwick sees the narrative as exemplifying Eliot's "gentle defense of the status quo" (145), I want to say again that this line of the narrative works to disrupt the defense and begins to lay out the possibility of cultural transformation. Where Eliot records Mrs. Poyser's powerful participation in the "household economy" of the farm (Tilly and Scott 227-28)—she makes "one quarter o' the rent" and saves "another quarter" (4, xxxii, 355)—Eliot also exposes the middle class's disempowering regulation of women's roles and opportunities in Dinah's exchange of her vocation for marriage to Adam. As Sedgwick argues, this "direct translation" from power to powerlessness is coincident with the transference of the gentry's "moral authority" (an authority, I would add, exemplified only in Arthur's narratively ironized *aspirations* to it) to the "newly bourgeois" Adam (157-58).

This narrative intertwining of reconfigured gender roles and class status signals the historicized weave of Eliot's text with its cultural context. As Marion Shaw asserts, "In this George Eliot accurately indicates the importance of an ideal marriage as a factor, perhaps the major factor, in the establishment of middle-class hegemony" (36).[19] And it also marks out a site for the possibility of cultural change. That is to say, while Barrett and Nancy Paxton, among others, are right, I believe, to see that Dinah's choice dramatizes Eliot's analysis of the incompatibility, for women in the emerging culture, of vocation and sexual fulfillment (Barrett 43; Paxton 68), I would want to add that the standing unease of the Epilogue was designed to foreground, and perhaps to promote, dissatisfaction with these culturally constrained options. While Adam congratulates himself for approving Dinah's submission to the Methodist Conference's prohibition against female preaching, Seth—a figure whom Eliot has used from the first to highlight truths that Adam neglects (see 1, i, 6, where Seth turns Adam's middle-class sermon on its head)—protests this bondage of "Christian liberty," and Dinah attempts to shift attention from this "standing subject of difference." Further, Dinah's translation from power to powerlessness is figured in her translation from the angel of the resurrection (Lisbeth and Adam remark on Dinah's likeness to a picture in the old family Bible [6, li, 509]) to the "angel in the house" of the Epilogue, a translation that at least some of Eliot's mid-Victorian readers noted.[20] Finally, this line of the plot, as I have been arguing, produces a parodic image of the central values of emerging middle-class culture. By disclosing the sacrifice of autonomy involved in Dinah's translation from itinerant preacher to housebound wife, Eliot reveals Adam's own illusion of self-sufficiency and the hollowness of the culture's individualist ethos that he exemplifies.[21]

Hetty's story, of course, enacts Eliot's middle-class critique of aristocratic morality. Arthur's seduction of Hetty provides an irrevocable image of the gentry's violation of their custodial obligations as trusted stewards of the community (Thompson 6; H. Perkin 277-90). But Hetty's story also registers Eliot's critique of middle-class patriarchal assumptions. It is after all the Poysers' treatment of their penniless niece as little more than a domestic servant that provokes Hetty's adolescent fantasies of luxurious rescue (1, ix, 98-99). Uneducated and offered no opportunity to become productive in the household economy, Hetty, as the narrator makes clear, both foolishly and understandably fashions her dreams around Arthur. And though severely limited by her moralistic judgments, Eliot's sympathy for Hetty, her understanding of Hetty's "woman's destiny" (3, xxii, 256), leads to a trenchant critique of the Poysers' refusal to "stand by her." "'They oughtn't to cast her off—her own flesh and blood,'" Adam proclaims, and his recently realized moral transformation doubly indicts the Poysers' culpability and the hypocrisy of middle-class respectability (5, xlii. 439).

Adam (whom Dinah likens to a "patriarch" [l, viii, 92]) is also shown as participating in the cultural discourse determining Hetty's fate; as Goode and others have argued, Adam reifies Hetty as the "prettiest thing God made" and marginalizes her in a realm of "dreams" outside his workday reality (32-35). But within the complex critique that Eliot initiates lie suggestions of potential cultural change. Modern critical theory has taught us to attend to a narrative's instances of "the male gaze" as an exemplification of gendered arrangements of power.[22] We find in ***Adam Bede***'s figures of reading Eliot's critical analysis of such appropriating perception. "Every man under such circumstances is conscious of being a great physiognomist," the narrator remarks on Adam's subjectifying (mis)reading of Hetty:

> The dear, young, round, soft, flexible thing! Her heart must be just as soft, her temper just as free from angles, her character just as pliant. If anything ever goes wrong, it must be the husband's fault there: he can make her what he likes—that is plain. . . . he wouldn't consent to her being a bit wiser. (1, xv, 154)

The obvious ironies of the free indirect discourse expose the inability of a patriarchal semiotics to underwrite a reading of the female body long before the narrator suggests "that there is no direct correlation between eyelashes and morals" (155). But when Adam visits Hetty in prison he has apparently learned to see ("he began to see through the dimness") with far different mediating assumptions, and this signals the possibility of cultural change. Instead of appropriating, Adam's eyes now return Hetty to herself: "When the sad eyes met—when Hetty and Adam looked at each other. . . . It was the first time she had seen any being whose face seemed to reflect the change in herself" (5, xlvi, 470). Marking, we could say, this "double change of self and beholder," Adam now feels "as if his brain would burst with the anguish of meeting Hetty's eyes" (471). And this extension of sympathy is the main emotional effect that the narrative has been designed to produce.

It is perhaps a just measure of Adam's transformation (and of the hopefulness of Eliot's analysis?) that his way of looking at Dinah too has been changed by his experience. As Kristen Brady points out, early on in the novel, "Adam is the only man whose 'dark penetrating glance' can create in Dinah Hetty-like blushes and 'self-consciousness'" (92). But, I would add, by book's end Adam can say to himself, "I shall look t'[Dinah] to help me see things right" (6, lvi, 542); and when Dinah returns to Adam, her "mild grey eyes turned on the strong dark-eyed man," they meet in mutual and unself-conscious desire (544).

The possibilities for change, of course, are severely circumscribed by the troublesome "happy ending." Although Eliot could faithfully record the contradictions of the emergent middle-class culture, she hesitates at a developed critique or an alternative vision. Unable to resolve, integrate, or critique those culturally informative contradictions, and pressed by the threat of cultural crisis, Eliot resorts at last to an unwarranted leap of faith in middle-class values. That leap, however, insofar as it can be seen as unwarranted, disruptive, or as contravening the narrative's ethics, manifests the very contradictions it was meant to conceal and thus mocks the celebratory functions of the narrative. There is no denying that Eliot's contemporary readers chose to concelebrate the narrative image of a consensually organized culture. To recall Dallas' comments, the narrative demonstrates "that there is not the mighty difference . . . usually assumed between high and low, rich and poor." But the narrative fracture originates in the "mighty difference" of the culture's gendered duties, opportunities, and liberties; and, disrupting the narrative's complicit messages of reassurance, that fracture of form and value will ultimately serve as a site of cultural transformation: it will lead Eliot to more critically active images, in ***The Mill on the Floss,*** especially, of the oppressions and disfranchisements operating in mid-Victorian England. As Eliot later remarked, "To my feeling there is more thought and profounder veracity in **'The Mill'** than in **'Adam'**" (*L* 3: 374). For all their conservative liberalism, Eliot's narratives from here on—even ***Felix Holt***—circulate a trenchant critique of the ethic of aspiration that Adam exemplifies.[23] In struggling against the ethical and political limits of the middle-class culture that her narrative records and celebrates, Eliot would come to realize in the interactions of text and context a consciousness that would make her narrative practice a much more critical "instrument of culture."

Notes

1. See, for examples, Geertz, Turner, MacIntyre, and Bellah.
2. Eliot once told Frederic Harrison that she "regarded the word 'culture' as a verbal equivalent for the highest mental result of past and present influences" (*L* 4: 395). Eliot would thus seem to share Matthew Arnold's definition of culture as a "pursuit of our total perfection by means of getting to know . . . the best which has been thought and said in the world." But, as Raymond Williams remarks, "Culture is one of the two or three most complicated words in the English language" (87), and Eliot's understanding of the term, as her mixing of "social conditions" and "moral tendencies" in the cultural metaphors of "roots" and "seed" suggests, was not limited to the Arnoldian sense. If, as Eliot claimed, language, minds, and societies "grow" (*E* 288), then "culture" for Eliot (as for us) signals a field of material, symbolic, and subjected relations, each element individually exhibiting a "process of development" which intervenes in or is intertwined with other developmental histories. In my use of the term I have tried to keep fairly close to the sense of "culture" as indicative of mid-Victorian "social environment." In that way I intend to emphasize the instrumentality of literature, a semiotic system expressive of and determined by communally shared understandings of human action, in bringing about certain social orders. While my working definition of culture lies squarely within the definition utilized by many social theorists and anthropologists (see n.1), I recognize my choice as arbitrary and, at best, pragmatic. Anyone acquainted with Williams's and Christopher Herbert's recent works will understand the difficulties of applying a term with rather dubious empiricist pretensions to an immaterial set of relations, ways of thought, or semiotic systems.
3. For all that I have learned from Goode's seminal essay, I still find his claim that Eliot presents a dehistoricized narrative to be logically incoherent. A narrative can be historicized by virtue of its historically accurate or resonant images—Arthur's return from Scotland fired with Young's plans for "drainage and enclosure," say, or the Poysers' "family economy"; by virtue of its references to "world historical" events—Adam's litany of the "great inventions" of the industrial revolution or the frequent imprecations on Bonaparte; by reference to cultural shifts—the narrator's prosopopoeia of "Old Leisure" (6, lii, 525) or what Sedgwick calls the "genealogy of the middle-class family" (145) represented by the differences between the Poysers' family structure and Dinah and Adam's; or by virtue of language, costume, recorded rituals, customs, habits, and so on, all of which *Adam Bede* provides in abundance. Goode mentions most of these features, and therein lies the incoherence, an incoherence that is not resolved by a further claim that these features are "merely decorative" (19). As we shall see, for Eliot's contemporary readers *Adam Bede* was an "authentic history"; that of course does not settle the matter, but its reminder that "history" is a contested term should prompt us to examine the narrative strategies that led Eliot's readers to read it as resolutely historicized. Finally, Goode's claim (which I obviously accept) that *Adam Bede*'s narrative process transforms "historical realities into an ideological fable" (36) suggests that just the sort of narrative process we have come to understand since Macaulay organizes all historical narratives. The universalizing humanism that invests Eliot's narrative was an active agent in the middle class's historic struggle for control of mid-Victorian England. See also Gregor; Palliser; and Widdowson, Stigant, and Brooker.

4. Victorian readers were well schooled in this kind of reading, and would have seen explicit adumbrations of the present in the pictured past. See Culler; and Anderson. Near the end of her career Eliot was to reflect on the narrative practice she had tried to institute. "The exercise of a veracious imagination in historical picturing," she wrote, "might help the judgment greatly with regard to present and future events. By veracious imagination, I mean the working out in detail of the various steps by which a political or social change was reached, using all extant evidence and supplying deficiencies by careful analogical creation" (*E* 446-47).

5. For another reading of the class-inflected habits of that handsome eight-day clock, see Dorothy Van Ghent (217-18).

6. Sarah Gilead, developing Victor Turner's concept of "ritual," focuses on Arthur's "failed" birthday feast as initiating "a risky liminoid period" culminating in Hetty's seduction and abandonment, a communal breach necessitating redress (240). For Gilead, redress comes through the "ritual dynamic of sacrifice-transformation-redemption" literally acted out in Hetty's trial, imprisonment, and transportation (243). I agree, and in a future article I plan to demonstrate the historically contingent dimensions of the "social drama" that *Adam Bede* represents par excellence.

7. Antonio Gramsci argues that in the early part of the nineteenth century a "suture" of the landowning and capitalist classes enabled the upper classes to retain political and economic control until the end of the century (18). See Tobin for an exploration of *Emma* as a narrative mirroring this "ideological fusion" (254).

8. Robyn Warhol explores Eliot's use of direct address from a somewhat different approach from the one I take here. Warhol convincingly analyzes the gendered differences between Eliot's engaging narratives and the distancing strategies employed by Thackeray and Trollope.

9. Compare Marx: "Owing to the extensive use of machinery and to division of labor, the work of the proletarians has lost all individual character, and consequently, all charm for the workman. He becomes an appendage of the machine ..." (*Manifesto* 16).

10. Drawing on Wayne Booth's notion of the "tacit contract" between readers and writers, Barbara Foley develops a theory of a "mimetic contract": in order for readers to comprehend stories at all, narratives must be constructed according to shared "paradigms for understanding reality" (43), that is, according to the culturally conditioned knowledge about the structures of everyday life.

11. Unlike instances in others of her novels, most notably *The Mill,* the textual reading performed by characters in *Adam Bede* is not, with one or two exceptions, significant. In addition to Adam's fondness for Franklin and Dinah's for the Bible, Eliot's depiction of Bartle Massey's students provides a potent metaphor for the transformative powers of reading. The workers struggling to apprehend print appear "as if three rough animals were making humble efforts to learn how they might become humans" (2, xxi, 240). This (de)humanizing trope is, not surprisingly, fortified by middle-class ideology; to become human here is to realize, among other things, one's competitive desires to be "prospering in the world" (238).

12. Knoepflmacher appears to have first noticed the connection (95).

13. Daniel Cottom presents a rigorously totalizing argument casting Eliot as an exemplary "liberal intellectual" whose social role is to interpret and disseminate systems of knowledge. For Cottom's Foucauldian analysis, this dissemination was a "technique of power" designed not so much to consolidate middle-class hegemony (although it did that), or even to enter into the culture-shaping debates of the period, as, rather, to produce an all powerful figure of the liberal intellectual. As much as I have learned from Cottom's argument, I find it too uncritical of its governing assumption that to reproduce an idea in discourse is necessarily an act of violence (see esp. 213). Such totalizing arguments neglect the contested, unstable, and incomplete debates that construct even such apparently consensual cultures as mid-Victorian England.

14. Widdowson, Stigant, and Brooker argue that the narrative progressively tames the historical radicalism of Methodism by moving Dinah from her status as Methodism's sole representative to become Adam's wife. But Dinah's Methodism, as we see here, is never portrayed as radical, except for its potential to subvert patriarchal assumptions about gender, seen as such by other characters.

15. The formal fracture of *Adam Bede* at Book 6 has long been recognized. Notable earlier accounts include Henry James (1866); and John S. Dieckhoff (1936). Among the many attempts to find unity in the disunity, one of the most interesting is Clayton's argument for Romantic vision requiring the cleaving addition.

16. Eliot records in her journal that her original plan was to bring the novel to a "climax" with the prison scene; this was the germ of the story she had heard from her aunt Elizabeth Samuel. It was Lewes's suggestion to bring Dinah and Adam together (*L* 2: 503).

17. Robin Gilmour reports a similar result in Smiles's *Self-Help.* While Smiles protested that his message emphasized the character-building virtues of improvement, the language of his narrative was shot

through "with the vocabulary of investment," and this always pointed to the external rewards of ostensibly intrinsic virtuous behavior (100).

18. Sedgwick makes a crucial distinction. Eliot's narrative, she argues, is "not a feminist one in its *valuations*" of characters and their choices, but it is thoroughly feminist in its "*analysis*" of them (emphasis in original; 140). I take that as an accurate description, but, as I will argue, Eliot's analysis in *Adam* leads to more intensely critical valuations in her subsequent narratives.
19. Shaw bases her assessment on Jeffrey Weeks's history of sexuality in nineteenth-century England.
20. The reviewer for the *Literary Gazette* (26 Feb. 1859): 282. Cited in J. Russell Perkin (56).
21. Davidoff and Hall comment on the culturally occluded network supporting such independent men as Adam: "The apparently autonomous individual man, celebrated in both political economy and evangelical religion, was almost always surrounded by family and kin who made possible his individual actions" (33). Adam's language articulates what Davidoff and Hall call the middle-class "ideological divide": men's public labor is "work" and women's private, domestic labor is not: "A working man 'ud be badly off without a wife to see to th' house and the victual, and make things clean and comfortable." As Bartle Massey's misogynistic response reveals, there's a world of difference between working and making things comfortable (2, xxi, 245).
22. For applications of this powerful explanatory theory to Eliot's narratives see Lefkowitz and Brady.
23. See Bodenheimer for an analysis of *Felix Holt* as Eliot's sustained attack on the entrepreneurial ideal and the conflation of gentry and middle-class power that it sanctioned.

Works Cited

Anderson, Olive. "The Political Uses of History." *Past and Present.* No. 36 (April 1967): 87-105.

Armstrong, Nancy. *Desire and Domestic Fiction: A Political History of the Novel.* New York: Oxford UP, 1987.

Bakhtin, M. M. "Discourse in the Novel." In *The Dialogic Imagination: Four Essays.* Ed, Michael Holquist. Trans. Holquist and Caryl Emerson. Austin: U of Texas P, 1981. Pp. 259-422.

———. "The Problem of Speech Genres." *Speech Genres and Other Late Essays.* Ed. Caryl Emerson and Michael Holquist. Trans. Vern W. McGee. Austin: U of Texas P, 1986. Pp. 60-102.

Barrett, Dorothea. *Vocation and Desire: George Eliot's Heroines.* New York: Routledge, 1989.

Bellah, Robert N., et al. *Habits of the Heart: Individualism and Commitment in American Life.* Berkeley: U of California P, 1985.

Bender, John. *Imagining the Penitentiary: Fiction and the Architecture of Mind in Eighteenth-Century England.* Chicago: U of Chicago P, 1987.

Bodenheimer, Rosemarie. *The Politics of Story in Victorian Social Fiction.* Ithaca: Cornell UP, 1988.

Booth, Wayne C. *The Rhetoric of Fiction.* 2d ed. Chicago: U of Chicago P, 1983.

Brady, Kristin. *George Eliot.* London: Macmillan, 1992.

Briggs, Asa. *The Making of Modern England, 1784-1867: The Age of Improvement.* New York: Harper, 1959.

Carlyle, Thomas. *Past and Present.* 1843. Ed. Richard D. Altick. New York: New York UP, 1977.

Carroll, David, ed. *George Eliot: The Critical Heritage.* New York: Barnes & Noble, 1971.

Clayton, Jay. "Visionary Power and Narrative Form: Wordsworth and *Adam Bede.*" *ELH* 46 (1979): 645-72.

Cottom, Daniel. *Social Figures: George Eliot, Social History, and Literary Representation.* Minneapolis: U of Minnesota P, 1987.

Culler, A. Dwight. *The Victorian Mirror of History.* New Haven: Yale UP, 1985.

Davidoff, Lenore, and Catherine Hall. *Family Fortunes: Men and Women of the English Middle Class, 1780-1850.* Chicago: U of Chicago P, 1987.

Dieckhoff, John S. "The Happy Ending of *Adam Bede.*" *ELH* 3 (1936): 221-27.

Dyhouse, Carol. *Feminism and the Family in England, 1880-1939.* Oxford: Basil Blackwell, 1989.

Eliot, George. *Adam Bede.* 1859. Ed. Gordon S. Haight. San Francisco: Rinehart, 1948.

———. *The George Eliot Letters,* 9 vols. Ed. Gordon S. Haight. New Haven: Yale UP, 1955-86. Cited as *L* in text.

———. "The Natural History of German Life." 1856. *Essays of George Eliot.* Ed. Thomas Pinney. New York: Columbia UP, 1963. Cited as *E* in text.

Foley, Barbara. *Telling the Truth: The Theory and Practice of Documentary Fiction.* Ithaca: Cornell UP, 1986.

Geertz, Clifford. *The Interpretation of Cultures.* New York: Basic, 1973.

Gilead, Sarah. "Barmecide Feasts: Ritual, Narrative, and the Victorian Novel." *Dickens Studies Annual* 17 (1988): 224-47.

Gilmour, Robin. *The Idea of the Gentleman in the Victorian Novel.* London: George Allen & Unwin, 1981.

Goode, John. "Adam Bede." In *Critical Essays on George Eliot.* Ed. Barbara Hardy. London: Routledge, 1970. Pp. 19-41.

Gramsci, Antonio. *Selections from the Prison Notebooks of Antonio Gramsci.* Ed. and trans. Quintin Hoare and Geoffrey Nowell Smith. New York: International Publishers, 1971.

Graver, Suzanne. *George Eliot and Community: A Study in Social Theory and Fictional Form.* Berkeley: U of California P, 1984.

Gregor, Ian. "The Two Worlds of *Adam Bede.*" In *The Moral and the Story.* Gregor and Brian Nichols. London: Faber, 1962. 13-32.

Herbert, Christopher. *Culture and Anomie: Ethnographic Imagination in the Nineteenth Century.* Chicago: U of Chicago P, 1991.

Hobsbawn, E. J. *Industry and Empire: From 1750 to the Present Day.* Harmondsworth: Penguin, 1968.

Hughes, J. R. T. "The Commercial Crisis of 1857." *Oxford Economic Papers* 8 (1956): 194-222.

———. *Fluctuations in Trade, Industry and Finance: A Study of British Economic Development, 1850-1860.* London: Oxford UP, 1960.

James, Henry. "The Novels of George Eliot." *Atlantic Monthly* (Oct. 1866).

Knoepflmacher, U. C. *George Eliot's Early Novels: The Limits of Realism.* Berkeley: U of California P, 1968.

Lefkowitz, Lori Hope. *The Character of Beauty in the Victorian Novel.* Ann Arbor: UMI Research P, 1987.

MacIntyre, Alasdair. *After Virtue.* 1981. 2d ed. Notre Dame: U of Notre Dame P, 1984.

Marx, Karl, and Friedrich Engels. *Karl Marx and Friedrich Engels; Collected Works,* 41 vols,, 1975-1983. New York: International Publishers, 1983, 40: 197-344.

Marx, Karl. *Manifesto of the Communist Party.* Ed. Samuel H. Beer. Arlington Heights, IL: Arlan Davidson, 1955.

Palliser, Charles. "*Adam Bede* and 'the story of the past.'" In *George Eliot: Centenary Essays.* Ed. Anne Smith. Totowa, NJ: Barnes & Noble, 1980. Pp. 55-76.

Paxton, Nancy L. *George Eliot and Herbert Spencer: Feminism, Evolutionism, and the Reconstruction of Gender.* Princeton: Princeton UP, 1991.

Perkin, Harold. *The Origins of Modern English Society, 1780-1880.* London: Routledge, 1969.

Perkin, J. Russell. *A Reception History of George Eliot's Fiction.* Ann Arbor: UMI Research P, 1990.

Sedgwick, Eve Kosofsky. *Between Men: English Literature and Male Homosocial Desire.* New York: Columbia UP, 1985.

Shaw, Marion. *Alfred Lord Tennyson.* Atlantic Highlands, NJ: Humanities International, 1991.

Shuttleworth, Sally. *George Eliot and Nineteenth-Century Science: The Make-Believe of a Beginning.* Cambridge UP, 1984.

Smiles, Samuel. *Self-Help.* London, 1859.

Stone, Lawrence, and J. F. C. Stone. *An Open Elite? England 1540-1880.* Oxford: Oxford UP, 1984.

Tholfsen, Trygve. *Working Class Radicalism in Mid-Victorian England.* New York: Columbia UP, 1977.

———. "The Intellectual Origins of Mid-Victorian Stability." *Political Science Quarterly* 86 (1971): 57-91.

Thompson, F. M. L. *English Landed Society in the Nineteenth Century.* London: Routledge, 1963.

Tilly, Louise, and Joan Scott. *Women, Work, and Family.* New York: Holt, 1978.

Tobin, Beth Fowkes. "The Moral and Political Economy of Property in Austen's *Emma.*" *Eighteenth-Century Fiction* 2 (April 1990): 229-54.

Turner, Victor. "Social Dramas and Stories about Them." *Critical Inquiry* 7 (1980): 141-68.

Van Ghent, Dorothy. *The English Novel: Form and Function.* New York: Harper, 1967.

Warhol, Robyn. *Gendered Interventions: Narrative Discourse in the Victorian Novel.* New Brunswick, NJ: Rutgers UP, 1990.

Watt, Ian. *The Rise of the Novel: Studies in Defoe, Richardson, and Fielding.* Berkeley: U of California P, 1957.

Weeks, Jeffrey. *Sex, Politics, and Society: The Regulation of Sexuality Since 1800.* London: Longman's, 1981.

Westminster Review 71 (April 1859): 269-83; American ed.

Widdowson, Peter, Paul Stigant, and Peter Brooker. "History and Literary 'Value': The Case of *Adam Bede* and *Salem Chapel.*" *Literature and History* 5 (Spring 1979): 2-39.

Wiesenfarth, Joseph. *George Eliot: A Writer's Notebook, 1854-1879, and Uncollected Writings.* Charlottesville: UP of Virginia, 1981.

Williams, Raymond. *Keywords: A Vocabulary of Culture and Society.* Rev. ed. New York: Oxford UP, 1983.

Caroline Levine (essay date 1996)

SOURCE: "Women or Boys? Gender, Realism, and the Gaze in *Adam Bede,*" in *Women's Writing,* Vol. 3, No. 2, June, 1996, pp. 113-27.

[*In the following essay, Levine analyzes the importance of the gaze as it questions the relationship between looking and loving in* Adam Bede.]

In the past two decades, critics from Laura Mulvey to Mary Louise Pratt have concerned themselves with the politics of looking.[1] They have compelled us to recognize that vision is not passive, but active—even *constitutive.* The world is not simply given to sight: it is shaped through the interested eyes of the tourist, the artist, the colonizer, the ordinary man—and yes, it may well be a man—on the street. Suddenly we find that it is crucial to consider who is looking, and how; who is seen, and for what reasons.

Looking, in ***Adam Bede,*** is an activity which reappears with startling persistence. From the anonymous stranger in the opening pages of the novel, whose only role is to gaze, to the famous treatise on realism, with its focus on visual art, we are repeatedly confronted with the surprisingly conspicuous act of seeing. And this is no accident: vision, Eliot tells us, is an integral element of an ethical education. She illustrates this point with her memorable example of Dutch painting, which offers us visual images of the homely and the ordinary, and thus invites us to focus sympathetically on the life around us, on "real breathing men and woman."[2] Images of the ideal are less beneficial: pictures of the lofty and sublime actually teach us to feel intolerant of the real, indifferent toward our "every day fellow-men" (p. 164). We learn to love our neighbours, then, by looking at certain pictures and disregarding others. Eliot's narrator urges us to dismiss the ideal and to pass—via representational realism—from looking to loving.

But the passage from one to the other is no simple matter when it comes to the narrative proper, where the vision of the beloved is problematic, if not downright dangerous: Hetty is much looked at, and meets only with catastrophe; Adam looks at Hetty and is perilously misled by her loveliness; Dinah stares at apparitions and absent faces, but becomes suddenly responsive to romantic love when she knows herself to be keenly observed by Adam Bede. All of this suggests that this text—"undoubtedly the most scopophilic of George Eliot's novels"[3]—is busily posing the same question in a number of ways: namely, what is the proper link between looking at the world and feeling love?

It will be my contention, here, that George Eliot's theory of ethical realism, with its paradigm of Dutch painting, is intertwined with a theory of gender. Both are concerned with the connection between aesthetics and ethics, between looking and loving. While critics have often considered the problem of female beauty in ***Adam Bede,*** they have failed to frame the problem as a question of *visual aesthetics.* Taken as a problem of aesthetics, it becomes clear that femininity occupies the same theoretical ground as the novel's explicit concerns about ideal beauty and sympathetic realism in chapter XVII. Beauty and sympathy are at odds for the women characters just as they are in the famous essay on aesthetics: Hetty's constant knowledge of her own visual beauty is a dangerous extreme of femininity, allowing her no room for an ethical recognition of the other, while Dinah's unconsciousness concerning her own appearance allows her to be sympathetic but, as we will see, perilously unfeminine. Judith Mitchell has written that George Eliot, in ***Adam Bede,*** identifies with a masculine narrator, and "basically endorses the idealization of beautiful women"[4]; while Nancy L. Paxton points out that "Eliot's treatment of Hetty's narcissistic sexuality . . . has often been read as an expression of her neurotic envy of the female beauty she did not personally possess."[5] These diametrically opposed readings—one based on an interpretation of a masculine narrator, the other on biographical speculation—have neglected to take account of the potentially polemical force of Eliot's two antithetical examples of femininity in ***Adam Bede***: neither the unself-conscious Dinah nor the excessively self-conscious Hetty, taken alone, can stand for Eliot's normative view of femininity. Critical of both examples, Eliot suggests that women, on display, must learn to negotiate their femininity through their roles as both subjects and objects of vision. In this context, ethics and the aesthetics of feminine beauty emerge as significantly related concerns: how can women, so much the beautiful objects of vision, become active, seeing, ethical subjects, capable of the kind of moral vision taught by Dutch painting?

Weaving together the strands of gender and aesthetics, I will argue, here, that Eliot's particular theorization of the link between ethics and vision allows her to launch a sophisticated critique of formalist aesthetics and the detached, impersonal eye—known to us as the "gaze." I am referring not to the explicitly gendered "male gaze," but rather to the term as it is employed by Norman Bryson, who argues that the gaze is predicated on a denial of the "locus of utterance": "*the disavowal of deictic reference* . . . the disappearance of the body as the site of the image."[6] This definition is concerned with an impersonal, *generalized* eye, and this model of vision, I will argue, is the object of Eliot's critique in ***Adam Bede.*** She urges, throughout the narrative, that we pay close attention to the particular embodiment of the spectator, located in time and space.

The refusal to accept the impersonal vision of the gaze is, as we will see, integral to Eliot's double critique: it is as essential to her rejection of an aestheticized feminine beauty as it is to her dismissal of an idealist aesthetics. And perhaps most importantly, it is fundamental to her unconventional theory of ethical realism, articulated through the model of Dutch painting. Realism and the gaze alike have been attacked for their pretensions to objectivity: as Bryson argues, the subject of the gaze always intends to be disembodied, aiming at a pure, universal perception, untroubled by the situated identities of bodies in all of their varied particularity; realism, too, has come under attack for its supposed goal of a universal, culturally uncontingent perspective. But Eliot's particularized realism repeatedly refuses the model of disinterested objectivity, and favours instead a careful self-consciousness about who is looking, and from what limited, embodied perspective each pair of eyes sees.

Boys to Women

Critics have rarely noticed that Dinah Morris is a spectacle. She is not only heard, after all, but looked at, and with real interest—a kind of visual curiosity. Everyone, from Arthur Donnithorne to Wiry Ben, has something to say about Dinah's appearance.[7] For all the talk, though, Dinah remains unruffled by the crowd of gazes that surrounds her. Her unselfconsciousness is one of her most marked characteristics, and one that surprises the many who gaze at her. Surely she knows how much attention she attracts? As Reverend Irwine asks: "'And you never feel any embarrassment from the sense . . . that you are a lovely young woman on whom men's eyes are fixed?'" (p. 83). Dinah responds firmly in the negative: "'No, I've no room for such feelings, and I don't believe the people ever take notice about that'" (p. 83).

But of course they do. Dinah is innocently wrong about how much notice is being taken of her, and it is worth bearing in mind that she is entirely mistaken about the extent to which the world is interested in her appearance. Importantly, too, it is not only her beauty, but also her unselfconsciousness that is apparent to all, perceptible even to those who have never seen her before. "The stranger was struck with surprise as he saw [Dinah] approach and mount the cart—surprise, not so much at the feminine delicacy of her appearance, as at the total absence of self-consciousness in her demeanor" (p. 17). Dinah's principal visual impact on a stranger is not her femininity: it is that she seems not to know that she is being looked at.

To see Dinah is to see a woman unaware of being seen—and this, it would seem, is strange in a woman. Adam Bede is likewise unaware of his appearance[8], but this is not marked for us as surprising: the text implies that unselfconsciousness is perfectly in keeping with a healthy masculinity. Most intriguing, perhaps, is that at two moments, Dinah's unselfconsciousness actually renders her boyish. "Dinah walked as simply as if she were going to market, and seemed as unconscious of her outward appearance as a little boy" (p. 17). *As unconscious of her appearance as a little boy*: in the realm of looks, unselfconsciousness belongs to boyishness. The second instance registers in Dinah's voice, which rings with "unconscious skill": "The simple things she said seemed like novelties, as a melody strikes us with a new feeling when we hear it sung by the pure voice of a boyish chorister" (p. 22).

Eliot's references to boys here are as perplexing as they are suggestive. It is not clear, in 1859, that little children are considered gendered subjects, and boys are certainly not the budding archetypes of hardy, intrepid, and vigorous masculinity that they will become by the end of the century. In fact, it is precisely in this period that the gendering of children seems to have been taking place, manifested in a growing institutional emphasis on the distinction between boys and girls. "After the passage of the 1870 Education Act, a child's experience of school was increasingly likely to be shaped by gender . . . The Board School curriculum was increasingly organized along sexist lines, with girls being taught domestic subjects such as home economics, sewing, cooking and child care, while boys were offered new options such as animal physiology, algebra, chemistry, and physics."[9] Similarly, children's books and stories generally specify an exclusively male or female readership only after 1870, with the publication of periodicals like the *Boy's Own Paper.*[10] It is not until the 1880s, according to some scholars, that a "tradition of . . . male-oriented juvenile fiction" is really in place.[11]

On the other hand, there is no question that Eliot, in 1859, is deliberate about her use of the figure of the boy for Dinah; she does not, as she well might have done, liken her character to a child or a girl. And we can draw from clear evidence in ***The Mill on the Floss,*** published just a year after ***Adam Bede,*** that Eliot was interested in the gendering of children. Tom Tulliver seems uncannily patterned on the enormously popular *Tom Brown's Schooldays* (1857), widely cited as the first example of the boys' fiction that would become standard by the end of the century.[12] Indeed, Eliot's picture of Tom Tulliver might be read as an exploration of the model of boyhood espoused in *Tom Brown's Schooldays.* Tom, aptly named, comes home from school in good Tom Brown fashion, filled with ideals of fair play ("I hate a cheat"), physical prowess ("I gave Spouncer a black eye, I know—that's what he got for wanting to leather me"), and honour ("Tom Tulliver was a lad of honour"), and entirely confident about the distinction between boys and girls. "Tom . . . was of the opinion that Maggie was a silly little thing; all girls were silly—they couldn't throw a stone so as to hit anything, couldn't do anything with a pocket knife, and were frightened at frogs."[13] These boyhood traits are of course in tune with Tom's rigid and exacting punishments of Maggie, which will last into adulthood, and ***The Mill on the Floss*** might be even read as a critique of the principled, manly boyhood represented in *Tom Brown's Schooldays.*

To return to ***Adam Bede,*** we can begin to contextualize Eliot's curious choice of a boyish model for Dinah. It is between the publication of *Tom Brown's Schooldays* in 1857 and the passage of the 1870 Education Act that boys become strictly associated with a masculine ideal, and thus ***Adam Bede*** is published at a transitional moment, a moment in which boys are being increasingly understood as those "who will be men."[14] In 1859, boys may not be strictly or prototypically masculine—with the connotations of physical strength, honour, and mastery that this term will come to imply—but they are a focus of gendered interest, and we know that Eliot will be concerned with this very question by the time she writes ***The Mill on the Floss*** in 1860. And, most importantly for our purposes, Dinah, in her unselfconsciousness, is likened neither to women nor to girls. At the very least, then, we can conclude that Eliot is dissociating Dinah from conventional femininity, and, in comparing her to boys rather than to children or girls, implies that Dinah crosses gender boundaries. Moreover, it is only in the context of her unselfconsciousness that Dinah seems so like a boy. It would seem that femininity and unselfconsciousness do not belong together.

Mentions of Dinah's unselfconsciousness reappear with almost alarming frequency in the first chapters of the novel. And it is telling, for our purposes, that her obliviousness informs Seth Bede that she is not in love. He looks for signs of reciprocated affection, only to find Dinah entirely unconscious of herself and of his presence: hers "was an expression of unconscious placid gravity—of absorption in thoughts that had no connexion with the present moment or with her own personality: an expression that is most of all discouraging to a lover" (p. 27). As we have seen, unselfconsciousness is typically masculine, but it would appear that it is also at odds with love: thus, lovers and women are self-conscious, while boys—and Dinah—are not.

At this point, we might come to a couple of eccentric conclusions. Firstly, we might say that Dinah, here, is *too much like a boy* to accept Seth Bede's love. Read thus, Eliot's text can be seen to reinforce a heterosexist norm in which love exists only between a man and a woman, *and* the woman must become sufficiently feminine for this love to emerge. Secondly, if Dinah is boyish because she is unselfconscious, then in order to shift from boyishness to mature womanhood she will have to become aware of her own appearance. And since such self-consciousness is also the stuff of love, she will then become a perfect candidate for romance—which is, of course, precisely what happens.

The Self-consciousness of True Love, or How to Blush Properly

Our conclusions about gender and self-consciousness have led us directly to the end of the narrative, where Dinah reaches adequate self-consciousness and falls in love with an equally self-conscious Adam Bede. Blushing furiously, each is transformed when beheld by the loving gaze of the other.

Blushing, as Margaret Homans has pointed out, is not just any signifier: in Adam Bede, it is the telling marker of sexuality.[15] It works as a revealing contrast between Hetty and Dinah: blushing is precisely what Hetty does with perfect complacency[16], and what she fails to do when she thinks of Adam, "Her cheeks never grew a shade deeper when his name was mentioned" (p. 90); but it is Dinah's only sign of sexuality, appearing only when she feels herself to be seen by Adam.[17] Indeed, the blush functions as the very first signal to the reader of a possibility of romantic love between these two, coming as a total surprise to Dinah when Adam first looks at her:

> *Dinah, for the first time in her life, felt a painful self-consciousness; there was something in the dark penetrating glance of this strong man so different from the mildness and timidity of his brother Seth. A faint blush came, which deepened as she wondered at it. (p. 107)*

The erotic suggestion of this passage would be hard to overlook, but it is important to recognize the place of the eye in the gendering of this scene: Adam's way of looking, marked as strong and penetrating, is clearly more masculine than that of his brother, and literally transforms Dinah from her boyish unselfconsciousness into a blushing femininity. The male gaze, we might conclude, is crucial to the construction of a feminine sexuality.

But then, Adam too blushes with self-consciousness. When he is first introduced to the idea that Dinah may be in love with him, "The blood rushed to Adam's face, and for a few moments he was not quite conscious where he was; his mother and the kitchen had vanished for him, and he saw nothing but Dinah's face turned up towards his" (p. 461). Reddening, he sees nothing but the image of Dinah, and it is a memory of her *looking at him*. Whether masculine or feminine, it would seem, consciousness and self-consciousness are bound up in the mutual look of romantic love. For Eliot, a reciprocal gaze is apparently fundamental to a mature sexuality in men and women alike.

Adam's love for Hetty remains remarkably unselfconscious and entirely unreciprocated, in both ways unlike his blushing love for Dinah. And it has nothing to do with consciousness, whether of self or other: it is an explicitly *impersonal* love of the beautiful. The narrator explains:

> *For my own part . . . I think the deep love [Adam] had for that sweet, rounded, blossom-like, dark-eyed Hetty, of whose inward self he was really very ignorant, came out of the very strength of his nature and not out of any inconsistent weakness. Is it any weakness, pray, to be wrought on by exquisite music?—to feel its wondrous harmonies searching the subtlest windings of your soul, the delicate fibres of life where no memory can penetrate . . . The noblest nature sees the most of this* impersonal *expression in beauty ... and for this reason, the noblest nature is the most often blinded to the character of the one woman's soul that the beauty clothes. (pp. 326-327, emphasis in text)*

"Blinded" by the impersonal nature of the aesthetic experience, Adam's noble nature fails to "see" and love anything in Hetty but beauty itself, a beauty as contentless and disinterested as a love of music. The separation of Hetty's impersonal beauty from her consciousness is clearly a serious obstacle to reciprocation. And Adam's love, it would seem, is entirely the affair of the spectator, gazing at the impersonal object of his vision. Adam's sentiment may be noble, perhaps, but it is not the stuff of true love and fruitful marriage. Or so the end of the narrative, with its rather different love, would have us believe.

It is tempting to argue that Adam's love for Hetty is Kantian, his love for Dinah Hegelian. Kant's theorization of the experience of the beautiful is that it is always impersonal, requiring no particular self-interest, no particular embodiment. It is a disinterested experience, occurring spontaneously within every human subject, and focused on the beauty of form. Kant writes: "The *beautiful* is that which pleases universally. . . ."[18] For Hegel, by contrast, the self is absolutely incapable of ethical judgment, community, or knowledge without a recognition of and by the other. This mutual acknowledgment is an absolute precondition of culture, political community, and ethical action. "Self-consciousness exists in and for itself when, and by the fact that, it so exists for another; that is, it exists only in being acknowledged."[19] From Kantian aesthetics to Hegelian self-consciousness: this movement could be said to describe the trajectory of Adam's *Bildung*, as he shifts from the love of Hetty's impersonal beauty to the reciprocal acknowledgment that comes with Dinah's love. Both are framed in terms of the visual: Kantian aesthetics "blinds" Adam, rendering him incapable of seeing Hetty's character and meeting Dinah's gaze.

If the end of the story is anything to go by, Eliot falls firmly on the side of a Hegelian self-consciousness; for her, proper love is distinguished by the reciprocal acknowledgment of self and other. And, in keeping with the novel's insistence on the visual, this self-consciousness is represented by a shared gaze, in which each party is both subject and object of vision, conscious of the other and conscious of the self through the eyes of the other. By stark contrast, the admiring sight of Hetty's "impersonal" beauty causes ethical blindness, blocking a real consciousness of the other and, consequently, of the self.

The Limits of Self-consciousness

With Adam and Dinah as our paragons of love, we begin to see that Eliot favours a love governed by a reciprocal self-consciousness, in which masculine and feminine, self and other, come to recognition through the gaze of the other. Thus, love is impossible between Dinah and Seth, since she is oblivious to his presence, and between Hetty and Adam, since he recognizes only her impersonal beauty, and without reciprocation.

But then, what is wrong with the love between Arthur and Hetty? By contrast to Dinah, Hetty is self-conscious indeed. There is no question that she is aware of her own appearance, and aware that others are conscious of her beauty. And she and Arthur are even given to reciprocal blushing when face to face: "If Arthur had had time to think at all, he would have thought it strange that he should feel fluttered too, be conscious of blushing too" (p. 119). Moreover, Hetty is clearly made more self-conscious by Arthur's attention, just as Dinah is by Adam's: "The vainest woman is never thoroughly conscious of her own beauty till she is loved by the man who sets her own passion vibrating in return" (p. 138).

The obvious obstacle to true love between Hetty and Arthur is class. But it would be naive to assume that there is no more to it than that. It is clear that theirs is not a love story destined to tragedy only by the differences in their social standing: such a tale would make ***Adam Bede*** a more radical text than it is.[20] Rather, the narrator insistently implies, Hetty is so self-conscious that she is incapable of love, and certainly of simple compassion.[21] She is explicitly resistant to sympathy ("as unsympathetic as butterflies sipping nectar" [p. 92]), and her heart is certainly far from warm: "Hetty would have been glad to hear that she should never see a child again; they were worse than the nasty little lambs that the shepherd was always bringing in . . . for the lambs were got rid of sooner or later" (p. 142). She rejects tenderness, compassion, and affection—all the emotions focused on the other. Indeed, her imagination is filled almost exclusively with visual images of herself. The narrator says: "of every [imaginary] picture she is the central figure, in fine clothes" (p. 141). Even when she thinks of Arthur, she sees herself through his eyes: "Captain Donnithorne couldn't like her to go on doing work; he would like to see her in nice clothes . . ." (p. 138). Concerned entirely with the reflected image of her own image, Hetty sees herself in precisely the same way that Adam and Arthur see her—as an object of visual beauty. She and her admirers alike are intent on looking in a single direction: at the "impersonal" beauty of Hetty herself.

Importantly, too, Eliot is careful to point out that Hetty's beauty appeals not only to the masculine eye, but to everyone: "there is one order of beauty which seems to turn the heads not only of men, but of all intelligent mammals, even of women . . . Hetty Sorrel's was that sort of beauty" (p. 75). Even Mrs Poyser is transfixed: "continually gaz[ing] at Hetty's charms by the sly, fascinated in spite of her self" (p. 75). Hetty's beauty, in good Kantian fashion, is universally pleasing, appealing regardless of the particular interests and character of the spectator. Her image appeals not to particular eyes, but to the eye in general—including even her own gaze, directed at herself. Consequently, she is incapable of seeing outward—toward the other—and equally incapable of recognizing herself as a seeing subject, able to look out on the world. It is clear that the gaze, internalized by Hetty and ignored by Dinah, has significant consequences for feminine subjectivity.

In this context, it will not be surprising that the mirror appears as Hetty's closest companion, mentioned even the first time we encounter her, part of the description of Mrs Poyser's immaculate house:

> *Hetty Sorrel often took the opportunity, when her aunt's back was turned, of looking at the pleasing reflection of herself in those polished surfaces, for the oak table was usually turned up like a screen, and was more for ornament than for use; and she could see herself sometimes in the great round pewter dishes that were ranged on the shelves above the long deal dinner-table, or in the hobs of the grate, which always shone like jasper. (p. 65)*

In polemical contrast to Dinah's boyish unselfconsciousness, Hetty's love of mirrors puts her at an opposite extreme. The mirror is Hetty's opportunity to gaze admiringly at her own beauty, but it also reveals her total identification with her own visual image. When we first encounter her before her bedroom mirror, she is admiring her own prettiness, consumed with the joy of self-regard. But later, when Arthur Donnithorne writes to tell her that their affair is over, the image is transformed: "when she looked up . . . there was the reflection of a blanched face in the old dim glass . . . Hetty did not see the face—she saw nothing—she only felt that she was cold and sick and trembling" (p. 307). A moment later, "she caught sight of her face in the glass: it was reddened now, and wet with tears; it was almost like a companion that she might complain to—that would pity her" (p. 307). Thus, Hetty's mirror image is, first, a delightful picture; second, total blankness, reflecting her virtual annihilation by Arthur; and third, a second self, a sympathetic other. It would seem that the mirror offers us our best access to Hetty's self-consciousness: her own reflected image is not only her greatest source of pleasure, but reflective of her whole vision of herself. It is suggestive that while Hetty loves her mirror, Dinah loves her window. At the very same moment that Hetty is dressing up before her bedroom mirror, Dinah is looking outside: "Dinah delighted in her bedroom window . . . the first thing she did, on entering her room, was to seat herself . . . and look out on the peaceful fields . . ." (p. 144).

An excess of self-consciousness, clearly, turns out to be no better than a deficit. We are faced with two striking extremes: Dinah, filled with ethical love from the outset, is not capable of romantic, sexual love until she sees herself through the eyes of Adam Bede; Hetty, self-conscious and demonstrative of a coquettish sexuality from the beginning, fails to feel love for any of those who surround her. It is a revealing contrast: Dinah must become self-conscious in order to fall in love, marry, and multiply, while Hetty's self-consciousness seems to make her incapable of loving anyone—Adam, Arthur, even her own child. Dinah is too boyishly unselfconscious for romantic love; she is so consumed with visions of the other that she fails to recognize herself; Hetty is so focused on the image of her own appearance that her only concern with others is her reflection through their eyes. If Dinah is too boyish then Hetty, perhaps, is too feminine.

The trajectory of the narrative brings us to a normative middle ground, where Dinah manages to reach the perfect combination of ungendered sympathy and feminine self-consciousness. But how, precisely, do these two reach their happy fusion? It is my contention that the crucial difference between Hetty's awareness of herself and Dinah's blush under Adam's keen stare is that Hetty responds to a *generalized* gaze, while Dinah answers to a specific pair of eyes. Adam, remember, is the only one who can make Dinah self-conscious. The same is not the case for Hetty. It is true that she blushes when beheld by Arthur Donnithorne, but he is not the only one whose eyes matter: "those other people didn't know how he loved her, and she was not satisfied to appear shabby and insignificant in their eyes even for a short space" (p. 231). Hetty is so dependent on a universal gaze of admiration that she sees the world only as that gaze, reflecting her back to herself.

If this self-consciousness gestures to a proper, mature femininity in Dinah, it is only, it seems, because Dinah's responds in this way *to a single gaze;* Hetty, by contrast, is given to a kind of promiscuous self-consciousness, an internalization of the impersonal gaze of all others. Hetty's sense of herself, all too feminine, is constructed through the indiscriminate gathering of looks that come her way, and this is perilous indeed; Dinah, by contrast, becomes feminine through the gaze of the single beloved.

In this context, Eliot's ideal turns out to be a bourgeois model *par excellence,* embracing the notion that a proper feminine sexuality appears only in the context of a single heterosexual couple: the woman is only feminized when faced with the dark, penetrating gaze of a particular man. Her foil, the woman who internalizes the generalized gaze of admiration, seeing herself as she is reflected in the eyes of all who look at her, meets only with catastrophe.

Other Beauty

The impersonal beauty of the Kantian aesthetic begins to look dangerous indeed, whether for spectator or for spectacle. This conclusion conveys us back to chapter XVII: after all, Hetty's beauty distracts Adam's attention from the reality of her character, much as idealist painting, in Eliot's disquisition on realism, deflects the viewer's attention away from the worthy but prosaic realities of everyday life. Perhaps impersonal beauty itself represents a dangerous distraction from the ethical life. In the famous treatise on painting, the reader, like Adam, is urged to put aside an admiration for formal beauty. In place of this idealist aesthetic, we are presented with the paradigm of Dutch painting:

> *All honor and reverence to the divine beauty of form! Let us cultivate it to the utmost in men, women, and children—in our gardens and in our houses. But let us love that other beauty too, which lies in no secret of proportion, but in the secret of deep human sympathy. (p. 164)*

Here, we are invited to favour that "other beauty"—human sympathy, which has nothing to do with perfect forms, and focuses instead on the virtuous but irregular realities of the world. Thus, "monotonous homely existence" (p. 163), "commonplace things" (p. 164), and "the common labourer" (p. 164) take the aesthetic place of the divine beauty of perfect proportions. Prompting us to "remember [the] existence" of "common, coarse people" (p. 164), Dutch pictures are best because they offer us the opportunity to see and therefore to know and contemplate the reality of the other, as vision and ethics are fused into a single experience. Significantly, too, this "other beauty" is not gendered: it is explicitly called human sympathy, and is directed, in chapter XVII, at images of both men and women alike.

In such a way, the narrative affirms a possible female gaze—a way for women to look out at the world. Dinah, always looking lovingly on her fellow beings, is sensitive to the "other beauty": in this context, the ethical gaze is clearly a look which women themselves can perform, no longer impersonal objects of vision but rather sympathetic, *seeing subjects*. Dinah's eyes themselves register this facet of her person: "they looked so simple, so candid, so gravely loving . . ." (p. 18). And this gaze is ultimately presented as if it transcended the gender barrier: readers and characters, masculine and feminine—all are urged to learn to look with love at the realities of the world, and thus to embrace an alternative model of the beautiful.

It is worth pausing to note that the phrase "other beauty" can be read in two ways. Sympathy is the "other" aesthetic: it is both an alternative to the beauty of form—*another kind of beauty*—and an aesthetic of the other, an attention to *the beauty of the other.* No wonder, then, that Dutch painting becomes a paradigm for the ethical realism of the text: "other beauty" has connotations at once both aesthetic and ethical. And Adam's shift from Hetty to Dinah can be seen in this context as a neat transformation from sensuous beauty to that "other beauty," from the ideal form of Hetty's appearance—a conventional aesthetic—to the intertwined consciousness of self and other—an *aesthetic of the other.*

In this context, the shift from a Kantian aesthetics to a Hegelian ethics is entirely framed under the larger rubric of aesthetics, the question of beauty. And it is formulated as a specifically visual problematic, Hetty's beautiful appearance and the "other beauty" of Dutch *painting.* Of course, vision is clearly a metaphor for a more general problem of consciousness, particularly ethical consciousness: seeing means illuminating, clarifying, comprehending the real. But it is not just any metaphor: it is the organizing problematic of this text. Under the aegis of the visual we find vanity, gender, love, ethics, realism—in short the many prominent thematic strands of this narrative.

The Aesth-ethics of Realism: Partial, Particular Visions

Our look at looking brings us to a series of conclusions, all having to do with the serious consequences of the visual in ***Adam Bede.*** Firstly, the generalizing gaze is responsible for Hetty's downfall, while the particular look of a specific man is the key to Dinah's sexual maturity. Feminine fortunes are thus contingent on the ways that women respond to their roles as seeing subjects and visual spectacles. Secondly, as we learned from Dutch painting, the universal admiration of perfect beauty is detrimental to an ethical appreciation of the imperfect reality of the other. And thirdly, both aesthetics and ethics are framed in terms of visual beauty—the one formal, ideal, and universally pleasing, and the other, well, simply *other.*

Taken together, these conclusions suggest a profound suspicion of the impersonal, universal eye—the disembodied gaze. When it is the basis of feminine sexuality, the gaze constructs a limited, self-absorbed, catastrophic consciousness; when it is the basis of art, it directs attention away from the world in which we live. This aesthetic diversion of our sympathies has tangible consequences: "you," the reader, will learn from idealist representations to "turn a harder, colder eye" on "real breathing men and women, who can be chilled by your indifference or injured by your prejudice; who can be cheered and helped onward by your fellow-feeling, your forbearance, your outspoken, brave justice" (p. 162). Representations not only refer to the world, they also operate in that world: "you" are implicated by them, trained by them, prompted by them to act with coldness or with sympathy and fellow-feeling. The aesthetic thus emerges as an ethical agent in the world.

We have seen that realism is identified with "human sympathy" and called an "other beauty." It is an alternative to the impersonal beauty of form, and an ethical one at that. We should recall, too, that realism claims a peculiar, ambivalent position in the history of aesthetics: it is a theory of art which repudiates artfulness, a deliberately *unaesthetic* aesthetic. It might seem odd, therefore, that Eliot frames it very deliberately as a species of the beautiful, to be understood as an alternative aesthetic, set against the formalist beauties of harmony and proportion. But read polemically, Eliot's visual model suggests a calculated critique of Kantian aesthetics: as we have seen, the *impersonal* beauty of form prompts the spectator to be blind to the reality of character, while ethical realism, focused on the reality of the other, is all about persons, about "human sympathy." Thus, a Kantian aesthetic allows women to be perceived not as persons but as forms—indeed, it blinds the spectator to their personhood—while a Hegelian ethics transcends the gender divide and invites men and women alike to look and be looked at in full recognition of self and other. Eliot displaces formalism as an *unethical* aesthetic, and pointedly supplants it with a radically unaesthetic aesthetic, the "rough," "stupid," "squat," and "ill-shapen" *beauty of the other* (pp. 163-164).

The consequences of this polemic against impersonal formalism are striking indeed when it comes to the novel's own realist practice. Most importantly, Eliot is absolutely scrupulous about locating vision—that crucial metaphor for consciousness—in persons. No visual impression is presented as an impersonal gaze: the seeing subject of realism in ***Adam Bede*** is always embodied, located in time and space. Thus, Eliot constantly affirms that it matters who is looking, and from what standpoint. What is striking about this choice is that it is not only an anti-conventional *aesthetics,* but it is also a surprising *realism,* suggesting that the real is not grasped by a detached, objective consciousness; it is in the domain of seeing persons, of embodied subjects whose vision is both partial and limited.

This point is best demonstrated by the voice of the narrator, who draws attention even to the specificity of "his" own perspective[22], frequently referring to "himself" as a particular, delimited consciousness. "I confess I have often meanly shrunk from confessing to these accomplished and acute gentlemen what my own experience has been," "he" claims (p. 168). And "he" presents opinions as if they belonged to a specific character: "For my own part . . . I think . . ." (p. 326). Descriptions of the novel's scenes are presented as if from a precise location in time and space: "We will enter very softly and stand still in the open doorway, without awaking the glossy-brown setter who is stretched across the hearth, with her two puppies beside her" (p. 47). In another example, the description of the Poysers' dairy is first presented as if from a neutral standpoint. The chapter begins: "The dairy was certainly worth looking at: it was a scene to sicken for . . . in hot and dusty streets" (p. 74). This voice then switches to speak for the eyes of Arthur Donnithorne, who has just come on the scene. The description breaks off: "But one gets only a confused notion of these details when they surround a distractingly pretty girl of seventeen . . . Hetty blushed a deep rose-color when Captain Donnithorne entered the dairy" (p. 74).

In the context of this careful embodiment of vision, it might seem peculiar that the text, like Hetty herself, is closely allied with the figure of the mirror. In good realist fashion, the novel poses as a mirror of the world it portrays: "With a single drop of ink for a mirror, the Egyptian sorcerer undertakes to reveal to any chance comer far-reaching visions of the past. This is what I undertake to do for you, reader" (p. 1). But what kind of a mirror is it? In one of the best known passages in the novel, the narrator claims "to give no more than a faithful account of men and things as they have mirrored themselves in my mind" (p. 161). And this mirror is far from perfect: "The mirror is doubtless defective; the outlines will sometimes be disturbed; the reflection faint or confused" (p. 161). Eliot's mirror is an image of the world, yes, but one explicitly located in the narrator's own mind, and "doubtless" reflecting imperfectly. This is indeed a curious realism, relying as it does on the mind of the subject, and refusing to promise either clarity or accuracy. But the reader will remember that Hetty's mirror, too, reflected the particularity of her own mind rather than a perfect, flawless reflection. It gave her back an image of her own absorbed self-consciousness. Thus, the apparently incongruous parallel between Hetty's unethical self-consciousness and the ethical realism of the narrative is ultimately a good one: both attest to the limited particularity of the spectator, refusing to claim universal, neutral, or *impersonal* status. And the difference between Hetty's mirror and that of the narrator is telling indeed: while Hetty sees and admires herself, the narrator reflects the other—"men and things." Notably, the novel's mirror also reflects the world *for the other*—that is, for the reader—in the interests of instructing us to see the world differently, with human sympathy. If Hetty's admiration of herself is circular, showing her to herself alone, the narrative's reflection traces a far more circuitous, productive, and *social* path: it travels from "men and things" to the mind of the narrator; from the narrator to the reader; and—with any luck—from the reader back to the world, with sympathy.

From Looking to Loving

True love, the end of the novel suggests, requires that a woman be able to see a man as an individuated, particular subject, rather than, as Hetty does, a generalized, impersonal eye—and also that she see *herself* through the eyes of that singular other. Similarly, the realist artist rejects the ideal and the typical in favour of the varied specificity of the real, and acknowledges the embodied particularity of the visual. In the end, Dinah, Adam, and the realist come to share the "proper" connection between looking and loving: they recognize the personhood of the other and recognize themselves, too, as seeing subjects. They repudiate impersonal form in favour of the visual aesthethics of "human sympathy," an appreciation of "that other beauty," which operates regardless of gender.

But we must not forget that Dinah is also feminized through her self-recognition in the eyes of Adam Bede. Love, whether sexual or ethical, may require an embodied spectator capable of appreciating the beauty of the other, but Eliot's ideal of heterosexual, bourgeois love also calls for the reciprocally (en)gendering gaze, masculine and feminine alike spellbound in the mutual recognition of self and other.

However, it must be said that this gendering of the eye, though strictly heterosexual, is not merely conservative; it also reveals radical undertones in ***Adam Bede.*** After all, there is an understated gesture toward equality in Eliot's model of sexual love: Dinah sees Adam as fully as Adam sees Dinah; the mutual look of true love is based on an equal interchange of gazes, requiring that both man and woman be at once spectator and spectacle. It is possible, too, to read Hetty's destruction as subversive: the story of her seduction and infanticide condemns the gaze, denouncing the impersonal vision of women as objects of aesthetic beauty and implying that this unidirectional admiration of feminine beauty poses a significant danger to women's self-consciousness. It is clearly crucial to Hetty's downfall, both moral and material, that she is incapable of considering the other, and this ethical failure is at least in part a product of the ways that she sees and is seen as an object of "impersonal beauty." Moreover, considered in the context of other representations of femininity, Hetty's destructive self-consciousness is all too obviously political: it implies that the beautiful heroine of fiction, myth, and even nineteenth-century science[23] is a cultural construct with potentially dire moral and social consequences.

If her own ideal had been less bourgeois, Eliot might perhaps have envisioned—pardon the pun—an embodied gaze which was not so entirely contingent on the individual, or on the opposition of masculine and feminine. She might have conceived of an erotic gaze, which, like her ethical gaze, acknowledged the other in his or her particularity, regardless of the strict gender dichotomy of heterosexuality. Or she might have theorized ways of seeing which belong to the group: the collective gaze, neither impersonal nor strictly individual, but culturally embedded, social-political. Falling short of such radical formulations, ***Adam Bede*** nonetheless launches an ethical critique of Kantian formalism and pushes its readers toward a recognition of the partial, embodied nature of the visual, pointing to the real consequences of the idealizing, impersonal gaze. Falling short of a revolutionary radicalism, perhaps, the textual exploration of the relations between aesthetics and ethics nonetheless reveals that ***Adam Bede*** is very much in tune with a critical understanding of the politics of looking.

Notes

1. See, for example, Laura Mulvey, "Visual Pleasure and Narrative Cinema," in *Visual and Other Pleasures* (London: Macmillan, 1989), pp. 14-26; and Mary Louise Pratt, *Imperial Eyes: Travel Writing and Transculturation* (London and New York: Routledge, 1992), especially pp. 201-219.
2. George Eliot, *Adam Bede* (New York: Harper and Brothers, 1859), p. 162. All subsequent quotations will refer parenthetically to page numbers from this edition.
3. Judith Mitchell, *The Stone and the Scorpion: The Female Subject of Desire in the Novels of Charlotte Brontë, George Eliot, and Thomas Hardy* (Westport and London: Greenwood Press, 1994), p. 97.
4. Ibid., p. 96.
5. Nancy L. Paxton, *George Eliot and Herbert Spencer: Feminism, Evolutionism, and the Reconstruction of Gender* (Princeton: Princeton University Press, 1991), p. 59.
6. Norman Bryson, *Vision and Painting: The Logic of the Gaze* (New Haven and London: Yale University Press, 1983), pp. 87, 89.
7. "'I'm half a mind ta'a look at her to-night . . . a uncommon pretty young woman,'" says Wiry Ben in the first pages of the novel (p. 4). "'She looked like St. Catherine in a quaker dress,'" says Arthur, "'It's a type of face one rarely sees among our common people'" (pp. 55-56).
8. "Adam, unconscious of the admiration he was exciting, presently struck across the fields" (p. 8).
9. Kimberley Reynolds, *Girls Only? Gender and Popular Children's Fiction in Britain, 1880-1910* (New York and London: Harvester Wheatsheaf, 1990), pp. 23-24.
10. See Joseph Bristow, *Empire Boys: Adventures in a Man's World* (London: Harper Collins, 1991), pp. 53-64.
11. Murray Knowles & Kirsten Malmkjaer, *Language and Control in Children's Literature* (London and New York: Routledge, 1996), p.9.
12. Both Bristow's *Empire Boys* and Reynolds's *Girls Only?* cite Thomas Hughes's *Tom Brown's Schooldays* as the first major text of boys' fiction.
13. George Eliot (1860) *The Mill on the Floss,* Ed. Gordon S. Haight (Oxford: Clarendon Press, 1980), pp. 45, 30, 33, and 35.
14. The epigraph to *Tom Brown's Schooldays* includes this phrase, apparently taken from the *Rugby Magazine.* Thomas Hughes, *Tom Brown's Schooldays* (Cambridge: Macmillan and Company, 1857), title page.
15. Margaret Homans, "Dinah's Blush, Maggie's Arm: Class, Gender, and Sexuality in George Eliot's Early Novels," *Victorian Studies,* 36, (1993), pp. 155-170.
16. "Hetty blushed a deep rose-color when Captain Donnithorne entered the dairy and spoke to her; but it was not at all a distressed blush, for it was inwreathed with smiles and dimples, and with sparkles from under long curled dark eyelashes" (pp. 74-75).
17. "Dinah's sexualization is limited to blushing," Homans, "Dinah's Blush," p. 168.
18. Immanuel Kant (1790) *Critique of Judgement,* tr. J. H. Bernard (London and New York: Hafner, 1951), p. 54.
19. G. W. F. Hegel (1807) *Phenomenology of Spirit,* tr. A. V. Miller (Oxford and New York: Oxford University Press, 1977), p. 111.
20. Homans makes a highly persuasive argument that the novel favours the marriage between Adam and Dinah as the realization of middle-class ideology, which Eliot "universalizes . . . by making its peculiar characteristics appear natural, generically human ones," Homans, "Dinah's Blush," p. 156.
21. Both Arthur and Adam are said to be "beguiled" when they see Hetty as "a dear, affectionate, good little thing" (p. 141), and the narrator tells us that it is "wonderful how little she seemed to care" about her family (p. 142).
22. I am using the masculine pronoun to describe the narrator in *Adam Bede,* following J. Hillis Miller, who writes: "I say 'his' to remind the reader that the putative speaker . . . is not Mary Ann Evans, the author of *Adam Bede,* but a fictive personage, 'George Eliot,' who narrates the story and who is given a male gender." J. Hillis Miller, *The Ethics of Reading: Kant, de Man, Eliot, Trollope, James, and Benjamin* (New York: Columbia University Press, 1987), p. 66.
23. Paxton offers a forceful case that Eliot's representation of Hetty is a polemical response to Herbert Spencer: "By describing Hetty's 'impersonal' beauty, Eliot questions Spencer's unexamined assumption that perfect beauty reflects intellectual perfection in men but moral virtue in women. Hetty's beauty, indeed, disguises the private and various secrets of her inner life." Paxton, *George Eliot and Herbert Spencer,* p. 47. This chapter as a whole considers the problem of beauty:

"Beauty, Sexuality, and Evolutionary Process: *Adam Bede* and 'Personal Beauty'" (Paxton, *George Eliot and Herbert Spencer*, pp. 43-68).

FURTHER READING

Criticism

Adam, Ian. "The Structure of Realisms in *Adam Bede*." In *Nineteenth Century Fiction* 30, No. 2 (September 1975): 127-49.

Looks at how the level of accuracy with which commonplace subject matter is presented has structural significance to *Adam Bede*.

Adams, Kimberly VanEsveld. "Feminine Godhead, Feminist Symbol: The Madonna in George Eliot, Ludwig Feuerbach, Anna Jameson, and Margaret Fuller." In *Journal of Feminist Studies in Religion* 12, No. 1 (Spring 1996): 41-70.

Argues that by placing Adam in the role of Christ figure and Dinah as the Madonna, *Adam Bede* becomes a representation of the Godhead's female qualities; through this configuration of the female earthly ideal, the Madonna figure becomes a means to criticize social oppression of women.

Anderson, Roland F. "George Eliot Provoked: John Blackwood and Chapter Seventeen of *Adam Bede*." In *Modern Philology* 71, No. 1 (August 1973): 39-47.

Examines Eliot's disagreement with publisher John Blackwood as the real-life impetus for her discussion of artistic realism and Dutch painting.

Brown, Monika. "Dutch Painters and British Novel-Readers: *Adam Bede* in the Context of Victorian Cultural Literacy." In *Victorians Institute Journal* 18 (1990): 113-33.

Looks at how Eliot's use of Dutch painting in *Adam Bede* establishes conventions for literary realism."

Cleere, Eileen. "Reproduction and Malthusian Economics: Fat, Fertility, and Family Planning in George Eliot's *Adam Bede*." In *Genders 24: On Your Left, Historical Materialism in the 1990s,* edited by Ann Kibbey, Thomas Foster, Carol Siegel, and Ellen Berry, pp. 150-83. New York: New York University Press, 1996.

Presents historical and economic information to support a reading of women as commodities within various family structures in *Adam Bede*.

Eifrig, Gail McGrew. "History and Memory in *Adam Bede*." *Soundings* LXXVI, Nos. 2-3 (Summer-Fall 1993): 407-20.

Examines Eliot's extensive familiarity with contemporary fiction, biographies, and histories, and discusses how this experience informs her treatment of character history in *Adam Bede*.

Erickson, Joyce Quiring. "Multiculturalism and the Question of Audience: *Adam Bede* as a Test Case." *The Victorian Newsletter* No. 85 (Spring 1994): 20-25.

Discusses the value of teaching *Adam Bede* in multicultural classrooms.

Herbert, Christopher. "Preachers and the Schemes of Nature in *Adam Bede*." *Nineteenth Century Fiction* 29, No. 4 (March 1975): 412-27.

Looks at *Adam Bede* as more than a simple country story but as a dialogue of the moral and religious issues circulating through Eliot's culture.

Homans, Margaret. "Dinah's Blush, Maggie's Arm: Class, Gender, and Sexuality in George Eliot's Early Novels." *Victorian Studies* 36, No. 2 (Winter 1993): 155-78.

A feminist reading of *Adam Bede* and *The Mill on the Floss* that discusses gender, sexuality, and how Eliot generalizes middle-class womanhood as all womanhood.

Hunter, Shelagh. "George Eliot: Adam Bede—the Bounds of the Idyll." In *Victorian Idyllic Fiction: Pastoral Strategies,* pp. 120-66. London: Macmillan Press, 1984.

Concentrating on rural people and their world as presented in nineteenth century fiction, this chapter considers *Adam Bede* to be Eliot's only idyllic novel, and explores its pastoral nature.

Knoepflmacher, U. C. "The Post-Romantic Imagination: *Adam Bede,* Wordsworth and Milton." In *ELH* 34, No. 4 (December 1967): 518-40.

Discusses the act of seeing as vital to the creation of reality in works by Milton and Wordsworth and examines their influence on Eliot's use of realism in *Adam Bede*.

Lewis, Robert P. "'Full Consciousness': Passion and Conversion in *Adam Bede*." In *Religion and the Arts* 2-4 (1998): 423-42.

Examines Eliot's religious influences and explores *Adam Bede*'s treatment of the failure of religious figures to save the truly lost sheep.

Martin, Bruce K. "Rescue and Marriage in *Adam Bede*." In *Studies in English Literature 1500-1900* XII, No. 4 (Autumn 1972): 745-63.

Discusses criticism of Eliot for *Adam Bede*'s happy ending, and seeks to understand authorial intent behind her use of rescue and marriage in a plot otherwise concerned with Adam's acquisition of sympathy.

Moldstad, David. "George Eliot's *Adam Bede* and Smiles's *Life of George Stephenson*." In *English Language Notes* XIV, No. 3 (March 1977): 189-92.

Draws comparisons between *The Life of George Stephenson* and *Adam Bede*. Also looks at Eliot's life experiences as models for *Adam Bede*.

Morgan, Susan. "Paradise Reconsidered: Edens without Eve." In *Historical Studies and Literary Criticism,* edited by Jerome J. McGann, pp. 266-82. Madison, Wis.: The University of Wisconsin Press, 1985.

Suggests that nineteenth-century British fiction explores the notion of paradise as a matter of history and gender intertwined, and describes the difficulty of performing a feminist reading of *Adam Bede* considering its male-centered plot.

Sadoff, Dianne F. "Nature's Language: Metaphor in the Text of *Adam Bede.*" *Genre* XI, No. 3 (Fall 1978): 411-26.

Examines the tension between transcendence and realism in Adam Bede through Eliot's theory of figurative language, and deconstructs the novel's assertions of coherence, stability, and symbolic unity.

Squires, Michael. "*Adam Bede* and the *Locus Amoenus.*" In *Studies in English Literature 1500-1900* XIII, No. 4 (Autumn 1973): 670-76.

Argues that with the use of locus amoenus (lovely place) Eliot combines pastoral conventions and Christian morality in *Adam Bede.*

Additional coverage of Eliot's life and career is contained in the following sources published by the Gale Group: *Concise Dictionary of British Literary Biography 1832-1890; Dictionary of Literary Biography,* Vols. 21, 35, and 55; *DISCovering Authors; DISCovering Authors: British; DISCovering Authors: Canadian; DISCovering Authors Modules: Most-studied Authors* and *Novelists; DISCovering Authors 3.0; Poetry Criticism,* Vol. 20; and *World Literature Criticism.*

Bayard Taylor
1825-1878

American travel essayist, poet, novelist, and translator.

INTRODUCTION

Bayard Taylor was a popular and prolific travel writer, although he always considered poetry his true calling. His eleven volumes of travel essays, including accounts of his adventures in the Middle and Far East propelled him to celebrity status. He immersed himself in other cultures, and although his portrayals are occasionally stereotypical and sometimes overly positive, they are never lacking in enthusiasm. Taylor's interest in travel was matched only by his love of poetry. He was a member of the Genteel Tradition, which emphasized conventionality and correctness in writing, and his poetry reflected the mores of 19th century society. Taylor was so well known and so well connected in the literary circles of the era that Herman Melville used Taylor as the basis for a character in *The Confidence Man,* and Bret Harte wrote a tribute to Taylor on the event of the latter's death. Much of Taylor's work has fallen into obscurity since his death, but his translation of Johann Wolfgang von Goethe's *Faust* (1871) has survived to this day, and is considered to be an excellent preservation of the original rhyme and meter.

BIOGRAPHICAL INFORMATION

Taylor was born on January 11, 1825, in Kennett Square, Chester County, Pennsylvania. His ancestry was English and German and he was raised as a Quaker. He was, however, never happy living on a farm, and relished his time in West Chester, where he apprenticed to a local printer. This apprenticeship allowed him to publish a volume of poems, *Ximena; or, The Battle of the Sierra Morena, and Other Poems* (1844). With the money he made from this volume, Taylor sailed to Europe, and truly began his career as a travel essayist and writer. *Views A-Foot; or Europe Seen with Knapsack and Staff* (1846), along with the newspaper essays which comprised the volume, propelled him to celebrity, and its success allowed him to travel for the rest of his life. In 1850 Taylor married his childhood sweetheart, but his bride died suddenly two months after the wedding; his grief prompted Taylor to embark on another voyage. He was quite taken with the cultures of Africa and the Middle East, describing them in *A Journey to Central Africa; or, Life and Landscapes from Egypt to the Negro Kingdoms of the White Nile* (1854) and *The Lands of the Saracen; or, Pictures of Palestine, Asia Minor, Sicily and Spain* (1854). He then joined Commodore Matthew Perry on his voyage to open Japan to the west, and chronicled the journey in *A Visit to India, China and Japan in the Year 1853* (1855). He also lectured prolifically throughout the period, until the Civil War broke out and reduced the demand for lecture tours. Searching for another source of income, Taylor began writing novels. He remarried in 1857 to Marie Hansen, the daughter of a German businessman, and was later appointed Minister to Germany. Taylor's connection to Germany and his growing interest in German literature prompted his translation of *Faust,* and he had planned on biographies of Schiller and Goethe before he died on December 19, 1878.

MAJOR WORKS

Taylor's travel essays were immensely popular in their time, with *Views A-Foot* going through six printings in its first year and a total of twenty by 1855. Despite their popularity, though, Taylor's travel essays have not withstood the test of time. These accounts express both his interest in immersing himself in other cultures and his belief in the superiority of European society; however, the breakneck pace at which he conducted his voyages, according to Richard Cary, prompted Park Benjamin to comment that "Taylor had traveled more but seen less than any man who ever lived." Taylor's greatest legacy is his translation of *Faust,* which is lauded to this day, although it has lost its status as the standard English translation of the work. Taylor's poetry is respected for its technical achievement, but has often been criticized as derivative. He is considered a good poet, but not a poetic genius. His novels have faced the same criticism, and are not held in so high regard as those of Mark Twain and other acquaintances of Taylor. Torn between his desire to write in the romantic vein and his reluctance to break with the conventional morality of the day, Taylor's indecision, in the view of some scholars, led to mediocrity. In the end, Taylor is more renowned for the quantity of his work than the quality.

CRITICAL RECEPTION

Taylor has received little critical attention in the twentieth century. Modern critics, such as C. W. LaSalle II, have focused on Taylor's poetry and novels, largely disregarding his travel works. Richard Cary sees Taylor's poetry and prose as mediocre at best, and few critics are impressed with his style and ability. He is considered a product of his environment, an example of his time rather than a ground-breaking figure, competent, but not especially gifted. Taylor's critical reception in his time, however, was extremely positive, owing partially to the practice by Genteel Poets of commenting favorably on each other's works. Many critics have considered the difference between Taylor's early critical and popular success and his relative obscurity one hundred years later. John T. Krumpelman pinpoints the imitative nature of his work, while Paul C. Wermuth blames both Taylor's lack of writing ability and a change in literary tastes for his diminished reputation in the twentieth century.

PRINCIPAL WORKS

Ximena; or, The Battle of the Sierra Morena, and Other Poems (poetry) 1844

**Views A-Foot; or, Europe Seen with Knapsack and Staff* (travel essays) 1848

Rhymes of Travel, Ballads and Poems Poetry 1849

Eldorado; or, Adventures in the Path of Empire: Comprising a Voyage to California, via Panama; Life in San Francisco and Monterey; Pictures of the Gold Region, and Experiences of Mexican Travel (travel essays, two volumes) 1850

A Book of Romances, Lyrics, and Songs (poetry) 1852

†*A Journey to Central Africa; or, Life and Landscapes from Egypt to the Negro Kingdoms of the White Nile* (travel essays) 1854

Poems of the Orient (poetry) 1855

‡*Lands of the Saracen; or, Pictures of Palestine, Asia Minor, Sicily and Spain* (travel essays) 1855

A visit to India, China, and Japan, in the Year 1853 (travel essays) 1855

Poems of Home and Travel (poetry) 1855

#*Cyclopaedia of Modern Travel: A Record of Adventure, Exploration and Discovery, for the Past Fifty Years: Comprising Narratives of the Most Distinguished Travelers Since the Beginning of This Century* (travel essays) 1856

||*Northern Travel; Summer and Winter Pictures of Sweden, Lapland, and Norway* (travel essays) 1858

At Home and Abroad: A Sketch-Book of Life, Scenery, and Men (travel essays) 1860

At Home and Abroad: A Sketch-Book of Life, Scenery, and Men, . . . Second Series (travel essays) 1862

The Poet's Journal (poetry) 1863

Hannah Thurston: A Story of American Life (novel) 1863

John Godfrey's Fortunes; Related by Himself. A Story of American Life (novel) 1864

The Poems of Bayard Taylor (poetry) 1865

The Story of Kennett (novel) 1866

The Picture of St. John (novel) 1866

§*By-Ways of Europe* (travel essays) 1869

The Ballad of Abraham Lincoln (poetry) 1870

Joseph and His Friend: A Story of Pennsylvania (novel) 1870

Faust: A Tragedy by Johann Wolfgang von Goethe; the First Part, Translated, in the Original Metres, by Bayard Taylor [translator] (drama) 1871

Faust: A Tragedy by Johann Wolfgang von Goethe; the Second Part, Translated, in the Original Metres, by Bayard Taylor [translator] (drama) 1871

Beauty and the Beast: And Tales of Home (poetry) 1872

The Masque of the Gods (drama) 1872

***Diversions of the Echo Club: A Companion to the "Autocrat of the Breakfast Table"* [anonymous] (parody) 1872

Lars: a Pastoral of Norway (poetry) 1873

The Prophet: A Tragedy (drama) 1874

††*A School History of Germany: From the Earliest Period to the Establishment of the German Empire in 1871* (history) 1874

Home Pastorals, Ballads and Lyrics (poetry) 1875

Boys of Other Countries: Stories for American Boys (stories) 1876

‡‡"The National Ode" (poem) 1876

Prince Deukalion: A Lyrical Drama (drama) 1878

Studies in German Literature (essays) 1879

Critical Essays and Literary Notes (essays, edited by Marie Hansen-Taylor) 1880

The Poetical Works of Bayard Taylor (poetry) 1880

*Augmented as *Pedestrian Tour in Europe. Views A-Foot; or, Europe Seen with Knapsack and Staff* 1848, revised 1855.

†Republished as *Life and Landscapes from Egypt to the Negro Kingdoms of the White Nile; Being A Journey to Central Africa* 1854.

‡Republished as *Pictures of Palestine, Asia Minor, Sicily and Spain; or, The Lands of the Saracen* 1855.

#Revised and enlarged as *Cyclopaedia of Modern Travel: A Record of Adventure, Exploration and Discovery, for the Past Sixty Years . . .* (two volumes) 1860.

||Republished as *Northern Travel: Summer and Winter Pictures of Sweden, Denmark, and Lapland* 1858.

§Also published as *Byeways of Europe* (two volumes) 1869.

**Augmented and republished as *The Echo Club, and Other Literary Diversions* 1876.

††Republished with an additional chapter by Marie Hansen-Taylor as *A History of Germany From the Earliest Times to the Present Day* 1894.

‡‡Republished as "The National Ode: The Memorial Freedom Poem" 1877.

CRITICISM

Richard Cary (essay date 1952)

SOURCE: *The Genteel Circle: Bayard Taylor and his New York Friends,* Cornell University Press, 1952, pp. 14-21.

[*In the following excerpt, Cary discusses Taylor's egotism and the effect it had on his work and on his role as a leader of the Genteel Tradition.*]

With complete justice Russell Blankenship calls Bayard Taylor "the crown prince of the Genteel Tradition under the benign despotism of the First Triumvirate, Lowell, Longfellow, and Holmes."[1] In Taylor may be descried all the traits of the romantic-sentimental school which culminates in a carefully cultivated academic isolationism despite its pretenses to rugged worldliness and manliness. His achievement was an inspiration to his three comrades, his popularity their hope, his sturdiness their rock in time of trouble. [Richard Henry] Stoddard, most clamorously self-sufficient of the four, paid Taylor this tribute after his death, "My nature is not a reverent one, I fear, but I looked up to Bayard Taylor."[2] [Edmund Clarence] Stedman, most dependent upon Taylor's spiritual largesse, and [Thomas Baileg] Aldrich, most equable of the quartet, also acknowledged their debts to him on frequent public and private occasions. He was all they were striving to be: well known, widely read, world-traveled, acclaimed by an indulgent audience, handsome, dashing, an inveterate idealist, and a solid family man. As long as he lived, he remained, discounting small disloyalties, the apex of their aspirations.

In his turn, Taylor revered the great Brahmins. He borrowed their themes and techniques, he aped their bookish urbanity, he longed for their Olympian status in the world of readers. He sought their praises avidly and quoted their favorable phrases exuberantly in his letters. He visited them as often as pretext would warrant (much to Stoddard's disgust), wrote eulogies on their flimsiest efforts, and associated himself with them in thought and print wherever and whenever possible. His fondest desire was to be mentioned in the same breath with them, to be entombed in the same future anthologies of American literature. He was to die disappointed, however, for he lacked that fund of human understanding which distinguished them from lesser practitioners of the genteel mode. They moved through the hearts of their readers in a surge of deep-felt sentiment; he hovered about their heads in a translucent mist of romance. His exteriority fell victim to winds of realism which could not affect the inward warmth induced by his elders.

Taylor's salient flaw, second in seriousness only to his essential mediocrity, was his hunger for fame. His quest for recognition was insatiable and, eventually, fatal. He diverted his energy into so many channels that his output was shallow in every respect. He substituted versatility and industry for originality and profundity. His subsidiary careers of journalist, traveler, writer of travel books, lecturer, diplomatist, and landed proprietor interfered with his prime ambition to become a distinguished poet. These secondary activities—true to the genteel code, he considered poetry the *highest* accomplishment of man—sapped his strength and finally brought him down. Taylor died twenty-five years before any of his three intimates, martyr to the "cheaper service" of which he wrote in **"Implora Pace."** His life was too full of excursion and he was too intent upon immediate fame to give the poetic sentiment sufficient time and quiet to mature.

The cult of the writer as gentleman was one of the most important genteel attitudes to which he subscribed. Remembering Scott and Burke in Great Britain, Irving and Cooper in America, he erected a gigantic country estate which he called Cedarcroft, near Kennett Square, Pennsylvania. He devoted a disproportionate part of the rest of his life supporting or trying to dispose of it. Ellis Paxson Oberholtzer,[3] Albert H. Smyth,[4] and other commentators testify to its severe drain upon his resources, mental and monetary. Mrs. Taylor reports additional tribulations:

> He was driven by the demands which his estate made upon him. He had a hearty, unaffected welcome for his friends, and they could not stay too long; but others, who had no claim upon his friendship, made one on his hospitality. He was vexed and teased by the petty gossip which assailed him, and by the direct assaults upon his freedom.[5]

The gossip and assaults upon his freedom of which Mrs. Taylor speaks sprang largely from the bucolic townsfolk of Kennett. They murmured against the frequent consignments of delicacies that passed through town on their way to Cedarcroft. Taylor affected an Eastern potentate's flair for entertainment, and it was particularly the spirituous nature of the refreshments that fostered hostile remarks.

Taylor's rage for recognition led him to solicit applause and to misconstrue the enthusiasm of celebrity-hunters for the sincere appreciation of literate readers. He delighted in the outward signs of his popularity evoked by his appearance on the lecture platform. Three letters written in February, March, and April, 1854, emphatically repudiate matinee idolatry, then continue contrarily to a confession of complete enjoyment.[6] He was happy to confuse the inquisitive and the critical faculties of the mobs who paid fifty cents to see his romantic profile and costume; it bolstered his belief in himself as an indestructible poet. He was "anxious for the roses,"[7] as George Edward Woodberry puts it, but he is not to be accused of petty egotism. His vanity was of the kind that took pleasure in achievement even if it were his own. His self-love was that of a child, supreme within his circumscribed universe. He repeated joyfully words of praise accorded to his works. But his manifest honesty and naïveté more than counterbalanced this offensive little habit.

Taylor was a man of infinite attraction, as his close friendship with such dissimilar personalities as Stoddard, Stedman, and Aldrich demonstrates. He had none of the repellent traits reputed to "the jealous, waspish, wrong-head, rhyming race." His willingness to forget a fault or patch up a difference is to be noted throughout his letters. His inclination to forgive was, in fact, sometimes embarrassing. He made his correspondent feel like a gamin who has hit an angel in the eye with a mud pie. And he was frequently too zealous in delegating the blame to the other party when, clearly, he was in the wrong himself. His expansiveness in these cases is amusingly ingenuous. But his sincerity is unquestionable. He praised unstintingly and was happy in his friends' happiness. He was a monument of good nature, giving freely of spiritual comfort and worldly goods. His ideal was peace on earth, good will.

Taylor's publicity-seeking and fraternizing with important international figures lend a distasteful savor to many of his letters. He practically bent his head to be patted by the Empress of Russia and Bismarck, relating his experiences in their company with ill-concealed effervescence to his friends in plebeian America. Woodberry attributes this parvenu trait of Taylor's to "a discomfortable doubt of his position."[8] There is much to commend this view, for Taylor was basically insecure; he did lack the sense of self-affirmation which usually goes with ripened genius. Four years before his death he was still grasping at outward signs of approval to reassure himself.[9] As so often before, he misinterpreted personal esteem for literary acclaim. It was a fortunate confusion for him; it prevented warping of his amiable nature and precluded bitterness or total disillusionment.

In order to assuage his thirst for fame he sought to encompass "cosmical experience," which, in his language, came to mean visiting musky regions of the world and inviting bizarre incidents. He penetrated darkest Africa, was with Perry at Japan's gate, had his nose frozen in Finland, ate the two-dollar table d'hôte in San Francisco during the gold rush, entered Indian temples and Chinese pagodas, sat in harems and conversed with eunuchs, crawled into the inner chambers of pyramids, tried on Cheops' signet ring, smoked hashish, and swam in the Dead Sea. No adolescent dream of grandeur has ever been more fully realized.

During the Quixotic Quarter-Century (1850-1875), the Hicks portrait of Taylor was as familiar a household object as a volume of Longfellow's verse. In the illustrated books and magazines of the period one may study the romantically bronzed profile, the lean cheek, the flashing eye, and the Asiatic accouterments of burnoose and narghile which thrilled a generation of prosaic Americans. He gloried in his virile role, extending it lustily into his literary activity.

In exemplifying his ideal of *mens sana in corpore sano,* he bounced about in foreign lands, arranging situations which would result in masculine adventures, then wrote and lectured upon these prefabricated hazards to enchanted audiences in America. He continually referred to his predilection for the natural man who drew his physical and spiritual sustenance directly from the earth. One is reminded of Whitman's overzealous manly pose, with the exception that Taylor, as always, drew genteel limits around his primitivism, which was practically all talk, talk calculated to create a myth. Taylor always took care to see that he was as comfortably fed, clothed, and housed as the occasion allowed.

His view of the author as well-muscled and virtuous athlete led to curious but comprehensible critical standards:

> No man of ordinary penetration can fail to detect, in the poems of Elizabeth Barrett Browning, or in the tales of Poe, the evidence of a diseased body. Byron, with all the shifting play of his wit, pathos, profanity and passion, cannot wholly purify the pages of *Don Juan* from the smell of gin; and Mrs. Radcliffe, in the nightmare horrors of her *Mysteries of Udolpho,* betrays the suppers of raw beef in which she indulged. Contrast the dark and sinful fascination of *Lucretia,* written by the exhausted and dyspeptic Bulwer, with the ruddy and healthy tone of *The Caxtons,* written by the same Bulwer after his system had been restored by the water cure.[10]

This canon of purity in mind and body, which stemmed partly from Taylor's Quaker heritage and partly from his reverence for the Brahmin code, betrayed him into the *ad hominem* fallacy. His refusal to acclaim Whitman and Swinburne—both of whom he admired as poets but contemned as men—was based on this guileless distortion of literary values. So successful was Taylor's output as "the expression of a genial, healthy mind,"[11] that it led John Macy to exclaim, "Bayard Taylor, a first-rate man but a fourth-rate littérateur."[12] It is a deserved rebuke; Taylor did become the logical conclusion to a fantastic theory of art.

He worked steadily, diligently, and without especial illumination at his chosen chore. Laura Stedman, wife of his colleague, characterized him as "a valiant example of enthusiasm, industry, scholarship, aspiration, unfaltering faith, and allegiance to the highest ideals of Art."[13] Encomiums aside, the truth of the matter is that Bayard Taylor killed himself prematurely by attempting to do more than his constitution would stand. His multifarious exploits outside of literature have already been commented upon. The variety and bulk of his literary production alone were enough to have severely strained him. His journalistic hack work included foreign correspondence, miscellaneous articles on popular subjects of the day, book reviews, editorials, and editing of materials submitted by other writers. Articles, poems, biographical sketches, and book reviews for the magazines flowed unceasingly from his pen. His bibliography reveals thirty-six published volumes: eleven travel books and one travel cyclopedia, four novels, fourteen books of poetry and poetical drama, one literary history, one translation, one history, one volume of collected short stories, one book of critical essays and literary opinions, and one of parodies.

The quantity is staggering; the quality unprepossessing. His prose is distinctive neither for its excellence nor for its badness; it is simply mediocre. The best of it may be found in his travel books which, despite Park Benjamin's quip that Bayard Taylor had traveled more and seen less than any man who had ever lived, are among the more satisfactory American volumes of the type. But to discuss Taylor's prose is not to discuss Taylor at all. He considered prose merely a breadwinner and tossed it off, so to speak, with his left hand. "His life," as Stedman explained, and every subsequent biographer and critic has echoed, "was consecrated to poetry."[14] It was through this medium that Taylor strove to express what was deepest and truest in him. Out of his sadly ineffectual efforts emerges the sincere, sensuous, prudent, thwarted personality that aspired to Helicon but had not the gifts to attain it.

His letters teem with expressions of optimism and, in time of defeat, of eventual victory. His friends turned to him often for courage and reassurance; his source of hope was seemingly inexhaustible. But, privately, he knew the pangs of failure and solaced himself with stratagems. When widespread recognition failed to materialize, he turned for comfort to the sympathetic critiques of his cronies and the like-minded Brahmins.[15] When critical opinion failed to justify his belief in himself, as in the case of his **"National Ode"** (1876), he took "rare pleasure in knowing that his lofty strains had fallen upon the delighted ears of the common people."[16]

For all of his fidelity and indefatigability, Taylor never achieved true distinction in poetry. Critics as diverse as Norman Foerster and Ludwig Lewisohn agree that he "aspired" to more than he "attained," and that the essence of his defect was diffuseness. Foerster blames Taylor's versatility and long hours:

> Taylor wrote lyrics, pastorals, idylls, odes, dramatic lyrics, lyrical dramas, translations, poems in German, poems in every mood and every meter, . . . poems on themes Oriental, Greek, Norse, American from coast to coast, poems classical, sentimental, romantic, realistic, poems of love, of nature, of art. . . . His poetry, again, is diffuse, as the poetry of a fifteen-hour-a-day journalist is likely to be.[17]

A short excursion into Taylor's verse will convince one that his biographer, Albert H. Smyth, was correct in classifying him as "a *meister-singer* . . . and master of the mechanics of his craft"[18] rather than a poet of first order. Taylor had poetic flair, gusto, talent, but not genius. He practiced Browning's dictum about a man's reach exceeding his grasp, but if he achieved Heaven, it was after his death.

Taylor's main difficulty rose from his disposition to compromise. He desired to be a romantic poet yet conform to the conventional modes of his day. The two, romance and convention, are mutually exclusive in a realistic period. As Beatty declares, "A conventional Shelley is inconceivable, as is a conventional Burns."[19] Conventional Taylor tried to be romantic Taylor but was incapable of bursting the bonds. He became, in his frustration, sentimental Taylor, pushing aside reality and cleaving to the myth. So his verse is a playground of romantic figments, sentimental clichés, and genteel techniques.

Perhaps the strongest genteel influence to be noted in his poems is the rigid adherence to form. He dallied with many line lengths and rhyme schemes but took care that each was an orderly, polished representative of its kind. He was no voyager into uncharted seas, no innovator of eccentric designs. His creed would not allow it. Writing to Stedman, who was himself a stickler for form, Taylor asserts: "Thought (in poetry) is subject to architectural rules."[20] The irregular metric and the slanted or absent rhyme were barbarisms not to be tolerated by writers in the great tradition. Taylor labored for hours, sometimes days, to eliminate crudity and asymmetry from his verse. Only such a votary of form would have planned and persevered in the translation of Goethe's *Faust* in the original meters.

The bookish phase of genteelism was triumphant in two other respects: the deliberateness with which Taylor conceived his poetry, and his conscious imitation of predecessors. He seems to have utterly lacked the intuitive fire—the sudden spiritual insight which informs the work of poets in the highest rank. His letters reveal the grocer-like calculation which preceded the production of a new poem. "He speaks of poems . . . as if they could be made to order: so many last week, so many to be ready by such a day next month."[21] One looks in vain for the spontaneity, the mystery which suffuses poetical creation. One finds only the pale glare of the intellect. An example of the mechanic method which brought so many of his poems into being is found in his letter to Boker in October, 1852:

> But two months ago, in Malta, I picked up a volume of the "Westminster Review," wherein I read, "B. T. has published a volume of Tennysonian imitations," etc. I fired up in an instant. "Damn the reviewer!" I said to myself. "Before he dies he shall tell another story," and in two days I had conceived at least six new poems.[22]

Job lots of poems born out of pique! What a grotesque approach to the conception of beauty.

Taylor's natural leanings led him to emulate the prominent romantics with whom he has already been linked. This congeniality of temper plus a prodigious memory—H. H. Boyeson[23] and Albert H. Smyth[24] affirm his amazing ability to remember long and obscure passages—made imitation inescapable in a man whose inventive powers were severely limited.

Dependence upon the library rather than life for poetic subject matter was another genteel failing which helped turn Taylor into a sentimentalist. He had travelled extensively in the Orient and knew its shoddiness as well as its glamour. But he chose to ignore the former in favor of a fairyland of intrepid men who loved horses as passionately as they did women. He recreated the enticement, the dream, and the dalliance proclaimed by sensualists of the past. But his gift was not so great as theirs; his ardor was forced, his rhetoric hollow. While he managed to shield these failings from most of the reading public during his lifetime, they have since become palpable.

Unwary critics have been misled by Taylor's habit of industrious revision. Noting numerous changes in poems from edition to edition, they have credited him with the capacity for ruthless self-criticism. It is true that Taylor applied new yardsticks to old poems and often altered them radically. But it is also true, as a reading of his letters will show, that he invariably considered his current work the *greatest* of his accomplishments so far. His urge to revise sprang less from an understanding of fundamental deficiencies than from a recognition of explicit limitations. His most grievous inadequacies persisted to the end. It would be unfair, however, to propose that Taylor did not improve with time: he progressively rid himself of his most flagrant affectations. But at the core he remained romantic and idealistic, exotic and unreal—a boy in a man's world.

Notes

1. *American Literature* (New York, 1931), p. 432.
2. Russell H. Conwell, *The Life, Travels, and Literary Career of Bayard Taylor* (Boston, 1881), p. 337.
3. *The Literary History of Philadelphia* (Philadelphia, 1906), p. 375.
4. *Bayard Taylor,* p. 121.
5. Taylor and Scudder, II, 515.
6. Taylor and Scudder, I, 270, 271, 276.
7. *Literary Memoirs of the Nineteenth Century* (New York, 1921), p. 242.
8. Page 243.
9. Taylor and Scudder, II, 661.
10. Richmond C. Beatty, "Bayard Taylor: A Mind Divided," *American Review,* III (April, 1934), 81.
11. John S. Hart, *A Manual of American Literature* (Philadelphia, 1878), p. 456.
12. *The Spirit of American Literature* (New York, 1913), p. 311.
13. "Bayard Taylor," *North American Review,* CCI (June, 1915), 907.
14. *Poets of America,* p. 409.
15. Leon H. Vincent, *American Literary Masters* (Boston, 1906), pp. 407-408.
16. Taylor and Scudder, II, 687.
17. "Later Poets," *Cambridge History of American Literature,* ed. by W. P. Trent (New York, 1921), III, 42.
18. Page 273.
19. *Bayard Taylor,* p. 102.
20. Taylor and Scudder, II, 634.
21. Woodberry, p. 245.
22. Taylor and Scudder, I, 240.
23. "Reminiscences of Bayard Taylor," *Lippincott's Magazine,* XXIV (August, 1879), 209-210.
24. Page 274.

John T. Krumpelmann (essay date 1959)

SOURCE: *Bayard Taylor and German Letters,* Cram, de Gruyter & Co., 1959, pp. 78-130.

[*In the following excerpt, Krumpelmann examines the degree to which Taylor's work imitates German literature.*]

As in his other works, so in his original literary compositions, Bayard Taylor shows the effects of his knowledge of and interest in German literature. If we examine these works chronologically, we find an ever increasing amount of German influence. As has been indicated above[1] Taylor's real acquaintance with German literature dates from his first trip to Europe (July, 1844—June, 1846). Consequently, his first little volume of poems, ***Ximena,*** published early in 1844[2], is entirely devoid of anything that might even suggest German poetry. His first prose volume, ***Views Afoot,*** which initiated the display of his German interest, has been sufficiently discussed.[3] Now we shall endeavor to demonstrate that some phase of his Germanic interest is displayed in every subsequent volume.

The poetical effusions which came into being during his first European sojourn and shortly thereafter were published in a volume, ***Rhymes of Travel, Ballads and Poems,*** which appeared coincident with the year of 1849. Those lines which Taylor prefixes to one section of this collection:[4]

> And many a verse of such strange influence,
> That we must ever wonder how and whence
> It came.
>
> —Keats

may be aptly applied to the whole volume. The "whence" of a goodly portion of the poetry is certainly German. The first four lines in the book are in that language.[5] They are the first stanza of Justinus Kerner's "Wanderlied"[6] and serve excellently to introduce that part of Taylor's volume called ***Rhymes of Travel.***

Several of the poems in the collection were written in Germany and are so designated.[7] A considerable number of them are on German subjects or have a German background, e.g. **"The Tomb of Charlemagne"**, **"To One Afar"**, **"The Wayside Dream"**, **"Starlight in the Odenwald"**, **"Steyermark"**, **"To a Bavarian Girl"**,[8] **"The Enchanted Knight"**, **"Re-union."** The last-named is a translation "from the German of Karl Christian Tenner."[9]

"The Enchanted Knight"[10] first appeared in *Graham's Magazine* for August, 1848. It was probably written considerably earlier.[11] In any event, we know that in the spring and summer of 1847 Taylor was engaged in reading Uhland's poems[12] and, as his own note to this poem points out:[13] "This old legend is told in Uhland's beautiful ballad, commencing:

> Vor seinem Heergefolge ritt
> Der alte Held Herald—"

Comparing the English poem with its German prototype, we find that Taylor has made rather free use of his material, save in the sixth to eighth stanzas inclusive, which are little more than a translation of the tenth to thirteenth of Uhland's composition. The moralizing tone of Taylor's last three stanzas is his own addition, typical of his youth and his Puritanical American schooling.

In form the poems are very much alike. Uhland's is written in a distinctive stanzaic form, Taylor's in imitation of it, his only variations being in the rime and the occasional substitution of an anapest or a trochee for an iambus. The following will illustrate the stanza structure.

Uhland		Taylor	
x'/x'/x'/x'	a	xx'/x'/xx'/x'	a
x'/x'/x'/	b	x'/xx'/x'/	b
x'/x'/x'/x'	c	x'/xx'/x'/x'	a
x'/x'/x'/	b	xx'/x'/x'/	b

This constitutes the German element in this volume for which we have proof, positive and direct, but we hope to show from internal evidence that other features owe their origin to German song.

We know that Taylor was reading Hauff's works in Germany in December, 1844.[14] His poem **"To One Afar"** is dated Heidelberg, 1844 which would indicate that it was written before December.[15] It may be that Taylor had become acquainted with some of Hauff's poems in Heidelberg, or, that **"To One Afar"** was conceived and sketched in that place and finished after Christmas in Frankfort.[16] Whatever may be truth of its genesis this composition bears undeniable resemblance to Hauff's "Sehnsucht."[17] The general theme of both poems is the same, a longing for a maiden who is afar, "in der Ferne," (L. 20). Although the general treatment by each author is very different, there are several details in common. First, each makes the banks of the Neckar the scene of his lamentations, "des Neckars sanfte Welle quillt." (L. 5); "Beneath, the sounding Neckar rolled." (L. 5). Second, each designates the season of the year in the third line of his poem. Third, Hauff's Neckar wells "an der Gestade Rebenhügel" (L. 6); Taylor's rolls "Through hills which bore him purple wine" (L. 6). Fourth, Hauff's river possesses a "silberreinen Spiegel" (L. 8); Taylor's glimmers like "a chain of gold." (L. 7). Fifth, Hauff pictures the landscapes from early morn until after the rising of the moon; Taylor also makes use of the landscape by daylight and by midnight. The close sequence of the above similarities, the first four corresponding almost line for line, makes them appear to be conscious. There are other points in common, which however might be accidental. Compare:

> Der Abend senket seinen Strahl, L. 21
> . . . . .
> und fernhin durch das holde Thal
> die Dörfer zu der Ruhe läuten

with:

> A vague sweet sense of lingering sound, L. 14
> Like echoes of the chimes of prayer,
> Hallowed the beauty-haunted ground—
> And, through the day's descending hours, etc.

and:

> Auf geht des Mondes Silberstrahl, L. 31
> . . . . .
> ihr Berge all, von Duft umhüllt, L. 35
> du Thal am Strome auf und nieder,

with:

> On the calm midnights' breezy tide, L. 49
> Came the sweet breath of flowers afar;
> . . . . .
> On the stream's bosom throbbed the star.

Then the similarity in form is striking. To be sure Taylor's composition (82 lines) is much longer than Hauff's (40 lines), but each author divides his poem into four stanzas. The meter, as is illustrated by the lines already quoted, is identical, iambic tetrameter.[18] But the rime scheme is the final and conclusive point of relationship. Hauff's stanzas rime regularly ababcdcdee. Taylor faithfully follows this rime scheme except that the last stanza does not end in a couplet.[19]

Any of the above similarities might in itself be accidental, but such a plethora of resemblance combined with the facts that we are positive that Taylor had Hauff's works in his hands by December, 1844,[20] and, that he on other occasions closely imitated German poems makes us feel certain that more than accident played a part in giving these poems so much in common.

The dependence of other pieces in this volume on German models, although probable, is not demonstrable by material proof. Poetry is after all subtile and Taylor was a poet. He did not always simply copy his model, he often merely created after it, perhaps unconscious of it. Therefore in the following instances we merely desire to suggest rather than to prove sources of Taylor's inspiration. In considering these cases one must not forget that Bayard Taylor was a poet in whom the "reminiscent note" is ever recurring. Mrs. Haskell has pointed out this feature in his writings,[21] but has, with one exception,[22] failed to look to German literature for the origin of these notes. The authors of *Life and Letters* are right when they say:[23] "The earliest efforts in poetry are necessarily more or less imitative, and it was inevitable that the poets whom he read should find an echo in his verse." Taylor himself wrote in later years (1863):[24] "Today the poems live in my memory which I read at the age of seven or eight years, and which drove me to desperate attempts at imitation."

With this in mind we think we hear in ***Rhymes of Travel*** other echoes, be they ever so faint, of Kerner, of Uhland, and one of Rückert. Taylor's articles in the *Tribune* of November 21 and 26, 1846, show that he was then familiar with the poems of these three authors. **"The Wayside Dream,"** probably conceived in June, 1845, was finished in March, 1847.[25] **"An Autumn Thought"** is dated 1845[26] and **"The Eagle Hunter"** dates from 1848,[27] hence all are subsequent to Taylor's acquaintance with the authors named.

"The Wayside Dream" is a wanderer's song very similar in mood and theme to that genre of poems found so often in Kerner and exemplified, not only by the poem from which Taylor took the first stanza with which to introduce this volume,[28] but also by "Der Einsame,"[29] "Alte Heimat," "Wanderer" and others. The meter of all three German poems, as well as that of Taylor's poem, is a little tripping iambic trimeter. All are written in short stanzas, Taylor's **"Dream"** and the "Wanderer" being in six line stanzas. In Taylor's stanzas the second, fourth and sixth verses are rimed, the first, third and fifth unrimed. In Kerner's "Der Einsame" the second verse rimes with the fourth, the odd verses are unrimed. Taylor has a given locality to describe[30] and cannot follow any one of Kerner's descriptions. The first four stanzas of the American poem describe his strange surroundings. This corresponds in a general way to the second and third stanzas of "Der Einsame." Then Taylor goes off into a day dream and, for five stanzas, dreams of the beauties of his home. The last lines of "Der Einsame" read:

> Ich schreite durch die düstre Nacht,
> In mir den hellsten Traum.

Kerner's "Alte Heimat" goes on to tell (to line eleven) of a wander's dream of home. In the twelfth stanza of Taylor's composition the dream of home vanishes. In the thirteenth the wanderer rises and journeys onward. The twelfth verse of "Alte Heimat" reads:

> Doch bald der Traum verschwand,

and the fourteenth and fifteenth:

> Da irrt ich weit hinaus
> Ins öde Land voll Sehnen;

There are minutiae in the two poems with bear resemblance, but they are neither numerous enough nor striking enough to prove anything, and could have arisen entirely independently of each other.

"An Autumn Thought" reminds of Rückert's "Herbstlied."[31] Both are written in stanzas of four lines with a rime scheme *abab*. The meter is unlike, both in the length of the lines and in cadence, but Taylor's treatment of the theme seems to be an answer to Rückert's pessimistic skepticism. Such details of expression as "golden" (verse one) applied to the landscape; and "den letzten Sonnenstrahl, / Der aus der düstren Wolke dringt." (L. 5) and "Save where a dim and lonely ray is stealing / The twining branches through." (L. 3 f.); and "brecht die Blume schnell, / Eh' ein Frost sie bricht" (L. 11 f.) and "The Summer's beauty, by the frosts o'ershaded." (L. 17) might be expected in any autumn poem. But, when Rückert interrogates

> Traut dem nächsten Lenze nicht,
> *Der die Blumen neu erweckt;*[32]
> Wißt ihr ob im Lenze nicht
> Erde schon euch deckt?

and Taylor replies,

> Hopes that round us in their beauty hover,
> Fall like this forest-rain;
> But, the stern winter of Misfortune over,
> *They bloom as fresh again!*
> The spring-like verdure of the heart may perish
> Beneath some frosty care,
> But many a bud which Sorrow learned to cherish
> Will bloom again as fair.

we are inclined to suspect that the German poem at least suggested the English one.

Finally the last two stanzas of **"The Eagle Hunter"** recalls, if not Uhland's "Des Knaben Berglied, at least Taylor's translation of it. I quote those lines which most nearly suggest the German poem and underline words and expressions especially worthy of comparison with the original poem or Taylor's translation thereof.

> *I* am come of nobler lineage,
> *And my realm is far above them,*
> Where the *cradles of the rivers*
> Have been hollowed in the snow;
> And *I drink their crystal sources.*
> . . . . .
> *In the meeting of the thunders.*
> When the solid crags are shivered,
> Firm and *fearless* and *rejoicing*
> *On the snowy peak I stand;*
> . . . . .
> *And my voice* has learned *the stormy music*
> *Of the lofty Mountain Land!*

In addition let me call attention to the boyish egotism of the speaker and the prevalence of the firstpersonal pronoun. It seems safe to conclude that these two stanzas would have taken quite a different form, or perhaps would have never come into being (for the story of the eagle hunter is really finished in the fifth stanza), except for Taylor's familiarity with Uhland's poem.[33]

The next volume of poems, ***A Book of Romances, Lyrics, and Songs*** appeared in 1851. In the summer of 1848 Taylor became acquainted with the poems of Shelley[34] "from whose weird and ethereal influence," E. C. Stedman assures us,[35] "Taylor never quite freed himself, nor desired to free himself, until his dying day." It was also of this period that Taylor wrote of himself and Stoddard: "I Shelley's mantel wore, you that of Keats."[36] It is, therefore, probably due in part to this interest in Shelley and his removal from immediate contact with German poetry that the volume of 1851 shows a falling off of the German influence. There is nothing in it which can be positively declared to be of German origin, but there is that which is probably to be attributed to Taylor familiarity with German poetry.

Speaking of Heinrich Heine, C. A. Bucheim writes:[37] "He stood in a sympathetic relation to all nature, particularly to the sea; perhaps, because it typified his agitated heart." It is peculiar that in the section of Taylor's volume which is devoted to **"Songs"**,[38] five of the eight pieces have to do with the sea. In some of them we meet with metrical forms which are common in Heine and the spirit of despondency which characterises so many of Heine's songs. Of course Taylor too was at this time in an agitated state of mind and despondent because he saw the death of Mary Agnew (Taylor) slowly and inevitably approaching. This may account for the pathos of his poems and, if we may follow Buchheim's conjecture, for his fondness for introducing the sea into his compositions. But when we realize that already in 1846 Taylor was well enough versed in the poems of Heine to express an intelligent opinion about them,[39] and when we recall the fact that in the volume which appeared immediately before the one under discussion, ***Eldorado,*** (May, 1850), we found evidence which led us that suspect that Taylor had then had Heine fresh in mind,[40] we have reason to consider more seriously the apparent similarity existing between the English and German poems. Taylor's **"Song" ("Upon a fitful dream of passion")**, **"The Waves"**, **"Storm Song"**, **"Song" ("From the bosom of ocean I seek thee")**, and **"March"** all deal more or less with the sea motive. Only the last three, however, are in meters which might be called characteristic of Heine. All three are in four line stanzas.[41] The structure of the stanza used in **"Storm Song"** is

x—/ x—/ xx—/ x—/ : a
x—/ x—/ x—/ x—/ : b
x—/ xx—/ xx—/ x—/ : a
xx—/ x—/ x—/ : b

with a rather free interchange of anapests and iambi. The poems **"March"**, and **"Song" ("From the bosom of ocean I seek thee")**, however, are more Heinesque in structure. They are written in *the* stanza of Heine:

Heine (Storm Song)
x—/ x—/ x—/ x : a
x—/ x—/ x—/ : b
x—/ x—/ x—/ x : a
xx—/ x—/ x— : b

Taylor (Song)
xx—/ xx—/ xx—/ x : a
x—/ xx—/ xx—/ : b
xx—/ xx—/ xx—/ x : c
x—/ xx—/ xx—/ : b

The **"Song"**[42] and **"March "** are also Heinesque in mood, the former, because it represents the lament of a lover separated from his beloved. In the latter (a better example), the singer, referred to by the first personal pronoun, of which Heine is so fond, is beside the gloomy, stormy sea. He wishes that the voice of the wind and waves might sing their dirge over his grave. The landscape is brown and bare and frosty. Night is approaching in sadness. His life is like the landscape, "bleak and withered." And then where Heine would, as a rule, have suddenly turned aside and destroyed the poetical illustration by humorously adding an ironical remark, Taylor also abruptly turns aside not, however, from despondency to humor, but to optimism and closes:

> Yet, through the cloud- racks gathered,
> Shines out the Evening Star!

Even **"March"**, which is, in my opinion undoubtedly after the manner of Heine, cannot be shown to be an imitation of any one individual poem of the German singer. Taylor has merely made use of the German poet's manner, his form, his cadence but has not slavishly copied minutiae.[43]

Speaking of the fall of 1863 the authors of *Life and Letters* tell us Taylor had conceived the idea of his Faust translation "nearly fifteen years before."[44] That would be about the end of 1848. We have seen that the first fragment of translation which Taylor published appeared in June, 1849.[45] This work must have been executed some weeks or months earlier. Therefore, when we find in the present volume suggestions of Goethe's *Faust* in two poems which Taylor must have composed about this time, **"Ariel in the Cloven Pine"** and **"The Summer Camp"**,[46] we are not surprised. There can be no doubt that the former poem owes its existence to Shakespeare's *Tempest,* on which Goethe has also drawn for the name of his airy sprite. The meter of the few snatches of song which Ariel sings in the English drama, that of the songs of Ariel and his "Chor" in Goethe's play[47] and that of Taylor's poem is essentially one, but the metrical resemblance existing between the two latter compositions is closer than that which either one bears to the lines of the English dramatist. The episode on which Taylor's poem is based is found only in Shakespeare and not even suggested in Goethe's Ariel scene. In the details of execution, however, the

American poem seems to have as much of that which suggests the verses Goethe's Ariel as it has echoes of Shakespeare's lines.[48] Since it is not my contention that Taylor's poem is an imitation of Goethe's lines, but rather that his reading of the German passage helped to inspire him to his composition, I shall cite passages from Taylor's poem and from his translation of Goethe's *Faust,* for this translation gives us what the German lines meant when translated into terms of the author of **"Ariel in the Cloven Pine"**. Italicized are those expressions which should be compared each with each.

Taylor's Ariel

> *All* the isle, *alive with Spring,*
> Lies, a jewel of delight,
> On the blue sea's heaving breast;
> Not a *breath* from out the *West,*
> But some *balmy* smell doth bring
> From the *sprouting* myrtle *buds,*
> Or from *meadowy vales* that lie
> Like a *green inverted sky,*

Faust

> When the *Spring returns*[49] serener
> *Raining blossoms* over *all;*
> When around the *green girt*[50] *meadow*
> *Balm* the *tepid winds exhale.*

Taylor (Dawn walks)

> Through his *vestibule of day*
> . . . . .
> *Now the* frosty *stars* are gone:
> I have watched them *one by one,*

Faust (Sunlight)

> Shuts the *golden gates of Day.*[51]
> *Now the* Night already darkles,[52]
> Holy *star succeeds to star.*

A perusal of the remainder of this scene in *Faust* discloses a similarity between it and **"The Summer Camp"** which is a few pages further along in Taylor's volume. Now this poem has been called a "description of California summer scenery on the plain, . . . a daguerrotype of nature as it exists there in the month of August".[53] Hence it cannot be an imitation of Goethe's description of Swiss scenery. Still, the poem betrays an infection acquired through its author's contact with *Faust.* Both poems describe a country abounding in its pristine beauty and innocence. In both poems the "Day comes on again" and with it awakes a new man, "Des Lebens Pulse schlagen frisch lebendig."[54] The old life is behind them. "Where is the life we led?" This fresh and refreshing land arouses thoughts of a new life after toil and defeat. Hence much of the American's poem is devoted to philosophizing, and the philosophy is Faustian. Might not these opening verses of one of Taylor's stanzas have been spoken by the awakening Faust?

> Other dreams are ours,[55]
> Of shocks that were, or seemed, whereof our souls
> Feel the subsiding lapse, as feels the sand
> Of tropic island-shores the dying pulse
> Of storms that racked the Northern sea. My Soul,
> I do believe that thou has *toiled* and *striven,*[56]
> And hoped and suffered wrong. I do believe
> Great aims were thine, deep *loves* and *fiery hates,*
> And though I may have lain a thousand years
> Beneath these Oaks, the baffled trust of Youth,
> The first keen *sorrow,* brings a gentle pang
> To temper *joy.*

With the latter part of the above passage compare the following from Faust's speech:[57]

> Is't *Love?* Is't *Hate?* that burningly embraces,
> And that with *pain* and *joy* alternate tries us.

The effect of the glorious landscape on Faust is a quickening one. He exclaims:[58]

> Du regst und rührst ein kräftiges Beschließen,
> Zum höchsten Dasein immerfort zu *streben.*

"Streben" is the key word to Faust. Taylor's poems ends with the resolution to leave the peaceful land of calm and beauty.

> "Rather set at once,[59]
> Our faces toward the noisy world again,
> And gird our loins for action. Let us go!"

Taylor accepts Faust's philosophy of action (Tätigkeit). It might also be noted that both the passages are written in iambic pentameter, Goethe's being rimed *abab,* etc.; Taylor's, unrimed.

It will have been observed that the very first scene of the Second Part of *Faust* contains the passages which we have compared with Taylor's poems. This evidence, if such it be, is the first we have of our poet's acquaintance with the Second Part of Goethe's poem. Two other passages in this volume may also be reminiscent of the Second Part of *Faust.* In **"The Soldier and the Pard"** written June, 1851[60] the following verses:

> but, take my word, (p. 55)
> Egyptian ruins are a serious thing:
> You would not dare let fly a joke beside
> The maimed colossi, though your very feet
> Might catch between some mumied Pharaoh's ribs.

suggest Mephistopheles' action in the "Classische Walpurgisnacht", and especially the sentiments he expresses in his speech beginning:

> Die nordischen Hexen wußt' ich wohl zu meistern,
> (7676 f.)
> Mir wird's nicht just mit diesen fremden Geistern.

Then on the following page of Taylor's poem we read:

> And floated off to slumber on a cloud
> Of rapturous sensation,

which perhaps indicates a progress to the fourth act of *Faust* where the hero speaks of "meiner Wolke Tragewerk" (10,041).

In Taylor's **"The American Legend"** which he composed in June—July, 1850,[61] the verse "And warlike Peter puts his harness on" (p. 16) cannot fail to call up at once Taylor's translation of Goethe's "Es mich sogleich in Harnisch bringt" (5466), viz., "I straightway put my harness on." *(Faust II,* p. 36, ed. 1882).

Each of these assumed echoes of the Second Part of *Faust* is in itself slight and, when one bears in mind that almost anything can be paralleled in *Faust,* none too convincing, but the appearance of a group of them just at the time when Taylor "began" his Faust-translation may be indicative. Taylor had to read the Second Part for the first time sometime. If it was not now, we have no evidence of when he first became acquainted with it. It seems certain that he must have learned to know the Second Part before entering upon his resolution to make his translation, which resolve dates from this period, 1849—1851.[62]

One of the results of Bayard Taylor's extensive travels in the East was the publication in 1854 of that volume which contains some of his best-known lyrics,[63] ***Poems of the Orient.*** Smyth informs us:[64] "He [Taylor] read, in the East, Rückert's 'Morgenländische Sagen und Geschichten' and Goethe's 'West-Oestlicher Divan'" and conjectures that: "The 'Westoestlicher Divan', had perhaps exerted some influence over him when he was writing ***Poems of the Orient***".[65] This is about as much as we get in critical writings of a possible influence of German poetry on this one of Taylor's volumes. But a closer investigation discloses that, in spite of all that has been said about echoes of Shelly and other English authors[66] found here, it is from the German poets, and especially from Rückert, that our poet has done most of his borrowing.

Taylor's travel in the East was broken by a short visit to Europe in the late summer and the autumn of 1852.[67] Before this European excursion he had been travelling in the Near East. One event of the excursion is important to our study. Taylor later wrote[68] (1866): "When I first visited Coburg, in October, 1852, I was very anxious to make Rückert's acquaintance. My interest in Oriental literature had been refreshed, at that time, by nearly ten months of travel in Eastern lands, and some knowledge of modern colloquial Arabic. I had read his wonderful translation of the Makamât of Hariri, and felt sure that he would share my enthusiasm for the people to whose treasures of song he had given so many years of his life." He relates that he was kindly received by the German poet and spent several interesting hours with him.[69]

From the visit to Coburg Taylor probably took away new inspiration for poetical composition and, positively material for that purpose in printed form, for in the Cornell collection[70] there is a short list of books owned by Taylor and therein is found the entry: "Rückert's Morgenländische Sagen und Geschichten, Bayard Taylor, October 5, 1852,"[71] probably an exact copy of the inscription in the fly-leaf of the book. It is easy to show exactly how, when and where Taylor made use of these two volumes[72] in his subsequent Oriental compositions.

Fortunately the dates of composition of most of the ***Poems of the Orient*** are at our disposal.[73] It will be noticed in what follows that none of the pieces composed prior to October, 1852 bears the least trace of resemblance to any of Rückert's poems. Of the *Makamât,* which Taylor says he read prior to this date, the ***Poems of the Orient*** show no influence, but at least five of the poems which were composed subsequent to October, 1852 exhibit positive proof of an almost direct use of the German volumes which Taylor acquired in October, 1852.

Attention has already been called to Taylor's reference to Rückert's "Mahmud, der Götzenzertrümmerer," *(Morgenländische Sagen und Geschichten)*[74] in his prose volume ***India, China and Japan.***[75] The scene which recalled Rückert's poem to the traveller's mind was witnessed in January, 1853.[76] The following are the poems which seem positively to be based on Rückert's "Sagen und Geschichten," **"The Arab Warrior,"** with a subtitle "From the Arabic," written March, 1853; **"The Birth of the Horse,"** subtitle, "From the Arabic," written September, 1853; **"The Bedouin Song, "** written October 29, 1853; **"The Shekh,"** subtitle "From the Arabic," written October 30, 1853; and **"The Wisdom of Ali,"** subtile, "An Arab Legend", for which a definite date cannot be ascertained.[77] It will be observed that this group embraces every poem in the volume which has a subtitle indicating an Arabic source. One other poem **"Gulistan"**, written October 24, 1853 has a subtitle which merely says "An Arabic Metre." It will further be recalled that Taylor himself knew next to no Arabic[78] and hence had to get his themes "from the Arabic" through an intermediary. This intermediary was Rückert.

Taylor's **"Arab Warrior"** is essentially a free translation of Rückert's "Antara singt, Desgleichen."[79] It corresponds to its model line for line, save that the American, by an extension of verbiage, gets in two lines not found in the German:

> And while the others idly feast
> I rub my harness bright.

Taylor possibly added these two lines to render his poem divisible into stanzas of equal length, since his composition consists of five four-line stanzas. The German poem has only eighteen verses and is not written in stanzaic form, but has full stops at the end of the fourth, eighth and twelfth lines. As regards meter and rime the English and German forms are practically identical, the odd lines being iambic tetrameter, the even iambic trimeter; the odd lines being unrimed, the even lines riming. Taylor, however, changes the rime from stanza to stanza, whereas Rückert, more in the manner of the Arabic, maintains the one rime throughout.

"The Birth of the Horse" is Rückert's "Die Geburt des Rosses."[80] The meter and stanza-length are the same in both versions. The rime-scheme, while similar, is not identical. Rückert rimes *abab,* Taylor, *abcb.* Again Taylor's version is little less than a free translation of Rückert. This time Taylor omits one stanza, the second of the German poem, and deviates from his model in one verse. He substitutes:

And fleetest with thy load,

for,

Und ohne Horn gehornet.

Otherwise the thought corresponds line for line.

While becalmed on the equatorial ocean between the coast of Borneo and the Mozambique Channel,[81] Taylor must have attempted to break the *ennui* by recourse to the second volume of *Morgenländische Sagen und Geschichten* for here on successive days were composed what has become his most popular lyric, **"The Bedouin Song"**, and **"The Shekh."** Strangely enough when Taylor, under the date of December 2, 1853, writes in his diary:[82] "I have done something in the way of reading also, as the following list, nearly complete, will show," and appends a list of twenty-eight titles, he here, as everywhere else, fails to make mention of Rückert's volumes. It almost seems as if he intended to keep concealed the source from which these poems sprang.

Of the **"Bedouin Song"** much has been written. It has become commonplace to point out its likeness to Shelley's "Lines to an Indian Air,[83] but no one seems to have detected its relationship to Rückert's "Die Liebeslieder und der Koranvers."[84] Had she detected this relation Mrs. Haskell would hardly have satisfied herself with the statement:[85] "Even the **'Bedouin Song'**, which apologists have made us regard as peculiarly Taylor's own, shows strongly the influence of Shelley." Had she suspected the ultimate source of the refrain of Taylor's poem, she would probably have agreed with Mr. Stedman[86] in calling the refrain "superb" rather than have pronounced the verdict that it "is prejudical to the illusion of sincerity, it degenerates readily into a jingle."[87] There can be no doubt that Taylor had Shelley's serenade distinctly in mind when he composed his **"Bedouin Song."** There can likewise be no doubt that he had recently had Rückert's second volume in hand. The two poems are similar neither in the treatment of theme, nor in form. But into Rückert's poem is introduced "ein beduinisch Lied"; hence the title of Taylor's poem. Also in Rückert's composition we find:

Ich las die Verse vom Gericht:
Wenn die Sonn' ist erkaltet,
Und die Sterne veraltet
Und die Berge gespaltet —
. . . . .
Und das Schuldbuch ist entfaltet.

These verses of the Koran, omitting the third, become Taylor's celebrated refrain:

Till the sands grow cold,
And the stars are old,
An the leaves of the Judgement
Book unfold![88]

In the original manuscript copy of this poem, written in pencil in a note book[89] and signed "B. T. Mozambique Channel, Oct. 29, 1853" the first line of the refrain reads,

the first time *"Till the sun grows cold,"*
the second time *"Till the sun grows cold,"*
and the third time *"Till the sun grows old"*

In the New York Public Library (Manuscript Division) there is a manuscript copy of the **"Bedouin Song"**, dated Oct. 29, 1853 with the following refrain:

Till the sun grows cold,
And the stars are old,
And the leaves of the Judgement
Book unfold!

Thus does the refrain resemble its model in form as well as in sense. Now it might be objected that each author took his verses independently from the Koran, but when we realize that out the dozen parallel verses which occur in the Koran, Taylor happens to use three out of just those four selected by Rückert, this objection loses its force. It vanishes entirely if we compare with Taylor's lines the passage in the Koran in which they are found, as given in the English translation. We know that Taylor "bought of Putnam Sale's Koran" in 1854[90] hence we shall quote from George Sale's[91] version.

When the sun shall be folded up; and when the stars shall fall; and when the mountains shall be made to pass away; and when the camel ten months gone with young shall be neglected; and when the wild beasts shall be gathered together; and when the seas shall boil; and when the souls shall be joined again to their bodies; and when the girl who hath been buried alive shall be asked for what crime she hath been put to death; and when the books shall be laid open; and when the heaven shall be removed; and when hell shall burn fiercely; and when paradise shall be brought near; *every* soul shall know what it hath wrought. Chap. lxxxi, vv. 1–14.

Surely each of Taylor's verses is nearer the German than it is to this version of the Koran. Thus whenever **"The Bedouin Song"** is read, recited or sung,[92] not only Taylor and Shelley, but also Rückert contributes to the entertainment of the readers and/or auditors.

The day after finishing the **"Bedouin Song"** Taylor, taking Rückert's "Nachtgespräch"[93] as his model, composed **"The Shekh"**. The first and the last stanza of the English poem represent a considerable departure from the German composition. The first and the three last stanzas of Rückert find no counterpart in Taylor's poem. But all the intervening verses of the "Nachtgespräch" have found expression in the prayer of Taylor's **"Shekh"**, almost line for line. In general the form of the two compositions is alike, stanzas of four verses of tetrameter, riming in Rückert, generally *abab,* but twice (stanzas four and five) *abcb;* in Taylor, generally *abcb.* The movement in the German is iambic, in the English, trochaic. Taylor has succeeded fairly well in keeping up the phenomenon of parallelism indicative of Rückert's Arabic fashion. He has, however, rendered Rückert's much repeated verb "Behüte" by "protect", "keep", "preserve." It is interesting to note that in the first draft of the poem,[94] he rendered "Behüte" three successive times by "keep". The line which now reads: "God preserve me from a spirit" originally ran "Keep my spirit from a feeling"; thus being, in form at least, nearer the German.

Although a definite date cannot be assigned to the composition of **"The Wisdom of Ali,"** we know that it was produced after Taylor's return to America, more definitely, between May 1st and June 12th, 1854.[95] Taylor now goes back to the first volume of *Morgenländische Sagen und Geschichten* and bases his poem on "Die Pforte der Weisheit."[96] Both the German and the English pieces are in riming couplets, but here again Taylor makes no attempt to imitate feminine rimes of the German. Both are in iambic measure, Taylor's lines having five feet, Rückert usually four. The English poem is some ten verses shorter than the German due to the fact that although Rückert uses the formula:

> Und als ihn so der, erste (zweite, etc.) fragte,
> War dis das Wort das Ali sagte:

ten times, Taylor uses a corresponding formula only twice, e.g.

> "And lastly when the tenth did question make,
> These were the words which Ali spake."

The two versions are exact in substance throughout most of their extent. Towards the end Taylor introduces some additional lines, not found in Rückert, but involving no new thought. Although it would not be possible to show conclusively that the English poem is a direct translation of the German, largely because the "legend" is made up of a series of short, direct quotations which hold any translation "from the Arabic" within rather narrow limits and, would compel a close similarity between all renditions into other languages, there seems no reason to doubt that Taylor's immediate source is Rückert.[97] This ends the elements which can be almost positively claimed to have arisen from Taylor's acquaintance with the *Morgenländische Sagen und Geschichten.* There are, however, at least two other points to which attention must be called.

At Grenada, Spain, in November, 1852, Taylor wrote **"The Garden of Irem"**. In the early pages of the Rückert volumes which he had then recently acquired is also found a piece called "Der Garten von Irem."[98] There is not enough similarity between the two compositions to warrant the assumption that the one is responsible for the existence of the other, but it is not at all unlikely that the American, reading his newly acquired volume, was seized with the idea of outdoing the effort of the German. The treatment of the theme is almost entirely different. The poems are unlike even in form. But in spite of the frequent variation of meter there are passages in each poem where the cadence is alike. It may be significant that each poem opens with a question. Taylor answers his own question immediately. Rückert answers the same question near the end of his poem but the answers are essentially the same,

> Keine Spur ist heut'ges Tages,
> Wo es mag gewesen sein.
> No mortal knoweth the road thereto.

I am of the opinion that Rückert's poem suggested the theme to Taylor whose execution is quite independent of the German production.

Just at that time when Taylor was making freest use of *Morgenländische Sagen und Geschichten,* October, 1853,[99] he wrote a **"Hymn to Air."** This poem has at least one point of contact with Rückert's "Der Wind unter der Erde."[100]

> Einst wird sie [die Schöpfung] sein zerschellt,
> Wenn er, [der Wind] zersprengt die Ketten,
> Wann jener Tag einfällt,
> Wo über den sündigen Städten
> Gott den Gerichtstag hält.
> And Thou [the air] dost hold, awaiting God's decree,
> The keys of all destruction:—in that hour
> When the Almighty Wrath shall loose thy power,
> Before thy breath shall disappear the sea,
> To ashes turn the mountain's mighty frame,
> And as the seven-fold fervors[101] wider roll,
> Thou, self-consuming, shrivel as a scroll,
> And wrap the world in one wide pall of flame!

These are the closing lines of the respective poems and represent a similarity of thought in compositions which are otherwise entirely different. This is probably an example of what critics delight in calling a "reminiscent note" in Taylor.

For reasons set forth hereinafter it is necessary it attempt to determine the relation which Taylor's volume ***Poems of the Orient*** bears to Rückert's *Oestliche Rosen.*[102]

POEMS OF THE ORIENT

> Da der West ward durchgekostet,
> Hat er nun den Ost entmostet.
>
> Rückert.

This, and this alone, appears on page thirteen of Taylor's volume.[103]

> Oestliche Rosen
> Erste Lese

is all that appears on page five of Rückert's volume.[104] Three of the pages preceding this title page contain a dedicatory poem, entitled "Zu Goethe's West-oestlichem Diwan," in the very first stanza of which occurs the above-quoted couplet. The use of this couplet makes it positive that Taylor was familiar with the *Oestliche Rosen* before he finished his ***Poems of the Orient.*** But that is not all. The twelve pages preceding Taylor's title-page are devoted to a **"Proem Dedicatory, An Epistle from Mount Tmolus to Richard Henry Stoddard,"** thus making the introductory topography of the two volumes practically identical. An examination of the contents of the poems of dedication yields the following: The "er" in Rückert's couplet, quoted above, refers, of course, to Goethe. The Orientalist goes on to say:

> Seht, dort schwelgt er auf der Ottomane.
> Abendröthen
> Dienten Goethen
> Freudig als dem Stern des Abendlandes;

and further down Rückert continues:

> Aus iran'schen Naphtabronnen
> Schöpft der Greis itzt, was die Sonnen
> Einst Italiens ihm, dem Jüngling, kochten.
> Jugendhadern
> In den Adern,
> Zorn und Gluth und Mild' und süßes Kosen;
> Alles Lieben
> Jung geblieben
> Seiner Stirne stehen schon die Rosen.
> Wenn nicht etwa ew'ges Leben
> Ihm verliehen ist, sei gegeben
> Langes ihm von uns gewognen Loosen.

In appropriating the couplet which Rückert had applied to Goethe, Taylor obviously refers to himself as the poet who, having made a trial of the west, is now turning his attention to the East. In the **"Proem"** he pictures himself "couched on Tmolus' side. In the warm myrtles, in the golden air Of the declining day." As Rückert had done for Goethe, so has Taylor begun his dedication by establishing himself in a seat of oriental ease. Then, after some intervening lines, our poet goes on:

> And now I turn, to find a late content
> In Nature, making mine her myriad shows;
> Better contented with one living rose
> Than all the Gods' ambrosia; sternly bent
> On wresting from her cup, whence flow
> The flavors of her ruddiest life—the change
> Of climes and races—the unschackled range
> Of all experience;—that my songs may show
> The warm red blood that beats in hearts of men,
> . . . . .
> Blame me not, that I
> Find in the forms of Earth a deeper joy
> Than in the dreams that lured me as a boy,"

And finally Taylor concludes:

> "Take them [these poems], and your acceptance, in the dearth
> Of the world's tardy praise, shall make them dear."

I would compare these lines with the second reference to Goethe quoted above and find in them an echo of Rückert. Because Goethe is presented as a "Greis" who dips from the Iranian "Naphthabronnen" what the sun of Italy had brought to maturity in him as a youth on whose brow the roses becomingly rest, so does Taylor represent himself as anxious to find "late content" (He was not yet thirty years of age!) in Nature, contented with one living *rose.* The cup which he would wrest from Nature and whence flows her ruddiest life, the change of climes and races, is suggested by Goethe's dipping from "iranschen" springs the ferment of his youthful Italian sojourn. If there were any doubt that Taylor had Goethe in mind when he shaped these lines the phrase "the unschackled range of all experience" would go far to dispel it. Here we have, not only an often expressed phase of Taylor's own nature, which was also to some extent characteristic of Goethe, but the very key note of *Faust* which Taylor had already planned to translate and with the execution of which plan he was now busy.[105] To proceed with our comparison: Is the desire that his "songs show the warm red blood that beats in hearts of men" anything other than a longing for that which Rückert's lines attributes to Goethe: "Jugendhadern In den *Adern*" "Zorn und Gluth und Mild' und süsses Kosen"? Then because Goethe, the "Greis", was compared with Goethe the "Jüngling", Taylor found it necessary to contrast the "deeper joy", which he now "*late* content" expects to find in the forms of Earth, with "the dreams that lured" him "as a *boy.*" Finally Rückert's appeal if immortality be not granted Goethe then: "sey gegeben Langes ihm von uns gewognen Loosen," is practically paralleled in Taylor's entreaty: "In the dearth of the world's tardy praise your acceptance shall make them dear." In addition to this, when we recall that years later (1866) Taylor said of this dedicatory poem of Rückert:[106] "I scarcely know where to look for a more graceful dedication in verse," we feel more inclined to believe that he used it as his model in composing his dedicatory verse for his Oriental poems.

Aside from this resemblance of the introductory pieces *Oestliche Rosen* and ***Poems of the Orient*** have nothing in common, unless we consider the pretty picture of the Nightingale and the Rose in the latter stanzas of **"The Poet in the East"** reminiscent of Rückert's work, for this sensuous figure occurs on practically every other of the four hundred and sixty odd pages which constitute the latter's volume. Taylor probably made use of the *Oestliche Rosen* only after he had practically completed his volume and was preparing it for the press.[107]

Despite Professor Smyth's statements that Taylor read Goethe's "West-Oestlicher Divan" in the East[108] and that this volume[109] "perhaps exerted some influence over him when he was writing ***Poems of the Orient,***" I have been unable to find any evidence of any influence of Goethe's *Divan* on Taylor's volume. There is among Taylor's poems **"A Pledge to Hafiz"** and in the *Divan* a poem "An Hafiz" but, aside from the titles, these two pieces have nothing in common. In the economy of Taylor's volume the idea of the introductory **"The Poet in the East"** may have been suggested by the "Hegira" in Goethe's *Divan.* Each affords the occidental poet an opportunity to make his bow to the Orient. Each is written in six-line stanzas. But here their similarity ceases. Likewise might Taylor have obtained the idea of closing his collection with a **"L'Envoi"** from Goethe's similar use of a "Gute Nacht." Taylor's exhortation to his songs.

> Go, therefore, Songs!—which in the East were born
> And drew your nurture—from your sire's control:
> Haply to wander through the West forlorn,
> Or find a shelter in some Orient soul.

might possibly be an echo of Goethe's

> Nun, so legt euch, liebe Lieder,
> An den Busen meinem Volke!

This is all that there is in the ***Poems of the Orient*** which even suggests the *Divan.* The nature of the two works, the spirit which pervades them, and all else about them is quite dissimilar. On such a meager suggestion of internal evidence and a total absence of external evidence—except for the statements of Smyth—I am unwilling to predicate an influence of this German work on Taylor's volume.

Returning once more to those days of abundant inspiration spent on the equatorial ocean, we find that on October 15, 1853, Taylor wrote **"The Angel of Patience"**.[110] Now American poetry knows another poem by this title from the pen of John Greenleaf Whittier. The latter's composition, which bears the subtitle "A Free Paraphrase of the German", was written in 1845 and first published in *The National Era,* May 13, 1847.[111] The composition of which the New Englander's poem is a paraphrase is Carl Johann Philipp Spitta's "Geduld." Taylor must have known Whittier's poem for "the friendship of the two poets dates from the publishing in *The National Era* of August, 19, 1847, and prefacing with hearty commendation, Taylor's poem, **'The Norseman's Ride'**".[112] There is no doubt that Taylor's **"Angel of Patience"** is another paraphrase of Spitta's "Geduld." The only question is: Did he make his adaptation directly from the German, or did he make it from Whittier's poem?

There is no external evidence to assist in answering this query. Nowhere do we find any hint that Taylor knew Spitta's poem. A glance at the Eastburn dissertation convinces one that Whittier was not a German scholar. Since Taylor was infinitely better acquainted with the language of the original, it might be expected that he familiarized himself with Whittier's source before attempting his own **"Angel of Patience."** This is exactly what a comparison of the three poems leads us to conclude.

In form no two of the three pieces are alike, but there are more features common to Spitta and Taylor than common to either Spitta and Whittier or Whittier and Taylor. An the length of the verses Whittier's tetrameters more nearly approach the German trimeters than do Taylor's pentameters. But in all other points, length of the poem, stanzaic form and rime-scheme, Taylor and Spitta are most nearly alike. Like Spitta's poem, Taylor's has forty versus; Whittier's has only twenty-four. Whittier's stanza is of six verses riming in couplets, Taylor's is of four lines with alternate rime (*abab*), Spitta's is of eight lines with a full stop at the end of each fourth, thus making the stanza essentially a four-line one, and also has alternate rime (*ababcdcd*).

Since neither American poet attempted a direct translation of the German, it is not always possible to compare individual verses each for each and thus determine which adaption is nearer the original. But in Taylor's poem frequent and striking similarities to the German lines occur, whereas in Whittier's piece the expressions which resemble the original are neither so strikingly similar nor so frequent. A few examples of these similarities will serve to illustrate the general relation in which the pieces stand to each other. Whittier's verses which most nearly resemble the original are:

> (1) Our dear and Heavenly Father sends him here.
> (2) there's quiet in the Angel's glance,
> (3) He kindly trains us to endure.
> (4) He walks with thee, that Angel kind,
> And gently whispers, "Be resigned."

In the German the corresponding lines read:

> (1) Hat ihn der Herr gesandt.
> (2) In seinem Blick ist Frieden,
> Und milde, sanfte Huld.
> (3) Sein Wahlspruch heißt: ertrage
> (4) So geht er dir zur Seite.

Taylor's renderings for these expressions are:

> (1) More than one Angel has Our Father given
> (2) (Not rendered).
> (3) (Not closely rendered).
> (4) And we . . . are led by her.
> Who walkest with us here.

In these cases Whittier is generally nearer the model. But notice the following likeness existing between Spitta and Taylor and not paralleled in Whittier.

> Zum Trost für Erdenmangel
> Hat ihn der Herr gesandt.
>
> To cheer, to help us, children of the dust,
> More than one angel has our Father given;
> But one alone is faithful to her trust.
>
> Den herbsten Herzenschmerz.
> Though with its bitterness the heart runs o'er.
>
> Er macht die finstre Stunde
> Allmählich wieder hell,
>
> But when the eye looks up for light once more,
> She turns the cloud and shows its golden side.
>
> Er tadelt nicht dein Sehnen.
> She doth not chide, nor in reproachful guise,
> The griefs we cherish rudely thrust apart.

Und wenn im Sturmestoben
Du murrend fragst: warum?
So deutet er nach oben,
Mild lächelnd, aber stumm.

Unto rebellious souls, that mad with Fate
To question God's eternal justice dare,
She points above with looks that whisper, "Wait" —

Er hat für jede Frage
Nicht Antwort gleich bereit

To the vain challenges of doubt we send,
No answering comfort doth she minister;

This evidence must suffice to show that Taylor made independent use of Spitta's "Geduld". A comparison of the second couplet of Whittier's poem with the similar thought negatively expressed in the first two lines of Taylor's second stanza, and the introduction of the figure of the Angel calming the care-worn brow, found in the first lines of the third stanza of both American poems and not present in the German model, makes us believe that Taylor likewise had Whittier in mind when composing his **"Angel of Patience"**.

In the second part of the volume ***Poems of the Orient*** is a piece which H. B. Sachs finds to be "somewhat in Heine's manner, repeating the favorite rhythm, reverie, subtle suggestiveness, and longing."[113] This poem **"A Picture,"** was written December 15, 1853.[114] Sachs finds this piece characterized by "the same smooth and quiet beginning, the vision, the passion and feeling of desolation that we so frequently find in Heine." He also calls attention to "the sudden recovery from reverie and revulsion of mood as expressed in the last strophe." Surely all these earmarks justify his conclusion that the poem is "somewhat in Heine's manner." Had Mr. Sachs examined the ***Poems of the Orient***[115] closely, he would have found a few pages further on **"In the Meadows"** and **"The Phantom"**, both written May—June 12, 1854,[116] which are also Heinesque. The former possess all the features claimed for **"A Picture,"** save that the poet's transition of mood is from happiness to sadness and the vision is mental rather than physical. The poem possess also an additional feature, so common Heine's songs, the continual recurrence of "I" and "me". In **"The Phantom"** the vision again plays its part, and the transition of mood (rather gloomy throughout) from hope to despair is accomplished rather suddenly in the last stanza. There is one Heinesque feature, however, which positively does not enter into any of these three compositions, irony, insincerity. These poems are the outpourings of Taylor's heart of hearts. They represent his disconsolateness over the death of his first wife, the sweetheart of his youth. It will be noticed that they were composed as he was nearing home and after he had arrived there, a time when the grief over Mary's loss would affect him most poignantly. For these reasons we may regard these lyrical outbursts as lamentations in the manner of Heine, with whose work, as we have seen, Taylor was already familiar, rather than compositions in conscious imitation of that singer.[117]

Because of a Faustian strain in Taylor's own nature to which he gave expression in his works in an ever increasing degree the more intimately he became acquainted with Goethe's masterpiece, it is dangerous to designate as an echo of the *Faust* every piece of Taylorian philosophy which may happen to smack of the German work. It is, however, worthy of notice that in one of those two pieces which seem to suggest the only possible link between the ***Poems of the Orient*** and the *West-Oestlicher Diwan*[118] and in the **"Proem Dedicatory"**, and in those two pieces alone, occurs much that is suggestive of *Faust.*[119] It is not always possible to catch hold of these elements and pin them down and exclaim: "Here, this line is the prototype of this one!", etc. *ad nauseam,* for it is the spirit of the pieces which is alike, and spirits are rather elusive. However, I shall subjoin a few excerpts from Taylor's pieces which seem to be most tangibly Faustian.

I at the threshold of the world have lain,[120]
. . . . but in vain.
And now I turn, to find a late content
In Nature, making mine her varied shows;
. . . . sternly bent
On wresting from her hand the cup, whence flow
The flavors of her ruddiest life—the change
Of climes and races—the unschackled range
Of all experience;[121]
For not to any race or any clime[122]
Is the completed sphere of life revealed;
He who would make his own that round sublime
Must pitch his tent on many a distant field.
Upon his home a dawning lustre beams,
But through the world he walks to open day,
Gathering from every land the prismal gleams,[123]
Which, when united, form the perfect ray.

This concludes the German element in the ***Poems of the Orient.*** R. H. Stoddard has written:[124] "If I had not been aware of the ease with which he wrote, I should have been surprised at the rapidity with which these poems succeeded each other," and:[125] "I doubt whether the genius of Byron ever produced more and better poetry than that of Bayard Taylor within the space of a single month." (October, 1853). Evidently Mr. Stoddard was not aware of the nature and amount of the inspiration furnished by German sources to facilitate the workings of his friend's genius and to accelerate his production. Truly Edward Engel words:[126] "Ähnlich wie Longfellow hatte Bayard Taylor aus allen fremden Dichtungsquellen zu reichlich getrunken, um einen ganz eigenen Gesang zu erzeugen," comes near being justified when applied to this volume.

In answer to a call for new editions of ***Rhymes of Travel*** and a ***Book of Romances, Lyrics, and Songs,*** Taylor issued late in 1855[127] a volume called ***Poems of Home and Travel*** in which he included what he considered the best of the two requested collections, supplemented by thirteen new poems.[128] The new element, small both numerically and in extent, possesses no outstanding poetic merit. In vain do we await any new echo from the German Parnassus. **"A Phantasy"**, because of its form, its elusive phantom and the erotic sentiments it expresses, does mildly suggest Heine, but it cannot safely be claimed to be a result of Heine's influence.[129]

Although Taylor's volumes ***At Home and Abroad,*** both the first and second series,[130] might have been treated with his work of travel, I chose to consider them with his more deserving productions, not because they possess any outstanding literary merit, but because they are not exclusively works of travel, but rather sketch-books, some of whose pieces possess literary value and are in no way concerned with travel. An examination of the earlier volume discloses that, of the forty sketches which constitute it, seventeen deal wholly or principally with German subjects, and of this number, four, **"Interviews with German Authors"**, **"Alexander von Humboldt"**, **"Weimar and its Dead"**, and **"The Three Hundredth Anniversary of the University of Jena"** deal in the main with German literature and its producers. The remaining articles, both those touching upon German subject matter, and some of those which are not based on German themes, display, in a lesser degree, Taylor's knowledge of and interest in German literature.

Since Taylor's personal relation to German authors will be treated in a subsequent chapter comment on the articles referring to that subject is deferred. Suffice it to remark here only the tender feeling which our poet bore in his heart for Germany and German institutions by directing our attention to such sketches as **"A German Idyl"**, **"A German Home"**, **"Life in the Thüringian Forest"**, **"The Castles of the Gleichen"** and **"Scenes at a Target-Shooting. "** Truly, Taylor has in these sketches done for rural Germany, if in a less polished form, nevertheless with no less fervor, what Washington Irving had done earlier for England in his *Sketch Book.*

The volume also abound in small snatches of translation mostly from folk songs and the songs of students. These are of no importance in themselves, but are interesting and are therefore enumerated in Appendix IV. One of these translation, however, must be given further consideration. Speaking of a woman minstrel, one of the folk, who was singing and distributing broadside, penny ballads, Taylor remarks:[131] "Here is one which, from the crowd of lusty young peasants who followed the raw-boned minstrel, to catch the air, must have been a great favorite." Then follows a translation of "Du hast Diamanten and Perlen" with a fourth stanza which I find in no edition of Heine's poems. Nor does Dr. August Walther Fischer in his monograph *Über die volkstümlichen Elemente in den Gedichten Heines*[132] make any mention of this additional stanza. The translation minus the last stanza has been published in *A Sheaf of Poems*[133] as a rendition of Heine's composition. It seems that the addition can be accounted for in only one of two ways. Either Taylor himself wrote the new stanza, which seems improbable, for he says of his volume:[134] "It is a record of actual experiences, and aims at no higher merit than the utmost fidelity," or the folk had already claimed Heine's song for its own and had begun revision.[135] In the latter event we have most valid evidence of the folklike nature of Heine's song. Even if this appendage be of folk origin, it is almost impossible to find any dissonance between it:

> And, because of thine eyes so tender,[136]
> Have I ventured more and more,
> And much, ah, so much have I suffered—
> My darling what would'st thou have more?

and the three original stanzas.

In the second volume of ***At Home and Abroad*** eleven of thirty-nine sketches deal with life in Germany and a twelfth piece, a short story, probably owes its origin to Taylor's readings in German literature. Even in the sketches on non-German subjects are to be found references to and quotations from German poetry, but such occurrences are of course more common in the ten pieces which Taylor wrote during the month of July (1861) which he spent in his **"Home in the Thüringian Forest"** and in **"A Walk Through the Franconian Switzerland"**.[137]

The most interesting thing about this volume, is the resemblance which much of the story **"The Confessions of a Medium"**[138] bears in general outline to Goethe's *Wahlverwandtschaften.* It is not possible to ascertain from direct statement whether Taylor had read this one of Goethe's works before the close of 1860. We know that he did read it at some time[139] before 1870, but mention of it occurs but seldom in his writings.[140] It is only fair to assume, however, that, having owned sets of Goethe's works since 1848,[141] Taylor had, ere May 12, 1860,[142] read the "*Wahlverwandtschaften.*" Be that as it may, all evidence for the dependence of the ground work of **"The Confessions of a Medium"** upon Goethe's novel must be of an internal nature.

It is a well known fact that the English-speaking countries considered Goethe's *Elective Affinities* as an immoral work.[143] Taylor's story intends to render both the idea of spiritualism and of elective affinities ridiculous, and hence stands, in its attitude toward the moral question involved, diametrically opposed to Goethe's thesis. The situation which develops in the same. Fredrich Theodor Vischer in *Das Schöne und die Kunst* analyzes the construction of the German plot thus.[144] "In Goethe's 'Wahlverwandtschaften' stehen sich die Figuren ungemein symmetrisch gegenüber, wie ausgezirkelt, fast zu fühlbar: Eduard und seine Frau, der Hauptmann und Ottilie. Die zwei Paare werden wie magnetisch übers Kreuz angezogen. Sie können das Skelett der Komposition mit Punkten und Linien konstruieren." The same chiasmic condition is found to obtrude itself in Taylor's plot. Mrs. and Mr. Stilton correspond to Goethe's married couple, Charlotte and Eduard; Miss Abby Fetters and John to Ottilie and the Captain. The solution of both plots may be represented by the chemical equation, AB + CD = AD + BC, in which in each case, A is the wife; B, the husband; C the young unmarried women and D the unmarried man. Of course Taylor's story concerns itself mainly with spiritualism, an element not found in Goethe's novel.

Aside from this basic structure of the stories, there is much in the individual thoughts expressed by Taylor's characters which seems to repeat Goethe. In addition to the frequent occurrence of the word "affinity"[145] and similar terms, such as "spiritual harmonies,"[146] such expressions as: "The soul had a right to seek a kindred soul. . . . Having found, they belonged to each other,"[147] and "The doctrine of affinities had sometime before been adopted by the circle,"[148] are entirely in the spirit of Goethe's work. I would compare especially the following passages:[149] "The elements of soul-matter are differently combined in different individuals, and there are affinities and repulsions, just as there are in the chemical elements. Your feelings are chemical not moral. A want of affinity does not necessarily imply an existing evil in the other party", with the material contained in the "Erster Teil," "Viertes Kapital" of the *Wahlverwandtschaften*[150] and more particularly with the lines:[151] "Lassen Sie mich gestehen, . . . wenn Sie Ihre wunderlichen Wesen verwandt nennen, so kommen sie mir nicht sowohl als Blutverwandte, vielmehr als Geistes- und Seelenverwandte[152] vor. Auf eben diese Weise können unter Menschen wahrhaft bedeutende Freundschaften entstehen: denn entgegengesetzte Eigenschaften machen eine innigere Vereinigung möglich."

Although Taylor's ***Poet's Journal*** did not appear until December, 1862,[153] its contents had been completed a year earlier. The manuscript form of the volume in the Harvard University library, which is identical with the printed form except that it does not contain **"Euphorion,"** is dated 1861. But even this date represents a lapse of six years since the appearance of ***Poems of Home and Travel.*** The contents of the ***Poet's Journal,*** which are in a large measure very personal and which the author himself admitted to be "a mixture of truth and poetry",[154] represent productions extending over the entire period from 1885—1861.

It is in this volume that H. B. Sachs has indicated the largest Heine element,[155] calling attention to the facts that **"On the Headland"** "repeats Heine's favorite rhythm and also his longing and sentimentality," and that: "The same rhythm is found in **'Exorcism,' 'Squandered Lives,' 'In Winter'**, etc." Now, Mr. Sachs knew that Taylor possessed a copy of Leland's translation of Heine's *Reisebilder* and had read it in company with Thackeray in 1855,[156] but he was probably not cognizant of the fact that of the four poems which he named as suggestive of Heine, the first three, and they alone of all the ***Poet's Journal,*** were composed in 1855.[157] This new observation dispels all doubt as to the connection between Heine's "Lieder" and Taylor's three compositions. As far as **"On the Headland"** is concerned such corroborative evidence was scarcely necessary. Anyone reading this poem and comparing it with the first sixteen of Heine's "Heimkehr" must perforce reach the conclusion already suggested by Sachs. Especially "Wir sassen am Fischerhause"[158] and "Die Möwe flog hin und wieder,"[159] recur to us in reading **"On the Headland."** And when Taylor, after a passionate lament:

I have a mouth for kisses,
But there's no one to give and take;
I have a heart in my bosom
Beating for nobody's sake, etc.

launches into the strain:

I could fondle the fisherman's baby,
And rock it into rest;
I could take the sunburnt sailor
Like a brother, to my breast, etc.

who would fail to hear therein echoes of Heine? So far Mr. Sachs must be commended for his detection, but he has allowed himself to evade a lot of difficulties by the use of the little *"etc"*. There is one other poem in the volume in which the disconsolate poet bemoans the loss of his beloved in exactly the same verse-form as that employed in the poems indicated by Sachs. This poem is **"Atonement"**. But the stanzas common to Heine, the above stanza with tetrametric lines or with the first and third lines tetrametric and the second and fourth in trimeter, characterize most of the lyrics in the ***Poet's Journal.*** Further, practically all of the lyrics of the first two evenings are likewise pervaded by a mood of longing and despondency. Taylor himself has unwittingly struck the key-note of most of the volume in the verses.[160]

The gift of Song was chiefly lent
To give consoling music for the joys
We lack, and not for those which we possess.

It would therefore seem that Sachs means to include some of these lyrics in the Heinesque element. It may be that, having a nucleus of the three oldest lyrics in this collection written in what we may call the stanza of Heine, Taylor was, for the sake of uniformity, somewhat influenced thereby in writing most of the remaining lyrics (1856—1860) to make use of this meter with variations, even as Heine had done. But, of course, this is not the whole story. It would seem that Taylor had learned consciously or unconsciously, partly from Heine, no doubt; partly from German song in general that this four line stanza, with verses tetrameteric or shorter and riming generally, not in couplets, but characteristically *abcb,* was a vehicle *par excellence* for the conveyance of lyrics which well from the common human heart and whose mood is sad.[161] It is noteworthy that in the lyrics of Taylor's third evening when the mood is no longer sombre, this type of stanza occurs less frequently.

A glance at the three translations appended to ***The Poet's Journal,*** "The Shepherd's Lament" from Goethe, "The Garden of Roses" and "The Three Songs"[162] from Uhland, shows Taylor's familiarity with this type of stanza in other German poets and its use in folk-like song of sorrow. Here, as elsewhere in his translations, Taylor, by adhering closely to the form of the original without doing violence to the sense, produced renditions worthy of his pen.

This volume contains also two snatches of translation from *Faust.* The **"Soldier's Song"**, already mentioned above,[163] and twelve lines from the **"Helena"**[164] which probably constitute Taylor's first publication of a translation from the Second Part of *Faust.* Unlike the **"Soldier's Song,"** this latter passage differs from the final version of 1871 by being less close to the original. These verses from *Faust* are prefixed to an original poem which Taylor wrote about the close of the year 1861 on the death of a young son of R. H. Stoddard and called **"Euphorion."** As Goethe had sung of Byron in the form of Euphorion, Taylor here sings of the Stoddard child.

The presence of the poems **"Icarus"** and the **"Passing of the Sirens"** in the same part of Taylor's volume in which we find **"Euphorion"** might lead one to believe that the lines

> Ikarus! Ikarus![165]
> Jammer genug.

in the Euphorion episode in *Faust* and the presence of the sirens in the "Classische Walpurgisnacht" in the act preceding that episode had induced Taylor to write on these themes. However, the chronology of the poems, the **"Passing of the Sirens"** (1859) and **"Icarus"** (1860), argues rather for the reverse operation, but does not perforce preclude the idea of a common origin of all three conceptions in the Faust drama. Then, too, the **"Passing of the Sirens"** is dramatic in form, a thing not common in Taylor's poems. It is written in blank verse. The main speeches in the scenes where the sirens occur in *Faust* are in iambic pentameter couplets. Taylor's siren chorus[166] is in the characteristic meter of Goethe's "Engelchor".[167] There are, however, no further points which might be said to be common to the two pieces. On the other hand there is much in Taylor's treatment of these two classical subjects which is entirely foreign to *Faust.* Moreover since Taylor had spent the winter of 1857 in Greece[168] he might be expected for this reason to have given poetical form to some Greek legend. It is, therefore, not necessary to conclude that these two poems grew out of his reading of *Faust.*

The volume contains two poems whose very titles at once suggest German literature, and whose themes are undoubtedly of German origin. With Taylor the expression "palm and pine" came to be a stock phrase to designate antipodal natures.[169] This idea is undoubtedly borrowed from Heine. Finally, in 1859[170] Taylor published his **"The Palm and the Pine"** which is reprinted in this volume. The treatment in no way resembles Heine "Ein Fichtenbaum steht einsam," but, peculiarly enough, Taylor seems to have here imitated the form of that poet's "Belsazar."

"The Count of Gleichen" is of course based on the well-known German legend. The poem recounts but briefly the legend of the Count of Gleichen and is an outgrowth of the material in the prose article, **"The Castles of the Gleichen,"** dated September, 1858, and published in ***At Home and Abroad.*** Of the many forms in which this legend is found I have not been able to discover any one that agrees in all points with Taylor's narrative, but the account given in Ludwig Bechstein's *Thüringer Sagenbuch* is the nearest to it. The place of publication and the date of appearance of this German volume also make it appear to be Taylor's probable source.[171]

It remains only to be noted that twice in the verses of this volume mention is made of a German poet. Each time it is of Goethe.[172] This together with the fact that the volume contains three translations from the German master-poet indicates the ascendancy of the Goethe cult in Taylor's life, which interest shall now be observed to assert itself continually until his end.

Near the end of 1861[173] Taylor set to work in a new field of literary endeavor. Between this time and November 24, 1870,[174] he produced four novels on American life. *A priori* one would not expect this genre of work to be influenced by the German models and an examination of Taylor's novels justifies this expectation. Only a few months before he began his composition of ***Hannah Thurston*** Taylor criticized the long-windedness of the *nine-volume* German novel in general and of Gutzkow's *Knights of the Mind* and *The Wizard of Rome* in particular.[175] This observation might at least have had the negative influence of causing Taylor to confine each of his novels to one moderate-sized volume.

Although no trace of influence from the German can be detected in the subject matter or structure of Taylor's novels, the first two contain numerous references, snatches of translation and other incidents which reflect their author's familiarity with German literature. Thus Taylor places in the library of Hannah Thurston "several volumes of Bettina von Arnim".[176] He has her speak of Carlyle's "Essay on Goethe" and his translation of *Wilhelm Meister.*[177] Woodbury lends Hannah translations of Jean Paul's *Siebenkäs* and *Walt and Vult.*[178] Reference is made to Schiller's *Maid of Orleans,*[179] Fouque's *Undine and Sintraim*[180] *[Sic!]* and to a hymn by Carl Maria Weber.[181] Finally we find, not only a reference to, but a translation of, Clärchen's song from Goethe's *Egmont.*[182] The rendition is below the level of Taylor's performances. In fine Taylor's eagerness to introduce German titles and the like almost destroys the illusion and lets the reader see the author behind the mask of the characters.

In ***John Godfrey's Fortunes*** one cannot fail to detect an autobiographical strain, Taylor's mild insinuation to the contrary not withstanding.[183] Hence John's early relation to German language and literature is, in the main, applicable to Taylor's own experiences.[184] In this volume too occur mentions and estimates of German literary artists and their works, but the opinions which the characters express, and the misstatements which they make, are those of the characters and not of the author. Here we find references to Heine,[185] to Schiller, "Goeethy", "Rikter",[186] "Hoffman",[187] "Richter"[188] and to "Peter Schlemihl".[189] There is also a short prose translation from Schiller,[190] four lines of a Latin drinking-song, which Taylor undoubtedly copied from his "Commersbuch",[191] and a verse rendition of a small passage from *Faust*[192] which, together with its setting, shows that Taylor had recently finished reading and was probably translating the first scene of Goethe's drama.[193]

There is another German author mentioned in this novel, Grillparzer. Anyone who reads ***John Godfrey's Fortunes*** is bound to realize at once that Taylor's **"Ichneumon"**, otherwise called the **"Cave of Trophonius"** or simply **"The Cave"**, is a sort of "Ludlamshöhle". The question arises: Did Taylor have Grillparzer's "*Selbstbiographie*" in mind when he invented his **"Ichneumon"**? Surely the two places, one real, the other fictitious, are in a general way alike, saloons, wine-rooms, beer-cellars, where the literary free lances meet and, inspired by the gifts of Bacchus, present and discuss the gifts bestowed upon them by the Muses. Such meeting-places are not necessarily rare phenomena, but not all of them happen to be called "Caves". Moreover, it is peculiarly significant that the only reference to Grillparzer in Taylor's works occurs at one of the assemblages in the "Cave" when, in answer to a suggestion that the first number of the proposed literary organ of the frequenters of the **"Ichneumon"** contain a philosophical article, the moving spirit of the group in his flippant manner objects:[194] "It might do in Vienna. When my old friend Grillparzer founded his light *Sonntagsblatt*—something like the *Oracle* in form—he began with articles on Hegel's philosophy, the Cretan-Doric dialect, the religion of the Ostiaks and a biography of Paracelsus."

Of course, Taylor does not intend that Brandegee's statements be in accordance with fact, nevertheless, it is noteworthy that in Grillparzer's *Selbstbiographie,* only a score of pages before the description of the "Ludlamshohle," is found an account of Grillparzer's first meeting with Hegel.[195] It thus appears as if the American author might have looked into the Austrian's autobiography and have found there a sort of prototype for his **"Ichneumon."** The two caves are very much alike. Since Grillparzer says of his Vienese cave that "es etwas Aehnliches, wenigstens in Deutschland, wahrscheinlich nie gegeben hat,"[196] we are inclined to wonder whether, in Taylor's novel there would ever have occurred anything so similar had he not known of the existence of the "Ludlamshöhle."[197]

Taylor's two later novels, ***The Story of Kennett*** (1866) and ***Joseph and his Friend*** (1870), show almost no indication of their author's interest in German. The lone reference in the former volume to the German proverb—"who loves, teases"[198] might possibly be an indication that Taylor also knew Grillparzer's *Weh dem, der lügt,* where we find: "Doch sagt man, was sich neckt, das liebt sich auch,"[199] but it is likely that the American had simply heard this as a current proverbial expression.[200]

Taylor's familiarity with the relation which exists between Marstrand and the outcast Afraja in Mügge's novel *Afraja* could not have failed to impress upon him the potential effectiveness which lay in a similar relation which he brought about between his hero, Gilbert Porter, and the outcast Deb Smith in ***The Story of Kennett.***[201]

In the autumn of 1864 appeared the so-called "Blue and Gold Edition" of Taylor's poems.[202] This collection contains, in addition to the introductory poem, only a few new compositions, the eight pieces constituting the final section of the volume, called *Since 1861.* Five of these are war pieces. **"Through Baltimore,"** with its refrain, might be called a war song. But the dates of composition[203] preclude the possibility of any of these poems being among those "war songs" which, we are told, Bayard Taylor busily wrote "to German melodies" in the fall of 1861.[204] It seems strange that none of these later "war songs" were printed in the "Blue and Gold" collection. Hence we find no German element in the new poems in this volume.

If every one of Taylor's works were prefaced with an "introductory note" like that which precedes ***The Picture of St. John,*** very little research would be required to determine the sources of the various components of the compositions. Here the author explains that, in endeavoring "to strike a middle course between the almost inevitable monotony of an unvarying stanza and the loose character which the heroic measure assumes when arbitrarily rhymed,"[205] there occurred to him "but one instance in which the experiment has ever been even partially tried,—the 'Oberon' of Wieland, wherein the rhymes are wilfully varied, and sometimes the measure, the stanza almost invariably closing with an Alexandrine."[206] Being "unable to detect any prohibitory rule in the genius of our language," Taylor decided to make this stanza the norm for his poem, except that he would avoid the final Alexandrine and "as frequently as possible use but three rhymes in a stanza."[207] The stanzaic form of the poem must therefore pay tribute to Wieland. Taylor's lines, however, are uniformly iambic pentameter, whereas Wieland's are of irregular length, hexameters being very frequent.

In regard to the subject matter, Taylor tells us that it grew naturally out of certain developments in his own mind, the story being "unsuggested by any legend or detached incident whatever."[208] Therefore, if the following fundamentals are common to the themes of ***The Picture of St. John*** and *Oberon,* such similarities must be ascribed to accident, or perhaps, to a remote, unconscious influence of the German romance. In both poems a man of the North, Bavaria in Taylor's, France in Wieland's poem, goes to the South, to Italy in Taylor's, to Babylon in Wieland's composition. He dreams of the daughter of a man of high estate, a Florentine nobleman, in the English, a Sultan, in the German poem; sees her, loves her and is loved by her in turn. She is about to be married to a native nobleman whom she does not love. The Northern stranger becomes her saviour, steals her away and becomes her husband. To each wife a son is born after she has passed several months in an unfriendly clime. In each poem the son is mysteriously carried away. Here the similarity ceases. In other respects, especially in spirit, the two compositions stand as far apart as the poles. Taylor's depiction of the struggle and the development of the soul of the artist is entirely devoid of anything that suggests the grotesquely supernatural element which pervades Wieland's Arabian-Nights-like fairy story.

There is too a suspicious likeness in the names of the principal personages. Wieland's hero is called Huon, Taylor's, Egon. Wieland's heroine, Rezia, after becoming a Christian is called Armanda. Taylor's heroine, Clelia, is also referred to by the name of Arminda. These resemblances in the forms of the names may be due only to the exigencies of meter, but the coincidence deserves notice.[209]

Mrs. Haskell has already called attention to an echo of *Faust* in ***The Picture of St. John.***[210] Surely the thought contained in Taylor's lines:[211]

> Two spirits dwell in us; one chaste and pale,
> A still recluse, whose garment knows no stain,

and the lines which follow them resemble Goethe's[212]

> Zwei Seelen wohnen, ach! in meiner Brust;
> Die eine will sich von der anderen trennen;
> Die eine hält in derber Liebeslust,
> Sich an die Welt mit klammernden Organen;
> Die andere hebt gewaltsam sich vom Dust
> Zu den Gefilden hoher Ahnen.

But is must be borne in mind that this thought of the dual nature of man is widespread in literature[213] and is also the theme of Schiller's "Das Ideal und das Leben" which Taylor undoubtedly knew.

Likewise, the thought expressed in the stanza LXVII (The Child)[214] seems to be a retort to the well-known lines of Mephistopheles:[215]

> Zwar sind auch wir von Herzen unanständig.
> Doch das Antike find' ich zu lebendig;

It is interesting to observe that the background of much of this poem is German scenery. Mrs. Taylor, speaking of the poet's activities in the spring of 1863, writes:[216] "Taylor again set out to see the Böhmerwald, where he hoped to find a background for his long poem, ***The Picture of St. John.***" She adds: "In Kötzingen my husband found what he had been seeking—the mountain valley that was to be the home of his hero, with

> Arber's head unshorn[217]

looming above."

The above constitutes the element which German poetry, in the printed work and in its animate forms of forests, valleys, and streams, contributed to Taylor's ***Picture of St. John.***[218]

In 1869 Taylor collected into a volume a series of articles which had already appeared in the *Atlantic Monthly,*[219] prefixed to them **"A Familiar Letter to the Reader,"** and called the collection ***By-Ways of Europe.*** Only three of these ***By-Ways*** are in German territory, but the articles in which Taylor has made use of his knowledge of German are three times that number.

In the introductory letter setting forth the general nature of all his travels the author not only admits that there was a "grain of truth" at the bottom of the statement falsely attributed to Humboldt—that Taylor had "travelled more and seen less than any man living,"[220] but goes on to show that he regarded the commendation of his travels by Humboldt, Dr. Petermann and Dr. Barth,[221] as the highest attainable reward for his ventures. It is here, too, that he says: "The idea hovered before my mind for a long time [to write] a *human* cosmos,"[222] and pronounces Goethe the only traveller in whom the scientific and literary, or creative, characteristics were thoroughly combined.[223]

The three articles on Russian life[224] contain nothing of importance for us. **"The Little Land of Appenzell"** is unimportant, save for the fact that it affords the author a chance to display his acquaintance with Schiller and *Wilhelm Tell*[225] and his knowledge of dialectal German and gives us an opportunity to observe that his occupation with Hebel's poems was not without results.[226]

As might be expected Montserrat leads Taylor to discourse[227] upon the "Bergschluchten" scene in the fifth act of the Second Part of *Faust.* Strange to relate, however, his generally quick mind does not seem to have recognized in the resurrected Riquilda who "rose up alive, with only a rosy mark, like a thread, around her neck,"[228] a possible source for Goethe's devise of causing the apparition of Gretchen to appear thus to Faust in the "Walpurgisnacht,"[229] so as to evoke from him the remark:[230]

> Wie sonderbar muß diesen schönen Hals
> Ein einzig rotes Schnürchen schmücken,
> Nicht breiter als ein Messerrücken!

In the article on **"The Republic of the Pyrenees"** there is no German element, but Taylor assures his readers "that the name of Andorra on the excellent German maps, which overlook nothing, was the first indication of the existence of the state"[231] which he had.

"The Kyffhäuser and its Legends" brings us into the midst of German lore. Here Taylor recounts the local legend of Peter Klaus which, he says, is "the source from which Irving drew his Rip Van Winkle," and adds: "It was first printed, so far as I can learn, in a collection made by Otmar, and published in Bremen in the year 1800."[232] Passing over for the present Taylor's meeting with the poet Friedrich Beyer,[233] we shall note his translation of Rückert's "Der alte Barbarossa"[234] and observe the fact that Taylor frankly admits: "Gustav Freytag, to whom I am indebted for some interesting information on this point [the legends of the Kyffhäuser] read to me, from a Latin chronicle of the year of 1050 . . ." etc.[235] Hence we may be quite sure that Freytag as well as Taylor is responsible for this essay. Also in this article Taylor displays his first interest to the "life" of Goethe. This probably marks the beginnings of his studies for the never-to-be-completed biography of Goethe of which we shall treat later.[236]

"A Week on Capri" may be looked upon as a collaboration of Taylor and Gregorovius. Not that the American was assisted by the German, but because of the amount of aid he obtained from the latter's little work, "The Island of Capri."[237] It is not possible to cite every detail of similarity that exists between these two works. It is only natural that two articles descriptive of the same island should possess many points in common. I shall, however, endeavor to prove by the citation of selected features of resemblance that these points of contact are not accidental.

In his very first paragraph Taylor tells of Jean Paul's and Gregorovius's conceptions of the general shape of Capri. Both these expressions are found in the second paragraph of Gregorovius's work. Taylor's article contains in ten lines of English verse,[238] a translation of a Greek inscription originally found in a grotto in Capri. Here he tells us himself that his translation is made, not from the original, but from the translation of Gregorovius.[239] These two mentions of the same German author, who had also written a work on Capri, at least inform us where to look for the source of some of Taylor's inspiration. A comparison of the two works discloses the following. Gregorovius wrote: "Even the far-famed wine of Capri is here called the Tears of Tiberius, as that of Vesuvius is called the Tears of Christ. I think the tears wept by a man like Tiberius must be exceedingly precious among the treasures of Nature."[240] Taylor varied this to: "A wine of the island is called the 'Tears of Tiberius' (when did he ever shed any, I wonder?), just as the wine of Vesuvius is called the Tears of Christ."[241] Gregorovius wrote: "The name Matromania, which the grotto bears, and which the people have with unconscious irony transformed into Matrimonio, as if Tiberius had here held wedding-ceremonies, may be derived from Magnae Matris Antrum, or perhaps from Magnum Mithrae Antrum."[242] Taylor writes thus: "The grotto of Mitromania—a name which the people, of course, have changed into 'Matrimonio,' as if the latter word had an application to Tiberius! . . . antiquarians derive from the name *Magnum Mithrae Antrum.*"[243] A coincidence of the facts might arouse suspicion, but a coincidence of both facts and "asides" establishes the conviction that Taylor was well acquainted with the work of Gregorovius.[244]

In **"A Trip to Ischia"** there is only one reference to German literature. Taylor takes issue with Jean Paul's "imaginary description" of the island[245] but it is interesting to note that once again he had to ascertain how a German author had described the place before writing his own article.

"The Land of Paoli" shows a reversion to Gregorovius. This time it is the latter's two volume work, *Corsica,* upon which Taylor draws. It might almost be declared that everything contained in Taylor's article can be found in Gregorovius' exhaustive work. On his second page Taylor quotes two verses from Seneca. These verses are also found in Gregorovius' work.[246] Taylor quotes Strabo in English.[247] The same passage is cited in German by Gregorovius.[248] A few pages further on, after giving some information found in the German work, Taylor quotes directly from the same page in Gregorovius on which that information is found.[249] On one page of Taylor's work we find a strophe in Italian of a Corsican lullaby and on the same page a stanza from another Corsican cradle song in an English translation.[250] This same lone strophe in Italian is found also in Gregorovius[251] and on the page immediately preceding it is a German translation of a "Corsisches Wiegenlied" which contains the stanza given by Taylor in English. Finally, at the very end of his article, our author submits seven couplets of verse. Concerning them he tells us:[252] "We took the words of our friend Gregorovius,[253] and made them ours." They are the final verses of a poem which concludes the German work *Corsica.*[254] This should suffice to establish the fact that Taylor's article owes much to the German traveller and poet, Ferdinand Gregorovius. The only question that remains is whether the reading of the German's work did not prompt not only Taylor's article, but even his very trip to Corsica.

In the essay **"The Island of Maddalena: with a Distant View of Caprera"** Taylor devotes most of his space to Garibaldi, who, he tells us,[255] "in features and complexion shows his Lombard and German descent," adding: "In fact, the best blood in Italy is German, however reluctant the Italians may be to acknowledge the fact." Such statements smack of German propaganda. Hence we are not surprised when Taylor, on the same page, writes:[256] "Before leaving his imprisonment at Varignano, he [Garibaldi] gave permission to the Frau von S—, an intimate friend, to publish a German translation from which I take the chief part of the narrative." Thereupon follow four pages of direct translation from the German work.

The only remaining essay, **"In the Teutoburger Forest,"** contains, in addition to historical and legendary accounts of personages and places, much idyllic description and personal narrative. The historical and legendary material Taylor naturally received from German sources. He himself relates that he "picked up a description of the Teutoburger Forest, written by the Cantor Säuerlander of Detmold[257]—a little book which no one but a full-blooded Teuton could have written. Fatiguingly minute, conscientious to the last degree, overflowing with love for the subject, exhaustive on all points, whether important or not."[258] This book, from which he makes one direct quotation,[259] may then be looked upon as the ultimate source of most, if not all, of Taylor's information. In addition to a comment which Detmold causes Taylor to make about Freiligrath,[260] the article contains short prose passages translated from Dr. Emil Braun[261] and from Goethe.[262]

The Masque of the Gods, which Taylor wrote "in four days, almost at a white heat"[263] (February 16–19, 1872), has been everywhere regarded as a result of Taylor's occupation with *Faust. The Philadelphia Evening Bulletin* called it "a thoroughly Goethean work."[264] Professor Smyth, who rightly regards this work as the beginning of the third stage of Taylor's poetic development, writes:[265] "He was soon absorbed in the study of Goethe, and his mind was taking on the cast of thought that was to determine his future literary product, the first fruit of which was ***The Masque of the Gods.***" Mrs. Taylor says?[266] "This drama marks the ripeness of the new intellectual development which had been preparing itself in the author's mind. It came after his translation of 'Faust,' that had taught him a masterly handling of form, and after a long and rare season of congenial labor and study." The critics generally were wont to center attention upon the metaphysical element in the work.[267] Taylor preferred to call this element "psychological."[268] It makes little difference whether we employ one of these terms, or call the work allegorical or cryptic, the fact remains that the supermundane theme is treated in a lofty manner involving much abstract speculation. It is, therefore, no wonder that in the light of the older criticism, which held up the *Faust* as an example *sui generis* of deep, abstract, metaphysical speculation, Taylor's ***Masque*** was immediately decreed to be "Faustian."

Undoubtedly there are elements in the ***Masque*** which are ascribable to Taylor's familiarity with Goethe's masterpiece. There are perhaps also reminiscences of Schiller's philosophical poems. But the work must not be called unqualifiedly Goethean. Speaking of the reception of the poem Taylor wrote in part:[269] "I feel, at last, that I have some qualities of my own, not simulated or borrowed." He also makes mention of a notice of his ***Masque*** in a German literary periodical wherein the critic, who probably would have been more apt to recognize echoes of Goethe than were the American critics, called the piece "one of the most remarkable and original poems which has ever been written in America."[270]

True, the ***Masque*** is, like *Faust,* a dramatic poem. It is, as Mrs. Taylor has said, rich in metrical form. Taylor's handling of the varied meters of Goethe's poem must have contributed to this feature of his own drama. In both poems there are choruses as well as dialogue parts. At the basis of both themes lies a breadth of view concerning religion, which Taylor designated for his poem as "not *un*christian, but *over*christian."[271] But in the general treatment of the subject matter the poems stand far apart. Whereas Goethe connects much of his lofty philosophy with quasi-real people, and has most of it spoken by persons who are real or purport to be real, Taylor allows his lines to be enunciated by mere spirits, abstractions, allegorical figures, and thereby gives to his work a sort of aloofness which makes it seem more metaphysical than Goethe's drama.

As concerns detail, the first part of Scene Two,[272] with its Doric setting, its personified trees, rivers and mountains, its mention of the death of the dryad, the disappearance of the nymphs and the god of the stream,[273] suggests Schiller's "Die Götter Griechenlands." When Taylor writes:[274]

> For Beauty is the order of the Gods.

he recalls a verse from the same German poem:

> Damals war nichts heilig als das Schöne.[275]

There are also other philosophical concepts in the ***Masque*** similar to those found in Schiller, but, of course, it would be unwise to assert that Taylor might not have come by the more general concept of his poem independently.

The problem of Taylor's poem is to make an exposition of the nature of the Deity. Not unlike the panentheistic conception held by Faust is the manner in which Taylor sets forth the Godhead. He finds in each of the most various gods of the most different religions and states of civilization a manifestation of the one true, higher Power whom man in his present state of development is incapable of comprehending.

> If we look up
> Beyond the shining form wherein Thy love
> Made holiest revelation, we must shade
> Our eyes beneath the broadening wing of Doubt,
> To save us from Thy splendor.[276]

The seed of this philosophy is contained in *Faust,* but, when "a voice from space," which represents the Most High, calls out:[277]

> Thou doest the work I set, yet nam'st thyself.
> I have no name.

we have a very translation of Goethe's[278]

> Ich habe keinen Namen
> Dafür!

used in a similar circumstance, an attempt to identify the Deity, but not by a corresponding character. When Taylor wrote his song of **"The Sea,"**[279] he may have had the last part of the "Classische Walpurgisnacht" in the background of his memory. That the same figures should appear in two scenes based on the same motive is, however, quite natural.

It may be concluded, therefore, that, in a general way, especially as regards the philosophical nature of the theme of his dramatic poem, Taylor was led by his occupation with Goethe; that, although some details resemble ideas found in Goethe and Schiller, and probably come from those sources, the poem is, after all, Taylor's own. The matter he may have borrowed, the manner he invented.

Taylor's next volume, ***Beauty and the Beast; and Tales of Home*** (1872), a collection of nine short stories which had appeared in magazines during the ten preceding years, shows little that is traceable to the German. Of course, there are throughout mentions of the German language, German characters, German society, German music[280] and the like, to an extent not to be expected in the works of the average American author, but the references to German literature are few and unimportant. One article, however, is essentially a German piece, **"Can a Life hide Itself?"** Taylor was very probably incited to write this detective story by his perusal of German works of a similar nature, for, in the very beginning of the narrative, the story-teller relates: "I had been reading, as is my wont from time to time, one of the many volumes of 'The New Pitaval',[281] that singular record of human crime and human cunning." The background of practically the whole story is German, as are its principal characters. Taylor must drag in German literature. Therefore, he makes an "old friend" of his, "an author from Coburg," an actor in the story. With this author Taylor, the narrator, sits and listens to the overture from Wagner's *Lohengrin*[282] and "hotly" discusses "the question of Lessing's obligations to English literature."[283]

In **"The Experiences of the A. C.,"** wherein Taylor pokes fun at the Transcendentalists of the Brook Farm type, he represents these good people as reading for hours at a time the works of Schelling or Fichte.[284] When we find among the frequent lyric outpourings of the sentimental Miss Ringtop a song beginning: "Thou, thou, reign'st in this bosom!",[285] we may be certain that the author has in mind the little German song, "Du, du liegst mir im Herzen."

In March, 1873, appeared Taylor's ***Lars: A Pastoral of Norway.*** Although the poem was written in Germany,[286] it in no way shows any influence of German literature. Taylor's statement:[287] "The story is wholly mine own invention, and seemeth unto me entirely original." may be taken at its face value. The "singularly truthful reproduction of Norwegian landscape, manners, and sentiment"[288] in this poem is, of course, ascribable to Taylor's travels in Norway in 1857 and his acquaintance with Mügge's *Afraja.*[289] We are surprised to hear Thomas Bailey Aldrich call **"Lars"** an "exquisite story, such as Goethe would have liked to tell," and add: "It made me think of Auerbach's peasant idylls."[290] But when we learn that Whittier "said that **'Lars'** ranked side by side with 'Evangeline' and 'Herrmann and Dorothea'—the three finest pastorals ever written,"[291] we recognize another link between the American "bourgeois" epic of the last century and its German forbears.

The Prophet (1874) was also written in Germany. Despite the fact that Taylor worked on this drama not only in Gotha and Leipzig,[292] but also in Weimar while pursuing his Goethe Studies,[293] not the least trace of German influence is present. This is positively due entirely to the fact that this is "a dramatic poem on a strictly American subject."[294]

When, in 1872, Taylor first proposed to bring out his "Pastorals" he called the poems to be contained in the collection "the waifs of ten years."[295] Hence, when the volume did finally appear in the autumn of 1875,[296] it comprised Taylor's minor compositions for a period of thirteen years, during most of which time he was intensively occupied with his study of Goethe, first with the translation of *Faust,* and then with the work preparatory to the proposed Goethe-Schiller biography. It is, therefore, natural that the ***Home Pastorals, Ballads and Lyrics*** should betray some results of his occupation with German literature.

The whole section of the volume which is called "Home Pastorals" is written in hexameter, unrimed.[297] Some of the "Ballads"[298] are written in the same meter, but with rime. Taylor's use of this meter, especially of the freer form without rime, is a result of his acquaintance with German hexametric writings.

Not only Taylor, but American authors rather generally, some of them in emulation of Taylor's example, turned their attention about this time to the German hexameter. Mr. Delmar G. Cooke in his *William Dean Howells, A Critical Study*[299] speaking of the latter's "The Pilot's Story", says:[300] "The poem came upon the mid-century revival of the hexameter, established in this country by Longfellow; and Howells never outgrew the penchant he then acquired for the metre." He then goes on:[301] "But Howells reinforced the impulse to write in hexameters given by Longfellow, going, as Bayard Taylor, directly to the eighteenth-century German popularizers of the measure. . . . The sketch entitled 'The Mowers' is reminiscent of *Hermann und Dorothea.*" In the *North American Review* for July, 1869,[302] in evaluating a new volume of E. C. Stedman's poems, no less a person than James Russell Lowell writes: "We are especially interested by the specimens of his translation of Theocritus. A good version of this truly charming and original poet is greatly wanted in English. Mr. Stedman, we feel sure, would succeed in giving us the standard one. We should only caution him to make his hexameters as easy of scansion as possible by the unlearned ear. The verse in English must follow German, not Grecian or even Roman models." Taylor saw and approved Lowell's comment and wrote to his friend Stedman:[303] "What he [Lowell] says of hexameters is exactly true. The Germans *have* discovered the best modern hexameter. I can rapidly give you an idea of it:—

Four feet dactylic, with an occasional trochee to vary the music.

The fifth *inevitably* a dactyl.

The sixth generally a trochee, but now and then a spondee, introduced when necessary to rest the ear.

No spondaic feet in the middle of the line. [. . .]

Evidently Stedman did make the experiment immediately, for within a week Taylor writes again:[304] "I gave you only *one* line as a specimen; of course the order of dactyls and trochees can always be varied in the first four feet, and an occasional spondee break the closing trochaic feet. The German hexameters—at least those of Goethe and Gregorovius[305]—are *never* monotonous. The October 'Atlantic' will have a **'Cedarcroft Pastoral'**[306] in hexameters, which I specially want you to read." The final statement is equivalent to an admission that his poem is an example of the German hexameter; and so it is, as an examination of its rhythm will demonstrate. Furthermore, the **"August Pastoral"**[307] is the earliest of the five pieces which constitute the first section of this volume.[308] The others are naturally modelled after the same metrical norm. Mrs. Taylor expresses the opinion that:[309] "these pastorals he conceived and wrote under the stimulus of this study of Goethe, whose 'Hermann and Dorothea' convinced him that the hexameter might be mastered in English no less effectively than it had been in German." Well might she venture this opinion, for it is a matter of record that "Taylor read 'Hermann and Dorothea' anew in the summer of 1869, while preparing his Notes for *Faust.*"[310]

Although Mrs. Taylor has pointed out that the reading of Goethe's rustic idyll may have influenced her husband's choice of meter, she has neglected another consideration which naturally presents itself: Did the reading of *Hermann und Dorothea* not suggest to Taylor the treatment of pastoral subjects? If such be the case, it is only the general theme that was thus suggested, for Taylor's pastorals are not like Goethe's epic in any other way. The fact that Taylor's three main poems treat three seasons, **"May-Time," "August," "November,"** recalls another German hexametric composition with which Taylor was thoroughly familiar, Goethe's "Vier Jahreszeiten,"[311] which he read about this time.[312] However, aside from the quasi-seasonal themes and the fact that both the German and the English compositions are more philosophical than descriptive, there is nothing to show a dependence of the newer upon the older composition.

Likewise written in hexameters and descriptive-philosophical is Schiller's "Der Spaziergang" which Taylor must have known.[313] This whole group of Taylor's poems is pastoral in the same way as the "Spaziergang" might be called a pastoral, the rustic description serves as a framework on which to spin fine philosophical discourse. It is impossible to establish the fact that Taylor had Schiller's poem in mind when he wrote his **"August,"** as there is no external evidence on this point. Nor are any details of technique or expression identical. But many resemblances occur in the general nature of the poems and in the general method of treatment. Furthermore, in his very first stanza Taylor, referring to his reading in the works of three German poets at this time, mentions first the author of the "Spaziergang:"

> Therefore be still, thou yearning voice from the garden in Jena,[314]

The poems are about the same length. An English translation of the Schiller's title would be just as appropriate to Taylor's piece as is the title **"August."** Both poets go forth into the blossoming nature; Schiller: "endlich entflohn des Zimmers Gefängnis Und dem engen Gespräch;[315] Taylor, from his library, for vain is one's commerce with books "when the world and the brain are numb in the torpor of August."[316] Schiller's road is "der ländliche Pfad," "ein schlängelnder Pfad" which "leitet steigend empor."[317] Taylor takes "the path by the pines, the russet carpet of needles, Stretching from wood to wood,"[318] which also leads upward, for soon he announces:

> Now from the height of the grove, between the irregular tree-trunks,
> Over the falling fields and the meadowy curves of the valley,
> Glimmer the peaceful farms, the mossy roofs of the houses,
> Gables gray of the neighboring barns, and gleams of the highway
> Climbing the ridges beyond to dip in the dream of a forest.

Schiller's path too had led to a height from which he could see, beyond the cultivated fields, "ein blaues Gebirg endigt im Dufte die Welt."[319] But compare with Taylor's lines above some details of Schiller's description of the intervening landscape![320]

> Aber in freieren *Schlangen* durchkreuzt die *geregelten Felder,*
> *Jetzt verschlungen vom Wald,* jetzt an den *Bergen* hinauf
> *Klimmend,* ein *schimmernder* Streif, die *länderverknüpfende* Straße.

Both poets traverse, either in person or in spirit, or in both, the intervening tilled lands and towards the end of the poem find themselves on another highland. Taylor gains "the top of the ridge, where stands, colossal the pin-oak."

"Yonder, a mile away, I see the roofs of the village."[321] Now Taylor observes:[322]

> Right and left are the homes of the slow, conservative farmers,
> Loyal people and true, ...
> Orderly, moral are they, ...

as Schiller had already observed:[323]

> *Nachbarlich wohnet* der Mensch noch mit dem *Acker* zusammen,
> Seine *Felder* umruhn *friedlich* sein ländliches *Dach.*

When Schiller contemplates the cultivated fields, the distant city and other signs of human achievement, he philosophizes upon the whole course of human civilization and deplores the loss of the "Golden Age" which for him was synonymous with Greek culture. Taylor, in a like situation, does not enter into a formal recitation of the history of civilization, but none the less deplores the loss of the culture of ancient Greece and bemoans the limitations imposed by civilization as the world now knows it. Thus, as he strolls reflecting, the sight of "a sylvan creature of Galway,"[324] nude and bathing in a brook, recalls to him the "bath of a nymph, the bashful strife of a Hylas" and suggests the contrast between the sight before him and the beauty of a similar incident in the "Golden Ages." Then the poet laments that he has been denied an Arcadian existence.

"Was it the spite of fate that blew me hither, an exile?"[325] He calls his "hunger unmeet for the times", an "anachronistical passion."[326]

> The record immortal[327]
> Left by the races when Beauty was law and Joy was religion

is entirely in harmony with Schiller's characteristic point of view. These and like Schilleresque expressions abound in this part of the poem.

Finally Schiller on the wild headland finds comfort in primaeval nature undefiled by the trace of modern civilization and concludes:

> Und die Sonne Homers, siehe! sie lächelt auch uns.

In closing, Taylor, in the twilight, afar from the dwellings of men, brings himself into a similar joyous mood, not by beholding in the sinking sun and in undefiled nature around him an ideal state, but by fleeing in the manner suggested by Schiller in "Das Ideal und das Leben," "aus dem engen, dumpfen Leben In des Ideales Reich!" Hence he closes:

> Thus, in aspiring, I reach what were lost in the idle possession;
> Helped by the laws I resist, the forces that daily depress me;
> Bearing in secreter joy a luminous life in my bosom,
> Fair as the stars of Cos, the moon on the boscage of Naxos!
> Thus the skeleton Hours are clothed with rosier bodies:
> Thus the buried Bacchanals rise into lustier dances:
> Thus the neglected god returns to his desolate temple:
> Beauty, thus rethroned, accepts and blesses her children!

It is safe to conclude that, had Taylor not known Schiller's "Der Spaziergang" and his other philosophical poems, the **"August Pastoral"** had never taken its present form. Again in the kindly satirical piece **"Cupido"** we find in the second stanza[328] a reference to the materialization of nature brought about by the scientific point of view. This immediately recalls once again Schiller's favorite theme.[329]

The dedicatory poem, **"Ad Amicos,"** initiates the Goethean element in this volume, for it resembles the "Zueignung" in *Faust,* which, too, is an "Ad Amicos." Both pieces are of approximately the same length; both are written in iambic pentameter with alternating rime, the rime of the odd lines being feminine, that of the even lines masculine.[330] Both are stanzaic, but the stanza length is not identical in the two pieces. The tone of each piece is that of a touching, but manly, emotion caused by recollections by the middle-aged poet of his youthful days. There is a contrast of situation presented by the two poems. Goethe addresses friends who have already passed beyond his world, Taylor addresses present friends. Yet we find in the latter half of Taylor's dedication echoes especially of the two final stanzas of the "Zueignung." I quote several stanzas and underline those passages which seem to be most similar.

> Sie *hören* nicht die folgenden *Gesänge,*
> Die Seelen, denen ich *die ersten* sang;
> *Zerstoben* ist das freundliche Gedränge,
> *Verklungen, ach! der erste Widerklang.*
> *Mein Lied ertönt der unbekannten Menge,*
> Ihr *Beifall* selbst macht meinem Herzen bang,
> Und was sich sonst an meinem Lied erfreuet,
> Wenn es *noch lebt,* irrt in der Welt *zerstreuet.*
> Und mich ergreift ein längst entwöhntes *Sehnen*
> Nach jenem stillen, ernsten Geisterreich,
> Es schwebet nun in unbestimmten Tönen
> Mein lispelnd Lied, der Äolsharfe gleich,
> *Ein Schauer faßt mich, Thräne folgt den Thränen*
> Das strenge Herz es fühlt sich mild und weich;
> Was ich besitze, seh' ich wie im Weiten,
> Und was verschwand, wird mir zu Wirklichkeiten.

Taylor:

> Ah, nevermore the dull neglect, that smothers
> The bard's dependent being, shall return;
> *Forgotten lines are on the lips of others,*
> *Extinguished thoughts in other spirits burn!*
> *Still* hoarded *lives* what seemed so *spent* and *wasted,*
> *And echoes come from dark and empty years;*
> Here brims the golden cup no more untasted,
> But *fame* is dim *through mist of grateful tears.*
> So *heard* and *hailed* by you, that, standing nearest,
> Blend love with faith in one far-shining flame,
> I hold anew *the earliest* gift and dearest,—
> The happy *Song* that cares not for its fame!

This last stanza seems to play the role in the economy of Taylor's poem which the first two stanzas play in the "Zueignung."

Mrs. Taylor finds a Goethean note in **"Notus Ignoto,"** written at the turn of the year 1868-1869, and discusses this at some length in *On Two Continents.*[331] Her remarks are quoted from manuscript notes prepared for an intended new edition of her husband's poems.[332] "The poem may possibly have been suggested by some verses of Goethe's which occur in his 'Four Seasons'. They are marked in a volume of 'Goethe's Poems, New Edition', given to Bayard Taylor by Berthold Auerbach in 1868. The following is a translation of them.[333]

> To invent is grand; but happy inventions of others
> Grasped and esteemed at their worth, are those not equally thine?
> Which is the happiest mortal? He that another man's merit
> Sees and another man's joy feels as though 'twere his own."

It is true that the theme found in these lines of Goethe as well as the thought contained in the distich preceding the first one quoted above:[334]

> Immer strebe zum Ganzen, und kannst du selber kein

Ganzes
Werden, als dienendes Glied schließ an ein Ganzes
dich an!

do pervade **"Notus Ignoto,"** but there is no nearer approach to coincidence of expression than the thought in Taylor's line: "Loss with gain is balanced"; and that in another of the distiches in the later added group:[335]

Vieles gibt uns die Zeit und nimmt's auch.

At best only the general theme of **"Notus Ignoto"** can be found in the "Vier Jahreszeiten."

Still another piece would Mrs. Taylor assign to her husband's interest in German literature. Again we quote from the notes to the proposed new edition of Taylor's poems.[336] "We may rightfully consider this little piece of verse as a result of the poet's studies in German literature at the time of Goethe. It was first entitled **'Distiches'** and later was given a place among the **'Improvisations'** as number IV."[337] There is nothing in this composition which justifies us in calling it an echo from the German. It may well be, but we cannot demonstrate the fact. The poem was published in *Harper's Monthly Magazine* for November, 1872, and hence must have been composed at a time when the distiches of Goethe were fresh in the mind of the author, for he quotes from the "Vier Jahreszeiten" in the notes[338] to the *Faust*[339] and also in his lecture on Goethe.[340]

Minor echoes of Goethe, and especially of *Faust,* are scattered throughout the volume. At times it is only a semblance of Goethe's voice which we detect, as:[341]

'Tis not for idle ease we pray,
But freedom for our task divine.

On other occasions the words of the master ring out clear and unmistakable, as in the lines:

Ah, moment. . . . .[342]
Stay—thou art all too fair!
And Art alas! is long.[343]
Our natures twofold are.[344]
How Art succeeds, though long.[345]

The Goethe element terminates with the very last piece in the volume, an ode to the German master dated August 28, 1875. The poem was finished shortly before that date, but it was on that day that its author read it when the Goethe Club of New York presented the bust of the sage of Weimar which was intended to adorn Central Park.[346] This composition is naturally permeated with strains from the poetry of Goethe.

At Gotha, Germany, in August 1873, Taylor wrote the piece entitled **"Summer Night. Variations of Certain Melodies."**[347] Mrs. Taylor, who was with him when he wrote it, explains:[348] "The latter points to the lyrical suggestion he received from the impassioned strains of Beethoven's immortal setting of 'Adelaida' and other verses of Matthison combined with echoes from Eichendorff's enchanting, dreamy 'Sehnsucht' and his verses:[349]

Sind's Nachtigallen
Wieder, was ruft
Lerchen, die schallen
Aus warmer Luft?

The mingling of these melodies furnish the theme of Bayard Taylor's **'Summer Night,'** which he clothes in the form of a 'Sonatina'."

The general atmosphere of the poem, the Klopstockian longing for an absent loved-one, has undeniably been inspired by the poems of Matthison and Eichendorff. The mention of Beethoven in the third division of the poem and its refrain "Adelaida" make it certain that Mrs. Taylor has correctly indicated its source. Were further proof necessary, several likenesses of expression might be adduced.[350]

It is likewise easy to detect the title and the first six verses of Taylor's poem in the first stanza of Eichendorff's "Sehnsucht."[351]

Es scheinen so golden die *Sterne,*
Am Fenster ich einsam stand
Und *hörte* aus *weiter Ferne*
Ein Posthorn im *stillen* Land.
Das Herz mir im Leib entbrennte,
Da hab' ich mir heimlich gedacht:
Ach, wer da mitreiten könnte
In der prächtigen *Sommernacht!*

Taylor:

Under the full-blown linden and the plane,
That link their arms above
In *mute,* mysterious love,
I *hear* the strain!
Is it the *far postilion's horn,*
Mellowed by *starlight,* floating up the valley, . . .[352]

'I have been unable to discover any other individual poems of either Matthison or Eichendorff which admit of being held up as direct models for Taylor's poem. Several of them possess the same *Stimmung* and the characteristic motives—nightingale, posthorn, etc., but such phenomena are only general. Furthermore, I am at a loss to understand why Mrs. Taylor has cited the four verses from "In der Fremde",[353] as a basis for her husband's poem. Any other of a score or so of Eichendorff's stanzas would have served just as well. Perhaps she knew that Mr. Taylor was especially fond of this stanza, or had marked it, or copied it. She must have had some reason. I think I can detect elsewhere a result of Taylor's intimacy with this stanza.

If the German verses quoted above be compared with the stanzas which constitute **"Improvisation VIII,"** it will be noted that Taylor has almost exactly imitated Eichendorff's form.[354] Then, too, the spirit and theme of both pieces are alike. A lover recalls the time when he, amid sylvan surroundings, was happy with his love. Now they are parted and happiness reigns no more. Witness their conclusions:

Ich hör' die Lieder,	Silence and shadow,
Fern, ohne dich,	After, might reign;
Lenz ist's wohl wieder	But the old life of ours
Doch nicht für mich.	Never again!

"Improvisation V," which was published in August, 1873,[355] and hence must have been written shortly before **"Summer Night,"** resembles in form Matthison's "Die neuen Argonauten." But here the similarity ceases and may, therefore, be a mere coincidence.[356]

We know that Taylor was acquainted with Eichendorff's poems[357] and "the splendid passion of 'Adelaida'"[358] as early as 1864. In 1868 he wrote.[359] "Eichendorff is the only poet to whom completely belongs the narrow borderland of moods and sensations." It seems that Taylor, whether induced thereto by Eichendorff or not, approached this "borderland" when, a couple of years later, he wrote his first **"Improvisation"**.

Before dismissing the volume, attention must be called to **"Napoleon at Gotha,"** because the subject matter is German. It relates the attempt by a boy at Gotha to assassinate the Emperor. Evidently the poem has an historical value, for Mrs. Taylor assures us:[360] "This incident actually occured. The youth was my great-uncle, Wilhelm Xaver von Braun."

Taylor's ***Echo Club,*** which was not published in America in book form until July, 1876,[361] more than two years after it had appeared in England,[362] was originally printed in slightly different form in the *New York Tribune* under the caption, **"The Battle of the Bards."**[363] Although some of the parodies contained in this work date back approximately two decades,[364] most of them, and all the dialogue parts were written in the autumn of 1871.[365]

Naturally, parody and criticism of non-English authors could not be offered to an English-speaking public with any hope of success. Therefore it is only in the dialogue that we find any display of Taylor's familiarity with German literature. The material which his knowledge of the German contributed to the composition of this volume is of no particular importance, but the frequency and variety of the references to, and quotations from, the authors of Germany suffice to mark the work as Taylor's. These elements therefore demand some consideration.

As early as 1854 we find Taylor writing impromptu imitations and parodies. Out of this sort of activity the ***Echo Club*** grew. It is, therefore, interesting to note his comment concerning his early endeavors.[366] "Dick, O'Brien, and I were talking the other evening about German ballads, and it was suggested, on the spur of the moment, that we should try our hands on something in the German vein. We chose 'The Helmet' as a subject, and had fifteen minutes to conceive and carry out our ideas. Dick wrote a very pretty thing. As for mine, I copy it as a curiosity which may divert you." Hence, although the printed volume, ***The Echo Club,*** contains no parodies on the German poets, it is certain that the "club" did at times concern itself with German themes.

The German atmosphere of the meeting place of the club has already been mentioned.[367] One of the members, "The Ancient," suggests that their new club is "a kind of Hainbund."[368] Taylor was careful to attribute all references to German, except one, to a single member of the club, "The Ancient," thus indicating that, although this member was very familiar with German literature, the others knew little about that subject. "The Ancient" represents Taylor himself. This being so, most references are naturally to Goethe. To that author Taylor goes to justify, so to speak, the activities of the "Echo Club."[369] "Young Goethe, we know, did many a similar thing. He was a capital *improvisatore,* and who knows how much of his mastery over all forms of poetry may not have come from just such gymnastics?" The work contains two brief quotations from Goethe, one in English,[370] the other in German.[371] There are two additional mentions of the same author.[372] Finally Zoilus proposes that the sessions of the club be closed "with a grand satirical American 'Walpurgis-Night' modeled on Goethe's Intermezzo in 'Faust',"[373] which proposal is eagerly accepted by all. Unfortunately the printed report ceases here, but "the Nameless Reporter" tells us: "The plan was carried out, and I think was not entirely unsuccessful."[374] This fiction indicates that Taylor would have liked to write such a satirical work modeled on Goethe's intermezzo.

Of Schiller we find but four mentions[375] in addition to one short citation in a translation by Coleridge.[376] In quoting once from Lessing, Taylor takes occasion to pay him the highest honor:[377] "Let me repeat to you what the greatest of critics, Lessing, said: . . . After Lessing, we can only accept Jeffrey with certain reservations until we come to Sainte-Beuve." Heine,[378] and Humboldt[379] are mentioned once each. There are several general references to German literature,[380] in one of which Geibel, Bodenstedt, Hamerling and Redwitz are called the most popular contemporary poets of Germany.[381]

An imitation of one of Uhland's pieces is found in the volume. "The Ancient" calls it "an American paraphrase of 'The Spring-Song of the Critic.'"[382] The paraphrase is not intended to be a parody of Uhland's piece, but is introduced because: "There never was a more admirable picture of that fine, insiduous egotism of the spurious critic, which makes him fear to praise, lest admiration should imply inferiority."[383] The paraphrase is in no way a very close rendition of the original. Rightly, "The Ancient" says:[384] "I have not translated any of Uhland's phrases." Even the form varies somewhat from that of the "Frühlingslied des Rezensenten" as the following stanza will illustrate.[385]

Hm! Spring? 'Tis popular we've heard,
And must be noticed therefore;
Not that a flower, a brook, or bird
Is what we greatly care for.

It is difficult to conceive of any other American author, who, in such a work as ***The Echo Club,*** would have interspersed references to German literature so freely as Taylor has done.

The plan for ***Prince Deukalion,*** which drama Taylor first intended to call *Eos,*[386] had matured in the author's mind early in 1875.[387] Actual writing began in March or April of the same year.[388] From then until the completion of the work, October 7, 1877,[389] Taylor always had the drama in mind, but actual composition seems to have been suspended between the spring of 1876 and autumn of 1877.[390] It is essential to bear these dates in mind, for, not only had Taylor been engaged for years previous with the *Faust,* but was even at this time revising his translation,[391] and pursuing his studies preparatory to writing the Goethe-Schiller biography.[392]

It seems that the charge of imitation gave Taylor some concern. Even before finishing his drama he wrote to Longfellow:[393] "You can imagine the interest with which I read your 'Pandora'. The choruses are as fine as anything you have ever done, and I read them three times before laying down the book. Their rhythmical character is another point of resemblance to my drama, and I anticipate the charge of imitation from the same refined and intelligent reviewers, when I shall come to publish. However, I shall not let that trouble me, since you know the truth." The authors of *Life and Letters* inform us:[394] "He was hastened . . . in his intention to publish by the discovery, after his poem was written, of two poems, an English[395] and a German,[396] which so nearly approached it in design as to convince him that he was in a wide current of thought, and that unless he published now he was in danger of finding his work received as if it were a follower instead of an *avant-courier.*" We know then that Taylor was influenced by none of these poems, but critics did immediately hail ***Deukalion*** as an offspring of his study of Goethe. The reviewer in the *New York Tribune* concludes thus:[397] "But as an artistic combination of poetical invention, philosophical reflection, and classical lore it gives authentic signs of a protracted date on the same line with the graver poems of Shelley and Goethe." In the *New York Times* appeared:[398] "Mr. Taylor flies higher than Goethe; but were it not for Goethe's broad back, where would ***Prince Deukalion*** be now? . . . ***Prince Deukalion*** is what we may only expect from a too frequent perusal of the second part of 'Faust'." The *Evening Post* comments in a similar vein.[399] "A work which one might easily fancy, has grown out of the author's study of the German masters. . . . The author has succeeded only in part . . . whether because there is too much or too little Goethe in the conception and execution of the piece, we shall not undertake to determine." Likewise does the *Boston Saturday Evening Gazette* find that:[400] "Strongly impressed by his recent study of Goethe, Mr. Bayard Taylor has written a poem that in form and treatment bears a closer relation to the German than to the English mode of thought." The reviewer in the *Atlantic Monthly*[401] comments thus on the form of the work: "In the varied management of his *Lieder,* Mr. Taylor reminds us of his master, Goethe, and doubtless has increased a rare natural gift by experience in translating the lyrical measures of 'Faust'."

This contemporary opinion of ***Deukalion*** has come to be the generally accepted one, and it is, in the main, correct. In form and in its general nature the poem betrays unmistakably the influence of Goethe. It is an error, however, to believe that the play is a result of Taylor's occupation with *Faust* alone. There is a similarity of theme in these two pieces. Taylor himself tells us of ***Deukalion:***[402] "The central design, or germinal cause of the Poem is to picture forth the struggle of Man to reach the highest, justest, happiest, hence most perfect condition of Human Life on this planet." This too is the theme of *Faust,* except that Goethe attempts to picture only the struggle of *a* man, and thereby attains a more human, less allegorical, effect. The critic of the *New York Times* is justified in saying that "Taylor flies higher than Goethe."[403] Taylor continues his argument: "But Knowledge, Religion, Political Organization, Art, and the manifold assumptions of the Animal Nature, by turns promote or delay the forward movement, make season after season of promise deceitful and cease not continually to assail the faith of Humanity in much that it possibly may, and rightfully should, possess." This, applied to the individual, is exactly what Faust experiences. Note, too, that the order in which Taylor enumerates the various provinces of activity is precisely that in which Faust encounters them, Knowledge, (Philosophie, Juristerei, Medicin), Religion (Und leider auch Theologie), Political Organization (*Faust* II, Act I, with a hold-over into Act IV), Art (Helena). There is enough in the poem which illustrates the "Wissensdrang" found in *Faust,* as for example,[404]

> But your concealed, undying woe
> Is this: ye have not sought to know.

as well as his "Tätigkeitsdrang":[405]

> Action, now,
> And waxing knowledge, destiny fulfilled,
> Restore the order of Titanic youth.

and:

> To find in endless growth all good—[406]
> In endless toil, beatitude.

or both:

> But I *accept,*—even all this conscious life[407]
> Gives in its fullest measure—gladness, health
> Clean appetite, and wholeness of my claim
> To knowledge, beauty, aspiration, power!
> Joy follows action, here, and action bliss,
> Hereafter. While, God-lulled, thy children sleep
> Mine, God-aroused, shall wake and wander on
> Through spheres thy slumberous essence never
> dreamed.

Likewise do we find the pantheistic view of Faust.[408]

What eye hath known Him? What fine instrument
Hath found, as 't were, a planet yet unseen,
His place among the balance of the stars?

To which we finally get the answer:[409]

Seek not to know Him; yet aspire
As atoms toward the central fire!
Not lord of race is He, afar,—
Of man, or earth, or any star,
But of the inconceivable All.

All these philosophical views are Goethean, not merely Faustian. Likewise common to a large number of Goethe's later dramatic productions, and by no means confined to the Second Part of *Faust,* is the richness and variety of metrical form which critics rightly designate as one of the acquisitions garnered by the author of ***Deukalion*** as a result of his occupation with the poetry of the German master.

In his commentary on Goethe's *Pandora,*[410] Otto Pniower observes: "Nach einem interessanten Bekenntnis in 'Dichtung und Wahrheit' (Bd. 25, 58 f.) hatte er jedoch das Gefühl, als zöge dieses Versmass [der fünffüssige Iambus] die Poesie zur Prosa herunter, und so suchte er eine neue Form, zu der 'Paläophron und Neoterpe' und das 'Vorspiel' von 1807 dem Rückschauenden wie Vorübungen erscheinen und die in dem Festspiel 'Des Epimenides Erwachen' und im zweiten Teil des 'Faust' wieder auflebt. Eigentümlich ist ihr ein Streben nach rhythmischer Mannigfaltigkeit, das in der 'Pandora,' wo beinahe für jede Stimmung und für jeden Charakter ein besonderer metrischer Ausdruck gesucht wird, bis zur Üppigkeit verschwenderisch erscheint. . . . Eine der Oper verwandte eigenartige Mischung von Drama und Lyrik ist das Resultat dieser Bemühung." The sense of these latter remarks might just as appropriately be applied to Taylor's ***Prince Deukalion, A Lyrical Drama.*** It is, moreover, a matter of record that Taylor was much interested in these later dramas of Goethe about the time of the writing of ***Deukalion.*** Mrs. Taylor says:[411] "Goethe's 'Natürliche Tochter' he considered 'a singularly neglected masterpiece,'[412] and 'Pandora' a wonderful poem." From a diary of Mrs. Taylor we acquire further information:[413] "1873 [Summer] we also read in Goethe's Works, and I remember that amongst his lyrical poems 'Prometheus' and amongst his dram. poems 'Des Epimenides Erwachen,' and especially 'Pandora'[414] were subjects of our interest and study. About this time also (but possibly before) the 'Protestantenbibel' which had been published recently occupied B's mind a great deal, and was of infinite interest to him.[415] It was in this year also that B. became acquainted with a work of my late uncle, Dr. Emil Braun, 'Griechische Götterlehre,' which had some influence on his ***Prince Deukalion.***" Albert H. Smyth is responsible for the statement:[416] "Now [circa 1873] it was his ambition to give to American literature a poem in the style of 'Faust' or 'Pandora'." Also discussing ***Prince Deukalion*** Smyth writes:[417] "He read little in metaphysics, but mediated much on Goethe's 'Pandora' and the second part of 'Faust.'" This evidence tends to confirm us in the belief that the form, style, and perhaps content, of the ***Prince Deukalion*** may be Pandorian to a greater extent than it is *Faustian.*

On the very title page of ***Prince Deukalion*** occurs the verse:

Bestimmt, Erleuchtetes zu sehen, nicht das Licht.

Goethe.

This line is, in essence, Faustian enough, but, in fact, it is Pandorian, and Taylor might have changed the color of the criticism of his drama, had he subjoined "Pandora, 958."

Of course the general subject of Taylor's ***Deukalion*** and Goethe's fragment is the same—the struggle of the Promethean descendents, the human race, to attain emancipation. Inasmuch as both authors are handling the same theme, there must needs be much in their works that would have been alike even if Taylor had never seen the earlier drama, but it can shown that at least some of the similarities are not accidental.

The *personae dramatis* of the two compositions correspond closely enough. Only those characters which are identical or corresponding in both pieces are here cited:

Goethe:	Taylor:
Prometheus	Prometheus
Epimetheus	Epimetheus
Pandora[418]	Pandora
Eos	Eos
Dämonen	Spirits
Hirten	Shepherd Shepherdess
Phileros, Prometheus' Sohn	Deukalion (son of Prometheus)
Epimelia, Epimetheus' Tochter (later wife of Phileros)	Phyrra (daughter of Epimetheus)(later wife of Deukalion)
Helios	Urania

The two poets do not follow the same course in developing the theme. Taylor has allowed his characters to run too much into types. He leads us through the development of the theological history of the human race, whereas Goethe confines himself, in a general way, fairly closely to the Pandora myth. It is because of the likeness of some details that we are inclined to believe that Taylor, having become acquainted with Goethe's fragment and the "Schema" for its completion, resolved to make use of the same theme.

It is noteworthy that both poets take occasion early in the composition to insult their audiences by explaining the name Epimetheus. Taylor:[419] "Only Epimetheus, the afterthoughted, who receiveth access of vigor in looking backward, and groweth reversely from age to youth,—etc." Goethe:

Denn Epimetheus nannten mich die Zeugenden
Vergangenem nachzusinnen, Raschgeschehenes
Zurückzuführen

(9 f.)

Further, it will be noticed that in both compositions the rejuvenation of Epimetheus is accomplished; Goethe, Schema; Z. 61. "Verjüngung des Epimetheus"; Taylor:[420]

> And locks of gray and gold are mixed above
> Their equal brows.

In Taylor's play Urania (Science) appears just when Epimetheus is entering upon his course of rejuvenation and instructs him:[421]

> The clear lamp, colorless,
> Of high Truth I possess.

In Goethe's plan we read "Helios" immediately before "Verjüngung des Epimetheus." It is hardly accidental that these spirits of light appear before the rejuvenation.

The third scene of the final act of ***Prince Deukalion*** presents what seems to be the nearest resemblance to Goethe's "Schema." We read in Goethe:[422]

> Schönheit.
> Frömmigkeit, Ruhe, Sabat. Moria

and further:[423]

> Tempel
> Sitzende Dämonen
> Wissenschaft, Kunst
> Vorhang

The following is the stage direction to Taylor's scene: *"The court of a grand, dusky temple, with beams as of cedar-wood, supported by gilded pillars. At the further end, a veil, through which sculptured cherubim are indistinctly seen. On each side are thrones, overlaid with gold, set in the interspaces of the colonades."* Here we have the "Tempel" and "Vorhang."[424] After the introductory soliloquy by Prometheus occurs another stage direction. *"The forms or phantasms of* Buddha, Medusa, Calchas *and* Urania *appear, and seat themselves upon opposite thrones.* Agathon *enters and advances to the center of the temple-court."* Now we have also the "Sitzende Dämonen."[425] Urania represents Science. This Taylor tells us himself.[426] Hence we have Goethe's "Wissenschaft." Only one other characters appears in Taylor's scene, Agathon. It is not possible to interpret Agathon as representing art, but he does represent something high and noble, and transcends all the "Dämonen" including Urania (Science) just as beauty transcends science in Schiller's order of things, which, as we shall see, was not without influence upon Taylor when he was writing ***Prince Deukalion***; so this more powerful spirit could represent nothing other than art. However, it seems best, and safest, to interpret Agathon as representing that which his name indicates—Good, and thus to make him analogous to, rather than identical with, Goethe's only remaining character,—"Kunst."

But that is not all. We must examine Prometheus's soliloquy in the temple.

> The sportive genii of illusive form,
> Of hidden color and divided ray,
> Have built me this, the ampler counterfeit
> Of thine, O Solomon! that lifted up
> Moriah into flashing pinnacles,
> And spoiled umbrageous Lebanon to roof
> Its courts with cedar!

Now why should Taylor introduce this temple as a second and greater Moriah? Look at Goethe's "Schema" and behold "Moria"! In a note on these lines of the "Schema" (37 f.) Düntzer says:[427] "Die nähere Bezeichnung der Schönheit 'Ruhe—Moria' soll nur die Seligkeit, welche die ideale Schönheit bereitet, in verschiedenen sich steigernden Bildern bezeichnen. Moria ist der von der Erscheinung des Herrn benannte Berg, auf welchem Salomo den schon von David vom Herrn befohlenen Tempelbau vollendete. Hier soll er, wie sonst Zion, die Burg Davids, die himmlische Seligkeit bezeichnen, wie Sabbath die stille Feier, Frömmigkeit, das andächtige Schauen, Ruhe, die völlige Ablösung von aussen und das innige Versenken."

Taylor's temple is not a material one; it may well "die himmlische Seligkeit bezeichnen" or represent a vision of the "new Jerusalem of the Apocalypse." The soliloquy continues:

> Less than air is mine, [temple]
> The ghost of thy barbaric fane, yet meet
> To hold the ghosts that deem themselves alive,
> As in a truce of spirit, when the Dead
> Float gray and moth-like through their wonted rooms,
> And send the hollow semblance of a voice
> To living ears,—the law that parts them both
> Being all inviolate.

The next verses of the speech introduce the element of "Ruhe," "Sabat."

> Such unconscious truce
> I now proclaim, as ever to large minds
> Holds back the narrower passion, and decides.
> The conflicts of the earth must sometimes pause,
> Breathless: some hour of weariness must come
> When each fierce Power inspects its battered mail,
> The old blade reforges, or picks out a new,
> While measuring with a dim and desperate eye
> The limbs of Man's new champion.

Then Prometheus apostrophizes Agathon.

> Agathon!
> Thy soul is yet outside the fiery lists:
> The trumpet hath not called thee: as a child
> Thou waitest, but the wisdom of a child
> Must first be spoken.

Despite these verses it is hardly possible to draw a parallel between Agathon and "Frömmigkeit," the only element in Goethe's scene which is not accounted for. Agathon may represent the good, but it is an active sort of goodness,[428] hardly to be designated as "Frömmigkeit." Hence the parallel is again imperfect. But we are not attempting to maintain that Taylor endeavored to carry out any of these scenes exactly as Goethe would have done, or as some commentator guesses Goethe would have done. We merely wish to demonstrate that Taylor had Goethe's *Pandora* more clearly in mind when he wrote his ***Prince Deukalion*** than has heretofore been realized.

Goethe originally intended to call his drama "Pandorens Wiederkunft."[429] The return of Pandora is the point about which the whole plot revolves. In Taylor's drama the return of Pandora plays no important part, but it is there in the background. Towards the end of the third act Prometheus says:[430]

> Now should Pandora speak!
> Withdrawn the demigoddess sits,
> And silent, yet there flits
> A flush across her cheek,
> A soft light o'er her eye,
> And half her proud lips smile:
> Unto thy hope, the while,
> Be this enough reply!

Finally, in the fourth scene of the final act, Pandora does appear for the first time in the earthly abode of her family,[431] and gives counsel to her daughter Phyrra.

It is evident that in Goethe's drama Phileros, son of Prometheus, was destined to wed Epimeleia, the daughter of Epimetheus and Pandora. In the "Schema"[432] we find the words:

> Phileros Epimeleia
> Priesterschaft

Now in Taylor's play the wedding, some day to be consummated between the son of Prometheus, Deukalion, and Phyrra, the daughter of Epimetheus and Pandora, is the thread about which the external, material action of the plot is woven. That Deukalion and Phyrra have a sort of mission to perform, which may be called a "Priesterschaft," is evident throughout the drama. This ideal man and this ideal woman are not to celebrate their nuptials until the dawn of the golden age. To them is entrusted the future of their race. Again we may quote a comment on Goethe's play to describe the situation in Taylor's.[433] "Deshalb [because they are "Antipoden"] empfangen nicht Prometheus und Epimetheus die himmlischen Gaben, sondern erst die nachfolgende Generation, ihre Kinder, sind reif für die göttliche Gnade. Phileros [Deukalion] und Epimeleia [Phyrra] werden zu Priestern des neuen Kultus geweiht."

There is a likeness in the thought expressed in the final lines of the third shepherd in *Pandora*[434]

> Reich' uns ein ehern Rohr,
> Zierlich zum Mund gespitzt,
> Blätterzart angeschlitzt:
> Lauter als Menschensang
> Schallet es weit;
> Mädchen im Lande breit
> Hören den Klang,

and that in the concluding verses of the Shepherd's song in Taylor's piece:[435]

> Too blest the hour hath made me
> For speech the tongue may know,
> But my happy flute shall aid me,
> And speak to my love below.

This likeness may be due to accident, but hardly a coincidence is the similarity existing between the closing lines of the two dramas. Goethe concludes:

> Was zu wünschen ist, ihr unten fühlt es;
> Was zu geben ist, die wissen's droben.
> Groß beginnet ihr Titanen; aber leiten
> Zu dem ewig Guten, ewig Schönen,[436]
> Ist der Götter Werk, die laßt gewähren.

and Taylor:

> Now as a child in April hours
> Clasps tight its handful of first flowers,
> Homeward, to meet His purpose, go!—
> These things are all you need to know.

There are a few isolated points in the American drama which suggest *Des Epimenides Erwachen.* ***Prince Deukalion*** begins with the awakening of a shepherd who beholds in the landscape around him destruction where formerly beauty had reigned. At the end of his soliloquy the shepherd hears the song of a nymph. This song is taken by the shepherd to be of ill omen. Then the shepherd hears "Voices *(from underground)*"[437] and says:

> What tongues austere are these that offer help
> Of loving lives?—that promise final good,
> Greater than gave the Gods,

All this is exactly what happens to the awakening Epimenides.[438]

> Wo bin ich denn?—In eine Wüstenei,
> Von Fels und Baum beschränkt, bin ich begraben.
> Wie war es sonst! etc.

At the close of his first speech Epimenides too hears an "Unsichtbares Chor" whose song seems evil to him.[439]

> Dämonen seid ihr, keine Genien!

After this shorter speech he hears the "Genien" who sing words of promise:[440]

> Komm! wir wollen dir versprechen
> Rettung aus dem tiefsten Schmerz—etc.

At another point in the American play Calchas, boasting of how he has made a bond-slave of Urania (Science), says:[441]

> Urania with forward-peering eyes,
> Saw not the vestments, which, to mark her mine,

I laid upon her shoulders: suddenly new,
Full-statured, with uplifted head she walks,
And drops her loosed phylacteries in the dust.

This reminds of how in *Epimenides Erwachen* the "Dämon der Unterdrückung" succeeds in enchaining "Glaube" and "Liebe" by flatteringly bestowing upon them bracelets, costly girdles and other ornamentations.[442]

In his little book, *Aus dem Amerikanischen Dichterwalde,* Rudolf Doehn, after summarizing the contents of Taylor's drama, writes:[443] "Dies ist in kurzen Zügen der Inhalt der Dichtung ***Prince Deukalion,*** die unzweifelhaft an manchen Stellen lebhaft an Schiller's 'Triumph der Liebe,' 'Götter Griechenlands' and 'Die Künstler' erinnert. In dem letzten Gedicht stellt Schiller die Wahrheit personificiert als Venus Urania dar, die sich aber für uns Menschen der strahlenden 'Feuerkrone' entkleidet, um uns als milde Göttin Cypria mit dem Gürtel der Anmuth, als Schönheit zu erscheinen. Nach einem Gespräche mit Wieland soll Schiller indess diesen Gedanken dahin modificirt haben, dass schon hienieden, wie Bayard Taylor es andeutet, die Menschheit eine Bildungsstufe erreichen werde, wo Schönheit und Wahrheit, Cypria und Urania, sich dem Menschen als ein und dasselbe Wesen darstellt." Such an insinuation may be contained in Taylor's drama, but it is only "angedeutet," not expressed, and by no means developed. Taylor was familiar with Schiller's "Die Künstler" and held it up as "an example of poetry crushed by philosophy."[444] He probably bore Schiller's Urania in mind when creating his own Urania, who is, however, a much more limited creature, and more material. She represents Science and cannot reveal the whole truth.[445]

No fond paramour
Shall woo me for my beauty, save as truth
Makes beautiful, or knowledge stands for love.
. . . . my serener light
Probes the dark closets of the mystic past,
And many a bat-like phantom, blinded, shrieks
For the last time, and dies: yet—one more step,
The final one, awaits me.
Agathon: Yea, and that
Thou canst not take.
Urania: What hinders me?—speak on?
Agathon: Then thou wert a God!
Urania: The Cause? the first impelling Force?
The Ages may yet make me so.

This is near as we get in the drama to an expression of the idea that Taylor's Urania may ultimately become absolute truth.

Was wir als *Wissenschaft* hier gekannt,
Wird *wohl* einst als Wahrheit uns entgegengehen

represents a deviation, equally great, from Schiller's lines and from his conception of Urania.

I find nothing that is common to "Der Triumph der Liebe" and ***Prince Deukalion.*** A shortcoming of Taylor's drama is it lacks a real human love element. The short song of Eros[446] is the nearest approach to an encomium to love.

Several mentions of Taylor's acquaintance with "Die Götter Griechenlands" have already been made[447] and there is no gainsaying that this drama gives further evidence of familiarity with it. Mrs. Taylor has pointed out the passage most like Schiller's poem,[448] compared it with that part of the German poem which her husband had translated[449] and made fitting comment. We cite the lines from ***Deukalion*** and the essential parts of Mrs. Taylor's remarks. Gaea addresses the nymphs:[450]

Ye highly live, more awful in the spell
Of unseen lovliness! No need to quit
Your dwellings, strike the dull sense of fear,
And win a shallow worship: Man's clear eye
Sees through the Hamadryad's bark, the veil
Of scudding Oread, hears the low-breathed laugh
Of Bassarid among the vine's thick leaves,
And spies a daintier Syrinx in the reed.
For him that loves, the downward-stooping moon
Still finds a Latmos: Enna's meadows yet
Bloom, as of old, to new Persephones;
And 'twixt the sea-foam and the sparkling air
Floats Aphrodite,—nobler far than first
These bright existences, and yours, withdrawn
To unattainable heights of half-belief,
Divine, where whole reflects the hue of Man.

Mrs. Taylor says:[451] "The author of our drama, in the lines before us, draws quite another conclusion from that which Schiller sets forth . . . ; and we feel very much inclined to accept the speech of Gaea as an answer to the . . . verses of Schiller."

When in her next speech Gaea says:

Fear not, sweet Spirits, what unflinching law,
Tracking creative secrets, Man may find
In my despotic atoms,

we at once recall Schiller's:[452]

Dient sie knechtisch dem Gesetz der Schwere
Die entgötterte Natur.

There are naturally scattered throughout the drama many minor points, philosophical ideas and shades of thought which seem reminiscent of Schiller's poems, but it is not possible to assert that they are the result of Taylor's study of Schiller. Any possible additional German element had best be designated as Mr. Henry Morford designates the Faustian element when he writes:[453] "***Prince Deukalion*** with its indefinable but actual resemblance to the weird 'Faust'." Not without some justification did Isaac Edwards Clarke call ***Prince Deukalion*** "perhaps the first direct result" of Taylor's occupation with *Faust.*[454]

After her husband's death Mrs. Taylor collected and published in 1880 in a volume called ***Critical Essays and Literary Notes*** a number of his minor compositions. These articles, which originally appeared in magazines and newspapers, form but a minute portion of all of Bayard Taylor's critical and editorial contributions,[455] but may serve as a representative cross section of the kind of thing that interested him and that he offered the public through the columns of the popular journals and monthlies.

It will be noticed that four of the eight main essays deal with German literature. Enough has already been said about the article on "The German Burns."[456] The one on **"Friedrich Rückert"**,[457] written in five days (April 15–20, 1866),[458] had to be condensed due to circumstanzes over which the author had no control. He wrote to James T. Fields:[459] "Here is the Rückert. . . . Had you allowed me 12 pages instead of 8, I could have made a more thorough article, with no more labor than this." This brief essay, occasioned by the death of Rückert, displays our author's familiarity with that poet's works, offers a number of laudable translations[460] from then, and, because of the personal relation which existed between the writer and the deceased, is such as Bayard Taylor alone of all American poets could write. Aside from the features mentioned, the piece has no distinctive merit. The two articles **"Autumn Days in Weimar"**[461] and **"Weimar in June"**[462] are pregnant with the literary atmosphere of the German Athens, but since they really constitute a study preparatory to the Goethe-Schiller biography, further discussion of their contents will be withheld for the present.

Other references to German authors and their works found in this volume have already been mentioned in this investigation. Still others will occur in the following pages. In order to illustrate how Taylor found it almost impossible to discuss literature at all without setting up a comparison with German letters, let us glance at some other passages. He points out how Victor Hugo in his *La Legénde des Siècles* endeavored to avoid "all reference to the achievements of the German race."[463] In discussing Heavysege's *Saul,* he informs his readers that the author "divides the subject into three dramas after the manner of Schiller's 'Wallenstein'."[464] With Thackeray he converses about Goethe.[465] There are other minor mentions of German authors and works.[466]

Among the shorter pieces we must not fail to call attention to Taylor's review of *The Christian Singers of Germany,* by Catherine Winkworth,[467] wherein Taylor demonstrates that he is also versed in German hymnology.

Again in the little story **"Who was She?"** which first appeared in the *Atlantic Monthly* for September, 1874,[468] are found elements which recall Goethe's *Die Wahlverwandtschaften.* The general situation in Taylor's story in no way resembles the plot in Goethe's novel, but there are at least two points which the American author may well have gotten from his German master. First, Taylor's story is based on the theory of affinities, which in this case act negatively. At the turning point in the plot we read:[469] "No mysterious magnetic force has drawn you to me and held you near me, nor has the experiment inspired me with an interest which cannot be given up without a personal pang." Secondly, the book of aphorisms which Ignotus finds in the dell and which belongs to Ignota certainly suggests "Ottiliens Tagebuch." It is not possible to match any of the American *sententiae* with those of the German, each for each, but a glance at the philosophy of Ignota discloses the general resemblance.[470] "It makes a great deal of difference whether we wear social forms as bracelets or handcuffs."[471]

"Can we not still be wholly our independent selves, even while doing, in the main, as others do? I know two who do so; but they are married."

"The men who admire those bold, dashing young girls treat them like weaker copies of themselves. And yet they boast of what they call 'experience!'"[472]

"I wonder if any one felt the exquisite beauty of the noon as I did today? A faint appreciation of the sunsets and storms is taught us in youth, and kept alive by novels and flirtations; but the broad, imperial splendor of this summer noon!—and myself standing alone in it—yes utterly alone!"

"The men I seek must exist: where are they? How make an acquaintance, when one obsequiously bows himself away as I advance? The fault is surely not all on my side."[473]

There is another point to which attention might be called. Taylor describes the lay of the land around Wampsocket very carefully and clearly.[474] In one of his only two references to *The Elective Affinities* he calls attention to the careful manner in which Goethe describes his landscapes and cites the description in *The Elective Affinities* as representing "almost topographical exactness."[475]

Mrs. Taylor, with the assistance of Mr. George H. Boker gave the public in 1880 a volume called ***The Poetical Works*** of Bayard Taylor.[476] The editors have included a not inconsiderable number of heretofore unpublished poems which were found among Taylor's manuscripts in a more or less finished state.[477] Of the thirty-three pieces which now make their initial appearance in book form, many of which had, however, previously appeared in periodicals, few are in any way concerned with German literature. This is explainable in part by the fact that a goodly proportion of those compositions are occasional poems, written on non-German subjects and three others are pieces in which Taylor sought to conceal his identity.[478] To betray a knowledge of German literature in the last-named group would have been to defeat the purpose of their composition. However, the additional stratum contains two translations from Goethe, "The Song of Mignon" and "Hartz-Journey in Winter."[479] The former is rendered in a manner which does Taylor no special honor. Its shortcomings are compensated for by the translation of the second piece which, both in form and meaning, closely follows the original line for line, losing little of the strange beauty of the German poem.

The lines entitled **"To Marie with a Copy of the Translation of Faust"** have already been referred to and quoted.[480] That the **"Epicedium,"** Taylor's last poem, composed for the Bryant commemoration in 1878, was written in Berlin was merely accidental, but the only other poem written during Taylor's last residence in Germany grew out of an incident peculiar to that country. "When driving from Gotha to Friedrichsroda he used to pass through the little village of Wahlwinkel, where he saw in the gable of a peasant's house a stork's nest which had been there from time immemorial."[481] Hence the theme for Taylor's last poem is on a German subject, "The Village Stork."

Thus, with the exception of two volumes, consideration of which has been deferred to a later chapter,[482] we have examined all of Taylor's publications in which there appears to be a German element. **"The National Ode"** (1876) has been passed over, for there the mention of Germany is only natural and incidental.[483] Likewise have we avoided mention of ***Boys of Other Countries,*** not only because of the juvenile nature of the work, but because the German story, "The Two Herd-Boys," is in no way more meritorious than the other tales contained in that volume.

Notes

1. P. 15.
2. See *Life and Letters,* p. 27 ff.
3. P. 17 ff., *supra.*
4. P. 116.
5. P. 13.
6. See *Dichtungen,* Stuttgart und Tübingen, I, 117.
7. See pp. 19, 23, 26, 28, 31, 40, 45.
8. See *Life and Letters,* p. 82 (Jan. 24, 1847).
9. P. 130.
10. P. 95.
11. E.g., *The Wayside Dream* was finished March 14, 1847 (Tay. 44, Cornell University), and first appeared in *Graham's Magazine* for December, 1847.
12. Taylor's diary (Tay. 44, Cornell University), under the date of Mar. 14, 1847, reads: "Uhland says: 'Schaurig süsses Gefühl—lieblicher Frühling du nahst.'"

    In a letter to Mary Agnes, June 29, 1847 (*Life and Letters,* p. 97), he writes: "*Morning.* My dreams were not of thee, but I had an inspiring vision. I thought old Ludwig Uhland sat beside me, leaning his silver head on my shoulder, and repeated some of his beautiful German ballads. It was a singular thought, but perhaps it had a mysterious connection with my waking reflections; for I was turning over in my mind the resolution to write no more poetry. . . . But there is no fear of it, I believe. A flower which has been planted by Nature, and cherished by years of thought, cannot die from such a slight neglect."

    From the data in hand and the nature of the opening stanza of Taylor's poem, I am inclined to believe that this composition was written about the time of this dream.
13. *Rhymes of Travel,* p. 116. In Tay. 65 (Cornell University) is a record of a translation thus: "Uhland's Harald Frankf., Nov. 14 1844." Also in Tay. 9.
14. *Views Afoot,* p. 126 (ed. 1872).
15. Taylor was in Heidelberg in September; note also the season represented in the poem is Autumn.
16. E.g., cf. *Views Afoot,* p. 250 f. and Taylor's statement that "The Wayside Dream" was written March 14, 1847 (Cornell, Tay. 44).
17. S. 74.
18. Except the final line of each of the first three of Taylor's stanzas, which is hexameter.
19. Taylor, of course, makes no attempt to imitate the feminine rimes when such occur in the German.
20. See *Views Afoot,* p. 126 (ed. 1872).
21. *Taylor's Translation,* p. 9 ff.
22. *Ibid.,* p. 11.
23. *Life and Letters,* p. 14.
24. *Life and Letters,* p. 14, Cf. *Orion,* hersg. von Adolf Strodtmann, I, 6, 450 (June, 1863).
25. See note 16, *supra.*
26. *Rhymes of Travel,* p. 109.
27. Smyth, *Bayard Taylor* p. 304.
28. See *supra,* p. 81.
29. S. 22, 25, 26, respectively. N. B. that these three poems stand close together near the beginning of the volume (ed. 1841), making it likely that Taylor learned them soon after his introduction to Kerner's lyrics.
30. Cf. *Views Afoot,* p. 250 (ed. 1872).
31. II, 8 (ed. 1843).
32. The underlining is mine.
33. In "The American Legend," written June-July, 1850, for the Phi Beta Kappa at Harvard, is found the line: "We swing their swords, we sing their lusty songs" (p. 16), which also seems reminiscent of Uhland's "Berglied."
34. See *Life and Letters,* p. 130 f.
35. *Scribner's Monthly,* XIX, 86.
36. *Home Pastorals,* p. 181.
37. *Heines Lieder und Gedichte* (Macmillan, 1897), p. xix f.
38. Pp. 137–151.
39. See p. 26, *supra.*
40. See p. 69 f., *supra.*

41. "From the bosom of ocean I seek thee" is printed as two eight line stanzas, but it is essentially four four-line stanzas.
42. P. 145.
43. The probability that this poem owes a debt to Heine is strengthened by the relation of Taylor to Heine. See p. 95 f., *infra.*
44. P. 418.
45. Cf. p. 36 ff., *supra.*
46. "The Summer Camp" was written in January, 1851 (see *Life and Letters,* p. 201 f.). Smyth assigns "Ariel" to 1849 (Smyth, p. 304.).
47. 4613–20; 4634–78; see also 4621–33.
48. The latter undoubtedly because of the very few lines which Shakespeare's Ariel sings, but compare Taylor, verses 7, 55, 56, 94, with Shakespeare.
49. *Faust,* II, p. 3 (ed. 1882); original, 4613 f.
50. *Ibid.,* p. 4; original, 4634 f.
51. *Ibid.,* p. 4; original, 4641.
52. *Ibid.,* original 4624 f.
53. *Life and Letters,* p. 202.
54. *Faust,* 1, 4679.
55. P. 88.
56. Underlining is mine.
57. Taylor's *Faust* II, 6 (ed. 1882).
58. 4684 f.
59. P. 61.
60. Cf. *Life and Letters,* p. 213, and note the date of "Summer Camp."
61. *Ibid.,* p. 173 ff. and also Bibliography.
62. P. 85, *supra.*
63. Cf. Stedmann, *Poets of America* (Boston and New York, 1886), p. 406.
64. *Bayard Taylor,* p. 98.
65. *Ibid.,* p. 202.
66. E.g., cf. Haskell, *Taylor's Translation,* 11 f.
67. See *Life and Letters,* p. 237 ff.
68. *Essays and Notes,* p. 95 f.
69. *Ibid.,* p. 96 ff.
70. Tay. 33 [larger]; see Appendix II.
71. Taylor left Gotha on October 8, 1852, after a stay of three weeks in the vicinity (*New York Tribune,* Dec. 2, 1852).
72. The *Morgl. Sagen und Geschichten,* as published in 1837, comprises two volumes.
73. Smyth, *Bayard Taylor,* p. 302 f.
74. II, 173 f.
75. P. 106; cf. also p. 288.
76. Cf. *India, China and Japan,* p. 92 and p. 161.
77. See p. 90, *infra.*
78. See p. 86, *supra.*
79. *Morgl. Sagen und Gesch.,* I, 135.
80. *Morgl. Sagen und Gesch.,* I, 56 ff.
81. See *India, China and Japan,* p. 508.
82. Cornell University, Tay. 49.
83. See Stedman, *Poets of America,* p. 408; Henry A. Beers, *Initial Studies in American Letters,* (New York, 1895), p. 178 f.; Haskell, *Taylor's Translation,* p. 12.
84. *Morgl. Sagen und Gesch.,* II, 315 ff.
85. P. 12.
86. *Scribner's Monthly,* XIX, 87.
87. P. 86 f.
88. The fact that Taylor prints these lines each time in italics does not indicate that they are a quotation, but that they constitute a song. See the songs in the *Faust* translation and elsewhere.
89. Tay. 37, Cornell University.
90. Cornell University, Tay. 67. See Appendix II.
91. London, 1825, II, 477.
92. The poem has been set to music by A. W. Foote. In this form it was repeatedly sung by Harvard Glee Club in the spring of 1923.
93. *Morgl. Sagen und Gesch.,* II, 295.
94. Cornell University, Tay. 37, a note-book of the Far Eastern journey: mostly financial accounts and poems.
95. Cf. *Life and Letters,* p. 277 and p. 274 ff.
96. S. 111.
97. It must not be forgotten that, although Taylor knew a little colloquial Arabic, he probably could not read that language and positively knew nothing of its literature from direct contact with the language.
98. *Morgl. Sagen und Gesch.,* I, 68.
99. Smyth, *Bayard Taylor,* p. 303; also Cornell University, Tay. 62, we read: "Oct. 7, 1853. I have just finished my 'Hymn to Air' and so got rid of a poem which has been troubling my mind for three years past."
100. I, 58.
101. "Ihn [den Wind] zu halten an Ketten Sind sieben Engel bestellt," occurs in Rückert's poem.
102. *Infra.,* pp. 93 ff.
103. Boston, 1854.
104. Leipzig, 1822.
105. See p. 36, *supra.*

106. *Essays and Notes,* p. 100.

107. In favor of his assumption is the fact that the "Proem Dedicatory—An Epistle from Mount Tmolus" was composed in May-June, 1854 (see Note 95, *supra.*). Against it argues Taylor's little lyric, "Persian Serenade," written at Grenada, Spain, November, 1852 (published, *Atlantic Monthly,* February, 1879; XLII, 247), which is thoroughly in the "Stimmung" of the *Oriental Roses.* It might be that Taylor acquired this volume when he acquired the *Morgenländische Sagen und Geschichten,* read it in Spain, and, when lightening his impedimenta for his Far-Eastern trip, sent it to his American home where he found it and used it on his return.

108. *Bayard Taylor,* p. 98.

109. P. 202.

110. Smyth, *Bayard Taylor,* p. 303, reads "The Angel of Patevin," which is an error for the above title. See R. H. Stoddard in *Atlantic Monthly* XLIII, 242 ff. (February, 1879).

111. A full discussion of Whittier's poem and its relation to the German will be found in Iola Kay Eastburn's *Whittier's Relation to German Thought and Life,* p. 96 ff.

112. *Ibid.,* p. 34.

113. *Heine in America, Americana-Germanica,* No. 23 (Philadelphia, 1918), p. 152.

114. Smyth, *Bayard Taylor,* p. 303.

115. Evidently he has used some collection of Taylor's poem and not the individual volumes. See Sachs *Heine in Amerika,* p. 152.

116. See *Life and Letters,* p. 277 and p. 274 ff.

117. The metrical form of these pieces is of frequent occurrence in Rückert's *Morgl. Sagen und Gesch.,* which Taylor had recently been reading.

118. "L'Envoi," see p. 93 f., *supra.* "Proem Dedicatory," May-June 12, 1854. See *Life and Letters,* p. 277 and p. 274 ff. "L'Envoi" was written even later than June 12th. *(Life and Letters,* p. 277). Taylor must have been reading *Faust I* at this time, for on August 10, 1854, he quoted from it in a letter to Stoddard. See *Life and Letters,* p. 278 and p. 175, *infra,* note 114.

119. Cf., however, "The Voyage of a Dream," p. 158.

Come down!

Come down! And let me quit this perilous height,
This icy royalty of thought, to glide.
Nearer the homes of men, the embowered nests
Of unaspiring, lowliest content.

with *Faust* "Von dem Thor", especially 937 ff.

120. "Proem Dedicatory," *Poems of the Orient,* p. 11. Cf. *Faust,* 354 ff. through 1770.

121. Cf. especially *Faust,* 1770 ff., and note that the lines Taylor quoted in his August letter are 2038 f., i.e., they follow this closely.

122. "L'Envoi," *Poems of the Orient,* p. 161. Cf. *Faust* 1770 ff.

123. Cf. *Faust,* 4705 ff.

124. *Atlantic Monthly* XLIII, 246 (February, 1879).

125. *Ibid.,* p. 247.

126. *Gesch. der engl. Lit.* (Leipzig, 1906, Sechste Auflage), S. 457.

127. Preface, dated October, 1855; published November. (See Smyth, *Bayard Taylor,* p. 300).

128. See *Poems of Home and Travel,* p. 3.

129. It seems probable that Taylor had already at least glanced over C. G. Leland's translation of Heine's *Reisebilder,* a presentation copy of which he had in his library (see Appendix III). We know he read this work soon after these poems were written (See note 156, *infra).*

130. 1859 and 1862, respectively. The sketches contained in both volumes appeared for the most part in periodicals at irregular intervals from 1851—1862.

131. "Scenes at a Target-Shooting," *At Home and Abroad,* p. 455. This incident occurred August, 1858.

132. Berlin, 1905, S. 33, 139 f.

133. P. 70.

134. *At Home and Abroad,* Preface.

135. It is peculiar that Taylor does not mention Heine in speaking of the song, for he was surely already acquainted with Heine's poems. See p. 26, *supra.*

136. *Ibid.,* p. 456.

137. See Appendix IV.

138. First published in the *Atlantic Monthly,* VI, 699 ff. (December, 1860).

139. See *Studies in German Literature,* p. 322.

140. Cf. *Faust I,* note 35, p. 242 (ed. 1882); *Studies in German Literature,* p. 322.

141. See p. 36, *supra.*

142. The date he began his "Confessions," etc. See Cornell University, Tay. 62.

143. Cf. *Goethejahrbuch,* V, 225.

144. *Stuttgart,* 1898, S. 134.

145. P. 451 (twice) 453, 459, 463 (twice), 464, 468, 469.

146. P. 463, 467.

147. P. 464.

148. P. 464.

149. P. 451.

150. See Jub. Ausg. XXI, 38 ff.

151. *Ibid.,* S. 40.

152. N. B. "soul-matter," *supra.*

153. See Smyth, *Bayard Taylor,* p. 300.
154. *Life and Letters,* p. 404; cf. Taylor always refers to Goethe's biography as "Wahrheit und Dichtung." *Faust I,* p. 230, 252, 264, 282, etc. (ed. 1882).
155. *Heine in America,* p. 152.
156. Sachs, *Heine in Amerika,* p. 81, 152. See also Appendix III, *infra.*
157. Cornell University has a copy of this volume designated as "Author's copy with his annotations." See also Tay. 65, in which the dates of the various poems are written in the margin in pencil by the author: "In Winter" bears the date June 11 (1860).
158. "Heimkehr," No. 7. Taylor translates stanza six of this poem in *Northern Travel* (1857). See p. 72 *(supra).*
159. "Heimkehr," No. 16, verse 6.
160. *Poet's Journal,* p. 81.
161. Cf. August Walther Fischer, *Über die volkstümlichen Elemente in den Gedichten Heines,* S. 52–62.
162. Here, however, the rime is in couplets.
163. P. 38.
164. *Faust,* 9723 ff.
165. *Faust,* 9901 f.
166. P. 132 f.
167. Verses 11726 ff.
168. *Life and Letters,* p. 336. See also p. 73, *supra.*
169. See p. 9, *supra.*
170. *Atlantic Monthly* III, 230 (February, 1859).
171. Coburg, 1858. It is not improbable that Taylor knew the Stolberg's poem, "Graf Gleichen." There is no evidence to show he did, but undoubtedly some of his friends had called his attention to the poem "Ritter Bayard," which stands almost next to "Graf Gleichen" in the Stolberg volume.
172. *Poet's Journal,* p. 78, p. 145.
173. *Life and Letters,* p. 374 f.
174. Smyth, Bayard Taylor, p. 301.
175. July 15, 1861, *At Home and Abroad,* Second Series, p. 257 ff.
176. P. 56.
177. P. 108.
178. P. 251.
179. P. 254.
180. P. 337.
181. P. 336.
182. P. 438. See Appendix IV.
183. *John Godfrey's Fortunes,* p. iii.
184. Pp. 6, 97. See also p. 9 f., *supra.*
185. P. 265.
186. P. 273.
187. P. 418.
188. P. 510.
189. P. 331.
190. P. 319. See also *Life and Letters,* p. 601.
191. P. 395. See "Mihi est propositum," *Commersbuch,* S. 231.
192. P. 413 f. See Appendix IV.
193. Cf. p. 38 f., *supra.*
194. P. 327.
195. S. 185 ff. and S. 161 ff., respectively (Cotta, 1874, Bd. X).
196. *Ibid.,* S. 187.
197. Be it also noted that the Latin song referred to above (p. 102) which the singer "had learned in Düsseldorf" (*John Godfrey's Fortunes,* p. 395), and which Taylor undoubtedly got from a *Commersbuch,* was sung in the "Ichneumon." This might indicate that Taylor had a German institution in mind when he invented his cave. Again, "The Echo Club," another such fraternity as that which met in "Ludlamshöhle" and in the "Ichneumon," has a meeting-place of the same kind. "In the rear of Karl Schäfer's lager-beer cellar and restaurant . . . there is a small room, with a vaulted ceiling, which Karl calls his 'Löwengrube,' or Lion's Den. Here in the Bohemian days Zoilus and the Gannet had been accustomed to meet and discuss literary projects, and read fragments of manuscript to each other. The Chorus, the Ancient, and young Galahad gradually fell into the same habit, and thus a little circle of six, seven, or eight members came to be formed. The room could comfortably contain no more: it was quiet, with a dim, smoky, confidential atmosphere, and suggested Auerbach's Cellar to the Ancient, who had been in Leipzig."

    "Here authors, books, magazines, and newspapers were talked about; sometimes a manuscript poem was read by the writer; while mild potations of beer and the breath of cigars delayed the nervous, fidgety, clattering-footed American Hours" *(Echo Club,* p. 14 f.). The very mention of "American" here implies that the author has in mind a similar situation which is non-American. Is the "Löwengrube" another "Ludlamshöhle?"
198. *Story of Kennett,* p. 76.
199. Act II, Sc. I, 15 (Cotta, 1874, VI, 58).
200. "Was sich neckt, das liebt sich." Franz Joseph Lipperheide, *Spruchwörterbuch* (Leipzig, 3. unveränderter Abdruck, 1935), S. 658.
201. The reference to the woman who drags the fisherman into the flood *(Joseph and his Friend,* p. 226) is an echo of Goethe's "Der Fischer." Cf.

Ferdinand Gregorovius, *The Island of Capri* (Boston, 1897), p. 87, which Taylor read about the time he was working on his novel.

202. Smyth, *Bayard Taylor,* p. 300. The *Cabinet Edition* (1865) is the same as this edition.

203. Most of them are dated. The dates of the others are ascertainable from *Life and Letters,* except that of "Through Baltimore." But the position of this poem in the volume and the manner in which it speaks of the incident described (April 19, 1861) seems to indicate that it was written about that date.

204. *Life and Letters,* p. 379.

205. P. iii f.

206. Wieland often ends his stanza in a rimed couplet. This couplet frequently introduces a fourth rime into the stanza, but because of the frequent variation in the length of either one or both of the lines, it is incorrect to call them Alexandrines. About 46

of Wieland's stanzas end in a couplet of any sort. Taylor is without justification in saying that Wieland's stanzas "almost invariably" close thus. The percentage of stanzas ending in a rimed couplet in Taylor's poem is also large (40%) in spite of his effort to resist "the temptation to close with an Alexandrine" (p. V).

207. P. v.

208. P. i.

209. When Taylor wrote his article "The Kyffhäuser and its Legends," which appeared in the *Atlantic Monthly* XXI, May, 1868, he had Wieland's *Oberon* fresh in mind. See *By-Ways* of Europe, p. 325.

210. *Taylor's Translation,* p. 11.

211. *Picture of St. John,* "The Artist," XLI, (XXXV, Haskell, p. 11, refers to *Poetical Works of Bayard Taylor,* Household Edition, 1880, p. 254.)

212. *Faust,* 1112 ff.

213. See Thomas's *Faust, I,* note to line 1112 and his Appendix III.

214. P. 153.

215. *Faust,* 7080-7092. See also Taylor's note to these lines, *Faust II,* note 66. These echoes of *Faust* are probably real ones as Taylor had gotten down to serious work on his translation before he finished *St. John.* Note also Clelia's prayer (p. 88 ff.) is to the "Mater Dolorosa" as Gretchen's had been. The former prays to the Virgin: "bend Thine ear" (XLVIII), "Incline Thy countenance . . . for Thou didst ne'er deny Compassion unto love" (L), as Gretchen had prayed: "Ach, neige, / Du Schmerzenreiche, / Dein Antlitz gnädig meiner Noth!" (3587 ff.).

216. *On Two Continents,* p. 142.

217. *The Picture of St. John,* Book I, stanza XVIII.

218. Taylor must have once thought of calling his poem *St. John of Sonnenheim.* A loose sheet in one of his scrapbooks (Cornell University, Tay. 35, Blank Book VII) contains the three first stanzas of *The Picture of St. John* in its original form with the title *St. John of Sonnenheim.* Although the stanzas are in Taylor's hand, the chirography of the title suggests another scribe.

219. From May, 1864–January 1869. One of the articles, "The Grande Chartreuse," is from the *New York Tribune,* November 14, 1867.

220. P. 13.

221. P. 14.

222. *Ibid.*

223. P. 16.

224. P. 23–112.

225. P. 143.

226. P. 122 f.

227. P. 166 f.

228. P. 168.

229. 4202 ff.

230. Like most commentators, Taylor, in his Faust translation, fails to give any note on this passage. For evidence suggesting that his story is a possible source of Goethe's inspiration, see John T. Krumpelmann, "Goethe's Faust, 4203-4205," *Modern Language Notes,* XLI, No. 2, 107 ff. (February, 1926).

231. P. 261.

232. P. 327.

233. P. 317.

234. P. 320.

235. P. 323.

236. On p. 433 is a translation from Goethe's *Zahme Zenien.* See Appendix IV.

237. This chapter from *Wanderjahre in Italien.* My citations and references are to the English translation by Lilian Clarke, Boston, 1879.

238. See Appendix IV.

239. By-Ways, p. 351; Gregorovius, *Capri,* p. 62.

240. P. 16.

241. P. 346.

242. P. 61.

243. P. 350.

244. For further evidence compare: Tiberius and Vesuvius, G., p. 15; T. p. 346; Napoleon and Tiberius, G., p. 72, T., p. 351; the order in which the description of the Blue Grotto is followed by that of the Green grotto, G., p. 87, T., p. 360 ff., and others *ad libitum.*

245. P. 377.

246. I, 207.

247. P. 397.

248. I, 9.

249. See Taylor, p. 400; Gregorovius, I, 160.

250. P. 414; see Appendix IV.

251. I, 200.

252. P. 417.

253. On August 19, 1868, Taylor announced that his Corsican article was half written *(Life and Letters,* p. 494). He had actually made the personal acquaintance of Gregorovius on March 28, 1868 (Cornell Univ., Tay. 63). The following evidence from an article in *Essays and Notes* (p. 25), dated May, 1877, seems to fix conclusively the source of the stanza referred to above. "In the delightful volume on Corsica by Ferdinand Gregorovius, there is a cradle-song of the Corsican mothers, the first stanza of which runs thus, in translation as literally as possible." Then follows the stanza exactly as found in *By-Ways.*

254. II, 264.

255. P. 439.

256. This work is probably Garibaldi's *Denkwürdigkeiten, nach handschriftlichen Aufzeichnun- gen desselben u. nach authentischen Quellen, bearb. u. herausg. 2 Bde., Hamburg,* 1851, *Hoff- mann und Campe,* XXIV, 474 S., Schwartz, Marie Esperance (Brandt) von, 1819–99 (alias, Melena Elpis).

257. H. Sauerländer, *Ein Fremdenführer durch Detmold und den Teutoberger-Wald* (Detmold, 1865).

258. P. 456.

259. *Ibid.*

260. P. 455.

261. P. 459; *Die Ruinen und Museen Roms* (Braunschweig, 1854), S. 175.

262. P. 463; *Werke,* Jub. Ausg. XXXV, 241, lines 11 ff.

263. *Life and Letters,* p. 572. See *Dramatic Works,* p. 332.

264. Clipping, Tay. 54 (147), Cornell University.

265. *Bayard Taylor,* p. 230 f.

266. *Dramatic Works,* p. 322.

267. Cf. *Life and Letters,* p. 653 and *On Two Continents,* p. 220.

268. *Ibid.*

269. *Life and Letters,* p. 584.

270. *Ibid.,* p. 592.

271. *Ibid.,* p. 575.

272. Pp. 20–26, incl.

273. P. 21; cf.

> But the nymphs of our fountains leave them untended,
> And the god of the stream is gone from his urn.

and:

> Aus den Urnen lieblicher Najaden
> Sprang der Ströme Silberschaum.

and see p. 107 f. The following passage of an unpublished letter of Taylor to J. B. Phillips (Cornell University), dated Mar. 8, 1871, is significant in this connection. "The other day in the street, I translated four lines which I copy as an imperfect specimen:

> Misty Oreads filled the nearer mountains,
> Yonder tree was then the Dryad's home;
> Where the Naiad held the urns of fountains
> Gushed the streams in silver foam.

and also this

> Where, as now our sages have decided,
> Soulless whirls a ball of fire on high,
> Helios then his golden chariot guided
> Grandly through the silence of the sky.

These are simply dashed off without second examination." Cf. also *Studies in German Literature,* p. 282 f.

274. P. 34.

275. P. 45.

276. P. 47. Cf. Am farbigen Abglanz haben wir has Leben. *Faust,* 4727 ff.

277. P. 40.

278. 3455.

279. P. 24.

280. Pp. 36, 162.

281. I.e., *Der neue Pitaval,* Hitzig und Häring (W. Alexis) (Leipzig, 1842–49).

282. P. 162.

283. P. 163.

284. P. 200.

285. P. 229.

286. Cf. *Life and Letters,* pp. 595 and 599.

287. *Ibid.,* p. 609.

288. *Ibid.,* 335.

289. See p. 72, *supra.*

290. T. B. Aldrich to Taylor, January 9, 1873 (Cornell University).

291. John Hay to Taylor, November 5, 1873 (Cornell University).

292. *Dramatic Works,* p. 325 ff.

293. *Two Continents,* p. 243–250.

294. *Ibid.,* p. 238.

295. *Life and Letters,* p. 582 f.

296. Smyth, *Bayard Taylor,* p. 301.

297. See also *Improvisations,* IV, p. 161.

298. E.g., *The Holly Tree, John Reed, Napoleon at Gotha.*

299. New York, 1922, p. 120 f.

300. P. 120 f.

301. P. 121.

302. CIX, 301. *The Blameless Prince and other Poems.*

303. Aug. 14, 1869; *Life and Letters,* p. 517.

304. Aug. 20, 1869; *Life and Letters,* p. 520.

305. "Euphorion," see *On Two Continents,* p. 204.

306. "An August Pastoral, " *Atlantic Monthly,* XXIV, 470 ff.

307. Finished August 12, 1869; Tay. 64 (Cornell University).

308. *On Two Continents,* p. 204.

309. *Poetical Works* (1902), p. vi.

310. *On Two Continents,* p. 204. Mrs. Taylor's statement that in addition to the poems of Goethe and Gregorovius, the "Amours de Voyage" of Clough had prepossessed her husband in favor of this metre (*On Two Continents,* p. 204) and Emerson's wondering "whether Clough had risen again and was pouring rich English hexametres" (*ibid.* See also *Life and Letters,* p. 543) must not induce us to consider that, in addition to the German models, our poet had an English one, for such is hardly in accordance with fact. An extract from Taylor's discussion of the hexameter about this time ("Bryant's Translation of the Illiad," *Essays and Notes,* p. 261 f.; dated February, 1870) will reveal his attitude in this respect. "In spite of the efforts of Longfellow, Clough and Kingsley to naturalize it, hexameter retains an artifical character for most English readers."

"In the German language the case is different. Hexameter has conquered its place, and now finds acceptance from the common as well as the classical ear. One cause of this success, we suspect, is the modification of the metre by the German poets, to adapt it to the genius of the language. Klopstock, Voss, Goethe and others write a hexameter which is German, not classic, in quantity and the arrangement of the cesural pauses."

311. Cf. *Faust II,* p. 332, note 19; p. 388, note 74 (edition of 1882).

312. Cf. p. 115, *infra.*

313. We have already seen that Taylor was familiar with the poems of Schiller in general (e.g., pp. 28, 71, 73). He knew the "Spaziergang" by the spring of 1870 (see note 340, *infra*). Mrs. Taylor tells us that in 1872 she and her husband followed the same path which Schiller had immortalized in this poem *(On Two Continents,* p. 225 f.).

314. *Home Pastorals,* p. 20.

315. "Spaziergang," 7 f.

316. P. 21.

317. Z. 14–24.

318. P. 22.

319. Z. 30.

320. Z. 43 ff. (Italics mine.)

321. P. 28; cf. "Spaziergang," 173 ff.

322. P. 28 f.

323. "Spaziergang," 51.

324. P. 25.

325. P. 27.

326. *Ibid.*

327. P. 29.

328. P. 171.

329. Dient sie knechtisch dem Gesetz der Schwere Die entgötterte Natur. "Götter Griechenlands," the first half of which Taylor translated sometime before April 1870. See *Studies in German Literature,* p. 281 ff. and Appendix IV, *infra.*

330. The last two lines of each Goethean stanza forms a couplet.

331. P. 196.

332. Treasure Vault, Cornell University.

333. These two distiches do not rightly belong to the "Four Seasons," but have been inserted in later editions, together with four others, between Nos. 45 and 46. See Jub. Ausg., I, 365.

334. Nr. 45.

335. Preceding Nr. 46. See Jub. Ausg. I, 365.

336. Treasure Vault, Cornell University.

337. See *Home Pastorals,* p. 161.

338. Written 1870–1871. See p. 41, *supra.*

339. Cf. note 19, *Faust II,* also note 73.

340. *Studies in German Literature,* p. 318 f. Written Spring, 1870.

341. "Implora Pace", *Home Pastorals,* p. 121.

342. "Sunshine of the Gods," *ibid.,* 95 f. Written, Summer, 1868.

343. "Penn Calvin," *ibid.,* p. 123.

344. "Canopus," *ibid.,* p. 170.

345. "Shakespeare's Statue," *ibid.,* p. 203.

346. *Life and Letters,* p. 668.

347. See *On Two Continents,* p. 237 f.

348. *Ibid.*

349. 2nd stanza of "In der Fremde" (5), *Sämtliche Werke* (Leipzig, 1864), I, 262, only a few pages from "Sehnsucht."

350. Taylor has equivalents from Matthison's "Nachtigallen" (5); "Im Gefilde der Sterne," (7); "im zarten Laube—im Gras," (9 f); and "Eine Blume der Asche meines Herzens," (14).

351. *Sämtliche Werke,* I, 267 f. The underlining is mine.

352. Commentary on the verse: "Is it the far postillion's horn?" Mrs. Taylor in an unpublished note states: "The original melody which suggested the *Variation* to Bayard Taylor is to be found in one of Joseph von Eichendorff's finest lyrics, entitled *Sehnsucht.* The refrain of the first and last stanza of the poem also suggested *Summer Night.*" ("Appendix to Editorial Notes for Bayard Taylor's Poems—by me [Mrs. Taylor] in 1895-96." Cornell University).

353. See note 349, *supra.*

354. I have not been able to ascertain the date of composition of "Improvisation VIII.", but it was almost certainly written later than "Summer Night" for all the "Improvisations" whose dates I know are arranged in the volume chronologically and No. VI was published in January, 1874.

355. *Harper's Monthly,* XLVII, 445 (1873).

356. Likewise probably attributable to accident is the coincidence in metrical form and cadence between "Improvisation VI" (first published *Harper's Monthly,* January, 1874) and Uhland's little "Waldlied."

357. Tay. 63, Cornell University; Jan. 25 (1864) "alone with B. in the eve. I read to him from Eichendorff's poems—" (Mrs. Taylor's diary.).

358. *John Godfrey's Fortunes,* p. 208.

359. *By-Ways of Europe,* p. 311.

360. *On Two Continents,* p. 201. See *New York Tribune,* Sept. 9, 1871.

361. Smyth, *Bayard Taylor,* p. 301.

362. *Echo Club* (1876), p. ix.

363. *On Two Continents,* p. 218.

364. Cf. *Echo Club,* p. v.; *On Two Continents,* p. 146 f.

365. *Life and Letters,* p. 564 ff.

366. *Ibid.,* p. 286; to G. H. Boker, Sept. 13, 1854.

367. See p. 103, *supra,* note 197.

368. *Echo Club,* p. 18.

369. *Ibid.,* p. 64.

370. *Ibid.,* p. 74.

371. *Ibid.,* p. 102.

372. *Ibid.,* p. 51 and p. 134.

373. *Ibid.,* p. 167.

374. *Ibid.*

375. *Ibid.,* pp. 43, 74, 79, 91.

376. *Ibid.,* p. 50.

377. *Ibid.,* p. 114.

378. *Ibid.,* p. 134.

379. *Ibid.,* p. 79.

380. *Ibid.,* pp. 55, 144.

381. *Ibid.,* p. 107.

382. *Ibid.,* p. 115 f.

383. *Ibid.*

384. *Ibid.,* p. 117.

385. A MS copy of the entire adaptation is found in Tay. 33, Cornell University.

386. *On Two Continents,* p. 257.

387. *Dramatic Works,* p. 334.

388. *Ibid.,* and *On Two Continents,* p. 257.

389. *Dramatic Works,* p. 334.

390. *Life and Letters,* p. 684 and p. 711.

391. *Ibid.,* p. 667.

392. See p. 135 ff., *infra.*

393. *Life and Letters,* p. 675; November 14, 1875.

394. P. 715 f.

395. See *Dramatic Works,* p. 335; A. A. Watts and Anna Mary Howett (?), *Aurora,* London, 1875. See *Eos,* note 386 *supra.*

396. *Ibid.;* Siegfried Lipiner *Der entfesselte Prometheus,* Leipzig, 1876. In Mrs. Taylor's diary (Tay. 64, Cornell Univ.) we read: "1878 Feb. 3. B. read me passages from the *Entfesselten Prometheus*—a new poem by a new German poet, which is surprising and startling."

397. Tay. 54 (Cornell Univ.); Dec. 17, 1878, p. 6, col. 4.

398. *Ibid.,* Dec. 2, 1878, p. 3, col. 1 f.

399. Tay. 54.

400. December 7, 1878.

401. XLIII, 119, January, 1879.

402. *Prince Deukalion,* p. ix.

403. P. 119 f., *supra.*

404. P. 123.

405. P. 125.

406. P. 171.

407. P. 150 f.

408. P. 154.

409. P. 171.

410. Jub. Ausg., XV, 377.

411. *On Two Continents,* p. 216.

412. See *Faust II,* p. 425 (edition of 1882).

413. Tay. 64, Cornell University.

414. It was also about this time that Taylor discussed *Pandora* with the Duke of Weimar. In *Essays and Notes* (p. 197) (See also *Atlantic Monthly,* XXXVI, 229 (1875), and XXXV, 26 ff. (1875)) we read: "The Grand-Duke remarked 'We have just been reading Goethe's Pandora, for the first time, now I suppose you have read it long ago.' 'Yes,' I answered, 'but I should like to hear, first, what impression it makes upon you.' 'It is wonderful!', he exclaimed, 'Why is such a poem not better known and appreciated?'"

415. This interest may be responsible for the prominence of the Biblical element in the *Prophet* (1874) and in *Prince Deukalion.*

416. Smyth, *Bayard Taylor,* p. 202.

417. *Ibid.,* p. 257.

418. Goethe's play being a fragment, we cannot tell exactly what part Pandora, Dämonen and Helios would have played, as they do not appear in the fragment.

419. P. x.

420. *Deukalion,* p. 131. See also p. 134.

421. P. 82 ff., especially p. 84 ff.

422. Z. 37 f.

423. Z. 50 ff.

424. Cf. Max Morris, *Goethe-Studien* (Berlin, 1902), 276 ff.

425. *Heinrich Düntzer, Erläuterungen,* XVII, 141, which commentary Taylor probably knew. Düntzer explains: "Dämonen, Geistige Mächte." Taylor's Buddha is Buddhaism; Medusa, the Papacy; Calchas, Protestantism.

426. *Life and Letters,* p. 716.

427. *Erläuterungen,* XVII, 139. Max Morris *(Goethe-Studien,* S. 263) says: "Es muss also doch wohl bei Moria = Jerusalem bleiben, nur dürfen wir darunter nicht das irdische Jerusalem verstehen, sondern das neue Jerusalem der Apokalypse. Wie der Sabbat der auf Erden für eine kurze Zeit sich verwirklichende Zustand von Friede, Schönheit, und Heiligkeit ist, so schaut Johannes ein solches vollkommendes Glück als eine in die Zukunft verlegte Vision in seinem neuen Jerusalem. Das Drama von Pandoras Wiederkunft ist eine verwandte Vision, und so können Sabbat und Moria dem Dichter hier als Merkworte dienen, die natürlich in der Dichtung selbst nicht genannt worden wären. Morris's words might without much *mutatis mutandis* be applied to Taylor's drama.

428. Cf. *Prince Deukalion,* p. 150 f.

429. Jub. Ausg. XV, 373.

430. P. 134.

431. P. 156.

432. Z. 55 f.

433. Otto Pniower, Jub. Ausg., XV, 375.

434. P. 285 ff.

435. P. 159.

436. Cf. the implied equation "Agathon = Schönheit," *supra.*

437. P. 17.

438. II, vi, Z. 696 ff.

439. Z. 753.

440. Z. 761 ff.

441. P. 112.

442. I, xiv, 470 ff. N. B. Taylor's *sententia* written circa September, 1874, "It makes a great deal of difference whether we wear social forms as bracelets or handcuffs" (cf. note 471, *infra.).*

443. (Leipzig, 1881) S. 277.

444. *Studies in German Literature,* p. 279.

445. *Deukalion,* p. 141 f.

446. P. 26.

447. See pp. 107–108.

448. *Dramatic Works,* p. 343.

449. See *Studies in German Literature,* p. 282 ff.

450. *Prince Deukalion,* p. 97.

451. *Dramatic Works,* p. 343.

452. "Götter Griechenlands," 111 f.

453. *Brooklyn Magazine,* February, 1880, p. 57. "The Best of Bayard Taylor."

454. *A Tribute to Bayard Taylor* (Washington, 1879), p. 3.

455. *Essays and Notes,* p. v.

456. P. 33 ff., *supra.*

457. Published, *Atlantic Monthly,* XVIII, 33 ff. (1866).

458. To J. T. Fields, Apr. 15 and Apr. 20, 1866 (Cornell University).

459. Apr. 20, 1866 (Cornell University).

460. See Appendix IV.

461. *Atlantic Monthly,* XXXV, 26 ff. (1875).

462. *Ibid.,* XXVI, 229 ff.

463. *Essays and Notes,* p. 47 f.

464. *Ibid.,* p. 120.

465. *Ibid.,* p. 136.

466. See also *ibid.,* pp. 38, 302, 305, 323, 343, 374.

467. *Essays and Notes,* p. 333 ff.

468. It was never collected into one of Taylor's volumes, but appeared in *Stories by American Authors,* I, Scribner and Sons, 1884.
469. *Stories by American Authors,* I, 31.
470. *Ibid.,* p. 10 f.
471. Cf. Goethe (Jub. Ausg. XXI, 188 f.), "Durch das, was wir Betragen und gute Sitten nennen, soll das erreicht werden, was ausserdem nur durch Gewalt, oder auch nicht einmal durch Gewalt zu erreichen ist." (See note 442, *supra.)*
472. Cf. Goethe (Jub. Ausg. XXI, 174). "Einem bejahrten Manne verdachte man, dass er sich noch um junge Frauenzimmer bemühte. Es ist das einzige Mittel, versetzte er, sich zu verjüngen, und das will jedermann."
473. Cf. *ibid.,* S. 225. "Ein Leben ohne Liebe, ohne die Nähe des Geliebten, ist nur eine Comédie à tiroir, ein schlechtes Schubladenstück."
474. P. 7 f.
475. *Faust I,* p. 242, note 35 (edition of 1882). It might also be borne in mind that "Who was She?" was written while Taylor was sojourning in Gotha, Germany (See *Life and Letters,* p. 640).
476. The edition of 1902 contains only one additional poem "The Centennial Hymn," which does not concern us here.
477. *Poetical Works,* p. iii.
478. "A Lover's Test," "My Prologue," "Gabriel." See note VI, 4, *infra.*
479. See Appendix IV.
480. See p. 56 f., *supra.*
481. *Life and Letters,* p. 762. See also letter of Sept. 18, 1878, *ibid.,* p. 759.
482. *A School History of Germany,* see p. 146 ff., *infra.* and *Studies in German Literatur,* see p. 140 ff., *infra.*
483. P. 40.

Paul C. Wermuth (essay date 1973)

SOURCE: "Critical and Other Works," in *Bayard Taylor,* Twayne Publishers, Inc., 1973, pp. 156-179.

[*In the following excerpt, Wermuth discusses Taylor's translation of* Faust, *his parodies, and other critical pursuits.*]

I Translations

The *Faust* translation is Taylor's most important work, and his only book which has survived. Still considered standard in some quarters, it is currently available in the Modern Library and in the Oxford World's Classics. Taylor seriously aimed at making it the standard version; indeed, he said that it was going to be "the" English *Faust* and that no one need translate it again after him. He compared all existing translations, mastered the scholarship (extensive even then), and studied the history of the Faust legend; he did all that sheer labor could do to contribute to a fine translation. In the process, he became an expert on Goethe, on *Faust,* and on some areas of German literature. And he did all this work in the midst of fulfilling other duties, for *Faust* did not bring in any money.

The origin of his interest in things German has already been suggested. His marriage to Marie Hansen was important; it is perhaps significant that her wedding gift to him was a copy of *Faust.* Of course, the influence of German culture, at this time, in America was beginning to be extensive—an influence to which Taylor was to contribute. Taylor's interest was probably stimulated also by the possibility of selling his own books in Germany. His wife translated many of them, and he did much to encourage the growth of his reputation there not only as an intermediary between Germany and America but also as a significant American literary figure. Even today, Taylor is probably better known in Germany than in the United States.

Taylor, however, did not actually do much translating. Over the years, he translated a number of lyrics or fragments of longer poems; but, except for *Faust,* he never undertook a complete work, with the possible exception of Friedrich von Schiller's *Don Carlos,* which he adapted for Lawrence Barrett in 1878. Apparently, Taylor wanted to be known as an American poet who, like Longfellow and Irving, had translated a great work to show his knowledge and skill; but he did not want to be a professional translator.

Taylor said he had started *Faust* twenty years before it was published. He did translate some passages in the early 1850's, but the translation as it exists was the work of the last six or seven years before its appearance in 1871; and the great bulk of it was done intensively during the last three years. The first part of *Faust* was published in December, 1870 (dated 1871); the second part, the following March.[1] Its format was uniform with Longfellow's Dante and with Bryant's Homer, making the work seem part of a great series of American translations and implying Taylor's equality with the great American poets of the day. This impression was reinforced by the treatment accorded him by his shrewd publisher, Fields, who gave a dinner to which were invited all the New England worthies whom Taylor had so assiduously cultivated. Sitting around a bust of Goethe were Longfellow, Lowell, Holmes, Howells, Aldrich, and Osgood; Whittier and Emerson, unable to come, sent regrets and compliments.[2] Such recognition, said Taylor's wife, went straight to his heart; "for he loved his work, he loved poetry and all art with a passion. . . ."[3] Later, he wrote proudly to his mother about his "glorious visit to Boston, and dinner with the authors. 'Faust' is everywhere pronounced a great success and will give me a permanent place in our literature."[4]

However much Taylor enjoyed the praise and recognition of his fellows, he did not intend to neglect promoting his work. He was a shrewd man; his frequent advice to Fields about format and price and about the number of copies to print, to give away, and to whom indicate he was vitally concerned with sales; though he insisted to friends that *Faust* couldn't sell, he did as much as an author can to ensure its success. To Fields, he wrote:

> If my "Faust" is what I mean it to be, it will have a permanent place in translated literature. No one is likely, very soon, to undertake an equal labor. An immediate success will be much more important to me than that of any work I have yet published. . . . I think the aspects are good just now. The German ascendency in Europe, Marie Seebach's acting here, and various similar influences, may all be so many indirect helps. I beg you, therefore, to take all usual measures to set the work fairly afloat, and catch up every little side-wind that may be turned towards its sails.[5]

Apparently, his care worked. Reviews were nearly unanimously favorable, but much of this response was probably due to a careful selection of reviewers. Krumpelmann reports that, of forty-seven reviews he examined, forty-five were favorable; one, middling; one, unfavorable.[6] Even if book reviewing in America at the time was rather corrupt (and Fields exerted influence in many journals), forty-five of forty-seven remains a little short of amazing.

The picture is somewhat blurred, however, by a copy of a suppressed review owned by the Harvard Library, which was to have been printed in the April, 1872, issue of the *North American Review.* The following note in longhand, signed by Henry Adams, is appended: "This notice, written originally by a strong admirer of Mr. Taylor, but much changed by me in tone, led to a protest from the author, and a request from Mr. Osgood that the notice should be suppressed. Which was done."[7] Since the review is not really unfavorable, it is difficult to see what Taylor objected to—probably to the fact that it was a twenty-five page article which Adams had cut to a ten-page review. The reviewer does say that translating in the original meters "is a devotion to principle which approaches fanaticism," complains that the work is "somewhat pedantic," and criticizes some inaccuracies; but he also calls it "a great achievement in this kind of translation."[8]

What is disturbing is that Taylor was able to suppress the review and that he desired to do so. How many other reviews Taylor or his publisher was able to suppress is not known, but such an episode leaves in doubt the value of reviews as a guide to the book's reception; however, it must be remembered that the *North American Review* was owned at this time by Fields's publishing house. Taylor was outraged; and he complained that the "course of the N.A.R. has been excessively clannish and narrow" by favoring New England authors over others. "If there is to be an exclusive Boston circle created in our literature," he said, "the sooner the rest of us know it the better."[9] He soon apologized, but he added that the *Review* "should have been prompt to notice, however briefly, the appearance of a work which has more than a personal character,—which is accepted, both in England and Germany, as one of the indications of our American culture. I think this ought to be done, independently of residence, and personal relations with the editor."[10] One can sympathize with Taylor's feelings, for Adams's snobbishness is well known, as was the tendency for New England writers to become ingrown. Yet Taylor's just complaint is somewhat vitiated by his own willingness to suppress a not too unfavorable review.

As to how good Taylor's translation of *Faust* is, the view that it was the best was widely accepted for a long time. Contemporary critics were strongly in its favor; so were German critics; but subsequent critics have raised doubts. One of the first to shatter this unanimity of opinion was Juliana Haskell, who, in a Columbia dissertation in 1908, attacked it vigorously.[11] But before noticing the basis of Miss Haskell's attacks, one should review some of Taylor's principles which he applied in his translation.

First, it should be noted that Taylor had a theory of translation, the first principle of which was that the translator should efface himself. Second, he argued that poetry should be translated in the same meters if possible, and it was possible with *Faust* because of similarities between the English and German languages—though he did not mean "a rigid, unyielding adherence to every foot, line, and rhyme . . . although this has very nearly been accomplished."[12] He was proud of his success in putting the poem into the original meters; but he has been accused of a mindless adherence to form, of a belief that form equals content, and of indulgence in padding, inaccuracy, and unnatural English.

Third, Taylor insisted that only a poet could translate another poet. He said the translator "must feel, and be guided by, a secondary inspiration. Surrendering himself to the full possession of the spirit which shall speak through him, he receives, also, a portion of the same creative power."[13] Finally, he made some odd remarks about English; for example, that English meter "compels the use of inversions" and "admits many verbal liberties prohibited to prose." But, as Beatty has pointed out, inversions have not been much used in English since the eighteenth century; and why Taylor thought they had been is somewhat puzzling. It should be noted, though, that his own poetry is full of inversions, so there was evidently some defect in his knowledge.

Miss Haskell's attack centered on these very points. Taylor claimed literalness; she lists (tiresomely) places where he departed from the sense, padded lines, distorted meaning, and even changed the meter. "He found himself unable at times to apply his theory," she says; "on the other hand he applied his theory, transferred the form and somehow the poetry was not transferred with it."[14] To his argument that only a poet can translate another poet, she replied that

Taylor was not a very good poet. She complained that he had Latinized Goethe; and, if this effect is unavoidable in English, then it denies his belief that the languages are similar. She quoted Barrett Wendell's remark that Taylor's *Faust* "in nowise resembles normal English," and she concluded that "Bayard Taylor had the intelligence of a well-trained journalist; he had not the emotions or the nice discrimination of a poet."[15] Concluding that Taylor's *Faust* is neither English nor Goethe, she holds that it is "an inadequate translation."

It has been alleged that this assault on Taylor's most famous work resulted in his widow's giving his papers to Cornell University rather than to Columbia.[16] Yet much of what Haskell says is obviously true, though her conclusion is not necessarily correct. The translation is frequently not good English; but it is, at times, very successful; and translating it in the original meters, while sometimes unnatural, was a *tour de force* which communicates something of the variety and vigor of the poem. Thorp argues that, despite its faults, the translation supplies the English reader with as much Goethe as he is likely to get.[17] Beatty agrees that it is "one of the best in English," and that leaning on Goethe supplied Taylor with a depth that was foreign to him.[18]

Krumpelmann objects that Haskell's criticism is largely structural and linguistic; that most of the faults she notes would not be noted by Germans; and that most of the "irregularities" are due "not to a conscious or unconscious imitation of the German order, but to the fact that finding that certain transpositions and the like facilitated his imitation of the form . . . he availed himself of these liberties. . . ."[19] Moreover, subsequent translators have leaned on Taylor, he says, and have been influenced by him "even down into the twentieth century."[20]

When *Faust* appeared, Taylor's translation was the most complete ever produced; he "succeeded as well as any translator, and better than any of his predecessors, in remaining faithful to the sense of the original," and in "preserving the music, rhythm and *Stimmung* of the German poem."[21] And his Notes, while to some extent antiquated, are still "not only interesting and instructive, but also essential." It should also be noted that Taylor was the first to translate the complete second part and to defend it as an integral part of the whole poem.

Obviously, there are many things about Taylor's *Faust* that are unsatisfactory and which one may find detailed in such criticism as that of Haskell. But, despite these flaws, critics of the twentieth century think the book has great value; and it is still one of the best translations available. Certainly, *Faust* is Taylor's one enduring work; it gave him the place in American literature that he so ardently sought; it became a standard. The fate of his own poetry would be disappointing to him, but he would probably be pleased with the reputation of his *Faust.*

Taylor's notes to *Faust* (1870), might well be included under "criticism." They are so extensive as to constitute a good-sized volume; with Prefaces and Appendices, they total some three hundred and fifteen pages of fine print. It is unfortunate that available reprints of Taylor's *Faust* do not include the notes, for they are quite valuable and show that Taylor was indeed an expert on this work. He had mastered the scholarship, consulted original manuscripts, knew all the translations that had been made, and for years debated fine points with friends and strangers. The result is that the Notes, as of 1870, constitute the most thorough summary of scholarship available—all of which, he said, "led me back to find in the author of *Faust* his own best commentator."

Sometimes the notes explicate, or give a brief biography of some person mentioned in the text, or quote parallel passages; sometimes they contain information about Goethe himself, explain his ideas or intentions, give alternative translations, or quote from other translations; and the appendices contain a history of the Faust legend. In sum, they constitute an extended commentary on *Faust;* marked by intelligence, taste, and interpretive ability, they are one of Taylor's most impressive achievements.

In the light of *Faust,* Taylor's other translations are not very important. He translated lyrics occasionally—eighty-six poems or portions of poems, according to Krumpelmann, from 1850 to 1877;[22] and the poets he was most attracted to were F. Freiligrath, Johann Uhlan, Schiller, Goethe, Heinrich Heine, Joseph von Eichendorff, and Friedrich Ruckert. (See p. 220) He was once commissioned by the actor Lawrence Barrett to translate and adapt Schiller's *Don Carlos* for the stage. But, since the official biography barely mentions this work, not much is known about it. It was neither acted nor published, and it seems to have been lost for some time. However, a scholar who saw Taylor's manuscript described it as containing roughly half the original, and he thought it might be actable; but this is pure speculation.[23]

II Parodies

That Taylor had a satirical streak can be seen in his novels and frequently in his letters. Though his poetry is serious, he had a good sense of humor. ***The Echo Club and Other Literary Diversions*** (1876)[24] is a group of parodies of contemporary poets, which originated (according to his wife) during his early life in New York when he and friends gathered for an evening's entertainment of poetic contests. In 1871, Taylor "conceived the notion of giving a certain body to the fun. He was half vexed, half entertained at the sudden rise in America of the dialect school of poetry," and he fancied that he "could make his parodies not only bits of fun, but sly criticisms as well."[25]

This idea, however, resulted in one of his many quarrels with Stoddard; for it was he who originally suggested collecting these pieces "as the work of a new poet." When Taylor used the material himself (dropping the "new poet" idea), Stoddard was miffed.[26] Of course, the minds of these men ran in the same channels so much of the time that it would not be accurate to say that Taylor borrowed the idea, for he might well have conceived it simultaneously. At any rate, the parodies were published as articles in the *Atlantic Monthly* over a period of eight months in 1872; and they appeared as a book four years later.

The material is arranged in eight "nights" during which several poets gather in a beer cellar; each takes from a hat the name of a contemporary whom he then proceeds to parody. Usually there are four each night, but a few "extras" are added from time to time. The four parodists supposedly have different viewpoints: the Ancient is "the calmer judicial temper, in literary matters, which comes from age and liberal study"; Zoilus, the "carping, cynical, unconsciously arrogant critic"; Galahad, the "young, sensational, impressive element in the reading public"; and the Gannet "represents brilliancy without literary principle, the love of technical effect, regardless of the intellectual conception of a work" (viii-ix). In fact, however, it is not easy to distinguish these differences; and the dominant voice is that of the Ancient, whose views seem to be Taylor's.

On the first night, the poets parodied are Morris, Poe, and Browning, the last one four different times. It should be mentioned that the Ancient defines parody as "a close imitation of some particular poem" characteristic of an author; but he also argues that something better would be to echo the author's tone and manner. Most of Taylor's parodies, however, are tied to specific poems of an author.

After the parodies, the Ancient comments on Poe's poetry; it "has a hectic flush, a strange, fascinating, narcotic quality. . . ." He adds that "there were two men in him: one, a refined gentleman, an aspiring soul, an artist among those who had little sense of literary art; the other . . . 'Built his nest with the birds of night.'" Browning, on the other hand, has a "wilfully artificial" manner. "Sordello" is "perplexity, not profundity"; but Browning has a "royal brain, and we owe him too much to bear malice against him."

The subjects of the parodies of the second night are an odd lot: Keats, Emerson, Swinburne, Mrs. Sigourney, and E. C. Stedman. These are prefaced by an argument from the Ancient defending the practice of deferring to English criticism. American critics are too partisan and prejudiced, he says; indeed, the lack of serious criticism is a familiar complaint of Taylor's. The Keats parody, **"Ode on a Jar of Pickles,"** while not bad, convinces the critics that they should stay with the poets of their own time. The Ancient's remarks on Swinburne are that he has no equal as a "purely rhythmical genius" but that one should wait for his ferment to settle; sensationalism means little in poetry. In an interesting defense of Emerson, the critic asserts that "barring a few idiosyncrasies of expression," there are few authors so clear as Emerson.

The third night covers Thomas Holley Chivers, Barry Cornwall, Whittier, D. G. Rossetti, and T. B. Aldrich. The Ancient complains that the chief fault of popular authors is "intensity of epithet," or striving for attention by odd diction, a habit not conducive to permanence. "There are eternal laws of Art, to which the moral and spiritual aspirations of the author, which are generally relative to his own or the preceding age, must conform, if they would become eternal."

The parody of Whittier is not only extremely mild but is embedded in praise. According to the Ancient, Whittier "deserves all the love and reverence" one can give him; his poetic art "has refined and harmonized the moral quality . . . which . . . made his poetry seem partisan." The alloy has been melted out "in the pure and steady flame of his intellect." The Gannett, who writes the parody, offers to go to Massachusetts to show the poet what he has done for his approval.

Bryant is parodied on the fourth night; his prominent characteristics "are all so evenly and exquisitely blended in his verse, that no single one seems salient enough to take hold of." Holmes is described as having brought the "playful element" to American literature. "O, how tired I am of hearing that every poem should 'convey a lesson. . . .' Why, half our self-elected critics seem to be blind to the purely aesthetic character of our art!"—this is the Ancient's outburst. The last poet discussed, Tennyson, causes a good deal of comment. "I yield to no one in the profoundest respect for his noble loyalty to his art," says the Ancient; Tennyson has understood the nature of his gift, and he has spent his energies perfecting it.

The following night the discussion of Tennyson continues; and he is absolved of all blame for the crimes of his imitators. Poets parodied this night are Henry Tuckerman, Longfellow, Howells, Stoddard, and Mrs. Stoddard. Naturally, Longfellow gets most of the space; and, like Whittier, he is very gently handled. He has "advanced the front rank of our culture," says the Ancient, who praises his "purity, his refinement, and his constant reference to an ideal of life which so many might otherwise forget." As a crude nation, the United States needs his "sweet and clear and steady" influence.

On the sixth night, which begins with complaints about American reviewing and criticism, the Ancient assures all that good work will ultimately triumph over pettiness. He adds that the best critics are Lowell, E. P. Whipple, and George Ripley. The poets parodied are Lowell, Taylor himself, Elizabeth Browning, and George Boker. Naturally, the Ancient has a hard time with Lowell since he likes him so much, but he manages to produce **"The Saga of Ahab Doolittle."** About the only critical remark he can manage is that Lowell's poetry is "over-weighted with ideas." Taylor's remarks about himself are not unexpected. He parodies one of his early Oriental poems, and the comments are that he hasn't any definite place yet; he has too many irons in the fire; his tendency to rhetoric is his chief weakness; and signs of a new form of development appear in his recent poetry. These clearly represent Taylor's idea of his own chief faults.

The topic of discussion on the seventh night is whether America is suffering a period of decline in literature, or is on the verge of a new outburst of genius. The Gannet argues for the renaissance, but the Ancient thinks a great era has just passed. Poets parodied this night are perfectly absurd subjects: Jean Ingelow, James B. Read, Julia Ward Howe, Mr. and Mrs. Piatt, and William Winter, all of whom seem to be a waste of time; perhaps Taylor deliberately chose them to support the view of the Ancient. Discussion rambles on about the need of American poets to forego metrical correctness in favor of developing an individual style. Bayard Taylor is complimented incidentally by the Ancient for seeking "the substance of poetry, rather than the flash and glitter of its rhetorical drapery."

The last night begins with a discussion of the relationship between quality and popularity; and, to the Ancient, the "genuine poet is always the best judge of his own works, simply because he has an ideal standard by which he measures whatever he does"—a favorite view of Taylor's. The poets parodied are the "dialect" group: Whitman, Bret Harte, John Hay, and Joaquin Miller. The Ancient suggests that the popularity of such poets in England is explained by the conventional nature of poetry there and by the subsequent desire for anything new and racy. Zoilus concedes that in Whitman "there are splendid lines and brief passages . . . there is a modern, half-Bowery-boy, half-Emersonian apprehension of the old Greek idea of physical life. . . ." Indeed, the elements of a fine poet exist in Whitman but "in a state of chaos." The Ancient replies: "The same art which he despises would have increased his power and influence. He forgets that the poet must not only have somewhat to say, but must strenuously acquire the power of saying it most purely and completely. A truer sense of art would have prevented that fault which has been called immorality, but is only a coarse, offensive frankness" (155).

The Echo Club is an interesting book for those who enjoy parodies, for many of them are quite well done. The faults of the volume, however, are several: first, some of the parodies are so mild as to be ineffective; and they are so because Taylor wanted to avoid offending people like the New England worthies. Second, the prose setting was not a good idea, chiefly because Taylor's opinions are not remarkably perceptive. Third, at least half the parodies are of poets who are now so dead that most readers have never heard of them. And, of course, Taylor, in his usual fashion, managed to get his friends into the book as a form of publicity—Mr. and Mrs. Stoddard, Stedman, Boker, and Aldrich, not to mention himself.

Unfortunately, the book did not draw much attention. Taylor reported from Rome in 1873 that the original articles were creating a stir among American painters there; and he quotes Browning, who had told a friend they were the best parodies he had ever seen.[27] But the book itself fell dead from the press in 1876. Beatty thought ***The Echo Club*** marked by an "irritating timidity." This is quite true; but the parodies are good when Taylor did not know the writers personally, or when he cared little about their opinion. Beatty also thought Taylor's literary opinions here were important, but their significance is less certain. It is nice to know that the permanent in art is worth striving for and that temporary fame is not the same; that the sensuous and sensational are not the best features of poetry; that simplicity is a virtue; that technical skill is important but not all-important; that American criticism was bad, and English better; that preaching in poetry is not a good thing; and that a poet is the best judge of his own work. But none of these views is either profound or surprising.

Professor Trent, in his history of American literature, said it was pathetic to find Taylor publishing parodies on popular poets.[28] On the other hand, W. D. Howells thought they were "the best parodies ever written."[29] One of the strongest supporters of ***The Echo Club,*** oddly enough, was Juliana Haskell, who argued that the book was "a classic of its kind," as good as the Bab Ballads, or Edward Lear, or Lewis Carroll, and certainly "the best of the works of Bayard Taylor."[30] This praise is rather high; but ***The Echo Club*** is surely *one* of his best works. It is significant that Dwight MacDonald, in his recent collection of parodies (1960), included three from ***The Echo Club***—on Poe, Browning, and Whitman.

III Studies in German Literature

As has been noted, Taylor achieved some status as a translator of *Faust,* and as an intermediary between Germany and America; he probably achieved a somewhat exaggerated reputation in Germany. The same may be true, to a lesser degree, of his friends, whose work he "puffed" in Germany—Stoddard, Stedman, Boker, and Aldrich. Taylor was also helped by the political influence exerted in America by German-Americans; therefore, when he was appointed ambassador to Germany, he had the solid support of the German-American community.

Outside of a few biographies, there is very little criticism or explication of Taylor's work. His poetry, fiction, and criticism have been largely ignored by modern critics and scholars, who seem to feel that he was not an important poet. His German work, however, has been the subject of considerable criticism, mainly concerned with the translations and the German elements in his work.

On result of his reputation as a Germanist was his appointment as a nonresident professor of German literature at Cornell University in 1869, a post that demanded he give a series of lectures but not regularly. Thus, in 1870, he gave the first six lectures on Lessing, Klopstock, Schiller, Goethe, and Humboldt. In 1871, he read a new series on early German literature. In 1875, he delivered lectures on Lessing, Klopstock, Herder, Wieland, Richter, Schiller, and Goethe, while in 1877 he repeated those on early German literature. He also used these lectures elsewhere—in 1876, at the Peabody Institute in Baltimore; in 1877, at the Lowell Institute in Boston he gave the whole series of twelve. He also gave them from time to time on his tours through the Midwest. He got a lot of usage from them, and their popularity may be one reason that his wife let them be published in 1879, shortly after his death.

Studies in German Literature (1879)[31] consists of these lectures; they were collected by George Boker, who said that he left them unchanged. He cautions the reader that Taylor aimed at no more than introducing his audiences to German literature. Yet, such was "the native power of his intellect and the depth of his knowledge" that he developed an admirable style of treatment;[32] and Taylor's style in these lectures is clear, simple, and unpretentious.

In Taylor's first six lectures about early German literature, one sees that, though Taylor knew Goethe and contemporary authors quite well, he was not at home with the earlier material. Indeed, Krumpelmann offers considerable evidence that Taylor cribbed most of this early material from the work of the German scholar Heinrich Kurz. For example, Krumpelmann says of the first lecture that, "although the manuscript copy contains no notes indicative of sources, all the German selections embodied in this lecture are contained in the selected passages found in the Kurz text and have been appropriated *Seriatum*."[33] Other sources are sometimes indicated, but it is plain that Taylor "was compelled to make quick acquaintance" with this material.

Nevertheless, such was Taylor's skill that he was able to make these early essays interesting to those who knew little of German literature. Taylor had the ability, from his journalistic experience, to pick out the salient features of material and to eliminate the rest. The best portions of these lectures are his translation of large swatches of poetry into reasonable English. He also spent much time on summary and historical background, and anyone who wants a brief survey of this material could do worse even today than read Taylor. Occasionally, he revealed an odd opinion such as that Luther's translation of the Bible is superior to the King James version because the "instinct of one great man" is better than the "average judgment of forty-seven men." But, for the most part, his opinions are not eccentric; and he sees German literature as advancing steadily toward the expression of the people and away from the values of court life.

George Boker singles out the essays on Goethe, *Faust,* and Richter as the best; for these are "filled with the light of discovery, and . . . with the most subtle and suggestive critical analysis." To these, Krumpelmann would add the lecture on Schiller; for, though it contains "little or nothing that is original or exceptional," it is the result of a "long familiarity with the life and works of that author."[34] These judgments are quite accurate.

Generally, Taylor's approach to a writer is to give a lengthy account of his life and career; then to describe his most important works, translating some passages to give the flavor; and, finally, to make a general judgment about the author's place in German literature. He is not devoted to analysis of text, but neither does he ignore the works themselves; indeed, his own strong interest in form makes him sound at times fairly modern. However, his criticism is likely to be intellectual—to center on the philosophical outlook of the author. Schiller, for example, had a "lofty, unceasing devotion to a noble literary Ideal." In his work, there was "an upward tendency—a lifting of the intellectual vision, a stirring as of unfolding wings. . . ." The highest rank cannot be awarded to Lessing "as a creative intellect"; but, as "a revolutionary power, as a shaping and organizing force, he has scarcely his equal in history."

For some years before his death, Taylor had been planning a combined biography of Goethe and Schiller. The two essays about these men are a foreshadowing of that interest, for they were in many ways bound together in Taylor's mind. The essay on Goethe is one of his best, and it succeeds in presenting Goethe (apart from his works) as a man of great variety and complexity. The essay on *Faust,* however, is somewhat disappointing in view of Taylor's great devotion to the poem. Of course, it is introductory; but his method is simply to summarize the story, with a running series of illustrative quotations from his own translation. This works fairly well, and the result is intelligent so far as the main lines of the poem are concerned; but one expects something more profound from a man who had devoted so much of his life to Goethe. Taylor's great contribution was, as has been noted earlier, his insistence on the integral relation of the second part to the whole; he argued that it completed and made meaningful the first part in a way that had not been appreciated. His statement of the essential meaning of the poem is this:

> The first lesson is that man becomes morbid and miserable in seclusion, even though he devotes himself to the acquisition of knowledge. He must also know the life of the body in the open air, and the society of his fellow-men. . . . He must fight, through his life, with the powers of selfishness, doubt, denial of all good, truth and beauty. . . . The passion for the Beautiful must elevate and purify him, saving him from all the meanness and the littleness which we find in Society and in all forms of public life. The restless impulse, which drives him forward, will save him. . . . Only in constant activity and struggle can he redeem himself—Only in working for the benefit of his fellow-beings can he taste perfect happiness. This is the golden current of wisdom which flows through "Faust" from the beginning to end. (386-87)

Studies in German Literature is, on the whole, an interesting volume. As an introduction to the subject, it is informative, accurate, and well written. Taylor was attracted to German literature by certain qualities of his own mind; and the influence of the Germans, particularly Goethe, was very strong on him. His belief in constant striving (which might seem an American trait), his passion for "The Beautiful," his belief in a vigorous physicality, his love of society—these may well be partially derived from *Faust.* At any rate, his interest in German literature was genuine, though reinforced by his marriage and his German friendships. These essays show he was at ease in German literature, at least of the "classical" period; they suggest too, something of his importance in the field. According to Krumpelmann, he was "the foremost literary intermediary between this country and Germany."

IV Other Criticism

Critical Essays and Literary Notes (1883)[35] was a posthumous collection of miscellaneous pieces edited by Taylor's wife, who bemoaned the fact in her preface that he was forced to return, late in his career, to daily journalism at the *Tribune.* Most of the short pieces (some thirty-three of them) are from the Book Notes section of that paper, which he edited during his last few years; and they represent, she says, only a "minute proportion" of his work of this type. The volume also contains eight long essays drawn from journals like *The Atlantic Monthly* and *Scribner's* on literary topics—two of these are really travel pieces dealing with his researches on Goethe and Schiller.

The essay on Tennyson is the best, and it demonstrates that Taylor had considerable critical ability when he had time to exercise it. A fervent admirer of the poet, he was still able to make critical judgments about him. Tennyson's great virtues have been two: "an exquisitely luxurious sense of the charms of sound and rhythm" and "an earnest if not equal capacity for sober thought and reflection." Taylor thought Tennyson succeeded only partly in trying to perfect these powers; his early delight in sound led to an "over-anxiety" about unimportant details which, in turn, led to a kind of obscurity. Tennyson's devotion to his art had been excessive, with a general "overrefinement of the artistic sense." His chief shortcoming was intellectual, according to Taylor; "his dream of progress is a vague and shining mist, his view of the Present narrow and partisan." Nor had he "ventured beyond the common level of speculation, nor fore-spoken the deeper problems which shall engage the generation to come." Still, he was not morbid; his teaching has "always been wholesome and elevating." Indeed, Taylor expects a reaction against Tennyson in which public taste will undervalue his achievement; but his place will finally be high.

The essay on Victor Hugo was one of Taylor's most astonishing feats, and it was quoted far and wide as an example of what he could do. He received one evening two fat volumes (seven hundred and forty pages) of *La Légende des Siècles,* and by the following evening he had not only read it but had also written a review of eighteen pages, including translations of five long poems in the original meter. This feat is certainly impressive, though his wife's claim that it was "as much greater than the mechanical exploits of journalism as the spirit of man is superior to a machine" is rather doubtful. The accomplishment attests, instead, to the machine-like efficiency with which Taylor could work; and it also gives a clue about how he was able to produce such a tonnage of printed material.

A major portion of two essays on German authors, Friedrich Hebbel and Friedrich Rückert, is devoted to Taylor's translations of their poems. Those by Hebbel, "The German Burns," are of some interest for they are written in the Alemannic dialect, which Taylor tries to reproduce. Hebbel's poetry, he says, teaches a "wholesome morality"; but Taylor admits that this approach is not a legitimate one for judging them. Rückert, on the other hand, was a scholarly poet, known for his translations and imitations of Oriental poetry. Since Taylor had met him a few times, this essay is more biographical and personal.

"The Author of 'Saul'" deals with a Canadian, Charles Heavysege, a workingman who wrote verse dramas. Taylor speculates about talent versus environment as a producer of poets; he is on the side of talent—the "mute, inglorious Milton" is, he says, a "pleasant poetical fiction." But many quotations from the poem do not support Taylor's assertion that its language is "fresh, racy, vigorous" and that it "might have been written by a contemporary of Shakespeare." It is, in fact, a mediocre biblical drama.

The essay on Thackeray, written in 1864, consists mainly of personal reminiscences. The English novelist was "essentially manly" and had a "sadness of the moral sentiment which the world persisted in regarding as cynicism"; but his nature was "immoveably based on truth." Taylor's admiration for Thackeray is great; he speaks of him as "the man whom I honor as a master, while he gave me the right to love him as a friend."

Two long essays on Weimar, from 1875 to 1877, are mixtures of travel observation, comments on life in the city, and accounts of the difficulties Taylor had in gathering information about Goethe and Schiller. Because of Taylor's charm, he gained the confidence of those who had control over Goethe's house. And he was thrilled when recognized by a count or duke or invited to a court ball. At one point, when he gave a lecture on American literature in German, he discovered that American poets, such as Whittier, Stedman, Stoddard, and Aldrich, interested his audience.

The Notes section of the book opens with two addresses given for the dedication of monuments to Fitz-Greene Halleck, but in them Taylor makes some interesting comments about American literature. "The destiny that placed us on this soil," he says, as had many other Americans, "robbed us of the magic of tradition, the wealth of romance, the suggestions of history, the sentiment of inherited homes and customs, and left us . . . to create a poetic literature for ourselves." Halleck himself was not important; he was genial and friendly, but his life "offers no enigmas for our solution." The monument symbolizes rather the "intellectual growth of the American people," and Halleck's life represents the "long period of transition between the appearance of American poetry and the creation of an appreciative audience for it."

In a review of Bryant's translation of the *Iliad,* Taylor repeats his own principles of translation, which have already been noted in his work on *Faust.* Though Bryant's translation doesn't always adhere to these principles, Taylor pronounces the translation very good, saying that blank verse will do until Americans become more accustomed to hexameters. Naturally, when comparing other translations of Homer, Taylor awards the palm to Bryant.

There are many short reviews of current books, sometimes by minor or obscure authors, and sometimes by his friends (who always get a good review; Stedman, for instance, is placed in the foremost rank of critics, beside Lowell and Matthew Arnold). When Taylor encounters a book of real merit, he is less certain; of George Eliot's *Daniel Deronda,* he says in a gingerly way that, when the crisis is reached in Eliot's novels and when her men and women "await a solution in which there shall be some ideal blending of the better possibilities of life, she closes her volume and turns away." This remark says more about Taylor than about Eliot, for he seems to desire an idealistic, or happy ending; yet he is able to see at least that her novels have substance and force.

The only other review of much interest today is of Henry James's *The American,* in which he complains that James is apparently untouched by sympathy for his characters. James habitually "gives us the various stages of a problem, and omits the solution." Taylor thinks Newman has utterly failed; and the only characters he cares for in the book are Valentin de Bellegarde and Mlle Noémie—all of which suggests that Taylor's comprehension of this novel was not total.

In short reviews like these an author cannot help appearing omniscient, and Taylor tends to fall into a pattern. He begins with comment on the author's life and career, makes a few remarks on his work generally, and then tries to fit the book into it, with occasional asides on art or poetry. Occasionally, Taylor indulges himself in wit, but he never attacks a book viciously. For example, he says of the popular author "Ouida": ". . . With a pace which is meant to be that of a choric dance, but rather suggests the 'hop, skip and jump' of school-children, she circles around a mutilated altar, casting into the flame upon it huge handfuls of strange gums and spices, some of which give up a momentary sense of perfume, while others blind, strangle, and set us coughing." As reviews, they are above average for his day; for Taylor at least had standards which he applied with reasonable consistency.

Two closing essays on **"Authorship in America"** add little to what he has said before on this topic. On the one hand, he complains of the poor remuneration and the lack of official recognition; on the other, he insists that one writes for the joy of writing, not for profit. Of course, these views are not mutually exclusive; he simply means that a writer ought to be able to write without worrying about subsistence. But he concludes that it will be some time yet before this situation would be possible in the United States.

V Juvenile Works

Taylor turned his hand to almost anything that promised a fair return; and, in a few instances, he produced work for children. These are not remarkable but are usually at least competent. ***The Ballad of Abraham Lincoln*** (1870),[36] however, is an exception. Printed as a small eight-page pamphlet with garish illustrations by Sol Eytinge, Jr., and published by Fields in 1870, it is terrible. Fields, who had started a series to which Stoddard and Stedman made contributions, invited Taylor, who was inclined to contribute because he wasn't lecturing that year. The poem is extremely sentimental; furthermore, it is eighty-six stanzas long.

Another of Taylor's most disappointing projects was his ***A School History of Germany*** (1874).[37] He referred to it as a piece of hackwork he had undertaken because it would "kindle a better fire under the household pot than all my good work has done." But, after working at it steadily for months, he ran into difficulty with Appleton's, which was having trouble with illustrations. Time passed, publication was delayed several times, and Taylor's wife said he never received any remuneration from it at all. A substantial work of nearly six hundred pages, Taylor said that the history was "based" on three recent German works by Dittmar, Von Rochau, and Dr. David Muller; from these, he constructed "an entirely new narrative," compressing the material into less than half the space. This description reads more like abstracting than original writing, but Taylor claimed that his was the "only German history in existence, as a connected, unbroken narrative." Being without condescension or childishness, it seems well written for schools.

The book had a curious fate. Reprinted in 1897 with an additional chapter by Taylor's wife, it ultimately became part of a twenty-five volume set called The History of Nations, edited by Henry Cabot Lodge, which was published in 1907.[38] Taylor's volume was revised and reedited by Sidney B. Fay. According to Krumpelmann, the work went through twelve editions; thus, in a curious way it became one of Taylor's most successful works—though not one, as he had intended it, for children.

Boys of Other Countries (1876)[39] has received less attention than any of Taylor's books. The official biography, which mentions its publication, says that it consisted of a series of sketches published in *Our Young Folks* and in *St. Nicholas* magazines. Smyth, who says it was Taylor's last published prose book, calls it a "children's classic." The reasons for the lack of comment are two: the book is now hard to find, suggesting that it didn't sell very well; and, when found, there is little one can think of to say about it. It contains five stories: **"The Little Post-Boy,"** about Sweden; **"The Pasha's Son,"** about Khartoum; **"Jon of Iceland,"** (for some reason three times longer than the others); **"The Two Herd-Boys,"** about Germany; and **"The Young Serf,"** about Russia. The tone is pleasantly informal, and the narrator is Taylor himself. The stories use his travel experiences, and they are not condescendingly written; indeed, they might be of interest to children even today. Another edition was published after Taylor's death, containing an additional story set in California.

Taylor produced hardly enough juvenilia for one to make generalizations about his talents as a writer for children. The Lincoln poem is terrible; the history, a compilation; and the short stories, moderately interesting. But all are examples of Taylor's versatility. He once made a clearcut distinction between his "professional" writing and his serious writing; these works clearly belong to the "professional" category.

Taylor's miscellaneous works constitute a large bulk of material, but much of it is unpublished. One might mention his lectures, for example, many of which are extant. There is also a large body of unreprinted periodical publication that might be delved into. An account of his many short translations would add little to one's assessment of him, nor would an account of his many lyrics that were set to music by various hands—**"The Bedouin Song"** no fewer than six different times. He also wrote introductions for several books by others; and, of course, he had an extensive correspondence with many people—thousands of his letters are extant in various libraries. But an account of this material would add little to what has already been said here—that he was an active and prolific journalist; a man of intelligence, taste, and skill who had to write for a living; and a writer who also wanted to be something more than a journalist—a literary man and a poet.

Conclusion

On the sum of Taylor's writings, not very much, admittedly, is worth preserving; but some of it is—and not only for historical reasons. Of the travel books, ***Eldorado*** is lively and well written; both volumes of ***At Home and Abroad*** are particularly interesting for their American material; and parts of the other books are lively and curious. Of Taylor's fiction, ***Hannah Thurston*** deserves resuscitation, but some critics would no doubt argue for ***The Story of Kennett. Poems of the Orient*** deserves a modest place on the shelf of minor verse of that age, as well as a handful of the romances and lyrics; one might choose also some of the verse in ***Prince Deukalion.*** The parodies of ***The Echo Club*** should be better known; and, of course, the *Faust* translation occupies even today an honored place among the best translations of difficult poems. These works constitute a reasonable quantity of good work.

Still, Taylor remains for us a figure of more historical than literary interest. His great popularity may seem puzzling; it seemed at times puzzling to him, too, for he thought of himself as a "highbrow" literary man, not as a popular journalist. Yet his success is clearly due to several factors. One was a powerful ambition and drive; no man could have done all the things he did, or written all the books that he wrote, without enormous energy and a thirst for fame. In a sense, it is remarkable that he lived for fifty-three years.

Another factor of great importance in Taylor's success was the close-knit, almost incestuous, nature of the literary world in Taylor's time. He knew personally nearly everyone of importance, or someone who knew the people he didn't know. One can't help feeling at times that some of his material didn't deserve publication and that it wouldn't have been published in a more critical atmosphere. Reading Taylor's short stories, for example, one is moved to wonder how in the world they ever got published at all; but the same observation could be made of multitudinous stories published in his era. The answer lies partly in his friendships with so many editors and literary men; for example, the editors of the *Atlantic Monthly* during the period Taylor published in it were James Russell Lowell (1857-1861); James T. Fields, Taylor's publisher (1861-1871); and William Dean Howells (1871-1881), with all of whom he was on friendly terms. Much the same was true of other periodicals to which he submitted material; it was seldom rejected, no matter how bad it may now seem. Therefore, he might be excused for thinking that his work was uniformly good.

But the third and perhaps most important reason for Taylor's success lies in the realm of taste, which, in mid-nineteenth-century America, was Genteel, in many ways reflecting English Victorianism. A central value of the Genteel tradition was an abstract ideal of beauty, one closely tied to an emphasis on purity and innocence and one usually symbolized by children and virgins. Of course, this emphasis ultimately derived from Christianity, which emphasized a clearly defined good and evil, chastity, asceticism, and so forth. Thus, the Genteel tradition's refusal to admit in literature the ugly and vulgar aspects of human existence suggests a kind of ascetic ideal. The tradition was not ignorant of crude reality; it simply chose to emphasize the perfection of an ideal. An etherealized woman, perfectly formed, was more to be tolerated than the animalistic possibilities of sex, childbirth, pain, and death.

But the values of the Genteel tradition were also essentially related to the upward mobility of the middle class. The values of money, hard work, and success—and its rewards, comfort and respectability—were all involved. They applied not only to the middle class, however, but also to those of the lower classes who aspired to rise. The price for this rise was very great, for it meant conformity to these principles, values, and attitudes. One accepted the proper values of reality, sex, marriage, family life, and of beauty, as well as the debt-paying conscience, the comfort, and the respect of society.

In a sense, Bayard Taylor was ruined by the Genteel tradition. He was a farmer's son who aspired to rise in society. This aspiration does not mean he lacked interest in literature; indeed, he was deeply absorbed in it, as it was understood by the Genteel. But the values of the tradition were those of wealth, comfort, and taste, which had no necessary relationship to literature, though the tradition could and did reward handsomely proper conformity to its principles. It is ironic to find Taylor so frequently condemning the public because he was conforming in fact to the Genteel public all the time. None of his work is very original or strikes out in new directions; he simply followed the forms, subjects, and themes of his time and of the era before him.

Obviously, there has been a fundamental change in taste between Taylor's time and the 1970's. Though some of the old views remain here and there in fragmentary form, the Genteel tradition was long ago routed not only in the sexual realm but also in regard to fundamental literary values. The literary life remains, and probably always will remain, an avenue of progress in society for poor boys with talent—as it should. Perhaps such persons still accept certain social values, but literary success now seems less dependent on social conventionality.

But the question of Bayard Taylor still nags at the mind. Would his work have been different in a different age? Why did he accept Genteel values so easily? Why couldn't he think his way through such superficiality toward some genuineness? Does his career mean that writers always reflect their age? Or is the only means one has of distinguishing between great writers and mediocre ones the fact that the great ones are intellectually free to rise above their age? The answers to these questions are not known; perhaps there are no answers to them; but this study of Taylor has tried to suggest some possibilities. On the other hand, the career of a minor author like Taylor—as well as those of his friends, too, Boker, Stedman, Stoddard, Aldrich—is interesting precisely because it is so typical of the age. In the last analysis, it is not their work which is interesting, but what it tells one about the taste of their age. In this sense, then, Taylor is important because he is typical of his age—its literary and social values—and because he embodies, both in his work and his person, the tenets of the Genteel tradition.

Notes

1. *Faust, A Tragedy,* by Johann Wolfgang von Goethe, translated in the original meters, by Bayard Taylor. Part I (Boston, 1870); Part II (Boston, 1871). References here are to the one-volume edition published by Houghton, Mifflin and Company (successors to Fields and Osgood) in 1900.
2. *Life and Letters,* II, 542.
3. *Ibid.,* II, 544.
4. *Ibid.,* II, 545.
5. *Ibid.,* II, 540.
6. Krumpelmann, p. 53.
7. A photocopy of this review, which was set in type, is also in the Yale University library.
8. Pp. 443 and 444 of the type-set copy.
9. Schultz, pp. 153-54.
10. *Ibid.,* p. 156.
11. Haskell, *Bayard Taylor's Translation of Goethe's Faust* (New York, 1908).
12. Preface to *Faust,* pp. xiv-xv.
13. *Ibid.,* p. viii.
14. Haskell, p. 34.
15. *Ibid.,* p. 83.
16. Krumpelmann, p. 177, note 170.
17. Spiller, ed., *Literary History of the United States,* p. 823.
18. Beatty, p. 280. On the other hand, Carl Van Doren, in the *Dictionary of American Biography,* said: "Its fidelity and sonorousness should not be allowed to hide the fact that Taylor rendered *Faust* in the second-rate English poetry which was all he knew how to write."
19. Krumpelmann, p. 54.
20. *Ibid.,* p. 55.
21. *Ibid.,* p. 46.
22. *Ibid.,* pp. 215-21.
23. *Ibid.,* p. 61. See also p. 166, note 4, to "Introduction."
24. (Boston, 1876).
25. *Life and Letters,* II, 566.
26. Beatty, pp. 257-58.
27. *Life and Letters,* II, 620.
28. W. P. Trent, *History of American Literature* (New York, 1903), p. 470; quoted in Haskell, p. 13.
29. In the *Atlantic Monthly* (January, 1877), quoted by Haskell, p. 13.
30. Haskell, p. 14.
31. *Studies in German Literature* (New York, 1879).
32. Introduction to *Studies in German Literature,* p. v.
33. Krumpelmann, p. 145.
34. *Ibid.,* p. 142.
35. *Critical Essays and Literary Notes* (New York, 1880).
36. *The Ballad of Abraham Lincoln,* Illustrated (Boston, 1870).
37. *A School History of Germany: From the Earliest Period to the Establishment of the German Empire in 1871* (New York, 1874).
38. *Germany* (Vol. 18 of *The History of Nations,* Henry Cabot Lodge, editor-in-chief), revised and edited from the work of Bayard Taylor by Sidney B. Fay (Chicago, Copyright 1907 by John D. Morris & Co.; Copyright 1910 by the H. W. Snow Co.).
39. *Boys of Other Countries. Stories for American Boys* (New York, 1876).

C. W. La Salle II (essay date 1973)

SOURCE: Introduction to *The Story of Kennett,* by Bayard Taylor, College & University Press, 1973, pp. 7-21.

[*In the following introduction to Taylor's* The Story of Kennett, *La Salle offers an overview of Taylor's career and provides background for the novel.*]

One hundred years ago, few serious readers in America would have thought it possible that Bayard Taylor would someday be an almost forgotten author, for he was one of the better-known writers of his period. Taylor's fate serves to remind us that two very different literatures were being written in the 1850's and 1860's. Among Taylor's contemporaries were Nathaniel Hawthorne, Herman Melville, Ralph Waldo Emerson, Henry David Thoreau, and Walt Whitman; but from another angle, the literary life was dominated by Henry Wadsworth Longfellow, James Russell Lowell, and John Greenleaf Whittier. The general devaluation of the "Genteel writers" of New England has consigned to obscurity such members of that tradition as Taylor, Thomas B. Aldrich, R. H. Stoddard, and George Henry Boker. Only by recalling the work of a writer such as Taylor, however, can the modern reader acquire a complete picture of American literature of the mid-nineteenth century.

I

Taylor's America was a country in flux. "Manifest destiny" was a popular doctrine, and the geography of America was being radically altered during Taylor's young manhood. While he was on his first voyage to Europe, the annexation of Texas took place. Within the next decade, that state's territory was substantially expanded, the territories of California and New Mexico were acquired, the border of Oregon was fixed along the forty-ninth parallel, and the Gadsden purchase was accomplished. This expansion accelerated the western drift of the population in the United States, and the census of 1850 revealed that fully forty-five per cent of the population resided west of the Alleghenies. More than most of his contemporaries, Taylor must have been conscious of this vast "other" America, for he made a trip to California in 1849 for Horace Greeley's newspaper, the *New-York Tribune.* The new literary market was one which Taylor would try repeatedly to tap on the lecture circuit tours of his middle years, although without complete success. This enlarged America would ultimately subscribe to values different from those associated with the New England literary establishment and with its heirs.

The other major historical event of Taylor's lifetime was, of course, the Civil War. For whatever reasons, Taylor himself did not go to war; but he secured a commission for his brother, gave speeches supporting the Northern cause, and was for a time a war correspondent for the *Tribune.* At the was's end, America was a country at once politically one and yet simultaneously ever more conscious of its cultural multiplicity. This heightened awareness of sectional peculiarities found expression in the "local color" movement in literature.

These historical occurrences encouraged the growth of a realistic, empirical American literature (as opposed to an idealistic one). And because of his involvement in these events, one could have expected Taylor to be a part of that development. Officially, he was not. It would remain for the next generation of American fiction writers—Bret Harte, Edward Eggleston, Mark Twain, William Dean Howells—to reflect the new modes of life to be seen in this enlarged America, and the ways in which the values of the new territories would conflict with those of the more traditional East. Only Whitman, at the time of Bayard Taylor's literary successes, was dealing with the expanded America as subject matter.

Despite Taylor's apprenticeship in journalism, much of his literature did not reflect his observations of the world about him; instead, it illustrated his commitment to the Genteel Tradition—the literary Establishment of his day. *The Literary History of the United States* (1948) phrases the problem tersely, as it identifies the choice which Taylor and his cohorts made: "The securities of Concord and Cambridge were gone, even though Longfellow and Lowell, Holmes and Emerson lived on. . . . The issue was sharply drawn: if one wishes to write, one must choose to defend the old order or to throw in one's lot with the new. There was no easy blending of ideality with reality in these uncertain times. . . . resentful of the claims of the realists, [Boker, Stoddard, Taylor, Aldrich, and Stedman] self-consciously proclaimed themselves the champions of Ideality in literature" (809).

What were the intellectual values of this tradition to which Taylor had bound himself? Its assumptions can be briefly summarized: that there was an "ideal" order which it was the writer's duty to express; that moral codes were of higher importance than, say, esthetic ones; that man was capable of virtually endless self-improvement in the ethical and cultural spheres; and that it was the social responsibility of literature to encourage this perfectibility. To be a useful, moral document, art should present a very disciplined experience, and call the reader's attention to the ideal, universal aspects of a present, specific situation.

V. L. Parrington in Volume II of his *Main Currents in American Thought* (1927-30) observes: "The essence of the Genteel Tradition was a refined ethicism, that professed to discover the highest virtue in shutting one's eyes to disagreeable fact, and the highest law in the law of convention. . . . The first of literary commandments was the commandment of reticence. . . . Any venture into realism was likely to prove libidinous, and sure to be common" (436). To take one specific example, the Genteel writers usually represented the "common man" in an idealized fashion, often in a semi-pastoral setting. For such a figure, contentment with one's social lot was a highly regarded virtue, although a certain measure of material ambition was acceptable. Sustained vernacular expression, physicality, and controversial ideas were avoided. Plot, in the mechanical sense, was an important element. The ideas which that plot projected were designed to flatter the social and moral preconceptions of the largest number of readers.

Ultimately, it is not surprising that the writers of the Genteel Tradition devoted an inordinate amount of attention to such minor literary forms as the more impressionistic kind of "local color" story, the historical romance, travel writing, and children's literature. It is of particular significance, however, that the tradition produced no major novelists, perhaps because the novel, more than other genres, has historically had social change as one of its basic subjects. The Genteel writers, in declining to have their work reflect the turmoils of their world, were really turning away from the major line of development of narrative fiction. Thus the writers of the Genteel tradition are usually remembered as poets or essayists rather than as novelists. Actually, they produced an appreciable amount of work more or less in that genre: Longfellow wrote two volumes of narrative fiction, Whittier one, Holmes three, Aldrich three, Taylor four. But—as Taylor undoubtedly noticed—most of the Genteel writers never achieved the popular success in the novel that they had enjoyed in other forms.

Such novelists of the period as Susan Warner, Maria Cummins, and Augusta Jane Evans Wilson were reaping financial rewards with a somewhat different kind of book. Alexander Cowie in *The Rise of the American Novel* (1948) comments that "When Holmes published *Elsie Venner* in 1861, the vogue of the historical romance and the Gothic tale was largely over or in abeyance, and the novel of domestic life was in ascendancy" (495). He defines the latter as "an extended prose tale composed chiefly of commonplace household incidents and episodes casually worked into a trite plot which involves the fortunes of characters who exist less as individuals than as carriers of moral or religious sentiment. The thesis of such a book is that true happiness comes from submission of suffering" (413). Virtually none of the practitioners of the "domestic novel" were considered serious writers by Taylor and his contemporaries, and he was certainly trying to go beyond the obvious limitations of such writing. Yet ***The Story of Kennett*** seems related to the "domestic novel" as it is defined by Cowley.

Kennett serves to remind us that the tradition of Melville and Hawthorne was not so dominant in the latter half of the nineteenth century as it is today. The decade of the 1850's had seen the publication of Melville's monumental *Moby Dick* and of Hawthorne's *The Scarlet Letter* and *The Blithedale Romance*. Hawthorne's *The Marble Faun* inaugurated the next decade in fiction, but no works in what might be called the Symbolist tradition followed it. To consider the American novel at its best in the 1860's is to be concerned with such Genteel items as Oliver Wendell Holmes's *Elsie Venner* and *The Guardian Angel,* Sidney Lanier's *Tiger Lilies,* Louisa May Alcott's *Little Women*—and the novels of Bayard Taylor.

The directions taken by the novel in the twentieth century allow us to forget the existence of Genteel narrative fiction. The modern American novel, as well as the tradition of American Realism in general, descended at least in part from the symbolic and allegorical interpretations of America written by Melville and Hawthorne; but it owes relatively little to the idealized depictions of the Genteel writers. The consequence is that Genteel novels have almost disappeared from the histories of American literature. Nevertheless, they are a part of America's literary history, and the present reprinting of a novel by Bayard Taylor will permit the examination of this sub-genre by a new generation of readers.

II

Richmond Croom Beatty's definitive *Bayard Taylor, Laureate of the Gilded Age* (1936) portrays the writer as one who embraced social and cultural values which led him to substitute activity for substantial achievement. Taylor was born in Kennett Square, Pennsylvania, in 1825. His formal education ended in his sixteenth year; an apprenticeship with a printer and newspaper publisher provided his introduction to writing as a profession. His first poem was published in the *Saturday Evening Post* in 1841, and his first volume of poetry, ***Ximena,*** appeared in February, 1844, under the name of "James Bayard Taylor." Shortly thereafter, he departed for a walking tour of Europe which lasted almost two years. His travel letters, originally sent back to Philadelphia magazines, were to published as ***Views Afoot*** (1846). The activities which were to claim the largest part of Taylor's attention—newspaper work, poetry, travel writing—were begun, therefore, by the age of twenty-two.

Taylor recommenced newspaper work upon his return from Europe, first in Phoenixville, Pennsylvania, and later in New York. Out of the already mentioned trip to the California gold fields came more travel letters (for the *New-York Tribune*), and an impressionistic book called ***Eldorado*** in 1850. Although Taylor had married that same year, his wife's death a few months later led him to embark on additional travels. He sailed for Africa in 1851, shortly before his first major volume of poetry, ***A Book of Romances, Lyrics, and Songs,*** was published. The trip through Egypt, Ethiopia, Turkey, and Palestine was extended, at Greeley's order, by a trek through India en route to Hong Kong, where Taylor joined Commodore Perry's expedition. Thus Taylor also visited Japan before returning to America at the end of 1853. His adventures were then recounted for an eager public in a series of travel books: ***A Journey to Central Africa*** (1854); ***The Lands of The Saracen*** (1854); ***A Visit to India, China and Japan in the year 1853*** (1855). ***Poems of the Orient,*** with "exotic" themes, was published in 1854.

In that same year, and in addition to performing miscellaneous editorial chores and preparing another volume of poems, Taylor entered the Lyceum circuit. He returned to Europe in 1865, and by the end of the year had made an extensive tour of Scandinavia; the resulting book was ***Northern Travel*** (1857). He remarried while abroad, and his growing responsibilities encouraged even more furious activity. Two books of miscellaneous essays, ***At Home and Abroad,*** were published in 1859 and 1862. ***The Poet's Journal*** appeared in 1862, and a collected edition of his poems in 1864. By this time, he had embarked on a new career in novel writing.

Taylor began his first novel, ***Hannah Thurston,*** while acting first as secretary, then as chargé d'affaires at the United States Embassy in St. Petersburg. This book, which dealt with his birthplace under the thin disguise of "Ptolemy, New York," and sold fifteen thousand copies within a few months of its publication in 1863, was soon issued in London, and later was translated into German and Russian. Its success led Taylor to work immediately on a second novel, ***John Godfrey's Fortunes,*** which appeared in England and in America in 1864. A first-person narrative, it is a satire on the literary life in New York City. ***The Story of Kennett,*** usually considered Taylor's most successful novel, was published in 1866.

III

Taylor's correspondence during the composition of this third novel (as quoted in Marie Hansen-Taylor and Howard E. Scudder's *Life and Letters of Bayard Taylor* [1884]) is interesting for what it reveals about the author's attitude toward the novel as a form. In a letter of January 6, 1866, to a Kennett Square friend, Taylor called the book his "pet novel," and described it as "totally different from the others—altogether objective in subject and treatment—" (451). By April, Taylor was anticipating good fortune: "My new novel . . . promises to be a marked success, so far as present indications go. Although the publishing business is as flat as possible, more than six thousand copies have been ordered in advance of publication, and the few who have read the book are unanimous as to its interest. . . . I . . . am entirely satisfied . . . with the experiment of writing three novels and am now sure that I can write a good and characteristic American Novel" (453). The two interesting implications in this letter are, first, that Taylor's measure of his novel's achievement was clearly a commercial one; secondly, in his view, the "characteristic American novel" would be something on the order of ***Kennett***—an idealized romance with a historical background and some Genteelly treated "local color" material.

Another letter, from the same volume, shows Taylor's concern with character psychology. When he replied to a protest about the impropriety of the funeral scene—a scene that is one of the best in the novel—he justified Mary Potter's actions in terms of logical character projection, not ideality or historical accuracy: "What you say of the order of the funeral in Kennett is quite true. Such an incident as I have described probably never occurred, but that makes no difference whatever. It is natural for Mary to do it; there could be no other culmination to her history. I was a year studying out the plot before I began to write, and the idea of the *denouement* at the funeral came to me like an inspiration" (456). He was not consistent, however. In too many other instances he imposed authorial values on his figures, rather than dramatizing those of the characters themselves.

Taylor's pleasure in the public acceptance of the book was expressed in a letter to Thomas Bailey Aldrich on April 16, 1866: "I had bestowed much preliminary thought upon the book, and I worked out the idea with the most conscientious care, hoping to make a stride in advance. It is a great joy and a great encouragement to be so unanimously assured that I have not failed in my aim. The moral is that labor pays, in a literary sense" (458).

Clearly, Taylor had high ambitions for ***The Story of Kennett;*** however, he also wanted a popular success. Thus he attempted in a single work to blend together several things: the material, settings, and melodramatic action associated with the historical romance; the theme of "patient suffering" and the housewifery of the domestic novel; and the didactic morality of the Genteel tradition.

The reader of ***Kennett*** is kept aware of the historical framework by a series of references to the Tories and their suspected sympathizers, one of whom is Old Man Barton. When Gilbert is being given advice on reporting his robbery to the proper authorities, one suggestion is that he write to General Washington demanding protection, "'and say the Tory farmers' houses ought to be searched'" (Chapter XXI). There are references to such local places and events as "Chadd's Ford," "the Hessian Burying Ground," and the "'Lammas flood o' '68'" (Chapter XXI). Gilbert's problem in borrowing money to pay off his farm's mortgage is explained in terms of the historical period: "In ordinary times he would have had no difficulty; but, as Mr. Trainer had written, the speculation in western lands had seized upon capitalists, and the amount of money for permanent investment was already greatly diminished" (Chapter XXVI). Finally, Taylor provides for us that standard figure of the historical melodrama, "Sandy Flash"—a flamboyant highwayman with overtones of Robin Hood.

A counterpart to the above is the love story of Gilbert and Martha, designed to attract the feminine audience. The tale is a conventional one: the young man of uncertain birth is inspired by his fair maid to triumph over his difficulties. A good deal of attention is devoted to various domestic arrangements and, in particular, to descriptions of the clothes worn by the female characters. This detail occurs throughout, but is particularly obvious in the descriptions of the wedding party in Chapter XXXIV. And Mary Potter, it should be noticed, is the perfect exemplification of the "domestic novel" heroine, as defined above.

But the book also exhibits the stylistic and intellectual characteristics of the Genteel literary tradition. Gilbert Potter, the "common man" protagonist, is heavily idealized—in his character and actions, as well as in his grammar. The heroine, Martha Deane, is without a single humanizing flaw. The plot is tightly constructed in a very mechanical way, and the suspense is situational rather than psychological. There is a clear implication that life in the past must have somehow been more pleasant, more meaningful than it was in Taylor's present. Vice and virtue are rather rigidly separated. The moral of ***The Story of Kennett,*** heavily underlined, is that the virtuous will always triumph—with patience—over their adversaries.

Taylor's novel is interesting, therefore, partly because it provides a sort of summary of trends current in American writing during the third quarter of the nineteenth century. Yet ***Kennett*** seems also to go beyond some of the contemporary Genteel literature; surprisingly, the movement is in the direction of greater realism and a more critical view of the society. For one thing, the reader is often given the sense of a dense cultural fabric such as one expects to find in the "novel of manners." The differences between the architectural styles of the Deane, Barton, and Potter homes are carefully rendered, for example; and the domicile is suggestive of the character within. The set-piece descriptions of fox hunt, barn raising, Quaker meeting, and country wedding correspond to the traditional "social gathering" scenes of that sub-genre. Even more striking is Taylor's attempt to render the intellectual, as well as the physical, landscape.

In his Prologue, the author calls attention to the fact that "the conservative influence of the Quakers was so powerful that it continued to shape the habits even of communities whose religious sentiment it failed to reach." Among the major characters, the only practicing Quaker is Dr. Deane, and his portrait is far from flattering. Taylor sees him as a humorous rather than a wicked villain, but the hypocrisy of his "plainness" is insisted upon. A similar irony is suggested by Taylor's rather rich vocabulary in his description of the Quaker meeting in Chapter VII. Again and again—through the figure of Martha Deane, for example—Taylor ironically ascribes the virtues associated with Quakerism to non-members of the sect.

The Quaker physician serves to introduce the question of "public opinion." Dr. Deane's concern for his reputation among the members of his sect also allows one to observe the extent to which the society is class-conscious. Gilbert Potter is constantly made aware of the gradations of a system which is prepared to make distinctions between "legitimate" and "illegitimate" human beings. For Gilbert, a great passion is the only excuse for his presumption in courting Martha Deane: "It might seen like looking too high, Mother, but I couldn't help it'" (Chapter XII). Viewed from this angle, Gilbert's real problem is with the caste system of his culture.

A third element is that, as rendered by Taylor, much of the society of rural Pennyslvania in the eighteenth century is money-fixated. Dr. Deane's criterion for a future son-in-law is largely financial, Alfred Barton's relationship with his father is totally governed by his anticipation of future inheritance, and Mary Potter confesses that it was Barton's prospects that led her to agree to their secret marriage. Even Gilbert Potter reacts to the symbolic value which money has taken on in his culture: "When Gilbert had delivered the last barrels at Newport and slowly cheered homewards his weary team, he was nearly two hundred dollars richer than when he started, and—if we must confess a universal if somewhat humiliating truth—so much the more a man in courage and determination" (Chapter IX).

Hypocrisy, snobbery, materialism—these are the values which Taylor seems to be ascribing to rural Pennsylvania in the eighteenth century. They are not the qualities which we immediately associate with that time and place; but they are exactly those that a writer like Mark Twain has taught us to associate with his—and Taylor's—nineteenth-century America.

It becomes important to realize that Taylor's knowledge of his own century did, in fact, surreptitiously enter the narrative. Albert H. Smyth in his biography (*Bayard Taylor* [1896]) assures us that the author based several of his eighteenth-century characters on people of his own day, some of whom he had known personally. Sandy Flash was based on an actual nineteenth-century highwayman; Gilbert Potter, Deb. Smith, Martha Deane, the farmer Fairthorne, and the boys Joe and Jake are modeled on people from Taylor's own period (167-73). Knowing this raises the possibility that Taylor was using his historical setting as a screen for critical comments about a culture which he knew at first hand.

But Taylor could not bring himself—or his protagonist, Gilbert Potter—to deal directly with the issues that he had raised. Both Gilbert and his friends plainly prefer to accept their society's values rather than question them. Only once in the narrative does Taylor have Gilbert come close to a critical look at the way in which his society operates—when the protagonist senses the analogy between his position and that of Deb. Smith:

> . . . her words hinted at an inward experience in some respects so surprisingly like his own, that Gilbert was startled. He knew the reputation of the woman, though he would have found it difficult to tell whereupon it was based. Everybody said she was bad, and nobody knew particularly why. . . . The world, he had recently learned, was wrong in his case; might it not also be doing her injustice? Her pride, in its coarse way, was his also, and his life, perhaps, had only unfolded into honorable success through a mother's ever-watchful care and never-wearied toil (Chapter VI).

Gilbert could have turned at this point to questioning the moral and social bases of his society—as Huckleberry Finn would do a few years later. From this possibility, Taylor felt it necessary to retreat. And the Genteel Tradition provided him with an easy escape route, through the sentimentality of the last sentence in the paragraph quoted above.

Perhaps because he sensed that prose fiction was a dangerous tool, Taylor wrote only one other novel: ***Joseph and His Friend*** (1870), his least interesting work in that genre. Taylor's real love was poetry, and he perhaps viewed his novels as distractions from what he considered his more serious work; indeed, he had stopped in the middle of writing ***Kennett*** to compose a long poem which he believed to be his masterpiece: ***The Picture of St. John,*** a narrative poem running to thirty-two hundred lines that appeared in 1866. His next major work was his translation of *Faust,* published in two parts in 1870 and 1871. Taylor's great feat was to render the poem in its original meter, and his translation is still admired. Various poems, stories, essays, editions, and travel books followed. Another long poem—***Lars: A Pastoral of Norway***—and two plays—***The Prophet*** and ***Prince Deukalion***—appeared between 1873 and 1878.

Public honors rewarded such prodigious activity. Taylor was invited to write and deliver the **"Ode"** at the Centennial Celebration in Philadelphia in 1876, and in 1878 he was named United States Minister to Germany. His death came less than a year after accepting that post. In the next two years, two collections of his work were published, and by the end of the century, three biographical studies had appeared: the previously cited Hansen-Taylor and Scudder volume, Smythe's work, and Russell H. Conwell's *The Life, Travels, and Literary Career of Bayard Taylor* (1884). To his large public, Bayard Taylor's literary reputation must have seemed firmly established.

IV

Taylor's letters and the magazine reviews show that ***The Story of Kennett*** was, in general, well received. Taylor summarized some of the praise in a letter to E. C. Stedman on April 15, 1866: "Whittier is enthusiastic about ***Kennett,*** ditto Howells. The former says it contains 'as good things as there are in the English language;' the latter, 'it is the best historical (historical in the sense of retrospective) novel ever written in America.' [George W.] Curtis said very nearly the same thing to me at our dinner. So, you see, my hope and your prophecy are in a way to be fulfilled. The people in this country are buying it like mad" (Hansen-Taylor and Scudder, 457).

In the literary journals, none of the anonymous reviewers found the plot of the book its most engaging aspect, nor the attempts at humor very telling. Most praised the portrayal of individual incidents and the characterizations to be found in Taylor's work. All seemed to accept the book as Taylor's attempt to depict the Quaker character within the framework of a regional portrait. The *Nation* (April 19, 1866) offered an unfavorable comparison to J. T. Trowbridge's New England novel, *Lucy Arlyn* (1866). The reviewer, who complained that Taylor's was not really a historical novel since it merely dressed contemporary events in the clothing of 1796, was particularly offended by the presentation of the Quakers: "We do not see real Friends. Perhaps we do see *Quakers.* Quakers are the sect beheld from the outside; but the Society of Friends can be known only by the most delicate interior affiliation, by spiritual rapport, or by the highest refinement of appreciation."

The reviewer concluded that the novelist simply did not comprehend the "inner life" of the Quakers—not allowing for the possibility that Taylor consciously might have chosen to concentrate on the sect's public aspect. A letter which Taylor wrote to Aldrich suggests that personal animus may have been involved: "Both the 'Round Table' and the 'Nation' seem to have a spite at me, altho' the managers of both papers want me to write for them" (Richard Cary, *The Genteel Circle: Bayard Taylor and His Friends* [1952], 33).

Interestingly, the reviewer for *The Athenaeum* of London (May 12, 1866) praises those elements which had offended the *Nation:* "Much of the population of Kennett is Quaker; and we can vouch for the fidelity of Mr. Bayard Taylor's portraits of Quakers at meeting or in their own houses."

A much more perceptive review was the unsigned one by William Dean Howells which appeared in the *Atlantic Monthly* (June, 1866). Significantly, the critic praised Taylor for the specificity of his material: "There is such a shyness among American novelists . . . in regard to dates, names, and localities, that we are glad to have a book in which there is great courage in this respect." The reviewer grasped the point that what other commentators had seen as a lapse of taste on Taylor's part in the funeral scene was actually a bit of psychological verisimilitude: "Considering her [Mary Potter's] character and history, it is natural that she should seek to make her justification as signal and public as possible."

Howells also held that the actions of Dr. Deane and Martha were intended by Taylor to represent opposite sides of the single coin of Quakerism: "In the sweet and unselfish spirit of Martha, the theories of individual action under special inspiration have created self-reliance, and calm fearless humility, sustaining her even in her struggle against the will of her father, and even against the sect to whose teachings she owes them. . . . [Dr. Deane] is the most odious character in the book, what is bad in him being separated by such fine differences from what is very good in others."

This point is a valid one. Whether Taylor's presentation of the religious sect is historically accurate, or even fair, is one question; whether or not the author has created believable psychological relations between his characters is quite another. What is worth noting is that the opposing characters of Dr. Deane and his daughter Martha are so created as to have additional meaning because of their contrast.

More recent critics have given Taylor's work in general, and his novels in particular, only passing reference. *The Literary History of the United States* comments tersely that he wrote "three creditable novels on social themes" (810). Arthur Hobson Quinn says in *The Literature of the American People* (1951) that "in ***The Story of Kennett*** (1866) . . . Taylor created a masterpiece." This surely overgenerous evaluation was made on the basis that Taylor wrote with affection of an era he knew well, that several characters were based on "real people," and that the novel has become a part of the "local life" (357).

Carl Van Doren in *The American Novel, 1789-1939* (1940) regards Taylor's work as an example of those sentimental narratives of the mid-nineteenth century which also reflected the rising interest in realistic literature: "During the sixties realism hovered in the air without definitely alighting. Oliver Wendell Holmes, for instance, in *Elsie Venner* (1861) worked his romantic problem of heredity upon a ground of shrewd realistic observation; Bayard Taylor employed a similar composition of elements" (177).

But only Alexander Cowie in *The Rise of the American Novel* (1948) attempts to define fully Taylor's place in the history of fiction in the United States. He describes Taylor's four novels as "useful links in any study of the evolution of fiction before the dawn of Howellsian realism" (475). Although he doubts that ***The Story of Kennett*** can accurately be called a "historical novel," the author's use of factual material "makes for authenticity in atmosphere and episode. . . . There are many homely illustrations of the quiet (Quaker) life of Kennett Square—social, religious, industrial—that ring true and that seem to be integral parts of the story . . ." Taylor was "on the whole . . . on the side of realism in fiction" and "anticipates Howells in protesting against the morbid tone of many novels of the 1850s and 1860s, but it remained for Howells to inaugurate a new regime in novel-writing" (481-86).

While Taylor's verse today seems irrelevant to the development of American poetry, ***The Story of Kennett*** appears to have been part of a growing realism in the American novel. In this novel about his birthplace, Taylor seems to be part of a tradition in the American novel of manners—one with James Fenimore Cooper for an ancestor, and George Washington Cable for a descendant. If Taylor sometimes relied on plot contrivances, idealized love stories, and melodramatic adventures, he differed from both his predecessors and some of his followers more in degree than in kind.

Much more than he seems to have done in his poetry, Taylor in ***The Story of Kennett*** was dealing with material which he knew in depth (even if he chose sometimes to concentrate on its superficial aspects). And he goes somewhat beyond a mere surface realism. The Quaker beliefs as a social force, the importance of money to one's status in the emerging American community, the tyranny of public opinion—all of these things are described and sorted out with the care, if not always the emphases, of the social historian.

Beatty comments "In his fiction, as in his other prose, he [Taylor] remained fundamentally a reporter" (238). The reporter and the romancer have an uneasy coexistence in ***The Story of Kennett.*** What one misses is the insistence on the inter-relationships within the social fabric which one gets on occasion from the novels of Cooper, and more certainly from a work like Cable's *The Grandissimes.* Some of the most interesting aspects of Taylor's novel for the modern reader are things which are only hinted at by the author—for example, the connections among the economic, social, and religious life in this small, culturally unified community. Why, one wonders, did he stop with these veiled suggestions? The answer lies in Taylor's relationship to the values of his own culture. Both in its achievements and in its limitations, ***The Story of Kennett*** is a document which implicitly defines the Genteel Tradition.

Luther S. Luedtke and Patrick D. Morrow (essay date 1973)

SOURCE: "Bret Harte on Bayard Taylor: An Unpublished Tribute," in *The Markham Review,* Vol. 3, No. 6, May, 1973, pp. 101-104.

[*In the following essay, Luedtke and Morrow offer a commentary on Bret Harte's obituary of Taylor, and examine the relationship between the two authors.*]

When Bayard Taylor died in Berlin on December 28, 1878, the one man who most fittingly could write his obituary for the German nation had just settled in the Ruhr town of Crefeld: his countryman, Francis Bret Harte. For Taylor, the German ambassadorship to which he had just been appointed culminated an affair with the heart of Germany which reached back beyond his acclaimed translation of Goethe's *Faust* in 1871-72 to the first appearance of his many travel books and poems in Germany in 1851.[1] Karl Bleibtreu's translation of eighty of Taylor's *Gedichte* in 1879, although inferior to earlier translations by Karl Knortz, Friedrich Spielhagen, and Adolf Strodtmann, was one sign of Germany's sadness at his passing.

The first two periods of American letters in Germany—the prose writings of Irving and Cooper, and the novels of Stowe—were succeeded in the late 1850's by the poetry of Longfellow and Bryant, and in the 1860's the reputation of American prose in Germany was maintained almost wholly by the travel literature of Taylor, Melville, and Richard Henry Dana, Jr. Taylor was best known in Germany as the author of lyrics and travel books, and, although his works appeared in German editions with moderate regularity through 1882, his major circulation there occurred in the sixties. In lyrics and travel narratives alike, Taylor's lively characterizations, his colorful descriptions of places seen, and his sympathetic portrayals of lower classes were well suited to broad German middle class tastes for the exotic and entertaining.[2]

Bayard Taylor's ambassadorship to Berlin closed a distinguished career of literary-cultural mediation. The less prestigious consulship which Bret Harte assumed in Crefeld in 1878, on the other hand, recognized a protege who had already surpassed his master and was on his way to becoming one of the all-time bestselling American writers in Germany. When Bret Harte and Mark Twain opened up the vistas of California and Nevada for the Germans in the early 1870's, a decade of American poetry was easily forgotten and a splurge of American local color tales and

"*Goldgräber Geschichten*" which was to dominate the last decades of the century had begun. Although difficult for our contemporaries to believe, until at least 1878, comparisons of Harte and Twain in Germany worked strongly in favor of the former. While Mark Twain was appreciated as a journalist, humorist, and good natured satirist, Harte was given the supreme accolade of *Dichter* for his mastery of the genre of the short story and for his smooth verses and popular tales. His infusions of the rough life of the mining camps with humor, sentimentality, and nobility amidst the depravity and squalor fed the same German tastes for exotic lands and strange peoples which Bayard Taylor had whetted. In 1872, the *Tauchnitz Verlag* published two volumes of Harte's *Prose and Poetry,* and in 1873—still a full year before the first appearance of Twain's *Jim Smiley's Beruhmter Springfrosch* in Germany—His *Kalifornische Novellen* and *Tales of the Argonauts* (1873-75) followed. German critics would gradually learn that Harte's development had ceased with his first successes while Twain gained stature as a social critic and philosopher.[3] But publication of Harte's works in Germany in the last three decades of the century continued to exceed Twain's, and by 1912 had reached a total of 109 separate editions of prose and poetry.[4]

Bret Harte and Bayard Taylor encountered each other several times during their lives. These two victims of forgotten stardom apparently first crossed paths in New York City at the occasion mentioned in Harte's tribute (late 1853 or 1854) when Harte, as a spellbound boy, listened to the most famous young traveler of his age tell about foreign lands. In 1870, Harte, then editor of *The Overland Monthly,* probably met Taylor again, on Taylor's third visit to California.[5] At that time Harte gave Taylor's most recent book, ***By-Ways of Europe,*** a generally favorable review for the *Overland.* In the review Harte objected to Taylor's "egotism" and "oppressive sense of oration" but praised the author's "honest descriptions" and "graphic realism."[6] A few years later Taylor wrote about Harte's work in ***The Echo Club,*** a collection of burlesques and parodies. Harte survived reasonably unscathed and even garnered a compliment. After a parody of "Truthful James" and scorn for Harte's "proported realism" and slavish imitation of Dickens, one of Taylor's characters said:

> He [Harte] never could have written that ["Plain Language from Truthful James"] if he had been only a humorist. His later work shows that he is a genuine poet.[7]

During the years 1871 to 1877, Harte and Taylor spent a good deal of time on the East Coast, although they did not see much, if any, of each other. But they had many mutual friends, including Mark Twain, who paid careful attention to the diplomatic appointments the new Rutherford B. Hayes administration made in 1878. By that year Twain and Harte were irreconcilably estranged, after their unsuccessful collaboration on the play, *Ah Sin,* despite their long friendship.[8] In 1878 the Clemens family was planning a European vacation with an extended stay in Germany, and Mark Twain went to great trouble to attend Taylor's American farewell banquet. On April 11, 1878, the Clemenses sailed for Europe with the Taylors aboard the *Holsatia.* In a letter to William Dean Howells on May 4, 1878, Twain praised Taylor highly, saying, "I tell you Bayard Taylor is a really loveable man."[9] At the same time Twain was far less enthusiastic about Bret Harte's German appointment, despite its low status. In an 1878 letter to Howells from Heidelberg, Twain made one of his most famous indictments of Harte, finally calling him "a liar, a thief, a swindler, a snob, a sot, a sponge, a coward, a Jeremy Diddler."[10]

In Germany Taylor seemed polite but distant to Harte, possibly the result of two weeks at sea with Mark Twain. Taylor wrote the publisher, James R. Osgood, concerning Harte's Crefeld appointment: "it's a capital place of a kind,—little work, next to no responsibility, and $3,000 a year, which is enough to live upon *well,* in Crefeld."[11] Harte, however, had a somewhat different view of life in the "capital" Crefeld. He wrote to his wife, Anna, who remained on the East Coast:

> . . . I've found out all about the cost of living in Germany, and my conclusion is this: you cannot live—*in any respectable or decent fashion—on less than you can live decently in America* [Harte's italics]. . . . Crefeld is a modern town. . . . Look any way, walk any way, north, east, south, and west, the same little blocks of stucco-fronted, shutterless houses, with windows from which no face ever shows through the muslin-shrouded panes. . . . The winter is here already—grim, black, bitter. . . . We have had two *earthquakes* at Crefeld, *since I've been here* [about six months; again Harte's italics][12]

With Taylor's unexpected death, Harte's critical feelings toward the Minister subsided. Within a few days of Taylor's death, Harte wrote a brief but important memorial essay for the influential *Berliner Tageblatt.* This tribute, entitled "*Zum Andenken Bayard Taylors*" ("In Memory of Bayard Taylor") has to our knowledge never been translated or republished since that date.[13] In January, 1879, Harte wrote to his wife:

> Mrs. Bayard Taylor has sent me a book of her late husband's and a very kind note, and it occurs to me to enclose today the letter I received from her in answer to one I wrote her after hearing of her husband's death. You remember that I did not feel very kindly toward him, nor had he troubled himself much about me when I came here alone and friendless, but his death choked back my resentment, and what I wrote to her, and afterwards in the 'Tageblatt,' I felt very honestly.[14]

Harte's essay appeared as three wide columns of *Fraktur* type in the December 29, 1878, issue of the *Berliner Tageblatt.* The article has biographical significance as one of the few extant sources about Harte's early reading, the literary influences on him, and his cultural activities. The article indicates that Harte heard several notable Lyceum lectures and that they impressed him greatly. (One recalls with irony Harte's own largely unsuccessful lecture career of the mid-1870's.) *Zum Andenken* also substantiates the claim that Harte left New York for California in early 1854.[15]

Published only ten days after Taylor's death, this article is hardly the carefully crafted, however sentimental, work that Harte typically produced. Nonetheless, characteristic touches do appear. Harte opens with a dramatic local color setting delivered in a tone of sentiment and patriotism typical of his most famous writings. He is highly conscious of the task at hand—to write about the nature of the American character, and eulogize a representative man. Hart tries to capture Taylor's essence as a speaker in metaphorical rather than critical terms, such as seeing in Taylor "a Robinson Crusoe incarnate, a Sinbad come to life." Yet, evidence of Harte's keen critical eye is present in the surprisingly accurate, if off-hand, biographical information, and in his estimate of Taylor as a cultural symbol and poet that is at once complimentary without being an outright lie. In the foreground is Harte's pose as eulogist, not literary critic. The elegaic effect is strongest at the end of the essay when Harte, having honored Taylor as a poet, traveler, and man, turns to Classical elegaic conventions. After meditating upon the nature of his subject in a mood of solemnity, Harte laments the loss in Pastoral terms: "In the workshop we miss his lofty figure; his sweet laughter no longer sounds in our ear." The tribute ends with acceptance, and mercifully without processions, refrains, or heavily rhetorical questions. Clearly Harte has been stunned and moved by Taylor's sudden death, and the occasion affords a downhill artist the chance to write some fresh insights and information about his subject and himself.

In Memory of Bayard Taylor[16]

A quarter of a century ago, in the audience which had gathered in America's largest city to hear the lecture of a famous young American, there also was a boy who was an omnivorous reader of newspapers, like almost the entire youth of America. The lecture gave a vivid description of personal experiences on trips in foreign lands. It was rich in exciting news, sharp and adroit in critical observations, and only moderately didactic; but it showed an energy which broke all opposition and a true American enthusiasm in combating obstacles. The audience had come to honor the victory of the traveler over difficulties such as used to put themselves obstructively in the path of each average young American: inexperience, insufficient wealth, lack of knowledge and models. The joy over the poetry of his language and the fortunate selection of his comparisons receded behind admiration for his energy. The audience was composed of regular visitors to the lecture series set up by the Lyceum; these were ladies and gentlemen accustomed to hearing Emerson; Sumner, Wendell, Philipp [Wendell Phillips] and Everth [Edward Everett]—popular and professional speakers. A few literary celebrities were also present who had taken the place of honor on the platform according to American custom and the wish of the assemblage; but it was soon clear, nonetheless, that the learnedness, the consummate form, and the profundity of the earlier lecturers did not influence opinion to the disfavor of the young traveler or make his lecture appear the less captivating.

Many in the hall were already acquainted with the subject matter of the lecture. They had had the opportunity to make themselves familiar with it, for in a series of electrifying articles which the traveler had sent to a distinguished journal during his wanderings, he had enlarged upon all his observations.[17] Curiosity, therefore, had contributed to the large attendance, and something of this curiosity might also have moved this boy, who had read the letters before, and to whom the speaker, with his captivating, romantic figure, appeared as an embodiment of the dreams of the future which warmed the heart of every American youth. The speaker appeared in the eye of the boy like a Robinson Crusoe incarnate, a Sinbad come to life—it's twenty-five years ago—but the memory has grown up with the child and today has a heightened meaning for the man; for this speaker was Bayard Taylor and to his youthful admirer has fallen the task of writing these lines. . . .

Twenty-five years in a land which makes history as quickly as America is an enormous time, and perhaps it's understandable that this lecture by Bayard Taylor and its success already belong to a vanished generation and appear to have been lost in the fulness of his present fame. For while he was admired by his countrymen even in such early youth as a characteristic expression of their energy and their spirit of enterprise, it was his lot in later years to turn attention to himself (successively and always successfully) as a journalist, poet, and translator of poets, and to bind that interest. Perhaps he has satisfied the insatiable hunger for the always new and unusual, which makes the American public simultaneously the most grateful and most dangerous, precisely in that he had already left the area of travel and adventure before a competitor had appeared, in order to distinguish himself effortlessly and successfully in so many other fields. The fact remains, however, that few (or none) of his countrymen have seen their versatility crowned by an equal success.

It has been maintained that there are a dozen different people planted in every American, a bundle of all conceivable talents, and that in the effort to realize all these potentialities his vital energy is often lost before it has succeeded in discovering its most developed talent. But in Mr. Taylor's various achievements nothing came out as an experiment or as dilettantism. He wrote poetry not to see if he could write poetry, but rather because he could do no other than to write poetry. He wrote a short story because he bore the living material within himself. His intimate knowledge of the German language, his poetic talent, and above all his innate impatience to be a pathfinder made him the admired translator of the greatest German poet [i.e., Goethe].

And yet his gaze was clear enough to recognize the worth of practical considerations. His love of travel finally became for him a rest after his work and ceased to be the literary bridge which connected him to his public. His knowledge of lands and people and geographic and climatic variations in manners of observation and thought, as well as his considerable skill with the pen, induced him to lay upon himself the yoke of editorial activity in the great journal of which he was part owner.[18] His adroitness in amiable small-talk also carried itself over onto the written word and often worked its charm at social and public gatherings as well. His political convictions—and like all sound men, Bayard Taylor was a man of firm political views which were not influencable by party pressures—he expressed in his lectures with such noble, fearless simplicity that in the days of agitation preceding the American rebellion he was hissed off the stage in the North by a fainthearted, irresolute, compromise-seeking audience.[19]

When the moment demanded it he made even poetry, his greatest and by far most distinguished gift, serviceable to utility. His Pegasus was bridled and ridden into the plowfield of translation, or, to the merriment of the unsuspecting audience, which noticed nothing of the folded wings under the many-colored caparison, made his jumps in the circus. His imitations of famous contemporary poets published by the Echo-Club are an exquisite example of his humor, but they delight more through the apparent pleasures which he had in invention and through technical adroitness than through any intention of satire, for this did not lie within the circle of his talents. The longing for battle, the heritage of the greatest spirits, was not among his character traits.

What he achieved in diverse and often difficult fields was always excellent and artistically perfect, but he didn't startle his readers into sudden admiration or snatch them into muddled raptures as less significant writers often do. He founded no school and discovered no new form of poetry, and therefore he has also been spared the doubtful honor of being imitated. He had no retinue of entranced women and men glowing with admiration, but he also provoked no jealousy. He demanded no partisans and did not arouse opposition. He remained relatively exempt from petty and spiteful criticism. He has stepped down into his grave unembittered by hate, and no leaf, no flower, has been withheld from him by envy.

The general admiration for his character and his greatness found in America its affectionate expression in the conferring of the honorary office which he filled so excellently, but for such a short time. It could almost appear an irony of fortune that death has followed so quickly upon the accumulation of honors in the flower of his manly vigor, but it has been granted to so few literary greats to die at the summit of their fame and honor—without blemishes on their name, without the strife between passion for creation and diminishing power—that such an end can perhaps be regarded as the best close of a life so blessed by fortune. Fifty-three years are not too little for the span of an American life. In this half-century there is repeated and compressed into his life the history of his fatherland. His childhood learned to know the conflict and perils which threatened his beloved republic. He learned at an early age to walk independently—and after fifty years his feet are weary—they have wandered around the globe—and he too must make room for a new champion, who was perhaps already on his heels in the race.

But however abstract yet to the point such a philosophy may be, it offers little solace for the loss of a personality who was as good, as gentle, as winning, as refreshing as Bayard Taylor. The world is always ready to forget the workman if his work remains behind; it undervalues the blessed influence of the example, and the witness and stimulation for all contemporary activity which proceed out of a noble spirit. Thus it is not enough for us that our fellow worker has completed his work, that it has been found good, and that it was rewarded. In the workshop we miss his lofty figure, his sweet laughter no longer sounds in our ear. Now that he is gone, our ambition and the desire for emulation have also gone; and sorrowfully we lay the tool aside, for with his death the soul has escaped from it. . . .

Only a few writers have found among comrades of all places such warm recognition as he; so that one of his oldest admirers, like the writer of these lines, in a strange land and a strange language, can scarcely say anything to the honor of his friend that will not have already been uttered much more strikingly.

Notes

1. In his survey of *American Literature in Germany, 1861-1872* ("University of North Carolina Studies in Comparative Literature," No. 35; Chapel Hill, 1964), p. 71, Eugene F. Timpe dated the first German publications of Taylor's travel books in 1853 (1) and 1858 (2). The *Hinrichs' Bucher-Catalog, 1851-1865* (Leipzig, 1875), Vol. 2, pp. 41, 367, however, lists the Taylor publications of the 1850's as *El-Dorado* (Weimar, 1851), *Eine Reise nach Centralafrika* (Leipzig, 1855), *Nordliche Reise* (Leipzig, 1858) and *Winterreise durch Lappland* (Leipzig, 1858).
2. Timpe, pp. 41, 72-73.
3. Lawrence Marsden Price, *The Reception of United States Literature in Germany* ("University of North Carolina Studies in Comparative Literature," No. 39; Chapel Hill, 1966), pp. 111-12.
4. Listed in Clement Vollmer, "The American Novel in Germany, 1871-1913," *German American Annals*, ns. Vol. 15 (1917), pp. 195-99.
5. *The Life and Letters of Bayard Taylor,* ed. Marie Hansen-Taylor and Horace E. Scudder (Boston, 1884), II, pp. 528-529.
6. *The Overland Monthly,* III (August, 1869), 195-196. No manuscript of this review survives, but it is generally thought to be by Harte. See George B. Stewart, *A Bibliography of the Writings of Bret*

Harte in the Magazines and Newspapers of California, 1857-1871 (Berkeley, 1933).

7. *The Echo Club* (Boston, 1876), p. 160.
8. George Stewart, *Bret Harte: Argonaut and Exile* (Boston, 1931), p. 245. See also Margaret Duckett, *Mark Twain and Bret Harte* (Norman, Okla., 1964), pp. 113-158.
9. *Mark Twain-Howells Letters,* ed. Smith, Gibson, Anderson (Cambridge, Mass., 1960), I, p. 227.
10. *Letters,* I, p. 235.
11. *The Unpublished Letters of Bayard Taylor in the Huntington Library,* ed. John R. Schultz (San Marino, 1937), p. 208.
12. *The Letters of Bret Harte,* ed. Geoffrey Bret Harte (Boston, 1926), pp. 83, 86, 115.
13. An early laudatory study of Taylor, *The Life, Travels, and Literary Career of Bayard Taylor,* by Russell H. Conwell (Boston, 1879), contains some sixty pages of tribute to Taylor from such figures as Longfellow, Emerson, Holmes, Tennyson, Stoddard, Bryant, and Whipple, as well as such lesser-known literary and publishing figures as James T. Fields. Harte's essay, however, is not mentioned.
14. *Letters,* p. 128. If Harte's letter to Mrs. Taylor survives, it has to our knowledge never been published.
15. Harte probably heard Taylor lecture in New York City in late December, 1853, or early in January, 1854. Taylor returned to New York from an around the world cruise on December 20, 1853. He was in and around New York City during January, 1854, setting up a lecture tour of major and minor cities to conclude with numerous appearances in rural Midwest towns. See *Life and Letters of Bayard Taylor,* I, pp. 262-268, and Schultz, *Unpublished Letters,* pp. 35-38. Still unpublished manuscript letters by Bayard Taylor in the Huntington Library place Taylor in New York City on January 12, 1854, and January 22, 1854. George Stewart and other Harte biographers agree that Harte and his fifteen year old sister, Margaret, left New York City for California aboard the *Brother Johnathan* on February 20, 1854. Their arrival in San Francisco on March 26, 1854, is verified only from haphazard passenger records printed in local newspapers.
16. The authors are indebted to Ms. Linda Barnett for uncovering a copy of *Zum Andenken Bayard Taylors* in the Willard S. Morse Collection of Bret Harte Materials housed in the Research Library, University of California, Los Angles. We are also indebted to Professor Hershel Parker for editorial assistance, and to Ms. Annelie Hagan for her suggestions and assistance with the translation.
17. Most of Taylor's travel exploits were serialized in Horace Greeley's *New York Tribune.*
18. Taylor owned *New York Tribune* stock most of his adult life.
19. This incident happened in Brooklyn shortly after Lincoln's 1860 election. Taylor was an uncompromising Abolitionist. See *Life and Letters of Bayard Taylor,* I, p. 373.

Hans Joachim Lang and Benjamin Lease (essay date 1977)

SOURCE: "Melville's Cosmopolitan: Bayard Taylor in *The Confidence Man,*" in *Amerikastudien,* Vol. 22, 1977, pp. 286-89.

[*In the following essay, Lang and Lease examine Herman Melville's portrayal of Taylor in* The Confidence Man.]

Shortly after finishing *The Confidence-Man,* Melville came down from the Berkshires to New York where he spent "a good stirring evening" with Evert Duyckinck (as Duyckinck described it in a diary entry dated October 1, 1856). According to Duyckinck, Melville was "charged to the muzzle with his sailor metaphysics and jargon of things unknowable" and overflowing with ironical wit. Duyckinck concludes his entry with a significant sentence that has been overlooked by commentators on *The Confidence-Man:* "[Melville] Said of Bayard Taylor that as some augur predicted the misfortunes of Charles I from the infelicity of his countenance so Taylor's prosperity 'borne up by the Gods' was written in his face."[1] Melville's characterization of Taylor as a darling of the gods is an important clue to the fact that the Cosmopolitan, the last avatar in *The Confidence-Man,* is in large part a portrait of Bayard Taylor—and that the sources for Melville's "dashing and all-fusing spirit of the West"[2] need not be exclusively Midwestern but could be Californian as well.

The thought and phraseology of Taylor's Preface to his ***Cyclopaedia of Modern Travel*** (dated July, 1856) are echoed in Melville's Masquerade. According to Taylor, the modern traveler "is characterized by scepticism rather than credulity" and, thanks to increased commerce and colonization, "is no longer obliged to masquerade in the disguises of other races than his own, but bears about him the distinguishing stamp of his nationality. He is thus less truly a cosmopolite than his prototype of two centuries back, and while his delineations of nature are in most cases as exact and faithful as possible, he gives us less of that extrinsic human nature which lends such a charm to the story of the latter."[3] Though he was one of America's most celebrated modern travelers, Taylor identified himself with those masquerading cosmopolites of the past who adopted the garb, customs, and point of view of the distant lands they visited. An extended passage from Taylor's account of his journeys in Egypt (published in 1854) will convey something of the Bayard Taylor who fascinated Melville—and who contributed much to Melville's portrait of the Cosmopolitan:

> I then sent out for a barber, had my hair shorn close to the skin, and assumed the complete Egyptian costume.

I was already accustomed to the turban and shawl around the waist, and the addition of a light silk *sidree,* or shirt, and trowsers which contained eighteen yards of muslin, completed the dress, which in its grace, convenience, and adaptation to the climate and habits of the East, is immeasurably superior to the Frank costume [. . .]. The legs [. . .] are even less fettered by the wide Turkish trowsers than by a Highland kilt [. . .].

After dinner, I seated myself at the tent door, wrapped in my capote, and gave myself up to the pipe of meditation. [. . .] The Nile had already become my home, endeared to me not more by the grand associations of its eldest human history than by the rest and the patience which I had breathed in its calm atmosphere [. . .]. "Achmet," said I to the Theban who was sitting not far off, silently smoking, "we are going into strange countries—have you no fear?" "You remember, master," he answered, "that we left Cairo on a lucky day, and why should I fear, since all things are in the hands of Allah?"[4]

Here is the original of Melville's "king of traveled good-fellows," a cosmopolitan who "ties himself to no narrow tailor or teacher, but federates, in heart as in costume, something of the various gallantries of men under various suns" (114–15). The Cosmopolitan's "style participating of a Highland plaid, Emir's robe, and French blouse" (114)—and other furnishings, including maroon-colored slippers—reflects Bayard Taylor's sartorial style in Egypt and in Khartoum, where he prepared for a visit to the Pasha's palace by dressing himself "in Frank costume with the exception of the tarboosh, shawl and red slippers."[5] Noteworthy among these parallels are the references to "a Highland kilt" in Taylor and "a Highland plaid" in Melville.

"I have been daguerreotyped in Arab dress, to be engraved for Putnam's Magazine [. . .]," Taylor wrote to his mother from New York on June 13, 1854.[6] Melville undoubtedly saw this portrait of a turbaned Taylor in flowing Arabian garb, right hand gripping a scimitar, for it served as the frontispiece of the same number (August, 1854) in which appeared the second installment of *Israel Potter.*[7] Melville was a regular contributor to *Putnam's* between November, 1853, and early 1856; numerous travel articles by Taylor (and references to him) were also being featured by that journal during the same period. "Our young friend, Bayard Taylor, is clearly *the* traveler of the nineteenth century," an editorial note of *Putnam's* proclaimed in September, 1854. The same number of *Putnam's* in which the seventh installment of *Israel Potter* appeared (January, 1855) included a laudatory review of Taylor's latest travel book in language that Melville would not overlook: "Bayard Taylor [. . .] gives us book after book, with as much facility as he steps from California to Cairo, or from Jersey to Japan." Since he himself was mentioned in it, Melville would probably have taken note of an omnibus review in the June number of that year, "American Travelers." The reviewer's opening gambit was that "the Englishman is at once the most rational and the most cosmopolitan of men," but two pages later he writes:

The American is the great national eclectic, and, in the sense of adaptability, he is more cosmopolitan than the Englishman [. . .] He learns easily, and accommodates readily. He has a more flexible accent, a more graceful taste, than any other traveler.

Taylor is singled out for praise as a traveler in the same sense that Mungo Park and John Ledyard were travelers—one who travels for the love of it.[8] *Putnam's* reviewer of Taylor's ***Poems of the Orient*** applauded the author's "cosmopolitan sympathy," and Taylor's ***India, China, and Japan*** was introduced in an editorial note as "the last of his cosmopolitan series."[9]

There is another feature which links Bayard Taylor to the cosmopolitan. As Merton M. Sealts has shown, "genial" with its cognates is a key word in Melville's work. In *The Confidence-Man* alone, there are more than seventy instances concentrated in chapters 9–11, 13, 23–24, 2–31, 34, 36—most of them chapters dominated by the cosmopolitan.[10] "A clear, simple, and truthful narrative, gives us confidence in our guide, while an undercurrent of strong yet genial enthusiasm keeps alive and animated" was the praise bestowed on Taylor in the editorial note of September, 1854, which also mentioned his "sort of imperturbable complacency."[11]

Bayard Taylor's glowing pictures of California and Californians in ***Eldorado*** (1850), so different from Yoomy's apocalyptic vision of avarice in *Mardi* (ch. 166), may also have contributed importantly to *The Confidence-Man* and the Cosmopolitan; one passage dealing with men and society during the gold rush is especially relevant:

The cosmopolitan cast of society in California, resulting from the commingling of so many races and the primitive mode of life, gave a character of good-fellowship to all its members; and in no part of the world have I ever seen help more freely given to the needy, or more ready cooperation in any humane proposition. Personally, I can safely say that I never met with such unvarying kindness from comparative strangers.[12]

It is scarcely necessary to add that Melville's Cosmopolitan is a man of many more meanings that any image of Bayard Taylor as a cosmopolitan, a genial traveler and flamboyant sartorialist could contain. Especially wanting in Taylor's personality are the more sinister traits of Melville's confidence-man. In this respect, another article in *Putnam's Magazine,* "The History of a Cosmopolite," is of interest.

A Cosmopolite has no country in particular, but makes himself at home in all. As he easily unlearns prejudices, he as easily adapts himself to the most varied practices [. . .]. He is never astonished at anything, for he has paid periodical visits to France since 1793 [. . .]. But, in forgetting his prejudices, he is apt to forget his principles: in becoming cosmopolitan, he generally loses love of country. [. . .] He is disposed to caricature—he has an eye considerably keener for faults than for virtues: he is not troubled by modesty: and his

> infacility for being humbugged has begotten in him a too general irreverence, incredulousness and distrust. He reverses our common law maxim, and supposes every man to be guilty until he has proved him to be innocent.

These general characteristics of a cosmopolite are illustrated "by some passages in the life of Mr. Vincent Nolte," whose memoirs are under review, and whose

> slight tailor's bill for one year, containing the items of twelve coats of all colors, and twenty-two pairs of small clothes, suggests the possibility of his being addicted to dress.[13]

It is important to realize that Melville, simply by reading *Putnam's Magazine,* could have found a conjunction of *motifs* basic to his novel-in-the-making: trust, cosmopolitanism and masquerade. The appropriately surnamed Taylor came in for some personal satire.

There was an aftermath, sufficiently ironic. As a failed novelist and struggling lecturer in the years immediately following the publication of *The Confidence-Man,* Melville found himself frequently and disadvantageously compared to the most popular lecturer in the lyceum circuit, the magnetic Bayard Taylor, "a famous man, the elect of lyceums, and the pride of booksellers."[14] "Lecturing is evidently not Mr. Melville's sphere," was one critic's response; another could not decide whether to blame Melville or consider him unlucky in having to follow "the matchless word-painting and the clear-ringing cadences of the handsome Bayard [. . .]." Several years later, on February 24, 1865, Taylor invited Melville to attend a sociable gathering of "The Travellers," a club made up of men who "had seen much of the earth's surface." There is no record of Melville's attendance and Elizabeth Melville Metcalf attributes his apparent failure to accept Taylor's invitation to poor health and low spirits.[15] Her explanation may be accurate but does not tell all.

Notes

1. Evert Duyckinck's diary, October 1, 1856, Jay Leyda, *The Melville Log: A Documentary Life of Herman Melville* (New York: Harcourt, Brace, 1951), II, 523. That *The Confidence-Man* had just been completed (or was almost finished) is indicated by Melville's agreement to deliver the manuscript to Dix and Edwards by October 11. Leyda, II, 525. A later contractual agreement postponed the promised delivery date until November 1; see Elizabeth S. Foster, Introduction to *The Confidence-Man: His Masquerade* (New York: Hendricks House, 1954), p. xxvi. For Melville's earlier involvement with Taylor, see Hugh Hetherington, *Melville's Reviewers* (Chapel Hill: Univ. of North Carolina Press, 1961), esp. pp. 120-21 and n. 28, 152. Taylor composed a valentine for Melville for Anne Lynch's party in 1848 and wrote favorable reviews of *Mardi* and *Redburn* for *Graham's Magazine* in May 1849 and January 1850, respectively.
2. *The Confidence-Man: His Masquerade,* ed. Hershel Parker (New York: W. W. Morton, 1971), p. 4. Subsequent references to this edition will appear parenthetically in the text. Critics have shown an awareness of Melville's use of real persons as models for some of the characters in *The Confidence-Man* but have neglected the Cosmopolitan. For a persuasive identification of a real person in the novel see Harrison Hayford, "Poe in *The Confidence-Man,*" *Nineteenth-Century Fiction,* 14 (December, 1959), 207–18. More recently, William Norris has presented a convincing case for a real-life counterpart of the "gentleman with gold sleeve-buttons" of Chapter 7; see "Abbott Lawrence in *The Confidence-Man:* American Success or American Failure?" *American Studies,* 17 (Spring 1976), 25-38.
3. (New York and Cincinnati: Moore . . ., 1860 [1856], I, viii.
4. *Life and Landscapes From Egypt to the Negro Kingdoms of the White Nile* (London: Sampson, Low, 1854), pp. 169-70.
5. *Life and Landscapes,* p. 288. In a letter to his mother from Egypt dated December 11, 1851 (perhaps accessible to Melville when incorporated into one of Taylor's numerous travel books or articles), Taylor includes a reference to "white baggy trowsers" very similar to those worn by the Cosmopolitan: "I am now wearing one of [my dragoman's] dresses: a green embroidered jacket, with slashed sleeves; a sort of striped vest, with a row of about thirty buttons from the neck to the waist; a large plaid silk shawl as belt; white baggy trowsers, gathered at the knee, with long, tight-fitting stokkings [. . .]." *Life and Letters of Bayard Taylor,* ed. Marie Hansen-Taylor and Horace E. Scudder (Boston and New York: Houghton, Mifflin, 1884), I, 223.
6. *Life and Letters of Bayard Taylor,* I, 277.
7. *Putnam's Magazine,* 4 (August, 1854). The frontispiece portrait of Taylor faces p. 121; the second installment of *Israel Potter* is on pp. 135-46. The same portrait of Taylor in Arab dress is also used as the frontispiece for *Life and Landscapes,* published the same year.
8. See *Putnam's Magazine,* 4 (September, 1854), 343; 5 (January, 1855), 109; 5 (June, 1855), 561-76, quotation 566. Among the many travel articles by Taylor that appeared in *Putnam's* while Melville was contributing to that magazine are "The Vision of Hasheesh," 3 (April, 1854), 402-8; "Experiences in Mount Lebanon," 6 (October, 1855), 396-401; "Notes in Syria," 6 (November, 1855), 493-500.
9. See *Putnam's Magazine,* 6 (July, 1855), 53; 6 (November, 1855), 551.
10. "Melville's 'Geniality'," in: Max F. Schulz, *et al.,* eds., *Essays in American and English Literature*

Presented to Bruce Robert McElderry, Jr. (Athens, Ohio: Ohio University Press, 1967), 3-26.

11. *Putnam's Magazine,* 4 (September, 1854), 343-44.
12. *Eldorado* (New York: Knopf, 1949 [1850]); the passage is on p. 79. For details about Taylor's Visits to California, see Nanelia S. Doughty, "Bayard Taylor: First California Booster," *Western Review,* 7 (1970), 22-27; and "Bayard Taylor's Second Look at California (1859)," *Western Review,* 8 (1970), 51-55.
13. *Putnam's Magazine,* 4 (September, 1854), 325-30.
14. *Putnam's Magazine,* 7 (May, 1856), 551. The following quotations are from Merton M. Sealts, Jr., *Melville As Lecturer* (Cambridge: Harvard Univ. Press, 1957), pp. 90, 82, 87, et passim.
15. Sealts, p. 82 n. 13; Elizabeth Melville Metcalfe, *Herman Melville: Cycle and Epicycle* (Cambridge: Harvard Univ. Press, 1953), p. 203.

Robert K. Martin (essay date 1979)

SOURCE: "Bayard Taylor's Valley of Bliss: The Pastoral and the Search for Form," in *The Markham Review,* Vol. 9, Fall, 1979, pp. 13-17.

[*In the following essay, Martin discusses Taylor's use of pastoral settings and classical themes in his treatment of homosexuality.*]

> I know . . . a great valley, bounded by a hundred miles of snowy peaks; lakes in its bed; enormous hillsides, dotted with groves of ilex and pine; orchards of orange and olive; a perfect climate, where it is bliss enough just to breathe, and freedom from the distorted laws of men, for none are near enough to enforce them! If there is no legal way of escape for you, here, at least, there is no force which can drag you back, once you are there: I will go with you, and perhaps—perhaps . . .[1]

Thus Joseph's friend Philip speaks to him in Bayard Taylor's novel, ***Joseph and His Friend,*** probably the first American novel to speak openly of love between men and of the search for a place where that love could be expressed. Philip's valley of bliss and freedom is clearly drawn from the pastoral conventions, which offered for the nineteenth century homosexual artist one of the very few possible models for the literary expression of deep friendship and love between men. In Theocritus, in Virgil, in Barnfield, and in Marlowe the homosexual artist might find some confirmation that his emotional needs were not unique, that they had been known by others, and had indeed been given a place of honor in the literature.

At the same time Taylor seems to have recognized that the pastoral dream is in fact no solution for mid-19th century America. He identified the pastoral with California, both in the passage above and in his poem **"On Leaving California,"** which evokes the famous "middle ground" of pastoral,[2] somewhere between civilization and the wilderness:

> Thy human children shall restore the grace
> Gone with thy fallen pines:
> The wild, barbaric beauty of thy face
> Shall round to classic lines.
>
> And Order, Justice, Social Law shall curb
> Thy untamed energies;
> And Art and Science, with their dreams superb,
> Replace thine ancient ease.[3]

Although he asserts that "Earth shall find her old Arcadian dream / Restored again in thee," his work as a whole clearly indicates that Bayard Taylor moved from a belief that happiness could be achieved by flight from America and by immersion in an alien culture to a conviction that the ideal state of the future might be found closer to home. The establishment of such an ideal state, which would include a place for homosexual love, required a change in men rather than a change in place.

Taylor's use of the pastoral theme in ***Joseph and His Friend*** reflects a modification of his earlier views, one that is important for a study of the development of a homosexual consciousness. Taylor established his reputation as a travel writer, and his reports from abroad filled a growing appetite for the exotic and the romantic. He provided landscapes of the Far North, the Orient, the Middle East, Africa, always with a sense of adventure and romance. In his homely fashion he did for American literature what French painters such as Delacroix were doing—offering the new bourgeoisie dreams of travel and excitement, ways of spending their new affluence, and of countering the boredom of everyday life. For Taylor travel fulfilled a moral purpose as well: it extended the moral options open to a mid-nineteenth century American man and permitted the expression of ideas that were inconceivable at home. (Taylor's rural, Pennsylvania Quaker background was stifling and repressive, to judge by his fiction, in part because his Quakers seem indistinguishable from the neighboring Amish.) Taylor's travel narratives permitted him to describe Turkish baths, hashish smoking, dancing girls, drunken brawls, and pretty Arab boys without fear of censorship: he was merely reporting on exotic customs. The travel books thus served a function not unlike some early forms of pornography. Under the guise of science, they offered erotic titillation.

Taylor's poetry often used similar strategies. His most successful book was his ***Poems of the Orient*** (1854), with its **"To a Persian Boy,"** subtitled **"In the Bazaar at Smyrna."**[4] The poem draws upon its Persian setting but also upon a tradition of Persian love poetry, often addressed to boys.[5] In other words, the poet indicates that his tribute to the beauty of a boy is a literary exercise, prompted by the scene. As a consequence of this strategy, the poem communicates on two levels: it appears as a minor literary exercise to the conventional reader, and at the same time conveys to the more observant reader Taylor's attraction for "the wonder of thy beauty." Still, in this very early poem (first published in 1851), Taylor does not concentrate on the specifics of the boy's beauty, but uses the poem as a means of expressing his taste for the East in terms that suggest a moral contrast with America: "From under thy dark lashes shone on me / The rich, voluptuous soul of Eastern land." But it is precisely the voluptuousness, the frank sensuality of the East that appeals. Taylor's own travels may well often have served as a means for him to experience such voluptuousness at first hand. For, like his friend Herman Melville, Taylor may have felt that true pleasure, particularly pleasure between men, could only be found in another land, where the burden of rigid moral codes was less heavy.

In another poem, **"Hylas,"** Taylor adopted a different strategy. Here the convention is Greek, not Persian, but Taylor is able to express a sensual response to a young man by appearing to imitate a classical legend. Since the story of Hylas is told by Theocritus (in *Idyll XIII*), Taylor can justify his loving portrayal of the boy by reference to the homosexual content of Theocritus's works and to the conventions of Greek romance. He can thus appear to be merely the translator, as it were, and so enjoy the sensuality without avowing it fully. Within the poem itself, the strategy of the poet is one we might call the "Leander" strategy, in honor of its most famous use by Marlowe. In this delightful, unfinished poem, Marlowe diverts the reader's attention from the story itself—the love of the youth Leander for the priestess Hero—to a subplot involving the rape of Leander by Jove, who mistakes him for Ganymede. The subplot is far more interesting than the plot itself, since it comes much closer to Marlowe's own sexuality, but it is still contained within an acceptably heterosexual frame. (Something of the same tension between heterosexual plot and homosexual subplot may be observed in Marlowe's plays as well, to a much smaller degree in Shakespeare's plays, and, more recently, in most of Forster's novels, including *The Longest Journey* and *Passage to India.*) In the case of the story of Hylas, the original legend is itself largely homosexual, concerned with the love of Hercules for Hylas and Hylas's drowning at the hands of the nymphs. But it also offers the possibility for the celebration of male beauty.

In fact, Taylor suspends his narrative long enough to linger over the form of young Hylas:

> Naked, save one light robe that from his shoulder
> Hung to his knee, the youthful flush revealing
> Of warm, white limbs, half-nerved with coming
> manhood,
> Yet fair and smooth with tenderness of
> beauty.

Taylor places Hylas at exactly the point preferred by the Greeks, the brief moment of flowering before the first signs of manhood (in Greek pederasty, the younger lover lost his charm the moment he began to grow a beard):

> manhood's blossom
> Not yet had sprouted on his chin, but freshly
> Curved the fair cheek, and full the red lips, parting,
> Like a loose bow, that just has launched its arrow.
> His large blue eyes, with joy dilate and beamy,
> Were clear as the unshadowed Grecian heaven;
> Dewy and sleek his dimpled shoulders rounded
> To the white arms and whiter breast between them.
> Downward, the supple lines had less of softness:
> His back was like a god's; his loins were moulded
> As if some pulse of power began to waken.[6]

There is considerable power in these lines and in their evocation of the barely confined erotic strength of the youth. Taylor's language is, as usual, highly uneven. His simile for the lips is, if extravagant, effective and sensual, but his image for the eyes, "dilate and beamy," can only be called awkward. The last line cited above, with its strong iambic beat and effective use of short, heavy words and the repeated *p,* conveys well the effect that Taylor is seeking, however. In such moments his verse almost seems to come alive, to be awakened from its own lethargy.

Taylor's most recent critic has argued that this poem is "about nothing important; it has no reverberating echoes or suggestions of larger meaning. It comes close to being 'pure poetry,' for it is unrelated to anything else, including human experience."[7] While one can understand the reasons for such a statement, and even see a certain truth in it, it is only a half-truth originating in the critic's inability to imagine what Taylor's poem tries to do. He apparently does not see that the story of the death-nymphs and their victory over the body of the beautiful boy is a major element in homosexual mythology. This story has remained one of the most important myths for homosexuals because it "explains" the transformation of the young lover into a heterosexual and hence his loss. Read mythically, the story says: Hercules loves Hylas until the day that Hylas is about to become a man; at that point he becomes attractive to women who seduce him and thereby kill him; Hercules is left mourning for a lost love. The myth blames women for their destruction of homosexual love, as in the story of Orpheus, or more recently in Eliot's "Prufrock." It also portrays homosexuality as a lost ideal, a state once enjoyed but now vanished, which one can only recapture in the imagination. Such a reading of the myth clearly underlies Taylor's adoption of it. Taylor's **"Hylas"** is indeed related to human experience: it is deeply related to Taylor's understanding of himself as a homosexual. His choice of the Hylas myth as a poetic subject is part of an attempt at self-definition as well as part of an attempt to situate himself in a poetic tradition which will justify his own emotional life. The failure of the poem comes from Taylor's inability to avow fully his real subject: the love of Hercules for Hylas, and, through that, the author's own love for young men. In Marlowe wit and humor carry the day. For the sentimental Taylor there can be no such baroque pleasures. His language is luxuriant but finally vague; unable to depict directly the body of love, it wanders off into a succession of similes.

The importance of the myth of Hylas for Taylor and his circle is clear. In 1852 Richard Henry Stoddard published his *Poems,* which he "dedicated to my friend, Bayard Taylor, whom I admire as a poet and love as a man." In that volume also appeared Stoddard's "Arcadian Idyl," depicting an encounter between Lycidas and Theocritus and illustrating the differences between two personalities and two poetic styles. Most of the poem is a dramatic monologue spoken by Lycidas, who recalls the rivalry between himself and his brother-poet, of whom he says: "I have a friend as different from myself, / As Hercules from Hylas, his delight."[8] Lycidas is the spirit of Pan—earth-bound, delicate, gentle, soft, compared to a fawn or a dove; Theocritus is the spirit of Apollo—stern, rugged, and wild, an eagle to Lycidas's nightingale. The idyl might seem a mere literary exercise if one did not remember that in the dedicatory **"Proem"** to Taylor's ***Poems of the Orient,*** addressed to Stoddard, Taylor declared that Apollo "is your God, but mine is shaggy Pan".[9] Thus it is clear that Stoddard and Taylor thought of themselves as Theocritus and Lycidas, both consciously pastoral models, and that they could also speak of their relationship in terms of Hercules and Hylas. Such references were no simple literary allusion, but functioned as an active part of the way these men saw themselves. The circle included others as well. In 1869 Edmund Clarence Stedman dedicated his *The Blameless Prince and Other Poems*[10] to Richard Henry Stoddard and included his "Hylas" (called a translation) as well as a sonnet to Bayard Taylor. Two years later Stoddard's *The Book of the East and Other Poems*[11] included his sonnet to Stedman, "With Shakespeare's Sonnets," regretting that they lived "an age too late" for the world Shakespeare evoked in his sonnet, "where love and friendship blend."

Although the homosexual circle of genteel poets to which Taylor, Stoddard, and Stedman belonged cast its work most often in classical and pastoral molds or exploited exotic scenes and Shakespearean allusions, Taylor increasingly moved away from these strategies toward a greater directness. This change was reflected in part by Taylor's shift, beginning in the 1860s, from writing poetry and travel narratives to writing distinctly realistic fiction. His fiction may have been influenced by a more general change in taste, as a concern for detail and the picturesque increasingly replaced a taste for the colossal and sublime. One can see this shift in the arts, for instance, in an important early work of realism such as Whistler's *Twelve Etchings From Nature* (1859). But there may also have been a more specific source in the work of Whitman, who seems likely to have influenced Taylor toward adopting a realistic form for his treatment of homosexual love. With the realistic treatment of character and setting came not only a new concern for social issues but also an interest in homosexual rights, which replaced what had previously been a concern simply for male beauty.

The world of the East had been an important element in Taylor's development and self-definition. As he put it in **"L'Envoi"** to ***Poems of the Orient,***

> I found among those Children of the Sun,
> The cipher of my nature,—the release
> Of baffled powers, which else had never won
> That free fulfillment, whose reward is peace.[12]

The theme of the Northerner discovering a land of warmth, beauty, and love is familiar, of course, and one that very often has homosexual meaning.

It is probably nowhere better expressed than in Mann's "Death in Venice," but Mann was himself drawing upon von Platen, and one could equally well cite Lawrence, Forster, von Gloeden, Gide, and many others, all of whose works link the ancient gods and an older, darker, civilization that remained in touch with the primitive sources of sensuality. For Taylor, journeys to the East provided a "cipher," a way to understand his own nature and to realize his own sexuality. In the first stage of his development these experiences led to a dream of the recovery of lost innocence, a pastoral reverie:

> The Poet said: I will here abide,
> In the Sun's unclouded door;
> Here are the wells of all delight
> On the lost Arcadian shore. . . .[13]

In ***Joseph and His Friend*** Taylor specifically considered the Arcadian dream and rejected it, calling instead for social and personal change to alter the condition of the homosexual in America.

In this novel, his fourth, Taylor turned to the subject matter he knew best: life in southeastern Pennsylvania, where a quiet, conservative Quaker faith survived only a short distance from the urban cultural center of Philadelphia. He subtitled his novel **"A Story of Pennsylvania,"** thereby leading a number of critics to imagine that "rural life" or "rural poverty" is the subject of the novel. The realistic depiction of life in rural Pennsylvania is, in fact, only a backdrop for a story of homosexual love and homosexual identity. (Perhaps the critics who saw only the superficial elements to the story are to be preferred to an earlier critic who wrote, "It is an unpleasant story of mean duplicity and painful mistakes. The characters are shallow and the surroundings shabby. There is not a single pleasing situation or incident in the book."[14] With this brief judgment, a 300-page study of Taylor dismisses the novel.) Taylor clearly states his intentions in the preface and on the title page. Twice he quotes Shakespeare's Sonnet 144, which begins "Two loves I have," citing the third and fourth lines,

> The better angel is a man right fair,
> The worser spirit a woman colour'd ill.

His novel is an elaboration on this theme, a young man torn between two lovers, the "better" a man, the "worser" a woman. And his preface declares his intention to demonstrate "the truth and tenderness of man's love for man, as of man's love for woman."[15]

The hero, Joseph Aster, who is undoubtedly partially autobiographical, is an early example of what would become a classic model for the homosexual in fiction well into the twentieth century. Joseph is "shy and sensitive," an orphan living with his aunt and attached to his dead mother, cut off from the larger community, which Taylor depicts as "coarse" and "rude." In the first section of the novel, Joseph yearns for companionship. But Taylor, significantly, does not view Joseph's timidity and awkwardness as failures in themselves, but as the products of a social and religious attitude that has taught him to reject his own body, which "they tell me to despise." Joseph senses the goodness of his body and rejects the attitude of the community for the "comfort and delight" of the body. (It is interesting at this point to compare Taylor's very Whitman-like "The Bath," with its opening lines:

> Off, fetters of the falser life,—
> Weeds, that conceal the statue's form!
>
> . . . . .
>
> Now fall the thin disguises, planned
> For men too weak to walk unblamed:
> Naked beside the sea I stand,—
> Naked and not ashamed.[16]

Here too Taylor recalls a symbolic undressing, which represents a conversion to the values of the truer, inner self.)

Joseph's extreme loneliness leads him to an engagement with Julia Blessing, a scheming, vain gold-digger. But on his way back from Philadelphia, where he is engaged, "All at once his eye was attracted by a new face," a stranger in the train—Taylor makes clear the sexual nature of this attraction: "Joseph dropped his eyes in some confusion, but not until he had caught the full, warm, intense expression of those that met them."[17] At this critical juncture the train derails, and Joseph awakens in the arms of the stranger. For whatever reason, Taylor could not depict realistically the interaction between the two men and so relies instead on the almost-comic conventional device of the derailment. The stranger, Philip Held (his surname is German for *hero*) becomes a spokesman for a much more conscious homosexuality than the rather vague yearnings of Joseph. Held explains to Joseph, "there are needs which most men have, and go on all their lives hungering for, because they expect them to be supplied in a particular form."[18] Lacking a "form" for the expression of their love, "most men" settle for an exclusively heterosexual life and remain permanently unsatisfied. Philip becomes Joseph's mentor, and, incidentally, the first fictional spokesman for gay liberation in American literature.

Despite Joseph's marriage and a series of parallel subplots on the theme of hopeless love, Philip's confidence in the future is unshaken, and he declares: "there must be a loftier faith, a juster law, for the men—and the women—who cannot shape themselves according to the common-place pattern of society,—who are born with instincts, needs, knowledge, and rights—ay, rights—of their own!"[19] In an age when homosexuals were not mentioned at all or were seen as repulsive sinners, Bayard Taylor created a hero who would defend the right to be different, different from birth on, and who would declare that such people have rights. "The world needs," says Philip, "a new code of ethics. . . . But it would need more than a Luther for such a Reformation."

At the end of the novel, Joseph goes off to the West in search of the valley of which he and Philip dream, an Edenic place of contentment and freedom where their love might finally find expression. But Bayard Taylor no longer believed that only one such place existed, nor that California alone offered it. And so Joseph writes back to Philip:

> Philip, Philip, I have found your valley!
>
> . . . there were lakes glimmering below; there were groves of ilex on the hillsides, an orchard of oranges, olives, and vines in the hollow, millions of flowers hiding the earth, pure winds, fresh waters, and remoteness from all conventional society. I have never seen a landscape so broad, so bright, so beautiful![20]

It is exactly the valley of which Philip had spoken, and if its "real" place is California, its literary place is Arcadia. But Joseph's spiritual growth has been such that he now recognizes the impossibility of believing that he and Philip can find love together by going there:

> Yes, but we will only go there on one of these idle epicurean journeys of which we dream, and then to enjoy the wit and wisdom of our generous friend, not to seek a refuge from the perversions of the world! For I have learned another thing, Philip: the freedom we craved is not a thing to be found in this or that place. Unless we bring it with us, we shall not find it.[21]

With those words, Joseph spoke also for Bayard Taylor himself. Taylor was recounting his own growth in understanding. He too had begun by believing in a valley of bliss, a place somewhere out there, a new world where men might love each other without fear of conventional society. He gave expression to that belief in a literature of escapism, which sought a primitive Paradise not unlike Melville's Typee, but with the beauty of Greece—and Greek love—as well. (Indeed Melville called his island Golden Lands "authentic Edens in a pagan sea.") One thinks of all the nineteenth-century, as well as twentieth-century, homosexuals travelling in quest of the great, good place: Melville in the South Seas, Stevenson in Samoa, T. E. Lawrence in Arabia, D. H. Lawrence in Mexico, André Gide in Tangiers, Oscar Wilde in Paris. Bayard Taylor recognized that homosexuals could only gain their freedom by creating a better world for themselves by daring to be free.

The search for a place for love had therefore to begin with the self. Taylor provides us with a memorable image of the two lovers:

> They took each other's hands. The day was fading, the landscape was silent, and only the twitter of nesting birds was heard in the boughs above them. Each gave way to the impulse of his manly love, rarer, alas! but as tender and true as the love of women, and they drew nearer and kissed each other. As they walked back and parted on the highway, each felt that life was not wholly unkind, and that happiness was not yet impossible.[22]

The image is undoubtedly romantic, even melodramatic by our standards, but how else was one to depict forbidden love? The convention of the time provided no form, no place for the love of two men, and so a writer who wanted to be honest found himself almost inevitably appealing to his readers' emotions as well as to their reason. One can see the same kind of thing in the romanticism of Forster's *Maurice,* written 40 years later and judged unpublishable, or that of Lawrence's novel of forbidden love, *Lady Chatterly's Lover.*

We can regret that we do not see Philip and Joseph together at the end of the novel, that Taylor can give us no idea of their life together. But we must also remember that this is because such a life was simply unimaginable. Taylor took the important first step. He liberated the literature of homosexuality from the pretense of Greek landscape. His characters are realistic and believable. They inhabit middle-class America. The birds that twitter above them are sparrows; not nightingales. He can bring Philip and Joseph to their "nest"; whether their offspring could learn to fly, he left to his successors.

Notes

1. Bayard Taylor, *Joseph and His Friend,* Household Edition (New York, 1875), p. 216. First edition published 1870.
2. See Leo Marx, *The Machine in the Garden* (New York, 1964) pp. 22-23.
3. "On Leaving California," in *Poetical Works of Bayard Taylor,* Household Edition (Boston, 1883), pp. 92-93.
4. *Poetical Works,* pp. 62-63.
5. Line 12, for example, cites Hafiz.
6. *Poetical Works,* pp. 72-75.
7. Paul C. Wermuth, *Bayard Taylor* (New York, 1973), p. 115.
8. Richard Henry Stoddard, *Poems* (Boston, 1852), pp. 70-73.
9. *Poems of the Orient* (Boston, 1855), p. 10.
10. *The Blameless Prince and Other Poems* (Boston, 1869).
11. *The Book of the East and Other Poems* (Boston, 1871), p. 178.
12. *Poems of the Orient,* p. 161.
13. "The Poet in the East," *Poems of Orient,* p. 21.
14. Albert H. Smyth, *Bayard Taylor* (Boston, 1896), p. 177.
15. *Joseph,* preface.
16. "The Bath," *Poetical Works,* pp. 90-91.
17. *Joseph,* pp. 90-91.
18. *Ibid.,* p. 95.
19. *Ibid.,* p. 214.
20. *Ibid.,* p. 355.
21. *Ibid.*
22. *Ibid.,* p. 217.

Paul C. Wermuth (essay date 1997)

SOURCE: Introduction to *Selected Letters of Bayard Taylor,* Bucknell University Press, 1997, pp. 17-31.

[*In the following introduction, Wermuth offers a survey of Taylor's career and his place in the literary climate of the 1800s.*]

> "Well—if I were to write about myself for six hours, it would all come to this: that Life is, for me, the developing, asserting and establishing of my own *Entelcheia*—the making all that is possible out of such powers as I may have, without violently forcing or disturbing them. You have often, no doubt, wondered at and condemned the variety of things I have either wilfully attempted or been compelled to do by the necessities of my life. I see the use of all these attempts now, when I am beginning to concentrate instead of scatter: if I am capable of good and lasting work, there is nothing I have hitherto done which will not now help me to achieve it. All's well that ends well: Yes, but the end is not yet come. it's enough that I'm not afraid of it."
>
> —Letter to E. C. Stedman, 16 Jan. 1874

This collection of Bayard Taylor's letters introduces the modern reader to an interesting, complex, and neglected figure in our literary history. Among other things, these letters form a sort of autobiography; most of the main events of Taylor's life are touched on here, and they are remarkably various and significant. In many ways, Taylor embodied the American dream, for he was a poor farm boy who rose through his own hard work, ambition, and talent to become one of the most famous Americans of his time, one who ultimately hobnobbed with kings and princes, presidents and politicians, and who knew all the literary men of his day.

The route to success that he chose (or that chose him) was not railroads, gold-mining, or retailing, but literature—an unlikely choice; for while literary persons may acquire fame within their circle, it seldom extends beyond to the larger world. Yet Taylor became acquainted with many famous persons outside of literature, and many of his works were widely popular with the general public. This was probably due more largely to his travel books and his lecture tours than to any other activity. In the midst of all this, however, he worked steadily and devotedly at his poetry, which he conceived was what he was really about.

Taylor insisted all his life that his real calling was poetry and that he cared much less about the prose work that constitutes the great bulk of his output and that actually supported him. His poetry, while technically skillful, has come to be thought often conventional and abstract, out of tune with the taste of our time. In fact, his prose is among his best work, highly professional and effective. These letters showcase his prose which, though hastily written, is nonetheless often sparkling, lively, humorous, and insightful. They bring him before the reader with force and intimacy, and remind us what a remarkable person he was. Taylor's mind was interesting in ways that ought to be significant to a modern reader, for he was widely read, intellectually curious, and had a subtle mind of great range, actively engaged with the ideas and movements of his time. As his letters to Charles M. Jones show, for example, he was aware of the latest information in biblical archaeology, and his religious views were advanced for his time.

These letters reveal a great deal about American life. Bayard Taylor was born into an exciting time. His career spanned the middle years of the nineteenth century, a period of rapid change, of growth and consolidation, of western expansion. He was "present at the creation" of the railroads, the change from sail to steam on the seas, the gold rush, the opening of Japan, the Civil War, the laying of the transatlantic cable, the growth of the big cities, the Indian wars in the west. Travelling to the far corners of the earth was a large part of his occupation for some years; but he also covered much of the United States, for his domestic travels were extensive and frequent.

The letters also provide much information about the literary world in the mid-nineteenth century. In many ways, Taylor's was a representative literary career; he frequently asserted his view of authorship as a vocation and a profession, exercised by brother poets around the world, no matter what the language. He had an exalted—some might say unrealistic—view of the importance of poetry in society, somewhat like that held by Shelley. At the same time, he claimed he was forced into the grubbiest sort of hack work in order to sustain himself and his family—"buying his time," as he often expressed it. No doubt his experience led him to qualify his expectations considerably, but he retained his cheerful faith in the importance and primacy of his poetic work throughout his life.

There is considerable information in these letters about how a writer earned a living during a time when writing alone could hardly sustain one. In our own time, writers appear to be doing well. The book-buying public is much larger compared with that of Taylor's time; and modern writers have outlets that didn't exist then—movies, television, and other sources. There are more magazines and newspapers today, too. Yet perhaps the leading patron of writers now is the university; any institution of higher learning with the least pretension has to have a resident poet and/or novelist, sometimes several, on generous stipend. How Taylor would have prized such a sinecure!

Beyond the university, however, some writers now live lives of comfort unimagined in the mid-nineteenth century. With a bit of luck, like a best-selling novel, movie rights, talk show appearances, even middling authors have become quite rich. Norman Mailer may not be typical, but he startled many when, during a recent court case, he asserted that he needed $400,000 a year just to make ends meet. Certainly the value of money now is not the same, but even allowing for that, Bayard Taylor's total income after a life of constant and assiduous labor never came close to such a sum. (According to a notebook in the Houghton Library at Harvard, to the end of 1872—six years before his death—Taylor had earned $185,241 from all sources: writing, lecturing, copyrights, and dividends.)

For the nineteenth-century writer, book publication was most desirable, though not often profitable unless lightning struck (as it did with Taylor's first travel book). Books were more prized then, but the audience was not nearly so large; a book that sold ten thousand copies (at $1 or $1.50) was considered a good success, though the author might earn only $1,000 or $1,500 on 10 or 12 percent of the list price. There were no modern agents, no million-dollar advances on books not yet written; an author generally dealt directly with his publisher and took the best terms he could get.

For most writers, other sources of income were necessary, and most easy to hand was journalism—newspapers and periodicals. Most did not pay very well—Taylor at the height of his career could get $25 to $50 for a poem, $50 to $200 for an article in a prestigious journal like the *Atlantic Monthly.* At such rates, one had to publish frequently; but there weren't many journals of quality, and one couldn't appear too often in the few that existed.

Many writers thus chose to become staff writers at a regular salary. Taylor was associated for most of his career with Horace Greeley's New York *Tribune,* and most of the writers he knew became associated with one or more papers or magazines. William Cullen Bryant edited and published the New York *Evening Post;* Walt Whitman wrote for and edited various newspapers; William Dean Howells edited the *Atlantic Monthly* and later, *Harper's Magazine;* Richard Stoddard, E. C. Stedman, T. B. Aldrich, G. W. Curtis, Donald Mitchell, William Winter, and many others of Taylor's friends were staff writers or editors at various times.

In an age without radio or television, the lecture circuit was a busy and lively activity, offering income to those with speaking skills and interesting experiences. Many writers derived some sustenance from it, including Emerson, Thoreau, Lowell, and many others. Lecturing became a mainstay of Taylor's income; he lectured assiduously for many years, sometimes giving two hundred lectures in a season. It was a grueling activity, however, dependent on train schedules, constant movement, bad food and housing, and—according to Taylor—much impertinent curiosity about one's personal life. He came to hate it passionately, and frequently announced his retirement from it, but he kept doing it because he needed the money.

Political appointment was a distant hope for a few. Best known was probably Nathaniel Hawthorne, who worked in the Salem Custom House and later became Consul at

Liverpool; he helped get Stoddard a job at the New York Custom House. Washington Irving, James Russell Lowell, Howells, George Boker, Motley, and of course Taylor himself secured posts of some sort, though the tenure in such diplomatic places was likely to be relatively brief, lasting only until the next change of administration in Washington. Bayard Taylor served as chargé d'affaires in St. Petersburg, Russia, for about six months, and it was helpful to his reputation, not to mention his bank account. Near the end of his life he secured the prize of ambassador to Germany; but unfortunately he died only a few months after assuming the post.

The university was not yet a haven for the creative writer. Longfellow, one of the few who did teach, worked at Bowdoin and Harvard; Lowell also taught during the later part of his career, and so did Henry Adams. Though Taylor had never attended college, the lengthy and serious work on his translation of Goethe's *Faust* gave him something of a scholarly reputation; and he was offered on the strength of it an appointment at Cornell as a nonresident professor of German, giving a series of lectures there, which were repeated in other cities.

Taylor had yet another source of income: an investment. With some of his profits from his first book, a best-selling travel book titled ***Views A-Foot: or Europe seen with Knapsack and Staff,*** he purchased several shares in the New York *Tribune,* which stood him in good stead for many years. The largest number he owned, I believe, was six and the fewest was three (he sometimes sold one when desperate, or might mortgage one.) Sometimes these shares paid him as much as $1300 each; sometimes they paid nothing at all. But it was a good investment, for the *Tribune* became one of the leading papers in the country, constantly expanding and developing a strong reputation under Horace Greeley.

Taylor used nearly all these sources of income at one time or another. He had to labor constantly to turn out material that would bring in money, so that he could have time in which to write his poetry. Along the way he developed middle-class virtues not always associated with writers: he did the work contracted for; he met his deadlines; he paid his debts; he was reliable. Though he detested some of the work he had to do, he always did the best work he was capable of. Publishers trusted him, and his friends did, too.

Taylor's career is instructive to those interested in the relationship between literature and journalism. He seems not to have actively disliked journalism, though he thought it inferior to his "real" work. Perhaps a distinction ought to be suggested between journalism and real "hack" work, like compiling cyclopedias and anthologies. Taylor usually described work as "hack" when he worked only for money; and he often used the word "literature" to refer to his general occupation as a writer. However, Taylor was an excellent journalist, and the *Tribune* trusted him with first-class assignments throughout his career.

Still, the transition from one to the other is not easy for some writers to make, and journalism is alleged to encourage habits of composition that may be fatal to serious and thoughtful literary work. One of the complaints against Taylor was that his work was facile, that he wrote easily and quickly, organizing pieces in his mind before he began to write. Considering the quantity of work he produced, such a technique must have been vitally necessary. The reader may see still other things in Taylor's work related to this conflict. Some journalists even today pass easily back and forth from the literary world to the journalistic one, as Taylor did, and how much each world affects the other is a matter for speculation.

> He is, unquestionably, the most terse, glowing, and vigorous of all our poets, young or old—in point, I mean, of *expression.*
>
> —Edgar Allan Poe

When Taylor moved to New York in 1848, an older generation of literary men was soon to pass from the scene. Edgar Allan Poe would die in 1849; James Fenimore Cooper in 1851. Washington Irving, in retirement at Sunnyside, had a few more years; William Cullen Bryant alone was still active as editor of the New York *Evening Post.* New England now held a firm grip on the literary world; the transcendentalists were prominent, with Emerson their leader; and the Genteel poets—Longfellow, Lowell, Holmes, Whittier—were fairly launched on their careers. Nathaniel Hawthorne was the leading novelist, at least critically. Taylor's generation was the next one, ten to twenty years younger, but generally respectful of the New England writers at the same time they hoped to better them.

The New York literary world was a confusing but lively cacophony of voices; a horde of writers worked for the various newspapers and magazines both there and in Philadelphia (though New York was rapidly eclipsing the latter city). Taylor was thus engaged in a competitive struggle with a host of would-be writers striving to make a name for themselves; it was a world in which, with his ambition and skill—and the head start he got from his early book—he quickly saw that he could compete and even succeed.

It was a close-knit world, where everyone knew everyone else, and reviewing was not often the objective judgment one would like to think. Authors often damned their enemies and praised their friends. Influence counted, too, in getting ahead. In his biography of Taylor, Albert Smyth says that at the time Taylor briefly edited the *Union Magazine* in 1848, Greeley handed him a manuscript with the admonition to "do something for this young man," who was named Henry Thoreau. Taylor paid $75 for the essay (on Ktaadn), only to suffer the wrath of Thoreau when it was published with a typographical error. Taylor's satirical account of the New York literary world makes up the best part of his novel ***John Godfrey's Fortunes,*** which conveys a keen sense of the time and circumstances.

Taylor knew all the important literary men of his day. He was friendly with Longfellow, Lowell, Whittier, Holmes;

he knew Bancroft and Prescott, Emerson and Thoreau, Melville and Whitman, Greeley and Dana and Hay; he knew Mark Twain and Henry James and William Dean Howells, and any number of lesser lights. A sketcher and painter himself, he was friendly with artists, too: Hiram Powers, William Wetmore Story, Jarvis McEntee, Eastman Johnson; and he knew famous persons, like Edwin Booth, Cyrus McCormick, and P. T. Barnum. Mark Twain refers to him several times in his books as though his name needed no footnote.

Taylor was also part of the transatlantic literary world. Through his travels he met most of the reigning literary lights of Europe. In England, he visited and was entertained by Tennyson and Browning and Arnold; Swinburne and Carlyle and Rossetti, and many others. He met Victor Hugo and Alexandre Dumas; he knew most of the contemporary German authors, and Scandinavian writers like Hans Christian Andersen were included in his large acquaintance. He was one of the most sophisticated men of his time, far beyond most American authors in his knowledge of foreign literatures and writers. He was also a translator, mostly from German. He served as an intermediary between American and German literature, and helped establish a firm connection between the two in an age when things German were coming rapidly to the fore. Many of his books were translated into various languages and published around the world.

All these constitute good reasons for printing these letters, most of which have not been published before, and those that have were never printed in their entirety. They bring before us a world in which there is no electricity, no radio, television, or telephone, no automobiles, and it was not easy to get from here to there. It is a fascinating world to a modern reader, for its inhabitants, despite what we might consider the shortcomings of their situation, managed nonetheless to live full and exciting lives, and to accomplish a great deal.

> When men who are now fifty years old were boys, there was not a youth in the country who did not know of Bayard Taylor and hope to do as he had done.
>
> —Theodore Dreiser

Although Bayard Taylor was one of the most famous and successful writers of his day, today he is almost unknown. Many writers vanish from public consciousness after their demise, only to have their reputations restored years later to some more deserving status. This has not happened to Taylor in the 117 years since his death in 1878. At that time, there was a flurry of appreciative articles, and two biographies followed soon after, as well as the standard *Life and Letters* by his wife and H. E. Scudder. Since that time, there has been only an occasional notice, although in the 1930s there was a small flurry of interest, not entirely favorable, which quickly faded. His virtual disappearance since that time seems unusual, since Taylor was not only one of the most productive of nineteenth-century authors, but was widely known through his travels; he lectured hundreds of times all over the country and was known to millions. He was, in short, what we today might call a "celebrity," but with a difference. While luck may form part of anyone's fame, and Taylor had luck, his career was sustained over many years by his intelligence, ability, and personality, all of which were considerable.

Indeed, his career illustrates much about the relationship between authorship and public life. Literary men in the nineteenth century had more of a chance than today of being appointed to a diplomatic post—possibly because literary activity was more widely appreciated among a smaller reading public. Washington Irving was ambassador to Spain, Motley to the Dutch Republic, Lowell was ambassador to England, Hawthorne was consul at Liverpool; Taylor's friend George Boker was ambassador, at different times, to Turkey, and to Russia; and William Dean Howells was consul at Venice. Taylor's political career might be said to have begun when he was sent by the *Tribune* to California to report on the gold rush, or shortly after, when he joined Admiral Perry's expedition to open Japan to Western trade. (Perry himself urged Taylor to apply for the job of Commissioner to Japan.) But those were essentially journalistic assignments. It was 1862 when he got his first real diplomatic post as secretary to the new Minister to Russia, Simon Cameron. Cameron did not stay long, and tried, in vain, to help Taylor succeed to the post. However, Taylor served as chargé d'affaires (and the only representative of the United States) for some months, and from all accounts, performed in an exemplary manner.

Next he was tantalized with a post in Persia, which did not materialize, and through the rest of his life he was rumored for other places—Brussels, Russia, Turkey. In the early 1870s he made some attempt to get appointed to Switzerland, but he finally landed the one job he most wanted—Minister to Germany—in 1878; unfortunately, by then his health was failing, and he died about six months after assuming the post, at the age of fifty-three.

It is not difficult to see why literary men coveted such positions. Generally, they paid well for little work (since any ambassador has secretaries to perform most of the hard work); and the job provides free time to write if managed properly. Those were the chief reasons Taylor was interested. However, the social requirements of the job occupy much of one's time, so the vision of being free to write often proves illusory—as it did for Taylor.

It is hard to say if his political career helped or hindered him. It helped in spreading his fame, in introducing him to many world figures; but at the same time it took away time he badly needed to plan out his work, to think about it, and to write more slowly and carefully. It did supply him with money which he usually needed badly. Taylor's life was a constant struggle between money and time, and the former usually won. Though he complained bitterly many times of the things he had to do to survive, that was to some extent due to the lifestyle he adopted, which was far above that of his compeers. After all, he did not *have* to build a large mansion and entertain friends there with some lavishness.

Toward the end of his life he began to realize this and made an effort to live more modestly, concentrating more on his poetry and scholarship. He gave up Cedarcroft to his family and lived in an apartment in New York city, returning to regular editorial work at the *Tribune,* and making fewer lecture forays.

In a relatively brief career of about thirty-two years, Taylor produced a remarkably extensive body of published material. He published nearly fifty books, and so much journalistic material—articles, reviews, criticism—that it would be a heavy task to collect it all. His poetry included odes, sonnets, pastorals, dramas, lyrics, in almost every conceivable form; he wrote occasional verse for the nation's centennial, for monuments to Goethe, to Shakespeare, to Fitzgreen Halleck, for the battle of Gettysburg and other events. He wrote novels and short stories, even a book of stories for boys; he wrote a history of Germany; he edited cyclopedias and a series of travel books; and he translated to and from German. And he lectured like fury, constantly; Smyth, in his biography, says that between January and May, 1854, Taylor filled ninety lecture engagements, and that fall delivered one hundred and thirty more. And in addition to all this, he carried on a huge correspondence; he told a friend once that he had written 150 letters over four days. Taylor letters available in libraries number around 4,000 with, probably, many more not yet discovered.

Indeed, diffuseness was one of the main criticisms of Taylor even during his lifetime. It was frequently asserted that he tried too many things without reaching excellence in any one of them. His answer to this was that he wrote to survive; that he didn't have the freedom to pick and choose what he wanted to do most.

> He was a very lovable man.
>
> —Mark Twain

Some of his success is accounted for by his personality, which by most accounts was unusually attractive. Readers of these letters cannot help seeing that his normal condition was cheerful and optimistic. He could not be down for long; even after his worst disappointments, he managed to find a bright side, quickly persuading himself that all was for the best, and looking eagerly to the next great event. He even talked that way about his books; the next one was always going to be the best. People liked him, and not only his intimate friends. He was helpful, generous, and kind to others; he loaned friends money (when he had it), praised their work, and often helped get it published, sometimes wrote favorable reviews of their books, constantly urged them on to greater tasks, shared his thoughts and failures as well as his successes. He had a keen sense of the camaraderie of authorship. Furthermore he recognized talent when he saw it, and constantly praised new writers, like Howells, John Hay, Bret Harte, and Sidney Lanier.

The question remains how someone who was so famous could pass into obscurity so quickly and completely. This collection of letters might suggest some answers; perhaps the reader may even decide that his neglect has been undeserved. But there ought to be some hope for a more just assessment of someone as talented and engaging as Bayard Taylor.

All this is not to say that Taylor was a paragon. He had his weaknesses, of course. He had a colossal ego, for instance, and an overweening ambition to succeed and make his mark. He was not beyond whining self-pity at times, or petulance, or pettiness. He had a desperate need for recognition, for approval by others, especially the established New England poets—as if he didn't really know if his work was good or not. He courted their praise at times in an almost sycophantic manner, and was irritated when his friends did not rush to praise his latest work. His letters illustrate various defenses and evasions, many of them ingenious and circuitous.

Some recent writers have tended to emphasize his shortcomings, as if they negated his many virtues. Fortunately, the reader will be able to judge, since here he will see complete letters rather than excerpts. These letters have not been selected to emphasize any particular view; they have been chosen for their intrinsic interest, and at times show Taylor at both his best and his worst.

> What he achieved in diverse and often difficult fields was always excellent and artistically perfect, but he didn't startle his readers into sudden admiration or snatch them into muddled raptures as less significant writers often do.
>
> —Bret Harte

From the great number of letters available, I have chosen about 276 as among the most interesting. The bases of such choice were several. I eliminated many that were brief replies to inquiries, invitations to lecture, making appointments, supplying autographs to collectors, and so forth. In addition, I passed over much early material, in favor of his more mature letters. There are some early letters here, to give the flavor of his youthful enthusiasm; but much of this material, including his letters to his first wife, Mary Agnew, which are sweet and sentimental, is sufficiently represented in *Life and Letters,* as are letters to his mother and most other relatives (except his sister Annie and his brother Fred).

I have tended to emphasize literary matters in most choices—opinions about other writers and works; advice on writing and verse forms; interpretations of his own work and of others; comments on the literary world and on ideas current; meetings with literary persons. Nevertheless, there is a good bit of personal information in the letters, too. And of course, the importance of the persons he was writing to is taken into consideration.

Financial information seemed important—how much he was paid for work, how much he earned at different times, how much income he had from Tribune shares, and so forth. Taylor was unusually open about such matters with his friends; perhaps he was boasting, but there are frequently times when he bemoans the fact that he is practically broke, and living from day to day.

The persons Taylor wrote to most extensively and often were George Boker, Richard and Elizabeth Stoddard, E. C. Stedman, Thomas Bailey Aldrich, John Phillips, and Jarvis McEntee. Often, he wrote to several of them at the same time, and thus the letters contain overlapping information. In such a case I chose one over others because it contained some interesting details. For example, in one of his letters to Aldrich he tells of having breakfast with Henry James in Italy, and expresses an opinion of James's work. This also partly accounts for the absence of letters to some of these persons over periods of time.

There were hiatuses in some of the correspondence. He wrote to George Boker all his life, but after Boker gave up literature, the letters are briefer and more perfunctory much of the time. After several quarrels with the Stoddards, there was a long hiatus in their correspondence. And after John Phillips moved to Minnesota, their correspondence dried up for some years, but was revived in the 1860s.

As younger generations came to the fore, Taylor forged friendships with them, too. Stedman and Aldrich and McEntee were younger than Taylor, as were Lanier, Howells, and Mark Twain. Correspondence with them begins years later than that with his earlier friends. Surprisingly, he managed to move, in his relatively brief life, from *enfant terrible* to *eminence grise.* In all, the wide variety of his correspondence is one of its most remarkable features. . . .

FURTHER READING

Biographies

Hansen-Taylor, Marie. *On Two Continents: Memories of Half a Century.* New York: Doubleday, Page & Company, 1905, 309 p.

Offers first-hand examinations of Taylor's life and writing process, written by Taylor's second wife.

Von Frank, Albert J. "Bayard Taylor and the Boston Millionaire: An Unpublished Letter." In *Resources for American Literary Study,* X, No. 2 (1990): 187-90.

Explores the question of how Taylor found financial backing for his many voyages.

Criticism

Sherbo, Arthur. "Tennysonia I: Bayard Taylor and C. V. Stanford in the Cambridge Review." In *The Tennyson Research Bulletin,* 5, No. 4, (November 1990): 182-95.

Examines Taylor's criticism on the works of Tennyson, and his interpretation of the latter's influences.

Wermuth, Paul C. "'My Full, Unreserved Self': Bayard Taylor's Letters to Charles Melancthon Jones." In *Resources for American Literary Study,* XVII, No. 2 (1991): 220-38.

Discusses Taylor's critical reaction to the work of Charles Melancthon Jones, as evinced by their correspondence.

Additional coverage of Taylor's life and career is contained in the following source published by the Gale Group: *Dictionary of Literary Biography,* Vols. 3 and 189.

How to Use This Index

The main references

Calvino, Italo 1923-1985 .... **CLC 5, 8, 11, 22, 33, 39, 73; SSC 3**

list all author entries in the following Gale Literary Criticism series:

BLC = *Black Literature Criticism*
CLC = *Contemporary Literary Criticism*
CLR = *Children's Literature Review*
CMLC = *Classical and Medieval Literature Criticism*
DA = *DISCovering Authors*
DAB = *DISCovering Authors: British*
DAC = *DISCovering Authors: Canadian*
DAM = *DISCovering Authors: Modules*
  DRAM: *Dramatists Module;* ***MST:*** *Most-Studied Authors Module;*
  MULT: *Multicultural Authors Module;* ***NOV:*** *Novelists Module;*
  POET: *Poets Module;* ***POP:*** *Popular Fiction and Genre Authors Module*
DC = *Drama Criticism*
HLC = *Hispanic Literature Criticism*
LC = *Literature Criticism from 1400 to 1800*
NCLC = *Nineteenth-Century Literature Criticism*
NNAL = *Native North American Literature*
PC = *Poetry Criticism*
SSC = *Short Story Criticism*
TCLC = *Twentieth-Century Literary Criticism*
WLC = *World Literature Criticism, 1500 to the Present*

The cross-references

See also CANR 23; CA 85-88; obituary CA116

list all author entries in the following Gale biographical and literary sources:

AAYA = *Authors & Artists for Young Adults*
AITN = *Authors in the News*
BEST = *Bestsellers*
BW = *Black Writers*
CA = *Contemporary Authors*
CAAS = *Contemporary Authors Autobiography Series*
CABS = *Contemporary Authors Bibliographical Series*
CANR = *Contemporary Authors New Revision Series*
CAP = *Contemporary Authors Permanent Series*
CDALB = *Concise Dictionary of American Literary Biography*
CDBLB = *Concise Dictionary of British Literary Biography*
DLB = *Dictionary of Literary Biography*
DLBD = *Dictionary of Literary Biography Documentary Series*
DLBY = *Dictionary of Literary Biography Yearbook*
HW = *Hispanic Writers*
JRDA = *Junior DISCovering Authors*
MAICYA = *Major Authors and Illustrators for Children and Young Adults*
MTCW = *Major 20th-Century Writers*
SAAS = *Something about the Author Autobiography Series*
SATA = *Something about the Author*
YABC = *Yesterday's Authors of Books for Children*

Literary Criticism Series Cumulative Author Index

Author Index

Author Index

Author Index

Author Index

Author Index

Author Index

Author Index

Literary Criticism Series Cumulative Topic Index

This index lists all topic entries in Gale's *Classical and Medieval Literature Criticism, Contemporary Literary Criticism, Literature Criticism from 1400 to 1800, Nineteenth-Century Literature Criticism,* and *Twentieth-Century Literary Criticism.*

NCLC Cumulative Nationality Index

FILIPINO

FINNISH

FRENCH

GERMAN

GREEK

HUNGARIAN

NCLC-89 Title Index

THE REICHSTAG FIRE

FRITZ TOBIAS

The Reichstag Fire

LEGEND AND TRUTH

Translated from the German by
ARNOLD J. POMERANS

With an Introduction by
A. J. P. TAYLOR

Secker & Warburg

LONDON

First published in England 1963 by
Martin Secker & Warburg Limited
14 Carlisle Street Soho Square W.1

Printed in England by
Bookprint Limited
London, Kingswood and Crawley

Contents

Illustrations

DIAGRAMS

The author gratefully acknowledges the help of:

the Wiener Library, London;
the International Institute for Social History, Amsterdam;
the Federal Archives, Koblenz;
the Federal Information Office, Bonn;
the State Office for Political Education, Hannover;
Chief Police Inspector J. C. Hofstede, Leyden;
Herr Ernst Torgler, Hannover;
Herr Gustav Schmidt-Kuester, Hannover;
Herr Karl-Heinz Dobbert, Berlin;
and many others.

The extracts quoted from *The Invisible Writing* and *The God That Failed* are printed by kind permission of Mr Arthur Koestler.

Introduction by A. J. P. Taylor

THE fire in the Debating Chamber of the Reichstag on 27 February 1933 has a place in all the history books. Historians, who find so much to disagree about, are for once in agreement, or were until the present book was published. National Socialists – Nazis for short – started the fire, we believed, in order to cause an anti-Communist panic in Germany and so to influence the general election, due on 5 March. The trick succeeded. The German electors took alarm. The Nazis got their majority, and Hitler was able to establish his dictatorship. The Reichstag fire not only explained the initial Nazi success. It also set the pattern for explanations of all Hitler's later acts. We saw at every stage – over rearmament, over Austria, over Czechoslovakia, over Poland – the same deliberate and conspiratorial cunning which had been first shown on 27 February 1933. Historians, writing about Nazi Germany, did not look closely at the events of that night. They took the central fact for granted: Nazis set fire to the Reichstag, and there was an end of it. Most historians were less sure how the Nazis did it. They used some equivocal phrase: 'we do not know exactly what happened'; 'the details are still to be revealed' – something of that sort. Much evidence was in fact available: police reports, fire inspectors' reports, large excerpts from the proceedings of the High Court at Leipzig, kept by Dr Sack, Torgler's counsel. Herr Tobias was the first to look at this evidence with an impartial eye. He took nothing for granted. He was not concerned to indict the Nazis, or for that matter to acquit them. He was that rare thing, a researcher for truth, out to find what happened.

His book sticks closely to the events of 27 February and to the legal or sham-legal proceedings which followed. Some knowledge of the political background may be useful. The republican constitution, created at Weimar in 1919, gave Germany an electoral system of proportional representation. No single party ever obtained an absolute majority in the Reichstag. A series of coalitions governed Germany between 1919 and 1930. Coalition broke down under the impact of the world depression. The Social

Democrats refused to carry through deflation; their former associates insisted on it. Brüning, a member of the Centre (Roman Catholic) Party, became Chancellor and imposed deflation by emergency decrees, without possessing a majority in the Reichstag. Discontent mounted. Nazis and Communists fought in the streets. In May 1932 Brüning proposed to dissolve the private armies of these two parties by emergency decree. The elderly Field-Marshal Hindenburg, President since 1925, refused. He feared that conflict with the private armies would bring the real army into politics; and this he was determined to avoid. Brüning was dismissed. Papen, another member of the Centre, became Chancellor. He, too, relied on emergency decrees. He dissolved the Reichstag in the hope of winning wider support. His hope was not fulfilled. The Nazis won 37.3 per cent of the votes cast on 31 July – their highest vote in a free election – and 230 seats in the Reichstag. Papen tried to tempt Hitler with an offer of subordinate office. Hitler refused. Papen dissolved the Reichstag again. This time the Nazis did not do so well. On 6 November they received only 33 per cent of the vote and 196 seats. Once more Hitler was offered office. Once more he refused. Papen now proposed to prorogue the Reichstag and to govern solely by Presidential decree. The army leaders declared that they would be unable to maintain order. Papen resigned. Schleicher, Hindenburg's military adviser, took his place.

Schleicher tried to strengthen his government by negotiating with trade union officials and with a few Nazis who had lost faith in Hitler. The negotiations came to nothing. On 28 January 1933 he confessed to Hindenburg that he, too, would have to rule by emergency decree. Meanwhile Papen, still intimate with Hindenburg though out of office, had been negotiating more successfully with Hitler. Hitler agreed to join a coalition government of National Socialists and Nationalists. On 30 January he became Chancellor. This was not a seizure of power. Hitler was intrigued into power by respectable politicians of the old order – principally by Papen and also by more obscure advisers round Hindenburg. Papen had, he thought, taken Hitler prisoner. There were only three Nazis in a cabinet of eleven; the key posts of foreign minister and minister of defence were in the hands of non-political experts, loyal to Hindenburg; and Hitler was not to visit Hindenburg except in the company of Papen, the Vice-Chancellor. Nazis and

Nationalists together did not have a majority. Hitler urged that yet another general election would give them a majority, and thus relieve Hindenburg from the embarrassment of issuing emergency decrees any longer. The constitutional system would be restored. This, after all, had been the object of making Hitler Chancellor.

Once more the Reichstag was dissolved. The Nazis now reaped the advantage of being in the government. Göring, Hitler's chief assistant, became head of the Prussian police; and the police naturally hesitated to act firmly against the Nazi ruffians in their brown shirts. Violence became one-sided. Communist and Social Democrat meetings were broken up. The Nazis made much of the Communist danger as an election cry. They alleged that the Communists were planning an armed rising. On 23 February the police, on Göring's orders, raided Communist headquarters in order to discover evidence of this plan. They found none. On 27 February the Reichstag went up in flames. Here, it seemed, was the decisive evidence against the Communists, provided perhaps by Heaven. Hitler announced the existence of a revolutionary conspiracy. Emergency decrees were passed, authorizing the arrest of dangerous politicians. Communists and others were sent to labour camps. As a matter of fact, the fire had singularly little effect on the general election of 5 March. The Social Democrats and Centre held their previous vote practically intact. The Communists had 70 deputies instead of 100. The National Socialist vote increased to 43.9 per cent. Even with the Nationalists, who also increased their vote a little, Hitler had only a bare majority in the Reichstag.

This was not enough for him. Hitler wished to carry an Enabling Law which would empower him to govern by decrees and thus make him a dictator by constitutional process. This Law needed a two-thirds majority in the Reichstag. The Communists were prevented from attending. The Social Democrats attended, and were solid against the Enabling Law. Decision rested with the 102 deputies of the Centre. They were lured by promises of security for Roman Catholic schools, and voted for the Law. Hitler obtained his two-thirds majority. He soon pushed aside the restrictions which Papen had tried to place upon him. He dislodged, or discredited, the Nationalist ministers; banned all parties in Germany except the National Socialist; and gradually engrossed all power in his own hands. The consequences for Germany and the world are known to us all.

On a cool retrospect, the burning of the Reichstag occupies a comparatively small place in the story of Hitler's rise to absolute power. He was Chancellor before the fire occurred; it did not much affect the electors; and they did not give him the crushing majority which he needed. The passing of the Enabling Law, not the general election, was the moment of decision. But these were not cool days. A democratic system was being destroyed in the full glare of publicity. Berlin was thronged with newspaper correspondents from foreign countries, eager for stories. With nerves on edge, everyone expected conspiracies by everyone else. The fire at the Reichstag supplied the most dramatic story of a dramatic time. It was naturally built up beyond its merits. For instance, we talk to this day as though the entire Reichstag, a great complex of rooms and building, was destroyed. In fact, only the Debating Chamber was burnt out; and the burning of a Chamber, with wooden panels, curtains dry with age, and a glass dome to provide a natural draught, was not surprising. Many other similar halls have burnt in an equally short space of time, from the old House of Commons in 1834 to the Vienna Stock Exchange a few years ago. A prosaic explanation of this kind did not suit the spirit of the time. People wanted drama; and there had to be drama.

There was, on the surface, no great mystery about the burning of the Reichstag. An incendiary was discovered: van der Lubbe, a young Dutchman. He gave a coherent account of his activities. This account made sense both to the police officers who examined him and to the fire chiefs who handled the fire. It did not suit either the Nazis or their opponents that van der Lubbe should have started the fire alone. Hitler declared, from the first moment, that the Communists had set fire to the Reichstag. They, knowing that they had not, returned the compliment and condemned the fire as a Nazi trick. Thus both sides, far from wanting to find the truth about the fire, set out on a search for van der Lubbe's accomplices. The German authorities arrested Torgler, leader of the Communists in the Reichstag, and three Bulgarian Communists. One of them, Dimitrov, was chief European representative of the Communist International, though the Germans did not know this. The four men were accused, along with van der Lubbe, before the High Court at Leipzig. The prosecution was not interested in establishing the guilt of van der Lubbe. This was both self-evident and unimportant. The prosecution was after the four Communists. It was essential to demonstrate that van der Lubbe could not have acted alone. Most of the evidence was directed to this point. It convinced the Court, and has continued to convince most of those who examined the case later. Van der Lubbe, everyone decided, had accomplices. The prosecution, however, failed to establish that the accomplices were the four men in the dock. All four were acquitted. Van der Lubbe was convicted, and executed by virtue of a special law, made retrospective for his case. His capital crime was not to have set fire to the Reichstag, but to have had accomplices in doing so.

The opponents of the Nazis outside Germany were quick to point the moral. Everyone now agreed that van der Lubbe had accomplices. The accomplices had not been found, despite all the labours of the German criminal police and the German High Court. From this it clearly seemed to follow that the accomplices were not being sought in the right place. They were, in fact, the Nazis themselves. Here was a splendid opportunity for anti-Nazi propaganda. Communist exiles used it to the full. They organized a counter-trial in London, and provided evidence for it as lavishly as Stalin did for the great 'purge' trials in Russia later. Many of those who manufactured the evidence did so in good faith. They argued that the Nazis were immeasurably wicked (which they were) and that they had set fire to the Reichstag. They must have done it in a certain way; and the evidence before the counter-trial, though actually conjecture not fact, merely showed what this way was. In those days many of us were passionately anti-Nazi, and were ready to believe any evil of them. We had, as yet, little experience of how the Communists manufactured evidence when it suited their purpose. Men of good will accepted the verdict of the counter-trial; and though they were later disillusioned by the 'purges', by the post-war trials in eastern Europe, or by the Hungarian rising in 1956, some are reluctant to admit that they were taken for a ride by the Communists as early as 1933. Much of the evidence accepted by the counter-trial has now been discredited. Everyone, for instance, now recognizes the Oberfohren Memorandum and the confession of Karl Ernst, both discussed in detail by Herr Tobias, as Communist forgeries. The central argument remains unassailed: van der Lubbe could not have set fire to the Reichstag alone. Yet the proof of this rests mainly on the evidence placed before the Leipzig High Court. The Nazis unwittingly convicted themselves; and anyone who believes in their guilt is relying on evidence which the Nazis provided – or manufactured.

Such is the background for this book. Herr Tobias has not produced new evidence. He has merely looked again at the evidence which always existed. His examination involves much detail. This is essential if we are to judge what the evidence is worth. He has had to follow many false trails, and it is exasperating when these lead to a dead end. In the original German edition, he ran after still more false trails. Some of these have been left out, in order to spare the English reader. They do not, in my judgement, affect the general picture. I do not know Herr Tobias. He was never a Nazi; nor was his book written to please the present authorities in Germany – very much the contrary. It was written in an endeavour, whether mistaken or not, to discover the truth. In my opinion, he has succeeded, so far as anyone can succeed with the evidence we have at present. The reader will, I hope, believe me when I say that I have no desire to 'acquit' the Nazis. I welcome the investigations by Herr Tobias, solely because their conclusions seem to me right.

The case against the Nazis rested on two arguments or rather assumptions: the first that van der Lubbe was a physical degenerate who was incapable of starting the fires alone; the second that it was impossible, in any case, for the fires to have been started by a single man. Herr Tobias has shaken both these assumptions. He shows that van der Lubbe was quick-witted, ingenious, and physically active. His defective eyesight was balanced, as often happens, by sensitivity in other ways. He described precisely how he had set fire to the Reichstag; and his description tallied with the evidence. The police took him through the Reichstag with a stop-watch. He covered the ground at exactly the right times. Herr Tobias also provides a convincing explanation of van der Lubbe's motives and of his later behaviour. Van der Lubbe despaired at the lack of fight shown by the Communists and other opponents of Hitler. He wished to give a signal of revolt. When his gesture failed, when indeed it helped to consolidate Hitler's dictatorship, he fell into despair. There is a cry of human tragedy in his repeated declaration to the High Court: 'I did it alone. I was there. I know.' No one believed him.

Herr Tobias shows too that the fires were not beyond the capacity of a single man. The opinion of the 'experts' against this rested on conjecture, not evidence. Thus, there is good ground for believing that van der Lubbe did it all alone, exactly as he claimed. We can go further. There is some evidence, though naturally more conjectural, that the Nazis did not do it. If they in fact started the fire, why did they so strikingly fail to provide any evidence against the Communists or even that van der Lubbe had accomplices? The Nazi leaders certainly behaved as though they were surprised when they arrived at the scene of the fire. Indeed everyone acknowledges that Hitler had no previous knowledge of the fire, and was genuinely surprised. Yet it was his spontaneous reaction in accusing the Communists which gave the Reichstag fire political significance so far as it had any. Hence even the believers in Nazi guilt must admit that Hitler's method was to grab at opportunities as they occurred, not to manufacture them beforehand. Again, there has been total failure to show how the Nazis were associated with the fire. The strongest point in Herr Tobias's book is perhaps the firm and final demonstration that neither the Nazis nor anyone else could have come through the famous 'tunnel' from Göring's house. Use of this tunnel by the Nazis was an ingenious Communist speculation, plausible only to those who knew nothing of the physical obstacles which the tunnel and its many locked doors provided. We are thus left with two conclusions. There is no firm evidence that the Nazis had anything to do with the fire. There is much evidence that van der Lubbe did it alone, as he claimed. Of course new evidence may turn up, though this is unlikely after thirty years. The full records of the proceedings before the High Court are locked away at Potsdam under Communist control. They would surely have been released before now if they had helped to convict the Nazis. I have an uneasy feeling that van der Lubbe talked about his intentions beforehand and that he may have been egged on by Nazi companions. This does not imply that the Nazi leaders knew anything of it, and it makes no difference to the story.

Should this book have been written and published at all? Many people have been indignant at any so-called attempt to 'acquit' the Nazis of any charge, true or false. It is easy to understand why people have been indignant in Germany. Nazi guilt means innocence for everyone else. In particular, present German Ministers, who, as members of the Centre, voted for the Enabling Law in 1933, can plead that they were cheated by Hitler into believing in a Communist danger. But why should people mind in England? They are reluctant, I suppose, to confess that they were taken in the other way round – by the Communists, not by Hitler. Writers and lecturers on German history are annoyed at having to change their texts or their lecture-notes. I do not sympathize with them. As a scholar, I am just as pleased at being proved wrong as at being proved right. The essential thing is to acknowledge one's mistakes. On the Reichstag fire I was as wrong as everyone else; and I am grateful to Herr Tobias for putting me right. The Nazi (and Communist) method is to stick to every charge against one's opponents, whether it be true or false. We sink to their level if we copy their methods. Every act of fair judgement against the Nazis – every 'acquittal' of them if you like – is a triumph for the free spirit. Herr Tobias has performed a great service for all those who believe in truly free inquiry.

An essay by Sir Lewis Namier on Open Diplomacy opens with the words: 'There would be little to say on this subject, were it not for the nonsense which has been talked about it.' This is true of many topics besides Open Diplomacy. It is true of the fire at the Reichstag. Taken by itself, merely as a fire, there is little to say about it. An unbalanced Dutch boy started the fire all alone, much as Martin set fire to York Minster in 1829. Martin wanted to stop the organ buzzing. Van der Lubbe wanted to give the signal for a rising against the Nazis. Both were disappointed. The organ of York Minster still plays. Not a single German responded to van der Lubbe's call. But then everyone talked nonsense. The Nazis accused the Communists of starting the fire. Communists and others accused the Nazis. The nonsense talked about the fire illuminates, perhaps better than anything else, the political climate of the nineteen-thirties. It illuminates Nazi methods and Nazi incompetence. It illuminates Communist methods and, by comparison at any rate, their competence – particularly their competence in manufacturing legends which deceived high-minded people all over the world. It was their best stroke since the affair of Sacco and Vanzetti, where, it now appears, Sacco, though probably not Vanzetti, was guilty after all. The legends about the Reichstag fire became a cardinal part of recent history. Like all legends, they should be demolished; and Herr Tobias has gone a long way towards demolishing them.

MAGDALEN COLLEGE
OXFORD

Author's Preface

LIKE so many evils, this book had its root in 1933, when, as a direct result of the Reichstag fire, I lost my job and my home. Born in 1912, the son of a ceramic artist who later became a Trade Union official, I was working as a bookseller in a shop in the Trade Union buildings in Hamburg by 1933. On the morning of 1 April 1933, Nazi thugs battered their way in, and when all the shooting and shouting was over, my father and I were jobless and homeless.

The fire trial, which I followed from a distance while struggling to find a new job, ended with a large question-mark. Everything seemed to show that Germany's new rulers had perpetrated a gigantic swindle. A government, I argued, that had promised to base its policies on honesty, decency and truth, and yet began with what appeared so transparent a deception, deserved neither credence nor respect.

When the end of the war found me in an Italian hospital, where skilful American surgeons patched me up and pumped me full of fresh blood, I learned from American papers of many other Nazi scandals and hoped that the real truth of the Reichstag fire would soon come to light.

For years I waited in vain, and when Rudolf Diels, the first chief of the all-knowing Gestapo, had to confess in his book *Lucifer ante portas* that he too considered the fire as mysterious as before, and when even the Nuremberg Trials produced no fresh evidence (only legends obviously designed to curry favour with the Occupation Authorities) I rashly resolved to try to find out for myself.

In 1946 I was made an honorary member of the Hanover Denazification Court, and soon afterwards I was asked to join the State Denazification Commission. Then, in 1953, I became a permanent member of the State Civil Service and began to have enough leisure to carry out my resolution and began the studies of which this book is the result.

As I pursued what at first were completely unsystematic attempts to get at the facts, a new picture began to emerge, first in outline and then in ever-greater detail. It differed radically from any that had been drawn before.

In the summer of 1956 I was approached by a member of the Federal Information Office who had heard by chance that I had been steadily amassing fresh evidence on the Reichstag fire, and who implored me not to keep my findings to myself. At first I refused to publish anything, partly because of laziness and partly because I knew what I should be letting myself in for. But in the end his persistence prevailed and I agreed to the publication of some extracts from this book in *Der Spiegel*.

I was not surprised when they were greeted with howls of rage, for in the course of my researches I had learned how tenaciously most people guard their familiar opinions. Many of those who attacked me in the correspondence columns of *Der Spiegel* and *Die Zeit* revealed that they are not nearly as interested in the truth as in preventing the acceptance of any facts that could possibly be interpreted as whitewashing the Nazis. In what follows I shall try to show that their fears are unjustified and that, as Kurt Stechert has put it, 'a democratic politician must declare war on all lies, for the humanitarian cause can only be advanced by the truth.'

Naturally, after all these years, including a total war and its aftermath, the picture I have been able to draw is somewhat blurred in places. On the other hand, I have managed to amass so large a volume of material that I have had to omit a great deal from a book addressed not only to the professional historian but also to the general reader. I must ask both to forgive me, and also to overlook my occasional inability to discuss sheer stupidity with the requisite scientific detachment.

F. T.

I

THE CRIMINAL CASE

1. A Case of Arson

SHORTLY before 10 p.m. on 27 February 1933, the telephone rang in Division IA, Police Headquarters, Berlin. When Detective-Inspector Heisig answered it, he was greeted by the voice of an extremely agitated Dr Schneider:

'Is that you, Heisig? Listen carefully, the Reichstag is on fire. The whole thing is a Communist job, because we've caught a Dutch Communist in the act. Göring has put the entire Prussian police on the alert, and I have just broadcast his orders over the Karlshorst police transmitter. Will you tell everyone in IA to get down to Headquarters as quickly as they can? The chief [Rudolf Diels] is bringing the criminal, and I want you to take a statement as soon as he arrives.'

Inspector Helmut Heisig had just turned thirty-one. Five years earlier, he had abandoned his theological studies to become a detective, first in Breslau, and later in Berlin. In the beginning, he had been assigned to criminal cases, but as the political tension mounted, he was increasingly drawn into the fight against Communist and National Socialist extremists. So impressed was Police President Albert Grzesinski with the work of his new inspector that he entrusted him with a number of extremely delicate and difficult political missions.

Heisig continued to do his duty by the Weimar Republic long after he realized that German democracy was doomed, that all the careerists in the force had long ago joined Nazi cells, and that they were now preparing black lists of 'unreliable elements'.

In fact, Heisig figured prominently on one such list, for in 1932 he had closed an election meeting of Captain Hermann Göring, the very man who, as Prussian Minister of the Interior, had meanwhile become his chief, and who was to complain to the Supreme Court on 4 November 1933: 'I was handed the Prussian Ministry of the Interior as a political instrument.... But the instrument turned out to be completely useless. What good were policemen who lived in the past, who had but yesterday beaten up our men...?'[1]

A typical opportunist, on the other hand, was the police officer who, on the historic 27 February 1933, attended a crowded Social Democratic election meeting in the Sportpalast. When the chief speaker, the editor of the *Vorwärts*, Friedrich Stampfer, explained the main difference between a Marxist and an anti-Marxist – 'While the former has to have a vast store of knowledge, the latter needs no knowledge at all' – the police officer leapt on to the platform and declared the meeting closed. The crowd was so incensed at this arbitrary intervention that the ushers had great difficulty in protecting the officer. There were shouts of: 'Down with Hitler', and: 'String him up'.[2]

The police had significantly counted on the sudden interruption of the meeting, and had accordingly placed the 32nd Precinct (Brandenburg Gate) on the alert. But when the door of the police station finally flew open, in came not the expected constable with an urgent request for reinforcement against the outraged demonstrators in the Sportpalast, but a panting young man in a brown raincoat.

'Come at once, the Reichstag is on fire!' he shouted.

And the duty officer, Lieutenant Emil Lateit, lost no time; together with Constables Graening and Losigkeit and the breathless young man, he jumped into the squad car whose engine had been kept running for quite a different purpose. The time was 9.15 p.m precisely.

Everything had happened so quickly that no one had found time to ask the young man for his name, let alone a signed statement. Back at the Reichstag, he kept standing about the street for a while and was then pushed back with the rest of the huge crowd which had meanwhile assembled. He went home, presumably satisfied that he had done his duty.

The squad car took no more than two minutes to reach the Reichstag building. When Lateit, whom the young man directed to the West Wing, observed a glow to the right of the main staircase, he hastily scribbled a note: '9.17 p.m. Reichstag blazing. Reinforcements needed', and sent Constable Graening back to the station. Graening returned a few minutes later with a large contingent of policemen who immediately cordoned off the area.

The Reichstag itself was quite deserted on this dull and wintry day – the temperature was 22 degrees F. and there was a sharp easterly wind. The last deputy to leave the building had been the chairman of the Communist parliamentary group, Ernst Torgler, who had passed through Portal Five (Northern Entrance) accompanied by the Communist deputy, Koenen, and the group secretary, Anna Rehme. Their late departure was not in the least unusual, for not only was Torgler a member of many Reichstag Committees, but his Reichstag rooms had become the Berlin Communist headquarters ever since the closure of the Karl Liebknecht House. The Reichstag was, in fact, the Communists' last legal refuge, for here alone did their leaders enjoy any kind of immunity. As Torgler passed through Portal Five he handed his keys to the night watchman, Rudolf Scholz. Scholz, who had known the affable and popular Torgler for many years, exchanged a few pleasantries with him before Torgler and his companions left the House.

Just under half an hour earlier, at 8.10 p.m. to be precise, Scholz had started on his customary round of inspection. It was his job to turn off any lights that had been left on and to close any open doors and windows. At about 8.30 p.m. he had passed the Session Chamber, and a quick look had showed him that everything was in order. Then he had heard footsteps in the dark, had switched on a light, but had continued on his round when he found that it was only Fräulein Anna Rehme on her way to the Communist Party rooms, where – as she explained – she wanted to pick up election material for Koenen. Scholz finished his rounds at about 8.38 p.m., just in time to take possession of Torgler's keys.

A few minutes later – at 8.45 p.m. – the Reichstag postman, Willi Otto, passed night porter Albert Wendt at Portal Five. Wendt told him that all the deputies had left. As was his custom, Otto lit his lantern and went up the main staircase leading to Portal Two (south), and to the Reichstag Post Office, where he emptied the post-boxes. Otto, too, neither heard nor noticed anything suspicious in the deserted building. Ten minutes later, at about 8.55 p.m., he left the Reichstag again through Portal Five, the only entrance still open.

At about 9.03 p.m., Hans Flöter, a young theology student, was making his way home from the State Library. As he turned the south-western corner of the dark and deserted Reichstag and headed across the square in front of the main entrance, he heard the sound of breaking glass. When he spun round to look in the direction of the noise, he saw a man with a burning object in his hand on the first-floor balcony outside a window to the right of the Main Portal. Flöter wasted no time but sprinted off to the north-western corner of the building where he knew he would find a police officer. The officer (Sergeant Karl Buwert) seemed unable to take in what Flöter was trying to tell him, so that Flöter, in his excitement, felt impelled to give him a thump in the back to emphasize his words. Then the policeman trotted off in the correct direction and Flöter – who was no friend of the new government – continued on his way home. As he later put it, he had pressed the button and had started the machine but was not at all concerned to watch it run its course. However, before he walked off, he looked at his watch. It was 9.05 p.m.

When Police-Sergeant Buwert reached the front of the building, he at once noticed a broken window and a red glow behind it. He thought that Flöter was still with him, when in fact he had been joined by someone else. The two men gaped speechlessly at the weird spectacle behind the Reichstag windows.

Then a third passer-by appeared on the scene. He was twenty-one-year-old Werner Thaler, a typesetter, who had rounded the south-western corner of the Reichstag on his way to the Lehrter Bahnhof. He had previously heard the noise of breaking glass, had jumped up on the balustrade in the centre of the carriageway, and had gained the impression that two persons, and not one, were trying to break in. (It appeared later that this might have been an optical illusion, caused by reflection.) Remembering that he had passed a policeman a short way back, he raced off in the direction of Portal Two (Southern Entrance) and shouted into the night: 'Quick. Someone's trying to break into the Reichstag.' Then he ran back to the carriageway where he found Buwert and his unknown companion. Thaler's wrist-watch, which was usually fast, read 9.10 p.m.

For a moment all three of them looked on in paralysed astonishment. Then, as the man inside could be seen rushing from window to window waving a flaming torch, the three men started after him. Buwert had meanwhile drawn his pistol, and as the flickering light appeared in the last window but one, Thaler shouted: 'For goodness' sake, man, why don't you fire?' Buwert aimed his gun, pulled the trigger, and ran towards the window. Seeing that the mysterious intruder had disappeared, he now turned to the (unidentified) second young man, and asked him to alert the Brandenburg Gate police guardroom:

'Tell them the Reichstag is on fire and to call the fire brigade.'[3]

The young man did as he was told, while Buwert himself ran off towards the Simsonstrasse. On the way he met a Reichswehr soldier and, having a rather poor opinion of civilians, he asked him, too, to report the fire to the Brandenburg Police Station. The soldier, who had no intention of doing anything of the kind, agreed, and – continued on his way. Later, a bus conductor, Karl Seling, recalled that a Reichswehr soldier had, in fact, boarded his bus at the Bismarck Memorial stop, at about 9.15 p.m.

Meanwhile Buwert had been joined by other passers-by: Messrs Karl Kuhl and Hermann Freudenberg, and their respective spouses. They had all been out walking, had noticed a suspicious glow from far away, and had rushed to the scene with loud shouts of 'Police! Fire!', arriving just in time to see the flames lick up the curtains. Buwert, who at last grasped the fact that someone was deliberately setting fire to the Reichstag before his eyes, now ordered Kuhl and Freudenberg to make sure that the fire brigade had been called.

Together with Frau Wally Freudenberg, the two men ran off down the Simsonstrasse. When they saw a number of people coming out of the German Engineering Institute (V.D.I.), they rushed up to the caretaker, Otto Schaeske, shouting:

'The Reichstag is on fire. Call the fire brigade!'

Completely taken aback, Schaeske opened the telephone book, and started a vain and nervous search for the right number. Eventually, Emil Lück, who had been helping out in the cloakroom that night, snatched the book from him, quickly found the correct entry, and dialled.

Meanwhile Buwert's shot had brought two patrolmen to the scene. When Buwert told them briefly what had happened, one of them decided to make absolutely certain, and ran off to sound the fire alarm in the near-by Moltkestrasse.

Buwert's shouting and waving had also attracted the attention of Constable Helmut Poeschel, who was on duty at the north-eastern corner of the Reichstag. When he heard Buwert's: 'Fire! Tell the doorkeeper of Portal Five,' Poeschel set off at a gallop. Gasping for breath, he ordered the completely stupefied Albert Wendt to pull the fire alarm which, as Poeschel knew, was kept in the door-keeper's lodge. But Wendt refused to believe the constable without seeing for himself. He rushed outside, carefully locking the door behind him. When he saw the blaze, he exclaimed: 'It's the restaurant!' and when Lieutenant Lateit, who had meanwhile arrived on the scene, told him that the fire brigade had already been called, he ran back to his lodge and tried to ring up Chief Engineer Eugen Mutzka and House-Inspector Alexander Scranowitz. In his excitement he must have misdialled, for he failed to get hold of either of them, though he did manage to contact the Chief Reichstag Messenger, Eduard Prodöhl, and Paul Adermann, the night porter at the Speaker's Residence. While he was still talking to Prodöhl, Wendt could hear the jangle of an approaching fire engine.

Adermann, for his part, immediately notified the Director of the Reichstag, Geheimrat Galle. Then he rang up the Prussian Ministry of the Interior to report the fire to Hermann Göring, the Speaker. The call was taken by Göring's secretary, Fräulein Grundtmann.

Immediately on his arrival at the Reichstag, Lieutenant Lateit asked Buwert whether the fire brigade had been called. When Buwert told him it had, he asked further whether the full-scale alarm had been sounded. Buwert said no, and Lateit told him to see to it, but also to keep a close watch on the Reichstag windows and to fire at anything suspicious.

Lateit then tried to enter the Reichstag, first through Portal Two (south) and then through Portals Three and Four (east), but found them all locked. He ran on to Portal Five (north), where Wendt, the porter, told him that House-Inspector Scranowitz was on his way with the keys to the inner doors.

Scranowitz had been having his supper in his near-by flat, when he suddenly heard the fire engines. Fearing the worst, he rushed to the telephone and called Wendt, quite unaware of the fact that Wendt had been trying to get hold of him. When Wendt told him that the restaurant was on fire, Scranowitz yelled at him: 'And why the dickens didn't you report it to me?'

He banged the receiver down and raced across to Portal Five. Once there, he opened the inner doors and rushed up the staircase, followed by Lieutenant Lateit, and Constables Losigkeit and Graening. As they dashed into the large lobby, they noticed a red glow coming from beyond the Kaiser Wilhelm monument. When Lateit looked through an open glass door into the Session Chamber, he saw a large flame. In the doorway he spotted a blazing 'cushion', which turned out to be a folded overcoat. In addition, the thick plush curtains on either side of the glass door were burning, and so was some of the wooden panelling.

It was about 9.22 p.m. when Lateit entered the Session Chamber. The whole Chamber was softly lit up by a steady, continuous sheet of flame over the tribune. The effect was that of a brightly illuminated church organ. (Lateit was unaware that its 'pipes' consisted of three blazing curtains.) He observed no other fires in the Chamber, nor did he notice any smoke. Constable Losigkeit, on the other hand, who went farther into the Chamber, saw other flames in the stenographers' well, below.

Lateit, now fully convinced that an incendiary was at work, ordered the two policemen to draw their revolvers. Meanwhile, House-Inspector Scranowitz had switched on the light in the corridors and in the lobby. Lateit, who had been present during the Blücher Palace fire in April 1931, was still firmly convinced that the Chamber could easily be saved by the fire brigade.

On his way back to Portal Five, Lateit noticed a number of small fires: here a carpet was in flames, there a wastepaper basket. Everywhere bits of material were lying about – he counted some twenty-five of these, each roughly the size of the palm of his hand. He thought 'they might have been the charred remains of table-cloths', for all of them were giving off a lot of smoke. On the floor of the lobby, he found a cap, a tie, and a piece of soap.

Near Portal Five he encountered a number of firemen who were busy extinguishing fires in the western lobby. To other firemen standing there he cried:

'It's arson. The place is one great mass of fires.'

He ordered one of the firemen to go back to the Session Chamber with Constable Losigkeit. Then he told his own men to make a careful search of the whole building for the intruder, while he drove back to the Brandenburg Gate for reinforcements. His arrival at the guardroom was recorded as 9.25 p.m. He had been away for a total of ten minutes.

While Lateit, Losigkeit, and Graening had been looking at the fire in the Chamber, they had been joined by Constable Poeschel. Lateit ordered him to accompany House-Inspector Scranowitz, who, after he had switched on the lights in the lobby and corridors, was about to light up the Chamber as well. Behind the Kaiser Wilhelm monument, Scranowitz noticed one of the many small fires Lateit had already observed, and stamped it out. Then he ran to the restaurant, opened the door, and was met by a mass of flames. When he made his way back to the lobby, he noticed that the curtains and a wooden panel leaning against the wall had caught fire.

Scranowitz, too, now looked into the Session Chamber – shortly after Lateit had done so. A single glance showed him that the curtains behind the Speaker's Chair had caught fire, but that the panelling was still untouched. But then he observed – or claimed that he observed – a completely different picture from that described by Lateit: on the first three rows of deputies' benches Scranowitz counted some twenty to twenty-five small fires, each about eighteen inches wide, and all of roughly the same shape. In addition, the Speaker's Chair and the Orators' Table were ablaze, and so were the curtains in the stenographers' well. Here the flames, however, were flickering and 'spluttering' violently. Scranowitz shut the door to the Chamber and, with Constable Poeschel, who had been looking over his shoulder, ran across the thickly carpeted southern corridor to the Bismarck Hall. Just as they passed under the great chandelier, a man, bare to the waist, suddenly shot across their path from the left, i.e. from the back of the Session Chamber. The man stopped dead in his tracks and then started to run back, but when Poeschel raised his pistol, shouting 'Hands up!', he obediently raised his arms. He was a tall, well-built young man, completely out of breath and dishevelled. All Poeschel found on him was a pocket knife, a wallet, and a passport. While Poeschel was leafing through this document, House-Inspector Scranowitz, shaking with rage, yelled at the stranger: 'Why did you do it?'

'As a protest,' the man replied.

Scranowitz, a tall, athletic man, hit out at him in blind fury.

Meanwhile, Poeschel had gathered from the man's passport that his name was Marinus van der Lubbe, that he came from Leyden in Holland, and that he was born on 13 January 1909.

The time was 9.27 p.m.

Then Poeschel marched his prisoner to Portal Five, where someone flung a rug over his naked shoulders, before they took him away to the Brandenburg Gate Police Station.

The fire alarm from the German Engineering Institute was received at Brigade Headquarters at 9.13 p.m. At 9.14, this call was duly transmitted to the Linienstrasse Fire Station, whence a section of pumps under Chief Fire Officer Emil Puhle was sent out at once. It arrived at the north-eastern corner of the Reichstag at 9.18 p.m. At 9.19 p.m. another section, led by Fire Officer Waldemar Klotz, drew up. It had been sent out from Turmstrasse Station in response to the fire call from Moltkestrasse. Each section consisted of four fire engines. At about 9.23 p.m., Puhle used ladders to climb up to, and break into, the restaurant; so great was his hurry that he failed to notice that one restaurant window was already broken. The door leading to the lobby and the entire panelling were now ablaze; the curtains had completely burnt down. There were a number of small fires – for instance, a window curtain which threatened to flare up in the draught from the broken window – and these were quickly extinguished. At 9.27 p.m., Puhle crossed to the Session Chamber where he was met by Fire Officer Waldemar Klotz. Klotz, who had seen Puhle's section parked at the western side, had not bothered to stop but had gone on to tackle the fire elsewhere. He made a brief stop at Portal Two (south) but, finding it locked, he drove right round the building to Portal Five (north), leaving Fire Officer Franz Wald and one vehicle behind.

At about 9.20 p.m., Klotz gave orders to make a hose ready, while he, with Firemen Kiessig and König carrying hand pumps, hurried into the lobby. Here they dealt with a burning carpet, the curtain of a telephone box, the telephone box itself, and the ornamental panelling of a door. At about 9.24 p.m., Klotz entered the Chamber, and noticed a tremendous draught and a tremendous wave of heat. The Chamber itself was full of thick smoke, so that all he could make out was a glow in the north-eastern corner. Since he was afraid of increasing the draught, he quickly shut the doors.

A little later, when he looked into the Chamber a second time, the whole place was a sea of flames. At 9.31 p.m., the tenth-grade alarm was given (each grade calling for one section of four pumps). A few minutes later, eight further sections started towards the Reichstag. With them came Chief Fire Director Gempp, the head of the Berlin Fire Department, accompanied by Fire Directors Lange and Tamm, and Chief Engineer Meusser. Quite separately, both Gempp and Lange gave the full-scale (15th grade or grand) alarm at 9.42 p.m. Within minutes, therefore, fifteen sections of pumps with more than sixty vehicles had been thrown into the fire-fighting. At the same time, a number of fire-boats began tackling the fire from the river Spree.

By the time the fire was finally put out at 11 p.m., the Session Chamber was completely gutted. The panelling was gone, and so were the three-tiered tribune, the glorious carvings, and the glass dome, which now offered an unimpeded view of the night sky.

It was also at about 11 p.m. that Paul Bogun, an engineer, reported to Lieutenant Lateit at the Brandenburg Gate Police Station. He told the lieutenant that, at about 9 p.m., he had come out of a lecture at the Engineering Institute, near the Reichstag, and finding that his tram had just left, he had decided to walk home. When he was some twenty yards from Portal Two, he heard a 'rattle', and then saw a man step out of the swinging doors. The man hesitated while looking across at two women, one of whom had appeared to give him a signal. The man had run off towards the Königsplatz, peering back at the Reichstag 'most suspiciously'.

Lateit told Bogun to report the matter to Police Headquarters at once. Bogun, however, preferred to wait for another three days before doing so.

Another person to come forward, Frau Kuesner, who passed the Speaker's Palace at about 8.55 p.m. on her way to the National Club, also alleged that she had seen a man running off. Later, it emerged that the man in question had, in fact, been an innocent pedestrian, who had taken shelter from the icy wind in Portal Two while waiting for a bus. When the bus came into sight he had made a dash for it.

2. The Arsonist

MARINUS VAN DER LUBBE

IN September 1955 – twenty-two years after the Reichstag fire – Johan van der Lubbe of Amsterdam petitioned the Berlin County Court to repeal the sentence passed by the Supreme Court in Leipsig on his brother Marinus on 23 December 1933. Three years later, his petition was dismissed for purely formal reasons.

Thus disappeared what little chance there still was of having the mysterious events of 27 February 1933, and the enigma of Marinus van der Lubbe, examined by an independent court.

What sort of man was this young Dutchman who, on the evening of 27 February 1933, was apprehended in the flaming Reichstag? Rarely has the life of any man been studied in such great detail, and yet been so deliberately distorted and misunderstood. To this day most people believe that van der Lubbe was:

1. A congenital idiot;
2. A juvenile delinquent;
3. A pathological vagrant;
4. A pathological liar;
5. A pathological boaster;
6. A homosexual prostitute in the service of the Nazis.

All attempts to describe the real van der Lubbe come up against two books published in 1933 and 1934 by Communist propagandists in Paris, with the sole aim of proving that the Reichstag was burned by the Nazis. In order to make that story stick, van der Lubbe had to be turned into a Nazi tool at all costs.

Part I, entitled *The Brown Book of the Hitler Terror and the Burning of the Reichstag*, appeared shortly after the fire; Part II, entitled *The Reichstag Fire Trial* or the *Second Brown Book of the Hitler Terror*, appeared after the trial and had a special introductory chapter by Georgi Dimitrov. In what follows, we shall refer to the two as *Brown Books I* and *II* respectively.

Soon after Inspector Heisig had given the alarm, officers of

Division IA started to report at Police Headquarters. When Diels and Schneider eventually arrived with the prisoner, everyone kept peering in to catch a glimpse of the half-naked Dutchman.

In his evidence to the Supreme Court, Heisig later described the strange situation as follows:

> The whole room was teeming with people. First of all there were the officers from my own and from near-by offices. Then there were Police President von Levetzow, the Vice-President, Ministerialrat Diels, Ministerialdirektor Daluege, together with a number of gentlemen from all sorts of Ministries. Altogether some forty to fifty people must have crowded into the little room, for it was completely packed.

All these men had come in, not only to catch a glimpse of the arsonist, but also to learn what further outrages might be expected that night. The presence of so many of his superiors naturally perturbed young Inspector Heisig, particularly when they kept interrupting his interrogation to fire questions of their own at the prisoner.

In general, the average Dutchman understands German far more readily than the average German understands Dutch, but in van der Lubbe's case Heisig had no difficulty at all in making him out, as he spoke German fluently, though with an unmistakable Dutch accent. Van der Lubbe himself insisted that he needed no interpreter, and spoke out quite fearlessly. Heisig had to interrupt him many times because most of his statements threatened to degenerate into political harangues. To begin with, Heisig asked him to explain his motives, so as to decide whether or not the crime fell within the province of the Political Branch. Van der Lubbe replied that his motives had been political: he wanted to encourage the German workers to fight for their freedom. His deed was meant as an example.

Heisig deduced that the man was a Communist, though van der Lubbe denied having any connection with the Communist Party.

During the discussion of his finances, van der Lubbe volunteered the information that he had used part of his extremely meagre resources to buy firelighters and matches for a number of other fires as well. When pressed by the astonished Heisig, van der Lubbe confessed that he had set fire to the Welfare Office in Neukölln, a Berlin suburb, two days before.

Detective-Inspector Walter Zirpins took over from Heisig. After another few hours, van der Lubbe grew visibly tired. By 3 a.m. he was completely exhausted, and Zirpins had him put in a cell for the night.

Meanwhile Heisig rushed off a letter to the police in Leyden, van der Lubbe's home town. Van der Lubbe was known so well there that the Dutch authorities were able to send back an immediate reply. In it Detective-Inspector N. G. Weyers confirmed that Marinus van der Lubbe was a dangerous Communist.

At about 8 a.m. next morning, van der Lubbe was fetched for further interrogation. Once again, a host of curious people popped in to have a look, but this time the atmosphere had grown a great deal less informal. All van der Lubbe's statements were now taken down verbatim. Because of the special interest the case was bound to excite, Heisig asked his secretaries to make as many copies as possible; van der Lubbe signed each page of every one.

The impression van der Lubbe made on his interrogators can be gathered from the police report dated 3 March 1933 and from the evidence of Inspector Heisig and Dr Zirpins before the Supreme Court. In the police report we read:

> He is endowed with a great deal of (admittedly very one-sided) intelligence, and, appearances to the contrary, he is a very bright fellow. His grasp of the German language is so good that he can follow even finger shades of meanings, though his own speech is slurred. Thus he could not only follow the examination but remember entire sentences and repeat them word for word. [Especially during the discussion of his motives] he kept correcting those phrases which, he thought, did not fully reflect his real meaning.

And this is what Dr Zirpins stated in evidence before the Supreme Court:

> . . . he corrected the statement, going into questions of style, and rejecting certain passages out of hand. In short he had no need of an interpreter.

Dr Zirpins also mentioned another characteristic:

> He had a remarkable capacity not only for repeating dates, but for remembering numbers in general. There are some people who cannot remember numbers, but he had, as it were, a genius for numbers, could remember dates and times, etc.

Few believed Zirpins when he went on to say:

> I gave him a small piece of paper to sketch on. First he drew a plan of the Welfare Office. At the time I did not know the layout, but, in fact, his plan was perfectly correct. . . . I had been in the Reichstag only twice before, and did not know the precise set-up, but van der Lubbe drew everything so perfectly that afterwards, when we inspected the scene of the crime, everything fell into place. I myself would – quite frankly – have been quite unable to reconstruct the scene nearly as well as he did. I gave him a red and a blue pencil with which he traced his path in and out of the building with perfect facility.

Marinus van der Lubbe was a bricklayer by trade and had learned drawing at night school. In addition he had an almost phenomenal memory. In the final police report we are told: 'He had a remarkable sense of direction, which he probably acquired in the course of his travels. Although he has been in Berlin for only eight days, he is able to describe long walks, street by street . . .'

During his evidence before the Supreme Court, on 27 September 1933, Heisig was asked whether he was present during the reconstruction of the crime. Heisig replied:

> Yes, and van der Lubbe led us. We neither indicated the direction nor influenced him in any way. He was almost delighted to show us the path he had taken. He said he had an excellent sense of direction because of his poor eyesight. Another sense had taken the place of his eyes.

All these statements by Heisig and Dr Zirpins were given little credence – they simply did not fit into the general scheme of things. For one thing, they ran counter to the public image of van der Lubbe as an apathetic moron; for another, they bore out van der Lubbe's claim that he was the sole culprit when all the experts said he could not have been.

We can form a good idea of Marinus van der Lubbe's real character from the statement he made to the police on 3 March 1933:

> At the outset, I must insist that my action was inspired by political motives. In Holland I read that the National Socialists had come to power in Germany. I have always followed German politics with keen interest and I read all the articles I could get hold of on Brüning, Papen and Schleicher. When Hitler took over the Government, I expected much enthusiasm for him but also much tension. I bought

all the newspapers on this subject, and found that they were of my opinion. I myself am a Leftist, and was a member of the Communist Party until 1929. What I did not like about the Party is the way they lord it over the workers, instead of letting the workers decide for themselves. I side with the proletariat in the class struggle. Its own leaders must stand at the head. The masses themselves must decide what they ought to do and what they ought not to do. [These were in fact the views of the *Rade* or International Communists, a tiny Dutch splinter group completely unknown in Germany.] In Germany a National Coalition has now been formed, and I think it holds two dangers: (1) it oppresses the workers, and (2) it refuses to submit to other countries so that it is bound to lead to war. I watched on for a few days and then I decided to go to Germany and to see for myself. I made the decision without anyone else, and I came to Germany all by myself. Once here, I intended to observe how the National Coalition affects the workers and what the workers think about the National Coalition. I started in Düsseldorf, where I spoke to workers in the street. I did the same thing in other towns. In Berlin, I also studied the pamphlets of the various parties and then went to the Welfare Offices in Lichtenberg, Wedding, and Neukölln. I also went to the Labour Exchange, but it was closed because of the elections. I found out that whereas the National Coalition has complete freedom in Germany, the workers have not.

Now, what the workers' organizations are doing is not likely to rouse the workers to the struggle for freedom. That is why I discussed better ways and means with the workers. The privileges which the National Socialists enjoy today must also be enjoyed by the workers. That is the reason why I asked the workers to demonstrate. But all I was told was to take the matter to the Party – the Communist Party. But I had heard that a Communist demonstration was disbanded by the leaders on the approach of the police, and that the people listened to these leaders instead of carrying out their own resolutions. I realized then that the workers will do nothing by themselves, that they will do nothing against a system which grants freedom to one side and metes out oppression to the other. In my opinion something absolutely had to be done in protest against this system. Since the workers would do nothing, I had to do something by myself. I considered arson a suitable method. I did not wish to harm private people but something that belonged to the system itself: official buildings, the Welfare Office for example, for that is a building in which the workers come together, or the City Hall, because it is a building belonging to the system, and further the Palace, because it lies in the centre of the city, and if it goes up, the huge flames can be seen from far away. . . . When these three

> fires failed to come off, that is to say when my protest did not come off, I decided on the Reichstag as the centre of the whole system. . . .

And finally, van der Lubbe's answer to the crucial question:

> As to the question whether I acted alone, I declare emphatically that this was the case. No one at all helped me, nor did I meet a single person in the Reichstag.[1]

Thus did the young radical explain his motives to the police, to the Examining Magistrate, the Public Prosecutor, and finally the Supreme Court Judges. Not one of them was prepared to listen to him, partly because his theories transcended their narrow political horizons, and partly because of their hatred of everything that smacked of Communism.

CHILDHOOD AND BACKGROUND

In the year 1904, Franciscus Cornelis van der Lubbe, a forty-one-year-old hawker, married Petronella van Handel-Peuthe, a divorcée, in Leyden. From her first marriage, she brought him four children – one girl and three boys – who were joined in time by three children from the new marriage: Johan, also called Jan; Cornelis and Marinus (Rinus). By the time Marinus was born on 13 January 1909, his parents had ceased to get on with each other. Soon afterwards they separated. The father took to the road and to drink, leaving his asthmatic wife to fend for her many children and herself. She opened a small shop in 's Hertogenbosch, and did all her housework, of which there was a great deal with so large a family, in the evenings. In short, her life would have been very hard for a healthy woman, let alone for a semi-invalid. As a result, the children were left to themselves most of the time and it was no wonder that Marinus, the youngest, ran wild and had to be sent to a home for neglected children – for a 'few weeks' as he himself put it. One of his teachers during that period, van der Meene, has described him as a 'talented boy of average application'. Marinus gave him little cause for complaint and at no time did he have to punish the boy severely.

Fate struck Marinus a severe blow in 1921: his mother died when he was only twelve years old and he joined the household of his stepsister, Annie Sjardijn, who lived in Oegsgeest near Leyden. She herself had three children of her own, aged two, four and six years respectively. Marinus, who, according to those who knew him at the time, was a charming, alert and respectful young lad, naturally acted the big brother to his small nephews.[1]

Marinus continued to attend the Christian School in Leyden for eighteen months after his mother's death, and then his brother-in-law apprenticed him to a builder. After work Marinus went to night school to continue his studies. At the age of sixteen Marinus was so healthy and strong that all his friends called him 'Dempsey'.

It was from his workmates that he first learned the new revolutionary gospel with which he quickly replaced all he had been taught by his Calvinist teachers, and which opened up to him an entirely new world of ideas, concepts and words.

Marinus, the boy who grew up with a minimum of parental authority and supervision, found it easy to dismiss all authority – individual or social – as completely unnecessary. He started his fight against 'bourgeois capitalism' by becoming a member of *De Zaaier* (The Sowers), a Communist Youth Organization. In it, he first proved his great ability to sway others.

Marinus worked hard at his job and earned good money. He spent much of his spare time reading and became a familiar figure in the Leyden Public Library. Among the heavy books he borrowed were *Philosophy and Labour* and *Today and Tomorrow* by Henry Ford, and Marx's *Das Kapital*. His longing to see the world was fed by Sven Hedin's books on Tibet and China, so much so that some years later he actually left for China – on foot. Needless to say, the foundation of his self-taught knowledge was rather shaky, so that his hatred of capitalism was based less on Marxist 'science' than on youthful enthusiasm and Utopian dreams of heaven and earth.

Then fate struck him yet another blow. During a lunch break he fell victim to what was meant to be a harmless joke. Two of his friends playfully pulled an empty lime sack over his head and a piece of lime got into his eye causing a painful inflammation. Since misfortunes never come singly, both eyes were damaged by more lime a short time later. He had to spend five miserable months in Professor van der Hoeve's eye-clinic. Despite three operations, his cornea turned opaque, his eyesight became weak, and his eyelids were ever afterwards subject to all sorts of infections.

This accident was a turning point in his life: he had to break off his apprenticeship and, not surprisingly, he is said to have toyed with the idea of suicide. He had no home, no parents, and now he was near-blind. The long months in the clinic in which he could do little but feel sorry for himself, were bound to increase his unrest and dissatisfaction with life, and he only saved his sanity by immersing himself completely in politics. He was awarded a very small weekly disability pension – seven gulden and forty-four cents – which was not nearly enough to live on, so that he had to do casual labour from time to time. During the intervals he lived on the dole. Among his many casual jobs, he was assistant waiter in the Railway Restaurant at Leyden (winter 1927), porter in the 'Hof van Holland' hotel in Nordwijk (summer 1928), and a potato trader on his own account. He also worked on a dredger, on a ferry plying between Nordwijk and Sassenheim, as a butcher, a messenger boy, and in the Dutch bulb trade. In short, he was anything but an idler.

In the Young Communist League, for which he worked indefatigably, his physical strength, intelligence, and lack of bourgeois prejudices marked Marinus out from the start. Very quickly he fell foul not only of the local police, but also of his ever-correct brother-in-law, Sjardijn. After countless political arguments, Marinus left Oegsgeest for good, and at the age of eighteen he moved back to Leyden to share a room with the Communist student Piet van Albada. Quite naturally, Albada and his political friends exerted a great deal of influence on him, so much so that Marinus soon attracted the attention of the Leyden police as well.

Despite his youth, Marinus was allowed to take the chair at a public meeting of the Leyden Communist Youth League on 15 November 1928. In October 1929 he rented an empty store-room, proudly baptized it Lenin House, and offered it as a meeting hall to the Youth Group. He wrote leaflets and edited factory and school pamphlets, in all of which he attacked militarism and capitalism; he was present at every strike meeting and political demonstration held in Leyden, and worked tirelessly for the revolutionary cause. His activities as public speaker and heckler soon made him a well-known figure, particularly among the unemployed, whom he led during a number of processions through the town.

Once, when his political opponents, the Dutch Social Democrats, held a rally, he organized a Communist counter-demonstration. On that occasion he launched his first direct attack on an institution against which he was afterwards to wage private war: the Welfare Office. For him the Welfare Office was the epitome of the hated capitalist system, a system in which petty officials pompously throw

crumbs from the opulent tables of the rich to the poor and dispossessed. Marinus 'hit back' by throwing bricks through the windows of the Welfare Office. He was arrested and sentenced to fourteen days in prison.

Though Marinus was quick to take offence, and quick to argue, he was no more truculent than most young radicals. Thus he repeatedly resigned from the Young Communist League, only to rejoin once his anger had abated. Finally, he broke completely with the Dutch Communist Party for reasons still shrouded in mystery but obviously related to his independent attitude and his spontaneous identification with the working class.

Through Piet van Albada, Marinus became familiar with the ideas of such 'left deviationists' as the LAO (Left Workers' Opposition) the AAU (General Workers' Union) and last but not least the PIC (Party of International Communists) or *Rade* Communists, as they were also called. This 'Party', which had only a handful of members in Holland, was opposed to the very idea of discipline and leadership, and saw the salvation of the working class in spontaneous, individual action alone.

THE 'PATHOLOGICAL VAGRANT'

None of the men who later cross-examined Marinus van der Lubbe had ever felt the urge to pull up their stakes and to go out into the world – without money or friends. No wonder therefore that they all looked down on him as a shiftless vagrant.

Like so many unemployed workers anxious to escape the sad monotony of their enforced indolence, Marinus van der Lubbe decided to change one kind of misery for what turned out to be another, and took to the roads of Europe. He was an exceptionally undemanding person; night after night he shared his quarters with the flotsam of human society, and he was content – because all of them applauded his scathing attacks on the State and on capitalism.

Marinus's first journey did not take him to Sven Hedin's mysterious East, but only to Northern France. Then, in 1928, he hiked through Belgium and spent a few days in the German city of Aachen. From August to November 1930 he was in Calais, where he conceived the idea of swimming the Channel one day. He was young and strong, used to exertions and unusually persistent once he made up his mind to do something. He returned to Leyden from his first trip, firmly resolved to see as much of the world as he possibly could.

In the spring of 1931, Marinus and his Communist friend, Hendrik Holverda, decided to raise money for another trip by what was then a favourite method with impecunious globe-trotters: they sold postcards bearing their own likenesses. On this particular photograph Holverda had raised his clenched fist in the Communist salute. The text, which was printed in French, Dutch and German, read: 'Workers' Sports and Study Tour of Marinus van der Lubbe and H. Holverda through Europe and the Soviet Union. Start of the tour from Leyden, April 14th, 1931'.

But they could not raise enough money and, on his way back to Holland, van der Lubbe was arrested by the Prussian police in Gronau (Westphalia) for selling postcards without a licence. On 13 May 1931, the court imposed a fine of fifty marks or ten days' imprisonment, and Marinus chose prison.

Naturally he was greatly disappointed, particularly since he knew that the Communists in Leyden would gloat over this set-back; yet he would not have been Marinus van der Lubbe had he given up completely. In fact, he tried time and again to reach his great goal – the Soviet Union, and it was this very persistence which enabled his detractors to say that van der Lubbe kept talking about fantastic projects which he never carried out.

On 29 September 1931, he made his first tour of the Balkans, and wrote to Koos Vink from Yugoslavia:

> If it is at all possible, I should like to fork left in Turkey, and go on to Tiflis (Russia). However, I anticipate great difficulties....

And on 14 October, he added the following reflections:

> I had intended, while on my way to China, to visit Tiflis in Russia. Since, however, I have not come far enough, I shall make, not for Tiflis, but for European Russia, say for Odessa or Rijeo [?] There I shall somehow try to smuggle myself across the Red border....

A week later – on 21 October – Marinus wrote to Koos Vink:

> I thought I might try to cross into Russia from Rumania but because that too is just another vast detour and because it's probably very difficult to get across the border, I have decided against it....

On 12 February 1932, when he had reached Vienna in the course of his second Balkan tour, he wrote to Koos Vink:

> I have just got a Hungarian visa and shall leave Vienna straight away, since otherwise the whole thing will take far too long. I shall probably go on to Russia, that is if nothing special happens. . . .

From his letter of 19 April it became clear that something 'special' had, in fact, happened:

> When you receive this letter, I shall have spent a whole week in a Polish prison. I was given three weeks, for illegal entry, and when my time is up I shall return to Holland.

Marinus himself never claimed that he had been to Russia; that claim was made 'on his behalf' by his former Party comrades anxious to show him up as a liar, particularly when it came to his attitude to the Soviet Union. It was to refute these and other slanders that Marinus's real friends, and especially the *Rade* or International Communists, published the *Red Book* (*Roodboek*) which, apart from a contemptuous and brilliant refutation of every Communist slander, also contained Marinus's diary for the period 6 September – 24 October 1931, together with a large number of his letters.

This brings us to his Channel-swimming attempts which even so sympathetic a man as Dr Seuffert, his counsel, has considered a clear sign of Marinus's boastfulness. However, we know from Mr Justice de Jongh that 'Marinus was a fine sportsman, who had swum from Noordwijk to Scheveningen'.[2] Now, a glance at the map will show that this was a very respectable achievement. Why, then, should his attempts to do what so many others have done – to swim the Channel – be considered a sign of boastfulness or a proof of his pathological need to impress others?

At the time, the Dutch newspaper, *Het Leven*, had offered a considerable prize – 5,000 gulden – to the first Dutchman to swim the Channel, and Marinus was a Dutchman and a good swimmer. And who could really have blamed him if, apart from the large prize, he was also attracted by the glory of it all?

In his diary or in his letters he never mentioned the Channel crossing in other than matter-of-fact terms:

> Having re-considered my plan once again this morning, I have come to the conclusion that I had best be back home at about the end of May or the beginning of June. Then I will have time to make up my mind whether I will take part in the Channel crossing or not. From now on,

I have decided not to rush about so much but – if possible at all – to go swimming every day.

How very seriously he took this business may be gathered from the fact that on 14 October, while he was still in Rumania, he sent a letter to a Dutchman he had met in Calais asking for work near the French coast, so that he could practise swimming every day. Even then he was not too optimistic about his chances, for on the same day he made the following entry in his diary: 'I have therefore decided to return so that I can be ready for the summer. But even when I return, things won't go as smoothly as all that.'

How very unboastful the whole scheme was is further borne out by the following entry, dated 21 October: 'By the way, I have tried to cross the Danube. But I failed, for the water was too cold. If I swam every day, things might be different.'

In his letter of the same day to Koos Vink, he returned to the Channel crossing once again:

> As regards the crossing, I should like to ask you if *Het Leven* has said anything at all about holding the prize open until next year. Please tell me if so, and if possible send me the article regarding the Channel crossing and the swimming. Incidentally, last week I wrote to the Dutch gentleman in France, asking about work and also if he would send his reply to your address. If you should hear from him . . .

The *Red Book* also published a postcard from an Austrian swimmer who had allowed Marinus to use her boat for his Channel training.

Shortly before his second journey to Hungary in January 1932, Marinus had another clash with the hated Welfare Office. Having been refused an increase in his unemployment relief, he once again smashed a few windows as a protest. Marinus was sentenced to three months' imprisonment *in absentia*.

On his return from Hungary, he was welcomed by a special reception committee: a police escort. On 15 June 1932, he sent the following cry for help to Koos Vink:

> As you can see from this letterhead I have landed in prison in Utrecht, because I was sentenced to three months on account of the windows . . . I can however appeal against the sentence which costs approximately 1.0 *fl.* Would you therefore be kind enough to send me a postal order for 1.50 *fl.* at once, so that I can appeal?

After hearing the appeal on 29 June 1932, the Court upheld the original three months' sentence. As a result, Marinus was in Scheveningen prison from 12 July until 2 October 1932. After his release he paid a number of brief visits: to his father in Dordrecht, to Amsterdam, and to The Hague.

Marinus's hatred of the Welfare Office also took forms other than smashing windows. When a further request for an increase was refused, he went on hunger strike and managed to last out for a full eleven days. Then he was carted off to hospital, but only when he was promised that his request would be met in full did he finally break his long fast.

Once again he had proved his remarkable strength of purpose. At the same time he had forged a new weapon which he was to use many times again: for example, during the preliminary investigation into the Reichstag fire. But there he met an equally determined opponent: the Examining Magistrate, Paul Vogt.

It has often been asked why Marinus should have gone back to Budapest so soon after his return from Hungary. Later, in the Supreme Court, he replied to the President's question: 'Why did you visit Hungary so often? Did you have special contacts there?' – by which, needless to say, the President meant political contacts – with a curt 'No', and there is, in fact, no evidence that any such contacts were made. Even so, the *Red Book* published a photograph of a Hungarian girl not, as the authors emphasized, to disprove the Communist slander that van der Lubbe was a homosexual, but '. . . in the hope that one of the readers of this book, which is printed in four languages, may recognize the woman in the photograph and may be able to provide us with her name and present address, so that we may turn to her for some explanation about her relationship with van der Lubbe.'

In an undated letter (published in the *Red Book*) which he must have posted towards the end of October 1931, van der Lubbe had written: 'Certain circumstances force me to leave Budapest tomorrow for Hódmezövásarhely. I think I shall probably be needing some money there . . .'

It must have been exceptional circumstances indeed which drove Marinus to ask for an urgent loan of 2.5 gulden, to be sent by express to that unpronounceable town, and it seems likely that the attractive original of the photograph was somehow involved in it all.

On his return to Holland, Marinus could not wait to find out whether a letter from Budapest was waiting for him. Though he knew he would be back in Leyden on Tuesday, 8 December 1931, he wrote to Koos Vink on Thursday, 3 December, from Enschede: '. . . in case a letter from Budapest should arrive before Sunday, would you please have it translated at once and send it on to me by express? If it should arrive after Sunday, please do nothing, I shall be able to deal with it myself.'

Quite obviously, Marinus treated his love affair with extreme discretion, for otherwise the editors of the *Red Book* should not have had to appeal to the world at large for the girl's name and address.

MARINUS VAN DER LUBBE'S LAST JOURNEY

On 30 January 1933, Dutch newspapers, in common with newspapers the world over, reported the Nazi victory in Germany in banner headlines. Adolf Hitler had been appointed Reich Chancellor. Subsequent issues were full of gory reports about Nazi outrages. Only the Communist papers consoled their readers with glib assurances that Hitlerism was nothing but the death rattle of expiring capitalism. Soon the victorious workers would sweep away even this excrescence and under the leadership of the 'vanguard of the proletariat' – the Communist Party of Germany – begin to build a better and more equitable society. Marinus van der Lubbe, who bought all the papers he could, had heated discussions with his friends, and particularly with Koos Vink, about the revolutionary possibilities which might, indeed which were bound to, result from the inevitable clash between the bourgeois-fascist hordes and the revolutionary proletariat. He felt that something tremendous, something unique, was happening in Germany and, after waiting for another few days, he set out on foot for Berlin, the great centre of political events. The date was 3 February 1933.

At first everything went according to plan. Passing Kleve, Düsseldorf, Essen and Dortmund, he reached Paderborn on 10 February. On the 12th, a Sunday, he was in Hameln. Then he continued via Braunschweig, Burg, and Genthin. He spent the night of 15 February in the small village of Morsleben, and the night of 17 February in the casual ward run by Frau Hedwig Wagner in Glindow near Potsdam. On the afternoon of the following day –

a Saturday – he reached Berlin, having hitched a ride in a lorry for the last stretch. He put up in the men's hostel in the Alexandrinenstrasse which he remembered from his first visit to Berlin.

Next morning (Sunday) he went to a concert arranged by the German Social Democratic Party in the Bülowplatz, and watched the police closing this innocent function without any explanation. In the afternoon he attended a demonstration of the *Reichsbanner* (Social Democratic Corps) in the Lustgarten, and in the evening he went to see *Rebellen*, a film starring Luis Trenker.

On Monday morning he cleared the snow outside the hostel, and then wrote a few letters to Holland, including one to Koos Vink, whom he asked to forward his disability pension.

It did not take Marinus long to abandon his rosy view of the situation – nowhere had he met the anticipated resolution to fight against the brown 'mercenaries of capitalism', and though he missed no opportunity of inveighing against Hitlerism, no one seemed to care. In the wintry streets of Berlin, at the Welfare Offices in Wedding and Neukölln, in the various labour exchanges he visited – everywhere he arrived at the same disappointing conclusion: there was not the slightest hope of mass revolutionary action. He suggested spontaneous protest marches, of the kind that had proved so successful in Holland, but people either took no notice of him or else treated him with suspicion. Why did this foreign busybody rant in the street, they wondered, instead of leaving things in the hands of the great German Communist Party, who, after all, knew best. No doubt the man was a Nazi spy.

Marinus spent Monday and Tuesday nights – 20 and 21 February 1933 – in the Fröbelstrasse hostel.

On Wednesday, 22 February, at about 10 a.m., he turned up outside the Welfare Office in 'red' Neukölln, where he harangued a number of unemployed who happened to be standing about. This harangue later provided the Examining Magistrate with the much-needed 'link' between van der Lubbe and his alleged Communist contacts (the indictment devoted no less than fifteen pages to what was said on that occasion). In fact, as we shall see, Marinus's remarks were no more 'significant' than any previous or subsequent comments he made on conditions in Germany. The only thing which distinguished this occasion from all the others was that it was here, in Neukölln, that van der Lubbe first suspected the truth: among the countless unemployed and Communists he had met in Berlin, not a single one was prepared to make even the slightest sacrifice for the cause. If anything at all could still be done, he would have to do it by himself.

On Thursday morning he got dressed, drank some coffee and then went to Schlaffke's Café. At about eleven o'clock he walked to the Alexanderplatz Post Office to pick up the three gulden which Koos Vink had forwarded to him. On a billboard he saw a placard announcing a Communist Party meeting in the Sportpalast, and he immediately made for it, after having asked a newspaper-seller the way. He arrived at the Sportpalast at about 2 p.m. and obtained a ticket. Then he walked back to the Alexanderplatz, and thawed out in the warm post office in the Königstrasse, while studying the pamphlets, newspapers and election manifestos he had meanwhile collected. As he intended speaking at the meeting he made a number of notes. Then he walked about the streets, and finally re-appeared at the Sportpalast at about 6 p.m. The main speaker was to be the Communist deputy Wilhelm Pieck.

As it happened, Marinus van der Lubbe was not given a chance to express his views – the meeting was closed by the police as soon as it started, and with no resistance on the part of the audience. Completely disgusted, van der Lubbe returned to his hostel, seething with impotent rage and unable to fall asleep for a long time. The great Communist Party of Germany had gone into voluntary liquidation!

On Friday morning he was back in Neukölln, a district with which he had by now become quite familiar. He had given up the idea of waiting for the German revolution, and took his leave of his new acquaintances. Then he walked back towards the Alexanderplatz. Quite suddenly he had the feeling that he must make one last attempt to persuade just a few workers to stand up to the Nazis. He retraced his steps to Neukölln and, in Prinz-Handjery Strasse, he came across a number of young people with whom he began to discuss his ideas. Again he was met with polite indifference. Dismayed, he turned his back on them and returned to the hostel in the Alexandrinenstrasse.

It was that Friday night that he finally decided to take matters into his own hands, and to begin by setting a number of public buildings on fire. Perhaps once the intimidated masses saw these strongholds of capitalism going up in flames, they might shake off their lethargy even at this late hour.

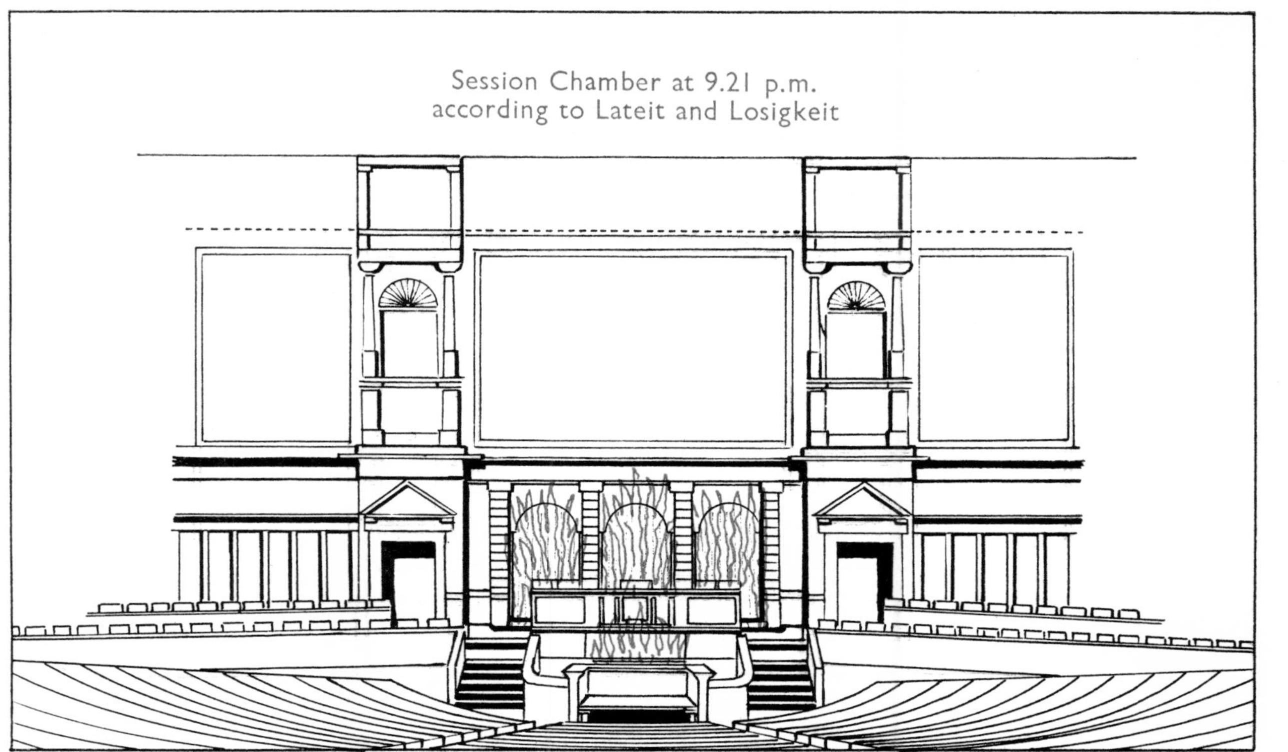

FIG 1. Bundesarchiv R43/294 after a photograph attached to Prof. Josse's affidavit.

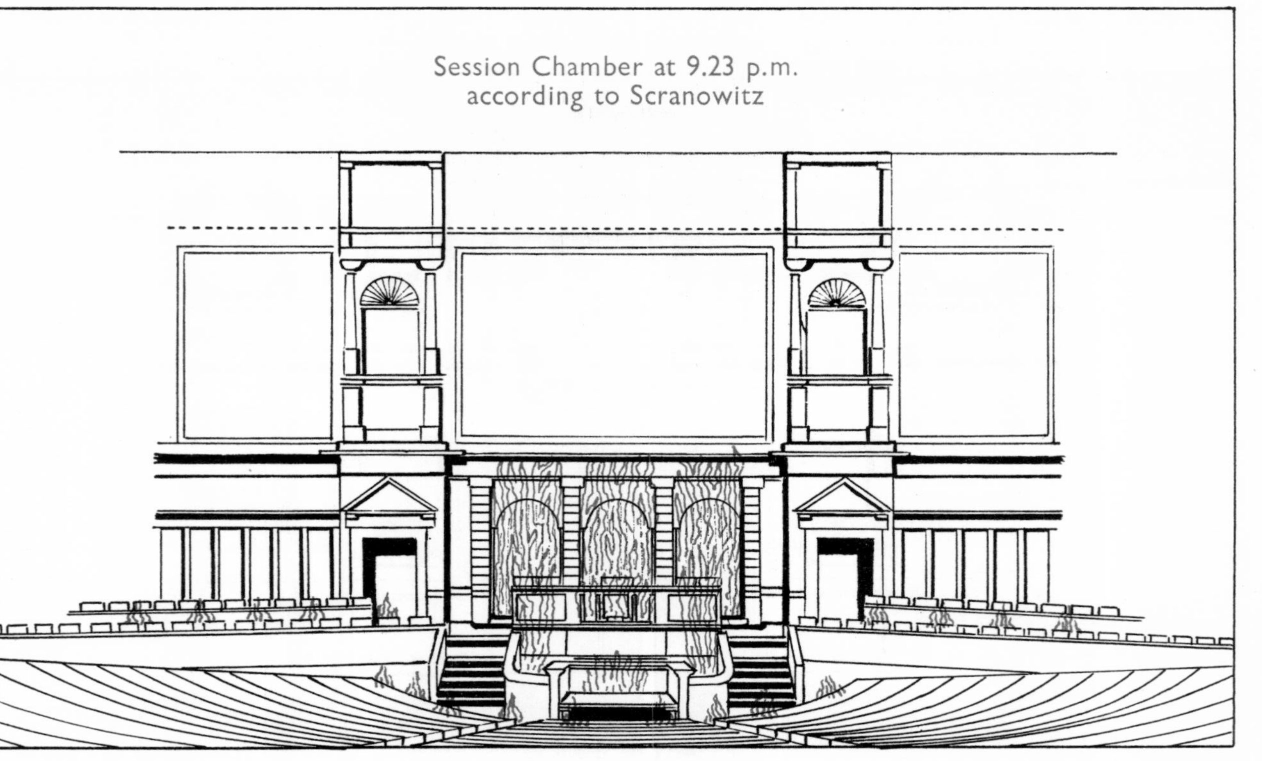

FIG 2. Origin as overleaf.

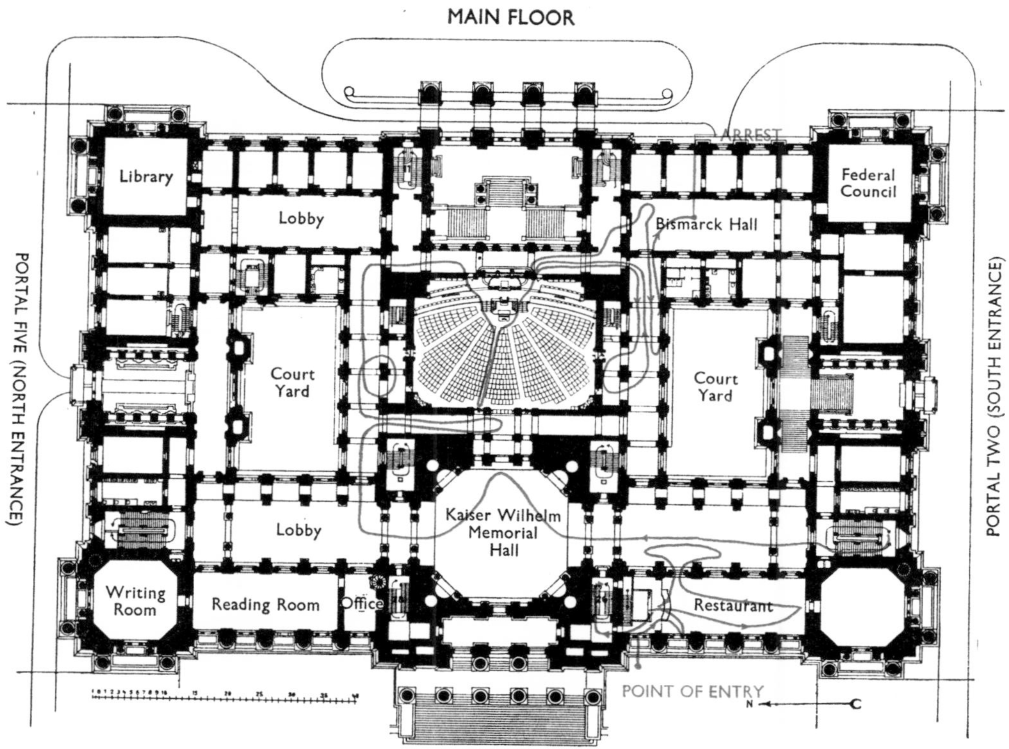

FIG 3. Van der Lubbe's trail through the Reichstag (main floor).

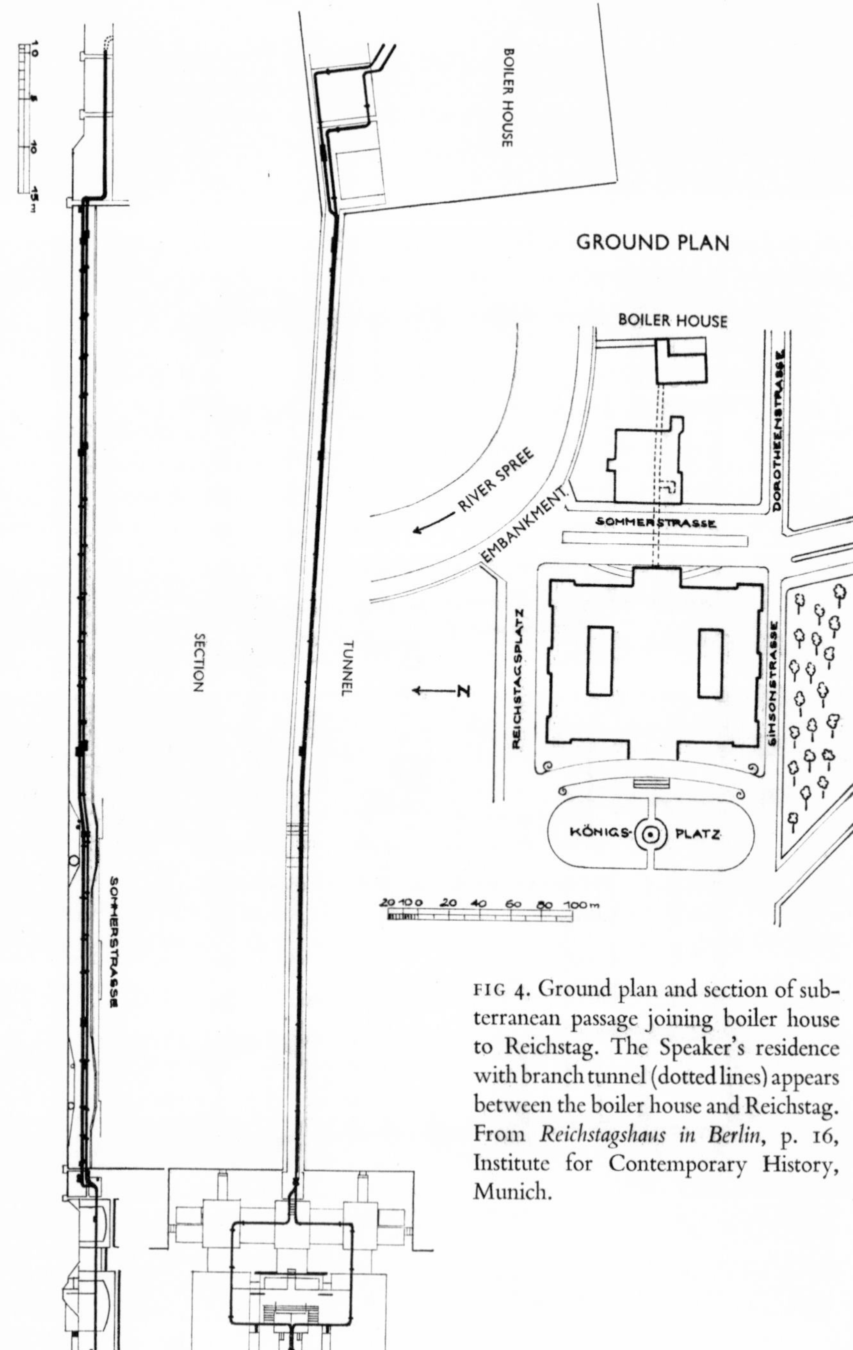

FIG 4. Ground plan and section of subterranean passage joining boiler house to Reichstag. The Speaker's residence with branch tunnel (dotted lines) appears between the boiler house and Reichstag. From *Reichstagshaus in Berlin*, p. 16, Institute for Contemporary History, Munich.

THE FOUR FIRES

On Saturday morning at about 10 a.m., Marinus left the hostel in the direction of Neukölln, passing the Town Hall and the Palace on the way. He then bought matches at Otto Zöchert's in the Annenstrasse, and two packets of firelighters at E. Brahl's in the Neanderstrasse. He specially asked for firelighters 'with a red flame' on the wrapper, i.e. for the 'Oldin' brand.

On leaving the shop, he at once opened the packets and looked at the contents very carefully.[3]

In yet another shop, Heleski's in the Liegnitzer Strasse, he asked for two more packets of lighters. As the shopkeeper did not understand him at once, he explained: '*Dinger zum Kacheln!*' (*Kachel* = 'stove' in Dutch, but 'tile' in German). Asked whether he was a Dutchman, he quickly replied that he came from the Rhineland.

At about 4 p.m. he turned the corner to the Neukölln Welfare Office, for he had decided to make a start right there.

The wooden hut was surrounded by a five-foot fence. While examining the layout very carefully, Marinus spotted an open window and, since it was still too light, he decided to return later. He was back at 6.30 p.m., swung himself over the fence, divided one packet of firelighters in two, lit one half, and then threw it through the open window at the back, into what turned out to be the ladies' lavatory. The firelighter landed on the concrete floor and charred the lavatory door before it burnt itself out. Van der Lubbe had meanwhile climbed up on a windowsill, where he lit the remaining half of the packet and threw it on to the snow-covered roof. Then he jumped down again, threw another half packet on to the eastern side of the roof, and made his getaway.

The lighter on the roof did its job so well that a fire was noticed soon afterwards by two passers-by. They summoned Police-Sergeant Albrecht who, with another passer-by, managed to put the fire out fairly quickly. As both witnesses stated later, the roofing had caught fire despite the snow. This alone shows the effectiveness of the sawdust-and-petroleum firelighters van der Lubbe was using.

Van der Lubbe had long disappeared by the time the fire was discovered and put out: he had made for the Hermannsplatz underground station to catch a train to the Alexanderplatz. From there, he walked through the Neue Königstrasse to the Town Hall which he reached at about 7.15 p.m. He had noticed an open basement window earlier during the day, and now threw a burning packet of firelighters through it – into the flat of Engineer Richard Kiekbusch.

Here, too, van der Lubbe ran away without awaiting the outcome. The fire cut a large hole into the floor, and also burned a coat-rack, the wallpaper and a large section of the skirting-board. The flames were so high that they scorched the ceiling. Kiekbusch, attracted by the smell, put out the fire just in time, for '. . . inflammable materials were stored in the adjoining rooms, and the fire might easily have eaten its way through the plasterboard walls into the other flats.'

Though he was extremely angry, Kiekbusch did not report the matter to the police. Instead he simply notified his own superiors next morning, and was told 'not to make a fuss about trifles'.[4] As Kiekbusch explained later, thoughtless or malicious passers-by had more than once thrown burning cigarette butts through the open windows, thus causing a number of minor fires.

Van der Lubbe next made for the old Imperial Palace, his third objective. As luck would have it, a scaffolding had been placed in front of the west entrance, which Marinus, the former bricklayer, had little difficulty in climbing. Once on top, he walked along the western edge of the roof, then along the southern edge until he came to a number of double windows with a common balustrade. One of the outer windows (the fourth) was slightly ajar, and he threw a burning packet of firelighters inside. It struck against the inner panes, fell down and burned the sill.

Next van der Lubbe discovered a kind of roof-arbour, belonging to a retired gentleman by the name of Schönfelder. Though he made repeated attempts to set fire to the wooden structure, the wind proved far too strong. In the end, Marinus climbed down the scaffolding and went back to sleep in the Alexandrinenstrasse hostel. At 10.10 p.m., Fireman Hermann Schulz of the Palace Fire Brigade noticed the smell of smoke during his round through the top of the Palace. He opened Room 42, and was met by thick clouds. He quickly climbed up on the roof, bent over, saw that the sill was ablaze, and immediately rang the Palace Fire Brigade, who sent up Fireman Waldemar Maass. Together they first broke a window and then put out the fire with a hose.

A report of this fire was published on 27 February:

> It has only now become known that a small fire broke out on Saturday in an office room on the fifth floor of the Berliner Schloss, which was quickly put out by a fireman stationed on the premises. The origin of the fire is not yet fully explained. But it is thought to have been an act of incendiarism.
>
> One hour before the fire started, the caretaker had made his round through the Schloss and had even passed through the room. At the time there was nothing suspicious to be seen. Soon afterwards the room was in flames. Investigation showed that there was a burning firelighter on the window-sill, and another under the window and also on the steam pipes.
>
> The police investigation has not yet been concluded.[5]

The origin of this fire might never have been discovered at all, had the amateur incendiary, van der Lubbe, not dropped so many spent matches on the roof, and had he not left the wrappers of his firelighters lying about.

At the Supreme Court Trial the Assistant Public Prosecutor, Dr Parrisius, had this to say about the first three fires:

> All the evidence suggests that he committed these crimes by himself. Had they produced the desired effect, the German capital would have been in a state of frenzied excitement as early as 25 February 1933.[6]

A comparison of the fires shows that they all had one remarkable thing in common: all three were started successfully despite the rather unorthodox methods used, and all three were discovered more or less by chance.

Next day, on Sunday, 26 February, van der Lubbe walked through Charlottenburg to Spandau. Shortly before midday, he watched a Storm Troop demonstration, and also spoke to a woman, who took pity on him and offered him some food. Afterwards he went on to Henningsdorf, where he reported his presence to the police in accordance with the Aliens Law. The police then gave him shelter for the night – a small cell in the police-station. According to the police records, he shared this cell with another man, to whom we shall return later.

On Monday morning, the two of them were put out very early, and were seen to cross the street to a café, where they were given a free cup of coffee each. It was well before eight o'clock when they started the march back to Berlin. Marinus arrived in the centre of the city at about 12 noon and went to Hermann Stoll's at 48a Müllerstrasse, where he bought four further packets of firelighters 'with the red flame on the wrapper'. He put one packet each into his overcoat and coat pockets, and then set off through Chausseestrasse, Friedrichstrasse, Unter den Linden, Neue Wilhelmstrasse and Dorotheenstrasse to the Reichstag where he arrived at about 2 p.m.

Walking round the vast building a number of times, Marinus discovered that there were quite a few ways of getting in. In the end he decided on the western front, because it was the least frequented. Richard Schmal, a junior official who was just leaving the Reichstag, remembered noticing van der Lubbe there, dressed in shabby clothes, a peaked cap, and ridiculously short trousers.

Since it was long before nightfall, van der Lubbe walked through the Tiergarten to the Potsdamer Platz and from there through the Leipzigerstrasse and the Königstrasse to the Alexanderplatz Post Office. There he stayed, in the warm, from 3.30 p.m. to 4 p.m., while reading some fresh pamphlets he had picked up in the street. Then he went to the Friedrich Gardens, and returned to the Reichstag at about 9 p.m. On the way he tore the wrappers off the firelighters, so as not to waste time later. The western front of the Reichstag was completely deserted. Marinus climbed up the balustrade to the right of the broad carriageway and expertly scaled the wall to the first floor. He landed on the balcony in front of the restaurant, i.e. in front of the window nearest the central portico on the southern side. (He left traces of his climb on the façade which were subsequently discovered and checked.) On the balcony, he took a packet of lighters out of his pocket and managed to light it, but only after he had used up half a dozen matches. As he explained later, he preferred lighting the packet outside in the strong wind to running the risk of being stopped by someone inside.

At 9.03 p.m. he kicked his foot through a pane 8 mm. thick – he had to kick more than once – and then dropped into the dark restaurant. There he flung the lighter, which had started to burn fiercely, on to a wooden table behind the bar. Then he took a second packet from his pocket, lit it from the remains of the first, snatched up the curtains over the door leading into the lobby, and set fire to them. (Both curtains were completely destroyed, and the wooden door and door-posts were badly damaged.) Then he ran back to the curtains over the second window, threw a firelighter on to a table and pulled the bottom of one curtain over it. Next he lit part of the third packet of lighters with the remains of the second, and set fire to the other curtain. Having lit the rest of the third packet from the burning curtain, he ran to the Kaiser Wilhelm monument and, finding nothing combustible there, he took off his overcoat, coat, sweater and shirt. Using the last as a firebrand, he doubled back to the restaurant, ran into the waiters' room to the left of the counter, and pulled a tablecloth out of a cabinet. He set fire to the tablecloth with his shirt, and ran down the stairs to the kitchen where he dropped the burning tablecloth. As he did so, he was startled by a shot outside (the shot fired by Buwert). Then he set fire to a number of towels in the cloakroom, and ran up the staircase back to the monument, where he picked up his coat and sweater, but left his cap, his tie and a piece of soap, all of which were later collected by Lieutenant Lateit. Near the door of the Session Chamber, he lit the sweater, and then, bare to the waist, raced through the lobby into the western corridor, saw a wooden panel leaning against a wall and tried to set fire to it. Next he set fire to a large desk standing between two doors in the northern corridor, opened the door to the Session Chamber, set fire to the curtains nearest the Speaker's Chair, tore down the curtain in the entrance of the stenographers' well, lit it from one of the other curtains, dragged it to the western corridor and dropped it. Then he went back to the Speaker's Chair for more burning material, ran out into the eastern corridor and then some yards into the southern corridor, where he set fire to a number of other curtains. At this point he suddenly heard voices, and made for the Bismarck Hall. On the way he dropped a burning brand which set fire to a door and a carpet. As he entered the Bismarck Hall, he was intercepted by Constable Poeschel and by House-Inspector Scranowitz.

Van der Lubbe surrendered quite happily, for he knew that his fourth fire had been a great success. He had shown the German workers that even one man could strike back at the Hitler régime, and that is why his answer to Scranowitz's furious 'Why?' was: 'As a protest!'

Van der Lubbe had stampeded through a vast building with such incredible speed that most people refused to believe his story. But later, even the most sceptical had to agree that when he was asked by the Court to reconstruct the crime, while an official clicked a stopwatch, he showed that he could, in fact, have been telling the truth all along.

The fourth fire differed from the other three by only one – admittedly essential – factor: it was the only one that was not detected in time, and hence the only one that did serious damage.

THE GREAT QUESTION

All the time van der Lubbe was in the Brandenburg Gate guardroom, he was surrounded by a wall of uniformed and well-nourished policemen, who looked on him with a mixture of curiosity and revulsion. Naturally the first question everyone wanted to ask him was why he had started the fire, and why in the Reichstag of all places. Van der Lubbe told them all that he had not intended to protest against parliamentary institutions as such, that he had already set fire to a number of other buildings, and that he would have set fire to more if he had not been stopped. He mentioned the Palace, and also the Cathedral.

When the duty officer, Lieutenant Emil Lateit, returned to the station a little while later, he asked van der Lubbe whether the cap and tie that had been picked up in the Reichstag were his. Lieutenant Lateit also asked whether van der Lubbe had really set fire to the Reichstag all by himself. Van der Lubbe said yes to both questions. Had he intended to set fire to the Palace and to the Cathedral as well? Van der Lubbe said yes again. To Lateit, the correct Prussian officer, any man who rebelled against order and discipline, let alone somebody who defied authority by running about half-naked in mid-winter and setting public buildings on fire, was quite obviously a raving lunatic. That is why, like Scranowitz before him and like everyone else after him, he kept on pressing van der Lubbe for the 'real' reasons – a question that was to break van der Lubbe's spirit in the end. As it gradually dawned on the unfortunate man that his captors, the guardians of the hated capitalist system, failed to understand him, not because they could not follow his peculiar German, but because they were quite incapable of grasping, however vaguely, what was in his mind, Marinus van der Lubbe lapsed into silence.

Unfortunately, Lateit was as incapable of understanding van der Lubbe's sudden silence as he had been incapable of understanding what preceded it. There was only one explanation: the fellow was no ordinary criminal but an obvious lunatic, one who deliberately courted notoriety and arrest, and one, what is more, who also threw his clothes away. Some kind of pyromaniac, no doubt, who liked to get his name into the papers. Shaking his head, Lateit gave up, and sent van der Lubbe to police headquarters in the Alexanderplatz.

The reader, too, may well shake his head at van der Lubbe's 'naïve' ideas, though few would care to argue that they were completely incoherent or senseless – under the prevailing conditions, they were, in fact, no more 'naïve' or 'adventurous' than those of the Nazis themselves. Ten years earlier, on the night of 8 November 1923, Hitler too had been convinced that his 'great deed' – the Munich putsch – would become a signal to all Germany and that the Weimar Republic would collapse as a result.

There are many other surprising similarities between Hitler and van der Lubbe. Each was one of seven children from different marriages. Both are said to have wanted to enter the ministry, both lost their fathers early in life – Hitler through death, van der Lubbe through desertion. Both had ailing mothers who died prematurely. Hitler was stricken with tuberculosis at sixteen, which changed the course of his life; van der Lubbe had an accident at sixteen with similar results. Both vacillated for years, unable to settle down to anything for long. Both were wild fanatics, and belonged to small political splinter groups. Both were penniless and spent much of their time drifting from one casual ward to another. Both had their heads stuffed with stupendous ideas, and both had nostrums for all mankind's major ills. Neither finished school; both had excellent memories and were excellent speakers. Both were avid readers of Sven Hedin's travel books. Both were too busy with politics and too poor to have steady girl friends, though neither was sexually abnormal. Both took political actions which, in the sober light of day, look like the actions of madmen. Finally, both Hitler and van der Lubbe died violent deaths, and saw the collapse of their most cherished political hopes.

Those who consider this comparison a little too far-fetched might do well to remember Frederick II's dictum:

> Courage and skill are shared by highwaymen and heroes alike. The difference is that the hero is a noble and famous robber while the other is an unknown rogue. One earns laurels and praise for his crimes, the other gets paid with the rope.

THE SÖRNEWITZ LEGEND

The widespread belief that van der Lubbe had close associations with National Socialists shortly before the Reichstag fire can be shown to be the result of deliberate Communist juggling with the facts. It all started with the following story, published in the *Brown Book* under the heading 'A Guest of the Nazis':

> On 1st and 2nd June (1932) he stayed the night at Sörnewitz (Saxony) where he was seen in company with the local councillor Sommer and also Schumann who owned a vegetable garden. Both are National Socialists. After the Reichstag fire, Councillor Sommer reported van der Lubbe's visit in 1932 to the Mayor of Brockwitz. This fact was recorded in a protocol, which was forwarded to the Saxon Ministry of the Interior, which notified Frick, Reich Minister of the Interior, of these facts. The facts became public as the result of an interpellation in the Saxon Diet by a Social Democratic deputy. They have not been denied by anyone. . . . Councillor Sommer disappeared a short time after he made the report.[7]

What was the basis of all this?

On 1 June 1932, on his way home from Hungary, van der Lubbe had asked the Sörnewitz parish authorities for permission to spend the night in the parish shelter. In the morning he left for Dresden, where his name was duly entered among those who spent the night of 3 June in the local poorhouse.

We shall see that, after the Reichstag fire, a reward of 20,000 marks was offered to anyone who could throw further light on van der Lubbe's 'real' motives and accomplices. Now, when this matter was discussed at a gathering of welfare officers in Meissen on 3 March 1933, the Mayor of Sörnewitz, Councillor Liebscher, told the meeting that van der Lubbe's name appeared in the register of his parish shelter. Franz Lindner, from neighbouring Brockwitz, then asked whether van der Lubbe was the crook who had also visited Brockwitz at that time, swindling the local Nazi leader Oskar Sommer. The man had given out that he was a National Socialist, and had muttered something about civil war and rebellion.

At the Supreme Court trial in Leipzig, the resulting comedy of errors took up so much time that van der Lubbe, who in any case could neither remember Sörnewitz nor fathom why they made such a fuss of his having spent the night there, had his first fit of laughter. The President and the Chief Public Prosecutor, who thought that the accused was holding them in contempt, interrupted the trial, to insist on an explanation. Naturally van der Lubbe found it extremely difficult to explain what he thought of their ridiculous efforts to reconstruct conversations that he had forgotten long ago, or of the way in which the Court blew up trivialities until they assumed quite ridiculous proportions. And when all this bluster went hand-in-hand with so much pomp and solemnity, with all the trimmings of German legality, what else could he do, poor fellow, but burst out laughing in their faces? He knew that he was no Nazi, had admitted that he had no accomplices, and simply could not understand what these ridiculous bunglers in purple were trying to do to him.

Still, all the Court's lengthy and laborious investigations eventually bore fruit: it was proved beyond the shadow of a doubt that the man who had swindled the Brockwitz Nazi leader could not have been van der Lubbe. What had happened was that on 7 August 1932, i.e. six weeks after van der Lubbe himself had been in Saxony, a young man had called on the Nazi Oskar Sommer, claiming that all his money and his papers had been stolen while he had taken a swim. He was foolish enough to show Sommer an envelope with his real name: Wilhelm Barge. As Sommer later told the Court, Barge kept boasting about his achievements, and even hinted that he was a member of Hitler's inner circle. According to Barge the Nazis were planning an armed uprising for 1 October and were quite ready for civil war. Sommer took his uninvited guest to the local inn, but being slightly suspicious of him, he asked the local policeman, Max Miersch, to keep his eye on the fellow. When Miersch turned up at the inn the next morning, Barge was still asleep, but half an hour later he disappeared without a trace. Sommer then lodged an official complaint. In December 1932, Wilhelm Barge was sent to prison for nine months for fraud and forgery.

But before Lindner's vague suspicion that Barge might be identical with van der Lubbe was finally refuted, the mere suggestion of such a possibility had proved most embarrassing to the Nazis, particularly after it was seized upon by their enemies.

When the Mayor of Brockwitz, Bruno Keil, first heard about Lindner's suspicions, he immediately summoned Sommer who, astonished though he was, admitted that Lindner might possibly be right. Keil picked up the telephone and reported the whole thing to the Chief Magistrate in Meissen, who in turn notified the Reichstag deputy Dobbert. Dobbert then rang up the Saxon Minister of the Interior, and also sent a telegram to the Public Prosecutor in Leipzig. The telegram, dated 4 March 1933, read as follows:

> Reichstag Incendiary Marinus van der Lubbe stayed night of 1 June 1932 in Sörnewitz as recorded in night register. Played National Socialist to leading National Socialists in Brockwitz, viz. Councillor Sommer and nurseryman Schumann. Entertained by Councillor Sommer and disappeared. Told Sommer Germany on eve of civil war, but that National Socialist Party fully prepared.

When Dobbert's telegram was forwarded to the Examining Magistrate, Judge Vogt, in Berlin, Vogt promptly dispatched his assistant, Dr Wernecke, to Brockwitz. It did not take Wernecke long to discover that the whole story was based on an almost incredible combination of errors and confusions.

THE MOST SHAMEFUL LIE OF ALL

Far more scandalous still was the *Brown Book* lie that Marinus was a homosexual. This is what the *Red Book* had to say on that subject:

> When, in their account of Marinus's youth, they come to his twelfth year or so, these red gentry begin to hint that Marinus was a strange sort of fellow, so strange, in fact, that he was certain to turn into a homosexual. . . . The victim gets his first jab on page 46 of the *Brown Book:*
>
> '[His comrades] also tease him on account of his fear of girls. This characteristic was so strong and so obvious that his former classmates talk about it to this day. He simply could not be made to consort with any girls, but found his love among schoolboys and other boys of his age.'
>
> The second injection with homosexuality germs comes on page 47:
>
> 'It was all the more inexplicable to the builders' apprentices, with whom he was working, why Marinus van der Lubbe was so afraid of women.'
>
> It would take us too far afield to refute the *Brown Book* story of van der Lubbe's youth point by point. We shall therefore single out the

lie that he was a homosexual, a lie that becomes the more brazen, the closer the *Brown Book* comes to Marinus's so-called 'experiences' with Dr Bell.

The *Red Book* then looks at the *Brown Book* story that '. . . Izak Vink told our reporter that he often shared a bed with van der Lubbe', and points out that though Vink said just that, he also added: '. . . without my ever noticing the slightest homosexual tendencies', a phrase which the *Brown Book* conveniently forgot to repeat.

Unlike the *Brown Book*, in which the main allegations were anonymous, i.e. completely uncorroborated, the *Red Book* published signed statements by many people who had known Marinus in Leyden. All were agreed that they had never noticed the slightest homosexual tendencies in him.

The *Brown Book*'s prize exhibit was provided by a Herr 'W.S.', the 'friend of Dr Bell'. This Dr Bell, a shady international adventurer, was alleged to have kept a list of all the boys whom he procured for his friend Röhm, the notorious Storm Troop Chief of Staff. Herr 'W.S.' had this to say:

> If I remember rightly, it was in May 1931 that Bell told me he met a young Dutch worker who made a very good impression on him. Bell was out in his car near Berlin or Potsdam, when he met a hiker, and offered him a lift. The hiker was a young Dutch workman, and he visited Bell later in Munich. Bell called him Renus or Rinus. He had frequent meetings with him. . . .
>
> Dr Bell fetched a number of papers from a secret cabinet. He pointed to a sheet and said: 'This is Röhm's love-list. If I ever publish it, Röhm is a dead man.' He showed me the list, which contained some thirty names. I remember very well that one of them was Rinus followed by a Dutch name beginning with 'van der'.[8]

'Unfortunately,' the *Brown Book* continued, 'this love-list was taken away by the Storm Troopers who murdered Bell near Kufstein.'

It is typical that this 'sworn statement of Herr W.S.' published in the *Brown Book*, differs in many respects from the testimony 'Herr W.S.' gave at the London 'Counter-Trial', and which was reported in *Het Volk* on 16 September 1933. According to that testimony, Bell's list consisted exclusively of Christian names, with only one exception which, as the reader will have guessed, was none other than: 'Marinus van der . . . and then one or two letters which I could not quite make out: S, T, L, or H and then . . . ubbe, and Holland.'

The *Red Book* rightly scoffed:

> Wasn't it clever of Dr Bell, to write the name of van der Lubbe out in full, when all the other entries were Christian names or nicknames, and even to add his country of origin! Obviously, the Germans must by then have grown so super-patriotic that they insisted on distinguishing between local homosexuals and alien imports.

The *Brown Book* also had other homosexual aces up its sleeve. Thus it claimed that:

> When van der Lubbe returned to Leyden in January or February 1932, he had a great deal to tell his friends about his tour. He claimed that he met a young journeyman whose sister worked in a Budapest brothel. Marinus van der Lubbe made it known that he had decided to save this girl. At her insistence he had spent one night with her but without touching her. This behaviour is so typical of homosexuals that Freud has called it the 'Parsifal-complex'.[9]

The reply of the *Red Book* was:

> If it is written in the *Brown Book*, so famed for its clarity and honesty, then, of course, it simply must be true. Particularly when its authority is propped up with Professor Freud's. However, the *Brown Book* might have added that – again according to Professor Freud – this 'complex' is found among heterosexual men, as well.[10]

During his travels in Europe, Marinus van der Lubbe had many clashes with the police. All his convictions are known, and it appears that, though male homosexuality is an offence in most European countries – with the notable exception of Holland – no charge sheet contains so much as a hint that he was ever suspected of being an invert. And yet, had he been a homosexual as well as a 'penniless vagrant' he would surely have tried to solicit male customers wherever he went.

3. The Police Investigation

THE FINAL REPORT

DETECTIVE-INSPECTOR Dr Walter Zirpins submitted his final report on the Reichstag fire on 3 March 1933. In Section C, he posed and answered a crucial question, when he said:

> There is no doubt that van der Lubbe committed the crime entirely by himself. This conclusion follows from the investigations, the objective facts, and the precise answers of the suspect.

In support of this view, which refuted the Nazi story of Communist complicity and hence was bound to earn him Government hostility, Dr Zirpins adduced the following facts:

> The scene of the crime and his activities there were described by van der Lubbe right from the start [i.e. before the official reconstruction of the crime on the spot] in such detail – seats of fire, damage caused, trails left, and paths taken – as only the incendiary himself could have supplied. Had he not been there himself, he could not possibly have described, and later demonstrated on the spot, all these facts and especially the smaller fires which he had lit at random.
>
> The reconstruction of the crime proved that all the details he gave were absolutely correct.

So accurate were van der Lubbe's descriptions and sketches that the astonished detectives were quite unable to catch him out in a single error or omission. Had there been accomplices, some signs of their presence would most certainly have come to light.

On 27 September 1933, when Dr Zirpins gave evidence before the Supreme Court, and hence before all the world, Torgler's counsel, Dr Sack, asked him to tell the Court why, in his final report, he felt so certain that van der Lubbe must have been the sole culprit.

Dr Zirpins's reply was:

> The method used was the same with all three fires. Marinus van der Lubbe has, as I have said, given us a signed statement, explaining the

whole matter. I believe – no, I am convinced – that he did it all by himself.

Now, the very fact that all those of van der Lubbe's statements which were verifiable proved to have been absolutely correct ought to have suggested to the worthy detective that van der Lubbe might also be speaking the truth about his motives. However, Dr Zirpins's objectivity did not stretch so far. Thus, in the last section of his report, he felt impelled to leave the safe foothold of established fact for the shifting sands of speculation, that is for the allegation that van der Lubbe had acted on the instructions of the German Communist Party. He based this allegation on the following 'evidence':

> During the police investigations he kept trying to develop his Communist ideas, so that it was only with great difficulty and after hours of conversation that we managed to get down to the real business.

And this was all the 'evidence' the police could muster to prove the story that van der Lubbe was a tool of the Communists. Oddly enough therefore, this slander, which the Communists soon turned against the Nazis, was not started by the National Socialists themselves, but by Zirpins, a police officer of the old school, one who at no time belonged to the Nazi Party. It was this man who said of van der Lubbe:

> A man who is willing to carry out revolutionary intrigues on his own account is just what the Communist Party needs. In the Party's hands, van der Lubbe became a willing tool, one who, while believing he was shifting for himself, was being shifted from behind the scenes. No wonder then that the Communist Party was so delighted to use him, particularly since they knew that they would be able to wash their hands of him completely.

And Zirpins added with quite remarkable assurance:

> The strong suspicion that van der Lubbe acted on the orders of Communist leaders, is confirmed by unequivocal facts.

And what precisely were these 'unequivocal' facts? One was that van der Lubbe had made 'contact', not with the Communist Party but '... with workmen in Welfare Offices, at meetings, etc., where he started discussions with them....'

Another 'unequivocal' fact was that '... on his arrest he was found to carry the appended Communist leaflets in his pocket.'

The third fact was even more 'unequivocal': 'When, after the interrogation on 2 March, he was taken back to the cells at 6 p.m., he promised cheerfully to deliver a stirring Communist speech to the Supreme Court.'

Then there came an 'unequivocal' incrimination of the Communist Party leadership:

> There is a great deal of circumstantial evidence to show that Communist deputies were the instigators of the crime, and especially the Deputies Torgler and Koenen, who in recent times used every conceivable occasion as an excuse for unusually frequent meetings in the Reichstag.

Quite apart from the fact that no evidence was produced to show that the two men used 'every conceivable occasion' for 'unusually frequent' meetings in the Reichstag, the fact that the President of the Communist Diet faction met the President of the Communist Reichstag faction in what, after the closure of the Karl Liebknecht House, remained their last legal refuge, was neither remarkable nor in any way suspicious, particularly at a time when a general election was being fought. No wonder that in all subsequent hearings these 'facts' were never mentioned again.

It was their Communist plot theory which encouraged the police to ignore the Criminal Procedure Code, and to allow hostile witnesses to have a good look at van der Lubbe first, and to 'describe' him afterwards. Their subsequent statements enabled Zirpins to claim:

> Three eye-witnesses saw van der Lubbe in the company of Torgler and Koenen before the fire. In view of van der Lubbe's striking appearance, it is impossible for all three to have been wrong.

Although police reports 'must restrict themselves to the established facts', Dr Zirpins's report continued:

> Witnesses who were in the vicinity of the Reichstag at the time, noticed a suspicious person fleeing the building during the fire. It seems likely that this person, whose identity remains unknown, was one of the principals keeping an eye on the progress of the crime.

Another bit of 'corroborative' evidence quoted by Zirpins was the following:

On 17 February 1933, a Russian was seen in the Potsdamer Platz in the company of two Dutchmen, to whom he handed bundles of bank-notes under suspicious circumstances.

Zirpins considered this last bit of 'evidence' so important that he quoted its sources in full:

We, the undersigned
1. Paul Merten
2. Walther Arlt
make the following statement:
A week ago we reported that on Friday, February 17th, 1933, between 11 p.m. and 11.30 p.m. we saw a Russian handing four bundles of banknotes to two Dutchmen in the Potsdamer Platz behind the news-paper kiosk (Post Office side).

We inferred the Dutch nationality of the two men from the fact that the word 'van' cropped up a number of times. The conversation was carried on softly in German, and we heard nothing of the subject matter the men were discussing. We did, however, watch the men and saw that they entered the Café Vaterland.... We also noticed that, as the Russian took the money from his coat pocket, he accidentally dropped a piece of paper. We picked it up later and made out a series of numbers, strokes, dots and punctuation marks. We handed this piece of paper over to the police.[1]

During the identity parade which was arranged at once, the two witnesses were unable to recognize van der Lubbe. He himself had this to say:

I am further told that on February 17th, 1933, a Russian was observed on the Potsdamer Platz handing [four bundles of banknotes] to two Dutchmen under suspicious circumstances. I myself did not arrive in Berlin until February 18th, 1933, and could obviously not have been there. I know no Dutchmen in Berlin, and have no acquaintances here.

Was Dr Zirpins dismayed? By no means! For this was his incredible conclusion:

Even though it has been established that van der Lubbe was not in Berlin on February 17th, 1933, and certainly not at the time in question – about 11 p.m., it nevertheless remains quite possible that these men were sent from Holland to pave the way for him.

The whole thing smacks of Gilbert and Sullivan, and not of a serious police investigation, particularly since the investigator-in-chief himself had only just stated that van der Lubbe had committed the crime without any assistance.

Further 'evidence' adduced by Zirpins was an unsigned newspaper article which the Police President of Essen had forwarded to him. Although even this article did nothing to prove the complicity of the other accused, Zirpins nevertheless used it against them. The article stated, *inter alia*, that:

> In the opinion of the Dutch police, the crime is undoubtedly the first of a series of individual outrages instigated by Moscow against Fascist Germany. These individual outrages are meant as substitutes for the old Communist method of starting riots, since, because of recent police measures, no great store can be set by mass actions.

Of similar validity was the next bit of 'incriminating' evidence, viz. the testimony of the ex-convict Otto Kunzack, a man whom the Supreme Court later described as an inveterate liar and informer. Yet this liar's statement was deemed worthy of being given great prominence in Zirpins's final report, where we can read:

> I knew van der Lubbe, the Reichstag incendiary, personally. He received his instructions from Cologne and Düsseldorf. Similar instructions were also received by Landtag Deputy Kerff, formerly a teacher in Cologne, and by one Josef Winterlich of Cologne.

As further evidence, Zirpins quoted a Nationalist press report alleging that the Communist Deputy Schumann had spoken of the Reichstag fire well before 8 p.m. on the eve of the fire. As it turned out, Schumann did not make the alleged remarks until after he had heard the ten o'clock news.

Yet all these bits of evidence which, taken singly or collectively, proved absolutely nothing, were deemed sufficient reason by Zirpins for '. . . suspecting that van der Lubbe acted on the orders of the Communist Party'.

Eighteen years later, Dr Walter Zirpins, now a senior Civil Servant, had this to say about his former theory:

> The question whether or not van der Lubbe acted under orders had to be left open by me, since my instructions were simply to examine van der Lubbe. Subsequently I have become firmly convinced that van der Lubbe had no principals.[2]

Had Dr Zirpins paused to reflect at the time, he would surely have reached the same conclusion much earlier. For when all is said and done, the very last thing German Communists wanted was to burn down their only remaining refuge in Berlin.

However, Zirpins's contentious and far-fetched conclusion, which earned him some ridicule even during the trial, was, in fact, just what Hitler needed in order to proscribe the Communist Party and to pour his brown hordes into the streets. That is, of course, the real reason why the story of van der Lubbe's untrustworthiness found its way into Zirpins's police report, whence it was handed on to the Examining Magistrate, the medical experts, the fire experts, the Public Prosecutor, and finally the Supreme Court judges.

Marinus van der Lubbe was committed for trial on the very day Inspector Zirpins published his report, and the case passed out of the hands of the police into those of Judge Vogt, the Examining Magistrate attached to the Supreme Court.

As one more astonishing example of the lengths to which the authorities were prepared to go to produce Communist 'accomplices', we need only tell the following story:

On the night of the fire, a large police force combed every conceivable nook and cranny of the Reichstag building for the alleged accomplices, and for any clues they might have left behind. All the policemen could discover, however, was the presence of some mysterious white crystals on the floor of one of Torgler's rooms. The crystals were carefully gathered up and rushed to the Prussian

Institute for Food, Drugs and Forensic Chemistry. Its director, Professor Dr August Brüning (now at Münster University) carried out an analysis and reported his findings to the Police President with all the pomp and circumstance demanded by the occasion. The conspiratorial particles were – granulated sugar.

HEISIG'S INVESTIGATIONS IN HOLLAND

On 4 March 1933 Inspector Heisig was sent to Holland by his chief, Rudolf Diels, with instructions to gather what evidence he could on van der Lubbe's background.

As Heisig told the Supreme Court on 29 September 1933, the Dutch authorities proved extremely helpful. He was able to speak to many of van der Lubbe's friends and acquaintances, including Piet van Albada, Jacob (Koos) Vink, the mayor of Oegsgeest, and Marinus's former teacher, van der Meene.

Albada, in particular, was concerned to defend his friend against Communist slanders, though, had he known with what disastrous results, he might not have said such things as:

> I have known van der Lubbe since about autumn 1929. I met him in the Dutch Communist Party. In the Party he gained his reputation by the work he did for the Young Communist League. In any case, even before he moved in with me, he was an exceptionally active member of the League. In the CPH [Communist Party of Holland] he attracted attention through discussions, lectures, and above all through his Communist work among the unemployed. The Party soon noticed his considerable influence among the unemployed, and entrusted him with ever more important tasks among them.[3]

Such explanations, far from vindicating van der Lubbe, merely confirmed Heisig's belief that Marinus was a Communist stooge and so, of course, did the following:

> After I left the CPH I became convinced that van der Lubbe was just the man the Party would use for special actions. He was always willing to start an agitation, without asking whether it had any chance of success or not.
>
> When I realized how the Party misused him, how they sent him into battle while they themselves remained safely in the background, and also that van der Lubbe was too decent to put any blame on the Party, I tried to make the whole thing clear to him and to gain him for my International Communist ideas. While he sympathized, he nevertheless refused to join us.

Once again, Albada had painted a picture of a zealot who would shield his so-called friends at any cost to himself. But Albada dealt Marinus an even worse blow when he went on to say:

> I know that the Party asked van der Lubbe to resign in case they were blamed for his activities. I have heard it said that the CPH has put van der Lubbe 'on ice'. But I know that he is still doing work for the Party, although not to the same extent as before.

With that statement Albada had completely discredited van der Lubbe's own statement and that of the Dutch police, namely that van der Lubbe had resigned from the Communist Party in 1929–31.

On 10 March 1933 van der Lubbe's friend Koos Vink made a similar statement, no doubt with the same good intentions, and with the same devastating results:

I am a member of the CPH. Marinus van der Lubbe is one of my best friends. Marinus van der Lubbe was a very hard-working and keen Communist and was very much respected in the Party. He frequently organized Communist meetings, at which he was a prominent speaker. He exerted a great deal of influence on the unemployed in Leyden; whatever he said always went down well with them and was done.

At the end of September 1933, when Heisig gave evidence on his investigations in Holland to the Supreme Court, and when the world press published his statement, the Communist Party put strong pressure on Albada and Vink, no doubt by telling them that their testimony might send van der Lubbe to the scaffold. As a result, Albada and Vink immediately retracted their statements, and the Communists were able to gloat:

No sooner was Heisig's evidence given than van Albada and Vink publicly protested. It appeared that not only had Heisig completely changed their statements but that he had included in them parts entirely of his own invention.[4]

Towards the end of his stay in Holland, the Chief of the Leyden police invited Heisig to hold a press conference which had been requested by a number of Dutch journalists. On this occasion, too, there were many questions about van der Lubbe's mysterious backers or accomplices. Now, had Heisig in fact been the Nazi hireling the Communists said he was, he could have hedged by claiming that the matter was *sub judice*, and thus have earned the gratitude of Göring and his other superiors. Instead, he gave what, in the circumstances, could only have been his honest opinion. This is how the Dutch press reported him next morning:

By treating him [van der Lubbe] considerately and by letting him feel that he would be deemed innocent until proved otherwise, the German authorities managed to get along with him extremely well. . . . Herr Heisig had the impression that van der Lubbe was being absolutely honest. . . . Though van der Lubbe lacked intellectual training, he proved exceptionally keen and shrewd whenever the discussion turned to anything he was particularly interested in. The German police officer was struck most of all by van der Lubbe's highly developed sense of direction. He knew Berlin almost as well as the inspector himself, and described his race through the Reichstag in every last detail. . . .

Herr Heisig was asked whether the fire might not have been started by political opponents of the Communist Party, and whether the police had not simply let the real culprits escape. That was all a lie, was the forthright answer of the German policeman. It was absolutely impossible for any accomplices to have escaped. In Herr Heisig's opinion, van der Lubbe had started the fire entirely by himself.[5]

This surprising opinion of someone in Heisig's position caused a tremendous stir in the Dutch press, for Heisig, who had been on the case from the start, and who ought to have known the facts better than anyone else, had denied the official German view that van der Lubbe had had countless Communist accomplices. The repercussions were fast, furious, and quite predictable: the Examining Magistrate, Judge Vogt, ordered Heisig to return immediately, while he himself published the following 'correction' in the official Government newspaper:

> Various newspapers have alleged that the Communist van der Lubbe burned the Reichstag by himself. In fact, the report of the Examining Magistrate shows there is good reason to believe that van der Lubbe did not act on his own. For the time being, all details must be withheld in the public interest.[6]

The *Red Book* rightly suspected that it was

> . . . probably not too sweeping an assumption that he (Heisig) was taken severely to task by his superiors for the careless views he had expressed. For how could they continue to hold the four Communists, once the inspector in charge of the investigation had himself declared that van der Lubbe was the sole culprit?[7]

In fact, Heisig was told by Judge Vogt that his press conference had helped to discredit not only the preliminary investigation but also the policies of the Third Reich. Accordingly, Judge Vogt made it known that all future press communiqués would be issued by him alone.

As Heisig spent the rest of his life under the spell of the Reichstag fire, we shall tell his story in brief.

After the events we have described, Heisig left Berlin, shortly before Division IA changed its name to Gestapo. As a petty official, and one who was politically 'unreliable' to boot, Heisig was careful to keep his mouth shut, which he found the easier to do in that no one would have believed him in any case: the Nazis because they were absolutely convinced of the guilt of the Communists; the Communists because they were as firmly convinced of the guilt of the Nazis.

Heisig took the first chance he had of resigning from the Prussian Police, and on 1 January 1934 became head of the Criminal Police in Dessau.

But even in the provinces he quickly got into hot water because of his political reticence which, under the Nazis, was bound to attract attention. His personal file which, it must be remembered, was compiled long before anyone thought of the possibility of denazification, contains the following statement:

> On January 1st, 1934, I took charge of the Criminal Police in Dessau (Anhalt), and on September 1st, 1934, I was appointed Chief Criminal Inspector.
>
> At the end of March 1936, I was accused of disrespect towards the local district leader of the National Socialist Party and was suspended on half pay.
>
> The Special Court in Halle referred my case to the District Court in Dessau which imposed a fine of 200 marks (or forty days) with the explanation that the status of the accused called for severe punishment.

At the beginning of May 1945, Heisig, who had meanwhile been promoted to the rank of Superintendent, was taken to the Regensburg Labour Camp by the Allies. Here he shared a cell with a particularly notorious prisoner, the former Chancellor, Franz von Papen. During their conversations Heisig told von Papen that, in his opinion:

> Van der Lubbe had fired the building, not at the instigation either of the Communists or of the Nazis, but on his own initiative. He had already attempted to burn the Schöneberg Town Hall, the Neukölln Welfare Office and the Berlin Palace.[8]

After Heisig's release from the internment camp, he ran into fresh difficulties. At the time of van der Lubbe's arrest in the Reichstag, Constable Poeschel had cursorily searched van der Lubbe without spotting a Communist pamphlet which was found on the Dutchman after a more thorough search in the police station. This pamphlet – 'Towards a United Front of Action'! – was later produced as evidence that van der Lubbe was a Communist (Exhibit 54).

When Poeschel, who knew nothing about this completely unimportant pamphlet, was asked about it during the trial, he was afraid to admit that he had overlooked anything, though no one would have blamed him if he had. He insisted blandly that, if he had not found the pamphlet at the time, then no pamphlet could have been there. In the end, the Court forced him to concede that 'perhaps it might have been there all the same'.

Now, in 1936 a former National Socialist and leader of the 'National Front against Bolshevist Excesses', Walther Korodi, who had left Berlin for Switzerland in 1935, published an anonymous article in which he alleged that Heisig had planted the pamphlet on van der Lubbe in order to prove his Communist connections. Though Heisig protested his innocence, which ought to have been clear from his record anyway, Communists made this slander the excuse for a vicious campaign against him in 1948, just after he had been released from the internment camp. One pamphlet called him a perjurer, adding that 'the whole story of the pamphlet was manufactured by the political police, and above all by Inspector Heisig'.[9]

As a result, Heisig was accused of complicity in the Reichstag fire and re-arrested. And so we have come full circle: Helmut Heisig, who had steadfastly opposed the Nazi thesis of Communist complicity at no small risk to himself, was now indicted as an accomplice by the very Communists he had tried to exonerate.

When he was first interned in May 1945, Heisig was already a broken and ailing man. The camp and the odious attacks by the Communists did the rest. After his final release he found that many of his former colleagues, who had shown themselves far more receptive to Nazi demands, had been reinstated long ago. On 23 August 1954, just before he, too, was due to be 'rehabilitated' at last, Heisig was killed in an accident.

In *Brown Book II*, Heisig is described as 'one of the confidants of the National-Socialist Party in the Berlin police headquarters', whose function it was 'to furnish convincing proofs of the guilt of the Communists'. It was further alleged that Heisig's interrogation of van der Lubbe was so irregular and that the record of it proved so embarrassing that '. . . from the beginning to the end of the trial the alleged statement was neither read nor shown to any of the other accused.'

Now, the authors of the *Brown Book*, who were apparently not familiar with the German criminal code, assumed that the statement must have disappeared simply because it was not read out in Court. However, according to German law, the Court is not entitled to consult police or other preliminary records, except in very special circumstances. Only direct evidence given in Court is considered admissible evidence.

But, in any case, the authors of the *Brown Book* knew perfectly well that the police records had not disappeared. In particular, they knew, or ought to have known from the Notes of Evidence, which they analysed with so much skill, that depositions made both to the police and to the Examining Magistrate were read out in Court, the moment van der Lubbe decided not to answer any more questions. Thus on 27 September 1933, the Presiding Judge, Dr Bünger, turned to Heisig with:

> I should like to recall to you the order in which your questions were put. You first asked what time it was when he [van der Lubbe] arrived at the Welfare Office. You recorded the answer: At 6.30 p.m.

Later, Dr Bünger told Heisig's colleague, Dr Zirpins:

> Now I shall tell you which interrogation we are concerned with – the one that took place on February 28th – probably well after midnight, was it not? This interrogation is incorporated in *Prel. Exam.* Vol. I, page 59. Did it take place early in the morning?

Dr Zirpins replied:

> Yes, it was in the morning. Herr Heisig had interrogated him for two hours during the night....

The depositions were further referred to on the 52nd day of the trial, i.e. on 6 December 1933. On that day Judge Rusch dealt with Dimitrov's request to be informed of what van der Lubbe had told the police about his (van der Lubbe's) alleged membership of the Dutch Communist Party. Judge Rusch said:

> As is generally known, the first interrogation was carried out by Inspector Heisig on the night of February 27th. The matter is reported in the form of questions and answers in *Prel. Exam.* Vol. V, page 48.

HITLER'S 'OVERSIGHT'

Hitler and his henchmen worked themselves into a lather of fury about van der Lubbe when really they ought to have been more than grateful to him. For was it not thanks to van der Lubbe's ill-considered action that they were given the chance of seizing power? Yet Göring, for instance, in his evidence to the Supreme Court on 4 November 1933 explained that the only reason he had refrained from 'making an example' of van der Lubbe was that he had hoped to catch the accomplices.

'The others are by far the worst,' he added.

Hitler himself kept harking back to this theme, particularly when world opinion laid the crime at his, or rather at Göring's, door. At a Cabinet Meeting held on 2 March 1933, Hitler explained that 'all these calumnies would have been stopped at source had the criminal been hanged on the spot'.

The subject was discussed again at the Cabinet Meeting of 7 March 1933 when Frick, the Minister of the Interior, argued that van der Lubbe should be hanged on the Königsplatz at once. Hitler concurred, and took the opportunity to deliver a harangue against those to whom nothing mattered except keeping to the letter of the law.

In his official address to the new Reichstag, on 3 March 1933, Hitler brought the matter up once again:

> The fact that a certain section of the press, particularly outside the German Reich, tries to couple the national resurrection of Germany with this evil deed, confirms my decision to wipe out the crime with the speedy public execution of the incendiary and his accomplices. (Loud applause from the National Socialist benches and the public.)[10]

Next day Hitler had an unpleasant surprise, for when Minister Frick demanded the death sentence for van der Lubbe in the Cabinet, Presidential Secretary Meissner told him: 'The Reich President [von Hindenburg] continues to have strong reservations about signing an order for the public execution of van der Lubbe.'

After this rebuff the President delivered an even more serious blow to 'that foreigner Hitler', when he said: 'The Reich President believes most strongly that public executions are not in keeping with German sentiments or with German history.'

After that, Hitler could not but proclaim that '... these views of the Reich President are naturally binding on the Cabinet'.[11] Eight years later, Hitler was still fuming about it all:

> Marinus van der Lubbe, the man who started the fire, ought to have been hanged within three days, if only because he was seen carrying a parcel from Torgler's house on the day of the fire. Had we made short shrift of him, we should also have been able to convict the real instigator, Dimitrov, who is now the head of the GPU in the Soviet Union.[12]

Today there seems little doubt that it was precisely by allowing van der Lubbe to stand trial that the Nazis proved their innocence of the Reichstag fire. For had van der Lubbe been associated with them in any way, the Nazis would have shot him the moment he had done their dirty work, blaming his death on an outbreak of 'understandable popular indignation'. Van der Lubbe could then have been branded a Communist without the irritations of a public trial, and foreign critics would not have been able to argue that, since no Communist accomplices were discovered, the real accomplices must be sought on the Government benches.

4. Wallot's Building

THE 'SYMBOL OF THE WEIMAR REPUBLIC'

MOST post-war accounts of the Reichstag fire repeat the legend that by destroying the Reichstag the incendiary or incendiaries intended to destroy the visible 'symbol' of German democracy – not only Parliament but parliamentary government as well.

Is it true to say, then, that the Reichstag building was the 'symbol' of German democracy? Was it really the embodiment of the democratic ideal of the Weimar Republic?

It is often forgotten that the unwieldy building on the Königsplatz was completed a quarter of a century before the young Weimar Republic moved in. Its architect, Paul Wallot, had worked away at it for ten long years – from 1884 to 1894 – at a cost to his country of 87 million gold marks. When he was finished, he had created a poor imitation of the Brussels Palace of Justice.

Its bombastic Prussian pomp, the banality of its sculptures, the clash of styles, were such that, immediately after the opening, voices began to clamour for the demolition squad, and for a new building more in keeping with the spirit and the needs of a modern state. Quite apart from the aesthetic aspects, the Reichstag's impressive façade soon proved to cover up a host of annoying shortcomings. For one thing, the mammoth structure was exceedingly short of working space, most of which had been wasted on display.

In order to remedy this glaring fault, the German Government offered a prize in 1929 for the best plan of rebuilding the Reichstag. However, all the entries had to be rejected – no satisfactory solution could be found. The deputies shrugged their shoulders, and forgot the whole business, particularly since Germany had come to feel the depression and no one could be bothered with parliamentary building experiments.

But it was not only architects who detested the building. Thus the former Minister of Justice, Gustav Radbruch, has said:

I have occasionally called the Reichstag 'a house without any weather'

> . . . for – no matter what the weather was outside, inside there was never anything but the insipid light of a cloudy sky.
>
> I am convinced that the excitability of the deputies . . . was based to some extent on the monstrous structure of the Reichstag.[1]

This so-called 'excitability of the deputies' was a reference to the many shameful scuffles by which German democracy was so often and so publicly degraded.

The ugliness of the Reichstag must have cushioned the blow of its destruction quite considerably. Thus when the Minister of Finance, Count Schwerin von Krosigk, was told about the fire he rejoiced at the fact that it was not a 'valuable monument'. The Nazi press officer, Dr Ernst Hanfstaengl, called the building a horror. The last Speaker of the Reichstag, Hermann Göring, said on many occasions that, though he bore no responsibility for the fire, he had no artistic objections to its results. On 13 October 1945 he astonished an American officer when, having emphatically denied his complicity in the Reichstag fire, he added that he himself would have burned the Reichstag for quite different reasons – simply '. . . because the large Session Chamber was so hideous, and because it had plaster walls. . . .'[2]

Before the Nuremberg Tribunal Göring also insisted that:

> There was no reason at all why I should have set the Reichstag on fire. True, from the artistic point of view I have no regrets that the Chamber was destroyed; I hoped to build a better one.[3]

The Reichstag building covered some two and three-quarter acres and was built of gigantic sandstone blocks. It faced true west, its road frontage was about 460 feet, and its central depth some 330 feet. Each corner had a tower, some 130 feet high. Right in the centre rose a gigantic glass cupola, which Berliners called the biggest round cheese in Europe; above it, rising almost 250 feet from the ground, shone a golden crown. From the Königsplatz which, at the time of the Weimar Republic, was turned into the Platz der Republik, a large flight of stairs led through the Main Entrance (Portal One) to the main floor. Beneath it lay the ground floor, the cellar, and two intermediate storeys, above it were two upper floors.

The main floor contained the Chamber, measuring some 95 feet by 72 feet. The three-tiered tribune (the Speaker's Chair above; the Orator's Table in the middle; and the stenographers' table below) faced the 600–700 deputies' seats, arranged in semicircles and divided into seven sectors. Successive rows were raised, in the manner of an amphitheatre. Opposite the tribune was the public gallery, with the press box, the former royal box, and the diplomatic box to the right. Daylight had to pass through the glass cupola and a glass ceiling, and was extremely faint by the time it reached the seats.

All the walls of the Chamber were richly panelled, and the panelling behind the tribune was lavishly hung with costly tapestries. In addition, there was a vast quantity of wood in the form of parapets, pillars, staircases, carvings, seats and desks. There were seven wooden doors, including a number of swinging doors. The stenographers' table stood in a well in the floor, which was reached by a small staircase, and had two doors of its own.

It was only because of the glass dome that the rest of the building was saved from destruction. For when the dome cracked, a natural chimney was formed, which sucked up all the flames and prevented the fire from spreading out.

This explains why the Session Chamber was 'cut out of the building by the fire as neatly as the stone from a peach' (Douglas Reed, *The Burning of the Reichstag*, p. 17), a fact which the former Reichstag President, Paul Löbe, was quite wrong to consider 'suspicious'.[4]

When the *Brown Book* alleged that the incendiaries – led by S.A. Colonel Heines with van der Lubbe 'fifth or sixth in line' – had entered the building through an 'underground passage', they started a rumour which grew as it fed on people's love of mystery and fable. In fact, the Reichstag tunnel was anything but mysterious: a tube six feet in diameter running some 450 feet from the Reichstag cellar to the boiler room on the Reichstag embankment. Wallot had placed the boilers at that distance from the main building 'in order that there should be no source of fire within Parliament itself', and had built the passage to carry the steam pipes across.

We know from Gustav Regler, an ex-Communist, how the *Brown Book* got hold of the plans of the Reichstag. With great (and quite unnecessary) secrecy, Regler copied the plans in the Strasbourg National Library – from Paul Wallot's *Das Reichstagsgebäude in Berlin* (Leipzig, 1899) and then offered them over the telephone to Willi Münzenberg, the leader of 'Agitprop' (Communist

Agitation and Propaganda Department), who had fled from Berlin to Paris.

> I explained my idea, and he grasped the importance of the documents at once. . . . A new publishing house would be founded, a *Brown Book* was to be published, and I, of course, would be expected to take part. The whole world would be aroused. 'Don't worry about money, bring all the photographs you can!' Next day I had a money order.
>
> Only in the train did I dare to study the photographs; I locked myself in the lavatory. They were precisely what we needed: in the cellar beneath the destroyed Parliament, a corridor ran towards Göring's residence; the incendiaries' secret entrance had been discovered.[5]

The *Brown Book* accordingly published a 'Central Section of the Reichstag Cellar' to show the 'secret' way in which the incendiaries must have entered the building.

> There is such a secret way into the Reichstag, namely the underground passage which connects the house of the President of the Reichstag (Göring) with the Reichstag building itself.[6]

The Communists themselves knew only too well that this Section Plan did not show the passage itself, but only a part of the Reichstag cellar. To my knowledge, no one has drawn attention to this deliberate deception.

The *Brown Book* also published a 'Section Plan of the German Reichstag Building' with the legend: 'The entrance to the underground passage leading to Göring's house is just above the word "Sitzungsaal".' The idea was to suggest to the reader (a) that the passage ran straight to, and only to, Göring's residence and (b) that it ended directly beneath the Session Chamber. Had they printed a genuine section of the passage, their colourful theories would quickly have been exploded, for Wallot's book, from which Regler had taken the plan, made no mention of a Speaker's residence, which was, in fact, built in 1903, nine years after the completion of the Reichstag. In order to join it to the central heating system, a special tunnel had then to be built, joining the main passage beneath the driveway of the Speaker's residence.

The passage, or tunnel, therefore, had three exits or entrances, one in the boiler house, a second in the Reichstag cellar and a third in the Speaker's residence. The Communists probably learned about this last entrance at the end of World War I when the revolutionary 'Reichstag' regiment gained a measure of notoriety:

> This 'Reichstag' regiment was made up of rather suspicious characters. They kept running up and down the passage. Machine-guns had been set up in the passage, and other arms were hidden there by members of the regiment and sold in secret. Once sold, they were taken out through the boiler room or the Speaker's residence. Ever since then the passage has been extremely popular in Left circles, at least to my knowledge.[7]

On 9 May 1933 the locksmith Wingurth testified before Judge Vogt, the Examining Magistrate:

> As for the rumour that the incendiaries entered and escaped through the underground passage, all I can say is that the whole thing strikes me as extremely unlikely, because too many doors would have had to be opened and shut, and I was told that all the doors were found properly locked after the fire.
>
> The door leading to the Reichstag cellar from the drive . . . can only be opened with a spanner. The iron door behind it must be opened with an ordinary key. In the cellar itself there is another, unlocked door. A bit farther along is the door into the Reichstag (the so-called black door). At the other end of the passage there is another iron door, the so-called red door, which is kept locked. The red door leads to the passage between the Reichstag and the boiler house and thence, through two other locked doors, to the courtyard.[8]

In other words, the cellar and the passage were sealed off by a number of doors, all of which were locked every night at 7 p.m. The keys were usually handed in to the doorkeeper of the Speaker's residence, or, less frequently, to the night porter of the Reichstag.

The tunnel itself was included in the rounds of the night porter, particularly since, in 1932, the police had been warned of an intended dynamite attack on the Reichstag. They were told that the dynamite had been hidden somewhere in the cellar, and that the criminals would try to enter the Reichstag through the underground passage. At the time the whole building was immediately searched – in vain. Nevertheless it was thought necessary to take additional precautions, and it was then that the red door was first put in.

How extremely difficult it really was to find the inconspicuous door to the passage in the maze of corridors and doors of the Reichstag cellar, was demonstrated during the trial. A police officer, whom the Court had sent into the passage in order to determine whether or not he would make a great deal of noise down there, failed to return. The judges waited with increasing impatience, and finally sent a search party to look for him. They found him wandering about in the labyrinth below, hopelessly lost.[9] These facts in themselves ought to have suggested how ridiculous it was to assume that a gang of foreign incendiaries could have rushed through that maze in record time.

The main passage formed a straight T at its junction with the subsidiary passage, so that no one could have hidden himself or anything in it without being discovered. In addition, it had a peculiarity which Douglas Reed described as follows: '. . . the tunnel was floored with loose metal plates which, as I was able to satisfy myself, made a din that must have been heard by him (the porter).'[10]

Reed was able to 'satisfy himself' of this din when, during the reconstruction of the crime, the Court was led through the passage by engineer Heinrich Risse:

> The judges, the Public Prosecutor and his collaborator, counsel for the defence, all laid aside their robes and made their way to the cellars. The five accused, the relevant witnesses, and the representatives of the international press followed. . . .
>
> The passage was a narrow brick one, floored with loose steel plates, and there was a clatter and a jangle as some sixty newspaper representatives made their way through it.[11]

These clattering and jangling plates made nonsense of the whole passage hypothesis for, as further experiments showed, the plates resounded noisily even when people walked over them in carpet slippers. A group of seven to ten men storming through the passage would have been heard by the night porter of Göring's residence even if they had walked on tiptoe. Now when the night porter, Paul Adermann, testified on oath that he heard no suspicious noises whatsoever, the Court had to believe him – the Presiding Judge himself had participated in the demonstration witnessed by Reed. The state of the window through which van der Lubbe had entered, the marks he left on the outside wall, and the evidence of the student, Flöter, left no doubt about the real path the incendiary had taken.

II

THE POLITICAL CASE

5. Brown *versus* Red

HITLER'S FIGHT WITH WINDMILLS

WHEN Marinus van der Lubbe fired the Reichstag, he could not have chosen a more crucial moment in Germany's history. A state of civil war, that had lasted for just under fifteen years and in which thousands had fallen, had culminated in victory for the one side. Henceforth battles would no longer be waged in the street, but old scores would be settled in S.A. barracks, in quickly erected concentration camps, and in prisons. The police, recently abused as the representatives of a hated system, were turned into the new Government's trusted henchmen, almost overnight.

Even though they had climbed into the saddle, the Nazis feared that their Communist enemies had, at best, suffered a severe setback. Judging by the past, they might hit back at any moment, and the only thing to do was to expect the worst, and to pounce on them on the slightest excuse.

That is why the fire started by a young fanatic was immediately turned into a major political issue, and why he was sacrificed in the struggle between brown and red. With van der Lubbe, the German police had caught, not an incendiary, but an immense red herring. . . .

When Dr Ernst Hanfstaengl, a guest in Göring's residence, heard the jangle of fire engines outside, he rushed to the telephone and called Dr Goebbels who, as he knew, was entertaining Hitler that evening. At first, Goebbels thought the whole thing was a practical joke – Hanfstaengl's way of paying him back for a recent hoax. Goebbels therefore told him not to be so damned silly and slammed the receiver down. A little while later, Goebbels had second thoughts and decided to ring Hanfstaengl back. Hanfstaengl was furious by now, and told Goebbels to come and see for himself. In the end, Goebbels called the Brandenburg Gate police-station, where he was told that the Reichstag was ablaze.[1]

While Goebbels the diarist had this to say about the beginning of that exciting evening: 'At nine o'clock the Führer is expected to dinner. We shall listen to music or chat'[2], Goebbels the propagandist gave out a different story next morning: 'Reich Chancellor Hitler rushed to the scene [the Reichstag] straight from his arduous work. He was accompanied by Dr Goebbels and Oberführer Ernst.'[3]

Göring was waiting for them in the Reichstag. Unlike Hitler, he had, in fact, been forced to interrupt his work. At 4.15 p.m. he had attended a Cabinet meeting and had then gone on to the Prussian Ministry of the Interior, where he was just having a discussion with Ludwig Grauert, an old air-force comrade and now his Under-Secretary, when the door was pulled open and Göring's adjutant, Police Captain Jacoby, rushed in with the news of the fire. Göring was completely taken aback, and exploded: 'What the hell is going on? Get me a car at once! I'm going straight there!'[4]

After telling his private secretary, Fräulein Grundtmann, that he wanted to see Sommerfeldt, his press chief, in the Reichstag as soon as possible, Göring raced off. Near the Reichstag his car was stopped a number of times by policemen who had meanwhile cordoned off the entire area. It was from one of them that Göring first heard the word arson, and that he first realized that 'the Communist Party had set the Reichstag on fire'.[5]

Göring first tried to enter the Reichstag through Portal Three, but finding it locked he made for Portal Two which had meanwhile been opened. There he and his party – all in mufti – were quietly joined by another civilian, the Berlin correspondent of the London *Times*, Douglas Reed. Reed's joy was, however, short-lived, for he was quickly recognized as a gate-crasher and put out by the police. The same happened to two other journalists whom Göring discovered in a telephone box.

Next, Göring gave orders to notify Hitler and the Chief of Police. He also told Chief Fire Director Gempp, who had rushed up to report to the Minister, not to bother about him but to carry on with the job of putting out the fire. Then Göring went to his own Reichstag rooms where he was soon afterwards joined by Vice-Chancellor von Papen, and a little later by Hitler and Goebbels.

Meanwhile Under-Secretary Grauert, who had come along in Göring's car, was told by Albert Wendt, the night porter, that the last people to leave the House had been Deputies Torgler and Koenen – two Communists. The day porter, Wilhelm Hornemann, made things even worse for Koenen when he alleged that Koenen had tried to sneak into the Reichstag at about 7 p.m., his coat collar suspiciously turned up and his face averted. Then Robert Kohls, cloakroom attendant at Portal Two, stated that he had rung up the Communist Party rooms at about 8 p.m., but that no one had answered. He had been most surprised, therefore, when Torgler's secretary rang down only a short while later to ask for Torgler's coat. Kohls was taken to Minister Göring, who considered his story so important that he asked Kohls to come along to the Ministry of the Interior.

Vice-Chancellor von Papen had spent the early part of the evening at the Conservative Herrenklub, where he was

> . . . giving a dinner in the President's honour. Suddenly we noticed a red glow through the windows. . . . The Field-Marshal got up, and all of us watched the dome of the Reichstag looking as though it were illuminated by searchlights.
>
> [Hindenburg] seemed rather unmoved and merely asked to be given further news as soon as possible . . . I went straight to the burning building . . . and found Göring in one of the badly damaged corridors, where as Prussian Minister of the Interior he was giving orders to the firemen. 'This is a Communist crime against the new Government,' he shouted to me.[6]

Papen, who had no reason to doubt Göring, expressed his disgust at this latest Communist outrage to the journalists waiting outside.

An official car had meanwhile brought Göring's press officer, Martin Sommerfeldt, to the Reichstag. This is how he remembered the scene:

> Göring was standing in the smoke-filled lobby, surrounded by officers of the fire brigade and the police. I reported to him, and found him quite calm. I gained the impression that, though he was worried about the fire, he did not attach too much importance to it. He told me quietly and briefly to get out full reports on the cause and the extent of the fire, and to draft an official communiqué.[7]

Sommerfeldt set to work at once.

Because of the size of the conflagration, no one present that night had the slightest doubt that a whole gang of arsonists – naturally Communists – must have been responsible for the fire. Imagine Göring's surprise, therefore, when he was told that, though the whole building had been sealed off and though every nook and cranny had been searched, not a single accomplice had been run to earth. It was then that Göring suddenly remembered the false alarm of 1932, when the political police had notified him, as the Speaker, of a threatened dynamite attack. Could not the criminals have followed the same route as the alleged dynamiters of last year? Göring immediately ordered a search of the underground passage, and his adjutant, Captain Jacoby, delegated the job to Göring's bodyguard, Walter Weber. With an escort of three policemen, chosen at random – as he testified before the Supreme Court and also told the author of this book in the spring of 1960 – Weber raced across to the Speaker's residence to fetch the keys from the housekeeper, Frau Puschke. The four of them then unlocked the door to the passage and found – absolutely nothing. Even so, Göring kept insisting that the passage must have been used by van der Lubbe's accomplices.

More fortunate by far than his colleague Douglas Reed was the Berlin correspondent of the London *Daily Express*, Sefton Delmer, who was allowed to enter the burning Reichstag with Hitler's party. Delmer heard Göring tell Hitler straightaway that the fire had obviously been started by Communists, that a number of Communist deputies had been seen leaving the Reichstag shortly before the fire was detected, that one of the Communist incendiaries had been arrested, that the entire Prussian police had been mobilized and that every public building had been specially garrisoned. 'We are ready for anything,' Göring said.

Then Hitler moved to one of the balconies to watch the raging inferno in the Chamber. Other Nazi leaders and Cabinet Ministers, including Dr Frick, Prince August Wilhelm, the Lord Mayor of Berlin, Dr Sahm, and Police President von Levetzow, had meanwhile joined their Führer, and so had the British Ambassador, Sir Horace Rumbold.

This is how Rudolf Diels described the scene:

> On a balcony projecting into the Chamber stood Hitler, surrounded by a band of his faithful. Hitler was leaning over the stone parapet, gazing at the red ocean of fire. When I entered, Göring stepped towards me. His voice conveyed the full pathos of the dramatic hour: 'This is the beginning of a Communist uprising. Not a moment must be lost . . .'
>
> Göring could not go on, for Hitler had swung round towards us. I

saw that his face had turned quite scarlet, both with excitement and also with the heat. . . . Suddenly he started screaming at the top of his voice:

'Now we'll show them! Anyone who stands in our way will be mown down. The German people have been soft too long. Every Communist official must be shot. All Communist deputies must be hanged this very night. All friends of the Communists must be locked up. And that goes for the Social Democrats and the *Reichsbanner* as well.'[8]

This outburst was anything but a well-rehearsed act on Hitler's part. Uncertainty about Communist plans had weighed heavily upon him ever since he became Chancellor on 30 January, and had increased daily as the Communists continued to lie low. Now, the enemy had struck at last – how could it be otherwise? This fire could have only one purpose – it was the signal for a Communist uprising, first in Berlin and then in the whole of Germany. Now the Communists would make common cause with the Social Democrats and with the millions of Trade Unionists. A general strike would be proclaimed, and Hitler's dreams of empire might be shattered once again. Was the 'national rebirth' to fare no better than the nationalist Kapp putsch in 1920? Had not the German Trade Union President, T. Leipart, called Hitler's appointment as Chancellor a 'declaration of war against the workers', adding: 'Because of their determination and love of freedom the German workers will wage a life-and-death struggle, the terrible consequences of which ought to be a warning to the new rulers.'[9]

And had not *Vorwärts*, the official organ of the Social Democratic Party, told the new rulers on 30 January 1933, that they would rue the day they decided to take illegal measures? Had they not threatened a general strike, claiming that:

> Striking is a legal weapon. . . . But tactical reasons tell us to be sparing with it, lest the crucial moment find us exhausted. . . . In times like these, things can change very quickly. There is only one answer to the alliance of the enemies of the working class: a United Front.

Goebbels recorded the reactions of the Nazi leaders when, on 31 January, he wrote in his diary:

> During discussions with the Führer we drew up the plans of battle against the red terror. For the time being, we decided against any direct countermeasures. The Bolshevik rebellion must first of all flare up; only then shall we hit back.[10]

Göring mentioned the same plan in 1933 and again after the war. Hence it was no wonder that, when Rudolf Diels gave Hitler his own view, namely that the fire must have been started by a madman, Hitler scoffed at his artlessness and said:

'This is a cunning and well-prepared plot. The only thing is that they have reckoned without us and without the German people. In their rat-holes, from which they are now trying to crawl out again, they cannot hear the jubilation of the masses.'[11]

Diels, who was a police expert on Communist activities, took a much more realistic view of the situation. He knew better than anyone else that the Communists had no intention of staging a rebellion – that much he had learned clearly from an army of Communist turncoats and traitors. However, not only Hitler but even Göring, who as Diels's chief, ought to have known the truth, refused to listen to him, and ordered

a state of alert for the entire police, merciless use of fire-arms, and what similar emergency measures there were in his great military arsenal. I repeated that I had sent a radio message to all police authorities ordering, in his name, a general alert and the arrest of all those Communist officials who had long ago been hallmarked for arrest in case the Communist Party was proscribed.[12]

Dr Schneider confirmed his colleague Diels's description of Hitler's furious outburst in the Reichstag:

After Hitler had shaken himself out of a kind of torpor, he started what seemed an unending stream of vituperations against 'Communist monsters'. He and Göring were absolutely convinced that the Communists had intended the 'shameless burning of Germany's palladium' as a signal for their boasted mass action. Hitler quite seriously gave the police orders to hang all Communist deputies and to take other drastic steps, though only some of his instructions were practicable and hence broadcast over all police transmitters, *viz*:

1. All Communist members of the Reichstag, the Landtag, Municipal Councils and all Communist officials are to be arrested;
2. All Communist newspapers are to be seized.[13]

Looking back at that hectic day, Dr Schneider today believes that:

What militates most against Nazi responsibility or complicity was the extraordinary agitation which the news of the fire sparked off among members of the Government and among leading Nazis. This shows better than anything that the fire was not pre-arranged by them. I was able to watch their agitation with my own eyes.

A third eye-witness of Hitler's dismay was Sefton Delmer:

> That evening, Hitler himself was not yet absolutely certain that the fire was a Communist plot. This became clear from what he said to me as we walked side by side through the burning building. 'God grant,' he said, 'that this be the work of the Communists. You are now witnessing the beginning of a great new epoch in German history.' That was the first clue. Hitler did *not* say, 'This *is* the work of the Communists', but, 'God grant this be the work of the Communists.' And a little later, when von Papen appeared, Hitler seized his hand, pumped it with much unbecoming enthusiasm, and said: 'This is a God-given signal, Herr Vice-Chancellor! If this fire, as I believe, is the work of the Communists, then we must crush out this murder pest with an iron fist.' Note the 'if'.

Like Dr Schneider, Delmer concluded:

> It must be granted that what I saw of Hitler's and Goebbels's behaviour in the Reichstag does not fit in with the theory that both were party or even privy to the Reichstag fire plot.[14]

Clearly, the Reichstag fire was no brilliantly conceived plan, no ingenious stratagem by the Nazis to destroy their opponents – on the contrary it was the Nazis' fear that the fire might let loose a flood of red terror that caused them to unleash a flood of brown terror first. The world was to learn time and again with what blind fury Hitler invariably reacted to real or imaginary threats.

The fantastic spectacle of Hitler's maniacal monologue on the night of the fire may well explain the remarkable fact that Hitler himself was never incriminated by even his worst enemies. So high-pitched was Hitler's voice, in fact, and so hysterical his tirade to his henchmen that Diels turned to his colleague and said: 'This is a real madhouse, Schneider.'

Hitler's delusions, which remind one so forcefully of Don Quixote's tilting against windmills or drawing his sword at empty wineskins, also stopped the Nazi leaders from realizing that the Communist threat existed only in their own minds. Moreover, it was this very misconception which gave birth to the legend of the 'Reichstag fire mystery' – a legend which has obstinately obscured the simple truth for three decades.

. . . . .

That very night, Division IA became the scene of feverish activity, as warrants were issued for the arrest of all Communist Party officials. The first squads – each consisting of a detective and two uniformed constables – set out at dawn, on 28 February 1933. At 3.15 a.m., a message was sent to the airport police in Tempelhof and at 3.25 a radio message was broadcast to German border patrols, warning them to intercept all Communist officials and deputies.

Meanwhile an improvised ministerial conference was being held in the Ministry of the Interior. Among those present were Hitler, von Papen and Göring, together with the Nationalist Under-Secretary von Bismarck, Under-Secretary Grauert, Police President von Levetzow, the Head of Division IA Rudolf Diels, and other high officials. On the agenda were the measures that must be taken to prevent the expected terrorist attacks by the Communists. Grauert, who was not a Nazi, insisted on an adequate legal basis for these measures, and Dr Frick undertook to provide it.[15]

Among the many curious spectators who gaped at van der Lubbe during the police interrogation on the night of the fire were the Nazi deputies, Berthold Karwahne and Kurt Frey and the Austrian Nazi official, Stefan Kroyer. They had been out on a spree, when they heard a late-night radio message that Torgler and Koenen had fled the Reichstag at about 10 p.m., and were wanted for questioning. Despite the late hour, Karwahne and his friends decided to call on Göring at the Ministry of the Interior. They told him that they had happened to pass the Communist Party rooms in the Reichstag a number of times that afternoon, and that on every occasion Torgler had been huddled together with extremely suspicious characters. Torgler himself had looked so guilty when he felt himself observed as to leave little doubt about what he was doing: he was briefing the others for arson.

Göring thereupon sent the Nazi trio straight to police headquarters, where a thoughtless detective led them to Heisig's room. In that way they were allowed to catch a glimpse of van der Lubbe, whom, needless to say, they 'identified' as one of the men they had seen with Torgler.

In their excitement the police had committed an irreparable blunder – they had allowed witnesses to look at a police suspect, and then to describe him as someone they had seen earlier. As a result, Torgler might easily have been hanged, had he not been saved by a series of fortunate circumstances, and by the devotion of his guardian angel and defending counsel, Dr Alfons Sack.

In the blazing Reichstag, Sommerfeldt had meanwhile carried out Göring's orders to gather what information he could about the fire and its causes. What the fire officials and Diels and Schneider told him was not much, but at least it had the advantage of agreeing with the facts fairly well:

> I learned that the fire was discovered at 9 p.m. by a civilian who notified the nearest policeman. The latter alerted a police patrol, the police-station alerted the fire brigade, etc. The policeman saw a man tugging wildly at a curtain over one of the large panes in the lobby, and fired a shot at him. When the police entered the building, they found burning firelighters everywhere, which suggested arson. They managed to collect about a hundredweight of this material, and arrested a man who seemed to be running berserk in the corridors. The man was carrying firelighters on his person.[16]

Apart from the weight of the firelighters, Sommerfeldt had been told the truth, and he immediately drafted a press communiqué:

> My draft ran to some twenty lines, and contained no facts other than those mentioned.
>
> In view of the tense political situation, and the coming elections, I deliberately refrained from dramatizing what struck me as a most mysterious affair.

When Sommerfeldt submitted his draft to Göring at about 1 a.m., he found to his surprise that '... whereas Göring had been completely composed in the blazing Reichstag, he was now in a state of great excitement.'

Sommerfeldt, who had not been there to see Hitler turning scarlet in the face as he shook Göring out of his composure, Diels out of his 'artlessness', and Goebbels out of his 'wait-and-see' policy, was even more surprised when Göring glanced at the report, flung all the papers on his desk to one side, thumped the table with his fist and thundered:

'That's sheer rubbish! It may be a good police report, but it's not at all the kind of communiqué I have in mind!'

Sommerfeldt, who knew he had done his job conscientiously, was deeply hurt: 'His tone was insulting; no one had ever dared to speak to me in that way.'

Göring, for his part, could not understand how anyone could produce that kind of insipid report after Hitler's prophetic outburst in the Reichstag. Rather than convince his stubborn press attaché, he seized a blue pencil and, shouting: 'This is sheer rubbish,' again, he went on: ' "One hundredweight of incendiary material? No, ten or even a hundred." And he added two noughts to my modest one.'

Now Sommerfeldt, too, became annoyed:

'This is quite impossible, Minister! No one can possibly believe that a single man could have carried that load . . .'

Göring snapped back:

'Nothing is impossible. Why mention a single man? There were ten or even twenty men! Don't you understand what's been happening? The whole thing was a signal for a Communist uprising!'

If he thought that would floor Sommerfeldt at last, Göring was quite wrong:

'I do not think so, Minister. No one has mentioned anything of the sort, not even Diels, whom I saw in the Reichstag. He merely thought that the Communists *might* have been responsible. I must insist, Minister, that my report is based on the official findings of the fire brigade and the police.'

Göring remained speechless for a moment, and then he flung his giant blue pencil furiously on to the desk.

'I shall dictate the report myself to Fräulein Grundtmann. You can insist all you want.'

Göring started dictating to his secretary without once stopping, but glancing at a piece of paper now and then. He gave it out as an established fact that the Reichstag fire had been intended as a signal for a Communist campaign of bloodshed and arson. He ordered the police to take all Communist officials into protective custody and to confiscate all Marxist newspapers. Göring multiplied my own figures by ten, with a side-long glance in my direction.

The additional nine culprits thus introduced became an integral part of the Reichstag fire 'mystery', and even Göring forgot its real origins. His ten criminals were welcomed by the Communists, who quickly turned them into Nazis.

When Göring had finished, Sommerfeldt asked him to sign the report.

'Whatever for?' Göring asked in astonishment.

'Because this is not an official report on a fire, Minister, but a political document. The news agencies will only accept it from me if you sign it officially.'

Silently, Göring wrote his distinctive large 'G' underneath the last line.

When Sommerfeldt took the communiqué to the Government agency (Wolffs Telegrafen-Büro – WTB) he discovered that the newly-appointed commissar, Alfred Ingemar Berndt, had already released a communiqué by Goebbels. Sommerfeldt mused:

> Now I realized what the piece of paper was which Göring kept looking at while he dictated his report.

At last, it dawned on him:

> While I was busy questioning the experts in the Reichstag, and writing my draft report, something must have happened to turn the Reichstag fire into a political event of the first importance.

Göring's full communiqué read as follows:

> *Results of the official investigation*
> Investigations of the fire which broke out in the German Reichstag have shown that the incendiary material could not have been carried in by less than seven persons, and that the distribution and simultaneous lighting of the several fires in the gigantic building required the presence of at least ten persons.
>
> The fact that the incendiaries were completely at home in the vast building suggests that they must have been people who have had free access to the House over a long period. Hence there are grave suspicions that the culprits were deputies of the Communist Party who have recently been assembling in the Reichstag under all sorts of pretexts.
>
> Their familiarity with the building and with the duty rota also explains why the police caught no one except a Dutch Communist, who, being unfamiliar with the building, was unable to escape after he had committed the crime. The arrested man, whom the Dutch police describe as a dangerous radical, is known to have been present during the deliberations of the Communist Action Committee, where he insisted on playing his part during the fire.
>
> Moreover, the arrested Dutch criminal was seen by three eye-witnesses in the company of the Communist deputies Torgler and Koenen a few hours before the fire.
>
> Since, furthermore, the Deputies' Entrance to the Reichstag is locked at 8 p.m., and since the Communist deputies Torgler and

Koenen had asked for their coats at about 8.30 p.m., but did not leave the Reichstag, through another exit, until 10 p.m., they are suspected of complicity in the crime.

According to a false rumour, Deputy Torgler has reported to the police of his own free will. All he did do was to apply for a safe-conduct the moment he realized that he could not escape. His application was refused, and Torgler was arrested.[17]

The figures quoted, and particularly the number seven, readily suggested that the police had obtained them after a scrupulous investigation. That figure was, however, merely the result of a spontaneous – and as he himself came to recognize soon afterwards – precipitate exclamation by House-Inspector Scranowitz, who had let slip during the night of the fire that at least six to eight persons must have been responsible. Now since 'six to eight' gives an average of seven, seven was the number which was generally adopted. Göring himself reported to the Cabinet on 2 March 1933 that, according to the experts, at least six to seven persons must have started the fire.

On the other hand, it seems incredible that as late as 1 March official reports still alleged that Torgler and Koenen had left the Reichstag at about 10 p.m., when that *canard*, based on a confusion of Torgler with the National Socialist deputy, Dr Albrecht, had already been exploded on 28 February. No wonder that official German reports were henceforth treated with so much scepticism abroad.

THE ARREST OF THE 'RINGLEADERS'

On leaving the Reichstag, Torgler, Koenen, and Torgler's secretary, Anna Rehme, who suffered from phlebitis, started walking very slowly to the Friedrichstrasse station. There Fräulein Rehme took her leave of them, and the two deputies went to dinner in the Aschinger Restaurant, where Torgler had arranged to meet the Communist deputy Birkenhauer. About an hour later, they heard the news that the Reichstag was on fire. At first Torgler thought that the whole thing was a joke, but he soon changed his mind, and tried to get back to the building. But trams were no longer allowed to stop near the Reichstag, and Torgler decided to return to Aschinger's. Meanwhile Koenen had left, but Torgler met him again at Stawicki's Beer Hall, near the Alexanderplatz, where they had previously arranged to play cards. Torgler, who was convinced the fire had been started by some careless fool, was completely stunned when he heard from Walter Oehme that he, Torgler, had just been described as an incendiary over the radio, and the fire as a signal for a Communist uprising. Torgler and his friends quickly put their heads together in Stawicki's Bar, and all of them concluded that, since the Government was blaming completely innocent people, the fire could only be a deliberate Nazi plot to prevent the Communist Party from fighting the coming elections. After a number of telephone conversations, Torgler decided to call the Nazis' bluff and to report to the police. He knew that he would have no difficulty in proving his complete innocence.

Had he had the least suspicion that the whole campaign, far from being a carefully planned provocation, was simply one of Hitler's many misjudgements against which it was useless to argue, Torgler, as he admits today, would have followed the example of Pieck, Ulbricht and Koenen, to mention only a few Communist leaders, and have fled abroad instead of bearding the brown lion in his den. Had he done so, however, his disappearance would have been considered a clear admission of guilt.

When Torgler eventually rang Division IA to announce his visit, he caused a tremendous stir, the ripples of which quickly reached Göring and Hitler. For meanwhile Detective Karl Spietz had reported that Torgler was away from home, that his wife claimed she knew nothing of his whereabouts, and that there was good reason to assume that he had made a quick getaway. And now the alleged fugitive had decided to turn up at police headquarters with two lawyers: Dr Kurt Rosenfeld and Rosenfeld's daughter, Frau Dr Kirchheimer. No wonder Goebbels felt impelled to dispel this 'rumour' in his press communiqué.

After he had been kept waiting for hours at the police-station, Torgler was told by Superintendent Reinhold Heller that he would have to stay there. And stay there he did.

While the Reichstag was still ablaze, the Munich-Berlin night express carried a passenger whose passport showed him to be a Dr Rudolf Hediger from Reinach. In fact, that passport was a forgery, one of many such churned out in a special Communist workshop in 48a Kaiserallee, Berlin-Wilmersdorf. Frau Rössler, from Berlin, would most certainly not have looked twice at the impressive middle-aged gentleman who was paying her compliments with so much southern dash, had she had the least suspicion that he was none other than Georgi Dimitrov, head of the West European Section of the Comintern. As it was, Frau Rössler declared her readiness to continue the acquaintance and agreed to a rendezvous in West Berlin.

Dimitrov's comrades and later co-accused, the Bulgarians Blagoi Simon Popov, and Vassili Tanev, spent the afternoon of 27 February 1933 in various Berlin cafés and finished the evening in an UFA cinema in the Nollenbergplatz, where they saw *Demon Islands*.

By the beginning of March, van der Lubbe's picture was plastered all over public hoardings and published in newspapers with the promise of a reward of 20,000 marks to anyone who could provide information leading to the capture of his accomplices.

On 3 March, Johannes Helmer showed the evening paper (*Nachtausgabe*) to his fellow-waiters in the Bayernhof Restaurant in the Potsdamerstrasse, and asked them whether they did not recognize van der Lubbe's picture. He reminded them about those 'Russians' who had repeatedly entered the restaurant – which was a Nazi haunt – by mistake. The other eight waiters shook their heads – not one of them could remember the face. Still, Helmer wanted the 20,000 marks badly, and he decided to go to the police. This is what he told them:

> In my opinion this man is certainly one of the guests who repeatedly came into the café with the Russians. All of them struck me as suspicious characters, because they all spoke in a foreign language, and because they all dropped their voices whenever anyone went past their table.[18]

Detective Walter Holzhäuser then showed Helmer a number of photographs, whereupon he readily picked out van der Lubbe's (which he had just seen in the evening paper). He went on to say: 'I am positive that this man came to the Bayernhof a number of times from the spring to the late summer of 1932.'

Since the police were being overrun with reports of this kind they merely asked Helmer to report back the moment the Russians appeared again.

Two days later – on 9 March – Helmer rang Holzhäuser.

'They are back,' he told them.

Holzhäuser and Detective Gast raced over to the Bayernhof, and sat down with such conspicuous indifference that the 'Russians' became suspicious and tried to leave. The whole scene was described by the Communist writer Ernst Fischer after the war:

> . . . Round the table sat a big, broad-shouldered man with a dark, lion's mane, and two younger men, slighter in build and less striking in appearance.
>
> The detective asked them to come along. The big, broad-shouldered man produced his papers. His real name was Georgi Dimitrov.[19]

True, that was the man's real name, but not the name he gave to the detective, or which appeared in his passport. The second 'Russian' carried a passport made out in the name of Penev. The third 'Russian' tried to escape through the revolving door, but was caught by Detective Gast. He then gave his name as Popov. Popov, who had no passport on him, tried to escape again, but in the end he gave up the struggle, and all three were taken to headquarters in a taxi.

Once there, the passports were quickly recognized as forgeries from the Berlin Communist forgers' shop which had recently been raided and whose stamps had been confiscated.

On the way to headquarters Dimitrov had tried to squeeze a piece of paper behind the taxi seat. When Holzhäuser had delivered his three charges, he went back to the cab and pulled out a Comintern appeal dated 3 March 1933. Clearly the 'Russians' were dangerous Bolsheviks, and Helmer had been quite right to report them.

Dimitrov and his two compatriots had a wild political past. After fleeing from his native Bulgaria in 1924, Dimitrov had lived in Yugoslavia, Austria, Germany and Russia, constantly changing his name. Like an experienced confidence man, he had played on the German respect for academic titles, calling himself Dr Jan Schaafsma-Schmidt, Dr Rudolf Hediger, Dr Stein, Dr Steiner and Professor Dr Jahn. When he insisted that he had obtained his last passport from a Swiss friend, he merely increased suspicion against himself, for the police knew perfectly well where his passport had been 'issued'.

Popov and Tanev were exiled Bulgarian Communists as well, and had lived in Russia and Germany. Tanev was the only one of the three who had been amnestied and who had been back to his native Bulgaria.

Dimitrov tried to excuse his false papers and the fact that he had failed to report regularly to the police, by claiming that his political opponents in Bulgaria, where he had been sentenced to death, would not hesitate to take his life even abroad. For that reason he had simply had to 'disappear'. He had no connection whatsoever with either the Reichstag fire or with the German Communist Party. His sole concern was with Bulgaria, and the moment a political amnesty was proclaimed, he would be returning home.

Not love alone, but distrust as well, is blind. How else explain police readiness to listen to Helmer's allegations? One fact alone ought to have given them pause for reflection: so oddly dressed an individual as van der Lubbe was bound to have been noticed by everyone in the Bayernhof, not only by one waiter.

Nor did the police bother to check whether van der Lubbe had been in Berlin at the time Helmer alleged he had seen him. This very neglect led to the ridiculous trial of the three innocent Bulgarians, and earned the German police world-wide scorn. In fact, van der Lubbe had spent the time in question at home, signing for his weekly disability allowance in his own hand.

True, Helmer's avarice provided the Nazis with a deceptively welcome increase in the number of culprits, but they were the first to regret it later. For when the 'Russian' Dimitrov was attacked in Court, he did not lie down meekly but gave his accusers and judges at least as good as he got.

THE ENABLING LAWS

In the weeks following the fire, the Government's unfounded fear of possible Communist outrages became the excuse not only for police raids and vicious excesses by Hitler's brown henchmen, but also for a wave of new laws and regulations. The first and most notorious of these, the 'Decree for the Protection of the People and the State' was promulgated on 28 February 1933.

The fact that this decree was passed only one day after the fire, has suggested to many historians that it must have been drafted well in advance. To obtain the sweeping powers this decree conferred on him, they said, all Hitler had to do was to send the Reichstag up in flames.

Today it can be shown that the decree was not drafted in advance, 'merely to be fetched out of a drawer'. It was during the *ad hoc* conference in the Prussian Ministry of the Interior on the night of the fire that the then Under-Secretary and former Attorney-General, Ludwig Grauert, insisted on the obvious fact that the emergency measures demanded by Hitler in the blazing Reichstag, and endorsed by all those present, must be put on a sound legal footing.

For that reason an Extraordinary Meeting of the Cabinet was called for next morning. The only point on the agenda was the political situation. After Hitler had called for the 'ruthless suppression of the Communist Party' which 'was determined to go to any lengths', he 'submitted' the following five points to the Cabinet: (1) to thank the Reichstag officials, the police and the fire brigade for their magnificent work; (2) to start rebuilding the Reichstag at once; (3) to leave the date of the general election unchanged; (4) to transfer the new Reichstag to the Potsdam Palace; and (5) to adopt Grauert's suggestion and to pass a law for the protection of the nation against the Communist danger.

The Cabinet was so unanimous in its fear of a Communist 'counter-revolution' that Hitler had no need whatever of bludgeoning them into signing his odious decree.

6. Counter-Attack

REFUGEES FROM NAZI TERROR

THE 60,000 unfortunate refugees[1] who had to flee their native land when Hitler came to power could console themselves with the fact that all they left behind in the Third Reich was one great concentration camp. Few carried away more than bitter hatred, and none believed a single word the Nazis ever spoke or published. The Communists among them, knowing that the very idea of a 'red uprising' was sheer nonsense, declared that the whole Reichstag fire was a Nazi pre-election stunt.

Furious because what they thought was a Nazi bluff had paid off, and sorely discountenanced at the ignominious collapse of the great German workers' movement, they decided to hit back as best they could from abroad. To start with, they knew that Göring's 'official communiqué' on the night of the fire had been a tissue of lies or, at best, of gross exaggerations – the German press itself had been forced to retract the story that van der Lubbe had been caught with a Communist Party membership card and that he had been in close touch with Social Democratic leaders. And since Göring had been caught out in two whopping lies, there was little reason to think that the rest of his pronouncements were any better. In vain did the 'Führer' of the 'German Legal Front', Dr Hans Frank, appeal to the world:

> We have done no harm to you, nor do we mean you any harm. All we ask is that we – who want peace through justice – be treated with the respect due to a cultured people.

Thirteen years later, a completely broken Dr Frank had to confess that not even by atoning during a thousand years could he wipe out his share in the inexpressible horrors and bestialities by which Germany's name had become besmirched for all time.

Quite understandably, German refugees fell easy prey to the Communists: common persecution called for a united front, and when Willi Münzenberg, Chief of the Communist 'Agitprop' in Paris, launched his 'anti-Fascist education campaign' he managed to ensnare a vast number of genuine democrats.

THE POT AND THE KETTLE

In fact, the Communists and the Nazis were like two brothers who had fallen out, swearing undying hatred to each other. Both were firmly convinced that the struggle for power would continue even after the Reichstag fire.

The Nazis were afraid, and rightly so, that if they failed to score immediate and spectacular economic successes, many of their unemployed and poverty-stricken converts would lose faith and desert *en masse*; the Communists, on the other hand, were counting on the Nazis' inability to steer Germany off the rocks – they still believed that Hitlerism was nothing but the brief death rattle of capitalism.

When news of the Reichstag fire struck both camps like a bolt from the blue, each immediately concluded that only the other was capable of so much malice and stupidity.

Not surprisingly therefore, each side was outraged when the other, in ringing tones of indignation, unscrupulously laid the crime at its door. While the Communists asked *cui bono*? and pointed out that only because of this dastardly plot had the Nazis been able to outlaw the otherwise 'unconquerable' Communist Party, the Nazis explained that the Communists, knowing their cause to be hopelessly lost unless they made some sort of spectacular show, burned the Reichstag as a last act of desperation.

In addition, brown and red alike claimed that blaming the fire on the other was a certain way of swinging votes in the forthcoming election.

The mirror symmetry between the two went further still. Thus, both Göring and the Communists claimed that the – red or brown – incendiaries had fled the Reichstag through the underground passage. Again, while the German press called van der Lubbe a Communist agitator, the Communist press called him a Nazi spy.

In short, even Solomon the Wise would have had great difficulty in deciding between the two, let alone the President of the Supreme Court, Dr Bünger, whose wisdom fell far short of the proverbial.

'ATROCITY PROPAGANDA' AND 'ANTI-ATROCITY DEFENCE'

This grotesque symmetry may perhaps explain why both sides became more and more ruthless as time went by. The Communists had the decided advantage over their opponents for they appeared before the world as the champions of freedom and democracy. Every sign of trouble, however slight, in the Third Reich was systematically blown up to gigantic proportions, and when there were no signs of trouble at all, the Communists would simply manufacture them.

Incensed and full of righteous indignation, the Nazis hit back. On 14 July 1933, they passed a law by which the Government was enabled to deprive 'disloyal' emigrants of their German citizenship and to confiscate their property.

However, it would be quite wrong to say that German refugees were the only detractors of Hitler's Third Reich, since a number of foreign journalists had also been privileged to watch the power-drunk brownshirts at work, and many of them – particularly those who looked Jewish – had felt the brown jackboot at even closer quarters. Thus it came about that even the most respected foreign papers lent their columns to what the Nazis called 'anti-German atrocity propaganda', and that Hitler and his henchmen came to be held in contempt by civilized men the world over.

Because Germany continued to be in the news, the world press sent its shrewdest and most capable reporters to Berlin. Meanwhile, German papers were growing more and more colourless, so that every German who could tried to get his news from abroad and particularly from Switzerland. The German circulation of foreign papers rose so steeply that Goebbels became exceedingly nervous and, as early as July 1933, he started to confiscate some of them and to arrest or expel their reporters.

Even before then, in March 1933, he had issued a warning against 'tendentious foreign reporting'. He claimed that, as a result, he had been promised better behaviour in the future, when no such promise was given by anyone.

Apart from press attacks, the German Government also had to brave military attacks, which did not help to soothe tempers in the Cabinet. Thus on 6 March 1933, Poland occupied the Westerplatte off Danzig – a fact that is generally forgotten – and encouraged the

French and the British to use force as well. Luckily for Hitler, the Western powers refused, in the mistaken belief that the collapse of the Nazi Government was only a matter of weeks away.

At the same time, anti-Nazi processions and demonstrations became a common sight in most European capitals. Demonstrators would gather outside the German Consulates or Embassies, shouting slogans, posting pickets, breaking windows, and disfiguring walls.

More unpleasant still for the Hitler Government were the anti-German boycotts and the constant attacks on Germany in the British Houses of Parliament. Time after time, members protested against acts of Nazi bestiality and political persecution, and the British Government had a hard time convincing a disgusted country that, short of going to war, there was little they could do about it.

Though the Nazis tried to refute the charges against them, in the end even Goebbels had to confess defeat.

MÜNZENBERG'S ANTI-SWASTIKA CRUSADE

It is mainly thanks to the recantations of ex-Communists that we know anything at all about the Communist 'Agitprop' (Agitation and Propaganda Department) in Paris, which spread anti-Fascist propaganda with so much skill. Arthur Koestler, in particular, has thrown much light on that charmed circle of Communist intellectuals, whose central star was Willi Münzenberg, or the Red Eminence as some have called him. According to Koestler, Münzenberg was '. . . a magnetic personality of immense driving power and a hard, seductive charm . . .'[2]

Margarete Buber-Neumann, Münzenberg's sister-in-law, took much the same view:

> Probably no leading German Communist was anything like as sparkling as Münzenberg. . . . Most [of his collaborators] were under the spell of his forceful personality, and admired his ability to subordinate everything to his central purpose, no matter whether it was collecting signatures from influential poets, artists and scientists, or the organization of a relief campaign.[3]

As a young artisan, Willi Münzenberg, who came of a very poor working-class family in Erfurt, had moved to Switzerland where he met a great many refugees from Tsarist Russia, including

Lenin, Trotsky and Zinoviev. After the end of World War I, Münzenberg, who had organized a number of successful strikes, was repatriated by the worried Swiss.

Back in Germany, he quickly came into his own. He was one of the founders of the German Young Communist League and was sent as their delegate to the 'Workers' Fatherland' in 1920. He was the brilliant organizer and leader of the 'International Workers' Aid Association', and the head of the huge Münzenberg Trust, which owned dailies and weeklies, illustrated journals, film companies and publishing houses. At the age of forty-four Münzenberg became one of the youngest Reichstag deputies.

On the evening of the Reichstag fire, chance threw Münzenberg near the Swiss frontier – luckily for him, because he was one of the Nazis' chief *bêtes noires*. He crossed into Switzerland where the police dug up his old file, and caused him so much trouble that he preferred to go on to Paris. In France, to which 25,000 of the 60,000 German refugees had fled, Münzenberg quickly established his Comintern propaganda headquarters and launched his world-wide anti-Fascist campaign, which, as Koestler put it, was 'a unique feat in the history of propaganda':

> This [World Committee] with its galaxy of international celebrities became the hub of the crusade. Great care was taken that no Communist – except for a few internationally known names such as Henri Barbusse and J. B. S. Haldane – should be connected in public with the Committee. But the Paris secretariat, which was running the Committee, was a purely Communist caucus, headed by Münzenberg and controlled by the Comintern. Its offices were at first in the Rue Mondétour near the Halles, and later at 83 Boulevard Montparnasse. Münzenberg himself worked in a large room within the World Committee's premises, but no outsider ever learned about this. It was as simple as that.[4]

Under the pretext of bringing relief to the victims of German Fascism, the Committee danced to Moscow's tune – and so did a great many other of Münzenberg's Communist front organizations:

> He [Münzenberg] produced International Committees, Congresses and Movements as a conjurer produces rabbits out of his hat: the Committee of Relief for the Victims of Fascism; Committees of Vigilance and Democratic Control; International Youth Congresses and so on. Each of these 'front organizations' had a panel of highly

respectable people, from English duchesses to American columnists and French savants, most of whom had never heard the name of Münzenberg and thought that the Comintern was a bogy invented by Goebbels.

Moreover:

> He organized the Reichstag Counter-Trial – the public hearings in Paris and London in 1933, which first called the attention of the world to the monstrous happenings in the Third Reich. Then came the series of *Brown Books*, a flood of pamphlets and *emigré* newspapers which he financed and directed, though his name nowhere appeared.

Koestler goes on to tell how Münzenberg enterprises came to assume 'truly dazzling proportions':

> He organized the Committee for Peace and against Fascism (the so-called Amsterdam-Pleyel movement) presided over by Barbusse; the Writers' Organization for the defence of Culture; the Committee of Inquiry into alleged Breaches of the Non-Intervention Agreement on Spain; and a series of other international mushroom growths.[5]

Across the Atlantic, Ruth Fischer added her voice:

> During the depression years, 1929–1933, the Münzenberg Trust burgeoned with every variety of anti-Fascist propaganda, with ballyhoo for Russian culture, films, literature, science, scenery. Progressives and liberals the world over, who wanted to join the fight against Fascism, but were reluctant to join a political party, found a haven in one of the numerous organizations Münzenberg founded. Of these the most important was the League against War and Fascism (in the United States, it [the League] changed its name successively to the American League for Peace and Freedom; in September 1939, to American Peace Mobilization; in June 1941, to American People's Mobilization; in April 1946, to National Committee to Win the Peace) which had the enthusiastic support of such prominent figures as Edo Fimmen, the secretary of the International Transport Union, and Ellen Wilkinson, a leader of the British Labour Party.[6]

Münzenberg's Trojan horses proved so effective that his successors are still trying to copy his methods today. It was Münzenberg's Paris office that spawned that gigantic forgery, the Oberfohren Memorandum, which took in practically the whole world. The Memorandum proved clearly that even non-Communists could be fooled very easily as long as the foolery was directed against the common enemy – Hitler. 'It was as simple as that.'

7. The Oberfohren Memorandum*

THE OBERFOHREN CASE

THE first published reference to the Oberfohren Memorandum appeared in April 1933 in the first of two articles, in the *Manchester Guardian*, on the Reichstag fire:

> A confidential memorandum on the events leading up to the fire is circulating in Germany. It is in manuscript, and the Terror makes any mention or discussion of it impossible. But it is a serious attempt by one in touch with the Nationalist members of the Cabinet to give a balanced account of these events. In spite of one or two minor inaccuracies, it shows considerable inside knowledge. While not authoritative in an absolute and final manner it is at least a first and a weighty contribution towards solving the riddle of that fire.[1]

The *Manchester Guardian*'s two articles, clearly based on this 'confidential memorandum', and accusing the Nazis of firing the Reichstag, aroused the bitter indignation of the Nazis:

> *Disgusting defamation of the German Government by English paper. Berlin, April 27th:*
> The English *Manchester Guardian* has been guilty of slandering the German Government in so shameless a way that a sharp protest has been lodged with the British Government.
>
> In an article, entitled 'Germany in April', which dealt with the Reichstag fire in an extremely provocative and slanderous way, the paper's so-called special correspondent has suggested that the incendiaries must be sought in the ranks of the German Cabinet. The article further alleged that a confidential memorandum on the fire is being circulated in Germany. This brazen and baseless attack on the

* For full text of *Oberfohren Memorandum*, see Appendix C, p. 293.

Government of a neighbouring state is without equal in the history of any Western nation. The German Government considers the article an act of unwarranted vilification and has, as we have already mentioned, ordered the German Legation in London to lodge a sharp protest against this kind of publication.[2]

However, only one day later, Goebbels was presented with yet another 'slanderous' article in the *Manchester Guardian* (see Appendix B). That article, too, was based on the Oberfohren Memorandum, and Goebbels replied with mounting fury:

Manchester Guardian continues its provocation.
The Liberal English *Manchester Guardian* continues its campaign of slander against Germany's National Government, even though a previous article forced the German Government to lodge a sharp protest in London. Regarding the second article on the burning of the Reichstag, official German sources today expressed their amazement that a leading English paper should open its columns to so monstrous a vilification of a foreign power. It is known that a clandestine press of the German Communist Party has been printing and circulating deliberate lies about the Reichstag fire ever since the middle of April. Oddly enough, these lying reports agree essentially with the articles published in the *Manchester Guardian*.

Those of us who have followed the methods of the Communist Party during the past years in various parts of the world know that setting the Reichstag on fire is completely in their line of country. Naturally, they now wish to blame their crime on a Government that has proved their relentless enemy. The *Manchester Guardian* has openly proclaimed itself a tool of the Communist propaganda machine.

It is in fact surprising that the *Manchester Guardian* should have allowed itself to be taken in by the Memorandum.

Sefton Delmer, the London *Daily Express* correspondent, who failed to report the Oberfohren affair to his paper, has explained:

My editor immediately wanted to know why I had not done the same. So I pointed out that apart from other improbabilities contained in the alleged Oberfohren document, I was particularly doubtful concerning the validity of one of the ten points it put forward as proof of the Nazi guilt. This 'point' was not in the *Manchester Guardian* version. But it was contained in the copy of the document I had seen.

'I think you will agree with me that it rather undermines the credibility of Herr Oberfohren's alleged revelations – if indeed he was their author. Listen to this!' And then I read him the passage.

'Hitler's constant companion and friend, the English journalist Delmer,' it said, 'telegraphed full details of the fire to his newspaper before it was discovered, and the name of van der Lubbe as being the culprit.'

The Editor agreed that perhaps we had not been scooped after all.[3]

Nevertheless the Memorandum, soon to be published in English by the so-called 'German Information Office' in London and in various other languages elsewhere, was widely regarded at the time as important evidence of Nazi guilt. Even after the war, in his report on the fire, Dr Wolff was to call it 'The fullest and most reliable report about the circumstances of the fire.'[4]

The Memorandum gained credence in the first place because of its supposed author's name. At the time the Nationalists, under the leadership of Hugenberg, were still in uneasy coalition with the Nazis. As chairman of the Nationalist deputies in the Reichstag, and because of his supposed close contact with Hugenberg, Dr Oberfohren might well be assumed to know the true inner story.

We shall therefore have to consider whether Oberfohren was indeed the author of the Memorandum, and also whether he was in fact on such close terms with Hugenberg as he was supposed to be.

Then we shall have to consider the credibility of the Memorandum itself. Its allegations about the fire have never received factual corroboration from any other source, but it also purports to give the inner story of various events leading up to the fire and shortly after it. As we shall see, its account of these matters not only conflicts with a great deal of credible evidence, but also contains a number of significant inherent improbabilities. An examination of these parts of the Memorandum will show us how little credence can be given to its uncorroborated statements about the fire.

Dr Ernst Oberfohren was a doctor of political science who, at the age of forty-three, had decided to abandon his teaching post in Kiel and to devote himself instead to politics. At the end of 1929, when Hugenberg became the national leader of the German Nationalist Party, Oberfohren was appointed its Parliamentary leader.

According to the *Brown Book*, as a confidant of Hugenberg's, he was fully informed of all that went on in the Cabinet. He set down in a memorandum what he knew of the preparations for the burning of the Reichstag, and sent the memorandum to his friends.[5]

But did Oberfohren, in fact, continue to enjoy Hugenberg's confidence after Hitler became Chancellor?

At the end of March 1933, the news that Oberfohren had resigned his seat caused a great deal of public speculation. The Nazi press reported the matter with suspicious brevity. A number of reasons were put forward for his resignation. One historian has said that he differed with Hugenberg over the Party's relationship to the National Socialists; a newspaper article claimed that there was disagreement within the German Nationalist Party on the monarchist issue, while another paper said Oberfohren's reasons were purely personal.

During a Nationalist caucus meeting on 11 April 1933, the leader of the Party, Hugenberg, also dealt with the Oberfohren case. According to the communiqué issued by the German Nationalist Press Agency, he explained that 'as everyone present knows, Oberfohren was opposed to the policy the Party adopted on 30 January'.[6]

Needless to say, this communiqué by Hugenberg makes nonsense of the *Brown Book*'s claim that Oberfohren continued to enjoy Hugenberg's confidence even after Hitler came to power.

At the same caucus meeting Hugenberg gave the real reasons for his break with Oberfohren. This is how the press reported the matter:

> He [Hugenberg] said he felt compelled to disclose a number of unpleasant facts to the caucus. The Prussian authorities had, without his knowledge, raided the house of Dr Oberfohren's Berlin secretary, who had made a formal declaration to the effect that two of the circulars which were found by the police and which attacked the Party Chairman [Hugenberg] had been composed by Dr Oberfohren and sent out on his orders. Dr Hugenberg was informed of this declaration, and made the contents of the circular known to the Parliamentary Party. . . . Immediately afterwards, Dr Oberfohren resigned his seat without any explanation. . . .[7]

There had obviously been a severe rift in the Nationalist Party. According to Dr Sack:

> Oberfohren killed himself because he was unmasked as a traitor to his Party leader Hugenberg, and because he saw the game was up. All these facts, however, were kept from the outside world, and that is why the so-called Oberfohren Memorandum was accepted as an

authoritative document, though only after Oberfohren himself was no longer there to disclaim it.[8]

Oberfohren's resignation caused a scandal, but the news of his suicide became a world sensation. One of the earliest reports was published in the *Hannoverscher Anzeiger* on 8 May 1933:

> On Sunday, the fifty-three-year-old former German Nationalist Deputy, Dr Oberfohren, shot himself in his own home.
>
> We learn that Oberfohren took his life at about twelve o'clock, before lunch, when his wife was not at home. The cause seems to be a conflict with his Party.

The very next day the German Nationalist Press Agency sent out the following correction:

> The death of Dr Oberfohren, which has shocked everyone who had worked with him in the German Nationalist Party, has led a section of the press to publish speculations which are quite incorrect, inasmuch as they associate Dr Oberfohren's death with the treatment meted out to him by the German Nationalist Party. We are therefore forced to publish a letter which Dr Oberfohren addressed to Dr Hugenberg on April 12th:
>
> Dear Dr Hugenberg,
>
> I have been told that despite all the trouble between us you could still speak up for me at a caucus meeting. This forces me to admit quite freely how wrongly I have acted. I sincerely regret the great damage my actions have done the Party. I can only add that it is my firm conviction that the [circular] letters were badly misused. I myself have suffered almost superhuman agonies during the last few weeks. Even before then, the course of political events almost overwhelmed me. My nerves are completely frayed, and I cannot bear the thought of further disputes. I beg you to forget the whole business, if only for the sake of our common struggles in the past. Herr Stein [Adolf Stein, the journalist] was kind enough to assure me that you would lend a ready ear to so open a recantation.

Although that letter ought to have proved to even the most confirmed sceptic that Oberfohren killed himself because he was caught trying to alter the ominous course of Nationalist Party politics by intrigue, the Communist legend that his suicide was connected with the Reichstag fire has persisted to this day. In vain did his widow, Frau Eda Oberfohren, declare:

> My husband was not killed by the Nazis. However, he felt he had become the object of a campaign of persecution, and realizing that the Nazi dictatorship was bound to lead to disaster for Germany and her people, he committed suicide in black despair.[9]

A similar view was expressed by a Social-Democratic journalist, who called on Oberfohren at his Kiel home on 3 May 1933, shortly after Oberfohren's return from a sanatorium:

> Oberfohren was quite alone, for he wanted to keep his wife out of all the scandal.
>
> 'Everything is hopeless,' Oberfohren cried whenever I mentioned the possibility of his standing up to the dictatorship. He was, in fact, a completely broken man.
>
> 'Everything is hopeless,' he repeated.
>
> He had pleaded with Hugenberg, he told me, but Hugenberg deluded himself that the Nazis could be taught better.
>
> Then he told me about the embarrassing police raids on his homes in Kiel and Berlin, the interrogations and the countless threats he had received. He prophesied the complete victory of bestiality.
>
> 'If it were not for my wife, I should have killed myself long ago. Because . . . we shan't see happy days again. What is happening now is merely the overture. Things are bound to get much worse.'
>
> Three days later, Oberfohren was dead![10]

Oberfohren's real downfall had been his own weakness, his lack of courage when, instead of following the light of political reason and breaking openly with Hugenberg, he preferred the questionable method of sending out anonymous circulars.

THE REAL AUTHORS

Shortly after the fire, the exiled Central Committee of the German Communist Party published a pamphlet with the title: 'The Reichstag is in Flames! Who are the Incendiaries?' According to Dr Sack, Torgler's counsel,

> . . . its approach, style and presentation were highly reminiscent of the so-called Oberfohren Memorandum. With some imagination and a great deal of ill will, this pamphlet became the basis of a crude forgery. All that was missing was a good author, and he was found on Oberfohren's death.[11]

Whereas the German edition of the resulting Memorandum called Oberfohren himself the author, the English edition explained:

So he [Dr Oberfohren] inspired a journalist to write a memorandum on the Reichstag fire, he himself supplying most of the necessary information. This is the now famous 'Oberfohren Memorandum'.

The reason for this difference was explained by Dr Sack, who attended the London Counter-Trial in September 1933 – just in time to hear Professor Georg Bernhard and Rudolf Breitscheid agree that '. . . while the so-called Oberfohren Memorandum might reflect Oberfohren's political views, he would never have used that particular style'.

In fact, the German text of the Memorandum was written by an uneducated hack, and could not possibly have stemmed from the pen of Dr Oberfohren, who had studied at the Universities of Berlin, Bonn and Kiel.

So much for the authorship; what about the contents?

One of the 'minor inaccuracies' referred to by the *Manchester Guardian* which was later incorporated into *Brown Book I*, p. 130, was the claim that the Nazi posse alleged to have burned the Reichstag was led by the notorious Storm Troop leader Heines. In fact, Heines spent the night of the fire at an election meeting in far-away Gleiwitz, as he was able to establish to the Supreme Court's entire satisfaction.[12]

Moreover the various editions of the Memorandum contain a number of major differences – a circumstance that does not speak highly for its authenticity. Nor are these differences due to improvements in style or corrections of linguistic errors, for all the changes have obvious political motives. Under the threadbare German Nationalist cloak, the red tunic blazes forth quite unmistakably.

If we analyse the Memorandum carefully, we discover the following main theses:

(1) The Nazis broke German Nationalist opposition in the Cabinet to the prohibition of the Communist Party by planting incriminating documents and arms in the Karl Liebknecht House, the Communist Party Headquarters;

(2) The Nazis burned the Reichstag as a pre-election stunt and as an excuse for a putsch.

Regarding the claim that the Nationalists in the Cabinet were opposed to Hitler's anti-Communist measures, Torgler's counsel, Dr Sack, had this to say:

> The Cabinet had no differences whatever of the kind mentioned in the Memorandum. It was not the National Socialists who urged the prohibition of the Communist Party, but the German Nationalists themselves. . . . The further allegation that the German Nationalists were against the prohibition of the Communist Party in order to prevent an absolute Nazi majority, runs counter to the general view taken by most foreign observers, according to whom the election prospects of the Nazis were bad. In that case, the prohibition of the Communist Party could not possibly have benefited the Nazis, but would have strengthened the Social Democrats. In other words, the combined size of the opposition would have remained the same. . . . Had they wanted an absolute majority, the Nazis would have left the Communist voters severely alone, and later disqualified their deputies.[13]

Even more preposterous was the allegation that the Nazis had planted large quantities of incriminating material in the Karl Liebknecht House. First of all, they could only have done so with the active support of a large number of policemen, and particularly of Police President Admiral von Levetzow, a staunch Nationalist, when the idea was allegedly to deceive the Nationalist Party. Secondly, the raid was first mooted, not by the Nazis, but by Superintendent Reinhold Heller, a policeman of the old school. Thirdly, the material could only have been planted if the Karl Liebknecht House had been deserted or closed beforehand by the police. In fact, the place was full of people at the time of the raid as the following article in a Communist paper showed:

> *Karl Liebknecht House raided again*
> Yesterday the Karl Liebknecht House was raided by the police once again. All those present had to leave the building, and a number of comrades were arrested. The police also raided the Communist Press Agency and confiscated the edition of February 23rd.[14]

Now, this article gave the lie to the whole story, for even had the police managed to smuggle the material in under the vigilant eyes of the Communist officials, they could not possibly have hidden it away in special caches during a fairly short raid. Here is Sommerfeldt's description of the finds:

> The first secret cache was discovered in the cellar, and, of all places, in the shower and washrooms. In one of the last cubicles on the courtyard side the police found a secret door, tiled over to look like the

other walls. This cubicle was ostensibly used for keeping supplies of towels, etc., for which purpose the walls and the secret door had been fitted with screw-on shelves. Now, one of the screws was, in fact, part of a secret lock: by removing it and introducing a fairly long screw-driver into the hole, one could press against a secret spring mechanism and unlock the door. The back of the door was bricked over so that it would sound solid. The door led into a room, some 16 ft. by 6½ ft., without any windows but provided with an electric light. Here the police found a small number of weapons, whose presence fully corroborated the widespread belief that the Karl Liebknecht House was stocked with arms for warding off surprise attacks.

Criminologists wondered whether these weapons were intended purely for defensive purposes or for equipping Communist shock troops. In the ground floor windows the large display shelves had been replaced with boxes which, at first glance, looked like the original shelves. They were heavy, had been nailed expertly and hooped, and were stuffed with compressed newspapers. Any soldier would have considered this type of box a kind of sandbag, behind which one could easily cover the entire Bülow Platz with machine-guns. This view was corroborated by the caretaker of the Karl Liebknecht House, the Communist Vorpahl:

'The boxes were made by a carpenter at the end of January, working partly in the courtyard and partly in a garage behind the courtyard. A few days later, I saw the boxes in the windows of the Karl Liebknecht House bookshop. As far as I know, these boxes were intended as barricades. They were so placed in the display windows that one could just see across them. They were built a few weeks before the Reichstag fire.'

The proof that the boxes were not built before the end of January, was provided by another incontrovertible fact: the Communists had stuffed them full of newspapers dated late January. The Central Office in the Karl Leibknecht House could not have shown more clearly that they were considering an armed uprising at the beginning of 1933, with the Karl Liebknecht House as one of their military strongpoints.

A second cache was reached through the goods lift in the courtyard. In order to get to it, the lift had to be taken down to the cellar, where the rear wall of the lift could be opened by a mechanical device. It gave into a room in which a wooden boarding, some 8 ft. by 5 ft., had been fixed between two pillars to form a secret cupboard. The cupboard itself, which was locked, contained about twenty bundles of important documents, some dated 1933.

Further well-hidden caches were discovered on the fourth floor, in a suite of rooms previously used by the Central Committee. These

> caches were reached by the removal of window sills. They, too, contained important documents.
>
> Similar caches were also discovered on the third floor, the former Berlin-Brandenburg district headquarters. These caches were intended for the sudden 'disappearance' of important Party documents during sudden police raids.[15]

Sommerfeldt's text was illustrated with a large number of photographs. In short, the claim that material was planted in the 'empty' Karl Liebknecht House seems to have just about as much substance in fact as the story about Nationalist opposition to the proscription of the Communist Party.

Now, who was interested in making these false claims? Surely not the Nationalist parliamentarian, Oberfohren, who, though appalled by his Party's alliance with Hitler, was as opposed to the Communists as he was to the Nazis! The very fact that the Communist Party was given so much prominence in the Memorandum shows clearly that neither Oberfohren nor any other German Nationalists could possibly have been its authors – German Nationalists were far too worried about other matters to give more than a fleeting thought to an anti-Communist raid.

THE ALLEGED NAZI PUTSCH

As for the thesis that the Nazis had planned a putsch for the night of 5–6 March (Oberfohren Memorandum, p. 9f.), it was so far-fetched that subsequent Communist accounts of the fire usually omitted it altogether. In fact the whole story, together with that of a Nationalist counter-putsch, came straight out of Münzenberg's head.

On 1 March 1933, the *Völkischer Beobachter* published the following story:

> We learn from official sources that, among the vast quantities of material discovered in the Karl Liebknecht House, the police also found orders with the forged signatures of high police officers and leaders of the S.A. and the S.S. . . . It is known that the evil genius behind these forgeries is the notorious Communist editor Münzenberg, who is still at large.

These sham S. A. orders were mentioned at length in Göring's radio address on 1 March:

In addition, numerous forged orders of the Storm Detachment and Stahlhelm leaders were found, in which the Storm Detachment were directed secretly to hold themselves in readiness for the night of March 6th in order to occupy Berlin, and they were to be prepared to use their arms and beat down all resistance, etc. These forged orders were then to be circulated to the authorities and among the citizens in order to create the fear of a National Socialist putsch.[16]

Göring returned to this question when he gave evidence to the Supreme Court on 4 November 1933:

These forged reports were sent first of all to President von Hindenburg with the polite comment that he, too, was to be removed on that occasion [the S.A. uprising on 5 March]. They were also sent to Minister Hugenberg, to the Stahlhelm and to the Reichswehr. They were even sent to me, with the impertinent suggestion that the Storm Troopers wanted to seize complete power, and that they intended to do away with the police and the Ministry of the Interior. Clearly these forgeries, though sometimes clumsy, were often devilishly clever. . . . One object was to incite the S.A. against their own leaders by suggesting to them, 'Why on earth don't you act on your own?' In other words, they [the orders] were an important and dangerous part of a well-planned propaganda campaign. . . .

Although we might be inclined to dismiss Göring's story as a simple attempt to whitewash himself after the event, there is, in fact, strong evidence that he was speaking the truth. This, for instance, is how Storm Troop Leader Karl Ernst described the forged orders in his inimitably stilted style:

As the official leader of S. A. Detachment Berlin-East, I was shown a yellow carbon copy by Herr Reichsminister Göring. It was alleged to be a copy of an order issued by me to the 8,000 men of my detachment.

Asked officially to swear on my honour whether or not I had ever issued that order, I was forced to say no, if only because such unmitigated rubbish could not possibly have been committed to paper by any S. A. leader; and secondly because the National-Socialist Party follows none but the orders of the Führer himself, who sets out all the steps to be taken to his corps of group leaders, in clear and unmistakable terms. Either the supreme S. A. leader gives the marching order and everyone obeys, or else there is no march at all, for no one in the German Freedom Movement ever marches out of step.

Again, from the purely tactical point of view, the order, logic, and sequence of the forgery attributed to me have been so incompetently botched that I would blush had I to sign such utter drivel. The heading of the 'order' is quite out of keeping with the usual S. A. procedure, so that it alone was bound to cause laughter. The same is true of the salutation.

Every order must be signed by the leader of the detachment, and not, as in this case, vouched for by someone with the name of Tetra, purloined from German mythology, and who was certainly never on my staff. The reference number has obviously been improvised, for my staff had never had a Division 22, a number which has been placed before the date.

If people forge documents, they ought at least to aim at making a credible impression. Now, even if we take the most favourable view of the work of these amateurs, we can adduce no evidence in their favour or in favour of their expert knowledge.

If I am further blamed because a Herr Wels from the Social Democratic Party has taken the trouble of blaming these ridiculous orders on an S. A. leader, all I can say is that Herr Wels, belonging as he does to a Party that is inimical to Germany's military honour, might be expected to come out with such allegations, though no one in good faith can tell me that Herr Wels himself believes in the validity of his claim. No doubt he took prior advice from a party comrade familiar with military matters, and then had the impertinence to dish up this 'alarming document' in feigned surprise and horror.

I accuse the Social Democratic Deputy Wels before German public opinion not only of belonging to a discredited party, but also of engaging in the vilest form of political struggle: the forgery of a political document in order to incriminate an opponent, to decry him before his compatriots and then to accuse him of incompetence in a sphere of which this rabble-rouser [Herr Wels] himself knows absolutely nothing. If Herr Wels wishes to refute this accusation (and nothing could be further from his mind!) all he has to do is to submit to the Reich President the original of this forged report, of which only a copy is at present available.[17]

With their story of dissension in the Nationalist camp, the Communists merely helped Hitler to re-arm while the foreign powers sat by, waiting confidently for an internecine massacre. But the Communist story had no substance in fact.

On 6 March 1933, for instance, when Sefton Delmer, the Berlin correspondent of the *Daily Express*, told Hitler that the wave of arrests in Germany had caused rumours to spread both in Berlin and abroad that he was planning a great slaughter of his enemies, Hitler replied:

I need no St Bartholomew's Night. Under the decrees for the Defence

> of the People and the State we have set up tribunals which will try enemies of the state and deal with them in a way which will put an end to conspiracies.

In any case there was little, if any, tension between Hitler and the Army. We have more than Hitler's own word for this – we know that General von Blomberg was anything but the anti-Nazi hero of the Oberfohren Memorandum: he was, in fact, one of Hitler's keenest admirers.[18]

Nor did Blomberg threaten to arrest Hitler, Göring, Goebbels and Frick, or to occupy public buildings, as the Oberfohren Memorandum claims. Moreover, in the spate of reminiscences published by officers of the Reichswehr since the war, there is not a single mention of any of the acts of resistance described in the Memorandum. It is amusing to learn from the alleged Nazi 'plan' in the Memorandum that Hitler would have been satisfied with the office of Reich President, leaving the far more important office of Chancellor to Göring. His later actions, particularly after Hindenburg's death, proved clearly how averse he was to sharing power with anyone else.

In short, the Oberfohren Memorandum was a tissue of Communist lies, and the most remarkable thing about it is that it managed – and continues even today – to take in eminent scholars when its sole and transparent purpose was to pave the way for Münzenberg's masterpiece: *The Brown Book of the Hitler Terror and the Burning of the Reichstag.*

8. The London Counter-trial

THE SIXTH DEFENDANT: THE *BROWN BOOK*

THE *Brown Book*'s very title was a brilliant stroke: it suggested the book was an official document, a kind of White Paper in disguise. To publish it and similar material, Münzenberg specially founded the 'Editions du Carrefour', in Paris.

In Alfred Kantorowicz's reminiscences about the preparation of the *Brown Book*, we read:

> The world at large learned of the history of this fire and of the true incendiaries from the *Brown Book of the Hitler Terror and the Burning of the Reichstag*, which contained a complete and irrefutable body of evidence, since then supplemented by captured Nazi documents, on this world-shaking criminal case.
>
> In Paris, all this evidence was ... carefully sifted, carefully checked, and put into order by a group of well-known writers and journalists, including André Simone, Alexander Abusch, Max Schroeder, Rudolf Furth, and the author of this report. The *Brown Book* is not a pamphlet, but a collection of documents.[1]

Just how carefully this 'collection of documents' was assembled is best gathered, not from Kantorowicz, but from Arthur Koestler:

> But how could we make the naïve West believe such a fantastic story? We had no direct proof, no access to witnesses, only underground communications to Germany. We had, in fact, not the faintest idea of the concrete circumstances. We had to rely on guesswork, on bluffing, and on the intuitive knowledge of the methods and minds of our opposite numbers in totalitarian conspiracy. The 'we' in this context refers to the Comintern's propaganda headquarters in Paris, camouflaged as the 'World Committee for the Relief of the Victims of German Fascism'.[2]

The real authors of the *Brown Book* preferred to hide behind the noble name of Lord Marley, whom no one could have called a suspicious Red. However, as the former Communist Reichstag Deputy Maria Reese, who knew both Münzenberg and Lord

Marley, has since explained, Lord Marley's real contribution was restricted to the loan of his title. 'It was as simple as that.'

Koestler continues his account as follows:

> The book contained the first comprehensive report on the German concentration camps (including statistics and lists of victims), on the persecution of the Jews, the repression of literature, and other aspects of the terror. The documentation had been assembled by the Comintern's intelligence apparatus. The *Brown Book* further contained the 'complete inside story' of the fire, starting with a detailed biography of Lubbe, unearthed by the *Apparat* in Holland, his contacts with the homosexual circles around the leader of the Brownshirts, Captain Roehm, and ending with a convincing description of how the incendiaries penetrated into the Reichstag through the underground tunnel. Several direct participants in the action were named: Count Helldorff, S.A. Leaders Heines and Schultz. All this was based on isolated scraps of information, deduction, guesswork, and brazen bluff. The only certainty we had was that some Nazi circles had somehow contrived to burn down the building. Everything else was a shot in the dark.

According to a former confidant and political friend of Münzenberg, Erich Wollenberg, Münzenberg told him in Paris

> . . . that in view of the panic which seized large masses of the German people after the Reichstag fire, he was forced to include a great deal of fantasy and invention which – like the alleged association between van der Lubbe and Ernst Roehm – were soon completely refuted.

Münzenberg also told him that '. . . all these inventions were sworn to by witnesses before the so-called London Counter-Trial . . .'[3]

Koestler describes his own share in the preparation of the *Brown Book* as follows:

> My part in it was a subordinate one. I had to follow the repercussions of the trial and of our own propaganda in the British press and in the House of Commons, to study the current of British public opinion, and draw the appropriate tactical conclusions. For a while I also edited the daily bulletins which we distributed to the French and British press.

These daily bulletins were swallowed by most of the bourgeois press, with few exceptions. One such was the *Morning Post* which suggested that the real identity of the authors emerged during the reading of the very first chapter.

Somebody else, too, had reservations – a man who knew Münzenberg and his methods as well as anyone. When Ernst Torgler was handed the *Brown Book* in prison, he felt 'a little shaken':

> I had never thought the whole thing had been so simple. Van der Lubbe an old acquaintance of Roehm and on his list of catamites? Could Goebbels really have planned the fire, and could Göring, standing, as it were, at the entrance of the underground tunnel, really have supervised the whole thing?[4]

Unencumbered by bourgeois inhibitions, Münzenberg even proclaimed Einstein one of the book's sponsors. This immediately prompted Goebbels to wield his poison pen:

> *Einstein in Trouble*
> Berlin, September 6th.
>
> Under the presidency of the notorious hack-writer and Communist, Albert Einstein, a so-called *Brown Book against the Hitler Terror* has recently been published. Two days after this forgery appeared, Herr Einstein was forced to disown his own literary creation. There seems no doubt that Einstein's denial was prompted by sheer panic, for nothing can disguise his personal responsibility. Numerous foreign papers, as well as the anonymous authors of the book, continue to hide behind Einstein's authority. During earlier discussions by the so-called World Committee for the Victims of German Fascism it was unanimously claimed that the book was a publication by Einstein and his circle.

One of Einstein's recent biographers, Catherine Owens Peare, tells how Einstein tried in vain to protest that he had absolutely no connection with the book, and that he had not even been told about its impending publication.

In fact, Münzenberg used names very freely, and the Nazis, quite impotent in the face of this onslaught from abroad, vented their rage on what friends and dependents of their detractors they could lay their hands on. Impotent rage was the reason why they threw five relatives of ex-Chancellor Philipp Scheidemann into concentration camps, as 'just retribution' for a 'slanderous article' Scheidemann had published abroad (*Völkischer Beobachter*, 15 July 1933); impotent rage drove them into launching an anti-Jewish boycott on 1 April 1933; impotent rage dictated most of their press and radio communiqués.

Now this is precisely what Münzenberg wanted. The world came to believe that a Government capable of reacting in this way was also capable of committing the vilest crimes, even those invented in Münzenberg's Paris 'Agitprop' office.

THE LONDON COUNTER-TRIAL

After his great success in harnessing good liberals as 'Trojan horses' to the Bolshevik cart, Willi Münzenberg, the inventive Ulysses from Thuringia, hit upon another brilliant propaganda idea. He remembered the secret revolutionary courts of pre-war Russia, and decided to transplant them to London. The World Committee for the Victims of German Fascism was quickly turned into a 'Commission of Inquiry into the Burning of the Reichstag', presided over by an 'International Committee of Jurists and Technical Experts'. In practice, these experts were recruited on Comintern recommendation. The men in question – internationally famous lawyers of liberal opinion, one and all – would one day receive a flattering letter inviting them to serve as impartial members on a committee investigating Nazi atrocities. Those who agreed to serve and who were finally selected were:

Dr Betsy Bakker-Nort (Holland)
Maître Gaston Bergery (France)
Mr Georg Branting (Sweden)
Mr Arthur Garfield Hays (U.S.A.)
Mr Vald Hvidt (Denmark)
Maître de Moro-Giafferi (France)
Mr D. N. Pritt, K.C. (England)
Maître Pierre Vermeylen (Belgium)

None of the Committee members was a Communist; all were respectable citizens. To this day, some of these honourable men have still not understood with what devilish skill Münzenberg and his pupils diverted their willingness to serve humanity into purely Communist channels. This is particularly true of the Chairman, the then forty-six-year-old K.C., Denis Nowell Pritt. In 1957, at the age of seventy, Pritt was given the freedom of the city of Leipzig, as a 'prominent member of the World Peace Movement'.

Originally, the Münzenberg Trust had appealed to a number of leading American jurists, including the famous lawyer (later Judge), Samuel S. Leibowitz of New York, Leo Gallagher of Los Angeles, Edward Levenson of Philadelphia, and also Paul Gravath, Clarence Darrow, and Felix Frankfurter of New York. In England, they had appealed not only to Pritt but also to Neil Lawson and many others; in France they had turned to Maîtres Henri Torrés, César Campinchi, Marcel Villard, and Vincent de Moro-Giafferi. Further they had invited Dr van 't Hoff-Stokk (Holland), Adolphe Jaeglé (Strasbourg) and the advocates Soudan, Graux, and Braffort (Belgium). Of all these, only Pritt and Moro-Giafferi ended up on the final list.

The American member, Arthur Garfield Hays, was to have the unique experience of seeing through both smoke screens – the red as well as the brown. In July 1933, Hays had just finished a dramatic case, and, as he tells us, had no plans for the immediate future, when to his utter surprise he received a telegram from Edward Levenson, an American lawyer. The telegram, which had been sent from Moscow, read:

> GEORGI DIMITROV CHARGED WITH COMPLICITY IN REICHSTAG FIRE. HIS MOTHER REQUESTS YOU DEFEND SON AS WELL AS OTHER COMMUNIST DEFENDANTS BEFORE GERMAN REICHSGERICHT. CHARGE IS A VICIOUS FRAME-UP AGAINST INNOCENT MEN. YOUR HELP NEEDED. TRIAL SEPTEMBER.

Hays cabled back: 'I shall be glad to join in defence provided German Government permits. Please bear in mind I am a Jew.'

Today Hays admits honestly that he can no longer tell whether his acquiescent reply was due to his emotional reaction at the time, a desire for change, or perhaps a thirst for adventure.

Hays – who was born in 1881 in the State of New York – was a most successful lawyer of liberal views. He was legal adviser to the American Civil Liberties Union, and one of the defence lawyers in the Sacco-Vanzetti trial. He could well afford to forgo fees, when the need arose, and had done so on a number of occasions. All these reasons must have made him appear an excellent choice to Münzenberg.

How very difficult the role was which Münzenberg expected the various members of his Commission to play is shown by the example of Georg Branting of Sweden, to whom the German Public Prosecutor wrote the following letter on 10 August 1933:

> Since – despite public appeals for information that might throw light on the matter and despite the offer of a very high reward for any information leading to the apprehension of the culprits – we have received no evidence beyond that set forth in the Indictment, and since the Court is extremely anxious to base its verdict on all the available facts, I should be most grateful to you if you would kindly let me know what documentary evidence the Commission has in its possession. I should be most obliged if you would reply at your earliest convenience, and if you could also let me have the names and addresses of any witnesses of the Reichstag fire, who might feel obliged, and who are willing, to appear before the Supreme Court.

Since even the worst lawyer must have realized that, compared with the boastful claims of the Committee, the evidence was extremely tenuous, Branting's reply to the Public Prosecutor (18 August 1933) was full of evasions:

> The best and most convincing evidence is futile if it may not be used to exonerate the defendant.
>
> I am not entitled to hand over documents at my own discretion, but I have no doubt that the Commission of Inquiry . . . will hand them over to counsel for the defence as soon as adequate guarantees are given that the accused will enjoy unrestricted legal representation.

As a result, Drs Sack, Seuffert, and Teichert, all of whom felt completely 'unrestricted', turned to the Commission and requested a sight of the famous evidence, but all in vain. Dr Sack even flew to Paris and later to London so as to leave no stone unturned in the defence of his client Torgler. In Paris, he and his assistants, Dr Hans Jung and Dr Kurt Wersig had a conference lasting five hours with Branting, Leo Gallagher and an 'Austrian journalist' who called himself 'Breda' but who was none other than Otto Katz, Münzenberg's chief lieutenant. When Dr Sack asked to see what evidence there was exonerating his client Torgler, he was told by Branting and his colleagues that they were not entitled to disclose the address of the attorneys to whom the material had been handed for safe keeping.

Instead of 'entitled' they ought to have said 'able', for the material never existed. Why else should they have made such a mystery of the whole business? For even if the Commission did not trust the German Supreme Court or its advocates with the material itself, there was no reason why photostats should not have been handed over, or published in the foreign press. Why then did the Commission agree to a conference with Dr Sack? Dr Sack and his colleagues soon discovered the real reason – it was to get information out of *them*. Disappointed, Dr Sack returned to Berlin on 9 September.

On 11 September 1933, 15,000 people crowded into the Salle Wagram in response to an appeal which the Münzenberg Trust had plastered all over Paris. The chief speaker was the French advocate and deputy Maître Vincent de Moro-Giafferi, who referred to his exhaustive study of all the documents bearing on the Reichstag fire, and who roused the audience to near-frenzy when he shouted: 'It is you, Göring, who are the real assassin and the real incendiary!'

It was certainly not mere solidarity with Göring that prompted Dr Sack to make the following objection: 'He [Moro-Giafferi] had seen neither the result of the preliminary examination nor the indictment (which, in cases of high treason, must be kept secret according to German law), yet this did not seem to weigh heavily on his legal conscience.'

A few months later, on 4 November 1933, Göring, whom Moro-Giafferi had denounced with so much emotion, followed suit when he, too, anticipated the Supreme Court verdict with: 'My sixth sense tells me that the fire was started by the Communists.'

Meanwhile Arthur Garfield Hays, accompanied by his daughter Jane, had arrived in Paris. In the Hôtel Mirabeau he was met by 'a self-effacing, apparently bewildered little lawyer who introduced himself as "M. Stephan Detscheff, *avocat bulgare*" '. With the help of an interpreter, Hays managed to find out that the *avocat* represented a committee of Bulgarians for the defence of Dimitrov, Popov and Tanev.

> I tried to find out who constituted the committee and asked: 'Who is the committee?' Answer: 'We'. I made further inquiry: 'Who are we?' Answer: 'A group of people interested in defending these innocent men.' 'What group of people?' The answer came back: 'Our Committee.' I gave up.

We can sympathize with Detscheff's reserve. Such unwelcome, inquisitive questions were not wanted, and were, in any case, rarely asked, for their 'panel of brilliant names' usually protected the Committee against any awkward questions.

In Paris, Hays also met his French colleague, Maître de Moro-Giafferi. 'My conference with him was unsatisfactory... One could not confer with him; one just listened. His rapid-firing comments did not even permit interruption for translation by my secretary.'[5]

With how little real knowledge Hays was expected to serve on the Committee is best shown by the fact that he arrived in Europe just one day before the beginning of the Counter-Trial and without any detailed briefing. He ought to have suspected straightaway that the Committee was far less concerned with his legal ability, than with using his name.

On 14 September 1933, the London Counter-Trial was formally opened in the courtroom of the Law Society. The inaugural address was delivered by Sir Stafford Cripps, to an audience including such famous men as H. G. Wells. Shaw, too, had been invited but he had declined with the remark: 'Whenever a prisoner is used as a stick with which to beat a Government, his fate is sealed in advance.'[6]

The whole trial was carefully staged with the 'bench' ranged on one side of the room. One of the 'judges' was Moro-Giafferi of whom Dr Sack had this to say:

> Legally-trained observers were unpleasantly surprised when they saw Moro-Giafferi on the bench. Four days earlier, this French lawyer had told all Paris that Hermann Göring was the real instigator of the Reichstag fire, and now he, whom every court throughout the world would have deemed an interested party, sat here as judge. He was judge and prosecutor rolled into one.[7]

Hays's comments were different, though no less telling:

> On the third day of the hearing, I saw my colleague, Moro-Giafferi, of France, apparently engaged in deep thought. He scribbled a note and pushed it to Bergery who sat at my right. I wondered what I had missed that this eminent French lawyer had caught. I glanced at the note. It read (translated into English): 'There isn't a good-looking woman in the courtroom.'[8]

Nor was the French lawyer the only one to be dissatisfied with the atmosphere at the Counter-Trial; the original sense of great excitement soon gave way to a general sense of great boredom. The reason was simple: the wirepullers, Münzenberg and Katz, were able to set the stage, but they could not keep control of it. One difficulty – and source of boredom for the ever-decreasing number of journalists – was the multi-lingual composition of the bench. Thus when a French 'judge' wished to put a question to a German witness, his question had first to be translated into English and then into German, and the German's reply had to be translated back into French via English. Most of the interpreters were ordinary members of the public and there were constant arguments about the correct translation of a given phrase. In the end, but only after a great deal of unpleasantness, it was agreed that an English-speaking German would put English questions to German witnesses and that a German-speaking Englishman would translate the German's reply, on the assumption that an ordinary person can understand a foreign language better than he can express himself in it. How closely the courtroom resembled the Tower of Babel can best be gathered from Hays's wry remark that, on one occasion, his own American idiom had first to be turned into the King's English before it could be translated into German.

Oddly enough, the Nazi press reported the Commission's original deliberation with surprising fairness:

> The International Legal Commission into the Burning of the Reichstag today heard the evidence of Georg Bernhard on the political position at the beginning of the year and his claim that stories about Communist responsibility [for the fire] were so many fables. Only if all their leaders had gone absolutely mad, could the Communists have hatched out so idiotic a plot.
>
> Bernhard went on to state that he knew the Communist Torgler extremely well. In his opinion, it is quite inconceivable that Torgler did anything so preposterous as setting the Reichstag on fire.
>
> After the noon recess, the Commission heard the Social Democrat Breitscheid. He, too, stated that he had known Torgler for many years and that he thought it impossible for Torgler to have had any connection with the Reichstag fire.

Then there is the story of how Albert Norden – editor of the *Rote Fahne* and, according to many people, the real author of the Oberfohren Memorandum – appeared before the Commission with a masked face, pretending he was a Storm Trooper from Germany. The mask was ostensibly worn so as to enable the Storm Trooper to return to Germany, when in fact it served to disguise Norden's 'pronounced Jewish features'. Even before producing his mysterious witness, Münzenberg had prepared the ground so well that, as Hays tell us,

> . . . one of the [London] papers reported that three of the fifteen witnesses whom we contemplated calling were on a 'Death List' posted on the bulletin of a London Nazi club. Under the names and photographs of those listed appeared the comment: 'If you meet one of them, kill him; if he is a Jew, break every bone in his body.'
>
> Often the doors to the hearing room would be locked before a witness was called and remain so until five minutes after the witness had testified. This in order to enable the witness to get away. . . . Many of the names of witnesses were kept secret.

But cleverly though Otto Katz played this cloak-and-dagger game, some of his schemes proved too hard to swallow even for the Commission. An example was the evidence of the witness 'W. S.' that Bell had shown him a list of thirty well-known homosexuals whom he had introduced to Röhm. Among these names, the witness went on to say, he 'particularly remembered' the name of Marinus van der Subbe or Marinus van der Lubbe and beneath it the entry: 'Holland'. Herr W.S. made so bad an impression, that the Commission had to dismiss him as 'not very reliable'. Still, there were many others no better than Herr W. S. whose monstrous lies the Commission saw perfectly fit to believe.

By means of the careful sifting of witnesses, the secretariat – that is, Otto Katz – made sure of one thing at least: the systematic exclusion of any real friends of van der Lubbe. Thus, when a special committee consisting of Dr Bakker-Nort, Mr Georg Branting and Maître Pierre Vermeylen heard the evidence of sixteen witnesses in Holland, all of these witnesses 'happened to be' hostile to van der Lubbe. One of them, the 'poet' Freek van Leeuwen, played a particularly odious role, for it was largely thanks to him that the London Commission accepted the story of van der Lubbe's homosexual relationship with Röhm.

On the evening of 19 September, members of the Commission assembled in a hotel suite. Hays tells us how the stolid and dignified Pritt sat in the bathroom with a typewriter, while Dr Kurt Rosenfeld (Torgler's former counsel) and other members of the committee straightened out exhibits. Others again were wandering about the rooms. Having finished his job and finding the bed covered with papers, the exhausted Hays, 'forgetting the dignity of the American bar', crept into a corner and fell asleep on the floor.

Next day, the Commission published its 'preliminary' findings, and it was in the nature of things that these were the mirror-image of the subsequent verdict of the German Supreme Court: where the former blamed the Nazis, the latter blamed the Communists.

The Final Conclusion of the Committee (formulated by Bergery) was:

(1) That van der Lubbe is not a member but an opponent of the Communist Party; that no connection whatsoever can be traced between the Communist Party and the burning of the Reichstag; that the accused Torgler, Dimitrov, Popov and Tanev ought to be regarded not merely as innocent of the crime charged, but also as not having been concerned with or connected in any manner whatsoever, directly or indirectly, with the arson of the Reichstag.

(2) That the documents, the oral evidence, and the other material in its [the Commission's] possession tend to establish that van der Lubbe cannot have committed the crime alone;

(3) That the examination of all the possible means of ingress and egress to or from the Reichstag makes it highly probable that the incendiaries made use of the subterranean passage leading from the Reichstag to the house of the President [Speaker] of the Reichstag; that the happening of such a fire at the period in question was of great advantage to the National Socialist Party; that for these reasons, and others pointed out in the third part of the report, grave grounds exist for suspecting that the Reichstag was set on fire by, or on behalf of, leading personalities of the National Socialist Party.

The Commission considers that any judicial organization exercising jurisdiction in the matter should properly investigate these suspicions.

Many lawyers have rightly objected to the German Public Prosecutor's absurd plea that the Court need not consider '. . . in which particular way each of the accused carried out the crime.' The London conclusions are open to precisely the same objection, for like the German Court verdict later, they were based on so many unverified political speculations.

As a known member of the London Commission, Hays was understandably reluctant when he was asked to go to Leipzig as an observer:

I tried to persuade some of the other lawyers to go with me. Most of them were too busy to go. Said Bergery: 'I can't go, I am a French deputy; if anything happened to me in Germany, it would create an international incident.'

Said I: 'Bergery, that wouldn't bother me. What bothers me is that if anything happens to me – nobody will pay a damned bit of attention to it.'

Hays started for Germany with trepidation, but he soon discovered that his fears were groundless. No one took the slightest notice of him – so much so that he confessed he was a 'little disappointed'.

> In general, much to my surprise, the trial was objective. Dr Sack was defending Torgler conscientiously and with ability. He made it clear that he had no sympathy for or with the Communist Party or with Torgler's political views, but that the man, not the party, was on trial. He left no doubt that he was sure of his client's innocence. Any lawyer, even though a non-Nazi, would in that atmosphere have taken the same position.

These remarks, which were published during the war, show not only that Hays was a man of outstanding honesty, but also why the Communists grew extremely chary of him. Thus he wrote:

> My committee, with headquarters in Paris, continually criticized Sack for not trying to prove that the arson was committed by the Nazis. Preposterous! Not only was that not his job, but it would have been inexcusably stupid.

Hays made it clear that he, the American Jew, was invariably treated with professional courtesy by Sack, the German Nazi, who was ready for conference at any time.

The Communists kept in touch with Hays in their own conspiratorial manner:

> Every few days I was visited by a Communist – usually a different individual – but always giving the name 'Mr Glueck'. I refused to go to out-of-the-way places, so Mr Glueck always came to my hotel.

The Paris Communists now thought it was high time to save poor Arthur G. Hays from the clutches of the Nazi devil, Dr Sack, and to lead him back to the straight and narrow path of anti-Fascism. To do so, they behaved with typical ruthlessness. After his return to Germany from a brief visit to Paris, where he had given an interview to a *Pravda* correspondent, Hays found that his words had been twisted out of recognition. Whereas he had told the reporter no more than

> . . . that the Nazis were not on trial, that Sack had based his defence on the innocence of his client rather than on the guilt of others, and that the only reason the Nazis came into the picture at all was because the

> court had gone out of its way to disprove the charges in the *Brown Book*....[9]

Pravda had reported him as saying:

> ... I had charged the Court with ignoring evidence pointing to the guilt of the Nazis, and had charged Sack with betraying his client.

With that 'interview' the Communists nearly attained their object – Dr Sack was deeply offended with Hays.

It was at about the same time that four foreign lawyers and observers at the trial, viz. the Bulgarians Grigorev and Detscheff, the Frenchman Marcel Villard, and the American Leo Gallagher, caused an incident which led to their temporary arrest and subsequent expulsion from Germany. Grigorev had tried to approach Dimitrov at the beginning of a noon recess, but the guards had pulled Dimitrov away. Enraged, Grigorev and the other foreign lawyers came to Hays's hotel and insisted that a protest be made immediately to the Court. Hays objected, stating with good reason that he had more important things to do than to make mountains out of molehills. A few days later, the Paris Committee sent him clippings from the French press to the effect that Dimitrov had been brutally handled in Court, and asked why Hays had ignored the matter.

Meanwhile, the others had lodged a protest with the Presiding Judge who referred them to Dr Teichert, Dimitrov's counsel. When their protest remained unheard, they wrote a letter to Dr Teichert calling him a Nazi stooge and the whole trial a frame-up. As a result, Grigorev, Detscheff and Villard were whisked across the border, while Gallagher, an American citizen and hence not so easily got rid of, was barred from Court. He stayed on in Germany and continued to bombard the President of the Court with letters of complaint.

The upshot of all this was that the stage-directors in Paris were left with no one at the trial except Hays, who kept letting them down badly:

> ... I had continually expressed resentment at their continued insistence that I urge Dr Sack to play up the Nazi angle. I had pointed out that the defence of the innocent was a big enough job and that this would be jeopardized by making charges we could not sustain in Court. ... The correspondence had become so heated that I had threatened to leave Berlin if the committee presumed to give me

> instructions. I had begun to feel that the committee might be controlled by 'leftists' who were more interested in anti-Nazi propaganda than in the fate of the defendants whom I was supposed to represent and that they were trying to use me as a pawn to further their political game.[10]

When all the factual evidence had been given at the trial, Hays felt that his job was ended, and he accordingly left Germany on 22 October 1933. Before his departure he wrote to Dr Sack:

> After a month of observing the trial I have the fullest confidence in the objectivity of your defence, and if anyone should criticize you abroad, you can always rely on my support.[11]

But Hays had not yet heard the last of the business. On 13 December 1933 the Public Prosecutor, in the course of a sharp attack on the *Brown Book* and the London Counter-Trial, which he called grotesque, charged Hays with hypocrisy, claiming he had told Soederman, a Swedish criminologist, that though he was convinced the Nazis were not involved, he had not had the courage to say so openly. This, the Public Prosecutor added, was typical of the manner in which the London Commission had set to work, and showed how much attention should be paid to its findings.

Hays immediately sent the following cable:

> DR KARL WERNER, REICHSGERICHT, LEIPZIG, GERMANY. ANSWERING NEWSPAPER REPORT YOUR SPEECH – I MADE THE SAME STATEMENT TO SOEDERMAN, TO LONDON COMMISSION, AND PUBLICLY, TO WIT – THERE IS NO DIRECT EVIDENCE THAT LUBBE HAD ACCOMPLICES BUT IF, AS YOU CLAIM, HE DID NOT ACT ALONE, THEN HIS ASSOCIATES MUST HAVE BEEN NAZIS. I HOPE YOU WILL MAKE THIS CORRECTION IN COURT BUT I DONT EXPECT IT.
>
> ARTHUR GARFIELD HAYS[12]

In other words, Hays was one of the few to realize that van der Lubbe had fired the Reichstag by himself. Small wonder, therefore, that he was not invited to attend the final session of the International Legal Commission (Caxton Hall, 18–20 December 1933), at the conclusion of which the Chairman, D. N. Pritt, K.C., read the verdict – three days before the Leipzig judgement. Once again the date had been chosen skilfully – if all the accused were sentenced there would be an international outcry, and if they were acquitted, the whole world would know that it was thanks to the efforts of Münzenberg's Commission.

The 'verdict' was largely a rehash of the 'final conclusions' of 20 September. In other words, it was based on evidence that most lawyers would have considered extremely slender, at best, and it was, once again, the German High Court verdict in reverse:

> (1) Marinus van der Lubbe could not have committed the crime alone.
> (2) Grave grounds exist for suspecting that the Reichstag was set on fire by, or on behalf of, National Socialist circles.
> (3) The Communist Party had no connection with the burning of the Reichstag.[13]

In addition the Commission found:

> That the retrospective application of the penal law of March 29th imposing the death sentence in cases of arson or high treason would constitute a monstrous violation of one of the principles of justice most universally recognized among all civilized nations;
>
> That the conviction of the accused Torgler, the accusation having been withdrawn against the three accused Bulgarians, will doubtless and rightly give rise to universal protest;
>
> That, bound by its terms of legal reference, the Legal Commission is not in a position to give expression to that protest in this report;
>
> BUT that it considers it its duty to proclaim that in these circumstances the sentencing to death of Torgler would constitute a judicial murder.[14]

In short, Münzenberg had made certain that the German Supreme Court always lagged one step behind the *Brown Book*, which Otto Katz correctly described as the 'sixth defendant' – the German Court sat for three months, most of which time it spent on desperate attempts to refute the *Brown Book* and the findings of the Counter-Trial.

As Koestler put it:

> It was a unique event in criminal history that a Court – and a Supreme Court to boot – should concentrate its efforts on refuting accusations by a third, extraneous, party. Hence the parade of Cabinet Ministers on the witness-stand, hence the fantastic request of the court to the Head of the Potsdam police, to furnish an alibi for his movements at the time when the crime was committed. . . .[15]

A German observer summed up the Court's 'fight against the sixth defendant' as follows: 'Their propaganda . . . was so widely believed that any failure to discuss their lies, however stupid, would have been considered an evasion'.[16]

Or, to quote Koestler again: 'Both Heines and Schultz had

produced fairly convincing alibis, and in some other respects, too, the guesses of the *Brown Book* had been wide of the mark. But that did not diminish the effects. In totalitarian propaganda details do not matter.'

In order to brazen it out with those who had seen through the *Brown Book*, Otto Katz produced a further masterpiece called *The Fight for a Book*. Here is a specimen of its methods:

> The *Brown Book* has been taken to task for calling Heines, Helldorff and Schultz the real criminals, when all three have protested that they were not. Now, that is the only 'proof' of their innocence. The so-called 'alibis' these men submitted were accepted by the Supreme Court without question – and that is now called a refutation of the *Brown Book*!

In fact, the three S.A. leaders had alibis that any court would have accepted. Thus Arthur G. Hays wrote:

> Heines, the Silesian Storm Troop chieftain and Reichstag deputy who, in the *Brown Book* and by the Oberfohren Memorandum, was said to have been the leader of the Nazis who had assisted van der Lubbe and had then left him alone in the burning building, presented an unimpeachable alibi. Not only he, but his wife, a nurse who attended his children, and others, testified to his whereabouts on the night of the fire, in a distant city, Gleiwitz, Silesia.

But facts had never bothered the *Brown Book* compilers: 'The Court failed to determine whether Heines had time to fly to and from his near-by constituency to Berlin.'[17]

But Hays closed even this loophole:

> More convincing, however, were clippings from local newspapers showing that Heines had made a speech at a public meeting on February 27th. Thinking this might have been planted, I had one of our Mr 'Gluecks' check up on newspapers of the town. Personally, I have no doubt that Heines was not involved. The same was true for Schultz, von Helldorff, and others who had been mentioned as Nazi accomplices.[18]

9. Münzenberg's Striking Success

THE CASE AGAINST GOEBBELS

THOUGH Münzenberg failed to take in Hays, he took in almost everyone else, particularly when the German Supreme Court agreed that van der Lubbe must have had accomplices. If the accused Communists were innocent, what could be more obvious than to seek the real incendiaries in the National Socialist camp? Oddly enough, Hitler himself was not implicated, either in the *Brown Book* or in the Oberfohren Memorandum. Instead, the Communists fastened suspicion on all sorts of leading Nazis, and especially on Goebbels and Göring.

Dr Goebbels became their favourite target simply because he, of all the Nazis, was the only one clever enough to have hit on the idea of burning the Reichstag as a means of seizing power. The whole thing was started in the Oberfohren Memorandum, where we read: 'The ingenious Goebbels, handicapped by no scruple, soon devised a plan . . .'

The *Brown Book*, which elaborated this argument with more enthusiasm than good sense, claimed: 'It was he [Goebbels] who first thought of a *grand coup* which would at one blow change the political position of the National Socialists.'[1] And elsewhere, in unmistakable Communist Party jargon: 'Goebbels provided the plans for the most outrageous provocation which a ruling class has ever used against the insurgent working class.'[2]

Goebbels himself scoffed at these accusations, when he gave his evidence before the Supreme Court:

> It came as a great surprise to me when I read that the *Brown Book* considers me the author of this plan. That is just one more proof of the complete lack of imagination with which the Communists trump up their charges. Can anyone really believe that I have no better way of fighting the Communists than starting a fire?[3]

Now, Goebbels would, in fact, have had to be a political idiot, and not the shrewd schemer he was, had he really hit upon so dangerous a plot. Let us, for the sake of argument, assume that a fire would have been needed by the Nazis in order to squash the Communist Party or 'the insurgent working class'. Let us further assume that the best plan would have been to set the Reichstag on fire. Then this is how Goebbels might have planned it:

A posse of Storm Troopers is returning from a victorious street battle. Singing a rousing song with throats hoarse from cheering for Germany, they are just rounding the Reichstag, full of the joys of life, when they are alerted by passers-by. The Reichstag is on fire! With their usual sang-froid the Storm Troopers rush into the burning building and catch the incendiaries red-handed. They are ten well-known Communists, carrying detailed instructions for a putsch and Communist Party membership cards in their pockets, and all are killed on the spot by the enraged Storm Troopers. Later, the press is allowed to inspect the gutted building, and the well-known faces of the Communist criminals. There is no lengthy trial, there are no foreign suspicions – just perfect co-ordination. And yet even this plan would have been studded with difficulties. First of all it would have involved a fairly large number of accomplices and hence a grave risk of betrayal. Secondly, most Reichstag officials, porters, etc., would have had to be replaced beforehand with reliable Storm Troopers.

But in any case Goebbels would have made certain that his men discovered real Communists – albeit dead – rather than Marinus van der Lubbe, who insisted he had left the Communist Party and had burned the Reichstag all by himself.

Torgler's counsel, Dr Sack, dealt with this question at some length:

> It is quite ridiculous to suggest that the National Socialists should have picked a tramp as the best person to carry out a plan whose discovery would threaten the whole nation....
>
> Only a fool would have allowed the intended arsonist to wander about alone, in rags and tatters, begging for food in the streets, and sleeping in the public shelters in Glindow, Berlin and Henningsdorf.
>
> Only a fool would have instructed van der Lubbe to scale up the wall of the Reichstag, to break windows, and thus to expose the whole plan to so many risks of discovery. After all, the shot fired by Sgt Buwert might easily have hit van der Lubbe and might thus have thwarted the 'whole plan'. This plan, allegedly invented by Goebbels, the undisputed master of the art of propaganda, would therefore have

been so full of flaws as to invite discovery deliberately. This suggestion alone shows that the Oberfohren Memorandum is a tissue of malicious lies. The Memorandum, which claims to know precisely what happened, is bound to be wrong, simply because its authors were, in fact, quite unaware of the real course of events. They did not know where van der Lubbe had spent the previous day, that he had climbed into the Reichstag instead of entering through the subterranean passage, or that a revolver was fired at him. They did not know all this because the records of the preliminary investigation had mercifully not been made public.[4]

All Dr Goebbels did do – and who would gainsay that he did it brilliantly? – was to exploit the *results* of the fire, the more so because he himself was fully convinced that the Communists were responsible.

Though neither Goebbels, Göring nor any other National Socialist had thought up the idea of burning the Reichstag as a pretext for starting an anti-Communist pogrom, Münzenberg's propaganda was so effective that the Nazi leaders themselves began to suspect one another. Thus one of Goebbels's collaborators, Werner Stephan, wrote after the war, when the burning of the Reichstag appeared a minor transgression in comparison with all the inhuman crimes the Nazis had committed, that Goebbels 'probably conceived the idea', and '... in any case, the burning of Parliament provided the main theme of his election campaign'.[5]

Dr Wolff's conclusion in his report on the fire was that

> Goebbels must be considered the evil genius behind and, thanks to his tremendous intelligence, the real perpetrator of, this devilish plan.

Also there is Sommerfeldt's highly informative *Ich war dabei* ('I was there') which threw a great deal of light on the circumstances surrounding the fire. In 1933 Göring had 'promoted' Sommerfeldt to the rank of Oberregierungsrat, and like many of Göring's minions, Sommerfeldt felt acutely suspicious of Goebbels, Göring's chief rival in the Nazi hierarchy. In his book, Dr Wolff published a letter from Sommerfeldt, from which we quote the following significant passage:

> From the night of the fire to this day, I have been convinced that the Reichstag was set on fire neither by the Communists nor at the instigation, let alone the participation, of Hermann Göring, but that the fire was the *pièce de résistance* of Dr Goebbels's election campaign,

and that it was started by a handful of Storm Troopers all of whom were shot afterwards by an S. S. commando in the vicinity of Berlin. There was talk of ten men, and of the Gestapo investigating the crime. This was reported to me on the one hand by the chief of the Berlin Storm-Detachment, Gruppenführer Ernst, who was filled with poisonous hatred of Goebbels, and also by Dr Diels who, at the time – it was the spring of 1934 – gave me exact details about the scene and of the crime and the identification of the ten victims.[6]

If Sommerfeldt did, in fact, claim that he knew all this in the spring of 1934, it seems most odd that he failed to disclose it in his *Ich war dabei* which was published in 1949. Moreover, if Sommerfeldt claims that he heard details of the crime and the victims from Diels, why did he not think fit to mention any of their names, thus helping to turn mere suspicion into certainty? But once again, it is more than accident that no names were mentioned, and it is not surprising that Diels's *Lucifer ante portas* contains no single reference to what would certainly have been a most important aspect of the Reichstag fire story – had the murder of the ten Storm Troopers ever happened, that is.

All Sommerfeldt wrote in 1949 was:

If we look back today across the ruins of Germany at the ruins of the Reichstag, we realize that that act of arson was no more than an act of malice and a 'masterpiece of agitation' of the kind for which Dr Goebbels was so well known. Today I am convinced of what I could only suspect at the time: that Goebbels administered this act of incendiarism as a shot in the arm of the floating or lazy voters. . . .

With his alleged signal for a Communist uprising, Goebbels flung Hitler and Göring into a whirlpool of profound and irrevocable decisions. And this master-psychologist showed that he knew what he was doing.[7]

It was in 1933 that Sommerfeldt first discussed his suspicions with his friend, Storm Troop Leader Prince August Wilhelm, who told him that the S.A. was in a state of great agitation because '. . . a number of Storm Troopers had been arrested and had since disappeared. S.A. Leader Ernst was prepared to swear any oath that Dr Goebbels was behind it all, and asked that Goebbels be paid out for his treachery.'

Sommerfeldt immediately asked whether there was any connection between these arrests and the Reichstag fire which, foreign rumour had it, was started by Ernst's gang. To Sommerfeldt's great disappointment, the Prince who, as a close confidant of Röhm and Ernst, ought to have known the truth '... denied categorically that he had heard anything on the subject except wild rumours'.[8]

Sommerfeldt also discussed his suspicions with Röhm:

> I dropped a gentle hint that the Reichstag fire trial had led to personal differences between Göring and myself, and Röhm asked in surprise:
>
> 'What on earth did Göring have to do with the whole business?'
>
> When I replied: 'Who else?' he said furiously:
>
> 'Well, who but that devil, Jupp [Joseph Goebbels]?'
>
> I must have evinced too much curiosity, for he quickly changed the subject . . .[9]

Now, all that this proves is that the Nazi leaders thought one another capable of any piece of villainy – quite rightly so, as all of us have had to learn to our cost.

Unfortunately, Sommerfeldt was not able to draw the only reasonable conclusion from these mutual recriminations, even though that conclusion stared him in the face:

> I had written a pamphlet on Göring and I had conducted the German and foreign press to the scene of the crime – for that was my job. This very fact was enough to stamp me an incendiary as well. It is understandable, therefore, why this stupid charge suggested to me that the accusations against the others might be just as false.[10]

And yet Sommerfeldt went on to blame Goebbels without producing a shred of real evidence against him. To this day, no such evidence has been brought forward by anyone, despite the fact that so gigantic a plot as the one Goebbels is alleged to have hatched out, must have involved a large number of accomplices, and despite the fact that accomplices invariably talk. In 1933, the Nazis were not nearly as well entrenched as they were, for instance, in 1939 when they attacked the Gleiwitz radio-station, pretending they were Poles. Yet, despite all their efforts to wipe out the evidence on that occasion, the real facts could be established without much difficulty, and far beyond mere rumour and speculation.

THE CASE AGAINST GÖRING

While not a single one of the many survivors from Göring's immediate circle considered it even vaguely possible that Göring could have had anything to do with the Reichstag fire, there are two men who claim to have heard Göring himself confess his guilt. These men are Hermann Rauschning and Franz Halder.

In 1940, Hermann Rauschning published a book in the United States which quickly became a best-seller and was translated into most European languages. The book was called *Voice of Destruction*.

Rauschning, who was elected President of the Danzig Senate in July 1933, left the Nazi bandwagon in the autumn of 1934. He stayed in Danzig for another two years, and then went abroad with his story of Hitler's intimate thoughts.

In his book Rauschning tells how, shortly after the Reichstag fire, Hitler asked him for a report on the Danzig situation, and how, while waiting in the lobby of the Chancellery, he got into conversation with some Nazi celebrities, including Göring, Himmler, Frick, and 'a number of Gauleiter from the western provinces':

> Göring was giving details of the Reichstag fire, the secret of which was still being closely guarded. I myself had unhesitatingly ascribed it to arson on the part of persons under Communist, or at any rate Comintern, influence. It was not until I heard this conversation that I discovered that the National Socialist leadership was solely responsible.
>
> The complacency with which this close circle of the initiated discussed the deed was shattering. . . . There is nothing more extraordinary than that this enormous crime, the perpetrators of which gradually became known in the widest circles, should not have been sharply condemned, even in middle-class quarters. Many people actually condoned this *coup*. Still more extraordinary is the fact that the incendiary himself has actually enjoyed a certain amount of sympathy in foreign countries, even till quite recently.

The incendiary Rauschning referred to was, not van der Lubbe, but Hermann Göring.

> Gratified laughter, cynical jokes, boasting – these were the sentiments expressed by the 'conspirators'. Göring described how 'the boys' had entered the Reichstag building by a subterranean passage from the President's Palace, and how they had only a few minutes at their disposal and were nearly discovered. He regretted that the 'whole shack' had not burnt down. They had been so hurried that they could not 'make a proper job of it'.

The many inverted commas round Göring's alleged phrases

suggest that Rauschning 'jotted them down under the immediate influence of what he had heard' – as he himself put it in the preface to his book. Hence it seems doubly surprising that, when asked to fill in some of the missing details, Rauschning was quite unable to do so. For instance, Rauschning was unable to identify the 'Gauleiter from the western provinces', though he continued to insist that '. . . after every such conversation he had made careful notes and that there was no doubt whatever about the general accuracy – though not necessarily the precise wording – of his reports.'

Rauschning added that the Reichstag fire discussion was dominated by Göring, who spoke 'very loudly and quite unashamedly'. However when he (Rauschning) approached the group, Gauleiter Forster (who had accompanied Rauschning from Danzig) gave a signal and the conversation stopped.

A few years later still, Rauschning described his experiences as follows:

> Göring did not describe these details to me or to Forster, but to a circle of confidants and friends in different sorts of uniforms, who surrounded him before we arrived. Forster and I heard no more than snatches of the conversation. When one of the group spotted me, the outsider, he gave Göring a sign and Göring stopped talking.

This version differs markedly from the one in Rauschning's book, in which Rauschning specifically stated that he 'got into conversation with the Nazi celebrities'. Also in the last version it was not Forster but one of the people round Göring who had signalled Göring to stop. Moreover, according to the book, Göring did not stop abruptly at all, but closed with the significant words: 'I have no conscience. My conscience is Adolf Hitler.'

True, Rauschning, when asked about these and other contradictions, insisted that his version of the conversation was the correct one, but it seems rather difficult to decide which of his versions he really meant. For in the end Rauschning himself had to admit that

> . . . detailed and careful investigations have shown certain contradictions in my evidence. . . . Indeed, I admit gladly that, as a result, I have grown less certain, not about my evidence, but in my previous attitude to the fire. . . . I declare with all emphasis that there had been no misunderstanding and that I vouch for the literal truth of Göring's closing words.[11]

And Rauschning went on to say:

> Whether Göring himself was speaking the whole truth, or indeed the truth, is quite a different matter. I myself have never fully believed Göring's version . . .

A far cry from the allegations made in his book!

Göring himself had, of course, read Rauschning's book, so that when he was asked by Mr Justice Robert H. Jackson, Chief Prosecutor at the Nuremberg Trial, whether he himself had not admitted to setting the Reichstag on fire, he knew at once what it was all about, and protested angrily:

> No. I know that Herr Rauschning said in the book which he wrote . . . that I discussed this with him. I saw Herr Rauschning only twice in my life and only for a short time on each occasion. Had I set fire to the Reichstag I would presumably have let that be known only to my closest circle of confidants, if at all. I would not have told it to a man whom I did not know and whose appearance I could not describe at all today. That is an absolute distortion of the truth.[12]

Now, Göring may have been too hard on Rauschning, for there is yet another possible explanation of the whole business: Rauschning might well have overheard, not a boastful outburst of Göring's, but one of Göring's frequent displays of his particular brand of twisted humour. For this is precisely what happened to the second 'star witness' against Göring, Franz Halder, the Chief of the General Staff:

> Jackson: 'Do you remember a luncheon in 1942, on Hitler's birthday, in the officers' mess, at the Führer's Headquarters in East Prussia?'
>
> Göring: 'No.'
>
> Jackson: 'You do not remember that? I will ask that you be shown the affidavit of General Franz Halder, and I call your attention to his statements which may refresh your recollection:
>
> ' "On the occasion of a luncheon on the Führer's birthday in 1943, the people round the Führer turned the conversation to the Reichstag building and its artistic value. I heard with my own ears how Göring broke into the conversation and shouted: 'The only one who really knows the Reichstag is I, for I set fire to it.' And saying this, he slapped his thigh." '
>
> Göring: 'This conversation did not take place, and I request that I be confronted with Herr Halder. First of all, I want to emphasize that what is written here is utter nonsense. It says: "The only one who really knows the Reichstag is I." The Reichstag was known to every

representative in the Reichstag. The fire took place in the general assembly room, and many hundreds of thousands of people knew this room as well as I did. A statement of this type is utter nonsense. How Herr Halder came to make that statement, I do not know. Apparently that bad memory, which let him down in military matters, is the only explanation.'

Göring had previously been examined on Halder's testimony by Dr Robert Kempner, Assistant Trial Counsel for the American Prosecution:

Kempner: 'A number of generals have alleged that you have boasted of your connection with the Reichstag fire.'

Göring: 'What the general says is not true. I should very much like to see him here, so that he can say it to my face. The whole thing is preposterous. Even had I started the fire, I would most certainly not have boasted about it. . . . These generals all talk utter nonsense. I object most strongly that people keep saying I did it. All I did was say, by way of a joke, that people will soon stop believing that Nero burned Rome, because the next thing they will say is that it was I who was fiddling in his toga.'

Now, even if Göring did make the remark Halder alleges he heard, the fact that he slapped his thigh suggests strongly that he must have been joking. Halder would certainly have missed the joke, for his lack of humour was proverbial.

The case against Göring also rested on the allegation by Diels and Gritzbach (Göring's Secretary of State) that their chief had told them about the Reichstag fire long before it started.

Kempner: 'Diels says that you knew exactly that the fire was to be started in some manner, and that he had prepared the arrest lists already previously, the lists of people that were to be arrested immediately the night after the fire.'

Göring: 'When did he say that?'

Kempner: 'He told that for the first time two days after the fire and he later repeated it.'

Göring: 'To whom did he say that two days after the fire?'

Kempner: 'To certain officials of the Ministry of the Interior'.

Göring: 'It is true that lists for the arrests of Communists quite independent of the Reichstag fire had already been prepared. The fire did not start for that. They would have been arrested anyway. If Diels said that I knew about the fire, then for some reason he must have spoken nonsense, and I can't explain it in any way, and it would be very interesting to me to be confronted with Diels so that he can tell it to my face.'

And elsewhere:

Göring: 'I cannot judge what people are saying now, but I should like to be confronted with Gritzbach so that he can tell it to my face that I knew about it. . . . I knew nothing about it and even they [Diels and Gritzbach] could have known nothing about it. Gritzbach, at the time, did not even belong to my personal staff. I never had such thoughts, and I must stress again that it would have been idiotic to deprive ourselves of the House, which was very important for us, and that afterwards I had great difficulties in finding a substitute for the Reichstag building.'

Kempner: 'You had nothing to do with it, and yet there were rumours that it was the Storm Troopers.'

Göring: 'No, I had nothing to do with it. I deny this absolutely, and am prepared to face anyone with whom you care to confront me. I can tell you in all honesty, that the Reichstag fire proved very inconvenient to us.'

Kempner: 'To whom?'

Göring: 'To the Führer and also to me as the President of the Reichstag. Had we given such a signal, we should have picked less essential buildings.'

Kempner: 'What buildings, for instance, would have been a better signal than the Reichstag? The Berlin Palace?'

Göring: 'Yes, the Palace or any other buildings. After the fire I had to use the Kroll Opera House as the new Reichstag. You must know that I took a keen interest in my state theatres, and that I found it bothersome, for the Kroll Opera was our opera number two, and the opera seemed to me much more important than the Reichstag.'

The International Military Tribunal apparently believed Göring rather than his accusers, for Diels's and Gritzbach's evidence was not pursued any further.

OR WAS IT KARL ERNST?

Before 30 June 1934 neither the *Brown Book* nor any other Communist publication contained even the slightest hint that Karl Ernst had played any active part during the fire. But when Hitler suddenly obliged them with three corpses: Gruppenführer Karl Ernst, and his associates Mohrenschild and Sander, the opportunity seemed far too good to be missed.

Immediately after the executions, in the summer of 1934, Münzenberg's Editions du Carrefour published a *White Book on the Shootings of June 30th 1934* (see Appendix D), containing a forged letter, ostensibly sent by Karl Ernst to Edmund Heines on 5 June 1934. The letter was written in what was assumed to be S.A. barrack-room style, and accompanied a signed confession to the effect that Ernst was 'Incendiary No. 1'.

Wisely the authors of the *White Book* refrained from telling their readers how they of all people had managed to get hold of this top secret Nazi document. Despite this omission, and despite the crude way in which they forged the letter, the Communists were, once again, able to take in a host of unsuspecting people.

Unfortunately for the forgers, two of the accomplices named by Ernst – S.A. Oberführer Richard Fiedler and Dr Ernst Hanfstaengl – survived 30 June 1934 and both men called the confession a complete fabrication.

Moreover, one of Münzenberg's former colleagues, Erich Wollenberg, published an article in Schulze-Wilde's *Echo der Woche* in which he stated that the Paris Communists forged documents so successfully that they managed to fool even the former Gestapo agent Gisevius. Among these documents was

> . . . the so-called Ernst testament, which was concocted by a group of German Communists in Paris – including Bruno Frei and Konny Norden – after Ernst's murder on June 30th, 1934, and only published after Dimitrov himself had edited it in Moscow. . . .[13]

Göring, who was in any case extremely sensitive about his alleged part in the Reichstag fire, was absolutely incensed when he heard that this forged document coupled his name with that of Karl Ernst. When Dr Robert Kempner asked him whether Ernst might have had a hand in the fire, he received the following reply:

> Göring: 'Yes, he is the man who could have done it. But I think the letter I was recently shown is absolute nonsense. . . .'
>
> Kempner: 'One of your friends told me that Ernst's part was discussed in your circle and that other people were also present. Will you tell us what was said on that occasion? There was talk in your

house that Ernst and the S.A. were involved. Will you tell us about that conversation?'

Göring: 'The matter was mentioned very briefly. There was no proof at all. Marinus van der Lubbe had admitted that he had taken these things into the Reichstag, and therefore nothing more was said about it.'

Kempner: 'Why did you mention Ernst's name and the S.A. in connection with the fire?'

Göring: 'Ernst played a part in it, but I don't remember who told me. From the start, I thought that Ernst was a man who would love to give us trouble, for he was responsible for savaging people in concentration camps. He was also a real live-wire and at one stage very important to Hitler.'

Kempner: 'We have some evidence to show that Goebbels and Ernst got on very well together at the time, that Goebbels knew something about the Reichstag fire, and that he talked about it.'

Göring: 'I do not believe that. Ernst was the leader of the S.A. and Goebbels did not get on with him. Goebbels was always suspicious of the Berlin S.A., because they staged a putsch in 1930, as a result of which our situation became very, very difficult.'

Kempner: 'Is Diels right to claim that you gave express orders to dig up evidence against the Communists but not to follow any trail leading to the S.A. or to Ernst?'

Göring: 'That is untrue. Ernst was not mentioned at all at the time.'

Kempner: 'How do you explain the fact that the whole world says you did it?'

Göring: 'Yes, that was said quite suddenly. They "just knew" it. The entire foreign press claimed two days afterwards that I had burned the Reichstag.'

Kempner: 'Why didn't they say it was Ernst and his men?'

Göring: 'They were not so well known abroad. I was the President of the Reichstag, and so it seemed more fitting to involve me.'

Kempner: 'Who were Ernst's friends or who do you think belonged to his circle at the time?'

Göring: 'I don't know who was close to Ernst. I don't know these people. I liked neither Ernst nor his tendencies.'

Kempner: 'Are you referring to his homosexual tendencies?'

Göring: 'Yes, but for political reasons.'

Kempner: 'But as a politician and as Prussian Prime Minister did you not know that those who constantly caused you trouble were Ernst's people?'

Göring: 'That's true of Ernst himself. But the names of his people – well, there were quite a few S.A. leaders outside Berlin, for instance,

Heydebreck in Pomerania, who were also making trouble. Ernst provided me with a comical S.A. guard, which was supposed to arrest me one day and of which I got rid with some excuse or other. I simply disbanded them.'

Kempner: 'What was said about Ernst's role? If his men burned the Reichstag, what motive could they have had? In criminal cases we have to ask: *Cui bono?*'

Göring: 'It was only discussed once, not immediately after the fire, but later. When all those allegations against me were being made, we wondered whether the S.A. had had anything to do with it, simply because that came out during the investigation.'

Kempner: 'In other words, you yourself had nothing to do with it, and it was merely rumoured that the S.A. was involved?'

Göring: 'No, I had nothing to do with it. I say so categorically and I look forward to any confrontation whatsoever.'

Kempner: 'There are these alternatives: either van der Lubbe did it, or else the S.A. did it for political reasons.'

Göring: 'In either case van der Lubbe was involved, for he, after all, was caught.'

Kempner: 'But van der Lubbe was half crazy, is that not true? Do you agree?'

Göring: 'Yes.'

Kempner: 'Is it therefore not possible that van der Lubbe was used by the S.A.?'

Göring: 'Yes, well, I have read the letter [he was referring to Ernst's letter]. As far as I know, van der Lubbe could not speak a word of German.'

Kempner: 'Yes, but there were interpreters who could have spoken to him.'

Göring: 'How could they have met van der Lubbe? But anything is possible.'

Kempner: 'Anything is possible, indeed. Do you think that Goebbels and the S.A. might have been jointly involved?'

Göring: 'I really cannot imagine it.'

Kempner: 'You cannot imagine it?'

Göring: 'No, I really cannot.'

Now Kempner urged Göring once again to recall who could possibly have been interested in starting the fire. Göring took the opportunity to put forward certain conjectures, but no more:

Göring: 'I must repeat that no pretext was needed for taking measures against the Communists. I already had a number of perfectly good reasons in the form of murders, etc. The fire served – or was supposed to serve – or could . . . well . . . I'm really wondering what motive Ernst might have had. Perhaps he argued: "We'll start the fire and then give it out that it was the Communists." Perhaps the S.A. thought in that way they might gain a larger slice of our power.'

Kempner: 'Well, now we're getting somewhere.'

Göring's reasons for harbouring vague suspicions against Ernst were obvious. After the Reichstag Fire Trial he, too, must have begun to wonder whether van der Lubbe's accomplices could have been Communists. Moreover, the S.A. outrages, and his growing dislike of Ernst and Ernst's gang must have made even Göring receptive to foreign and local rumours.

However, Göring himself gave his word to Count Schwerin von Krosigk and also to Presidential Secretary Otto Meissner, who was interned with him and who asked him about his share in the Reichstag fire, that he (Göring) was completely innocent. All he did was grant the possibility that '. . . some "wild" National Socialist commando, and possibly even the Berlin S.A. leaders Count Helldorff and Karl Ernst, might have been responsible for the Reichstag fire, and might have used van der Lubbe as their tool'.[14]

And why, after all, should Göring have thought Karl Ernst, the man who, in his opinion, had prepared a putsch against Hitler in 1934, incapable of setting fire to the Reichstag? Or for that matter Count Helldorff, who had participated in the anti-Hitler revolt of 20 July 1944?

But that is all Göring did – admit that these men *might* have started the fire. Yet unlike most of his detractors, he left it at that, and refrained from whitewashing himself by making direct accusations against others.

Finally, let us listen to a witness whose evidence is more than speculation or surmise: the former S.A. Obersturmführer and subsequent Detective-Inspector, Dr Alfred Martin. This is what he had to say:

> At the time of the Reichstag fire, I was an S.A. Obersturmführer on the personal staff of Gruppenführer Helldorff and Ernst, which made me a sort of general factotum. The reason for my promotion was simply that my doubts had caused me to keep clear of politics and also that – as one of the few trained men among a whole lot of rowdies – I was more presentable than such types as Schweinebacke. In my S.A. work I enjoyed the complete confidence of Ernst and of his

lieutenants, and I am quite certain that I should have known, had Ernst, Schweinebacke, etc. – all those names were later mentioned by anti-Fascist circles as having been involved in the Reichstag fire – really had anything to do with it. In particular, I had highly confidential conversations with them – and also with Walter von Mohrenschild, a debonair young man of very good family and Ernst's second in command. At the time I had already joined the Resistance and whenever these men were in their cups I made a point of returning to the subject of the fire. Moreover, von Mohrenschild and I were both dragged by S.A. gendarmes before the summary court of that fine gentleman Herr Fritsch and sentenced to death [June 30th, 1934]. Until Mohrenschild's execution, we shared a cellar of the Lichterfelde Kaserne, and had many long and serious conversations, during which I referred to the part he was alleged to have played in the Reichstag fire. All these men steadfastly denied S.A. or Party responsibility for the fire. I, personally, have gained the conviction that the Party and the S.A. had absolutely nothing to do with it. Moreover, during my training with the criminal police in Berlin in autumn 1933, I had occasion to glance at the files and I also had long conversations with the man in charge of the investigations and above all of van der Lubbe's interrogation. . . . This man [Dr Zirpins], whom I knew very well, was anything but a Nazi. He told me that there was no doubt that van der Lubbe had burnt the Reichstag by himself.

The reliability of this witness is vouched for by Diels, who wrote:

This organization [Division Ic of the S.A.] also contained a number of decent young men, some of them students, who had joined the S.A. merely in order to fight Communism. But when all sorts of sordid desperadoes from the gutters of Berlin started flocking into Ic, the better elements left in horror. Among them was the group round young Dr Martin, who made contact with the 'anti-militarist machine', thus probably saving the lives of many intended Storm Troop victims.[15]

THE MASS ARRESTS

One weighty reason for blaming the Reichstag fire on the National Socialists was that they had ostensibly prepared a huge number of warrants, with only the date missing, against the night of the fire, when they hauled thousands of Communists out of bed and dragged them off to police-stations and S.A. barracks.

Now, there is no denying the arrests themselves, but they do not necessarily imply Nazi complicity in the Reichstag fire.

First of all, the large-scale arrests and raids involved the full co-operation of the Political Branch (Division IA) of the Prussian police and ready access to their documents. Hence the whole plan hinged on the silence of men, many of whom, as we saw, were still so filled with 'old-fashioned' notions that Göring was forced to create the more reliable Nazi 'auxiliary' police on 22 February 1933. These men kept silent, simply because there was nothing to reveal. This fact alone exonerates the Nazis even if we choose to ignore the statements by Diels, Dr Schneider, and other high-ranking officers of Division IA, that the Reichstag fire took them completely by surprise.

During his evidence to the Supreme Court on 4 November, Göring himself had this to say:

> Many people have wondered how it came about that my orders to arrest the ringleaders were carried out so promptly. Far from proving my prior knowledge of the fire, this merely shows how efficient our measures were.... Now, for the reason why: on the night of the fire, I knew all about the whereabouts of leading Communists because my predecessor had already prepared a full list of their addresses and hide-outs. On coming into office, I immediately checked and completed that list, and that is why I was able to arrest thousands of Communist officials immediately after the Reichstag fire.[16]

Göring's explanation was fully corroborated by Diels:[17] a list of the names and addresses of leading Communists had been prepared under Police President Severing, together, of course, with a similar list of Nazis and rightist extremists – a fact which Diels did not mention. In other words, the mass arrest of Communist officials could have been ordered any time the Minister saw fit to do so.

When Göring was asked about the matter in 1933 and again in 1945, he kept insisting:

> I very much regret – and I confess it openly before all the world – that the Reichstag fire saved certain Communist leaders from the gallows, when it had always been my intention to smash them completely the moment they gave the slightest hint of rebellion....

There were many other 'regrettable' mistakes during Göring's action, including one which caused great amusement in Court, viz. the abortive attempt to arrest Ernst Torgler. This is how Torgler himself remembers the occasion:

> Because I expected them to come for me next morning, if not that night, I decided to spend the night [of the fire] with our parliamentary secretary, Otto Kuehne, at his house in Berlin-Pankow. While he himself was arrested there next morning, I was left severely alone. This fact caused some amusement in the court-room because of the light it cast on the 'shrewdness' and 'intelligence' of the police officers. When a policeman opened the door to the room in which I had slept, I was just dressing and bade him good morning politely. He returned the greeting with equal politeness, and closed the door.[18]

Really though, there was no reason to laugh at dapper detective Franz Hohmann, for like so many of his colleagues, he had been summoned to police headquarters in the early hours of the morning, and ordered to bring in a whole lot of men. Naturally he realized that all of them were Communists, but he never even thought of arresting anyone for whom he had no warrant. After all, he was a policeman and not a politician.

Thus Hohmann is our best witness for the fact that 'outmoded' police methods were still being used at that time and, beyond that, that the black list had been compiled by Göring's predecessors. For Torgler's host for the night, Otto Kuehne, had moved house a year before, yet Hohmann had been sent to look for him at his old address, where he wasted hours trying to dig him up. In fact, Hohmann did not arrive at the correct address until seven o'clock in the morning.

But while the police were going about their business, the Storm Troopers were making another, quite independent, series of mass arrests which has often been confused with the police action. This wave of arrests was completely improvised, as many former Nazis have since testified. Dr Taube, for instance, an 'anti-Communist propaganda expert, spent the evening of the fire in the Berlin Nazi headquarters, from which the Reichstag blaze could be seen. Since no one thought the fire had any political implications, Dr Taube eventually went home to bed. An hour later, he was ordered back to headquarters, where he found everyone in a state of great agitation. He was told that the police had caught a Dutch Communist, that a Communist putsch might start at any moment. A senior S.S. officer – the S.S. was a branch of the S.A. until 30 June 1934 – was poring over a list of 'suspicious political elements' compiled by Nazi blockwardens and by Heydrich's intelligence service. The S.S. officer then ticked off all 'dangerous' names, on the principle that members of the intelligentsia were particularly noxious. That is how it came about that such non-Communists as Ludwig Renn, Erich Mühsam, Carl von Ossietzky, Otto Lehmann-Russbüldt and many like them were hauled out of their beds in the middle of the night.

The Nazi lists, like those of the police, were out of date, and included names of people who had died some time earlier. Moreover, former Nazis have admitted that individual S.A. leaders and men made hay while the sun shone, and started settling personal scores with people who were not on the list. On 20 October 1933 the Supreme Court asked Count Wolf von Helldorff, Police Chief of Potsdam and Berlin S.A. Chief, to describe his movements on the night of the fire. He testified:

> On the day of the Reichstag fire, I worked in my office until about 7 p.m. Then I joined Professor von Arnim, the then Chief of Staff of the Berlin S.A., for dinner at Klinger's in the Rankestrasse. When we were at table, someone rang us up and told us about the Reichstag fire. I asked Herr von Arnim to get to the Reichstag as quickly as possible, and to ring me at home in case I was needed. At about 10 p.m. I was told that my presence in the Reichstag was not required. At about 11 p.m. I drove to my offices in Hedemannstrasse where I had a conference with my staff. The subject of the Reichstag fire was broached. Next day, I gave orders for the arrest of a large number of Communist and Social Democratic officials.[19]

(This statement was corroborated by Professor von Arnim and the owner of the restaurant.)

After his testimony, Helldorff was greatly embarrassed by Torgler, who asked him: 'Did you give the orders for the arrest of the Communist and Social Democratic leaders in your official capacity [as Chief of the Potsdam police] or in your capacity as S.A. leader?'

Helldorff started hedging; he was not quite sure what Torgler was getting at. The Public Prosecutor immediately rushed to his assistance, objecting that Torgler's question was irrelevant and immaterial inasmuch as it had no bearing on Helldorff's movements. However, the Presiding Judge overruled the objection, and Helldorff was compelled to answer. He preferred to sacrifice the truth and incriminate himself rather than throw the blame on Göring, the Minister of the Interior:

I gave the orders entirely on my own responsibility. As Gruppenführer of the Berlin S.A., I felt fully entitled to arrest enemies of the state, particularly since the Reichstag had been set on fire and since we all knew who the culprits were.

Fourteen days later Hermann Göring tried to correct Helldorff's damaging admission, and told the Court:

> We threw in the entire police force. Because that was not enough, I naturally deployed the S.A. and the S.S. as well. That is why I summoned Count Helldorff. I know he has told the Court that he acted entirely on his own initiative, but I must add the small proviso that, though I left him a free hand in details, I gave him the clear order to use his Storm Troops and arrest every Communist vagabond he could lay his hands on. That was a measure which I supported one hundred per cent. Without the praiseworthy help of our S.A. and S.S., the colossal success of that night, during which 5,000 Communist leaders were taken behind lock and bar, would not have been possible.

Clearly, either Göring or Helldorff had committed perjury. The truth came out much later, when Göring was forced to admit, under Dimitrov's piercing questions, that Helldorff had ordered his S.A. henchmen out into the street before he (Göring) had a chance to sanction the order, thus giving it a semblance of legality.

Unable to grasp that the only reason why the Communists made no effort to hit back was that they had made no plans to do so, Göring and Helldorff both boasted to the Court that it was the Government's speedy measures which had thwarted a Communist rebellion. Goebbels was under a similar misapprehension: 'No resistance was shown anywhere; the enemy was apparently so taken aback by our sudden and drastic measures that he lifted no finger in his defence.'[20]

Diels has described the confusion resulting from Helldorff's ill-prepared action: a large number of prisoners caught by the S.A. could not be found on the blacklists – and had to be released, only to be caught again by the Storm Troopers. This explains why the figures varied so much: Göring spoke first of 4,000 prisoners and then of 5,000; Diels mentioned 1,800 arrests in Prussia, when the official figures gave 10,000.[21]

All in all, there is little doubt that, when Hitler ordered the arrests on the night of the Reichstag fire, he did so on the spur of the moment, and in genuine fear that a Communist rebellion was imminent. That is also the reason why Göring was able to complain that far too many Communist leaders had managed to elude his net.

THE PRE-ARRANGED DATE

A further Communist argument for Nazi responsibility is that all Nazi leaders kept 27 February suspiciously free of election engagements. Instead, they all seemed to have repaired to Berlin for a grandstand view of the fire.

This story saw the light of day in the Oberfohren Memorandum:

> 'All was prepared. On Monday 27th February, for some extraordinary reason, not one of the National-Socialist Propaganda General Staff was engaged in the election campaign. Herr Hitler, the indefatigable orator, Herr Goebbels, Herr Göring, all happened to be in Berlin. With them was the *Daily Express* correspondent Sefton Delmer. So, in a cosy family party, these gentlemen waited for the fire.'*

What happened in fact on the night of the fire was that Göring was at work in the Prussian Ministry of the Interior; Hitler and Goebbels were listening to music in the company of a group of people including Professor Hoffmann; von Papen was entertaining President von Hindenburg in the Herrenklub; the Foreign Office spokesman, Dr Hanfstaengl, was in bed with influenza; Count Helldorff was having supper in a restaurant in the Rankestrasse; and Himmler was in Munich. Seen thus, the evening of 27 February seems considerably less suspicious than the Oberfohren Memorandum made it out to be.

Moreover, there was no need, even had the Nazis planned the fire, for all the leaders to assemble in Berlin – suspiciously and quite pointlessly. True, in his testimony to the Supreme Court in November 1933, Goebbels did not produce the preceding explanation, but argued instead that the pause in the election campaign had been chosen at random in order to enable the Nazi leaders to attend a Cabinet Meeting.

And oddly enough, no one seems to have wondered why men who had ostensibly planned so gigantic a pre-election stunt as the fire should have spent the whole afternoon discussing such prosaic

* Delmer was not in fact 'with' the Nazi leaders, in this 'cosy family party'. He met them at the fire. See *Trail Sinister*, p. 185.

topics as changes in the milk law, the national insurance regulations, etc. Neither did anyone wonder why the Nazi leaders were so obviously astonished when they first heard of the fire: Goebbels slammed down the receiver on what he thought was one of Hanfstaengl's silly hoaxes; Hitler, too, refused to believe the news at first, and we know from Ludwig Grauert that Göring's surprise was not shammed. In any case, both Goebbels and Göring expressed the view that somebody's carelessness was to blame, and Göring repaired to the scene of the crime, where he wasted precious hours staring at the flames and speculating about their causes and consequences, instead of pulling his prepared plans out of his breast pocket, or issuing his prepared newspaper and radio communiqués.

Now, it is precisely the remarkable confusion and the many contradictions in the Nazi press after the fire, that ought to have suggested how little Hitler, Göring and Goebbels were expecting the fire. For if the Reichstag had really been burned by the highly organized Nazis, their press would have thrown the blame on the Communists from the start, instead of publishing a host of contradictory rumours, allegations and denials. Dr Goebbels proved often enough that he could order the entire German press to speak with one drab voice. It may be argued that at the time of the Reichstag fire Goebbels was not yet Minister of Propaganda and could therefore not yet order the non-Nazi press to dance to his tune. However, the Nazi press itself was completely under his thumb, so that there was no reason why the *Völkischer Beobachter*, for instance, should give the name of the incendiary as van Durgen, and why the man who left the Reichstag with Torgler was variously said to have been Wilhelm Pieck, Otto Kuehne and Wilhelm Koenen. The Nazi press even mentioned the presence in the burning Reichstag of a man who 'was identified as an American'.[22]

WAS THE FIRE BRIGADE CALLED IN TIME?

The suspicion that the Reichstag fire was started by mysterious criminals gave rise to a series of legends about the Berlin Fire Brigade and its chief, Fire Director Walter Gempp, particularly after Gempp was suddenly dismissed from his post. Once again, the real source of these legends was the Paris Agitprop office, and once again the German Supreme Court had to refute them. Still, we ought to be thankful since otherwise we should never have been able to discover what measures the fire brigade took on the night of the fire – all the brigade records were destroyed during the war.

Dr Wolff has repeated the legend that Gempp, during a meeting of fire brigade officers held in Berlin early in March, complained that the 'grand alarm' was given too late when, as the former Police President of Berlin, Albert Grzesinski, told the London Commission of Inquiry: '. . . any fire in the Government quarters of Berlin automatically calls for the highest-stage alarm, unless there is a specific order to the contrary.'

The *Brown Book* wondered who gave that order, and in whose interest it was that

> . . . the highest stage of alarm was not given to the fire brigade until half an hour too late . . . by which time the flames had attained considerable dimensions. . . . The delaying of . . . the highest alarm, coupled with the non-compliance with the fire regulations was responsible for the disastrous effects of the fire in the Session Chamber, the devastation in which was made good use of by the National Socialist propagandists.[23]

In fact, the existence of automatic regulations of the kind mentioned by Grzesinski has never been proved. Instead, Berlin, then as now, had a special Decree for the Alarm and Deployment of Fire Fighting Forces, according to which fire calls from public buildings, theatres, warehouses, factories, etc., were given various priorities. Thus the report that the Reichstag was on fire automatically set off the third-stage alarm. In other words, Grzesinski was quite wrong to claim that every fire in the Government quarters automatically called for the grand (fifteenth-stage) alarm. In any case, such automatic rules would have been quite preposterous, since even the smallest fire in the Government quarters would have left the rest of the gigantic city of Berlin denuded of fire engines. Even today, the highest-stage alarm sounded automatically for any public building in West Berlin is the fifth-stage.

If then the first report of the Reichstag fire called for 'no more than the third-stage alarm', the question still remains why the three sections of pumps associated with that stage were not automatically sent to the fire. Was there perhaps a deliberate plot to sabotage the fire-fighting arrangements?

As with so many historical events, here, too, the combination of a series of quite independent accidents led to the strangest consequences. However, the fact that there was no organized attempt to interfere with the work of the fire brigade is proved, not only by the evidence of firemen, but above all by the Court's reconstruction of the actual events:

First alarm, 9.05 p.m.

At 9.05 p.m., the police officer on duty outside the Reichstag, Sergeant Buwert, was told by two passers-by (Flöter and Thaler) that incendiaries had climbed into the Reichstag. After dithering for a few minutes (until 9.09 p.m.), Buwert requested another passers-by to alert the police at the Brandenburg Gate. One minute later – at 9.10 p.m. – he also requested the passers-by Kuhl and Freudenberg to call the fire brigade. These two sprinted to the Engineering Institute, whence Brigade Headquarters, Linienstrasse, were alerted at 9.13 p.m. Headquarters transmitted the call to the 'Stettin' Brigade, in the Lindenstrasse. A minute later, Section 6 pulled out, commanded by Chief Fire Officer Puhle. Puhle arrived at the Reichstag at 9.18 p.m. Passers-by directed him first to the northern front, whence he drove on to the restaurant (western front).

Second alarm, 9.15 p.m.

At 9.15 p.m., a patrolman pulled the fire alarm in the Moltkestrasse. Section 7, under the command of Fire Officer Klotz immediately left the 'Moabit' Brigade in the Turmstrasse, reaching the Reichstag four minutes later. When he saw the four vehicles of Section 6 outside the Western Entrance, Klotz drove on with three of his vehicles, leaving the fourth, commanded by Fire Officer Wald, at the south-western corner. Klotz stopped briefly outside Portal Two (south) which was locked, and then went on to Portal Five (north), the only entrance which was kept open at night. He arrived there at about 9.20 p.m.

Third alarm, 9.19 p.m.

At 9.17 p.m., immediately after his arrival at the Reichstag, Police Lieutenant Lateit ordered Sergeant Buwert not only to watch the windows and to fire at anything suspicious, but also to give the 'grand alarm'. Since Buwert could not possibly carry out both orders, he decided to remain where he was until a fellow policeman arrived on the scene. By that time the fire brigade had decided to sit tight, since two sections of pumps had already been sent out, and since, in any case, the 'grand alarm' had no precise technical significance. During the trial, Buwert was given a severe dressing down by the Public Prosecutor for having carried out the first part of his order first: 'Should you not have known that the last order always takes precedence?'[24]

Fourth alarm, 9.31 *p.m.*

Fire Officer Wald gave the tenth-stage alarm by telephone from Portal Five at 9.31 p.m.

Fifth alarm, 9.32 *p.m.*

Immediately afterwards – at 9.32 p.m. – the tenth-stage alarm was given, once again from Portal Five. Altogether eight sections of pumps were now on the way to the Reichstag, in addition to the two sections that had meanwhile arrived. With them came Chief Fire Director Gempp, Fire Directors Lange and Tamm, and Chief Government Surveyor Meusser.

Sixth alarm, 9.33 *p.m.*

Chief Fire Officer Puhle ordered Fireman Trappe to give the fifth-stage alarm from the Engineering Institute, but when Trappe did so he was told that the tenth-stage alarm had already been sounded.

Seventh alarm, 9.42 *p.m.*

Immediately after his arrival at the Reichstag, Chief Fire Director Gempp consulted Fire Director Lange and then gave orders for the fifteenth-stage alarm to be sounded. Chief Government Surveyor Meusser gave the same orders on his own authority.

Since every section consisted of four vehicles, no less than sixty fire-fighting vehicles were now drawn up round the Reichstag. At the same time a number of fire-boats had begun to fight the fire from the River Spree.

The time-table we have just drawn up shows why Dr Sack, Torgler's counsel, was able to speak with some justification of the 'exceptionally quick mobilization of the fire brigade'. Still, the question remains why the very first telephone call did not lead to the automatic and prompt dispatch of at least the three sections which the regulations demanded.

From the study of all the evidence given at the preliminary examination and at the trial, the following explanations emerge:

1. When the fire was reported to Brigade Headquarters from the Engineering Institute, the caller apparently said it was a minor fire. In order not to deplete the central brigade of all its pumps for the sake of a minor fire, only one section was sent out.

2. When the second alarm was sounded from the Moltke-strasse fire alarm, the call went automatically to Brigade Headquarters, and hence to the 'Moabit' Brigade which sent out Section 7. Headquarters still felt that two sections were more than enough to deal with an insignificant fire.

3. From that moment – 9.15 p.m. – until the tenth-stage alarm was given at 9.31 or 9.32 p.m., no further alarm was received by Brigade Headquarters. It seemed reasonable to assume, therefore, that the two sections were quite adequate.

4. Brigade Headquarters also inferred that the fire was under control from the fact that none of the fire-alarms in the House itself had been pulled. Had that been done, three sections would undoubtedly have gone out straightaway.

Night porter Albert Wendt, whom Constable Poeschel had asked to pull the fire alarm in his lodge, had not done so for the following reasons: firstly he simply refused to believe Poeschel's story before he had checked it; then, when he saw the blazing restaurant, Lateit told him the fire brigade had already been called; finally, as he returned to his lodge, he could hear the jangle of the approaching fire brigade. Wendt could not have known that there was a difference between calling the brigade from inside and outside the House.

The time-table shows that the fire officers themselves gave the tenth-stage alarm thirty minutes after the arrival of the first section. During that interval, the fire in the Session Chamber had grown to unmanageable proportions. The alleged 'omission' of the fire officers to give the tenth-stage alarm sooner was due to the following reasons:

At 9.22 or 9.23 p.m., Section 6 under Chief Fire Officer Puhle, used ladders to enter the restaurant. There they found a burning window curtain draped over a table, a burning door, and another burning curtain.

All these fires were immediately put out. Then Puhle walked through the scorched door into the lobby where he met men from Section 7. The restaurant and the lobby were filled with smoke which he thought came from the restaurant. He therefore concluded that two sections were more than enough. When the remains of van der Lubbe's firelighters were discovered in the restaurant, Puhle ordered a search of all the neighbouring rooms. During the search Puhle himself entered the Session Chamber. Recently, he described his impression as follows:

> When I entered the Chamber, I saw much the same picture as on the other floors and rooms: a thin veil of smoke, but no sign of fire. . . . When I returned to the Chamber after a further inspection, I was suddenly faced with a large fire, and I immediately ordered Trappe to give the fifth-stage alarm.[25]

Meanwhile, many smaller fires – for instance bits of carpet that had caught fire when van der Lubbe's burning firelighters or burning rags had dropped on them – were quickly stamped out or extinguished. As a result, many of these minor fires were surrounded with moist spots, which gave many journalists and particularly Pablo Hesslein the wrong impression that they were so many 'pools of petrol'.

Douglas Reed, who followed all the evidence most carefully, came to the following conclusion:

> The firemen, ignorant of what was happening in the Session Chamber, devoted their attention to the small fire in the restaurant which they quickly extinguished, so that Thaler, looking back from the Victory Column, thought they were already packing up to go home. Firemen, then, were already in the Reichstag when the fire in the Session Chamber was in its first beginnings, but were busying themselves with the insignificant outbreak in the restaurant. By the time they reached the Session Chamber, it was too late.[26]

Reed's reference to Thaler is explained by the latter's testimony to the Supreme Court on 10 October 1933:

> I remained on the spot for a brief time, after which I and the other passers-by who had meanwhile gathered there were pushed back by officers of the flying squad. All the passers-by dispersed, and I crossed towards the Lehrter Bahnhof. . . . When I reached the end of the Victory Column, I turned round once again. Quite suddenly I noticed

a deep red glow in the dome of the Reichstag. I assumed that the fire had grown to large proportions, ran back to the Reichstag building, and reported my observation to the fire brigade.[27]

In a 'radio report from the desolate chamber', Fire Director Gempp also explained that the fire brigade had at first thought the fire was restricted to the restaurant alone: 'The first section from the Linienstrasse found nothing except the two fires in the restaurant. Only when they were ready to leave again, did they hear of a third fire.'

Not only the fire officers, however, had the impression that the fire was relatively harmless, for Police Officers Lateit and Losigkeit were of precisely the same opinion. Lateit later told the Court that, in his view, the Chamber could easily have been saved, had the fire in it been discovered in time.

None of these factors – except the last one, of course – might have been crucial by itself, but coming as they did on top of one another, they led to the complete destruction of the Chamber.

Oddly enough, Douglas Reed was the only observer to have considered the actual evidence – most other observers were completely taken in by the *Brown Book* allegations which, for their part, rested on the flimsiest of speculations.

In short, the firemen did their best in difficult circumstances, and there is not the slightest shred of evidence that anyone tried to obstruct them in their work.

THE GEMPP AFFAIR

At about the same time that Dr Oberfohren made his exit from the political stage, another prominent personality suddenly left his job: the Chief of the Berlin Fire Brigade, Herr Walter Gempp. He, too, was seized upon by the *Brown Book*, which turned him into yet another poor victim of the Reichstag fire 'conspiracy'. However, the real facts of the Gempp case were far less flattering to the Herr Direktor.

After the Reichstag fire, Chief Fire Director Gempp, an extremely popular man, was hailed by the Berlin press for the speed with which he had acted. No one blamed him for the loss of the Chamber, for it was generally appreciated that, once the glass dome had cracked, it acted as a giant chimney, spitting fire and heat into the dark night. That was also the reason why the fire was controlled so quickly once the flames had consumed everything combustible in the Chamber.

Hence the *Völkischer Beobachter* could speak of the 'quick and decisive intervention of the fire brigade' and add that its handling of this fire had been exemplary. On 1 March, the *Völkischer Beobachter* further published Hitler's motion in the Cabinet (28 February 1933), 'that this Cabinet expresses its gratitude to all Reichstag officials, the police and the fire brigade, for their unstinting efforts in subduing the flames.'

Next day, Hitler sent a special letter to Hermann Göring, the Minister responsible for the German fire-fighting services. That letter, which was published in all German papers, read as follows:

> The foul attack launched yesterday by Communist criminals against the Reichstag was thwarted within a few hours, thanks only to the swift action of the Berlin fire brigade, and the resolute leadership and personal courage of individual firemen.[28]

Though Gempp had received similar praises (and the Kronenorden) from Kaiser Wilhelm II, and from President Hindenburg, he was not allowed to bask in the favour of the new rulers for long – zealous brown rats began quickly to gnaw at his reputation. Göring's noisily promulgated 'Anti-Corruption Law' was encouraging a growing army of Nazi job-hunters to denounce their superiors. Every day the newspapers were full of sensational 'revelations' about the alleged misdeeds of the great – including such respectable and honourable men as, for instance, Dr Adenauer, and the former Prussian Ministers Braun and Severing, who were said to have embezzled millions of marks.

On 25 March 1933, the *Völkischer Beobachter* published the following laconic note:

> At the request of State Commissioner Dr Lippert, Chief Fire Director Gempp and Chief Clerk Drescher were given indefinite leave of absence. Gempp is succeeded by Fire Director Wagner, and Drescher by Inspector Feind. Other staff changes are expected.

Though sudden dismissals had become the order of the day, Gempp's case was bound to attract very special attention: unlike most of the other victims, he had never played the slightest part in politics so that there was no possible reason why he should have focused National Socialist resentment on himself. The *Vossische*

Zeitung expressed its dismay on 25 March 1933 in a brief report entitled 'Chief Fire Director Gempp Dismissed':

> It is still not known what motives swayed the State Commission to dismiss the tested leader of the Berlin Fire Brigade, a man who has devoted twenty-seven years to the service of the City of Berlin. This much alone we know: Gempp, who is fifty-five years old, helped to make the Berlin Fire Brigade the pride of all Berliners. The thousands of foreigners who come to us in order to study fire-fighting are full of admiration for Gempp's work.

Once this article was published, the authorities could no longer keep quiet, and published the following communiqué:

> Director Gempp, Chief of the Berlin Fire Brigade, who was provisionally granted leave of absence by State Commissioner Dr Lippert, was accused of having tolerated Communist intrigues in the service under his control. Gempp then requested that disciplinary proceedings should be started against him. This request was not granted at the time, in view of the fact that Gempp was suspected of other offences. Disciplinary proceedings have now been opened against him; he is charged with dereliction of duty under Section 266 of the Criminal Code in connection with the purchase of a motor car by an ex-official, the Social Democratic councillor Ahrens.

Needless to say, most people preferred to believe a different story. Thus ex-Reichspräsident Löbe explained that Gempp was hounded to death 'because he was the only one to look into the real causes of the Reichstag fire',[29] and according to Pablo Hesslein,[30] Gempp was punished for what he said at a press conference shortly after Hitler left the burning Reichstag:

> Chief Fire Director Gempp, who spoke first, was visibly excited. He stated quite openly that the fire was a well-planned affair involving a number of people, and that he had counted some 25–30 specially prepared areas which were meant to catch fire but did not. A Dutchman had been caught in the act, and had been described as the sole incendiary, but it was quite impossible for a single man to have started so many fires within so short a space of time. The last Reichstag officials had left the building some time after 8 p.m. and the first alarm was received at 8.45 p.m.; consequently van der Lubbe, who entered the building in a most mysterious way, would have had, at most, 20–35 minutes in which to do his work.

Now, even this brief report contains a series of errors which

Gempp was unlikely to have committed. Firstly, there were no specially 'prepared areas' that failed to catch fire, nor was the first alarm received at 8.45. Marinus van der Lubbe entered the Reichstag through a window in a most unmysterious manner, and the last Reichstag officials left the building well before and not 'some time after' 8 p.m.

Hesslein continues: 'Gempp was immediately suspended and placed under house arrest. A few months later, after he had sworn an oath of silence, he was finally dismissed.'

This allegation, too, is false, just as false as the many lies about Gempp which the *Brown Book* published at the time. Because of his alleged refusal to let the Nazis get away with it, Gempp was even elevated to the role of Resistance fighter by many misinformed observers:

> The Reichstag fire faced this man, who was respected at home and abroad as an outstanding engineer and a conscientious official, with a decision that was to cost him not only his job but also his life. Because his conscience was not for sale, Gempp felt impelled, during a conference with his inspectors and officers, to correct the official story.[31]

At this conference Gempp is alleged to have told his officers:

1. that the fire brigade had been summoned too late;

2. that he – Gempp – had met an S.A. detachment when he arrived at the scene of the fire;

3. that Göring had expressly forbidden him to circulate a general call and to summon stronger forces to fight the fire;

4. that undamaged parts of the building contained enough incendiary material to fill a lorry.

And, having made these 'corrections' which clearly refuted the Nazis' claim that the Reichstag had been burned by Communists, Gempp simply had to disappear.

As one historian, who believed the *Brown Book* story that Gempp was one of those people who knew too much and whom the Nazis had to get rid of, put it:

> Not even his dismissal was enough to satisfy the new rulers. They uttered the vilest slanders, persecuted him, and finally arrested him in September, 1937. At a put-up trial he was charged with misdemeanour, and duly convicted. Gempp appealed, but shortly before the appeal was heard, on May 2nd, 1939, he was found dead in his cell.

The *Brown Book* added that Councillor Ahrens was dismissed and arrested for exactly the same reasons. Now, had Gempp and Ahrens really been such dangerous witnesses, one wonders why the Nazis did not use their tested method of shooting them 'while trying to escape', why Ahrens was set free soon after his arrest so that he could survive Hitler's glorious Third Reich (he died in West Berlin in 1957), and why Gempp was given the chance of refuting the 'trumped-up' charges against him, and hence of exposing his detractors in open Court.

Gempp's alleged 'corrections' were first published on 21 April 1933 in *La République* and four days later in the *Saarbrückener Volksstimme*.

At the time, it was extremely risky to publish such dangerous stories abroad, for they were likely to jeopardize the lives of men who were completely at the mercy of a ruthless dictator. Luckily for Gempp and for Ahrens, they could easily prove that the whole article was a fabrication.

As a result, the *Brown Book* was forced to 'explain':

> Göring, who had not the courage himself to deny what the *Saarbrückener Volksstimme* reported, compelled Gempp to issue a *démenti*. Gempp seems to have refused to do so for a long time. It was only on June 18th, 1933, that a statement by him appeared in the German press, in which he declared that the report published in the *Volksstimme* was false. . . . Under the pressure of the charges made against him, and from fear of imprisonment with which he was threatened, Gempp gave way to Göring's threats.[32]

On the very day when Gempp was alleged to have held his staff conference and to have criticized the official story of the fire, he gave an interview to the *Berliner Lokalanzeiger*:

> The fire brigade came across two main fires and countless little fires. The fires had all been started with firelighters, paraffin and petrol. One fire was discovered in the immediate vicinity of the Chancellor's office. The carpet was charred. A large fire was also blazing in the restaurant. In the Session Chamber, the Speaker's Chair, the deputies' benches and the tribunes were almost completely destroyed. Fragments of the cracked wall had fallen down. The dome itself did not collapse, only the glass ceiling. Individual girders were melted by the heat.[33]

Moreover, a Swiss journalist, Ferdinand Kugler, wrote on the subject of the 'Gempp affair' during the Leipzig trial:

Of special interest is the evidence of Berlin's ex-Fire Chief Gempp, who was dismissed shortly after the Reichstag fire, and who was supposed to have been murdered.

First he declared with a broad smile that he was, of course, the same Herr Gempp who had directed the fire brigade on February 27th. . . . He was then questioned by the President of the Court:

Dr Bünger: 'You have been asked to appear before this Court because of certain newspaper articles and remarks in the *Brown Book*. The *Brown Book* alleges that, after the fire, you held a conference with inspectors and officers of the fire brigade during which you said that the fire brigade had been summoned too late, that 20 Storm Troopers were at the scene of the fire by the time the fire brigade finally appeared, that the Prussian Minister of the Interior, Göring, had expressly forbidden you to circulate a general call, and that those parts of the Reichstag building which were not destroyed were found to contain large quantities of unused incendiary material which would have completely filled a lorry. I request your comments on these points.'

Gempp: 'I have been heard on these points more than once, first by a representative from State Commissioner Dr Lippert's office, and again by the Secret State Police. In both cases I have declared that all these allegations are pure nonsense. I found no Storm Troopers on my arrival – at least not in large numbers, for one or two might have been there whom I cannot remember – neither did I find large quantities of incendiary material. As for my discussion, or rather meeting, with Minister Göring, this is what happened: roughly fifteen minutes after I arrived at the Reichstag, I spotted the Minister and some gentlemen in the southern wing. I immediately approached him in order to give him a full report, for he was my highest superior. The Minister walked with me towards Portal Two. I described the damage, the fire-fighting forces we had deployed, and soon. The Minister then asked me if I had seen the Director of the Reichstag, Herr Galle. That was the only question he put to me. When I asked if he had any instructions for me, the Minister replied: "Please don't let me detain you. You are in charge here." '

Gempp went on to say that the conference he held with his inspectors had been pure routine. Such conferences were convened after every large fire.

Gempp further declared that no pressure had been brought to bear on him to deny the *Brown Book* allegations, and that the *démenti* he had issued to the press on 18 June had been given quite freely. Neither had he ever been placed under arrest or in any way attacked in connection with the Reichstag fire.

In this connection we must now refer to the subsequent statement of Councillor Ahrens whom the *Brown Book* was forced to turn into the 'real' source of the corrections once Gempp had let the Communists down so badly. Ahrens not only repeated Gempp's explanation of what had really happened at the official conference on the morning after the fire, but added that he thought Gempp far too intelligent to call Göring a liar before so large a crowd, even had he believed that a correction was called for.

After the war, ex-Chief Fire Officer Emil Puhle, who had also attended Gempp's conference, confirmed that only ordinary routine questions were discussed. He added: 'It is nonsense to suggest that Göring prohibited the circulation of a general call, when, in fact, the tenth-stage alarm was given fairly early on.'[34]

In fact, though Gempp smiled when he told the Supreme Court that he was the man who had extinguished the Reichstag fire, he could not have been very happy. His vaunted conscience was anything but clear, and he would very much have liked not to be in the limelight of public attention right then.

It is quite true that Gempp was originally charged with tolerating Communist intrigues in the Berlin Fire Brigade, and later with a dereliction of duty in connection with the purchase of a motor car. However, the real charges against him were being kept secret at the time, because they might have shaken public confidence in Göring's great pet: the Prussian Civil Service.

In the summer of 1932, Dr Pitzschke, a former chief adviser to Minimax, the internationally renowned makers of fire-extinguishers, started a legal action against his erstwhile employers. *Inter alia* he alleged that Minimax were on the verge of bankruptcy because they had spent 'vast sums of money on bribing public servants'. Though the Court ruled that Dr Pitzschke had no case, the Presiding Judge nevertheless informed the Public Prosecutor of Dr Pitzschke's allegations. This happened on 24 January 1933, i.e. before Hitler came to power.

The whole affair culminated four years later in a monster trial which had far-reaching repercussions but not the slightest political background. Gradually more and more leading fire officers were inculpated, some of whom later took their lives. The trial, which started on 29 September, was concluded on 1 July 1938, when Judge Böhmer read the verdict: Friedrich Gunsenheimer, a director of Minimax, was found guilty on sixteen charges of bribery and sentenced to two-and-a-half years' imprisonment. Chief Fire Director Walter Gempp was sentenced to two years' hard labour, loss of civic rights for three years and confiscation of 15,600 marks. Because of repeated acceptance of bribes, seventeen of the eighteen accused fire directors, engineers, fire officers, etc., from Berlin, Cologne and Munich, were sentenced to hard labour or imprisonment.

Gempp himself cut rather a poor figure during his trial. It appeared that although he lived rent-free, and earned a monthly net salary of 1,000 marks, an annual bonus of 2,000 marks from the City of Berlin and of 1,200 marks from the Prussian Fire Department – not to mention his consultant's fees and royalties – he nevertheless allowed Gunsenheimer to press quite a number of envelopes containing from 1,500 to 1,800 marks into his greedy hands. Gunsenheimer had carefully and discreetly kept a record of all these sums, using the secret code:

1 2 3 4 5 6 7 8 9 0
u n i v e r s a l o

Though Gempp had learned of the charges against him well before the trial, he steadfastly refused to admit to his shady dealings with Minimax. Even after the police raided Gunsenheimer and discovered his meticulously kept records, Gempp merely admitted to having been Minimax's official adviser – for a fee of 300 marks a month.

However, all these evasions proved of no avail. The Court not only found against him but even refused to take his excellent record into consideration:

> The accused Gempp was Head of the Berlin fire service which – thanks largely to him – was famed far beyond the boundaries of Berlin and the borders of the Reich. As Chief Fire Director, he held a respected and highly-paid position which together with his considerable other earnings – quite apart from his own and his wife's private incomes – guaranteed him so high a standard of living that he and his family went short of absolutely nothing. And yet Gempp saw fit to accept bribes from Minimax over the years, and to render to Minimax services incompatible with his office. By accepting sums amounting to 15,600 marks, Gempp received the third highest sum of money Minimax spent on bribery. The Court has not taken into account the many lavish presents he was given in addition to this. A

chief of the Fire Brigade who, despite his excellent income, sees fit to lend himself to such corrupt practices, to set his subordinates so bad an example, and to sully the reputation of the Berlin Bire Frigade in the way he has done, must be punished with the full severity of the law.

The Court also takes a most serious view of the fact that the accused showed no signs of remorse, but tried to cover up his actions with all manner of stupid and mendacious excuses, as for example the fable that he was a bona fide consultant to W. G. [Managing Director of Minimax].

Others to be pilloried by the Court included such well-known 'patriots' as Fire Director P., who was sentenced to only one-and-a-half years' imprisonment because 'the Court took into account the part he played in Germany's rebirth', and Chief Engineer R., 'who had shown so much devotion to the national cause'.

All this explains why the Nazi press was so anxious to play this gigantic scandal down. None of the accused was a Jew, a Marxist, a Freemason – all were tested Prussian officials whose blood was as unobjectionable as their politics.

No more need be said about the 'mysterious' circumstances surrounding Gempp's death – like so many of his co-accused he committed suicide before the sentence became legally binding. The allegation that he was killed because he might have betrayed the Nazi Reichstag incendiaries is absurd: the Minimax trial lasted for a total of 123 days, during which time Gempp had ample opportunity to say what he liked. In fact, Gempp was turned into a martyr for purely political reasons, and it is sad – but unavoidable – that we have had to strip him of his halo. Gempp's suicide – and there is no doubt whatever that it was suicide – was the last act of a man who, though brilliant at his job, would not resist the temptation to which all successful public servants are continuously exposed.

THREE FURTHER *BROWN BOOK* SUSPECTS

In 1957, when the journalist Curt Riess tried to repeat one of the many *Brown Book* slanders, he was threatened with a libel action and withdrew the charge, viz. that:

Amongst Göring's confidential men was a certain Dr Lepsius, who later gave evidence at the trial. Although he occupied a high position in the Air Ministry, Dr Lepsius certainly had no official authority or

> competence, and it may be doubted whether he possessed the qualifications requisite to conduct the interrogation of a political incendiary [van der Lubbe]. . . . On the fourteenth day of the trial he told the Court how, afterwards, he had retraced with van der Lubbe the route which the latter had taken in firing the Reichstag. . . . What precise interest Dr Lepsius – not a police or judicial official – had in interrogating van der Lubbe, much more in retracing his path in the Reichstag, remained unexplained. Perhaps it was that Dr Lepsius was better acquainted with the geography of the Reichstag than van der Lubbe and so was able to assist him in the choice of route.[35]

Dr Lepsius, an internationally renowned chemist and one of a long line of scholars, could not possibly allow this libel to go unanswered. He had never even met Göring, and he held no position at all in the Air Ministry, let alone a high one. His only connection with flying – and this shows what mental acrobatics the *Brown Book* authors were capable of – was that, as a chemist, he had been co-opted to the Air Defence League. On behalf of that body, he had requested Under-Secretary Schmid to admit him to the Reichstag on the day after the fire, so that he could pursue his studies of the effects of incendiary bombs on massive buildings.

The detectives – including Heisig and Dr Zirpins – who had just been going over van der Lubbe's route – were so impressed with Dr Lepsius's letter of introduction that they immediately acceded to his request and asked van der Lubbe to retrace his steps once again. Dr Lepsius then asked van der Lubbe a number of questions about each individual fire, and came away with the firm conviction that the fires had been started precisely in the way van der Lubbe had told him.

In particular,

> . . . the witness [Dr Lepsius] took the occasion to ask van der Lubbe whether he had specially set fire to the curtains over the door in order to burn the Session Chamber. Van der Lubbe said no, and explained that the Session Chamber had probably caught fire because the flames from the curtains had leapt across to the panelling.[36]

Dr Lepsius thereupon examined the Reichstag curtains more closely and learned from the Director of the Reichstag, Geheimrat Galle, that they had been put up dozens of years earlier. He concluded correctly that they were extremely inflammable. We shall have to return to this point again.

. . . . .

It was Dimitrov's persistent questions which threw suspicion on Dr Herbert Albrecht, Nazi deputy and 'standard-bearer of Troop 33', as he proudly described himself in the Reichstag handbook.

On the night of the fire, Dr Albrecht, who was staying in a boarding-house some fifty yards from the Reichstag, had retired to bed with influenza. He was suddenly alerted when a maid shouted through the open door: 'The Reichstag is on fire.' Despite his illness, he immediately got up, for he remembered to his horror that important family papers including, of all things, the proof of his 'Aryan' descent were kept in the Reichstag offices of the National Socialist Party. He dressed quickly and, not bothering to put on a collar, a tie, or a hat, rushed across to the burning House. At Portal Five he was challenged by a police official, and allowed to pass when he showed his deputy's card. Dr Albrecht raced up the stairs, collected his papers and stormed out of the building 'as if in flight'. When he had just passed Portal Five, he was challenged and – because he did not obey at once – fetched back by a policeman. A Reichstag official then told the officer:

'He's all right. I know him.'

When Dr Albrecht tried to return to the Reichstag a little later, perhaps to salvage other valuables, he was turned back, for Göring had meanwhile given orders not to admit anyone.

This incident had already been discussed in the Police Court, when Albert Wendt, the porter who had been on duty at Portal Five on the night of the fire, told an attentive audience – including Douglas Reed – that a collarless and hatless deputy had rushed out of the Reichstag at 10 p.m., and that he, Wendt, could swear that he had not let him in through the only open Portal.

However, even while the fire had still been raging, detectives had checked Albrecht's alibi, and found that it was unshakeable. As a result, Judge Vogt decided quite rightly that there was no need to subpoena Dr Albrecht to the main trial.

. . . . .

Alexander Scranowitz, Reichstag House-Inspector from 1930 to 1945, was another favourite *Brown Book* suspect.

In 1904, Scranowitz, who held an honourable discharge from the German Navy, was given a job in the Reichstag. He slowly worked his way up the ladder: in 1927 he became Assistant House-Inspector, and in 1930 – on the death of his predecessor – he was promoted to the position he held at the time of the fire.

Scranowitz was a tall and powerfully-built man, who chose to wear his Kaiser moustache even under the Republic. Though he had served the Reichstag most faithfully for thirty years, the *Brown Book* saw fit to accuse him of dereliction of duty, and to stamp him a Nazi for good measure.

> On February 27th, the National Socialist inspector of the building released the officials on duty at one o'clock in the afternoon. The staff told him that it was contrary to the terms of their employment to leave before the end of their spell of duty.

Crude though this slander was, it must nevertheless have caused Scranowitz a great deal of anguish. Thus the Presiding Judge asked Scranowitz on 14 October 1933:

> I have seen a press report to the effect that you took the unusual step of dismissing all the officials before they had completed their duty, to be precise at 1 p.m., and that the staff lodged a protest with you. Is that really so?

Scranowitz replied that he had neither dismissed the staff nor had he had the power to do so. He added that, even if he had, it seemed most unlikely that the staff would have objected. In any case, it had by then been fully established that not a single one of Scranowitz's many subordinates had been sent home.

In answer to a question by Dr Sack, Scranowitz replied that most of the officials on duty at the time of the fire were old-timers, and that the Nazis had not sacked a single one of them.

Because Scranowitz had been called a National Socialist in the *Brown Book*, the Assistant Public Prosecutor, Dr Parrisius, asked him whether he would care to tell the Court what his political opinions were. Scranowitz replied:

> When I came to the Reichstag in 1904, I met an old Reichstag official, Maas by name. He told me: 'Scranowitz, as Reichstag employees, we have to serve every party alike. Take my advice and don't join any of them.' And that is precisely what I have done. To this day I have not belonged to a party. Still, you may say I hold Rightist views.

Accordingly, the *Brown Book* changed its original account into:

> The suspicions against this official, of decided National Socialist leanings (*sic!*) were shortly indicated in the *Brown Book*. Scranowitz's denial in Court cannot be regarded too seriously inasmuch as he stated

that he himself had gone home at 3 p.m., which was not his usual hour.[37]

In fact, Scranowitz left the Reichstag at 2.45 p.m., for the simple reason that he had a doctor's appointment. Later, while he was sitting at dinner, he was alarmed by the noise of fire engines. He sprang to the window, and seeing that the fire brigade had stopped across the road, he immediately rang the porter's lodge to find out what was happening. The telephone was answered by Albert Wendt, who told Scranowitz that the restaurant was on fire. Whereupon Scranowitz roared at him:

> 'And why the dickens didn't you report it to me?', slammed down the receiver . . . dashed into the bathroom, grabbed my shoes and shouted to my wife and my son: 'Notify the Speaker and the Director,' slipped on my jacket and coat and rushed out of the house. I finished dressing as I ran.

Dr Wolff has attacked Scranowitz because

> . . . shortly before his death [1955] he published two newspaper articles in which he still asserted that van der Lubbe had no accomplices and burned the Reichstag alone. This self-confessed Rightist played a very strange role in the whole affair.

And Dr Wolff went on to mention the observations of firemen, according to whom Scranowitz's

> . . . only concern was to get the brigade to save a precious Gobelin tapestry. When a number of people asked the House-Inspector why he was less worried about the House than about the tapestry, he explained that this valuable piece was one of the articles that France had claimed as part of the German reparation payments after World War I.

What the firemen could not have known, but what Dr Wolff himself could have read in Dr Sack's book (op. cit., p. 20) would have made Scranowitz's 'only concern' far less suspicious than it looked:

> Göring knows that the House contains two irreplaceable treasures: the library and the Gobelin tapestries which were kept in a room behind the diplomats' box. 'The Gobelins must be saved,' the Minister cried. His first care was for these irreplaceable works of art.

Dr Wolff went on to quote from a truly astonishing article by his friend, the late Pablo Hesslein.[38] Apparently Hesslein heard of the fire as early as 8.30 p.m., and saw the fire from the Victory Column at 9 p.m. – before van der Lubbe had even entered the building! He then witnessed the arrival of the Cabinet, and heard Papen's indignant denunciation of the Communists. Hitler and the rest apparently left the building in complete silence.

Then Hesslein and other journalists were invited by a Reichstag official – obviously Scranowitz – to join a conducted tour of the building: 'In the lobby leading to the Reichstag restaurant, we noticed that the thick carpets had been soaked in petrol. In the restaurant, too, we found similar pools ...'

In fact, the 'petrol pools' were pools of water, squirted on the carpets by the fire brigade. While this was a forgivable error, the rest of Hesslein's story is not. Thus, no one will believe his claim that he heard the Director of the Reichstag, Geheimrat Galle, assert that:

> Göring had ordered all Reichstag officials without exception to leave the House punctually at 8 p.m. This order applied to him, Galle, as well, so that ... the Reichstag was completely deserted from 8 p.m. onwards.

Once again we have the assumption that the Speaker of the Reichstag – even had he wanted to set fire to the House – would have been stupid enough to give away his intentions by such blatant orders. Then we are asked to swallow the claim that Geheimrat Galle, the very prototype of a conservative official' (*Neue Zürcher Zeitung*, 21 October 1933), would have obeyed an order of that kind.

This sensational article by Hesslein caused Dr Wolff to write to Galle's widow, who quite naturally replied that she thought the whole story unlikely, and that '... although her husband had never discussed official business with her, he would certainly have dropped a hint about this particular matter during the long years of his retirement'.

In footnote 36 of his Reichstag fire report, Dr Wolff further mentions a letter by the former Director of the Reichstag library, Professor Fischer Baling, which included the following sentence: 'I was present at his [Scranowitz's] interrogation and did not gain the impression that he was telling everything he knew.'

Now that impression was absolutely correct, for at the time it would have been extremely dangerous for Alexander Scranowitz to tell what he knew or – rather – what he thought he knew. He came out with it long after the war, when he admitted 'quite openly' that he had said nothing about the ridiculous official theories to anyone except a small circle of close friends 'because he had believed that the truth would come out anyway, once all the stored-up bitterness gave way to quiet objectivity. Now, however, he felt he could keep quiet no longer'.[39]

And the old gentleman – he had recently turned seventy-two – added in broad Berlin dialect:

> It's not that I don't think Adolf and his gang couldn't have done it, it's just that they didn't happen to have anything to do with the Reichstag fire. And when your paper published all that stuff about a secret passage and about Storm Troopers blundering about in the burning building, I really did feel my gorge rise.

Scranowitz went on to call himself the 'chief witness' in the Fire Trial, and, in fact, that is precisely what he was, though only in a certain sense: he was responsible for the commonly held idea that the fire had spread with 'supernatural' speed, or as he himself put it at the trial:

> I looked into the Session Chamber for a mere fraction of a second. The whole top of the Speaker's Chair was blazing away. Behind the Speaker's Chair, three curtains were burning quite steadily. The individual flames were quite distinct. In addition, I saw flames on both the Government and the Federal Council benches, though I cannot state with certainty whether in the first or second row. These flames represented individual, completely independent, fires, bunched together into pyramids, each twelve to twenty inches at the base, and some twenty to twenty-five inches in height.
>
> I made out similar bundles of flames on the first rows of deputies' seats – fifteen of them in all. I also spotted a fire on the Orator's Table, flanked by the burning curtains of the stenographers' well below. I quickly slammed the door shut.

As a result of this evidence, based on observations during 'a fraction of a second', the judges and experts alike underplayed the testimony of the police officers who saw something far less dramatic:

> When Lateit pushed the door open, and looked across the downward sloping rows of benches, he saw a fire which he estimated at some ten feet wide by twelve feet high. The fire was topped by tongues of

> flame so that it looked like a 'flaming church organ'. The flames themselves were extremely steady. Lateit saw no flames to the right or left of this 'organ', i.e. on the Government or Federal Council benches, nor could he detect any smoke. Poeschel and Losigkeit, who were looking over Lateit's shoulder, observed the same picture.[40]

Hence Lateit had every reason to think that the fire could be put out very quickly. Moreover, his testimony tallied with van der Lubbe's.

One Swiss correspondent had this to say on the difference between Scranowitz's and Lateit's evidence:

> Not even the late Edgar Wallace could have hit upon a more intricate plot than the one that came out at this trial. Who is the magician? In this trial the great dénouement does not coincide with the dramatic climax. On the contrary, at 9.22 p.m., one minute after Police Lieutenant Lateit saw the lonely 'fire organ' on the Speaker's Chair [actually: behind the Speaker's Chair] a second witness looked into the Chamber, and saw a completely different picture: the first three rows of the semicircular deputies' seats were aglow with twenty to twenty-five small pyramid-shaped fires, each about twenty inches wide, all of equal height, and neatly placed at regular intervals of five feet from one another, just as if an assembly of fiery spirits were holding a meeting. Other flames of equal height and of the same bright-red colour were neatly distributed over the government benches to the right and the left of the Speaker's Chair. A similar fire was blazing on the Orator's Table. At its feet another flame had leapt across the solid oak 'Table of the House'. But the palm of this parliamentary Walpurgis Night went to a larger fire, some thirty inches high, above the Speaker's Chair; behind it three curtains were ablaze but the fire had not yet reached the panelling. In addition, the curtains on either side of the stenographers' places had caught light. And all this was stated on oath, not by a crystal-gazer, but by Herr Scranowitz, the tried, tested, and pensionable inspector of the Reichstag, a man who had gone on his nightly key-rattling rounds of the House, under the Kaiser, the Republic, and the Third Reich. This good man, who must consider appearing in court a welcome break in his otherwise unusually monotonous life, likes to hear the sound of his own voice.[41]

Unfortunately, nobody – not even the fire experts – suspected that Scranowitz, who, after all, knew the Reichstag better than anyone else, might have been wrong. Now if the fire had in fact changed from a minor into a major conflagration within the one minute that separated Scranowitz's and the police officers' inspection of the Chamber, then the flames could not possibly have spread spontaneously; then accomplices and plotters must indeed have been at work.

And yet there is no need to dismiss Scranowitz as a deceitful or extravagant witness, for there is a completely natural explanation for his mistake: in that 'fraction of a second' during which Scranowitz peered into the Chamber, all he did, in fact, see was the burning curtains – all the other 'flames' were reflections from the highly polished desks.

The police officers, on the other hand, who watched the fire for a much longer time, were able to distinguish clearly between the burning curtains and their flickering reflections.

In short, Scranowitz was sincere but – utterly confused.

Unfortunately the President of the Court chose to ignore this obvious fact, and adopted Scranowitz's erroneous story, simply because it fitted in much better with the accomplice theory. Scranowitz himself told the Public Prosecutor:

> I said one man couldn't possibly have started all the fires by himself; no less than six to eight people must have done it. That was my guess at the time, though I didn't actually see anybody. All I knew was that one person couldn't possibly have done it all in so short a time.

Luckily for Scranowitz, no one asked him to give any reasons for these guesses and assumptions. Later, when he realized the truth, he admitted publicly that van der Lubbe must have been the sole culprit. Since he is dead, he can no longer speak for himself.

III

THE TRIAL

10. The Preliminary Examination

THE EXAMINING MAGISTRATE

ONCE the police endorsed Hitler's 'inspiration' that the Reichstag fire was a call to Communist rebellion and hence to high treason, the case against van der Lubbe and 'accomplices' had to be referred to the Supreme Court.

One man who did not like these developments was Hermann Göring. On 2 March 1933, he told the Cabinet:

> The police will soon have to hand the case over to the Supreme Court. The examining magistrate is Dr Braune, who used to investigate charges against members of the National Socialist Party, and who has always been most ruthless with us. Even if he did his work objectively, he would hardly be the right man to handle so important a case. Thus he might restrict his investigations to the criminal alone, when all the experts agree that six to seven persons, *at the very least*, must have been involved. He might even give orders to set Deputy Torgler free. Any slips now would have extremely grave consequences later. Hence it is advisable to see if another, more suitable, magistrate could not be put in charge of the investigation of the Reichstag fire, considered not as an act of common arson but as one of high treason.

Hitler, too, objected to Dr Braune, so that Under-Secretary Schlegelberger had to hunt up an examining magistrate more to his liking. He found him in the person of Judge Paul Vogt, a man who responded with such alacrity and who set to work with such zeal that Torgler, for one, became convinced the Government had offered him a chance of 'rehabilitating' himself.

Vogt, who had investigated many other political cases, had joined the Supreme Court in 1931. By all accounts, he was the very model of a Prussian judge: conservative, correct, unrelenting once he had arrived at a decision, unwilling to temper justice with mercy, and self-assured to the point of arrogance. A Swiss correspondent described him as follows: 'His bearing is that of a typical Prussian reserve officer. His legal knowledge and loyalty are beyond question.'[1]

For simplicity's sake, Vogt ran the examination from the Reichstag itself. At his own request, Detective-Inspectors Heisig and Dr Braschwitz, and Detective-Sergeant Raben were allocated to him. His legal assistant – also appointed at his own request – was Dr Wernecke.

When most of the information supplied by willing members of the public proved completely useless, Vogt asked the entire German press to publish photographs of Marinus van der Lubbe together with a reward of 20,000 marks – a tremendous sum at that time – to anyone offering useful information. Similar photographs were pasted up on countless hoardings and walls.

The high reward helped to lend wings to the public's sporting instincts and fantasy. Of the many who came forward, a large number were eventually unmasked for what they were: petty crooks and informers out to feather their own nests or to blow their own trumpets.

But far-fetched though all their stories were, none of them produced any further accomplices, so that Judge Vogt felt he must hang on at any cost to the five suspects he already had.

Because of the official thesis that a Communist rebellion had been quashed at the last moment, Vogt asked police chiefs throughout Germany to supply him with information about Communist activities. The results were condensed and included in the Indictment, from which every unbiased person would have been forced to conclude that the Communists had been lying low. Yet Judge Vogt held fast to his Communist putsch theory, though – according to Diels – he did realize that, were he to arraign the leaders of the Communist Party on the basis of the 'documentary evidence' he had gathered, his whole case might collapse. Hence he decided to argue that, though there was insufficient direct evidence to show that there had been a central plan to fire the Reichstag as a signal for rebellion, the existence of such a plan could nevertheless be inferred from Communist acts of terror and arson in the past. When Göring heard of this development, he exploded. The Führer himself had blamed the Communist leaders directly – hence there just had to be an organized plot.

And indeed, at first the whole case had seemed quite cut and dried. Had a Communist not been caught red-handed? Was it likely that he had acted alone? Would not a thorough police investigation and the offer of a high reward bring the other culprits to book? And could van der Lubbe's accomplices be anything but Communists? Had not the Communist deputy, Ernst Torgler, been incriminated by a number of quite independent witnesses? And was there not weighty evidence against the three Bulgarian Communists?

Thus when Vogt set to work it was quite reasonable to assume that the Government thesis of a Communist putsch was the right one. But by the time he had heard more than five hundred witnesses, and had filled twenty-four volumes with depositions and documents, he ought to have realized that Göring's first press communiqué on the night of the fire had been quite wrong. Far from doing that, Vogt held fast to the spirit, if not to the letter, of the official thesis, and continues to do so to this day. Still, not even he could close his ears to the persistent rumours that the Nazis themselves had fired the Reichstag as an election stunt. Thus, on 3 March 1933, Walter Lassmann, a merchant from Apolda, petitioned the Court to investigate the rumour that the National Socialist Party had set the Reichstag on fire. He added:

> Those arrested so far are said to have been paid by the National Socialist Party, and to have been instructed to blame the crime on the Communist Party. . . . Only the National Socialist Party is in favour of governing without a Parliament and hence without a House.[2]

On 2 March 1933, one Baron von der Ropp humbly petitioned the President of the Supreme Court

> . . . to instruct the Public Prosecutor to put on record the names of the real incendiaries. At the moment, these men are still employed in Göring's Residence, whence they carried the incendiary material into the underground passage. It would be an irreparable loss if future German historians were kept in ignorance of the names of the real incendiaries.[3]

While Baron von der Ropp merely repeated a general rumour, the Communists themselves were careless enough to mention the actual names of the alleged Nazi accomplices. When all of these had supplied Vogt with perfectly good alibis, he quite understandably concluded that the Communists were merely trying to pass the buck. That, by the way, was also the view of the Public Prosecutor.

On the other hand, Vogt saw no reason to protest against the equally unsubstantiated Nazi claim that the Communist Party was implicated. He accordingly dismissed van der Lubbe's protestations that he had fired the Reichstag by himself as so many further Communist lies, all of which were meant to whitewash the real culprits. Hence the good magistrate was able to promise Dr Taubert, an emissary of the anxious Dr Goebbels, that he would somehow manage to get the Communists convicted.

Although Vogt was obliged to submit regular reports to the Minister of Justice, there is not the slightest evidence that he was under any direct political pressure. Vogt was allowed to fill his twenty-four volumes of records as he chose. Early in June 1933, he handed them over to the Public Prosecutor's office, whence they were returned to him briefly for a number of factual emendations. He completed the work at the end of June 1933.

THE NEUKÖLLN 'LINK'

As we saw, Vogt shared Dr Zirpins's view that van der Lubbe's real principals were the leaders of the Communist Party, and Torgler and Koenen in particular. However, when he tried to substantiate this thesis and the Government thesis that the Reichstag fire had been the signal for a Communist uprising, he came up against an insurmountable obstacle: how could van der Lubbe, the unknown Dutch tramp, have got hold of the leaders of the German Communist Party within so short a time of his arrival in Berlin? After all, these leaders were ostensibly planning a major civil war, and must have been terribly busy. All Vogt could say was that van der Lubbe must have managed it somehow.

Then, on 6 March 1933, he was apparently proved right when, duly encouraged by the reward of 20,000 marks, a worker by the name of Ernst Panknin reported from Neukölln. Panknin claimed that on the Wednesday before the fire he had seen van der Lubbe in 'conference' with the metalworker Paul Bienge, the labourer Paul Zachow, and the shoemaker Herbert Löwe – all three men with known Communist leanings – outside the Neukölln Welfare Office.

The Indictment devoted fifteen long pages to this 'conference', which was to have such tragic consequences: the three men were arrested, threatened, and subjected to torture when they refused to confess something of which they were completely innocent.

According to Panknin, this is what had happened:

Zachow began by complaining very bitterly that a horde of Storm Troopers had torn off 'Iron Front' badges from Socialist passers-by in the Sonnenallee. He, Zachow, had been forced to restrain his friend Bienge since otherwise there would have been a fight. Bienge then said:

'If all of us were like you, we shouldn't ever amount to anything.'

Marinus van der Lubbe, who was listening to all this, then asked the way to the Sonnenallee; he wanted to go there at once, and was very disappointed when he learned that the whole story had happened the day before. Van der Lubbe was very excited and said that the workers ought to be encouraged to hit back, and to start a revolution after the great Russian model; it was now or never. Zachow, for his part, suggested that the best way of shaking up the people and of inciting them to revolution was firing public buildings. To which Bienge had added: 'Well, let's start with the Reichstag and the Palace. For either we come to power and we shan't need the Reichstag, or else the others will come to power and won't let us in anyway.'[4]

Bienge went on to say that special groups would have to be formed, whose job it would be to catch single Storm Troopers, pour petrol over them, and then set fire to them.

Zachow argued in favour of burning 'the lot', and not just individual buildings. When Marinus van der Lubbe agreed with all their plans, Bienge gave Zachow a dig in the ribs and said:

'This lad is all right; we can use him.'

At that point, Marinus van der Lubbe confessed that he was an experienced and active Communist and pulled a red booklet out his pocket. This, according to Panknin, had to be a Communist Party membership card because it was red. Then van der Lubbe asked to be directed to Communist Party headquarters.

On 30 March 1933, when Panknin was confronted with van der Lubbe, he repeated the whole story, adding:

> When the conversation was over, I mean their discussion about setting public buildings on fire, van der Lubbe asked if he could join in, and all the others agreed readily.[5]

With that the fate of the three men from Neukölln was sealed, and it did not help van der Lubbe to protest:

> I can only repeat again and again that I heard no conversation whatsoever on the subject of burning public buildings. When I first decided to set public buildings on fire, I was thinking of the Neukölln Welfare

Office because it seemed the best place to me. If I am told it is unlikely that my actions should accidentally have agreed with what was allegedly discussed outside the Welfare Office, I can only reply that it was, in fact, a sheer coincidence. And if I am further alleged to have asked for the address of Communist Party headquarters, all I can say is that I did nothing of the kind. On the contrary, I insisted that the Communist Party was using the wrong kind of tactics. True, I asked whether the Communist Party was still active in Neukölln, and was told that it was very difficult to do anything at all these days.[6]

Of course, van der Lubbe's words went unheard. The Neukölln link, or rather the Neukölln fantasy, was something to which Juge Vogt had to cling like a leech, for that fantasy was the cornerstone of the Communist conspiracy theory, and hence of the whole trial. Thus when the President of the Court, Dr Bünger, asked Vogt later whether van der Lubbe had admitted inciting the others to arson, the following dialogue ensued:

Vogt: 'Yes, I believe he did at the beginning . . . no, to the best of my knowledge he denied it.'

President: 'He has kept repeating: "I did not say it; I merely heard it." '

Vogt: 'I believe the records will show the contrary. I think he merely denied that he himself was the one to say that public buildings must be burned. I seem to remember that it was Bienge who said that.'

President: 'Did you say that he admitted having asked the way to Communist Party headquarters?'

Vogt: 'Oddly enough, he denied everything that might constitute a link with Party headquarters. He was afraid of admitting that link.'[7]

The witness Ernst Panknin still dreams of the 20,000 marks which, despite his efforts, slipped through his fingers. The fate of his poor victims was less happy: Paul Zachow died soon afterwards from the treatment his captors meted out to him; Paul Bienge had all his teeth broken and was beaten mercilessly to confirm the fable of the Neukölln link – but in vain. The shoemaker Herbert Loewe, too, was 'imprisoned' for a whole year without obliging his tormentors with a confession. Bienge and Loewe are still alive.

Nor was Panknin the only pretender to the reward of 20,000 marks: a second claimant of the same sort appeared on the scene soon afterwards, and actually provided the grateful Judge Vogt 'direct evidence' against the Communist Party leaders. The name of that witness was Willi Hintze.

During those sad February days which Marinus van der Lubbe had spent in Neukölln, an unemployed man, Fikowsky by name, decided to put an end to the miserable life he had been forced to live.

When Fikowsky's sobbing widow was taken to Schlaffke's, a near-by bar, by her brother, Willi Hintze, she sobbed out that her husband had committed suicide because he could no longer bear to look on while his family starved. Thereupon Walter Jahnecke, a member of the Unemployeds' Executive, suggested a demonstration against the Welfare Office. Hintze went one step further and called for an armed attack, offering to supply the requisite arms himself. At first, everyone was enthusiastic, but soon Jahnecke and the rest of the unemployed grew suspicious. All of them knew that Hintze had been to prison, not for his political work, but because he was a member of a notorious gang of criminals. He was also said to be a police informer. In any case, instead of an armed attack on the Welfare Office there was a police raid on Schlaffke's. Jahnecke and some other 'ringleaders' were arrested – very luckily for them, as it later turned out, for otherwise they would most certainly have been implicated in the Reichstag fire.

The Director of the Welfare Office, Stadinspektor Frank, told the Supreme Court on 28 September 1933, that Hintze had warned him of an impending attack. He had immediately notified the police who, on Friday morning, sent him an officer and eight constables to guard the Welfare Office. At about 10 a.m., the police raided Schlaffke's, but found no arms – simply because Hintze had not brought any along.

Judge Vogt swallowed the whole story hook, line and sinker, particularly when Hintze, or 'Swindle-Hintze' as he was generally called, told him that the details of the attack on the Welfare Office had been planned by Communist Party headquarters in Neukölln, that he had seen van der Lubbe in Schlaffke's back room, and that Torgler's name had been mentioned in connection with the planned attack on the Welfare Office.

At the trial, it was this last, quite gratuitous, embellishment, which brought Torgler's counsel, Dr Sack, to the fore – much to Hintze's discomfiture. Referring to Hintze's many previous convictions, his well-deserved nickname, and the rest of the evidence, Dr Sack argued that it had been Hintze himself who had hatched out the whole plan of attacking the Welfare Office. Hintze tried to deny everything at first but in the end he confessed that he 'had played along with the police'. A newspaper report on Hintze's court performance concluded with the observation: 'The character of this witness is such that even the Public Prosecutor ignored his evidence against Torgler.'[8]

VAN DER LUBBE'S 'UNTRUSTWORTHINESS'

One of the experts whom Judge Vogt consulted about the fire was the proud owner of the Halle 'Private Institute for Scientific Criminology', Dr Wilhelm Schatz. At the time, Dr Schatz was as little known to the public as he was to his fellow-scientists.

At the end of May 1933, the experts performed a series of tests on the curtains, tablecloths, and towels which van der Lubbe had used as additional firelighters. This is what they found:

The restaurant door-curtains burned with astonishing speed.
Time: about thirty seconds.
The restaurant tablecloth burned quickly.
Time: fifty-five seconds.
The towel lit with a firelighter burned quickly.

Then came the first surprise:

> A piece of the curtain from the western corridor did not catch fire even when it was held in the flame of a firelighter for five minutes.[9]

This bit of curtain was immediately turned into a prize exhibit for, if the experts were right, van der Lubbe could only have set fire to it if it had been 'prepared' well in advance. It followed that the curtain had been '. . . soaked in a . . . petroleum derivate, i.e. benzine or gasoline.'[10]

To what extent Judge Vogt allowed himself to be blinded by science, and how badly he misjudged poor van der Lubbe as a result, can be seen from his own evidence to the Supreme Court on 27 September 1933 when he testified:

> Finally, van der Lubbe was greatly embarrassed when I put it to him that we had tried in vain – the experts will describe all the details – to light the curtain over the exit to the western corridor with a firelighter. . . . I told him: 'Marinus van der Lubbe, there can no longer be any doubt that, at least as regards the complicity of other persons, you have not spoken the truth.' He replied: 'Well, the experts can say what they like, but I know that it caught fire all the same.' Then

I pointed to the curtain once again and said to him: 'You can see for yourself, if it can't even be lit with a firelighter, then you could not possibly have lit it by brushing against it with bits of material.' Then he thought hard and said: 'Yes, perhaps it wasn't me after all!' I persisted: 'But how did the curtain catch fire in that case?' Then he shrugged his shoulders and said: 'Well, perhaps I tried to burn it after all.'

I could get absolutely nothing definite out of him, and I became convinced that the more I drove it home to him that his statements did not tally with those of the experts, the more determined he became to say nothing further.[11]

With the last sentence, the ingenuous judge had hit the nail squarely on the head, for van der Lubbe, who had kept repeating the simple truth, gave up in despair when he realized that Judge Vogt was far less interested in the facts than in his own pet theory.

In fact, Vogt believed that van der Lubbe lied 'at every opportunity':

Whenever it was a question of determining whether others had helped him, he invariably told deliberate lies. Only when it came to explaining that he – Lubbe – was the big hero who had started the fires all by himself, did he speak quite openly.[12]

Here we can see by what criterion Vogt judged van der Lubbe's trustworthiness: everything that did not fit in with the official views was dismissed as a lie. Since Marinus van der Lubbe knew perfectly well that he had set fire to the curtain, no amount of expert evidence could convince him of the contrary. All the experts did manage to do was to make him feel confused.

In contradistinction to Judge Vogt, Detective-Inspector Heisig told the Supreme Court that van der Lubbe had always struck the police as a reasonable man:

It was quite remarkable how much interest he showed in the investigation, and how he tried to explain every last detail. When he was asked to sign the statement we had taken from him, he insisted on making a number of corrections, and explained at length why he preferred particular turns of phrase.

And Heisig, who was only too familiar with Vogt's fatal bias, added: 'He remained interested for as long as he stayed with the police.'

Heisig also insisted that van der Lubbe's description of the path he had taken through the Reichstag had never changed, while Judge Vogt told the Supreme Court that van der Lubbe had made a number of contradictory statements about his movements. For once, the Supreme Court refused to listen to Vogt, finding instead that there was

> . . . no doubt that the accused took the path he described in the preliminary examination and which he was asked to retrace on a number of occasions during the trial. It would have been impossible for a man whose eyesight is as poor as van der Lubbe's to describe time and again the complicated trail he followed on the night of the fire, had he invented the whole story.

On the essential points, however, the Supreme Court agreed with Vogt rather than with Heisig. Thus, when van der Lubbe shook off his 'torpor' on 23 November 1933, to repeat that he had used his jacket to set fire to the curtains in the Session Chamber, the President reproached him, saying:

> 'All that is quite untrue, for the experts tell us that the curtain could not have been set on fire that way.'
>
> Van der Lubbe: 'But it did catch fire!'
>
> President: 'The Court does not believe you. The fire could not possibly have started in the way you have described.'[13]

The same attitude was also reflected in the Court's verdict:

> The Court holds that the curtains were not set on fire by van der Lubbe, the more so because his vagueness on that point is in marked contrast to his lucid and uniform description of the path he took through the Reichstag. At the preliminary examination he explained that he did not know whether, or precisely when, he had set fire to these curtains.

And yet van der Lubbe had spoken the truth, the whole truth, and nothing but the truth. Unfortunately for him, the Supreme Court chose to listen instead to the director of the 'Private Institute for Scientific Criminology'.

There were many other reasons why Vogt doubted van der Lubbe's truthfulness. First of all, van der Lubbe had been a Communist, and Communism was anathema to the Judge. Then van der Lubbe seemed to be a shiftless vagabond, one who preferred cadging his way through Europe to a respectable existence in his native Holland. Third, the Bulgarians' and Torgler's insistence that they had never met van der Lubbe was most suspicious, when so many witnesses had come forward to assert the contrary.

Vogt had strong private reasons for hating all Communists, for in 1928 an attractive Communist woman, Olga Benario, had persuaded him to send for her alleged fiancé, Otto Braun – whose real name was Karl Wagner and who was a leading Communist conspirator – in Moabit prison. While the two 'lovers' were reunited under Vogt's watchful eyes, a band of Communists carried Wagner off by force. There was a tremendous scandal, and poor Vogt was made to look an absolute fool.[14]

He must have been thinking of this when, on 27 September 1933, he told the Supreme Court: 'I believe I have some experience in interrogating and dealing with Communists.'

What made things particularly difficult for Vogt now was that the five Communist 'incendiaries' were so completely unlike one another. For one, there was van der Lubbe, who had been caught red-handed, and who confessed his crime quite freely; then there were the three Bulgarians who travelled with false papers and who thought it their duty to deceive the 'Fascist' police; and finally there was Torgler who could so easily have been mistaken for a gentleman. All Vogt knew was that he must not allow himself to be taken in by any of them.

He never guessed how little Dimitrov thought of him from the very start – as early as 3 April 1933, the Bulgarian scribbled the following entry in his diary: 'Vogt – small stature – Jesuitical. Good for petty crimes. Too small for historical trial, for world publicity. Petty; an idiot.' And Dimitrov added an observation which most observers of the trial came to share: 'Had he had even a modicum of intelligence, he would have fought tooth and nail to keep me out of the courtroom.'[15]

THE ACCUSED IN CHAINS

On the very first day of the preliminary examination, Judge Vogt ordered the accused to be put in chains. Torgler and the Bulgarians had to endure this torture for five long months, until 31 August 1933; van der Lubbe was forced to drag his chains into the courtroom as late as 25 September.

Dimitrov later described '. . . the agony of their fetters, the unbearable pain caused by the gashes on their ankles and wrists where the chains cut into them; the sleepless nights which they passed. What Vogt's intentions were in this respect passes almost beyond conjecture.'[16]

Torgler raised a similar outcry: 'It was left to the warders' discretion either to tighten our chains until the blood circulation was gravely impeded, and the skin broke, or else to take pity on us and to loosen the chains by one notch.'[17]

To make things worse, the summer of 1933 was exceptionally hot, so that the poor wretches had to drag their chains in an unbearably stifling atmosphere.

Vogt later told the Supreme Court that he had ordered fetters 'in accordance with the regulations'. He added:

> When he [van der Lubbe] complained about the chains I told him – and, by the way, the other accused as well – that much as I regretted this step . . . I had to act in accordance with the regulations. I suggested that he petition the Supreme Court.

As Dimitrov was quick to point out, Vogt's 'regulations' (Article 116, Section 4 of the Criminal Procedure Code Act) had nothing to do with the case, for:

> The Criminal Procedure Code prescribes circumstances in which accused persons may be put in fetters. This course should be taken only when they are specially dangerous to other persons or when they have attempted or have prepared to attempt suicide or escape.

In his testimony to the Supreme Court, Vogt claimed that he had told Dimitrov's counsel, Dr Werner Wille:

> I cannot help myself; it is my bounden duty to put them in chains but I have no objection to your petitioning the Supreme Court, thus releasing me from a grave responsibility.

When the Presiding Judge asked why no such petition had been lodged, Vogt replied:

> 'Wasn't it? I really do not know. Wille told me that he fully appreciated the necessity of the step I had taken, and that he personally would never even dream of petitioning the Supreme Court.'

Whereupon the Presiding Judge said quite pointedly:

> 'In this connection, I should like to have it established that the chains were subsequently removed on the instructions of this Court.'

In short, Vogt's so-called 'regulations' should never have been applied.

What the Presiding Judge did not point out was that it had been Vogt's moral, if not his formal, duty to submit all petitions to the Supreme Court personally. In other words, there was no need to wait for Dr Wille to 'release him from this grave responsibility'. In fact, when the Supreme Court first heard about the chains from Dr Sack, the learned Judges not only ordered the chains to be removed forthwith, but instructed Judge Vogt to submit a written explanation of the reasons which had prompted him to take this unusual step. Vogt's answer, dated 18 August 1933, betrays his bias and his bad conscience: to him all the accused were dangerous criminals even before they were convicted, and had to be treated as such. In addition, van der Lubbe had attacked an official, Tanev had attempted suicide, and Dimitrov had once come towards him with clenched fists!

At the time, it was suggested that Vogt had been given orders to chain the prisoners lest they commit suicide in prison. (In fact, Tanev tried to kill himself precisely *because* of the fetters.) The *Manchester Guardian* had warned that any such suicide would be looked upon as deliberate murder and an admission of Nazi guilt in the Reichstag fire.

But when Paul Vogt was asked in January 1957 whether he had, in fact, been ordered to put the prisoners in fetters, he insisted that he had not. In fact, he could remember nothing about the whole episode. This gap in his memory is most surprising, for Dimitrov had made a great point of taunting him with the chains.

In particular he ought to have remembered the following clash in Court:

President (to Dimitrov): 'This is not the place to accuse the Examining Magistrate. This is no Court of Appeal, Dimitrov.'

Dimitrov: 'Of course not. . . . But isn't it true that I lodged at least ten oral and written protests, and that I asked to have the chains removed in accordance with the Criminal Code. Is that true or not?'

Vogt: 'Yes.'

Dimitrov: 'Were all these protests and requests summarily dismissed, without my receiving any explanation or reason?'

President: 'Did you examine his requests?'

Vogt: 'No. No written request was ever submitted to me.'

Dimitrov: 'I sent you three!'

Vogt: 'Just one minute! Quite possibly he did. He certainly kept referring to the matter, for at almost every interrogation Herr Dimitrov asked me to remove his shackles. It is also quite possible – I am ready to concede that – that he put it in a letter. I can't possibly remember any more.'

Vogt, who considered every lapse of memory on the part of the accused an admission of their guilt and dishonesty, quite obviously applied different standards of probity to himself.

'I AM A GERMAN JUDGE AND MY NAME IS VOGT'

The trial brought to light many of Judge Vogt's other exceedingly strange methods.

The reader will remember that the three Bulgarians were arrested and brought to trial on information lodged by the waiter, Johann Helmer. His evidence was one long fiasco for the Examining Magistrate and the prosecution; Helmer proved only one thing – his absolute untrustworthiness. Or as Counsel for the Bulgarians, Dr Teichert, put it:

> Helmer's testimony is highly improbable. If we are to believe him, the Bulgarians met van der Lubbe in the Bayernhof at least four to six times from the summer to the winter of 1932. . . . They engaged in mysterious conversations and carried suspicious pamphlets on their persons. The clear implication of his evidence was that they and van der Lubbe were plotting an attack on the Reichstag, and perhaps other crimes as well. Now, the Reichstag did, in fact, go up in flames and Lubbe was caught. His picture was published in all the newspapers and pasted up on advertising pillars. In addition, a high reward was offered for further information. I ask the Court, does it seem likely that, after all this had happened, the Bulgarians would have gone back to the very place where they had formerly hatched their plots with a man who had meanwhile been arrested?

Torgler's Counsel added:

> I should like to draw attention to some other blunders which have been allowed to come up during the trial; blunders which hinge on the allegation that the accused van der Lubbe was seen in the Bayernhof. One witness, Helmer, was suddenly turned into a star witness for the prosecution. And why? Simply because no one bothered to ask what sort of place the Bayernhof really was, and how van der Lubbe was dressed at the time he was supposed to have been in the place. Had I

> been asked to investigate the crime, I should surely have said: I do not know what sort of place the Bayernhof is, so I shall go and have a look. I shall find out whether they have a doorkeeper who bars shabbily-dressed customers. Only then will I be able to tell whether the accused van der Lubbe could have met Dimitrov and the others in that place.

And yet it was left until the trial for this point to be cleared up.[18]

Dr Teichert then pointed out that inquiries in Holland had shown beyond a shadow of doubt that van der Lubbe could not have been in Berlin at the times mentioned by Helmer. This fact, too, ought to have been established, not at the trial, but during the preliminary examination.

Though Dr Teichert generally left all the talking to Dimitrov, he simply could not contain himself when, on 7 November, Helmer came out with the further fable that he had seen the three Bulgarians with van der Lubbe on the day before the fire:

> This is so improbable an allegation that I can only express my regret that the Examining Magistrate should have followed this witness who, I am convinced, is absolutely mistaken, on to a path that has proved so disastrous for the German people.

When the Public Prosecutor objected to this remark, Dr Teichert explained that it was his acceptance of Helmer's evidence which had made Judge Vogt, and hence German justice, an easy target for attacks from abroad. The acquittal of all three Bulgarians fully proved the justice of Dr Teichert's remark.

During the trial, it also came out that, although the three accused had repeatedly insisted on their right to be confronted with witnesses, Judge Vogt had just as insistently refused them. Hence the *Brown Book* was able to say:

> Vogt declined to accede to the requests of Dimitrov, Popov and Tanev to be confronted with van der Lubbe. Popov and Tanev had stated, quite independently of each other, that at about 9 p.m. on the evening of February 27th they were in the UFA pavilion in the Nollendorfer Platz seeing a film. Popov stated that he had left his gloves behind, had gone back later to look for them and had searched with the help of an attendant. His request to be confronted with the attendant Vogt refused. Popov and Tanev gave detailed accounts of their movements on February 27th. They asked to be confronted with the waiters at the Aschinger Restaurant in the Bülowstrasse where they had dinner that evening. Vogt declined to do this. He

failed to confront Torgler with Karwahne, the most serious of the witnesses against him. Had this been done, Torgler would have been able at an early stage to demonstrate the falsity of Karwahne's statements. By refusing to hold any of these confrontations, Vogt deliberately deprived the accused men of the benefit of their legal rights.[19]

And Dr Sack added in his final address:

The Examining Magistrate, having first shown the witness photographs, ordered a confrontation, but not with the witness Karwahne, because in the Magistrate's opinion Karwahne knew the accused Torgler extremely well. I, however, as Counsel for the Defence, take the view that it was quite irrelevant whether or not Karwahne was previously acquainted with the accused Torgler. It was the Examining Magistrate's duty to confront the two with each other.

By contrast, Vogt allowed repeated confrontations between the witness Bogun and Popov, during each of which Bogun 'remembered' fresh details. Apparently Vogt made a clear distinction between the needs of the prosecution and the defence, so much so that Popov was forced to complain:

The Examining Magistrate refused to confront me with the waiters at the [Aschinger] restaurant. When I repeated my request, he merely told me that Tanev had already admitted he had been there with me.[20]

Dr Sack rightly objected to Vogt's bluffing the witnesses with the story that their alleged accomplices had already confessed. When he cross-examined Vogt on that point, the Magistrate was stung into quick fury and betrayed a highly exaggerated sense of his own importance:

Dr Sack: 'Did you ever try, by alleging that Torgler had already confessed, to get the other accused to admit that Torgler was an accomplice in burning the Reichstag?'

Vogt: 'I should have hoped . . .'

Dr Sack: 'I am in duty bound to put that question to you. . . .'

Vogt: '. . . that I would have been spared that question. For first, as I have already said, I am a German judge and second my name is Vogt.'

Sack: 'Might I then ask you another question? The man who made the allegation [that Vogt had bluffed the witnesses] is also a German lawyer. Why did he accuse you?'

Vogt: 'I do not know. But since you insist, and so as to avoid any misunderstanding, I hereby declare most emphatically that nowhere and at no time did I ever do anything incompatible with the honour of a German judge.'[21]

The *Brown Book* added the following laconic comment: ' "First, I am a German judge; second my name is Vogt!" This is perhaps unique amongst Vogt's statements in that it cannot be contradicted.'[22]

The *Brown Book* also took up a number of other complaints by the defence. For instance, it stressed the importance of a list of Torgler's appointments, which had been found in the office of the Communist Party Parliamentary Group, and which Vogt claimed had 'disappeared'. This list, the defence had argued, was important evidence for Torgler's innocence: 'A man intending to burn the Reichstag so as to bring about a political upheaval would hardly go to the trouble of working out a complete list of ordinary engagements to follow the deed.'[23]

This is what Dr Sack had had to say on this subject:

> 'There is one thing that has made me sit up and think. I submit, Your Honours, that I, as Torgler's counsel, should have been in no position to adduce proof of Torgler's plans on and after February 27th, 1933, had I not hunted through the Court's dossiers. Is it counsel's job to go to such lengths, to say "I would rather see for myself" when he is told a document is missing? I ask you, Your Honours, what would have happened, had I been unable to find this list and to place it before you? Your Honours, I could mention many further oddities of this kind.'[24]

In view of the importance of the preliminary investigation and the keen interest the world press took in it, Judge Vogt saw fit to publish communiqués from time to time. Some of his press handouts proved rather premature – to put it very mildly. A typical example was the following, which appeared thirteen days after the Bulgarians were taken into custody:

> The investigations so far have shown that the Dutch Communist incendiary who was arrested in the Reichstag at the time of the fire has been in touch not only with German Communists but also with foreign Communists, including some who have been condemned to death or to long terms of penal servitude in connection with the blowing up of Sofia cathedral in 1925. The men in question have been apprehended.[25]

What had happened was that Dr Ernst Dröscher, a Nazi press

officer, had 'identified' Dimitrov as the man who blew up the cathedral, and that Judge Vogt had not bothered to ask any questions. In fact, as Dr Teichert later found out from the German Legation in Sofia, the cathedral was blown up by one Stefan Dimitrov Todorov, a man who had no connection with, or any resemblance to, Georgi Dimitrov.

On 27 September 1933, when – very angrily – Dimitrov asked Vogt whether or not he had issued a press statement on 1 April, i.e. before the start of the preliminary investigation, to the effect that Dimitrov, Popov and Tanev had been in touch with van der Lubbe, Vogt was so taken aback that he stammered out the completely irrelevant, though highly revealing, answer:

> It is correct that a statement was issued to the press which implied that the three arrested Bulgarians had taken part in the setting on fire or blowing up of the Sofia cathedral. At a later date I told Dimitrov that this information was apparently incorrect. He himself, however, is responsible for the error, since he failed to correct me when I connected the commencement of the Bulgarian insurrection in 1923 [in which Georgi Dimitrov had participated] with the outrage in Sofia Cathedral which did not, in fact, take place until 1925.

This odd claim on the part of a judge that the accused is to blame for the Court's blunders, is all the more incomprehensible because Vogt went on to admit that Dimitrov had, in fact, tried to put him right. But then Judge Vogt was singularly deaf when it came to any protests on the part of the accused, no matter whether their protests were concerned with points of fact or with the wearing of chains.

In any case, Dimitrov's original question, which had so flustered Judge Vogt, had been about the Bulgarians' alleged meetings with van der Lubbe and not about his own part in the Sofia bombing. However, before Dimitrov had time to point that out, Vogt had gone on to make an even greater fool of himself. Having just agreed that Dimitrov did not take part in the bombing, he now went on to say: 'The accused Dimitrov *was* involved in the blowing up of Sofia Cathedral. Yes! Mr Dimitrov, we are a little confused. But you wait a while for there will be a witness who will swear that you had a part in that affair.'

(Vogt's witness was Dr Dröscher, who contradicted himself so much and so often that the Court had to dismiss his evidence.)

When Dimitrov finally managed to get a word in edgeways, he began very quietly:

> 'I did not ask about the Sofia cathedral, but I did ask, and I ask again about our alleged association with van der Lubbe. I shall prove that Judge Vogt has conducted the judicial investigation in a biased manner, and that he has deliberately misled public opinion.'
>
> President: 'Hold your tongue! I cannot permit you to conduct your defence in this disgraceful manner!'

When Dimitrov thereupon pulled Vogt's 'premature' press release out of his pocket and passed it across to the President,[26] the President was forced to ask:

> 'I take it, this is the report which the Examining Magistrate issued at the time, and on which he has already testified?'
>
> Vogt: 'Yes. That is quite correct. Not only did I have the right to issue this statement, but the statement was proved right by the subsequent investigation. After all, we only caught the three Bulgarians because we could prove they had been in touch with van der Lubbe. Otherwise we should never have been able to arrest them.'

During the trial, Dr Sack asked Vogt:

> 'What were you trying to establish when you interrogated van der Lubbe? Did you think he was the sole culprit? Or did you think he must have had other accomplices?'
>
> Vogt: 'I never come to a case with preconceived ideas. I thought I have made that perfectly clear.'

Dr Sack returned to the problem of Judge Vogt in his final address:

> 'Even magistrates are in danger of becoming confused . . . particularly those who never have the slightest doubt that they are in the right.'

The very same judge who would not forgive the accused their most trivial lapses, himself perpetrated a number of terrible blunders. Torgler inferred from Vogt's great zeal that he was trying to ingratiate himself with the new masters. Heisig gained much the same impression, for, as he told von Papen during their common internment in Regensburg:

> Those chiefly responsible for trying to turn this criminal offence into a political one were Göring and Goebbels. They found a useful ally in

Judge Vogt, whose chief purpose was to gain a position of influence in the National Socialist Party.[27]

Heisig was probably too hard on Vogt. True, Vogt had no sympathy for Socialists and Liberals, let alone for Communists, but he was not so much corrupt, as misguided in thinking that the Nazis were serving his country's best interests. This is borne out by his subsequent career. In June 1937, Vogt was appointed President of the Second Criminal Court of Appeal. Seven years later he was summoned to Berlin and censured for political misconduct. When he refused to go into voluntary retirement, he was forcibly placed on the retirement list.

Vogt's 'crimes' were that he had given a clergyman, Dr Jannasch, leave to appeal against a sentence of two months' imprisonment for 'misuse of the pulpit' (the clergyman had prayed for Dr Niemöller), and that he had allowed the appeal of a German Nationalist leader, Joachim von Rohr-Demmin, against a sentence of eight months' imprisonment. Von Rohr-Demmin's misdemeanour had been very grave indeed: he had refused to throw two dead Russian prisoners into a pit and had given them a decent funeral.

Six months later, the Americans marched into Leipzig. After weeks of contradictory rumours, they finally withdrew and left Saxony and Thuringia to the Russians. Within days, a Russian commission called on the Supreme Court and took the fifty-two volumes constituting the records of the preliminary examination. One day later, on a Sunday, the Commission called on Judge Paul Vogt and questioned him very politely about the trial.

Vogt was arrested a short while later and taken to Dresden together with Judges Brandis, Wernecke and Frölich. Wernecke had been Vogt's assistant during the preliminary investigation and Frölich an Assistant Judge at the trial itself.

When the arrested men were told that their help was needed at the Nuremberg Tribunal to discover the real culprits of the Reichstag fire, they recommended that the records be consulted, and that all those witnesses at the trial who were still alive be re-examined.

The Russian legal experts immediately took up this suggestion, only to return empty-handed: none of the witnesses they could discover was able or willing to change his original testimony, none had apparently given his evidence under Nazi pressure.

Now Vogt was asked to write a 'Memorandum on the Reichstag Fire', and he submitted a thirty-two-page summary of everything he could remember. Naturally, he produced no fresh evidence inculpating the Nazis.

This caused the Russians so much embarrassment that they proposed a face-saver: they asked the former judges to write an affidavit to the effect that, although the Nazis could not be directly incriminated, their other outrages made their complicity seem highly probable. The judges merely shrugged this suggestion off. Nor could they satisfy the Russians that they had really told all they knew. Time and again they referred their captors to the records, and though Russian legal experts must have gone through these with more than one fine-tooth comb, they were quite unable to pin anything fresh on the Nazis. No wonder then that no Third Brown Book has ever been published in Moscow or East Berlin.

The treatment of the arrested judges had been scrupulously correct, indeed polite and friendly, and their quarters and their food had been unexceptionable. All that was changed the moment the Russians realized that the judges could not or would not help them. Vogt, Wernecke, and Frölich were sent to internment camps in August 1945. Their treatment there would require a book in itself; suffice it to say that Dr Walter Frölich, whose bearing during the Reichstag fire trial had attracted a great deal of favourable attention abroad, died within a few months of his arrest. Judge Wernecke died of malnutrition in a hospital in 1946.

Paul Vogt, who was sent from camp to camp, remained unbroken, taciturn and unrepentant. To this day he is convinced that the Communists set the Reichstag on fire. For the rest he wants to be left alone.

Still the old gentleman, who now lives in West Germany, cannot really object when people criticize the part he played in the Reichstag fire trial. He, who drove innocent men to the depth of despair, who shackled prisoners without justification, and blustered his way through the trial, must not complain if he himself is now put in the dock by historians and found wanting.

TORGLER'S COUNSEL

Many people have wondered how it came about that Ernst Torgler, the Communist Deputy, was defended by an avowed National Socialist.

In early June 1933, after the preliminary examination, Judge Vogt told Torgler to obtain the services of a barrister. Dr Kurt Rosenfeld, who had been Torgler's lawyer for many years, and who had even accompanied him to police headquarters on the day after the fire, had decided to leave Germany, and such well-known advocates as Dr Puppe, Walter Bahn, and Count Pestalozza politely declined the brief. Torgler's wife ran from lawyer to lawyer, and finally discovered one whose courage had not entirely evaporated. He was Dr H. R. Habicht of Berlin, and he wanted to be paid handsomely: from a letter reproduced in the *Brown Book* it appears that he asked Frau Torgler (who was completely destitute) for an initial fee of fifteen thousand marks with an additional thousand marks a day if the trial lasted for more than ten days. Needless to say, that demand was as good as a refusal.

August was drawing near, and Torgler was still without a lawyer. At this point the Supreme Court stepped in and nominated a Dr Huber as his official counsel. Weeks later, a terrified old gentleman appeared in Torgler's cell and complained bitterly about his brief. In his opinion, things looked very black – at best Torgler would get a life sentence. No wonder that Torgler

> . . . thanked him for his reassuring opinion and thought that, in these circumstances, I would rather do without his help. Rescue came a few days later, in the uniform of a prison warder:
>
> 'Do you know Dr Sack?' he asked me rather unexpectedly.
>
> And then he told me that Sack was a well-known member of the criminal bar who had got 'quite a few people off in his time'. He advised me to fill in a printed card, and gave me Sack's address.[28]

On hearing Dr Sack's name, Torgler was vaguely reminded of 'patriotic' and other Nazi murder trials, but what choice did he have in the matter? He filled in the card and sent it off. As Dr Sack explained later, he was completely taken aback when he received it:

> Knowing that the new laws forced Torgler to brief a Nationally-minded layer, I was concerned with only one question: is the man guilty or is he innocent? Only if I could be reasonably certain that Torgler had entered politics for idealistic reasons and not for selfish motives and that he had never made personal capital out of his political beliefs, would I find it within me to accept his defence. When my partner, Pelckmann, returned from his visit to Torgler, all he said was: 'You will have to go to him!'[29]

At the end of August, Dr Sack moved to Leipzig with eight juniors and began to plough through the thirty-two volumes of depositions. He also took the earliest opportunity to demand that Torgler's chains be removed. As a result, the Court ordered the unshackling of all the accused – except van der Lubbe.

Having once undertaken to stand by Torgler, Dr Sack kept faith with him through thick and thin. Not only did he stand up to the Public Prosecutor, but he mercilessly attacked National Socialist witnesses, no matter how prominent, once his client's interests were at stake. Thus he could say with perfect honesty:

> Thank God that all these underhand activities did not succeed in sowing mistrust between the Communist Torgler and myself, his National Socialist counsel. All they did do was to bring me closer to the accused. . . . And this trial has proved me right: I have gained the firm conviction that Torgler always told me the truth.

These brave words nearly cost Dr Sack his life:

> Dr Sack was unable to shake off the odium of having appeared for Torgler, and after the great purge of June 30th, 1934, he was kept behind bars for some considerable time, ostensibly so that he could 'adjust' his views.[30]

Dr Sack's dignified and noble bearing in Court was praised by all objective reporters. Douglas Reed, for instance, wrote:

> It was no enviable task that Dr Sack undertook, and his acceptance of it – at a fee which learned counsel, accustomed to enormous retainers and to subsequent payments not rare but eminently refreshing, would have regarded with the same feelings as a Savoy waiter a tip of two-pence – did him great credit. He was reproached from the bench with challenging the trustworthiness of official National Socialist witnesses; he was reproached in the press with the vigour of his final speech in Torgler's defence: and he was vilified abroad for his lack of activity in that same cause. Actually, he did all he could for his client.[31]

In his final speech, the courage of which was greatly praised by the *Neue Zürcher Zeitung*, Dr Sack exposed the lies that had been told by witnesses to whom common sense, logic, and reason meant little if anything. In particular, he exposed the Nazi deputy Karwahne and the methods of Judge Vogt, thus arousing the Nazi press to a high pitch of fury.

Nor did the Communists show any gratitude:

No thanks to Sack's defence, Torgler was acquitted. The transparent weakness of the case against him, his own courage and the bold defence of Dimitrov furnished the conditions for his acquittal. The moral pressure of world opinion secured it.

Yet, Dr Sack had been the only man to volunteer for the job, and the only German lawyer to protest against the *lex Lubbe*, i.e. the decree of 29 March 1933 which enabled the Government to impose the death sentence retrospectively. And had he not paid for two expensive trips to Paris and London out of his own pocket? According to Torgler:

> I once again made inquiries whether the Party had any objections to this lawyer. The reply was: 'Everything is in order.' And my wife added: 'They have even given me money for Dr Sack.'[32]

But soon after the main trial opened in Leipzig, the Communists changed their minds. One day, just after he had told foreign correspondents that he was fully satisfied with Dr Sack and therefore did not require the services of Arthur Garfield Hays,[33] Torgler noticed his ailing mother among the spectators: 'She was given permission to exchange a few words with me, and used the occasion to slip me a note from my comrades. We were nearly caught at it.'

That evening, when Torgler, who as we saw had just expressed his confidence in Dr Sack, read the note, he was utterly perplexed:

> I simply failed to understand. One moment they told me everything was in order, and now they wrote: 'The Central Committee asks you to take the first opportunity to disown Dr Sack as an agent of Hitler.' Added was a rather stilted paragraph instructing me to tell the Court that Goebbels and Göring had set the Reichstag on fire. The thing was signed by Wilhelm Pieck. I argued with myself for at least twenty-four hours. If I complied, I would cause a sensation, and that would make an extremely good headline. But what would happen to me...?

And, indeed, it does not require too much imagination to realize what would have happened to Torgler had he carried out the orders Pieck sent him from his safe refuge abroad. But then, the Communist Party, realizing that they could no longer use Torgler in Parliament, had only one use left for him: to let him be a martyr for the cause.

> I had fallen between two stools: Fascism and Bolshevism. . . . If I really told the Court that Göring and Goebbels had set the Reichstag

on fire – without being able to produce a shadow of a proof for this allegation – was I not simply signing my own death warrant . . .? I must frankly confess that these Party orders broke my spirit. I had resolved to throw myself into the struggle with enthusiasm, now I was paralysed, and without friends. . . .[34]

THE PUBLIC PROSECUTOR'S DILEMMA

After the lengthy preliminary investigation, the Public Prosecutor was handed thirty-two volumes of depositions, and the task of weeding this unwieldy mass of papers into a convincing indictment proved extremely onerous for even such experienced lawyers as Dr Werner and his assistant, Dr Parrisius.

Dr Karl Werner, who had come to the bar in 1926, was 'a zealous, somewhat dry official who had grown grey in the service of the law'.[35] Whereas Torgler still thinks that Werner was not at all cut out to play the part of Torquemada, Otto Braun, remembering his own bitter experiences, called him a reactionary with a blind eye to the errors of the Right, and with pitiless clear-sight when it came to those of the Left.[36]

Though Werner had previously acted as Public Prosecutor to the Supreme Court, the Reichstag fire trial was his most important – and most embarrassing – case by far. He might not have realized it at first, but as the trial proceeded he must often have wished most fervently that someone else were in his shoes. Here the sketchy witnesses for the prosecution stepped out of the dry pages of Judge Vogt's record, were made flesh, and – one and all – turned into miserable swindlers, psychopaths and hardened criminals. An old German saying has it that only a rogue can give more than he owns, and it did not take the Public Prosecutor long to realize that most of his witnesses owned nothing at all. Some were such transparent liars – for instance Anna Meyer and the chauffeur Theel, who had sworn they had seen Dimitrov near the Reichstag on the night of the fire – that they had to be dropped without further ado, and none of the others were very much better either. As a result, Dimitrov was able to keep jeering at Dr Werner and his 'classical indictment'. Indeed, the *Brown Book* was right to assert that the only remarkable thing about that legal document was its impressive size of 235 pages.

In any case, we can understand why Dimitrov wrote to his lawyer:

It is most regrettable that the indictment has not been published to this day, for its publication would be my best defence. I am certain that my position, as the accused, is incomparably sounder than that of the Public Prosecutor who must substantiate his indictment before the Court and before public opinion. I don't envy him at all.

No, the Public Prosecutor was in a truly unenviable position, for though Diels had warned Hitler and Göring repeatedly against trying to involve the Communist Party leaders, Göring had insisted on taking just that course.

Only because poor Dr Werner had to carry out the orders of his superiors, was Dimitrov able to proclaim that Göring and Goebbels had rendered yeoman service to Communism by pressing their ridiculous charges in the Supreme Court.

All these facts must be borne in mind by anyone wondering how so paltry a document as this indictment could ever have been presented in a court of law. Because he had to uphold Göring's and Hitler's thesis that the Reichstag fire was a desperate attempt on the part of the Communists to stop the irresistible march of National Socialism, Werner had to clutch at even the most fragile straws. No wonder that all the pieces of evidence assembled by Judge Vogt and the Prosecution collapsed like a house of cards under the merciless probing of the defence, and particularly of Torgler's lawyer, Dr Sack. It was largely thanks to him that all Judge Vogt's witnesses were unmasked as hardened criminals, pathetic liars, Nazi fanatics, police informers, Communist renegades, hysterical old women, and psychopaths.

It did not help Dr Werner that he fought a desperate struggle on behalf of every one of them – no single witness was able to establish that the Communists had, at the time in question, made any plans for an organized uprising, in which case the Reichstag fire could not have been a Communist 'signal' for anything. To save his case from utter collapse, Dr Werner himself was forced to ask for the acquittal of the three Bulgarians. His fiasco was complete when the Court acquitted Torgler as well. The Court's verdict was, at the same time, a verdict on Judge Vogt and his preliminary examination.

What the Court was left with was only one man who had done his utmost to incriminate himself without any prompting from the police, from the Examining Magistrate, or from the Public Prosecutor. That man was Marinus van der Lubbe.

11. The German Court and its Shadow

THE COURT

WHEN the case against 'Van der Lubbe and Accomplices' was duly sent for trial to the Fourth Criminal Chamber of the Supreme Court in Leipzig, the accused found themselves before the very same Bench which, in September 1930, had tried three army officers – Ludin, Scheringer and Wendt – for National-Socialist subversion in the army. One of the witnesses on that occasion was Adolf Hitler who stated on oath that he intended to come to power by legal means.

The President of the Court, since 1931, had been Dr Wilhelm Bünger. Before then, Dr Bünger was a well-known National Liberal politician who had served as Saxon Minister of Justice, and even as Prime Minister of Saxony. His appointment to the Supreme Court was frowned upon by his professional colleagues, most of whom considered him a political failure rather than a legal success – possibly out of jealousy.

Dr Bünger's associate judges were Dr Coenders, Dr Rusch, Dr Lersch and Dr Froelich. Coenders was described by Douglas Reed[1] as having 'a massive, finely carven head surmounted by masses of waving silver hair' and as having a voice 'with the vibrant resonance of a cathedral bell'. Another observer, however, disapproved of Coenders's behaviour during Göring's testimony on 4 November: 'The judges listened to [Göring's] deliberations quite expressionlessly; the only exception was Dr Coenders who kept nodding with satisfaction, and beaming all over his face.'[2] However, most permanent observers praised the strict impartiality of Dr Froelich.

The tensely awaited trial opened on 21 September 1933, in the presence of eighty-two foreign correspondents. So large was the rush for press tickets that a system of 'rationing' had to be instituted. Naturally, Dr Goebbels saw to it that his 'Marxist enemies' and the hated *Manchester Guardian*, were sent away empty-handed. However, two Soviet representatives of Tass and *Izvestia* were admitted later.

We owe the description of the strange procession in which the accused were led into the courtroom to Douglas Reed:

> A being of almost imbecile appearance, with a shock of tousled hair hanging far over his eyes, clad in the hideous dungarees of the convicted criminal, with chains around his waist and wrists, shambling with sunken head between his custodians – the incendiary taken in the act. Four men in decent civilian clothes, with intelligence written on every line of their features, who gazed sombrely but levelly at their fellow men across the wooden railing which symbolized the great gulf fixed between captivity and freedom. . . . Torgler, last seen by many of those present railing at the Nazis from the tribune of the Reichstag, bore the marks of great suffering on his fine and sensitive face. Dimitrov, whose quality the Court had yet to learn, took his place as a free man among free men; there was nothing downcast in his bold and even defiant air. Little Tanev had not long since attempted suicide, and his appearance still showed what he had been through, Popov, as ever, was quiet and introspective.[3]

The general appearance of the incendiary-in-chief, van der Lubbe, caused a tremendous stir among the observers. Was this shadow of a man really so dangerous that he had to be put in chains like a common murderer? Sitting in the dock with downcast head, he looked far more like a terrified child than a terrorist:

> According to the affidavit and also to the police witnesses, van der Lubbe was intelligent, mentally alert, and quick to respond. But the van der Lubbe whom we were now shown was a mental wreck, completely broken and dull-witted.[4]

The proceedings were opened by Dr Bünger promptly at 9.15 a.m., with a dignified speech which, with slight modifications, was reported in the *Völkischer Beobachter* of 22 September 1933, and also in *Brown Book II*:

> The enormous repercussions of the event which constitutes the background of this trial have had the consequence of elevating the subject-matter of these proceedings to the rank of universal interest. It has formed the object of passionate discussion and speculation in the press of the whole world. Attempts have been made to anticipate the results of these proceedings. It does not, however, follow that this Court is entering upon its task with preconceived views or with its mind already made up. So far that has never been the custom either in Germany or abroad. Nor has prejudgment of the issues of a trial in the press been usual.

> The struggle between these various conflicting theories has not affected the Court before which these issues come to be tried. This Court will pass sentence solely upon the results of the proceedings within its cognizance. For the purpose of this Court's decision only facts which are revealed in the course of the proceedings before it can have weight. Not only is this trial open to the public of all lands without restriction but the prisoners are represented by counsel without let, hindrance or condition. It has been said that no foreign lawyer has been permitted to appear for the defence. In this connection it must be observed that the law only permits such a course in exceptional circumstances. In the present case, the Court in the free exercise of its unfettered discretion has not seen fit to permit the admission of foreign lawyers. Not only has the Court seen no occasion for their admission but it holds the view that such applications as were made for this purpose were not directed to serve exclusively the interests of the prisoners, but were chiefly intended to cast doubt on the independence of German justice.

In this connection, it might be worth quoting Professor Friederich Grimm:

> The question has been raised abroad why no foreign lawyers were admitted to this trial. In van der Lubbe's case, the answer was simple for he had expressly refused the services of a Dutch lawyer; in the case of the other accused, and particularly the Bulgarians, it was obvious that the briefing of foreign counsel could only serve the ends of propaganda.... No court in the world would have admitted foreign lawyers to a political trial once there was even the slightest risk that their admission might endanger the safety of the state.[5]

The generally objective Swiss correspondent, Kugler, however, had grave doubts: 'I am completely baffled. The renown of German jurisprudence would clearly have been enhanced had foreign lawyers been admitted.'[6]

Now, though Kugler had every right to be baffled, particularly as his native Switzerland had often admitted foreign lawyers, it seems doubtful whether anyone could have served his clients better than the German advocates. Arthur Garfield Hays, for instance, had nothing but praise for Torgler's counsel, Dr Sack, and van der Lubbe, though he steadfastly refused to accept legal assistance and though he would not exchange a single word with his state counsel, Dr Seuffert, was extremely well served by the latter – it was certainly not his fault that he failed. Nor is there any doubt that Dr Teichert, the Bulgarians' lawyer, defended his clients as best he could in the circumstances.

Moreover, most correspondents were agreed that Dr Bünger, the President of the Court, set to work with great patience and perfect courtesy to all. It was only as the trial proceeded that he gradually succumbed under the tremendous cross that had been placed on his somewhat too slender shoulders.

To begin with, the Nazis had begun to 'clear up' the Department of Justice and all 'politically unreliable officials' were in danger of instant dismissal. Now, Bünger had been made a judge under the Weimar Republic, and knew full well that the new Government expected him to atone for his 'evil' past. Needless to say, he became increasingly nervous as the trial failed to produce the expected results. To make things worse, Associate Judge Coenders thought very little of his forensic gifts and made many caustic comments on Dr Bünger's clumsiness, absent-mindedness, and frequent mistakes.

In fact, as the trial ran its difficult course, Bünger got more and more out of his depth. Nothing seemed to make any sense or to hang together in any way. All the evidence was contradictory; van der Lubbe refused to play by the rules, and the other accused kept holding the Court in contempt. Worst of all, two of the accused needed interpreters who muddled things further still.

On the very first day of the trial, Bünger earned Coenders's understandable strictures when he asked van der Lubbe: 'Have you ever been an active National Socialist, I mean have you ever pretended to be one except in Sörnewitz?'

As Coenders noted laconically, van der Lubbe had not even been active as a National Socialist in Sörnewitz. Moreover, that whole business had already been cleared up when Bünger asked his leading question.

A typical sample of the President's bungling was his examination of Constable Poeschel:

Bünger: 'You started giving your evidence yesterday during the inspection.'

Poeschel: 'No, not yet.'
President: 'Not yet?'
Poeschel: 'No.'
President: 'How is that?'
Poeschel: 'I merely took the oath.'
President: 'You took the oath? Well, that's splendid. When I asked

you last night I thought you said that you had not taken the oath.'
Poeschel: 'On the contrary, I said that I had taken the oath.'

Bünger's time-consuming excursions into irrelevant issues are best appreciated from the following sample:

Bünger: 'You said that there were four officers. Who were they?'
Poeschel: 'Lieutenant Lateit, Constable Losigkeit, another officer and myself.'
Bünger: 'But that only makes three. Who was the fourth officer?'
Poeschel: 'I don't know him by name.'
Bünger: 'Ah, so there was another one!'

With this and other clumsy interrogations, Bünger kept leading the Court into one blind alley after another, wasting not only hours and days, but weeks and months.

A tragi-comical scene was enacted on 18 October 1933, when the Court examined the evidence of the Reichstag official Robert Kohls. Kohls had alleged that, on the night of the fire, Torgler failed to answer his telephone. When Krueger, a telephone expert, testified that the ringing tone recurred every ten seconds, Bünger remarked:

'In that case, Herr Kohls must have misinformed us. He said the sound was ss – ss – ss.'
Dr Sack: 'May I remind the Court that it was I who made that sound. I said "Was it sss?" and the Public Prosecutor said: "Wasn't it mmm?" It was you, Mr President, who suggested "sss" and the witness Düsterhoeft who suggested "rrrrrr".'

These edifying reflections on possible ringing tones covered many pages of the Court's records. Another illustration of Dr Bünger's legal prowess was given on 6 December, when the Court rose to consider a motion by Dimitrov, and returned after a brief recess.

Bünger: 'Please be seated. The Court refuses the request of the accused Dimitrov that the sentence passed on the leaders of the uprising on November 9th 1923 [the Hitler putsch] be read out here. Or was that a motion of yours, Mr Public Prosecutor?'
Dr Werner: 'I have submitted no such motion.'

Clearly Dr Bünger's memory was such that it did not even last him from his chambers to the courtroom.

. . . . .

In his address to the Court, the Public Prosecutor, Dr Werner, expressed his thanks to all those 'thousands of fellow-Germans' who felt obliged to report what observations they thought might have been relevant to the case, first to the police, then to the investigating magistrate and finally to the Public Prosecutor's office or the Court.

The combined chance of attracting world attention as a witness, of currying favour with the new German masters, and of carrying off the rich reward of 20,000 marks, proved quite irresistible to a host of shady and self-seeking characters. All of them felt that even if their evidence did no good it certainly could do no harm. Naturally, no one volunteered to appear as a witness for the defence; in fact those defence witnesses who were subpoenaed proved rather reluctant and – sometimes – rather untruthful. One of these was Ernst Torgler's 'friend', the journalist Walther Oehme, who lied about the time he had visited Torgler on the day of the fire.

In contrast to the hesitant and vague witnesses for the defence, the witnesses for the prosecution all took the stand with amazing self-confidence. What they had to say, they said with perfect assurance. Thus the star witness Helmer, who swore that he had seen van der Lubbe in the Bulgarians' company, identified van der Lubbe with an emphatic: 'I would sooner mistake my own wife than the accused van der Lubbe.'

So definite were the witnesses for the prosecution, and so unsure those for the defence that foreign journalists kept remarking on the striking distinction between the two categories. In every other trial, this very distinction would have made the Court sit up and take notice, particularly when the general quality of the prosecution witnesses was as poor as it proved to be here. Yet Dr Werner, the Public Prosecutor, could not afford to be very discriminating since, as he confessed, he had been unable to dig up '. . . a single person who had direct evidence that the four accused [Torgler and the Bulgarians] had participated in the crime'.[7]

Clearly, in a totalitarian state, justice stands on feet of clay.

And so the trial dragged on under the critical eyes of Nazis and Communists alike. Like a blind man in a maze, Dr Bünger followed every possible trail, clinging to every possible clue as Theseus did to Ariadne's thread. Yet the more he tried, the more he became engulfed in a yawning abyss of boredom, and the more he revealed the absolute aimlessness of the whole trial.

To make things worse, Bünger adopted quite a different manner to the two classes of witnesses, so much so that it was easy to tell from his tone alone whether a given witness appeared for the prosecution or the defence. Understandably enough, Bünger, who must have come to realize that he was making no headway whatever, vented his spleen on the 'obdurate' and persistent causes of his failure, the accused and their witnesses. On the other hand, all those witnesses for the prosecution who obviously tried so hard to help the 'truth' to victory, naturally needed every kind of encouragement and sympathy.

As a result, witnesses for the defence, who in any case were afraid to open their mouths, had their slightest slips treated with utmost scorn and severity, while witnesses for the prosecution were encouraged to come out with the wildest feats of fantasy. Time and again the Public Prosecutor and the President intervened to help witnesses for the prosecution out of their difficulties.

A Dutch newspaper summed it all up as follows:

> National Socialist witnesses quite especially, are protected against every kind of reprimand. All of them are handled like unboiled eggs, indeed with every consideration and politeness. This distinction has become so blatant that the tone in which the Court addresses a witness is a clear indication of the latter's political colour.[8]

Douglas Reed took much the same view. Thus he tells us that, when Dr Sack wished to lay bare the discrepancies in the witness Karwahne's testimony, Dr Bünger intervened with: 'There will always be discrepancies in such statements, and I must protect the witness against the suggestion that he intentionally, or through negligence, concealed anything.'[9]

THE 'SUBSTITUTE INCENDIARY'

Douglas Reed – undoubtedly one of the shrewdest and best-informed observers of the Leipzig trial – has described the court appearance of Georgi Dimitrov:

> His exchanges with Dr Bünger – who told him sharply at the start that he came into Court with the reputation of indiscipline during the preliminary examination and had better comport himself differently now – were the beginning of a duel which lasted fifty-seven days. In

> vain did the little judge . . . seek to subdue Dimitrov, to compel him by admonition, by threat of expulsion, by repeated expulsion itself, to be meek, to behave himself as a disreputable Bulgarian Communist should who is under grave suspicion of tampering with the edifice of the Reich. Dimitrov felt himself not only innocent, but as good as any man in Court, and was not prepared to have an inferiority thrust on him which he did not feel. Nothing could stop him. At the end, the Court itself had a certain rueful affection for the disarming and dauntless man.

The great pomp with which the trial was conducted did not impress Dimitrov for a single moment. His intelligence was razor-sharp and, unlike his two compatriots, he had a good command of the German language, and was therefore able to expose the prosecution's case for the sham it was.

When he was first arrested, Dimitrov had been afraid that the 'Fascist police' might have recognized him as the leader of the West European Branch of the Comintern. Imagine his surprise when instead he discovered that they were seriously trying to blame him for a crime that had been committed at a time when he had a perfect alibi! No wonder that he refused to believe his enemies would be stupid enough to make him stand trial before the Supreme Court.

When Dimitrov presented his alibi to Judge Vogt, the Examining Magistrate neatly countered that in that case Dimitrov must certainly have prepared the fire and then gone off to Munich for the sake of the alibi, leaving van der Lubbe to take the blame. That was also the view adopted by the Public Prosecutor.

Now, Dimitrov had an inestimable advantage over his judges: he knew that the Communist Party was completely innocent of the Reichstag fire. Only in one respect was there complete agreement between him and the prosecution: both were absolutely convinced that van der Lubbe must have had accomplices.

Once Dimitrov recognized the shallowness of the case for the prosecution, he used his quick wit with unerring skill. A man whose name few people had heard when the trial opened, had become an international celebrity, and a godsend to the Communists, by the time the trial was over.

To Dr Bünger, on the other hand, Dimitrov's behaviour proved a constant provocation, and a test beyond endurance. As Dimitrov continued flinging veiled insults at the Court, Bünger increasingly lost his original composure. In the end, he looked for poisonous barbs in even the most innocent remarks and repeatedly excluded Dimitrov from the trial. The only result was an increase in Dimitrov's popularity with the press.

Bünger was, in fact, treating Dimitrov much as Judge Paul Vogt had done before him. The Bulgarian's very bearing was an affront to both, for he would miss no opportunity of exposing his judges.

After every expulsion Dimitrov came back into the courtroom with renewed vigour. He was always most careful to behave with formal courtesy; what made him so insufferable, indeed so terrifying, was the biting irony with which he attacked his accusers, often to the great amusement of the public gallery.

A typical example of how tense Dr Bünger became every time Dimitrov opened his mouth, is the following incident. Dimitrov was recalling his previous request that Detective-Inspector Heisig be cross-examined on the evidence of a witness, and added:

> 'As I remember, I was completely taken aback when the Public Prosecutor agreed to this request.'
>
> President: 'You were taken aback! You really must omit these gratuitous remarks which, almost without exception, are affronts to this Court. I am telling you so for the last time.'

After further skirmishes, during all of which Dimitrov remained completely unruffled, while the President could barely control his temper, Dimitrov said quite unexpectedly and very quietly:

> 'And furthermore, Herr President, please allow me to say so – you are extremely nervous today, I don't know . . .'
>
> President: 'I am not at all nervous; it is just that your constant repetitions and impertinent interjections force me to cut you short. In fact, I never get nervous, I should like to reassure you on that point, but I cannot possibly let you go on. I cannot and I will not. You simply do not respond when you are spoken to in civil tones. That is the simple truth of the whole matter. Well, let us proceed.'
>
> Dimitrov: 'You can, of course, throw me out, Herr President, I know you have the right to do so, but please allow me, the accused, to say a word or two about the documents presented today . . .'
>
> President: 'Provided you are not just taking another liberty. If that is the case, I shall simply refuse to hear you.'
>
> Dimitrov: 'I merely call a spade a spade.'
>
> President: 'It's for me to decide that.'

Dimitrov: 'Of course, it's sheer bad luck for the prosecution that a whole series of important witnesses are psychopaths, opium addicts and thieves.'

President: 'I object to the expression "bad luck", and therefore will not hear you further.'

Dimitrov: 'That would be quite wrong of you, Herr President.'

Once again things had come to a head. The Court retired, and returned with the warning that Dimitrov would be automatically ejected if he were guilty of the least impropriety. It added that he would have been expelled even earlier, had this not been the last day of the trial.

After the luncheon recess, the remorseless Dimitrov started plaguing the harassed Court with yet another petition.

Dimitrov: 'May I request, Herr President, that, for the sake of completing the judgment you have just read out, you also read out the verdict on the Rightist putsch in Munich on the 8th and 9th November, 1923. If it should be necessary to give reasons for this request, I ask for permission to do so.'

President: 'No. We shall decide about this and the other petitions afterwards.'

Dimitrov: 'A National Socialist putsch.'

President: 'I heard you. I am not deaf.'

Dr Werner: 'I object to the petition, for clearly it has no bearing on the question of who burned the Reichstag.'

Here we have another perfect illustration of the double standard applied by a Court which saw fit to admit as evidence Communist outrages that had no earthly connection with the Reichstag fire, but refused point-blank to allow Dimitrov to introduce evidence about similar National Socialist acts of subversion.

On the last day of the trial, Dimitrov also settled his score with House-Inspector Alexander Scranowitz, who had originally alleged that he had seen the three Bulgarians in the Reichstag but who later recanted. Dimitrov's reference to the matter once again brought out the incompetent worst in Dr Bünger:

President (to Scranowitz): 'You can no longer say so with any certainty?'

Scranowitz: 'No, not with the same certainty.'

Dimitrov: 'With what certainty?'

President: 'You say you can no longer say so with the requisite degree of certainty?'

Scranowitz: 'Not with enough certainty to state on oath: "It was him." '

President: 'You cannot do that?'

Scranowitz: 'No, I cannot.'

Dimitrov: 'Herr President, I should like to point out that when I saw Herr Scranowitz in the courtroom for the first time I immediately said to myself, this must be the Macedonian terrorist who murdered ten Communists. But as I could not believe my eyes, I did not tell the Court that Herr Scranowitz was this Macedonian terrorist, and even less that . . .'

The rest of Dimitrov's sentence was drowned in laughter.

From all these dialogues and arguments, one thing emerges quite clearly: the greater Dimitrov's composure, the greater Dr Bünger's discomfiture. Dimitrov's very presence gave the President palpitations. In this connection a Swiss journalist reported the following characteristic incident:

> Someone made an interjection in an undertone, and the President . . . turned irately to Dimitrov: 'Be silent! Hold your tongue!' It turned out that Dimitrov had not so much as opened his mouth. . . .[10]

THE FIRST FOUR EXPULSIONS

Dimitrov's first expulsion from the courtroom occurred on 6 October 1933, when, according to the foreign press, he was ejected for 'quite inexplicable reasons'[11] or 'on a ridiculous pretext'.[12]

On that day, the President put it to Dimitrov that the documents which the police had removed from his briefcase and from his suitcase seemed to belie his protestations that he was exclusively concerned with Bulgarian affairs. Afraid that if his real position in the Comintern were ever discovered all would be up with him, Dimitrov kept insisting that all these documents had been planted by the police. For instance, when Dr Bünger produced a pamphlet issued by the Central Committee of the German Communist Party dated 3 March 1933, and entitled: 'The Burning of the Reichstag', Dimitrov simply claimed that he had 'neither seen, possessed, nor read such a document' and that he had certainly never been asked about it by the police. Thereupon Dr Bünger read Dimitrov's own statement of 9 March 1933, the day of his arrest, in which Dimitrov admitted having obtained this pamphlet from 'Inprecorr' (International Press Correspondence) for which he had allegedly been working. Now Dimitrov became excited: 'Impossible! This statement is not the one that was read out to me at the time.' (Dimitrov had consistently refused to sign any statements.)

The President now called Detective Officer Kynast to tell the Court about a 'Pharus' map of Berlin found among Dimitrov's effects. Kynast stated that he had found crosses on this map and corresponding crosses on the street index. The crosses referred to the Palace, the Reichstag and the Dutch Embassy.

Dimitrov immediately asked to see the map, looked at it, and exploded with: 'At the time of the police investigation these crosses were very thick. Now they are very thin!'[13]

Somewhat taken aback, the President then asked him for what reason he thought the crosses might have been altered, to which Dimitrov replied mysteriously that he would come back to the matter.

When the Public Prosecutor, who had introduced the map as a possible link between Dimitrov and van der Lubbe, asked whether Dimitrov admitted that it was his own, Dimitrov replied: 'I admit that I bought a map. Whether it is this particular one, I cannot say.'[14]

He added that, in any case, he himself had certainly not made the crosses; the whole thing was a police fraud.

When the President warned him not to make offensive remarks about police officers, Dimitrov, disgusted at the stupid manner in which the police were trying to manufacture a link between him and van der Lubbe, burst out with: 'I can't give any guarantees for the police.'

Half incensed and half amused, the President replied: 'We shall just have to make do without your guarantees.'

Whereupon Dimitrov

> . . . took it upon himself to deliver an elementary lesson on deciphering code to the ignorant police officers. What he had learned during his illegal stay in Berlin, might be of great use to those Nazis who, at this very moment, were carrying on their nefarious activities in Czechoslovakia and in Austria, using false names and codes.[15]

When he added: 'The police have shown great incompetence and incomprehension,' the President sprang to his feet and the Court filed out in solemn procession. On their return, Dr Bünger announced that Dimitrov would be removed 'for disobeying repeated admonitions to desist from insulting police officers'.[17]

Furiously, Dimitrov snatched up his briefcase, shouting: 'Monstrous! Monstrous!'

And while two policemen hustled him out he added: 'My sentence has already been pronounced in another place.'[11]

Dimitrov had been somewhat impertinent, but when all was said and done, his head was hanging by these idiotic and, to say the least, suspicious pencil crosses on the map. Moreover, Dimitrov's remark that he could not give any guarantees for the police had a very serious, indeed a highly embarrassing, background, for when they searched his room the over-zealous police officers had quite clearly exceeded their powers: they had not produced independent witnesses (Article 105, Crim. Code); they had not carried out the search in the presence of the suspect or of his representative (Article 106); they had not handed the suspect a list of all confiscated articles (Article 107); they had not placed all confiscated documents in sealed envelopes or asked the suspect or his representative to seal them (Article 110).

It was only because of these undeniable errors and omissions, that Dimitrov could stand up in Court and allege that the police had tampered with his papers and the 'Pharus' map. This embarrassing fact was quite specifically referred to in the verdict where we read that 'it is impossible to establish the truth [about the crosses on the map, etc.] since no inventory of the confiscated documents was made.'

On 11 October Dr Bünger announced that the Court would move from Leipzig to the Reichstag for an on-the-spot inspection. Dimitrov immediately requested permission to put a question to the Court.

> Dr Bünger: 'No, Dimitrov, it's no use at all. I have told you more than once that the Criminal Code does not allow you to keep asking questions or making long statements and you can hardly expect that I should allow you, of all people, who – to put it very mildly – have repeatedly tried to abuse the Court's indulgence, at least with respect to the putting of questions and the making of statements, to do something to which the Rules of Procedure do not entitle even you. Please calm yourself.'

From a purely formal point of view, the President was completely in the right. Dimitrov's persistent refusal to allow his

Government-nominated counsel, Dr Teichert, to act on his behalf, was, in fact, a technical breach of the Rules of Court. But Dimitrov was not dismayed by such trifles.

Dimitrov: 'Herr President . . .'

Dr Bünger: 'No, I don't want to hear another word. Please don't bother me, it's no use at all. Sit down.'

Dimitrov: 'I should like to . . .'

President: 'I cannot allow you to speak!'

Dimitrov: 'I am here not only as Dimitrov the accused but also as the defender of Dimitrov.'

Once again the Court rose in a flurry and, on its return, made known that Dimitrov was expelled from Court until further notice (and hence barred from attending the reconstruction of the fire which was to be enacted on the following night).

Before he was led out of the courtroom, Dimitrov quickly handed a note to Dr Teichert, saying: 'I had wanted to ask these questions, ask them for me!'

After his second expulsion, Dimitrov sent a letter of protest to Dr Bünger which deserves to be quoted in full:

Berlin, October 12th, 1933.

To the President
Fourth Criminal Chamber of the Supreme Court.
Mr President,

When the Supreme Court rejected every one of the eight lawyers chosen by me, I had no option but to defend myself as best I could. As a result I have been compelled to appear in Court in a double capacity: first as Dimitrov, the accused, and second as the defender of the accused Dimitrov.

I grant you that both as the accused and also as my own defender, I may have proved annoying and awkward to my accusers and their principals. However, I cannot help that. Once the Prosecution has been careless enough to put me, a completely innocent man, in the dock as a substitute incendiary, they must also be prepared to accept the resulting annoyance. They have called the tune, now they must dance to it. Whether they like it or not is neither my affair, nor is it my problem. I am a political suspect appearing before a Supreme Court, and not a soldier in barracks or a prisoner-of-war in an internment camp.

I am firmly convinced that, in this trial, van der Lubbe is no more than what one may call the Reichstag-fire Faust, manipulated by the Reichstag-fire Mephistopheles. The miserable Faust now stands before the bar of the Supreme Court, but Mephistopheles has disappeared.

As an innocent suspect, and particularly as a Communist and as a member of the Communist International, I have the utmost interest in discovering every last detail of the Reichstag-fire complex, and in bringing the vanished Mephistopheles to justice. My questions serve this one object and nothing else. I have no need to make Communist propaganda before the Supreme Court, the more so since the best propaganda for Communism has already been made, not by me, but by the mere fact that Dr Parrisius' classical indictment accuses innocent Communists of burning the Reichstag.

I have the natural right to defend myself and to participate in the trial both as the accused and my own defender. Expulsions from sessions of the Court or from inspections of the scene of the crime are quite incapable of intimidating me. These expulsions from what are the most important sessions and reconstructions are not only an open violation of my right to defend myself, but also serve to show the world that my accusers are not at all sure of their own case. The expulsions thus only serve to add further substance to existing Communist allegations about this trial.

If this insupportable treatment of myself is continued, I confess quite openly that I shall feel compelled to reconsider whether there is any purpose at all in my reappearing before the Court, irrespective of the consequences.

Dimitrov's brilliant use of a foreign language, his controlled tone, particularly in the last paragraph, his natural dignity – all these did not miss their effect on Dr Bünger. Dimitrov was henceforth given access to (at least some of) the Court files, and was allowed to petition the Court, albeit to have most of his petitions rejected. In other words, the Court gave him tacit permission to perform his double act of accused and defender. In addition, Dimitrov was explicitly granted the right to deliver a final address.

On 31 October 1933, one of the least reliable witnesses of all, the glazier Gustav Lebermann, was put on the stand.

When Dimitrov tried to discover why this witness had been fetched out of prison at such short notice, Dr Bünger told him that Lebermann had only come forward on 13 October. Dimitrov insisted on being told who had called Lebermann as a witness.

Dr Bünger: 'The Public Prosecutor. But I must order you straight away not to enter into completely pointless arguments. After all, you cannot stop the Public Prosecutor or the Court from hearing any witnesses or any kind of material evidence.'

Dimitrov: 'I merely wished to point out that the chain of witnesses is now closed. After giving us National Socialist deputies and journalists, the Public Prosecutor now gives us criminals and thieves.'

When Dimitrov ignored Dr Werner's objection, and started again on the 'chain of witnesses', the irate Dr Bünger snapped at him:

'Dimitrov, I have told you on more than one occasion that though you may put questions to witnesses, you cannot address the Court on all sorts of subjects. There is a time and a place for doing that. You may ask questions now, but nothing else. Do you wish to put any questions? To the witness, mind, and not to the Public Prosecutor!'

Dimitrov: 'I should like to put a question to the witness of Dr Parrisius' [Dimitrov obstinately refused to address the Assistant Public Prosecutor by his full title].

President: 'No! Anyway, what question do you want to put to the witness?'

Dimitrov: 'I should like to ask the following question, Herr President . . .'

President: 'You have no questions, then?'

Dimitrov: 'I have the following question . . .'

President: 'Then for goodness' sake ask your question.'

Dimitrov: 'He made a statement on October 13th, that much is clear, after he had read the newspaper reports on the Reichstag fire trial. He has said that much here. He was in prison, he was not at large. He was given the third degree. He had hopes of being discharged on the basis of the lies he has told. I ask who influenced him to utter these shameless and disgraceful . . .'

Dr Bünger: 'Keep quiet! I will not have you insult witnesses.'

Even so, Dr Bünger, to whom Lebermann's character was no more of a mystery than it was to anyone else in Court, turned to the witness with: 'Has anyone at all influenced you?' Naturally Lebermann replied: 'No one at all!' and Dr Bünger was able to tell Dimitrov: 'Your question has been answered.' But Dimitrov had the last word: 'May I congratulate you on this witness, *Herr Reichsanwalt?*' he asked Dr Parrisius. And this time he used the full title.

This skirmish was to have grave outside repercussions on Dr Bünger. On 1 November 1933 the *Völkischer Beobachter* objected that neither the President nor the Public Prosecutor saw fit to rebuke Dimitrov for his malicious remark that the chain of National Socialist witnesses was now closed. The paper concluded with a massive threat:

> We National Socialists hope that even Dr Bünger's Court will find some means of preventing such unseemly and insulting attacks by a Communist criminal on National Socialist witnesses.

One can understand why Dr Bünger got cold feet immediately, and why, the very next day, he emphasized that, had he fully understood Dimitrov's unseemly remarks, he would most certainly have intervened at the time. He added that the accused would in future be kept under even stricter control, whereupon Dimitrov quipped back:

'The *Völkischer Beobachter* has every reason to be satisfied now.'

And with this he cut Bünger to the quick. Once again he ordered the police to take Dimitrov out of the courtroom, and once again Dimitrov cried:

'Monstrous! And this is supposed to be a fair trial!'

In the general uproar, the rest of his unflattering remarks were lost.

On 3 November, Dimitrov was back again, as aggressive as ever. A number of witnesses from the Soviet Union were testifying that they had met Popov and Tanev in Russia. One of the witnesses was a Frau Weiss, whom the Public Prosecutor treated with great suspicion, suggesting, *inter alia*, that Weiss was not her real name.

Dimitrov, who had obviously been spoiled by success, intervened to remark that, in the Soviet Union, anyone could choose any name he liked. He added: 'I am extremely surprised to see how ignorant the Public Prosecutor is of Soviet law.'

Dr Werner whispered something into the ear of Dr Bünger, who immediately rebuked Dimitrov for his impertinence. Dr Bünger then apologized to Dr Werner, saying that he had not understood what Dimitrov had been saying.

Dimitrov, for his part, objected to Dr Werner's whispers and exclaimed: 'You still have a lot to learn, Herr Oberreichsanwalt!'

Once again the Court filed out, and once again it decreed that Dimitrov, the incorrigible, be excluded from the trial – this time for two days.

This last expulsion was particularly annoying to Dimitrov, since next day a very special witness – Hermann Göring – was to appear in Court. For most observers of the trial, it had been a great sensation when, on 17 October 1933, Dr Werner had asked for leave to call the Storm Troop leaders and Police Chiefs Helldorff and Heines, together with Ministerpräsident Göring and Reichsminister Dr Goebbels. The reason for this unusual step was that

> . . . the *Brown Book* had made the monstrous allegation – without trying to produce a shred of evidence – that Minister Goebbels was the indirect, and the Prussian Ministerpräsident Göring the direct, instigator of the plan [to burn the Reichstag]. Once such impudent and unsubstantiated slanders were put abroad, the victims must be given the opportunity of clearing their names.[18]

Now, any other Court would, of course, have dismissed Dr Werner's request out of hand, since what the Court had to establish was not the guilt or innocence of Göring or Goebbels, but that of the five accused. Moreover, by acceding to this request, the Court helped not only to introduce the noisy atmosphere of the hustings into the hushed solemnity of the courtroom, but also to drag out the trial quite unnecessarily. As if to revenge this outrage on her dignity, Justice dealt the Nazi ministers, who had hoped to use the courtroom as a forum for cleansing their sullied names, a resounding blow. As her tool she chose a man whose courage more than stood up to the bullying of even his mightiest enemies.

THE FIFTH EXPULSION

Next day, on 4 November 1933, to everybody's surprise, a nonchalant Dimitrov took his place in the Court from which he had only just been banished for two days. Since it seemed unlikely that Dr Bünger had reversed his own decision by himself, the general feeling was that he had been given a 'hint' from above. Obviously Göring did not wish to give the impression that he had deliberately avoided a meeting with the wily Bulgarian.

A Swiss correspondent has described the dramatic climax of the trial as follows:

> Whole swarms of policemen, armed with carbines, surrounded the Reichstag building [where the Court was meeting at this stage], checking every visitor with unusual vigilance.
>
> The improvised courtroom was completely packed long before the judges arrived. People kept craning their necks to catch a glimpse of such well-known personalities as the American Ambassador, Minister

1. The Burning Reichstag.

2. The Nazi Leaders at the scene of the fire. Hitler talking to Prince August Wilhelm, Göring (second from left) and Goebbels (second from right).

3. The Burnt-out Sessions Chamber.

4. Marinus van der Lubbe
before the fire.

5. Dimitrov, Popov and Tanev

6. Van der Lubbe giving evidence.

7. Göring giving evidence.

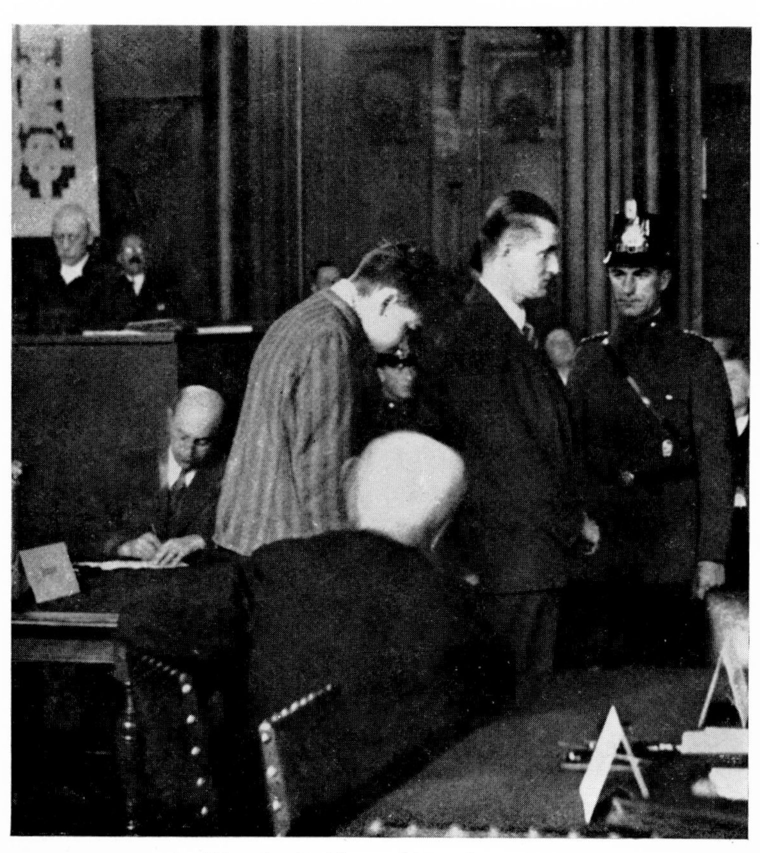

8. Van der Lubbe and Torgler in court.

of Trade Schmidt, the two Prussian Ministers, Russ and Kerrl, Minister of Justice Frank, and Under-Secretary Koerner. The tension was tremendous.

And the tension mounted the longer Göring kept his expectant audience waiting. At 10.30 a.m. – over an hour late, and thereby expressing his contempt for the highest German court—

> . . . Göring entered the room in the brown uniform, leather belt and top boots of an S.A. leader. Everyone jumped up as if electrified, and all Germans, including the judges, raised their arms to give the Hitler salute.

When all the arms had dropped again, the President addressed the following harangue to Göring:

> 'Herr Prime Minister, in naming you and Herr Reichsminister Dr Goebbels as witnesses whom he desired to summon before the Court, the Public Prosecutor stated that you could not be deprived of the right to express yourselves under oath concerning accusations and slanders which have been directed against your Excellencies from certain quarters, particularly in the so-called *Brown Book*, regarding the subject matter of this trial. The Supreme Court desires to express its concurrence in this statement.'[19]

Bünger's view of Göring's role did not suit the latter in the least. In a completely 'unministerial' tone, he explained his own views of the matter:

> 'Herr President, you have just said that I was summoned as a witness in order to clear my name of accusations and slanders made by the *Brown Book*. I should like to emphasize that I consider my evidence important in two quite other respects . . .'

And the President of a German Supreme Court meekly allowed a witness not only to instruct him in court procedure, but also to launch an election address lasting for over three hours. After every jibe at his enemies, Göring's fans roared out their approval while the President who, at the beginning of the trial had expressly forbidden 'all expressions of approval, of disapproval, or even of astonishment', sat by without a murmur.

The great clash between Göring and Dimitrov began with Dimitrov's rising from his seat '. . . with as much unconcern as if he were about to cross-examine an insignificant grocer or publican from Neukölln and not the Prussian Prime Minister'.[20]

As Dimitrov faced Göring, it became apparent that neither would give way. At the time, the Bulgarian was a hounded alien and in the hands of his political opponents; twelve years later the tables were turned – as Göring's political star reached its nadir, Dimitrov's rose towards its zenith: by the time Göring had to answer for his war crimes to the victors' tribunal at Nuremberg, Dimitrov had become premier of Bulgaria. Though no one could have predicted these developments in 1933, Dimitrov behaved all along as if there were not the least doubt about the final outcome.

Dimitrov started by trying to rattle Göring with a host of minor questions. Then, quite suddenly, he brought out his big guns:

> Dimitrov: 'On February 28th, the morning papers published a statement or an interview by Ministerpräsident Göring on the Reichstag fire. This report alleged – I remember its general sense very clearly – that the fire had been started by the Communist Party, that Torgler was one of the culprits, and that the arrested "Dutch Communist" van der Lubbe carried his passport and a membership card of the Communist Party on his person. I should like to know how Ministerpräsident Göring could have known at the time that van der Lubbe had a Communist Party membership card on him?'
>
> Göring: 'I must admit that, so far, I have not bothered unduly about this trial, that is, I haven't read all the reports. I did gather, however, that you are an exceptionally bright fellow and hence I should have expected even you to know the correct answer to this question, which was given long ago. I have already testified that I don't rush round pulling things out of people's pockets. In case you don't know, I have a police force to do that sort of thing and – in case you don't know that either – the police search every criminal and – in case you don't know even that – they report their findings to me. The whole thing is really quite simple.'
>
> Dimitrov: 'Herr Ministerpräsident . . . ' (President: 'Dimitrov!') 'If I may speak quite freely . . .'
>
> President: 'First listen to what I have to say. I should like to draw your attention to the fact that this question has been fully answered.' (Dimitrov: 'If I may speak quite freely . . .') 'The question has been answered I tell you. If you want to ask a further question then please do so, but in such a way as to make its purport quite clear from the start.'
>
> Dimitrov: 'Yes, quite clear. I should like to put it to the Herr Ministerpräsident that the three police officers who arrested and searched van der Lubbe all agreed that no Communist Party member-

ship card was found on him. I should like to know where the report that such a card was found came from.'

Göring: 'I can tell you that very easily.' (Dimitrov: 'Please do!') 'I was told by an officer. Things which were reported to me on the night of the fire, particularly those which cropped up in the course of explanations by officials, could not all be tested and proved. The report was made to me by a responsible official and was accepted as a fact. As it could not be immediately tested, it was announced as a fact. When I issued the first report to the press on the morning after the fire, the interrogation of van der Lubbe was not concluded. In any case, I do not see that anyone has anything to complain of, because it seems to have been proved in the trial that van der Lubbe had no such card on him.'

Dimitrov: 'As Prussian Ministerpräsident and Minister of the Interior, did you order an immediate police investigation?'

President: 'I could not understand a word of what you were saying, so please repeat the last sentence.'

Dimitrov: 'I was saying, did Herr Göring, as Prussian Ministerpräsident, as Minister of the Interior and as Speaker of the Reichstag, give immediate orders for the apprehension of van der Lubbe's accomplices?' (Göring: 'Yes, of course.') 'After all, he is the one – and he has said so himself – who bears the full responsibility for his department and for his police. Is that not so?' (Göring: 'Quite so!') 'I would like to ask the Minister of the Interior what steps he took on February 28th and 29th or on the following days to make sure that van der Lubbe's route to Henningsdorf, and his stay and meetings with other people there, were investigated by the police in order to assist them in tracking down van der Lubbe's accomplices?'

President: 'Your question is quite long enough!'

Dimitrov: 'Quite clear enough!'

Göring: 'I have already acknowledged my responsibility. You didn't even have to ask your question. If you had only paid attention, you would have heard me say that, as a Minister, I don't have to track criminals like a detective, and that I leave it to the police to make detailed investigations. . . . I merely gave orders to carry out the investigation with the utmost speed and with the utmost care. Of course, I, too, was fully aware that van der Lubbe must have had accomplices' (Dimitrov: 'Quite true!') 'and I ordered their speedy arrest.'

Dimitrov: 'When you, as Prussian Ministerpräsident and Minister of the Interior, let it be known in Germany and abroad that the Communists burned the Reichstag' (Göring: 'Exactly!') 'that the Communist Party' (Göring: 'Quite so!') 'was responsible, that the

Communist Party of Germany conspired with van der Lubbe and other alleged foreign Communists, did you not, in fact, influence the police and judicial investigations in a particular direction, thus preventing the apprehension of the real incendiaries?'

Göring: 'I know what you are getting at, but there is really no problem at all. The police were from the start given orders to pursue their investigations in every possible direction, no matter where these investigations led them. But as I am not a detective myself but a responsible Minister, it was not important that I should trouble myself with trifling details. It was my business to point out the Party and the mentality which were responsible for the crime. All I had to determine was: is this a civil offence, or is it a political offence? Now it was clearly a political offence and at the same time it became clear to me, and it remains just as clear today, that your Party were the criminals.'

President (to Dimitrov): 'Regarding your reference to influencing the judges . . . you did refer to that, didn't you? To influencing the judges?'

Dimitrov: 'No. What I said, Herr President, was that the police inquiry and later the preliminary examination could have been influenced by these political directives, and mainly in one direction. That is why I am asking my question.'

Göring: 'Herr Dimitrov, that, too, is admitted. If the police were allowed to be influenced in a particular direction, then, in any case, they were only influenced in the proper direction.'

Dimitrov: 'That is your opinion. My opinion is quite different.'

Göring: 'But mine is the one that counts.'

Dimitrov: 'I am only the accused, of course.'

President: 'You may only ask questions.'

Dimitrov: 'I am doing that, Herr President. Does Herr Ministerpräsident Göring realize that those who possess this alleged criminal mentality are today controlling the destinies of a sixth part of the world, namely the Soviet Union?' (Göring: 'Unfortunately.') 'The Soviet Union has diplomatic, political and economic contacts with Germany. Her orders provide work for hundreds of thousands of German workers. Does the Minister know that?'

Göring: 'Yes, I do.' (Dimitrov: 'Good!') 'I also know that the Russians pay with bills and I should prefer to know their bills are met. In that case Russia's orders would really provide work for our workers. But that is not the point here. I don't care what happens in Russia. Here, I am only concerned with the Communist Party of Germany and with the foreign Communist crooks who come here to set the Reichstag on fire.'

(Loud 'bravos' from the public.)

Dimitrov: 'Yes of course, bravo, bravo, bravo! They have the right to fight against the Communist Party, but the Communist Party of Germany has the right to go underground and to fight against your Government; and how we fight back is a matter of our respective forces and not a matter of law.'

President: 'Dimitrov, I will not have you making Communist propaganda here.' (Dimitrov: 'But he is making National Socialist propaganda!') 'I most emphatically order you to desist. I will not have Communist propaganda in this courtroom!'

Dimitrov: 'Herr President, arising out of my last question, there is just one further question that needs explaining in any case: the question of party and philosophy. Herr Ministerpräsident Göring has stated that he is not concerned with what happens in the Soviet Union, but only with the criminal mentality of the Communist Party. Is the Minister aware that this criminal mentality rules the Soviet Union, the greatest and best land in the world?'

Göring: 'Look here, I will tell you what the German people know. They know that you are behaving in a disgraceful fashion. They know that you are a Communist crook who came to Germany to set the Reichstag on fire, and who now behave yourself with sheer impudence in the face of the German people. I did not come here to be accused by you.' (Dimitrov: 'You are a witness.') 'In my eyes you are nothing but a scoundrel, a crook who belongs to the gallows.' (Dimitrov: 'Very well, I'm most satisfied. . . .')

President: 'I have repeatedly warned you not to make Communist propaganda . . .' (Dimitrov tries to speak on.) 'If you continue in this vein I shall have you put outside. I have told you not to make Communist propaganda, and you cannot wonder that the witness gets angry when you continue to do so. I order you most emphatically to desist from doing so. If you have any questions, then let them be purely factual and nothing more.'

Dimitrov: 'I am highly satisfied with Herr Göring's explanation . . .'

President: 'Whether or not you are satisfied is a matter of complete indifference to me.' (Dimitrov: 'Most satisfied. I am merely asking questions.') 'After your last comment, I must ask you to sit down.' (Dimitrov: 'I'm asking questions.') 'I am asking you to sit down. Do so!'

Dimitrov: 'I am asking a purely factual question.'

President: 'I have asked you to sit down.'

Dimitrov: 'You are greatly afraid of my questions, are you not, Herr Minister?'

Göring: 'You will be afraid when I catch you. You wait till I get you out of the power of this Court, you crook!'

President: 'Dimitrov is expelled for three days. Out with him!' (Dimitrov is hustled out.)

A Swiss comment was:

The public applauded enthusiastically. They did not appreciate the full significance of what had just been happening: the whole trial had been turned into a farce. For the world had been told that, no matter whether the accused was sentenced or acquitted by the Court, his fate had already been sealed.[21]

GOEBBELS

Dimitrov's meeting with Goebbels promised to produce another highlight of the trial. It took place four days later, on 8 November.

Unlike Göring, Goebbels arrived in Court very punctually, and declared his willingness to answer all questions. After a preliminary skirmish, Dimitrov dropped his bombshell: he asked whether or not Goebbels had made a broadcast in which he had blamed the Reichstag fire not only on the Communists but also on the Social Democrats. Dimitrov's purpose in asking this question was quite plain: if Goebbels now admitted he had been wrong about the Social Democrats, might he not have been equally wrong about the Communists? The following dialogue then ensued:

Goebbels: 'I shall gladly answer this question. I have the impression that Dimitrov is using this Court as a platform for making propaganda for the Communist or the Social Democratic Party. Now I know what propaganda means, and he is quite wrong to think that he can trip me up with such questions. If we accuse the Communists, we do not forget their close relationship with the Social Democrats...'

Dimitrov: 'In the autumn of 1932, under the Papen and Schleicher government, a series of bomb attacks took place in Germany. As a result, there were trials and a number of death sentences were passed on National Socialists. I should like to know if these terrorist acts in 1932 were not committed by National Socialists?'

Goebbels: 'It is possible that *agents provocateurs* might have been planted in the National Socialist Party to commit such acts. The National Socialist Party has always used legal means; that is why it preferred running the risk of an internal crisis to coming to terms with its violent Stennes wing.' [This part of the evidence was not published by the German press.]

Dimitrov: 'Is the witness aware that National Socialists, who were condemned to death for the murder of an opponent, were released and demonstratively greeted by Chancellor Hitler?'

Goebbels: 'I know that Dimitrov is referring to the Potempa case [where five Nazis were sentenced to death for killing a man in his bedroom]. The National Socialists involved felt they were right to do away with a Polish insurgent who had betrayed Germany under the guise of being a Communist official. They were condemned for this. The Führer felt he could not desert these men, who thought they acted in the interest of the Fatherland, on the foot of the scaffold, and sent them telegraphic greetings.'

Dimitrov: 'Does the witness realize that many political murders were committed in Germany? That the Communist leaders Karl Liebknecht and Rosa Luxemburg were murdered . . .'

President: 'Silence! We are trying to find out who set the Reichstag on fire. We can't possible delve back so far into the past.'

Goebbels: 'We might as well talk about Adam and Eve. When these murders you complain of were committed, our movement had not even been born.'

Dimitrov: 'Were not the assassins of German statesmen like Erzberger and Rathenau the associates of the National Socialist Party. . . ?'

President: 'I cannot allow this question unless the Minister wishes to answer it specifically.'

Goebbels: 'I do not wish to evade this question. The murders of Erzberger and Rathenau were not committed by associates of the National Socialist Party. At the time, our movement was still very small and restricted to Munich. I am a National Socialist, and I am ready to answer for everything the National Socialist movement has done and omitted to do. At the time, Hitler was in the military hospital in Pasewalk, suffering from war-blindness. I cannot tell who the culprits were. Some fled abroad, some were shot by the Prussian police or committed suicide. Most of these people are no longer alive, and I am not particularly interested in them.'

Dr Werner: 'I consider it extremely courteous of the Minister to answer this question, but I submit that it would be far better not to allow such questions to be answered at all, for they are only asked for propaganda purposes.'

Goebbels: 'I am merely answering Dimitrov's questions in order that the world press shall not be able to say that, in the face of his questions, I remained downcast and silent. I have given reason and answer to greater men than this little Communist agitator.'

Dimitrov: 'All these questions arise out of the political case against me. My accusers allege that the Reichstag fire was meant to overthrow the German constitution. I now ask what sort of constitution was in force on January 30th and which on February 27th?'

Goebbels: 'The Weimar Constitution – for better or for worse. It was legal and we recognized it as such. What changes in it had to be made we did not wish to leave to the Communists but reserved for ourselves. I consider that constitutional changes are necessary.'

Dimitrov: 'That is clear proof that you have no respect for the German Constitution.'

President: 'Leave the Constitution alone!'

Dimitrov: 'Are you aware, Herr Minister, that your spiritual brothers, the National Socialists in Austria and Czechoslovakia, have also to work with illegal methods, with false addresses and false signatures?'

Goebbels: 'It seems to me that you are trying to insult the National Socialist movement. I will answer you with Schopenhauer: Every man deserves to be looked at but not to be spoken to.'

There followed a brief duel between Goebbels and Torgler, who reminded the Court that strikes and not violence had always been the chosen weapons of the German working class. He himself had always tried to keep the political struggle to one of intellectual weapons.

Then Dr Goebbels turned, ostensibly to the Court, but in reality to the world press, and revealed the true reason for his and Göring's performances in Court:

> 'Herr President, I have been at the greatest pains to contradict the accusations which are made against the German Government and the National Socialists with minute scrupulosity. That is the reason why I have gone to such lengths in describing all the circumstances surrounding the crime, and all the known facts. On behalf of the German Government I express regret that the lying accusations made in the *Brown Book* are still being circulated abroad and that the foreign press has done nothing to remedy this state of affairs. I expect the foreign press to be decent enough to report the facts I have given, and to cease publishing vile slanders about a decent, diligent and honourable people.'

Goebbels's attempt to administer an antidote to the *Brown Book* misfired altogether, not least thanks to Dimitrov's refusal to put the 'right' kind of questions. *Le Temps*, for instance, wrote on 10 November 1933:

> In his evidence yesterday, in the trial against the alleged incendiaries of the Reichstag, Dr Goebbels seems to have addressed himself to the foreign press. He requested that his statements should be fully reported. The Minister of Propaganda is deceiving himself if he imagines that he has contributed anything new to the content of the trial.[22]

And the *Brown Book* concluded gleefully:

> For the most part, the foreign press was not satisfied with Goebbels's 'real' account of the facts. His appearance before the Court was received with as little favour as his colleague's had been. In his foreword to Dr Sack's book on the trial (*Reichstagsbrandprozess*, p. 12) Professor Grimm openly expresses regrets that despite Goebbels's appeal the results in the foreign press were and remain unfavourable. He particularly pointed to the treatment of Göring's evidence by the foreign press and complained that instead of being accepted as contradicting the accusations of the *Brown Book* it was largely taken as confirming them![23]

Clearly Dr Goebbels, too, had lost his battle against Münzenberg and Dimitrov.

When it became clear that neither Göring's heavy broadsword nor Goebbels's nimble foil had succeeded in subduing the irrepressible Dimitrov, the atmosphere in the courtroom changed perceptibly. Foreign observers like Douglas Reed suggested that the Court felt it could obviously not be expected to succeed where such great men as Göring and Goebbels had so signally failed. The lawyers, and particularly Dr Sack who had continually asked Dimitrov to refrain from making remarks behind his back, were suddenly on smiling terms with him: 'Dr Bünger at times became almost paternal in his altercations with Dimitrov; Dimitrov was occasionally seen roaring with laughter at some joke he shared with his police custodians.'[24]

This relaxation of the courtroom atmosphere was greatly helped by Dimitrov's correct manner. Thus, on 25 November 1933, he had the following brief exchange with Dr Bünger:

> President: 'Dimitrov, a foreign newspaper has said that it is you who are really conducting this trial. I must gainsay this, but you will see that your manner makes this impression on public opinion. You must submit yourself to my authority and I desire that in future you restrict yourself to asking questions.'
>
> Dimitrov: 'As defendant, I recognize only one superior, and that is

the President of the Court. But I beg my superior to give me the possibility of defending myself and elucidating the truth.'

He had the last word once again.

DIMITROV'S 'SATANIC CIRCLE'

Just as famous as Dimitrov's description of van der Lubbe as the 'Faust of the Reichstag fire' who danced to the tune of an unknown Mephistopheles (an unmistakable allusion to Dr Goebbels with his club foot) was his reference to a 'satanic circle of prosecution witnesses'.

The whole thing was based on a ring Dimitrov had drawn to illustrate the roles played in the Reichstag fire by:

1. Berthold Karwahne
2. Kurt Frey
3. Dr Ernst Dröscher
4. Major Hans Weberstedt.

Berthold Karwahne, who was born in Silesia on 3 October 1877, and whom nature had underendowed with scruples and over-endowed with a love of brutality, threw himself into politics at an early age. At first, he joined the Social Democrats, but at the end of World War I he moved further and further to the Left, ending up with the Communist Party in 1920. In 1927, he made a complete volte-face and went over to the National Socialists, who always received reinforcements from that quarter with open arms.

That same year Karwahne was appointed an alderman; shortly afterwards he was elected a Member of the Diet, and in 1930 a Member of Parliament. The Reichstag Handbook wisely refrained from mentioning anything other than his date and place of birth – clearly a full *curriculum vitae* would have proved extremely embarrassing to himself and to his political friends.

Over the years Karwahne managed to climb higher and higher up the Nazi ladder. In 1933, he was made Head of the State Chemical Syndicate in which capacity he persecuted his political opponents with such atrocity that his name still makes his former colleagues wince today.

After the collapse of the Third Reich, which had helped Karwahne to amass a small fortune, a well-known Hanover lawyer said of him: 'He is the most despicable and infamous man I have ever met – and I have met many despicable characters in my job! He is a bully lacking any sense of fairness, decency or morality.'

Others have called him a 'petty but sadistic man' and 'a spineless, brutal fellow'. To Torgler's Counsel, Dr Sack, Karwahne must have been anathema, not only because of his political past but also because of his bearing in Court. Thus while Dr Sack never disguised his personal respect for the Communist Ernst Torgler, no one in Court was left in any doubt about the contempt in which he held his fellow National Socialist Karwahne.

On one occasion, Dr Sack asked Karwahne why, on allegedly seeing van der Lubbe in the company of Torgler, he had immediately said to himself: 'That is one of the typical criminals Torgler always has round him.'

Karwahne, taken unawares, denied the whole thing, and Dr Bünger intervened at once to say that he, too, could not remember having heard the witness say anything of the sort. When the record proved Dr Sack right and the President wrong, Karwahne conceded quite nonchalantly: 'If it's in the record and if the stenographers have put it down like that, then I might easily have said it. No doubt it's slipped out of my mind.'

In the verdict, the evidence of Karwahne (and of his two companions) was described as being of little value, 'the more so because they might have been involuntarily influenced by the [police] remark: "That one [van der Lubbe] is the incendiary", and because they were already convinced the man they had seen in the Reichstag must be the culprit.' Moreover, whereas they had described van der Lubbe's features (which they had had every opportunity of studying at police headquarters) in exact detail, they were unable to say anything at all about the most unusual clothes van der Lubbe had worn – no wonder, for when they saw him in the police station he was wearing a rug over his shoulders! And yet, Karwahne and his companions were no more to blame than the police, who had quite unlawfully allowed them to take a good look at the criminal and then to 'identify' him later.

It was this very police misdemeanour which probably saved Torgler's life, for Karwahne would have been quite capable of 'identifying' van der Lubbe as Torgler's companion without ever having seen him anywhere. In that case, however, Dr Sack might not have been able to call Karwahne's bluff.

. . . . .

The Austrian Nazi, Stefan Kroyer, fared no better in Court than his friend Berthold Karwahne. The Court had this to say of his alleged identification of van der Lubbe:

> Kroyer was and remains under the spell of his original statement, for he himself admits that any retraction of his statement to the police is hardly possible inasmuch as – for better or for worse – he wrote an article about it three days after his return to Austria.

All that can be said in favour of this witness is that he was a simpleton, one whom Dimitrov found particularly good bait:

> Dimitrov: 'The witness lives in Austria. We all know that the National Socialist Party is illegal in Austria, and that the members live and work illegally.'
>
> President: 'These remarks are uncalled for.'
>
> Dimitrov: 'Does the witness know that National Socialists are living in Austria using false names and failing to report to the police?'
>
> President: 'I cannot allow this question.'
>
> Dimitrov: 'Does the witness know that National Socialist refugees live in Germany with false passports?'
>
> President: 'I cannot allow this question.'
>
> Dimitrov: 'Do not Austrian National Socialists print newspapers and leaflets abroad and send them to Austria?'
>
> President: 'What has all that to do with the Reichstag fire?'
>
> Dimitrov: 'In the indictment, Herr Parrisius has accused me, a Bulgarian Communist, of living in Germany illegally on a false passport and working illegally for the Bulgarian Communist Party.'

When Kroyer objected that there is a great difference between a Bulgarian meddling in German affairs and an Austrian working in the Fatherland, Dimitrov retorted:

> 'Of course, there is a difference between my Communism and your National Socialism. It is the difference between heaven and hell.'

. . . . .

The Nazi Deputy, Kurt Frey, from Munich, came off slightly better in the verdict.

Frey, too, had alleged that, when showing Kroyer over the Reichstag, he had noticed Torgler in the company of a badly dressed individual with a 'curly shock of hair and a coarse, common face'.[25] But when Frey was first confronted with van der Lubbe, he was unable to maintain his original identification, and he was accordingly commended on his honesty in the verdict.

Now, though Frey corrected one error, he persisted in a second, viz. that he had seen Popov and Torgler huddled together on a sofa outside the Communist Party rooms in the Reichstag.

In the verdict, the Court agreed with Torgler that he had shared the sofa not with Popov but with the Communist Deputy, Dr Neubauer, who, from a distance, could easily be mistaken for Popov. Frey's evidence in that respect lacked 'inner probability'. Unfortunately, the Court forgot this question of probability when, in the absence of any tangible evidence, it nevertheless insisted that van der Lubbe must have had accomplices.

The testimony of the National Socialist Press Officer, Major Hans Weberstedt, proved to be a most unseemly mixture of sheer fantasy and parade-ground swagger.

It was he who had 'immediately identified' two men waiting outside Judge Vogt's chambers – van der Lubbe and Tanev – as the two men he had seen together on the day of the fire. This fable was seized upon by Vogt, who at once issued a press communiqué to the effect that van der Lubbe's 'association with foreign Communists was an established fact'.

When the major repeated this fable in Court, Tanev protested that Weberstedt was either mistaken or telling an untruth, whereupon Weberstedt roared at him in his most solemn parade-ground voice: 'I wish to declare that a German officer neither lies nor makes mistakes.'

Tanev then pointed to the many contradictions in the major's evidence, and stressed the fact that, since he (Tanev) did not speak a word of German, let alone Dutch, he could not possibly have carried on a conversation with van der Lubbe.

When Tanev sat down, Dimitrov put the following question to the major:

> 'Did you discuss these things with Dr Dröscher?'
>
> Weberstedt: 'Of course.'
>
> Dimitrov: 'Very well, then. Weberstedt and Dröscher talked the thing over. Weberstedt saw Tanev, Dröscher saw Dimitrov. At the risk of being expelled from the Court again, I should like to ask the following question. I am my own defender. Did these two witnesses divide the parts between them? Is that how German officers behave?'

Though Dimitrov was strongly rebuked by the President, the verdict nevertheless dispelled the myth that a German officer does not lie or err, for it stated that Weberstedt probably fell victim to an unwitting act of self-deception when he identified Tanev after he had had a good look at him first. 'His belief that Tanev was the right man was not spontaneous, but the result of long reflection. . . . Weberstedt probably confused Tanev with the witness Bernstein, especially as he claimed to have seen Tanev in the Reichstag frequently when, in fact, Tanev had only entered Germany on 24 February.'

Torgler was able to refute another of the major's allegations, namely that Communists – including a striking number of foreigners – were always congregating in the Communist Party rooms in the Reichstag. As Torgler explained, any such meetings could only have taken place with the express permission of the Speaker. That was particularly true of one meeting which Weberstedt had considered 'most suspicious'. In fact,

> Göring, the Speaker of the Reichstag, gave us permission to hold this meeting; Göring, the Minister of the Interior, later prohibited the meeting by special decree. I then lodged a complaint against Göring the Minister of the Interior with Göring the Speaker of the Reichstag.

The verdict also dismissed the evidence of the journalist, Dr Ernst Dröscher, the man who had first spread the rumour that Georgi Dimitrov had been responsible for the bombing of Sofia cathedral – a rumour which Judge Vogt had handed on to the press without bothering to check its accuracy.

Dröscher had also alleged that he had seen Torgler in the company of a man whom he had 'recognized' as the Sofia assassin from a photograph, adding: 'The man had so typical and expressive a face that I could not possibly have mistaken him.'[26]

Now, as we saw, the photograph was not of Georgi Dimitrov, who had had to flee Bulgaria after the abortive uprising of 1923, but of the lawyer Stefan Dimitrov Todorov, who wore a beard while Georgi Dimitrov was clean-shaven.

With such witnesses the Public Prosecutor and the National Socialists were quite unable to make an impression on the Court, let alone on world opinion. The zeal with which, according to the Court, these witnesses tried to 'contribute to the elucidation of the truth' was rightly considered by most observers to be zeal in quite a different direction.

THE 'RED' SATANIC CIRCLE

On 27 February 1934 – the anniversary of the Reichstag fire – Dimitrov held a press conference in Moscow. In it he said:

> . . . in prison and in Court we were heartened by the knowledge that the great German Communist Party continued to stand firm. Loyalty and devotion to their Party could be read on the faces of the working-class witnesses who had been dragged into the Court from the concentration camps . . .

In a subsequent interview, Dimitrov paid similar compliments to the 'indomitable' Communist witnesses, and the *Brown Book*, too, eulogized their heroic stand in Court.

All these praises were meant to hide the awkward truth – the 'bankruptcy of Communist solidarity' as the *Neue Zürcher Zeitung* called it on 23 October 1933.

True, there were quite a few witnesses from the concentration camps who, to the utter dismay of the Presiding Judge, insisted on speaking the truth now that their oppressors were no longer standing over them. Bünger blustered and interrupted them at every conceivable opportunity, for they proved a source of extreme embarrassment to the Court.

But it was, in any case, not by prisoners dragged from concentration camps against their will, but by ex-Communist volunteers that the moral bankruptcy of the Communist Party was laid bare. These men formed a circle no less repulsive than Dimitrov's circle of Nazi witnesses.

In October 1933, the glazier Gustav Lebermann from Hamburg, who was serving a prison sentence for theft and fraud, told the Court that he had been a secret Communist courier before resigning from the Party.

He went on to tell a hair-raising story made up of odd pieces of information which he had obviously gleaned from reading reports of the trial. Thus he alleged that he had met Torgler in Hamburg on 25 October 1931, and again in January 1932, when Torgler had told him to keep himself in readiness for a 'big job'. Torgler would meet him in Berlin on 6 March and take him to the Reichstag where Lebermann would receive detailed instructions. All Lebermann was told at the time was that he would be expected to rush about the Reichstag like a lunatic in order to focus attention on himself, to allow himself to be caught, and to 'admit' that he was a National Socialist incendiary. Meanwhile the two real incendiaries – 'Arthur' and 'Black Willy' – would quickly make their getaway.

When Lebermann refused to have anything to do with so 'mean' a trick, Torgler promised him a reward of 14,000 marks. In July 1932, Torgler visited Lebermann again, and when Lebermann persisted in his refusal, Torgler punched him in the abdomen. He had suffered from abdominal haemorrhages ever since.

While in prison in Lübeck, Lebermann tried to smuggle a letter to his wife. In it he told her he was pretending to be mad in order to be released. He also referred to his chronic stomach disorder. Clearly Torgler's 'punch' had had nothing to do with his haemorrhages.

Lebermann's evidence was so preposterous that even Torgler could not help smiling at it. He told the Court:

> All I can say regarding this evidence is how astonished I am that anyone should utter such lies before the highest Court of the land. I have never seen this man in my life. I have never been in Hamburg for any length of time, and when I did go to Hamburg it was merely to attend meetings of the Union of Post Office Workers, of the Union of Municipal Officials and to address public meetings. Not a single word the witness has spoken is true. Everything he says is a lie, from start to finish.

The impression Lebermann made on the Court was so bad that the President expressed his reluctance to put him under oath.

Even the journalist Adolf Stein, who was highly prejudiced against Torgler, was forced to admit that

> ... the witness Lebermann really does not look as if he would allow himself to be ill-treated by so slightly built a man as Torgler. Moreover, Lebermann, good anarchist that he is, only remembered the whole business on October 13th, 1933, after he had been reading reports of the Reichstag trial in prison.

Yet so catastrophic was the lack of honest witnesses for the prosecution that the Public Prosecutor could not afford to dispense with even the most disreputable of them. He therefore argued rather lamely:

> 'Admittedly this witness has many previous convictions, and he is

certainly not what the Prosecution could have wished him to be. But that is no reason for doubting his credibility . . . Lebermann's testimony belongs to that category of statements of which I have said that, though they point strongly to Torgler's guilt, they are not in my opinion sufficient by themselves to establish that guilt conclusively.'[27]

Acquitting Torgler, the Court itself found that

. . . no credence whatsoever can be given to the evidence of the witness Lebermann . . . whom the Hamburg County Court has previously described as being of weak character and a morally inferior person . . .

And that was the man whose credibility the Public Prosecutor saw no reason for doubting!

Popov had insisted all along that he had only come to Germany on 3 November 1932. It was to refute this claim that the Public Prosecutor 'found' the locksmith Oscar Kämpfer in a concentration camp. Kämpfer, too, was an old convict whose previous convictions added up to six and a half years' hard labour and one and a half years' preventive detention. He admitted that he had been a member of the Communist Party and a Berlin district leader of the 'Red Aid' organization.

Kämpfer alleged that he had put up Popov at his home, albeit under a false name, from May to July and again in November 1932, both times on Communist Party instructions. One day someone brought Popov a case of bottles, and on one occasion Popov poured a glass of brown fluid down the kitchen sink. The sink smelt of benzol for hours afterwards. Another foreigner, whom Kämpfer identified as Tanev, had also called on Popov.

These allegations brought Popov, who had remained composed throughout the trial, to his feet:

'Even my patience can be exhausted. I have proved with official documents and with witnesses from Russia that I could not have been in Germany at that time. The witness Kämpfer, who has four previous convictions, is trying to buy his release from the concentration camp. His whole testimony is one barefaced lie.'[28]

The Public Prosecutor, however, thought otherwise:

'Kämpfer used to be a well-known member of the Communist Party. A number of witnesses have testified that, whenever the Communists made trouble in his district, he was one of the ringleaders – not that he often went out in front, for he generally preferred to egg others on from the rear. But he is certainly not one to level false accusations against a fellow Communist. In short, there can be no doubt that Popov came to Germany in 1932 and that he tried to conceal his stay.'[29]

The Court produced a still less flattering picture of Kämpfer:

Kämpfer, who has many previous convictions and who is a very untrustworthy witness, has identified the foreigner who allegedly stayed with him from May onwards as Popov. Now the fact that he also alleged that Tanev asked him for Popov, makes his entire testimony suspect. Tanev did not even have a smattering of German. Kämpfer's fantastic story about a brown fluid . . . merely suggests that he must have read newspaper reports of Dr. Schatz's evidence . . .

To the same category of witnesses as Lebermann and Kämpfer there also belonged the bricklayer, Otto Grothe, a former leader of the Red ex-Servicemen's Union, and since 1921 a member of the Communist Party. He was also Agitprop leader of the 'Red Aid' in the Wedding district of Berlin.

Grothe, who remained a Communist Party member until May 1933, became one of the prosecution's star witnesses, so much so that the indictment devoted no less than eleven pages to his preliminary examination. The crux of his testimony was that, during a meeting on 23 February 1933, a fellow Communist by the name of Kempner had told him that Torgler was planning to burn the Reichstag, with the help of foreigners. Grothe further alleged that Torgler, Thälmann, Popov and other Communists had met on 27 February for a dress rehearsal. This secret meeting had taken place on 'a small bench in the Tiergarten'.

Though Grothe kept changing the names of those who had allegedly attended this secret meeting, Judge Vogt saw no reason at all to distrust him. As a result, Grothe was allowed to take the stand in the Supreme Court, and much time and effort was wasted on what turned out to be a 'psychopathic case, subject to hysteria and psychological disturbances'.[30]

Judge Vogt's credulity is the more surprising in that Grothe had alleged that the meeting at which he was told about Torgler's plans took place in the Karl Liebknecht House on 23 February, a day on which, as Judge Vogt must have known perfectly well, the

Karl Liebknecht House had already been closed by the police.

Characteristically, Grothe had made his first 'confidential reports' to the police while he was still a self-confessed member of the Communist Party.

The Communists, of course, could not swallow the fact that one of their own number should have behaved so despicably, and they accordingly disowned Grothe by claiming he had joined the 'Red Aid' organization as a police spy 'before Hitler came to power'. And indeed he had joined the Communists before that time, – in 1921, to be precise.

When two days of the Supreme Court's deliberations had been wasted on Grothe, Dr Sack's junior, Horst Pelckmann, caused a sensation by charging Grothe with perjury. The Public Prosecutor tried to avert disaster, and argued that Grothe, far from committing perjury, had merely been guilty of an understandable confusion of dates. Even so, the President could not simply ignore Pelckmann's request, and agreed to look into Grothe's evidence.

So weak was the Public Prosecutor's case that he put forward the following, absolutely ridiculous, argument:

> Grothe's testimony has now been checked, above all against that of Kempner from whom Grothe claimed he had received his information. Now, Kempner's outright denial of Grothe's story does not really convince me. Kempner, who is in prison on suspicion of having played a part in the events which form the substance of this trial, has very good reason to deny these allegations; they might easily incriminate Kempner himself.

The Court once again dealt a severe blow to the Public Prosecutor when it dismissed Grothe's testimony as utterly unreliable. In particular, Grothe's story of the meeting in the Tiergarten was called improbable in the highest degree.

In short, Grothe had utterly discredited the Examining Magistrate, the Public Prosecutor, and the Communist Party to which he had belonged.

The miner, Otto Kunzack, another important prosecution witness, had a record of sentences for crimes of violence and sexual offences. At the time of the trial he was in Naumburg Penitentiary.

Kunzack testified that he had been a member of the Communist

Party until March 1932. From 1921 to 1927 he was a secret Communist courier, in which capacity he had attended a secret conference in Düsseldorf in 1925. The conference was presided over by the well-known Communist Heinz Neumann, and attended by no less a person than van der Lubbe. He could remember the latter's name so clearly because it reminded him of the town of Lübben. The young Dutchman had taken part in the discussion and had been so violent that Kunzack had gained the impression he was quite capable of committing any kind of outrage.

Van der Lubbe had further declared his willingness '... to go out in front bearing the banner of the revolutionary proletariat'.[31]

Later, Kunzack was forced to admit that van der Lubbe had not delivered his 'fiery speech' in German, as he had originally alleged, but in Dutch. A Swiss reporter mused: 'How fortunate for Kunzack that the Court decided not to put him on oath. For this witness tells the most brazen lies in the most incredibly transparent manner.'[32]

Kunzack stuck to his story even when he was told that, had van der Lubbe really been present at the conference, he would only have been sixteen years old at the time.

When Kunzack, who had boasted that he had been a secret courier, *inter alia* to Heinz Neumann, was asked by Associate-Judge Coenders to identify a photograph, Kunzack looked at it for a long time, and then shook his head. He had fallen into a trap, for the photograph was of Heinz Neumann.[33]

Kunzack's honesty as well as the gullibility of the Examining Magistrate are best appreciated from the fact that Kunzack wrote to Judge Vogt from prison on 24 May 1933, offering to root out the Communist terrorists with the help of their 'female associates', and adding: 'And once I have proved myself, the rest of my sentence will be remitted. And moreover I ask that what time I lose during my interrogation be made good.'[34]

Kunzack's further fantasies included the claims that he had met Torgler in the latter's 'office in the Karl Liebknecht House', when Torgler had no office in that building, and that Torgler and the Deputy Wilhelm Kasper had attended dynamite tests outside Berlin. Torgler's retort that he had never even met Kunzack was dismissed by the Public Prosecutor with: 'Though the accused Torgler denies his part in the events described by the witness Kunzack ... the Court must accept the latter's testimony.'[35]

Once again, the Court was forced to take a different view – it described the witness Kunzack as a completely untrustworthy person who had tried to gain financial and other advantages from his testimony.

Tanev, too, was falsely accused by two ex-Communists: the merchant Bruno Bannert and the blacksmith Adolf Kratzert.

Bannert alleged that in 1927 and 1928 he had met Tanev every month or so in the 'Red Aid' offices where he (Bannert) had worked as Agitprop leader for the Brandenburg region; and Kratzert alleged he had met Tanev in the Karl Liebknecht House.

All these ex-Communist witnesses proved to be completely consistent in one respect: they all refused to withdraw any part of their baseless denunciations. The collapse of Communist solidarity would therefore have been quite devastating, had Dimitrov and Torgler not helped so much to redress the balance.

FALSE FRIENDS AND BABBLERS

On 28 October, the Supreme Court heard the evidence of the journalist Walther Oehme. It was Oehme who had been mainly responsible for convincing Judge Vogt that Ernst Torgler was a liar, for whereas Torgler had explained that Oehme had called on him in the Reichstag shortly after 3 p.m., and that it was Oehme with whom Karwahne, Kroyer and Frey must have seen him, Oehme insisted that he had not met Torgler before 4 p.m. at the earliest.

Since Torgler had no reasons for believing that Oehme was lying, he desperately searched his memory for another visitor in whose company the three Nazis might have seen him, and suggested that it could have been Communist Deputies Florin or Dr Neubauer. The Public Prosecutor then accused him of trying to change horses in midstream.

In the end, however, Oehme was forced to admit the real truth: he had, in fact, been with Torgler at the time Torgler had originally stated. The incensed Public Prosecutor, who felt Torgler slipping from between his fingers, vented his disappointment in Court: 'Oehme's alleged reason for withdrawing his previous testimony is that he lied in order to protect his own valuable person and therefore betrayed Torgler, whom he is proud to call his friend.'[36]

This might have been the right moment for the Public Prosecutor to ask himself whether the 'liar' Torgler might not have been speaking the truth all along.

When Torgler's counsel, Dr Sack, addressed the Court on the Oehme incident, he said:

> I refrain from telling the Court what I think of the witness Oehme, a man who has said he considers it an honour to be called a friend of the accused, Torgler . . . I could sympathize with Torgler if he lost faith in mankind now, if he completely despaired of humanity. But perhaps the accused Torgler must bear his cross, perhaps he will have to drain his cup of bitterness to the last drop.[37]

When Dr Sack spoke these words, he was also thinking of another of Torgler's 'friends' – the Communist deputy Erich Birkenhauer – who, for much the same reasons as Oehme, had lied about Torgler during the preliminary examination, thus enabling the Public Prosecutor to say:

> At the preliminary examination, Birkenhauer testified that he had tried to get in touch with the accused Torgler on the day of the fire and that – as the accused Torgler admits himself – he managed to reach him over the telephone at about 4 p.m. It was arranged that Birkenhauer would ring later in the evening. According to Birkenhauer: 'When I rang again at about 7 p.m., I was told by a woman that Torgler was not available for the moment . . .' Now, it seems most unlikely that a Party secretary should say her chief is not available, had he been next door, in the antechamber, or anywhere near by. In my opinion, it follows that the accused Torgler was not anywhere near the telephone, that the witness Rehme had no idea where he was, or that she did know but did not care to tell. I therefore conclude that Torgler was away from his Party offices at about 7 p.m., i.e. at just about the time that the preparations for setting the Reichstag Session Chamber on fire would have been made.[38]

Torgler kept insisting that Birkenhauer's story about the second telephone call could not possibly be true. However, Birkenhauer had meanwhile fled Germany, and Torgler's counsel could not challenge his testimony in Court. As a result, Judge Vogt became even more convinced that Torgler was a brazen liar.

The Communists tried to cover up Birkenhauer's betrayal by alleging that the Public Prosecutor had deliberately falsified his testimony. Birkenhauer testified before the London Commission that, far from telling him that Torgler was not available, the woman had merely informed him that Torgler was not yet ready to fix the time for a meeting and had asked him to ring again at 8 p.m.

In that case, however, Birkenhauer must have told yet another lie, for the record shows that he declared before Judge Vogt on 17 May that:

> I remember that I rang the Reichstag once before, an hour or so earlier, say at about 7 p.m. . . . The telephone was answered by a woman. . . . She told me – as far as I can remember – that Herr Torgler was at a conference or at a meeting. I then told her that I would ring again . . .[39]

Birkenhauer's story that he had rung Torgler, not at 4 p.m., as Torgler alleged he had, but at 7 p.m., was denied outright by Fräulein Anna Rehme, Torgler's secretary. The Court found:

> Finally no proof has been adduced that Fräulein Rehme told Deputy Birkenhauer at 7 p.m. that Torgler was at a meeting. In fact, there is no evidence that any call was made at that time. Birkenhauer has fled the country and did not testify before the Supreme Court; his deposition at the preliminary examination is not considered admissible evidence. The witness Rehme does not remember the call, but does remember that Torgler was expecting Birkenhauer's call and that she would certainly have called Torgler to the telephone.

In fact, Birkenhauer made his second call shortly after 8 p.m. Since the telephone exchange had closed down by then, Torgler had to run down to Portal Five where he arranged a meeting with Birkenhauer at Aschinger's. Obviously, Birkenhauer, too, had tried to clear himself of suspicion at the expense of his 'friend'.

The newspaper report that Torgler was suspected of complicity in the fire produced a spate of 'witnesses' who felt they had some helpful contribution to make. Among them were Frau Helene Pretzsch and her stepson Kurt Moeller, both of whom suddenly remembered that they had seen Torgler carrying two large brief-cases on the morning of the fire.

Both witnesses testified that Torgler looked as if he were carrying an exceptionally heavy load. They also noticed that Torgler had a 'shifty' look. Next day, when Frau Pretzsch learned about the Reichstag fire, she immediately said to her stepson: 'Now I know what Torgler was doing with those heavy brief-cases last night!'[40]

Torgler explained that, far from carrying incendiary material, he had filled his brief-cases with large quantities of newspapers, which he had intended reading over the week-end. One of these brief-cases was, in fact, found in his Reichstag rooms, but when it was first shown to the witnesses, they insisted that it was not one that Torgler had been carrying on 27 February. At the trial Moeller was allowed to inspect the ominous brief-case and admitted: 'Well, now that I have seen the brief-case packed with newspapers and have felt its weight, I must admit that there was nothing extra-ordinary in the way Torgler carried it.'[41]

What strikes us as odd today is that such 'classical witnesses', as Dr Sack called them, or such 'slight evidence', as the verdict had it, should have been admitted in the first place.

The palm, however, went to the daytime porter Wilhelm Hornemann, whose evidence earned him a roar of laughter from the public. Hornemann tried to throw suspicion on Torgler by alleging that he had noticed Herr Koenen, Torgler's subsequent companion, 'sneaking' into the Reichstag on the day of the fire at about 6.30 p.m., with his coat-collar turned up and with his glance averted to the left.

The whole thing was, of course, utterly absurd. What well-known deputy of long standing would have thought of sneaking into the Reichstag past the porter, when he knew that the porter had instructions to challenge all strangers?

Nor did Hornemann leave it at that, for he also alleged that on the same afternoon he had seen three men leaving the Reichstag, one of whom – later 'identified' by Hornemann as Dimitrov – had said in broken German: 'The Reichstag is going up in the air in fifteen to twenty minutes.'

Quite obviously Hornemann had not been told of Dimitrov's unshakeable alibi. No wonder that Dimitrov's face was wreathed in smiles through most of Hornemann's evidence.

But who knows what would have happened to Dimitrov had he not, by pure chance, been away from Berlin on 26 and 27 February, had he not returned in a sleeper, whose attendant Otto Wudtke remembered him clearly, and had he not started a mild flirtation with Frau Irmgard Rössler, who was returning from a ski-ing holiday, and to whom Dimitrov had introduced himself as Dr Hediger?

. . . . .

Another to take pride of place among the 'show-offs and confirmed liars', as Dr Sack called them, was the drunkard Leon Organistka. Organistka went to the police with the 'important' news that he and a friend, Oskar Müller by name, had met van der Lubbe and another Dutchman on 15 October 1932, in the vicinity of Constance. They had talked, Organistka alleged, of many things, and he particularly remembered van der Lubbe saying: 'There will soon be no more Reichstag in Germany,' and: 'If we Communists don't soon have a turn there's going to be fire and brimstone in Germany.' He greatly impressed the public by turning to van der Lubbe during their confrontation with: 'Come on, van der Lubbe, old mate, surely you haven't forgotten me?'

His friend Müller confirmed Organistka's testimony and basked in the latter's glory – until an official report from Leyden established that van der Lubbe had spent the entire October of 1932 in Holland and that he had regularly fetched his weekly allowance at the Leyden Post Office in person. The same report also invalidated the testimony of Helmer who claimed he had frequently seen van der Lubbe and the two Bulgarians in the Bayernhof.

As moths are attracted to the light, so the witnesses for the prosecution were attracted by the dazzle of publicity, and by the glitter of silver. And, like moths, most of them got singed in the process.

During the appearance of this weird procession of witnesses, there was much hearty laughter in Court. This laughter must not, however, let one forget the frightful reality: all these fawning and servile men were falling over one another in their eagerness to send innocent men to their death. Sober workmen, good mothers, chauffeurs, waiters, locksmiths and housewives, babblers and fools, no less than professional criminals, were doing their utmost to make their fantasies, lies, or delusions stick at any cost.

DIMITROV'S FINAL SPEECH

On 16 December 1933, one week before judgement was given, Dimitrov was granted the right to address the Court on his own behalf.

At last the moment had come for which Dimitrov had worked throughout the long months of his imprisonment, and though Dr

Bünger interrupted him from time to time, Dimitrov proved more than a match for him. After one such interruption, Dimitrov said:

'I admit that my tone is hard and sharp. But my life has been hard and sharp. However, my tone is frank and open. I seek to call things by their correct names. I am not a lawyer appearing before this Court defending just another client....

'I can say with an easy conscience that everything which I have said to this Court is the truth. I have refused to testify on my illegal party. I have always spoken with seriousness and from my deep convictions. . . .'

President: 'I shall not permit you to indulge in Communist propaganda in this Court. You have persisted in it. If you do not refrain, I shall have to prevent you from speaking.'

Dimitrov: 'I must deny absolutely the suggestion that I have pursued propagandist aims. It may be that my defence before this Court has had a certain propagandist effect. . . . If the question of propaganda is to be raised, then I may fairly say that many utterances made in this Court were of a propagandist character. The appearance here of Goebbels and Göring had an indirect propagandist effect favourable to Communism, but no one can hold them responsible because their conduct produced such results (laughter in Court). I have not only been roundly abused by the press – something to which I am completely indifferent – but my people have also, through me, been characterized as savage and barbarous. I have been called a suspicious character from the Balkans and a wild Bulgarian. I cannot allow such things to pass in silence. . . . Only Fascism in Bulgaria is savage and barbarous. But I ask you, Mr President, in what country does not Fascism bear these qualities?'

President: 'Are you attempting to refer to the situation in Germany?'

Dimitrov: 'Of course not, Mr President. At a period of history when the "German" Emperor Karl V vowed that he would talk German only to his horse, at a time when the nobility and intellectual circles of Germany wrote only Latin and were ashamed of their mother tongue, Saint Cyril and Saint Methodius invented and spread the use of old Bulgarian script in my "barbarous" country.... During the preliminary inquiries I spoke with officials, members of the investigating authority, concerning the Reichstag fire. Those officials assured me that we Bulgarians were not to be charged with complicity in that crime. We were to be charged solely in connection with our false passports, our adopted names, and our incorrect addresses.'

President: 'This is new matter. It has not been mentioned in the proceedings hitherto and you have no right to raise it at this stage.'

Dimitrov: 'Mr President, during that time every circumstance could have been investigated in order to clear us promptly of any charge in relation to the fire. The indictment declares . . .' (Dimitrov began to quote from the indictment at some length.)

President: 'You must not read the whole of the indictment here. In any case, the Court is quite familiar with it.'

Dimitrov: 'As far as that goes, I must state that three-quarters of what the counsel for the prosecution and defence have said here was generally notorious long ago. But that fact did not prevent them from bringing it forward again (laughter in Court). Helmer stated that Dimitrov and van der Lubbe were together in the Bayernhof restaurant. Now permit me again to refer to the indictment, which says: "Although Dimitrov was not caught red-handed on the scene of the crime, he nevertheless took part in the preparations for the burning of the Reichstag. He went to Munich in order to supply himself with an alibi. . . ." That is the basis of this precipitate, this aborted indictment.'

[Here the President intervened again and warned Dimitrov not to refer disrespectfully to the indictment.]

Dimitrov: 'Very well, Mr President, I shall choose other expressions.'

President: 'In any case you must not use such disrespectful terms.'

Dimitrov: 'Göring declared before the Court that the German Communist Party was compelled to incite the masses and to undertake some violent adventure when Hitler came to power. . . . He stated that the Communist Party had for years been appealing to the masses against the National Socialist Party and that when the latter attained power the Communists had no alternative but to do something immediately or not at all. The Public Prosecutor attempted more clearly and ingeniously to formulate this hypothesis.'

President: 'I cannot permit you to insult the Supreme Court.'

Dimitrov: 'The statement which Göring as chief prosecutor made, was developed by the Public Prosecutor in this Court . . .'

And now Dimitrov really set to work. In particular, he developed the view that the Communist Party could confidently look forward to the speedy collapse of the Hitler Government, and that the glorious example of the Russian revolution was an example to be followed by all mankind.

'. . . What is the Communist International? Permit me to quote from its programme:

'"The Communist International, an international association of workers, is the association of the Communist Parties of individual lands; it is a united world Communist Party..."

'. . . A copy of the appeal of the Executive Committee of the Communist International was found in my possession, I take it that I may read from it.'

Dimitrov then read the appeal, and stressed that it made no mention of any immediate struggle for power. He went on to argue:

'The point is simply this: was an armed insurrection aimed at the seizure of power actually planned to take place on February 27th, 1933, in connection with the Reichstag fire?

'What, Your Honours, have been the results of the legal investigation? The legend that the Reichstag fire was a Communist act has been completely shattered. Unlike some counsel here, I shall not quote much of the evidence. To any person of normal intelligence at least this point is now made completely clear, that the Reichstag fire had nothing whatever to do with any activity of the German Communist Party, not only nothing to do with an insurrection, but nothing to do with a strike, a demonstration, or anything of that nature. The Reichstag fire was not regarded by anybody – I exclude criminals and the mentally deranged – as the signal for insurrection. No one observed any deed, act, or attempt at insurrection in connection with the Reichstag fire. The very stories of such things expressly appertain to a much later date . . . But it was shown that the Reichstag fire furnished the occasion and the signal for unleashing the most terrific campaign of suppression against the German working class.'

When Dr Bünger interrupted: 'Not the German working class but the Communist Party,' Dimitrov quickly retorted that Social Democratic and Christian Democratic workmen had been arrested as well, and went on to say:

'The law which was necessary for the proclamation of the state of emergency was directed against all the other political parties and groups. It stands in direct organic connection with the Reichstag fire.'

President: 'If you attack the German Government, I shall deprive you of the right to address the Court.'

Dimitrov: '. . . One question has not been in the least elucidated either by the prosecution or the defending counsel. This omission does not surprise me. For it is a question which must have given them some anxiety. I refer to the question of the political situation in Germany in February, 1933 – a matter which I must perforce deal with now. The political situation towards the end of February, 1933, was such that a bitter struggle was taking place within the camp of the "National Front".'

President: 'You are again raising matters which I have repeatedly forbidden you to mention.'

Dimitrov: 'I should like to remind the Court of my application that Schleicher, Brüning, von Papen, Hugenberg and Duesterburg should be summoned as witnesses.'

President: 'The Court rejected the application and you have no right to refer to it again.'

Dimitrov: 'I know that, and more, I know why!'

President: 'It is unpleasant for me continually to have to interrupt your closing speech, but you must respect my directions. . . . You have always implied that your sole interest was the Bulgarian political situation. Your present remarks, however, show that you were also keenly interested in the political situation in Germany.'

Dimitrov: 'Mr President, you are making an accusation against me. I can only make this reply: that as a Bulgarian revolutionary I am interested in the revolutionary movement all over the world. I am, for instance, interested in the political situation in South America, and although I have never been there, I know as much about it as I do of German politics. That does not mean that when a Government building in South America is burned down, I am the culprit.'

He then proffered his own theory of the part played by van der Lubbe, which was merely a copy of the Nazi theory, but with the 'link' shifted from Neukölln to Henningsdorf and with a change of principals:

'Is it not probable that van der Lubbe met someone in Henningsdorf on February 26th and told him of his attempts to set fire to the Town Hall and the Palace? Whereupon the person in question replied that things such as those were mere child's play, that the burning down of the Reichstag during the elections would be something real? Is that not probably the manner in which, through an alliance between political provocation and political insanity, the Reichstag fire was conceived? While the representative of political insanity sits today in the dock, the representative of political provocation has disappeared. Whilst this tool, van der Lubbe, was carrying out his clumsy attempts at arson in the corridors and cloakrooms, were not other unknown persons preparing the conflagration in the Session Chamber and making use of the secret inflammable liquid of which Dr Schatz has spoken?

'The unknown accomplices made all the preparations for the conflagration and then disappeared without a trace. Now this stupid fool, this miserable Faust, is here in the dock, but Mephistopheles has disappeared. The link between van der Lubbe and the representatives of political provocation, the enemies of the working class, was forged in Henningsdorf.'

Dimitrov went on to complain that no attempt whatever had been made to trace the man with whom van der Lubbe passed the night in Henningsdorf. He further complained that the identity of the civilian who first reported the fire to the Brandenburg Gate police station had never been revealed:

'The incendiaries were sought where they were not to be found. . . . As the real incendiaries could not and must not be found, other persons were taken in their stead.'

President: 'I forbid you to make such statements and I give you another ten minutes only.'

Dimitrov: 'I have the right to lay my own reasoned proposals for the verdict of the Court. The Public Prosecutor stated that all the evidence given by Communists was not worthy of credence. I shall not adopt the contrary view. Thus I shall not declare that all the evidence given by National Socialist witnesses is unreliable. I shall not say they are all liars, for I believe that amongst the millions of National Socialists there are some honest people.'

President: 'I forbid you to make such ill-intentioned remarks.'

Ordered by the President to conclude, Dimitrov finally proposed the following verdict:

'1. That Torgler, Popov, Tanev and myself be pronounced innocent and that the indictment be quashed as ill-founded;

'2. That van der Lubbe be declared to be the misused tool of the enemies of the working classes;

'3. That those responsible for the false charges against us be made criminally liable for them;

'4. That we be compensated for the losses which we have sustained through this trial, for our wasted time, our damaged health, and for the sufferings which we have undergone.

'. . . The elucidation of the Reichstag fire, and the identification of the real incendiaries is a task which will fall to the People's Court of the future proletarian dictatorship . . .'

Since Dimitrov gave no sign that he had any intention of concluding – the notes which he published subsequently indicate that he would have gone on for a very long time – the President, whose patience was completely exhausted, adjourned the Court, and Dimitrov had to be removed by force.

When the Court returned, Popov and Tanev delivered lengthy addresses which had to be translated sentence by sentence. Then it was Torgler's turn, whose final speech was as brief as it was to the point. Before he rose at 9 p.m. to adjourn the Court for a week, Dr Bünger had this to say:

'When I opened the proceedings nearly three months ago, I said that it was the custom, not only of the German press, but of newspapers the world over, not to prejudge the issues which this Court has been called upon to decide....

'Unfortunately my remarks have not been fully heeded. The foreign press has not been alone in attempting to anticipate these proceedings in a manner which does no credit to its noble calling. I can only repeat, once again, that the clash of opinions cannot influence this Court.'

When Dr Bünger admonished 'not only the foreign press' he was clearly alluding to a recent interview Göring had given to the *Berliner Nachtausgabe*. In it Göring had complained that the Supreme Court trial was a great disappointment to the German people. When it came to dealing with vile political criminals, it was simply not good enough to keep to the letter of the law. Göring had added that the authority of the state and the safety of Germany would be undermined if this lengthy trial were allowed to continue much longer.[42]

Göring's outburst presented the judges with a terrible dilemma. How could they possibly satisfy the irate new rulers of Germany, and yet let it appear that justice was not being flouted too flagrantly? After nine long months of collecting depositions and testimonies, could they now admit that they had been quite unable to form any kind of reasonable picture of the real course of events on that icy night of 27 February?

The result was a blatant compromise, so blatant, in fact, that only because no one at the time was interested in the plain truth, could it be put forward at all.

12. The Experts

TWO FIRE EXPERTS

ONCE the Court had made up its mind to disbelieve van der Lubbe, it was willy-nilly driven into the arms of the so-called 'fire-experts'.

When the Public Prosecutor began to bore his way through the mountain of papers which the Examining Magistrate had bequeathed to him, he discovered to his dismay that no two of Dr Vogt's experts had agreed on the origins or the development of the Reichstag fire. To make things worse, each of the experts had tried to reconcile his particular opinion with the incompatible statements of various prosecution witnesses.

When Professor Emil Josse, a lecturer on thermodynamics at the Berlin Technical College, produced his opinion in May, he became the first of a series of experts who hid their profound ignorance of the facts behind a barrage of words. What had 'struck him so particularly' was the 'explosive disintegration of the Session Chamber', from which he concluded:

> Had there been no explosion or rather had the Session Chamber not been filled with an explosive mixture of gases, the small fires could quickly have been extinguished by the fire brigade – just as they were in the restaurant – so that the damage would have remained relatively small.

One week later, Fire Director Wagner, Chief of the Berlin Fire Brigade, came out with quite a different view when he said:

> If we bear in mind the special conditions prevailing in the Chamber, we shall find that the development of the fire, as the witnesses have described it, fits in perfectly with our experience of the development of fires in general. During the three minutes under discussion, from 9.18 to 9.21 p.m. that is, there was still quite enough oxygen in the large chamber to allow for complete and smokeless combustion . . .

Professor Josse, who remained firmly convinced that the whole fire had been carefully planned, kept cudgelling his brain as to why the incendiaries should have bothered to set fire to the restaurant, thus 'giving the whole game away'. He concluded that there were two possibilities:

1. The restaurant was set on fire at random, which seems unlikely in view of there having been a complete plan, and which could only have happened had van der Lubbe started the fire by himself, or

2. The incendiaries hoped that, by starting the fire in the restaurant, they would obtain particularly quick results and wreak maximum havoc, so much so that they decided to run the risk of being discovered.

Professor Josse thought the key to this mystery was an 'extra' ventilator, However:

> 'If we postulate that, by starting the fire in the restaurant, the incendiaries hoped to take advantage of the fanning effects of the additional ventilator, then we must also postulate that an unforeseen circumstance led to a change in the plan since . . . the additional ventilator was apparently not working . . .'

Only Lewis Carroll could have thought up a more preposterous argument than that, or, for that matter, than the one with which Dr Josse came out on 23 October 1933: 'The main purpose of starting the fire outside the Session Chamber was to divert attention from the latter.'

This was too much even for the Public Prosecutor who pointed out that had the restaurant not been fired, the fire in the Session Chamber might not have been discovered until very much later.

Professor Josse was also the first to propound the theory that the incendiary material had been smuggled into the Reichstag long before the fire, and that it had been stored in the stenographers' well. That was also the view of Dr Schatz.

Imagine, then, the surprise of these two great experts and the disappointment of all those others who believed in their simple theories, when it appeared that the suspected well had been cleaned from top to bottom on the afternoon of the fire, that it had been personally inspected by Scranowitz, and that the liftman Fraedrich, who had wound up the clock there at 4 p.m. had seen nothing suspicious.[1]

After Professor Josse had finished giving his evidence, the President addressed the following remarks to van der Lubbe:

> 'Raise your head, van der Lubbe. Did you understand what has been said here? The expert, who is a learned professor, has told us that you

could not have fired the Reichstag all by yourself. Who helped you? Answer me that!'

But Marinus van der Lubbe had long ago decided not to enter into any further useless and senseless discussions. He kept silent.

Afraid that van der Lubbe might have had no Nazi accomplices after all, Dimitrov put the following question to Professor Josse:

'Is it at all possible that van der Lubbe could have laid the fire trail within a quarter of an hour, or that he himself could have started the fire in the Session Chamber?'

To Dimitrov's disappointment, Professor Josse replied without any hesitation:

'I have reflected on this question at length. For a time I believed that he could not have done so; but when, during the on-site inspection, I saw the speed with which Lubbe crashed through the windows and was told that he was in a lather of sweat when he was arrested, I came to the conclusion that he might have done it with adequate preparation.'[2]

When Dr Teichert, the Bulgarians' counsel, next asked Josse what van der Lubbe had done with the containers of the 50 lbs of liquid fuel with which, according to the Professor, he had started the fire (the debris had been searched immediately after the fire and no traces of any such containers had been found), Dr Josse was at a loss for an answer. Nor, as Professor Urbain of the Sorbonne rightly objected, could he tell on what scientific data he had based his estimate of 50 lbs. Professor Urbain also attacked Josse and particularly Dr Schatz for putting forward the view that

. . . the Session Chamber was set on fire by means of a liquid hydrocarbon. . . . Tables and chairs were covered with rags soaked in petrol or paraffin. . . . The rags were then sprinkled with a self-igniting fluid or joined to one another by means of fuses or celluloid strips, probably the latter.

As Professor Urbain pointed out, petrol and paraffin do not produce the kind of flames all the witnesses had described. Fire Director Wagner added the view that no volatile liquids could have been used, since otherwise all the rags would have flared up simultaneously. In that case, no separate bundles of flames would have been produced or observed. According to Wagner, experiments in the Reichstag had shown that a large number of separate fires could not have been started with reels of celluloid film, or with petrol and paraffin.

Dr Ritter, a Government technical officer, agreed with Wagner:

> It seems unlikely that mineral oils, for instance petrol, were used to start the fire. During the lengthy preparations a large part of the petrol would have evaporated, later to be precipitated as heavy vapour. Had the incendiary tried to run a fuse through that vapour, flames would quickly have spread over the entire incendiary system, possibly with explosive effects.

With commendable honesty Dr Ritter concluded:

> On the available evidence it is quite impossible to decide how the fire in the Session Chamber was started.

No wonder he was dropped out of the experts' and the Court's further deliberation.

On 23 October 1933, when Professor Josse, Dr Wagner and Dr Schatz were cross-examined in open Court, the public was astonished to learn how radically they differed on even the most elementary questions. As a Dutch newspaper put it at the time:

> This has been a very important day, for it has shown how shaky are the foundations which these experts have erected.
>
> Being poets and dreamers, they do not try to justify their respective theories with facts, but simply produce the theories and leave it to the Court and the prosecution to do the rest. They keep shooting arrows into the blue, and if mistakes occur – well, van der Lubbe must have made them, for compared with these gentlemen, he is a mere tyro when it comes to starting fires. They are all agreed that he could not have done it by himself. For the rest they beg to differ. But that is their privilege – they are the experts, after all.[3]

DR SCHATZ

Chemical discussions in Court paved the way for the appearance of that remarkable chemical expert, Dr Wilhelm Schatz, the man whose astonishing performance, mental acrobatics, and sleights of hand, left an indelible impression on all who watched him.

At the time, Dr Schatz was Head of the 'Private Institute for Scientific Criminology'. He was an extremely busy and versatile man: a court-expert on chemistry, fingerprints, type, a graphologist, a pharmacist, a food expert, a botanist, a toxicologist, and a scientific criminologist – in short, a Jack-of-all-trades. Another remarkable thing about him was that he usually wrote his opinions on the inside of used envelopes or on the backs of old letters, all of which he hid from his assistants and collaborators with a great show of secretiveness.

Despite – or perhaps because of – his great versatility, Dr Schatz did not enjoy a particularly good name in chemical and scientific circles. For one thing, his manner was most unprepossessing, for another he was generally considered to be a pompous and disputatious ass. The highly-respected chemist Dr Brüning called him a fantasy-monger, and the *Neue Zürcher Zeitung* a 'malicious expert'. Berlin chemical circles wondered why on earth the Court should have called in a dubious provincial chemist in the first place, and there were rumours that he was not a disinterested party. There certainly was no doubt that Judge Vogt had 'briefed' Dr Schatz carefully on van der Lubbe's so-called accomplices.

Now, by that time even Judge Vogt had come to appreciate that Torgler could not have been in the Reichstag at the time of the fire. However, he had apparently been out of his rooms between 7 and 8 p.m., during which time he might have been 'preparing' the fire, that is sprinkling petrol or some other inflammable fluid over curtains, carpets, chairs, etc.

Unfortunately, no one at all could be found who was willing or able to testify that Torgler had smelt of any of these pungent substances, nor was Professor Brüning able to detect any signs of such substances having been used. To help Judge Vogt out of the resulting impasse, Dr Schatz obligingly invented a mysterious igniting fluid, which Torgler might easily have sprinkled about between 7 and 8 p.m.

At the request of Dr Sack, Schatz, who had previously told the Court that he would not mention the name of that mysterious fluid lest other incendiaries came to hear of it, now described one of its properties: it smelt strongly of chloroform.

But, alas, no one had noticed Torgler smelling of chloroform either; hence Dr Schatz was forced to ask all sorts of silly questions. On 14 October, for example, he asked Chief Fire Director Gempp whether the liquid which Gempp alleged he had detected in the Bismarck Hall, had not smelt like rotten cabbage. Gempp, who had previously 'smelt' petrol, said he could not remember.

One day before, on 13 October, Dr Schatz had put the following question to Lieutenant Lateit: 'You have stated that you saw no smoke, but that you smelt smoke. Did you notice a peculiar smell or taste in your mouth or throat?'

When Lateit said no, Dr Schatz coaxed him with: 'Not at all?' Again the witness said no, but Dr Schatz refused to give up:

> Dr. Schatz: 'Do you know the smell given off by a smoky lamp – for instance by an old-fashioned oil lamp? Was the smell like that?'
>
> Lateit: 'No.'
>
> Dr. Schatz: 'You testified that your eyes were smarting.'
>
> Lateit: 'That was downstairs, when we came in through Portal Two, and were met by thick smoke. My men were completely blinded; our eyes were smarting and streaming so much that we had to cover our faces with handkerchiefs.'
>
> Dr. Schatz: 'Do you know the smell of the old kind of matches, you know the ones with phosphorus and sulphur? When you struck them, you got a strange prickling sensation in the nose and a taste resembling the one you get when you eat eggs with a silver spoon. Did you have that sensation?'
>
> Lateit: 'No.'

When Patrolman Losigkeit and House-Inspector Scranowitz corroborated Lateit's evidence, it became obvious that no one at all had smelt anything in support of Dr Schatz's theory. On the contrary, Dr Brüning's analysis had established that the trail which Gempp had described was not due to any inflammable or self-igniting fluid. Only one witness swore to the theory of the great expert Dr Schatz. That witness was the expert Dr Schatz himself.

But even he was left with the problem of why Torgler had not smelt of the miracle-fluid whose odour was supposed to stick to one for hours. He accordingly had a new inspiration and performed a secret experiment. The result was quite astounding:

> He explained that though he had rubbed his hands with the self-inflammatory fluid, two policemen and two Reichstag officials were quite unable to detect any smell even when he held his hands very close to their faces.[4]

Suddenly the strong and persistent smell was no longer; suddenly the smell of chloroform and rotten cabbage had evaporated, and – Torgler could remain a suspect.

Then Dr Schatz produced his second bombshell: van der Lubbe had never even set foot in the Session Chamber; the Chamber was fired by his accomplices. Asked by Dr Sack how these accomplices had managed to get in and out of the Reichstag, the great expert replied that he preferred to keep his own counsel on that subject since, after all, he was merely a scientific expert.

When Torgler thereupon implored Dr Schatz to forgo his scientific modesty for the sake of four innocent men, Dr Schatz could do no better than rehash an old theory: van der Lubbe's conspicuous behaviour in the restaurant could only have meant that he was trying to divert attention from his accomplices in the Chamber.

Douglas Reed has described the conclusion of Dr Schatz's testimony:

> 'If I have understood this interesting address aright,' said Dimitrov gravely, addressing himself to Dr. Schatz, 'a certain technical knowledge must be assumed on the part of persons employing this method of incendiarism?'
>
> 'The people who deal in these things know what they are about,' answered Dr. Schatz.
>
> 'And if they are not acquainted with the interior of the Reichstag?' asked Dimitrov.
>
> 'Some knowledge of the place is necessary,' Dr. Schatz replied.
>
> 'And when must this self-igniting liquid have been distributed?'
>
> 'At most an hour or two before the fire,' said Dr. Schatz.[5]

And Dr Schatz went on to say that van der Lubbe's accomplices had

> '... the kind of knowledge which is found only among employees of chemical concerns and laboratories, pharmacists or pharmaceutical assistants.'[6]

It seems incredible that Dr Schatz should have been allowed to develop his unsubstantiated theories without anyone seriously challenging him. Not only did these theories imply the utter incompetence of all the police officers who had checked van der Lubbe's movements, but they also ran counter to all the other evidence.

On 15 October 1933, for instance, the upholsterer Otto Borchardt had testified that a piece of material adhering to van der Lubbe's coat came from a curtain behind the stenographers' table.

But why should Dr Schatz have worried about such trifles when he was not only helping the German authorities, but was also attracting the attention of the rest of the world? For the international press, too, was humming with the name of Dr Schatz and his mysterious 'self-igniting liquid'.

On 23 October 1933, Dr Schatz demonstrated his liquid to the Court during a special session from which the public was excluded. And lo! the liquid did burst into flames, though not after an hour, as Dr Schatz had predicted in order to 'explain' Torgler's absence between 7 and 8 p.m., but after eight minutes. However, the mere fact that the mixture had burst into flames at all so impressed the Court that it took the rest on trust.

Only one voice protested – that of Georges Urbain, the irrepressible Professor of Chemistry at the Sorbonne:

> 'What are we to think of someone who postulates that the accused, none of whom are chemists or trained in laboratory techniques, should have succeeded in performing an experiment in the Session Chamber where they were pressed for time, and probably afraid of being caught, which he, the acknowledged chemical expert, could not perform successfully under far more favourable conditions?'

Luckily for Torgler, no amount of juggling with the facts helped Schatz to pin the blame on him, for Dr Sack had established Torgler's innocence beyond the shadow of a doubt. What Schatz did succeed in doing was to seal van der Lubbe's fate. For since van der Lubbe could not describe the mysterious ingredients for the secret fluid, it 'followed' that these were handed to him by his principals and that he was one of a highly organized gang of insurrectionists.

No other Court would have listened to an expert whose every statement was so blatantly refuted by the facts.* Moreover, if van der Lubbe had, in fact, had Communist accomplices who carried the liquid into the Reichstag, why did he refuse to do an essential part of his job, i.e. blame the fire on the Nazis? Was not van der Lubbe's obstinate insistence that he started all the fires by himself proof positive of his complete veracity?

As Dr Seuffert, Douglas Reed and Mr Justice de Jongh among others realized at the time, van der Lubbe failed to confess anything simply because he had nothing to confess. Moreover, had a self-igniting liquid been used, van der Lubbe would not have been

* Dr Schatz was also called to give evidence as a graphological 'expert'. He made no better an impression in that role.

needed at all – why divert attention from accomplices who had finished their work long before?

Douglas Reed expressed his complete bewilderment in the following words:

> Van der Lubbe's part, then, was, at the most, to touch off the fire; possibly not even that. What function remained for this enigmatic figure with the sunken head than that of a scapegoat, a dupe, a cat's-paw, a tool, a whipping boy for others? Why the spectacular entrance from outside, the crashing glass, the waving fire-brands, the crazy dash through the rooms beneath the restaurant, with their windows facing the Königsplatz? . . . How was van der Lubbe brought, or prompted, or induced to enter the Reichstag at the vital moment, and to remain there to be taken? Did he know who prompted him and why did he not say? As far as this, the fundamental issue, was concerned, the evidence brought no enlightenment whatever; the world was confirmed in its opinion that van der Lubbe was the tool of others, but was further than ever from the truth about them.[7]

WAS THE REICHSTAG FIRE REALLY MYSTERIOUS?

When Dimitrov, in the course of his final speech, said:

> Whilst this fool, van der Lubbe, was carrying out his clumsy attempts at arson in the corridors and cloakrooms, were not other unknown persons preparing the conflagration in the Session Chamber and making use of the secret inflammable liquid of which Dr Schatz here spoke?

van der Lubbe could no longer contain himself. He suddenly burst into laughter.

> He laughed almost soundlessly but with such lack of self-control that his whole body was shaking and he almost fell off the bench. Once again everybody gaped at him. His whole face was distorted into a grin.
>
> One wonders what sort of a man he really is, and if he will still be laughing up his sleeve when they lead him and his secret to the scaffold.[8]

In fact, Marinus van der Lubbe was not laughing up his sleeve at all; he was laughing because he could not help himself. He must have used a great deal of self-control during Dimitrov's wild speculations, starting with the unknown man in Hennigsdorf who allegedly asked van der Lubbe: 'Why such a small fire? I'll be able to put you on to something really big,' and ending with this ridiculous self-igniting liquid, and it was only a question of time before he would erupt into helpless laughter.

As early as 9 March 1933, Dr August Brüning, the highly respected director of the Prussian Institute for Food, Drugs and Forensic Chemistry, had corroborated van der Lubbe's testimony. At the request of the police, i.e. long before the whole business was turned into a political issue, Dr Brüning had gone to the scene of the crime, where he carried out a most careful examination and found '. . . no evidence that such substances as petrol, paraffin or methylated spirits had been used.'

The Professor had gone on to say that what traces of extraneous combustible substances he could discover, were all explicable in terms of firelighters or drippings from firemen's torches.

Having identified the mysterious 'incendiary substance' with van der Lubbe's humble firelighters, Dr Brüning – like Dr Ritter – was, of course, dropped by Judge Vogt.

Now these firelighters did, in fact, have a considerable power of destruction. Thus van der Lubbe used them to set the snow-covered roof of the Neukölln Welfare Office ablaze, to cause a fire in the Town Hall and another one on the roof of the Palace, where – as Dr Bünger confirmed – a massive window frame was set alight by half a packet of firelighters.

Moreover, the same lighters could easily have set fire to that crucial bit of evidence – the curtain in the western corridor whose alleged flame-resistance Dr Schatz had 'proved'. This proof, which was an essential link in the accomplice theory, shows better than anything else what manner of scientist the Director of the 'Private Institute for Scientific Criminology' really was. It took a quarter of a century – to be precise until 26 January 1957 – before the mystery of this curtain which was flame-resistant and yet burst into flames was solved: during a conversation Judge Vogt let it slip out that Dr Schatz had performed his experiments not with the actual curtains, but with remnants that had been stored away in heavy chests.

Now, if one could not expect Judge Vogt to know that fire-resistant treatment by impregnation wears off after years, let alone after decades, of use, one could certainly have expected this knowledge from a fire expert. In particular, Dr Schatz ought to have known that if pieces of curtain, which had been kept in practically air-tight chests where their original impregnation was preserved, did not burn, that did not mean the actual curtains would behave in the same way. For Dr Schatz ought to have been familiar with the decree passed by the Berlin Police President on 5 June 1928, stipulating that the impregnations of all theatre curtains must be checked yearly and, if necessary, renewed. The reason for this decree was quite simple: experience had shown that such materials as velvet, velour, baize, or plush, in particular, gradually lose their fire-resistance through the unavoidable accumulation of dust, constant changes of temperature and humidity, and finally through natural deterioration. Now, the Reichstag curtains, as the Director of the Reichstag, Geheimrat Galle, told the chemist Dr Lepsius on the day after the fire, had been hanging undisturbed for decades. No wonder, therefore, that they caught fire so quickly and so easily.

On 4 October 1933, Dr Sack – a lone voice in the wilderness – objected that the expert opinions '. . . are faulted because the experiments were not carried out under the original conditions.'[9]

Needless to say, this objection was overruled.

We shake our heads when we read to what lengths Fire Director Wagner went in his vain attempts to set fire to massive chairs and desks with firelighters, petrol and filmstrips, while forgetting that only a full reconstruction of the original conditions could produce conclusive results. We know that van der Lubbe did not start the fire in the Chamber by burning an odd chair or an odd desk; what he did was to set fire to the curtains over the tribune, whence the fire leapt across to the tapestries and panelling behind. As a result, so much heat was generated that the glass ceiling cracked in a number of places, and a tremendous updraught was created. Moreover, the wooden walls needed no special preparation to catch fire, for, as Chief Fire Director Walter Gempp stated on the morning after the fire: 'The desiccated old panelling offered the fire excellent food, and that is the reason why the fire spread so quickly in the Session Chamber.'[10]

But it was not only the relative fire-resistance of the chairs in the Session Chamber which confused Professor Josse and Dr Schatz; what misled them even more was the difference between the development of the fire in the restaurant and the one in the Chamber. From the fact that the former was easily extinguished, and the latter was not, they concluded that the two could not have been started in the same way.

This thesis seemed highly plausible to Dimitrov and the Public Prosecutor, both of whom were looking for accomplices, albeit of different shades of political opinion. And yet the main difference between the two fires was the difference in updraught, as anyone who knew anything about fires ought to have realized at once.

We need only recall the fire which destroyed the imposing Vienna Stock Exchange on Friday, 13 April 1956:

> The fire which, for unexplained reasons, started in the cellar shortly after midnight, spread like lightning over the rest of the building, despite desperate attempts by the fire brigade to confine it . . . The flames shot very high into the air and turned the night sky an uncanny red. Thousands had gathered to witness this horrifying but impressive spectacle.[11]

In *Brandschutz*, the official journal of the Vienna Fire Brigade, Engineer Priesnitz explained the catastrophic development of the fire as follows:

> The great hall with its inflammable contents [panelling and furniture] could be compared to a huge oven. Once a fire had started in it and was not extinguished immediately, the fire was bound to spread with such speed that every attempt to extinguish it was doomed to utter failure.

The Reichstag, too, blazed up quite suddenly – the moment the glass ceiling of the Chamber burst. This set up so tremendous an updraught that one of the firemen – Fire Officer Klotz – had to cling to the door for fear of being sucked in.

As early as 1 March 1933, Dr Goebbels gave his own impression of the fire:

> The great Session Chamber is about to cave in. With every bit of debris, an ocean of fire and sparks shoots 250 ft to the dome, which has turned into a chimney.[12]

Engineer Foth of the Berlin Fire Brigade also referred to the updraught phenomenon at the time:

> The glass of the 250 ft dome had burst in places so that the flames could shoot through the cracks. The result was a considerable updraught which . . . caused the air to be sucked through all the passages into the burning Chamber.[13]

Since no such updraught was created in the restaurant and in other parts of the Reichstag, it is not surprising that they escaped thc fate of the Chamber.

The ventilation expert, M. J. Reaney, has pointed out that it was one small spark that destroyed the General Motors factory in Lavonia, Michigan, a building that was almost exclusively constructed of fire-resisting materials. Reaney also explained that it was a spark from a neighbouring building which completely destroyed India House in London, a steel and concrete structure, in 1940. The reason was simple: India House contained enough paper, curtains, and furniture to superheat the air. Now superheated air surrounds the fire and dries out everything in its path. Even at small temperature differences, air may circulate with a speed of 1,000 ft per minute, but when air is superheated that speed is greatly increased. That is the reason why a tiny spark may cause even the largest fires – the concrete shell of a building does not, of course, burn, but will collapse under the pressure.[14]

Ever since Prometheus brought us fire, flames have been mankind's most faithful friends and bitterest enemies. With the rise of cities, fire damage has grown to gigantic proportions, yet the cause of most fires is usually a mere trifle – a stupid accident, a tiny omission, one spark, one cigarette end, and a forest, a skyscraper or an ocean liner is destroyed.

For example, a 1913 survey showed that of 1,200 theatre fires, thirty-seven per cent were caused by naked flames, twenty-one per cent by faulty lights, sixteen per cent by faulty heaters, twenty-three per cent by fireworks, firearms and similar explosive matter, and three per cent by arson. In no case were highly inflammable fluids involved, and in most cases, once the fire had started, the theatres were completely destroyed.

Or take another historical example:

> On October 16th, 1834, between six and seven o'clock in the evening, the sky over Westminster turned an exceptionally bright colour. Fire alarms echoed throughout the south-east of London, while thick red smoke poured out of the front windows of the House of Lords.
>
> Archivists had been burning old records when, quite suddenly, the Debating Chamber was on fire. Before help could come, the Lords' resplendent Hall with all its glorious furniture, was ablaze. Even the House of Commons was seized by the flames, which spread as far as Westminster Hall.[15]

Another historic fire, in the Tower of London, was discovered in much the same way as the Reichstag fire:

> On October 30th, 1841, at about 10.30 p.m., a passer-by noticed a strong glow in the Tower. He notified a policeman who fired a shot, as a result of which the whole garrison was alerted and 500 people came to the rescue. Pumps proved quite useless, partly because of the lack of water, and partly because the Tower was full of fabrics.[16]

In the case of Parliament, it was ordinary paper which had caused the conflagration, and no one so much as suggested that self-igniting liquids, petrol, paraffin, or, for that matter, pitch or resin had been used. Paper was quite enough to burn the fire-resisting furniture, and that was that. But then no one was trying to make political capital out of the London fire.

The Reichstag Session Chamber was set ablaze, not by paper, but by the old, heavy velvet curtains behind the tribune. From these musty curtains the fire quickly spread to the richly hung wooden panelling near it.

As every fireman knows, large fires radiate heat over fairly large distances, and this fact partially explains why the Court 'experts' failed to set light to the same kind of furniture that the actual fire consumed so quickly.

Firemen also know that the most dangerous fires are those which start in such vaulted buildings as cinemas, theatres, and – the Reichstag. Hence the Reichstag fire did not puzzle them at first:

> According to the fire office, a ventilation shaft in the Session Chamber acted as a chimney, sucking the fire upwards and impeding its lateral development. The roof girders suffered little damage since the panes burst very quickly, leaving the air free access and the flames free escape.[17]

Had the fire not broken out at a critical point in Germany's history, the experts would not have been expected to propound any of their far-fetched theories, or to perform any of their pointless experiments. They would have simply told the Court – what every housewife knows in any case – that once you light a fire in a stove with an unobstructed chimney, it will blaze away until all the fuel has been consumed. And that is precisely what happened in the Reichstag Session Chamber.

13. The Verdict

THE VERDICT

ON 23 December 1933, Dr Bünger solemnly read the judgement of the Supreme Court:

> The accused Torgler, Dimitrov, Popov and Tanev are acquitted. The accused van der Lubbe is found guilty of high treason, insurrectionary arson and attempted common arson. He is sentenced to death and to perpetual loss of civic rights.

This verdict was received with satisfaction abroad. The fact that four of the five accused had been acquitted, not because of their innocence but merely for lack of evidence against them, was considered a minor flaw, and van der Lubbe's death sentence caused only a flicker of revulsion. For there had never been any question about his guilt; what was in doubt was his sanity.

The National Socialist press, on the other hand, foamed with rage:

> The acquittal of Torgler and the three Bulgarian Communists for purely formal reasons is, in the popular view, a complete miscarriage of justice. Had the verdict been rooted in that true law on which the new Germany is being founded and in the true feeling of the German people, it would surely have been quite different. But then the entire manner in which the trial was conducted, and which the nation has followed with increasing displeasure, would have been quite different too.[1]

A less prejudiced German paper wrote:

> The highest German court has spoken. It has . . . shown the qualities which the new Germany expects of a 'royal' judge: an unflinching will to justice, the utmost objectivity in the discovery and assessment of the facts, complete independence.[2]

That view was no less objectionable for, as Erich Kuttner has rightly pointed out:

> The verdict is an abuse of logic and of reasonable thought. It is not by the acquittal of four innocent men, but by its specious attempt to

prove, despite the acquittal, what could only have been proven by a verdict of guilty, that we must judge this Court and assess its subservience to the political rulers of the Third Reich.[3]

In fact, the judges were paralysed from the moment Hitler made his fateful pronouncement in the blazing Reichstag. In addition, most German judges were Nationalists, and inclined to side with the Nazis against the Communists and Social Democrats as a matter of course. Thus, in 1923, when Adolf Hitler made a seditious attempt to overthrow the elected Government, and caused the death of many people, he was merely confined in Landsberg fortress, from which he was released soon afterwards.

Dr Bünger's Court, too, was no exception to the general rule; it openly paid homage to the Nazi masters when it declared:

> On January 30th, 1933, the Reichspräsident expressed his confidence in Adolf Hitler, the leader of the National Socialist Party, by appointing him Chancellor . . . thus paving the path for the building of the Third Reich and for our political rebirth. . . . A wave of confidence met our Führer Adolf Hitler and held out the promise that the new elections, set down for March 5th, would ensure the overwhelming success of the National Socialist Party. . . . [Hence there was] not the slightest reason why the National Socialists should have burned the Reichstag and blamed the fire on others as a pre-election stunt. Every German realizes full well that the men to whom the German nation owes its salvation from Bolshevik anarchy and who are now leading Germany towards her rebirth and recuperation, would never have been capable of such criminal folly. The Court therefore deems it beneath its dignity to enter into these vile allegations, all of which have been spread by expatriated rogues, who stand condemned by their own words. It is sufficient to state that all these lies have been completely refuted in the course of the trial . . .

Inasmuch as the Court acquitted the accused Communists, it proved that it still enjoyed a measure of independence, but inasmuch as it upheld the absurd thesis of Communist complicity, it showed how small that measure really was – dazzled by the national firework display, the judges turned a blind eye to the most basic principles of jurisprudence. It was their subservience to Hitler which constantly forced them to shelter behind such evasions as 'possibly', 'apparently', 'probably', 'presumably', and so on. A summary of the verdict might have read: Somehow and somewhere, some unknown – but certainly Communist – criminals entered the Reichstag with some substance that somehow served to prepare the Chamber for the fire. Somehow, somewhere, and at some time, these Communist criminals made contact with van der Lubbe, and somehow, somewhere and at some time, they disappeared again after the crime was committed.

Though not a single accomplice was run to earth despite all the efforts of the famous German police, and despite the offer of a large reward, the Court nevertheless found that there could be

> . . . no doubt about the objects which van der Lubbe and his accomplices were pursuing, or about the camp in which the criminal's accomplices and principals must be sought. Their intention was clearly to give the signal for a Communist rebellion.

And on what evidence did the Court base this conclusion, when it could not even establish how these accomplices got in and out of the building? It seems quite incredible but the answer is: On evidence which the Court itself found hard to swallow, viz. on Paul Bogun's claim that he saw one of the accomplices leave the Reichstag shortly before or just after 9 p.m. This is what the verdict said on the subject:

> . . . While the Court has no reason to distrust the witness Bogun, and while the Court does not doubt that what Bogun saw outside Portal Two was the escape of one of the accomplices, the Court was able to satisfy itself that light conditions outside Portal Two were such that no positive identification of the clothing and appearance of the accomplice was possible from where the witness Bogun stood.

Bogun, who had become the star witness after most of the others had proved such transparent liars, came out rather poorly himself when the defence had finished with him. This is how the *Neue Zürcher Zeitung* described his appearance in Court:

> A barrage of questions fired at the witness by Dr Teichert and Dr Sack, counsel for the defence, revealed that his evidence is full of loopholes and contradictions. His times differ by quarter-hours; minutes are changed into seconds, and vice versa. The witness, who is short-sighted and wears thick glasses, had originally stated that it was too dark to tell the colour of the stranger's hair. Later he alleged that the stranger had dark hair, just like Popov. Bogun also gave five different descriptions of the stranger's headgear. The stranger's shoes changed colour; his face and eyebrows only assumed definite shape after Bogun had been confronted with Popov.

The witness has begun to twist and turn so much that, in his own interest, one would wish that the floor would swallow him up. Yet all Bogun can say is that details do not matter. He even swore on oath that he had spoken the whole truth.[4]

Dimitrov, too, turned his full scorn on Bogun:

German engineers are usually as precise as mathematics. Why, then, are Bogun's powers of observation so much better three months after the fire than they were at the time? How does he explain that Popov's light trousers have become blue? Bogun is not an engineer, he is a romancer.[5]

Another witness, Frau Elfriede Kuesner, who also alleged that she had seen the 'accomplice' escape from Portal Two, was known to have entered the National Club at 9 p.m. She therefore had to time her 'observation' at 8.55 p.m., i.e. a few minutes before Bogun did. On top of that, she had watched the 'getaway' from an extremely poor vantage point, at least 165 feet away from Portal Two, and against the light.

Now we know that Portal Two had been duly locked by Wocköck, an old and trusted Reichstag servant, because House-Inspector Scranowitz had to unlock it for the fire brigade. Moreover, the police had established that the lock had not been tampered with in any way, and that there were only two keys: the one Wocköck had handed to Wendt in Portal Five, and the other which was kept in a locked cupboard in Scranowitz's (locked) office.

In other words, some of the accomplices would have had to steal Wendt's key, race from Portal Five to Portal Two, unlock and lock the door to allow their friends to escape, race back to Portal Five to return the key, thus wasting much time and risking discovery, when all of them could have escaped by the mysterious and undetectable route by which they had allegedly come in.

All these strange facts did not apparently worry the Court, nor, for that matter, did the discrepancy between the evidence of the witnesses Bogun and Kuesner, or the internal contradictions in Bogun's own evidence. For Bogun had presented the Court with a much-needed accomplice, and the Court was determined to hang on to his gift through thick and thin. All that remained to be done was to link the accomplice to van der Lubbe, and linked to him he was:

> The very fact that he [van der Lubbe] betook himself to Neukölln, the Communist stronghold, is extremely suggestive. His conversations outside the Welfare Office, at Schlaffke's and at Starker's are equally suspicious. . . . Even though his demand to be shown to Communist headquarters was refused, he was nevertheless taken to Neukölln Communist haunts. . . . In the view of the Court, it was here that van der Lubbe made contact with Communist circles. The precise nature of these contacts, their subsequent effects, and their precise relevance to van der Lubbe's participation in the crime could not be established. However, that the crime was preceded by other actions than lonely walks through the streets of Berlin, sudden unmotivated decisions, and the purchase of a few firelighters, is proved by the obstinate silence which the accused van der Lubbe maintained, even during the preliminary examination, on the subject of his movements on February 23rd and 24th, and from February 27th until the time of the fire. Undoubtedly it was during these times that the preparations were made. . . . Although the details of these preparations remain unknown, all the evidence points to the fact that van der Lubbe's accomplices are to be found in the ranks of the German Communist Party. In this respect it is not without interest that Hennigsdorf . . . was an industrial town with a Communist majority, and that it was here that van der Lubbe was seen in the company of known Communists and with the sister of a Communist leader . . .

And this compilation of idle speculations and bad logic was the basis on which the highest German Court decided the fate of van der Lubbe! But then the Court needed these crutches, for without them it could never have sentenced van der Lubbe to death – not even as a favour to Hitler.

The Court's remarkable arguments about van der Lubbe's movements were followed by no less remarkable arguments about the fire itself. When all was said and done, the allegation that van der Lubbe could not have started the gigantic fire with mere firelighters stood and fell by the fire-resistance of the curtains in the Session Chamber. Now the verdict declared all Reichstag curtains fire-resistant, even those which had caught fire easily during the experiments. The reason was simple: the idea that the curtains were fire-resistant had been so widely adopted that Dr Schatz thought it best not to confuse the issue with fine academic distinctions. Hence, when the witnesses, Thaler, Buwert, Freudenberg and Kuhl all testified how quickly the restaurant curtains had burned, Dr Schatz alleged that these curtains, too, must have been soaked in his famous liquid. Now, since the Court had established that van der Lubbe was the only person who could have 'prepared' the restaurant, he must somehow have procured a bottle or can of the mysterious substance between 2 p.m., when the witness Schmal saw him without a container, and 9 p.m., when he was seen breaking into the Reichstag. Moreover, he must have carried the large container (Dr Schatz spoke of one gallon of liquid) on his person while scaling the Reichstag wall, jumping over the parapet, kicking in the thick panes, lighting the first firelighters in the wind – the first five matches were blown out – and then climbing in through the broken window. Even Dr Schatz realized that to do all this van der Lubbe had to have both hands free, and he accordingly 'invented' a large container that could fit into an overcoat pocket. Needless to say, no traces of such a container were ever discovered. Even so, the Court found that

> Dr. Schatz's examination of van der Lubbe's charred coat has proved conclusively that the accused van der Lubbe carried the inflammable liquid on his person. The coat pocket had a clear burn-mark running inwards, and chemical investigations of the pocket revealed the presence of phosphorus and carbon sulphide in different stages of oxidization together with traces of hydrated phosphoric acid and hydrated sulphuric acid.

Moreover, whereas Lateit had testified that he saw the curtains burning from the bottom to the top, as they would have done had they been lit with firelighters, the Court preferred Dr Schatz's speculations on the subject:

> Both curtains burned diagonally from the inside top to the outside bottom. This fact is further evidence in favour of Dr Schatz's opinion that the curtains had been sprinkled with liquid.

According to the verdict, therefore, van der Lubbe not only sprinted through the Reichstag in record time, lighting firelighters, tablecloths, papers, shirts, and other pieces of clothing, but he also spent much additional time sprinkling curtains, carpets, etc.

> It seems reasonable to assume that van der Lubbe shed his clothes . . . not, as he alleged, in order to supplement his supply of lighters, but simply because, as a result of contact with the self-igniting liquid, they had themselves caught fire.

Yet this dangerous liquid, which had allegedly consumed massive oak furniture in a matter of seconds, was unable to destroy van der Lubbe's poor coat, remnants of which Dr Schatz had therefore been able to submit to his far-reaching examinations. In any case, it seems odd that neither van der Lubbe's hands nor his trousers and shoes showed the slightest burn-marks.

At first, Dr Schatz had argued that the inflammable liquid had been smuggled into the Reichstag well in advance. However, the trial soon showed that this view could not be maintained. The time available for preparing the fire kept shrinking until the Court had to face the remarkable fact that even the Session Chamber must have been 'prepared' immediately before the fire. For a brief moment, it looked very much as if the Court would have to believe van der Lubbe's story after all, and it was at this point that Dr Schatz came to the rescue with his self-igniting substance. He explained that it was merely in order to give this substance time to work that van der Lubbe had drawn attention to himself in the restaurant.

The Court offered no explanation of how the container or containers of the liquid had disappeared without trace. Moreover, whereas the Public Prosecutor admitted that there was no evidence to show that such inflammable liquids as paraffin, petrol, benzol or ether had ever been used, the Court preferred to listen to Dr Schatz once again:

> Since the soot in the ventilators and underneath both the Speaker's Chair and also the Table of the House contained simultaneously residual naphthalene and mineral oil, it seems likely that the [self-igniting] liquid and the sawdust-and-naphthalene firelighters were used in conjunction with petrol or benzol.

Again, whereas the Indictment had stressed that Professor Brüning's examination of the alleged 'fluid trail' in the Bismarck Hall had revealed no trace of an inflammable liquid, the Court (and Dr Schatz) believed that:

> It seems likely that the accomplice or the accomplices, having performed their allotted task in the Session Chamber, used the remaining liquid for firing the curtains in the western corridor, the southern corridor and the Bismarck Hall, on the carpet of which the incendiaries left a clear trail of fluid which, according to the chemical examination by the expert, Dr Schatz, consisted not only of mineral oil, but also of self-igniting liquid.

In other words, the Court saw no need for having the contradictory opinions of two of its experts checked by a third one. It sided with a provincial chemist against a scientist of international renown.

Now, had a highly inflammable liquid been used in fact, the fire would have spread like lightning over the entire liquid-soaked area, leaving a great deal of soot, when all the eyewitnesses were agreed that the flames looked steady and that there was no inordinate amount of soot.

How blindly the judges followed Dr Schatz is best shown by their argument that the self-igniting fluid caught fire at a predetermined moment. The reader will remember that even the great Dr Schatz was quite unable to fix that interval under laboratory conditions; how likely is it, then, that van der Lubbe's alleged accomplices should have been able to compound the mixture with so much greater precision?

Moreover, while agreeing that van der Lubbe himself was carrying the fatal liquid on him, the Court nevertheless found that he could not possibly have burned the Chamber:

> Fully refuted is van der Lubbe's allegation that he himself started the fire in the Chamber . . .
>
> In any case, there was no need for van der Lubbe to have fired the Chamber with firebrands, etc., when the Chamber had been prepared beforehand with the self-igniting substance . . .
>
> The part which the accused van der Lubbe was apparently expected to play was to deflect attention from his accomplices. . . . In the opinion of the Court, this is borne out by his conspicuous waving of a firebrand outside the restaurant window, for such behaviour is quite incompatible with common arson. . . . In fact, van der Lubbe's accomplices or principals did achieve their object, for though they ran the risk of discovery, they did manage to divert the fire brigade from the main fire. . . . It was also in order to divert the fire brigade from the main fire that van der Lubbe laid a blazing trail through the corridors. . . .

And the only basis for all these 'findings' was the rich fantasy of Dr Schatz. For if, as the Court claimed, van der Lubbe did not even set foot in the Chamber, how was it that he was able to lead the detectives straight there on the very next day? And what must we think of a Court which finds that 'the detectives were *originally* convinced that van der Lubbe fired the Reichstag by himself' when neither (Heisig or Zirpins) had changed their original views in the slightest?

Even the fact that van der Lubbe chose 9 p.m. as the best time to climb into the Reichstag was twisted into an argument supporting the accomplice theory, for at that time the Reichstag was ostensibly deserted. In fact, had the Reichstag postman not accidentally started on his round a few minutes before his normal time, he would certainly have spotted any 'accomplices' that might have been at work.

Having made the most of Dr Schatz's fantastic gifts, and having twisted the facts to exhaustion, the Court easily arrived at the truly amazing conclusion that:

> It has been established that van der Lubbe's accomplices must be sought in the ranks of the Communist Party, that Communism is therefore guilty of the Reichstag fire, that the German people stood in the early part of the year 1933 on the brink of chaos into which the Communists sought to lead them, and that the German people were saved at the last moment.

In sentencing van der Lubbe to death for insurrectionary arson, the Leipzig Court ignored two legal maxims, without either of which justice becomes a mere sham: *in dubio pro reo* (the accused has the benefit of the doubt) and *nulla poena sine lege* (no punishment without law). To put it more plainly, when the Court convicted van der Lubbe of complicity in a non-existing plot and sentenced him to death for a non-capital offence, it chose political expediency and deliberately jettisoned the law.

THE MYSTERY OF VAN DER LUBBE

According to the French Ambassador, François-Poncet, van der Lubbe was 'the feeble-minded, mentally deficient, and probably drugged tool of the real criminals'.

In fact, drugging van der Lubbe would only have made sense had he, in fact, provided the Nazis with what they needed: the confession that he had acted on behalf of the German Communist Party. This he steadfastly refused to do.

But if not drugged, why did van der Lubbe, whom Inspector Heisig had described as being so alert after the fire, appear in Court speechless, bowed, slavering, with a running nose and, in general, wretched-looking?

Part of the answer was given by Kugler who wrote: 'It is quite possible that, having been kept in shackles for seven long months, the twenty-four-year-old van der Lubbe . . . was so exhausted that he had a nervous breakdown.'[6]

And it should not require too much imagination to realize the effects of a form of inhuman torture which had driven tough Tanev to attempt suicide and Dimitrov to the limits of his endurance. Van der Lubbe, unlike the other accused, had not a single friend, and was thus a singularly defenceless butt of Judge Vogt's sadistic attacks. To make things worse, his intended protest against the enemies of the working class had helped those very enemies to power, and his former associates were now calling him a Nazi stooge.

All these facts were mentioned in a medical opinion which two well-known authorities, Professor Karl Bonhoeffer, of the Psychiatric Clinic of the University of Berlin, and Professor Jurg Zutt, now Director of the Neurological Clinic in Frankfurt, submitted to the Court at the time.

What had caused Judge Vogt to call in the two psychiatrists as early as March 1933, was van der Lubbe's decision to go on hunger-strike. When asked about this, van der Lubbe told the doctors quite simply that, though he had been held for three weeks and though he had done his best to help the authorities, the trial was dragging on and on and he was trying to hurry things up, not only for his own sake but also for the sake of his innocent fellow-sufferers, Torgler and the Bulgarians. He also volunteered the information that he had found hunger-strikes most effective with the Dutch authorities.

Now, if three weeks was too long for him, how must he have felt after another forty-four weeks, for twenty-nine of which he was kept in chains day and night? In any case, the two psychiatrists, far from considering him an imbecile, found him

> . . . an individual who knows what he wants and who tries to say what has to be said and no more. . . . [Because of his eye injury] he gives the impression of staring into space at times; in reality, however, he pays careful attention to what goes on around him. Little seems to escape his attention.

It did not take van der Lubbe long to find out why the two psychiatrists had been called in:

> He laughed quite naturally, perhaps somewhat arrogantly, though not impudently. So that was what it was all about! He had burned the

Reichstag and now he had gone on hunger-strike, so, obviously, they all thought he was mad!

When the doctors tried to assess his intelligence with general knowledge and mathematical questions, he told them that

> . . . he was far more interested in things he had experienced by himself. . . . He considered religion just one branch of knowledge among many. . . . When asked what he thought about life after death, he replied that it was a bourgeois mistake to expect an answer to that question. Either life continues after death or it does not, and that's that. Death and the beyond were, after all, no more than concepts, and all concepts are lodged in our heads; they only exist when we think about them . . .
>
> He was inclined to burst into youthful laughter, especially when he was asked questions that seemed to be paradoxical, or others which, in his opinion, complicated simple things quite unnecessarily.

Van der Lubbe's youthful laughter repeatedly caused observers to shake their heads at what they could only assume were the antics of a lunatic. On the very first day of the trial, for instance, van der Lubbe started shaking with laughter after the pointless Sörnewitz-Brockwitz discussion had been going on for what seemed an eternity. In great perplexity, Dr Bünger asked him:

> 'Are you feeling ill or is something the matter with you? You must not laugh here.'
>
> Dr Werner: 'He is shaking with laughter.'
>
> President: 'Lubbe, will you stand up! What is the meaning of this? Why are you suddenly laughing when you are normally so serious? Is it because you find the subject matter of this trial amusing, or is there any other reason? Do you think our deliberations are ridiculous?'
>
> Van der Lubbe: 'No.'
>
> President: 'Do you understand everything? Do you understand this trial?'
>
> Van der Lubbe: 'No.'
>
> President: 'So it is not the subject matter of this trial which makes you laugh. What is it then? Why do you laugh? Out with it!'
>
> Van der Lubbe: 'Because of the trial.'
>
> President: 'Do you think the trial is a joke?'
>
> Van der Lubbe: 'No.'
>
> President: 'If it is not a joke, then please don't laugh!'

But how could van der Lubbe help laughing when so much pomp and circumstance was being wasted by the highest Court in the land to establish who said what to whom in Sörnewitz, a little backwater that had absolutely nothing whatever to do with the Reichstag fire?

Next day, Sörnewitz was still on the agenda, and van der Lubbe was told once again not to laugh.

> President: 'Why do you laugh? These matters are of extreme gravity. I am warning you, van der Lubbe!'

A few days later, van der Lubbe burst into laughter once more, when Tanev replied to the question whether he had known van der Lubbe: 'Where should I have met him? I don't understand a single word of German. What should I have wanted with him?'

In short, van der Lubbe laughed whenever he was given cause for laughter. His was a special kind of morbid humour which grew as he watched the Court's blustering attempts to obscure the simple truth and to manufacture accomplices out of thin air.

In any case, Professors Bonhoeffer and Zutt found that '. . . during all our visits we never saw him laugh unless he saw something funny in the situation.'

But as the trial dragged on, van der Lubbe's humour began to wilt visibly. In the end, when he came to realize that these hopeless old fools in their fine robes were not in the least interested in what he had to tell them, he stopped smiling and wasting his breath.

When the two doctors asked van der Lubbe why he had set fire to the Reichstag, he replied that, as the German working class had done nothing to protest against the Nazis, he had felt it his duty to make an individual protest on their behalf.

The learned gentlemen confirmed that van der Lubbe could express himself in reasonably good German, and that he needed no Dutch interpreter. Moreover, the Court interpreter, J. Meyer-Collings, told Judge Coenders who had asked him about van der Lubbe's Dutch: 'It is an odd fact, but van der Lubbe does not talk like an ordinary Dutch worker; he uses the idiom of educated people.'

In March 1933, the two medical experts concluded: 'We found no indications of mental unbalance. Marinus van der Lubbe strikes us as a most intelligent, strong-willed and self-confident person . . .', but when they saw him again at the beginning of the

Leipzig trial, they found him a broken man. They described the results in purely medical terms, and wisely kept their own counsel on the causes: van der Lubbe's strength had been sapped by his fetters, and his morale undermined by the realization that nothing he might say to these pompous judges would make the slightest difference.

In order to kill the story that his transformation was due to drugs, the Court asked Professor Karl Soedermann, Lecturer in Criminology at the University of Stockholm, to examine van der Lubbe. On 28 September 1933, Soedermann reported:

> I can only say that they treat him better than they do the other prisoners, for instance as regards food. The moment he saw me, Marinus van der Lubbe asked: 'Why are you examining me?' I said: 'Because foreign papers allege that you are being badly treated here.'
>
> Van der Lubbe laughed and shook his head. I gained the impression that we could have conversed for hours, and that I would invariably have received intelligent and logical answers. . . . I also asked him if he had at any time felt anything strange after eating or drinking and he told me emphatically that he had not.[7]

Professor Soedermann also examined van der Lubbe's body, but found no marks of ill-usage (e.g. injections) of any kind.

The two German psychiatrists, too, felt compelled to refer to the drug rumours:

> . . . Then there are the many strange 'diagnoses' which no doctor would accept, but which are repeated by the public and above all by the suspicious foreign press, viz. that Marinus van der Lubbe has been hypnotized in prison, and that his odd behaviour is the result of his having been drugged with scopolamine.
>
> Even if it were feasible that medical men should lend themselves to such criminal practices, and even if someone could be kept under hypnosis for weeks and months on end, van der Lubbe's attitude, behaviour, and intransigence are by no means those of a hypnotized or drugged subject.

On 20 October 1933, the Court heard the evidence of S. A. Gruppenführer Wolf von Helldorff. When van der Lubbe was asked to step forward for the usual confrontation, the President, the interpreter and counsel tried in vain to make him look up at the Nazi. It was only when Helldorff yelled at him: 'Put your head up, you! And jump to it!' that van der Lubbe slowly did as he was told.

Helldorff and his applauding cohorts in the public gallery now felt that firmness was all van der Lubbe had needed, and that his downcast mien had been sham all along. In fact, van der Lubbe had merely been shaken out of his resigned boredom by the parade-ground voice of a professional bully.

Helldorff himself must have regretted his courtroom success the next day, when he read in the foreign press that van der Lubbe had obviously obeyed the voice of his master, or as the *Brown Book* put it: 'Had the shrill command penetrated through the mists of van der Lubbe's memory: had it cleaved the fog in his brain for one transient second?'[8]

The *Brown Book* even offered a 'scientific explanation' based on the findings of an 'eminent toxicologist': 'There is one poisonous drug with such qualities that comparatively minute doses will produce symptoms exactly similar to those produced in van der Lubbe.'[9]

In fact, as Professor Zutt had already pointed out, 'there is no drug that can completely silence a man'. Moreover: 'His behaviour is a natural reaction to his external circumstances. . . . True, he has grown apathetic, but he often glances up and round, though without appearing to move his head.'

Then, on 13 November 1933, van der Lubbe suddenly 'woke up' once again, sat upright, and looked attentively at everyone in Court. More miraculously still, he broke his long silence and answered all questions that were put to him.

One of his answers caused a sensation in Court, for when the President asked him whom he had gone to see in Spandau, he burst out with: 'The Nazis!' However, the excitement quickly subsided when it appeared that he had merely gone to watch a Nazi demonstration.

Van der Lubbe caused an even greater sensation on 23 November, the forty-third day of the trial, when he rose to his feet, raised his head, and faced the Court.

> The judges, startled, gazed across at him. Defending counsel turned in their seats and hung on his words. His fellow-prisoners shed the weariness of two months like a garment and sat forward, straining their ears to hear what he should say. The public craned its neck. The few newspaper correspondents who had both followed the trial to Leipzig and risen early enough to be present at van der Lubbe's

awakening – a brief awakening it was to be – congratulated themselves on their own perseverance and thought without compassion of their absent colleagues.[10]

Van der Lubbe explained that he had risen in order to ask a question. When Dr Bünger said he might, the following discussion ensued:

Van der Lubbe: 'We have had three trials now, the first in Leipzig, the second in Berlin, and the third in Leipzig again. I should like to know when the verdict will be pronounced and executed.'

President: 'I can't tell you that yet. It all depends on you, on your naming your accomplices.'

Van der Lubbe: 'But that has all been cleared up. I fired the Reichstag by myself, and there must be a verdict. The thing has gone on for eight months and I cannot agree with this at all.'

President: 'Then tell us who your accomplices were!'

Van der Lubbe: 'My fellow defendants have all admitted that they had nothing to do with the fire, were not even in the Reichstag, and did not fire it.'

President: 'I have told you repeatedly that the Court cannot accept your statement that you were alone. You simply must tell us with whom you did it and who helped you.'

Van der Lubbe: 'I can only repeat that I set fire to the Reichstag all by myself. After all, it has been shown during this trial that Dimitrov and the others were not there. They are in the trial, that is quite true, but they were not in the Reichstag.'

Dr Seuffert: 'And what about Herr Torgler?'

Van der Lubbe: 'He wasn't there either. You (turning to Torgler) have had to admit yourself that you weren't there. I am the accused and I want to know the verdict, no matter if it is twenty years in prison or the death penalty. Something simply has to happen. The whole trial has gone wrong because of all this symbolism and I am sick of it.'

Dr Werner: 'What does the accused mean by the term "symbolism"?'

Dr Seuffert: 'He objects to the Reichstag fire being called a signal.'

Van der Lubbe: 'What sort of deed was it anyway, this Reichstag fire? It was a matter of ten minutes, or at most, a quarter of an hour. I did it all by myself.'

And then he poured out his own feelings: what had troubled him so sorely was the fact that his dignified inquisitors were apparently determined to spin out their comedy of errors for as long as they could. He, for one, would rather die than have this sordid farce continue. How could they blame him for delaying the proceedings by not betraying accomplices he had never had? Though he knew that arguing with these senile old fools was a sheer waste of time, he tried once again:

> Van der Lubbe: 'The Court does not believe me, but it's true all the same.'
>
> President: 'Have you read the opinions of the experts who say one man could not have started the fire?'
>
> Van der Lubbe: 'Yes, I know that is the personal opinion of the experts. But then, I was there and they were not. I know that I set fire to the Session Chamber with my jacket.'

What followed merely shows how right van der Lubbe had been to save his breath.

> President: 'You have confessed to the crime and there is therefore no argument on that point. But it remains a fact that other persons have been accused and that the Court must now decide whether or not these person are guilty. It would help us greatly if you now admit with whom you committed the crime.'
>
> Van der Lubbe: 'I can only admit that I started the fire by myself; for the rest I cannot agree with what this Court is trying to do. I now demand a verdict. What you are doing is a betrayal of humanity, of the police, and of the Communist and the National Socialist Party. All I ask for is a verdict.'

And when Dimitrov, too, said: 'In my opinion no one person could have started this complicated fire . . .' Van der Lubbe interrupted him with: 'There is nothing complicated about this fire. It has quite a simple explanation. What was made of it may be complicated, but the fire itself was very simple . . .'

When the President thereupon suggested that his poor fire-lighters could not have caused a major conflagration, van der Lubbe replied: 'In that case, the Session Chamber must have been far more inflammable than the experts believe.'

The Court's persistent blindness was referred to by Mr Justice de Jongh:

> Why does it not enter anyone's head that both the National Socialists and the Communists might be innocent, and that the unhappy Marinus van der Lubbe committed the crime by himself, or, for that matter, with antisocial elements belonging to neither of the two parties?[11]

Another foreign observer to voice his doubts at the time was Douglas Reed, who wrote:

> Attempts from all sides of the court to wrest from van der Lubbe the secret of his accomplices, however, were parried in a manner that indicated either great cunning or the sincere conviction that he had none. . . . There remained only two possibilities – that van der Lubbe had no accomplices or that he did not himself know who they were. The one man from whom, it had been thought, the secret might yet be wrested, either would not yield it or had none to yield.[12]

When the death sentence on van der Lubbe was finally pronounced on 23 December 1933, the Dutch Ambassador in Berlin appealed for clemency, and countless petitions poured into Germany from all over the world. Mr Justice de Jongh, in adding his voice, pointed out that with van der Lubbe's execution there would disappear the last chance of ever solving the mystery of the Reichstag fire.

On 9 January 1934, when the Public Prosecutor informed van der Lubbe that his appeal for clemency had been rejected, and that he was to be beheaded the following morning, van der Lubbe answered with great composure:

'Thank you for telling me; I shall see you tomorrow.'

Marinus van der Lubbe wrote no farewell letters to relatives or friends. On 10 January 1934, when he was led out of his cell, he looked calm and peaceful. A large company had assembled to witness the last act of an apalling tragedy. President Bünger and three of his assistant judges had come, and so had Dr Werner, Dr Parrisius, Dr Seuffert, the Court interpreter, the prison chaplain, the governor of the prison, two doctors, and twelve selected Leipzig citizens. The executioner was dressed in tails, top hat and white gloves.

The Public Prosecutor explained that the Herr Reichspräsident had decided not to exercise his prerogative of clemency, and then ordered the executioner to do his duty. There were no complications, no tears, no belated confession. A few moments later Marinus van der Lubbe was dead.

Appendix A

THE MANCHESTER GUARDIAN
26 April 1933

THE REICHSTAG FIRE

I. *Who was Guilty?*

THE CASE AGAINST THE NAZIS

Germany, April.

WHEN Hitler became Chancellor – with von Papen as Vice-Chancellor – at the end of January, the Nazis and their partners in office, the Nationalists, had antagonistic ambitions. The Nazis, above all Captain Göring and Dr Goebbels, wanted absolute and undivided power. Von Papen, as well as the Nationalist leader, Dr Hugenberg, and the President, von Hindenburg, wanted the Nazis, with their enormous following, to provide a 'National' Government with the popular support which was denied to the Nationalists themselves. The Nazis, in other words, were to share power with the Nationalists while being denied that preponderance which, by virtue of being by far the biggest party in the Reich, they considered their due.

The Nationalists, though a very small party, had certain sources of strength. They represent all that is left of Imperial Germany; they, and not the Nazis, incarnate old Prussian traditions. They were supported by a large part of the higher bureaucracy, by the higher ranks of the Reichswehr, by the Stahlhelm, a powerful conservative league of ex-servicemen, and by President von Hindenburg, whose personal authority was still considerable. Nor were they, in case of need, disinclined to negotiate for the support of the trade unions and even of the Reichsbanner, a strong militant force (made up chiefly of workmen) whose leaders had developed certain militarist and nationalist tendencies.

The Nazis were showing signs of disintegration. The Brown Shirts were growing mutinous in different parts of the Reich; several units had to be disbanded, and in the electorate there were symptoms of waning enthusiasm. Another election might (if sufficient time were allowed to lapse) mean a heavy loss of votes. And would not a movement that had arisen so rapidly and so high suffer a correspondingly precipitous decline?

NAZIS AND NATIONALISTS

Thus the Nazis were under a strong compulsion to take a share of power, lest the time might come when even a share would be denied to them. Hitler had become Chancellor of the 'Government of National Concentration' only on condition that there would be no changes in the Cabinet without the sanction of President Hindenburg. Thus the Nazis, although in a position of great influence, achieved nothing comparable with that complete transformation of the whole economic and social order to which they and the millions of their enthusiastic followers had aspired. Had they respected the terms imposed on Hitler, the disappearance of those millions would only have been a matter of time. They were indeed in a trap.

The Nationalists had no particular faith in Hitler's word, which had been broken more than once before. But they were vigilant, and on the slightest sign of bad faith they were ready, with the sanction of the President and the army, to proclaim a military dictatorship (in which case they could have counted on the support not only of the Stahlhelm but also of the police, amongst whom Socialist influences were still strong). How were the Nazis to get out of the trap? If there were a general election without loss of time they might still increase their vote, for Hitler's Chancellorship had the appearance of almost absolute power without the substance, and new hope had revived the ardour of his followers, though, with the inevitable emergence of the reality, it was bound to cool in a very short time. He therefore demanded a general election at the earliest possible date. His promise to the President was, it is true, binding, irrespective of the result of that election. At the same time, an increase of his already heavy vote could only be welcome. Indeed, if he obtained an absolute majority, could his promise be considered binding against the manifest 'will of the people'? Or would not Hindenburg give way before that 'will'?

But the chances that he would get such a majority were small, and as the election campaign developed it seemed probable that revived enthusiasm was ebbing once again and that the elections would show a loss in the Hitlerite vote. This would have bound

Hitler to his promise and the Nazis permanently to the Nationalists. It was clear to their more adventurous and ambitious leaders, Captain Göring and Dr Goebbels, that 'something' must be done to keep Nazi enthusiasm at its height, indeed to drive it still higher, and to precipitate a new situation in which Hitler could either be freed from his promise or that promise would lose its meaning. The election campaign promised to be violent, there was a tense atmosphere, extravagant rumours were abroad. The moment was favourable to men of imaginative daring and unscrupulous ambition.

NOT A SURPRISE

Everyone – including the correspondents of British, French, and American newspapers in Berlin – expected 'something' – a staged Communist uprising, a fictitious attempt to murder Hitler, or a fire. The Reichswehr warned the Communists, through an intermediary, that they must not allow themselves to be provoked into any rash action. On no account must they provide an excuse for raising an anti-Bolshevik scare.

When on 27 February the Reichstag burst into flames no serious observer of German affairs was at all surprised. Nevertheless, there was widespread horror and panic. Many understood the signal well and fled the country forthwith, fearing to wait until they should be arrested or until the frontiers should be closed. There were workmen who, with shrewd foresight, at once buried their 'Marxist' literature. It was the Reichstag fire, not the Chancellorship of Hitler nor his electoral victory on 5 March, that began the Brown Terror.

The fire was instantaneously attributed to the Communists by the Government, which at once began to manufacture false evidence, thereby not inculpating but rather exculpating the Communists and deepening the suspicion felt by all objective observers that the real incendiaries were to be found within the Cabinet itself. Before the tribunal of history it is not the Communists, not the wretched van der Lubbe (their alleged instrument, whose public execution Hitler has threatened before his guilt has been proved, before he has even been tried), but the German Government that is arraigned.

A confidential memorandum on the events leading up to the fire is circulating in Germany. It is in manuscript, and the Terror makes any open mention or discussion of it impossible. But it is a serious attempt by one in touch with the Nationalist members of the Cabinet to give a balanced account of these events. In spite of one or two minor inaccuracies it shows considerable inside knowledge. While not authoritative in an absolute and final manner, it is at least a first and a weighty contribution towards solving the riddle of that fire. The memorandum contains certain allegations of high interest that will be discussed in the next article.

Appendix B

THE MANCHESTER GUARDIAN
27 April 1933

THE REICHSTAG FIRE

II. *Nazis Guilty?*

A NATIONALIST VERSION

Storm Troopers Accused

Germany, April.

THE 'Karl Liebknecht Haus', the headquarters of the Communist Party, and editorial office of the 'Rote Fahne', had been searched again and again by the police, but no incriminating matter had been found. The Nationalists were opposed to the suppression of the Communists, for without the Communist members the Nazis would have had an absolute majority in the Reichstag. This the Nationalists wished to avoid at any cost.

But the chief of the Berlin Police, Melcher, a Nationalist, resigned under Nazi pressure. He was replaced by Admiral von Levetzow, a Nazi. On 24 February the Karl Liebknecht Haus was again searched. On the 26th the 'Conti', a Government news agency, issued a report on the sinister and momentous finds that were supposed to have been made 'in subterranean vaults' and 'catacombs' that had long been cleared of everything by the forewarned Communists. The report also hinted darkly at plans for a Bolshevik revolution. The confidential Nationalist memorandum mentioned in the first article describes the annoyance of the Nationalist members of the Cabinet over the clumsiness and transparent untruthfulness of this report. They refused to allow the suppression of the Communist Party.

On 25 February a fire started in the old Imperial Palace. It was quickly extinguished. The incendiary escaped, leaving a box of matches and some inflammable matter behind. From various parts of the country came news – all of it untrue – of arson and outrage perpetrated by Communists. On the 27th, according to the memorandum, the chief Nazi agitators, Hitler, Göring, and

Goebbels, all three of whom are members of the present German Government, were, 'strangely enough', not touring the country to address election meetings, although the campaign was at its height, but were assembled in Berlin 'waiting for their fire'.

THE ACCUSATION

The Reichstag is connected with the Speaker's residence by a subterranean passage. Through this passage, according to the memorandum, 'the emissaries of Herr Göring (the Speaker) entered the Reichstag'. Each of these emissaries – they wore civilian clothes – 'went to his assigned place, and in a few minutes sufficient inflammable matter was distributed throughout the building' (after the fire had been quenched several heaps of rags and shavings soaked in petrol were found unburnt or half-burnt).

The Storm Troopers then, so the memorandum continues, withdrew through the passage to the Speaker's residence, put on their brown uniforms, and made off. They left behind them in the Reichstag building Van der Lubbe, who, so as to make sure that the Communists could be incriminated, had taken the precaution to have on his person his Dutch passport, a Communist leaflet, several photographs of himself, and what seems to have been the membership card of some Dutch Communist group.

THE OFFICIAL STORY

On the following day, the 28th, the fire was announced by the official 'Preussische Pressedienst' as intended to begin the Bolshevik revolution in Germany, the plans for this revolution having been discovered amongst 'the hundreds of hundredweights of seditious matter' found in the 'vaults and catacombs' of the Karl Liebknecht Haus. According to these plans 'Government buildings, museums, palaces, and essential plant were to be fired', disorders were to be provoked, terrorist groups were to advance behind screens of 'women and children, if possible the women and children of police officers', there were to be terrorist attacks on private property, and a 'general civil war' was to commence.

It is peculiar that no preparations for this civil war had been made by the German Government – there had been time enough, for the alleged plans had been discovered on the 24th. Whenever there has been the slightest reason to suspect violent action against the State, carbines are served out to the police, Government buildings are specially guarded, and the Wilhelmstrasse is patrolled night and day. No precautions of this kind were taken against the 'general civil war', not even after the fire in the Imperial Palace.

The 'Angriff', of which Dr Goebbels is editor, announced that the documents found in the Karl Liebknecht Haus would be 'placed before the public with all speed'. Eight weeks have passed and this has not been done.

FALSE REPORTS

The full political effects of the Reichstag fire could not be achieved merely by the presence of a Communist (with leaflet and membership card) in the Reichstag building. The Nazis have all along been bent on the destruction of 'Marxism' as a whole – that is to say, of Social Democracy as well as Communism. The communiqué of the 'Preussische Pressedienst' therefore added that 'the Reichstag incendiary has in his confession admitted that he is connected with the Socialist Party. Through this confession the united Communist-Socialist front has become a palpable fact.' Since then the Nazi press has repeatedly published false reports that arms and ammunition have been found hidden in rooms owned by the Socialist trade unions.

So as to incriminate the Communists still further, it was announced (in the 'Deutsche Allgemeine Zeitung') that their leaders Torgler and Koenen had spent several hours in the Reichstag on the evening of the 27th, and had been seen not only with van der Lubbe but also with several other persons who were carrying torches, these persons having eluded arrest by escaping through the passage to the Speaker's residence. Why did no one telephone to the Speaker's residence to have them arrested there? The question remains unanswered.

Two persons happened to get into the Reichstag almost immediately after the fire broke out. One of them rang up the 'Vorwärts' with the news. He was promptly cut off at the exchange, and was, together with his companion, arrested. Neither has been heard of since – the memorandum describes the one as a member of the staff (*Redakteur*) of the 'Vorwärts', but this is an error. The arrest of Stampfer, the editor, was at once ordered, and the editorial office was occupied by police within an hour (Stampfer eluded arrest by flight). The entire Socialist press throughout Prussia was suppressed on the night of the fire. The first edition of the 'Vorwärts' was already out, but all copies were confiscated by the police. On the morning of the 28th, Torgler gave himself up to the police of his own free will, accompanied by his solicitor, Dr Rosenfeld, and prepared to face and answer any charges that might be brought against him. This was most inconvenient – 'his flight', according to the memorandum, 'would have been much more desirable'.

A SCARE CREATED

But the fire made a deep impression on the electorate. The elimination of the Socialist press in Prussia and the rigorous censorship on all other papers allowed hardly a suspicion to get into print. The Nationalists could not speak up, for even if they did not want the Nazis to have the mastery they could not afford to see them collapse – and the truth about the fire, if publicly known, would have meant the collapse of the Nazi movement. The scaremongering story of the impending Bolshevik revolution was supplemented by others – an alleged plot to assassinate Hitler, the alleged discovery of Communist arsenals and munition dumps, and so on. Such stories are still being invented and appear in the Nazi papers almost every day.

A Bolshevik scare was created, especially in the country districts (stories of burning villages were calculated to impress the imagination of the peasantry). Hitler seemed the one saviour from anarchy and red revolution. That scare not only gave the Nazis and Nationalists a joint majority, it also unleashed that inhuman persecution of Communists, Socialists, Liberals, pacifists, and Jews which is still going on. It made the complete suppression of the Communist Party possible, thus eliminating its members from the Reichstag and giving the Nazis the absolute and overwhelming majority which the elections alone had not given them.

Despite the clumsiness with which it was staged, and despite the grossness of the falsehoods with which facts and motives were concealed, the fire turned out to be a big success. The legend that it was the work of Communists and Social Democrats is the main foundation of the Hitlerite Dictatorship and of the Brown Terror.

Appendix C

THE OBERFOHREN MEMORANDUM

As published by the German Information Office, London, in 1933, except for minor alterations where the original English translation made poor sense. A. J. P.

INTRODUCTION

GERMAN Conservatives had for years encouraged and supported the Nazis. They did not think much of Hitler – he was too big a demagogue for them, besides being a foreigner (it was only later on that he exchanged his Austrian nationality for German). But the impoverished, demoralized middle-class was rallying round him and, in the villages and smaller towns, he was not only pushing back the local Socialists and Communists but was creating a movement that would, in time, challenge Socialism and Communism in their strongholds, the big industrial cities.

The Nazis, with immense propagandist skill, an instinctive sense of what would work on the German imagination, and with a new colourful romanticism and glittering martial display, roused long-dormant emotions and fired the youth of middle-class Germany into a revivalist mass-activity against organized labour.

To the German Conservatives – notably the German-National People's Party which is (or rather was, for it has gone down in the storm it helped to raise) roughly what right-wing Tories are in England – the new movement was more than welcome. At last, they thought, there was hope of achieving what years of vain effort by the gentry, the bankers, the industrial leaders, the judiciary, and the army, had failed to achieve, namely to thrust organized labour back to where it had been before the war.

And so they helped the Nazis where they could – they openly admired their martial spirit, applauded their idealism, and helped to fill the capacious and insatiable Nazi purse.

The Conservative calculation was not only accurate – it was too accurate. The Nazis did all that was expected of them – and much more. They developed a contagious fervour that swept the nation. They claimed to represent a new generation, they preached a kind of romantic, middle-class Socialism, and adopted the phraseology of revolution. They became by far the biggest of the political parties, thus ousting the Socialists from a position they had held for years.

Though financed by the same people and representing, as their decrees since gaining power have clearly shown, the same interests as the Conservatives, the Nazis had no intention of being the docile agents of the Conservatives – if they were victorious, then victory was to be theirs and theirs only.

Even in 1932, the Conservatives were getting alarmed. They still hoped that, together with the Nazis, they would have a majority in the Reichstag, they themselves just making up the difference between majority and minority, and so holding the balance of power. But the Nazis were not submitting to tame partnership in a conventional coalition.

So with incomparable audacity and imaginative cunning, they set fire to the German Parliament, the Reichstag, and, by putting the blame on the Communists and Socialists, they raised a Bolshevik scare and started an anti-Labour drive, creating an entirely new situation in which they could set their Terror going. They had long been training their militants, the Brown Shirts and Black Shirts, for this Terror. While winning a great electoral victory on the 5th March, they carried out arrests, beatings, and shootings, thus laying the foundations of the dictatorship that is still in power.

The Parliamentary leader of the German-National People's Party was Dr Oberfohren. He had been a hater of Socialism and Communism. The Nazis had filled him, too, with hope that they would stem its progress. But he was a man of decency. He could honour an honest opponent, like the Communist leader, Ernst Torgler, even when he fought him ruthlessly.

To him the triumph of the Nazis soon came to mean the triumph of barbaric violence and the end, not only of Socialism and Communism, but of law, order, and morality.

The burning of the Reichstag was to him an abomination. The world, he thought, should know about it and should be told what the Nazis really are. Only thus, he believed, could their influence be counteracted and, perhaps, their sweeping advance held up.

So he inspired a journalist to write a memorandum on the Reichstag fire, he himself supplying most of the necessary information (being in touch with the Cabinet in which his own Party was represented, he knew more than most). This is the now famous 'Oberfohren Memorandum', which contains the fullest existing account of circumstances surrounding the fire. Every newspaper being in Nazi hands, it was impossible to secure its publication in the ordinary way. Typewritten copies were secretly circulated in Germany towards the end of March.

One of these copies was brought out of Germany by an English journalist in April and so it reached the outside world, the first extracts being published in the *Manchester Guardian* on 27 April.

The genesis of the Memorandum was kept a secret, but one day a detachment of Brown Shirts raided Dr Oberfohren's house (he was growing more and more suspect). A copy of the Memorandum was found there. He was given a brief period to take the only course left open to him. After writing a heart-broken letter to his friend, Dr Hugenberg, the chairman of the German-National People's Party, he committed suicide.

HITLER'S HANDS TIED

The conditions under which the General Field Marshal (Hindenburg) conferred the Chancellorship on Adolf Hitler were very hard for the N.S.D.A.P. (the Nazi Party). They had to agree that the German-Nationalist Ministers were given a clear majority in the National Coalition Cabinet. They were also forced to agree to the appointment of a Vice-Chancellor with equal rights in the person of Herr von Papen. The very day after their accession to office, the N.S.D.A.P. were obliged to accept the transfer of the powers of the Commissioner for Prussia, conferred upon the Chancellor by the emergency decree of 20 July 1932, to the Vice-Chancellor Herr von Papen. The Prussian Executive had been deprived of all authority. It retained purely advisory functions.

Another thorn in Hitler's flesh was the promise he had been forced to make to Hindenburg that without the latter's consent no changes whatever would be made in the National Coalition Cabinet, no matter what the results of the elections demanded by the N.S.D.A.P.

Hindenburg had already had unpleasant experiences with a similar undertaking. At the time of Herr von Papen's nomination to the Chancellorship – in summer, 1932 – Hitler had tried to break his promise following his electoral victory in August, 1932, and had demanded the leadership of the Cabinet. His demand, as is well known, was met by a sharp refusal on the part of the General Field Marshal.

On 30 January Hitler had had to give a specific promise in the presence of all the other members of the Cabinet. During the election campaign that followed, individual members of the Cabinet, especially the Stahlhelm* leaders repeatedly referred to this pledge, and assured their supporters that the leader of the N.S.D.A.P. was bound to keep his word of honour.

GÖRING AND GOEBBELS TRY TO FREE HITLER

National-Socialist circles round Göring and Goebbels tried desperately to find a way out of this impasse. This section of the N.S.D.A.P., particularly the ambitious Dr Goebbels, had not the smallest intention of playing second fiddle to anyone. They regarded the hegemony of the N.S.D.A.P. as absolutely indispensable. A situation in which the relationship of forces within the Cabinet was distributed was intolerable to them. Further, Goebbels and his friends recognized that the authority of the General Field Marshal had grown enormously throughout the Nationalist ranks. They were also conscious of the fact that the greater part of the Stahlhelm and the Reichswehr† stood solidly behind the General Field Marshal and his Nationalist friends. Nor could Göring and Goebbels count on the police in the German States. In the largest State, Prussia, the police force was honeycombed with Social Democratic sympathizers.

Goebbels and his circle paid special attention to recent trends among the working classes. They could not help noticing, and fearing, the emergence of a Social Democrat-Communist United Front among the workers, in spite of all the resistance of the Social Democratic leaders, and in spite of many mistakes on the part of the Communist leadership.

The National-Socialist minority in the Cabinet had already tried in vain to force the prohibition of the Communist Party at one of the very first Cabinet meetings. But Herr Hugenberg had pointed

* Ex-Servicemen's organization; paramilitary and German-Nationalist in sympathy.

† The regular army.

out the likelihood of public disorder by uncontrolled and uncontrollable acts of terror on the part of the Communists or Left Radical elements once the restraints imposed by preserving the legality of the Party had been removed.

The Police President,* Melcher, had made repeated raids on the Karl Liebknecht Haus.† At the beginning of February, yet another of these thorough searches was made. The result of this search showed that the building was as good as abandoned by the Communist Party. All documents, typewriters and stationery had been cleared out of the office, and all that was left in the bookshop and storerooms was a small number of pamphlets. Only the so-called City Press was still functioning and producing election material. All that was left in the former Party Secretariat was a man to answer the telephone.

GÖRING AND GOEBBELS CONCOCT A PLAN

Göring and Goebbels, the two most active champions in the fight for the hegemony of the N.S.D.A.P., took counsel. The ingenious Goebbels, handicapped by no scruple, soon devised a plan, the realization of which would not only overcome the resistance of the German-Nationalists to the demands of the N.S.D.A.P. for suppression of Social Democratic and Communist agitation, but, in case of its complete success, also force the actual prohibition of the Communist Party.

Goebbels considered it essential to plant such material in the Karl Liebknecht Haus as would establish the criminal intention of the Communists, the impending threat of Communist insurrection, and the grave danger of delaying. Since Melcher's police could find nothing in the Karl Liebknecht Haus, a new Police President had perforce to be appointed, and from the ranks of the National-Socialists. Only reluctantly did Herr von Papen let his henchman Melcher go from the Police Presidium. The proposal of the N.S.D.A.P. to nominate as Police President the leader of the Berlin S.A.,‡ Count Helldorff, was rejected. Agreement was finally reached on the more moderate Admiral von Levetzow, who certainly belonged to the N.S.D.A.P., but who had preserved certain connections with German-Nationalist circles. The

* Of Berlin.

† Communist Party Headquarters.

‡ *Sturmabteilung*, the private army of the Nazis.

smuggling of material into the vacant Liebknecht Haus was simplicity itself. The police had blueprints of the building, and the necessary documents could easily be brought in.

Goebbels had been perfectly aware from the first that it would be necessary to emphasize the seriousness and the credibility of the documents he had forged by some incident or other, even if only an indirectly suggestive one. This question, too, was not neglected.

THE PLAN PUT INTO EXECUTION

On 24 February the police entered the Karl Liebknecht Haus, which had now been standing empty for weeks, searched it and sealed it.* On the same day the discovery of a mass of treasonable material was officially announced.

On 26 February, 'Conti', a Government news agency, issued an exhaustive report of the results of the search. There is no point in reproducing this report word for word; the blood-and-thunder style of the announcement must have struck every impartial reader of it. Secret corridors, secret trapdoors and passages, catacombs, underground vaults, and similar mysteries were all listed in detail. The whole make-up of the report appeared the more ridiculous, in that, for example, the cellars of an ordinary building were described, literally, in such fantastic terms as 'underground vaults' and 'catacombs'. People must have wondered how it was that many tons of the most exact instructions for carrying out the supposed revolution had ostensibly been hidden in well-concealed annexes to the cellars. Particularly ridiculous was the announcement that these hidden discoveries provided clear proof 'that the Communist Party and its subsidiaries maintained a second, illegal, underground existence'!

Within the Coalition Cabinet the results of the search of the Karl Liebknecht Haus gave rise to the most lively controversy. Papen, Hugenberg and Seldte reproached Herr Göring in the sharpest possible manner for making use of such a common swindle. They pointed out that the documents supposed to have been found were so crudely forged that in no circumstances must they be made public.† They held that much more care should have been taken,

* The only search of the Karl Liebknecht Haus ever carried out at which the Secretary of the Communist Party was not present and at which receipts were not given for material taken away; see evidence London Commission of Inquiry.

† Today, seven months later, they have not yet been made public.

after the fashion of the English Conservatives at the time of the Zinoviev-letter forgery. The clumsiness of the communiqué issued to the Conti agency was attacked. German-Nationalists and the Stahlhelm both maintained that no one could be expected to believe that the Communists would have chosen, of all places, the Karl Liebknecht Haus as their illegal headquarters. The forgeries would have looked far more convincing had the illegal headquarters been 'unearthed' in some other district.

However, once the whole affair had been made public, the German-Nationalists had no alternative but to agree to the anti-Communist decrees. They had never been motivated by any regard for the Communists; what they criticized was the clumsiness of the whole proceedings. And, moreover, they were particularly anxious that, come what may, the Communist Party should be allowed to contest the forthcoming elections, lest the National-Socialists obtain a clear majority in the Reichstag.*

The German-Nationalist paper *Montagszeitung* did in fact publish an announcement to the effect that the Government had been forced, in view of the material found, to take stern defensive measures. Among the proposed measures to be discussed on Tuesday, 28 February, one of the most striking was the prohibition of the printing† of foreign press reports injurious to the Government.

GOEBBELS AND GÖRING TAKE FURTHER COUNSEL

Goebbels and Göring were furious at the obstinacy of their German-Nationalist ally. They wanted at all costs to force the prohibition of the Communist Party. In order to increase the plausibility of the material found, they had already organized, with the help of devoted confidants, acts of arson in various parts of the city. On 25 February, for example, No. 43 of the Berlin evening paper *Tempo* announced in gigantic four-column headlines the discovery of a fire in the former Imperial Palace. In the course of their controversy with their German-Nationalist ally, the National-Socialists had come to understand that obtaining the prohibition of

* Reichstag election, November 1932 (before the fire): Nazis 196, Nationalists 51, total 247; all others 337, less 100 Communists, 237. New election, March 1933 (after the fire): Nazis 288, Nationalists 52, total 340; all others 307, less 81 Communists, 226.

† In Germany.

the Communist Party was no easy task. Consequently a more prominent building had to be set on fire. A blow could then be dealt to the Communists and Social-Democrats and the German-Nationalist ally faced with a *fait accompli*.

All was prepared. On Monday, 27 February, for some extraordinary reason, not one of the National-Socialist Propaganda General Staff was engaged in the election campaign. Herr Hitler, the indefatigable orator, Herr Goebbels, Herr Göring, all happened to be in Berlin. With them was the *Daily Express* correspondent, Sefton Delmer.* So, in a cosy family party, these gentlemen waited for their fire.

THE FIRE

Meanwhile the agents of Herr Göring, led by the Silesian S.A. leader, Reichstag-deputy Heines,† entered the Reichstag through the heating-pipe passage leading from the palace of the President of the Reichstag, Göring. Every S.A. and S.S.‡ leader was carefully selected and had a special station assigned to him. As soon as the outposts in the Reichstag signalled that the Communist deputies Torgler and Koenen had left the building, the S.A. troop set to work. There was plenty of incendiary material, and in a few minutes it was prepared. All the men withdrew into the President's Palace, where they resumed their S.A. uniforms and whence they could disappear unhampered. The only one to be left behind was their creature, van der Lubbe, whom they had thoughtfully provided with a Communist leaflet on the United Front, a few odd photographs of himself, and even, it appears, a membership carrd of some Dutch Communist splinter group.

CONFUSION

The incendiaries, Goebbels and Göring, had thought out everything very cleverly, but they had none the less made far too many mistakes, mistakes that are very difficult to understand considering

* *Sic.* But Mr Delmer was not in Hitler's company *before the fire*. He learnt of its outbreak from a colleague who lived near the scene and arrived within a few minutes. Accordingly, the imputation in the memorandum is clearly unjustified. It is, however, easy to see how Oberfohren became mistaken. Mr Delmer in his account relates that, while hastening to the Reichstag, he was overtaken by Hitler's car and passed through the police cordon in his company. Thus he arrived with Hitler *just after the fire*.

† A self-confessed and convicted murderer, now Chief of Police of Breslau.

‡ *Schutzstaffeln*, another section of the N.S.D.A.P. private army.

the skill and ingenuity of the present Minister of Propaganda. Let us look at some of them. In the official announcement of 28 February (Prussian Press Service) we can read, *inter alia*: 'This fire is the most monstrous act of terror yet committed by Bolshevism in Germany. Among the many tons of subversive material that the police discovered in their raid on the Karl Liebknecht Haus were instructions for running a Communist terror campaign on the Bolshevik model. According to these documents, Government buildings, museums, palaces and essential buildings were to be set on fire. Further, instructions were given to place women and children, if possible those of police officials, at the head of terrorist groups in cases of conflict or disorder. The burning of the Reichstag was to have been the signal for bloody insurrection and civil war. Widespread looting was to have broken out in Berlin as early as 4 a.m. on Tuesday. It has been established that for today (28 February) acts of terror were planned against certain individuals, against private property, against the life and safety of the population.'

The astonished reader may well ask how it was that the police authorities and the Minister of the Interior waited until after the burning of the Reichstag on 27 February to take their anti-Bolshevik steps, when they had 'discovered' the plans for the insurrection as early as the 24th. Further, as early as Saturday, 25 February, an act of arson was discovered in the former Imperial Palace. But Herr Göring and Herr Levetzow did nothing at all to guard Government buildings, palaces or museums. That was one of the mistakes they made in their hurry.

But it was certainly not the only one. Who in his right senses can believe the fairy tale they have spread about the incendiary van Lubbe? A hiker arrives from Holland. He spends the night of 17–18 February in Glindow near Potsdam. In the 'Green Tree Inn' he produces his Dutch passport and signs the visitors' book with his full name, birthplace, and place of usual residence. He is poorly dressed in a grey coat and soft hat, and in no way distinguishable from any of the other hikers that throng the roads. On 18 February, he leaves Glindow in the direction of Werder-Berlin. On the 19 February or so, he reaches Berlin, and lo and behold, he immediately succeeds in joining the Action Committee of the plotters and is assigned a most important part in helping to fire the Reichstag barely ten days later. Whereupon this fine revolutionary sticks a Dutch passport, a United Front leaflet and so on in his pocket, stays behind in the Reichstag and is the only one to get himself arrested by the police. 'Look, everybody, here's the Communist who set fire to the Reichstag.' Herr Goebbels and Herr Göring have badly overestimated the credulity of world public opinion. It is an even happier chance that this van Lubbe also volunteered the information that he was in touch with the S.P.D.* In the Press Service† report mentioned above we read: 'The Reichstag incendiary has admitted his contacts with the S.P.D. By this admission, the Communist-Social Democrat United Front has been implicated.' Goebbels and Göring went further still, although, on the whole, perhaps a little too far. For they also produced three scoundrels who had allegedly seen Deputies Torgler and Koenen in the Reichstag with van Lubbe. The *Deutsche Allgemeine Zeitung* declared that Herr Torgler had spent several hours before the fire in the company of the incendiary who was later arrested, and also with a number of other individuals, some of whom were seen carrying torches. The only reason why these individuals were not caught was because they managed to escape through the subterranean heating passage leading to the palace of the Reichstag President.

The astonished reader may well wonder once again why Herr Torgler was allowed to run about the Reichstag with several persons, all equipped with torches, for several hours. And he may also marvel at the smartness of Herr Göring, or at least of his police, who discovered, even before the fire was extinguished, that the incendiaries must have got away through the subterranean heating passage.

It may, perhaps, be worth mentioning further that two reporters from the *Vorwärts* managed to slip through the cordon round the Reichstag, to get into a telephone booth in the Reichstag and to ring up the *Vorwärts* with the news that Herr Göring had set the Reichstag on fire. Naturally, they were both caught in the telephone booth, if only as 'proof' that it was the Social Democrats who had started the rumour that Göring had set fire to the Reichstag. Again, Mr Sefton Delmer of the *Daily Express*, who had waited with Göring, Hitler and Goebbels for the conflagration to break

* Social Democratic Party.

† Official Prussian Press Service, under the direct control of Göring.

out,* wired to his newspaper that shortly after the news of the fire became known, he met his friends in the Reichstag. When Hitler saw von Papen there, he said to Papen: 'If this fire, as I believe, turns out to be the handiwork of Communists, then nothing can now stop us crushing this murder pest with an iron fist.' A little later, Göring joined them as well and said to Herr Hitler: 'This is undoubtedly the work of Communists. A number of Communist deputies were in the Reichstag twenty minutes before the fire broke out. We have succeeded in arresting one of the incendiaries.' Alas, how obvious this dispatch of Mr Sefton Delmer makes it why the Reichstag was burned!

How beautifully, too, they had prepared the lists of people to be arrested by the police! Hundreds of addresses had been got together, not only of Communists, but also of bourgeois journalists who might have added their voices to the protest. . . .†

THE GERMAN-NATIONALISTS AND THE FIRE

Though the German-Nationalist Party was in full agreement with the severe measures against the Communists, it was as fully opposed to the act of arson carried out by its partner in the Coalition. Thus the Cabinet endorsed the severest measures against the Communists and also against the Social-Democrats, but voiced the opinion that the fire would seriously damage the reputation of the National Front‡ abroad. So outraged were the Nationalists that the National-Socialist ministers failed to obtain the prohibition of the Communist Party. They§ needed the Communist deputies to prevent the National-Socialists securing a clear majority in Parliament. The Cabinet also told Herr Göring not to publish the forgeries he had 'found' in the Karl Liebknecht Haus. It was pointed out to him that the publication of these clumsy forgeries would damage the Government even further. Particularly embarrassing to the Government was the fact that the Communist deputy Torgler, Chairman of the Communist fraction in the Reichstag, had surrendered to the police on the Tuesday morning. It would have been far preferable had he fled abroad. The mere fact

* *Sic.* But Mr Delmer was not with Hitler before the fire. (In fact, Delmer won a libel action against one retailer of this completely unsubstantiated rumour. A. J. P.)

† This sentence was incomplete in the original.

‡ The coalition of the Nationalist groups.

§ *Sic.* 'They' refers to the German-Nationalist Ministers.

that, accused though he was of so grave a crime, after the arrest of thousands of Communist officials, and in peril of execution under martial law, he yet placed himself at the disposal of the police, was in the highest degree annoying to the Government. Herr Göring was instructed to deny that Torgler had surrendered voluntarily. The world press was, however, so unanimous in ascribing the fire to leading members of the Government, that the National Government's reputation was seriously undermined.

GÖRING AND GOEBBELS TAKE FURTHER COUNSEL

Much as Göring and Goebbels welcomed the paralysis of the Communist and Social Democratic election machinery, though they knew that broad masses of the petty bourgeoisie, white-collar workers, and peasants would believe their tales about the burning of the Reichstag and consequently vote for the N.S.D.A.P. as the vanguard against Bolshevism, they were not at all pleased with the position taken up by the German-Nationalist Ministers in the Cabinet. Approval continued to be withheld from the prohibition of the Communist Party. With increasing bitterness they felt that their boundless ambition was hemmed in by German-Nationalists, Stahlhelm and Reichswehr. It was obvious to them that they must break this grip as soon as possible. They plotted and schemed.

At last, this group decided on a bid for power during the night of 5–6 March. The plan was to occupy the Government buildings and to force Hindenburg to reconstruct the Cabinet. Should he refuse, his abdication was to be demanded. In that case, Hindenburg was to hand the Reich Presidency over to Hitler, and Hitler would appoint Göring as Chancellor. There was some talk that this might perhaps be effected on the occasion of the great propaganda march of the S.A. and the S.S. through Berlin, combined with the ceremonial paying of homage to Hitler, which had been fixed for Friday, 3 March. This great propaganda march was now being prepared with every possible dispatch. Already numerous battalions of S.A. men from districts outside Berlin were camped within the city, the streets along the route of the procession were cordoned off by the police, traffic was diverted, and thousands waited in the Wilhelmstrasse* for the demonstration.

As rumours were spreading that this march was to lead to seizure of the Government buildings, the German-Nationalist Ministers

* The quarter in which the Government buildings are situated.

managed, at the eleventh hour, to obtain Hitler's agreement to abandon the route through the Wilhelmstrasse. The thousands in the Wilhelmstrasse were suddenly informed, to their astonishment, that the S.A. procession was to take another route not touching the Wilhelmstrasse, but going west through the Prinz-Albrechtstrasse. The German-Nationalists had to bind themselves in return to renounce the march of the Stahlhelm through the Government quarter. The Stahlhelm march had been proposed as a march of homage to Hindenburg. To this change, the Stahlhelm leaders agreed.

A GERMAN-NATIONALIST COUNTER-MARCH

The German-Nationalist Ministers were in a very serious position. The election results in Lippe-Detmold had shown how real was the danger of the German-Nationalist voters going over bag and baggage to the Nazis. Their propaganda was no match at all for the Nazis'. The Herrenklub,* the Stahlhelm groups and the German-Nationalist leaders consulted together. Nazi occupation of the Government buildings having only just been averted on Friday afternoon, reliance could not be placed on the Stahlhelm and Reichswehr alone keeping the Nazis at bay on the night of 5–6 March. It was clear that the masses stood, not behind Hindenburg, but behind their idol Hitler. It would have been futile to fight alone against these masses and their mass enthusiasm. The only thing left was to act as unscrupulously as Göring and Goebbels had acted when they set fire to the Reichstag. The following plan was devised. The public would be told officially about the results of the investigation into the Reichstag fire, but the announcement would be so worded that, in case of need, it could be used against the Nazis. An official announcement of this kind could be used to exert pressure on the Nazi Ministers, if they really persisted in their plan to occupy Government buildings. In that way it was intended to fill the Nazi masses with doubt and to win them over for the National Front under the leadership of the German-Nationalists and Hindenburg. An appeal was prepared to nationalist Germany, in which Hindenburg would reveal the plot for the violent seizure of power,† accuse Göring, Goebbels and Hitler of arson, referring to the earlier, ambiguous communiqué, and summon the Nazi

* A group of *Junkers*, landowners and militarists – the Papen circle.

† By the National-Socialists.

masses to rally behind Hindenburg as the only effective answer to Marxism. Hindenburg himself was not to be present at the Stahlhelm's ceremony of homage to him, but was to spend the night of the 5th–6th outside Berlin under the protection of the Reichswehr. The Reichswehr itself would be put on the alert.

THE OFFICIAL ANNOUNCEMENT OF FRIDAY, 3 MARCH

The chief of the political police, Dr Diels, a man who, in spite of his membership of the N.S.D.A.P., was very close to the German-Nationalists, summoned, in the late evening hours of Friday, a press conference to receive and make public the results of the investigation, as far as it had gone, into the burning of the Reichstag. The Nazis were told that this communiqué was being issued to support their election campaign. Besides the communiqué, Diels gave out photographs of the incendiary, of his passport, of a Communist leaflet found on him, and of the gutted Session Chamber. At the same time a reward of 20,000 marks was promised for information leading to the discovery of those implicated in the burning. The significant passages in the official announcement ran as follows:

> 'There can be no question of van der Lubbe's having been in contact with the K.P.D.* Van der Lubbe is known to the police as a Communist agitator.'

Exact consideration of these two sentences reveals their ambiguity, indeed, rather, their single significance. Van der Lubbe's contact with the K.P.D. is said not to be in 'question'; now, this can mean that such contact has been proven; but it can also mean the exact opposite. Now, this very ambiguity could – if the need arose – be used to exonerate the K.P.D. Or take the following sentences:

> 'Van der Lubbe admits his own participation in the crime. How far the investigations have proved the complicity of other persons cannot at the moment be revealed in the interests of the pending proceedings and the safety of the State.'

It is perfectly obvious that the security of the State could be no ground for concealment of serious evidence against Communists. For election purposes, it would have been far better to say: 'The investigations have shown cause for serious suspicions against persons either belonging to or closely associated with the K.P.D.'

* German Communist Party.

But had the K.P.D. been accused straight out, the purpose of this press conference and of this communiqué as means of pressure against the Nazi Ministers would have been defeated. Further, one must not forget Diels's evasive answer – again in the interests of security – to an inquisitive journalist, who asked *how far* grounds existed for serious suspicions that there had been contacts between van der Lubbe and other Communists. How could the safety of the State have been endangered if Diels had merely declared that grounds *existed* for such suspicions?

Diels also refused to say anything about the discovery of seditious instructions in the Karl Liebknecht Haus, 'lest their content be made known to Communists throughout the Reich'. (This although Göring had already published the most essential part of this 'incriminating' material in an official announcement on the night of the fire.) At this moment, declared the ingenious Dr Diels, he would rather not make any statement about the assertion that van der Lubbe had been seen in the Reichstag with the Communist deputy Torgler or else with Koenen. (Why not?)

THE 5TH OF MARCH

Election day had come, and the police had taken a multitude of precautions. In particular, public buildings were guarded, far more carefully even than had been decreed after the fire. The authorities gave out that preparations had been made for every possible eventuality. None the less, it was said that demonstrations of some kind must be expected as soon as the definite results of the election became known.

With streets strongly guarded by police patrols on horseback, on foot and in motor vans, election day passed off unusually quietly in the capital. The Stahlhelm demonstration in honour of Hindenburg took place in Hindenburg's absence. In Hindenburg's message to the Stahlhelm we find the following remarkable passage: 'Your wish to convey to me the greetings of former Front soldiers cannot, unfortunately, be gratified for reasons which I have given verbally.' On the advice of his friends, Hindenburg was spending the day in Doeberitz with the Reichswehr, and not in the Government quarters. Hitler, however, had been told that Hindenburg was ill and unable to leave his palace. The Nazis thought that the President was in the Wilhelmstrasse on the night of 5 March. The Stahlhelm had already announced that its country contingents would move into Berlin for the night of the 5th–6th. In a Stahlhelm communiqué dated 12 March ('Die junge Front', No. 11) it is stated that after the demonstration, the field-grey Stahlhelm companies waited in readiness for further orders until midnight before they were dismissed.

Shortly after the close of the ballot, between 6.30 and 8.30, picked S.A. troops poured into Berlin in squadrons of brand-new motor vans. One of these detachments, consisting of six vans, each carrying about thirty to forty men, drove from the Heerstrasse across the Reichskanzlerplatz and down the Neue Kantstrasse and Tauentzienstrasse at about 6.45 p.m. The occupants of the vans were newly equipped, wore dark breeches and dark S.S. caps, and brown shirts with brassards. Silently, without cheers, without slogans, these detachments rushed with extreme speed into the city, behind a special car carrying the leaders.

The Reichswehr, too, was not idle. The Reichskanzlerplatz was patrolled by an armoured radio car, and so were all roads leading into the city. In that way the Reichswehr command was given an exact picture of the forces pouring in as well as of their subsequent movements.

Midnight was the hour fixed for seizing the Government buildings. The Nazi leaders, including Hitler, Göring, Goebbels and Frick, waited in the Reich Chancellory. Shortly before eleven a strong detachment of Reichswehr officers, led by General von Blomberg, called on Hitler. They requested Hitler to order the immediate withdrawal of his private army. Hitler was also informed that Hindenburg was in Doeberitz with the Reichswehr and that the Reichswehr would quash any attempt at a violent seizure of power on the part of the Nazis.

For this purpose the Stahlhelm was stationed ready for action in a ring round the centre of the city and at other strategic points. In addition, the most important public buildings were occupied by the Reichswehr. Hitler was required further to announce to the press that, in spite of the great electoral victory of the Nazis, which even at this hour was already certain, no change would be made in the composition of the Government. In case of refusal, General Blomberg declared, shortly and firmly, that Hitler, Göring, Goebbels and Frick would be arrested on suspicion of arson. Hindenburg would then issue an appeal to all Nationalists, and especially to the millions of Nazi voters, to stand firm behind him. The fight against Bolshevism called for the greatest determination, but the national cause must not be allowed to be soiled by such criminal acts as those committed by a number of the Nazi leaders. General Blomberg referred briefly to the equivocal communiqué of the political police issued on Friday night, which made it possible now for the Cabinet to denounce the Nazis as the true Reichstag incendiaries.

The gamble for power, which Hitler, Göring and Goebbels had imagined to be so easy, was lost. The torches they had lit had been snatched away by the German-Nationalists and their military allies. No time for reflection was granted. Motor cars bearing the adjutants of the Reichswehr and the S.A. and S.S. leaders accompanying them left the Wilhelmstrasse *en route* to all the action stations of the S.A. and S.S. The detachments of S.A. and S.S. men from outside the city which had been intended to occupy the Wilhelmstrasse left the city forthwith and returned to their camp in the Mark.* The Stahlhelm was told about midnight that no special orders were likely to be issued and that the men in field-grey could at last turn in.

NEW PLANS BY GÖRING AND GOEBBELS

Furious at being outwitted by their allies, Göring, Goebbels, and their cronies considered what next might be done. Should so gigantic an electoral success still bring them no nearer sole hegemony? They had 288 deputies and the German-Nationalist ally only fifty-two – a clear majority; yet the Cabinet still remained in the hands of the German-Nationalists.† This was really a bit too much for the pride of those who had already seen themselves as sole dictators of Germany. All that had taken place during this week in the way of illegal acts, private arrests by S.A. and S.S. men, private killings, bestial treatment of captured political opponents in the private prisons of the S.A.‡ – all had been organized by the Nazi leadership to create further disturbances and to provide the excuse for stealing further slices of power. Quick action was needed. In a

* Brandenburg.

† Before the Communist Party was prohibited, the Reichstag stood: National Front 340, Opponents 307; without the Communists: Nazis 288, all others (including Nationalists) 280.

‡ This is not the first protest by a German Conservative against Nazi brutality. See letter of Count Reventlow (an N.S.D.A.P. member) reprinted in the *Manchester Guardian*.

speech at Stettin, Göring expressly declared that he assumed full responsibility for every illegal act that might be committed during the week. The seizure of the newspaper offices of the Centre Party,* interference in administrative and judicial matters by S.A. troops, destruction of trade union buildings, in short everything that happened, all happened because the Leader so wished it. Goebbels busied himself with attacks on department stores and one-price shops.† Forgeries, like the letter from Messrs Hermann Tietz (a large department store) to the Central Committee of the Communist Party, were published to inflame the masses, and particularly the petty bourgeoisie. A deputation of S.A. men appeared outside the Stock Exchange, and as a climax to the disorder, Göring delivered the famous incitement speech of Essen, in the course of which he said: 'Go, rob and plunder far and wide. Break into houses, shoot – never mind if you shoot too far or too short – the main thing is, shoot! and don't come back to me without any booty.' This in short was the context of his infamous speech. A brigand chief could not have urged his bandits on more eloquently. During the night following this speech the S.A. seized the printing works of the Centre Party's newspaper and forced the editors, at gun point, to print Göring's speech verbatim on the front page. Two hundred thousand copies of the Centre Party newspaper were printed on the Friday morning and rushed by car for distribution to all towns and villages.

But the echoes of the speech had scarcely died away, when the Leader issued a new decree directly opposed to Göring's incitement.

Hitler, driven into a corner by the far more powerful and stronger forces of the German-Nationalists and Reichswehr, demanded, only a few hours after Göring's speech, in an appeal to his Party comrades of the S.A. and S.S., the strictest possible discipline, immediate cessation of all individual action, particularly the molestation of foreigners, the dislocation of motor traffic and the disturbance of business. Whoever promoted such acts was irresponsible and malicious. It was well-known that Communist spies were trying to incite Germans to such action. The further course of the national uprising must henceforth be directed from above. The effect of this appeal was like a thunderclap. A moment

* Catholic Centre Party.

† Shops like our Woolworths.

previously Göring had said: 'I refuse to regard the police as watchmen for Jewish department stores. There must be an end to the nuisance of every swindler detected in his swindles calling the police. The police will protect anyone in Germany who earns an honest living; they are not here to protect swindlers, bandits, usurers and traitors. To all those who say, that somewhere, some time, somebody has been seized and ill-treated, we can only reply: "You can't plane a board without shaving splinters." We live in exceptional times. For years we have been promising to settle accounts with these traitors.'

And a few hours later, Herr Hitler: 'Only unscrupulous individuals, and especially Communist spies, will seek to compromise the Party by individual action.' It was all too obvious.

GOEBBELS AND GÖRING STILL UNSATISFIED

Once more a shackled Hitler had been forced to call off the masses. Goebbels and Göring were frustrated. They now proposed to make a last attempt on Sunday 12 March. S.A. and S.S. men were equipped with cars and arms, ready to strike. They waited in vain – as they had waited in vain after the first Presidential election of 1932, as they had waited in vain in August 1932, and as they had waited in vain through the night of 5th–6th March.

As early as 10 a.m. the radio announced that the Reich Chancellor would make an important appeal at 2 p.m. And at two o'clock Adolf Hitler announced nothing more revolutionary than the Reich President's 'flag decree'* and added an energetic and extremely sharp appeal to his Party comrades for blind obedience to his orders. Every individual action must be suppressed. He, as Leader, appealed to them, the German people, in the name of the National Revolution. The economy must be put on a sound footing. Interference with the administration and with business must stop forthwith. All paltry desire for revenge must be checked. Hitler's appeal was repeated over the wireless almost hour by hour. S.A. and S.S. men all over the Reich listened to the impressive voice of the man they idolized. Goebbels, Göring and their cronies were powerless.

THE FIGHT GOES ON

Goebbels and Göring must postpone the realization of their dreams to some distant day. Goebbels is Reich Propaganda

* Making the Swastika Germany's new flag.

Minister. He keeps trying to undermine the Reichswehr, and to detach the Stahlhelm as well as the Reichswehr from the German-Nationalists. The Reichswehr is still exempt from hoisting the swastika flag, it still salutes the black-white-and-red banner with the iron cross. For how long? And who will prove stronger in the struggle? When will Hitler be unshackled?

This is the full text of the memorandum. The [original] translator has thought it better to preserve the irregularities and unclarities of what was obviously a very hastily typed sheet. Oberfohren has not had to wait long for the answers to his questions. Within three months the German-Nationalist Party had dissolved, the Stahlhelm had been incorporated into the ranks of the S.A., the Cabinet had been reconstructed and, as a climax, Göring has been promoted from Captain to General by Hindenburg! But rapid as has been this march of events, it has been too slow for Oberfohren, who was found dead on May 7th.

Had he lived, he would have seen Hitler still bound, as he and his Party must always be bound within the framework of its determination to preserve the national interests which the old German-Nationalists represent. But the mock-struggle he described has been resolved – the Nazis have bought power by endorsing in practice the substance, *e.g. the whole social programme and decrees of the German-Nationalist landowning, military and big business interests; and the remaining German-Nationalists have bought tolerance by endorsing in silence the* form, *e.g. the brutalities of Göring, the demagogic falsehoods of Goebbels and what, as we see here, they know well to be the crowning infamy of tyranny of all time – the Leipzig trial.*

Appendix D

EXTRACTS FROM THE WHITE BOOK ON THE EXECUTIONS OF 30 JUNE 1934

(*Editions du Carrefour, Paris*, 1935.)

THE REICHSTAG INCENDIARIES

THE spectre of the Reichstag fire cannot be exorcized. In vain did the Hitler Government try to clear its name before the whole world at a trial lasting three months. In vain is Ernst Torgler being kept imprisoned even after his acquittal, lest he raise his voice against the true incendiaries. In vain did the Nazis hope that van der Lubbe's secret would die with him. The accusing voices cannot be silenced.

Whenever Göring raises his voice, he is answered with an echo of: 'Incendiary!' Whenever Goebbels addresses the world, the reply resounds: 'Incendiary!' The flames of the Reichstag fire continue to scorch the guilty.

In the Nazi camp itself, the fire has become a blackmail weapon. The names of the incendiaries were known to eleven people. Three of the incendiaries – Ernst, Fiedler and Mohrenschild were murdered on 30 June, and the accessories to the crime – Röhm, Heines and Sander – were also sent to their death. All of them paid with their lives for their knowledge of the Reichstag fire, and for the great service they had rendered to National Socialism.

Fear of persecution and murder are rife as never before inside the leading Nazi clique. Whenever we are shown pictures of Nazi leaders, we invariably see them flanked by huge men, right hands bulging in coat pocket, in the manner of American gangsters. But not even these bodyguards are thought adequate, for, in addition, every Nazi leader has thought fit to compile a dossier inculpating all the others: Göring against Himmler; Himmler against Göring; Goebbels against Göring; Ley against Goebbels – and all against Hitler.

The S.A. Gruppenführer Karl Ernst was another to compile a dossier and to deposit it in a safe place. In it, Ernst dealt with the Reichstag fire and gave a full account of the actual events. He named the incendiaries and their accomplices. Ernst was counting on the fact that, in case of his arrest or dismissal, the mere threat of publishing the document abroad would persuade Göring and Goebbels to rescind any measures they might have decided to take against him. Another reason why he compiled his dossier was that he needed a safeguard against his own assassination, or a means of revenge against his murderers. Ernst laid it down that the dossier was to be made public only in the event that he died an unnatural death or if Fieldler or von Mohrenschild authorized the publication. He deposited the document with a lawyer – probably the same Advocate Voss to whom Gregor Strasser, too, had entrusted his papers. Voss was murdered on 30 June, before he had a chance of taking the document abroad.

Ernst also sent a signed copy of his document and a covering letter of explanation to Heines, whom he advised to put his own knowledge about the Reichstag fire on record as well.

We cannot tell whether Heines followed Ernst's advice, but we do know that Heines sent Ernst's letter and confession, together with some other papers, to a friend in Breslau. It is this man, who still lives in Germany, who has sent us Ernst's confession. That confession explains the course of the Reichstag fire and bears out what was stated in the two *Brown Books* and the entire world press, and what was proved at the London Counter-Trial, viz. that the Reichstag was burned by the National Socialists.

We are now publishing Ernst's confession, in the hope that the National Socialist leaders may feel compelled to contest our case against them before an unprejudiced Court. We accuse the Prussian Prime Minister, Hermann Göring, Reichsminister Joseph Goebbels, the Saxon Prime Minister, Manfred von Killinger, and Potsdam Police President Graf Wolf Heinrich von Helldorff of having played a part in planning or in staging the Reichstag fire. We accuse the Nazi press attaché, Ernst Hanfstaengl, of being an accessory. We accuse the assassins of 30 June, of the murder of the S.A. leaders Ernst, Fiedler, von Mohrenschildt and Sander, all four of them men who had dangerous knowledge of the Reichstag fire.

The following were murdered:

Karl Ernst, S.A. Gruppenführer, Berlin-Brandenburg, Member of the Reichstag, Member of the Prussian State Council, Reichstag incendiary; Fiedler, S.A. Oberführer, Berlin-Brandenburg, Reichstag incendiary; Von Mohrenschild, S.A. Führer, Berlin-Brandenburg,

Reichstag incendiary; Sander, Standartenführer, Berlin-Brandenburg, accessory to the Reichstag fire.

With their deaths the Nazi leaders hoped to remove all traces of National Socialist guilt in the Reichstag fire.

We now publish two documents, viz. Ernst's covering letter to Heines, and his account of the Reichstag fire. These documents prove conclusively that the National Socialist leaders stand for everything that is vile and treacherous in political life.

On 5 June, when the battle for the S.A. had already been lost, Ernst wrote the following letter to Heines:

June 5th, 1934.

Dear E,

The Chief has been round at last. Long discussion. The Chief told me they were at it for hours. 'He' set up his usual howl and implored the Chief to believe that He would much rather see the Chief at the head than an old geezer from Neudecker. But it didn't work. General difficulties, fear of foreign opinion, a meeting in Venice and the like. But you will meet the Chief yourself and will hear all about it from him. The upshot of it all was a mutual promise to do nothing until the old chap croaks. Then we shall see.

But that means getting down to brass-tacks. Anyone can see that, if we wait until the Egyptian bastard makes common cause with the cripple and the tailor's dummy, the three of them are going to do us in. So we must act first. Hermann is out to skin us alive, and though he can't stand the cripple, when it comes to fighting us he would even make friends with Black Boy. We shall have to explode a bomb right up their backsides. I would do anything to get hold of the cripple alone. A pity R. stopped me smashing his skull that time when he spread that muck about my marriage. I've told the Chief about your letter. You know I'm usually not much of a speaker and writer. He agrees with you that we must be prepared for the worst. The cripple will stop at nothing. The Chief has sent all the most important documents to a place of safe keeping. After my chat with him, I, too, signed an account of the events in February which M had typed out for me. It is now in safe hands. If anything nasty should happen to me, the whole balloon will go up. I'm enclosing a signed copy just in case. Look after it carefully, and put your own things in a safe place, as well. Read it through. It is the strongest weapon we have and our last resort. Perhaps it will help, but perhaps it won't. You know that the cripple can outwit us any time. Our strength lies elsewhere, and we are determined to use it.

But this time you'll have to stick with us through thick and thin. I have thought up a plan to smash the cripple once and for all, but we must lie low until everything is settled. The main thing is to hit the cripple where it hurts him most. That is my own aim but the Chief is more concerned with skinning Hermann alive. But then why not do them both in? Still, the first thing is to drive a wedge between the two bastards. If only we can get 'Him' on our side for a while, everything will be fine. Fi will tell you more about my plan. You can rely on him blindly. It's a pity that I'm not with you while you two are fixing things up. I agree with everything the Chief says but I insist on having the cripple to myself, nobody can rob me of that pleasure. He is the bastard who got me into this mess, and then laughed up his sleeve at me.

The Chief thinks we must not start before the Party Conference. He has news that the old boy will live for another ten years. I don't believe that, but since everybody agrees with the Chief, I can't do a thing about it. But after the Party Conference, we simply must get cracking. I'm going on leave within the next few weeks. I've just got to get away with her for a bit. Get Fi to send me a copy of your documents, don't put the thing off, and be careful with Sch. People are talking. Don't be seen with him so often. The Chief tells me 'He' has dropped a remark about it.

Clear up your den. Our friend from the Albrechtstrasse informs me that Black Boy is thinking of looking us all up; I myself am looking forward to the visit because I've prepared a lovely surprise for him.

Keep your chin up,
Yours,
Carlos.

[KEY: 'He' = Hitler; the Chief = Röhm; the Cripple = Goebbels; the tailor's dummy and Hermann = Göring; the Egyptian = Hess; Black Boy = Himmler; Fi is probably Fiedler; 'M' is probably von Mohrenschild; the 'friend from the Albrechtstrasse' is a Gestapo official (the headquarters of the Gestapo are in the Prinz Albrechtstrasse); 'Sch' is probably another adjutant of Heines.]

ERNST'S CONFESSION

'I, the undersigned, Karl Ernst, S.A. Gruppenführer, Berlin-Brandenburg, Prussian State Councillor, born on September 1st 1904 in Berlin-Wilmersdorf, herewith put on record a full account of my part in the Reichstag fire. I am doing so on the advice of friends who have told me that Göring and Goebbels are planning to betray me. If I am arrested, Göring and Goebbels must be told at once that this document has been sent abroad. The document itself may only be published on the orders of myself or of the two friends who are named in the enclosure, or if I die a violent death.

I hereby declare that, on February 27th, 1933, I and two *Unterführer* named in the enclosure, set fire to the German Reichstag. We did so in the belief that we should be serving the Führer and our movement. We hoped that we might enable the Führer to deliver a shattering blow against Marxism, the worst enemy of the German people. Before this pestilence is completely smashed, Germany cannot recover. I do not regret what I have done, and I should do the same thing all over again. What I do regret deeply is that our action helped scum like Göring and Goebbels to rise to the top, men who have betrayed the S.A., who betray our Führer every day, and who use lies and slander to destroy the Chief of Staff and the S.A. The S.A. is the strongest weapon our movement has.

I am a National Socialist. I am convinced that National Socialism stands and falls with the S.A.

A few days after we seized power, Helldorff asked me to go with him to Göring's that evening. On the way, Helldorff told me that the idea was to find ways and means of smashing the Marxists once and for all. When we got there, I was surprised to see that Goebbels, too, had turned up, and that he had worked out a plan: when the Führer's plane touched down in Breslau, where he was to address an election meeting, two 'Communists' would attack him, thus providing the pretext for a campaign of retribution. Heines had been summoned to Berlin to discuss all the details. The Berlin-Brandenburg group of the S.A. was to stand ready. Helldorff would be told all the details within the next two days.

Two days later, we met again at Göring's, but this time without Goebbels. Göring had decided against the whole plan; he felt it might give undesirable elements the wrong ideas. He added that Goebbels disagreed with him, and implored us to do our best to talk him round. He had advised Heines to postpone his trip to Berlin for a few days.

Next day, I was ordered to report to Goebbels. I arrived last, and found that the others had all agreed to drop the original plan. Göring suggested a number of alternatives including the firing of the Palace and the bombing of the Ministry of the Interior. It was then that Goebbels said with a smile that it would be far better to set the Reichstag on fire, and then to stand up as the champions of parliamentarianism. Göring agreed at once. Helldorff and I were against the plan because we thought the practical difficulties involved were far too great. We pointed out that starting a fire in the Palace was much easier, because there was hardly anyone on guard there. But in the end, we were won over by Göring and Goebbels. We spent hours settling all the details. Heines, Helldorff and I would start the fire on the 25th February, eight days before the election. Göring promised to supply incendiary material of a kind that would be extremely effective yet take up very little space. On February 25th, we would all hide in the Reichstag Party rooms until everyone had left, and then set to work. The technical arrangements were left to me. When I called on Göring next day, he had suddenly grown less confident. He was afraid that our hanging about was bound to be noticed on a Saturday, when the Reichstag closed earlier than usual. He also felt that it would be wrong to let known S.A. leaders do the actual work. If one of us were caught, everything would be lost. He telephoned Goebbels, who turned up soon afterwards. Göring mentioned his objections, but Goebbels pooh-poohed them all.

Even so, we had to give up our plan in the end, when we realized that the Communists, whose Party rooms were opposite ours, kept very late hours. There was every reason to fear that they might spot us.

In the meantime Röhm had come to Berlin, and Heines, Killinger, Helldorff and I discussed the whole question with him over a meal. It was decided that none of us must take any part in the fire because the danger to the Party was far too great. Killinger recommended leaving all the dirty work to a few S.A. men who could later be got out of the way. Röhm felt he must make absolutely sure he was appointed State-Security Commissar before the fire.

At the next discussion which, I believe, took place in Göring's house, Helldorff was absent because he was addressing an election meeting. I suggested to Göring that we use the subterranean passage leading from his residence to the Reichstag, because that would minimize the risk of discovery. I was ordered to pick my men. Goebbels insisted on postponing the fire from February 25th to February 27th, because February 26th was a Sunday, a day on which no evening papers appeared so that the fire could not be played up sufficiently for propaganda purposes. We decided to start the fire at about 9 p.m., in time for quite a number of radio bulletins. Göring and Goebbels agreed on how to throw suspicion on the Communists.

Helldorff and I paced out the subterranean passage three times in order to get our precise bearings. In addition, Göring had given us a section plan and also a precise time table of when the officials made their rounds of inspection. During one inspection of the subterranean passage we were almost caught – the watchman, who probably heard our footsteps, made an unscheduled round. We hid ourselves in a dead-end branch of the passage which the watchman fortunately overlooked – else he would not be alive today. Two days before the fire, we stowed the incendiary material which Göring had procured for us in the same dead-end branch. The material consisted of small canisters of a self-igniting phosphorus mixture together with a few litres of paraffin. During all our visits to the passage we always went in through the boiler-house to which we had been given keys. Whenever we went in and out, Göring would call the watchman so that we could come and go unnoticed.

I wondered for a long time whom I could trust with the execution of the plan and came to the conclusion that I would have to join in after all, and that I could only rely on men from my closest circle. I convinced Göring and Goebbels and they both agreed. I now think that they merely agreed because they thought they would get me more firmly under their thumb that way. My choice fell on two men in whom I had complete confidence, and to whom I am most grateful. I made them swear an oath of personal loyalty, and they kept it. I knew that I could rely on them. They themselves must decide whether or not their names, which are indicated in the covering letter, should be made public.

During our discussion, Göring told us that he had confided our plan to Hanfstaengl. Hanfstaengl, who lived in Göring's residence, would, on the 27th, divert the watchman's attention while we slipped in through the residence. We had keys to all the doors. Göring himself was going to be away – in the Ministry of the Interior.

A few days before the fixed date, Helldorff told us that a young fellow had turned up in Berlin of whom we should be able to make good use. This fellow was the Dutch Communist van der Lubbe. I did not meet him before the action. Helldorff and I fixed all the details. The Dutchman would climb into the Reichstag and blunder about conspicuously in the corridor. Meanwhile I and my men would set fire to the Session Chamber and part of the lobby. The Dutchman was supposed to start at 9 o'clock – half an hour later than we did.

The main difficulty was keeping to a precise timetable. The Dutchman had to climb into the Reichstag after we had left, and after the fire had already started. In order to familiarize him with the place, Helldorff sent him on a tour of inspection into the Reichstag. Apart from that he was made to learn the plan of the whole Reichstag by heart with the help of a very accurate map and with Sander's constant prodding. We decided that van der Lubbe must climb into the Reichstag restaurant, not only because that was the simplest way in, but also because, if he were caught, we should still have plenty of time to get away. To make perfectly certain that van der Lubbe would not take fright or change his mind at the last moment, Sander would not leave his side all afternoon. He would escort him to the Reichstag and watch him climb in from a safe distance. As soon as he was sure that van der Lubbe was in, he was to telephone Hanfstaengl and Göring. Van der Lubbe was to be left in the belief that he was working by himself.

I met my two helpers at eight o'clock precisely on the corner of Neue Wilhelmstrasse and Dorotheenstrasse. We synchronized our watches with Sander's. We were all dressed in civilian clothes. A few minutes later we were at the entrance to Göring's residence. We slipped into the passage unnoticed. Hanfstaengl had diverted the watchman. At about 8 o'clock we reached the dead-end branch. Here we had to wait until 8.40 p.m., i.e. until the guard had finished his round. Then we pulled galoshes over our shoes and walked on as silently as we could. We entered the Session Chamber at 8.45 p.m. One of my helpers went back to the dead-end branch to fetch the rest of the incendiary material. We started with the

Kaiser Wilhelm Memorial Hall and the Session Chamber, where we prepared a number of fires by smearing chairs and tables with the phosphorus mixture and by soaking curtains and carpets in paraffin. At exactly 9.5 p.m. we had finished, and started on our way back. It was high time – the phosphorus was fixed to go off within 30 minutes. At 9.12 we were back in the boiler-house and at 9.15 we climbed across the wall.

The allegations published abroad against any others are false. We three did the work entirely by ourselves. Apart from Göring, Goebbels, Röhm, Heines, Killinger, Hanfstaengl and Sander, no one knew about our plan.

The Führer, too, is said not to have known until later that the S.A. set the Reichstag on fire. I do not know about that. I have served the Führer for eleven years, and I shall remain faithful to him unto death. What I have done every other S.A. man would gladly have done for his Führer. But I cannot bear the thought that the S.A. was betrayed by those it helped to bring to power. I confidently believe that the Führer will destroy the dark plotters against the S.A. I am writing this confession as my only insurance against the evil plans of Göring and Goebbels. I shall destroy it the moment these traitors have been paid out.

Berlin, June 3rd, 1934
Signed Karl Ernst
S.A. Gruppenführer

The confession had the following addendum:

'This document may only be published on my orders, on the orders of my comrades Fiedler and von Mohrenschild, or if I die a violent death. My comrades Fiedler and Mohrenschild who have helped to set fire to the Reichstag must themselves decide whether their names can be made public or not. By our deed, the three of us have rendered yeoman service to National Socialism.'

Sources Consulted

OFFICIAL DOCUMENTS:

The case against van der Lubbe and accomplices (15 J 86.33).

Notes of Evidence, dated Sept. 21, 27 and 29, Oct. 10, Dec. 6 and 23; 1933.

Copy of Verdict (2P Aufh. 473.55; Public Prosecutor's Office, Berlin).

The Chancellory Records: 'Reichstag Fire' (Federal Archives, Koblenz R 43 II/294); 'Jews and the National Movement' (Public Records Office, London, Series E 611 913 – 612 666); 'Cabinet and Foreign Office Decisions' (Public Records Office, London, Series No. 3598, 4620, 8510, 2339, 2860, 8593, 8539, 8542, 9140, K 1052, 9094).

Records of the Berlin Fire Brigade (Institute of Contemporary History, Munich).

The Case against Gunsenheimer *et al.* (503) 77 KLs 16/37 (165.36); Public Prosecutor's Office, Berlin.

Dr Sack's extracts from the 32 volumes of Records of the Preliminary Examination.

Trial of the Major War Criminals before the International Military Tribunal, Nuremberg, 1947–1949.

WRITTEN AND VERBAL STATEMENTS TO THE AUTHOR BY:

Former members of the Berlin Fire Brigade;
Former officers of the Berlin Police;
Judge Paul Vogt, Cadenberger-Niederelbe;
Ernst Torgler, Hanover;
Paul Bienge, West Berlin;
Former S.A. staff-officers under the command of Karl Ernst;
Former Under-Secretary Ludwig Glauert, Hubbelrath-Mettmann;
Police officers, Leyden, Holland;
Ferdinand Kugler, Basle;
Dr Eberhard Taubert, Bonn;
Otto Schmidt, Hanover;
Dr Horst Pelckmann, now German Consul in Philadelphia;
Dr Hermann Rauschning, Portland, Oregon;
Dr Richard Lepsius, Baden-Baden;
Various ex-associates of Willi Münzenberg;

Prof. Dr Grimm;
Former Chief Clerk of the Reichstag, Ludwig Krieger, Bonn;
Prof. Robert M. W. Kempner, Lansdowne, Philadelphia, Pennsylvania;
et al.

BOOKS AND ARTICLES:

Abusch, Alexander: 'Das Braunbuch über den Reichstagbrand'. *Die Weltbühne*, Berlin, 1947.

Bergsträsser, Ludwig: *Geschichte der politischen Parteien in Deutschland.* (Isar) Munich, 1952.

Blagojewa, S.: *Georgi Dimitroff.* (Dietz) Berlin, 1954.

Bley, Wulf: Text of broadcast from the gutted Session Chamber as published in *Völkischer Beobachter* on 3rd March 1933.

Bonhoeffer, Karl and Zutt, Jürg: 'Über den Geisteszustand des Reichstagsbrand-stifters Marinus van der Lubbe'. *Monatsschrift für Psychiatrie und Neurologie*, Berlin, April 1934.

Borchmeyer, W.: *Hugenbergs Ringen in deutschen Schicksalsstunden*, 1949.

Borkenau, Franz: *Der europäische Kommunismus.* (Francke) Bern 1952.

Bracher, Karl Dietrich: 'Stufen totalitärer Gleichschaltung'. *Viertel-jahreshefte für Zeitgeschichte*, Stuttgart 1/1956.

Brandes, Peter: 'Feuer über Deutschland'. *Der Stern*, Hamburg, 43/1957–52/1957.

Braun, Otto: *Von Weimar zu Hitler.* (Hammonia) Hamburg, 1949.

Brecht, Arnold: *Vorspiel zum Schweigen.* Vienna, 1948.

Bross, Werner: *Gespräche mit Göring.* (Wolff) Flensburg, 1950.

The Brown Book of the Hitler Terror and the Burning of the Reichstag. (Victor Gollancz) London, 1933.

The Second Brown Book of the Hitler Terror. (Bodley Head) London, 1934.

Buber-Neumann, Margarete: *Von Potsdam nach Moskau.* (Deva) Stuttgart, 1957.

Bullock, Alan: *Hitler.* (Odham's Press) London, 1952.

Crankshaw, Edward: *Gestapo.* (Putman) London, 1956.

Czech-Jochberg, Erich: *Vom 30. Januar zum 21. März.*

Dahlem, Franz: *Weg und Ziel.* Berlin, 1952.

Diels, Rudolf: *Lucifer ante portas.* (Deva) Stuttgart, 1950.

Dimitroff contra Göring. Die Vernehmung Görings als Zeuge im Reichstags-brandprozess am 4. November 1933. (Tribune Druckerie) Leipzig n.d.

Dimitrov, Georgi: *Der Reichstagsbrandprozess.* (Neuer Weg) Berlin, 1946.

Dodd, William E.: *Ambassador Dodd's Diary*. (Victor Gollancz) London, 1945.
Duesterberg, Theodor: *Der Stahlhelm und Hitler*. Wolfenbüttel, 1949.
Effenberger, Gustav: *Welt in Flammen*. Hanover, 1913.
Ehrt, Adolf: *Entfesselung der Unterwelt*.
Ernst, Franz J.: *Der Reichstagsbrand*. Würzburg, 1948.
Eschenburg, Theodor: *Staat und Gesellschaft in Deutschland*. (Schwab) Stuttgart, 1956.
Fischer, Ernst: *Das Fanal*. (Stern) Vienna, 1946.
Fischer, Ruth: *Stalin and German Communism*. Harvard, 1948.
Flechtheim, Ossip: *Die KPD in der Weimar Republik*. Offenbach, 1948.
Forsthoff, Ernst: *Deutsche Geschichte seit 1918 in Dokumenten*. (Kröner) Stuttgart, 1938 (2nd edition).
François-Poncet, André: *Als Botschafter in Berlin*. (Kupferberg) Mainz, 1948.
Friedrich, G. and Lang, F.: *Vom Reichstagsbrand sur Entfachung des Weltbrandes*. (Promethée) Paris, 1938.
Frischauer, Willi: *Ein Marschallstab zerbrach*. (Münster) Ulm, 1951.
Gisevius, Hans Bernd: *Bis zum bitteren Ende*. a: (Claasen & Goverts) Hamburg, 1947. b: (Fretz & Wasmuth) Zürich, 1954.
Goebbels, Joseph: *Vom Kaiserhof zur Reichskanzlei*. (Eher) Munich, 1934.
Goebbels, Joseph: *Wetterleuchten*. (Eher) Munich, 1943. (5th edition).
Görlitz, Walter and Quint, Herbert A.: *Adolf Hitler*. (Steingrüben) Stuttgart, 1952.
Grimm, Friedrich: Politische Justiz. *Die Krankheit unserer Zeit*. (Bonn Univ. Press) Bonn, 1953.
Hager, Alfred: *Lehrbuch der Kriminalistik. Verhörtechnik und taktik*. (Hagedorn) Hanover, n. d.
Halle, Felix: *Wie verteidigt sich der Proletarier vor Gericht?* (Mopr) Berlin, 1929.
Hammerstein, Kunrat Freiherr von: 'Schleicher, Hammerstein und die Machtübernahme 1933'. *Frankfurter Hefte*, Frankfurt 1/1956–3/1956.
Hanfstaengl, Ernst: *Unheard Witness*. (Lippincott) Philadelphia, 1957.
Hays, Arthur Garfield: *City Lawyer*. (Simon & Schuster) New York, 1942.
Hegner, H. S. (Schulze-Wilde, Harry): *Die Reichskanzlei* (Frankfurter Bücher) Frankfurt, 1959.
Hegner, H. S. (Schulze-Wilde, Harry): 'Hinter den Kulissen der Reichskanzlei'. *Frankfurter Illustrierte*, Frankfurt 50/1948–8/1959.
Heiden, Konrad: *Die Geburt des Dritten Reiches*. (Europa) Zürich, 1934.

Hesslein, Pablo (Paul): 'Ich war im brennenden Reichstag'. *Stuttgarter Zeitung*, Stuttgart, 27th February, 1953.

Heydecker, Joe J. and Leeb, Johannes: *Der Nürnberger Prozess.* (Kiepenheuer) Cologne, 1958.

Hoegner, Wilhelm: *Die verratene Republik.* (Isar) Munich, 1958.

Hofer, Walther: *Der Nationalsozialismus. Dokumente 1933–1945.* (Fischer-Buch) Frankfurt, 1957.

Hohlfeldt, Johannes: *Dokumente der deutschen Politik.* (Juncker & Dünnhaupt) Berlin, 1933–1943.

Horkenbach, Cuno: *Das Deutsche Reich von 1918 bis heute.* (Presse-u. Wirtschaftsvlg.) Berlin, 1935.

Jäger, Hans: *Das wahre Gesicht der NSDAP.* Prague, 1933.

Jenke, Manfred: 'Die Wissenden schweigen'. *Frankfurter Rundschau*, Frankfurt, 25th February, 1956.

de Jong, G. T. J.: *De Brand.* (Blik) Amsterdam, 1934.

Kantorowicz, Alfred: *Deutsches Tagebuch.* (Kindler) Munich, 1959.

Kantorowicz, Alfred: 'Der Reichstagsbrand – Auftakt zur Weltbrandstiftung'. *Aufbau*, Berlin, 2/1947.

Katz, Otto: *Der Kampf um ein Buch.* (Carrefour) Paris, 1934.

Kaufhold, Friedrich: *Verbrennen und Löschen.* (Kohlhammer) Stuttgart, 1956.

Keesing's Contemporary Archives.

Knickerbocker, H. R.: *Deutschland so oder so?* (Rowohlt) Berlin, 1932.

Koestler, Arthur: *The Invisible Writing.* (Collins) London, 1954.

Koestler, Arthur: *The God that Failed.* (Hamish Hamilton) London, 1950.

Krivitsky, W. G.: *I was Stalin's Agent.* Amsterdam, 1940.

Kugler, Ferdinand: *Das Geheimnis des Reichstagsbrandes.* (Munster) Amsterdam, n. d.

Kuttner, Erich (Justinian); *Der Reichstagsbrand.* (Graphia) Karlsbad, 1934.

Last, Jef.: *Kruisgang der Jeugd.* (Brussel) Rotterdam, 1939.

Leber, Annedore: *Das Gewissen steht auf.* (Mosaik) Berlin, 1956.

Löbe, Paul: *Der Weg war lang.* (Arani) Berlin, 1949.

Lochner, Louis P.: *Stets das Unerwartete.* (Schneekluth) Darmstadt, 1955.

Lucian: *Die Abenteuer der Samosata.* (Allg. Verl. Anst.) Munich, 1924.

'Ludwig': *Der Reichstagsbrand. Ursachen, Wirkungen und Zusammenhänge.* (Défense) Paris, 1933.

Mantell, Ferdinand (Schneider, Wilhelm): 'Der Reichstagsbrand in anderer Sicht'. *Neue Politik*, Zürich, 20th January – 18th March, 1949.

Meissner, Otto: *Als Staatssekretär unter Ebert, Hindenburg und Hitler.* (Hoffmann & Campe) Hamburg, 1950.

Meissner, Hans Otto and (Schulze-) Wilde, Harry: 'Ein Toter spricht . . .' *Weltbild*, Munich, 23/1957–2/1958.

Meissner, Hans Otto and (Schulze-) Wilde, Harry: *Die Machtergreifung.* (Cotta) Stuttgart, 1958.

Mengering, Bob: '*Das Wahrheitsserum*'. (Kinau) Lüneburg, 1957.

Misch, Carl: *Deutsche Geschichte im Zeitalter der Massen.* (Kohlhammer) Stuttgart, 1952.

Niekisch, Ernst: *Das Reich der niederen Dämonen.* (Rowohlt) Hamburg, 1953.

Obbergen, Paulus van (Leers, Johannes von): 'Vom Reichstagsbrand zum Untergang des Reiches'. *Der Weg*, Buenos Aires, 12/1954.

The Oberfohren Memorandum. (German Information Bureau) London, 1933.

Papen, Franz von: *Der Wahrheit eine Gasse.* (List) Munich, 1952.

Picker, Henry: *Hitlers Tischgespräche im Führerhauptquartier* 1941–1942. (Athenäum) Bonn, 1951.

Rauschning, Hermann: *Conversations with Hitler.* (Butterworth) London, 1939.

Reber, Charles: 'Toxikologisches zum Fall van der Lubbe'. *Neues Tagebuch*, Paris, 1933.

Reed, Douglas: *The Burning of the Reichstag.* (Cape) London, 1934.

Reed, Douglas: *Fire and Bombs.* (Cape) London, 1940.

Regler, Gustav: *Das Ohr des Malchus.* (Kiepenheuer) Cologne, 1958.

Reitlinger, Gerald: *Die SS.* (Desch) Munich, 1956.

Roodboek (The Red Book). (Intern. Uitgeversbedrijf) Amsterdam, 1933.

Sack, Alfons: *Der Reichstagsbrandprozess.* With a foreword by Prof. Dr Friedrich Grimm. (Ullstein) Berlin, 1934.

Sauerbruch, Ferdinand: *Das war mein Leben.* (Kindler) Munich, 1956.

Schacht, Hjalmar: *Abrechnung mit Hitler.* (Rowohlt) Hamburg, 1949.

Scheringer, Richard: *Das grosse Los.* (Rowohlt) Hamburg, 1959.

Schlange-Schöningen, Hans: *Am Tage danach.* (Hammerich & Lesser) Hamburg, 1946.

Schulthess' Europäischer Geschichtskalender. (Beck) Munich, 1934.

Schulze-Wilde, Harry: 'Zur Geschichte der Technik der Nationalsozialistischen Machtergriefung'. *Frankfurter Hefte*, Frankfurt, 6/1957.

Schulze-Wilde, Harry: 'Van der Lubbes Rolle beim Reichstagsbrand'. *Süddeutsche Zeitung*, Munich, 25th–26th February 1956.

(Schulze-) Wilde, Harry: 'Der erste Schauprozess'. *Politische Studien*, Munich, 104/1958.

Schützinger, Hermann: 'Der Reichstag brennt'. *Neuer Vorwärts*, Bad Godesberg, 27th February, 1953.

Schwerin von Krosigk, Lutz Graf: *Es geschah in Deutschland*. (Wunderlich) Tübingen, 1951.

Sommerfeldt, Martin H.: *Ich war dabei*. Darmstadt, 1949.

Sommerfeldt, Martin H.: *Kommune*. (Mittler) Berlin, 1934.

Stampfer, Friedrich: *Die ersten vierzehn Jahre der Weimarer Republik*. (Auerdruck) Hamburg, 1953. (3rd edition).

Stampfer, Friedrich: 'Die Nacht des Reichstagsbrandes'. *Vorwärts*, Bad Godesberg, 20th December, 1957.

Stampfer, Friedrich: *Erfahrungen und Erkenntnisse*. (Politik und Wirtschaft), Cologne, 1957.

Stechert, Kurt: *Wie war das möglich?* (Bermann-Fischer) Stockholm, 1945.

Stein, Adolf (Rumpelstilzchen): *Gift, Feuer, Mord*. (Brunnen) Berlin, 1934.

Stephan, Werner: *Joseph Goebbels. Dämon einer Diktatur*. (Union) Stuttgart, 1949.

Sternberg, Fritz: *Kapitalismus und Sozialismus vor dem Weltgericht*. (Rowohlt) Hamburg, 1951.

Studnitz, Hans Georg von: 'Leben zwischen Macht und Gefahr'. *Christ und Welt*, Stuttgart, 5th December, 1957.

Taylor, A. J. P.: 'Who burnt the Reichstag?' *History Today*, London, August, 1960.

Thälmann, Ernst: *Der revolutionäre Ausweg und die KPD*. Quoted in *Wissen und Tat*, Düsseldorf, 5/1952.

Torgler, Ernst: 'Der Reichstagsbrand und was nachher kam'. *Die Zeit*, Hamburg, 21st October – 11th November, 1949.

Valtin, Jan (Krebs, Richard): *Out of the Night*. (Heinemann) London, 1941.

Wallot, Paul: *Das Reichstagsgebäude in Berlin*. (Cosmos) Leipzig, 1899.

White Book on the Executions of the 30th June, 1934. (Carrefour) Paris, 1934.

Wolff, Richard: 'Der Reichstagsbrand 1933. A Special Investigation'. Supplement to *Das Parlament*, Bonn, 18th January, 1956.

Wollenberg, Erich: 'Dimitroffs Aufstieg und Ende'. *Echo der Woche*, Munich, 12th August, 1949.

SOURCES CONSULTED

NEWSPAPERS AND JOURNALS:

Algemeen Handelsblad, Amsterdam
Amtl. Preussischer Pressedienst Berlin
Der Angriff, Berlin
Arbeitertum, Zeitung der DAF, Berlin
Berliner Börsen-Courier
Berliner Börsenzeitung
Berliner Lokalanzeiger
Berliner Nachtausgabe
Braunschweiger Neueste Nachrichten
Braunschweigische Staatszeitung
Christ und Welt, Stuttgart
Daily Express, London
Deutsche Allgemeine Zeitung, Berlin
Deutscher Reichsanzeiger, Berlin
Deutsche Rundschau, Stuttgart
Deutsche Woche, Munich
Echo der Woche, Munich
Feuerschutz
Frankfurter Hefte
Frankfurter Illustrierte
Frankfurter Rundschau
Das freie Wort, Bonn
Germania, Berlin
Hannoverscher Anzeiger
Hannoverscher Kurier
Hannoversche Presse
Het Volk, Amsterdam
History Today, London
Internationale
Kommunistische Internationale
Lichtpfad, Lorch
Lubecker Nachrichten
De Maasbode, Rotterdam
Manchester Guardian
Ministerialblatt für die Preussische innere Verwaltung, Berlin
Monatsschrift für Psychiatrie und Neurologie, Berlin
Morning Post, London
Nationalsozialistische Partei-Korrespondenz, Munich
Neue Arbeiter-Zeitung, Hanover
Neues Deutschland, Berlin
Neue Politik, Zürich
Neue Weltschau, Stuttgart
Neue Zürcher Zeitung, Zürich
Neues Tagebuch, Paris
New York Evening Post
Niedersächsische Tageszeitung, Hanover
Niedersächsische Volksstimme, Hanover
Das Parlament, Bonn
Politische Studien, Munich
Prager Montagsblatt
Pravda, Moscow
Reichsgesetzblatt, Berlin
La République, Strasbourg
Die Rote Fahne, Berlin
Saarbrückener Volksstimme
Safety at Work, London
Salzburger Nachrichten
Sender Freies Berlin
Der Spiegel, Hamburg
Der Stern, Hamburg
Stuttgarter Zeitung
Süddeutsche Zeitung, Munich
Der Tag, Berlin
De Telegraaf, Amsterdam
Telegraphen-Union, Berlin
The Times, London
Vierteljahreshefte für Zeitgeschichte, Stuttgart

Völkischer Beobachter, Berlin-Munich
Vorwärts, Berlin
Neuer Vorwärts, Berlin
Neuer Vorwärts, Bad Godesberg
Vorwärts, Bad Godesberg
Vossische Zeitung, Berlin
Die Welt, Hamburg
Weltbild, Munich
Die Weltbühne, Berlin
Der Weg, Buenoes Aires
Wiener Arbeiterzeitung
Wissen und Tat, Düsseldorf
Wolffs Telegraphen-Büro, Berlin
Die Zeit, Hamburg

References

CHAPTER I

1. Martin H. Sommerfeldt: *Kommune*, p. 45.
2. *Vorwärts*, 20 December 1957.
3. Reported to the author by Buwert, now a police inspector.

CHAPTER 2

1. *Prelim. Exam.*, Vol. I, p. 57f.
2. De Jongh: *De Brand*, p. 54.
3. De Jongh: op. cit., p. 54.
4. *Prelim. Exam.*, Vol. I, p. 50.
5. *Niedersächsische Tageszeitung*, 29 September 1933.
6. *Brown Book I*, p. 112.
7. *Brown Book I*, p. 58f.
8. *Brown Book I*, German ed., pp. 55 and 57.
9. *Brown Book I*, German ed., p. 57.
10. *Red Book*, p. 52.

CHAPTER 3

1. *Prelim. Exam.*, Vol. I., p. 33.
2. Statement by Dr Zirpins on 26 December 1951.
3. *Prelim. Exam.*, Vol. II, p. 142.
4. *Brown Book II*, p. 47.
5. *Algemeen Handelsblad*, 11 March 1933.
6. *Völkischer Beobachter*, 15 March 1933.
7. *Red Book*, p. 36.
8. F. von Papen: *Der Wahrheit eine Gasse*, p. 303.
9. Franz J. Ernst: *Der Reichstagsbrand*, p. 12.
10. *Niedersächsische Tageszeitung*, 25 March 1933.
11. *Proc.*, 24 March 1933.
12. Picker, *Hitlers Tischgespräche*, p. 211.

CHAPTER 4

1. *Die Welt*, 24 August 1957.
2. Appendix to Dr Wolff's report, op. cit., p. 22.
3. IMT, Vol. XI, p. 489.

4. *Erinnerungen eines Reichstagspräsidenten*, p. 148f.
5. Gustav Regler, *Das Ohr des Malchus*, p. 21.
6. *Brown Book I*, p. 134.
7. *Prel. Exam.*, Vol. G, p. 46, Evidence of Engineer Krug.
8. *Prel. Exam.*, Vol. G, p. 48f.
9. Douglas Reed: *The Burning of the Reichstag*, p. 151.
10. Douglas Reed: *Fire and Bomb*, p. 20.
11. Douglas Reed: *The Burning of the Reichstag*, p. 150f.

CHAPTER 5

1. Cf. Ernst Hanfstaengl: *Hitler – the Missing Years*, p. 201f.
2. Goebbels: *Vom Kaiserhof zur Reichskanzlei*, p. 269.
3. *Völkischer Beobachter*, 28 February 1933.
4. Reported to the author by Ludwig Grauert on 3 October 1957.
5. *Völkischer Beobachter*, 5 November 1933.
6. Papen: op. cit., p. 302.
7. Martin H. Sommerfeldt: *Ich war dabei*, p. 25.
8. Rudolf Diels: *Lucifer ante portas*, p. 193.
9. Quoted in N. Hoegner: *Die verratene Republik*, p. 345.
10. J. Goebbels: op. cit., p. 254.
11. Rudolf Diels: op. cit., p. 194.
12. Rudolf Diels: op. cit., p. 195.
13. Dr Wilhelm Schneider: *Neue Politik*, Zürich, Nos. 2–5, 1949.
14. *Der. Spiegel*, 25 November 1959.
15. Reported by Grauert on 3 October 1957.
16. Martin H. Sommerfeldt: *Ich war dabei*, p. 26.
17. *Niedersächsische Tageszeitung*, 2 March 1933.
18. Sack: *Reichstagsbrandprozess*, p. 32.
19. Ernst Fischer: *Das Fanal*, p. 37.

CHAPTER 6

1. Keesing's Contemporary Archives, 11 December 1933.
2. Arthur Koestler: *The God that Failed*, p. 71.
3. M. Buber-Neumann: *Von Potsdam nach Moskau*, p. 199.
4. Arthur Koestler: *The Invisible Writing*, p. 198.
5. Arthur Koestler: *The God that Failed*, p. 71f.
6. Ruth Fischer: *Stalin and German Communism*, p. 613.

CHAPTER 7

1. *Manchester Guardian*, 26 April 1933.
2. *Völkischer Beobachter*, 28 April 1933.

3. Sefton Delmer, *Trail Sinister*, p. 198.
4. Wolff: op. cit., p. 36.
5. *Brown Book I*, p. 82.
6. *Völkischer Beobachter*, 12 April 1933.
7. *Völkischer Beobachter*, 12 April 1933.
8. Dr Sack: op. cit., p. 40.
9. Dr Wolff: op. cit., p. 35.
10. *Neuer Vorwärts*, 29 October 1933.
11. Dr Sack: op. cit., p. 46.
12. Cf. Wolff, op. cit., note 63.
13. Dr Sack: op. cit., p. 49.
14. *Neue Arbeiter Zeitung*, Hanover, 25 February 1933.
15. Martin H. Sommerfeldt: *Kommune*, p. 85ff.
16. As reported in *Brown Book I*, p. 75.
17. *Völkischer Beobachter*, 3 March 1933.
18. Cf. Papen: op. cit., p. 291.

CHAPTER 8

1. *Aufbau*, No. 2, 1947.
2. A. Koestler: *The Invisible Writing*, p. 197f.
3. *Echo der Woche*, 12 August 1949.
4. *Die Zeit*, 4 November 1948.
5. Hays: *City Lawyer*, p. 341.
6. Dr Sack: op. cit., p. 240.
7. Dr Sack: op. cit., p. 116.
8. Hays: op. cit., p. 345.
9. Hays: op. cit., p. 377.
10. Hays: op. cit., p. 378.
11. Dr Sack: op. cit., p. 149.
12. Hays: op. cit., p. 388.
13. Dr Sack: op. cit., p. 154.
14. *Brown Book II*, p. 244.
15. Koestler: *The Invisible Writing*, p. 200.
16. Dr Sack: op. cit., preface.
17. *The Fight for a Book*, p. 16.
18. Hays: op. cit., p. 373.

CHAPTER 9

1. *Brown Book I*, p. 82.
2. *Brown Book I*, p. 52.
3. *Hannoverscher Kurier*, 8 November 1933.

4. Dr Sack: op. cit., p. 48.
5. Werner Stephan: *Joseph Goebbels*, p. 61.
6. R. Wolff: op. cit.
7. Martin H. Sommerfeldt: *Ich war dabei*, p. 30.
8. Martin H. Sommerfeldt: *Ich war dabei*, p. 57.
9. Martin H. Sommerfeldt: *Ich war dabei*, pp. 60–61.
10. Martin H. Sommerfeldt: *Ich war dabei*, p. 30.
11. Letter to *Der Spiegel*, 30 November 1959.
12. IMT, Vol. IX, p. 196.
13. *Echo der Woche*, 12 August 1949.
14. Meissner: *Staatssekretär*, p. 283.
15. Rudolf Diels, op. cit., p. 324.
16. *Völkischer Beobachter*, 5–6 November 1933.
17. Rudolf Diels: op. cit., p. 204.
18. *Die Zeit*, 21 October 1948.
19. *Niedersächsische Tageszeitung*, 20 October 1933.
20. J. Goebbels: op. cit., p. 271.
21. Keesing's Contemporary Archives: 19 April 1933.
22. *Völkischer Beobachter*, 28 February 1933.
23. *Brown Book II*, p. 303.
24. Douglas Reed: *The Burning of the Reichstag*, p. 121.
25. Letter dated 8 November 1957.
26. Douglas Reed: *The Burning of the Reichstag*, p. 122.
27. *Völkischer Beobachter*, 11 October 1933.
28. *Amtl. Preuss. Pressedienst*, 2 March 1933.
29. *Erinnerungen eines Reichstagspräsidenten*, p. 151.
30. *Ich war im brennenden Reichstag*, Stuttgarter Zeitung, 27 February 1933.
31. Annedore Leber: *Das Gewissen steht auf*, p. 106.
32. *Brown Book I*, p. 123.
33. *Berliner Lokalanzeiger*, 28 February 1933.
34. Letter by Puhle, 29 November 1957.
35. *Brown Book II*, p. 45.
36. *Niedersächsische Tageszeitung*, 12 October 1933.
37. *Brown Book II*, p. 298.
38. *Das freie Wort*, 21 February 1953.
39. *Lübecker Nachrichten*, 21 July 1954.
40. *Verdict*, p. 24.
41. *Neue Zürcher Zeitung*, 14 October 1933.

CHAPTER 10

1. *Neue Zürcher Zeitung*, 28 September 1933.
2. *Prelim. Exam.*, Vol. I, pp. 103–5.
3. *Prelim. Exam.*, Vol. I, p. 100.
4. *Indictment*, p. 33.
5. *Prelim. Exam.*, Vol. VI, p. 62.
6. *Prelim. Exam.*, Vol. VI, p. 63.
7. *Notes of Evidence*, 27 September 1933, p. 171.
8. *Neue Zürcher Zeitung*, 23 October 1933.
9. *Prelim., Exam.*, Vol: Reichstag III, pp. 156–7.
10. *Prelim. Exam.*, Vol: Reichstag IV, pp. 27–46.
11. *Notes of Evidence*, 27 September 1933, pp. 150–151.
12. *Notes of Evidence*, 27 September 1933, p. 155.
13. *Hannoverscher Kurier*, 23 November 1933.
14. cf. Buber-Neumann: op. cit., p. 238.
15. cf. S. Blagojewa: *Georgi Dimitroff*, p. 99.
16. *Brown Book II*, p. 57.
17. *Die Zeit*, 21 October 1948.
18. Dr Sack: op. cit., p. 218.
19. *Brown Book II*, p. 53f.
20. F. Kugler: *Geheimnis des Reichstagsbrandes*, p. 85.
21. *Notes of Evidence*, 27 September 1933.
22. *Brown Book II*, p. 59.
23. *Brown Book II*, p. 55.
24. Dr Sack: op. cit., p. 92.
25. C. Horkenbach: *Das Deutsche Reich;* entry of 21 March 1933.
26. *Neue Zürcher Zeitung*, 28 September 1933.
27. F. von Papen: op. cit., pp. 303–4.
28. *Die Zeit*, 28 October 1948.
29. Dr Sack: op. cit., pp. 96 and 288.
30. R. Diels: op. cit., p. 203.
31. Douglas Reed: *The Burning of the Reichstag*, p. 35.
32. *Die Zeit*, 4 November 1948.
33. *Niedersächsische Tageszeitung*, 24 September 1933.
34. *Die Zeit*, 4 November 1948.
35. *Neue Zürcher Zeitung*, 14 December 1933.
36. Otto Braun: *Von Weimar zu Hitler*, p. 100.

CHAPTER 11

1. op. cit., p. 41.
2. *Neue Zürcher Zeitung*, 5 November 1933.

3. Douglas Reed: *The Burning of the Reichstag*, p. 40f.
4. F. Kugler: op. cit., p. 29.
5. Dr Sack: op. cit., Preface, p. 9.
6. F. Kugler: op. cit., p. 23.
7. Dr Sack: op. cit., p. 155.
8. *Maasbode*, 31 October 1933.
9. Douglas Reed: *The Burning of the Reichstag*, p. 198.
10. *Neue Zürcher Zeitung*, 15 November 1933.
11. *De Telegraaf*, 7 October 1933.
12. *Het Volk*, 7 October 1933.
13. *Hannoverscher Anzeiger*, 7 October 1933.
14. *Hannoverscher Anzeiger*, 7 October 1933.
15. *Neue Zürcher Zeitung*, 8 October 1933.
16. F. Kugler: op. cit., p. 81.
17. *Neue Zürcher Zeitung*, 8 October 1933.
18. F. Kugler: op. cit., p. 100.
19. *Brown Book II*, p. 178.
20. *Neue Zürcher Zeitung*, 6 November 1933.
21. *Neue Zürcher Zeitung*, 6 November 1933.
22. Quoted in *Brown Book II*, p. 258.
23. *Brown Book II*, p. 193f.
24. Douglas Reed: *The Burning of the Reichstag*, p. 255f.
25. *Indictment*, p. 141.
26. Dr Sack: op. cit., p. 140.
27. Dr Sack: op. cit., p. 184ff.
28. *Neue Zürcher Zeitung*, 15 November 1933.
29. Dr Sack: op. cit., p. 198.
30. Army Medical Opinion quoted by Dr Sack: op. cit., p. 242.
31. *Indictment*, p. 160.
32. *Neue Zürcher Zeitung*, 1 November 1933.
33. *Neue Zürcher Zeitung*, 1 November 1933.
34. Kugler: op. cit., p. 136.
35. *Indictment*, p. 162.
36. Dr Sack: op. cit., p. 167.
37. Dr Sack: op. cit., p. 317.
38. Dr Sack: op. cit., p. 162.
39. *Prelim. Exam.* Vol. T III, p. 43.
40. *Indictment*, p. 136.
41. Dr Sack: op. cit., p. 310.
42. *Berliner Nachtausgabe* and *Neue Zürcher Zeitung*, 12 December 1933.

CHAPTER 12

1. *Prelim. Exam.* G. p. 53ff.
2. *Völkischer Beobachter*, 23 October 1933.
3. *De Telegraaf*, 24 October 1933.
4. *Niedersächsische Tageszeitung*, 24 October 1933.
5. Douglas Reed: *The Burning of the Reichstag*, p. 187.
6. *Neue Zürcher Zeitung*, 24 October 1933.
7. Douglas Reed: *The Burning of the Reichstag*, p. 298f.
8. *Neue Zürcher Zeitung*, 13 November 1933.
9. *Neue Zürcher Zeitung*, 5 October 1933.
10. *Berliner Lokalanzeiger*, 28 February 1933.
11. *Hannoversche Presse*, 14 April 1956.
12. *Völkischer Beobachter*, 1 March 1933.
13. *Feuerschutz*, 1933, p. 50.
14. See M. J. Reaney: 'Give the Fire Air' in *Safety at Work*, London.
15. Effenberger: *Welt in Flammen*, p. 266.
16. ibid., p. 272.
17. *Völkischer Beobachter*, 1 March 1933.

CHAPTER 13

1. *Nationalsozialistische Partei Korrespondenz*.
2. *Berliner Börsen-Courier*, 23 December 1933.
3. Erich Kuttner: *Reichstagsbrand*, p. 34.
4. *Neue Züricher Zeitung*, 19 October 1933.
5. Adolf Stein: *Gift, Feuer, Mord*, p. 27f.
6. Kugler: op. cit., p. 25.
7. *Niedersächsische Tageszeitung*, 28 September 1933.
8. *Brown Book II*, p. 215.
9. *Brown Book II*, p. 173.
10. Douglas Reed: *The Burning of the Reichstag*, p. 264.
11. De Jongh: op. cit., p. 96.
12. Douglas Reed: *The Burning of the Reichstag*, p. 265f.

Index